Lecture Notes in Computer Science 3306

Commenced Publication in 1973
Founding and Former Series Editors:
Gerhard Goos, Juris Hartmanis, and Jan van Leeuwen

Editorial Board

David Hutchison
Lancaster University, UK

Takeo Kanade
Carnegie Mellon University, Pittsburgh, PA, USA

Josef Kittler
University of Surrey, Guildford, UK

Jon M. Kleinberg
Cornell University, Ithaca, NY, USA

Friedemann Mattern
ETH Zurich, Switzerland

John C. Mitchell
Stanford University, CA, USA

Moni Naor
Weizmann Institute of Science, Rehovot, Israel

Oscar Nierstrasz
University of Bern, Switzerland

C. Pandu Rangan
Indian Institute of Technology, Madras, India

Bernhard Steffen
University of Dortmund, Germany

Madhu Sudan
Massachusetts Institute of Technology, MA, USA

Demetri Terzopoulos
New York University, NY, USA

Doug Tygar
University of California, Berkeley, CA, USA

Moshe Y. Vardi
Rice University, Houston, TX, USA

Gerhard Weikum
Max-Planck Institute of Computer Science, Saarbruecken, Germany

Xiaofang Zhou Stanley Su
Mike P. Papazoglou Maria E. Orlowska
Keith G. Jeffery (Eds.)

Web Information Systems – WISE 2004

5th International Conference on
Web Information Systems Engineering
Brisbane, Australia, November 22-24, 2004
Proceedings

Volume Editors

Xiaofang Zhou
Maria E. Orlowska
University of Queensland
School of Information Technology and Electrical Engineering
Brisbane QLD 4072, Australia
E-mail: {zxf, maria}@itee.uq.edu.au

Stanley Su
University of Florida
Database Systems Research and Development Center
P.O. Box 116125, 470 CSE, Gainesville, FL 32601-6125, USA
E-mail: su@cise.ufl.edu

Mike P. Papazoglou
Tilburg University
INFOLAB room 304, P.O. Box 90153, 5000 LE, Tilburg, The Netherlands
E-mail: mikep@kub.nl

Keith G. Jeffery
CCLRC Rutherford Appleton Laboratory
Chilton, Didcot, Oxon OX11 0QX, UK
E-mail: k.g.jeffery@rl.ac.uk

Library of Congress Control Number: 2004115150

CR Subject Classification (1998): H.4, H.2, H.3, H.5, K.4.4, C.2.4, I.2

ISSN 0302-9743
ISBN 3-540-23894-8 Springer Berlin Heidelberg New York

This work is subject to copyright. All rights are reserved, whether the whole or part of the material is concerned, specifically the rights of translation, reprinting, re-use of illustrations, recitation, broadcasting, reproduction on microfilms or in any other way, and storage in data banks. Duplication of this publication or parts thereof is permitted only under the provisions of the German Copyright Law of September 9, 1965, in its current version, and permission for use must always be obtained from Springer. Violations are liable to prosecution under the German Copyright Law.

Springer is a part of Springer Science+Business Media

springeronline.com

© Springer-Verlag Berlin Heidelberg 2004
Printed in Germany

Typesetting: Camera-ready by author, data conversion by PTP-Berlin, Protago-TeX-Production GmbH
Printed on acid-free paper SPIN: 11354482 06/3142 5 4 3 2 1 0

Message from the General Co-chairs

It is a great pleasure to introduce the proceedings of WISE 2004 with a few remarks. Following the success of WISE in Hong Kong (2000), Kyoto (2001), Singapore (2002) and Rome (2003), Brisbane was honored to host the fifth conference in the series in November 2004.

It is with sadness that we acknowledge the untimely death of Yahiko Kambayashi; he was a great supporter of WISE and, indeed, we both knew him well through our involvement in the VLDB Endowment Board and in other areas of the international scene in information systems. His lifework is a testament to his contribution to the world.

Turning to this year's conference, the quality of the program speaks for itself and we are sure that the attendees enjoyed the hospitable social atmosphere of Brisbane.

It only remains for us to thank the key persons who, with their teams to whom we are also very grateful, ensured WISE 2004 was a success. They are: Program Committee Chairs: Mike Papazoglou, Stanley Su and Xiaofang Zhou; Workshops Chair: Christoph Bussler; Tutorials Chair: Fabio Casati; Publication Chair: Yanchun Zhang; and the Local Organizing Chair: Xue Li.

September 2004

Maria E. Orlowska
Keith G. Jeffery

Message from the Program Co-chairs

This volume contains papers selected for presentation at the 5th International Conference on Web Information Systems Engineering (WISE 2004), which was held in Brisbane, Australia during November 22–24, 2004. WISE is the premium forum for researchers, professionals and industry practitioners to share their knowledge and experiences in the rapidly growing area of Web technologies, methodologies and applications. Previous WISE conferences were held in Hong Kong (2000), Kyoto (2001), Singapore (2002) and Rome (2003).

WISE 2004 received 198 submissions from 27 countries and regions worldwide. After a thorough review process for each submission by the Program Committee and specialists recommended by Program Committee members, WISE 2004 accepted 45 regular papers and 29 short papers (the acceptance ratios were 22.7% and 14.6%, respectively). This volume also includes invited keynote papers, given by three leading experts at WISE 2004: Prof. Alistair Moffat (University of Melbourne), Prof. Vijay Varadharajan (Macquarie University) and Dr. Wei-Ying Ma (Microsoft Research Asia).

Two workshops were held in conjunction with WISE 2004. The workshop papers were published in a separate volume of proceedings also published by Springer in its Lecturer Notes in Computer Science series.

The conference received financial support from the Australian Computer Science Society and the Australian Research Council (ARC) Research Network in Enterprise Information Infrastructure (EII). We, the conference organizers, also received help and logistic support from the University of Queensland, City University of Hong Kong, the Web Information Systems Engineering Society (WISE Society), and Mark Hau and the Conference Management Toolkit Support Team at Microsoft. We are grateful to Xue Li, Miranda Lee, Yanchun Zhang and Qing Li for their great effort in supporting conference organization. Finally, we would like to take this opportunity to thank all Program Committee members and external reviewers for their expertise and help in evaluating papers, and to thank all authors who submitted their papers to this conference.

September 2004

Mike Papazoglou
Stanley Su
Xiaofang Zhou

Conference Organization

General Co-chairs

Maria E. Orlowska, University of Queensland, Australia
Keith G. Jeffery, BITD, UK

Program Committee Co-chairs

Mike Papazoglou, Tilburg University, The Netherlands
Xiaofang Zhou, University of Queensland, Australia
Stanley Su, University of Florida, USA

Workshops Chair: Christoph Bussler, DERI, National Univ. of Ireland, Galway
Tutorials Chair: Fabio Casati, HP Labs, USA
Publication Chair: Yanchun Zhang, Victoria University, Australia
Local Organization Chair: Xue Li, University of Queensland, Australia

WISE Steering Committee

Yanchun Zhang (Chair), Victoria University, Australia
Qing Li, City University of Hong Kong, China
Xiaofang Zhou, University of Queensland, Australia
Katsumi Tanaka, Kyoto University, Japan
Xiaohua Jia, City University of Hong Kong, China
Roland Wagner, University of Linz, Austria
Klaus R. Dittrich, Universität Zürich, Switzerland
Tosiyasu L. Kunii, Hosei University, Japan
Marek Rusinkiewicz, Telecordia Technologies, USA

Program Committee Members

Dave Abel, Australia
Witlod Abramowicz, Poland
Marco Aiello, Italy
Ken Barker, Canada
Boualem Benatallah, Australia
Sonia Bergamaschi, Italy
Arne Berre, Norway
Alex Borgida, USA
Tiziana Catarci, Italy
Sang Kyun Cha, Korea
Arbee L.P. Chen, Taiwan
Guihai Chen, China
Phoebe Chen, Australia
Andrzej Cichocki, USA
Vincenzo D'Andrea, Italy
Anindya Datta, USA
Valeria De Antonellis, Italy
Flavio De Paoli, Italy
Alex Delis, Greece
Gill Dobbie, New Zealand
Schahram Dustdar, Austria
Johann Eder, Austria

David Embley, USA
Dimitrios Georgakopoulos, USA
Angela Goh, Singapore
Paul Grefen, The Netherlands
Wook-Shin Han, Korea
Manfred Hauswirth, Switzerland
Sushil Jajodia, USA
Manfred Jeusfeld, The Netherlands
Dimitris Karagiannis, Austria
Kamal Karlapalem, India
Martin Kersten, The Netherlands
Hiroyuki Kitagawa, Japan
Masaru Kitsuregawa, Japan
Manolis Koubarakis, Greece
Herman Lam, USA
Haifei Li, USA
Jianzhong Li, China
Qing Li, China
Xue Li, Australia
Ee Peng Lim, Singapore
Xuemin Lin, Australia
Tok Wang Ling, Singapore
Chengfei Liu, Australia
Ling Liu, USA
Mengchi Liu, Canada
Richard Liu, USA
Hongjun Lu, China
Jianguo Lu, Canada
Kalle Lyytinen, USA
Wei-Ying Ma, China
Sanjay Madria, USA
Pat Martin, Canada
Massimo Mecella, Italy
Rubens Melo, Brazil
Michele Missikoff, Italy
Mukesh Mohania, India
San Murugesan, Australia
Anne H.H. Ngu, USA
Moira C. Norrie, Switzerland
Beng Chin Ooi, Singapore
Jeff Parsons, Canada
Barbara Pernici, Italy
Colette Rolland, France
Stefano Paraboschi, Italy
Dimitris Plexousakis, Greece
Depei Qian, China
Louiqa Raschid, USA
Thomas Risse, Germany
Michael Rys, USA
Keun Ho Ryu, Korea
Shazia Sadiq, Australia
Wasim Sadiq, Australia
Klaus-Dieter Schewe, New Zealand
Karsten Schulz, Australia
Heng Tao Shen, Australia
Ming-Chien Shan, USA
Keng Siau, USA
Eleni Stroulia, Canada
Kian Lee Tan, Singapore
Katsumi Tanaka, Japan
Frank Tompa, Canada
Peter Trianatfillou, Greece
Aphrodite Tsalgatidou, Greece
Willem-Jan van den Heuvel, The Netherlands
Vijay Varadharajan, Australia
Benkt Wangler, Sweden
Roel Wieringa, The Netherlands
Jian Yang, Australia
Ge Yu, China
Jeffery Yu, China
Philip Yu, USA
Osmar Zaiane, Canada
Carlo Zaniolo, USA
Aoying Zhou, China

External Reviewers

Ioannis Aekaterindis
Reema Al-Kamha
Denniz Altintasli
Yuan An
Samuil Angelov
George Athanasopoulos
Per Backlund
Donald Baker
Roberta Benassi

Daniela Berardi
Avneesh Bhatnagar
D. Bianchini
Alessia Candido
Belinda Carter
Shermann S. Chan
Syin Chan
Shiping Chen
Ding-Ying Chiu
Bin Cui
Aasa Dahlstedt
Maya Daneva
Fulvio D'Antonio
Antonio De Nicola
Drew Devereux
Yihong Ding
Riccardo Dondi
Kaushik Dutta
Claudio Ferretti
Hans-Georg Fill
Bugra Gedik
Jonathan Gelati
Francoise Gire
Daniela Grigori
Michael Grossniklaus
Francesco Guerra
Zhimao Guo
Sven Hartmann
Peter Höfferer
Sangyong Hwang
Noriko Imafuji
Yoshiharu Ishikawa
George Karabatis
Neeran Karnik
Yutaka Kidawara
Stephen Kimani
Markus Kirchberg
Yong Sik Kwon
Alexander Lazovik
Jeonghoon Lee
Ki-Hoon Lee
Marek Lehmann
Kees Leune
Changqing Li
Xueming Li
Sebastian Link
Johannes Lischka
Ning-Han Liu
Qing Liu
Carlos Lopez
Marco Loregian
Qiang Ma
Michele Melchiori
Diego Milano
Hyun J. Moon
Myo Myo Naing
Satoshi Nakamura
Zaiqing Nie
Nikos Ntarmos
Alex Palacios
Massimo Paolucci
Thomi Pilioura
Paul Ralph
Sankardas Roy
Takeshi Sagara
Maneesha Sahasrabudhe
Chad Saunders
Monica Scannapieco
Jun Shen
Quan Z. Sheng
Norihide Shinagawa
Anoop Singhal
Halvard Skogsrud
Eva Söderström
Panagiotis Stamatopoulos
Mattias Strand
Jianmin Su
Subbu Subramaniam
Aixin Sun
Katsumi Takahashi
Takayuki Tamura
Cui Tao
Kerry Taylor
Alessandro Termini
Dimitrios Theotokis
Helen Thomas
Dian Tjondronegoro
Giovanni Toffoli
Masashi Toyoda
Alexei Tretiakov
J.M. Turull-Torres
Pascal van Eck
Maurizio Vincini
Fusheng Wang
Hongzhi Wang
Lingyu Wang
Stella L. Wang
Yitong Wang
Rob Warren
Ji-Rong Wen
Darrell Woelk
Guy Wood-Bradley
Li Xu
YongSIk Yoon
Yidong Yuan
Jane Zhao
Xin Zhou
Bin Zhu
Sencun Zhu

Table of Contents

Keynote Papers

Session 1: Web Information System Modelling

Session 2: Payment and Security

Session 3: Information Extraction

Session 4: Advanced Applications

Session 5: Performance Issues

Session 6: Linkage Analysis and Document Clustering

Session 7: Web Caching and Content Analysis

Session 8: XML Query Processing

Session 9: Web Search and Personalization

Session 10: Workflow Management and Enterprise Information Systems

Session 11: Business Processes

Session 12: Deep Web and Dynamic Content

Session 13: Web Information System Design

Session 14: Ontology and Applications

Session 15: Multimedia, User Interfaces, and Languages

Session 16: Peer-to-Peer and Grid Systems

What Does It Mean to "Measure Performance"?

Alistair Moffat[1] and Justin Zobel[2]

[1] Department of Computer Science and Software Engineering
The University of Melbourne, Victoria 3010, Australia
[2] School of Computer Science and Information Technology
RMIT University, Victoria 3001, Australia

Abstract. The purpose of much computer science research is to invent algorithms, and generate evidence to convince others that the new methods are worthwhile. All too often, however, the work has no impact, because the supporting evidence does not meet basic standards of rigor or persuasiveness. Here the notion of "experiment" is explored, with reference to our current investigation into distributed text query processing on a cluster of computers. We describe some of the issues that we encountered, and lessons that can be applied by researchers designing experiments in other areas of computing.

1 Introduction

Research into practical systems is often intended to yield what the investigators believe to be new structures and algorithms. Having established via the research literature that an invention is indeed novel, the investigators seek to establish its worth. In most papers, the demonstration of worth is by some combination of experiment, simulation, or analysis. Sometimes the demonstration is entirely absent.

For the great majority of practical algorithms the most reliable form of demonstration is by experiment. The alternatives are interesting, but not compelling. In some papers, the "proof" of validity or superiority rests entirely on rhetoric – known in less intellectual circles as "hand-waving". Such papers have little impact in either an academic or practical sense.

In other papers, the demonstration is by mathematical analysis, or simulation using a model, or a combination of both. But such approaches typically involve simplifications such as representing data by statistical distributions, and can fail to capture the complexity of a realistic computing environment. Asymptotic superiority can also be illusory. The difference between a $\log n$ factor and a $\log \log n$ factor in an analysis can be completely swamped by constant factors, and many algorithms that appear strong analytically have not survived the test of a practical implementation.

In the traditional sciences, theories are working hypotheses whose applicability is validated by experiments designed to distinguish between competing proposals. An experiment that confirms a theory does not prove that theory to be true – it merely adds weight to the likelihood that it is true. This "accepted until demonstrated incorrect" methodology has evolved over hundreds of years, and has itself stood the test of time.

The same scientific method underlies algorithmic computer science [Tichy, 1998]. The algorithms that are regarded as significant are those that have been shown to work in practice, with evidence strong enough to convince skeptics. And because computing

X. Zhou et al. (Eds.): WISE 2004, LNCS 3306, pp. 1–12, 2004.
© Springer-Verlag Berlin Heidelberg 2004

is a discipline in which innovations are valued as much for their economic merits as for their intrinsic elegance, new techniques tend to be regarded as of only curiosity value until they have been carefully evaluated in realistic settings.

After inventing a new indexing structure or query processing algorithm, we should, therefore, seek to implement it and measure its behavior. First, we form a hypothesis, that is, make a statement of belief about the algorithm, such as identifying what it is expected to be superior to and in what circumstances it is expected to be superior. Such hypotheses are often highly general. Rather than make claims about behavior on specific hardware, for example, we might claim that one algorithm is always faster than another for sufficiently large volumes of input data. Second, we design an experiment to distinguish between our hypothesis and previous ones. Third, we impartially carry out the experiment. The final step is to communicate the structure of the experiment, the outcomes of the experiment, and the conclusions we draw from those outcomes, usually as a written paper or report. Importantly, that description should allow an independent expert to undertake similar experiments and validate our claims.

In the long term, this scientific model is effective, and only the most successful algorithms are remembered and used. The work in individual computer science papers, however, is often remote from the ideal. In the specific areas of indexing and searching – used in this paper to illustrate the difficulties of experimentation – testing an algorithm often consists of implementing the simplest baseline that the investigators think is worth considering; implementing the "improved" algorithm; running both on some test data; and measuring the amount of CPU or elapsed time that was consumed. Using this evidence, the researchers draw both graphs and conclusions, often rather more of the former than the latter.

Such experiments almost always demonstrate improvements, and researchers rarely admit to having invented inferior techniques. In computing, reviewers tend to react negatively to papers that have as their rationale a further verification of the status quo, and an experimental refutation of the implicit hypothesis that "the new idea is better" is generally deemed to be not worthy of communication. As a result, researchers all too often construct experiments in which their new method is identified as a success.

Many research papers fail to earn any citations. A key reason, we believe, is that the evidence does not meet basic standards of rigor or persuasiveness, or is simply inadequate [Tichy et al., 1995]. Perhaps the experiments were flawed, the data inadequate, the baselines inappropriate, or, in extreme cases, the investigators deliberately chose to overlook the parts of the results that shed a bad light. Another issue is that, often, insufficient thought is given to the experimental design. In many cases it is far from clear how improvements in performance should be measured. Such failings mar many experimental papers [Johnson, 2002].

In this paper the notion of "experiment" is explored, with reference to the task of distributed text search on a tightly-coupled cluster of computers. Our intention is, as a case study, to explore the rigor that we believe is necessary in experimental computer science, in the hope that the lessons learnt in our experiments will be helpful to others.

It is also worth reflecting on what can happen when rigor is neglected. Physical scientists know well how costly careless experiments can be – thousands or millions of dollars worth of effort wasted, and possibly reputations destroyed. Consider for example the cold fusion saga, in which hundreds of scientists unsuccessfully attempted to reproduce work that had been announced without appropriate experimental validation. More

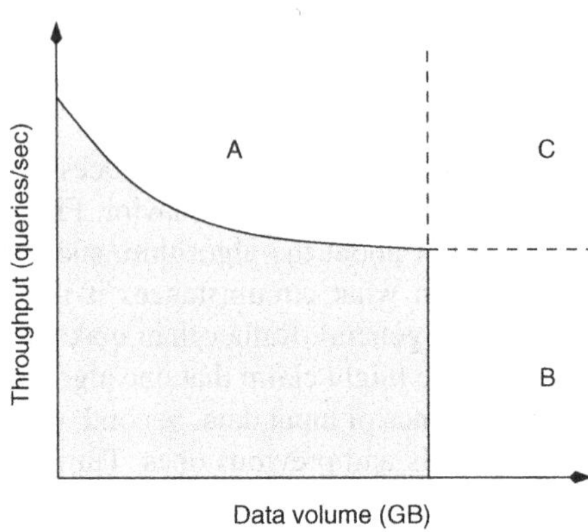

Fig. 1. The relationship between data volume and query throughput rate for a standard "unit cost" computer. Points in the shaded region are feasible; points above and to the right are not. The regions labelled A, B, and C are discussed below.

recently, a claimed link (based on flimsy and now disproven evidence) between autism and a common childhood vaccine has led to unnecessary suffering. Arguably the Y2K "bug", whose effects were largely unsubstantiated yet cost many billions of dollars, is an example of similar carelessness in computing. Competent scientists applying robust methods in an open manner are unlikely to cause such incidents.

2 Storing and Accessing Data

Consider Figure 1, which depicts a computer – with a processor, main memory, and disk storage – applied to a data management task. The horizontal axis shows schematically the size of problem that can be handled on this machine, with the vertical line crossing it representing the physical storage capacity of the given hardware. For example, on a machine with 1 TB of disk storage, we might (certainly with a straightforward implementation) suppose that problems involving more than 1 TB of data are not feasible.

The vertical axis in Figure 1 shows a processing rate – measured in queries per second – and is an independent measure of the system. The curve represents the peak processing load for that hardware combination. In most retrieval applications, the effort per query increases as the data volume increases, hence the downward trend.

The shaded region bounded by the two lines is the *feasible* zone. Combinations of data volume and query arrival rate that fall within the feasible zone are sustainable on the hardware, whereas combinations outside the region are not. In practice the exact positions of the lines depends on many factors, not all of which are easy to quantify:

- the processor speed and other characteristics, such as cache size and type;
- the amount of main memory available;
- the amount of disk storage available, and its access speed;
- the quality of the compiler;
- the skill of the programmer; and
- the fundamental nature of the algorithm and of the task that it supports.

When circumstances dictate a combination of data volume and query arrival rate that lies outside the feasible region, we must shift the bounding lines so that the feasible region includes the desired performance point. Reflecting the list above, this might be done by increasing the processor speed or cache speed or size; increasing the amount of main memory; increasing the disk capacity or speed; using a better compiler; improving the quality of the implementation; or by using a better algorithm.

The goal of research in areas of this type is almost always to achieve the last of these: we seek recognition by devising better techniques, and use our science to recognize circumstances in which adding more resources is unlikely to be helpful. In contrast, a supplier of commercial solutions more often than not simply scales the hardware.

Figure 1 is simplistic in several ways, not the least of which is the lack of scale on either axis. Another way in which it is potentially misleading is that the bounding curve is portrayed as a sharp line, whereas in practice there is a blurred transition between the feasible region and the infeasible region. When the query load is close to the maximum that can be supported, the system may begin to thrash or behave chaotically, and average query response time will increase markedly. In practice, systems are typically operated well below their peak capability, so as to meet a quality-of-service guarantee.

As an example of the type of improvements that can alter the feasible region, consider the role of compression. If we suppose that the data being manipulated can be stored compressed, then the data volume limit (the vertical boundary in Figure 1) shifts to the right, widening the feasible region. On the other hand, depending on the nature of the transformation used, and the type of processing required for each query, compression might slow query response rates rates, and lower the horizontal boundary of the feasible region. Note, however, that in some circumstances compression can boost query processing rates, thereby extending the feasible region in both dimensions [Zobel and Moffat, 1995, Williams and Zobel, 1999].

3 Distribution

Another way to extend feasibility is via distribution – by harnessing the power of multiple computers, we are able to tackle problems that are orders of magnitude larger than might be handled on a single machine. For example, much of the impressive performance achieved by the Google search engine arises as a consequence of the more than 10,000 computers used to support querying operations [Barroso et al., 2003].

Looking again at Figure 1, several distinct situations might occur. If the data volume fits the machine profile, but the anticipated query volume is too high, then we are in region A. To meet the required query load, the correct response is *replication* of the system, since a single computer is able to support the data volume, and, assuming that queries are read-only, multiple computers operating independently in parallel with mirrored data sets have no need for any synchronization overhead. In this scenario, a query is routed to a server by a *receptionist* process, and the server that resolves the query communicates the output directly back to the initial client.

On the other hand, in region B of Figure 1, one server could possibly carry the query load, but is unable to hold the necessary volume of data. Multiple computers are again required, but now it is the data that must be divided into manageable chunks, rather than the workload. Systems that partition the data are inherently more complex than replicated

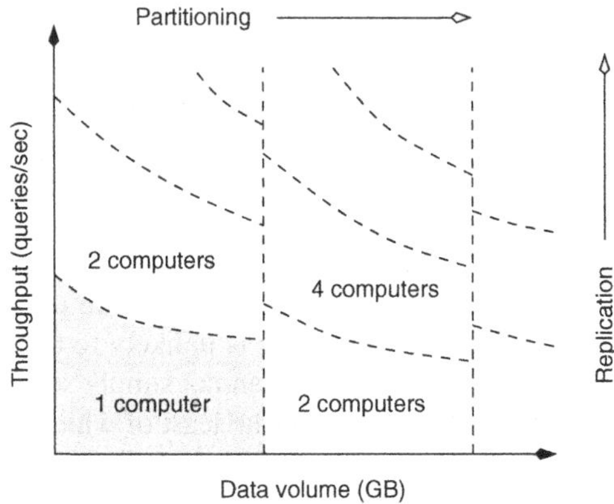

Fig. 2. Use of multiple unit machines to handle data volumes or query loads larger than can be handled by a single unit machine.

systems – the receptionist process must split each query according to the data distribution, invoke multiple servers on sub-queries, and then combine the partial answers that they return. There are two places in this arrangement where *drag*, or redundant computation, might be introduced. First, it might not be possible to perfectly split the query or data, making the sum of the effort involved in the sub-queries greater than the cost of executing the original query. Second, there may be non-trivial effort involved in combining the partial answers to make a global answer.

Finally, in region C of Figure 1, the data must be partitioned across several machines, and then replicated to obtain the required query processing capability.

One interesting question is whether it is more effective to double the volume of disk and memory on a given machine or to add another machine with the same memory and disk capacity. If the aim is to increase throughput, disk is unhelpful but memory could make a massive difference; if the aim is to increase the volume of data supported, further disk and memory can do so but at some cost in throughput and response time. If the aim is to fully explore the space depicted in Figure 1, all three resources must be added – hence our interest in distribution using idealized unit computers.

Figure 2 shows, again for a hypothetical unit computer of some fixed configuration, the zones that describe the resources required when data partitioning and replication must be combined. The shapes of the regions are a direct consequence of the factors discussed. Twice the number of machines used to manage twice the volume of data result is unlikely to result in the same query throughput rate being possible. On the other hand, a data split across multiple machines reduces the load on each, so total query load can, in theory, also increase – but not beyond what could be attained by placing a proportionate fraction of the data on a single machine.

For these various reasons, any algorithmic challenge lies in the area of partitioning rather than of replication. An immediate consequence is that experiments to test a distributed mechanism must be on a scale that warrants data partitioning. Taking any fixed volume of data and executing a software system using $k = 1, 2, 3, \ldots$ computers does not supply any inherent evidence as to the scalability of the technique in question. Such an experiment represents an implausible situation.

Given a new algorithm, then, the question arises as to how the benefit it offers might be measured. A typical experiment involves selecting some sample data sets and measuring, say, query processing times as the number of processors used is varied. But do changes in processing time tell us anything about the position of the feasible regions (Figure 2), or about potential throughput? And do the results have any lessons for other hardware, or other data, or other implementations? We explore such questions below, after reviewing issues and challenges for experimental design.

4 Designing an Experiment

The purpose of an experiment is to seek confirmation of a hypothesis. Having accepted that experimentation is essential for robust science [Tichy, 1998], there are many issues that an investigator needs to confront [Zobel et al., 1996, Zobel, 2004, chapter 11]. The following paragraphs summarize a set of minimum standards that a skeptical reader (and a good reviewer) will apply before accepting the validity of any experiments.

Baselines. There needs to be a clear, interesting hypothesis. It isn't particularly meaningful, for example, to claim that an algorithm is "fast" or "efficient". Efficient compared to what? Such a claim implies the existence of a baseline – a method against which the new algorithm is being compared. It follows that the baseline should be the best previous method for computing the same task. Comparison against a poor baseline makes little sense, since there are many different ways of gaining initial improvements. And is the new method faster on all kinds of data, on all machines, at all scales?

More typically, it is the trend of behavior that is relevant. A technique is most interesting if, as the data volume increases, the improvement offered by the new algorithm increases by a greater fraction.

The use of baselines presents other challenges. If the implementations are not of similar standard, then the results are meaningless; yet, during a research program, investigators tend to focus on developing their contribution and not on reimplementing the work of others. In some cases, other investigators have made their code available – allowing results directly comparable to those previously published. (Note that if you do use the source code or data of others, you should both cite the paper in which the techniques are described and also as a separate note indicate the source and authorship of the software you have made use of. The two works may involve quite different sets of people, and both sets should have their work acknowledged.)

An experiment might also be used to show that an algorithm provides a feasible method for solving a problem, for example when expected asymptotic costs have been reduced from quadratic to linear. In such cases, a baseline might be of less interest, and absolute performance sufficient to defend the hypothesis. Nevertheless, measuring performance across a range of scales of data is crucial. Performance at a single data point is (singularly) uninformative.

Data and software. Measurement of performance requires use of input data. It is important for sensible data to be used, and explained carefully. If the data is artificial in some way, the justification for using it needs to be very careful indeed – results on synthetic data rarely generalize to realistic cases.

Once you have finished with your data and software, it is good practice to make them publicly available. By all means add any caveats that you wish – "may be used for research purposes only", "no warranty", and so on – but do allow them to be used by your colleagues. The field that you are a member of will benefit, and your work is more likely to be accurately recognized. Being overly protective of your intellectual property hints that there are limitations in your code or data that would undermine or contradict your published results.

In some fields, there are data sets that have become so widely used that they have the status of "gold standards". Even if you wish to give results for, and then make public, more specific data sets that show the behavior you wish to comment on, you should also give comparative values for previous data sets that have been widely quoted.

Occasionally an investigator argues that, because the cost of undertaking a full-scale experiment is prohibitive, a limited or artificial experiment should be used. Perhaps two computers running multiple processes are assumed to resemble a grid; or a gigabyte of data is used where a terabyte would be the likely volume in practice; or querying is simulated by random accesses into an index; or documents are simulated by random strings of fixed length; or queries are randomly-sampled strings from documents. Doing so is perfectly reasonable, but only if the conclusions make it clear that the results are no more than preliminary and may have no implications for realistic implementations.

Any extrapolations from results on a limited data set are likely to be flawed. For example, search amongst a few thousand documents does not present the challenges of search across the web. Similarly, performance on a data set that fits into a CPU cache has no implications for performance on a memory-sized data set. Nor does performance on data that fits in memory have any lessons for larger data sets on disk.

Measurement. Another important issue is deciding what to measure. Candidates include – but are not limited to – response time, CPU time, query throughput, memory usage, number of simultaneous users, network activity, disk volume, and, in the case of text search, effectiveness as indicated by the ability to retrieve relevant documents.

These various facets are often in tension, and can be traded against each other. Giving an overall feel as to the viability of a technique is just as useful as giving precise results in one axis of measurement. For example, a new data compression technique that obtains improved compression effectiveness may be of considerable interest, but the excitement would be greatly tempered if the computational costs and memory requirements mean that in practice it can only be applied to small files.

Measurement is rarely straightforward. Even simple cases present issues, such as startup costs and questions such as whether it makes sense to average costs over widely varying inputs. A common error is to report reductions in size and gains in speed, but to fail to note that they could not be achieved at the same time.

Another common error is to introduce a large number of variables, then fail to determine which are responsible for the observed performance. Fixing key variables while exploring others is essential for thorough analysis of behavior. However, be aware that variables may be correlated with each other; for example, considering the example in the previous section, fixing the size of the data set while varying the number of machines may lead to meaningless results.

A key issue is that any training must be separated from testing. It is enticing to play around with your implementation until you are sure it is properly tuned, and then report a "best" run and claim it as evidence of success; but in a production environment such settings might be impossible to determine. In contrast, if tuning or training on one set of data leads to excellent performance on another, it is clear that the results are indeed strong. Even better is if a wide range of training data gives rise to consistent and stable parameter settings. That is, the more independent cross-checks that can be performed, the more robust the claims. Conversely, results from a single data set should be treated with suspicion – and if there is any doubt about replicability, statistical tests should be applied to the output of multiple independent experiments, and confidence estimates reported to lend credence to claimed relativities.

Finally, it is perhaps worth commenting that it can also be valuable to carry out experimentation on a tractable rather than industrial scale, or using assessment methodologies that have known flaws but still provide some useful guidance. Not everyone has the resources to operate – referring to our distributed text querying case study – a network of dozens of computers and terabytes of data.

Reporting. A final aspect of measurement is considering what to report. For example, what units will convey the most general information? How might the numbers be standardized across different data sets to eliminate unimportant information? And are they presented as graphs, or tables, or both? This aspect of experimental design is beyond the scope of this paper, and the reader is instead referred to the advice given by, for example, Johnson [2002], and Zobel [2004].

5 Distributed Text Querying

We now return to our case study: distributed text retrieval. We suppose that there are k processors, that the data is being split k ways, and that the data is sufficiently voluminous that a k-way split is sensible on the target hardware.

In a text retrieval system, queries are sets of words or phrases, and the records being searched are unstructured. For example, in a web search engine, a large number of web pages are indexed, and users supply queries typically containing just a few words. To answer a query, the retrieval system identifies the r documents in the collection that are assigned the highest scores by a similarity heuristic. In web applications $r = 10$ or perhaps 100, and in other document search environments $r = 1{,}000$ is a reasonable upper limit. In both situations, the system is implemented using an *inverted index*, consisting of a *vocabulary*, and a set of *inverted lists* [Witten et al., 1999].

Two different types of data partitioning have been proposed for text searching. In a *document-partitioned* index, each server contains an index for a fraction of the documents, and can answer queries for that subset of the documents. Queries for the collection as a whole are only answered when all servers have computed their top r answers, at which time the top r of those rk answers can be identified by the receptionist. Document-partitioned systems have been described by, amongst others, Harman et al. [1991], Tomasic and García-Molina [1993], and [Cahoon et al., 2000]. Google uses both document-partitioning and replication [Barroso et al., 2003].

In an *index-partitioned* index, each server contains the full index information for a subset of the terms. Queries for the collection as a whole can only be answered when all servers that store information for query terms have returned the corresponding inverted lists to the receptionist. Index-partitioned indexing has been considered by, among others, Jeong and Omiecinski [1995], Ribeiro-Neto and Barbosa [1998], and Badue et al. [2001]. In effect, an index-partitioned system uses the additional computers as data stores only,

Table 1. Comparison of costs associated with document-partitioned text retrieval and index-partitioned text retrieval, when a query of q terms is processed with a k-way data partition, to determine a ranked list of r answers. Note that q is assumed to be less than k. Quantity I is the sum of the lengths of the inverted lists for the query terms, counted in pointers.

Performance indicator	Monolithic system	Index partitioned	Document partitioned
Number of servers active on query	1	q	k
Per processor			
Disk seeks and transfers	q	1	q
Index volume transferred from disk	I	I/q	I/k
Number of documents scored	r	0	r
Plus			
Computation load at receptionist	n/a	$I + r$	kr
Network volume	n/a	I	kr
Total cost	$I + q + r$	$I + q + r$	$I + kq + kr$

rather than as auxiliary computation devices. In the event of two terms being stored on the same machine, local operations can take place, but for large text searching systems the usual relationship is $k \gg q$, and only one term per processor is active in any given query.

Each of the alternatives has disadvantages. In a document-partitioned system, each query is executed in full on each of the machines, including the disk seeks to retrieve inverted lists. Over the k processors, a query of q terms involves kq seeks and data transfers. Moreover, if the top-ranking r documents for the whole collection are to be correctly determined, each of the subcollections must also identify its top r documents. In total, more computation is performed than in a monolithic system. Conversely, in an index-partitioned system, all of the computation is undertaken on the receptionist, which is then a potential bottleneck.

Table 1 summarizes the relative performance of document- and index-partitioned systems, and compares them to a non-partitioned system (assuming it to be feasible) for the same volume of data. In a non-partitioned system, there is one seek per query term, and a total computation load dominated by the processing of I pointers, and then extracting the top r answers. Note that, in practice, I is directly proportional to the volume of indexed data.

An interesting aspect of performance not directly captured in the table is elapsed time per query, which is best approximated as the sum of the per processor section of the table, plus the receptionist cost. In the case of the index-partitioned system, the sum is proportional to $I + q + r$ still, as the receptionist must collate all inverted lists to determine the final answer. On the other hand, for a document-partitioned system, the elapsed sum time is proportional to $I/k + q + kr$, and it is clear that the elapsed time will be less, since $r \ll I$ for a typical query.

Table 1 suggests that index-partitioning is more *scalable* than document-partitioning, because the per-query cost using the latter is dependent on k. In this argument, as the data is split over more and more machines, the drag associated with document-partitioning becomes greater, and index-partitioning is more efficient.

However, we observed above that partitioning should only be used when the volume of data exceeds the capacity of one machine. That is, there is a relationship between I and k that must be allowed for, and any "scaling up" discussion must take account of the fact that doubling the number of processors k is only required when the volume of data being manipulated doubles, and hence when the volume of data I per query is doubled. Thus the bottom line of Table 1 shows that both document- and index-partitioned text retrieval costs can be expected to scale almost linearly with data volume, and hence with the number of processors.

Elapsed time per query suggests another perspective. Since I grows with data volume, increasing the number of processors is of little benefit to index-partitioning, as the receptionist must become a bottleneck. In contrast, for document-partitioning addition of further processors increases total costs but can reduce elapsed time.

6 The Challenge

We recently developed a new *pipelined* distributed query evaluation method, and sought to compare it to the document- and term-partitioning approaches. The new method is a variant of index-partitioning, with the bottleneck at the receptionist circumvented by transferring queries amongst servers. Each query still has elapsed time roughly proportional to I, compared to roughly I/k for document-partitioning, but k queries can be processed in about the same elapsed time as can k queries with document-partitioning. Thus, intuitively, individual elapsed times might be higher but throughput should be similar. We also expected pipelining to scale better with additional data and processors due to the elimination of some of the per-processor costs.

But how to evaluate relative performance experimentally? In the context of the criteria identified in Section 4, the *baselines* are clear. We can regard pipelining as successful if the trend is to better throughput and response time than document- or index-partitioning. Regarding *software*, we developed all of the necessary code in-house, and the same libraries underpin our implementations of all three approaches. The result is a full-scale search engine, and even with just one standard desktop workstation, the monolithic implementation can process 5–50 queries per second on 100 GB of data. Regarding *data*, artificial sources would clearly be inappropriate, and would lead to unrealistic results. Fortunately, large volumes of real web data are available, and we made use of 100 GB of text from the TREC project [Bailey et al., 2003], and some millions of queries from the logs of search engines such as Excite. We are not comparing retrieval effectiveness in these experiments, so have no need for query sets that have matching relevance judgements. Whether or not 100 GB of data is sufficient is arguable, but use of more would imply a significant escalation of costs, both for data acquisition, and for experimental hardware.

Measurement, in our context, is far from straightforward. We wish to investigate scalability as the volume of data and the number of processors is increased, and must also consider the number of simultaneous users, which are supported in different ways in the different approaches.

One important facet of our experiments was that we removed start-up effects, by measuring the elapsed time for 10,000 queries; then some time later measuring the elapsed time for 20,000 queries; and then finally attributing the difference in elapsed time to the second tranche of 10,000 queries. We also experimented carefully with intra-query parallelism, allowing multiple execution threads to be simultaneously active.

In terms of *reporting*, we used units "GB × queries/machines × seconds", where "GB" is the volume of indexed data and "seconds" is elapsed time measured over a large set of queries. In these units, a low number corresponds to inefficient use of machines. The measure provides an indication of whether a system scales with number of machines and with data volume. It does not show absolute throughput ("queries/seconds"), though this can be deduced; and nor does it provide an indication of averaged elapsed time per query, which needs to be measured separately.

Some previous work in the area of distributed text retrieval is unconvincing because of failings with respect to these issues. One paper, for example, extrapolates results from a small number of processors and 160 MB of data, to 1 TB of data – based on synthetic documents and synthetic 10-term queries. In several papers, only small numbers of queries are used to compare approaches; however, since the different methods cache re-used data in different ways, the results cannot be applied to a system with an aggregate non-trivial volume of memory. In many cases, the volume of data is unrealistically small; given that the amount of disk activity is one key discriminator between the approaches, a small data set that resides in memory is uninformative.

More subtly, in many of the past papers the power of distribution was demonstrated by choosing a fixed-size data set and increasing the number of machines. It should be clear from the discussion above that little can be learnt from such an experiment. If the volume of data is well within the capacity of a single machine, spreading it among many machines does no more than allocate additional memory and disk – strategies that would also improve performance on a single machine. Bottlenecks in the system are not revealed, nor is there evidence of scaling. More worrying is that in only a few of these papers is there evidence that queries were allowed to proceed in parallel; in many cases, the measurement was of sequential query processing, an uninteresting task in a distributed environment. Our pipelined method, for example, would perform poorly in such a context, despite higher potential for scaling with data volumes and with number of servers than is offered by other approaches.

7 Summary

This article has, in no small part, arisen by our being asked to read very many papers in which experimentation has been neglected, or handled poorly. Good experimentation can be tedious, and expensive to mount; but is the ultimate test of our science – and of the usefulness of our ideas. As a consequence, we should not hesitate to undertake careful experimentation, and as readers (and referees) should expect that claims of usefulness will be empirically defended by rigorous and plausible experiments.

Having said that, out final observation is that experimentation is extraordinarily hard to do well, but very rewarding when accomplished. Our investigation into distributed searching was criticized by the referees as being on too little data and using insufficient machines, and the paper was rejected. Our challenge now is to design and execute further experiments that do pass the twin tests of rigor and persuasion.

Acknowledgement. We thank Ricardo Baeza-Yates (University of Chile) and William Webber (RMIT University) for their participation in the development and measurement of pipelined distributed retrieval. Bruce Croft (University of Massachusetts) also provided helpful input. This work was supported by an RMIT VRII grant, by the Australian Research Council, and by the ARC Center for Perceptive and Intelligent Machines in Complex Environments.

References

C. Badue, R. Baeza-Yates, B. Ribeiro-Neto, and N. Ziviani. Distributed query processing using partitioned inverted files. In G. Navarro, editor, *Proc. Symp. String Processing and Information Retrieval*, pages 10–20, Laguna de San Rafael, Chile, Nov. 2001.

P. Bailey, N. Craswell, and D. Hawking. Engineering a multi-purpose test collection for web retrieval experiments. *Information Processing & Management*, 39(6): 853–871, 2003.

L. A. Barroso, J. Dean, and U. Hölzle. Web search for a planet: The Google cluster architecture. *IEEE Micro*, 23(2): 22–28, Mar. 2003.

F. Cacheda, V. Plachouras, and I. Ounis. Performance analysis of distributed architectures to index one terabyte of text. In S. McDonald and J. Tait, editors, *Proc. 26th European Conference on IR Research*, volume 2997 of *Lecture Notes in Computer Science*, pages 394–408, Sunderland, UK, Apr. 2004. Springer.

B. Cahoon, K. S. McKinley, and Z. Lu. Evaluating the performance of distributed architectures for information retrieval using a variety of workloads. *ACM Transactions on Information Systems*, 18(1): 1–43, Jan. 2000.

D. Harman, W. McCoy, R. Toense, and G. Candela. Prototyping a distributed information retrieval system using statistical ranking. *Information Processing & Management*, 27(5): 449–460, 1991.

B.-S. Jeong and E. Omiecinski. Inverted file partitioning schemes in multiple disk systems. *IEEE Transactions on Parallel and Distributed Systems*, 6(2): 142–153, 1995.

D. S. Johnson. A theoretician's guide to the experimental analysis of algorithms. In M. Goldwasser, D. S. Johnson, and C. C. McGeoch, editors, *Proceedings of the 5th and 6th DIMACS Implementation Challenges*, Providence, 2002. American Mathematical Society.

B. A. Ribeiro-Neto and R. R. Barbosa. Query performance for tightly coupled distributed digital libraries. In *Proc. 3rd ACM Conference on Digital Libraries*, pages 182–190. ACM Press, New York, June 1998.

W. F. Tichy. Should computer scientists experiment more? *IEEE Computer*, 31 (5):32–40, May 1998.

W. F. Tichy, P. Lukowicz, L. Prechelt, and E. A. Heinz. Experimental evaluation in computer science: a quantitative study. *J. Systems and Software*, 28 (1): 9–18, Jan. 1995.

A. Tomasic and H. García-Molina. Performance of inverted indices in shared-nothing distributed text document information retrieval systems. In M. J. Carey and P. Valduriez, editors, *Proc. 2nd International Conference On Parallel and Distributed Information Systems*, pages 8–17, Los Alamitos, CA, Jan. 1993. IEEE Computer Society Press.

H. E. Williams and J. Zobel. Compressing integers for fast file access. *The Computer Journal*, 42 (3):193–201, 1999.

I. H. Witten, A. Moffat, and T. C. Bell. *Managing Gigabytes: Compressing and Indexing Documents and Images*. Morgan Kaufmann, San Francisco, second edition, 1999.

J. Zobel. *Writing for Computer Science*. Springer-Verlag, London, second edition, 2004.

J. Zobel and A. Moffat. Adding compression to a full-text retrieval system. *Software – Practice and Experience*, 25(8):891–903, Aug. 1995.

J. Zobel, A. Moffat, and K. Ramamohanarao. Guidelines for presentation and comparison of indexing techniques. *ACM SIGMOD Record*, 25(3):10–15, Oct. 1996.

Trustworthy Computing
(Extended Abstract)

Vijay Varadharajan

Macquarie University, Australia
vijay@ics.mq.edu.au

The notion of trust has been around for many decades (if not for centuries) in different disciplines in different disguises. In particular, the concept of trust has been studied extensively in various disciplines such as psychology, philosophy, sociology as well as in technology. Yet we do not have a clear handle on this concept of trust which is increasingly becoming significant in our information economy and the Internet world. In this talk, we will take a journey through the concept of trust in the secure computing world and see how it has evolved and then raise some of the challenges and pitfalls involved in trustworthy computing.

To begin with, we will briefly discuss some of the diverse views on what trust is. From a social perspective, trust is a common phenomenon. It has been pointed out by Luhman [1] that we as humans would not be able to face the complexity of the world without resorting to trust, because trust enables us to reason sensibly about possibilities of every day life. Another notion that is generally accepted is that trust implies a risk of some sort. In the words of Deutsch [2], "one trusts when one has much to lose and little to gain". Another one of the widely quoted notions of trust arises from the classic work of Gambetta [3]: "Trust is the subjective probability by which an individual, A, expects that another individual, B, performs a given action on which its welfare depends". This definition contributes to the notion of treating trust as an opinion, an evaluation and thus a belief. Trust can also be defined from a malicious point of view. One can argue that if there is no malicious behavior in the world, then trust would no longer be a useful concept because everyone could then be trusted without exception. This can be used to categorize entities into two types for defining trust [4]: passionate entities which posses human-like free will to choose between benevolent and malicious behavior and rational entities that lack such human-like free will. From a computer science point of view, software agents and computing machines are representatives of the human owner(s) and they reflect the complex trust relationships and exhibit the behaviors of human social interactions.

Though the concept of trust is used in many contexts, precise definitions of trust are still somewhat rare. At one level, trust can be thought of in terms of relationships between a trustor (which is a subject that trusts a target entity) and a trustee (which is an entity that is being trusted). We would argue that it should be further refined to include the following: trust as the belief of honesty, competence, reliability and availability of an entity within a context of interaction and co-operation in social and technical settings. Honesty captures characteristics such as intentions and actions for intended interactions and co-operations.

X. Zhou et al. (Eds.): WISE 2004, LNCS 3306, pp. 13–16, 2004.
© Springer-Verlag Berlin Heidelberg 2004

Competence captures the ability to perform an action in a particular situation. Reliability represents the degree of ability to perform the actions correctly and fulfill the commitments faithfully. Availability indicates the proper allocation of resources that are necessary for the intended interactions and co-operations.

Let us now look at the traditional notions of trust in security.

Trust has played a foundational role in security over a quite along period of time. Perhaps the most notable one is in the development of Trusted Computer System Evaluation Criteria (TCSEC) [5] in the late 70s and early 80s. The way trust is used is in the process of convincing the observers that a system (model, design or implementation) is correct and secure. A set of ratings is defined for classification of systems and the claim is higher the level, greater the assurance that one has that the system will behave according to its specifications. Then there is the notion of "trusted" processes. These processes are trusted in that they will not do any harm even though they may violate the security policies of the system, which all the other processes are required to satisfy. This notion is still being used in secure systems particularly in the operating system context.

In the context of distributed system security, trust has also played a key role, leading to the formulation of trusted authorities involved in the management of security services. We talk about several trusted authorities such as authentication and key management authority, certification authority, access control authority and trusted third party for dispute resolution. All these authorities are "trusted" by the population of entities that use them to provide guarantees and assurance about the security information and services that they are providing. In mid 90s, the idea of trust management [6] became popular. It is fair to say this notion as it was originally proposed is limited in scope, primarily addressing the management of identity and authentication information. It is clear that two people do not trust each other on the identity alone. There are a range of other attributes and credentials that come into play. In the case of mobile agents, there have been different types of trust such as a host trusting the agent (based on a number of parameters such as who created it, who sent it and which hosts it traversed etc.) as well as the agent trusting the host to perform its execution. Recently we have introduced the notion of reflexive trust in the context of mobile agents, which is concerned with A's view of B's trust on A [7].

Another important development in the security space over the last few years has been the notion of "trusted platform". This notion of trusted platform (TCPA [8], currently known as TCG) was backed by a broad spectrum of companies including HP, Compaq, IBM, Microsoft and Intel and many others. We will discuss the notion of "trusted platform", which is a platform that "contains a hardware based subsystem devoted to maintaining trust and security between machines". A trusted platform has some "special processes", which dynamically collect and provide evidence of behaviour. These special processes themselves are "trusted" to collect evidence properly. So there is a combination of social (static) trust on the mechanisms and a behavioural (dynamic) trust based on the information collected. There are also third parties endorsing platforms which underlie the confidence that the platform can be "trusted".

More recently, we have seen the appearance of the term "trustworthy computing" in various circles in the security industry. This has helped to broaden the discussion on trust to where we started at the beginning. The questions raised in this debate include the following: Is the technology available when it is needed? Does it do what it is supposed to do? Does it offer proper protection? What can we say about the intentions and behaviour of the providers of these technologies? One such initiative is the Trustworthy Computing Initiative [9] by the Microsoft Corporation. We will briefly discuss how this initiative addresses the issue of trust.

We will conclude the talk by considering some possible directions for further research in the area of security and trustworthy computing. At the modeling level, I believe there is a need to expand the scope of the trust models, instead of the limited scope that we have seen so far in authentication and access control based trust management. For instance, the trust relationship should be able to include a set of conditions and properties that allow one or more trustors to trust trustees that they will do a set of actions or have a set of attributes. Such a general structure will enable us to investigate some emergent properties, in addition to the traditional ones such as transitivity. We have been exploring such an extended trust model that can capture some of these properties [10]. There is also a need to further develop what I call "hybrid" trust models, which bring together the so called "hard" trust (based on traditional security mechanisms) with the "soft" trust based on social control aspects such as recommendations, observations and experience. At the system level, there is a need to integrate the trust decisions and recommendations as part of the overall system decision process. For instance, they could be used to enhance the quality of security (e.g. access control) decision making. We have been doing some work in this area of combining hard and soft trust and integrating them to provide a trust enhanced security management in the context of mobile agent based Internet applications. Another opportunity lies in the area of utility maximization. Although traditionally this has been left to the business modeling processing that is outside the scope of technical model, I believe that there is potential in linking such a trust enhanced security process with maximizing utility or wealth growth in areas such as electronic commerce. Finally, in addition to expanded trust model and their integration into system architecture and business modeling, in my view, there is a need to do further research work from the user perspective side; for instance, the need to understand better users' mental models of trust relationships, thresholds and constraints. These need to be captured effectively and then translated into suitable representations that can be manipulated by computers. Without this, all our trust models and management systems will stay in the cupboards or remain in prototype form and will not be widely used.

References

1. N. Luhmann, Trust and Power. Chichester: Wiley, 1979.
2. M. Deutsch, Cooperation and Trust: Some Theoretical Notes, in Nebraska Symposium on Motivation, Nebraska University Press, 1962.
3. D. Gambetta, Trust. Oxford: Basil Blackwell, 1990.
4. A. Josang, "The right type of Trust for Distributed Systems", Proc. Of the New Security Paradigms Workshop, 1996.
5. Dept of Defense, "Trusted Computer System Evaluation Criteria", (TCSEC), DoD5200.28- STD Dec.1985.
6. M. Blaze, J. Feigenbaum and J. Lacy, "Decentralized Trust Management", IEEE Conference on Security and Privacy, 1996.
7. C. Lin, V. Varadharajan, "Trust Relationships in Mobile Agents - A Reflective Approach", International Conf. on Agent based Technologies and Systems, ATS'03, Aug. 2003.
8. TCPA, "Trusted Computing Platform Alliance", Building a Foundation of Trust in the PC, Jan. 2000, http://www.trustedcomputing.org (now known as Trusted Computing Group, https://www.trustedcomputinggroup.org/home)
9. C. Mundie et al, "Microsoft's Trustworthy Computing", White Paper, Microsoft Oct. 2002.
10. W.Zhao, V.Varadharajan, G.Bryan, "Modelling Trust Relationships in Distributed Environments, International Conference on Trust and Privacy in Digital Business, TrustBus04 (in conjunction with DEXA2004), Aug. 2004.

Towards Next Generation Web Information Retrieval

Wei-Ying Ma, Hongjiang Zhang, and Hsiao-Wuen Hon

Microsoft Research Asia

Abstract. Today search engines have become one of the most critical applications on the Web, driving many important online businesses that connect people to information. As the Web continues to grow its size with a variety of new data and penetrate into every aspect of people's life, the need for developing a more intelligent search engine is increasing. In this talk, we will briefly review the current status of search engines, and then present some of our recent works on building next generation web search technologies. Specifically, we will talk about how to extract data records from web pages using vision-based approach, and introduce new research opportunities in exploring the complementary properties between the surface Web and the deep Web to mutually facilitate the processes of web information extraction and deep web crawling. We will also present a search prototype that data-mines deep web structure to enable one-stop search of multiple online web databases.

In contrast with current web search that is essentially document-level ranking and retrieval, an old paradigm in IR for more than 25 years, we will introduce our works in building a new paradigm called object-level web search that aims to automatically discover sub-topics (or taxonomy) for any given query and put retrieved web documents into a meaningful organization. We are developing techniques to provide object-level ranking, trend analysis, and business intelligence when the search is intended to find web objects such as people, papers, conferences, and interest groups.

We will also talk about vertical search opportunities in some emerging new areas such as mobile search and media search. In addition to providing information adaptation on mobile devices, we believe location-based and context-aware search is going to be important for mobile search. We also think that by bridging physical world search to digital world search, many new user scenarios that do not yet exist on desktop search can potentially make a huge impact on the mobile Internet. For media search, we will present those new opportunities in analyzing the multi-typed interrelationship between media objects and other content such as text, hyperlinks, deep web structure, and user interactions for better semantic understanding and indexing of media objects. We will also discuss our goal of continually advancing web search to next level by applying data mining, machine learning, and knowledge discovery techniques into the process of information analysis, organization, retrieval, and visualization.

X. Zhou et al. (Eds.): WISE 2004, LNCS 3306, p. 17, 2004.
© Springer-Verlag Berlin Heidelberg 2004

Making XML an Information Modeling Language

Mengchi Liu[1], Guoren Wang[1], and Tok Wang Ling[2]

[1] School of Computer Science, Carleton University, Ottawa, Ontario, Canada, K1S 5B6

[2] School of Computing, National University of Singapore Lower Kent Ridge Road, Singapore 119260

Abstract. With the wide adoption of XML, the goal for XML has been expanded far beyond data representation and exchange over the Internet. However, XML is not an expressive language for information modeling. In this paper, we describe what is needed for an information modeling language. Then we discuss how to extend XML to make it suitable for information modeling.

1 Introduction

XML is now widely used for data representation and exchange over the Internet. Unlike HTML in which tags are mainly used to describe how to display data, XML tags describe the data so that XML data is self-describing and thus suitable for machine processing. DTD is one of the schema languages for XML documents. It is used to specify the structure of an XML document using element and attribute declarations. With the wide adoption of XML, the goal for XML has been expanded far beyond data representation and exchange. However, XML is not an expressive language for information modeling.

To deal with information modeling, classification, specialisation and generalisation are fundamental constructs [7,11,12]. Classification means to classify objects with common properties into various categories. Classification establishes an *instance-of* relationship between objects and categories. There are two kinds of classification: *single classification* and *multiple classification*. Single classification only allows an object to be a direct instance of one category. Multiple classification allows an object to be a direct instance of more than one category. Most conceptual models only allows single classification.

Specialisation means to specify a category (sub-category) as a refinement of another one (super-category). It establishes an *ISA* relationship between categories. Sub-categories inherits properties of super-categories and instances of sub-categories are indirect instances of super-categories. There are two kinds of inheritance: *single inheritance* and *multiple inheritance*. Single inheritance means that a category can only have at most one super-category while multiple inheritance means that a category can have more than one super-category. Multiple inheritance is obvious more natural but much more difficult to implement than single inheritance.

X. Zhou et al. (Eds.): WISE 2004, LNCS 3306, pp. 18–28, 2004.
© Springer-Verlag Berlin Heidelberg 2004

Generalisation is the reverse of specialisation. It means to specify a category (super-category) to be more general than a set of categories (sub-categories). A generalisation is *covering* if every instance of the super-category is also an instance of at least one sub-category. Otherwise, it is *incomplete*; that is, there exists an instance of the super-category that is not an instance of any sub-category. A generalisation is a *disjoint* if instances of sub-categories are disjoint. Otherwise, it is *overlapping*. A *partition* is a generalisation that is both complete and disjoint. It is one of the most used generalisations in information modeling [3].

Using generalisation and specialisation, we can organise categories into a category hierarchy so that information being model becomes more meaningful.

Unfortunately, XML and its schema languages do not support these important information modeling constructs. In this paper, we extend XML into an information modeling language. Since tags in XML are used to describe the data, we treat tags as categories of the data and allow data to have multiple tags to support multiple classification. The specialisation/generalisation relationships between categories are represented using extended DTD.

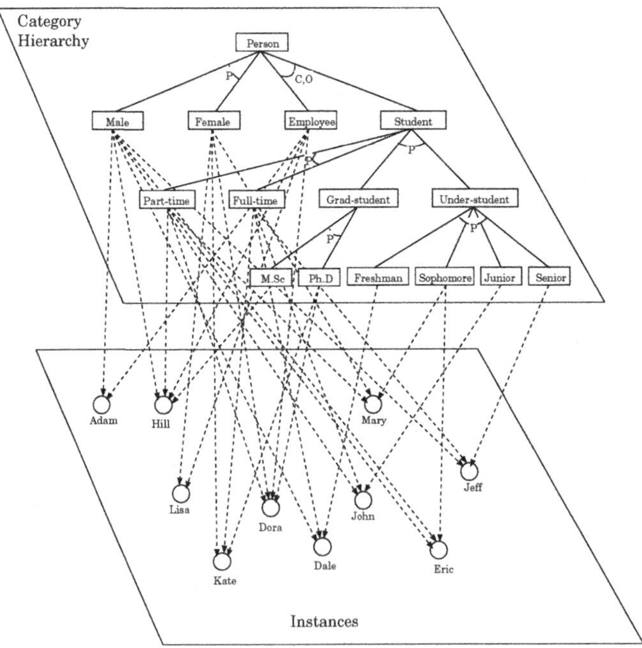

Fig. 1. Category Hierarchy Example

2 Information Modeling

Figure 1 shows a category hierarchy in the upper layer and multiple classifications from the upper layer to the lower layer. Category *Person* is partitioned into categories *Male* and *Female*, denoted graphically with *p*, and it is a covering and overlapping generalisation of *Employee* and *Student*, denoted with *c,o*.

Category *Student* is partitioned into *Full-time* and *Part-time*. It is also partitioned into *Grad-student* and *Under-student*. Category *Grad-student* is further partitioned into categories *M.Sc* and *Ph.D* while *Under-student* into categories *Freshman*, *Sophomore*, *Junior* and *Senior*.

Now consider classifications that link categories in the upper layer to objects in the lower layer. Category *Male* has direct objects *Adam, Hill, Dale, John, Eric, Jeff.* Category *Employee* has direct objects *Lisa, kate, Dora, Mary.* Their direct objects are indirect objects of category *Person.* The rest are self-explanatory.

Note that Figure 1 shows multiple classifications: *Adam* belongs to *Employee* and *Male*, *Lisa* to *Employee* and *Female*, *Kate* to *Ph.D* and *Female*, etc.

Now let us see how to represent the category hierarchy and classification in major conceptual models.

With object-oriented data models [2,4,5], we have to introduce one superclass *student* and 4 subclasses *full-time-grad-student*, *part-time-grad-student*, *full-time-under-student*, and *part-time-under-student.* If we want to further partition the students into *male-student* and *female-student*, then we have to use 8 subclasses. Obviously, the number of subclasses increases exponentially based on the number of multiple classifications. What is worse, queries based on these categories are complex to express due to the poor information modeling.

If specialisation and inheritance are considered, then it become much more complex to implement. This problem has been addressed in [1].

In a category hierarchy, a sub-category inherits all attributes and component categories of its super-categories. For example, besides its specific category *salary*, category *Employee* inherits attribute *id* and component categories *name* and *sex* from its super-category *Person.* Besides the inheritance of attribute and category, a sub-category also inherits the categories from its super-category. For example, a category *Male* and *Female* is declared in category *Person* and is inherited by its sub-categories *Employee* and *Student.* Thus, *Employee* is classified into two classes *Male* and *Female* and *Student* is classified into two classes *Male* and *Female.* Thus, category *Student* has three category declarations, from which 20 more specific classes may be inferred, for examples, *Male Grad-student*, *Part-time Under-student*, *Female Full-time Grad-student* and so on and so forth.

In a category hierarchy a sub-category inherits all attributes, categories and category declarations from its super-category. For example, sub-category *Grad-student* inherits attribute *id*, categories *Name*, *Sex* and *GPA*, and the category declarations *Male* and *Female*, *Part-time* and *Full-time.*

3 Extension of XML

In this section, we first extend *DTD* with several new element declarations. Then we extend XML with multiple tags to support multiple classifications.

Extension 1. The syntax for sub-element declaration is as follows.

<!ELEMENT sub-element ISA super-element>

The sub-element inherits elements and attributes declarations from the super-element. See Section 5 for details.

The following examples declare elements *Employee* and *Student* to be sub-elements of element *Person.*

<!ELEMENT Employee ISA Person>

<!ELEMENT Student ISA Person>

Note that the above two element declarations only specify that *Person* is an incomplete and overlapping generation of *Employee* and *Student.*

To support covering generations, we introduce the following extension.

Extension 2. The syntax for covering generalisations is as follows.

<!ELEMENT super-element COVER sub-element-list>

The following example specifies that *Person* is a covering generalisation of *Employee* and *Student.*

<!ELEMENT Person COVERS Employee, Student>

When it is combined with the declarations above, then *Person* is a covering and overlapping generation of *Employee* and *Student.*

To support disjoint and covering generalisation, we introduce the partition declaration.

Extension 3. The syntax for partition declaration is as follows.

<!ELEMENT super-element PARTITION sub-element-list>

The following are examples of partition declarations.

<!ELEMENT Person PARTITION Male, Female>

<!ELEMENT student PARTITION Part-time, Full-time>

<!ELEMENT student PARTITION Grad-student, Under-student>

Figure 2 shows the complete declarations in extended DTD for categories in Figure 1.

As discussed earlier, multiple classification allows an object to belong to more than one category without introducing most specific category. For example, *Hill* in Figure 1 belongs to both employee and Ph.D categories. In order to support multiple classification in XML, we extend XML so that an element can have more than one tag, each of which specifies a category of the element belongs to.

Extension 4. The syntax for elements in XML documents is as follows.

(1) element ::= EmptyElemTag | StartTag content EndTag
(2) StartTag ::= '<' TagNames (Attribute)* '>'
(3) EndTag ::= '</' TagNames '>'
(4) tagNames ::= Name (',' Name)*

Figure 3 shows a sample XML document that corresponds to the sample DTD in Figure 2.

```
<DOCTYPE Persons[
    <!ELEMENT Persons (Person *)>
    <!ELEMENT Person (Name, Age)>
    <!ATTLIST Person id ID #REQUIRED>
    <!ELEMENT Name (#PCDATA)>
    <!ELEMENT Age (#PCDATA)>
    <!ELEMENT Person PARTITION Male, Female>
    <!ELEMENT Person COVER Employee, Student>
    <!ELEMENT Employee (Salary)>
    <!ELEMENT Employee ISA Person>
    <!ELEMENT Salary (#PCDATA)>
    <!ELEMENT Student (GPA)>
    <!ELEMENT Student ISA person>
    <!ELEMENT Student PARTITION Part-time, Full-time>
    <!ELEMENT Student PARTITION Grad-student, Under-student>
    <!ELEMENT GPA (#PCDATA)>
    <!ELEMENT Grad-student PARTITION M.Sc, Ph.D>
    <!ELEMENT Under-student PARTITION Freshman, Sophomore, Junior, Senior>
    <!ELEMENT Male EMPTY>
    <!ELEMENT Female EMPTY>
    <!ELEMENT Part-time EMPTY>
    <!ELEMENT Full-time EMPTY>
    <!ELEMENT M.Sc EMPTY>
    <!ELEMENT Ph.D EMPTY>
    <!ELEMENT Freshman EMPTY>
    <!ELEMENT Sophomore EMPTY>
    <!ELEMENT Junior EMPTY>
    <!ELEMENT Senior EMPTY>
]>
```

Fig. 2. Extended DTD

4 Querying

In this section, we discuss how to query XML documents that confirm to the Extended DTD discussed in the previous section. We use XQuery for our examples as it has become the standard for querying and extracting data from XML documents. Also we assume the sample XML document in Figure 3 is stored in the file *sample.xml.*

Extension 5. In a query statement, a super-element can be substituted with its sub-element or its sub-categories; that is, sub-element or sub-category can appear anywhere super-element or super-category is expected and the query statement is still meaningful.

The following query finds the names of all *Employees.*

```
<Result>
    FOR $a in document("sample.xml")/Persons/Employee
    RETURN <name> $a/name/text() </name>
</Result>
```

```
<Persons>
  <Employee,Male id="Adam">
    <name> Adam </name> <age> 45 </age> <salary> 1500 </salary>
  </Employee,Male>
  <Employee,Female id="Lisa">
    <name> Lisa </name> <age> 40 </age> <salary> 3500 </salary>
  </Employee,Female>
  <Employee,M.Sc,Part-time,Male id="Hill">
    <name> Hill </name> <age> 26 </age>
    <salary> 800 </salary> <GPA> 98 </GPA>
  </Employee,M.Sc,Part-time,Male>
  <Ph.D,Full-time,Female id="Kate">
    <name> Kate </name> <age> 31 </age> <GPA> 95 </GPA>
  </Ph.D,Full-time,Female>
  <Employee,Ph.D,Part-time,Female id="Dora">
    <name> Dora </name> <age> 33 </age>
    <salary> 800 </salary> <GPA> 97 </GPA>
  </Employee,Ph.D,Part-time,Female>
  <Freshman,Full-time,Male id="Dale">
    <name> Dale </name> <age> 18 </age> <GPA> 94 </GPA>
  </Freshman,Full-time,Male>
  <Sophomore,Part-time,Female id="Mary">
    <name> Mary </name> <age> 19 </age> <GPA> 89 </GPA>
  </Sophomore,Part-time,Female>
  <Junior,Full-time,Male id="John">
    <name> John </name> <age> 20 </age> <GPA> 92 </GPA>
  </Junior,Full-time,Male>
</Persons>
```

Fig. 3. Sample XML document

According to the extended DTD in Figure 1, element *Persons* consists of 0 or more *Person* elements. Thus, the path expression */Persons/Person* is meaningful. According to Extension 5, the path expression */Persons/Employee* is also meaningful since *Employee* is sub-element of *Person* and therefore can substitute *Person*.

Because we extend tag name to support multiple classification, the above path expression */Persons/Employee* should be executed in a way different from the usual way. It should work as follows.

(1) If the name of root element does not match *Persons*, then the result is empty.
(2) Otherwise, for each component element or the root, if *Employee* is contained in the tag of the element, then the element is one of the result of the path expression.

Therefore, the result of the query is as follows.

```
<Result>
  <Name> Adam </Name>
```

```
    <Name> Lisa </Name>
    <Name> Hill </Name>
    <Name> Dora </Name>
</Result>
```

The following query finds the names of all *full-time* students.

```
<Result>
    FOR $a in document("sample.xml")/Persons/Full-time
    RETURN <name>$a/name/text() </name>
</Result>
```

Sometimes, users want to find information of an element as well as all its sub-elements. For example, find information of all *Persons* including *Person*, *Student*, *Employee*, *Grad-student*, *Male*, *Freshman*, etc. The query can be represented as union of several queries similar to the first query above, but it is not concise and has no good performance. To address this problem, we introduce the notion of *inclusive element.*

Extension 6. In a query statement, an inclusive element, denoted by $E\downarrow$, represents element E and all its sub-elements.

The following query finds all students' names:

```
<Student>
    FOR $a in document("sample.xml")/Persons/Student↓
    RETURN <name> $a/name/text() </name>
</Student>
```

In the above query statement, the path query *"/Persons/Student↓"* is used to find the set of *Student* elements and its sub-elements *Grad-student*, *Under-student*, etc.

In the extended XML documents, we introduce set of tag names to support multiple classification. Similarly, we extend XQuery so that set of element names can be used to support more powerful querying ability.

Extension 7. In a query statement, a set of element names can appear anywhere a single element is expected in XQuery.

The following query finds the names of all female part-time student.

```
<Student>
    FOR $a in document("sample.xml")/Persons/(Female,Part-time)
    RETURN <name> $a/name/text() </name>
</Student>
```

In an element hierarchy, there is an *overlapping* constraint between sub-elements. For example, *Employee* is overlapping with *Student* in Figure 1. Thus, some objects belong to both *Employee* and *Student*. The following query finds such objects.

```
<Result>
    FOR $a in document("sample.xml")/Persons/(Employee,Student)
    RETURN <name> $a/name/text() </name>
</Result>
```

Note that some queries may be illegal with respect to the extended DTD. Due to space limitation, we omit this part in this paper.

5 Formalization

In this section, we first discuss how to formalize the extended DTD, and then discuss how to check whether or not an XML document conforms to an extended DTD; that is, validation of semantics.

We assume the existence of the following notations.

(1) Notations for attributes: $attr_i$ is used to represent an attribute; ai_i for an attribute instance; $\mathcal{AN}$ for the set of all attribute names; $\mathcal{AT}$ for the set of built-in attribute types;
(2) Notations for elements: se_i is used for simple element; ce_i for complex element; sei_i for simple element instance; cei_i for complex element instance; $\mathcal{EN}$ for the set of element names; $\mathcal{ET}$ is used to represent the set of element types;
(3) Notations for document schemas and instances: *dsch* is used for a document schema; *dins* for document instance; $\mathcal{E}$ for the set of elements; $\mathcal{EI}$ for the set of element instances; $\mathcal{A}$ for the set of attributes; $\mathcal{AI}$ for the set of attribute instances; $\mathcal{V}(ae)$ for the set of values of attribute or simple element *ae*;
(4) Notations for functions: $f_t(val)$ is used for the function returns the type of the value *val*; $f_{se}(ce)$ for the function which returns the set of sub-elements of the element *ce*; $f_{len}(s)$ for the function which returns the length of the set or ordered set *s*;

We first define formally basic concepts for element hierarchy, including *schema*, *complex element*, *simple element*, *attribute*, *document instance*, *complex element instance*, *simple element instance*, and *attribute instance*.

Definition 1. An attribute *attr* is defined as a 3-tuple *attr* = <*attr_name*, *attr_type*, *elem*>, where *attr_name*$\in\mathcal{AN}$ is an attribute name, *attr_type*$\in\mathcal{AT}$ is an attribute type, *elem* is used to specify the element attribute *attr* belongs to.

Definition 2. A simple element *se* is defined as a 3-tuple *se* = <*elem_name*, *elem_type*, *attrs*>, where *elem_name*$\in\mathcal{EN}$ is an element name; *elem_type*$\in\mathcal{ET}$ is the type of the simple element *se*; *attrs* is a set of attributes of the simple element *se*;

Definition 3. A partition is defined as a set of element names.

Definition 4. A complex element *ce* is defined as a 6-tuple *ce* = <*elem_name*, *super_elems*, *constraint*, *partitions*, *component_elems*, *attrs*>, where *elem_name*$\in\mathcal{EN}$ is the name of the complex element; *super_elems*$\subseteq\mathcal{E}$ is an ordered set consisting of the direct super-elements of the element *ce*; *constraint* is used to represent the constraint over the element hierarchy and there are four kinds of constraints: *covering* and *overlapping*, *covering* and *disjoint*, *uncovering* and overlapping, and *uncovering* and *disjoint*; *partitions* is a set of partitions; *component_elems*$\subseteq\mathcal{E}$ is an ordered set consisting of the *component elements* of the element *ce*; and *attrs* is a set of attributes of the element *ce*;

Definition 5. A schema *dsch* is defined as a 4-tuple *dsch* = <*root*, *ces*, *ses*, *attrs*>, where *root*$\in\mathcal{E}$ is the root element, *ces* $\subseteq\mathcal{E}$ is the set of all complex elements, *ses* $\subseteq\mathcal{E}$ is the set of all simple elements and *attrs* $\subseteq\mathcal{A}$ is the set of all attributes.

Definition 6. An attribute instance *ai* is defined as a 3-tuple *ai* = <*attr_name*, *attr_value*, *elem_instance*>, where *attr_name*$\in\mathcal{AN}$ is the name of the attribute, *attr_value*$\in\mathcal{V}$(*attr_name*) is the value of the attribute, *elem_instance* is the element instance *ai* belongs to.

Definition 7. A simple element instance *sei* is defined as a 3-tuple *sei* = <*elem_name,elem_value,attr_instances*>, where *elem_name*$\in\mathcal{EN}$ is the name of the simple element, *elem_value*$\in\mathcal{V}$(*elem_name*) is the value of the simple element *sei* and *attr_instances* $\in\mathcal{AI}$ is the set of attribute instances of the simple element *sei*.

Definition 8. A complex element instance *cei* is defined as a 3-tuple *cei* = <*elem_name*, *elem_instances*, *attr_instances*>, where *elem_name*$\in\mathcal{EN}$ is the name of the complex element defined as; *elem_instances*$\subseteq\mathcal{EI}$ is the ordered set of the sub-elements of the complex element *cei*, and the sub-elements may be either complex or simple; *attr_instances*$\subseteq\mathcal{AI}$ is the set of attribute instances of the complex element *cei*.

Definition 9. A document instance *dins* is defined as a 4-tuple *dins* = <*root*, *ceis*, *seis*, *ais*>, where *root*$\in\mathcal{EI}$ is the instance of a root element, *ceis*$\subseteq\mathcal{EI}$ is the set of all complex element instances, *seis*$\subseteq\mathcal{EI}$ is the set of all simple element instances and *ais*$\subseteq\mathcal{AI}$ is the set of all attribute instances.

Next, we discuss how to check whether or not a document instance conforms to a schema; that is, validation of semantics. Assume that *dsch* = <*root*, *ces*, *ses*, *attrs*> is an *Extended DTD* schema and *dins*=<*root,ceis,seis,ais*> is a document instance. The validation rules of semantics to support element hierarchy are defined as follows.

Rule 1. Let *attr*$\in$*dsch.attrs* be an attribute of an *Extended DTD* schema and *ai*$\in$*dins.ais* be an instance of an attribute. The instance *ai* is valid with respect to attribute *attr*, denoted by *attr*$\models$*ai*, if and only if

(1) the attribute name of the instance *ai* conforms to the name of the attribute *attr*; that is, *ai.attr_name* = *attr.attr_name*;
(2) the type of value of the instance *ai* conforms to the type of the attribute *attr*; that is, f_t(*ai.attr_value*) = *attr.attr_type*;
(3) the parent element name of the instance *ai* conforms to the parent element name of the attribute *attr*; that is, *ai.elem_instance.elem_name* = *attr.elem.elem_name* or *ai.elem_instance.elem_name* is the sub-element of *attr.elem.elem_name*;

Rule 2. Let *se*$\in$*dsch.ses* be an simple element of an *Extended DTD* schema and *sei*$\in$*dins.seis* an simple element instance. The instance *sei* is valid with respect with the simple element *se*, denoted by *se*$\models$*ssei*, if and only if

(1) the element name of the instance *sei* conforms to the name of the simple element *se*; that is, *sei.elem_name* = *se.attr_name*;
(2) the type of value of the instance *sei* conforms to the type of the simple element *se*; that is, f_t(*sei.elem_value*) = *se.attr_type*; and

(3) *sei.attr_instances* is valid with respect with *se*, denoted by $se \models sei.attr\_instances$; that is, $(\forall x)(x \in sei.attr\_instances)((\exists y)(y \in se.attrs \wedge y \models x))$

Rule 3. Let $\{ce_1, ce_2, ..., ce_n\} \subseteq dsch.ces$ be an complex element of an *Extended DTD* schema and $cei \in dins.ceis$ an complex element instance. The The instance *cei* is valid with respect with the complex element *ce*, denoted by $\{ce_1, ce_2, ..., ce_n\} \models cei$, if and only if

(1) For any pairwise $ce_i, ce_j \in \{ce_1, ce_2, ..., ce_n\}$ and $i \neq j$, there is an *overlapping* constraint applied over one of the common super-elements of ce_i and ce_j.
(2) The element name of the instance *cei* must match the set of the names of the complex elements $\{ce_1, ce_2, ..., ce_n\}$, that is,
   1. cei.elem_name = $\{ce_1$.elem_name, ce_2.elem_name, ..., ce_n.elem_name$\}$
(3) The elem_instances of the complex element instance *cei* must conform to the closure component elements of the complex elements $\{ce_1, ce_2, ..., ce_n\}$ one by one; that is,
   1. Assume that $C = ce_1$.component_ele*ms*$^* \cup ... \cup ce_n$.component_ele-*ms**. And ce_k.*component_elems** can be computed as follows.
      a) For (i=1; i$\leq f_{len}(ce_k$.super_elems)) $tmp = tmp \cup super\_elems[i].component\_elems^*$;
      b) For (i=1; i$\leq f_{len}(ce_k$.partitions)) $tmp = tmp \cup partitions[i].component\_elems^*$;
      c) $tmp = tmp \cup ce_i.component\_elems$;
      d) $ce_i.component\_elems^* = tmp$.
   2. $f_{len}($ cei.elem_instances $) = f_{len}(C)$ and
   3. For (i=1; i$\leq f_{len}$(cei.elem_instances)) C[i]$\models$cei.ele_instances[i]
(4) *cei.attr_instances* is valid with respect with $\{ce_1, ce_2, ..., ce_n\}$, denoted by $\{ce_1, ce_2, ..., ce_n\} \models cei.attr\_instances$; that is, $(\forall$ x)(x $\in$ cei.attr_instances) $((\exists y)(y \in (ce_1.attrs^* \cup ... \cup ce_n.attrs^*) \wedge y \models x))$.
   The computation of $ce_k.attrs^*$ is similar to $ce_k.component\_elems^*$.

Rule 4. Let *dsch*= *<root,ces,ses,attrs>* be an *Extended DTD* schema and *dins*=*<root,ceis,seis,ais>* be a document instance. The document instance *dins* is valid with respect with the schema *dsch* if and only if $dsch.root \models dins.root$.

6 Conclusions

With the wide adoption of XML technologies, more sophisticated needs arise, such as information modeling, manipulation, integration, etc. In this paper, we first discussed what is needed for information modeling. We then extended XML by incorporating several powerful information modeling constructs. We also extended XQuery to support queries based on various categories. We formalized our extensions and discussed validation of XML documents.

We would like to investigate how to manipulate extended XML documents. One of main problems is object migration. There has been a lot of work done for object-oriented data models so far [6,8,9,10]. We will investigate this problem in the context of the extended XML. Also, we would like to find out whether the extended XML helps in the XML document integration.

References

1. E. Bertino and G. Guerrini. Objects with Multiple Most Specific Classes. In *Proceedings of the 9th European Conference (ECOOP'95)*, pages 102–126, Aarhus, Denmark, 1995.
2. R. G. G. Cattell, editor. *The Object Database Standard: ODMG-93, Release 1.2.* Morgan Kaufmann, Los Altos, CA, 1996.
3. C. Gómez and A. Olivé. Evolving partitions in conceptual schemas in the uml. In *Proceedings of the 14th Conference On Advanced Information Systems Engineering*, pages 467–483, Toronto, Ontario, Canada, May 2002. Springer.
4. W. Kim. *Introduction to Object-Oriented Databases.* The MIT Press, Cambridge, MA, 1990.
5. C. Lecluse and P. Richard. The O_2 Database Programming Language. In *Proceedings of the International Conference on Very Large Data Bases*, pages 411–422, Amsterdam, The Netherlands, 1989. Morgan Kaufmann.
6. T. Ling and P. Teo. Object migration in isa hierarchies. In *Proceedings of the 4th International Conference on Database Systems for Advanced Applications*, pages 292–299, Singapore, 1995. World Scientific.
7. R. Motschnig-Pitrik and J. Mylopoulos. Classes and Instances. *International Journal of Intelligent and Cooperative Information Systems*, 1(1):61–92, 1992.
8. E. Odberg. Category classes: Flexible classification and evolution in object-oriented databases. In *Proceedings of the 6th Conference On Advanced Information Systems Engineering*, pages 406–420, Utrecht, The Netherlands, June 1994. Springer.
9. A. Olivé, D. Costal, and M. Sancho. Entity evolution in isa hierarchies. In *Proceedings of the 18th International Conference on Conceptual Modeling*, pages 62–80, Paris, France, 1999. Springer.
10. Z. Peng and Kambayashi Y. Deputy mechanisms for object-oriented databases. In *Proceedings of the 4th International Conference on Database Systems for Advanced Applications*, pages 333–340, Taipei, Taiwan, 1995. IEEE Computer Society.
11. J. M. Smith and D. C. P. Smith. Database Abstraction: Aggregation and Generalization. *ACM Trans. on Database Systems*, 2(2):105–133, 1977.
12. M. Snoeck and G. Dedene. Generalization/specialization and role in object. *Data and Knowledge Engineering*, 19(2):171–195, 1996.

Web Information Exchange Diagrams for UML

David Lowe and Rachatrin Tongrungrojana

University of Technology, Sydney
PO Box 123 Broadway NSW 2007, Australia
{david.lowe, rachatrin.tongrungrojana}@uts.edu.au

Abstract. A crucial aspect in the development of Web systems is the ability to ensure that the relationships between the system design and the business models, processes and workflows are understood. By representing these relationships and defining transformations between them we support the joint evolution business and web systems and ensure their compatibility and optimisation. In previous work we have developed and evaluated a model (called WIED) which creates this bridge. The existing model is generic, but the notations and transformations have been based on mappings between specific models - namely the e^3-value and WebML models. In this paper we illustrate how the WIED model can also be represented using a UML-compliant notation.

1 Introduction

In the span of a decade, the Web has transformed entire industries and entered the mass culture. It has created new expectations on ease of access, freshness, and relevance of information accessed via the Internet. Online Web-enabled systems have become increasingly crucial to both business success and to the provision of social and government services [1]. These systems are much more complex than simple web sites containing static pages. They typically employ Web technologies to provide a complex distributed front-end combined with high-performance back-end software systems that integrate new components with existing legacy applications to support critical business processes [2,1].

One crucial aspect in the development of these complex systems is the ability to understand the relationships between system designs and business models, processes and workflows. (Good discussions in regard to this issue can be found in [3,4,5]). Further, by representing these relationships and defining transformations between them we potentially support the joint evolution of business and web systems and ensure their compatibility and optimization [6].

In response we have proposed an information model – the Web Information Exchange Diagram (WIED). This concept has been evaluated by a series of empirical studies and the results have provided evidence that WIED is a useful tool in supporting an understanding of ways in which business models affect the information design, but also ways in which the systems designs and changes to these designs affect the business model. This work has been published in [7,8,9].

The design of WIED is based around an abstract model which has been formalized as an XML DTD (Document Type Definition). In our previous work we

X. Zhou et al. (Eds.): WISE 2004, LNCS 3306, pp. 29–40, 2004.
© Springer-Verlag Berlin Heidelberg 2004

showed how this model could be operationalized as a notation and associated diagram that are consistent with WebML [10]. We also developed a set of transformations between e^3-value (a business modelling notation [11]) and WIED, and then between WIED and WebML [12]. These related models were chosen as typical exemplars of business models and detailed design models rather than because of any particular strength these models may have. This has allowed us to evaluate the approach and ensure its effectiveness in linking typical modelling notations. We do however recognise that other modelling languages are also widely used - particularly UML.

In this paper we look at how the formal WIED model can be mapped into the UML notation, and show that the result is a new UML diagram that can capture the relationship between high-level business models and processes, and lower level information designs. We begin by providing, in the next section, a background of the development of WIED, followed by a brief overview of WIED. We then go on to look at the details of how WIED maps into UML. Following that we discuss how the WIED (UML-compliant) can be linked to other UML-based modelling approaches. We finish the paper with conclusions and present some ideas for further work.

2 Background

2.1 Web System Modeling

As discussed above, over the last decade we have seen the rapid emergence of systems that utilize web technologies to support the integration of complex functionality with rich information handling. This emergence has been accompanied by the development of modelling languages capable of capturing some – though not all – of the aspects of these systems. To model these systems there are a number of elements that we would like to represent. At the highest level of abstraction we have a business model showing the essential aspects (such as the strategic intent) of the way of doing business. Often this will be represented in terms of the value exchange between the organization and other entities that enable the organization to achieve its business goals. A typical example of a relevant modeling notation is the e^3-value notation [11,13]. This model focuses on the core concept of value, and expresses how business value is created, interpreted and exchanged within a multi-party stakeholder network.

Conversely, at lower levels of abstraction we have models of the detailed system design. These models typically capture design elements that have a direct correspondence to specific implementation artifacts. Functional design models are relatively well-established, with the dominant model (arguably) now UML [14]. UML can be used to model both detailed design and higher-level designs through a complex suite of diagrams that are all treated as views onto a consistent underlying model. Whilst UML is effective in terms of modelling system functionality as well as data relationships, in terms of modelling the information design the situation is somewhat less mature. Typically we wish to model not only the data (i.e. content) itself, but also the relationship between the underlying content and the user-perceived views of that content, and the interactions with those views (such as navigational aspects). Given that UML has not been as successful at modelling these aspects, there has been an emergence of a number of informational modelling approaches specifically developed for Web (or hypermedia) applications. Example approaches include RMM (Relationship Management Methodology) [15] and OOHDM (Object Oriented Hypermedia Design Methodology) [16], and more recently WebML (Web Modeling Language) [12]. These models have typically focussed on modelling at a relatively low-level and have failed to address architectural and even business process modelling issues.

In between modelling the business operations and the detailed system designs we have models of the high level system architecture that capture the functionality and information that need to exist in order to support the business value exchanges. As discussed previously, functional aspects at this level are well supported by UML. A set of UML models can be used to represent the business and operational workflows (process) of a system. Examples of this include activity diagrams for presenting the sequential flow of activities and data flow diagrams for presenting the flow of data from external entities into and within the system.

However, modelling informational aspects at this intermediate level is more problematic – particularly in terms of explicitly showing the relationships between business models and processes as well as detailed information designs. For example, UML activity diagrams focus on the representation of activities and events (which can be seen as the functional aspects of business processes [17]), but are unable to accurately capture the rich domain context that is important in understanding information relationships and flows (as distinct from data flows) that support value exchanges in business. This includes the relationships between underlying content and the user-perceived views of that content, the interactions with those views, and the ways in which information is represented and presented to the users. Interesting discussions on gaps in modelling can be found in [3].

2.2 WIED

In response to this problem, we have proposed a new modelling notation (which we call WIED - Web Information Exchange Diagram) aimed at representing information flows that occur between actors for supporting value exchanges in businesses [7,8,9]. The proposed model also represents the relationships between the underlying information and the actor interaction with the information. In effect, our model forms the bridge between business concerns and detailed information designs which we have argued is largely lacking in existing models [10].

The abstract WIED model has been formalized as an XML DTD. To illustrate the application of the model we mapped it into a custom diagram and notation that is consistent with WebML. In this context it can be considered as a companion model to the existing WebML diagrams (and hence, in our earlier work, we referred to it as WebML+).

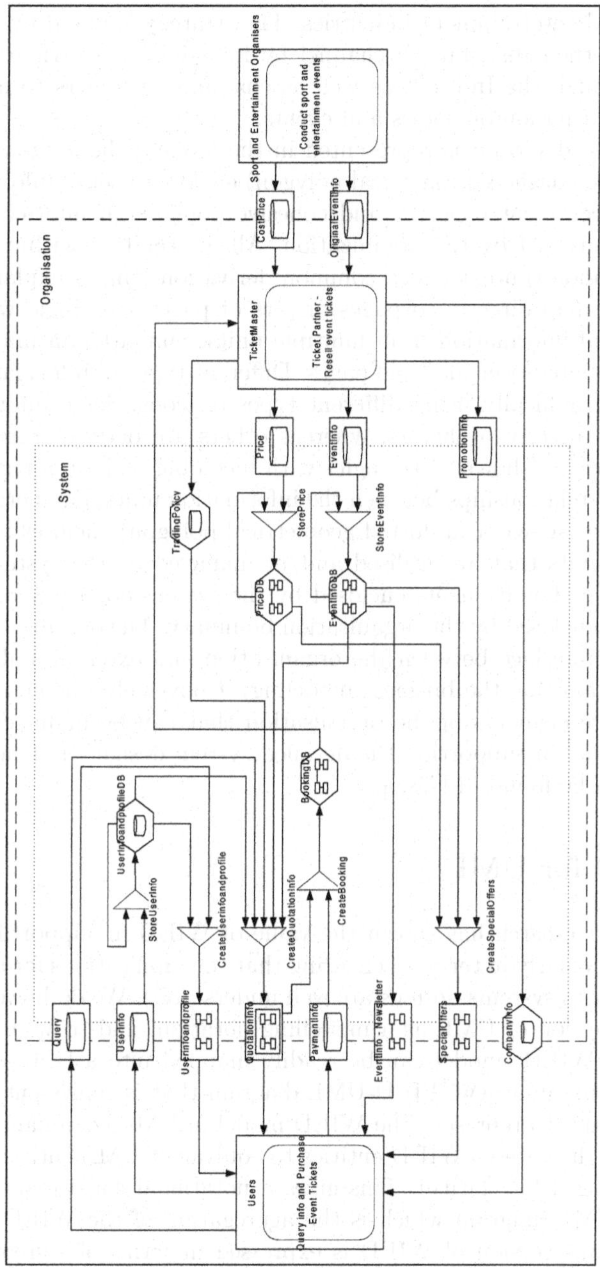

Fig. 1. Typical Web System represented using WIED

Figure 1 shows an example of a WIED model (using the WebML-compliant notation) for a hypothetical example: TicketMaster is a ticketing partner for the sports and entertainment industries. The strategy adopted by TicketMaster is to expand their distribution channel by introducing real-time transactional ticketing through the Internet as well as enabling customers to enquire about the latest information on shows and events.

Let us consider what is represented in the model. The organization boundary (shown as a dashed geometrical polygon) encloses a set of information units. These units represent coherent and cohesive domains of information that are managed or utilized by the organization. All information within a single unit shares a common context and a common derivation (this is explained shortly). They do not map directly to pages or sets of pages – a single web page may contain partial information from multiple units. Similarly, an information unit may be distributed over multiple pages. Different types of information units are represented graphically using different types of icons. Some information units are provided directly by actors, whereas others are derived from other units. These derivations (shown as triangles with incoming and outgoing arrows) capture the inter-relationships between the information units. Furthermore, the system boundary (shown as a dotted geometrical polygon) encloses only the set of information units that are utilised and/or managed by the system under consideration. (i.e. The elements enclosed by the system boundary are a subset of the elements enclosed by the organisation boundary. The organisation boundary captures the interface between the organisation and external stakeholders (i.e. crucial in supporting the business modeling). Conversely, the system boundary captures those elements of the organisation that can be managed by the system (i.e. crucial in supporting the detailed system design). Further details and examples can be found in [7,8,9].

3 WIED for UML

Our previous research has shown the value of WIED in supporting the design process (particularly in terms of ensuring that the implications for business models of changes to systems designs are well understood). We do however recognise the wide adoption of UML as a modelling notation, and so wish to show how the abstract WIED model can be readily mapped into a UML-compliant notation, resulting in a new WIED-UML diagram that is consistent with existing UML diagrams. To represent the WIED model in UML-compliant notations we need to map the various WIED entities to equivalent UML entities (which have been stereotyped for clarity). This gives a notational consistency with UML - but a new UML diagram which is the aggregation of the WIED entities. The UML-compliant version of WIED is expressed in terms of stereotypes, tagged values and constraints. Next, we present the various WIED entities represented by UML-compliant notations. In discussing the WIED UML notations we will also show the original WIED WebML notations for the purpose of demonstrating the one-to-one mapping between these notations.

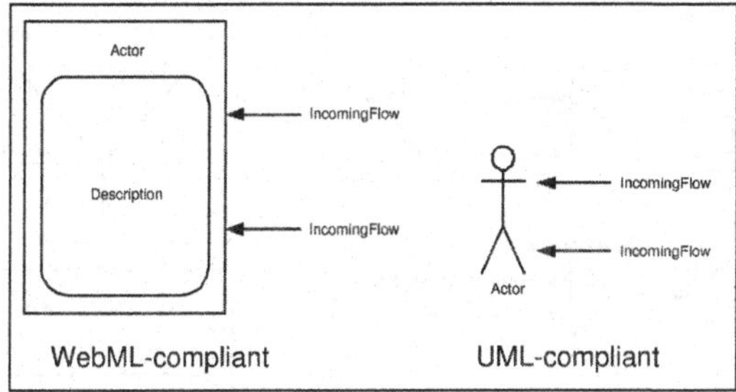

Fig. 2. Actor Units

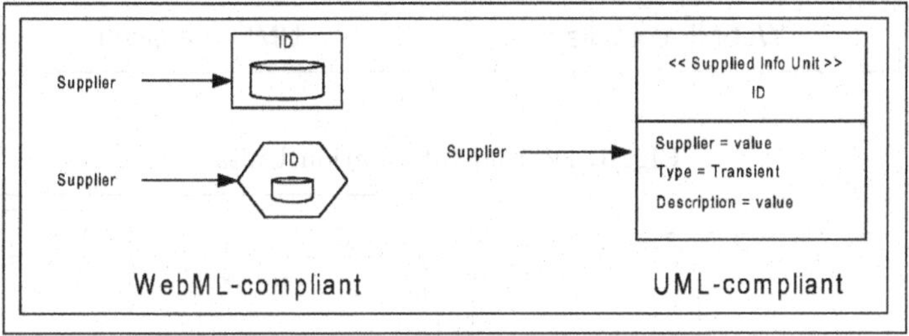

Fig. 3. Supplied Information Units

Actor Units: Actor units are defined to show the roles that the users play with respect to the system. In WIED, actor units show how users participate with information flows. Figure 2 shows actor units represented in WebML-compliant notation and UML-compliant notation.

Supplied Information Units and Derived Information Units: In general, an information unit represents a single information object in an organization business process. To represent information units using UML, classes are used since they describe the types of objects in the system and the relationships that exist between them. Two types of information units are defined in WIED: supplied information units and derived information units. A supplied information unit presents information about a single information object that is provided by a supplier actor. A stereotype "SuppliedInfoUnit" (with attributes such as supplier, type and description) is used for representing a supplied information unit (as illustrated in Figure 3). A derived information unit presents information that is derived from other information units. This derivation may ultimately be implemented as a process that generates the underlying content. To specify a derived information unit we provide both the unit itself (represented again using a stereotype: "DerivedInfoUnit") and an indication of the source of the information (represented using a transition, since a transition describes a change of an object from one state to another). This is illustrated in Figure 4.

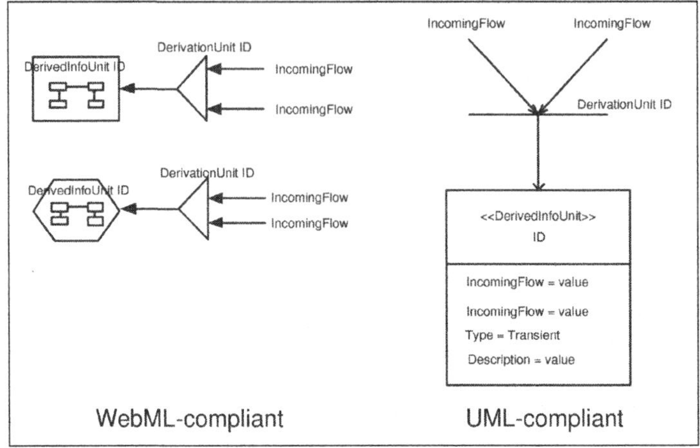

Fig. 4. Derived Information Units

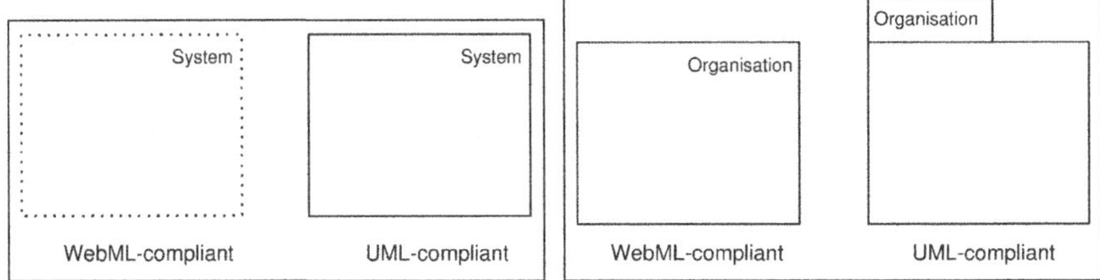

Fig. 5. Systems and Organisations

Information flows: An arrow represents flow of information in both WIED custom notations (WebML compliant) and UML compliant version of WIED.

System and Organisation: The system boundary encloses the set of information units that are utilized and/or managed by the system under consideration, and the organisation encloses the set of information units that are utilised and/or managed by the organisation. The system can be considered as a super class of a set of information units, and so can also be represented as a class. The organization on the other hand can be considered as a superset of the system where some information units are exchanged within the organization (and with external actor) but not in the system. A UML package is preferred for representing the organization since in some cases more than one system are used in the organization and a system can be distributed across multiple organisations. Figure 5 shows system and organisation units represented in WebML-compliant notation and UML-compliant notation.

Figure 6 shows an example of a WIED model for the same hypothetical example discussed earlier: TicketMaster.

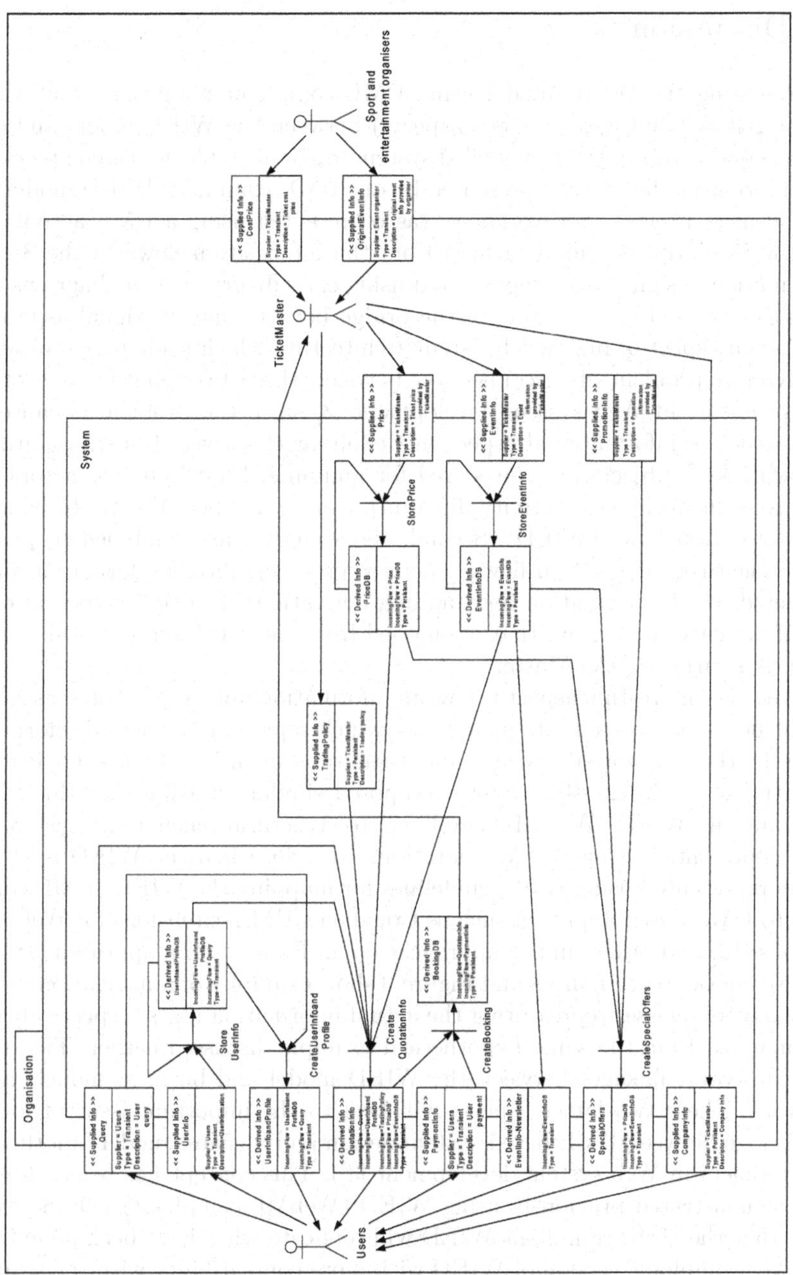

Fig. 6. Typical Web System represented using WIED-UML

4 Discussion

Representing the WIED model using UML compliant notations enables us to create relevant linkages (in some aspects) between the WIED model and other aspects of the overall UML-modelled systemm. For example, we can map between the information flows (as represented by our UML-compliant WIED model) and the business process and workflows (as represented using a UML activity diagram). Similarly we can then map from the information flows to the detailed information designs (often represented using class diagram, state diagrams, etc.) This can be seen as a forming of the bridge between informational aspect and functional aspect of high level system architecture which leads to a solution for resolving a problem of disconnection between these two aspects (one of crucial problems in Web system development [3] since the problem is caused by an absence of informational aspect modelling at this level of abstraction). The following key subjects are considered for mapping. First, business actors, who play roles in workflows (activity diagram), can be mapped directly to be actors in information flows (WIED). Second, the scenarios are combined to produce comprehensive information flows. Then, where a significant information unit is triggered by an information flow, adding derivations. Figure 7 shows an example of an activity diagram that is mapped from the same hypothetical example discussed earlier: TicketMaster.

Another interesting aspect is how an information unit (represented as a class) might be deconstructed into sub-classes which represent the actual information units in the conceptual schema and then subsequently into the navigational structure [18]. Previously, we have proposed similar guidelines for this aspect, mapping the WIED (WebML-compliant) to structural schema and system siteview represented using WebML notations [10]. So, when the WIED is alternatively represented using UML, guidelines for mapping the WIED (UML compliant) to UML-based approach such as Conallen's UML extensions for Web applications [19] and other similar approaches (e.g. Baumeister's approach [18]) will be also considered. Figure 8 and Figure 9 show examples of a navigational structure and sub-classes representing the actual information units respectively,these are mapped from the same hypothetical example discussed earlier: TicketMaster. Moreover, linkages between the WIED model and business models is also relevant. These two latter aspects will lead to the important issue of forming the bridge between UML-based system design and business model (another crucial problem in Web system development [3]). This concept has been addressed and demonstrated previously using WIED (WebML-compliant) [10]. So we believe that the UML compliant WIED will replicate what have been done by the WebML compliant version of WIED with more compatibility with the standard modelling, UML (i.e. be operationalized as a notation and associated diagram that are improved consistent with UML).

Space limitations preclude us from including the detailed procedures how to map the WIED (UML compliant) to other UML-based modelling approaches. These will be published elsewhere.

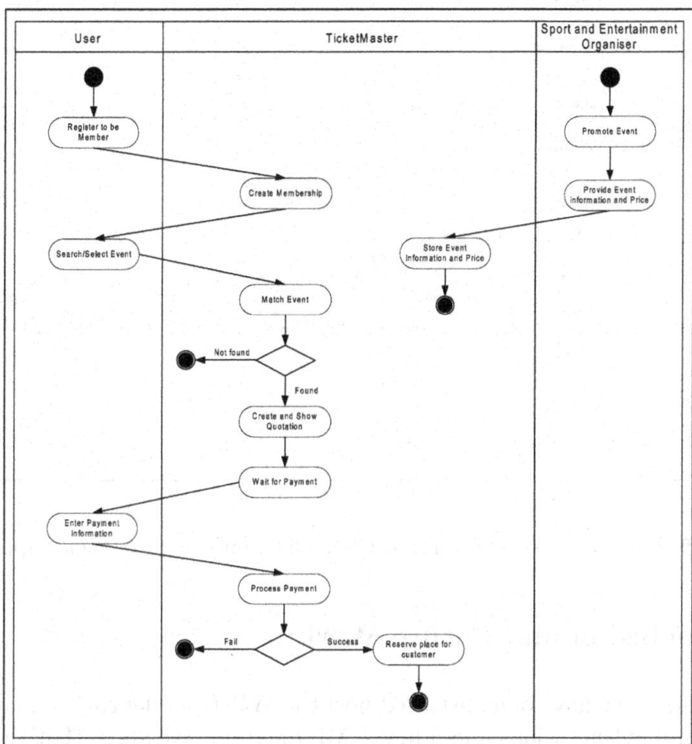

Fig. 7. Typical Activity Diagram representing Business Processes

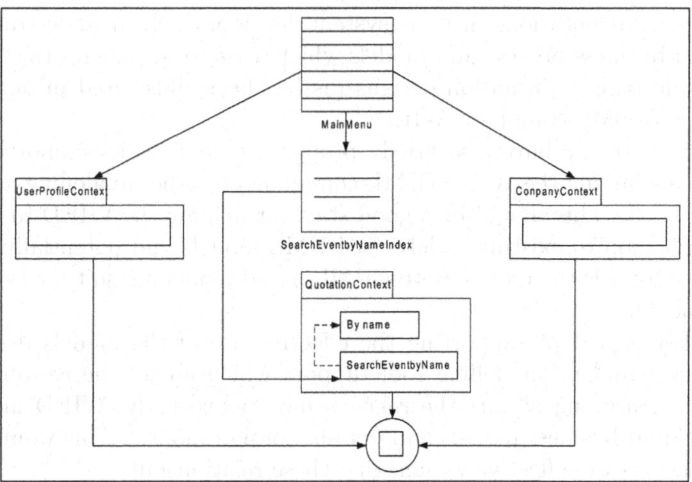

Fig. 8. Partial Navigational Structure represented using Baumeister's approach

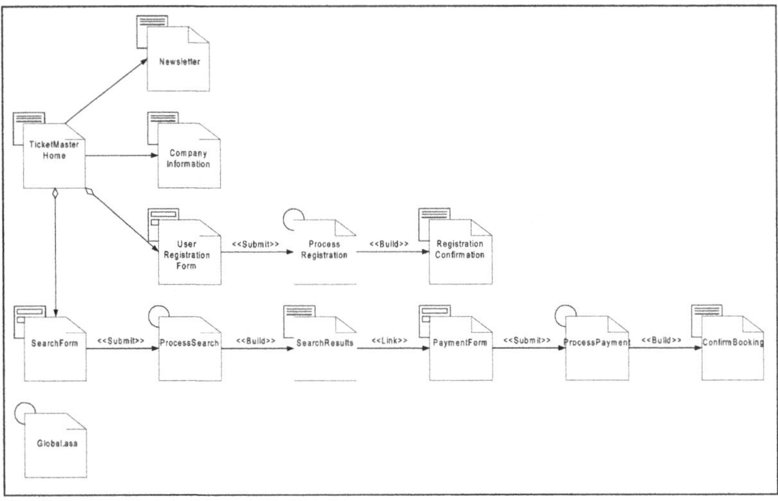

Fig. 9. Partial Browsing Overview Class Diagram using Conallen's approach

5 Conclusion and Future Work

In this paper, we have demonstrated how the WIED model can be mapped into UML compliant notations and a new UML diagram. We argue that this enables WIED to be compatible with UML and provide improved connections between WIED and other models that are typically constructed. Therefore, it will lead to a more standardized WIED and subsequently enhance the design process of Web-enabled systems. We believe that this will also assist developers and clients, who use UML-based notations in their system developments, in understanding the impact on business process and models which arise from changes that are made to the underlying information designs (as has been illustrated in our previous work with WebML-compliant WIED.

In this work, we have also briefly proposed guidelines to support the mapping process linking the WIED (UML-compliant) to other modelling approaches based on UML. This should be a good start for making the WIED to be practically companion to existing widely-used UML models and potentially integrate with those models to create a better UML-based modelling suit for Web system developments.

One key aspect of supporting the effective use of the models described in this paper would be modelling tool support which allows the capture of (and ultimately reasoning about) the relationships between the WIED models and the associated business models and detailed design models. This would support developers in more effectively managing these relationships.

Ongoing work is focusing on clearly defining and improving linkages between the WIED (UML-compliant) and UML-based modelling approaches. We will also possibly conduct an empirical study for evaluating the WIED (UML-compliant)

model. The outcomes of improved mapping between modelling approaches and the evaluation will be reported elsewhere.

References

1. Shelford, T.J., Remillard, G.A.: Real Web Project Management: Case Studies and Best Practices from the Trenches. 1st edn. Addison Wesley Professional (2002)
2. Powell, T.A.: Web Site Engineering. Prentice-Hall (1988)
3. Gu, A., Henderson-Sellers, B., Lowe, D.: Web modelling languages: The gap between requirements and current exemplars. In: AusWeb02, Gold Coast, Australia (2002)
4. Kappel, G., Proll, B., Retschitzegger, W., Hofer, T.: Modeling ubiquitous web applications - a comparison of approaches. In: The International Conference on Information Integration and Web-based Applications and Services, Austria (2001)
5. Christodoulou, S., Styliaras, G., Papatheodourou, T.: Evaluation of hypermedia application development and management systems. In: ACM Hypertext'98 Conference, Pittsburgh (1998)
6. Lowe, D.: Web requirements: An overview. Requirements Engineering Journal (2003)
7. Lowe, D., Tongrungrojana, R.: WebML+ for communication of information flows: An empirical study. In: the Third International Conference on Web Engineering, Oviedo, Asturias, Spain (2003)
8. Tongrungrojana, R., Lowe, D.: Modelling forms of information derivation in modified WebML+. In: the Ninth Australian Web Conference, Gold Coast, Australia (2003)
9. Tongrungrojana, R., Lowe, D.: WIED: a web modelling language for modelling architectural-level information flows. Journal of Digital Information (2004)
10. Tongrungrojana, R., Lowe, D.: WebML+: a web modeling language for forming a bridge between business modeling and information modeling. In: the Fifteenth International Conference on Software Engineering Knowledge Engineering, San Francisco (2003)
11. Gordijn, J., Akkermans, J.: e^3-value: Design and evaluation of e-business models. IEEE Intelligent Systems **16** (2001) 11–17
12. Ceri, S., Fraternali, P., Bongio, A.: Web modeling language (webml): a modeling langauge for designing websites. In: the Proceeding of WWW9 Conference, Amsterdam (2000)
13. Gordijn, J.: e^3-value in a nutshell. In: International workshop on e-business modeling, Lausanne (2002)
14. OMG: Introduction to omg's unified modeling language (uml) (2003)
15. Isakowitz, T., Stohr, E., Balasubramanian, P.: RMM: A methodology for structured hypermedia design. Communications of the ACM **38** (1995) 34–44
16. Schwabe, D., Rossi, G.: Developing hypermedia applications using oohdm. In: Workshop on Hypermedia Development Processes, Methods and Models (Hypertext'98), Pittsburgh, USA (1998)
17. Lieberman, B.: Uml activity diagrams: Detailing user interface navigation (2001)
18. Baumeister, H., Koch, N., Mandel, L.: Towards a UML extension for hypermedia design. In: "UML" 1999: The Second International Conference on The Unified Modeling Language, Fort Collins, Colorado, USA, IEEE (1999) 614–629
19. Conallen, J.: Modeling Web application architectures with UML. Communications of the ACM **42** (1999) 63–70

A User Service Oriented Method to Model Web Information Systems

Valeria de Castro, Esperanza Marcos, and Paloma Cáceres

Kybele Research Group
Rey Juan Carlos University
Madrid (Spain)
{vcastro,emarcos,pcaceres}@escet.urjc.es

Abstract. Nowadays it is possible to develop Web Information Systems (WIS) that allow us to buy a fly ticket or to book a hotel, as well as to get specific information through the Internet. However, due to the lack of suitable methods to build the navigation model of WIS, frequently the users are lost while navigating through the system, because they do not know how to use it. Traditional methodologies for WIS development usually propose to obtain the navigation model from the conceptual data model, without taking into account the behavior of systems. Unlike these methodologies, we propose to address the problem of navigation model construction from a *user service oriented* perspective. In this work we explain, through a case study, the hypertext modeling method proposed by MIDAS. It allows to build more intuitive and user friendly WIS. Moreover, we present a comparative study in which we remark the main benefits and advantages of our method with regard to the traditional methodologies for hypertext modeling.

1 Introduction

Usually in Web Information Systems (WIS) development it is the client who defines the requirements of the WIS, because he knows the IS and what he wants to show or to sell to the users. Unlike the traditional IS, in WIS, the client and the users are not the same people. In the Web scope, when the user accesses to the WIS he does not know how to use it. The user only knows what he wants to do, but not how to do it. For this reasons, the users often are lost while navigating through the system. Therefore, the WIS and its navigation model should be clear and intuitive to guide to the user.

The construction of the navigation model is a problem addressed by most of the methodologies for WIS development [1,3,5,7,8,9,10,11]. Despite the differences found between them, most of them follow a similar approach to obtain the navigation model: they start from the conceptual data model [9,10]. At best, they make reference to the need to consider use cases model [9,11] but only as a recommendation, without indicating how to do it. Unlike the mentioned methodologies which follow a *structural* approach to build the navigation model, we propose to address the problem of the systematic construction of the navigation model from a *user service oriented* perspective [3]. That is, we will mainly take into account the services required by the user, called from now on *conceptual user services*. We propose a method to obtain the

X. Zhou et al. (Eds.): WISE 2004, LNCS 3306, pp. 41–52, 2004.
© Springer-Verlag Berlin Heidelberg 2004

navigation model starting from the *user services model*, a use cases model in which we identify conceptual user services as stereotyped use cases. We also take into account the conceptual data model, but in a second step.

In previous works [12,13] we have presented a first approach to a systematic method (from now on hypertext modeling method) to obtain a navigation model. The method includes the process, the models and the mappings between them. In this work we explain, through a case study, how the hypertext modeling method proposed by MIDAS allows to build more intuitive and user friendly WIS. The navigation model obtained with our approach will present a main menu with the services required by the user. Moreover, for each service, the navigation model will specify the sequence of steps to properly carry out the service. This sequence of steps will be called *route*, and allows guiding the user when navigating through the WIS.

Moreover, in order to validate the proposed method, we present a comparative study remarking the main benefits provided by a *user service oriented method* with regard to a structural one. The comparative study analyzes the advantages in the navigational model obtained as well as the benefits of the method itself.

The hypertext modeling method is part of MIDAS, a model driven methodology for WIS development which proposes to model the WIS according to the three basic aspects: hypertext, content and behavior. This work focuses on the MIDAS method to model the hypertext aspect whose output is the navigation model.

The rest of the paper is structured as follows: Section 2 is an overview of the model driven architecture of MIDAS, which makes up the framework of this work. Section 3 describes, through a case study, the hypertext modeling method of MIDAS, including the process, the models and the mapping rules. Section 4 presents a comparative study in which we analyze the main benefits of our method with regard to the traditional methodologies for hypertext modeling. Finally, in section 4, we conclude underlying the main contribution and the future work.

2 MIDAS Framework

MIDAS is a methodological framework for agile development of WIS, which proposes a Model Driven Architecture [2] based on the MDA proposed by the Object Management Group [17]. MIDAS proposes to model the WIS according to two orthogonal dimensions (see Figure 1). On the one hand, taking into account the platform dependence degree (based on MDA approach): first, specifying the whole system by Computation Independent Models (CIMs), Platform Independent Models (PIMs) and Platform Specific Models (PSMs); and second, specifying the mapping rules between these models. And on the other hand, according to three basic aspects [12]: *hypertext*, *content* and *behavior*. Besides, MIDAS suggests using the Unified Model Language (UML) [18] as a unique notation to model both PIMs and PSMs.

The MIDAS framework has been partially presented in [14,15,16,20]. In this paper we focus on the PIM models involved in the hypertext aspect modeling of a WIS and we introduce four new models, shadowed in Figure 1: the *user services model*, the *extended use cases model*, the *extended slices model* and the *extended navigation model*. These new models have been introduced in [3]. The next section presents the process for the hypertext modeling method of MIDAS and the guides to build the new proposed models, by means of a case study.

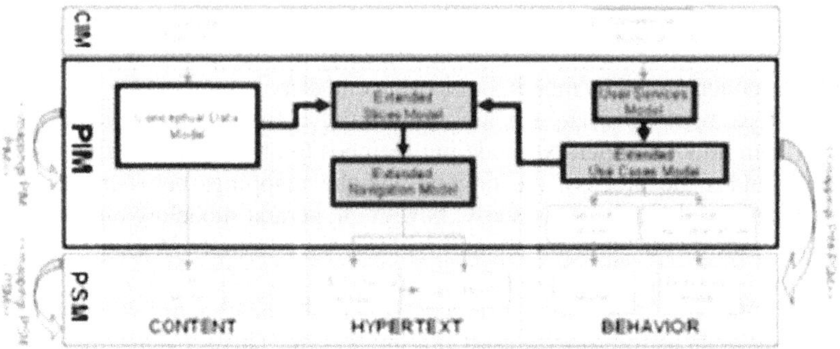

Fig. 1. Model Driven architecture of MIDAS

3 The Hypertext Modeling Method of MIDAS

The hypertext modeling method of MIDAS proposes a process to get the navigation model of a WIS from a user service oriented approach (see Figure 2), that is to say, a process guided by the user services.

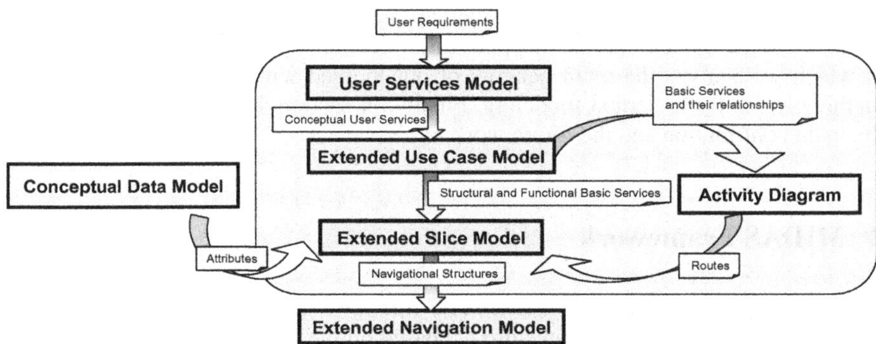

Fig. 2. The Process for the Hypertext Modeling Method

The inputs of the method are the *user requirements* and the *conceptual data model*; and the output is the *extended navigation model*. Our method defines four new models (shadowed in Figure 2): the *user services model*, the *extended use cases model*, the *extended slices model* and *extended navigation model*; and mapping rules between them. Moreover, we propose to use an a*ctivity diagram* to model the services composition and to obtain the route. This route will guide to the user when he navigates through the WIS.

In next subsection we present through a case study, the hypertext modeling method of MIDAS, explaining in depth how to build the proposed models. Before describing the method, we are going to introduce a new set of concepts. The *user services model* and the *extended use cases model* are extensions of the traditional use cases model

[18] in which different types of use cases are identified. In [3] the use case taxonomy that we propose was presented.

A *use case* is defined as "the specification of a sequence of actions performed by a system which yields an observable result that is, typically, of value for one or more actors or other stakeholders of the system. [18].

A ***conceptual user service*** is a special type of use case, identified in the *user services model*, which represents a service required by the user.

Each conceptual user service must be decomposed in simpler use cases that we have called ***use service***. A use service is a functionality required by the system to carry out the conceptual user service. Therefore, a user conceptual service is an aggregation of use services. Note that, a use service could be implemented by means of Web services or not. Based on the Web service classification provided in [19], a use service can be either a basic or a composite service. A ***basic use service*** is an atomic functionality of the WIS, for example, viewing a book catalogue. A ***composite use service*** is an aggregation of either basic or composite use services. Finally, from a presentational point of view, a basic use service can be functional or structural. A basic use service is ***structural*** when its functionality is only to provide a data view (i.e. viewing a catalogue, viewing the author's data, etc.). A basic use service is ***functional***, if it implies some interaction with the user, generally requiring some input data (i.e. searching a book, adding a product to the shopping cart, paying, etc.). The basic (structural and functional) and composite use services are also a type of use case identified in the *extended use case model*.

3.1 A Case Study

The process, models and mapping rules of the hypertext modeling method of MIDAS are illustrated in depth, through a case study. The case study we are going to present is the *ConfMaster WIS* [6], a WIS to support the organization of conferences. It allows the nomination of the Program Committee (PC) members, paper submission, assignment of papers to reviewers, etc Note that in this application there are at least four roles played by a user (Author, PC Chair and PC Member) that interact with the systems. Each one of these roles is represented in a use case model as an actor [18]. We propose to model one *user service model* to each actor implied in the system, and then we going to obtain one navigation model for each role that interact with the system. For sake of space in this work we will focus on the services that an author requires of a system and we will obtain the *extended navigation model* for him.

In previous work [13] we have modeled the *ConfMaster WIS* just as it appears in the Web, now we present a similar application with the same requirements of *ConfMaster* but following a user service oriented approach. In section four we compare the navigation model obtained from our approach with regard to the navigation model of *ConfMaster WIS*.

User Services Model. As we have mentioned before, we propose the build the navigation model from a user service oriented approach. Then, we generate the *user services model* taking into account this approach. The ***user service model*** is an extension of the use case model in which the conceptual user services, stereotyped with <<*CUS*>>, are represented.

In Figure 3 you can see the user service models to each actors of *ConfMaster WIS*. As we said before, we will focus on the services required by the authors (a). In our example, the real aims of an author are: to submit a paper, to view their papers or to edit the author data. They are the specific services required by the author; so in a user services model (a) we have identified Submit Paper, View own Papers and Edit User Data as conceptual user services.

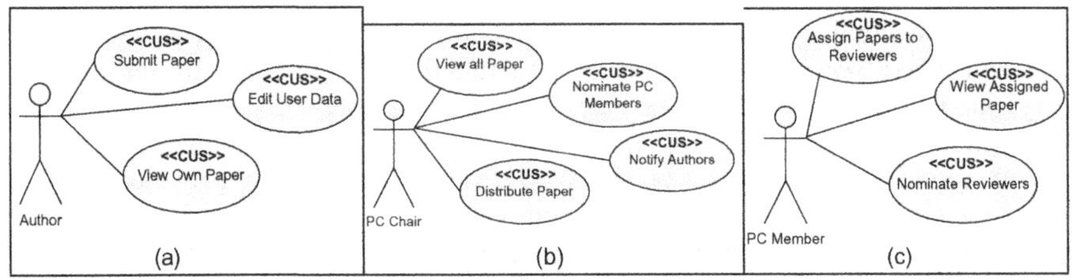

Fig. 3. User Services Model for Author *(a)*, PC Chair *(b)* and PC Member *(c)*

Extended Use Cases Model. The ***extended use cases model*** is obtained from de user services model. An extended use cases model includes: actors; include and extend relationships; and use services. Include and extend relationships have the same semantics as in the use cases model. UML defines the stereotypes <<include>> and <<extend>> to identify these relationships. As we said, a use service is a kind of use case. To identify (basic or composite) use services we have defined the following stereotypes: *<<CS>>* to represent a *composite use service*, *<<FBS>>* to represent a *functional basic use service* and *<<SBS>>* to represent a *structural basic use service*. We propose to model this composition of use services with a UML activity diagram.

To build the extended use cases model we start *identifying the basic and composite use services* taking into account the functionality required by the WIS to carry out the conceptual user services previously identified. Next, we *specify in detail the composite services* identified previously and finally we *identify the include and extend relationships*.

In Figure 4 the extended use case model for the author is depicted. An author must be register as a new author and then he obtain a login. Then the author can submit a paper, can edit his data and can view his submitted papers. From now on we will focus on the *View own Paper* conceptual user service, the basic use services involved in this conceptual user service are shadowed in Figure 4. To view his papers the author must be logged in, if the author has one or more papers he will view a list of his papers, then the author can view the paper data in the screen or can download the file. In Figure 5 you can see the activity diagram associated to the *View own Paper* conceptual user service.

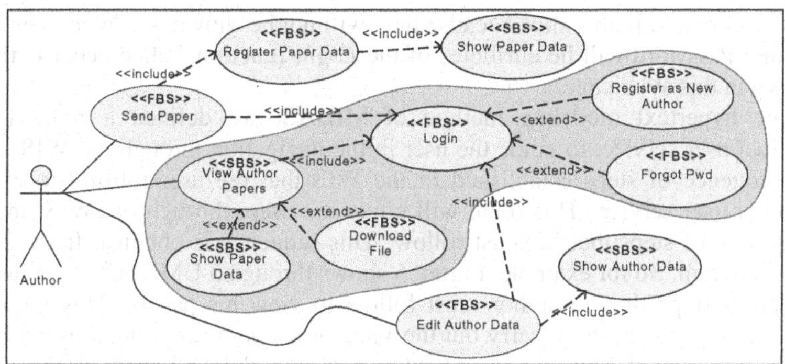

Fig. 4. Extended Use Cases Model

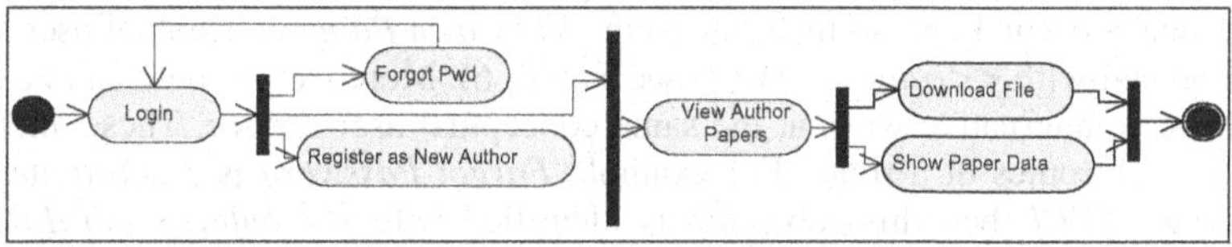

Fig. 5. Activity Diagram for the *View Own Paper* Conceptual User Service

Extended Slices Model. The *extended slices model* is obtained from the extended use cases model and taking into account the conceptual data model and the activity diagram associated with each conceptual user service. The *slices model* is defined in [10] as the decomposition of the system into meaningful units, called slices, and the hyperlinks between them. Our approach proposes to obtain: the slices from the extended use cases model and the information about each slice from the conceptual data model. As the extended use cases model represents two kinds of basic use services, (structural and functional) we also have to introduce two types of slices. A *structural slice* is a slice as defined above. A *functional slice* also represents a Web page, but an interactive one. Therefore, a functional slice allows the interaction with the user to be represented. ***An extended slices model*** is defined as a slices model in which the functional and structural slices are represented. To identify the different slices, we introduce the <<*SS*>> and <<*FS*>> stereotypes that represent structural and functional slices, respectively.

To build the extended slice model first, each structural and functional basic service from the extended use cases model will give rise to a structural and functional slice respectively in the extended slice model; and second, the relationships between basic use services will give rise to the hyperlinks between slices. The attributes of the slices generally come from the attributes of the conceptual data model. For the sake of space limitation, the conceptual data model has been omitted. This model presents two classes: *Author* and *Paper*. So for example, attributes of the *Show Author Data* come from the class *Author*; however, some attributes of this class as Login and Password, are not represented in this slice because they will not be shown in a Web page. In fact, Login and Password will be attributes of the *Login* functional slice because they will be shown in this Web page.

In the hypertext modeling method of MIDAS, we defined a *route* for each conceptual user service, to guide the user in the navigation through the WIS. A ***route*** is the sequence of steps established in the WIS that the user follows to execute a conceptual user service. This route will guide the users through the WIS, indicating the sequence of steps that he must follow. This sequence is obtained from the UML activity diagram. So for example, Figure 5 shows through a UML activity diagram the sequence of steps that an author must follow to view his papers. This sequence of steps represents the route to carry out the *View own Paper* conceptual user service. A route is represented first in the extended slices model and then in the extended navigation model.

In the *extended slices model,* each route is composed by a set of slices linked between them. Each link between two slices is represented by an arrow stereotyped with *<<route>>*. Moreover, a route has a tagged value to identify the conceptual user service that is carried out; so the route to the *View own Paper* conceptual user service is stereotyped with *<<route>> {VP}* (see Figure 6). Moreover, a route can be forked giving rise to alternative ways at the same conceptual user service. These alternative ways are sub-routes of a route. For example *Forgot Password* is a sub-route of the *<<route>> {VP}* then this sub-route is identified with *<<route>> {VP.FP}* as is shown in Figure 6.

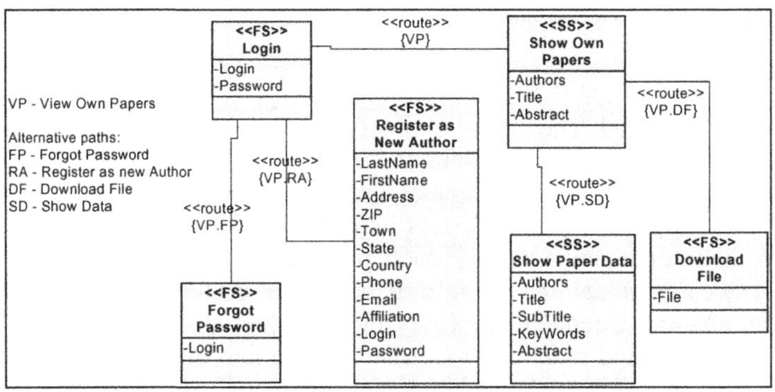

Fig. 6. Extended Slices Model to the *View own Papers* Conceptual User Service

Extended Navigation Model. The *extended navigation model* is the result of introducing the navigational structures (index, menu, etc.) into an extended slices model. An *extended navigation model* is an extended slices model plus the navigational structures, that is, a navigation model which includes functional slices and structural slices and routes. Both, extended slices model and extended navigation model are represented using the UML extension proposed in UWE [9]. So, in this model, each route is composed by the slices, the links between them plus the navigational structures. In Figure 7 the extended navigation model for the author role is depicted and we have remarked the *View own Papers* conceptual user service.

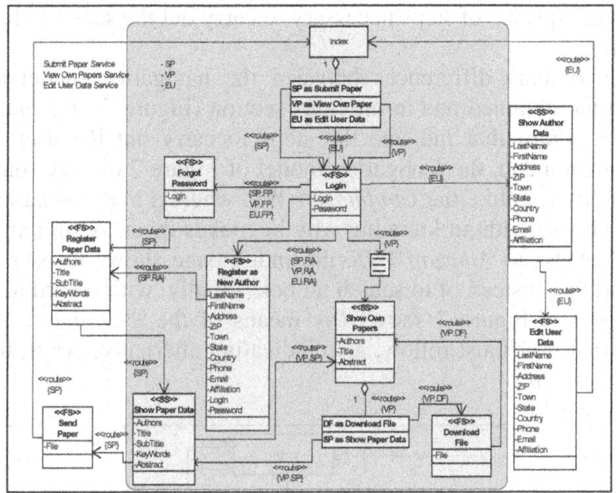

Fig. 7. Extended Navigation Model

We propose to introduce a main menu with the services required by the user that represents the beginning of each route. As you can see in Figure 7, we represent a main menu with three entries, one per each conceptual user service: *Submit Paper*, *View Own Paper* and *Edit User Data*. Besides, the route of *View Own Paper*, stereotyped as *route {VP}*, also has two alternative paths for representing the *Download File* and the *Show Paper Data* slices. Then, we also represent a menu with two entries, one per each slice. The navigational structures should be introduced according to the guidelines proposed in [9].

4 Benefits of the User Service Oriented Approach: Comparative Study

In this work we have presented the hypertext modeling method proposed by MIDAS and, taking as case study the *Confmaster WIS*, we have obtained a more intuitive and user friendly navigation model for this system. In order to validate the proposed method we present a comparative study in which we analyze on the one hand, difference between the navigation model obtained from a user service oriented perspective and the present navigation model of *Confmaster WIS*; and on the other, we analyze the main benefits of our method with regard to the traditional methodologies for hypertext modeling.

The navigation model obtained from a user service oriented approach contains the routes to navigate through the WIS. This sequence of steps is unknown to the user, because he doesn't know the steps, required by the WIS, to carry out the service. So, in our example, if the user chooses View own Paper in the main menu, the WIS will force him to login before to allow him download a file. In this way, the user is guided through WIS, giving rise to a more intuitive and user friendly WIS. The user simply chooses what to do (through a main menu that only includes the user services) and then follows the sequence of steps necessary to carry out the service, that is to say, the associated route.

There are two main differences between the navigation model of *Confmaster* (Figure 8) and the obtained one in previous section (Figure 7): *the main menu* of the system and *the routes* that indicate the steps to carry out the user services. With regard to the main menu, the navigation model of Figure 7 displays only the services required by the user, unlike the *Confmaster WIS* where a main menu has options that the user must choose without knowing why he makes them. A similar case would be that when we access to *Amazon WIS*, the index page shows to users the option to register as costumer instead of to search a book. Finally, with regard to the routes, the navigation model of Figure 7 shows (by means of the <<*route*>> stereotype) the specific route that user must follow, also indicating alternative ways, to carry out the services of the system.

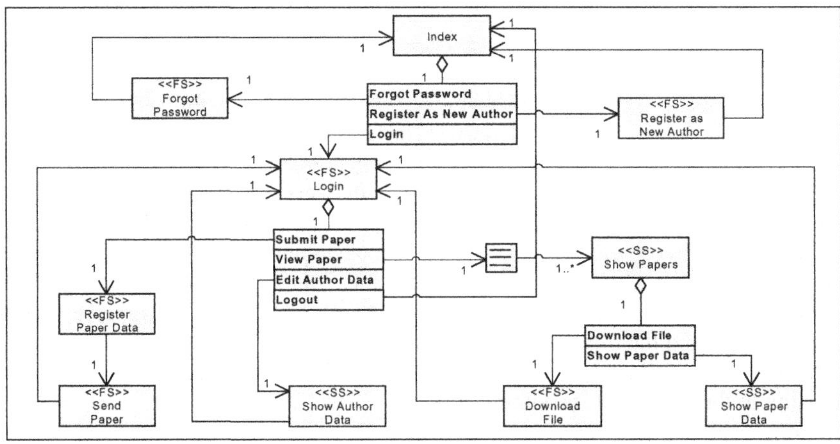

Fig. 8. Extended Navigation Model of *ConfMaster WIS*

Now, comparing the user services oriented method with regard to the traditional methodologies for the hypertext modeling we notes that there are three important advantages of our method with regard to the traditional ones: *the new user service oriented approach* to the WIS development, *the incorporation of behavior aspects* in navigation model and *the method* itself that defines guides to build more intuitive and user friendly WIS.

The method proposes to model the hypertext starting from an extended use case model called user service model. In figure 9 the use case model (for Author role) of *Confmaster WIS* is depicted. As we said, unlike traditional use case model, the user service model (Figure 3 (a)) presents only the use cases that represent services required by the users. In our example, the real aims of an author are: to *submit a paper*, to *view own papers* or to *edit the author data*. These use cases (shadowed in Figure 9) are the conceptual user services that will be represented in a user service model. *Register a new author* is a previous step to submit a paper; *Login* is functionality required by the system for accessing security purpose and finally, *forgot password* is a functionality that the system offers to the users.

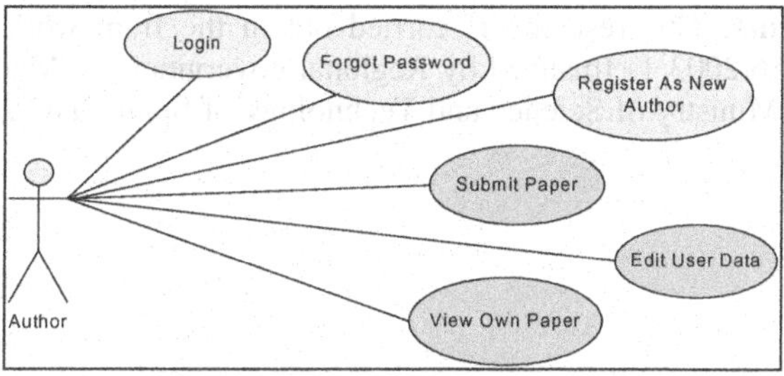

Fig. 9. Use Case Model of *ConfMaster WIS*

After obtain the user services model, the hypertext modeling method of MIDAS is centered in the conceptual user services; first, identifying functionalities involved in each one and then representing the composition of theses functionalities. The composition model is represented by means of activity diagram, obtaining next the routes for each conceptual user service.

5 Conclusions and Future Work

In this paper we have presented a method for the systematic construction of the navigation model in the framework of MIDAS, a model-driven methodology for WIS development. Unlike traditional methodologies for WIS development, that follow a *structural* approach to build the navigation model, we propose to address the problem from a *user service oriented* perspective. That is, we will mainly take into account the services required by the user, that we have called *conceptual user services*.

Usually in the Web scope when a user access to a WIS he does not know how to use it. The user only knows what he wants to do, but not how to do it. Therefore, the WIS and its navigation model have to be clear and intuitive to guide the user. The navigation model obtained with our approach will present a main menu with the services required by the user. Moreover, for each service, the navigation model will specify the sequence of steps to properly execute the service. This sequence of steps will be called *route*, and allows guiding the user in the navigation through the WIS. Beside, we have presented a comparative study in which the benefits of our approach had been summarized.

At the present time, we are working on the integration of this method with other models proposed by MIDAS and the inclusion of business process modeling into MIDAS Framework. One of the main benefits of this proposed approach will undoubtedly be maximizing the automation of the WIS development process. Thus, in future work we are going to implement the proposed models and mappings in a CASE tool that supports MIDAS to generate the WIS (semi-)automatically.

Acknowledgments. This research is carried out in the framework of the projects: EDAD (07T/0056/2003 1) financed by Regional government of Madrid and DAWIS financed by the Ministry of Science and Technology of Spain (TIC 2002-04050-C02-01).

References

1. Atzeni, P., Merialdo, P., Mecca, G.: Data-Intensive Web Sites: Design and Maintenance. World Wide Web 4(1-2), pp. 21-47, 2001.
2. Cáceres, P., Marcos, E., Vela, B.: A MDA-Based Approach for Web Information System Development. Workshop in Software Model Engineering (WiSME) in UML'2003. Retrieved from: http://www.metamodel.com/wisme-2003/.
3. Cáceres, P., De Castro, V., Marcos, E.: Navigation Modeling from a User Services Oriented Approach. AVDIS Conference 2004. Accepted to be published.
4. Castano, S., Palopoli, L., Torlone, R.: A General Methodological Framework for the Development of Web-Based Information Systems. Conceptual Modeling for E_Business and the Web. Liddle, S. W., Mayr, H. C., Thalheim, B. (eds.) ER 2000. Berlin (Germany), October, 2000. LNCS-1921. Springer Verlag. October, 2000.
5. Conallen, J.: Building Web Applications with UML. Addison Wesley, 2000.
6. ConfMaster. Available in http://confmaster.net/phpwebsite_en/index.php, 2003.
7. Fraternali, P.: Tools and approaches for developing data-intensive Web applications: a survey. ACM Computing Surveys, Vol. 31, nº 3, 1999.
8. Gómez, J., Cachero, C., Pastor, O.: Conceptual Modeling of Device-Independent Web Applications. IEEE Multimedia, 8 (2), pp. 26-39, 2001.
9. Hennicker, R., Koch, N.: A UML-based Methodology for Hypermedia Design. UML' 2000, LNCS 1939, pp.410-424, 2000.
10. Isakowitz, T., Kamis, A., Koufaris, M.: The Extended RMM Methodology for Web Publishing. Working Paper IS-98-18, Center for Research on Information System. Retrieved from: http://rmm-java.stern.nyu.edu/rmm/, 1998.
11. Koch, N., Kraus, A., Cachero, C., Meliá, S.: Modeling Web Business Processes with OO-H and UWE. In Third International Workshop on Web-oriented Software Technology (IWWOST03). Schwabe, D., Pastor, O., Rossi, G., Olsina, L. (eds.), 27-50, July 2003.
12. Marcos, E., Cáceres, P., De Castro, V.: An approach for Navigation Model Construction from the Use Cases Model. The 16th Conference On Advanced Information Systems Engineering. CAISE'04 FORUM, pp. 83-92.
13. Marcos, E., Cáceres, P., De Castro, V.: Modeling the Navigation with Services. IADIS International Conference WWW/Internet 2004. Accepted to be published.
14. Marcos, E., Cáceres, P., Vela, B., Cavero, J.M.: MIDAS/DB: a Methodological Framework for Web Database Design. DASWIS 2001. H. Arisawa, Y. Kambayashi, V. Kumar, H. C. Mayr, I. Hunt (eds.). LNCS-2465. Springer Verlag. September, 2002.
15. Marcos, E., De Castro, V., Vela, B.: Representing Web Services with UML: A Case Study. The First International Conference on Service Oriented Computing (ICSOC03). M.E. Orlowska, S. Weerawarana, M.P. Papazoglou, J. Yang (eds.). Springer Verlag, pp.15-27, 2003.
16. Marcos, E., Vela, B., Cavero, J.M.: Methodological Approach for Object-Relational Database Design using UML. Journal on Software and Systems Modeling (SoSyM). Springer-Verlag. France, R., Rumpe, B. (eds.). Volume SoSyM 2, pp.59-72, 2003.
17. Object Management Group. OMG Model Driven Architecture. Miller, J., Mukerji, J. (eds.) 2001. Document number ormsc/2001-07-01. Retrieved 2003, from: http://www.omg.com/mda.

18. Object Management Group. UML Superstructure 2.0. Draft adopted Specification. Retrieved from: http://www.uml.org/.
19. Papazoglou, M.P., Georgakopoulos, D.: Serviced-Oriented Computing. Communications of ACM, Volume: 46, 10, October 2003, pp. 25-28.
20. Vela, B., Marcos, E.: Extending UML to represent XML Schemas. The 15th Conference On Advanced Information Systems Engineering. CAISE'03 FORUM. J. Eder, T. Welzer (eds.). Short Paper Proceedings, 2003.

The Power of Media Types

Klaus-Dieter Schewe

Massey University, Information Science Research Centre
& Department of Information Systems
Private Bag 11222, Palmerston North, New Zealand
k.d.schewe@massey.ac.nz

Abstract. Media types are extended views on some underlying database schema. They permit the detailed formal specification of the data used in the scenes of the story space, i.e. the definition of information portfolios for the actors, and the concretisation of pre- and postconditions for actions. In this paper we show that this leads to higher-order dynamic logic as a basis for formally reasoning about the system specification. In particular, we address the problems of static and dynamic consistency. Furthermore, it refines the level of detail for the personalisation of systems.

1 Introduction

The codesign approach in [4] emphasises a development method for web information systems (WISs) that is oriented at abstraction layers and the co-design of structure, operations and interfaces. Among others this comprises a theory of *media types*, which covers extended views, adaptivity, hierarchies and presentation style options. This theory is coupled with *storyboarding*, an activity that addresses the design of an underlying application story. Storyboarding is supported by the language `SiteLang` [2], which in fact is a process algebra.

In [7] we showed that story algebras are indeed many-sorted Kleene algebras with tests [6] (KATs). They can be used to reason about the story space on a propositional level, which we applied to WIS personalisation. In addition, each user activity requires some data. Therefore, each scene in the story space is supported by a media type [4], i.e. an extended view on some underlying database schema.

The focus of this paper is on advanced reasoning about WISs by exploiting media types. The presence of media types refines the activities in the story board to dialogue operations that update the database and delete or create new media objects, i.e. instances of the media types. Furthermore, the pre- and postconditions of the activities are refined into logical conditions on the database and the media types. As a consequence, reasoning with KATs changes to reasoning with higher-order dynamic logic [5]. In this paper we particularly address static and dynamic consistency. Furthermore, we reconsider the personalisation of WISs in this stronger context.

X. Zhou et al. (Eds.): WISE 2004, LNCS 3306, pp. 53–58, 2004.
© Springer-Verlag Berlin Heidelberg 2004

In Section 2 we first recall briefly the concept of media types, then review story spaces going beyond the propositional level and towards an application of dynamic logic. Finally, in Section 3 we show how the more detailed specification of WISs using dynamic logic can be exploited for reasoning about consistency and enhanced personalisation. We conclude with a brief summary.

2 Media Types for Information Portfolios

Each user of a WIS has information needs that have to be satisfied by the system. These information needs are usually not known in advance. Part of the needed information may depend on other parts, on decisions made while navigating through the WIS, and even on the information provided by the user him/herself. That is, the information portfolio of a user depends on the path through the WIS, i.e. in our terminology on the story.

Therefore, assuming that there is a database for the data content of the WIS with database schema $\mathcal{S}$, the information need on a scene s definitely accounts for a *view* V_s over $\mathcal{S}$. That is, we have another schema $\mathcal{S}_V$ and a computable transformation from databases over $\mathcal{S}$ to databases over $\mathcal{S}_V$. Such a transformation is usually expressed by a query q_V.

This leads us to media types [4]. In principle, it is not important what kind of database we have as long as there exists a sufficiently powerful query mechanism that permits to define views. So assume we are given a database schema $\mathcal{S}$, which itself is based on some underlying type system such as (using abstract syntax)

$$t = b \mid (a_1 : t_1, \dots, a_n : t_n) \mid \{t\}.$$

Here b represents an arbitrary collection of *base types*, e.g., $BOOL$ for boolean values $\mathbf{T}$ and $\mathbf{F}$, $\mathbb{1}$ for a single value $\mathbf{1}$, $TEXT$ for text, PIC for images, $MPIC$ for video data, $CARD$ and INT for numbers, $DATE$ for dates, ID for object identifiers, URL for URL-addresses, $MAIL$ for e-mail-addresses, etc. The constructors $(\cdot)$ and $\{\cdot\}$ are used for records and finite sets.

For each type $R \in \mathcal{S}$ we have a representing type t_R. In a $\mathcal{S}$-database db each type $R \in \mathcal{S}$ gives rise to a finite set $db(R)$ consisting of pairs (i, v) with i of type ID and v of type t_R. Using this we may set up a powerful query language adapting a logic programming approach as in [1].

Thus, a query will be expressed as a set of rules (precisely: a sequence of such sets). Evaluating the rule body on a given database will result in bindings of variables, and the corresponding bindings for the head together with the creation of new identifiers for unbound variables results in an extension to the database. These extensions are iterated until a fixed point is reached. Due to space restrictions we have to abstain here from formalising this.

An *interaction type* has a name M and consists of a content data type $cont(M)$ with the extension that the place of a base type may be occupied by a pair $\ell : M'$ with a label ℓ and the name M' of an interaction type, a defining query q_M with type t_M, and a set of *operations*. Here t_M is the type arising from $cont(M)$ by substitution of URL for all pairs $\ell : M'$.

Finite sets $\mathcal{C}$ of interaction types define *content schemata*. Then an $\mathcal{S}$-database *db* and the defining queries determine finite sets $db(M)$ of pairs (u, v) with URLs u and values v of type t_M for each $M \in \mathcal{C}$. We use the notion *pre-site* for the extension of *db* to $\mathcal{C}$. The pair (u, v) will be called an *interaction object* in the pre-site *db*. A boolean query on $\mathcal{S} \cup \mathcal{C}$ defines a *condition* φ.

A *media type* extends an interaction type M in two ways: It adds *adaptivity* and *hierarchies*, which can be formalised by a cohesion pre-order $\preceq_M$ (or a set of proximity values) and a set of hierarchical versions $H(M)$, respectively. For our purposes here we concentrate on the operations that already come with the interaction types, for the extensions see [4].

In general, an *operation* on a type R consists of a *signature* and a *body*. The *signature* consists of an operation name O, a set of input-parameter/type pairs $\iota_i : t_i$ and a set of output-parameter/type pairs $o_j : t'_j$. The *body* is an *abstract program* using the following constructs:

- 1 and 0 are abstract programs meaning `skip` and `fail`, respectively.
- An *assignment* $x := exp$ with a variable x and an expression of the same type as x is an abstract program. The possible expressions are defined by the type system. In addition, we permit expressions $\{\mathcal{P}\}$ with a logic program $\mathcal{P}$, assuming that $\mathcal{P}$ contains a variable *ans*. The expression $\{\mathcal{P}\}$ is interpreted as the result of the logic program bound to *ans*.
- If p, p_1 and p_2 are abstract programs, the same holds for the *iteration* p^*, the choice $p_1 + p_2$ and the sequence $p_1 \cdot p_2 = p_1 p_2$.
- If p is an abstract program and φ is a condition, then the *guarded program* φp and the *postguarded program* $p\varphi$ are also abstract programs.
- If x is a variable and p is an abstract program, then the *selection* $@x \bullet p$ is also an abstract program.

With respect to the connection to the story space, the propositional conditions φ now have to be refined to conditions on $\mathcal{S} \cup \mathcal{C}$, while each action α on a scene s is refined by an operations associated with the media type that supports s.

3 Correctness, Consistency, and Personalisation

With the introduction of media types to support scenes we can no longer rely on simple equational reasoning. Therefore we introduce a higher-order dynamic logic, where the order comes from the intrinsic use of the set constructor and the logic programs in queries. In fact, instead of using logic programs with a semantics defined by inflationary fixed-points, we could directly use higher-order logic enriched with a fixed-point operator (see e.g. [3]).

As a consequence, we may consider a logic program $\mathcal{P}$ as a representative of a higher-order logical formula, say $\varphi_{\mathcal{P}}$. If $\{\mathcal{P}\}$ is used as the right-hand side of an assignment, then it will correspond to a term $\mathbf{I}ans.\varphi_{\mathcal{P}}$ denoting the unique *ans* satisfying formula $\varphi_{\mathcal{P}}$. That is, all conditions turn out to be formulae of a logic $\mathcal{L}$, which happens to be a higher-order logic with an inflationary fixed-point operator. From the point of view of expressiveness (see [3]) the fixed-point operator is already subsumed by the order, but for convenience we do not emphasise this aspect here.

Furthermore, by adding terms of the form $\mathbf{I}x.\varphi$ with a formula φ and a variable x all assignments in operations are just "normal" assignments, where the left-hand side is a variable and the right-hand side is a term of $\mathcal{L}$.

We now extend $\mathcal{L}$ to a dynamic logic by adding formulae of the form $[p]\varphi$ with an abstract program p and a formula φ of $\mathcal{L}$. Informally, $[p]\varphi$ means that after the successful execution of p the formula φ necessarily holds (see [5]). In addition, we use the shortcut $\langle p\rangle\varphi \equiv \neg[p]\neg\varphi$, so $\langle p\rangle\varphi$ means that after the successful execution of p it is possible that the formula φ holds.

Using our recursive definition of abstract programs the following rules apply to $[p]\psi$ for a complex abstract program p:

$$
\begin{aligned}
[1]\psi &\equiv \psi \\
[0]\psi &\equiv 0 \\
[x := t]\psi &\equiv \psi\{x/t\} \text{ (substitute all free occurences of } x \text{ in } \psi \text{ by } t) \\
[p_1 p_2]\psi &\equiv [p_1][p_2]\psi \\
[p_1 + p_2]\psi &\equiv [p_1]\psi \wedge [p_2]\psi \\
[p^*]\psi &\equiv \text{ the weakest solution } \varphi \text{ of } \varphi \leftrightarrow \psi \wedge [p]\varphi \\
[\varphi p]\psi &\equiv \varphi \rightarrow [p]\psi \\
[p\varphi]\psi &\equiv [p](\varphi \rightarrow \psi) \\
[@x \bullet p]\psi &\equiv \forall x.[p]\psi
\end{aligned}
$$

The equivalence for the iteration operator refers to the implication order, i.e. if $\varphi \models \psi$ holds, then ψ is called *weaker* than φ. Further rules looking also at the structure of ψ are given in [5].

With these preparations we can rethink the reasoning about the story space. In the sequel we will discuss three applications of dynamic logic:

- We take a look at proof obligations for the operations that result from the the specification of the story space.
- We take a look at proof obligations for the operations that arise from static and dynamic integrity constraints on the underlying database schema.
- We reconsider WIS personalisation in the light of dynamic logic as opposed to KATs.

Story Space Proof Obligations. Let p denote the KAT expression that represents the complete story space. If all conditions in p are replaced by conditions on the pre-site and all actions are replaced by the abstract programs defining the realising operations, we obtain an abstract program, which by abuse of notation shall still be denoted p.

As a WIS has a general purpose, this can be formalised by some postcondition ψ. Thus, $[p]\psi$ describes the weakest condition, under which the purpose of the system can be achieved. If φ characterises a precondition that should be sufficient for the achievability of the WIS purpose, then we obtain $\varphi \rightarrow [p]\psi$ as a *general story space proof obligation*. In most cases we should expect $\varphi \equiv 1$.

Similarly, we may concentrate on fragments p' of the story space expression of the form $\varphi p \psi$, which corresponds to a Hoare triplet $\{\varphi\}p\{\psi\}$ and thus gives rise to a *special story space proof obligation* $\varphi \rightarrow [p']\psi$.

Consistency Proof Obligations. A *static constraint* on the underlying database schema $\mathcal{S}$ is a condition ζ, in which the free variables are among the $R \in \mathcal{S}$. Such constraints give rise to the request that whenever an operation is started in a database satisfying ζ, then the database reached after successfully completing the execution of the operation, must necessarily satisfy ζ, too.

That is, for all operations p that are defined on a pre-site and all static constraints ζ we obtain a *static consistency proof obligation* $\zeta \rightarrow [p]\zeta$.

A *dynamic constraint* on the underlying database schema $\mathcal{S} = \{R_1, \dots, R_n\}$ is a condition ζ, in which the free variables are among in $\mathcal{S} \cup \mathcal{S}'$ with $\mathcal{S}' = \{R'_1, \dots, R'_n\}$ and each R'_i having the same type as R_i. The additional variables R'_i are used to distinguish between $\mathcal{S}$-databases db, on which an operation p is started, and $\mathcal{S}'$-databases db' resulting after p has been successfully executed.

Obviously, a dynamic constraint ξ has to be interpreted on a pair (db, db') of databases. Following a standard approach to dynamic consistency we associate with ξ an abstract program

$$p(\xi) = @R'_1, \dots, R'_n \bullet \xi \; R_1 := R'_1 \dots R_n := R'_n.$$

Then dynamic consistency of an operation p with respect to ξ means that p must "specialise" $p(\xi)$, i.e. we require that $[p(\xi)]\psi \rightarrow [p]\psi$ for all conditions ψ on $\mathcal{S}$. Fortunately, this proof obligation can be rephrased using a renaming p' of $p(\xi)$ given by

$$p' = @R'_1, \dots, R'_n \bullet \xi\{R_1/R''_1, \dots, R_n/R''_n\} \; R''_1 := R'_1 \dots R''_n := R'_n.$$

Then the *dynamic consistency proof obligation* for p with respect to ξ becomes

$$([p']\langle p\rangle(R_1 = R''_1 \wedge \cdots \wedge R_n/R''_n))\{R''_1/R_1, \dots, R''_n/R_n\}.$$

Personalisation Proof Obligations. The general approach to personalisation that was outlined in [7] is still the same, i.e. we can assume a set Σ containing general constraints on $\mathcal{S} \cup \mathcal{C}$ and specific constraints that refer to preferences of a particular user type. Examples of such preferences are the following:

- An equation $p_1 + p_2 = p_1$ expresses an unconditional preference of operation p_1 over p_2.
- An equation $\varphi(p_1 + p_2) = \varphi p_1$ expresses an conditional preference of operation p_1 over p_2 in case the condition φ is satisfied.

- Similarly, an equation $p(p_1 + p_2) = pp_1$ expresses another conditional preference of operation p_1 over p_2 after the operation p.
- An equation $p_1p_2 + p_2p_1 = p_1p_2$ expresses a preference of order.
- An equation $p^* = pp^*$ expresses that in case of an iteration of operation p it will be executed at least once.

Furthermore, personalisation assumes a postcondition χ that expresses the goals of the particular user. Then personalisation of story space p aims at a simpler story space p' such that $[p]\chi \leftrightarrow [p']\chi$ holds.

4 Conclusion

In this paper we used media types to refine story spaces for WISs. This adds a detailed level of views on an underlying database. The refinement impacts on the story space in such a way that we may now reason with dynamic logic. We emphasised proof obligations for static and dynamic consistency, and enhanced personalisation. We demonstrated the significantly increased reasoning power that results from the introduction of media types.

In our presentation we omitted actors, i.e. abstractions of classes of users with the same role, rights, obligations, intentions and preferences. In particular, the rights and obligations that are associated with the role of an actor give rise to deontic constraints. By taking media types into consideration we have to use a rather complex semantics. Same as for the dynamic logic the expressive power will significantly increase. The investigation of deontic logic and reasoning pragmatics constitute the major areas for future research.

References

1. Abiteboul, S., and Kanellakis, P. Object identity as a query language primitive. In *Proceedings SIGMOD 1989* (1989).
2. Düsterhöft, A., and Thalheim, B. SiteLang: Conceptual modeling of internet sites. In *Conceptual Modeling – ER 2001*, H. S. K. et al., Ed., vol. 2224 of *LNCS*. Springer-Verlag, Berlin, 2001, pp. 179–192.
3. Ebbinghaus, H.-D., and Flum, J. *Finite Model Theory.* Springer-Verlag, Berlin Heidelberg, 1999.
4. Feyer, T., Kao, O., Schewe, K.-D., and Thalheim, B. Design of data-intensive web-based information services. In *Proceedings of the 1st International Conference on Web Information Systems Engineering (WISE 2000)*, Q. Li, Z. M. Ozsuyoglu, R. Wagner, Y. Kambayashi, and Y. Zhang, Eds. IEEE Computer Society, 2000, pp. 462–467.
5. Harel, D., Kozen, D., and Tiuryn, J. *Dynamic Logic.* The MIT Press, Cambridge (MA), USA, 2000.
6. Kozen, D. Kleene algebra with tests. *ACM Transactions on Programming Languages and Systems 19*, 3 (1997), 427–443.
7. Schewe, K.-D., and Thalheim, B. Reasoning about web information systems using story algebras. In *Proceedings ADBIS 2004* (Budapest, Hungary, 2004). to appear.

Scenario Matching Using Functional Substitutability in Web Services

Islam Elgedawy, Zahir Tari, and Michael Winikoff

RMIT University
School of Computer Science and IT, Melbourne, Australia
{elgedawy,zahirt,winikoff}@cs.rmit.edu.au

Abstract. Existing web services discovery techniques mainly match the services' descriptions using keyword-based techniques. This leads to a low service discovery precision as the semantics of services and their domains are ignored. To overcome this problem, we propose a matching approach that matches web services based on their goals as well as their expected *external behavior*. Scenario-networks are used to partially describe the external behavior of web services. A many-to-many semantic-based matching approach for scenario networks is proposed adopting the concept of *functional substitutability*.

1 Introduction

Locating web services in WWW (World Wide Web) without a-priori knowledge is known as a service discovery process. This involves examining descriptions of services in order to find the required service. As the number of web services increases on the Internet, the current keyword-based syntactic services matching techniques are not appropriate due to their low matching precision [2,10,4,11,3].

In order to improve matching precision we need to enrich service descriptions with semantic information. Specifically, we focus on services' *goals* and *contexts* [8,5], and have proposed the G^+ model [5] which explicitly models these concepts. A service goal is modelled by one of the domain operations as well as a group of scenarios that roughly describe how the goal will be achieved. Such group of scenarios is known as the goal scenario network. This describes in an informal manner the expected external behavior of a web service[1]. Therefore, the matchmaker can use this information to match web services based on their functional specifications. Later the matched services could be filtered based on their nonfunctional specifications (e.g QoS). Much work has been done in matching services based on their nonfunctional specification (e.g. [9]). However, this is out of the scope of this paper as it focuses on matching services using their functional specification.

Unfortunately, existing scenario matching techniques are purely syntactic as they match scenarios' components using a one-to-one matching without adopting any semantics provided by either the service model or the service domain [1]. This paper deals

[1] An external behavior of a service represents the sequence of interactions with the user from moment the service is invoked till the user goal is accomplished.

X. Zhou et al. (Eds.): WISE 2004, LNCS 3306, pp. 59–65, 2004.
© Springer-Verlag Berlin Heidelberg 2004

with this problem by proposing a many-to-many semantic matching technique for scenario networks adopting their functional contexts[2]. The proposed technique matches two web services by first constructing partial behavior models from their scenario-networks specifications, and later matching the constructed behavior models based on the functional substitutability [6] of the generated states.

2 Background

G$^+$ Model [5]. This is a hierarchical goal-behavior model providing modelling constructs for functional semantics of web services. Every node represents the corresponding goal/sub-goal, the goal functional context (the goal pre- and post- constraints) and the execution scenarios for achieving this goal/sub-goal. Figure 1 depicts a partial description of a holiday booking application. The booking operation represents the required basic goal, while the hotel room booking operation and the flight booking operations represent the sub-goals.

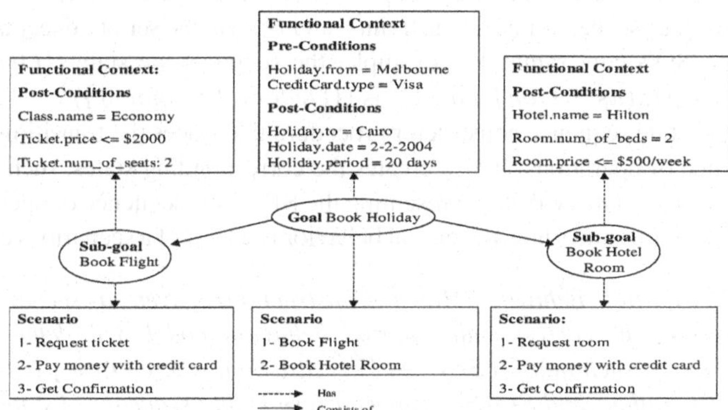

Fig. 1. An Example based on the G$^+$ Model

G$^+$ elements are defined using any ontology following a specific meta-ontology, which has three domain[3] element types: *concepts*, *operations* and *roles*. More details about the G$^+$ model and the proposed meta ontology can be found in [5].

Functional Substitutability. The principle of matching entities using functional substitutability can be summarized as follows: *two entities are said to be matching if they can perform the same required task to achieve a given goal.* For instance, if the goal is to move a group of three people from Melbourne to Sydney, then transportation methods like Car, Bus or Airplane could be used to accomplish the goal. However, according to the required goal achievement constraints (e.g. cost and availability constraints), not

[2] A functional context represents the pre- and post- constraints of achieving the web service goal
[3] By domain we mean the application domain for web services such as tourism, sport.

all these transportation methods could be used for achieving the goal. The use of functional substitutability [6] will establish the matching as follows: Car matches Airplane iff both of them could be used to accomplish the goal without violating the required constraints. It is important to note that Car matches Airplane only with respect to the specified goal and constraints. Implementation details of how functional substitutability concept is used to semantically match web services contexts can be found in [6].

3 Partial Behavior Model Construction

The behavior model of a scenario is represented by the sequence of states that model the transitions that occur due to the invocation of the scenario's operations. A scenario represents a single behavior usage pattern (BP) for a web service.

Definition 1. *(State) A state S_x between two operations Op_{x-1} and Op_x is defined as $\langle SI, SO \rangle$, where SI is the set of post-constraints of Op_{x-1} and SO is the set of pre-constraints of Op_x.*

Every state has a corresponding scope $\langle SI_c, SO_c \rangle$, where SI_c is the set of concepts appearing as scopes for SI's constraints, and SO_c is the set of concepts appearing as scopes for SO's constraints. For example, the scope of the state $\langle \{Order.Qty > 0\}, \{Payment.status = Confirmed\} \rangle$ is $\langle \{Order\}, \{Payment\} \rangle$[4].

SSC is the state sequence constructor procedure that traces the transition points in a given sequence of operations. It also creates the corresponding states, such that the resulting sequence of states will be representing the BP of this sequence of operations. The following definition shows how the partial behavior model β of a scenario is constructed.

Definition 2. *(Partial Behavior Model Construction) Given a scenario $SC = \langle Cntxt,\ OpSeq \rangle$, its corresponding partial behavior model β is defined as: $\beta = \langle Cntxt, StatSeq \rangle$ such that $OpSeq \longrightarrow^{SSC} StatSeq$, where $OpSeq$ is the scenario sequence of operations and $StatSeq$ is the corresponding sequence of states.*

Let us consider a scenario SC_i having its goal as "Selling Books" and its context represented by the complex pre-constraint (Payment.method = Credit-card $\vee$ Payment.method = Check $\vee$ Payment.method = bank-transfer). Its operation sequence is defined as follows:

Operation	Pre-Constraints	Post-Constraints
0- Create-Order(DB):Order	DB.size >0	Order.qty > 0 Order.items ≠ Null Order.status = created Order.delivery ≠ Null
1- Submit-Payment(Order, Payment):Payment	Payment.method = Null Payment.details = Null Order.status = created	Payment.method ≠ Null Payment.details ≠ Null Payment.status = valid
2- Confirm-Order(Order, Payment): Order	Payment.status = valid Order.status = created	Order.status = confirmed

[4] The functional substitutability of the scope's concepts is determined based on the defined substitutability and transformation graphs [6].

Using Definition 2, the state sequence of the corresponding behavior model could be built, as depicted in the table below. For instance, S_0 represents the transition point before Op_0. Therefore S_0 has no SI constraints, however it has SO constraints (which are the Op_0 pre- constraints).

No	State
0	$\langle\{\}, \{DB.size > 0\}\rangle$
1	$\langle\{Order.qty > 0, Order.items \neq Null, Order.status = created, Order.delivery \neq Null\}$, $\{Order.status = created, Payment.method = Null, Payment.details = Null\}\rangle$
2	$\langle\{Payment.method \neq Null, Payment.details \neq Null, Payment.status = valid\}$, $\{Order.status = created, Payment.status = valid\}\rangle$
3	$\langle\{Order.status = confirmed\}, \{\}\rangle$

Scenario networks[5] are used to describe complex service behavior. The behavior model for a scenario network is a collection of the behavior models that correspond to every behavior pattern in the scenario network (i.e. every path from the initial node to the final node in the network). To obtain a behavior model for a behavior pattern, every scenario node belonging to the behavior pattern is replaced by its operation sequence linked in tandem forming a decompressed behavior pattern (DBP). The behavior pattern functional context will be the conjunction of functional contexts of the scenarios belonging to the pattern. SSC is then applied to every decompressed pattern to generate the corresponding behavior model. Thus, the web service behavior model will be formally represented as $\langle Cntxt, DBPS\rangle$, where $Cntxt$ is the service functional context and the $DBPS$ is a set of decompressed behavior pattern. Each decompressed behavior pattern is formally defined as $\langle PCntxt, StatSeq\rangle$, where $PCntxt$ is the functional context of the pattern and $StatSeq$ is the state sequence resulting from applying SSC over the corresponding operation sequence.

4 Behavior Model Matching

As the concept of functional substitutability is used in the matching process, the matching behavior models should substitute each other in the achievement process of a given goal such that the goal is still achieved. This occurs when their contexts are functionally substitutable as well as their corresponding DBP.

Definition 3. *(Behavior Model Matching) Let* $\beta_i = \langle Cntxt_i, DBPS_i\rangle$ *and* $\beta_j = \langle Cntxt_j, DBPS_j\rangle$ *be two behavior models and G a given goal. Then* β_j *can be functionally substituted by* β_i *with respect to G (denoted as* $\beta_i \rhd_G \beta_j$*) iff (a)* $Cntxt_i \rhd_G Cntxt_j$*; and (b)* $\forall DBP_k \in DBPS_j, \exists DBP_q \in DBPS_i$ *such that (1)* $PCntxt_q \rhd_G PCntxt_k$*, where* $PCntxt_q$ *and* $PCntxt_k$ *are respectively the functional context of* DBP_q *and* DBP_k*; and (2)* $StatSeq_q \rhd_G StatSeq_k$*, where* $StatSeq_q$ *and* $StatSeq_k$ *are respectively the state sequence (See Definition 7) of* DBP_q *and* DBP_k*.*

The behavior model matching problem could then be addressed by determining when a sequence of states functionally substitute another sequence of states, which implies

[5] Scenario network is a group of scenarios temporally organized in a form of and/or graph

many-to-many state matching. Many-to-many state matching is feasible if we know which states should be merged together and when. To develop further this idea, we first introduce the concepts of merging and matching states.

Definition 4. *(State Merging) Given a sequence of states StatSeq = S_0, S_1,..., S_n. The resulting state of merging StatSeq's states is $S_m = \langle \bigcup_{i=0}^{i=n} SI_i, \bigcup_{i=0}^{i=n} SO_i \rangle$, where SI_i is the SI of state S_i and SO_i is the SO of state S_i.*

The following definition provides the necessary requirements for two states to be matched based on their functional substitutability.

Definition 5. *(State Matching) Let $S_i = \langle SI_i, SO_i \rangle$ and $S_j = \langle SI_j, SO_j \rangle$ be two states and G a goal. S_j can be functionally substituted by S_i with respect to G (denoted as $S_i \rhd_G S_j$) iff (a) $\forall Pc_k \in SI_j$, $\exists Pc_q \in SI_i$ such that $Pc_q \rhd_G Pc_k$, where Pc_k, Pc_q are primitive constraints; and (b) $\forall Pc_u \in SO_j$, $\exists Pc_v \in SO_i$ such that $Pc_v \rhd_G Pc_u$, where Pc_u, Pc_v are primitive constraints.*

Let us consider the following states: $S_1 = \langle \{City.name = Cairo\}, \{Trip.date = 1/10/2004\} \rangle$ and $S_2 = \langle \{Country.name = Egypt\}, \{Trip.\ Date > 1/1/2004\} \rangle$. S_1 can functionally substitute S_2 because (City.name= Cairo) functionally substitutes (Country.name = Egypt) and (Trip.date = 1/10/2004) functionally substitutes (Trip.Date > 1/1/2004). It is important to note that S_2 does not functionally substitute S_1 because (Country.name = Egypt) does not functionally substitute (City.name = Cairo)[6], also (Trip.date = 1/10/2004) can not be substituted by (Trip.Date > 1/1/2004). More details about primitive constraint matching can be found in [6].

Adopting the proposed state matching definition, how will many-to-many state matching be accomplished and which states should be merged? To answer this question we introduce the concept of an "expandable" state. An expandable state is a state that could be merged with other states in its sequence such that a given state in other sequence can be functionally substituted by the new merged state.

Definition 6. *(Expandable State) Let $S_x \in StateSeq_i$ and $S_y \in StateSeq_j$ be states and G a goal. Then S_x is expandable with respect to S_y and G iff (a) Scope(S_x) $\neq$ Scope(S_y); and (b)$\exists S_q \in StatSeq_i$: $(q > x) \wedge (S_w \rhd_G S_y)$, where S_w is a new state resulting from merging the states S_i such that S_w matches S_y, where $x \leq i \leq q$ along $StatSeq_i$.*

We propose a procedure, called *sequence augmenter* (SEQA) that determines which states should be merged and when. SEQA accepts two sequence of states, say $StatSeq_s$ (source) and $StatSeq_t$ (target), and checks whether the target can be functionality substituted by the source with respect to G without violating the constraints of its functional context. SEQA generates two augmented sequences of states, denoted as $AStatSeq_i$ and $AStatSeq_j$, as well as their corresponding matching peers. Figure 2 depicts the flow chart that indicates how the SEQA procedure works, where T represents the current target state to be matched in $StatSeq_t$ and S represents the current proposed matching state in $StatSeq_s$. If a state expansion occurs in a given state sequence, the state sequence is changed into its augmented version. Reaching "finish" in the flow chart means we have

[6] Egypt has many cities, not just Cairo.

the final augmented sequences stored in $StatSeq_t$, $StatSeq_s$ and their corresponding matches.

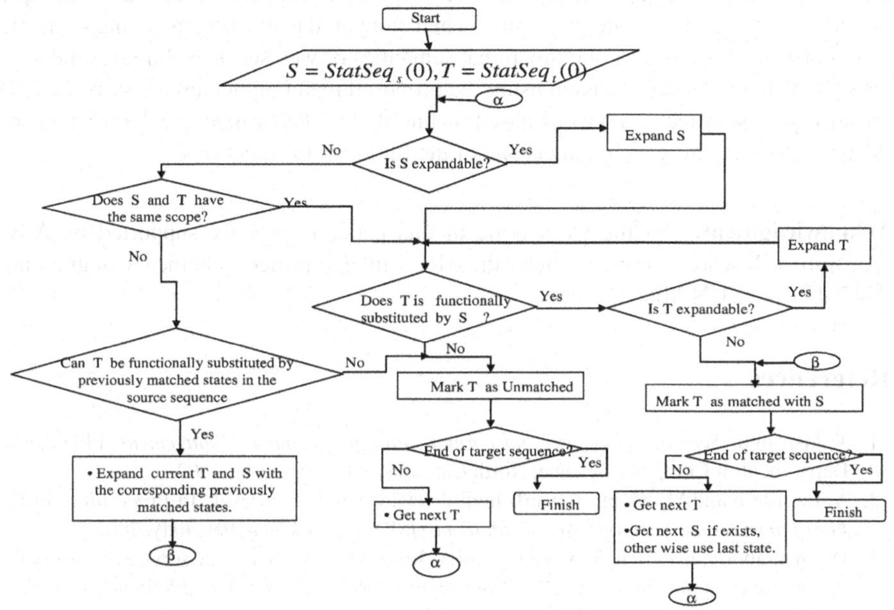

Fig. 2. SEQA Flow Chart

For every state expansion, state S is merged with it successor until $Scope(S) \supseteqq Scope(T)$ such that the new merged state scope subsumes the target state scope.

In case a target state T matches a previously matched state (the extreme left branch in the flow chart), all the corresponding previously matched states in both sequences are merged.

The question now is, when do two state sequences match? The answer is provided in the following definition.

Definition 7. *(State Sequence Matching) Let $StatSeq_i$ and $StatSeq_i$ be state sequences and G a given goal. Then $StatSeq_j$ is functionally substituted by $StatSeq_i$ with respect to G (denoted as $StatSeq_i \rhd_G StatSeq_j$) iff (a) $(AS_{0i} \rhd_G AS_{0j}) \wedge (AS_{fi} \rhd_G AS_{fj})$; and (b) $(\forall AS_{xj}, AS_{yj} \in AStatSeq_j : x < y, \exists AS_{ui}, AS_{vi} \in AStatSeq_i : (AS_{ui} \rhd_G AS_{xj}) \wedge (AS_{vi} \rhd_G AS_{yj}) \wedge (u < v))$, where AS_{0i}, AS_{0j} are the initial augmented states belong to $AStatSeq_i, AStatSeq_j$ respectively and AS_{fi}, AS_{fj} are the final augmented states belong to $AStatSeq_i, AStatSeq_j$ respectively.*

This definition is a strict definition as it assumes every state in the target behavior model should have a matching peer. However a less strict matching could be achieved if the second condition in Definition 7 is neglected.

5 Conclusion

Matching web services based on their goals and their expected external behavior provides a new way of matching web services. We believe the proposed matching technique provides a more precise matching results when compared to existing matching syntactic techniques, as it is based on the functional semantics of web services. Initial simulation tests show that retrieval precision using the proposed matching technique surpasses the retrieval precision using keyword-based technique [7]. Performance enhancement for the proposed matching technique is one of the future work directions.

Acknowledgment. All the work done in this paper is proudly supported by ARC (Australian Research Council), under the ARC Linkage-project scheme (with grant no. 0347217) and SUN Microsystems.

References

1. T. Alspaugh. *Scenario Networks and Formalization for scenario Management.* PhD thesis, Department of Computer Science, North Carolina State University, 2002.
2. A. Bernstein and M. Klein. Towards high-precision service retrieval. In *Proceedings of the First International Semantic Web Conference (ISWC)*, pages 84 – 101, Italy, 2002.
3. D. Chakraborty, F. Perich, S. Avancha, and A. Joshi. Dreggie: Semantic service discovery for m-commerce applications. In *20th Symposiom on Reliable Distributed Systems: Workshop on Reliable and Secure Applications in Mobile Environment*, 2001.
4. K. Decker, M. Williamson, and K. Sycara. Matchmaking and brokering. In *Proceedings of the Second International Conference in Multi-Agent Systems(ICMAS)*, Japan, 1996.
5. I. Elgedawy. A conceptual framework for web services semantic discovery. In *Proceedings of On The Move (OTM) to meaningful internet systems*, pages 1004–1016, Italy, 2003. Springer Verlag.
6. I. Elgedawy, Z. Tari, and M. Winikoff. Functional context matching for web services. Technical Report TR-04-3, RMIT University, Australia, 2004.
7. I. Elgedawy, Z. Tari, and M. Winikoff. Scenario networks matching using functional substitutability in web services. Technical Report TR-04-7, RMIT University, Australia, 2004.
8. D. Fensel and C. Bussler. The web service modeling framework WSMF. *Electronic Commerce Research and Applications*, 1(2):113–137, 2002.
9. J. Klingemann, J. Wäsch, and K. Aberer. Adaptive outsourcing in cross-organizational workflows. In *Proceedings of the the 11th Conference on Advanced Information Systems Engineering (CAiSE)*, pages 417–421, Germany, 1999.
10. M. Paolucci, T. Kawamura, T. Payne, and K. Sycara. Semantic matching of web services capabilities. In *Proceedings of the First International Semantic Web Conference (ISWC)*, Italy, 2002.
11. K. Sycara, J. Lu, M. Klusch, and S. Widoff. Matchmaking among heterogeneous agents on the internet. In *Proceedings AAAI Spring Symposium on Intelligent Agents in Cyberspace*, 1999.

Three Kinds of E-wallets for a NetPay Micro-Payment System

Xiaoling Dai[1] and John Grundy[2, 3]

[1] Department of Mathematics and Computing Science
The University of the South Pacific, Laucala Campus, Suva, Fiji
dai_s@usp.ac.fj

[2] Department of Computer Science and [3] Department of Electrical and Electronic Engineering
University of Auckland, Private Bag 92019, Auckland, New Zealand
john-g@cs.auckland.ac.nz

Abstract. We have developed NetPay, a micro-payment protocol characterized by off-line processing, customer anonymity and relatively high performance and security using one-way hashing functions for encryption. In our NetPay prototypes we have identified three kinds of electronic wallets to store e-coins – a server-side wallet, client-side wallet application, and cookie-based wallet cache. We describe the motivation for NetPay and describe the three kinds of e-wallets and their design. We report on prototype implementations of these wallets and end-user perceptions of their use.

1 Introduction

Macro-payment systems used by most E-commerce sites are not suitable for charging per-page for web site browsing. Such systems typically use complex encryption technologies and require communications with an authorisation server to request and confirm payment. Micro-payment systems offer an alternative strategy of pay-as-you-go charging, even for very low cost, very high-volume charging. There are a number of micro-payment systems [8], [11]. Most existing micro-payment technologies proposed or prototyped to date suffer from problems with communication, security, and lack of anonymity or are vendor-specific. In addition, they usually adopt a single strategy for managing the electronic coinage, not always the one customer requires or desire.

We have developed a new micro-payment protocol called NetPay to address these problems. The NetPay protocol allows customers to buy E-coins, worth very small amounts of money, from a broker and spend these E-coins at various vendor sites to pay for large numbers of discrete information or services of small value each. NetPay shifts the communication traffic bottleneck from a broker and distributes it among the vendors by using transferable E-coin Touchstones and Indexes. We have identified three different strategies for managing these E-coins: a server-side E-wallet that is exchanged among vendor sites as the customer buys information or services; a

X. Zhou et al. (Eds.): WISE 2004, LNCS 3306, pp. 66–77, 2004.
© Springer-Verlag Berlin Heidelberg 2004

client-side E-wallet application that resides on the customer's PC and from which vendors debit coins; and a hybrid, cookie-based E-wallet cache.

In this paper, we give an overview of existing micro-payment models and point out the problems with these models. We then briefly describe the NetPay micro-payment protocol. We then describe the three kinds of e-wallets we have designed and prototyped for the NetPay system. We describe the designs for the two NetPay e-wallets and illustrate their usage. We conclude with an outline of our further plans for research and development in this area.

2 Motivation

With the development of Internet businesses, more and more content providers are switching once free content or services to a paid subscription model or pay-per-click model, eliminating the revenue relying on only an advertisement market [10]. Today there are already many newspapers and journals in electronic form. Most of newspapers and journals allow their regular subscribers to read the articles on the net for free while they also get a normal paper copy of them. Such a procedure seems to waste resources since the subscribers can print the articles in which they are interested on net and thus there is no need to read the paper copy. Micro-payment systems could be used to make things different for online contents or services. You could read and download an article and only pay a small amount of money e.g. 5c, 10c or 20c. Other forms of emerging on-line content provision include purchase of music and video clips, clip art, stock market and other financial data, and so on [9]. For example, online music can be downloaded as a single at a time from an on-line music site by paying small amounts of money per single.

There are a number of micro-payment systems in various stages of development from proposals in the academic literature to systems in commercial use [8], [5], [6], [11]. Though micro-payment protocols have received a lot of attention from researchers and cryptographers, only one micro-payment system, Millicent [12], exists in general public use in Japan. All existing protocols for micro-payments have their strengths and weaknesses in practical applications [2]. In Millicent [8], the third party must be online whenever the user wishes to interact with a new vendor, i.e., the system places a heavy real-time burden on the third party. In Mpay [7], customers can pay nothing to access services for a full day and also the customer's anonymity is not protected. In PayWord [11], the payword chain is customer and vendor specific, i.e., the system locks customers to some sites that they have the payword chains. Most micro-payment approaches provide customers with E-coin scripts or payword chains, or require customers to log onto a vendor web site to access a stored collection of e-coins. Most do not support inter-vendor spending of E-coins.

Most existing micro-payment approaches use a single mechanism for managing the electronic coinage they use. The majority store these e-coins in (usually) encrypted files on the client PCs. They need a specialized application with which this e-coin database is accessed and updated. This approach often requires installation of client-side "e-wallet" applications to manage the e-coins. Some approaches are susceptible to fraudulent alteration of the e-coins while others require heavyweight, expensive encryption technologies to decode the e-coins each time they are used. Some on-line micro-payment approaches use a server-side approach where an on-line broker manages the e-coins for each customer and decrements the coins available on each spend. This provides a single point of failure or bottleneck for the micro-payment system as a whole and often removes the anonymity of the customer.

3 NetPay Protocol

We have developed a new protocol called NetPay that provides a secure, cheap, widely available, and debit-based protocol for an off-line micro-payment system [1]. NetPay differs from previous payword-based protocols by using touchstones that are signed by the broker and an e-coin index signed by vendors, which are passed from vendor to vendor. The signed touchstone is used by a vendor to verify the electronic currency – paywords, and signed Index is used to prevent double spending from customers and to resolve disputes between vendors. In this section, we describe the key transactions in the NetPay protocol.

Suppose an e-newspaper site wants to use the NetPay micro-payment system to sell articles on a per-page usage basis. The system involves four parties – a NetPay broker site; e-newspaper vendor sites; customer PCs; and a bank macro-payment system. The customers can be classified as registered customers and unregistered customers. Only registered customers can buy e-coins from a broker's site and click-buy an article with a newspaper site. Both types of customers can search and view article titles on line. Initially a customer accesses the broker's web site to register and acquire a number of e-coins from the broker (bought using a single macro-payment). The broker creates an "e-wallet" that includes the e-coin ID, touchstone, and e-coins for the customer. This e-wallet may reside on the client PC (via a special application) or be passed to vendor servers.

The customer browses the home page of the newspaper web site and finds a desired news article to read. Each article will typically have a small cost e.g. 2-10c, and the customer would typically read a number of these. When wishing to read the details of an article, the customer clicks on the article heading and the vendor system debits the customer's e-coins by e.g. 10c (by taking 1, 2 or more e-coins from their payword chain, depending on the monetary value of each, up to 10c in value).

The newspaper system verifies that the e-coin provided by the customer's e-wallet is valid by use of a "touchstone" obtained once only from the broker. If the payment is valid (coin is verified and sufficient credit remains), the article is displayed on the screen. The customer may browse other articles, their coins being debited (the index of spent coins incremented) each time an article is read. If coins run out, the customer is directed to the broker's site to buy more. The vendor keeps copies of the spent e-coins.

When the customer changes to another online newspaper (or other kind of vendor using the same e-coin broker currency), the new vendor site first requests the current e-coin touchstone information from previous vendor's site. The new vendor contacts the previous vendor to get the e-coin touchstone and "spent coin" index and then debits coins for further news articles.

When the previous vendor system is "down", a backup server in the system sends the e-coin ID, the touchstone, and the index to the broker. The new vendor could also contact the broker to get the e-coin touchstone and the "spent e-coin" index. At the end of each day, the vendors all send the spent e-coins to the broker, redeeming them for real money (done by macro-payment bank transfer from the broker to vendor accounts).

4 NetPay E-wallets

We have designed three kinds of e-wallets to manage e-coins in the NetPay system. One is hosted by vendor servers and is passed from vendor to vendor as the customer moves from one site to another. The second is a client-side application resident on the client's PC. The third is a hybrid that caches E-coins in a web browser cookie for debiting as the customer spends at a site.

4.1 Server-Side E-wallet

Some people prefer to access the Internet from multiple computers (e.g. a business person who often travels around). A Server-side hosted e-wallet is suitable for these people. The server-side e-wallet is stored on the vendor server and is transferred from the broker to each vendor when required.

Fig. 1 shows how a vendor application server debits e-coins from the server-side e-wallet. When a customer clicks title of an article on his/her browser (1), the web server sends the request to the vendor application server (2), which then debits e-coins from the customer's e-wallet (3) paying for the content. Customers can buy articles using the server-side e-wallet anywhere in the world and the e-coin debiting time is very fast on the server-side e-wallet system. However customers are required to remember e-coin IDs and password in order to log into a newspaper site when changing vendor. When a customer moves from one vendor to another, their e-wallet contents must be passed from the previous vendor site to the new one. If the first vendor site becomes unavailable, the customer temporarily does not have access to their e-wallet.

4.2 Client-Side E-wallet

Some people prefer to access the Internet using one machine (e.g. those who stay home most of the time or access sites from their work PC only). A Client-side e-wallet is more suitable for these kinds of people. The client-side e-wallet is an application running on the client PC that holds e-coin information.

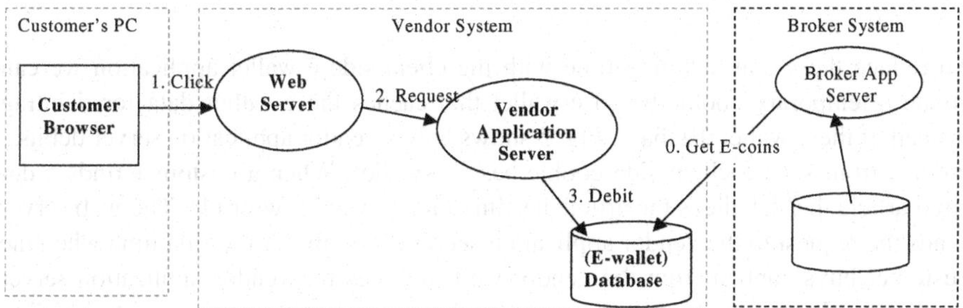

Fig. 1. Server-side e-wallet conceptual model.

Fig. 2 shows how a vendor application server debits e-coins from the client-side e-wallet. When buying an article content a customer clicks the title of the article on the web browser (1) and then the web server sends the request to the vendor application server (2). The vendor application server sends the price of the article to the e-wallet application (3) and then the e-wallet application returns the e-coins, paying for the content to the vendor application server (4-5).

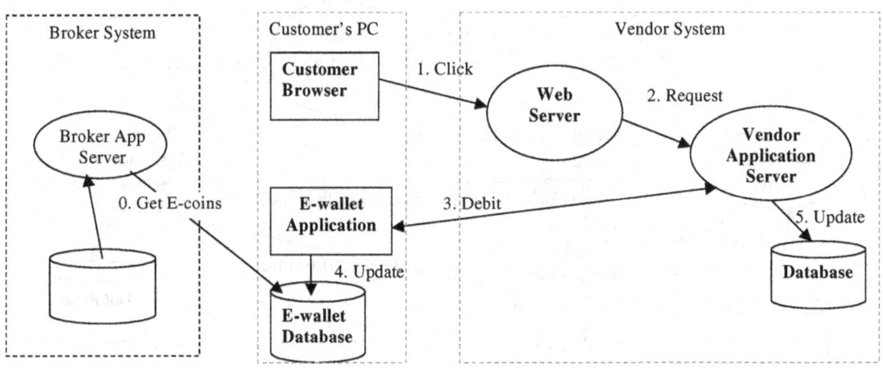

Fig. 2. Client-side e-wallet conceptual model.

Customers can buy article content using the client-side e-wallet at different newspaper sites without the need to log in after the e-wallet application is downloaded to their PC. Their e-coins are resident on their own PC and so access to them is never lost due to network outages to one vendor. The e-coin debiting time is slower for a client-side e-wallet than the server-side e-wallet due to the extra communication between vendor application server and customer PC's e-wallet application.

4.3 Client-Side Cookie-Based E-wallet

To reduce the e-coin debiting time with the client-side e-wallet application we can create a temporary cookie-based e-wallet that caches the e-wallet data for debiting instead of the e-wallet database. Fig. 3 shows how a vendor application server debits e-coins from such a client-side cookie-based e-wallet. When a customer finds a desired article, he/she clicks the article heading on the web browser (1). The web server sends the request to the vendor application server (2). Only for the first time when the customer buys content from the vendor web site does the vendor application server need to get the e-coins from the e-wallet application (3). It then creates a "cookie" to cache the remaining customer e-coins, stored in a cookie file on the customer PC (4). Once the cookie is created, the vendor application server debits e-coins from the cookie directly after each HTTP request to buy content (5). The e-wallet application can read the cookie file information to know how many e-coins are left when the customer wants to check the balance of the e-wallet or after the customer has moved to access another vendor site (6). This reduces the need for the vendor application server to communicate with client PC-based e-wallet, caches the e-coins in HTTP request that holds cookies.

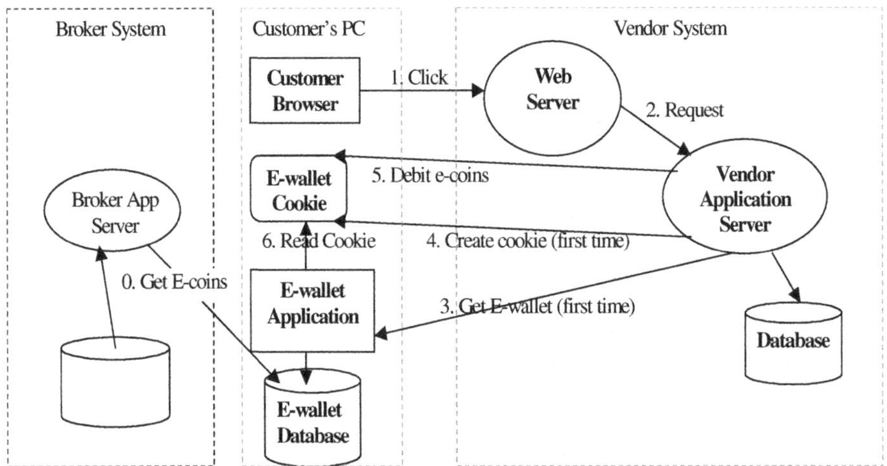

Fig. 3. Client-side cookie-based e-wallet

When the customer changes to another vendor, the new vendor contacts the previous vendor to request the touchstone and the index of the e-wallet, and the previous vendor application server gets the remaining e-coins from the cookie file, storing them back into the e-wallet database. It then deletes the cookie. This approach is suitable for a customer performing many purchases from a single vendor, and then changing to another vendor.

5 NetPay E-wallet Design

In our current NetPay prototype we have implemented two kinds of e-wallet, a server-side e-wallet and a client-side e-wallet. The broker application sets the e-wallet that stores the e-coins in the server-side or client-side.

5.1 Server-Side E-wallet NetPay Design

The server-side e-wallet should be transferred from the broker to each vendor in turn that the customer is buying content from. Vendor systems need to know the location of the customer's e-wallet and to get the e-wallet contents. To do this we designed the broker application server so that it provides a set of CORBA interfaces with which the vendor application servers communicate to request an e-wallet location or to get an e-wallet. The vendor application servers also provide a CORBA interface in order for another vendor application server to get the e-wallet if it has been passed to one of them. The e-wallet is thus passed from vendor to vendor as needed. The major problem with this approach is that the new vendor cannot get the e-wallet when the previous vendor crashes or becomes unavailable.

When a customer first clicks the Login&Buy button to purchase e-coins on the browser, the HTTP server runs JSPs handling the request. The Broker application server communicates with a macro-payment system to debit money from the customer bank account and stores the e-coins information in the database.

When the customer goes to a vendor site, he/she needs to login by entering the e-coin ID and the password. A JSP page handles the login request. If the e-wallet does not exist, the vendor's application server communicates with broker application server via CORBA to get the e-wallet location, including host and port of the broker or previous vendor. Then it communicates with the broker/previous vendor via CORBA to get the customer's refreshed e-wallet. This includes ecoinID, touchstone, index, paywords, and amount. After the customer clicks the article handing, a JSP page deals with a display content request. The vendor application server debits e-coins from the server-side e-wallet paying for the content. The key components of the NetPay server-side e-wallet design as illustrated in Fig. 4.

5.2 Client-Side E-wallet NetPay

The client-side e-wallet is implemented as a Java application runs on the client PC. According to our protocol, a touchstone and an index (T&I) of a customer's e-coin should be passed from the broker to each vendor. To do this we have the broker application server provide a CORBA interface for vendor application servers to communicate with to get the T&I to verify e-coins. The vendor application servers also provide a CORBA interface in order for another vendor application server to communication with it to pass the T&I, avoiding use of the broker where possible.

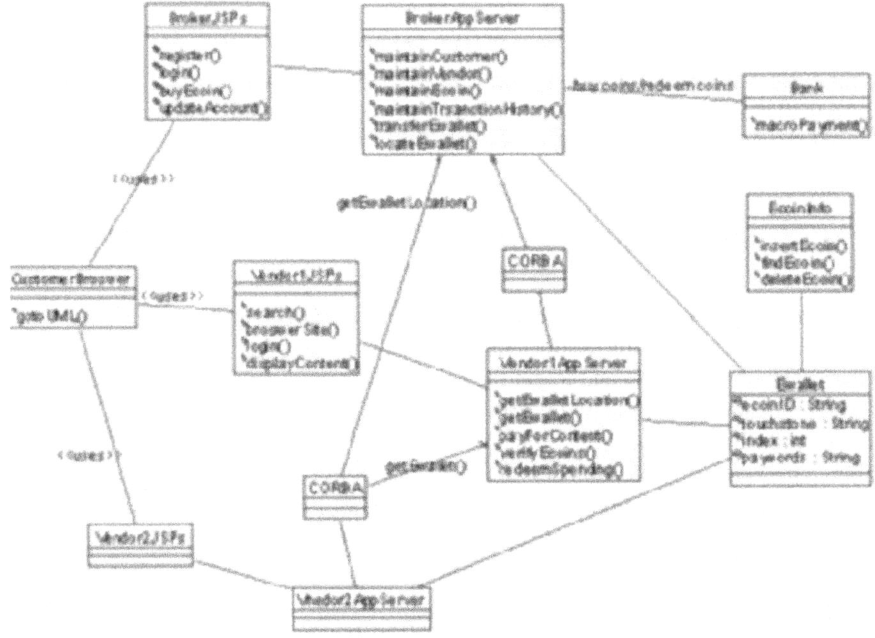

Fig. 4. An overview of the NetPay server-side e-wallet design.

When a customer first clicks the Login&Buy button to purchase e-coins on the browser, JSPs running on the web server handle the request. The Broker application server communicates with macro-payment system to debit money from the customer bank account and then sends the e-coins to the customer's e-wallet on the customer machine.

A JSP page deals with displaying content when the customer clicks on the title of an article. The vendor application server connects with the e-wallet application and sends the price of the article. The customer's e-wallet returns with the e-coins and the location of the T&I to the vendor application server. The vendor application server communicates with the broker or previous vendor via CORBA to obtain the T&I, which are used to verify the e-coins. The main client-side NetPay e-wallet design features are illustrated in Fig. 5.

The cookie-based E-wallet design is an extension to the client-side e-wallet design that uses browser-based cookies as a temporary cache. When the Vendor application server first communicates with the client PC-hosted e-wallet application, it reads the e-coins from the e-wallet and stores them in a browser cookie. The e-wallet updates its database to indicate the e-coins are now cached by the local browser in a cookie file for the vendor. Each subsequent pay-per-click from the same vendor has one or more e-coins from the cookie removed and stored in the vendor's redemption database. If

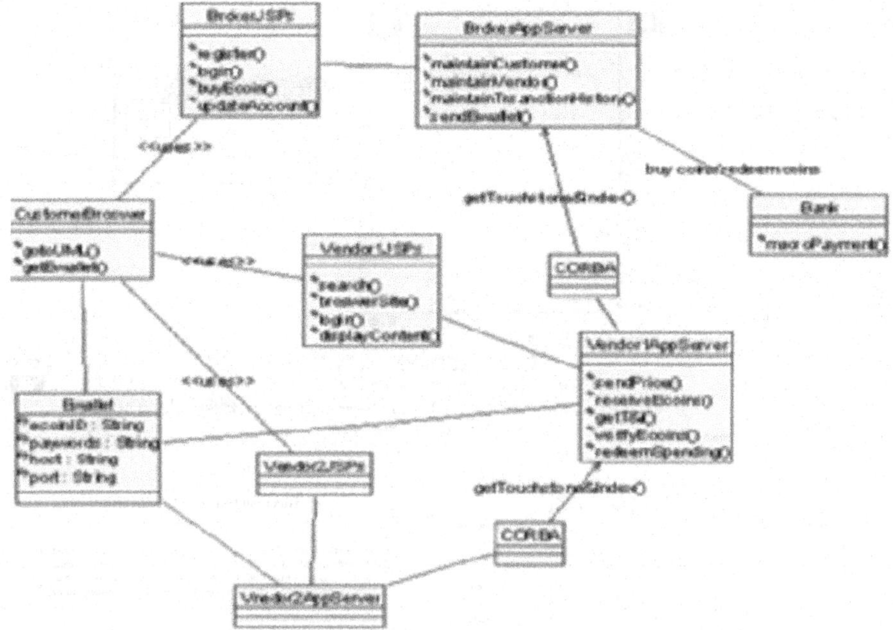

Fig. 5. An overview of the NetPay client-side e-wallet design.

the customer moves to another vendor, the first new vendor access to the e-wallet application causes an update of the e-wallet e-coins from the cached cookie file from the previous vendor. This cookie file is then deleted by the client PC-hosted e-wallet.

6 Example Usage

We briefly illustrate the usage of our E-wallet prototypes for a simple E-newspaper system enhanced with NetPay. Fig. 6 shows an example of NetPay in use for this prototype E-newspaper application. The customer first buys e-coins from a broker (1-2), and these are stored in a client-side E-wallet (3) or requested by a vendor on customer login.

The customer visits a NetPay-enhanced vendor site (4), and if using a server-side E-wallet logs in providing an E-wallet ID and password generated by the broker. The customer accesses articles on the E-newspaper site, each time their E-wallet being debited (5). The server-side E-wallet held by the vendor site server is debited and the remaining credit displayed to the user after each article is presented, as shown in (5). The client-side E-wallet is held by an application resident on the customer PC, and its balance can be accessed when desired or displayed periodically, as shown in (3). The

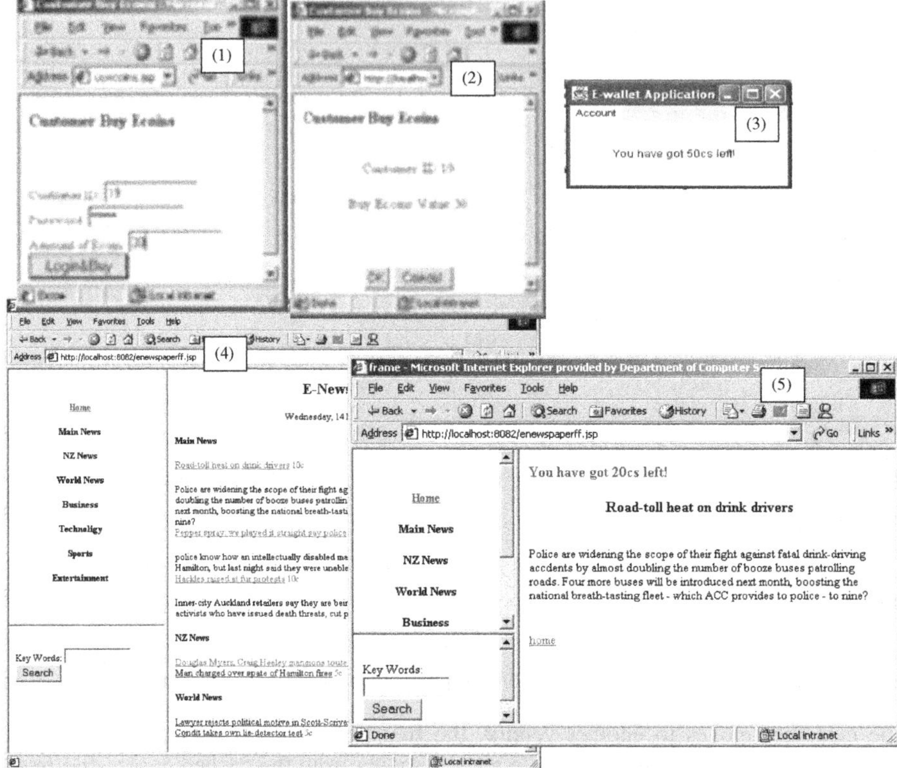

Fig. 6. Example of NetPay and e-wallets in use

cookie-based E-wallet provides the same look-and-feel as the client-side E-wallet, with caching of the remaining E-coins in a browser cookie done by the vendor's Net-Pay-enhanced web server.

7 Discussion

We focused on designing three kinds of "E-wallets" for NetPay broker and vendor prototypes using a CORBA-based approach. Each approach has advantages and disadvantages. The first requires uses of e-coin ID and password to login to a vendor system. The later two require that the customers download an e-wallet application and install it on their PC. The e-coin debiting time is slower for a client-side e-wallet than for a server-side e-wallet system due to extra overhead communicating to the client PC. A firewall installed on the customer PC may also interfere with this communication from the vendor server. We implemented two kinds of the NetPay e-wallet and "hard-coded" this support into a prototype vendor application to enhance it with Net-

Pay mcro-payment support. We used these prototype client-side and server-side e-wallets to carry out an evaluation of NetPay usability and performance.

We used three prototypes, one providing macro-payment style subscription-based payment, a second server-side NetPay micro-payment and the third client-side NetPay micro-payment. We carried out some basic usability testing via a survey-based approach with representative target users of NetPay [4]. This survey found that the article content at different newspaper sites was found by users to be easy to access and read without logging into client-side NetPay system. However, users found that this approach could incur a distracting extra delay in page display over the other systems. The server-side NetPay system allowed users to read articles anywhere in the world, but customers needed to remember e-coin Ids in order to use the system. The conventional macro-payment based system was found to be less appealing to our users than the NetPay-enhanced micro-payment implementing e-newspaper vendors.

Our three e-newspaper prototypes have also been tested for application server performance and client response time under heavy loading [4]. The key aim was to test how long a newspaper site takes to serve client requests when extended to use each of the three payment systems, from the time the customer clicks the title of an article to the time the article is fully displayed on screen.

The results of the set of performance impact tests are shown in Table 1. The response time measures how long it takes for a page to be returned from the vendor site.

Table 1. Initial prototype performance

System	Response Delay Time (average)
Subscription-based	16ms
Server-side NetPay	80ms
Client-side NetPay	950ms

From Table 1, the server-side NetPay takes 64ms for e-coin debiting per article and Client-side takes 934ms total time, though the time to debit coins is taken by the client's e-wallet application, not the vendor's application server. The large response time overhead in the server for the server-side NetPay prototype is due to the database transactions it carries out to record coin updates and debits to redeem to the broker. Note that multi-threading in the server allows the vendor to serve other clients during NetPay debits but the server-side e-wallet incurs heavy update overhead. We enhanced the NetPay vendor server components to use a redemption transaction log file with over night update of the vendor redemption database from the log file. This markedly improved server-side performance and reduced server CPU and database overhead by nearly 40%. Further enhancements, such as the use of a server-side memory database for managing e-coins for redemption and server-side e-wallets could further reduce the impact of NetPay components on vendor server performance.

8 Summary

We have described the development of a new micro-payment system, NetPay, featuring different ways of managing electronic money, or e-coins. NetPay provides an off-line, anonymous protocol that supports high-volume, low-cost electronic transactions over the Internet. We developed three kinds of e-wallets to manage coins in a NetPay-based system: a sever-side e-wallet allowing multiple computer access to e-coins; a client-side e-wallet allowing customer PC management of the e-coins, and a cookie-based e-wallet cache to improve performance of the client-side e-wallet communication overhead. Experiences to date with NetPay prototypes have demonstrated it provides an effective micro-payment strategy and customers welcome the ability to manage their electronic coins in different ways.

References

1. Dai, X. and Lo, B.: NetPay – An Efficient Protocol for Micropayments on the WWW. Fifth Australian World Wide Web Conference, Australia (1999)
2. Dai, X., Grundy, J. and Lo, B.: Comparing and contrasting micro-payment models for E-commerce systems, International Conferences of Info-tech and Info-net (ICII), China (2001)
3. Dai, X., Grundy, J.: Architecture of a Micro-Payment System for Thin-Client Web Applications. In Proceedings of the 2002 International Conference on Internet Computing, Las Vegas, CSREA Press, June 24-27, 444--450
4. Dai, X. and Grundy J.: "Customer Perception of a Thin-client Micro-payment System Issues and Experiences", *Journal of End User Computing*, 15(4), pp 62-77, (2003).
5. Gabber, E. and Silberschatz, A.: "Agora: A Minimal Distributed Protocol for Electronic Commerce", *Proceedings of the Second USENIX Workshop on Electronic Commerce, O*akland, California, November 18-21, 1996, pp. 223-232
6. Gabber, E. and Silberschatz, A.: "Micro Payment Transfer Protocol (MPTP) Version 0.1". *W3C Working Draft*, 1995. http://www.w3.org/pub/WWW/TR/WD-mptp
7. Herzberg, A. and Yochai, H. : Mini-pay: Charging per Click on the Web, 1996 http://www.ibm.net.il/ibm_il/int-lab/mpay
8. Manasse, M.: The Millicent Protocols for Electronic Commerce. First USENIX Workshop on Electronic Commerce. New York (1995)
9. MP3 Web Site: http://www.mp3.com
10. Posman, "Would You Pay for Google?", 2002. http://www.clickz.com/media/agency_start/article.php/1013901
11. Rivest, R. and Shamir, A.: PayWord and MicroMint: Two Simple Micropayment Schemes. Proceedings of 1996 International Workshop on Security Protocols, Lecture Notes in Computer Science, Vol. 1189. Springer (1997) 69—87
12. Welcome to MilliCent WORLD Homepage, 2001. http://www.mllicent.gr.jp

Information Assurance in Federated Identity Management: Experimentations and Issues *

Gail-Joon Ahn[1], Dongwan Shin[1], and Seng-Phil Hong[2]

[1] University of North Carolina at Charlotte, Charlotte, NC 28232, USA
{gahn,doshin}@uncc.edu
[2] Information and Communications University, Taejon, Korea
philhong@icu.ac.kr

Abstract. Identity management has been recently considered to be a viable solution for simplifying user management across enterprise applications. When users interact with services on the Internet, they often tailor the services in some way for their personal use through their personalized accounts and preferences. The network identity of each user is the global set of such attributes constituting the various accounts. In this paper, we investigate two well-known federated identity management (FIM) solutions, *Microsoft Passport* and *Liberty Alliance*, attempting to identify information assurance (IA) requirements in FIM. In particular, this paper focuses on principal IA requirements for Web Services that plays an integral role in enriching identity federation and management. We also discuss our experimental analysis of those models.

1 Introduction

Surveys and polling data confirm that the Internet is now a prime vehicle for business, community, and personal interactions. The notion of identity is the important component of this vehicle. Identity management (IM) has been recently considered to be a viable solution for simplifying user management across enterprise applications. As enterprises have changed their business operation paradigm from brick-and-mortar to click-and-mortar, they have embraced a variety of enterprise applications for streamlining business operations such as emailing systems, customer relationship management systems, enterprise resource planning systems, supply chain management systems, and so on. However, a non-trivial problem has been compounded by this reinforcing line of enterprise applications, *the problem of managing user profiles.* The addition of such applications has proved to be subject to bringing in a new database for storing user profiles, and it was quite costly and complex to manage all those profiles, which were often redundant. Considering business-to-business environments, where a set of users consists of not only their employees or customers but also those of

* The work of Gail-J. Ahn and Dongwan Shin was supported by the grants from Bank of America through e-Business Technology Institute at the University of North Carolina at Charlotte.

X. Zhou et al. (Eds.): WISE 2004, LNCS 3306, pp. 78–89, 2004.
© Springer-Verlag Berlin Heidelberg 2004

their partners, this problem became even worse. As a set of underlying technologies and processes overarching the creation, maintenance, and termination of user identities, IM has attempted to resolve such issues.

Furthermore, the prevalence of business alliances or coalitions necessitates the further evolution of IM, so called federated identity management (FIM). The main motivation of FIM is to enhance user convenience and privacy as well as to decentralize user management tasks through the federation of identities among business partners. As a consequence, a cost-effective and interoperable technology is strongly required in the process of federation. Web Services (WS) can be as a good candidate for such requirement as it has served to provide the standard way to enable the communication and composition of various enterprise applications over distributed and heterogeneous networks.

Since identity federation is likely to go along with the exchange of sensitive user information in a highly insecure online environment, security and privacy issues with such exchange of information are key concerns in FIM. In this paper, we describe a comparative study of FIM to investigate how to ensure information assurance (IA) for identity federation. We first discuss key benefits of FIM and how WS can play an integral role in enriching IM through federation. Then, we investigate two well-known FIM solutions, *Liberty Alliance* [HW03] and *Microsoft Passport* [tr103], attempting to identify IA requirements in FIM. In addition, we describe our experimental study on those models.

The rest of this paper is organized as follows. Section 2 overviews three approaches involved in IM, along with the prior research works related to our work. Section 3 describes FIM, particularly, Liberty and Passport in detail. Section 4 discusses the role of WS in federating identities in the two models. Section 5 articulates IA requirements for FIM followed by the experimentation details in Section 6. Section 7 concludes this paper.

2 Identity Management and Related Works

In this section, we start with the discussion of IM approaches. We categorize IM approaches into the following three styles: *isolated IM*, *centralized FIM*, and *distributed FIM*. Thereafter, we discuss the core components of WS architectures.

The isolated IM model is the most conservative of the three approaches. Each business forms its own identity management domain (IMD) and has its own way of maintaining the identities of users including employees, customers, and partners. Hence, this model is simple to implement and has a tight control over user profiles. However, it is hard to achieve user convenience with this model since different IMDs are likely to have different authentication processes or mechanisms for their users and corresponding authentication policies may vary between players.

The centralized FIM model has a single identity provider (IDP) that brokers trust to other participating members or service providers (SP) in a Circle of Trust (CoT). IDP being a sole authenticator has a centralized control over the identity management task, providing easy access to all SP domains with simplicity of management and control. The drawback of this approach is a single point of failure within a CoT infrastructure in case that IDP fails to provide authentication service. User convenience can be also achieved partially in that the single sign-on (SSO) for users is only effective within SPs which belong to the same CoT.

The distributed FIM model provides a frictionless IM solution by forming a federation and making authentication a distributed task. Every member agrees to trust user identities *vouched for* by other members of the federation. This helps users maintain their segregated identities, making them portable across autonomous policy domains. It also facilitates SSO and trust, thereby allowing businesses to share the identity management cost with its partners. Microsoft Passport is based on the centralized FIM model, while Liberty Alliance aims to be the distributed FIM model.

Earlier works related to user identity management were mostly focused on a user-centric approach [DPR99], where users have control over IM functions. A simple idea of managing user identities is described in [Cha85]. They proposed the use of personal card computers to handle all payments of a user, thereby ensuring the privacy and security of the user's identity on the Web. Hagel and Singer [HS99] discussed the concept of *infomediaries* where users have to trust and rely on a third party to aggregate their information and perform IM tasks on their behalf while protecting the privacy of their information. The Novell digitalme technology [Cra] allows users to create various identity cards that can be shared on the Internet according to users' preferences. Users can control both what information is stored in each card and conditions under which it may be shared.

3 Federated Identity Management

In this section, we discuss FIM in general, Liberty Alliance and Microsoft Passport in particular. Federated identity gives the ability to securely recognize and leverage user identities owned by trusted organizations within or across CoTs, and identity federation allows organizations to securely share confidential user identities with trusted ones, without requiring users to re-enter their name and password when they access their network resources. Additionally, identity federation provides the ability to optionally and securely share user information such as their profiles or other data between various trusted applications which is subject to user consent and organizational requirements.

Two well-known FIM solutions, Liberty Alliance and Microsoft Passport have fundamentally the same goal of managing web-based identification and authentication. Both enable organizations to build IM systems that can be federated across many disparate sources. Therefore, each user can have a single network identity that provides SSO to the web sites that have implemented either or both of the systems.

3.1 Liberty Alliance

Liberty Alliance is a consortium of more than 150 companies working together towards developing an open, interoperable standard for FIM. It is aimed towards realizing the notion of a cohesive, tangible network identity, which can facilitate SSO and frictionless business operations. It is a distributed FIM model, relying on the notion of IDP and SP, as we discussed earlier. IDP is responsible for carrying out identity federation. Authentication messages or authentication requests are passed between IDP and SP. IDP and SP in Liberty Alliance Model actually facilitate WS to discover service locations and handle incoming messages from other IDP and SP.

3.2 Microsoft Passport

Microsoft Passport provides authentication services for Passport-enabled sites called participating sites. It was initially released as a service and not an open specification and precedes Liberty Alliance by at least a year. It is the underlying authentication system of Microsoft Hotmail and Microsoft Network, and it is integrated for use in Windows XP. A centralized Passport server is the only IDP in Passport model and contains users' authentication credentials and the associated unique global identifier called Passport Unique Identifier (PUID). Passport is an example of a centralized FIM model. Unlike Liberty Alliance, cookies play a major role in Passport architecture where Passport server stores and reads identity information in the form of session and browser cookies stored securely at a client side.

4 Role of Web Services in FIM

In this section, we describe the role of WS in identity federation. Identity federation usually involves three actors: IDP, SP, and users. IDP in a CoT performs the task of authentication and SP relies on IDP for authentication information of a user before granting the user access to its services. Identity federation occurs with the user's consent to federate his local identity at SP with his identity at IDP which further facilitates SSO. In this process of federation, WS architecture has four key components: consumer, SOAP, WSDL and UDDI and provides SOAP/HTTP-based standard communication vehicles among the providers [tr201]. SP can discover IDP either statically or by querying a UDDI registry. Afterwards, SP communicates with IDP by reading its WSDL from UDDI, whereby SP can exchange authentication request/response through service endpoints (SEP) specified in WSDL.

4.1 Web Services in Liberty Alliance

In Liberty Alliance, each CoT has one or more providers using SOAP/HTTP based communication channels for exchanging authentication-related information between WS endpoints. Both SP and IDP follow agreed-upon schema for federation and SSO. Security Assertion Markup Language (SAML) [HBM02] is an essential component in this process for the purpose of asserting authentication status of users between the providers. A federated sign-in at IDP would provide users with a valid session that is respected by all the SPs in its CoT. Figure 1(a) shows the WS-enabled FIM architecture for Liberty Alliance which hosts two WS components, SSO Login and Global Logout.

Federation requires a user to opt-in by providing consent for mapping his identities at IDP and SP. As a result, both IDP and SP store a *pseudonym* as a name identifier for the user. Pseudonyms are used by IDP later when the user requests an SSO. IDP vouches for SAML-based user authentication request from SP by providing SAML-based authentication response.

Global Logout WS endpoints, also called Single Logout endpoints, receive and process logout events from SP and IDP. Typically, when a user logs out from one provider, the user's SSO session which is active at the rest of providers is invalidated by sending a message to these WS endpoints. The user agent accesses Global Logout WS at IDP and indicates that all SPs, which the IDP has provided authentication for during the current session, must be notified of the session termination. Then, the user agent receives an HTTP response from IDP that confirms the completion of a global logout.

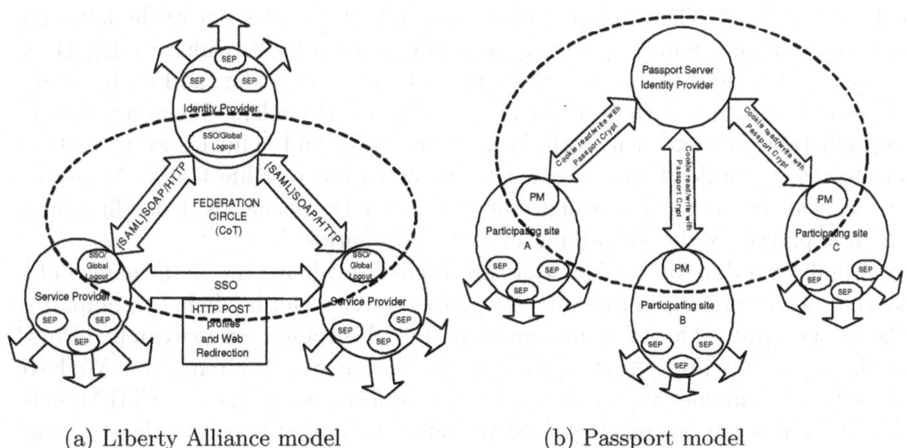

(a) Liberty Alliance model

(b) Passport model

Fig. 1. FIM Models

4.2 Web Services in Microsoft Passport

Figure 1(b) shows the Passport architecture with WS endpoints. There are WS components that make up Passport authentication service and involve the implementation of the authentication service [tr103]. The primary WS component for Passport authentication model is Login Service.

As implied by its name, Login WS is mainly in charge of the user authentication service. For instance, a user logging in to any Passport-enabled site is automatically authenticated by all other Passport-enabled sites, thereby enabling SSO. Subsequent sites receive the authentication status of the user from Login WS through a Component Configuration Document (CCD). CCD is an XML document used by Passport to facilitate the synchronization of the user's authentication status in participating sites.

5 Experimentations for Information Assurance: Metrics and Details

In this section, we describe our experimentations and results. Our goal is to measure the performance of the two models of federated identity management, particularly focusing on authentication issue which is a critical component to maintain information assurance. To measure the performance of *LibertyAlliance* and *MicrosoftPassport* models, we developed a set of tools to generate and monitor loads. The performance for various key operations or services–such as federation of identities and SSO–are measured for the generated workload.

To identify those key operations, we first introduce an imaginary company, called *MegaBank*. Then we attempt to have *MegaBank* play one of the following three roles as shown in Figure 1: a) MegaBank as Identity Provider, b)MegaBank as Service Provider with single third-party Identity Provider, and c)MegaBank as Service Provider with two third-party Identity Providers. There are various unpredictable factors such as the delay from user's end, which prevent us from producing a workload that is exactly similar to the real life traffic. Moreover, the workloads that we are using may differ over the scenarios depending upon the role played by the MegaBank in various scenarios. [1]

Finally we develop metrics that are used to evaluate the performance of a system. The comparison and analysis of the systems can be done by comparing the values obtained for these measured metrics. Therefore, metrics can be termed as the key points that reflect the impact of the changes in system state. We have identified certain metrics for measuring the performance of the two FIM Models. These metrics are common for both models. The measurement of these metrics is performed by applying monitors at various locations in the systems. Those monitors are embedded in the codes as software modules. A typical dialog that

[1] Workload can be categorized into test workload and real workload. Real workload is observed on a system being used for normal operations. Test workload denotes any workload used in performance studies.

occurs between the communicating parties in each FIM model consists of various time factors. The dialog between a service provider and identity provider may consist of different time factors as follows:

- *Communication Time*, $Tc_{[from,to]}$: The time an entity takes to send a request to another entity and get a response back from that entity. $Tc_{[from,to]}$ denotes where "from" is the entity at which the time is measured and "to" is the entity which sends back a response to the request made by a "from" entity. The response sent back by the "to" entity completes the communication cycle.
- *Data Access Time*, Td_{at}: The time that a service provider or an identity provider takes to retrieve a user's information or attributes from the local storage for the purpose of authentication is called the Data Access time. In Td_{at}, "at" signifies the entity at which data access time is measured. The data access time may vary depending upon the type or directory servers and data access mechanism employed.
- *Message Processing Time*, Tm_{at}: The time taken by the entities to process the message received. In Tm_{at}, "at" denotes the entity or the communicating party at which message processing time is measured.
- *Request Redirect Time*, $Tr_{[sp1,sp2]}$: The time required for redirecting a service request from one service provider to another service provider. $Tr_{[sp1,sp2]}$ denotes the time between the source service provider $sp1$ and the destination service provider $sp2$.

This section describes additional metrics, their significance, and the composition. By composition, we mean that one or more of these metrics may be composite. They may contain one or more of the time factors and the actual measurement of these time factors may depend upon the case scenario. The steps for measuring these metrics are different for Liberty Alliance and Microsoft Passport because of the differences in their architecture. Though there are a number of sub-factors that we can measure, we have limited our scope to the most important, required and relevant factors to the scope of our research.

- *Local Login Time/Service Provider Authentication Time*, A_{sp}: A_{sp} is the time taken by a principal to get authenticated at the Service Provider. This time neither facilitates federation nor SSO. The measurement of this metric is important in situations where one wants to measure the data access time at the Service Provider.
- *Identity Provider Authentication Time*, A_i: When a principal chooses to logon using the identity providers credentials, the service provider directs the principal to the identity provider site, which is one time process, when the principal signs in for the first time. A_i is the time taken by a principal to get authenticated just after when he signs in at the identity providers' site. In other words, it is obtained from Td_{sp}
- *Federation Time*, $F_{i,sp}$: For attempting a single sign-on, a principal is required to federate her/his identity at the service provider with its identity at the Identity provider. $F_{i,sp}$ consists of A_i and $Tc_{[sp,idp]}$the communication time, data access time and the message processing time.

– *Single Sign-On Time,* $S_{[idp,sp]}$: Once principal's identities at various service providers are federated with her/his identity at the identity provider, s/he can access the resources at any of the service providers without re-logging within a common authentication context. This is a very important metric and is the most crucial in studying the performance of the two systems. $S_{[idp,sp]}$ consists of the communication time, the message processing time and the data access time including A_i, $Tc_{[sp1,idp]}$, $Tc_{[sp2,idp]}$ and $Tr_{[sp1,sp2]}$.

Figure 2 shows our experimentation results on authentication and federation issues based on the aforementioned metrics.

As we mentioned earlier, our experimental analysis represents a proportion or a sample of the population that may exist in the real life for both the models. Moreover, the factors that affect the performance of the system may vary with location and deployments across enterprise applications. In such cases, definitive statements cannot be made about the characteristics of all systems, but a probabilistic statement about the range in which the characteristics of most systems would fit can be made. Therefore, we have adopted a statistical approach for performance evaluation. Rather than making any directive statement about the superiority or inferiority of one of the two models, we are summarizing the results based on their characteristics. We have adopted a statistical approach whereby we can state with a certain amount of confidence that the values of the proposed metrics can lies within a specified range. Moreover, we can compare these confidence intervals (CIs) for various metrics with respect to the two models. We use the method to calculate the CIs for unpaired observations. The brief steps for calculating the CIs that we used in this work are as follows:

1. We first calculate the sample mean X_{lam} and X_{pm} for Liberty and Passport, where n is the number of observations.
   $X_{lam} = \frac{1}{n}\sum_{i=1}^{n} X_i$, $X_{pm} = \frac{1}{n}\sum_{i=1}^{n} X_i$
2. Next, we derive the sample standard deviations S_{lam} and S_{pm} and it gives us the standard deviation S of the mean difference.
   $S = \sqrt{(\frac{S_{lam}^2}{n} + \frac{S_{pm}^2}{n})}$
3. Using the standard deviation, we compute the effective number of degrees of freedom V.
   $V = \left[\frac{(\frac{S_{lam}^2}{n} + \frac{S_{pm}^2}{n})^2}{\frac{1}{(n+1)}(\frac{S_{lam}^2}{n})^2 + \frac{1}{(n+1)}(\frac{S_{pm}^2}{n})^2}\right]$
4. Finally we identify the confidence interval CI for the mean that can be used to determine the performance characteristics.
   $CI = (X_{lam} - X_{pm}) \pm t_{[1-\frac{a}{2},v]}S$

Unfortunately our results are not permitted to be available in public but we briefly describe lessons learned from this work. Our analysis demonstrated the followings: a) FIM leads us to consider several trade-offs between security and

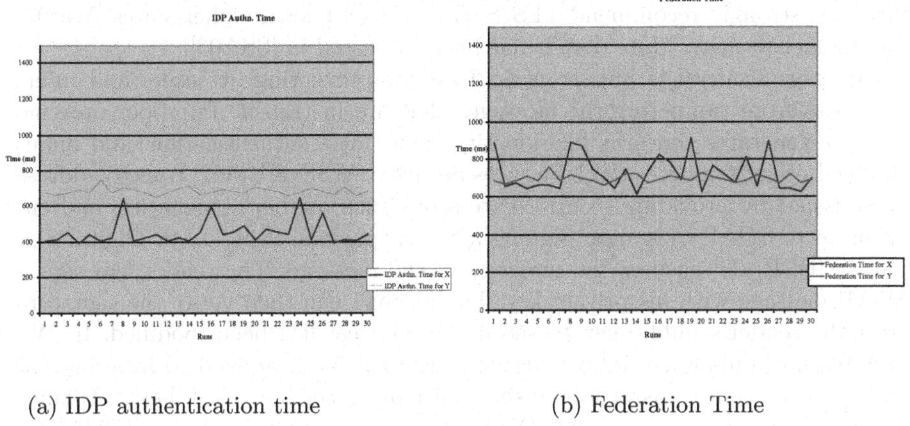

(a) IDP authentication time

(b) Federation Time

Fig. 2. Experimentation Results

system overheads; b) organizational roles in FIM are very important to identify additional requirements related to performance factors; and c) it gives us an idea on which system and workload parameters mostly affect the performance of FIM models in given case scenarios. We believe this work can be helpful to IA practitioners for designing the enhanced FIM architectures.

6 Information Assurance Issues in FIM

As an effort to identify principal IA requirements for FIM, we discuss security and privacy concerns relevant to WS in FIM in this section. We also describe how Liberty Alliance and Microsoft Passport deal with these concerns to fulfill such requirements in their architectures.

6.1 Security Concerns in FIM

Security concerns in FIM can be observed from the perspective of the general objectives of information security: availability, integrity, and confidentiality. In addition, authorization is also an important aspect to be considered in that controlled access to federated identity information is strongly required.

The *availability* of information in FIM models concerns system reliability and timely delivery of information. In FIM models, the availability of information can be ensured by not only having a common protocol or mechanism for communicating authentication and other information between parties but also securing communication channels and messages. Channel security can be achieved using protocols like TLS1.0/SSL3.0 or other protocols like IPsec with security characteristics that are equivalent to TLS or SSL. However, these protocols can only provide security at the transport level and not at the message level. Liberty specifications strongly recommend TLS/SSL with well-known cipher suites [Wat03] for channel security. More details has been discussed in [SSA03].

Message security is important in FIM for preventing attackers and intermediaries from tampering the messages that are in transit. Improper message security generates concerns like identity theft, false authentication, and unauthorized use of resources. Web Services Security (WSS) [IBM02] tries to address these issues by providing security extensions such as digital signature and encryption to SOAP messages. Signing a SOAP payload using XML Digital Signature [ERB+02] ensures the integrity of the message. The sender can sign a SOAP message with his private key. The receiver can then verify the signature with the sender's public key to see if the message has been modified. In WS architecture, public key infrastructure (PKI) can be leveraged to have organizations sign security assertions instead of issuing certificates. Liberty Alliance specifications recommend XML Digital Signature and Encryption [IDS02] for encrypting a complete SOAP message or a part of the SOAP message to maintain the *integrity* and *confidentiality* of its contents. Microsoft Passport takes an approach to encrypting cookies for securing data contained within them. Cookies store sensitive information like user profiles that can be securely accessed by authorized parties.

FIM requires communicating parties to provide controlled access of information to legitimate users. *Authorization* deals with what information a user or an application has access to or which operations a user or an application can perform. Proper authorization mechanisms are necessary in WS communication especially when the communication endpoint is across multiple hops. Liberty specifications recommend a permission-based attribute sharing mechanism, which enables users to specify authorization policies on their information that they want to share. Similarly, Microsoft Passport allows users to have their choices regarding the information they want to share with participating sites.

6.2 Privacy Concerns in FIM

Privacy is a growing concern with FIM models due to the voluminous exchange of sensitive information that occur across enterprises. Securing communication channels and encrypting messages may help preserve the privacy of relevant information only up to some extent. The security concerns that we discussed in the previous section are obviously applicable to privacy as well. In WS-enabled FIM where the receiver of a message may not be its ultimate destination, improper security measures may result in unauthorized access of user's personal information which leads to violation of privacy.

Protection of user identities and personal information can be achieved by using the principle of pseudonymity. Obfuscating message payloads can also preserve their privacy by making them accessible only by authorized parties having proper credentials or keys [MPB03]. Privacy enhancing technologies like Platform for Privacy Preference (P3P) [CCL+02] provide a solution for point-to-point privacy protection based on user preferences. However, such solutions do not scale for a more open, interoperable WS architecture.

Liberty's SAML implementation uses pseudonyms constructed using pseudo-random values that have no discernable correspondence with users' identifiers at IDP or SP. The pseudonym has a meaning only in the context of the relationship between the two communicating parties. The intent is to create a non-public pseudonym so as to contravene the linkability to users' identities or activities, thereby maintaining the privacy.

Organizations using FIM models is required to follow four key principles of fair information practices which are discussed in [tr102]:

- *Notice*: Users should receive prior notice of the information practices.
- *Choice*: Users have a choice to specify what information will be used and the purpose for which the information is collected.
- *Access*: Users should be able to access and modify their personal information as and when needed.
- *Security*: Users should be assured that the organizational system is capable of securing their personal information.

Liberty specifications have recently proposed an approach to sharing user attributes on the basis of user's permission. The specifications also provide a set of guidelines that will help businesses adhere to these principles. Microsoft Passport's approach to online privacy is also based on adherence to these aforementioned principles.

7 Conclusion and Future Works

Information security and privacy issues are the key concerns in FIM because identity federation requires the exchange of sensitive user information in a highly insecure and open network. In this paper, we discussed two well-known FIM solutions, Microsoft Passport and Liberty Alliance and how WS can play an integral role in FIM. In addition, we have identified certain metrics that are crucial when considering a FIM model. These metrics are composite metrics which may consist of measuring one or more of the time factors. Also, we identified and discussed core IA requirements in FIM focusing on WS-relevant issues. We believe our work can be leveraged by the research and industry communities working on issues in identity management.

Our future work will focus on a privacy attribute management framework within Liberty Alliance which can provide users with a high level of confidence in the privacy of their personal data. Developing IA metrics for FIM is another issue that we intend to work on in the near future. It is generally believed that no single perfect set of IA metrics can be applied to all systems. Thus, we would attempt to investigate IA metrics specifically designed for FIM systems.

References

[CCL+02] Lorrie Cranor, Lorrie Cranor, Marc Langheinrich, Massimo Marchiori, Martin Presler-Marshall, and Joseph Reagle. The platform for privacy preferences 1.0 (p3p1.0) specification. Technical report, www.w3.org/TR/2002/REC-P3P-20020416/, 2002.

[Cha85] David Chaum. Security without identification: Card computers to make big brother obsolete. *Communications of the ACM*, 28(10):1030–1044, 1985.

[Cra] Lorrie Faith Cranor. Agents of choice: Tools that facilitate notice and choice about web site data practices.

[DPR99] Herbert Damker, Ulrich Pordesch, and Martin Reichenbach. Personal reach ability and security management - negotiation of multilateral security. In *Proceedings of Multilateral Security in Communications*, Stuttgart, Germany, 1999.

[ERB+02] D. Eastlake, J. Reagle, J. Boyer, B. Fox, and E. Simon. XML - signature syntax and processing. Technical report, http://www.w3.org/TR/2002/REC-xmldsig-core-20020212/, 2002.

[HBM02] Phillip Hallam-Baker and Eve Maler. Assertions and protocols for OASIS SAML. Technical report, http://www.oasis-open.org/committees/security/docs/cs-sstc-core-01.pdf, 2002.

[HS99] John Hegel and Marc Singer, editors. *Net Worth: Shaping Market When Customers Make the Rule.* Harvard Business School Press, 1999.

[HW03] Jeff Hodges and Tom Watson. Liberty architecture overview v 1.2-03. Technical report, http://www.sourceid.org/docs/sso/liberty-architecture-overview-v1.1.pdf, 2003.

[IBM02] IBM. Web services security (WSS) specifications 1.0.05. Technical report, http://www-106.ibm.com/developerworks/webservices/library/ws-secure/, 2002.

[IDS02] Takeshi Imamura, Blair Dillaway, and Ed Simon. XML encryption syntax and processing. Technical report, http://www.w3.org/TR/2002/CR-xmlenc-core-20020304/, 2002.

[MPB03] Marco Casassa Mont, Siani Pearson, and Pete Bramhall. Towards accountable management of identity and privacy: Sticky policies and enforceable tracing services. Technical report, http://www.hpl.hp.com/techreports/2003/HPL-2003-49.pdf, 2003.

[SSA03] Prasad Shenoy, Dongwan Shin, and Gail-Joon Ahn. Towards IA-Aware web services for federated identity management. In *Proceedings of IASTED International Conference on Communication, Network, and Information Security*, pages 10–15, New York, USA, December 2003.

[tr102] Federal Trade Commission. online profiling - a report to congress, part 2. Technical report, http://www.ftc.gov/os/2000/07/onlineprofiling.htm, 2002.

[tr103] Mircrosoft Corporations. Microsoft .Net Passport Review Guide. Technical report, http://www.microsoft.com/net/services/passport/review_guide.asp, 2003.

[tr201] W3C note: Web services description language (WSDL) v 1.1. Technical report, http://www.w3.org/TR/wsdl12/, 2001.

[Wat03] Tom Watson. Liberty ID-FF implementation guidlines v 1.2.02. Technical report, Liberty Alliance Project, 2003.

Query-Log Based Authority Analysis for Web Information Search

Julia Luxenburger and Gerhard Weikum

Max-Planck Institute of Computer Science
Stuhlsatzenhausweg 85, 66123 Saarbrücken, Germany
{julialux,weikum}@mpi-sb.mpg.de

Abstract. The ongoing explosion of web information calls for more intelligent and personalized methods towards better search result quality for advanced queries. Query logs and click streams obtained from web browsers or search engines can contribute to better quality by exploiting the collaborative recommendations that are implicitly embedded in this information. This paper presents a new method that incorporates the notion of query nodes into the PageRank model and integrates the implicit relevance feedback given by click streams into the automated process of authority analysis. This approach generalizes the well-known random-surfer model into a random-expert model that mimics the behavior of an expert user in an extended session consisting of queries, query refinements, and result-navigation steps. The enhanced PageRank scores, coined QRank scores, can be computed offline; at query-time they are combined with query-specific relevance measures with virtually no overhead. Our preliminary experiments, based on real-life query-log and click-stream traces from eight different trial users indicate significant improvements in the precision of search results.

1 Introduction

1.1 Motivation

State-of-the-art web information search is based on two orthogonal paradigms, traditional textual similarity (e.g., tf*idf-based cosine similarity between feature vectors), on one hand, and link-based authority ranking, on the other hand. The most prominent approach for the latter is the PageRank method by Brin and Page ([5]) that measures the (query-independent) importance of web pages by analyzing the link structure of the web graph. The key idea of PageRank scoring is to grant a web page higher prestige the more high-quality pages link to it. The rationale behind this is that the outgoing links of a web page exhibit an intellectual endorsement of the page creator who judges the linked pages valuable. This kind of intellectual user input can be generalized to analyzing and exploiting entire surf trails and query logs of individual users or an entire user community. These trails, which can be gathered from browser histories, local proxies, or Web servers, reflect implicit user judgements. For example, suppose a user clicks on a specific subset of the top 10 results returned by a search engine

X. Zhou et al. (Eds.): WISE 2004, LNCS 3306, pp. 90–101, 2004.
© Springer-Verlag Berlin Heidelberg 2004

for a multi-keyword query, based on having seen the summaries of these documents. This implicit form of relevance feedback establishes a strong correlation between the query and the clicked-on documents. Further suppose that the user refines a query by adding or replacing keywords, e.g., to eliminate ambiguities in the previous query; the ambiguity may be recognized by the user by observing multiple unrelated topics in the query result. Again, this establishes correlations between the new keywords and the subsequently clicked-on documents, but also, albeit possibly to a lesser extent, between the original query and the eventually relevant documents. The problem that we study in this paper is how to systematically exploit user-behavior information gathered from query logs and click streams and incorporate it into a PageRank-style link analysis algorithm. We believe that observing user behavior is a key element in adding intelligence to a web search engine and boosting its search result quality. Of course, these considerations and the results presented in this paper can also be applied to search in intranets or digital libraries where explicit hyperlinks are much more infrequent and can usually not be exploited that well [10].

1.2 Our Approach and Contribution

The key idea of our approach is to extend the Markov chain structure that underlies the PageRank model (see Section 2) by additional nodes and edges that reflect the observed user behavior extracted from query and click-stream logs. Just like PageRank models visits to web pages to states of a Markov-chain random walk, we model all observed queries and query refinements as additional states, and we introduce transitions from these states to the pages that were clicked-on in the user histories. The transition probabilities are chosen in a biased way to reflect the users' preferences. Then we employ standard techniques for computing stationary state probabilities, yielding the query-log-enhanced authority scores of web pages, coined *QRank* scores. The QRank procedure consists of three stages:

1. We extract information from the browser histories of users. We recognize all URLs that encode queries (i.e., with query keywords being part of the URL of an HTTP GET request) and all URLs that are subsequently clicked on within a specified time window. In addition to mining these pairs of queries and clicked-on documents, we also aim to recognize entire user sessions, based on heuristics about the user's timing, and identify refinements of a previously posed query.
2. From the observed queries, query refinements, and clicked-on documents we construct an extended web graph by adding extra nodes and edges to the hyperlink-induced graph. We also compute document-document similarities to construct additional associative links for pages with high content similarities.
3. We now solve the extended Markov chain for its stationary state probabilities, i.e., the QRank scores of the indexed web pages. At query time we merely combine the offline precomputed QRank score of a page with the

page's content relevance for a given set of query keywords, e. g. , by weighted linear combination for the overall scoring and final result ranking.

The contributions of this paper are twofold. First, we present the novel QRank model that generalizes random-surfer behavior into a random-expert model that mimics the behavior of an expert user in an extended session consisting of queries, query-refinements, and result-navigation steps. Second, we show how QRank can be efficiently implemented and demonstrate its practical viability and benefits for query result quality in an experimental study using the Wikipedia web-page collection and browser histories from eight different trial users. The rest of the paper is organized as follows. Section 2 discusses prior work on link analysis and data mining of query logs and click streams. Section 3 develops the query-log-enhanced PageRank model, coined QRank. Section 4 presents our prototype implementation and discusses specific efficiency issues. Section 5 presents the results of a preliminary experimental evaluation.

2 Related Work

An intuitive explanation of the PageRank method [5] assumes a random surfer who starts at page v with probability $\boldsymbol{p}_0(v)$ according to the initial probability distribution $\boldsymbol{p}_0$ with $\sum_v \boldsymbol{p}_0(v) = 1$. Then at each state the random surfer either performs a random jump to any other page with small probability ϵ (usually between 0.1 and 0.2) or chooses an outgoing link uniformly at random with probability $1 - \epsilon$. This yields the homogeneous Markov chain (V,t) on the finite set of states V (web pages) with the transition probability function $t : V \times V \rightarrow [0,1], v \mapsto \begin{cases} \epsilon \cdot \boldsymbol{r}(\mathrm{v}) + (1-\epsilon) \cdot \frac{1}{\mathrm{outdegree(u)}} & , \text{ if (u,v) } \in E \\ \epsilon \cdot \boldsymbol{r}(\mathrm{v}) & , \text{ otherwise} \end{cases}$ where E is the set of edges (hyperlinks) and $\boldsymbol{r}$ is the random jump vector with $\boldsymbol{r}(v) = \frac{1}{|V|}$.

Other approaches to link analysis proceed along similar lines. They include the HITS method by Kleinberg [14] and a variety of extensions and generalizations of both PageRank and HITS [3,1,9,13].

Query-dependent link analysis has been explicitly addressed by Richardson and Domingos [16], inspired by and extending work of Cohn and Hofmann [7] on a predictive probabilistic model for document content and hyperlink connectivity. An algebraic, spectral-analysis-type, approach to such predictive models has been developed by Achlioptas et al. [2]. Among these, only Richardson and Domingos provide a practical algorithm for query-dependent authority ranking. They use a "directed surfer" model where the probabilities for following links are biased towards target pages with high similarity to the given query. None of these methods considers query-log or click-stream information.

Exploiting query logs for an improvement of search results is not a completely new idea. Wen, Nie, and Zhang [21] introduced various query clustering methods on server-side query logs to identify frequently asked questions, partially building on an earlier bidirectional query clustering algorithm developed by Beeferman and Berger [4]. However, the benefit of their techniques for web search has not been shown explicitly and no method has been suggested to overcome the huge effort of manually editing the result sets of FAQs. A recent approach of Cui, Wen, Nie, and Ma [8] exploits data from user logs for query expansion. This is achieved by reasoning on the conditional probabilities of a document term $w_j^{(d)}$ occurring in a clicked document given that the query contains the term $w_i^{(q)}$, i. e. , $P(w_j^{(d)}|w_i^{(q)})$. Modifications of HITS, respectively PageRank, that incorporate user click streams have also been studied. Wang, Chen, Tao, Ma, and Wenyin [20] generalized HITS based on the assumptions that: 1) the importance of a web page can be infered from the frequency and expertise of the visiting users, and 2) the importance of a user can be infered from the quality and quantity of web pages he has visited. In contrast Xue, Zeng, Chen, Ma, Zhang, and Lu [24] modified PageRank by replacing the hyperlink-based web graph with an implicit link graph where edges connect subsequently visited pages.

None of the above work fully integrates query-log and click-stream analysis with PageRank- or HITS-style link analysis and authority scoring. To the best of our knowledge, the approach presented in this paper is the first method to fully address the issue of query-log-enhanced link analysis and provides a complete solution.

3 The QRank Model

We exploit the implicit relevance feedback contained in query logs by adding the notions of query nodes and appropriately chosen edges to the PageRank model. We first discuss how we extract this information from the query and click-stream logs in subsection 3.1; then we present the QRank model itself in subsection 3.2; finally we discuss some properties of QRank in subsection 3.3.

3.1 Analyzing Browser Histories

The browser history of a user can be extracted from the browser's internal files using special tools such as UrlSearch [19]. An excerpt of a browser history is shown in table 1. Here the user query "france highest mountain" is refined by the query "france highest summit" and a page on the Mont Blanc is clicked on. A slight complication is the storage-saving policies of most browsers that erase multiple occurences of the same web page and only store a page once with the time it was last visited. This becomes especially crucial with the common navigation via a browser's back button. However, by either encoding server-supplied timestamps into URLs and thus making URLs unique or by timestamp-based and other heuristics one can still extract all relevant click-stream information from the browser history. In contrast, server log files are known to be problematic because of difficulties of identifying the same user in a series of requests (see, e.g., [25],[23],[21]), unless all users enable the use of cookies (which many users would hate for privacy concerns). Therefore and because we wanted to use query logs for both our own prototype search engine (for which we could also access the server log) and big Web search engines such as Google, we used browser histories on the client side. We simply asked a number of voluntary trial users to provide us with their histories extracted by the UrlSearch tool.

Table 1. Browser history

URL	Timestamp
http://139. .../index. jsp?query=france+highest+mountain	2004/05/28, 15:24:04
http://139. .../index.jsp?query=france+highest+summit	2004/05/28, 15:24:14
http://139. .../wiki/wiki.phtml?title=Mont_Blanc	2004/05/28, 15:24:44

By gathering the queries users posed and the documents they subsequently visited, we can deduce frequently asked questions as well as the answers that were regarded (at least upon first glance) as relevant. Interpreting *every* user click as an endorsement would, of course, be an overstatement, but clicks are meaningful with high probability. Certainly users do not follow links at random, but have a certain intention they act upon. In contrast to users being explicitly asked to give feedback, implicit relevance judgement does not suffer from the likely reluctance and laziness of users (at the cost of some small inaccuracy in the extraction process depending on the extent to which heuristics are used in the browser history mining).

By analyzing the timestamps of HTTP requests, variations of queries representing the same search intention can be extracted. This situation most likely occurs whenever the user is not satisfied by the search results and tries to achieve an improvement by reformulating or refining her original query. We define a *query click stream* to be a pair consisting of a query and the set of subsequently visited documents, i. e. , query click stream $:=<$ query, $\{d_1, d_2, \ldots, d_n\}$ $>$. Analogously, a *query refinement* is a pair consisting of a query and its reformulation, i. e. , query refinement $:=<$ query, refined query $>$. Finally, a *query session* is an initial query together with its reformulations, each with its own set of visited documents, i. e. , query session $:=<$ query, {refined query click stream$_1$, $\ldots$, refined query click stream$_k$} $>$. The demarcations of query sessions, i.e., when one session ends and the next one starts, are identified using heuristic rules on time intervals. When a user is inactive for more than a specified timespan (e.g., 1 minute), it is assumed that a new query session is started. This is certainly not a foolproof technique, but is empirically found to work with high probability.

3.2 Incorporating Queries into PageRank

As despicted in Figure 1 queries are added in a natural manner to the web graph by introducing query nodes. Thus the set of nodes V is the union of the set of document nodes D and query nodes Q. We introduce a number of edge types that represent various relationships between queries and documents:

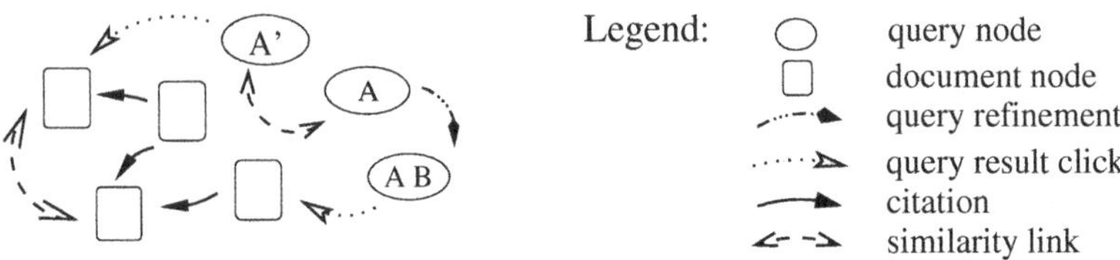

Fig. 1. QRank Graph

Explicit links are represented by directed edges reflecting different kinds of recommendation information. We distinguish three explicit link types:

Query Refinement. An edge (q_1, q_2) represents a situation, observed in the query history, that a user did not obtain satisfying search results for her query q_1 so that she reformulated q_1 and posed query q_2.

Query Result Clicks. An edge (q, d), obtained from the query and click-stream log, indicates that a user posed query q and then clicked on the document d after having seen its summary in the top-10 result list.

Citation. An edge (d_1, d_2) represents a hyperlink that points from d_1 to d_2 and thus indicates that the author of d_1 appreciates the contents of d_2.

Implicit Links. In addition to the various forms of explicit links, we introduce implicit links that capture associative relationships between graph nodes, based on content similarity. These relationships are bidirectional, so the implicit links are undirected edges. We introduce an implicit link from node u to node v if the query-query or document-document similarity, in terms of the tf*idf-based cosine measure [15,6], exceeds a specified threshold.

For the definition of the QRank model some notation needs to be introduced. Let $v, v' \in V, d \in D$ and $q, q' \in Q$. Then

$\mathbf{E_{in}(v)}$ denotes the set of predecessors of node v via *explicit* links

$\mathbf{E_{out}(v)}$ dentotes the set of successors of node v via *explicit* links

I(v) denotes the set of neighbors of node v via *implicit* links. As implicit links are undirected we cannot distinguish between predecessors and successors.

outdeg(v) denotes the number of *explicit* links leaving node v

docOutdeg(v) denotes the number of *explicit* links leaving node v and pointing to a document node

queryOutdeg(v) denotes the number of *explicit* links leaving node v and pointing to a query node

sim(v',v). Overloaded similarity function symbol $sim : Q \times Q \to [0,1], sim : D \times D \to [0,1]$ with $\sum_{v' \in I(v)} sim(v, v') = 1 \quad \forall v \in V$

click(q, d). Normalized click frequency, that reflects the probability that a user clicks on document d after posing query q.
$click : Q \times D \to [0,1]$ with $\sum_{d \in E_{out}(q) \wedge d \in D} click(q, d) = 1 \quad \forall q \in Q$

refine(q, q'). Normalized refinement frequency, that reflects the probability of a user posing query q after query q': $refine : Q \times Q \to [0,1]$ with $\sum_{q' \in E_{out}(q) \wedge q' \in Q} refine(q, q') = 1 \quad \forall q \in Q$

Now we are ready to introduce the equations of the QRank Markov model. We model a random expert user as follows. The session starts with either a query node or a document node (i.e., a web page). With probability ϵ the user makes a random jump to a uniformly chosen node, and with probability $1-\epsilon$ she follows an outgoing link. If she makes a random jump, then the target is a query node with probability β and document node with probability $1-\beta$. If the user follows a link, it is an explicit link with probability α or an implicit link with probability $1-\alpha$. In the case of an implicit link, the target node is chosen in a non-uniform way with a bias proportional to the content similarity between nodes which is either a document-document similarity or a query-query similarity. When the user follows an explicit link, the behavior depends on whether the user currently resides on a query node or a document node. In the case of a document node, she simply follows a uniformly chosen outgoing link as in the standard PageRank model. If she currently resides on a query node, she can either visit another query node, thus refining or reformulating her previous query, or visit one of the documents that were clicked on (and thus implicitly considered relevant) after the same query by some other user in the overall history. From the history we have estimated relative frequencies of these refinement and click events, and these frequencies are proportional to the bias for non-uniformly choosing the target node in the random walk. This informal description is mathematically captured in the following definition.

Definition 1 (QRank). *Let $v \in V$, $d \in D$ and $q \in Q$. Then the QRank vector $\mathbf{p}^{(QRank)}$, in the following called $\mathbf{p}$ for the sake of simplicity, is recursively defined as*

$$\mathbf{p}_0 = \boldsymbol{r}$$

$$\mathbf{n > 0:} \quad \mathbf{p}_n(v) = \epsilon \cdot \boldsymbol{r}(v) + (1-\epsilon) \cdot \left[\alpha \cdot \sum_{v' \in E_{in}(v)} \mathbf{p}_{n-1}(v') \cdot w(v', v) + (1-\alpha) \cdot \sum_{v' \in I(v)} \mathbf{p}_{n-1}(v') \cdot sim(v', v) \right]$$

In full detail, with documents and queries notationally distinguished, this means:

$$\mathbf{p}_n(d) = \epsilon \cdot \boldsymbol{r}(d) + (1-\epsilon) \cdot \left[\alpha \cdot \sum_{d' \in E_{in}(d) \wedge d' \in D} \mathbf{p}_{n-1}(d') \cdot w(d', d) \right.$$

$$\left. + \alpha \cdot \sum_{q' \in E_{in}(d) \wedge q' \in Q} \mathbf{p}_{n-1}(q') \cdot w(q', d) + (1-\alpha) \cdot \sum_{d' \in I(d) \wedge d' \in D} \mathbf{p}_{n-1}(d') \cdot sim(d', d) \right]$$

$$\mathbf{p}_n(q) = \epsilon \cdot \boldsymbol{r}(q) + (1-\epsilon) \cdot \left[\alpha \cdot \sum_{q' \in E_{in}(q) \wedge q' \in Q} \mathbf{p}_{n-1}(q') \cdot w(q', q) \right.$$

$$\left. + (1-\alpha) \cdot \sum_{q' \in I(q) \wedge q' \in Q} \mathbf{p}_{n-1}(q') \cdot sim(q', q) \right]$$

with

$$w(v',v) = \begin{cases} \frac{1}{outdeg(v')} & , \quad if\ v',\ v\ \in D \wedge v' \in E_{in}(v) \\ \frac{queryOutdeg(v')}{outdeg(v')} \cdot refine(v',v) & , \quad if\ v',\ v\ \in Q \wedge v' \in E_{in}(v) \\ \frac{docOutdeg(v')}{outdeg(v')} \cdot click(v',v) & , \quad if\ v'\ \in Q, v \in D \wedge v' \in E_{in}(v) \\ 0 & , \quad otherwise \end{cases}$$

and

$$\boldsymbol{r}(v) = \begin{cases} \frac{\beta}{|Q|} & , \quad if\ v \in Q \\ \frac{1-\beta}{|D|} & , \quad if\ v \in D \end{cases}$$

3.3 Properties of QRank

We give some fundamental properties of the QRank Markov model. For lack of space we omit all proofs.

Lemma 1. $\forall d \in D: \quad \sum_{d' \in D} w(d,d') = 1$

Lemma 2. $\forall q \in Q: \quad \sum_{d \in D} w(q,d) = \frac{docOutdeg(q)}{outdeg(q)}$

Lemma 3. $\forall q \in Q: \quad \sum_{q' \in Q} w(q,q') = \frac{queryOutdeg(q)}{outdeg(q)}$

Lemma 4. $\sum_{v \in V} \boldsymbol{r}(v) = 1$

Theorem 1. *QRank defines a probabilistic transition matrix T, i.e.* $\forall v \in V$: $\sum_{v' \in V} T(v,v') = 1$, *thus a time-discrete finite-state homogeneous Markov chain.*

Theorem 2. *For* $\epsilon \neq 0$, $\beta \neq 0$ *and* $\beta \neq 1$ *QRank converges.*

By the following theorem we show that our QRank approach contains the original PageRank model as a special case.

Theorem 3. *For* $\alpha = 1$ *and* $\beta = 0$ *QRank converges to PageRank.*

Theorem 2 proves that the QRank model has a unique and computable solution, and we can compute QRank scores by the standard method of power iteration for the QRank transition matrix (see, e.g., [6] for this standard method).

4 Implementation

We integrated our query-log enhanced authority model, the computation of QRank scores, into the BINGO! toolkit [17] that already comprises the capabilities for crawling and indexing web data as well as searching the indexed documents. BINGO! runs upon an Oracle9i database so that the integration was easily done by extending the underlying database schema. Our implementation mainly consists of three components: 1) a parser that mines the browser histories obtained from the UrlSearch tool for query sessions and refinements, 2) an implicit link constructor that computes weighted correlations between queries or documents, and 3) the actual QRank computation. All components store intermediate results in the database for modularity and reuse of computations. After the pre-processing steps (history mining, associative link generation) the actual QRank computation proceeds in three steps: first the enhanced web graph is loaded into memory, then QRank is computed by power iteration using 100 iterations, and finally the resulting QRank score vector is written to the database. Some crucial implementational issues arise in the computation of similarity between queries or documents. Standard textual similarity measures like tf*idf-based cosine yield no reasonable results for query-query similarities because queries contain only very few keywords. On the other hand, the alternative of defining query-query similarity via their clicked-on documents in the history would only add redundant information to the enhanced web graph which already reflects these relationships by explicit links. We decided to make use of an ontology for first mapping the query keywords onto concepts and then aggregating the semantic similarities between the corresponding concepts. The ontology that we are using captures hypernym/hyponym and other relationships in a graph structure. The nodes and edges are derived from the WordNet thesaurus [12]; in addition, the ontology quantifies edges by computing Dice similarities between concepts and their descriptions based on a large corpus. Details of this ontology service can be found in [18].An efficiency problem is that the pairwise computation of all document-document similarities would have quadratic complexity in terms of computation and database accesses running time, and this high cost is unacceptable. Therefore we restricted ourselves to a reasonably small set of source documents, and for each of these we computed the k most similar documents. The selection of source documents is based on the rationale that only authoritative documents have high enough QRank scores to be propagated along associative links. Introducing implicit links between "insignificant" documents would result in a negligible overall effect. Thus, we choose the set of clicked-on documents as well as the top-m documents with the highest standard PageRank scores as our set of source documents. Then an approximative top-k search is performed for each source document S according to the following procedure: first the **n** terms of S with highest tf*idf scores are retrieved , then the top-k ranked documents with respect to these terms are efficiently computed using *Fagin's Median Rank Algorithm* [11], and finally, for each document in the top-k result set and S a tf*idf-based cosine similarity score is computed, using all document terms, and stored in the database.

5 Experiments

5.1 Testbed

Experiments were carried out on an Intel Pentium 3 GHz computer with 1 GB working memory under Windows XP with an Oracle 9i database and an Apache Tomcat 4.1 server running on the same computer. The experiments consisted of two phases. In the first phase, eight test persons were asked to generate query logs by searching the data indexed by our prototype search engine. In the second phase, four test persons evaluated the rankings for some independently selected queries. Here we compared the original ranking, which resulted from a combination of tf*idf-based cosine similarity and standard PageRank, against the ranking produced by a combination of tf*idf-based similarity and our QRank scores. As test data we used the web pages of the Wikipedia Encyclopedia [22]. This open-content encyclopedia started in January 2001 and contains, in the English version as of January 2004, 226346 articles on a wide variety of subjects. Test users could freely choose their queries, but to provide some guidance about what interesting information one could search we gave them a number of quiz questions from the popular Trivial Pursuit game.We obtained all the browser history files of all test users, and extracted a total of 265 different queries with a total of 429 clicked-on documents and 106 query refinements. The test users in the second phase provided the intellectural quality assessment on the result rankings produced by the standard method versus QRank. We initially considered only one variant of QRank with parameters set as follows: $\epsilon = 0.25$, $\alpha = 0.5$, $\beta = 1.0$. Studies with parameter variations are underway; the bottleneck in conducting these additional experiments is the intellectual quality assessment by unbiased test persons. For each query the test users were shown an HTML page that displays the query and in two columns the top-10 results under the two methods we compared. The two rankings were randomly placed in the left and right column without any explicit labels; so the assessors did not know which method produced which ranking. The users were then asked to mark all documents that they considered relevant for the given query (possibly after looking at the page itself if the summary on the HTML overview page was not informative enough), and also to identify the one of the two rankings that they generally considered of higher quality.

5.2 Results

We first focused on the assessor's preferences about which of the two rankings had higher quality results. For 32.9% of the evaluated queries the assessors preferred standard PageRank, whereas QRank was considered better in 61.4% of the cases. 5.7% of the query rankings were perceived as fairly similar so that no preference could be stated. This result clearly shows that QRank outperformed PageRank significantly.

Table 2. Standard PageRank vs. QRank

Query	mars	giraffe	bolivar	virtual reality	anthrax bacteria	guatemala	Average
PageRank	0.06	0.4	0.2	0.5	0.75	0.1	0.30
QRank	0.16	0.6	0.35	0.55	0.75	0.5	0.38

From the relevance assessments we also computed the precision (for the top-10 results) for each query and the micro-average (which is equal to macro-average for the top-10 results) [15] over all queries. The results are shown in Table 2 for selected queries and the average. We see that QRank yields an improvement of search results with respect to precision although the extent depends on the

Table 3. Top-5 result sets

Query 1: "Expo"		Query 2: "Schumacher"	
PageRank	QRank	PageRank	QRank
1998	World's fair	1969	Michael Schumacher
1992	EXPO	Michael Schumacher	German Grand Prix
Computer	International Expositions	Joel Schumacher	Formula 1
1967	World Fair	Toni Schumacher	Ralf Schumacher
World's Fair	World Exhibition	Ralf Schumacher	Joel Schumacher

actual query. The precision for some queries is for both PageRank and QRank quite low due to the restricted data set.

Table 3 provides some anecdotic evidence by giving the top-5 results (titles of web pages; on the Wikipedia data the title of a page is a good descriptor of its content) for each of the two rankings for two example queries. For the query "expo" QRank produced clearly better results than standard PageRank that boosts summary pages of years because of them being highly linked. The second query "schumacher" shows how a strong user interest in "formula 1" (car racing) can influence the result for such an ambiguous term. This effect might be a strength with respect to personalized search. However, in the general case, such a topic drift might be undesirable. We perceived similar, partially more serious, phenomena due to the limited number of search topics the trial persons could consider in the first phase. With a broader query spectrum we hope to weaken this effect. Nevertheless these preliminary experiments revealed the high potential of QRank that is subject of ongoing further experiments.

6 Conclusion and Future Work

We presented a new method that naturally integrates query-log and click-stream information into the automated process of authority analysis. Ongoing and future work aims at underpinning our preliminary results by further experiments with long-term user histories and a wider spectrum of queries. Moreover, we want to study generalizations of the QRank model with more sophisticated probabilistic models for computing edge weights and with consideration of negative user feedback.

References

1. Serge Abiteboul, Mihai Preda, Gregory Cobena: *Adaptive on-line page importance computation.* WWW Conference 2003: 280-290
2. Dimitris Achlioptas, Amos Fiat, Anna R. Karlin, Frank McSherry: *Web Search via Hub Synthesis.* FOCS 2001: 500-509
3. Krishna Bharat, Monika R. Henzinger: *Improved Algorithms for Topic Distillation in a Hyperlinked Environment.* 21st ACM SIGIR 1998: 104-111

4. Doug Beeferman, Adam Berger: *Agglomerative clustering of a search engine query log*. 6th ACM SIGKDD 2000: 407 - 416
5. Sergey Brin, Lawrence Page: *The Anatomy of a Large-Scale Hypertextual Web Search Engine*. WWW Conference 1998
6. Soumen Chakrabarti: *Mining the Web: Discovering Knowledge from Hypertext Data*. Morgan Kaufmann, 2002
7. David A. Cohn, Thomas Hofmann: *The Missing Link - A Probabilistic Model of Document Content and Hypertext Connectivity*. NIPS 2000: 430-436
8. Hang Cui, Ji-Rong Wen, Jian-Yun Nie, Wei-Ying Ma: *Query Expansion by Mining User Logs*. IEEE Trans. Knowl. Data Eng. 15(4) 2003
9. Chris H. Q. Ding, Xiaofeng He, Parry Husbands, Hongyuan Zha, Horst D. Simon: *PageRank, HITS and a Unified Framework for Link Analysis*. SDM 2003
10. Ronald Fagin, Ravi Kumar, Kevin S. McCurley, Jasmine Novak, D. Sivakumar, John A. Tomlin, David P. Williamson: *Searching the workplace web*. WWW Conference 2003: 366-375
11. Ronald Fagin, Ravi Kumar, D. Sivakumar: *Efficient similarity search and classification via rank aggregation*. ACM SIGMOD 2003: 301-312
12. Christiane Fellbaum (Editor): *WordNet: An Electronic Lexical Database*. MIT Press, 1998
13. Taher H. Haveliwala: *Topic-Sensitive PageRank: A Context-Sensitive Ranking Algorithm for Web Search*. IEEE Trans. Knowl. Data Eng. 15(4) 2003: 784-796
14. J. M. Kleinberg: *Authoritative Sources in a Hyperlinked Environment*. J. ACM 1999 46(5): 604-632
15. Christopher D. Manning, Hinrich Schütze: *Foundations of Statistical Natural Language Processing*. MIT Press, 1999
16. Matt Richardson, Pedro Domingos: *The Intelligent surfer: Probabilistic Combination of Link and Content Information in PageRank*. NIPS 2001: 1441-1448
17. Sergej Sizov, Michael Biwer, Jens Graupmann, Stefan Siersdorfer, Martin Theobald, Gerhard Weikum, Patrick Zimmer: *The BINGO! System for Information Portal Generation and Expert Web Search*. CIDR 2003
18. Martin Theobald, Ralf Schenkel, Gerhard Weikum: *Exploiting Structure, Annotation, and Ontological Knowledge for Automatic Classification of XML Data*. WebDB 2003: 1-6
19. H. Ulbrich: *UrlSearch 2.4.6* http://people.freenet.de/h.ulbrich/
20. Jidong Wang, Zheng Chen, Li Tao, Wei-Ying Ma, Liu Wenyin: *Ranking User's Relevance to a Topic through Link Analysis on Web Logs*. WIDM 2002: 49-54
21. Ji-Rong Wen, Jian-Yun Nie, Hong-Jiang Zhang: *Query Clustering Using User Logs*. ACM Trans. Inf. Syst. 20(1) 2002: 59-81
22. *Wikipedia, The Free Encyclopedia*. http://en.wikipedia.org/wiki/Main_Page
23. Yi-Hung Wu, Arbee L. P. Chen: *Prediction of Web Page Accesses by Proxy Server Log*. World Wide Web 5(1) 2002: 67-88
24. Gui-Rong Xue, Hua-Jun Zeng, Zheng Chen, Wei-Ying Ma, Hong-Jiang Zhang, Chao-Jun Lu: *Implicit Link Analysis for Small Web Search*. SIGIR 2003: 56-63
25. Osmar R. Zaiane, Jaideep Srivastava, Myra Spiliopoulou, Brij M. Masand: *WEBKDD 2002 - MiningWeb Data for Discovering Usage Patterns and Profiles*. 4th International Workshop 2002, Revised Papers Springer 2003

XML Signature Extensibility Using Custom Transforms

Laurence Bull and David M. Squire

School of Computer Science and Software Engineering,
Monash University, Caulfield East 3145, Australia
{Laurence.Bull, David.Squire}@infotech.monash.edu.au

Abstract. The XML Signature specification defines a set of algorithms to be used to ensure security and application inter-operability for content signed using an XML Signature. We discuss a limitation of the XML Signature that arises from its extensibility to cater for new algorithms, and that is likely to be encountered in real-world implementations. We propose two ways to use and disseminate newly defined, or custom, transformation algorithms to address this limitation. These involve downloading the algorithm on-demand, or embedding the algorithm in the signature itself. Finally, we highlight a possible vulnerability to attack in the existing XML Signature Core Validation process when using custom transforms, and suggest an extension to the XML Signature standard to remedy this.

Keywords: XML Signatures; XML Signature Custom Transforms.

1 Introduction

The security and privacy of electronic interactions and transactions are an integral factor in consumer trust of the Internet, and hence, its ever-increasing use. They are one of the pillars of the emergent electronic society. Contributions to the field of information security and privacy will only gain widespread adoption in a web-based world when included in widely adopted international standards.

The XML Signature (XMLsig) is emerging as a web standard for digital signatures to protect digital content. It is backed by major research institutions, government and major industry-based organisations such as IBM, Sun, and Microsoft. The XMLsig standard provides an extensible framework for the signing and verification of structured and potentially distributed digital content. It has been designed with extensibility in mind, so that it can cater for the emergence of new algorithms. In particular, it furnishes a mechanism through which custom transforms, to be applied to the data before verification, may be specified.

It is with the XMLsig extensibility and attendant trust that the focus of this paper lies. We revisit the notion of dynamically downloaded transforms [3], and introduce a method for embedding custom transform code in an XMLsig. We highlight a potential weakness in the current XMLsig standard, and propose extensions to remedy it.

1.1 Motivation

The XMLsig, like the standard digital signature, involves the use of *a priori* specified, publicly available algorithms, as well as matching private and public keys. The standard defines a set of algorithms that must be implemented and provides extensibility

X. Zhou et al. (Eds.): WISE 2004, LNCS 3306, pp. 102–112, 2004.
© Springer-Verlag Berlin Heidelberg 2004

by allowing for the use of newly defined or user specified algorithms [12, §2.1, §2.1.1, §6.1, §6.2]. Section 6.2 explicitly states that additional algorithms are expected: "... it is expected that one or more additional strong digest algorithms will be developed in connection with the US Advanced Encryption Standard effort.". Indeed, over time, the XMLsig standard will likely want to embrace stronger, faster, more capable or comprehensive algorithms for digesting, encrypting, XML processing etc., or perhaps, to address emergent weaknesses in existing algorithms.

The deployment of newly defined or user specified algorithms gives rise to a limitation on the inter-operability of content signed with an XML Signature. This limitation arises due to the nature of the traditional software life-cycle and user inertia in the face of regular upgrade cycles. New versions of the XMLsig standard, or algorithms, require the updating of the vendor XMLsig API (Application Programming Interface). This in turn necessitates an updated version of XMLsig application software in order to utilize the new version of the XMLsig standard. The newer XMLsig applications begin to circulate content signed using the new algorithms contributing to a mixture of content signed with different versions of XMLsig. Users of XMLsig application software who do not upgrade to the latest version will not be able to verify content signed using the new algorithms. Further, depending on vendor and application implementation, it is likely that old versions of XMLsig software will give a 'verification failure' response when trying to verify content signed using new algorithms. This would result in reduced confidence in the XMLsig standard and its inter-operability.

1.2 Contents of This Paper

Section 2 provides a background to signing digital content, the XMLsig and previous work with respect to custom transforms. Custom transform implementation models involving dynamic downloading and embedding in the XMLsig itself are covered in Section 3. In Section 4, we discuss a possible vulnerability to malicious code in the XML Signature Core Validation process when using custom transforms from a signer. This is followed by some proposed extensions to the XML Signature specification to redress the vulnerability, followed by some closing comments in Section 5.

2 Background

In order to improve the security and integrity of digital data, Diffie and Hellman conceived the idea of public key cryptosystems [4], that was later implemented by Rivest, Shamir and Adleman [9]. Thus an effective content-dependent digital signature could be used for electronic documents and digital content. Beth, Frisch and Simmons [2] suggest that this development heralded a change in the information security field, and its primary focus, from secrecy alone to include broader notions of authentication, identification and integrity verification. With the steady rollout of the Public Key Infrastructure (PKI), and its legal recognition in many countries, public, corporate and governmental confidence in, and acceptance of, digital signatures has steadily grown.

2.1 Prior Work

The XML Signature. The World Wide Web Consortium (W3C) [12] and the Internet Engineering Task Force (IETF) [5] formed the XML Signature Working Group (XML-sig WG) to develop the XML-Signature Syntax and Processing Specification through substantial involvement of interested parties from industry, academia and government. This became a core W3C recommendation and was published in February, 2002 [1].[1]

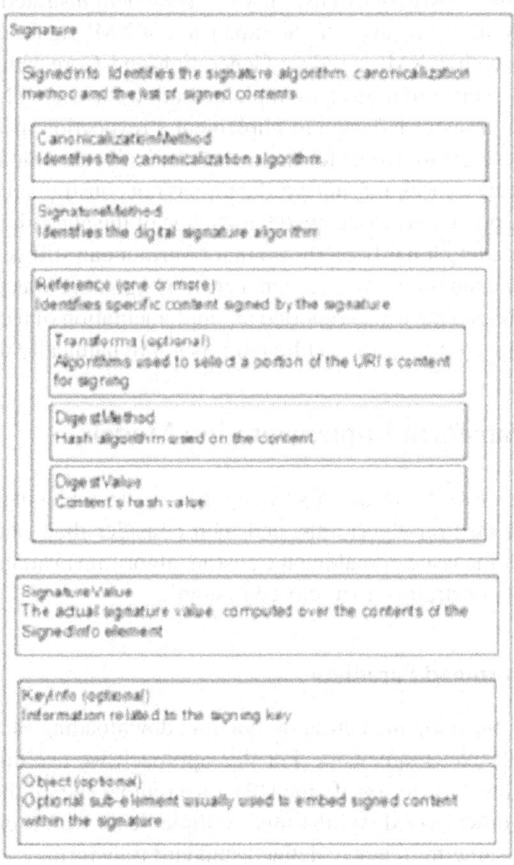

Fig. 1. Main components of an XML Signature showing where the various algorithms are deployed (adapted from [6, p.710] and [7])

An XMLsig is comprised of four top level components or elements, as depicted in Fig. 1. The first component, the `<SignedInfo>` element, includes all of the content or resources to be signed. Each item of content to be signed has a corresponding `<Reference>` element that identifies the content. All of the elements in the `<SignedInfo>` element,

[1] Available as RFC3275 from http://www.ietf.org/rfc/rfc3275.txt

which includes the <CanonicalizationMethod> and <SignatureMethod> elements as well as all of the <Reference> elements, are digested and cryptographically signed in a manner similar to signing when using a standard digital signature. The resulting signature value is stored in the <SignatureValue> element. The <KeyInfo> and <Object> elements are optional. The XMLsig defines algorithms for elements and attributes in four main areas as follows: DigestMethod, Transforms, SignatureMethod and CanonicalizationMethod. For a detailed description of the XMLsig standard see [12].

Custom Transforms. XMLsig extensibility has been demonstrated by developing and implementing custom transforms with the expansion of XMLsig functionality to include CES functionality within XMLsig Core Generation and Core Validation [3]. Further reported in [3] was a custom transform implementation for use with non-XML content as well as a custom transform design to implement a revocation mechanism for signed content. All of these custom transforms are dynamically downloaded from the web demonstrating that custom signing and verification is not constrained to a 'closed system' of parties that have previously exchanged knowledge of the algorithms. Through the use of dynamic downloading it has been shown that a verifier can still verify a custom XML Signature compliant signature even though a custom signature was produced.

Polivy and Tamassia have also reported an implementation of a custom transform to validate an Authenticated Skip List, although it is not dynamically downloaded [8].

3 Custom Transform Implementation Models

Using the XMLsig we will now discuss two approaches to achieving more functionality through the use of custom algorithms, and then consider their characteristics. These approaches address the issue of making the custom algorithm available so that the added functionality is not constrained to a 'closed system'.

3.1 Dynamic Download Paradigm

In [3] we reported our implementation of dynamic downloading of a custom transform using the Microsoft .Net Framework. For this approach we use the <Transform> element's `Algorithm` attribute to specify the URI, on a remote site, of the custom transform code that is to be downloaded. Whilst this example deals with a custom transform, it nevertheless is the same for a newly defined standard transform.

Discussion. The dynamic downloading and execution of an algorithm from a remote location enables the verification of an XMLsig that has been produced according to the custom requirements of the signer. A downside to this is that the verifier must be online to download the algorithm, and perhaps the signer's public key, if it is not available locally. In some cases, the required bandwidth—predominantly for the algorithm—may be an important consideration. There is also likely to be a noticeable latency depending upon the usual suspects, such as the size of the algorithm, the speed of the network connection, network congestion, server load etc., as well as the absence of a connection in the case of mobile devices. In one-off cases this may well be acceptable, while with frequent occurrences a significant improvement may be gained by using a locally cached version.

The downloading of code for execution immediately raises security concerns. As the Internet is a public medium and typically insecure, the code may be subject to such attacks as server redirection through DNS spoofing [10], proxy server interceptions, as well as being modified on the server and while in transit. The use of SSL can enable the secure downloading of the code and can be simply specified by the signer when signing the content by using an HTTPS URI for the transform. To combat the risk of the code being modified or replaced with malicious code, we can use either another `<Reference>` element, to include the code along with the content being signed, or sign the code with a digital signature. Since the code is signed one way or the other, it is not possible to modify it *without detection*.

The flexibility of signing the custom transform code with another digital signature, or of including it along with the content being signed, has implications with respect to the content. If the custom transform is signed using another digital signature, then there is no binding between the content being signed and the custom transform itself. On the other hand, if the custom transform is also included in the signature, the custom transform is bound to the content through the signature. Binding the custom algorithm to the signed content means that if the custom algorithm is upgraded or changed in any way, then all of the signed documents in circulation will have to be re-signed using the new custom algorithm and re-issued. Assuming the practicality and feasibility of re-signing, this would usually entail significant overheads. On the other hand, the lack of binding of the custom algorithm code to the signed content may be an attractive option, since changes to the custom algorithm will not require the re-signing of the already signed documents in circulation. The need to upgrade a custom transform could easily arise over time due to changing circumstances, or requirements, not foreseeable at the time of signing.

While dynamic downloading enables the use of new or custom algorithms in an 'open system' that is not XMLsig version sensitive, it is not inherently platform-independent. However, the use of a virtual machine (VM) and compatible byte code for the custom algorithm, such as the Java VM commonly shipped with web browsers, may render this workable.

3.2 Embedded Paradigm

An alternate approach to furnishing the new or custom transform is for the signer to make it available with the signature by embedding it in the signature itself.

This approach entails base64-encoding the algorithm and placing it an `<Object>` element in the signature along with some adjustments to the XMLsig design used for dynamic downloading [3, §3]. Thus the `<Reference>` element in the new XMLsig structure is now as follows:

```
<Reference URI="#obj1" Type="...#Object">
  <Transforms>
    <Transform Algorithm="#VerifyPolicy"/>
```

```
    </Transforms>
    ...
  </Reference>
...
<Object Id="VerifyPolicy"> ... </Object>
```

The `<Transform>` element's `Algorithm` attribute now refers to an element with the `ID` attribute value 'VerifyPolicy'. We add a new `<Object>` element containing the base64-encoding of the VerifyPolicy transform.

For this approach, the implementation detailed in [3, §4.1] has an important variation. Instead of downloading the algorithm from the Internet, it is now retrieved from within the XMLsig.

Discussion. The embedding of the transform in the signature eliminates the issues involved with downloading the code. However, this is at the cost of a larger signature. While it could be argued that the verifier does not use any extra bandwidth, as the verifier has to get the transform one way or another, it does mean that more storage is required for storing the document. Although the downloaded transform may be stored locally, it is only stored once, even though there may be more than one document. The use of the 'embedded' paradigm sees the transform stored with every document that uses it. The document owner also has extra bandwidth and storage costs due to the embedded custom transform. In the case of CES-XML signatures, the document owner doesn't need to use the transform when extracting a subdocument and corresponding CES-XML signature.

To ensure trust in the integrity of the embedded custom transform the only option is to sign it together with the content being signed. This can be achieved by inserting a new `<Reference>` element—prior to the `<Reference>` elements that use the transform—to include the algorithm in the signature.

The 'embedded' paradigm means that the transform algorithm code is bound to the signed content. It also means that if the public key of the signer is well known and frequently used, hence available locally, the verifier can verify the content and its signature offline. This may have appeal for some applications. There is no involvement of the signer in the verification process, thus affording good privacy and anonymity with respect to use of the signed content. The 'embedded' paradigm shares the platform sensitivity associated with the 'downloading' paradigm.

3.3 Transform Trust

The issue of trust in the transform that is either downloaded or embedded is an important concern, since the code is executed on the verifier's machine. This is analogous to the concern with models for trusting code, and indeed hosts, in the mobile agent domain [11]. More generally, modern electronic documents, unlike their paper predecessors, can contain *active content*. This can be either explicit, such as JavaScript or PHP embedded in an HTML page, or more subtle: an XML document with an associated XSLT (Extensible Stylesheet Language Transformations) stylesheet is also active. Indeed, XSLT is a very general programming language, including loops, conditionals, and file loading. Trusting active content is a general problem in our increasingly networked world.

The transform may be constrained by sandboxing in, say, a Java virtual machine. Nonetheless, whilst the verifier may be prepared to trust the content that is signed, they may not trust, or have sufficient confidence in, the signer regarding the custom transform. This may be addressed by certifying the custom transform. For example, the existing Certification Authorities (CA) could expand their services to include the certifying and then signing of custom transforms, as well as hosting them for downloading. In the case of embedded custom transforms, there could be a slight variation to the signature so that the CA's signature for the custom transform is also embedded in the `<Object>` element. This would enable the verifier to use the public key of the CA to verify the custom transform to gain confidence in the custom transform prior to using it.

3.4 Summary and Comparisons

To highlight the similarities and differences between the 'downloading' and 'embedded' paradigms, to make the new or custom algorithm available, we present the following brief summary.

The 'Downloading' paradigm

- doesn't impact the size of the signature for the document owner, even though the verifier uses extra bandwidth to download the algorithm,
- may have a larger latency when verifying due to the download time of the algorithm,
- means that the transform may be either bound to, or independent of, the signed content, and can therefore support algorithm upgrade/replacement without recall of signed documents,
- requires homogeneous platforms for algorithm execution,
- provides good privacy for the document owner, although the IP address of verifier might be trackable, and
- requires an online connection to perform verification, unless the transform is available locally.

The 'Embedded' paradigm

- increases storage and bandwidth requirements for the document owner and verifier, as the signature now includes the transform,
- has no latency as the transform is immediately available from the signature itself,
- transform is always bound to the signed content, thus algorithm upgrade/replacement requires re-issue and re-signing of signed documents,
- requires homogeneous platforms for algorithm execution,
- requires no interaction with the signer, so privacy is good for both document owner and verifier, and
- verification does not require an online connection if the signer's public key is available locally.

4 Potential Vulnerability

Our discussion in Section 3.1 regarding the signing of the transform raises a very important issue involving a possible vulnerability to malicious code in the XMLsig Core

Validation process when using new or custom transforms from a signer. While we have described two methods for signing the code to ensure integrity and assurance, concern remains about how verification failures, in particular, exploitation by potentially malicious code, are dealt with.

XMLsig Core Generation involves the mandatory steps of Reference Generation first, followed by Signature Generation [12, §3.1]. Signature Generation can only occur *after* Reference Generation is complete, as the `<Reference>` element information is included in the signature. On the other hand, the Core Validation process, Reference Validation and Signature Validation, are not so constrained. Signature Validation may be performed *either* before or after Reference Validation. The specification states for Core Validation:

> The REQUIRED steps of core validation include (1) reference validation, the verification of the digest contained in each `<Reference>` in `<SignedInfo>`, and (2) the cryptographic signature validation of the signature calculated over `<SignedInfo>`. [1, §3.2]

This seems to imply an order of operations, although it is not explicitly stated. We note that Microsoft's implementation in the .Net Framework uses this implied order to perform Reference Validation and *then* Signature Validation [6, p.760].

There is also the question of what happens when a validation failure occurs. For example, if Reference Validation is performed first, what happens if a `<Reference>` element fails validation? Does it automatically exit the whole verification process, as does Microsoft's implementation [6, p.760], or does it continue on, checking all of the `<Reference>` elements and then attempt a Signature Validation? The XMLsig specification appears to be silent on this matter. These are important considerations when using custom transforms, as we will now discuss.

First, we will consider the approach of signing the transform by adding an additional `<Reference>` element to include it before the content being signed. An attack could see the transform being swapped for malicious code and the digest in the `<Reference>` element replaced with a digest for the malicious code. We assume Core Validation proceeds with Reference Validation first, followed by Signature Validation, and that an early exit to the Core Validation process is taken upon the first validation failure. Reference Validation of the first `<Reference>` element, which contains the malicious code, processing would verify the digest over the code, proceeding to verify the following `<Reference>` elements for the signed content. This would see the malicious code gain execution control in the transform chain for the first `<Reference>` element processed for the signed content. This vulnerability could occur for both a downloaded algorithm or an embedded algorithm.

The transform *must* be validated prior to its execution. The above attack can easily be thwarted by simply performing the Signature Validation before the Reference Validation, as it will detect the swapped digest for the malicious code, fail Signature Validation and abort Reference Validation.

The other approach, pertinent only for the 'downloading' paradigm, of signing the transform with another digital signature, means that the digital signature must be verified before the transform is executed. Rather than relying upon the operating system to enforce verification of the algorithm prior to its execution, the XMLsig specification should ensure that it occurs. In order to verify the signature for the transform, we need to provide some information about the digital signature. This information can be provided as follows by the signer:

```
<Reference URI="#obj1">
  <Transforms>
    <Transform Algorithm=".../VerifyPolicy">
      <SignatureMethod />
      <KeyValue />
      <SignatureValue />
    </Transform>
  </Transforms>
  <DigestMethod />
  <DigestValue />
</Reference>
```

Here we overload the operation of input arguments to the transform algorithm by adding three child elements to the `<Transform>` element. This information is intended as input for what we propose is a signature verification process that must occur prior to a algorithm being allowed to execute. The `<SignatureMethod>` element specifies the signature algorithm to be used, while the `<KeyValue>` element contains the public key to be used for the verification and the `<SignatureValue>` element contains the signature to be checked against the transform.

In order to combine the two different verification approaches for transforms and their required information, we propose a new `<Transform>` element attribute called '`VerificationMethod`' and a new `<VerificationValue>` child element as follows:

```
<Reference URI="#obj1" Type="...#Object">
  <Transforms>
    <Transform
         Algorithm=".../CustomTransform"
         VerificationMethod="">
      <VerificationValue />
          (<SignatureValue />)?
    </Transform>
  </Transforms>
  ...
</Reference>
```

where: `?` denotes zero or one occurrences.

The `<Transform>` element's `VerificationMethod` attribute can be used to specify any of the digest or signature methods supported by the XMLsig. The `<VerificationValue>` element contains either a digest value or public key value and a `<SignatureValue>` child element, according to what VerificationMethod is specified. As this information is protected by the signature over the `<SignedInfo>` contents, once Signature Validation has been confirmed, then the contents can be used as a basis for verifying the algorithm prior to its use. Thus we have provided a simple, flexible mechanism for specifying the transform verification information that affords the signer flexibility when signing content according to whether they want the transform bound to the signed content or not.

Finally, we propose the following processing rules when using transforms not known to the XMLsig API:

i. It is MANDATORY for custom transforms to be verified before they are executed,
ii. Signature Validation is MANDATORY *before* Reference Validation,
iii. It is MANDATORY to specify the VerificationMethod attribute for `<Transform>` elements *and* the `<VerificationValue>` child element when signing the document.

5 Conclusion

We have shown how to embed a custom transform in the signature itself, and revisited our earlier work on their dynamic downloading, and discussed the implications of these approaches. We have highlighted a possible vulnerability in the existing XML Signature Core Validation process when using new or custom transforms, and suggested an extension to the XML Signature standard to remedy this. Finally, we have proposed processing rules that any implementation using new or custom transforms should obey.

Acknowledgements. The authors would like to thank Dr Brian LaMacchia of Microsoft Corporation for his time and effort reviewing draft manuscripts, along with his helpful comments.

References

1. M. Bartel, J. Boyer, B. Fox, B. LaMacchia, and E. Simon. XML-signature syntax and processing. In D. Eastlake, J. Reagle, and D. Solo, editors, *W3C Recommendation*. World Wide Web Consortium, 12 February 2002. [Last accessed: 21 May, 2004]. `http://www.w3.org/TR/2002/REC-xmldsig-core-20020212/`
2. T. Beth, M. Frisch, and G.J. Simmons, editors. *Public-Key Cryptography: State of the Art and Future Directions*, volume 578 of *Lecture Notes in Computer Science*. Springer, 3–6 July 1992. E.I.S.S. Workshop Oberwolfach Final Report.
3. Laurence Bull, Peter Stanski, and David McG. Squire. Content extraction signatures using XML digital signatures and custom transforms on-demand. In *Proceedings of The 12th International World Wide Web Conference (WWW2003)*, pages 170–7, Budapest, Hungary, 20–24 May 2003. ACM Press. [Last accessed: 21 May, 2004]. `http://www2003.org/cdrom/papers/refereed/p838/p838-bull.html`
4. W. Diffie and M.E. Hellman. New directions in cryptography. *IEEE Transactions on Information Theory*, IT-22(6):644–54, 1976.
5. IETF. The Internet Engineering Task Force. Available online. [Last accessed: 21 May, 2004]. `http://www.ietf.org/`
6. B. LaMacchia, S. Lange, M. Lyons, R. Martin, and K. Price. *.NET Framework Security*. Addison-Wesley, Boston, MA, USA, 2002.
7. Brian LaMacchia. Personal communication, 25 March 2004.

8. Daniel J. Polivy and Roberto Tamassia. Authenticating distributed data using web services and XML signatures. In *Proceedings of the 2002 ACM workshop on XML security (XMLSEC-02)*, pages 80–89, New York, USA, 22 November 2002. ACM Press.
9. R.L. Rivest, A. Shamir, and L. Adleman. A method for obtaining digital signatures and public-key cryptosystems. *Communications of the ACM*, 21(2):120–8, 1978.
10. Doug Sax. DNS spoofing (malicious cache poisoning). Available online, 12 November 2000. [Last accessed: 21 May, 2004]. `http://www.giac.org/practical/gsec/Doug_Sax_GSEC.pdf`
11. U. G. Wilhelm, S. Staamann, and L. Buttyán. On the problem of trust in mobile agent systems. In *Proceedings of the Network and Distributed System Security Symposium (NDSS'98)*, pages 114–124, San Diego, CA, USA, 11–13 March 1998. Internet Society.
12. World Wide Web Consortium. The World Wide Web Consortium. Available online. [Last accessed: 21 May, 2004]. `http://www.w3.org/`

Extraction of Cognitively-Significant Place Names and Regions from Web-Based Physical Proximity Co-occurrences

Taro Tezuka, Yusuke Yokota, Mizuho Iwaihara, and Katsumi Tanaka

Kyoto University
Graduate School of Informatics
tezuka@dl.kuis.kyoto-u.ac.jp, {yyokota, iwaihara, ktanaka}@i.kyoto-u.ac.jp

Abstract. The cognitive significances of geographic objects play an important role in optimizing a set of place names presented on a map interface. The aim of this research is to assign a value for cognitive significance to each place name in GIS, based on regional documents collected from the Web. The assigned values could be used in GIS applications including regional information searches, path findings, and car navigation systems. We will compare different criteria for cognitive significance and discuss a system already in use, before presenting our experimental results.

1 Introduction

Geographic information systems (GIS) have expanded their range of applications from analysis tools for natural resources and social activities to everyday tasks such as car navigation systems, regional information searches, and tour planning assistances [1][2].

In these new GIS applications, users expect map interfaces to display cognitively significant place names, such as landmarks, famous districts, important paths, etc. In other words, in addition to physical information, cognitive information on GIS is gaining importance.

Maps are easier to understand if the significant place names are placed properly. Imagine a map without any place names. Such a map would be inconvenient to use.

Although the cognitive significance of place names plays an important role in new GIS applications, there has not yet been much analysis on this subject, except for purely social-scientific reasons. Such research has often employed labor-intensive questionnaires, and was too costly and impractical for use in practical applications.

Today, many GIS applications already contain some sets of significant place names. For example, regional information search systems, path-finding systems, and car navigation systems all contain sets of significant place names for their map interfaces. In many cases, a map editor selects the place names manually. This is particularly cumbersome for cities where landmarks change rapidly. We propose an automated method of extracting such place names using large regional information texts, especially from the Web.

Our aim is to measure cognitive significances of place names, and also to extract networks of such place names which give rise to cognitively significant districts. A list

X. Zhou et al. (Eds.): WISE 2004, LNCS 3306, pp. 113–124, 2004.
© Springer-Verlag Berlin Heidelberg 2004

of place names and their locations taken from regular GIS are used basic data set. Web mining is applied to measure their frequencies, and also their cooccurrences.

In Section 2 we will discuss related work. Section 3 defines notions used in the paper. Section 4 discusses methods for extracting significant place names, and in Section 5 we will look at the extraction of k-edge connected components. In Section 6 we will show an implementation, and in Section 7 the experimental results are described. We will conclude the paper with a brief summary in Section 8.

2 Related Work

There are many related works on the subject of significant place name extraction using web resources.

In the text-mining research field, term frequency-inverse document frequency (TF-IDF) is the most widely used measure for significance of a term in a document [3]. The number of times a given term appears in a given document is DF. The log of the whole document set size divided by the document set size containing the given term is IDF. We will show that this measure is unsatisfactory for geographic place names, due to frequent ambiguities.

There are also linguistic approaches to the extraction [4], but they have the same problems as TF-IDF, when used to extract geographic information. In most cases, people can resolve the place-name ambiguity through a context. Unfortunately, most natural language processing systems are weak in the area of contextual analysis.

Currently, many researchers are working on organizing the massive amount of geographic information available on the Web. There are systems that require human intervention, such as the InfoMap [5] and Geo-Portal[6], and others that are in fully automated schemes [7]. Our research differs from those approaches in that our ultimate goal is not to enhance searches for information that already exist on the Web, but to create a whole new set of cognitive cityscape information by analyzing the existing data.

Georeferenced Information Processing SYstem (GIPSY)[8] is a system similar to ours in that it parses through documents and retrieves place names and their characteristics. Yet their final aim was to assign geographical coordinates to a given set of documents, and not to measure the significance of each place name.

Tung et al. proposed an algorithm for clustering spatial objects under various constraints. Yet, unlike our method of clustering place names based on co-occurrences between the names, their system handles obstacles in space, or type differences between the entities [9].

Kevin Lynch, an urban engineering researcher, has written a classic work on the cognitive cityscape, entitled "The Image of The City" [10]. Here, residents of three U.S. cities were asked to give the basic geographic elements of their residing cities.

He observed that city image is basicly formed from five basic elements: landmarks, edges, paths, nodes, and districts. Lynch writes that "Landmarks are another type of point-reference, but in this case the observer does not enter within them, they are external." This statement is related to comparison of "nodes" to another group of cognitively significant elements, which were "strategic spots in a city into which an observer can enter, and which are intensive foci to and from which he is traveling." On the other hand, he defines districts as, "the medium-to-large sections of the city, conceived of as having two-dimensional extent, which the observer mentally enters 'inside of', and which are recognizable as having some common, identifying character."

Unfortunately, his method is not directly applicable for regional information systems, since the research was based on a labor-intensive task of collecting questionnaires. One of our research aims is to automatically extract social information without using questionnaires, from large sized document sources such as the Web.

Koiso et al. extracted landmarks based on categorical attributes and visual significances [11]. An object surrounded by other objects with different attributes is more likely to be a landmark, while its volume also works as a positive factor. This approach aims at estimating how each object is "seen" by observers, whereas in our method, the focus is on how each object is "expressed" on web resources.

3 Definition

Place names are the names of immovable objects on a geographic scale, and includes buildings, regions, roads, rivers, etc. For our analysis, each place name must have coordinates. For place names with extensity, we used the centers of gravity of their minimum bounding rectangles (MBR) for their coordinates. A **target region** is the whole area under discussion. A **location** is a set of specific coordinates in physical space. A location can be expressed as a vector x. Due to the ambiguities in place names, many place names indicate several locations. **Significant place names** are well known place names with high cognitive significance. It is difficult to set the threshold between significant and insignificant place names. We prefer to concentrate on assigning each place name a value that indicates the level of significance.

4 Extraction of Significant Place Names

In this section, we will discuss various methods for measuring the cognitive significance of each place name. We will discuss three different measures. They are document frequency, physical proximity co-occurrence sum, and the adjusted physical proximity co-occurrence sum.

4.1 Document Frequency

In the field of text mining, **document frequency** has been widely used as a measure for term significance. The value indicates the number of documents in which the term appears.

Experience shows that document frequency is not a satisfactory measure for the cognitive significance of place names because place names have ambiguities. Some words are used for place name, peoples' names, and general nouns. The fact that place names are proper nouns makes the ambiguity much more common than in cases of general nouns. Therefore document frequency does not often match the number of cases in which it was used to refer to a specific location. Therefore, it does not express the level of significance for designating certain locations. Document frequency does not provide a suitable criterion for measuring cognitive significance.

4.2 Physical Proximity Co-occurrence Sum

The simplest way to deal with the ambiguity problem is to affirm the location assumption by finding two or more place names in documents that indicate locations close to one another. In other words, suppose that a place name a indicates two different locations x_a and $x_{a'}$ due to ambiguity, while place name b indicates a location x_b, and $|x_a - x_b| < |x_{a'} - x_b|$. If a and b co-occur in a document, then the document is more likely to be discussing a on the location x_a, rather than $x_{a'}$. For example, suppose that a document contains the term "Paris". If the document also contains "Versailles", then we can assume that the document is discussing about Paris, France. On the other hand, if the document also contains "Texarkana", then the document is likely to be discussing Paris, Texas.

In this method, we must first define how far "physical proximity" will stretch. One way is to set a threshold distance. However, this will not work if the target region discussion covers areas that contain both high and low concentrations of place names. This would not be fair, if, for some place names, there are more matches for finding co-occurrences, while there are only few for others.

In our proposed measure of **physical proximity co-occurrence sum**, or PPCS, we define **physical proximity** as a set of n, the closest place names from the target place name. This is obtained by sorting the place names by their distance from the target place name, as shown in Figure 1. In the expressions, P_i and P_j are then place names of which the cognitive significances are to be measured, with i and j as the index numbers. C_{ij} indicates the number of documents in which the place names i and j co-occur.

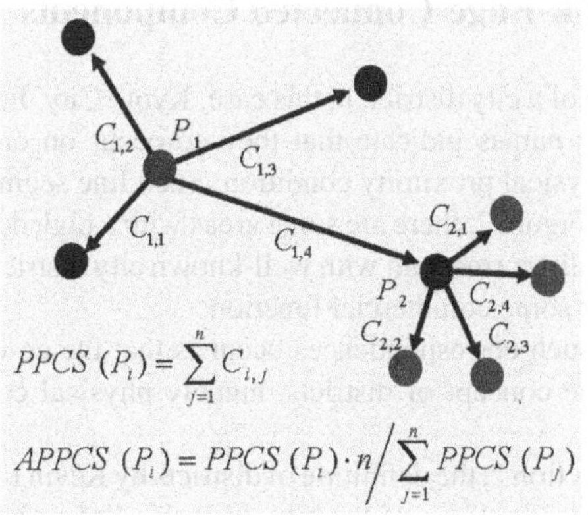

Fig. 1. Physical proximity, PPCS, and APPCS

PPCS is the sum of the number of co-occurrences between the target place name and its physical proximity. Because PPCS expresses how often each place name co-occurs with the surrounding place names, it should reduce misplacings caused by place name ambiguities.

One problem with PPCS is that place names surrounded by other significant place names are likely to have high PPCSs, because those co-occurrences are affected by the original document frequency. This will be explained in Section 7, when we present the experiment results.

4.3 Adjusted Physical Proximity Co-occurrence Sum

To avoid a PPCS bias caused by the surrounding environments, the effects from the accumulations of significant place names in physical proximity should somehow be compensated.

We define another measure, **adjusted physical proximity co-occurrence sum**, or APPCS, by dividing PPCS by the sum of PPCSs of the place names in physical proximity. The expression for APPCS is also expressed in Figure 1.

A comparison between the three methods is shown in Table 1.

Table 1. Merits and demerits of DF, PPCS, and APPCS

Methods	Merits	Demerits
DF	Less calculation time	Can not handle ambiguity in PNs
PPCS	Reduces ambiguity	Deviates from significance of PNs in proximity
APPCS	Avoids bias from PNs in proximity	Deviates if too many significant PNs in proximity

5 Extraction of k-Edge-Connected Components

Figure 2 shows a map of a city district, in this case, Kyoto City, Japan. The line segments connecting two place names indicate that they co-occur on one or more web pages and also fulfill the physical proximity condition. Such line segments will be called **co-occurrence links**. In Figure 2, there are some areas with a high density of co-occurrence links. Such areas usually correspond with well-known city districts that have a historical or cultural interest, or some commercial function.

The reason why such correspondences occur is that the co-occurrence links fulfill two conditions for the concept of districts, namely physical coherence and semantic relationships.

As described in Section 2, the definition of districts by Kevin Lynch was that "districts are the medium-to-large sections of the city, conceived of as having two-dimensional extent, which the observer mentally enters 'inside of', and which are recognizable as having some common, identifying character." If a set of place names has identifying characteristics, the members of the set are likely to co-occur on web documents. Also if the place names constitute a district, then they fulfill the physical proximity condition required for co-occurrence links. Even if there is a strong relationship between place names, if they are far apart, no link will be established. Therefore, a densely connected set of place names fulfills the both of the district criteria defined in Section 2.

Our hypothesis is that such sets of place names often correspond to the actual districts of a city.

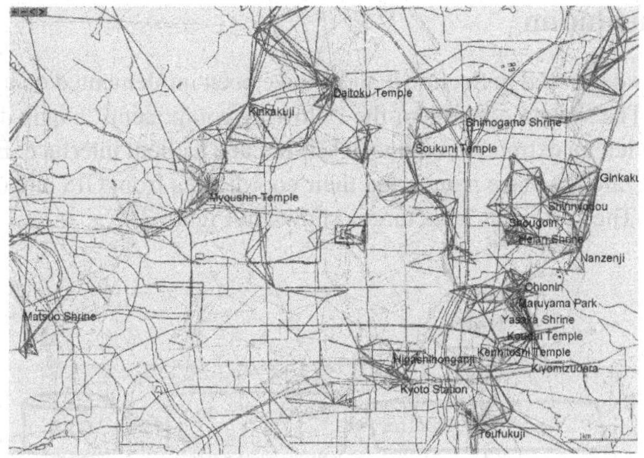

Fig. 2. Co-occurrence Link Network

We have performed a k-edge-connected component extraction algorithm on the co-occurrence link networks [14][15][16][17].

Input: a network N, a constant k.
Output: k-edge-connected components of the network N.
Step 1. N(0,0)=N; i=0.
Step 2. j=0.
Step 3. For the vertex set N(i,j), get MAO(maximum Adjacency Ordering).
Step 4. The cut between last two elements of MAO is equal to the last element's degree, so store that value.
Step 5. Merge the last two elements of MAO into one vertex, and obtain a new network N(i,j+1).
Step 6. j++.
Step 7. If N(i,j) has more than one vertex, go back to Step 3.
Step 8. Get the minimum from all of the stored values. That is the minimum cut for N(i,0).
Step 9. Cut the network N(i,0) into two, using the minimum cut.
Step 10. i++.
Step 11. For each new networks, if minimum cut is larger than k-1, go back to Step 2.
Step 12. The obtained networks are the k-edge-connected components of N.

In addition to extracting k-edge-connected components, the following processes can create coherent regions, rather than sets of place names. The regions obtained resemble the districts.

– Obtain k-edge-connected component.
– Get convex hull of the graph.
– Broaden the region around the edge, so that all vertices are included in the region.

6 Implementation

The algorithms described in Section 4 and 5 have been implemented on a system named **PLACES2C**. The system consists of the following components: a map database (GIS), a focused crawler, an extraction engine, a servlet, and a client interface. Basic data used by PLACES2C are (1) place names and their coordinates from GIS and (2) text content from the Web. The system architecture is shown in Figure 3.

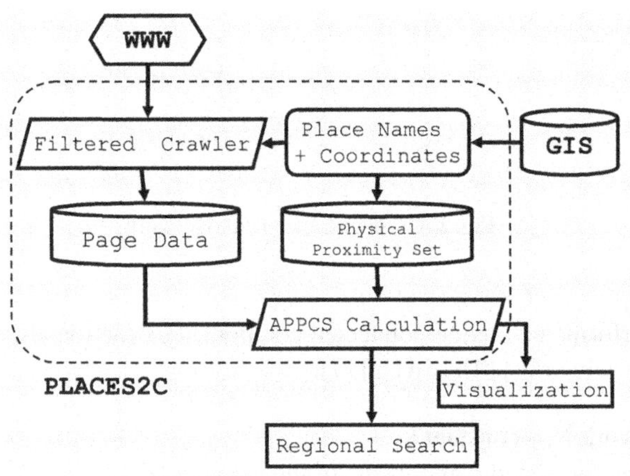

Fig. 3. The architecture for PLACES2C

Descriptions of each component in the system are as follows.

A focused crawler is a special type of web crawler that collects pages that fulfill certain conditions only. The links are traced only when a page satisfies the condition. The conditions can be the existence of certain keywords or a high similarity to given example pages. In many cases focused crawlers are reported to have a higher efficiency in retrieving web pages under certain topics[13]. The underlying assumption is that pages concerning certain topics are more likely to be linked to pages discussing the same topic.

Because our objective was to extract significant place names for a certain target regions, we used a focused crawler for efficient retrieval. The condition is that pages must contain any of the place names within the region. Due to the ambiguity of place names, not all of the retrieved pages discuss the target region. Yet the ratio of all related pages increased, in comparison with using a regular crawler.

Using the algorithm discussed in the Section 4 and 5, each place name had an APPCS calculated. The map interface presents place names with top 20 APPCS values, grouped into regions based on k-edge connected components.

7 Experiments

We performed experiments using PLACES2, to compare the validity of DF, PPCS and APPCS.

For map data, we used a digitalized residential map provided by Zenrin, Ltd.[12]. The target region was Kyoto, Japan. Zenrin's map data was divided into many layers. Each layer contained geographic objects under certain category. There was a "significant objects" layer, which contained 7,234 place names. Their significance varies. Both famous temples and ordinary elementary schools are included in this layer. By itself, this set of place names is unsatisfactory as an indicator of cognitive significance. No quantitative value is given either. Our goal in this experiment was to assign a value to each place name found in this layer.

For a document set, we used 157,297 web pages collected by a focused crawler. Each page contained one or more place name in the target region. The results of the experiments are described in the following subsections.

7.1 Extraction of Significant Place Names

To calculate document frequency, we used the full-text search engine, Namazu [18]. Prior to the search, we added place names taken from GIS to the Namazu indexing-word-list. As a result, 2,552 place names (out of 7,234) appeared more than once in the set of 157,297 web pages. The average and the standard deviation for the document frequencies (DFs) were $\mu = 47.64, \sigma = 217.16$.

The place names with the highest DFs were as follows: Shijo (Commercial Street) - 5,166, Gion (Nightlife District) - 4,202, Kyoto Station - 3,715, Sanjo (Street of Kyoto) - 2,790, Kawaramachi (Commercial Street of Kyoto), Nishijin (District) - 2,617, Arashiyama (Tourism District) - 2,485, Hankyu (Train and Department Store Company), Nijo Castle - 1,331. Because the universities had such high frequency in a non-geographic sense, we excluded them from the list.

For PPCS, the proximity limit (=n) was set at 50. Out of 7,234 place names, 1,343 place names were found to have more than one co-occurrence with its physical proximity, although the number of analyzable place names decreased by 1,343/2,552 = 0.526 (about one half). If we use larger web page collection, however, this problem may well be compensated. The average and the standard deviation for PPCS was $\mu = 52.20$ and $\sigma = 120.82$.

The average distance to their physical proximity was 795 m. This is neither too far nor too close to the physically proximate place names, when we are discussing urban areas. Thus, we considered n=50 to be an appropriate threshold.

The place names with the highest PPCSs were as follows. Arashiyama (Tourism District) - 1,738/2,485, Kohdaiji (Temple) - 999/586, Kiyomizudera (Temple) - 922/972, Yasaka Shrine - 891/623, Tenryuji (Temple) - 863/418, Nison-in (Temple) - 826/86, Joujakkouji (Temple) - 781/81, Chion-in (Temple) - 758/449, Giohji (Temple) - 688/64, Sanzen-in (Temple) - 683/397. The first number indicates PPCS, and the latter is DF. Many points of interests (especially temples) are now in the list, which indicates that significant place names from visitors are extracted.

In Figure 4, the place names were lined in descending order of the PPCS. The solid line is the PPCS of each place name, and the pale line is the sum of the PPCS of the surrounding place names. The values are all standardized ($Z = (x - \mu)/\sigma$).

The graph shows that there is a co-occurrence between the two measures. This co-occurrence indicates that the place names with high PPCS are likely to be surrounded by

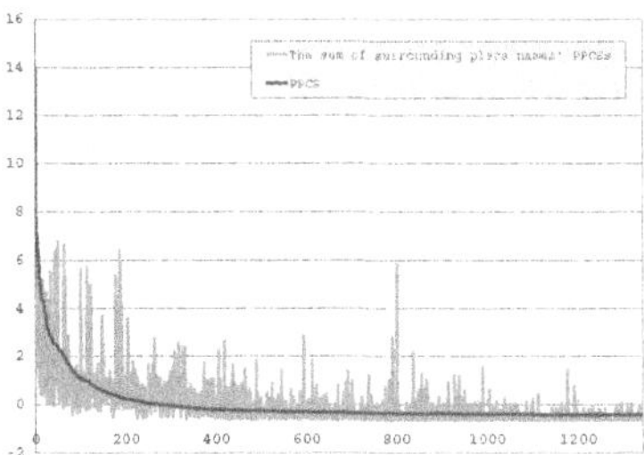

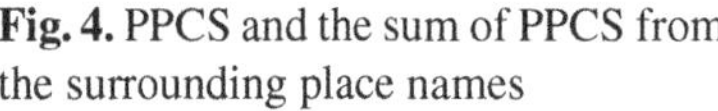

Fig. 4. PPCS and the sum of PPCS from the surrounding place names

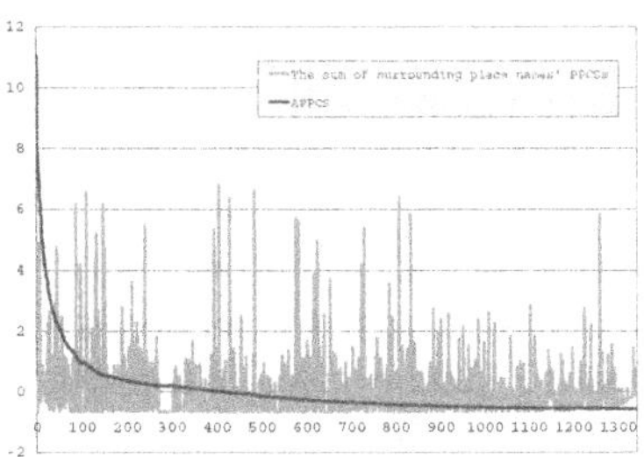

Fig. 5. APPCS and the sum of PPCS from the surrounding place names

place names with high PPCS. In a more realistic sense, it indicates that the surrounding environments raise the PPCS value.

In Figure 5, the solid line is the APPCS of each place name, and the pale line is the sum of PPCS of the surrounding place names. They show that there is less sign of a correlation between APPCS and the sum of PPCSs by the surrounding place names, compared to Figure 4. In other words, the APPCS value is less affected by its surrounding environment. The APPCS is more intrinsic to the place name itself.

The APPCS can be calculated for any place name with PPCS. Therefore, the number of place names with APPCS is again 1,343. The average and the standard deviation for APPCS were $\mu = 0.74, \sigma = 1.33$.

The place names with the highest APPCSs were as follows: Tohfukuji (Temple) - 15.40, Shoukokuji (Temple) - 11.25, Vivre (Department Store) - 11.00, Myoushinji (Temple) - 10.41, Nanzenji (Temple) - 10.24, Nishihonganji (Temple) - 10.03, Arashiyama (Tourism District) - 9.24, Kiyomizudera (Temple) - 9.20, Kuramadera (Temple) - 8.78, Tohji (Temple) - 8.46. Extracted place names are mostly more significant than any other place name in their surroundings. In PPCS, some place names scored higher than more significant place names near by.

Figures 6 and 7 show examples of how the PPCS handles ambiguous place names. The place names shown on Figure 6 have high document frequencies (DF). "Shoutoku Temple" appears on the left side. 30 pages out of the collected 157,297 web pages contain the term "Shoutoku Temple". However, Shoutoku Temple is not a well-known landmark in the target region, according to various guidebooks of the area. This discrepancy resulted because Shoutoku Temple is a common name for temples and is used throughout the country. Not all 30 pages discussed the Shoutoku Temple in the target region.

Figure 7 shows the same region, except that place names were selected using PPCS, and the line segments indicate that there are co-occurrences between the connected place names.

The PPCS for "Shoutoku Temple(A)" is 3, which means Shoutoku Temple does not often co-occur with its surroundings. It also indicates that Shoutoku Temple is not as important when compared to other place names with a similar document frequency order, such as "Nishihonganji Temple(B)" (DF=, PPCS=, APPCS=), "Koshoji Temple(C)"(DF=95, PPCS=63, APPCS=1.028), and "Tanbaguchi Station(D)" (DF=76,

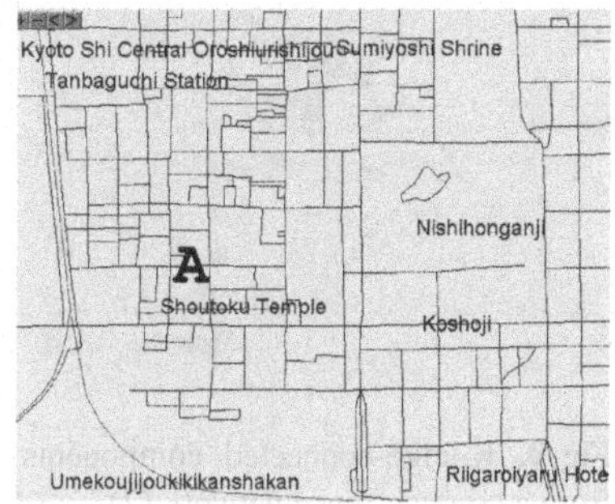

Fig. 6. DF, without co-occurrence links

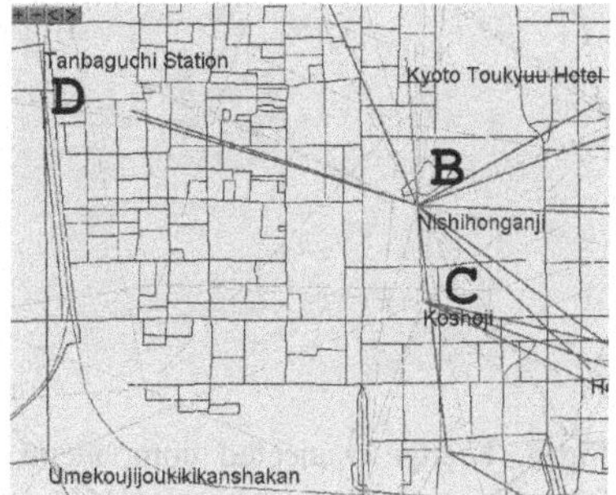

Fig. 7. PPCS, with co-occurrence links

PPCS=49, APPCS=0.683). Figure 7 shows that Shoutoku Temple has only a small number of co-occurrence links with its physical proximity.

Pages containing "Shoutoku Temple(A)" were checked manually to test the above observation. Only 1 out of 30 were relevant to the target region (=Kyoto). Table 2 shows a comparison with Nishihonganji Temple(B), Koshoji Temple(C), and Tanbaguchi Station(D). These place names appear in both Figures 6 and 7, unlike Shoutoku Temple. Although there were some temples named Koshoji, the Koshoji in the target region (Kyoto) was significant enough to dominate the appearance ratio. This comparison shows how PPCS and APPCS give a good cognitive significance criterion, especially when there are ambiguities in the place names, which is usually the case. Precision were checked manually whether the place names refer to the locations in the target region. For Nishihonganji Temple(B), the check was performed only partially, due to the large DF.

Table 2. Results of DF, PPCS, APPCS, and Manual Judgement

Place Name	A	B	C	D
DF	30	712	95	76
PPCS	3	326	63	49
APPCS	0.111	10.031	1.028	0.683
Precision	1 / 30	197 / 200	67 / 95	76 / 76

7.2 Extraction of k-Edge-Connected Components

We also performed experiments to extract the k-edge-connected components of co-occurrence link networks. The results are shown in Figures 8 and 9. Each k-edge-connected component is shown in a different color.

The figures show that the k-edge-connected components correspond with districts in the target region. This was confirmed by comparing these components with districts described in regional guidebooks. As in Lynch's definition of districts in Section 2, those place name sets are "recognizable as having some common, identifying character."

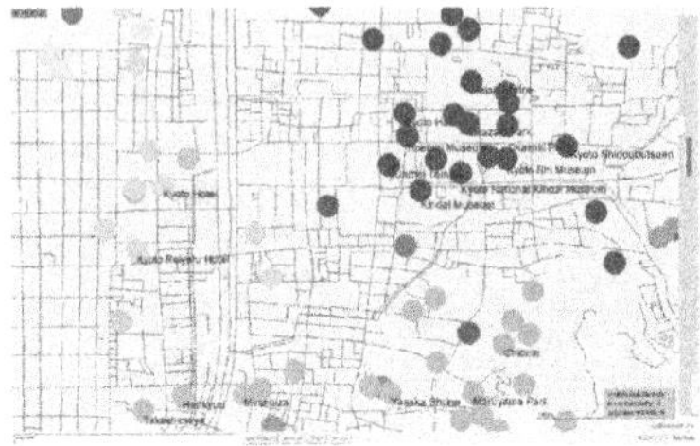

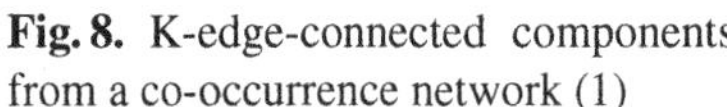

Fig. 8. K-edge-connected components from a co-occurrence network (1)

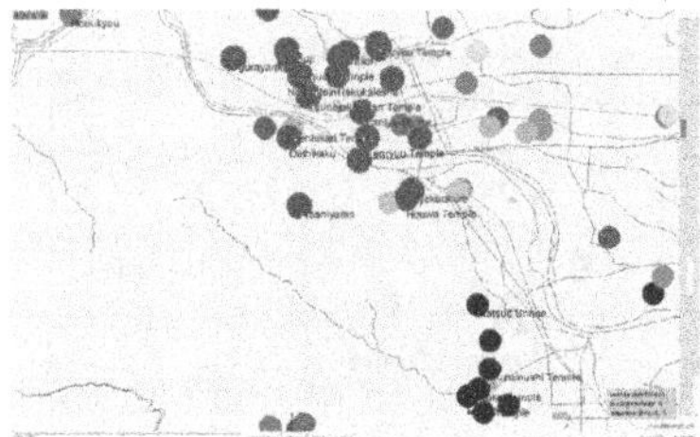

Fig. 9. K-edge-connected components from a co-occurrence network (2)

Because the optimal value for k is dependent on the scale of the map being presented, the user interface has a slider to dynamically change k. In the experiments, we used $2 \leq k \leq 6$. If k rose higher, the graph was divided into smaller components, and partitions became trivial.

8 Conclusion

In this paper, we described methods of measuring the cognitive significances of place names and presented the implementation and results of experiments. The comparison between the three measures show that the adjusted physical proximity sum (APPCS) avoids ambiguity problems and are less affected by place names' surrounding environments.

The extraction of significant place names is an attempt to bring GIS closer to actual human cognition of geographic space. Such exploration will become more important as the GIS applications expand and become more closely related to our daily lives.

Maps are so common in our daily lives and fundamental to our thinking that the word "map" is often used to describe different types of information visualization. However, in order to maximize vast digitalized data available now, we need an entirely new user-friendly interface with expanded functionality. Our proposed system provides one answer to this concern. Unlike many digitalized map interfaces that simply provide copies of traditional maps, our system provides a new, easy to use interface with more utility.

Our future work will include a semantic analysis on how each pair of place names co-occur. The extraction of either the homogeneous or functional relationships hidden behind the co-occurrence links could be used in a wide range of applications.

References

1. Y. H. Chou, Exploring Spatial Analysis in Geographic Information Systems, OnWordPress, 1997
2. C. Harder, Serving Maps on the Internet, Environmental Systems Research Institute, Inc. (ESRI), 1998
3. G. Salton, Developments in Automatic Text Retrieval, Science, Vol. 253, pp. 974-979, 1991
4. T. Strzalkowski, "Natural Language Information Retrieval", Information Processing and Management, Vol.31, No.3, pp. 397-417, 1995

5. K. Hiramatsu, K. Kobayashi, B. Benjamin, T. Ishida, and J. Akahani, “Map-based User Interface for Digital City Kyoto”, in Proceedings of the 10th Annual Internet Society Conference, Yokohama, Japan, 2000
6. E.P. Lim, D. Goh, Z. Liu, W.K. Ng, C. Khoo, S.E. Higgins, "G-Portal: A Map-based Digital Library for Distributed Geospatial and Georeferenced Resources," in proceedings of the 2nd ACM+IEEE Joint Conference on Digital Libraries (JCDL 2002), Portland, Oregon, 2002
7. N. Yamada, R. Lee, H. Takakura, and Y. Kambayashi, “Classification of Web Pages with Geographic Scope and Level of Details for Mobile Cache Management” , in Proceeding of the 3rd International Workshop on Web and Wireless GIS, Singapore, 2002
8. A. G. Woodruff and C. Plaunt, “GIPSY: Automated geographic indexing of text documents”, Journal of the American Society for Information Science, Vol. 45, No. 9, pp.645-655, 1994
9. A. K. H. Tung, R. T. Ng, L. V. S. Lakshmanan and J. Han, “Geo-spatial Clustering with User-Specified Constraints”, Proc. of the Int. Workshop on Multimedia Data Mining, in conjunction with ACM SIGKDD Conference, Boston, 2000
10. K. Lynch, The Image of the City, The MIT Press, Cambridge, Massachusetts, 1960
11. Kengo Koiso, Takehisa Mori, Hiroaki Kawagishi, Katsumi Tanaka, and Takahiro Matsumoto, “InfoLOD and LandMark: Spatial Presentatino of Attribute Information and Computing Representative Objects for Spatial Data”, International Journal of Cooperative Information Systems, Vol.9, No.1-2, pp.53-76, 2000
12. ZENRIN CO.,LTD,
http://www.zenrin.co.jp/
13. S. Chakrabarti, M. van den Berg, B. Domc, “Focused crawling: a new approach to topic-specific Web resource discovery”, in Proceedings of the 8th International World-Wide Web Conference (WWW8), Toronto, Canada, 1999
14. A. V. Karzanov and E. A. Timofeev, “Efficient algorithm for finding all minimal edge cuts of a nonoriented graph,” Kibernetika, 2, pp. 8-12, 1986 (translated in Cybernetics, pp. 156-162, 1986)
15. H. Nagamochi, T. Watanabe, “Computing k-Edge-Connected Components of a Multigraph”, IEICE Trans. Fundamentals, Vol. E76-A, No. 4, 1993
16. S. Fujishige (Eds), Discrete Structure and Algorithms II, Kindai-Kagakusha, 1993 (in Japanese)
17. K. Sugihara, T. Ibaraki, T. Asano, and M. Yamashita (Eds), “Algorithm Engineering”, Kyoritsu Shuppan, 2001 (in Japanese)
18. Namazu: a Full-Text Search Engine,
http://www.namazu.org/index.html.en
19. T. Tezuka, R. Lee, H. Takakura, and Y. Kambayashi, “Web-Base Inference Rules for Processing Conceptual Geographical Relationships”, Proc. of the 2nd Int. Conf. on Web Information Systems Engineering, The 1st Int. Workshop on Web Geographical Information Systems, Kyoto, 2001
20. T. Tezuka, R. Lee, H. Takakura, and Y. Kambayashi, "Acquisition of Landmark Knowledge from Spatial Description", in Proceedings of 2002 IRC International Conference on Internet Information Retrieval, pp. 214-221, Koyang, Korea, 2002
21. T. Tezuka, R. Lee, H. Takakura and Y. Kambayashi, "Cognitive Characterization of Geographic Objects Based on Spatial Descriptions in Web Resources," in Proceedings of the Workshop on Spatial Data and Geographic Information Systems (SpaDaGIS), Milano, Italy, 2003

Query Based Chinese Phrase Extraction for Site Search

Jingfang Xu, Shaozhi Ye, and Xing Li

Department of Electronic Engineering, Tsinghua University
Beijing 100084, P.R.China
xjf02@mails.tsinghua.edu.cn, ys@compass.net.edu.cn, xing@cernet.edu.cn

Abstract. Word segmentation(WS) is one of the major issues of information processing in character-based languages, for there are no explicit word boundaries in these languages. Moreover, a combination of multiple continuous words, a phrase, is usually a minimum meaningful unit. Although much work has been done on WS, in site web search, little has been explored to mine site-specific knowledge from user query log for both more accurate WS and better retrieval performance. This paper proposes a novel, statistics-based method to extract phrases based on user query log. The extracted phrases, combined with a general, static dictionary, construct a dynamic, site-specific dictionary. According to the dictionary, web documents are segmented into phrases and words, which are kept as separate index terms to build phrase enhanced index for site search. The experiment result shows that our approach greatly improves the retrieval performance. It also helps to detect many out-of-vocabulary words, such as site-specific phrases, newly created words and names of people and locations, which are difficult to process with a general, static dictionary.

1 Introduction

Information retrieval(IR) systems select relevant documents by matching index terms with the query. The selection of index terms affects both precision and efficiency of retrieval systems. An ideal indexing term should be a meaningful unit, expressing the concept documents contain and the information user need[1]. Words, the minimum meaningful units, are selected as index terms in most IR systems. Phrases, comprising several continuous words, are usually also inseparable combinations, i.e., they might be misunderstood when broken into words. Therefore, phrases should also be kept as index terms. In the retrieval of alphabet-based languages, such as English and French, it has been proved that choosing both words and phrases as indexing terms is more efficient than indexing words only[2]. Unlike words, phrases have no explicit separator, thus phrase extraction turns out to be a challenge. It becomes more complex when processing character-based languages, such as Chinese, which have neither word boundary nor phrase separator. To deal with these languages, word segmentation has to be done before phrase extraction.

X. Zhou et al. (Eds.): WISE 2004, LNCS 3306, pp. 125–134, 2004.
© Springer-Verlag Berlin Heidelberg 2004

The basic approaches of word segmentation in character-based languages can be partitioned into two categories: statistic-based and dictionary-based[3]. Statistic-based approaches make use of statistical properties, such as frequencies of characters and character sequences in the corpus[4]. Mutual information(MI) is usually employed by these approaches[4][5]. Dictionary-based approaches use a dictionary to identify words. When matched with a word in the dictionary, a sequence of characters will be extracted as a word. For match approaches, there are maximum match, minimum match and hybrid approach. The maximum match approach can be further divided into forward maximum match approach and backward maximum match approach. Ideally, the dictionary-based approach can detect all the words if the dictionary is complete. In practice, however, a static dictionary that contains all possible words is unfeasible, costly and unnecessary[6]. A corpus usually contains only part of words in the dictionary, and on the other hand, a static dictionary is lack of many out-of-vocabulary words, e.g., site-specific words, newly created words and names of people and locations. A dynamic, topic-specific dictionary of a corpus will alleviate the problem by eliminating irrelevant words and providing special words.

Phrase extraction is similar to word segmentation. There is already some work on the statistics-based phrase extraction[7][8]. Previous statistics-based phrase extraction approaches consider all possible phrases in the corpus as potential phrase candidates and calculate the statistical information of all these phrases, which is costly and time consuming. Moreover, the extracted phrases are often non-meaningful or never concerned by users. In this paper we propose a method applying MI to phrase extraction based on user query log. We obtain the phrase candidates only from user queries and calculate their MI scores in both document space and query space. The experiment result shows the efficiency of our method and the extracted phrases are really needed by users.

To evaluate our phrase extraction algorithm, we build a phrase enhanced index, which is supposed to improve both precision and efficiency of retrieval. Phrase index terms provide more accurate information, thus help to select more relevant results. On the other hand, indexing phrases accelerate phrase search. When searching a phrase, e.g., "AB", if "AB" is not an index term, all the documents that contain both A and B have to be chosen to check whether "A" is followed by "B". It will be much faster if the phrase "AB" is an index term.

In this paper, we choose a Chinese web site search engine for our experiment platform and use 69,680 web documents and 508,464 query requests as training set. First, with a static, general dictionary, we segment the training set into words and extract phrases based on MI. Then we combine these phrases with a general dictionary to construct a dynamic, site-specific dictionary. This dictionary is used to parse all web documents into words and phrases and finally build a phrase enhanced index. The experiment result shows that when queries of testing set match the general word only index, the average number of index terms per query hits is 2.61 and with our enhanced index, it can be reduced to 1.93. Although the results presented in this paper are all based on Chinese documents, our method can be easily adopted in other character-based languages with just a little modification of character encoding.

The rest of this paper is organized as follows. First we propose our phrase extraction method in Section 2 and analyze the experiment dataset in Section 3. Then experiment results and evaluation are presented in Section 4. Finally we review the previous work in Section 5 and conclude this paper with Section 6.

2 Mutual Information and Phrase Extraction

Mutual information(MI) can be used to measure the coherence of the adjacent characters and is applied widely in statistic-based WS, where the adjacent characters with high MI score are identified as a word. In our approach, similarly, we identify the adjacent words as a phrase if its MI score is higher than a predefined threshold.

Consider a string of words "$...c_0c_1c_2c_3...$", the MI of words c_1 and c_2 is computed by Equation 1:

$$MI(c_1c_2) = \log_2 \frac{p(c_1c_2)}{p(c_1)p(c_2)} \tag{1}$$

Where $p(c_1c_2)$ is the occurrence probability of the words sequence "c_1c_2", which is estimated by the times that c_1 is followed by c_2, normalized by N, the total number of words in the corpus. $p(c)$ is the probability of word c, which is estimated by the total occurrences of the word c normalized by N. Therefore, Equation 1 is represented as Equation 2:

$$MI(c_1c_2) = \log_2 \left(\frac{\frac{freq(c_1c_2)}{N}}{\frac{freq(c_1)}{N}\frac{freq(c_2)}{N}} \right) = \log_2 \left(N \frac{freq(c_1c_2)}{freq(c_1)freq(c_2)} \right) \tag{2}$$

The previous phrase extraction methods select all the potential phrases in documents, while we only consider the potential candidates which have appeared in the user query log. More precisely, three methods to calculate MI are compared in this paper.

2.1 MI in Query Space

The query space is constructed by all the user queries. In query space we tend to extract the phrases which interest users while their separated constituent words do not. Here N in Equation 2 is the total number of words in query log, and the $freq(c)$ is estimated by the times of word c appears in the log.

2.2 MI in Document Space

The document space is constructed by all the web documents. In this space, we consider the occurrences of phrase candidates in web documents. For all the candidates, we compute their MI scores in the document space. Here N is the total number of words in web documents and the $freq(c)$ is estimated by the times of word c appears in the web documents.

2.3 MI in Hybrid Space

Method 1 extracts the phrases that usually queried by users and method 2 extracts the phrases that frequently appear in the documents. This method integrates them, i.e., extracts the phrases that occur frequently in both user queries and web documents. We first compute MI scores of the candidates in query space, and discard the phrases whose MI scores are lower than a threshold. Then, we compute MI scores of the phrases extracted from query space in document space to select the high MI score phrases.

Combined with the general dictionary, the extracted phrases construct a site-specific dictionary. As we track the dynamic query log, the site-specific dictionary with extracted phrases is also dynamic.

3 Dataset Analysis

We choose a Chinese web site, the homepage of *China Education and Research Network(CERNET)*[1], and its site search engine as our experiment platform. Table 1 summarizes the web documents of this site and training query log from its site search engine. Forward maximum match method is used to segment 69,680 web documents and 508,464 Chinese requests into words, according to a general dictionary from *On-Line Chinese Tools*[2] which contains 119,804 unique Chinese words.

Table 1. Summary of Web Documents and Query Log

Web Documents	69,890
Words in Documents	40,889,563
Unique Words in Documents	82,186
Log Days	Aug. 13, 2003 - Jan. 31, 2004
Total Queries	627,920
Chinese Queries	508,464
Unique Queries	82,078
Words in Queries	1,335,151
Unique words in Queries	13,808

The analysis of the training set shows that:

1. Neither web documents nor queries contain all the words in the general dictionary. Web documents contain 69% and the query log contains only 9%, which means that many words in the general dictionary never appear in web documents or queries.

[1] http://www.edu.cn

[2] http://www.mandarintools.com/

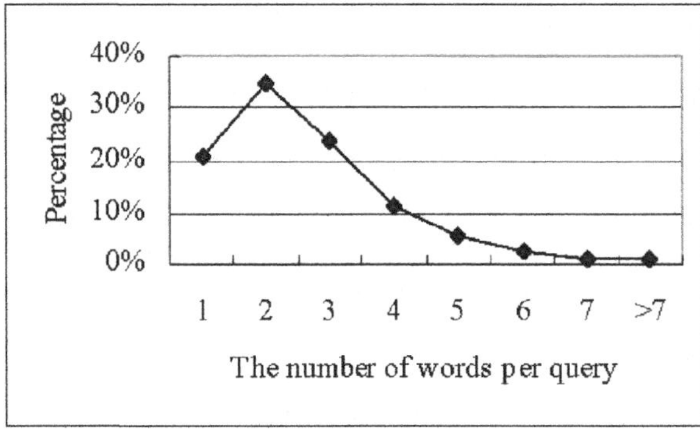

Fig. 1. Words Per Query in the Log

2. Most queries contain more than one word. As shown in Figure 1, only 20.93% queries contain just one word and 34.67% queries are made up of two words. Searching multiple words is more complex and time consuming than searching a single word[9]. So indexing phrases will greatly improve retrieval performance. Moreover, many query phrases are site-specific or newly created, which can not be dealt with a general, static dictionary. These phrases may be related to many other documents when broken into words, which hurts both precision and efficiency. Thus these specific query phrases should be extracted and indexed directly. In this paper, the notion phrase enhanced index is used for indexing both words and phrases, comparing with the original index which indexes only words.
3. The distribution of words in web documents differs from that in query log. Removed stop words, the top 10 most frequent words in the web documents are totally different with the top 10 most frequently queried ones, as shown in Figure 2. There are two possible reasons. First, many words in the web document are not interested by users. Second, web documents and queries may use different words to describe the same thing. The words in web documents are usually written and official, while those in user query are mostly spoken and informal. Moreover, users may also use different queries to search just the same information. For an IR system, it may be not interested in what the documents contain, but it may concern what the user want to search. Those extracted phrases, never searched by user, are useless to the system and should not be indexed as an index term. So it is unnecessary to extract phrases through full document.

4 Experiment Results and Evaluation

First of all, all the web documents and Chinese queries are segmented into words according to the general dictionary. 400,477 queries which occur in the log and

Most Frequent Words in Document Space	Most Frequent Words in Query Space
教育(Education)	公务员(Official)
中国 (China)	成人高考 (Adult College Entrance Exam)
稿件 (Contribution)	专升本 (Upgrade from Junior College Student to University Student)
转帖(Outside Post)	成绩查询(Grade Enquiry)
科研(Research)	论文(Paper)
大学(University)	公务员考试(Offical Examination)
评论(Comments)	成绩(Grade)
问题(Question)	简历(Resume)
注明 (Indicate)	计算机等级考试 (Computer Rank Exam)
学生(Student)	答案(Answer)

Fig. 2. Most Frequent Words in Documents and Queries

contain more than one word are selected as phrase candidates. Their MI scores in three spaces are computed separately. In hybrid space, we first eliminate the phrases whose MI scores in query space are lower than 13[3], and then compute MI scores of the rest candidates in document space. Figure 3 lists top 15 phrases with highest MI scores in each space. In each space we extract the top 8,000 MI score phrases and combine them with the same general dictionary to construct a dynamic dictionary for the corresponding space.

To evaluate three phrase extraction methods, phrase enhanced indices are built which index both words and phrases in the corresponding dictionaries. The general dictionary and three dynamic dictionaries are used to segment web documents and queries individually. Then we build a general word only index and three phrase enhanced indices. The notions query index, document index and hybrid index are used for phrase enhanced indices built with the query space, document space and hybrid space dictionaries respectively.

Table 2. Summary of Test Queries

Log Days	Feb.1 - Feb.29,2004
Total Queries	75,499
Chinese Queries	60,235
Unique Queries	24,083

[3] We check the phrases with high MI scores manually and select this threshold.

Query Space	Document Space	Hybrid Space
课件(Courseware)	新婚姻(New Marriage)	新婚姻(New Marriage)
雅思 (International English Language Test)	民族团结 (National Unity)	民族团结 (National Unity)
三个代表 (Three Representatives)	中国青年政治学院 (China Youth University for Political Sciences)	通货紧缩 (Deflation)
八级 (Eighth-band Test for English Majors)	通货紧缩 (Deflation)	实话实说 (Tell the Truth)
申论(State)	实话实说(Tell the Truth)	中国青年政治学院 (China Youth University for Political Sciences)
亿唐 (Etang Name of a Website)	新世纪 (New Century)	珠江三角洲 (Delta of Zhujiang River)
说课(Teaching)	未就业(Not Employed)	新世纪(New Century)
六级(College English Test 6)	乙型肝炎(Hepatitis B)	未就业(Not Employed)
自我鉴定 (Appraise Oneself)	完形填空 (Cloze)	给水排水 (Supply Water and Drain off Water)
英语学习(English Study)	近世代数(Modern Algebra)	乙型肝炎(Hepatitis B)
特长生(Students Having Specialty)	神州数码(Digital China)	完形填空(Cloze)
北外(Beijing Foreign Studies University)	线性代数(Linear Algebra)	近世代数(Modern Algebra)
课讯(course information)	期末考试(Final Exam)	化学方程式(Chemical Equation)
非典(SARS)	居里夫人(Mrs. Curie)	神州数码(Digital China)
查分 (Grade Enquiry)	同等学力 (Same Educational Level)	敦煌莫高窟 (Mogao Grottoes of Dunhuang)

Fig. 3. Top 15 MI Score Phrases in Each Space

The user queries of CERNET from Feb. 1, 2004 to Feb. 29, 2004 are used as our testing data. Table 2 summarizes the testing queries. These testing queries are matched by four indices, general index, query index, document index and hybrid index. The hit ratios are shown in Table 3 and Figure 4.

When retrieval, if queries hit fewer index terms, there will be fewer index operations. For example, if the query is segmented into just one index term, we can directly return the record of this index term. While if the query is segmented into three index terms, the records of these three index terms have to be retrieved and compared to generate the final results for user. Multi-index term accesses will be prohibitively expensive especially when the index is large, thus reducing index term accesses is vital to alleviate the overhead of retrieval. Table 3 shows that all the three phrase enhanced indices outperform the original word only index in one index term hit ratio, which means a direct hit and no operation for multi index terms comparison. The hybrid index gets a 22.93% higher direct hit ratio than the general index. The average number of index terms per query is 2.61 with the general index and it is reduced to 1.93 with the hybrid index.

Table 3. Query Hit Ratios of Different Indices

Index Terms Per Query	General Index	Query Index	Document Index	Hybrid Index
1(direct hit)	20.93%	32.26%	43.55%	45.86%
2	34.67%	34.57%	30.46%	30.91%
3	23.49%	19.24%	15.74%	13.91%
4	11.10%	8.16%	6.07%	5.64%
5	5.48%	3.21%	2.34%	2.58%
6	2.35%	1.39%	0.96%	0.08%
7	1.03%	0.55%	0.41%	0.46%
>7	0.95%	0.68%	0.46%	0.56%
Average	2.61	2.25	2.00	1.93

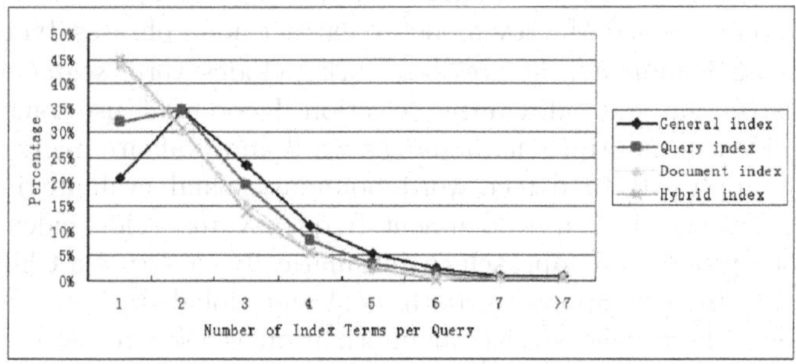

Fig. 4. Index Terms Hit by Queries to Different Indices

The results show that our phrase enhanced indices can serve queries with fewer index operations, which greatly improves the retrieval performance.

Among the three phrase enhanced indices, the query index improves least, which may be caused by the dynamic and informality of user queries. Some queries occur rarely in the web documents, and there are also some typos and abbreviations. The hybrid index is lightly better than the document index for it makes use of the knowledge of user queries.

Our approach can also detect many site-specific phrases, newly created words, and names of people and locations. Some examples are shown in Figure 5. These out-of-vocabulary words and phrases are difficult to deal with a general, static dictionary. With the user query log, our method can find the newly rising phrases. Also the phrases from queries will be removed from the dictionary when they are out of popularity, say, after one or two months, if these phrases are never or seldom queried, they are removed from the dictionary. Thus our method can keep track of phrases popularity to make the dictionary fresh and small.

非典(SARS)
三个代表(Three Representatives)
中国青年政治学院(China Youth University for Political Sciences)
专升本(Upgrade from Junior College Student to University Student)

Fig. 5. Some Special Phrases Detected by Our Approach

5 Related Work

Much work has been done on statistics-based English phrase extraction. Shimohata et al. extract phrases from plain text according to the co-occurrence frequency of words[7]; with maximum entropy, Feng and Croft use Viterbi algorithm based on a trained Markov model to extract noun phrases dynamically[8].

For Chinese documents, the previous work includes words segmentation, dictionary construction and index terms selection. Khoo et.al. use some statistical formulas to identify multiple characters as word and evaluate many factors[10]; Yang et al. apply MI to detect word boundaries and evaluate its effect to indexing[5]. Takeda et.al. use document frequency to decide index strings[1]. Jin and Wong propose an approach to automatically construct a Chinese dictionary for IR[2]. In their approach, both local and global statistical information is considered, where local statistical information is used to select candidates and global statistical information is used to extract words based on occurrence frequency. Although this approach uses local statistical information for lower computation cost and higher accuracy, it still computes statistical information through full text just like others.

In all, there are two limitations in these previous approaches, high cost of computation and some non-meaningful extracted phrases. Different with these priori methods, our method makes use of the knowledge of user query log to select phrase candidates, which improves both precision and efficiency of retrieval.

6 Conclusion

In this paper we propose a method to extract Chinese phrases by computing MI in both user queries and web documents, which does not extract phrases through full document. It is simple to implement and the experiment results have shown its improvement on both precision and efficiency in retrieval.

Word segmentation and phrase extraction are important to character-based language IR. Using the phrases in the query log as candidates can reduce the cost of calculation and improve retrieval performance. We use these extracted phrases to construct dynamic dictionaries and build phrase enhanced indices to evaluate three MI selection methods. The result shows that the hybrid space method does the best. And our dynamic dictionaries can also alleviate the out-of-vocabulary problem which is difficult to deal in dictionary-based natural language processing.

Although only Chinese documents are used in our experiments, we believe our approach can be easily implemented in other character-based language IR systems. We also intend to apply our approach to alphabet-based languages, such as English.

Acknowledgement. The authors are grateful to Shuguang Zhang of CERNET to provide the user query log. The authors would also like to thank the anonymous reviewers for their helpful comments in improving the paper.

References

1. Takeda, Y., Umemura, K., Yamamoto, E.: Determining indexing strings with statistical analysis. IEICE Transactions on Information and Systems **E86-D** (2003) 1781–1787
2. Jin, H., Wong, K.: A chinese dictionary construction algorithm for information retrieval. ACM Transactions on Asian Language Information Processing **1** (2002) 281–296
3. Nie, J., Brisebois, M., Ren, X.: On chinese text retrieval. In: Proceedings of the 19th Annual International ACM SIGIR Conference on Research and Development in Information Retrieval, ACM Press (1996) 225–233
4. Lua, K., Gan, G.: An application of information theory in chinese word segmentation. Computer Processing of Chinese and Oriental Languages **40** (1994) 115–124
5. Yang, C.C., Luk, J.W., Yung, S.K., Yen, J.: Combination and boundary detection approaches on chinese indexing. Journal of the American Society for Information Science and Technology(JASIST) **51** (2000) 340–351
6. S.Foo, H.Li: Chinese word segmentation and its effects on information retrieval. Information Processing and Management **40** (2004) 161–190
7. Shimohata, S., Sugio, T.: Retrieving collocations by co-occurrences and word order constraints. In: Proceedings of the eighth Conference on European Chapter of the Association for Computational Linguistics. (1997) 476–481
8. Feng, F., Croft, W.: Probabilistic techniques for phrase extraction. Information Processing and Management **37** (2001) 199–200
9. Zhou, M., Tompa, F.: The suffix-signature method for searching phrase in text. Information System **23** (1997) 567–588
10. Khoo, C.S.G., Dai, Y., Loh, T.E.: Using statistical and contextual information to identify two- and three-character words in chinese text. Journal of the American Society for Information Science and Technology(JASIST) **53** (2002) 365–377

Extracting Business Rules from Web Product Descriptions

Mizuho Iwaihara[1], Takayuki Shiga[1], and Masayuki Kozawa[2]

[1] Department of Social Informatics, Graduate School of Informatics, Kyoto University, Kyoto 606-8501, JAPAN
[2] Toppan Co. Ltd., Osaka 553-8580, JAPAN
iwaihara@i.kyoto-u.ac.jp, {tshiga,kozawa}@db.soc.i.kyoto-u.ac.jp

Abstract. Products sold in e-commerce sites are usually attached with conditions, policies and provisions, which are sometimes important criteria for buyers to compare products. Although logical languages dealing with business rules have been proposed, most of business rules on the Web are still given in natural language texts only. In this paper, we discuss technologies for locating those rules in product descriptions, categorizing them, and translating them into a formal constraint language. We take airline tickets as an example, and discuss what processes in this translation can be automated. By translating into the constraint language, we can search, compare and verify complex conditions.

1 Introduction

A variety of goods sold in e-commerce sites are usually attached with descriptions which define various types of conditions, terms, and policies. They provide important information for buyers to choose appropriate goods and their options. We use the generic term *business rule* for such conditions, rules, and policies. In business-to-consumer (B2C) markets, business rules frequently appear in configurable goods, such as PCs and travel plans, where buyers pick up components and configure a product of their own needs. Here, business rules describe possible combinations of components, and pricing of components. There are also rules for discounts, cancellation policies/penalties, qualification for discounts, and so on.

In the e-commerce sector, various EDI-fashioned industrial standards for XML schemas are proposed or recommended, such as TravelXML[16] by Japanese Travel Bureau Association and OTA Specification by Open Travel Alliance[13], for the travel industry. However, in those standards, business rules are required to be written in a natural language. Natural language descriptions of business rules hinder computer processing of those rules. Thus understanding and checking business rules should be done by human.

It is quite popular in e-commerce sites to provide programs for checking business rules. For example, PC vending sites check whether configurations entered by users satisfy combination constraints, and airline ticket sites check basic constraints such as seat availability and pricing rules. The problem of rule checking by embedded programs is that (1) rules handled by programs are limited to simple ones; comprehension of

X. Zhou et al. (Eds.): WISE 2004, LNCS 3306, pp. 135–146, 2004.
© Springer-Verlag Berlin Heidelberg 2004

complex rules are left for humans, (2) programs are hard-coded, so that business rules can be checked only by a predefined manner; flexible reasoning, comparison, or verification of business rules are not provided, and (3) since the programs define semantics of those business rules but those programs are not open, exchange of those rules between e-commerce sites for flexible product search is not possible.

One approach for realizing advanced processing of business rules is to establish a formal model for business rules, which has a clear logical semantics and provides reasoning capabilities, at the same time offering user-friendly natural language descriptions of rules. Such rules can be easily exchanged and shared for advanced business rule processing, such as cooperation between e-commerce sites, and computer assistance in searching and comparing business rules, and agent-based negotiations[5]. Our previous work[7] showed a classification of business rules, and formal modeling and querying by dynamic constraint algebra[11].

Capturing and handling logic in web information is considered to be important in the framework of semantic web[2]. DAML+OIL and its successor OWL[14] are description-logic based languages for web ontologies. Rules belong to the fourth layer in the seven-layered model of semantic web[2], and RuleML[3][4] is one of approaches for providing rule descriptions for semantic web. Unifying logic programs and description logic is discussed in [8]. BRML[5] and IBM Common Rules are also targeted for processing business rules. Trastour et al.[15] discussed processing business rules by utilizing DAML+OIL. However, these approaches assume business rules are written in their formal languages.

In this paper, we discuss extracting business rules from product descriptions on the web. Providing a tool for authoring business rules in a logical language is one direction. Extracting rules for shipping costs from an online bookstore web site and translating them into XRML is discussed in [6]. However, their approach requires costly manual processes for marking up natural language texts.

Overall, the most desired technology is automatic conversion of informal product descriptions into formal ones. If that is difficult, then at least we should provide semi-automatic conversion with user directives. The conversion can be divided into the following steps:

1. Capture the structure of product descriptions in web pages. Here, product descriptions can be semi-structured data such as HTML or XML. Find attributes and their values in the data.
2. Capture business rules from the above attribute-value pairs. Here, business rules in the descriptions might be structured using HTML or XML tags, or written in a natural language.
3. Translate the captured business rules into formal descriptions.

As for (1), extracting attribute-value pairs from program-generated web pages is proposed in [1], and this technology can be utilized for our purpose. As for (2), capturing business rules from structured/unstructured product descriptions will be our main challenge. Machine translation of natural language descriptions is inevitable. However, business rules mentioned in product descriptions are rather simplified and specialized form of sentences, where pricing rules, policies and others have some fixed patterns. We also note that business rules are supposed to be written in unambiguous expressions.

Therefore we can just focus on specialized classes of natural language sentences, where similar patterns are frequently used. In this circumstance, we can find a practical translation algorithm. As for (3) above, we provide a mapping from captured business rules in an intermediate format into logical expressions on equality logic.

In this paper, we take up the case of airline tickets and show a series of methods for extracting business rules from web product descriptions. Airline tickets contain a wide variety of business rules, such as combination rules, discount rules, and cancellation policies. In addition to such typical business rules of airline tickets, we consider tickets sold by discount ticket retailers who resell tickets with their own added policies, giving a more challenging target than tickets sold directly by airline companies.

Business rules in web pages are often expressed in succinct and semi-fixed forms, so that translation from natural language sentences is possible. However, resolving irregularities and diversities of sentences is an important issue. We show extracting token sequences while removing synonyms, and then clustering rule sentences having the same token sequence patterns. Then we show two ways of transformation, called semantic transformation and generic transformation. Semantic transformation converts rule sentences through full interpretation by predefined templates. On the other hand, generic transformation shallowly checks occurrences of token sequences, but still can safely translate into logical expressions, without predefined templates. We show experimental results in which real business rules of airline tickets are successfully converted into logical expressions.

The rest of the paper is organized as follows: In Section 2, we explain the problem of extracting business rules. In Section 3, we describe separating business rule sentences from web pages. In Section 4, we describe our method of transforming business rules into logical expressions, and in Section 5, we show evaluation results. Section 6 concludes this paper.

2 Business Rules in Web Product Descriptions

2.1 Business Rule Model

In this section, we describe a model for business rules. A *product description* consists of a set of *clauses*. A clause has a name and a set of *business rules*. A business rule is a constraint stating relationships between *attributes* and *values*. A business rule can be in either a natural language or a formal language. We call a business rule in a natural language a *rule sentence*. A product description is a logical conjunction of clauses.

As for a formal language for business rules, we employ *equivalence constraints*. An equality is of the form $x =$ "USD 120" or $x = y$, where x and y are variables from a set $\mathcal{V}$ of variable names, and "USD 120" is a constant from a constant domain $\mathcal{C}$. We assume that each variable x has a type $type(x)$ such that the domain of x is restricted to $type(x) \subseteq \mathcal{C}$. A *logical expression* is equalities combined by Boolean operations $\wedge$ (AND), $\vee$ (OR), $\neg$ (NOT), $\rightarrow$ (IMPLICATION). The class of equivalence constraints can represent Boolean combinations of possible constants, which are frequent in selling and buying conditions.

The above logical expressions are quantifier-free formulae over equalities. For a

Table 1. Sample of airline ticket descriptions (translated from Japanese descriptions)

Clause	Business rules
Destination cities	Atlanta, Boston, Buffalo, Seattle, Salt Lake City, Vancouver, Toronto
Max. number of destinations	Maximum of three destinations from cities listed above
Valid term	three days to one month (no reservation change for return trip)
Additional fares	Weekend rates: JPY4,000 up for departure from destinations on Fri, Sat, Sun.
Maximum stop-overs	Free up to two stop-overs. Maximum three stop-overs, costing JPY10,000.

formalism for querying or inferencing over such logical expressions, we can translate them into formulae of semantic web languages, such as description logic based OWL[14] and rule-based RuleML[3][4]. On the other hand, the logical expressions can be also well handled by the framework of *constraint databases*[12], where ordinary tuples of the classical relation database model are replaced by *constraint tuples*, which are quantifier-free formulae. Constraints can have infinite solutions. For example, constraint tuple $(x \neq \text{"c"}) \wedge (x \neq \text{"d"})$ is allowed. A query calculus for a constraint database introduces first-order quantifications over constraint tuples, and query processing is essentially equivalent to quantifier elimination. An answer for a query over a constraint database is again quantifier-free constraints. Business rules could have many variables and it is hard to anticipate all the variables in rule processing. In that case, the *dynamic constraint database model*[10][11] is suitable, since it does not require predefined schemas. In the rest of the paper, we do not stick to any specific rule processing paradigms, but we focus on extracting formal business rules. Translating extracted business rules into the above mentioned frameworks is not a hard task.

2.2 Airline Tickets

In this section, we describe benchmark data of product descriptions. We have extracted airline ticket descriptions in HTML files from http://www.arukikata.com/, which contains pricelists, discount rules, additional costs, cancellation penalties, rules on combination of destinations, remarks, etc, written in Japanese. Tickets in this site are resold by a travel company, which added a number of their own discounts and restrictions to wholesaled tickets. A sample of airline ticket descriptions is shown in Table 1. We have collected about 2,000 ticket data that correspond to a catalog for a quarter of the year. Although the original descriptions are in Japanese, the process of extracting business rules described in this paper is language independent, and solutions can be applied to other languages.

3 Separating Business Rules

In this section, we discuss a series of techniques for extracting business rules from product descriptions.

3.1 Clause Separation

The product descriptions are in the form of HTML pages, where formatted texts, tables, and tags are used. There are upto seventeen clauses per one ticket. Each clause contains text descriptions and/or cells of an HTML table, where a number of attributes and values are mentioned in a sentence, constituting a business rule.

Separating clauses from one product description in HTML is carried out by ad hoc scripts, and those separated clauses are stored in a relational database. Extracting schema information from document instances has been discussed in the literature[1], and these technologies can be utilized. However, our focus is rather on the steps after this clause separation.

There are 18,482 clauses in the 2,000 product descriptions. Duplications caused by literally identical clauses are removed by string comparison, and the total number of distinct clauses is 3,766. This number is too large for manual extraction, and thus a sophisticated extraction method is required.

3.2 Similarity and Irregularity of Business Rules

Table 2 shows business rules of the benchmark data regarding weekend surcharge costs. As we can see, quite similar, but slightly different rules exist in the table.

- The symbols "*" and "·" are used as line heads. Such symbols are chosen by human authors, or coming from different sources, and like HTML pages, they are not following a fixed format.
- Rules 4,6,10,12,13,14,23,24,26,27,29,30,41,45,50 and 57 have the identical meaning that "if return trip is starting on Friday or Saturday, then weekend surcharge of 5,000 yen is applied." But their expressions are slightly different.
- The difference of Rule 19 and Rule 20 is just the price of surcharge.
- The number of days of the week on which surcharge is applied varies from one to three.
- Rules 11, 17, 18, and 32 present two combinations of days of the week, having a different structure from others.

As we can find in Table 2, irregularities of expressions are common. For example, the same word such as "Saturday" is expressed as "Sat" or "Sa". We found that those business rules are written by a number of people, and each individual uses slightly different expressions. More irregularities could happen if we collect product descriptions from multiple sources.

4 Transforming Business Rules into Logical Expressions

4.1 Functional Dictionary

We resolve irregularities in terminology mentioned above by providing a *functional dictionary*. The dictionary should contain registered words and their *word types*, or simply *types*, define the category or domain name of each registered word. For example, City

Table 2. Rules sentences containing irregularities (original is in Japanese)

1	*Weekend: JPY3,000UP for return trip departing on Fri or Sat.
2	*Weekend: JPY5,000UP for return trip arriving in Japan on Sun.
3	*Weekend: JPY3,000UP for return trip arriving in Japan on Sun.
4	*Weekend: JPY5,000UP for return trip departing on Friday or Satday.
5	*Weekend: JPY5,000UP for return trip departing on Sat.
6	*Weekend: JPY5,000UP, for return trip departing on Fri or Sat.
7	*Weekend: JPY3,000UP, for return trip departing on Fri, or Sat.
8	*Weekend: JPY4,000UP, if return trip is departing on Fri, Sat or Sun.
9	*Weekend: JPY3,000UP for return trip departing on Fri or Sat.
10	*Weekend: JPY5,000UP for return trip departing on Fri, or Sat.
11	*Weekend: Return trip JPY5,000UP departing on Friday , JPY8,000UP on Saturday.
12	*Weekend: JPY5,000UP for return trip departing on Fri or Sat.
13	*Weekend: Return trip JPY5,000UP, departing on Fri or Sat.
14	*Weekend: Return trip JPY3,000UP, departing on Fri or Sat
15	*Weekend: Return trip JPY3,000UP, departing on Fri or Sat.
16	*Weekend: Return trip JPY5,000UP, departing on Fri or Sat.
17	*Weekend: Return trip, JPY5,000UP if departing on Friday, JPY8,000UP if departing on Satday.
18	*Weekend: Return trip, JPY5,000 if departing on Friday, JPY15,000UP if departing on Satday.
19	*Weekend: Return trip, JPY3,000 if departing on Satday.
20	*Weekend: Return trip, JPY5,000 if departing on Satday.
21	*Weekend: Return trip, JPY2,000UP, departing on Fri or Sat.
22	*Weekend: Return trip, JPY3,000UP, departing on Fri or Sat.
23	*Weekend: Return trip, JPY5,000UP departing on Fri or Sat
24	*Weekend: Return trip, JPY5,000UP departing on Fri or Sat.
25	*Weekend: Return trip, JPY8,000UP departing on Fri or Sat.
26	*Weekend: Return trip, JPY5,000UP, departing on Fri or Sat
27	*Weekend: Return trip, JPY5,000UP, departing on Friday or Saturday.
28	*Weekend: Return trip, JPY3,000UP departing on Sunday.
29	*Weekend: Return trip, JPY5,000UP depart on Fri or Sat
30	*Weekend: Return trip, JPY5,000UP, depart on Friday or Saturday.
31	*Weekend: Return trip, depart on Friday JPY5,000UP, Saturday JPY8,000UP.
32	*Weekend: Return trip, arriving in Japan on Sat or Sun JPY3,000UP.
33	*Weekend: Return trip, arriving in Japan on Sat or Sun is JPY3,000UP.
34	*Weekend: Return trip, arriving in Japan on Sun, JPY3,000UP.
35	*Weekend: Return trip, arriving in Japan on Sun is JPY2,000UP.
36	*Weekend: Return trip, arriving in Japan on Sun JPY3,000UP.
37	*Weekend: Return trip, arriving in Japan on Sun, JPY2,000UP.
38	*Weekend: Return trip, arriving in Japan on Sun, JPY3,000UP.
39	*Weekend: Return trip, arriving in Japan on Sun is JPY3,000UP.
40	*Weekend: Return trip, arriving in Japan on Sun is JPY5,000UP.
41	*Weekend: Return trip depart on Fr Sa JPY5,000UP.
42	*Weekend: Return trip depart on Fri or Saturday, JPY3,000UP.
43	*Weekend: Return trip departing on Saturday, JPY3,000UP.
44	*Weekend: Return trip departing on Saturday, JPY5,000UP.
45	*Weekend: Return trip departing on Friday or Saturday, JPY5,000UP.
46	· Weekend: Return trip departing on Fri, or Sat, JPY3,000UP
48	· Weekend: Return trip departing on Fri or Sat JPY3,000UP
49	· Weekend: Return trip departing on Fri, Sat, Sun, JPY4,000UP
50	· Weekend: Return trip departing on Friday Saturday, JPY5,000UP
51	· Weekend: Return trip departing on Saturday, SundayJPY3,000UP
52	· Weekend: Return trip departing on Saturday, JPY2,000UP
53	· Weekend: Return trip departing on Sunday: JPY3,000UP
54	· Weekend: Return trip departing on Sunday is JPY3,000UP
55	· Weekend: Return trip departing on Sunday is, JPY2,000UP
56	· Weekend: Return trip departing on Sunday is, JPY3,000UP
57	· Weekend: Return trip departing destination on Fri or Sat, JPY5,000UP
58	· Weekend: Return trip departing destination on Sat, JPY3,000UP
59	Weekend: Departing destination on Fri or Sat, JPY3,000UP
60	Weekend: Departing destination on Fri or Sat: JPY3,000UP

Name, DayOfWeek, and Price are word types. By looking up the functional dictionary, we can find the word type of a given word. Also, since product rule sentences contain irregularities, we register a *standard form* for each word. For example, Table 2 contains "Satday," "Sat," and "Saturday,"and all of them are synonyms of "Saturday." Therefore we register one of them, and here we choose "Saturday," as the standard form.

4.2 Flow of Extracting Logical Rules

1. **(token extraction)** For each product rule, replace registered words into their standard forms using the functional dictionary. By this token extraction, irregularities of words are resolved.
2. **(token repetition folding)** In rule sentences, words of the same type are often listed with punctation. In the case of airline tickets, possible days of the week or possible destination cities are listed in this way. In a more complex case, pairs of days of the week and price are listed. In token repetition folding, such a listing is recognized and marked as a *token sequence*, and word types and the number of elements are also recorded.
3. **(rule clustering)** After token repetition folding, some rule sentences become identical if we ignore the differences of actual words in each toke sequence and compare them just by word types. Such rule clauses are grouped into one by rule clustering.
4. **(rule transformation)** For each rule sentence, a rule transformation template which matches with the folded token sequence of the rule clause is searched, and the sentence is converted into a logical expression as specified in the template. We propose the following two types of rule transformation:
   a) **(semantic transformation)** In this transformation, a rule transformation template which matches with the natural language part of the rule is selected, and the rule is transformed into an accurate logical expression. We assume that such templates are provided by a programmer.
   b) **(generic transformation)** In this transformation, each rule is transformed into a logical expression without using the meaning of the entire rule sentence. However, the meaning of folded token sequences is recognized, and mapped into a logical expression by a conservative method.

The semantic transformation can produce accurate logical expressions, assuming that each template is correctly constructed. On the hand, if the number of rule clusters is large, providing all the necessary templates is costly. In this case, we adopt fully automated generic transformation to produce (shallowly interpreted) logical expressions. The generic transformation does not capture the entire logical structure of rule sentences, but extracted partial knowledge on rule sentences can be utilized for rule processing.

4.3 Token Extraction from Rule Sentences

In token extraction, notations containing irregularities are converted into their standard forms. Table 3 shows the result of token extraction applied to Rules 3,4,17 and 41 in Table 2. In the result, type names have prefix "#", standard forms are underlined, and the original expressions are doubly quoted. Rules having an identical meaning, such as Rules 4 and 41, (and also Rules 6,10,12,13,14,23,24,26,27,29,30,45,50, 57) have the same word types and standard forms, and they can be detected. Thus irregularities are absorbed.

Table 3. Rule sentences after token extraction

	(#type, standard form,"expression in rules")
3	(#weekend_surcharge, Weekend Surcharge, "Weekend Surcharge") (#return_trip_arriving_in_Japan, return trip arriving in Japan, "for return trip arriving in Japan") (#DayOfWeek, Sunday, "Sunday") (#Price, JPY3000, "JPY3,000")
4	(#weekend_surcharge, Weekend Surcharge, "Weekend Surcharge") (#return_trip_departing, return trip departing, "for return trip departing") (#DayOfWeek, Friday, "Fri") (#DayOfWeek, Saturday, "Sat") (#Price, JPY5000, "JPY5,000")
17	(#weekend_surcharge, weekend surcharge, "Weekend Surcharge") (#return_trip_departing, return trip departing, "if departing") (#DayOfWeek, Friday, "Friday") (#price, JPY5000, "JPY5,000") (#DayOfWeek, Saturday, "Saturday") (#price, JPY8000, "JPY8,000")
41	(#weekend_surcharge, weekend surcharge, "Weekend Surcharge") (#return_trip_departing, return trip departing, "Return trip depart") (#DayOfWeek, Friday, "Fr") (#DayOfWeek, Saturday, "Sa") (#price, JPY5000, "JPY5,000")

Table 4. Word types of folded token sequences

	type of folded token sequences
a	$\text{"Weekend surcharge"}^1, \text{"return trip departing"}^2 ({}_1({}_2\text{weekday}^3)_2^+ \text{price}^4)_1^+$
b	$\text{"Weekend surcharge"}^1, \text{"return trip arriving in Japan"}^2 ({}_1({}_2\text{weekday}^3)_2^+ \text{price}^4)_1^+$

4.4 Token Repetition Folding and Rule Clustering

In this section, we describe token repetition folding. For each token sequence $S = s_1 s_2 \ldots s_l$, examine word type t_i of each token s_i, and if there is a subsequence of types $t_j t_{j+1} \cdots t_{j+k}$ that has no less than one repetition, then replace the subsequence by *folded token sequence* $(t_j t_{j+1} \ldots t_{j+k})^+$. Apply this operation from the head of S repeatedly, until there is no more replacement.

Rule clustering is to classify a set of rule sentences into groups such that their folded token sequences consist of the same word types. By rule clustering, rule sentences having different values or different number of repetition in token sequences but the word types in folded token sequences are identical are clustered into one group. Note that rule sentences having different meaning may also be classified into the same group. Distinguishing those sentences are done at rule transformation.

In Table 4, we show the result of token repetition folding applied to Table 3. Rule 3 has the folded token sequence **b** of Table 4, while Rules 4, 17 and 41 have the folded token sequence **a**. Likewise, all the rules shown in Table 2 have either **a** or **b**. Namely, all the rules are classified into two groups **a** and **b**.

4.5 Rule Transformation

In rule transformation, rule sentences having folded token sequences are transformed into logical expressions, following a *transformation template*. A transformation template τ is a function from rule sentences to logical expressions. We assign numerical identifiers to open and close parentheses in the token sequences. We also assign numerical identifiers to token types. In Table 4, identifiers for parentheses are shown as subscripts and identifiers for tokens are shown as superscripts.

We assume that logical expressions transformation templates produce are in *negation normal form*, namely all the negations ($\neg$) are pushed down to literals by De Morgan's Law. Here, literals are either equality ($v =$"c") or non-equality ($v \neq$"c"). The transformation template τ specifies either AND ($\wedge$), OR ($\vee$), NOR ($\oplus$), or SEQUENCE (σ).

The transformation template τ also assigns a variable to each token sequence. Variable names are assigned according to their template IDs and types of tokens. Each constant c appeared in the original rule sentence is replaced by its standard form $std(c)$. For example, suppose that a token sequence of cities $c_1, c_2, \ldots, c_k$ is folded into $({}_i w_j)_i^+$. Also suppose that $\tau((.)_i) = \vee$ and $\tau(w_j) = city1$. Then the rule sentence is transformed into the following disjunction:

$$(city1 = std(c_1) \vee city1 = std(c_2) \vee \cdots \vee city1 = std(c_k))$$

On the other hand, if the logical connective $\tau((.)_i)$ is $\oplus$ (NOR), then the following conjunction of non-equalities is produced:

$$(city1 \neq std(c_1) \wedge city1 \neq std(c_2) \wedge \cdots \wedge city1 \neq std(c_k))$$

Note that we do not have to consider the case of NAND for token sequences, because the expression $(city1 \neq std(c_1) \vee \cdots \vee city1 \neq std(c_k))$ is always true for $k \geq 2$. Likewise, AND on a token sequence of a single variable, such as $(city1 = std(c_1) \wedge \cdots \wedge city1 = std(c_k))$, is always false for $k \geq 2$. Therefore AND shall be used for combining disjunctions or combining equalities on different variables. We also note that not all token sequences can be converted into AND, OR, or NOR logical connectives. For example, a token sequence may be specifying an order, not a logical connective. In such cases, we use SEQUENCE. In SEQUENCE, transformation is done by an ad hoc script.

We consider the following two modes of transformations:

(semantic transformation) In semantic transformation, the transformation template τ_s has a *sentence format* $< t_1, t_2 \ldots, t_k >$, where each t_i is either a string or a folded token sequence. The template can be applied to a (token-folded) rule sentence T if T exactly matches with the concatenation $t_1 t_2 \cdots t_k$. The template τ_s defines a function that assigns each folded token sequence t_i logical operations (AND, OR, NOR) or SEQUENCE, and variable names.

(generic transformation) In generic transformation, there is only one "generic template" τ_{gen} and all the rule sentences are transformed by τ_{gen}. The transformation proceeds in the following way:

1. If a folded token sequence contains a specific phrase that indicates a logical operation, then transform the token sequence according to the logical operation. The following phrases are typical in English and can be transformed into the logical operations shown left: $c_1, \ldots,$ and, $c_k \Rightarrow$ AND
$c_1, \ldots,$ or, $c_k \Rightarrow$ OR
except $c_1, \ldots, c_k \Rightarrow$ NOR
2. If there is no matching phrase for a token sequence, then the sequence is regarded as SEQUENCE, and transformed into a conjunction of equalities where each equality has a different variable name. For example, suppose that the sequence $c_1, \ldots, c_k$ has sentence id i and word type wt. Then it is transformed into the following conjunction:

$$i\_wt\_1 = std(c_1) \wedge i\_wt\_2 = std(c_2) \wedge \cdots \wedge i\_wt\_k = std(c_k)$$

The idea of generic transformation is that each rule sentence is conservatively transformed into a "tuple" which is a conjunction of equalities $i\_wt\_i = std(t)$, where t is a registered token of word type wt. Token sequences whose logical operation (AND, OR, NOR) is apparent from the context are converted into that operation.

Semantic transformation can produce accurate transformation of rule sentences, under the assumption that transformation templates for specific rule sentence patterns are given. However, providing all the necessary templates are costly. On the other hand, generic transformation is universal and there is no need for providing specific templates. Generic transformation shall be applied when there is no matching semantic transformation. Generic transformation does not capture all the semantics of rule sentences; it recognizes only folded token sequences and explicit logical connectives. However, we can safely argue that there is "some" dependency between variables assigned to a rule sentence, and such existence or non-existence of dependencies can be utilized for selecting business rules. If precise query processing is required, the original rule sentence should be presented to the user in a dialog for confirmation.

For rule sentences of Table 3, we show semantic transformation templates τ_a and τ_b, respectively, in Table5. By template τ_a, the (first occurrence of) word type "#DayOfWeek" is mapped to variable v_a, which should carry the meaning that "the weekday on which return trip departs," and the word type "#price" is mapped to variable p, which should carry the meaning of "the price of weekend surcharge." In template τ_b, the word type "#DayOfWeek" is mapped to variable v_b, which should carry the meaning that "the weekday on which return trip arrives in Japan."

The result of applying templates τ_a and τ_b to the rule sentences in Table 2 is shown in Table 6.

5 Evaluation

We have implemented the logical rule extraction method described in Section 4, using Perl. The program was executed by a 3.2GHz Pentium 4 Processor with 512MB memory.

For the 3,766 rule sentences extracted from airline ticket data, 495 clusters having the same folded token sequences are extracted. This process took 9,745 seconds. In Table 7, we summarize distribution of cluster size. Most of clusters contain less than 10 rule sentences, and average number of rules per cluster is 7.639. However, large clusters

Table 5. Transformation templates

τ_a	τ_b
$(.)_1 \mapsto$ '∨'	$(.)_1 \mapsto$ '∨'
$(.)_2 \mapsto$ '∨'	$(.)_2 \mapsto$ '∨'
$(.)_2$#price$^4 \mapsto$ '∧'	$(.)_2$#DayOfWeek$^4 \mapsto$ '∧'
#DayOfWeek$^3 \mapsto v_a$	#DayOfWeek$^3 \mapsto v_b$
$textrm\#DayOfWeek^4 \mapsto p$	#price$^4 \mapsto p$

Table 6. Result of transformed logical expressions

1,7, 9, 14, 15, 22, 42, 46, 48, 59, 60	$(v_a =$ Friday $\vee\ v =$ Saturday$) \wedge (p =$ JPY3000$)$
2,40	$v_b =$ Sunday $\wedge\ p =$ JPY5000
3, 34, 36, 38, 39	$v_b =$ Sunday $\wedge\ p =$ JPY3000
4, 6, 10, 12, 13, 14, 16, 23, 24, 26, 27, 29, 30, 41, 45, 50, 57	$(v_a =$ Friday $\vee\ v_a =$ Saturday$) \wedge (p =$ JPY5000$)$
5,20,44	$v_a =$ Saturday $\wedge\ p =$ JPY5000
8, 49	$(v_a =$ Friday $\vee\ v_a =$ Saturday $\vee\ v_a =$ Sunday$) \wedge (p =$ JPY5000$)$
11, 17, 31	$v_a =$ Friday $\wedge\ p =$ JPY5000 $\vee\ v_a =$ Saturday $\wedge\ p =$ JPY8000
18	$v_a =$ Friday $\wedge\ p =$ JPY5000 $\vee\ v_a =$ Saturday $\wedge\ p =$ JPY15000
19,43,58	$v_a =$ Saturday $\wedge\ p =$ JPY3000
21	$(v_a =$ Friday $\vee\ v_a =$ Saturday$) \wedge (p =$ JPY2000$)$
25	$(v_a =$ Friday $\vee\ v_a =$ Saturday$) \wedge (p =$ JPY8000$)$
28, 53, 54, 56	$v_a =$ Sunday $\wedge\ p =$ JPY3000
32, 33	$(v_b =$ Saturday $\vee\ v_b =$ Sunday$) \wedge (p =$ JPY3000$)$
35, 37, 55	$v_a =$ Sunday $\wedge\ p =$ JPY2000
51	$(v_a =$ Saturday $\vee\ v_a =$ Sunday$) \wedge (p =$ JPY3000$)$
52	$v_a =$ Saturday $\wedge\ p =$ JPY2000

Table 7. Number of rules in cluster

number of rules in a cluster	clusters
1 to 10	457
11 to 50	24
51 to 100	5
101 to 200	3
201 to 600	4
avg. number of rules per cluster	7.639

containing more than 100 rules exist, and they occupy more than half of the entire rules. Transformation by templates is effective for such large clusters. Clustering by types of folded token sequences also allows users to identify rules similar but having slightly different meaning. Thus clustering can assist users to design appropriate templates.

As for the functional dictionary, eleven word types including day of the week, price, date, and city were necessary. We have populated the functional dictionary by scanning the ticket data. There were a number of transformation errors when the dictionary was not completed. But as the dictionary approached completion, the accuracy of token extraction and token repetition folding was improved. Most of encountered folded token sequences are OR-type.

We have provided semantic transformation for 117 clusters. Computation time for semantic transformation by those templates took 1,600 seconds. On the other hand, generic transformation took 331 seconds to process the entire 493 clusters.

6 Conclusion

In this paper, we discussed extracting business rules in the form of logical expressions from web product descriptions. This is an important step toward providing logical inference capabilities to web information. We showed a number of techniques for translating natural language business rules into logical expressions. Among them, semantic transformation produces logical expressions by predefined templates, while generic transformation executes without predefined templates, through shallow interpretation of rule sentences. The experimental system successfully translated real airline ticket descriptions. As for future work, user assistance for authoring transformation templates, and automatic generation of interactive queries from logical expressions are planned.

References

1. A. Arasu, H. Garcia-Molina, "Extracting Structured Data from Web Pages," Proc. ACM SIGMOD Conf. 2003, pp. 337-348, 2003.
2. T. Berners-Lee, "The Semantic Web-LCS seminar," http://www.w3.org/2002/Talks/09-lcs-sweb-tbl/
3. H. Boley, S. Tabet, and G. Wagner, "Design Rationale of RuleML," *A Markup Language for Semantic Web Rules, Semantic Web Working Symposium*, Stanford, July/ August 2001.
4. H. Boley, "The Rule Markup Language: RDF-XML Data Model, XML Schema Hierarchy, and XSL transformations," *INAP2001*, Tokyo, Oct. 2001.
5. B. N. Grosof, Y. Labrou, and H. Y. Chan, "A Declarative Approach to Business Rules in Contracts: Courteous Logic Programs in XML," *E-COMMERCE 99*, Denver, 1999.
6. J. L. Kang, K. Jae, "Extraction of Structured Rules from Web Pages and Maintenance of Mutual Consistency: XRML Approach," *Proc. of RuleML 2003*, Springer-Verlag, LNCS2876, pp. 150-163, 2003.
7. M. Kozawa, M. Iwaihara, and Y. Kambayashi, "Constraint Search for Comparing Multiple-Incentive Merchandises," *Proc. of EC-Web 2002*, Springer, LNCS2455, pp.152-161, Sep. 2002.
8. B. N. Grosof, I. Horrocks, R. Volz, and S. Decker, "Description Logic Programs: Combining Logic Programs with Description Logic," Proc. Int. Conf. WWW, 2003.
9. IBM Common Rules, http://alphaworks.ibm.com.
10. M. Iwaihara, "Supporting Dynamic Constraints for Commerce Negotiations," *2nd Int. Workshop in Advanced Issues of E-Commerce and Web-Information Systems* (WECWIS), IEEE Press, pp. 12–20, June 2000.
11. M. Iwaihara, "Matching and Deriving Dynamic Constraints for E-Commerce Negotiations," *Proc. Workshop on Technologies for E-Services*, Cairo, Sep. 2000.
12. G. Kuper, L. Libkin, J. Paredaens (eds.), "*Constraint Databases,*" Springer-Verlag, 2000.
13. Open Travel Alliance, OTA Specification. http://www.opentravel.org/.
14. OWL Web Ontology Language Guide. http://www.w3.org/2001/sw/WebOnt/.
15. D. Trastour, C. Bartolini and C. Preist, "Semantic Web Support for the Business-to-Business E-Commerce Lifecycle," Proc. WWW2002.
16. TravelXML. http://www.xmlconsortium.org/wg/TravelXML/TravelXML_index.html

Wrapping HTML Tables into XML

Shijun Li[1], Mengchi Liu[2], and Zhiyong Peng[3]

[1] School of Computer, Wuhan University, Wuhan 430072, China
shjli@public.wh.hb.cn
[2] School of Computer Science, Carleton University,
1125 Colonel By Drive, Ottawa, ON, Canada K1S 5B6
mengchi@scs.carleton.ca
[3] State Key Lab of Software Engineering, Wuhan University,
Wuhan 430072, China
peng@whu.edu.cn

Abstract. HTML tables are information rich and are used frequently in HTML documents, but they are mainly presentation-oriented and are not really suited for database applications. To wrap HTML tables, in this paper, we introduce a conceptual model for HTML tables, and based on it, we present a new approach to wrap HTML tables into XML documents. It can automatically convert basic HTML tables, nested tables, composite HTML table and the tables without marked headings, into XML documents.

1 Introduction

Tables are used frequently in HTML documents and are information rich. They are intended for human users, rather than for computer applications. Being able to capture the meanings of HTML tables automatically has many potential applications. In HTML documents, the cells in HTML tables may span multiple rows or columns. So HTML tables may have nested heading; and each row or column may have different number of data cells that may not aline. Also the cells may be not atomic as the cells may contain nested table, list etc. It is not trivial to automatically wrap them into XML document, which escribes contents of data and can be processed by database applications.

As the number of rows or columns spanned by a cell is set by *rowspan* or *colspan* attributes, we can normalize HTML tables by inserting redundant cells into them. Based on their normalized tables, we introduce a conceptual model for HTML tables, in which an HTML table consists of seven elements: captions, ULC (upper-left corner), row headings, column headings, the affiliation of ULC (affiliating to row headings or column headings), data, and attribute-value pairs. Based on the conceptual model, we introduce a mapping rule to map the normalized HTML tables to XML documents. Since the mapping rule uses recursive function, it is well-suited for capturing the nested table, list and the nested structure marked by formatting information, in cells of HTML tables.

For some complex HTML tables that consist of sub-tables, we introduce the notion of *composite table* and wrap them into XML by decomposing them into sub-tables, and then wrap each sub-table by the mapping rule.

X. Zhou et al. (Eds.): WISE 2004, LNCS 3306, pp. 147–152, 2004.
© Springer-Verlag Berlin Heidelberg 2004

Table 1. The normalized HTML table

ULC			$h_{1,q+1}$	...	$h_{1,n}$
			$\vdots$		$\vdots$
			$h_{p,q+1}$	...	$h_{p,n}$
$v_{p+1,1}$	...	$v_{p+1,q}$	$d_{p+1,q+1}$	...	$d_{p+1,n}$
$\vdots$		$\vdots$	$\vdots$		$\vdots$
$v_{m,1}$	...	$v_{m,q}$	$d_{m,q+1}$	...	$d_{m,n}$

The paper is organized as follows. Section 2 introduces a conceptual model for HTML tables. Section 3 presents the approach to wrapping HTML tables. Section 4 introduces the approach to wrapping composite HTML tables. Section 5 compares our work with other related work. Finally we conclude in Section 6.

2 Conceptual Model for HTML Tables

In HTML, table cells generally contain heading information via the *th* element and data via the *td* element. Table cells may span multiple rows and columns, which cause complex nested heading structure. To capture the attribute-value pairs in an HTML table, we need to normalize the HTML table. In an HTML table, if a *th* or *td* element contains $colspan = k$ or $rowspan = k$, it means that the particular cell of the *th* or *td* is to be expanded to $k - 1$ more columns or $k - 1$ more columns, starting from the current cell in the current row or collumn. By using the attributes colspan and rowspan in *th* or *td* elements, that is, by inserting redundant cells into an HTML table, we can normalize the HTML table in the form of Table 1.

Based on the general form of the normalized HTML tables as show in Table 1, we introduce a conceptual model for HTML tables as follows.

Definition 1. An HTML table T is denoted by
$T_{m \times n \times p \times q}(C, ULC, RH, CH, F, D, AD)$
where C is the content of the caption of T; ULC is the content of the upper-left corner of T; $ULC = \phi$, if $p = 0$ or $q = 0$; RH is the row headings of T; if $q = 0$, then $RH = \phi$, otherwise $RH = \{V_{p+1} = (v_{p+1,1}, \ldots, v_{p+1,q}), \ldots, V_m = (v_{m,1}, \ldots, v_{m,q})\}$; CH is the column headings of T; If $p = 0$, then $CH = \phi$, otherwise $CH = \{H_{q+1} = (h_{1,q+1}, \ldots, h_{p,q+1}), \ldots, H_n = (h_{1,n}, \ldots, h_{p,n})\}$; F is the affiliation of ULC; $F \in \{F_{RH}, F_{CH}, \phi\}$; if $ULC = \phi$, then $F = \phi$; if ULC is affiliated to row headings, then $F = F_{RH}$, otherwise $F = F_{CH}$; D is the data part of T; $D = \{d_{ij} \mid i = p+1, \ldots, m;\ j = q+1, \ldots, n\}$; AD is the attribute-value pairs of the table; if $p \neq 0$ and $q \neq 0$, then $AD = \{((V_i, H_j), d_{ij}) \mid V_i \in RH, H_j \in CH, d_{ij} \in D\}$; if $p = 0$ and $q \neq 0$ then$AD = \{(V_i, d_{ij}) \mid V_i \in RH, d_{ij} \in D\}$; if $q = 0$ and $p \neq 0$, then$AD = \{(H_j, d_{ij}) \mid H_j \in CH, d_{ij} \in D\}$.

If $p \neq 0$ and $q \neq 0$, then the table is called *two dimensional* tables. Otherwise it is called *one dimensional* tables. In the case of one dimensional table, if $p = 0$, the table is called column-wise table; if $q = 0$, the table is called row-wise table. If $p = 0$ and $q = 0$, the table is called *no-attribute* table.

3 Mapping Nested Structure of HTML Tables to XML

In the above conceptual model for HTML tables, if $F = F_{RH}$ (i.e. the ULC is affiliated to the row headings), then the nested structure of an HTML table can be expressed as (denoted in path expressions in XPath):
captions/ULC/row headings/column headings/data cell;
if $F = F_{CH}$ (i.e. the ULC is affiliated to the column heading), then the nested structure of an HTML table can be expressed as:
captions/ULC/column headings/row headings/data cell.
So we can map this nested structure of an HTML table to the corresponding XML document as follows.

Rule 1. Let an HTML table T be $T_{m\times n\times p\times q}(C, ULC, RH, CH, F, D, AD)$, let the value of C, ULC be c, ulc, respectively, and RH, CH, F, D, AD take the form in Definition 1. Let the rows that contain data be $r_{p+1}, r_{p+2}, \ldots, r_m$, and the columns that contain data be $c_{q+1}, c_{q+2}, \ldots, c_n$, where $0 \leq p \leq m$, $0 \leq q \leq n$. If $F = F_{RH}$ or $F = \phi$ and T is a two dimensional tables or T is a column-wise table (i.e. $p = 0$), then we use row-priority conversion as follows:
$\psi(T) =< c >< ulc > \psi(r_{p+1}) \oplus \psi(r_{p+2}) \oplus \ldots \oplus \psi(r_m) < /ulc >< /c >.$
Otherwise we use column-priority conversion as follows:
$\psi(T) =< c >< ulc > \psi(c_{q+1}) \oplus \psi(c_{q+2}) \oplus \ldots \oplus \psi(c_n) < /ulc >< /c >,$
where ψ is the converting function which converts an HTML document into XML one, and $\oplus$ is the operation that concatenates two character strings and

$$
\begin{aligned}
\psi(r_i) = & < v_{i,1} > \quad \ldots \quad < v_{i,q} > \\
& \quad < h_{1,q+1} > \ldots < h_{p,q+1} > \psi(d_{i,q+1}) < /h_{p,q+1} > \ldots < /h_{1,q+1} > \\
& \quad \ldots \\
& \quad < h_{1,n} > \ldots < h_{p,n} > \psi(d_{i,n}) < /h_{p,n} > \ldots < /h_{1,n} > \\
& < /v_{i,q} > \ldots < /v_{i,1} > \\
\psi(c_j) = & < h_{1,j} > \quad \ldots \quad < h_{p,j} > \\
& \quad < v_{p+1,1} > \ldots < v_{p+1,q} > \psi(d_{p+1,j}) < /v_{p+1,q} > \ldots < /v_{p+1,1} > \\
& \quad \ldots \\
& \quad < v_{m,1} > \ldots < v_{m,q} > \psi(d_{m,j}) < /v_{m,q} > \ldots < /v_{m,1} > \\
& < /h_{p,j} > \ldots < /h_{1,j} >
\end{aligned}
$$

where $i = p + 1, \ldots, m;\ j = q + 1, \ldots, n;\ 0 \leq p \leq m;\ 0 \leq q \leq n.$

After an HTML table is converted into an XML document by using above rule, we need to refine the XML document by merging the content of the same XML element, i.e. by using the following equation:
$< t1 >< t2 > s2 < /t2 >< /t1 >< t1 >< t3 > s3 < /t3 >< /t1 >$
$=< t1 >< t2 > s2 < /t2 >< t3 > s3 < /t3 >< /t1 >.$

Rule 1 covers not only two dimensional tables but also one dimensional tables. In Rule 1, we use F (i.e. the affiliation of ULC) to determine if using row-priority or column-priority conversion. Generally, the ULC is affiliated to the row headings except that it ends with a colon. So we use the following heuristic approach: If the ULC ends with a colon, then the ULC is affiliated to the row headings. Otherwise it is affiliated to the column headings.

There are some HTML tables without marked headings via *th* element in HTML documents. To convert them, the key is to recognize their headings. For HTML tables without marked headings, the authors generally use different formatting information, which are mainly font (size, bold and italic), to mark headings for visual easy recognition by uses. So we can recognize their headings by formatting information implied by HTML tags [9].

The mapping rule Rule 1 use recursive function so that it is particularly well-suited for converting the nested structure in cells of HTML tables. Given the conversion rules for text-level elements and list elements, which are introduced in [9], by using Rule 1, we can wrap nested tables, nested lists and the nested structure marked by formatting information in cells of HTML tables into XML.

4 HTML Composite Tables

For the HTML tables that have separate headings and more than one caption, we introduce the notion of *composite table.*

Definition 2. Let T be an HTML table, and T have n rows: $r_1, r_2, \ldots, r_n$, where r_i is the ith row of table T, $i = 1, 2, \ldots, n$. If T has at most one caption and no separate headings, we call T a basic table. If the rows of T can be grouped as: $r_1, \ldots, r_{k_1}; r_{k_1+1}, \ldots, r_{k_2}; \ldots; r_{k_{p-1}+1}, \ldots, r_{k_p} = r_n$; where $0 \leq k_1 < k_2 < \ldots < k_p = n$, and the row set of each group composes a basic table called sub-table, then we call T a row-wise composite table.

We can similarly give the definition of column-wise composite tables. Table 2 is a sample of row-wise composite tables. For the rows of a table T that contain only one cell, if it is the first row, then we can take it as the caption of T; otherwise we can take it as the *sub-caption* of T. For example, in Table 2, the first row is the caption of the Table 2, and the fourth row and the seventh row are the caption of the second and third sub-table of Table 2, respectively. It is much more difficult to capture the nested structure in the row-wise composite tables than the basic tables discussed in Section 3, since the column heading of the first sub-table is shared by the other sub-tables, and the caption and ULC of the first sub-table are the caption and ULC of the composite table. For example, in Table 2, the second row is the column heading, which is shared by the second and third sub-table. To convert row-wise composite table, we need add column heading of the first sub-table to the other sub-tables.

Rule 2. Let T be a row-wise composite table which consists of n sub-tables: $T_1, T_2, \ldots, T_n$, and the column heading of T_1 be h. Then dismiss the caption (let its value be c) and ULC (let its value be ulc) from the first sub-table, and add h to each of $T_2, \ldots, T_n$ as headings. After that, let we turn $T_1, T_2, \ldots, T_n$ into $T_1', T_2', \ldots, T_n'$, respectively.
Then $\psi(T) = < c >< ulc > \psi(T_1') \oplus \ldots \oplus \psi(T_n') < /ulc >< /c >$,
where $\psi(T_1'), \ldots, \psi(T_n')$ can be computed by Rule 1 using row priority conversion.

Table 2. A sample composite table

Percentage of children enrolled				
Characteristic	1991	1995	1999	2001
Total students	52.8	55.1	59.7	56.4
Poverty status				
Below poverty	44.2	45.1	51.4	46.7
At or above poverty	55.7	58.8	62.3	59.1
Race/ethnicity				
White	54.0	56.9	69.0	59.0
Black	58.3	59.5	73.2	63.7
Hispanic	38.8	37.4	44.2	38.8

Example 1. Consider the row-wise composite table T in Table 2, which consists three sub-tables. By using Rule 2, the heading of the first sub-table, that is the second row need be added into the second and the third sub-table. After that its three sub-tables are turned into the following three sub-table: T_1', which consists of tw0 rows: the second and third row of Table 2; T_2', which consists of four rows: the forth, the second, the fifth and the sixth row of Table 2; and T_3', which consists of five rows: the seventh, the second, the eighth, the ninth and the tenth row of Table 2. By using Rule 2, as c = Percentage of children enrolled, ulc =Characteristic,

$\psi(T)$ =<Percentage-of-children-enrolled>
<Characteristic> $\psi(T_1') \oplus \psi(T_2') \oplus \psi(T_3')$ </Characteristic>
</Percentage-of-enrolled>.

By using Rule 1, we can easily get the results of $\psi(T_1')$, $\psi(T_2')$, and $\psi(T_3')$, and then the result of $\psi(T)$, that is, the wrapped XML document of Table 2.

5 Comparison with Other Work

The manual approaches w4f [6], Tismmis [3], XWrap [7], and DOM-based approach [5] have strong expressive capability, but they often involve the writing of complicated code. Lixto [10] manage to avoid the writing of code by providing a fully visual and interactive user interface. The induction approach [1] uses machine-learning techniques to generate wrappers automatically which need to be trained under human supervision. Ontology-based approach [2] also involves the writing of RDF code. [4] presents an automatic approach to converting HTML tables. However, it cannot convert the tables without marked heading and composite tables. [8] presents an automatic approach to extracting attribute-value pairs. But it gives no formal approach to capture the attribute-value pairs in HTML tables with nested headings, and cannot capture nested structures in table cells. In this paper, we present a new approach to wrapping HTML tables into XML, and have implemented it using java and performed experiment on HTML tables on the web related to car selling, national statistic information, etc., with the average precision being about 93% and the recall about 98%. We must stress the fact that some of the presented rules are based on heuristics and might fail. Compared with the other related approaches, our approach introduces a conceptual model for HTML tables, which is the basis of our approach so that it is more formal and precise. And it uses recursive function, so that it can wrap nested HTML tables. In addition, it introduces the notion of HTML composite tables and the approach to wrap them. While the other approaches cannot apply the HTML composite tables or just cover part of them.

6 Conclusion

We have introduced a conceptual model for HTML tables, and based on it, we present a new approach that automatically captures the nested structure in HTML tables and converts them into XML documents, and a system implementing this new approach, which can automatically wrap the selected tables, including nested tables, composite HTML table into XML documents with a good performance. It can be used as an efficient auxiliary tool in recycling HTML tables as XML documents.

References

1. Nicholas Kushmerick, D. Weld, and R. Doorenbos. Wrapper Induction for Information Extraction. In proceedings of IJCAI (1997), 729–737
2. David W. Embley, Cui Tao, and Stephen W. Liddle. Automatically Extracting Ontologically Specified Data from HTML Table of Unknown Structure. In proceedings of ER (2002), 322–337
3. Joachim Hammer, Hector Garcia-Molina, Svetlozar Nestorov, Ramana Yerneni, Markus M. Breunig, and Vasilis Vassalos. Template-Based Wrappers in the TSIMMIS System. In proceedings of SIGMOD Conference (1997), 532–535
4. Seung Jin Lim, Yiu-Kai Ng, and Xiaochun Yang. Integrating HTML Tables Using Semantic Hierarchies And Meta-Data Sets. In proceedings of IDEAS (2002), 160–169
5. Suhit Gupta, Gail E. Kaiser, David Neistadt, and Peter Grimm. DOM-based content extraction of HTML documents. In proceedings of WWW (2003), 207–214
6. Arnaud Sahuguet and Fabien Azavant. Building Intelligent Web Applications Using Lightweight Wrappers. Data and Knowledge Engineering (2001), 36(3): 283–316
7. L. Liu, C. Pu, and W. Han. XWrap: An Extensible Wrapper Construction System for Internet Information. In proceedings of ICDE (2000) 611–621
8. Yingchen Yang and Wo-Shun Luk. A Framework for Web Table Mining. In proceedings of WIDM'02 (2002), 36–42
9. Shijun Li, Mengchi Liu, Tok Wang Ling, and Zhiyong Peng. Automatic HTML to XML Conversion. In proceedings of WAIM (2004), 714–719
10. R. Baumgartner, S. Flesca and G. Gottlob. Visual Web Information Extraction with Lixto. In proceedings of VLDB (2001), 119–128

Vague Event-Based Related News Detection

Wei Hu, Dong-mo Zhang, and Huan-ye Sheng

Computer Science Dept, Shanghai Jiao Tong Univ,
200030 Shanghai, China
no_bit@hotmail.com
zhang-dm@cs.sjtu.edu.cn
hysheng@sjtu.edu.cn

Abstract. The task of related news detection is to find news articles which discuss events that have been reported in earlier articles. In this paper the notion of "event" in news is extended to be "vague event" and news article is represented using a vector of vague event trees. Then an approach to vague event-based related news detection is presented and an experiment for Chinese sports news detection is designed.

1 Introduction

An important force of event detection is Topic Detection and Tracking (TDT) [1]. The primary participants were Carnegie Mellon University, Dragon System, and the University of Massachusetts at Amherst. CMU takes an approach based on group average agglomerative text clustering [2]. The UMass approach is similar to the extent that it uses a variant of single-link clustering and builds up (clusters) groups of related stories to represent events [3]. Dragon approach is based on observations over term frequencies, but using adaptive language models from speech recognition [1].

In most of the methods above, events are not explicitly extracted but are implicitly hidden in vectors of (weighted) terms which can be either words or phrases. In this paper the notion of an "event" is modified to be a "vague event", and an article is represented using a vector of vague event trees based on which an approach to related news detection is developed.

2 Notion of Event

In the TDT pilot study the definition of "event" is "something that happens at a particular time and place" [1]. But in our application, this notion could be extended

2.1 Events Readers Interested in

Consider, for example, we have three sentences:

X. Zhou et al. (Eds.): WISE 2004, LNCS 3306, pp. 153–158, 2004.
© Springer-Verlag Berlin Heidelberg 2004

Four-Star General may run Iraq transition. (Yahoo News)
Four-Star General will run Iraq transition next week.
Four-Star General will not run Iraq transition next week.

The meanings of these sentences are different. Even the second sentence is opposite to the third one. But to the readers, whether Four-Star General will run Iraq transition is the event they concern and these three sentences just cover this event. They will not complain about poor consistency. On the contrary, reports from different media are welcome. In such situation, triple *<run, Four-Star General, Iraq transition>* is capable of summarizing the event, regardless of modifiers in each sentence.

Consider another example:

The Spurs beat New Jersey 88-77. (NBA Official Site)
The Spurs 88-77 win over New Jersey. (NBA Official Site)
The Spurs lost to New Jersey.
The Spurs is beat by New Jersey.

Event mentioned in the first sentence is similar to that in the second sentence, and opponent to that in the third sentence. The fourth sentence is a passive voice, which express opponent meaning to the first sentence. Also readers will be interested in the gather of these fours reports.

2.2 Vague Event

Now, we find that ignoring modifiers and voice will not affect our related news detection task. On the contrary, modifying the notion of "event" to a triple will bring us some advantages. "vague event" and related notions are defined as follow:

Suppose A is an article in the Web news collection. A_t is the title of A and A_f is the first paragraph of A. E_{A0} is the set of events which are both mentioned in A_t and A_f.

Event 1 (Vague Event): The set of A's events 1 is denoted by E_{A1}.

$E_{A1} = \{<v,n_1,n_2> |$ v is the main action of event e, n_1 is the subjective of action v, n_2 is the objective of action v, e belongs to $E_{A0}\}$

Event 2 (1-extended Vague Event): The set of A's events 2 is denoted by E_{A2}.

$E_{A2} = \{<v',n_1,n_2> |$ v' is v's synonym or antonym in dictionary, $<v,n_1,n_2>$ belongs to $E_{A1}\} \cup \{<v,n_1,n_2> | <v,n_2,n_1>$ belongs to $E_{A1}\} - E_{A1}$

Event n+1 (n-extended Vague Event): The set of A's is E_{An+1}.

$E_{An+1} = \{<v',n_1,n_2> |$ v' is v's synonym or antonym in dictionary, $<v,n_1,n_2>$ belongs to $E_{An}\} \cup \{<v,n_1,n_2> | <v,n_2,n_1>$ belongs to $E_{An}\} - (\cup_{i:1\text{-}n} E_{Ai})$

The union set of E_{Ai} is called article A's *Extended Vague Events*. The tree, with one vague event as root and synonym or antonym or interchanging relation as farther-son relation, is called *Vague Event Tree*. Then article A can be represented using a vector of vague event trees. $A=<T_1,T_2,\ldots,T_n>$.

3 Vague Event Tree Extraction

In this section, we will discuss the vague event tree extraction approach. Before discussion, a Chinese lexical knowledge dictionary and taxonomy will be introduced.

3.1 HowNet

HowNet is a common-sense knowledge base unveiling inter-conceptual relations and inter-attribute relations of concepts in Chinese lexicons. About 1500 sememes are defined and organized into 7 basic taxonomies. More than 60,000 Chinese words are defined in about 110,000 entries. Each entry has an expression comprised of sememes and operators which express the semantic information of the word. In the extraction approach, *HowNet* is used to extract lexical knowledge in Chinese.

3.2 Vague Event Extraction

To extract vague event (event 1) from the title and the first paragraph of (Chinese) articles, several Natural Language Processing (NLP) modules are used first: (1) Word Segmentation & Part-Of-Speech (POS) Tagging; (2) Named Entity Recognition; (3) Syntactical Parsing.

The event 1 extraction algorithm is described as follow:

```
Algorithm 1.  E1E ( T, F, E1 )
for all t such that t is a tree in F do
  for all v such that v is a word tagged verb on t do
    if ( ExistRelatedV ( v, T )) then
      L = R = Φ
      for all l such that l is a word left to v on t do
        if ( l's tag is noun or named entity ) then
          AddWord ( l, L )
        else if ( l's tag is pron ) then
          AddTree ( p, L )   p is a tree previous to t
        end if
      end for
      for all r such that r is a word right to v on t
        do
        if ( r's tag is noun or named entity ) then
          AddWord ( r, R )
        else if ( r's tag is pron ) then
          AddTree ( p, R )   p is a tree previous to t
        end if
      end for
      for all l in L do
        for all r in R do
          AddEvent ( < v, l, r >, E1 )
        end for
      end for
    end if
  end for
end for
```

The formal parameter *T* is the segmented, tagged, and named entity recognized title. *F* is the list of parser trees. Every sentence in the first paragraph corresponds to one tree. *E1* is the set of event 1 and is empty initially.

The predicate *ExistRelatedV* (*v*, *T*) will judge whether there is a word *u* tagged verb and related to verb *v* on the tree *T*. Here, "related" means:

(1) *u* is the synonym or antonym of *v* according to *HowNet* or

(2) *u* is the prefix of the *v*'s synonym or antonym

The function *AddWord* (*w*, *S*) will add the word *w* into the set *S*. *AddTree* (*t*, *S*) will add all the word tagged noun or named entity on the tree *t* into the set *S*. *AddEvent* (*e*, *E*) will add the event *e*, which is a triple, into the event *E*.

3.3 Extended Vague Event Extraction and Vague Event Tree Construction

Given a root of vague event tree (a vague event), we can generate all its sons which are belong to 1-extended vague event (event 2). The algorithm is listed in pseudo as follow:

```
Algorithm 2.  E2E ( < v, l, r >, E2 )
for all u such that u is synonym of v in HowNet do
  AddEvent ( < u, l, r >, E2 )
end for
for all u such that u is antonym of v in HowNet do
  AddEvent ( < u, l, r >, E2 )
end for
AddEvent ( < v, r, l >, E2 )
```

The formal parameters $<v,l,r>$ is a vague event and *E2* is the set of event 2 which is empty initially.

The algorithms for extracting *n*-extended vague event are similar to algorithm 2. Having introduced extended vague events extraction approach, we can present the algorithm of vague event tree construction easily.

4 Related News Detection

Given that each news article can be represented using a vector of vague event trees, clustering algorithm appears to be a proper approach to news detection.

4.1 Distance Measure

Assume that vague event tree vectors $A = <T_{A1},T_{A2},\ldots,T_{An}>$ and $B=<T_{B1},T_{B2},\ldots,T_{Bm}>$ are learned form news article *A* and news article *B* respectively. The distance between *A* and *B* can be defined as follow:

First a vector of vague event trees is considered to be as a character string and the first part of distance is $D_1(A, B) = |A|+|B|-2|LCS(A, B)|$, where *LCS* stands for the longest common subsequence of string *A* and string *B*.

Then suppose that $S_A = <T_{A(1)},T_{A(2)},\ldots,T_{A(l)}>$ and $S_B = <T_{B(1)},T_{B(2)},\ldots, T_{B(l)}>$ are common subsequences of *A* and *B*. The distance between S_A and S_B is $D_S(S_A, S_B) = \sum_{i:1-l} Step\ (T_{A(i)}, T_{B(i)})$, where *Step* stands for the minimum extended steps required from root of $T_{B(i)}$ to root of $T_{A(i)}$. Assume that there are k such pairs of (S_{Ai}, S_{Bi}), the second part of distance between vector A and vector B is $D_2(A, B) = min_{i:1\text{-}k} \{D_S(S_{Ai}, S_{Bi})\}$.

The distance between A and B is defined to be $D(A, B) = 4\, D_1(A, B) + D_2(A, B)$.

4.2 Clusters and Related News Detection

Having defined the distance between news articles, we can judge whether a news article A is related to B through calculating the distance between A and B.

In this application, we introduce a threshold θ. If the minimum distance between A and B is below the θ, then article A is consierd to be realted to article B; otherwise A is not realted to B.

To some extent, it is the threshold θ that restricts the notion of related news. If given related news clusters, can we consider the threshold is just the lower boundary of distances between two centroids? In this opinion, we can estimate value of θ by formula $\theta = min_{i,j:1\text{-}n}\{D(c_i,c_j)\}$, where n is the number of clusters, c_i, c_j are centroids of cluster S_i, S_j respectively and $D(c_i,c_j)$ is the distance between two centroids.

5 News Detection Evaluation

To testify the validity of our approach, we have performed an experiment on it. Also we have borrowed some ideas from Topic Detecting and Tracking (TDT) in evaluation.

5.1 Corpus

A corpus of sports news has been developed to support the evaluation. This corpus spans the period from Nov. 1, 2003 to Nov. 20, 2003 and includes nearly 16,073 news articles, with taken from 166 media [4].

The corpus is divided into four samples. Sample 1 contains 3667 news articles. Sample 2 contains 3969 articles. Sample 3 contains 4343 articles. Sample 4 contains 4094 articles. Each sample will be processed before being used in experiment in the following manner. Assume that sample 1 is to be processed. Firstly, we randomly draw 10% (377) articles from sample 1 and manually classify these articles into 98 sets. Each of 377 articles is assigned a label of S_i (i from 1 to 98) to show which set it belongs to. Then, we draw another 377 articles from remaining (90%) articles. Among these articles, 52 articles belong to 98 sets. Then 52 articles are positive examples of related news articles while 325 articles are negative examples.

5.2 Experiment and Results

Assume that we use sample 1 for experiment. The procedure is listed as follow:

(1) Calculate centroid coordinates of 98 sets.

Suppose that there are n_i articles labeled S_i in sample 1. First map the distance space to Euclidean space and then set i's centroid coordinate c_i the average of n_i articles' coordinates.

(2) Calculate threshold.

$\theta = min_{i,j:1\text{-}98}\{D(c_i,c_j)\}$

(3) Detect related new articles.

For all article A_i is the second time drawn from sample 1, calculate $Score(A_i) = min_{j:1\text{-}98}\{D(A_i,c_j)\}$. Article A_i is assigned a label "R" if $Score(A_i)$ is less than θ while is assigned a label "U" if $Score(A_i)$ is greater than θ.

Table 1 lists the results of new articles detection using sample 1.

Table 1. Detection results using sample 1

	Negative Example	Positive Example
Labeled U	256	6
Labeled R	69	46

Table 2 summarizes the performance of related news detection.

Table 2. Performance of detection using different samples

	Sample 1	Sample 2	Sample 3	Sample 4
Recall	78.8%	74.2%	66.9%	82.5%
Precision	97.7%	98.6%	94.7%	97.6%
Miss	21.2%	25.8%	33.1%	17.5%
False Alarm	11.5%	13.3%	22.6%	10.4%
F_1	87.2%	82.1%	78.4%	89.4%

6 Conclusion

We have presented our work on event notion extending, vague event trees extracting, Chinese sports news detection and some evaluation. And the proposed detection approach is proved to be effective.

References

1. J. Allan, J. Carbonell, G. Doddington, J. Yamron, and Y. Yang. Topic detection and tracking pilot study: Final report. In *Proceedings of the DARPA Broadcast News Transcription and Understanding Workshop*, 1998
2. Y. Yang, T. Pierce, and J. Carbonell. A study on retrospective and on-line event detection. In *Proceedings of SIGIR'98*, 1998
3. J. Allan, R. Papka, and V. Lavrenko. On-line New Event Detection and Tracking. In *Proceedings of the 21th AnnInt ACM SIGIR Conference on Research and Development in Information Retrieval (SIGIR'98)*, pages37-45, 1998
4. Sina Sports News. From *http://sports.sina.com.cn/normal/oldnews.shtml*

A Web Based Platform for the Design of Administrational Reference Process Models

Jörg Becker, Lars Algermissen, Patrick Delfmann, and Björn Niehaves

Westfälische Wilhelms-Universität Münster
ERCIS - European Research Center for Information Systems
Leonardo-Campus 3, D-48149 Münster
{becker, islaal, ispade, bjni}@wi.uni-muenster.de

Abstract. Public administrations are increasingly confronted with a modernization and service gap. Within the scope of eGovernment initiatives in the last few years, administrations try to overcome this gap by reorganizing and automating their business processes. In order to increase the quality of operations and processes, reference process models can be used as a valuable design support. Reference process models show a high level of reusability and thus allow for an extensive exploitation of synergy potentials as well as a reduction of redundancies. For the design of reference process models public administrations need to identify the best practice or common practice within the regarded domain. In order to support the identification of best practice or common practice a communication platform is needed that contains process descriptions of the specific administrations that can be provided by the administrations themselves. The aim of our paper is to propose a conceptual framework of such a web based platform as well as application scenarios in the German public administration domain.

1 Knowledge Deficits in Municipalities as a Driver for Reference Process Models in eGovernment

Public administrations are increasingly confronted with a modernization and service gap which results from a rising task load at simultaneous decreasing liquid funds [1]. E. g., extra tasks arise from accepting competencies from higher administration instances, increasing requirements from citizens and organizations as well as the handling of more complex administration-specific information systems.

Administration performance downgrades due to a continuing bad economic situation, decreasing tax gains, increasing encumbrance and problematic demographical development. In order to close the modernization and service gap, municipalities start to take part in a national and international competition and adopt business management concepts (New Public Management) [8]. On the technical layer, public administrations try to increase efficiency as well as "citizen-friendliness" by applying innovative technologies. In order to handle the resulting complexity many municipalities join regional software choice and user groups. Nevertheless, the

X. Zhou et al. (Eds.): WISE 2004, LNCS 3306, pp. 159–168, 2004.
© Springer-Verlag Berlin Heidelberg 2004

economic situation of the public administrations is keeping on getting worse. One cause are knowledge deficits on supra-municipal, intra-municipal and inter-municipal layer.

1.1 Supra-municipal Knowledge Deficits

Public administrations are not aware of the requirements they have to fulfill in terms of future establishments and laws. They do not know which responsibilities or even new freedoms for process execution they will face, and how organizational and technical requirements can be realized in an efficient way [2], [3]. From the legislator's point of view, the effectiveness of laws and establishments cannot be controlled adequately. Moreover, it is difficult to quickly put innovations across to the concerned municipalities.

1.2 Inter-municipal Knowledge Deficits

Many municipalities "re-invent the wheel", because they do not possess the knowledge how other municipalities solve similar problems or have already solved problems respectively [12]. Furthermore, there is no awareness of existing problems because information of structure and process quality is missing and optimization potentials are remaining unrevealed. Municipality comparison communities seem to provide a solution of these problems. These are so far based on business ratios and hence provide indications, who is doing something better, but do not show why and under which conditions (comparison of symptoms, not of causes). Specific characteristics of municipalities are not taken into account. For the same reason, the creation of regional software choice and user groups is not always reasonable. The basis of these communities should not be spatial nearness, but rather similar structures and processes.

1.3 Intra-municipal Knowledge Deficits

In terms of organizational design, a structured and transparent preparation of relevant information about administrational processes is missing. Besides a user group-adequate visualization of processes and their interdependencies, organizational units within and between public administrations as well as performance ratios belong to this information. In fact, performance ratios are used in product catalogues. Because the ratio instances do not provide inferences of their cause in the business processes, they can not always be used to generate action recommendations for the organizational design. Knowledge is rarely provided in a transparent and structured form in order to support employees in the execution of operational routine processes. At the same time, employees do not possess the knowledge about the placement of their own tasks in an overall business process, as well as legal interdependencies and process and organizational relationships.

In terms of application design, CIOs are confronted with a complex market of domain-specific applications, server technologies and standards. Many CIOs are overstrained with the choice of new software and the adoption of new technologies.

They shy at radical changes, because they do not want to commit without the required knowledge.

A compensation of the mentioned knowledge deficits promises a high improvement potential of municipality process performance [10]. In order to provide the required knowledge, an adequate knowledge base is needed. A great knowledge base for public administrations is their own business processes, or the business processes of many public administrations respectively [6]. Especially by learning from other public administrations that might perform the "best practice processes" in the public domain, the above mentioned modernization and service gaps and the resulting deficits can be overcome. In this paper, we propose a conceptual framework of a web based platform which will be able to support the identification of best practice processes in the public administration domain. For this purpose, the platform is designed to host process descriptions of the specific administrations that can be provided, viewed and compared by the administrations themselves.

2 Structure of a Knowledge Base for Reference Process Models

The framework which delivers the structure for the knowledge bases is divided in 4 different layers [7]. Within each layer the level of refinement raises (see Fig.1).

Layer 1 contains a functional-contextual framework which serves as an entry point in the total model and allows the navigation within the knowledge-base. For the presentation of a large number of model based knowledge on a high level of abstraction a structure according to management processes, core processes and support processes has proven valid. The elements of the framework link certain functions according to their contextual dependencies and can be compared to organisational units like departments.

On layer 2 the different functions are decomposed and hierarchically structured (e.g. by the use of function decomposition diagrams). The elements on layer 2 refer to certain services how they can be found for example in municipal product catalogues [9].

On layer 3 the processes are examined which underlie the different services. The complete process is presented as a combination of different process modules (e.g. by the use of value chain diagrams). In cooperation with a set of innovative municipalities these modules can be identified, consolidated and saved in the knowledge base in different variations. Application domain specific modules belong (e.g. for the evaluation of building applications) to the process modules as well as domain spanning process modules (e.g. payment applications, signature applications etc.).

On layer 4 different specifications or variations of the process modules are provided which fit the application context best (e. g. manual or electronic archiving process). In order to create the process modules a certain modelling language has to be selected. There are various and diverse model types for modelling (business) processes. Petri-nets [4] and event-driven process chains (EPC) [11] are amongst the

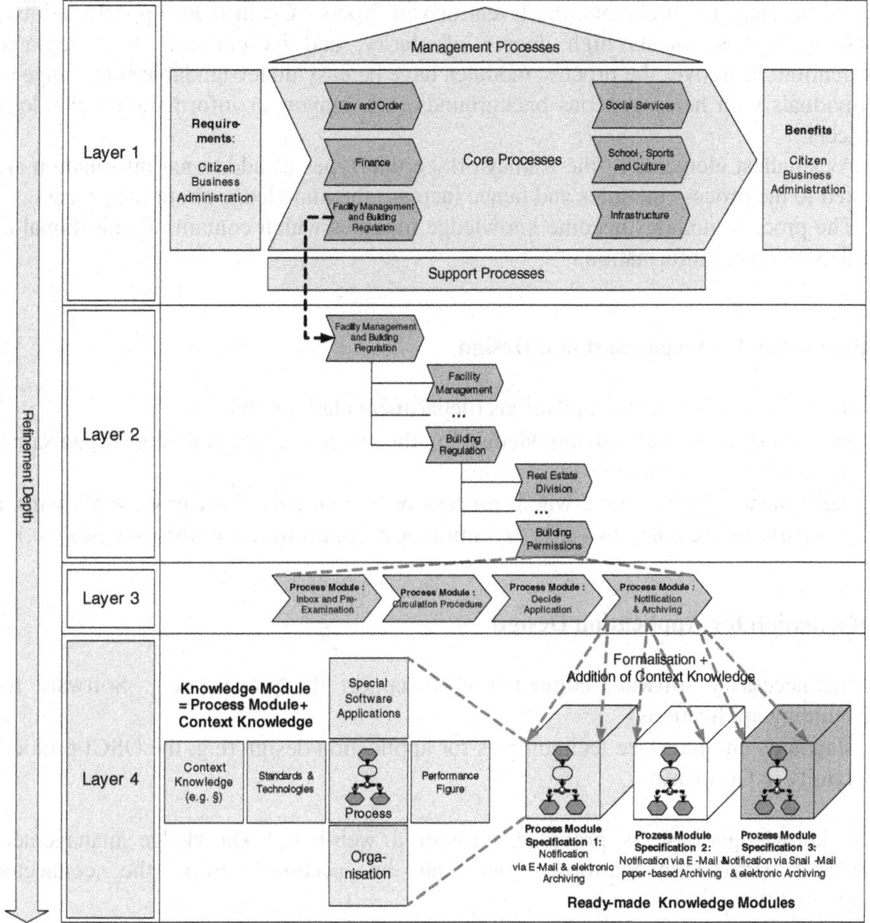

Fig. 1. Structure of a Knowledge Base for Reference Process Models

best known. Application aims, such as simulation and workflow management, require model types which produce detailed, precise, formally itemised models. This excludes, for example, the use of added-value chain diagrams. Application objectives such as process-oriented reorganisation require less formal models. The most important requirements of a modelling method in the given context are summarised below:

- Simple principle, clear presentation
- Comparability between various models
- Presentation of information systems
- Presentation of organisation units and places
- Presentation of information flow

Based on these requirements, the Event-driven Process Chain (EPC) is selected as a method, because of its high degree of clarity, and its potential for integrated evaluation. Moreover the process modules have be easy understandable for a range of individuals with heterogeneous backgrounds (e.g. mayor, or information technology officer).

As smallest elements in the framework certain types of additional information are linked to the process modules and hence increase the knowledge about the process.

The process modules become knowledge modules which contain organisational as well as technical information.

Information for Organisational Design

- the organisation units and positions (department clerk or chief)
- the necessary contextual knowledge for the process execution (e.g. organisation rules or law regulations)
- performance figures for a whole process or certain parts of a process allowing a comparison or evaluation (e. g. execution or transport time, number of cases etc.)

Information for Application Design

- the necessary software components to support the process (e.g. Software for building applications)
- standards and interface technologies for application design (e.g. the OSCI protocol family in Germany)

The knowledge base is provided through a web-based knowledge management platform (ProKMuni-Platform) and can be accessed from the connected municipalities.

3 The Application of a Knowledge Base for Reference Process Models – The Web-Based ProKMuni-Platform

The possibilities of the knowledge base are made applicable by means of a web-based knowledge management platform [5], called ProKMuni-Platform (process oriented knowledge management for municipalities) (see Fig. 2). We aim at the following application scenario:

A municipality can use multimedia based manipulation tools in order to construct their as-is processes (e.g. a specific building application procedure) based on ready-made knowledge modules. Furthermore they can perform certain adaptation procedures to enhance the reproduction quality (e.g. by changing the sequence of the process modules).When implementing the tools is has to be made sure that on the one hand the functionality is powerful enough to describe the problem area adequately. On the other hand the modelling tools have to be easy and intuitive enough to allow a high number of users and get their acceptance. The modelling of the processes can for example be done with graphical drag and drop-techniques (like the web based ARIS Easy-Design) or interactive surveys.

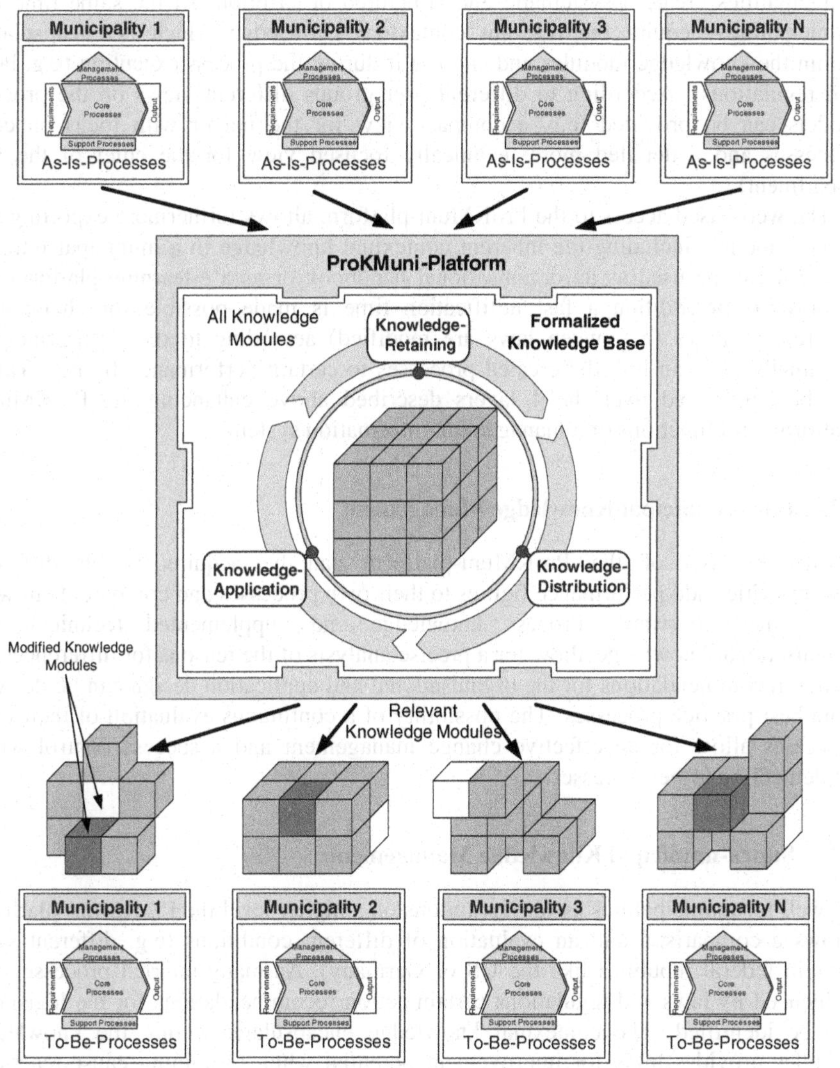

Fig. 2. The Application of the ProKMuni-Platform

The as-is-processes are the base for a knowledge management on different levels:

3.1 Intra-municipal Knowledge Management

With the web based reconstruction of processes using knowledge modules municipalities create a systematic and structured description. At the same time the municipalities acquire the relevant contextual knowledge which is encapsulated within the knowledge modules and can use it during the process execution (e.g. laws and regulations). According to different user groups different views on the process models can be provided (e.g. a compact view for the mayor with focus on core processes and a detailed more technically focused view for the chief of the IT-department).

The web-based access to the ProKMuni-platform allows furthermore exporting the process models including the inherent contextual knowledge in a municipal intranet where it can be used as an organisational handbook or as a e-learning-platform for employees. In addition a fast notification time is made possible for changes in different modules (e.g. when laws are modified) according to the push-principle. Eventually one can link the created processes to certain performance figures. These can be aggregated over the 4 layers described above enhancing the ProKMuni-platform with functions of a management information system.

3.2 Inter-municipal Knowledge Management

Further benefits of the ProKMuni-platform can be acquired when different municipalities add performance figures to their own processes and compare them with each other afterwards Process knowledge and supplemented technical and organisational knowledge allow for a precise analysis of the reasons for differences. Action recommendations for the organisational and application design can be derived from best-practice processes. The possibility of a continuous evaluation of their own processes allow for an effective change management and a success control when implementing to-be-processes.

3.3 Supra-municipal Knowledge Management:

As well for municipalities as for institutions on a higher level the ProKMuni-platform allows a comparison and an evaluation of different conditions (e.g. different state laws in federal republics like the US or Germany). As many internal processes are influenced by laws and regulations certain action recommendations for the legislator can be identified. The contextual knowledge encapsulated within the knowledge modules provides hints for improvement potential when examining cause-reaction-chains.

Summarized the ProKMuni-platform can help in answering many questions regarding the organisational or application design which helps to reduce knowledge deficits on an intra-municipal, an inter-municipal and a supra-municipal level (see table 1).

Table 1. Benefits of the ProKMuni-Platform

	Organisational Design	Application Design
Intra-municipal	• How do different processes in a certain administration look like and how do they fit together? • What organisational units are involved in which processes? • What effects had organisational changes on certain assessment figures?	• What software applications support what processes? • How does the actual software architecture look like? • What effects had the introduction of a new software on certain assessment figures?
Inter-municipal	• What municipality has the fastest, qualitatively best or most cost efficient processes? • Are differences caused by the process execution? • Are differences caused by the organisational structure?	• Can differences in success be justified on the software applications? • What software is the best for a certain process? • What standards and technologies have proven best?
Supra-municipal	• What effects have changes in law on the organisation? • Are differences in processes caused by different laws and regulations in certain states?	• What effects do changes in law and regulations have und software applications (e. g. Digital Signature)?

4 The Generation of the Knowledge-Base

The manual creation of an initial knowledge base can be done through the examination of innovative processes in municipalities known to be best practice.

Therefore in a first step the process and contextual knowledge is acquired and consolidated according to the structure of the knowledge base (see figure 1).

The automated addition of new knowledge takes place during the continuous usage of the platform by the participating municipalities.

On the one hand side existing process module specifications can be composed differently and hence create new knowledge through combination which is then added to the knowledge base. On the other hand existing process module specifications can be modified either by manipulating or enhancing the process itself or the contextual knowledge. The modified modules are also added to the knowledge base as a new specification variant.

As municipalities, in contrast to companies, do not compete to each other one can project a wide acceptance for participation throughout the municipalities. That is also the most important reason why this domain is the most suitable for the idea of the platform.

Hence the ProKMuni-platform becomes a learning system which increases in quality and quantity during the duration of usage and therefore makes itself more attractive for new participations through the well known network effect.

When adding all the different modules certain mechanisms to ensure syntactical consistency have to be implemented. In addition the correctness of the knowledge can be supervised by creating an institution which has the certain competencies (e.g. one big municipality is responsible for the building permission procedure).

5 Summary

Reference processes are created, supplemented with organisational and technical information and then stored in a web based knowledge base called ProKMuni as so called knowledge modules.

Using certain modelling methods and tools municipalities are able to model their own as-is-processes in a formal way and compare them to other municipalities in order to identify potential for improvement. Processes which have been evaluated as good many times can hence be considered as best-practice and therefore added to the knowledge base as a new knowledge module.

The platform allows, that innovative organisational and technical knowledge which has been decentrally developed by different municipalities can be centrally presented in a structured manner therefore enabling other municipalities to adapt that knowledge.

Hence a standardisation of administrational processes can be reached on a high level. By disseminating the innovative knowledge which has been stored on the ProKMuni-platform as knowledge modules the previously described knowledge deficits can be significantly reduced. Hence the efficiency of public administrations rises. At the same time the conditions for the economy and hence for more growth and employment are enhanced.

References

1. Budäus, D.; Schwiering, K.: Die Rolle der Informations- und Kommunikationstechnologien im Modernisierungsprozeß öffentlicher Verwaltungen. In: A.-W. Scheer (Hrsg.): Electronic Business und Knowledge Management. Heidelberg 1999, S. 143-165.
2. Falck, M. (2002) Business Process Management - As a Method of Governance. In: Lenk, K. and Traunmüller, R. (Eds.): Electronic Government, First International Conference, EGOV 2002, Aix-en-Provence, Proceedings, Lecture Notes in Computer Science, Berlin et al.: Springer, pp. 137-141.
3. Hammer, M. and Champy, J. (1993) Reengineering the Corporation: A Manifesto for Business Revolution, New York, NY: Harper Collins Publishers.
4. Jensen, K. (1985) An Introduction to High-Level Petri Nets, Int. Symp. on Circuits and Systems, Proceedings, Kyoto, Japan, Vol. 2,New York, IEEE, pp. 723-726.
5. Klischewski, R. (2001) Infrastructure for an e-Government Process Portal. In: Remenyi, D. and Bannister, F. (Eds.) European Conference on e-Government, MCIL. Reading, UK, pp. 233-245.
6. Klischewski, R. and Lenk, K. (2002) Understanding and Modelling Flexibility in Administrative Processes. In: Traunmüller, R., Lenk, K. (Eds.): Electronic Government. Proceedings EGOV 2002. Springer Lecture Notes. Berlin et al.: Springer, pp. 129-136.

7. Peristeras, V. and Tarabanis, K. (2000) Towards an enterprise architecture for public administration using a top-down approach. European Journal of Information Systems Vol 9 No 3, pp. 252-260.
8. Porter, M. E., (1990), The Competitive Advantage of Nations, London: The Macmillan Press Ltd.
9. Preston, H. (2001) Managing Electronic Services - A Public Sector Perspective. European Journal of Information Systems, Vol 10 No 4, p. 178.
10. Tarabanis, K.; Peristeras, V. and Koumpis, A. (2003) Towards a European Information Architecture for Public Administration: The InfoCITIZEN project. http://www.eurice.de/infocitizen/Paper_Venice_Oct2001.htm. Date of retrieval 2003-02-01.
11. van der Aalst, W. (1999) Formalization and Verification of Event-driven Process Chains. Information and Software Technology, Vol 41 No 10, pp 639-650. [in German]
12. Wetzel, I. and Klischewski, R. (2002) Serviceflow beyond Workflow? Concepts and Architectures for Supporting Inter-Organizational Service Processes. In: Advanced Information Systems Engineering. Proceedings 14th CAiSE. Springer Lecture Notes in Computer Science. Berlin et al.: Springer, pp. 500-515.

Technologies for Online Issuing Service of Documents

Jongweon Kim[1], Kyutae Kim[2], and Jonguk Choi[1, 2]

[1] College of Computer Software and Media Technology, Sangmyung University
7, Hongji-dong, Jongno-gu, Seoul, 110-743, Korea
{jwkim, juchoi}@smu.ac.kr
http://swc.smu.ac.kr/

[2] MarkAny Inc.,
10F, Ssanglim Bldg., 151-11, Ssanglim-dong, Jung-gu, Seoul, 100-400, Korea
{jedam, juchoi}@markany.com
http://www.markany.com/

Abstract. With the wide spread use of Internet, many government organizations are trying to implement e-government projects to provide on-line service and to improve productivity of public service. Because not all services are performed electronically, however, it is necessary to development technologies for enhancing the convenience of services for citizens by linking online digital documents and offline printed documents. This study investigated technologies and frameworks for issuing online documents such as certificates in e-Government, and examined cases of service to which the technologies and frameworks were applied.

1 Introduction

With the wide spread use of internet, many countries are planning e-government projects in which main targets are to shift offline public services for citizens to online service, to reduce service cost, to enhance service quality, and to improve productivity of government people. Especially, governments in Eastern Asia have keen interest in implementing on-line public service in order to improve work efficiency, save cost, and reduce citizens' time consumption for civil affairs the government of each country is making efforts to improve its services for citizens by planning e-Government. The basic purpose of e-Government is to shift offline services for citizens into online in order to improve work efficiency, save cost, and reduce citizens' time consumption for civil affairs. The main reasons for citizens to visit governmental offices are to report and to get issued permits or certificates. Governmental offices have to provide these services with limited number of people, which lowers the quality of services and cause citizens' complaints because of long waiting time.

E-Government projects are very knowledge intensive in that it requires participations of knowledge workers and improvement of efficiency and productivity involved in work processes of service organizations by reforming all administrative processes using communication technologies, database and information systems. Final goal of

X. Zhou et al. (Eds.): WISE 2004, LNCS 3306, pp. 169–180, 2004.
© Springer-Verlag Berlin Heidelberg 2004

the project is to provide high quality administrative services to the citizens. In a narrow sense, e-government should provide public services through online networks in which many government organizations are interlinked to each other to provide streamlined service to meet the final goal. Interactions between government organizations are through mutual organic electronic interaction among three aspects, namely, the aspect of services for citizens, the aspect of internal administrative process and policy-making, and the aspect of procurement[1].

The concept of e-Government was introduced first by Clinton Administration in the U.S. in 1993 with the object of upgrading the quality of people's life and activating economy using information technologies. America now provides integrated internet service through which integrates all of around 20,000 websites related to the federal government [2]. Other countries are planning various e-government projects in which many different purposes and targets are pursued with different schedules.

In Korea, the Ministry of Information and Communication takes charge of national society informatization projects including the administration computerization project in 1978, the administration computer network project in 1987, the information super highway project in 1994, and the introduction of the concept of e-Government in 1995. In 1999, the government established visions and strategies for e-Government including 24-hour one-stop administration service aiming at the implementation of e-Government until 2002.

However, this project in Korea is different from those in foreign countries including the U.S. While in U.S. and Japan local self-governing bodies pursue distributed informatization projects, in Korea the central government leads projects focused on strengthening the ruling system and most projects are executed by governmental departments.

This study purposed to develop technologies for security and preventing forgery and alteration in order to provide effective services for citizens, and introduce the service frameworks based on cases of services provided in Korea.

2 Functional Requirements of Issued Certificates

The idea of 'providing public service on line' or 'possibly mobile service' is fancy. The citizens need not visit government offices. They just drags pull-down menu and finish everything at home. However, as always there are a tradeoff between convenience of the citizens and security of government organizations. Because convenience and security are mutually exclusive sitting on both ends of seesaw bar, if one is considered as benefits, then the other is disadvantage. For the convenience of public services citizens shall be provided with online services such as registration and certificate issuing even though they do not have to visit government offices. However, from the perspective of ensuring security, citizens' personal information should be protected from disclosure, authentication process should be guarded, and civil affair documents should be prevented from forgery and alteration.

Providing service on line is vulnerable to various attacks such as theft of personal information stored in DB or network, and cracking document DB of civilian services, and thus on-line services should be provided under a near-perfect security. If security is emphasized too much, however, public services for citizens will be limited. Thus the two aspects of public services, convenience and security, should be traded off. Current e-Governmental online services for citizens are no more than administrative information inquiry services, on-line application and inquiry for processing status through e-mail correspondence. These services are easily manageable from the view of information security, but insufficient to meet citizens' demand for highly sophisticated services. Accordingly, it is necessary to adopt technologies that minimize the change of established systems and enhance security in order to deliver civilian data using existing systems safely to users and to issue online documents such as public certificates.

The followings are functions commonly required in online services for citizens, which are currently provided or are planned in Korea.

- Minimizing change of existing systems
- Authorization of issued certificates
- Prevention of forgery or alteration
- Safe deliver of the documents on the network

First of all, most organizations preparing online services are running existing public service information systems. It is necessary to establish an on-line certificate issue system without modifying existing system's architecture and coding. Thus, the certificate issue system should be modularized for easy migration into the existing system.

Second, certificates issued to civilians should be authorized by valid stamp. In off-line processing of government's certificates authorization is conducted by putting unique seals on documents, proving that the document issued by the organization is valid and authentic and preventing surreptitious uses of the organizations. In online document service, however, users are supposed to print out the certificates using ordinary papers and printers, so there should be a mechanism showing that the documents printed through user's printer is authentic and authorized. To realize authorization process, the printed certificates should have organizations' stamp on it.

Third, to implement online document service including issuing certificates the contents of documents issued should be prevented from being forged or altered. This requirement is the most serious and important issue that government officers are concerned with. Officers are worried about possible alteration or forgery by malicious users. Thus, because digital data is very easy to manipulate and modify using graphic tools and scanners, the on-line document service system should meet the requirement of preventing possible forgery and alteration.

Lastly, various types of personal information are transmitted between government organizations and users, and information included in the printed documents might be stored in computers and printers. For the reason, it is necessary to prevent illegal users from accessing the information at each stage of transmission and printing.

Printer spool control and access control of temporary files generated in the process of printing are examples of such functions.

3 Technologies of Online Document Printing

This section discusses technologies newly developed and included to implement on-line document printing described in Section 2. The first requirement, namely, the minimization of the change of existing information systems, including database, information processing programs, and networks systems, can be met easily by using modularized programming in system implementation. However, to meet the other three requirements new technologies should be developed and old technologies should be modified for adoption. Essentially, DRM (digital rights management) technology is employed for secure delivery of the document to the right person. In addition, many technologies are employed and combined in the implementation: high density 2D barcode technology that can store original documents in order to prevent the forgery and alteration of official documents, PKI (Public Key Infrastructure) authentication mechanism to confirm issuing organizations, electronic signature technology that can determine the forgery and alteration of original documents, and watermarking technology to protect official seals of issuing organizations. The other technologies in on-line document service include technologies of preventing screen capture and of printer control to prevent cracking in the transmission of original documents from servers to clients.

3.1 High-Density 2D Barcode

If users can print out official documents issued online, they do not need to visit public offices. However, there is high possibility of forgery and alteration in on-line printing. If there is no way to determine if official documents printed out at home or offices are forged or altered, there can be many frauds and goodwill victims. This problem may be solved if there is information on original copies for documents printed out offline and the users cannot create the information. Thus there should be a method of recording contents of the original document on an off-line printed document, and 2D barcode is a suitable solution for this.

Barcode has already been widely used in the area of products distribution, and it is evolving into 2D barcode in order to store a larger quantity of information. There are 4 international standards of 2D barcode [3].

Because the international standards of 2D-barcodes were developed for easy decoding and widespread use, they have very low recording density so that any device can easily decode barcode contents and read it. The barcode systems cannot be directly used in on-line issuing government, because of the large data size of the document, frequently up to 4KB or more. For the reason of low density, there is a need to develop high-density 2D Barcode system in which maximum recording density should be more or less 200Byte/cm^2. To achieve the goal, a new 2D barcode system should be designed in consideration of basic layout for data recording and control code for correcting distortion caused by scanning.

In this research a new algorithm of high-density 2D barcode system was developed. Design principles are as follows. The 2D barcode, which is named Watercode, has a recording density of 436Byte/cm^2, so it can record a 4KB-sized government document into a 10 blocks of barcode scheme. 10% of barcode space is set aside for control code and error correction code. Error correction code is needed when some parts of the barcode are damaged and cannot be easily deciphered. In Watercode system, error correction is possible even when 20% of the barcode is destroyed. Consequently, the net data recording density is 320Byte/cm^2. The new barcode system (Watercode) is composed of multiple basic blocks. Size of one basic block is 1 cm^2. Figure 1 shows a basic block of 2D barcode.

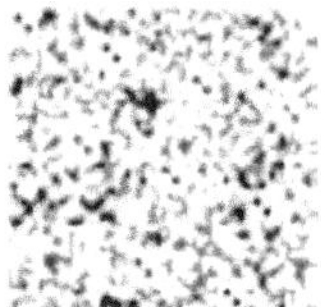

Fig. 1. Developed high-density 2D barcode

2D barcode includes contents of the document, PKI certificates of the organization that issued the documents, and digital signature for proving the integrity of the contents.

3.2 Digital Signature Embedded into 2-D Barcode

Digital signature is a message digest to authenticate identity of institution or the person who created documents or messages, as well as the integrity of the contents. Digital signature usually employs a method of public key mechanism. Instead of encrypting whole document of a message, the message is digested using hash algorithms. The hash value of message digest is encrypted using private key of signing institution or person that created the message. The reason of encryption using private keys is to prove that the signature belongs to the corresponding institution or person that created the message, with the assumption that only the corresponding institution or person possesses the private key. In other words, the third parties cannot create the same signature that will be decrypted by public keys of the message creators. Figure 2 shows the flow diagram of digital signature.

In this research, purpose of employing digital signature is to confirm the identity of document issuing organizations and to verify the integrity of the documents. It can be achieved using part of PKI (public key infrastructure) mechanism in which public keys and private keys are used with digital signature. In PKI, data confidentiality is achieved by using two different keys between encryption and decryption. Even though public key algorithms of cryptography can secure confidentiality of the message between two parties, the number of encryption/decryption keys increases exponentially with increase of users. To solve the problem of key distribution and control, the public key algorithm was suggested in which two different keys are used for encryption and for decryption.

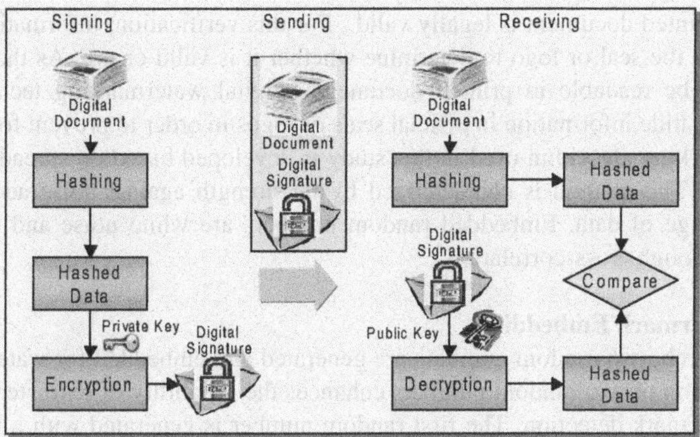

Fig. 2. Flow Diagram of Digital Signature

Of a pair of keys, the signing person or institution keeps private key, while public key is opened to the public. The two-key mechanism can easily verify message sender or used in sending a message to a specific receiver. In order to eliminate the possibility of the forgery of private or public keys, however, there should be reliable third party institutions, which issue private and public keys as well as certificates for the keys. Such institutions are called certification agencies and there are higher certification agencies that certify certification agencies. The highest agency is called root CA[4]. Figure 3 shows the outline of PKI certification.

In this research a part of PKI mechanism is employed to prevent possible forgery and digital alteration. Certificates of message creators are embedded into 2D barcode for later verification. The contents of government documents are encoded by high-density 2D barcode algorithm and encrypted with private key of document issuing organization. Certificate of the issuing organization is also encoded into high-density 2D- barcode.

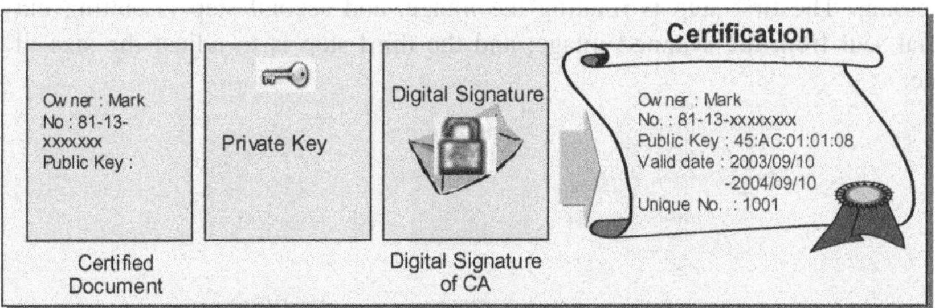

Fig. 3. Outline of PKI Certification

3.3 Digital Watermarking Technology

Traditional official seals or logos representing document-issuing organization can be easily forged. Therefore, it is necessary to verify that the official seal or logo printed in offline-printed document is legally valid. For this verification, information should be hidden in the seal or logo to determine whether it is valid or not. As the information should be readable in printed documents, digital watermarking technology is employed to hide information in official seals or logos in order to prevent forgery.

Watermarking algorithm used in this study is developed based on spread spectrum method [5]. The method is characterized by its strength against noise addition and partial damage of data. Embedded random numbers are white noise and they were extracted through cross-correlation.

3.3.1 Watermark Embedding

In this research, two random numbers are generated and embedded for watermarking. The generation of two random numbers enhances the reliability of extracted information in watermark detection. The first random number is generated with a fixed seed value, and the second random number is generated using an input certificate number as the seed. When the position of the maximum value that is detected in measuring cross-correlation (CC) is identical for the two random numbers, it is considered that watermark has been detected. The reliability of detected information is higher when the random numbers are longer. For example, if the number of digits of the random numbers is 16, the probability that the position of the CC maximum value is identical for the two random numbers is 1/196. Equation 1 below represents the method of embedding watermark and Equation 2 shows error rate.

$$I' = I + \alpha(W_1 + W_2) \tag{1}$$

$$Err = \frac{1}{(random\_number\_length)^2} \tag{2}$$

3.3.2 Watermark Detecting

Watermarking detection in offline-printed document requires three steps of preprocessing. The first step is rotating the image, and second step is cutting out the official seal from the scanned image, and the third step is to adjust the size of the image.

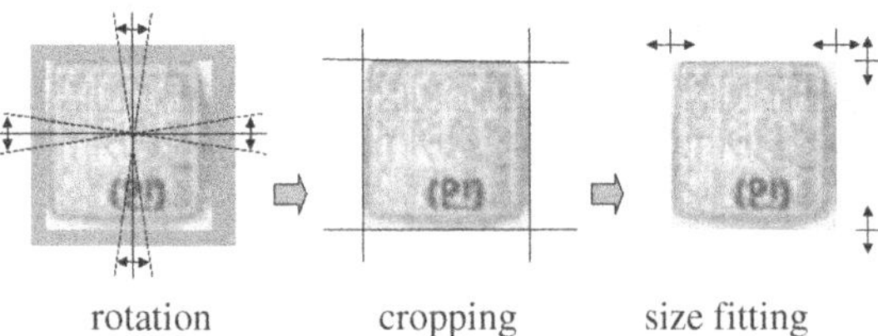

Fig. 4. Preprocessing for Watermark Detection

After preprocessing as in Figure 4, cross-correlation value is calculated and whether the position of the maximum value is identical is determined. If it is identical, watermark is considered to have been detected, and otherwise it is not.

$$
\begin{aligned}
&PosW_1 = Max\_pos(REAL(fft(fft(I') \times fft(W_1)))) \\
&PosW_2 = Max\_pos(REAL(fft(fft(I') \times fft(W_2)))) \\
&\begin{cases} PosW_1 == PosW_2, & Detection \\ \quad otherwise, & Not\ Detection \end{cases}
\end{aligned}
\tag{3}
$$

3.4 Screen Capture Prevention Technology

On-line public service provides commonly its service through web sites which is displayed on screen of users. Document image displayed on the screen of users are vulnerable to various attacks. First of all, document image can easily captured by inherent functions of operating systems. For example, the documents displayed on the screen can be easily captured using ‘Print Screen’ into image editing tools and easily altered using image editing tools. Second, there are so many image capturing tools in web environment such as ‘snap-it’ program. Because web technology relies on TCP/IP protocols for data communications, tools that employ TCP/IP protocols easily capture multimedia contents residing in the web sites. Sometimes, it is possible to capture documents images in cache directory by clicking web objects the users have visited. For the reasons, there is a need to develop technology that can prevent screen capture and protect web contents by controlling video memory calls and mouse popup menus.

In this research, a new technology of screen capture prevention is developed. Web contents are displayed on the user’s screen and it is possible for the user to scroll up and down to read the documents. However, it cannot be copied into video memory for ‘saving into new file’. Thus, the function of ‘screen capture’ provided by Window OS cannot properly make an image copy of the document and other image capture tools are not working properly. Images stored in cache directory are immediately erased as soon as the user terminates web operation.

3.5 Print Control and DRM Technology

One of the important things in offline document printing service is controlling printer for preventing image capturing and forgery. Government documents that are issued free of charge do not require printer control, but paid documents service requires controlling printer. First of all, the number of printing should be controlled. In other words, the number of printing should be limited according to the amount of paid fees, because government documents are a source of public service income and useful asset of the government organization. Second, there should be a mechanism that can prevent creation of temporary files in printer. As the documents to be printed are stored into the ‘printer spool’ in the form of image file at the stage of document printing, it is necessary to prevent creation of temporary files. Thus file management using DRM technology can keep users from generating illegally temporary files.

DRM technology was developed for safe multimedia contents services, but its application is being expanded to security for internal data and security for files existing inside computers. In this research, DRM technology is employed and printer control technology was developed to prevent creation of temporary files. Also, controlling number of printing can be done using this new technology.

4 E-government Service in Korea

In Korea, on-line public service has been successfully provided since 1998. However, people should visit government offices at least 5 times a year to get government issued certificates, because people cannot print certificates at home or their offices, even though applications of government certificates can be done using on-line services. The first off-line printing service of government certificates was initiated by a local government, Gannam-gu, in 2001. Using the service people can request government certificates and print the certificates at home or offices using normal printers. When the request of certificates is sent to government organization through web site operation, for example Gannam-gu government, the certificates are displayed on the screen. When the user pays printing fee to the government organization using home telephone number, mobile telephone number, or credit card number, he/she can print displayed certificates through his/her own printer.

Since 2003 various organizations have introduced off-line printing services. In 2003, the Ministry of Government Administration and Home Affairs began to provide printing service for public information such as residential information, birth certificates, and others. Then, the Supreme Courts began to provide services for real-estate registration transcripts in the early 2004, while the National Tax Service started to provide service for tax payment certificates. Currently, many government organizations are preparing off-line printing service: certificates of construction contracts at the Ministry of Construction and Transportation, certificates of software contracts at the Association of Korea Software Promotion, and etc.

This section introduces technologies employed by the Supreme Court to provide certificate off-line printing services for real-estate registration, which are used by the largest number of people in Korea. The Korean Supreme Court issues on-line certificates of real estate registration transcripts and corporation registration transcripts. To bring registration transcript services to home and offices, the Supreme Court established an online inquiry system and on-line service of registration transcripts that is issued through off-line printing. The off-line printed certificates are legally valid for designated period, because the law of electronic document was past in the Korea Assembly to provide legal validity for on-line issued certificates.

The Supreme Court is currently providing register transcript inquiry service, and the structure is shown in Figure 5. A citizen can access the website that takes inquiry of registration transcripts by entering ID and password. The certificates the citizen wants to see will be displayed on the screen just for viewing. Then, when the citizen requests printing the certificates, the system authenticates the user, takes payment, fetches relevant documents from the register transcript database, displays it on the screen, and sends the documents to users for printing at the user's sites. There are many different ways of paying the service fees that are charged to: home telephone number, mobile telephone number, credit card number, or cash certificates.

The off-line printing at on-line public service goes through the following steps. When a user accesses web site of the public service systems for the first, a client module is automatically installed at the user's computer through active-X. The process of user authentication is done with user ID and password. Payment is done by charging to home telephone number, mobile telephone number, or by cash certificates. When the service system retrieves the document user wants to print from the database, the system generates an electronic signature using HSM (hardware security module) and delivers it to the printing module along with PKI certificate of the Supreme Court. HSM equipment is a hardware module for protection of the private key of the Supreme Court and PKI certificates. Then, 2D barcode is generated with the document, the electronic signature and the PKI certificate. In other words, contents of the document, electronic signature, and PKI certificate are included in the generation of a 2D barcode. The barcode is delivered to the user's computer with the image of original document. In the process of delivery, a secure channel is established in order to prevent cracking. The image of original document and 2D barcode are encrypted. The documents displayed on the screen of users can be viewed but cannot be printed. If the user clicks 'print' button in the displayed document, the user should pay for the printing. When the user completes payment for printing, the system goes through printing processes. Figure 6 shows architecture of the service system.

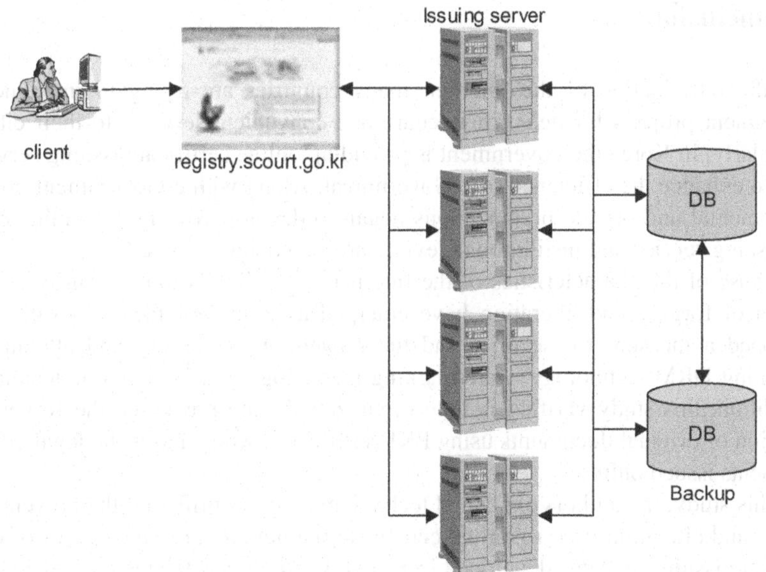

Fig. 5. The Structure of Supreme Court Register Transcript Inquiry Service

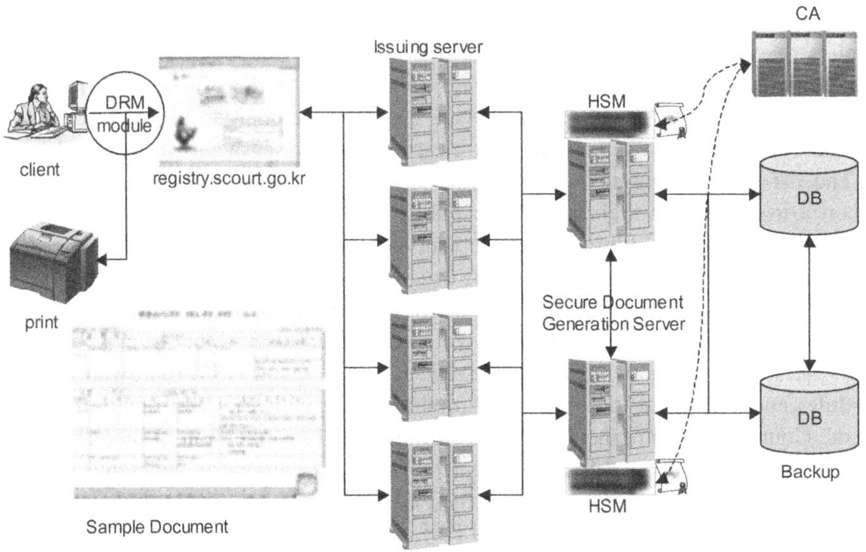

Fig. 6. The Structure of Supreme Court Register Transcript Issuing Service

Through the system, citizens can get issued certificates in any place without visiting public offices.

5 Conclusions

With the introduction of the Internet, many countries are trying to implement e-Government projects for delivering secure and convenient services to their citizens. Particularly, in Korea the government is providing online certificate issuing service in order to enhance the efficiency of e-Government. Along with e-Government projects, governmental and private organizations began to develop systems for online certificate issuing service and institutional devices are also being prepared.

Because of the characteristics of the Internet and online issuing, security and prevention of forgery and alteration have emerged as important factors, so this study developed a measure for security and the prevention of forgery and alteration by integrating DRM technology, watermarking technology and 2D barcode technology. In addition, this study verified issuing organizations and prevented the forgery and alteration of original documents using PKI certificates, which bases the legal effect of documents issued online.

In this study, the authors explained technologies for security and the prevention of forgery and alteration used in online certificate issuing and presented cases of online certificate issuing systems developed in Korea. Until all certificates are issued online and digital document systems are established, the necessity of certificates issued in paper will continue. Accordingly, technologies for security and the prevention of forgery and alteration in printing online certificates as paper documents are still highly useful.

If technologies such as the recognition of 2D barcode using a camera are developed to provide services fit for ubiquitous environment, they will greatly improve the quality of e-Government's services for citizens.

Acknowledgement. Solideo Gloria. This work was supported by National Research Laboratory project(2000N-NL-01-C-286) of Ministry of Science and Technology in Korea

References

1. KyungSup Kim, "Analysis of Structure Elements to Implement Successful e-Government", Information & Communication Policy Issue (15:1), 2003, pp.1-51.
2.
3.
4. Shimshon Berkovits, Santosh Chokhani, Judith A. Furlong, Jisoo A. Geiter, and Jonathan C. Guild. "Public Key Infrastructure Study: Final Report", Produced by the MITRE Corporation for NIST, April 1994.
5. I. J. Cox, J. Kilian, T. Leighton, and T. Shamoon, "Secure spread spectrum watermarking for multimedia" NEC res. Insti., Princeton, NJ, Tech. Rep., (95-10), 1995.

AutoDBT: A Framework for Automatic Testing of Web Database Applications

Lihua Ran, Curtis E. Dyreson, and Anneliese Andrews

School of Electrical Engineering and Computer Science
Washington State University, USA
lran,cdyreson,aandrews@eecs.wsu.edu

Abstract. The complex functionalities and high demands of software quality make manual testing of a web application ineffective. Automatic software testing methods can help to determine if a web application is working correctly, but existing methods are unable to test whether such an application interacts correctly with a back-end database. This paper elaborates an approach, called the Automatic Database Tester (AutoDBT), that extends the functional or black-box testing of a web database application to include database updates. AutoDBT takes as input a model of the application and a set of test criteria. The model consists of a state transition diagram showing how a user navigates among pages in the application, and a data specification which captures how data flows in the application and how the database is updated. AutoDBT uses the model along with the test criteria to generate test cases for functional testing of the application.

1 Introduction

Web applications are increasing in importance as consumers use the web for a wide range of daily activities such as online shopping and banking. Though web applications differ widely in their functionality and in the technologies used in their implementation, at heart, these applications share a common architecture in which a web application interfaces with users through a set of (HTML) forms. The forms collect input data that is processed by the application. Typically, a web application is supported by a back-end *application database* (AD), which is updated in response to user actions.

Testing is critically important in ensuring that a web application has been implemented correctly. Several methods have been developed for testing web applications (see Sect. 5), but current testing methods do not adequately incorporate testing of the application database. Surprisingly, relatively little attention has been given to developing systematic techniques for assuring the correctness of the interactions between a database management system (DBMS) and an application program. Given the critical role that web applications play in e-commerce, there is a need for new approaches to assess their quality.

This paper presents a framework for the functional or black-box testing of web database applications called AutoDBT. Functional testing evaluates the correctness of an application by judging whether the application passes or fails selected test cases. Previously, we developed an approach to perform functional testing of web applications [1]. In this paper, we extend our previous work to include the interaction of the application with a database. Additional problems that emerge from this interaction are listed below.

X. Zhou et al. (Eds.): WISE 2004, LNCS 3306, pp. 181–192, 2004.
© Springer-Verlag Berlin Heidelberg 2004

Evolving database state: An in-memory application can start a test from a known, clean state by restarting the application for each test. But when a database is involved, the state of the database might be different at the start of each test since database modifications accumulate over time as individual tests update the database. AutoDBT automatically generates a *guard* query for each test case. The guard determines whether the test can be performed given the current state of the database.

Modeling of database updates: As the application executes, it will update the database. AutoDBT allows a software tester to specify, at a high-level, the database updates associated with page transitions.

Correctly choosing test data: Each test case is self-contained in the sense that it contains all of the test data that is input to the set of forms during evaluation of the test. A test of an in-memory application can manufacture the test data as needed since the application does not store data between tests. But when testing a web database application, the test data must be carefully selected. Some tests are based on data that must be present in a database (e.g., a test to modify an existing car reservation needs that reservation to be in the database prior to the test) while other tests require that the same data be absent (e.g., a test to create a car reservation demands that the reservation be new to the database). AutoDBT distinguishes between data that should be drawn from the application database, and data that is not present in the application database, and should instead be chosen from a database of synthesized test data, called the *synthetic database* (SD).

The next section introduces an example that is used to illustrate the AutoDBT framework. An overview of the framework is given in Sect. 3. The section also describes how to model the page navigation, how to specify the input data in each transition, and how the database is updated. Section 4 outlines the test sequence generator. The generator is used to generate test cases for testing of the application. Section 5 compares our contribution to related work, both in the area of database technology and in the area of testing of web applications. Finally, the paper concludes and presents a few ideas for future work.

2 An Example Web Application

This section presents a fragment of a web application that will be used to illustrate the ideas in this paper. The example application is an online car rental system (OCRS). On the main page shown in Fig. 1(a), there are buttons to enable a customer to make a new reservation, to view a current reservation, and to modify or cancel an existing reservation. For instance, consider the third button, "Modify Reservation." When this button is activated, the customer is led to a new page as shown in Fig. 1(b). After entering the required data and activating the "Continue" button, the desired car reservation is shown the page corresponding to Fig. 1(c). This page allows the car reservation data to be updated. After activating the "Confirmation" button, the updated reservation information is displayed in Fig. 1(d). The modification process can be terminated at any point by activating the "Cancel" or "Back to Main Page" button, which transfers the customer to the main page (Fig. 1(a)).

One common feature of web database applications such as OCRS is the frequent interaction between customers and an application database. An important component

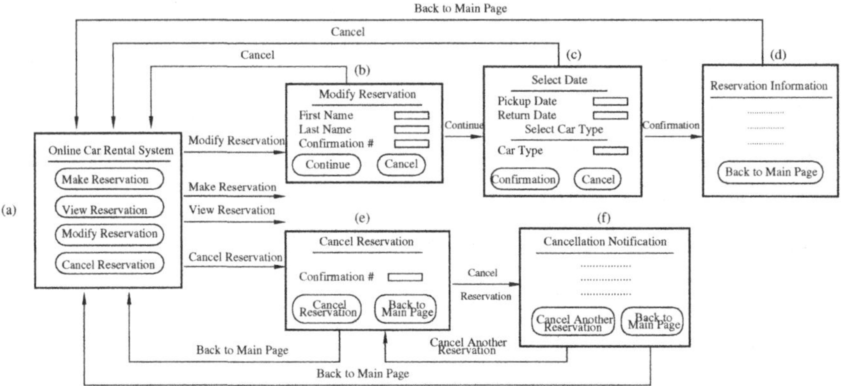

Fig. 1. The online car rental system (OCRS)

to testing this type of application is verifying whether the database has been correctly updated in response to the customers' inputs. For instance, in the previous example, a customer provides required information through the GUI in Fig. 1(b) and changes some data in Fig. 1(c). After clicking the "Confirmation" button, the database should be updated. Therefore, the application needs to be thoroughly tested to determine whether the database has been successfully updated.

3 The AutoDBT Framework

This section describes the AutoDBT framework for testing a web database application. We present an overview of the architecture first. Then, each component in the architecture is described.

3.1 Overview

AutoDBT is a framework for testing web database applications. The framework is depicted in Fig. 2(a). AutoDBT has three main steps. The first step is to specify the expected behavior of the application. We have found that finite state machines (FSM) are a suitable tool for modeling this behavior [1]. In this step, a modeler develops an FSM specification for the web application. As shown inside the top-most component of Fig. 2(a), the FSM consists of two parts: a *state transition diagram* and a *data specification*. The state transition diagram is a directed graph that models the user navigation between forms in the interface (see Fig. 2(b)). The data specification articulates input constraints and database updates associated with each transition in the state transition diagram. In the second step the Test Sequence Generator automatically generates a set of *test sequences*. A test sequence traces a path in the FSM. The *test coverage criteria* dictate the range of test sequences that are generated. Meanwhile, a Dynamic Data Specification Generator automatically generates a *dynamic data specification* based on the data specification given in the first step. The dynamic data specification captures how the application database is updated during evaluation of a test. The third step performs the testing process which takes as input the dynamic data specification, the generated test sequences, data sources and test data selection criteria, and generates a report about the test result. The testing process is described in detail in Sect. 4. The rest of this section illustrates the framework in detail using the OCRS example.

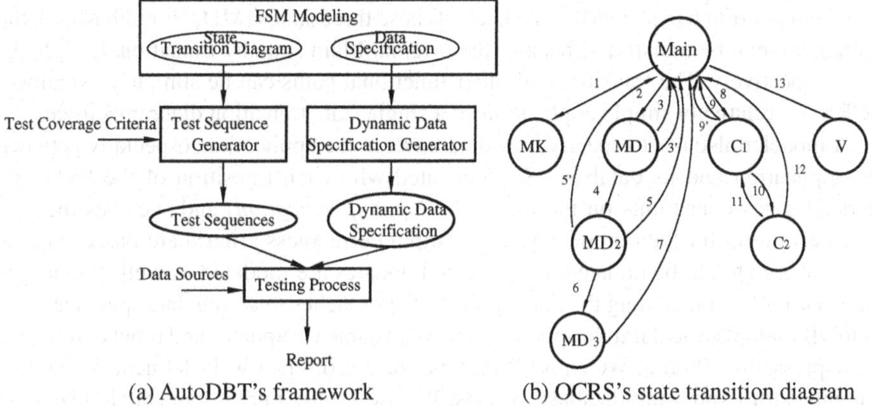

(a) AutoDBT's framework (b) OCRS's state transition diagram

Fig. 2. Modeling of a web application

3.2 FSM Modeling

Finite state machines (FSM) provide a convenient way to model software behavior in a way that avoids issues associated with the implementation. Several methods for deriving tests from FSMs have also been proposed [5,6,14]. Theoretically, (in-memory) web applications can be completely modeled with FSMs, however, even simple web pages can suffer from the state space explosion problem. There can be a large variety of possible inputs to text fields, a large number of options on some web pages, and choices as to the order in which information can be entered. Factors such as these mean that a finite state machine can become prohibitively large, even for a single page. Thus, an FSM-based testing method can only be used if techniques are found to generate FSMs that are descriptive enough to yield effective tests yet small enough to be practically useful.

The technique in [1], FSMWeb, addresses the state explosion problem with a hierarchical collection of aggregated FSMs. The bottom level FSMs are formed from web pages and parts of web pages called logical web pages, and the top level FSM represents the entire web application. Application level tests are formed by combining test sequences from lower-level FSMs.

AutoDBT extends FSMWeb to include testing of the application database. The first step of using AutoDBT is to model the page navigation with an FSM. Part of the FSM is a state transition diagram that captures the expected behavior of a given web application at an abstract level. We assume that the modeler who builds the FSM has a thorough knowledge about the requirements and behavior of the application.

The modeler specifies a state transition diagram. The diagram is a directed graph in which each node represents a (logical) web page and each edge represents a possible page transition (button or hyperlink). For the OCRS example, the diagram is given in Fig. 2(b). In this paper we focus only on the Modify Reservation and Cancel Reservation paths, so in Fig. 2(b), only those paths are drawn in detail. According to this diagram, the web application begins in the Main state. There are four paths that emanate from the Main state. Through transition 2, the application is transferred first to state (MD_1) of the Modify Reservation path, then through transition 4 to state MD_2, and finally through transition 6 to state MD_3. At each of these three states (MD_1 through MD_3), the application can be transferred back to the original Main state by transition 3, 3', 5, 5', or 7, respectively. The transitions of other functional paths can be similarly explained. OCRS is a relatively simple application so a single state transition diagram suffices.

A modeler also has to specify how data flows in the application, especially between the application and its database. So associated with each transition of the FSM, the modeler gives constraints on the input (the *input specification*) and sketches the correctness criteria for the output. Since the output correctness criteria are based on how the database should be updated, the expected updates are modeled as well (the *update specification*). From among the many potential approaches to giving data specifications, AutoDBT adopts a declarative approach, in which database updates and input constraints are expressed in *Prolog*. We chose Prolog because it offers a well-defined, declarative semantics for expressing database queries. We use Prolog rather than Datalog because we generally need to evaluate our queries using a top-down, tuple-at-a-time evaluation technique, i.e., using Prolog's evaluation model. In the rest of this section, we illustrate how the input and output are specified in Prolog through the OCRS example.

Web applications have many different kinds of input widgets, such as drop down menus. For simplicity, this paper focuses only on text boxes and buttons. The input specification consists of two related parts. The first part is to specify the source of the test data. For a web database application, the input data can be drawn from two sources: the application database (AD) and the synthetic database (SD). The SD contains data that is not in the AD. For instance, in a test of the page in Fig. 1(b), the customer's last name, first name and confirmation number should be drawn from the AD since the data should already exist in the application database. However, in a test of Fig. 1(c) some "new" data, which is not resident in the AD, is needed when the customer changes an existing reservation. The new data is chosen from the SD.

The second part of the input specification captures the data flow on transitions in the FSM.

Definition 1 (Input data flow specification). *The input data flow specification for transition i is either a button name or a Prolog rule of the following form followed by a button name:*

$$\text{input}_i(I_1, \ldots, I_n) \text{ :- } \text{Predicate}_1, \ldots, \text{Predicate}_m.$$

where

- input_i *is a predicate with a list of variables* $(I_1, \ldots, I_n)$ *denoting all of the required input parameters; and*

– $\text{Predicate}_1, \ldots, \text{Predicate}_m$ *is a list of predicates of the following form:*

$$\text{Database\_Relation}(A_1, \ldots, A_k) \textit{ or } \text{input}_j(J_1, \ldots, J_k).$$

where Database ∈ {*AD, SD*} *and* Relation ∈ $\{R_1, ..., R_n\}$*;* $A_i \in$ {*constant, variable,* '_'}*(*$1 \leq i \leq k$*), where constant* ∈ *domain of the* i^{th} *column; and the rule is safe which means all variables in the head appear in some predicate in the body.* ∎

Table 1. Input data flow specification for the Modify Reservation and Cancel Reservation paths

Transition	Input Data Flow Specification
2	Button(Modify Reservation).
3	$input_3$*(Fn, Ln, C#)* :- AD_Customer(*Fn, Ln, Cid*), AD_Reserves (*Cid, C#*). Button(Cancel).
3'	$input_{3'}$*(Fn, Ln, C#)* :- SD_Customer(*Fn, Ln, Cid*), SD_Reserves (*Cid, C#*). Button(Cancel).
4	$input_4$*(Fn, Ln, C#)* :- AD_Customer(*Fn, Ln, Cid*), AD_Reserves(*Cid, C#*). Button(Continue).
5	$input_5$*(Pd, Rd, Ct)* :- AD_Reservation(_, *Pd, Rd, Ct*). Button(Cancel).
5'	$input_{5'}$*(Pd, Rd, Ct)* :- SD_Reservation(_, *Pd, Rd, Ct*). Button(Cancel).
6	$input_6$*(Pd, Rd, Ct)* :- SD_Reservation(_, *Pd, Rd, Ct*). Button(Confirmation).
7	Button(Back to Main Page).
8	Button(Cancel Reservation).
9	$input_9$*(C#)* :- AD_Reservation(*C#*, _, _, _). Button(Back to Main Page).
9'	$input_{9'}$*(C#)* :- SD_Reservation(*C#*, _, _, _). Button(Back to Main Page).
10	$input_{10}$*(C#)* :- AD_Reservation(*C#*, _, _, _). Button(Back to Main Page).
11	Button(Cancel Another Reservation).
12	Button(Back to Main Page).

To help explain the input data flow specification, consider the OCRS example. Table 1 shows the specification for transitions of the Modify Reservation path and the Cancel Reservation path in Fig. 2(b). According to the specification, on transition 2, a "Modify Reservation" button is required. On transition 4, the customer's first and last names, and the confirmation number of an existing reservation are required before a "Continue" button is activated. The FSM modeler uses *Fn, Ln, C#* to denote the required input. The *Fn* and *Ln* are chosen from the Customer relation while *C#* comes from the Reserves relation of the AD. The meaning of the input data flow specification for the other transitions can be similarly explained.

Before the testing process commences, the AD and SD need to be populated. Initially the SD is empty, while the AD might already contain some data (if the web application has been running prior to testing). Since the testing process will change values in the AD, the AD should be copied prior to testing and the copy used for testing. The SD will need to be populated with *synthetic data*, that is data generated strictly for testing purposes. Gray et al. present several techniques to populate a database with synthetic data [7]. In particular they show how to quickly generate, in parallel, a large database that obeys certain statistical properties among the records generated. Using their techniques we can populate the SD (and the AD if needed) with synthetic data.

In addition to the input specification, the modeler also needs to specify how the database should be updated. This specification is used to evaluate whether the application correctly updates the AD. There are three kinds of updates: insertion, deletion, and modification. We treat a modification as a deletion followed by an insertion. To model deletions from AD_*Relation*, we add a relation, delete_AD_*Relation*, that is used to store tuples that should be deleted. For insertions, we introduce insert_AD_*Relation* which buffers tuples that should be inserted. The schema of each relation is the same as that of AD_*Relation*.

In the update specification, the modeler gives a specification of what should be deleted or inserted during an update.

Definition 2 (Update specification). *The update specification is one or more Prolog rules of the following two forms.*

1) delete_AD_*Relation($A_1, \ldots, A_n$) :-* Predicate$_1$, ..., Predicate$_m$.
2) insert_AD_*Relation($A_1, \ldots, A_n$) :-* Predicate$_1, \ldots,$ Predicate$_m$.

The form of each Predicate$_i$ *is given in Definition 1.* ∎

Table 2. The update specification for the Modify and Cancel Reservation paths

Trans.	**Update Specification**
6	delete_AD_Reservation(*C#, Pd, Rd, Ct*) :- *input*$_4$(_, _, *C#*), AD_Reservation(*C#, Pd, Rd, Ct*). insert_AD_Reservation(*C#, Pd, Rd, Ct*) :- *input*$_4$(_, _, *C#*), *input*$_6$(*Pd, Rd, Ct*).
10	delete_AD_Reservation(*C#, Pd, Rd, Ct*) :- *input*$_{10}$(*C#*), AD_Reservation(*C#, Pd, Rd, Ct*). delete_AD_Reserves(*Cid, C#*) :- *input*$_{10}$(*C#*), AD_Reserves(*Cid, C#*).

Table 2 shows the update specification for transitions of the Modify Reservation and Cancel Reservation paths. There is no update associated with most of the transitions so only a few of the transitions have update specifications. Transition 6 modifies the AD while transition 10 involves a deletion. The modification is modeled as a deletion followed by an insertion, so two rules are associated with transition 6. Transition 10 deletes a tuple from the AD_Reservation relation. In order to maintain referential integrity, the corresponding tuple which has the same *C#* in the AD_Reserves relation has to be deleted as well.

Finally, we should note that the modeler has to be careful when developing an update specification to associate updates only with transitions that reflect transaction commit points.

3.3 Test Sequence and Dynamic Data Specification Generator

Based on the state transition diagram, for any given test coverage criteria, we can automatically generate a *test sequence*. A test sequence is a sequence of transitions. It describes which transitions need to be tested and in what order. Common kinds of coverage criteria include testing combinations of transitions (switch cover) [5], testing most likely paths [18], and random walks. For instance, after applying a New York Street Sweeper algorithm [2] to the Modify Reservation path, the following test sequence is generated.

2→3→2→3'→2 →4→5→2→4→5' →2→4→6→7

Finally, a *dynamic data specification* is automatically generated based on the data specification. The dynamic data specification consists of two components: *Data Inheritance Graph* (DIG) and *Dynamic Input Specification* (DIS). The DIG captures the data dependencies between transitions, while the DIS specifies both how new versions of the database are created in response to user inputs and database update and the data inheritance based on the DIG.

3.4 Summary

The first step to using AutoDBT is to construct a model of the web application to be tested. The model consists of an FSM and a data specification. The data specification is a high-level description of the data flow in the application. AutoDBT automatically generates a dynamic data specification, which is a low-level, precise description of the data flow. The second step to using AutoDBT is to decide on test coverage criteria. The criteria are input to the Test Sequence Generator to generate a list of test sequences. Each test sequence is a list of FSM transitions. The next step is to generate and run individual test cases as described in detail in the next section.

4 The Testing Process

Figure 3 diagrams the testing process. The testing process starts with a *test sequence scheduler*. The scheduler schedules all of the test sequences, forming a queue of test sequences. Next, a test sequence is chosen from the queue and a *guard* is generated. The guard checks whether a test sequence can generate a *test case* given the current AD and SD states. A test case is an instantiation of the input parameters for an entire test sequence. If the guard fails, then the current AD and SD states can't build a test case for the entire test sequence, and the test sequence is placed at the end of the queue. Possibly, a future database state will be conducive to generating the test case. If the guard succeeds the test case is generated, as well as a *test oracle* to determine whether the test succeeds or fails. The test case is subsequently evaluated on the web application. During evaluation of the test case, the oracle is consulted after each transaction. If the oracle fails then the database was updated incorrectly, and the testing process aborts with a failure message. Finally, some test sequences involve more than one test case, so if more tests are needed for this particular test sequence, then the guard will be re-evaluated to generate more test cases. The process completes when the queue of test sequences becomes empty or the guard fails for every test sequence in the queue. Due to space limitations we discuss only guard generation and evaluation in detail in this section.

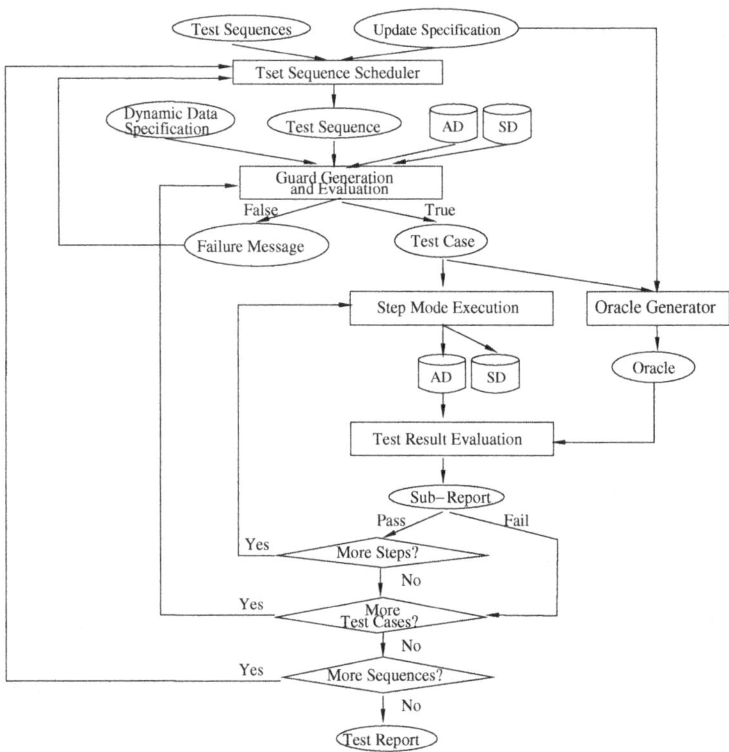

Fig. 3. Framework of the testing process

A guard is a query to determine whether a test sequence can be instantiated to produce a test case. A guard is automatically constructed for a test sequence by concatenating the head of each DIS rule corresponding to a transition in the sequence. In the following, we explain how to form a guard through an example.

Consider the test sequence generated for Modify Reservation path in Sect. 3.3. Ignoring the button inputs, the guard for this given test sequence is given below.

$$
\begin{aligned}
&?\text{-}\ input_3(Fn_1, Ln_1, C\#_1, AD_{in}, AD_1),\ input_{3'}(Fn_2, Ln_2, C\#_2, SD_{in}, SD_1),\\
&\quad input_4(Fn_3, Ln_3, C\#_3, AD_1, AD_2),\ input_5(Pd_1, Rd_1, Ct_1, AD_2, AD_3),\\
&\quad input_4(Fn_4, Ln_4, C\#_4, AD_3, AD_4),\ input_{5'}(Pd_2, Rd_2, Ct_2, SD_1, SD_2),\\
&\quad input_4(Fn_5, Ln_5, C\#_5, AD_4, AD_5),\ input_6(Pd_3, Rd_3, Ct_3, C\#_5, AD_5, AD_6, SD_2, SD_3).
\end{aligned}
$$

The following two points are important in generating the guard.

1. Variable Renaming - Variables should be renamed to be unique in the guard, even though they are the same in the DIS. The exception is variables that are inherited from a previous transition (the inheritance is part of the FSM modeling). If a later transition inherits a variable from an earlier transition then the same variable is used. For example, $C\#_5$ is passed into transition 6 from transition 4.
2. Database versions - The database is (potentially) modified in each transition, so the output version of a database in one transition, e.g., AD_2, is passed as input into the next transition.

To generate a test case, the guard is evaluated. In a successful evaluation, values will be bound to the variables. The binding produces a test case. An unsuccessful evaluation implies that the initial AD/SD is not in a good state, so the test sequence is put back to the queue.

5 Related Work

Much of the literature on testing web applications is in the commercial sector and tests non-functional aspects of the software. An extensive listing of existing web test support tools is on a web site maintained by Hower [8]. The list includes link checking tools, HTML validators, capture/playback tools, security test tools, and load and performance stress tools. These are all static validation and measurement tools, none of which support functional testing or black box testing.

Several papers have looked at in-memory testing of web applications. Kung, Liu, and Hsia [10,11] developed a test generation method based on multiple models of the applications under test. Their research assumes that the source code for the application is available, whereas our research does not. Lee and Offutt [12] describe a system that generates test cases using a form of mutation analysis. It focuses on validating the reliability of data interactions among web-based software components. Their approach tests web software component interactions, whereas our research is focused on the web application level. Ricca and Tonella [15] proposed a UML model of web application for high level abstraction. The model is based entirely on static HTML links and does not incorporate any dynamic aspects of the software. Yang et al. [19,20] present an architecture for test tools that is directed towards testing web applications. The architecture consists of five subsystems including test development, test measurement, test execution, test failure analysis and test management. The FSM modeling-based tool proposed in [1] satisfies the test development and test measurement portion of Yang et al.'s test architecture. Jia and Liu [9] proposed an approach for formally describing tests for web applications using XML and developed a prototype tool, called WebTest. Their XML approach could be combined with the test criteria proposed in [13] by expressing the tests in XML. Benedikt, Freire and Godefroid [3] presented VeriWeb, a dynamic navigation testing tool for web applications. VeriWeb explores sequences of links in web applications by nondeterministically exploring action sequences, starting from a given URL.

None of the above papers deal with testing of an application database. Database testing research has focused primarily on techniques to automatically populate a database with synthetic data for testing purposes [4,7]. These approaches are complementary to our research in modeling and testing the interaction of a web application with a database. Database benchmarks like TPC are popular for assessing the performance of DBMSs [17,16]. However, DBMS benchmarks aren't useful for functional testing of database applications, though they could play a role in the future if we extend AutoDBT to performance testing.

6 Conclusions and Future Work

There is a need for strategies to automate testing of web database applications since relying on manual testing is ineffective for many such applications. AutoDBT extends the functional testing of a web application to include database updates. To use AutoDBT, a modeler develops a model of the application. The model consists of a state transition diagram that shows how users navigate from page to page in the application, and a Data Specification that describes how data is input and the database is updated. Once the model is complete, a tester decides on test coverage criteria. AutoDBT uses the model and the coverage criteria to generate test cases. Each test case is a self-contained test of the web application. AutoDBT selects test case data from either the application database or the synthesized database as needed. AutoDBT also generates a guard for each test. The guard checks whether the current state of the database is conducive to running the test case, since previous tests may have modified the database to an extent that renders the test invalid.

The main contributions of this paper are a design of AutoDBT and the identification of testing as an important, open issue for web database applications. Much remains to be done. We plan to complete the implementation of AutoDBT. We have yet to build tools for many of the components in the framework. We designed AutoDBT for functional testing, but we'd like to investigate other kinds of testing of web database applications, such as performance testing. Finally, we'd like to improve the guards. A guard checks whether a test case can be attempted, but it would be better if the guard populated the database with the data that is needed to perform the test.

References

1. A. A. Andrews, J. Offutt, R. T. Alexander. Testing Web Applications By Modeling with FSMs. Accepted by *Software and System Modeling*, Springer-Verlag.
2. L. Bodin, A. Tucker. Model for Municipal Street Sweeping Operations. In *Modules in Applied Mathematics Vol. 3: Discrete and System Models*, pp. 76-111, 1983.
3. M. Benedikt, J. Freire, P. Godefroid. VeriWeb: Automatically Testing Dynamic Web Sites. In *Proceedings International WWW Conference(11)*, pp. 654-668, Honolulu, Hawaii, USA. 2002.
4. D. Chays, S. Dan, P. G. Frankl, F. I. Vokolos, E. J. Weyuker. A Framework for Testing Database Applications. In *Proc. of the International Symposium on Software Testing and Analysis*, pp. 147-157, 2000.
5. T. S. Chow. Testing Software Design Modeled by Finite-State Machines. In *IEEE Transactions on Software Engineering*, SE-4(3), pp. 178-187, May 1978.

6. S. Fujiwara, G. Bochmann, F. Khendek, M. Amalou, and A. Ghedasmi. Test selection based on finite state models. *IEEE Transactions on Software Engineering*, 17(6), pp. 591-603, June 1991.
7. J. Gray, P. Sundaresan, S. Englert, K. Baclawski, P.J. Weinberger. Quickly Generating Billion Record Synthetic Databases. In *Proc. ACM SIGMOD*, pp. 243-252, 1994.
8. R. Hower. Web site test tools and site management tools. Software QA and Testing Resource Center, 2002. `www.softwareqatest.com/qatweb1.html` (accessed November 2003).
9. X. Jia, H. Liu. Rigorous and Automatic Testing of Web Application. In *Proceedings of the 6th IASTED International Conference on Software Engineering and Applications (SEA 2002)*, Cambridge, MA, USA. pp. 280-285, November 2002
10. D. Kung, C. H. Liu, and P. Hsia. A model-based approach for testing Web applications. In *Proc. of Twelfth International Conference on Software Engineering and Knowledge Engineering*, Chicago, IL, July 2000.
11. D. Kung, C. H. Liu, and P. Hsia. An object-oriented Web test model for testing Web applications. In *Proc. of IEEE 24th Annual International Computer Software and Applications Conference (COMP-SAC2000)*, pp. 537-542, Taipei, Taiwan, October 2000.
12. S. C. Lee and J. Offutt. Generating test cases for XML-based Web component interactions using mutation analysis. In *Proceedings of the 12th International Symposium on Software Reliability Engineering*, pp. 200-209, Hong Kong China, November 2001. IEEE Computer Society Press.
13. J. Offutt and A. Abdurazik. Generating tests from UML specifications. In *Proceedings of the Second IEEE International Conference on the Unified Modeling Language (UML99)*, Lecture Notes in Computer Science Volume 1723. pp. 416-429, Fort Collins, CO, October 1999.
14. J. Ofutt, S. Liu, A. Abdurazik, and P. Ammann. Generating test data from state-based specifications. *The Journal of Software Testing, Verification, and Reliability*, 12(1):25-53, March 2003.
15. F. Ricca, P. Tonella. Analysis and Testing of Web Applications. In *23rd International Conference on Software Engineering (ICSE)*, Toronto, Ontario, Canada. pp. 25-34, 2001
16. D. Slutz. Massive stochastic testing of SQL, In *Proceedings of the Twenty-Fourth International Conference on Very-Large Databases*, Morgan Kaufmann, pp. 618-622, 1998
17. Transaction Processing Performance Council. *TPC-Benchmark C*. 1998
18. J. Whittaker, M. Thomason. A Markov Chain Model for Statistical Software Testing. In *IEEE Transactions on Software Engineering, Vol. 20*, pp. 812-824, 1992.
19. J. Yang, J. Huang, F. Wang, and W. Chu. An object-oriented architecture supporting Web application testing. In *First Asian-Pacific Conference on Quality Software (APAQS '99)*, pp. 122-129, Japan, December 1999.
20. J. Yang, J. Huang, F. Wang, and W. Chu. Constructing an object-oriented architecture for Web application testing. *Journal of Information Science and Engineering*, 18(1):59-84, January 2002.

Web-Based Surgical Simulation of Craniofacial CT Data

Sun K. Yoo[1], Jin Ho Jo[2], Sung Rim Kim[3], and Yong Oock Kim[4]

[1] Dept. of Medical Engineering, College of Medicine Yonsei University, Seoul Korea
sunkyoo@ yumc.yonsei.ac.kr
[2] Graduate program in Biomedical Engineering, Human Identification Research Institute, Yonsei University, Seoul Korea, jhjo@yumc.yonsei.ac.kr
[3] Dept. of Internet Info. Seoil College, Seoul, Korea
srkim@seoil.ac.kr
[4] Dept. of Plastic Surgery, College of Medicine Yonsei University, Seoul Korea
sgm625@yumc.yonsei.ac.kr

Abstract. The goal of this study was to represent medical two-dimensional (2-D) sectional images to three-dimensional (3-D) volumes over the Web using VRML (Virtual Reality Modeling Language) and JavaScript. Furthermore, a virtual surgical operation with craniofacial CT data has been suggested. The mandible and Lefort I, II and III of maxilla in the CT volume were segmented and rendered to VRML polygonal surfaces by a marching cube algorithm, as well as a surface specified morphing route which animated the surgical procedures. An embedded user interface tool, with JavaScript routines, enabled the display, adjustment of transparencies and optional animated motion of 3-D models. The developed application has several advantages. First, the user can easily connect to this application on the Web and obtain intuitive information more efficiently. Secondly, the virtual surgical operation is simpler than osteotomy when using cephalometry or rapid prototyping. Finally, the doctor can simulate without restriction of the simulation times.

1 Introduction

The World Wide Web (WWW) facilitates information sharing on the Internet. In particular, the WWW allows a variety of three-dimensional (3-D) visual resources to be commonly retrieved through a standardized Virtual Reality Modeling Language (VRML), independent of the specific computer systems used to access the Internet. The dynamic and interactive visualization capabilities of the VRML have attracted increasing attention with regard to medical education and surgical planning.

Typical computer images used in medical fields include Computerized Tomography (CT) and Magnetic Resonance Imaging (MRI). Both of these methods of diagnoses are taken by computers and stored, transmitted and imaged in the forms of digital data. Consequently, these images have been effectively used for medical diagnosis, education and follow-up evaluation of treatments.

Although some applications have been developed in the visualization of simple anatomical 3-D images [1], few studies have been performed on the simulation of

X. Zhou et al. (Eds.): WISE 2004, LNCS 3306, pp. 193–198, 2004.
© Springer-Verlag Berlin Heidelberg 2004

craniofacial surgery performed frequently in the area of plastic surgery. Therefore, in this paper, VRML-based surgical simulation routine of craniofacial surgery was designed using CT images and embedded Java-script to visualize and manipulate it on the Web.

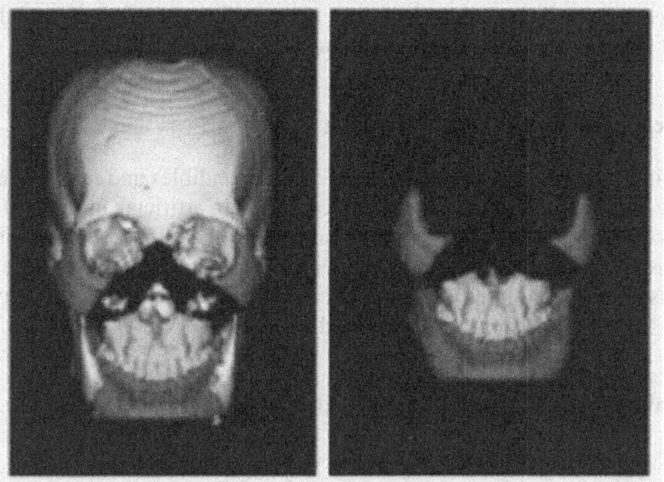

(a) Segmented skull (b) Isolated Mandible, Lefort I, II and III.

Fig. 1. Volume visualization of the skull and isolated sub-structures

2 Method and Materials

2.1 Segmentation and Surface Extraction

The visualized 3-D images of CT were reconstructed by the Volume Render property of the Analyze AVW 5.0 program and segmented to close-up the major focus of the facial cranium structures (Fig. 1-(a).). This segmentation method uses a thresholding method to isolate the cranial structures by setting the threshold level to between 85 and 255. The segmented image of the visualized 3-D facial cranium was then arranged along the Frankfort Horizontal plane (a surface that passes through both the porion & inferior orbital) line [2]. In the arranged image, a total of four major focuses, including the distal mandible from the osteotomy of mandibles and the Lefort I, II and III from the osteotomy of maxillae, were segmented and stored as an object map. Then, using a Marching Cube Algorithm [3], the volumetric parts of organs were transformed into 3-D surface objects consisting of 3-D surface polygons.

2.2 Polygon Reduction

An important limiting factor for Web-based 3-D visualization is the bandwidth of the WWW. The number of polygons dictates both the speed and downloading performance of the VRML browser on the WWW. Sufficient numbers of polygons are important for high quality display of 3D objects on the Web, but adversely affect on the downloading time of the polygonal objects, which can result in cumbersome Web operations. However, the drawback of the Marching Cube Algorithm used for surface extractor was the creation of too many surface polygons [3]. The polygon reduction operation is implemented using an optimization modifier [4-5]. The number of polygons is iteratively reduced until a reasonable tradeoff between the display quality and the number of polygons is obtained.

2.3 Surgical Simulation Using Morphing

The morphing targets of the bone segments of the mandibles and maxilla segments of Lefort I, II and III osteotomies are obtained by their artificial movement along the animated trajectories. The surgical simulation along the simulation path is based on the progressive transformation of segmented objects into others using the morphing function based on spatial interpolation. All of the polygonal objects are converted into an indexed face set consistent with the VRML format.

2.4 Visualization and Manipulation on the Web

The VRML-type file of surface images is viewed using Cosmo player 2.1. VRML, with JavaScript, was chosen to support the 3-D visualization and platform-independent development of the modeled craniofacial surgery on the Web using Microsoft Internet Explorer. Java script routines are embedded in VRML to set the transparency of the craniofacial appearance and control the craniofacial surgery simulation.

When the arrangement of the mandible was made along the morphing route, the exact recognition of the route and location was sometimes difficult due to the overlapping of skin cells or osseous tissues. Therefore, a method for adjusting the transparency was designed for controlling overlapped display of multiple objects. User interface tools, including seven buttons with different colors and eleven slide bars, were embedded into the VRML file for interactive manipulation on the Web. Seven slider bars were organized in the upper right corner to adjust the morphing route for surgery simulation, and control the amount of transparency for the visualization effect. Also, seven buttons were added to remove unnecessary parts whenever needed.

3 Results

Figs. 2 and 3 show the selected morphing sequences along the simulation path for the surgical simulation of the Maxilar movement of the Lefort I, II and III, and the mandible. Additionally, adjustment of the transparency of the skull can be used to change the visualized appearance to effectively control the appearance of opaque object, as shown in Fig. 4. Ten loading tests also showed that the downloading time for the Web display of the VRML file was on average five seconds (Fig. 5), which as a delay can be compromised for the Web-based operation of the surgical simulation.

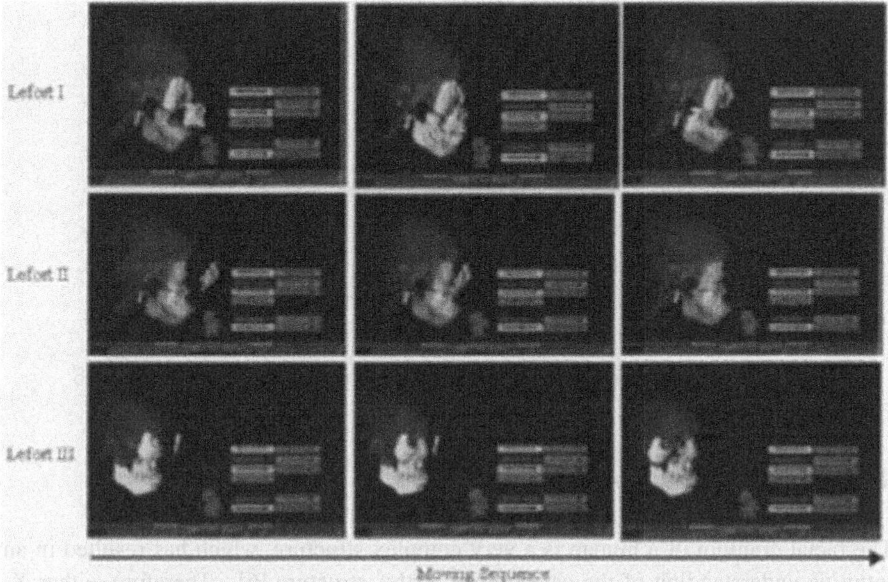

Fig. 2. Simulation Sequence of the Maxilla of the Lefort I, II and III

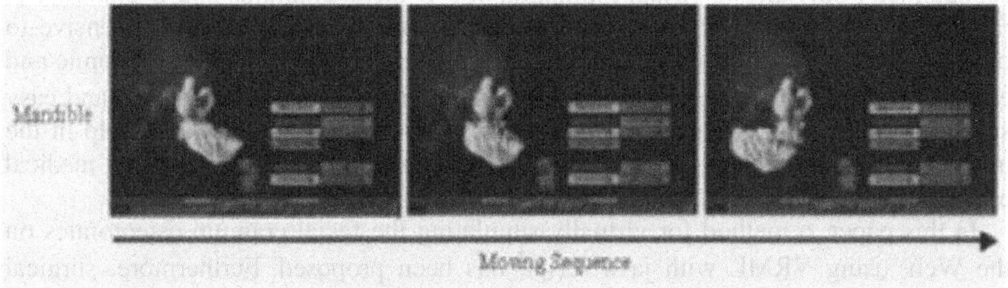

Fig. 3. Simulation Sequence of the Mandible

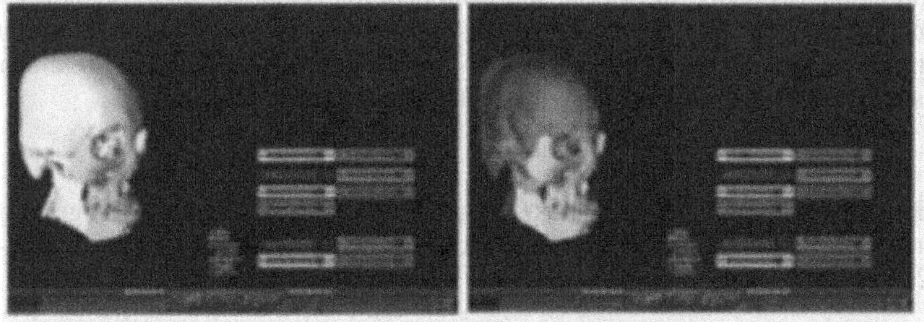

Fig. 4. Transparency Control of the Skull to Adjust the Visual Appearance

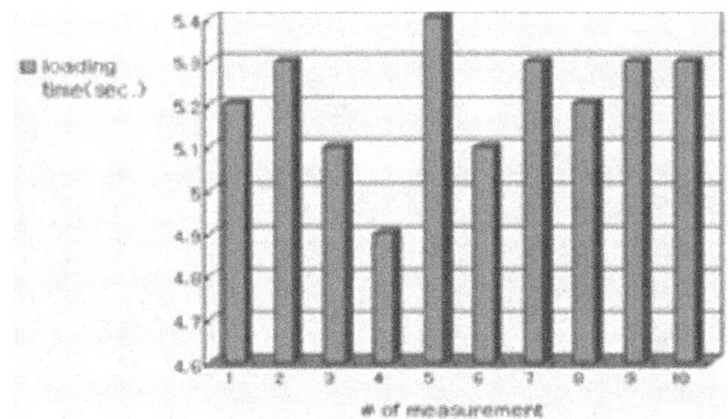

Fig. 5. Measurements of the Loading Time of the Surface Images on the Web

4 Discussion and Conclusion

The facial cranium of a human is a very complex structure, which has resulted in an intuitive understanding of the osteotomies of this structure [6]. Therefore, either X-ray cephalometry or rapid prototyping, based on CT, has been applied for the education and simulation of possible occurrences during osteotomies. However, cephalometry only allows virtual estimation of 3-D facial craniums in 2-D planes. The rapid prototyping model can allow for intuitive comprehension, but is expensive to produce. Therefore, our proposed method is relatively simple, accurate, economic and educational for 3-D surgical simulation of osteotomies. The visual images and easy surgical simulations through a Web-browser with simple graphical tools help in the understanding of medical procedures. It is also suitable for high-quality medical education in addition to the anatomical knowledge relating to the surgery.

In this paper, a method for virtually simulating the facial cranium osteotomies on the Web, using VRML with java script, has been proposed. Furthermore, surgical simulation using craniofacial CT data was designed using morphing combined with polygon reduction. The developed application has several advantages. First, the user can easily connect to this application on the Web and more effectively obtain intuitive information. Secondly, the virtual surgical operation is simpler than osteotomy when using cephalometry or rapid prototyping. Finally, the doctor can simulate without restriction on the simulation times. Our suggestion will be helpful for diagnostic plastic surgery, and in the interest of patients and surgical operations.

Acknowledgement. This work was supported by the Basic Research Program of the Korea Science and Engineering Foundation (KOSEF) under Grant R01-2002-000-00205-0(2002).

References

[1] Brooke N. Steele, Mary T. Draney, Joy P. Ku, Member, IEEE, and Charles A. : Taylor Internet-Based System for Simulation-Based Medical Planning for cardiovascular Disease IEEE Transactions on information Technology in Biomedicine, VOL. 7, NO. 2, JUNE 2003

[2] Kim KW and Lee DJ: A Cephalometric and Computerized Study of the Craniofacial Pattern in Adult with Normal Occlusion; Korean journal of orthodontists; 20(1):87-99, 1990

[3] Lorensen WE, Cline HE, Marching cubes: A high resolution 3D surface construction algorithm; Computer Graphics; 21(4) 163-169, 1987

[4] Yoo SK, Kim NH, Lee KS: Polygon reduction of 3D objects using Strokes' theorem", Computer Methods and Programs in Biomedicine, Vol.71, pp.203-210, 2003.

[5] Yoo SK, Wang G, Rubinstein JT, Skinner MW, Vannier MW : Tree-dimensional modeling and visualization of the cochlea on the internet IEEE Trans Inf Technol Biomed 4(2):144-51, 2000

[6] Jung H, Kim H, Kim D, et. al. : Quantitative Analysis of Three-Dimensional Rendered Imaging of the Human Skull Acquired from Multi -Detector Row Computed Tomography; Journal of Digital Imaging; vol. 15, No4 pp232-239, 2004

Applications of Data Mining in Web Services

Richi Nayak and Cindy Tong

Centre for Information Technology Innovation, School of Information Systems
Queensland University of Technology, GPO Box 2434, Brisbane, QLD 4001, Australia
{r.nayak, c.tong@}qut.edu.au

Abstract. The success of Web services in business relies on the discovery of Web services satisfying the needs of the service requester. In this paper we discuss the use of data mining in the service discovery process. We recommend a set of applications that can leverage problems concerned with the planning, development and maintenance of Web services.

1 Introduction

Web services have recently received much attention in businesses [3, 6, 8, 9]. However, a number of challenges such as lack of experience in predicting the costs; lack of service innovation and monitoring; strategies for marketing Web services and service location are need to be resolved. One possible approach is by learning from the experiences in Web services and from other similar situations. Such a task requires the use of Data mining (DM) to represent generalizations on common situations. Data mining identifies the valid, novel, potentially useful and ultimately understandable patterns and trends in data that are unknown to its keeper [5]. This research examines how some of the issues of Web services can be addressed through DM.

Table 1. Various DM Tasks

Mining Task	**Goal**	**Approaches**
Predictive Modelling (Classification, Value prediction)	To predict future needs based on previous data	Decision tree, Neural networks
Clustering or Segmentation	To partition data into segments	Demographic, Neural networks
Link Analysis (Association, Sequential, Similar time discovery)	To establish association among items	Counting occurrences of items such as Apriori Algorithms
Deviation Analysis	To detect any anomalies, unusual activities	Summarization and Graphical representation

Prior to commencing the mining process, businesses identify and define the goals. Accordingly, data is gathered and collated from multiple sources. Now quality of the data is ensured by removing noise, handling missing information and transforming to an appropriate format. A reduced volume of the data set - representative of the overall

X. Zhou et al. (Eds.): WISE 2004, LNCS 3306, pp. 199–205, 2004.
© Springer-Verlag Berlin Heidelberg 2004

processed data - is derived by applying data reduction techniques. An appropriate DM technique or a combination of techniques is applied to the pre-processed data for the type of knowledge to be discovered (Table 1). The discovered knowledge is then evaluated and interpreted. When the mined results are determined insufficient, an iterative process of performing pre-processing and mining begins until adequate and useful information is obtained. Lastly the information is presented to user to incorporate into the company's business strategies.

2 Data Mining Applications in Web Services

DM applications can be used by management to assist in making strategic decisions; or by human resource in maximising staffing levels while minimising costs; or by technical staff in devising new services or in improving existing services.

2.1 Web Services Cost and Savings Prediction

It is difficult for businesses to gauge the costs and savings of a Web service deployment with having little or even no experience in deployments. However, from the data collected by research firms such as Nemertes [8], businesses can learn from the experiences of similar organizations and get a good approximation of these values.

Value prediction is suitable in this instance to model the investment versus return functions for the prediction of figures for costs and savings. Regression techniques derive the predicted continuous values obtained from functions that best fit the case [4]. For predicting the costs, the input data required consists of, for each deployment, the number of staff member involved, the time it took, and the complexity of the deployment. The complexity of the deployment can be quantified in terms of the lines of code used in the programs, and the annual revenue from the operations that the deployment oversees. The costs of the proposed deployment can be predicted based on these parameters.

Once the costs are known, prospective savings can be predicted. Using inputs such as the cost of the deployment, and the original and new cost of the operation, savings can be determined. Having determined the costs and the savings that can be gained, the return of investment for Web services deployments can be calculated based on these figures. Businesses can then identify the size of Web services deployment that is best suited for them and turn the discovered insights into action.

2.2 Performance Monitoring

Strategic placement of human resource plays a crucial role in the effective monitoring of performance and handling of events. This leads to the need to prioritise tasks. A service being used by many clients at the time when a problem occurs should have a higher priority than a service being used by few clients at the same time. By knowing the usage pattern of services, training programs on groups of services with similar usage patterns can be developed. This allows staff monitoring the services at certain times to have a more in depth knowledge of particular services.

To identify services with similar usage patterns, similar time sequence analysis can be used [11]. The input for such an operation is time-series data recording the number of clients using a particular service at any moment in time. Although such data is not normally collected explicitly, it is implicitly recorded in the web server access logs. The steps in generating this time-series data from web server logs are as follows:

1. Select from the web server log all entries related to the offered Web services by extracting all entires containing the web service's URL in the URL field.
2. Group the entries by Web services and client IP addresses, and then order the entries by time. This gives a set of a client's interaction with a web service.
3. Calculate the time between each interaction to determine separate client sessions with the web service. A client session is one 'use' of the web service. The duration of a client session for different services varies depending on the nature of the service. Setting the threshold of session boundaries thus requires the knowledge about the individual services.
4. For each service, count the number of clients using it at specified time intervals. This can then be used to construct the time- series graph for each service.

Algorithms [4, 11] for approximate subsequence matching in time-series now can be applied to find Web services that have similar usage patterns. These patterns can then be used to help in the design of roster schedules that optimise staffing levels and skill requirements while minimising the number of employees that need to be present.

2.3 Service Innovation

It is important for service providers to establish themselves in the market by offering a range of quality services. The set of queries used by potential clients to find suitable Web services is a rich source for finding clues about what the clients want. If an unusual search term is used with other common search terms in the queries, and that the search terms are all related, then it is a good indication that there is a demand for a new service. The unusual search term may represent a new concept, or a specialisation of a general service currently being offered. As an example, SMS (Short Message Service) sends text messages to mobile phones while a more recent technology MMS (Multimedia Message Service) sends multimedia messages. SMS is a frequently used search term but MMS is not. As the technology becomes more prevalent, demand for MMS Web services will emerge and the appearance of MMS in query data will be evidence of this.

The simplest approach in discovering uncommon search terms is by deviation analysis [4]. Having counted the frequencies of the search terms appearing, simple measures such as median, quartiles and inter-quartile range (IQR) can be calculated. Then using the common heuristic that outliers fall at least 1.5 * IQR above the third quartile or below the first quartile, the unusual search terms can be identified [4]. An alternative measure is the use of support [1] to count the number of times the term appeared in total terms. If a search term has very low support, then it can be classified as an outlier. Given that the demand for different services varies, applying these measures to the raw frequency count will produce biased results towards less popular services, producing many false positives. The solution to this is to group searches into search areas and then find the outliers for each search area. This can be done by:

1. Grouping the queries into search sessions
2. Joining all search sessions that are similar to form search areas
3. Form search term pools for each search area.
4. Within each search term pool, apply statistics to find the uncommon search terms that suggest demands for a new web service.

2.4 Service Recommendation

Web services providers can recommend services to clients based on the services that other similar clients have used in the past with the use of DM. This is because similar clients are likely to have similar service needs. Since service providers have information such as the line of business, size of business and what services their clients use, they can use these as inputs for predictive modelling operations and make recommendations to new clients. Inputs such as the interfaces, functionality and security offered by the service, as well as the cost, and other resources required by the service should also be considered in analysis.

Classification techniques such as decision trees [10] can be used to build rules on service subscriptions. Since the only information service providers have about clients are those for billing purposes, the number of attributes available is small. Consequently, the structure of the resulting decision tree will be relatively simple and easily comprehensible to a human analyst. To further enhance the success rate of recommendations, service providers can find dissociations among the services they offer. Dissociations [13] capture negative relationships between services with rules such as the use of service X and Y implies that it is unlikely service Z will also be used, even though service X and Z are often used. That is, $X \Rightarrow Z$; $X \wedge Y \Rightarrow Z$. By incorporating these dissociations in the recommendation process, more specific recommendations can be made.

2.5 Search Term Suggestion

The location of Web services using existing Web services search engines (keyword based) can be a lengthy endeavour. This method of service discovery suffers from low recall, where results containing synonyms concepts at a higher or lower level of abstraction to describe the same service are not returned. This problem can be approached in two ways, either by returning an expanded set of results to the user with the use of ontology, or by suggesting the user with other relevant search terms based on what other users had used in similar queries [2, 15].

Whilst previous approaches capture the intra-query relationships by clustering queries on a per query basis, they omit the inter-query relationships that exist between queries submitted by a user in one search session. A better option is to group the similar search sessions and provide suggestions of search terms from search sessions that belong to the same cluster.

The first task is to consolidate the data from the user query and web server logs. This is done by matching the query recorded in the query log with the subsequent service descriptions viewed by the user recorded in the web server log. The next task is to form search sessions to arrange a set of queries in sequence by a user to locate a particular service [12]. Search session similarity now can be calculated based on the similarity of the set of search terms used and the set of service descriptions viewed between two search sessions. The Jaccard coefficient [5, 7] can be used to calculate the similarity of the search terms, and service descriptions sets.

Search sessions are assigned to the same cluster if they have many queries and service descriptions that are the same from the entire query and service description pool. The type of clusters desired is therefore globular in nature. Also the algorithm must be resistant to noise and outliers. The agglomerative hierarchical clustering [7] is well suited to generate these types of clusters.

After the clusters are formed, the support [1] for each of the search terms in each cluster is counted and then assigned weights. The weights can be used to predict a user's service need by suggesting search terms from the cluster with the largest weight for the user's search term. Depending on the size and number of search terms that make up the clusters, the suggested terms can either be all search terms within the cluster, or be limited to those from a predefined number of most similar search sessions. A test was conducted for evaluating the effect of the measure combining both keyword and service description similarity (Table 2). The results show that the search sessions clustered using the combined measure is more similar internally and thus the clusters are more compact. This is essential in the suggestion of search terms as users would only be interested in suggestions that are highly similar to those submitted.

Table 2. Similarity based on keywords and service descriptions viewed

Cluster	# of Objects	Avg. Internal Similarity	Std. Dev. of Internal Similarity	Avg. External Dissimilarity	Std. Dev. of External Dissimilarity
0	24	+0.675	+0.103	+0.073	+0.043
1	16	+0.538	+0.098	+0.100	+0.089
2	10	+0.535	+0.099	+0.064	+0.043

3 Data Mining Challenges in Web Services

Data Fusion. With businesses spanning their operations across the entire globe, as well as having multiple servers that provide mirrored services, the Web server access logs from Web servers located at different sites must be consolidated to facilitate DM. There is a need for controlled and reliable data collection to co-ordinate the transfer and storage of the data, while keeping the associated costs down. By compressing the data before sending and scheduling transfers during off-peak hours of the network, the impact of data transfer and the volume to be transported can be greatly reduced.

Analysis results interpretation. To maximise the end user's understanding, the outputs of a DM operation must be easy to comprehend ignoring unnecessary complexities and displaying only the relevant details. For example, in the search term suggestion application, the end users are service requesters trying to locate a particular service.

Instead of graphical clusters showing which queries are similar, the contents of the clusters in simple rules should be shown. In the performance monitoring application, the users would find it useful to see the similar sub-sequences in the time-series represented graphically when determining services with similar usage patterns.

Data reliability. Mining for Web services usage from Web server logs may not produce accurate results. Although in Web services mining, caching is not a problem, the use of firewalls does distort the overall picture of service usage patterns. Implementations of firewalls often involve the masking of internal IP addresses by substituting this with the IP address of the server that connects the network to the Internet. When a Web service client accesses a Web service, the Web server of the Web service provider logs the communication from the service client. If a firewall is used at the client side, then multiple accesses to the same service from different clients within the network may be recorded as one client – that of the server. This in effect masks the service usage in terms of how many clients are using this service. A solution is to modify the Web application services to write log information. This log files will determine session information much better and can be analysed better than simply Web server logs.

Proprietary nature of data. Data is a valuable asset for businesses and so is not normally shared. Therefore, unless there are mutual agreements between the businesses, obtaining the data in sufficient volume may be a problem. If insufficient data is used in the operation, poor data models may be produced. Therefore the quality of the input data is a key factor in determining the quality of the final model. Reputable research companies such as IDC (stencilgroup.com) may provide an answer to this. With the resources to arrange the necessary legal agreements, these research firms can perform DM on data collected from multiple businesses to discover knowledge that cannot be gained from other ways.

Privacy and security. Although DM produces generalisations of data, it does have the problem that some sensitive information can be inferred. This is called the inference problem and arises when users submit queries and deduces sensitive information from the legitimate response they receive [14]. This can be a hindrance when collecting data from many businesses for mining, as well as a problem when mining Web server access logs that record the services used by certain clients. Therefore, even if data can be collected, measures must be in place to ensure that businesses contributing to the DM operations such as the service recommendation application are not disadvantaged.

4 Conclusions and Future Work

In this research, a number of DM applications that that would directly facilitate and improve the use of Web services have been proposed. The DM tasks that find applications in Web services mining include value prediction, similar time sequence analysis, deviation analysis, classification and clustering. These applications range from delivering business value that can be used by management for strategic decision making, to providing technical benefits that target specialist end users.

Several avenues for further improving and extending the work are required. Firstly, further testing should be performed to identify the real value of the applications. Secondly, because some applications such as search term suggestion require real-time responses, techniques for providing results efficiently need to be developed. These may include new algorithms for scheduling the processing of requests and delivery of responses to multiple users so the information is returned at close to real time as possible.

References

1. Agrawal, R., & Srikant, R. (1994). *Fast Algorithms for Mining Association Rules*. IBM Research Report RJ9839, IBM Almaden Research Center.
2. Beeferman, D., & Berger, A. (2000). *Agglomerative clustering of a search engine query log*. Paper presented at the Sixth ACM SIGKDD International Conference on Knowledge Discovery and Data Mining, Boston, Massachusetts.
3. Bernstein, A., & Klein, M. (2002). *Discovering Services: Towards High Precision Service Retrieval*. Paper presented at the CaiSE workshop on Web Services, e-Business, and the Semantic Web (WES): Foundations, Models, Architechture, Engineering and Applications, Toronto, Canada.
4. Devore, J. L. Probability and Statistics for Engineering and the Sciences, 4th Ed. New York: Duxbury Press, 1995.
5. Han, J., & Kamber, M. (2001). *Data Mining: Concepts and Techniques*. San Francisco: Morgan Kaufmann.
6. Hoschek, W. (2002). *Web Service Discovery Processing Steps*. Paper presented at the IADIS International Conference WWW/Internet 2002, Lisbon, Portugal.
7. Jain, A. K., Murty, M. N., & Flynn, P. J. (1999). Data Clustering: A Review. *ACM Computing Surveys (CSUR), 31*(3), 264-323.
8. Johnson, J. T. (2003). *State of the Web services world*. Retrieved 17 April, 2003, from http://www.computerworld.com.au/index.php?secid=1398720840&id=622609517&eid=-180
9. Larsen, K. R. T., & Bloniarz, P. A. (2000). A cost and performance model for Web service investment. *Communications of the ACM, 43,* 109-116.
10. Lim, T. S. & Loh, W. Y. (2000). A comparison of prediction accuracy, complexity and training time of thirty three old and new classification algorithms. *Machine Learning, 40*(3), sep. 203-228.
11. Perng, C. S. , H. Wang, S. R. Zhang, and D. S. Patker. Landmarks: A new model for similarity-based patterns querying in time-series databases. In Proce. 2000 Int Conf Data Engineering, 33-42, San Diego, CA.
12. Srivastava, J., Cooley, R., Deshpande, M., & Tan, P.-N. (2000). Web Usage Mining: Discovery and Applications of Usage Patterns from Web Data. *SIGKDD Explorations, 1*(2), 12-23.
13. Teng, C. M. (2002). *Learning from Dissociations*. Paper presented at the Fourth International Conference on Data Warehousing and Knowledge Discovery DaWaK 2002, Aix-en-Provence, France.
14. Thuraisingham, B. (2002). Data mining, national security, privacy and civil liberties. *ACM SIGKDD Explorations Newsletter, 4*(2), 1-5.
15. Wen, J.-R., Nie, J.-Y., & Zhang, H.-J. (2002). Query clustering using user logs. *ACM Transactions on Information Systems (TOIS), 20*(1), 59-81.

A Framework for the Relational Implementation of Tree Algebra to Retrieve Structured Document Fragments

Sujeet Pradhan

Kurashiki University of Science and the Arts, Kurashiki, JAPAN
sujeet@soft.kusa.ac.jp

Abstract. Naive users typically query documents with keywords. The problem of retrieval unit when keyword queries are posed against a structured document consisting of several logical components has been studied in the past. We developed a new query model based on tree algebra, which successfully resolves this problem. However, one important issue any such effective theoretical model has to deal with, is the difficulty in its equally effective implementation. In this paper, we overview our query model and explore how this model can be successfully implemented using an existing relational database technology. Tree nodes representing logical components of a structured document are indexed with their pre-order and post-order rankings and stored as a relation. We then show how the basic algebraic operation defined in our query model can be transformed into a simple SQL query against this relation. We also discuss various issues regarding query optimization on the implementation level of the model.

1 Introduction

With the growing number of XML/XHTML-based structured documents in the World Wide Web, there has been a lot of interest and effort on developing new mechanisms to query structured documents. While extensive studies have been carried out on structure-based queries, relatively little work has been done on a formal framework for keyword-based queries. Naive users typically query documents with keywords and it is important that database-style formal approaches to keyword-based queries are taken into consideration to ensure definitive results. However, the semantics of keyword-based queries are generally regarded to be ambiguous. This ambiguity becomes even more conspicuous when retrieving portions of structured documents consisting of multiple components. This is due to the fact that not all the keywords specified in a query may be contained in a single component. In such a case, an answer needs to be composed from several logically related components.

In [9], we stated this *problem of retrieval unit*, when keyword queries are posed against a structured document consisting of several logical component. We proposed a theoretical framework that successfully resolves this issue by providing a novel query mechanism. Our mechanism enables users to find relevant portions in a structured document simply by specifying a set of keywords. A structured document was modelled as a rooted ordered tree and several algebraic operations were defined. Keyword queries were transformed into algebraic expressions and relevant document fragments corresponding to the specified keywords were composed dynamically from several inter-related

X. Zhou et al. (Eds.): WISE 2004, LNCS 3306, pp. 206–217, 2004.
© Springer-Verlag Berlin Heidelberg 2004

component units. Since the query semantics is imprecise, the operations produce *every* computable answer that can be considered relevant to a query.

One of the key issues any such effective theoretical model has to deal with, is the difficulty in its equally effective implementation. In this paper, we overview our query model and demonstrate how this model can be successfully implemented using an existing RDBMS (Relational Database Management System) technology. The potential advantages of using a RDBMS is well-understood. Having data indexed and stored in a conventional RDBMS provides us an opportunity to manipulate various functionalities supported by a mature technology for effective and efficient processing of the data.

In order to store the information about a structured document in a conventional RDBMS, one needs an appropriate encoding method that is amiable to RDBMS norms. Recently, various numbering schemes have been proposed for encoding XML data, which is essentially tree-shaped data[12][4][7][13]. One method, frequently adopted by the database community, uses a numbering scheme based on the preorder and postorder rankings of tree nodes for capturing the inter-relationship information among the nodes. In this paper, we follow this numbering scheme to index tree nodes representing logical components of a structured document and store this index information in a relation. We then show how the basic algebraic operation defined in our query model can be transformed into a simple SQL query against this relation. We also discuss various issues regarding query optimization on the implementation level of the model.

The rest of the paper is organized as follows. We next briefly describe the problem of retrieval unit in a typical structured document, which is the motivation for our previous work. Section 3 gives an overview of our theoretical framework of the query mechanism. In section 4, we explain our implementation of the proposed model in detail. We discuss several issues regarding query optimization in the implementation level in Section 5. Related work is provided in section 6, and finally we conclude by highlighting our contributions and providing some directions for future work.

2 Problem of Retrieval Unit

In a typical structured document, there are mainly two reasons why a meaningful portion of a document does not always necessarily mean one physically indexed component.

1. The size and nature of the logical components, which constructs the document is heterogeneous. Some components such as a movie clip may be self contained while others such as a text paragraph may not be.
2. The query keywords may split across multiple components. For example, when a query $\{\mathtt{k}_1, \mathtt{k}_2\}$ is posed against a document modelled by a tree as shown in Figure 1 (a), at first glance, there appears no node satisfying the query. However, many intuitive answers consisting of interrelated components as shown in Figure 1 (b),(c),(d) can be considered relevant to this query.

It is obvious that simple boolean transformation of keyword-based queries cannot always produce desired intuitive answers. Such a naive approach would either produce no result at all or produce many separate results which would lack any semantical relationship among the document components. We need a mechanism that enables dynamic composition of *every* intuitive answer from various logical components based on the keywords specified in a query.

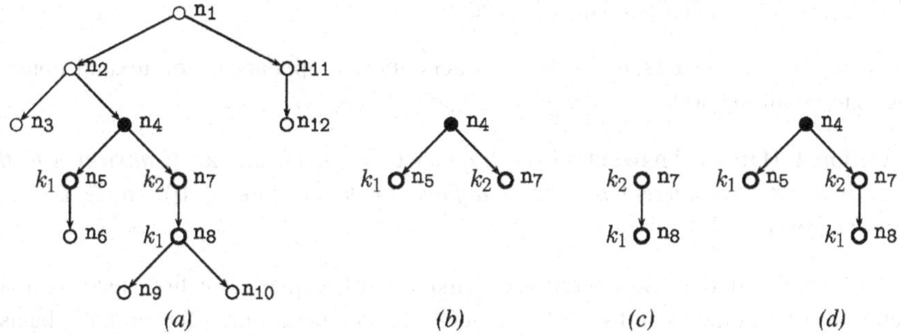

Fig. 1. A document tree and three possible answers to the query $\{\mathtt{k}_1, \mathtt{k}_2\}$

3 Model Overview

Before we define and discuss the implementation of our query mechanism, here we present an overview of the formal definitions of the data and query model based on our tree algebra.

Definition 1 (Digital Document). *A digital document, or simply a document, is a rooted ordered tree* $\mathcal{D} = (\mathtt{N}, \mathtt{E})$ *with a set of nodes* N *and a set of edges* $\mathtt{E} \subseteq \mathtt{N} \times \mathtt{N}$. *There exists a distinguished root node from which the rest of the nodes can be reached by traversing the edges in* E. *Each node except the root has a unique parent node.*

Each node n of the document tree is associated with a logical component of the document. There is a function keywords(n) that returns the representative keywords of the corresponding component in n. The nodes are ordered in such a way that the topology of the document is preserved. We write nodes($\mathcal{D}$) for all the nodes N and edges($\mathcal{D}$) for all the edges E.

Definition 2 (Document Fragment). *Let* $\mathcal{D}$ *be a document. Then* $\mathtt{f} \subseteq \mathcal{D}$ *is a document fragment, or simply a fragment, iff* $\mathtt{nodes(f)} \subseteq \mathtt{nodes}(\mathcal{D})$ *and the subgraph induced by* nodes(f) *in* $\mathcal{D}$ *is a tree. In other words, the induced subgraph is connected and has a distinguished root node.*

A fragment can thus be denoted by a subset of nodes in a document tree – the tree induced by which is also a rooted ordered tree. A fragment may consist of only a single node or all the nodes which constitute the whole document tree. In Figure 1, the set of nodes $\langle \mathtt{n4}, \mathtt{n5}, \mathtt{n7}, \mathtt{n8} \rangle$[1] is a fragment of the sample document tree. Hereafter, unless

[1] For clarity, we use '⟨' and '⟩' instead of conventional '{' and '}' to enclose the nodes of a fragment

stated otherwise, the first node of a fragment represents the root of the tree induced by it. For clarity, we refer to a single noded fragment simply as a node.

Definition 3 (Query). *A query can be denoted by* $\mathtt{Q} = \{\mathtt{k}_1, \mathtt{k}_2, ..., \mathtt{k}_m\}$ *where for all* $j = 1, 2, \ldots, m$ $\mathtt{k}_j$ *is called a query term.*

We write $\mathtt{k} \in \mathtt{keywords(n)}$ to denote query term $\mathtt{k}$ appears in the textual contents associated with the node $\mathtt{n}$.

Definition 4 (Query Answer). *Given a query* $\mathtt{Q} = \{\mathtt{k}_1, \mathtt{k}_2, ..., \mathtt{k}_m\}$*, answer* $\mathtt{A}$ *to this query is a set of document fragments defined to be* $\{\mathtt{f} \mid (\forall \mathtt{k} \in \mathtt{Q}).\exists \mathtt{n} \in \mathtt{f} : \mathtt{k} \in \mathtt{keywords(n)}\}$.

To formally define the operational semantics of a query, we first need to define operations on fragments and sets of fragments. These operations will eventually be used to compute the intuitive answers that we discussed in our motivating example. The operations can be basically classified as (1) *selection* and (2) *join* operations.

Definition 5 (Selection). *Supposing* $\mathtt{F}$ *be a set of fragments of a given document, and* $\mathtt{P}$ *be a predicate which maps a document fragment into* $true$ *or* $false$*, a* selection *from* $\mathtt{F}$ *by the predicate* $\mathtt{P}$*, denoted by* $\sigma_\mathtt{P}$*, is defined as a subset* $\mathtt{F}'$ *of* $\mathtt{F}$ *such that* $\mathtt{F}'$ *includes all and only fragments satisfying* $\mathtt{P}$*. Formally,* $\sigma_\mathtt{P}(\mathtt{F}) = \{\mathtt{f} \mid \mathtt{f} \in \mathtt{F}, \mathtt{P}(\mathtt{f}) = true\}$.

Hereafter, the predicate $\mathtt{P}$ is also called a filter of the selection $\sigma_\mathtt{P}$.

The simplest filter is for the keyword selection of the type 'keyword $= k$' which selects only those document fragments having the word 'k'. Another selection predicate of the type 'size $< c$' is to have control over the size of the fragment. The size of a fragment is measured in terms of the number of nodes included in it. This means the predicate 'size < 5' would select only those fragments constituted by less than 5 nodes. Other complex but practically useful filters were introduced in [9]. Next, we define various *join* operations on document fragments.

Definition 6 (Fragment Join). *Let* $\mathtt{f}_1, \mathtt{f}_2, \mathtt{f}$ *be fragments of the document tree* $\mathcal{D}$*. Then, fragment join between* $\mathtt{f}_1$ *and* $\mathtt{f}_2$ *denoted by* $\mathtt{f}_1 \bowtie \mathtt{f}_2$ *is* $\mathtt{f}$ *iff*

1. $\mathtt{f}_1 \subseteq \mathtt{f}$,
2. $\mathtt{f}_2 \subseteq \mathtt{f}$ *and*
3. $\nexists \mathtt{f}'$ *such that* $\mathtt{f}' \subseteq \mathtt{f} \wedge \mathtt{f}_1 \subseteq \mathtt{f}' \wedge \mathtt{f}_2 \subseteq \mathtt{f}'$

Intuitively, the fragment join operation takes two fragments $\mathtt{f}_1$ and $\mathtt{f}_2$ of $\mathcal{D}$ as its input and finds the minimal fragment $\mathtt{f}$ in $\mathcal{D}$ such that the resulting fragment would contain both the input fragments $\mathtt{f}_1$ and $\mathtt{f}_2$, and there exists no other smaller fragment $\mathtt{f}'$ contained by $\mathtt{f}$ in $\mathcal{D}$, which would also contain the input fragments $\mathtt{f}_1$ and $\mathtt{f}_2$. Figure 2 (b) shows the operation between two fragments $\langle \mathtt{n5}, \mathtt{n6} \rangle$ and $\langle \mathtt{n8}, \mathtt{n10} \rangle$ (see Figure 2 (a)) which finds its minimal subgraph fragment $\langle \mathtt{n4}, \mathtt{n5}, \mathtt{n6}, \mathtt{n7}, \mathtt{n8}, \mathtt{n10} \rangle$ (fragment inside dashed line in Figure 2 (b)). By its definition, the fragment join operation between arbitrary fragments $\mathtt{f}_1$, $\mathtt{f}_2$ and $\mathtt{f}_3$ have the following algebraic properties.

Idempotency $\mathtt{f}_1 \bowtie \mathtt{f}_1 = \mathtt{f}_1$

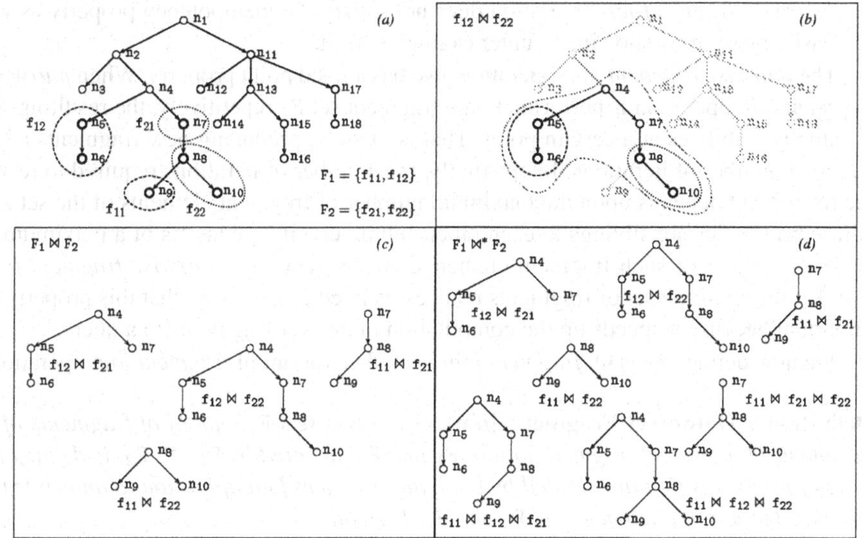

Fig. 2. (a) A Document Tree (b) Fragment Join (c) Pairwise Fragment Join and (d) Powerset Fragment Join Operations

Commutativity $\mathtt{f}_1 \bowtie \mathtt{f}_2 = \mathtt{f}_2 \bowtie \mathtt{f}_1$
Associativity $(\mathtt{f}_1 \bowtie \mathtt{f}_2) \bowtie \mathtt{f}_3 = \mathtt{f}_1 \bowtie (\mathtt{f}_2 \bowtie \mathtt{f}_3)$
Absorption $\mathtt{f}_1 \bowtie (\mathtt{f}_2 \subseteq \mathtt{f}_1) = \mathtt{f}_1$

These properties not only enable an easy implementation of the operations but also reduce the cost of query evaluation, as explained in [9].

Next, we extend this operation to a set of fragments. called *pairwise fragment join*, which is the set-variant of fragment join.

Definition 7 (Pairwise Fragment Join). *Given two sets* $\mathtt{F}_1$ *and* $\mathtt{F}_2$ *of fragments of a document* $\mathcal{D}$, *pairwise fragment join of* $\mathtt{F}_1$ *and* $\mathtt{F}_2$, *denoted by* $\mathtt{F}_1 \bowtie \mathtt{F}_2$, *is defined as a set of fragments yielded by taking fragment join of every combination of an element in* $\mathtt{F}_1$ *and an element in* $\mathtt{F}_2$ *in a pairwise manner. Formally,*

$$\mathtt{F}_1 \bowtie \mathtt{F}_2 = \{\mathtt{f}_1 \bowtie \mathtt{f}_2 \mid \mathtt{f}_1 \in \mathtt{F}_1,\ \mathtt{f}_2 \in \mathtt{F}_2\}$$

Figure 2 (a),(c) illustrates an example of *pairwise fragment join* operation. For given $\mathtt{F}_1 = \{\mathtt{f}_{11}, \mathtt{f}_{12}\}$ and $\mathtt{F}_2 = \{\mathtt{f}_{21}, \mathtt{f}_{22}\}$, $\mathtt{F}_1 \bowtie \mathtt{F}_2$ produces a set of fragments $\{\mathtt{f}_{11} \bowtie \mathtt{f}_{21}, \mathtt{f}_{11} \bowtie \mathtt{f}_{22}, \mathtt{f}_{12} \bowtie \mathtt{f}_{21}, \mathtt{f}_{12} \bowtie \mathtt{f}_{22}\}$.

For arbitrary fragment sets $\mathtt{F}_1$, $\mathtt{F}_2$, and $\mathtt{F}_3$, *pairwise fragment join* has the following algebraic properties.

Commutativity $\mathtt{F}_1 \bowtie \mathtt{F}_2 = \mathtt{F}_2 \bowtie \mathtt{F}_1$
Associativity $(\mathtt{F}_1 \bowtie \mathtt{F}_2) \bowtie \mathtt{F}_3 = \mathtt{F}_1 \bowtie (\mathtt{F}_2 \bowtie \mathtt{F}_3)$
Monotony $\mathtt{F}_1 \bowtie \mathtt{F}_1 \supseteq \mathtt{F}_1$

The *pairwise fragment join* operation does not satisfy the idempotency property as we can easily prove it by showing counter examples for it.

The *pairwise fragment join* operation also has a fixed point property. When *pairwise fragment join* operation is performed on a fragment set F_1 repetitively, the resulting set eventually stabilizes at a certain point. That is, it stops producing new fragments after a certain number of iterations. Interestingly, this number of iterations required to reach the fixed point depends upon the maximum number of fragment elements of the set F_1, whose root nodes are siblings to each other. Intuitively, if F_1 consists of a maximum m ($m \geq 2$) number of such fragment elements, after m repetitive *pairwise fragment join* over F_1, the resulting set of fragments reaches its fixed point[2]. Note that this property is important because it speeds up the computation of answer fragments to a query.

We now define *powerset fragment join* – another variant of *fragment join* operation.

Definition 8 (Powerset Fragment Join). *Given two sets F_1 and F_2 of fragments of a document $\mathcal{D}$, powerset fragment join of F_1 and F_2, denoted by $F_1 \bowtie^* F_2$, is defined as a set of fragments that are yielded by applying fragment join operation to an arbitrary number (but not 0) of elements in F_1 and F_2. Formally,*

$$F_1 \bowtie^* F_2 = \{\bowtie (F_1' \cup F_2') \mid F_1' \subseteq F_1, F_2' \subseteq F_2, F_1' \neq \phi, F_2' \neq \phi\}$$

$$where \bowtie \{f_1, f_2, \ldots, f_n\} = f_1 \bowtie \ldots \bowtie f_n$$

The above definition can be expanded as:

$$\begin{aligned} F_1 \bowtie^* F_2 = {} & (F_1 \bowtie F_1) \cup (F_1 \bowtie F_1 \bowtie F_2) \cup (F_1 \bowtie F_2 \bowtie F_2) \cup (F_1 \bowtie F_1 \bowtie F_1 \bowtie F_2) \cup \\ & (F_1 \bowtie F_1 \bowtie F_2 \bowtie F_2) \cup (F_1 \bowtie F_2 \bowtie F_2 \bowtie F_2) \cup \ldots \end{aligned}$$

Figure 2 (a),(d) illustrates an example of *powerset fragment join* operation. It should be noted here that for the same two sets of fragments $F_1 = \{f_{11}, f_{12}\}$ and $F_2 = \{f_{21}, f_{22}\}$ in Figure 2 (a), *powerset fragment join* produces more fragments than *pairwise fragment join* (see Figure 2 (c)). It should also be noted that some of the fragments are produced more than once due to the algebraic properties of *fragment join* and *pairwise fragment join*.

Although the operation *powerset fragment join* looks complex, in many cases, it can be transformed into a simpler equivalent expression. The transformed expression would involve a *pairwise fragment join* operation between two fragment sets, which are the fixed points of *pairwise fragment join* operation over F_1 and F_2 respectively. For example, in each F_1 and F_2, if the maximum number of elements whose root nodes are siblings to each other are two, then the above operation can be transformed into the following equivalent expression.

$$F_1 \bowtie^* F_2 = (F_1 \bowtie F_1) \bowtie (F_2 \bowtie F_2)$$

The transformation of the *powerset fragment join* into three *pairwise fragment join* operations in this manner is possible due to certain algebraic properties that both *fragment*

[2] For $m = 1$, the required number of iterations to reach fixed point would still be two.

join and *pairwise fragment join* hold. Intuitively, the generalized transformation can be expressed as

$$F_1 \bowtie^* F_2 = FP(F_1) \bowtie FP(F_2)$$

where $FP(F_1)$ and $FP(F_2)$ are two fixed points of *pairwise fragment join* operation on F_1 and F_2 respectively. For space constraints, we do not provide the formal proof.

One must note here that the transformed *powerset fragment join* is the operation that we actually use to compute all the document fragments relevant to a query. It is obvious that the transformation allows us to compute the answers in polynomial time.

For example, a query represented by $\{k_1, k_2\}$ can be evaluated by the following formula.

$$Q = \{k_1, k_2\} = \sigma_{\text{keyword}=k_1}(F) \bowtie^* \sigma_{\text{keyword}=k_2}(F) = FP(F_1) \bowtie FP(F_2)$$

where $F_1 = \sigma_{\text{keyword}=k_1}(F)$ and $F_2 = \sigma_{\text{keyword}=k_2}(F)$.

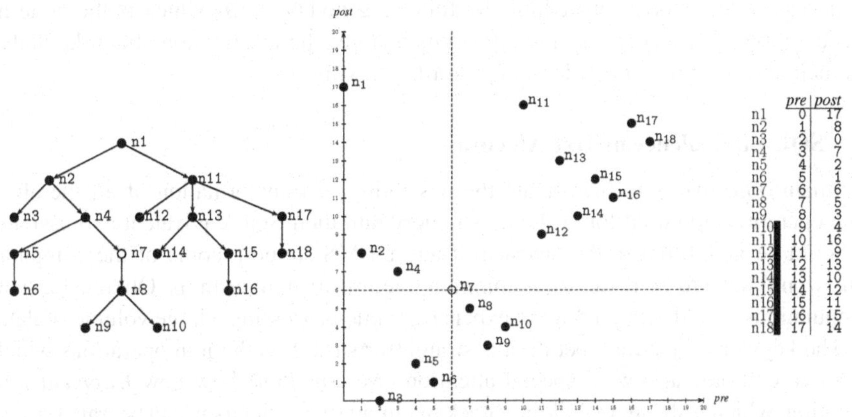

	pre	post
n1	0	17
n2	1	8
n3	2	0
n4	3	7
n5	4	2
n6	5	1
n7	6	6
n8	7	5
n9	8	3
n10	9	4
n11	10	16
n12	11	9
n13	12	13
n14	13	10
n15	14	12
n16	15	11
n17	16	15
n18	17	14

Fig. 3. (i) Tree representation of a structured document (ii) Nodes mapped onto Pre-post plane (iii) Relation of pre-post

4 Relational Implementation

Data in XML format is ubiquitous. Extensive studies are in progress to discover new methodologies and techniques for encoding XML data, which would enable the data to be indexed and stored in a conventional RDBMS. Having stored data in a database, especially in a relational database, has many advantages, the primary one being the effective and efficient processing of the data.

Since XML data is basically a tree-shaped data, one common technique of encoding it is by using a number scheme based on the preorder and postorder ranking of the tree nodes. This technique has been frequently adopted by database community for storing tree-shaped data using a RDBMS technology[4]. A preorder ranking of a node is determined according to the preorder traversal of the tree in which a tree node is marked visited before its children are recursively traversed from left to right. Similarly, a postorder traversal ranking of node is determined according to the postorder traversal of the tree in which a tree node is marked visited after all its children have been traversed from left to right. Encoding based on preorder and postorder rankings defines the inter-relationship of the nodes in the tree in such a way that given a node, its ancestors, descendants, preceding nodes and following nodes can be easily mapped into four distinct regions in a two dimensional plane[4].

We begin by following this technique to encode our structured document data. Figure 3 (i) shows a tree representation of a structured document. Each node in the tree represents a logical component of a document. Figure 3 (ii) shows its transformation into two dimensional plane based on the preorder and postorder ranks of the nodes in the tree. It can be seen that the two horizontal and vertical straight lines drawn through the node `n7` divides the plane into four distinct regions. Each region distinctly contains the ancestor, descendant, preceding and following nodes of `n7`, which is the node in consideration. Figure 3 (iii) is a relation which stores the information about the nodes and their corresponding preorder and postorder rankings.

4.1 SQL Equivalence of Tree Algebra

Our main objective is to investigate the possibility of transformation of all the algebraic operations required for evaluating a query into their SQL equivalent expressions. It should be noted that in the absence of any DBMS support, some of the computations would have to be done using common tree traversal algorithms. Obviously, such computations would turn out highly expensive while processing a large volume of data.

The keyword selection operation is straightforward. It is the join operations which are more complex and need special attention. We will first show how *fragment join* operation, which is the main building block of our query mechanism, can be transformed into region queries in the pre/post order plane of the tree. Since both *pairwise fragment join* and *powerset fragment join* operations are simply the set variants of the *fragment join* operation, they can be easily incorporated into the system.

Here, we first explain why encoding based on preorder/postorder numbering scheme is appropriate to our query mechanism. Basically, what *fragment join* operation between any two fragments of a document does is that starting from the roots of the two fragments, it goes on finding their ancestor nodes all the way up to their least common ancestor. Therefore, intuitively the operation between two fragments can be defined in terms of

- first retrieving the nodes in the top left region (region of ancestor nodes) in the two dimensional plane for the root node of each fragment and
- then performing conventional set operations among these retrieved nodes.

To be more specific, in order to evaluate *fragment join* operation, we only need to perform the following four region queries (three region queries and one node query to be precise).

1. The region containing the nodes of the two input fragments themselves, denoted by the set S_1. See the dashed area in Figure 4 (ii).

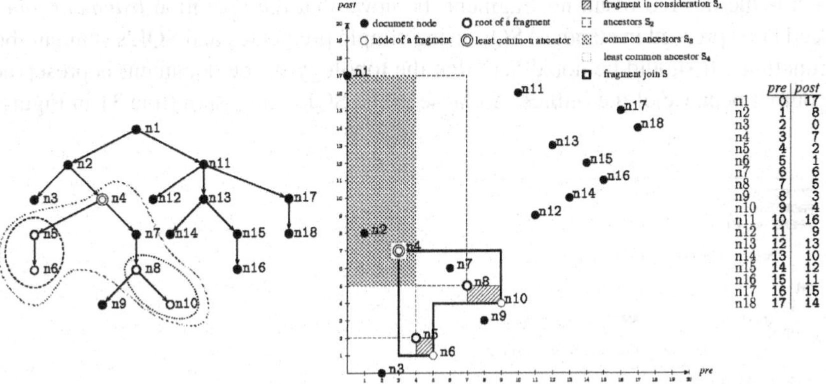

	pre	post
n1	0	17
n2	1	8
n3	2	0
n4	3	7
n5	4	2
n6	5	1
n7	6	6
n8	7	5
n9	8	3
n10	9	4
n11	10	16
n12	11	9
n13	12	13
n14	13	10
n15	14	12
n16	15	11
n17	16	15
n18	17	14

Fig. 4. (i) Fragment Join Operation on a Tree (ii) Fragment Join Operation in Pre-post plane (iii) Relation of pre-post

2. The region containing all the ancestor nodes of the two input fragments, denoted by the set S_2. See the area enclosed by the dashed line in Figure 4 (ii).
3. The region containing all the common ancestor nodes of the two input fragments, denoted by the set S_3. See the grey area in Figure 4 (ii).
4. The [region containing] nearest common node from the two input fragments. Let us denote it by a singleton set S_4. See the area enclosed by the dotted line in Figure 4 (ii).

Intuitively, the SQL equivalence of *fragment join* operation should then be expressed in terms of usual set expressions such as union, intersection, and difference between sets of nodes.

$$S = ((S_1 \cup S_2) - S_3) \cup S_4$$

Figure 5 gives the general pseudo SQL expression for the operation between any two arbitrary fragments `f1` and `f2`. We assume that various user-defined functions such as `nodes`, `pre`, `post`, and `root` are available. Figure 4 (i) and (ii) depicts the *fragment join* operation between two input fragments ⟨n5, n6⟩ and ⟨n8, n10⟩. In Figure 4 (ii), the fragment induced by the nodes contained in the area enclosed by the dark line will be the resulting fragment of the operation. For this particular example, the SQL expression when evaluated against the relation in Figure 4 (iii) will produce:

1. $S_1 = \{4, 5, 7, 9\}$.
2. $S_2 = \{0, 1, 3, 6\}$.
3. $S_3 = \{0, 1, 3\}$.
4. $S_4 = \{3\}$.

Consequently,

$$S = S = ((S_1 \cup S_2) - S_3) \cup S_4 = \{3, 4, 5, 6, 7, 9\} \equiv \langle n4, n5, n6, n7, n8, n10 \rangle$$

which is the desired resulting fragment. It shows that the operation *fragment join* can indeed be expressed in standard SQL using simple predicates and SQL's standard built-in functions. It should be noted here that the topology of the document is preserved in the output because of the ORDER BY clause in the SQL expression (line 31 in Figure 5).

```
1  SELECT pre
2  FROM tree
3  WHERE pre IN
4    (
5      (nodes(f1)) OR (nodes(f2))
6    )
7  OR
8    (
9      (pre < pre(root(f1)) AND post > post(root(f1)))
10   OR
11     (pre < pre(root(f2)) AND post > post(root(f2)))
12   )
13 AND pre NOT IN
14   (
15   SELECT pre
16   FROM tree
17   WHERE
18       (pre < pre(root(f1)) AND post > post(root(f1)))
19     AND
20       (pre < pre(root(f2)) AND post > post(root(f2)))
21   )
22 OR pre IN
23   (
24   SELECT max(pre)
25   FROM tree
26   WHERE
27       (pre < pre(root(f1)) AND post > post(root(f1)))
28     AND
29       (pre < pre(root(f2)) AND post > post(root(f2)))
30   )
31 ORDER BY pre
```

Fig. 5. SQL equivalent expression for fragment join operation between two arbitrary fragments f1 and f2

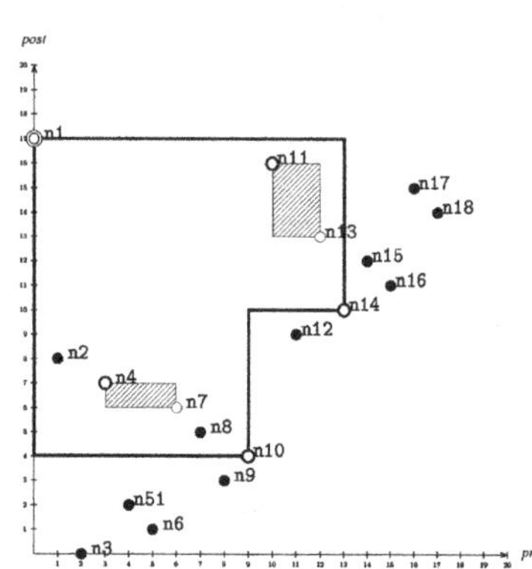

Fig. 6. Generation of duplicate fragments

5 Discussion

Some optimization issues need to be considered while implementing our model in a conventional RDBMS in order to take full advantages supported by a RDBMS. One negative aspect of our *fragment join* and subsequently *pairwise fragment join* and *powerset fragment join* operations is that they may produce a large number of duplicate fragments under certain conditions. The problem is mainly due to the algebraic properties that these operations possess. For example in Figure 6, the *fragment join* operation 1. $\langle \mathtt{n10} \rangle \bowtie \langle \mathtt{n14} \rangle$, 2. $\langle \mathtt{n10} \rangle \bowtie \langle \mathtt{n14} \rangle \bowtie \langle \mathtt{n4}, \mathtt{n7} \rangle$, and 3. $\langle \mathtt{n10} \rangle \bowtie \langle \mathtt{n14} \rangle \bowtie \langle \mathtt{n4}, \mathtt{n7} \rangle \bowtie \langle \mathtt{n11}, \mathtt{n13} \rangle$ would all produce the same resulting fragment $\langle \mathtt{n1}, \mathtt{n2}, \mathtt{n4}, \mathtt{n7}, \mathtt{n8}, \mathtt{n10}, \mathtt{n11}, \mathtt{n13}, \mathtt{n14} \rangle$. However, we believe that the information provided by the numbering scheme to encode our structured data can be effectively manipulated to minimize the number of join operations required to produce the desired result. One idea is to prepare two lists of the root nodes of the fragments to be joined – one sorted by preorder rankings of the nodes and another by postorder ranking. What we wish to do then is that if operations involve several fragments, ideally, we select a subset of fragments by scanning these two lists and perform the join operation without affecting the end result.

Another issue to be considered here is the generation of duplicate nodes while performing the join operation involving a large number of fragments. In [5], techniques such as pruning, partitioning and skipping have been introduced for minimizing production of duplicated nodes when joining several nodes of a tree. Our problem here is slightly different from the one stated in [5], since we are joining fragments and not simply nodes. Therefore, in addition to taking advantage of specific properties of tree data, we must also take algebraic properties of our operations into consideration for an effective optimization plan.

Our ultimate goal, however, is to develop a strong theoretical groundwork for an efficient query optimization. The key idea is to enable pushing down of several selection predicates during the optimization plan. Several such practically useful selection predictions were introduced in [9].

6 Related Work

In recent years, there has been a growing interest in storing and indexing XML data in a conventional database management system. Most of these work proposes various methods for encoding XML data[12][4][7][13]. While work by [7] focuses on efficient support for sequences of regular path expressions, [12] emphasizes the ordering of XML data. A path-based indexing for storing XML data in a relational database and transforming XPath query expressions into corresponding SQL queries has been proposed in [13]. The relational implementation of our query mechanism is largely inspired by the work introduced in [4][5]. However, the underlying key issue discussed in [4][5] is a database index structure to support the evaluation of XPath queries, which is different from the one we have addressed in this paper.

Research on database systems for structured documents has been done in the past[10]. Extensive studies have been done on retrieval of logical units from structured documents based on region algebra[11][1][2][8][6]. Most of these studies, however, are concerned with integration of content and structure in text retrieval. There is also a proposal for integrating keyword queries in conventional XML queries[3]. To the best of our knowledge, no database-like formal approach has been taken to queries solely based on keywords for retrieving relevant fragments of a structured document.

7 Conclusion

Naive users typically query documents with keywords and it is important that database-style formal approaches to keyword-based queries are not overlooked. Our tree algebra is a theoretical model that resolves the problem of retrieval unit when keyword queries are posed against a structured document consisting of several logical components. The main contribution of this paper is the proposal of a framework for the relational implementation of our tree algebra. The topological information and the relationship among the logical components of a structured document is captured by a numbering scheme based on the preorder and postorder rankings of tree nodes. By storing this information in a conventional RDBMS, we showed how the basic algebraic operation defined in our query model can be transformed into a simple SQL query against this relation. We believe this paper has laid the strong foundation for an effective query processing for our model. Further investigation is required into the several issues we discussed above regarding query optimization.

Acknowledgements. We would like to thank the anonymous referees for their useful remarks. We would also like to thank Katsumi Tanaka of Kyoto University for his helpful comments on this work. This work was partially supported by the Ministry of Education, Culture, Sports, Science and Technology, Japan, under the grant 14780337.

References

1. Forbes J. Burkowski. Retrieval activities in a database consisting of heterogeneous collections of structured text. In *Proc. of the 15th annual international ACM SIGIR conference on Research and development in information retrieval*, pages 112–125. ACM Press, 1992.
2. Charles L. A. Clarke, G. V. Cormack, and F. J. Burkowski. An algebra for structured text search and a framework for its implementation. *The Computer Journal*, 38(1):43–56, 1995.
3. D. Florescu, D. Kossman, and I. Manolescu. Integrating keyword search into XML query processing. In *International World Wide Web Conference*, pages 119–135, 2000.
4. Torsten Grust. Accelerating XPath location steps. In *Proc. of the 2002 ACM SIGMOD International Conference on Management of Data*, pages 109–120. ACM, June 2002.
5. Torsten Grust, Maurice van Keulen, and Jens Teubner. Staircase join: Teach a relational DBMS to watch its (axis) steps. In *Proc. of the 29th VLDB Conference*, pages 524–535, September 2003.
6. Jani Jaakkola and Pekka Kilpelainen. Nested text-region algebra. Technical Report C-1999-2, Department of Computer Science, University of Helsinki, January 1999. Available at http://www.cs.helsinki.fi/TR/C-1999/2/.
7. Quanzhong Li and Bongki Moon. Indexing and querying XML data for regular path expressions. In *Proc. of 27th International Conference on Very Large Data Bases*, pages 361–370. Morgan Kaufmann, September 2001.
8. G. Navarro and R.A. Baeza-Yates. Proximal nodes: A model to query document databases by content and structure. *ACM Transactions on Information Systems*, 15(4):400–435, 1997.
9. Sujeet Pradhan and Katsumi Tanaka. Retrieval of relevant portions of structured documents. In *To appear in DEXA04*, 2004.
10. R. Sacks-Davis, T. Arnold-Moore, and J. Zobel. Database systems for structured documents. In *International Symposium on Advanced Database Technologies and Their Integration*, pages 272–283, 1994.
11. A. Salminen and F. Tompa. Pat expressions: an algebra for text search. *Acta Linguistica Hungar*, 41(1-4):277–306, 1992.
12. Igor Tatarinov, Stratis Viglas, Kevin S. Beyer, Jayavel Shanmugasundaram, Eugene J. Shekita, and Chun Zhang. Storing and querying ordered XML using a relational database system. In *Proc. of the 2002 ACM SIGMOD International Conference on Management of Data*, pages 204–215. ACM, June 2002.
13. Masatoshi Yoshikawa, Toshiyuki Amagasa, Takeyuki Shimura, and Shunshuke Uemura. XRel: a path-based approach to storage and retrieval of XML documents using relational databases. *ACM Transactions on Internet Technology*, 1(1):110–141, August 2001.

An Efficient OLAP Query Processing Technique Using Measure Attribute Indexes*

T.S. Jung[1], M.S. Ahn[2], and W.S. Cho[2]

[1] Department of Information Industrial Engineering, Chungbuk National University, 361763 Choungju, Chungbuk, Korea
[2] Department of Management Information Systems, Chungbuk National University, 361763 Choungju, Chungbuk, Korea
{mispro, epita55, wscho}@chungbuk.ac.kr

Abstract. We propose an index structure, called *measure attribute (MA) index*, and a query processing technique to improve OLAP query performance. OLAP queries are extremely complicated due to representing the intricate business logic of the company on a huge quantity of data. This is why the efficient query evaluation becomes a critical issue in OLAP systems. Proposed query processing technique supports an efficient evaluation of the star joins and grouping operators known as the most frequently used but very expensive operators in OLAP queries. The MA index is a variation of the path index in object databases and supports index-only processing for the star joins and grouping operators. Index-only processing is a well known efficient technique in the query evaluation area. We implemented the MA index on top of an object-relational DBMS. Performance analysis shows that the MA index provides speedups of orders of magnitude for typical OLAP queries.

1 Introduction

Data warehouse is a collection of integrated, subject-oriented, nonvolatile, time-variant information for decision making in an organization[10,15]. The data warehouse is becoming an essential infrastructure in most organizations such as business companies, hospitals, and government organizations.

OLAP (On-Line Analytical Processing) is the process that end users directly analyze the data warehouse in an interactive mode for various decision making applications[3]. Conventional OLAP systems can be implemented either MOLAP (multidimensional OLAP) or ROLAP (relational OLAP)[3]. In this paper, we assume another type of OLAP implementation, called OOLAP (object-relational database OLAP). Recently, the necessity of OOLAP is increasing by the emergence of ORDBMSs as the next generation DBMSs[1,4,6,7,14].

* This research was supported by the Program for the Training of Graduate Students in Regional Innovation which was conducted by the Ministry of Commerce, Industry and Energy of the Korean Government.

X. Zhou et al. (Eds.): WISE 2004, LNCS 3306, pp. 218–228, 2004.
© Springer-Verlag Berlin Heidelberg 2004

OLAP queries are extremely complicated due to representing the intricate business logic of the company. They also require long response time because of the complex queries on a huge quantity of data. This is why the efficient query evaluation is an important issue in OLAP systems.

In this paper, we propose an index structure, called *MA* (*measure attribute*) *index*, and a query processing technique to improve the performance of OLAP queries. The MA index is a variation of the path index in object databases and supports index-only processing for the star joins and grouping operators. Note that they are the most frequently used operators in OLAP queries[5]. An MA index directly associates the values of the measure attribute with OIDs (or RIDs) of the dimension class (or table) for index-only processing of the star joins and groupings. Index-only processing is a well-known query processing technique in the database performance area. We also propose algorithms for index-only processing of the star joins and groupings.

Proposed query processing technique with the MA indexes supports an efficient evaluation of the star join and grouping operators. We have implemented the MA index on top of an object-relational DBMS, and the query performance analysis shows speedups of orders of magnitude for typical OLAP queries. Although the idea has been implemented in the OOLAP environment, it can be applied to the ROLAP environments with no modification.

The paper is organized as follows. In Section 2, we discuss OOLAP systems and the existing index structures. In Section 3, we propose the MA index and a query processing technique utilizing the index. In Section 4, we describe mathematical analysis and performance evaluation results. In Section 5, we present conclusions and future work.

2 Related Work

We discuss about the star schema and OLAP queries in OOLAP environments. We then present existing indexes to speedup OLAP query evaluation.

2.1 Star Schema and OLAP Query

There are some differences between ROLAP and OOLAP environments. First, OOLAP uses Object DBMSs instead of Relational DBMSs. Second, relationships between primary key and foreign key in ROLAP are replaced by attribute-domain relationships in OOLAP. Each class in the OOLAP may have subclasses, and the domain of an attribute may be another class. Figure 1 shows a star schema in OOLAP. Various analyses can be done on Figure 1 by using OLAP queries. Query 1 is a typical OLAP query on the star schema.

In query Q1, star joins of Sales, Store, Time, and Product are represented by the path expressions in the object SQL. Note that the cost of the star joins is very expensive because the fact class Sales contains a huge number of objects in most cases.

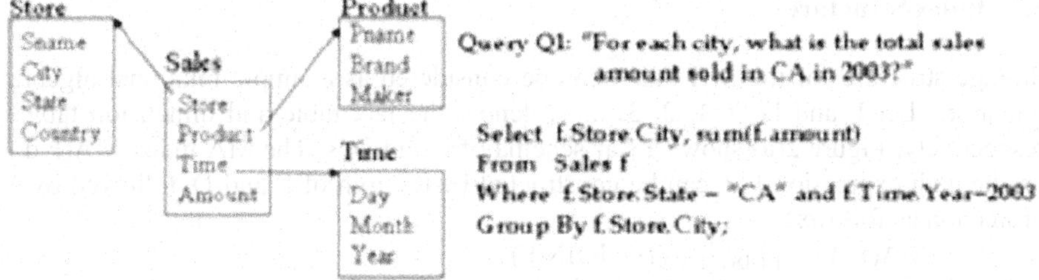

Fig. 1. A Star schema for sales information

2.2 Conventional Index Structures for OLAP Query Processing

For efficient OLAP query processing, various indexes such as *Bitmap* (BM for short) index and *Bitmap Join* (BJ for short) index have been proposed in OLAP systems[2,8,9,12,13,18,19]. Generally, BM index is superior to the B^+-Tree index in space and retrieval efficiency. BJ[12] index is an integration of the Join Index[17] and BM index for efficient star joins.

However, space overhead of the indexes BM index and BJ index becomes serious as the number of distinct values in the attribute increases[18]. *Encoded Bitmap* (EB for short) index is a solution for the space overhead[19]. In Figure 1, let assume 1,000,000 tuples in the fact table *Sales*, 12,000 tuples in the dimension table *Store*. The BJ index between *Sales* and *Store* requires 12,000 bit vectors, each of which has 1,000,000 bits (12Gbits). However, the EB index requires just $\lceil \log_2 12000 \rceil = 14$ bit vectors, each of which has 1,000,000 bits (14Mbits) [19].

Although these indexes provide a reasonable space overhead and reduced access time compared with conventional indexes, their query evaluation cost is still expensive especially when a large number of objects have to be accessed from the fact table. Note that the index provides not the objects themselves but the locations of the qualified objects. So the query processor should access the qualified objects from the fact table via the locations obtained from the indexes. Our experiments show that the latter activity (i.e., accessing qualified objects via the locations) requires a significant time overhead when a great number of objects should be accessed from the fact table. We confirm this situation in Sections 4.2 and 4.3.

3 The MA Index and Query Processing Technique

We present the MA index which intends to minimize the access cost even though the query processor accesses a great number of objects from the fact table. We then propose an efficient query processing algorithm that fully utilizes the MA indexes.

3.1 Index Structure

Storage structure for the MA index can be considered as a simple relational algebra operators. Let F and D_i, i=1, 2, 3, ..., n denote the fact table and dimension tables respectively. Figure 2(a) shows a star schema of F and D_i's. The MA index $MA(F.d_i)$ on the path expression $F.d_i$ can be constructed by the join of F and D_i followed by a projection as follows:

$$MA(F.d_i) = \prod_{Di.oid,\ MA} (D_i \text{ JOIN } F)$$

For the star schema in Figure 2(a), we create four MA indexes for the joins (D_i JOIN F), i=1, 2, 3, 4. Each index $MA(F.d_i)$ is conceptually a binary relation whose attributes are *oid* of D_i and the *measure attribute (MA)* of F. Figure 2(b) shows the structure of $MA(F.d_i)$, i=1, 2, 3, 4. In the implementation, all the MA indexes share the MA values stored in the file MAF rather than duplicating them in each index.

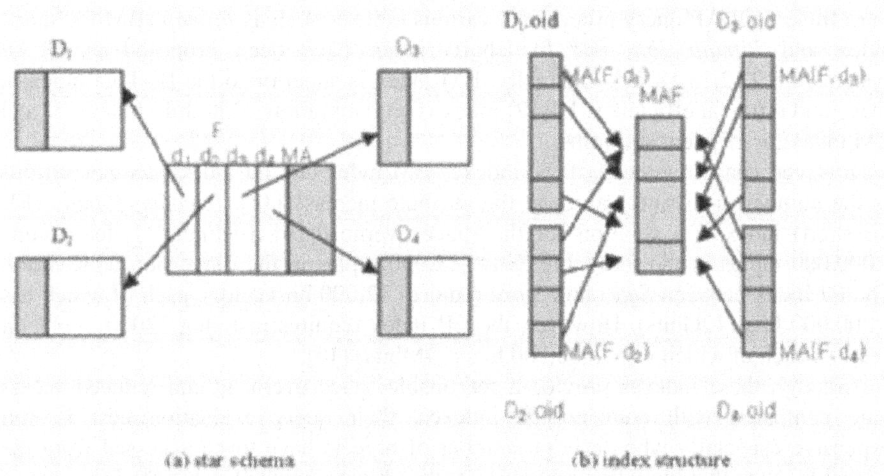

Fig. 2. MA Index Structure

(Example 1)
Figure 3 is showing the example of storage and index structures for the classes Sales, Store, and Time for the star schema in Figure 1. Figure 3 (b) shows the states of Sales, Store, and Time classes and Figure 3 (a) shows two measure index on the attributes Sales.Store and Sales.Time : MA(Sales.Store) and MA(Sales.Time). Note that objects in the fact class are not stored in the original form; only measure attribute(s) is physically stored in the file MAF(measure attribute file). And the relationships between fact and dimension classes are stored in the index MA. For example, MA(Sales.Store) includes two fields; one for the search key, and the other for the offsets of the values in MAF. The key of the index MA(Sales.Store) is the OID of Store, and the pointer field has the offsets of the values in the MAF file. For example, Amount values related to the Store OID 3312 are 5, 10, 45, … because their offset in MAF are 1,3,5,… respectively. In MA(Sales.Store), we can see the index entry [3312|1,3,5,…] denoting this information. MA(Sales.Time) can be constructed in the same way. We can access Amount values sold by a specific Store object from the

index MA(Sales.Store), and this leads a significant advantage in the processing of star joins and grouping operators.

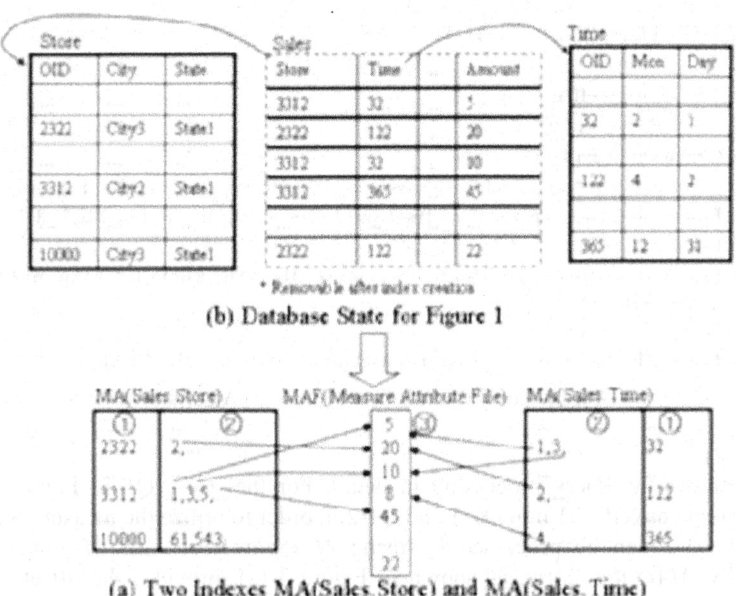

Fig. 3. Database State and Index Structure

Note that the user interface is Figure 3(b), not Figure 3(a). That is to say, users see the star schema in the form of Figure 1, and issue OLAP query as the form of Query Q1 in Section 2.1. The OLAP engine described in Section 3.2 decomposes the OLAP query for the star schema in Figure 3(b) into a number of small queries in accordance with the storage structure in Figure 3(a).

Although conventional EB and join indexes also support star joins of F and D_i, they still need significant access costs for the measure attributes. However, the MA indexes overcome this overhead by containing the measure values directly in the index. For example, we can aggregate measure attribute values (*5, 10, 45, …*) in MAF after joining store (*OID = 3312*) and sales objects by using the index *MA(Sales.Store)*. I.e., index-only processing for the joins and aggregations is possible.

3.2 Query Processing Algorithm

Here, we describe a query processing algorithm for utilizing the MA indexes. We assume the star schema in Figure 2. For the following Query Q in Figure 4, the algorithm QueryDecompAndProc() shows the query transformation process.

```
[Query Q]
Select      d1.a1, d2.a2, ..., dk.ak, Agg_Func(f.m1)
From        F
Where       σ(d1.a1), σ(d2.a2), ..., σ(dN.aN)
Group by    d1.a1, d2.a2, ..., dk.ak

[QueryDecompAndProc( )]
Input: OLAP Query Q
Output: Query Result
Step1: Convert Q into Qi, i=1,2,...,N where Qi is the query on the dimension Di
Step2: For each Qi, compute the offset list Li by using the index MI(F.di)
Step3: L = L1 ∩ L2 ∩ ... ∩ LN
Step4: For each group attribute dj.aj, generate the offset list GLj by using the
       index MI(F.dj)
Step5: GLj = L ∩ GLj
Step6: For each GLj , compute aggregation by accessing the MAF
```

Fig. 4. Query Q and Query Processing Algorithm

(Example 2)
Figure 5 shows the query processing in detail. For the query Q1 in Figure 1, the OLAP system converts Q1 into Q1-1 and Q1-2 in order to utilize the measure indexes. Q1-1 and Q1-2 can be processed by using *MA(Sales.Store)* and *MA(Sales.Time)* respectively. *MA(Sales.Store)*, as shown in Figure 3 (a), provides the offsets which point to the amounts sold by the state "*CA*". Similarly, *MA(Sales.Time)* generates the offsets for the amounts sold in *2003*. Two sets of the offsets (described by L_1={1,3,5,7,9,21,33} and L_2={1,3,5,21,34,45}) are merged into the set L={1,3,5,21} to process the logical AND operator in the WHERE clause. Each offset in L denotes the location where the qualified measure value is stored in MAF. If there are grouping attributes, the list L is decomposed into the group lists GLs by using the MA indexes: GL_1 and GL_2. Finally, measure values corresponding to GL_i are accessed and aggregated into the find results.

4 Performance Analysis

In this section, we analyze the space and time complexity for the measure attribute indexes. We first describe mathematical analysis and then query response time for a large data warehouse. Symbols in Table 1 show the parameters used in the mathematical analysis.

4.1 Space Comparison

In Figure 2, we assume the following statistics for space analysis. Here the length of OID is 8 bytes.

$$n(D_i) = 10{,}000,\ n(F) = 100{,}000 \sim 100{,}000{,}000$$

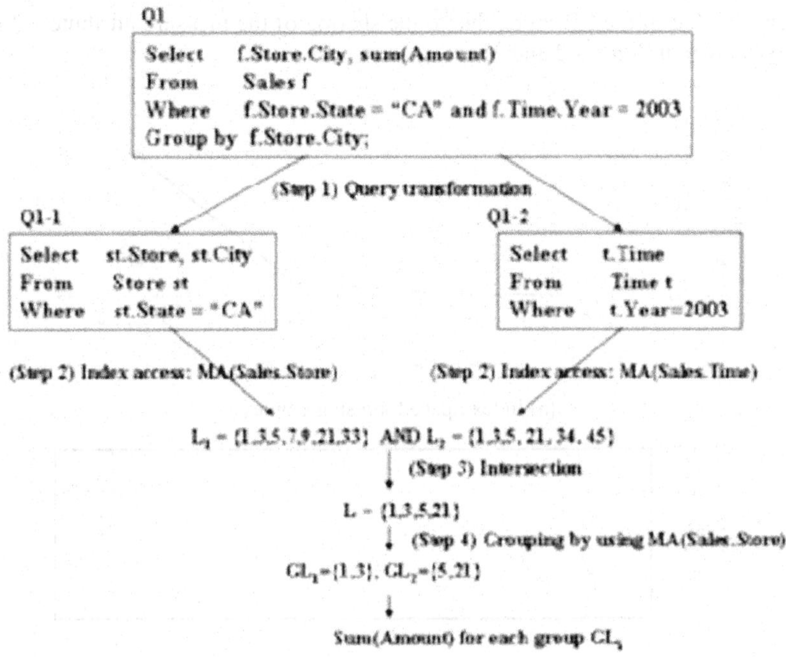

Fig. 5. Query Processing by Transformation

Table 1. The parameters used in the analysis.

Symbols	Meaning
n(C)	Number of objects in the class C
p(C)	Number of blocks in the class C
s(pred)	Selectivity for the condition *pred*
s(C)	Selectivity of the class C
B(b, bf, k)	The expected number of block I/Os when *k* records are accessed in the address order from the file composed of *b* blocks with *bf* blocking factor [20]
c(I)	Index access cost for the index I
bf(C)	Blocking factor for the class C
G(I, attr)	Grouping cost using the index I

From these statistics, we compute the space requirements for B^+-Tree, Encoded Bit-map(EB) index, and Measure Attribute (MA) indexes. Figure 6(a) shows the comparison of the space requirements for one index. As *n(F)* increases, space requirements of B^+-Tree and the MA index increase rapidly compared with EB index. Figure 5(b) shows the space of each index structure as the number of indexes to be created increases. If we create more than 4 indexes, the space of the MA index is smaller than that of the EB index due to the sharing of the measure attribute values in MAF as shown in Figures 2 and 3.

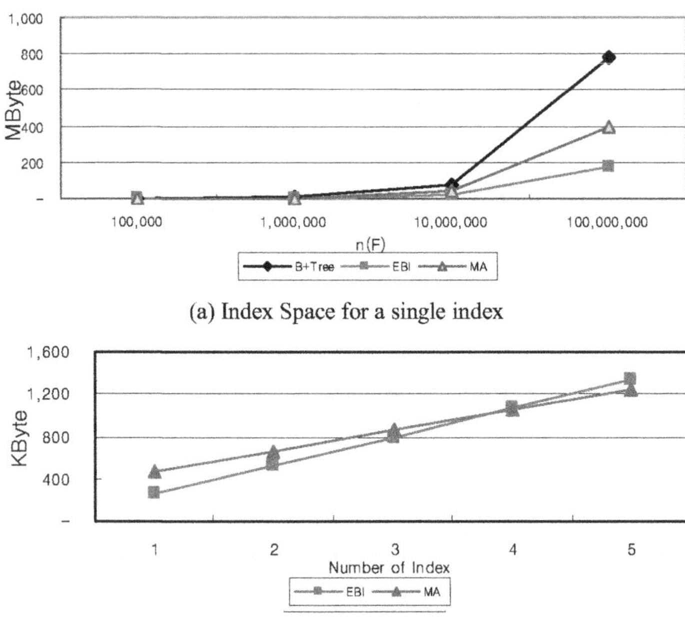

(a) Index Space for a single index

(b) Index Space as the number of indexes to be created increases

Fig. 6. Index Space Comparisons

4.2 Query Evaluation Cost

Here, we compare query evaluation costs for B^+-Tree, EB, and MA indexes. Various parameters shown in Table 1 are used in the mathematical cost modeling.

For query Q in Section 3.2, equations (1), (2), and (3) are the cost formulas when we use B+-Tree index I_1, EB index I_2, and MA index I_3, respectively. Aggregation cost is excluded because it has the same cost regardless of the index types. Here, we measure the query evaluation cost in the number of disk block IOs.

$$Cost1(Q) = p(D_i) + n(D_i) \times s(C) \times c(I_1) + b(\, p(F),\, bf(F),\, n(F) \times s(C)\,) + G(I_1, attr\text{-}list) \quad (1)$$

$$Cost2(Q) = p(D_i) + n(D_i) \times s(C) \times c(I_2) + b(\, p(F),\, bf(F),\, n(F) \times s(C)\,) + G(I_2, attr\text{-}list) \quad (2)$$

$$Cost3(Q) = p(D_i) + n(D_i) \times s(C) \times c(I_3) + b(\, p(MAF),\, bf(MAF),\, n(F) \times s(C)\,) + G(I_3, attr\text{-}list) \quad (3)$$

In the formula, $p(D_i)$ is the access cost for the dimension table D_i to evaluate the local conditions. The next item $n(D_i) \times s(C) \times c(I_j)$ is the index access cost for qualified objects in D_i. The third item $b(\, p(F),\, bf(F),\, n(F) \times s(C)\,)$ represents the access cost for the fact table F. The last item $G(I_j,\ attr\text{-}list)$ denotes grouping cost by using the index I_j.

We assume that the query processor evaluates the conditions of each dimension table at first and obtains OIDs of the qualified objects in the dimension tables. In the next, an index is used to find OIDs of the qualified objects in the fact table. In Equation (1) and (2), the query processor accesses the fact table by using the OIDs of the fact table returned from the index. However, in Equation (3), the values in the measure attribute can be obtained from MAF instead of the fact table.

In Equations (1), (2), and (3), the first and the second items have almost the same cost for all indexes; but, the third and the fourth items have a great difference as the number of qualified objects in the fact table increases. The parameter $b(\,p(MAF), bf(MAF), n(F)*s(C)\,)$ is much smaller than $b(\,p(F), bf(F), n(F)\times s(C)\,)$ in Equations (1) and (2) since MAF is small compared with the fact table F. Furthermore, group by operator can be processed by the index-only fashion in the MA index. Therefore, $G(I_3, attr\text{-}list)$ in Equation (3) is much smaller than those of Equations (1) and (2).

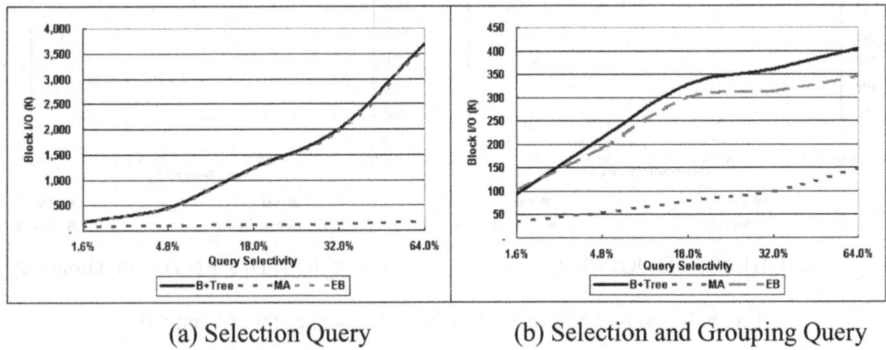

(a) Selection Query (b) Selection and Grouping Query

Fig. 7. Comparison of query evaluation costs for various indexes

Figure 7 shows the costs of Equations (1), (2), and (3) in a graphical form. Figure 7(a) compares the costs of queries where group by operators are not included; but Figure 7(b) shows the costs of queries having group by operators. In Figure 7(a), there is a little difference between B^+-Tree and EB indexes in the query evaluation cost. In Figure 7(b), the difference between B^+-Tree and EB is not significant due to the dominant grouping cost. This is because the conventional query processor does not utilize B^+-Tree or EB indexes in the evaluation of the grouping operators. Note that the MA index provides a superior performance regardless of the query selectivity. There are two reasons for this superiority; (1) the third item in Equation (3) is very small since it accesses the smaller MAF file instead of the huge fact table F. (2) the fourth item in Equation (3) is also very small due to the index-only processing of the grouping operators.

4.3 Experimental Results

For performance comparison, we create a data warehouse for Figure 3 containing 1,000,000 objects and 5,000,000 objects in the fact table F(Sales). Two queries Q1 and Q2 are used : Q1(F JOIN D_1) and Q2(F JOIN D_1 JOIN D_2 with Grouping). B^+-Tree and MA indexes are compared. Remind that B^+-Tree and EB indexes have almost the same cost as shown in Figure 7, especially for the queries having grouping operators. Figure 8 shows that the MA index provides a significant performance advantage compared with B^+-Tree. For small query selectivity, there is relatively little performance difference. However, as the query selectivity increases or if the query includes group by operators, the MA index has a significant performance advantage. This performance advantage comes from the index-only processing for the expensive star joins and grouping operators. Since most OLAP queries include grouping operators with high query selectivity compared with the OLTP queries[16], this performance advantage is especially valuable.

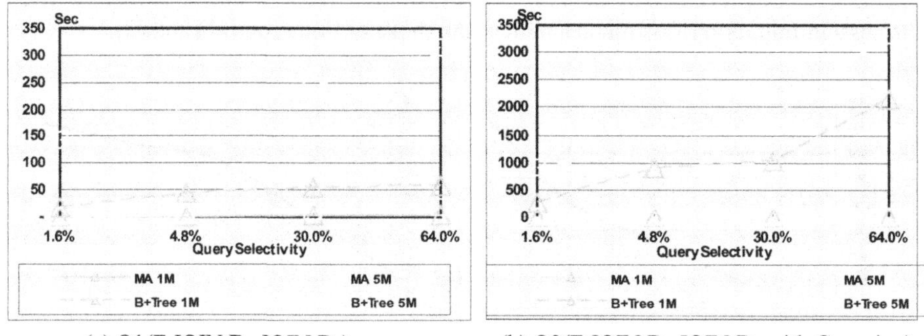

(a) Q1(F JOIN D_1 JOIN D_2) (b) Q2(F JOIN D_1 JOIN D_2 with Grouping)

Fig. 8. Response times of B^+-Tree and MA indexes for 1M and 5M

5 Conclusions

We proposed a new index structure, called *measure attribute(MA) index*, and a query processing technique to improve the performance of OLAP queries. OLAP queries are extremely complicated due to representing the intricate business logic of the company on a huge quantity of data. That is why the performance is an important issue in the OLAP queries.

The MA index supports an efficient evaluation of the star joins and groupings that are frequently used but most expensive operators in the OLAP queries. The MA index is a variation of the path index in object databases and it supports index-only processing of the star join and grouping operators. We have implemented the MA index on top of an object-relational DBMS. The performance analysis shows that the MA index provides speedups of orders of magnitude for typical OLAP queries.

References

1. Y. Zhao, et al., "Array-based evaluation of multi-dimensional queries in object-relational database system," In Proc. Int'l Conf. ICDE, 1998.
2. C. Y. Chan and Y. Ioannidis, "Bitmap index design and evaluation," In Proc. ACM SIGMOD Conference, pp. 355-366, 1998.

3. G. Colliat, "OLAP, relational and multidimensional database system," In Proc. ACM SIGMOD Record, 25(3), 1996.
4. B. D. Czejdo, et al., "Design of a data warehouse over object-oriented and dynamically evolving data sources," DEXA Workshop, pp. 128-132, 2001.
5. R. Elmasri and S. B. Navathe, Fundamentals of database Systems, Addison-wesley, 2000.
6. V. Gopalkrishnan, et al., "Star/snow-flake schema driven object-relational data warehouse - design and query processing strategies," DaWaK, pp. 11-22, 1999.
7. J. Gu, et al., "OLAP++: Powerful and easy-to-use federations of OLAP and object databases," In Proc. Int'l Conf. on VLDB, pp. 599-602, 2000.
8. T. Johnson, "Performance measurements of compressed bitmap indices," In Proc. Int'l Conf. on VLDB, pp. 278-289, 1999.
9. M, Jurgens and H. J. Lenz, "Tree based indexes vs. bitmap indexes : a performance study," In Proc, Int'l Workshop on DMDW, 1999.
10. L. Do, et al., "Issues in developing very large data warehouse," In Proc. Int'l. Conf. on VLDB, pp.633-640, 1998.
11. C. Mohan, et al., "Single Table Access Using Multiple Indexes: Optimization, Execution, and Concurrency Control Techniques," In Proc. EDBT, pp. 29-43, 1990. 3
12. P. O'neil and G. Graefe, "Multi-table joins through bitmapped join indics," In Proc. ACM SIGMOD Record, 24(3), pp. 8-11, Sept, 1995.
13. P. O'neil and D. Quass, "Improved query performance with variant indexes," In Proc. ACM SIGMOD, pp. 38-49, 1997.
14. F. Ravat and O. Teste, "A temporal object-oriented data warehouse model," In Proc. DEXA Workshop, pp. 583-592, 2000.
15. Stanford Technology Group, "Designing the data warehouse on relational database," White Paper.
16. TPC-D, http://www.tpc.org, 2002
17. P. Valduriez, "Join indices," ACM Trans. on Database Systems, 12(2), pp.218-246, 1987.
18. K. L. Wu and P. S. Yu, Range-based bitmap indexing for high cardinality attributes with skew, Research Report, IBM Waston Research Center, May, 1996.
19. M. C. Wu and A. P. Buchmann, "Encoded bitmap indexing for data warehouses," In Proc. Int'l Conf. ICDE, 1998.
20. S. B. Yao., "Approximating block accesses in database organizations," Comm. of the ACM, 20(4), pp. 260-261, 1977.

Preserving Aggregation Semantic Constraints in XML Document Update

Eric Pardede[1], J. Wenny Rahayu[1], and David Taniar[2]

[1] Department of Computer Science and Computer Engineering
La Trobe University, Bundoora VIC 3083, Australia
{ekpardede, wenny}@cs.latrobe.edu.au
[2] School of Business System
Monash University, Clayton VIC 3800, Australia
{David.Taniar}@infotech.monash.edu.au

Abstract. In this paper we propose a methodology to accommodate XML Update without violating the original document's constraints. The method takes form as a set of functions that perform checking mechanism before updates. The main focus is on the aggregation relationship, which is further differentiated based on the constraints: cardinality, adhesion, ordering, homogeneity and share-ability. The proposed method can be implemented in many different ways, and for example we use XQuery language. We also propose the mapping of the aggregation relationship in the conceptual level to the XML Schema. We use XML Schema for structure validation, even though the algorithm can be used by any schema language.

1 Introduction

In the last few years the interest in storing XML Documents in the native XML Database (NXD) has emerged rapidly [1][10]. The main idea is to store the documents in their natural tree form. However, many users still prefer to use the RDBMS for their document storage. One reason of not using the NXD is the incompleteness of its query language. Many proprietary XML query languages and even W3C-standardized languages still have limitations compared to the Relational Model SQL. One of the important limitations is the lack of support for update operation [10].

Different NXD applies different update strategies. Very frequently after updates, an XML document losses the conceptual level semantic. To the best of our knowledge, there is no XML query language that has considered the semantic problems emerged from the updates such as the insertion of duplicated content, deletion of a key, etc. We suggest this as an important issue to raise and to investigate further.

In this paper we propose a new methodology providing checking mechanism, which works like triggers in any DBMS. The methods take form as a set of functions that checks, for example, deletion of a refereed key node, insertion of duplicated

X. Zhou et al. (Eds.): WISE 2004, LNCS 3306, pp. 229–240, 2004.
© Springer-Verlag Berlin Heidelberg 2004

attribute, etc. The functions ensure that the operations do not violate the conceptual semantics of the XML document.

This paper focuses on the checking update for the aggregation relationship. We distinguish the aggregation constraints in XML document, analyze the potential update integrity problems and propose the method to avoid these problems. For the implementation, we use a W3C-standardized query language XQuery [14].

XML update operations will require structure validation. For that purpose we apply XML Schema [12][13]. Therefore, a part of the paper is allocated to developing a transformation on the aggregation relationship into XML Schema. It is important to mention that it should not limit the usage of the proposed method. The transformation can be conducted in any standardized or proprietary schema language.

2 Background: Aggregation Relationship in XML Document

By nature, XML document is structured as a set of aggregation relationship. In this relationship, a "whole" component has one or more "part" components related to it. A "part" component on the other side can only has one "whole" component related to it.

Semantically, this relationship type can be distinguished by different constraints such as *cardinality*, *adhesion*, *ordering*, *homogeneity*, and *share-ability*. Each influences how the "part" components relate to the "whole" component. Except the share-ability, the constraints can be identified in XML data model such as in Semantic Network Diagram [2]. The following diagram (see Fig.1) depicts different aggregation constraints in XML document as our running example.

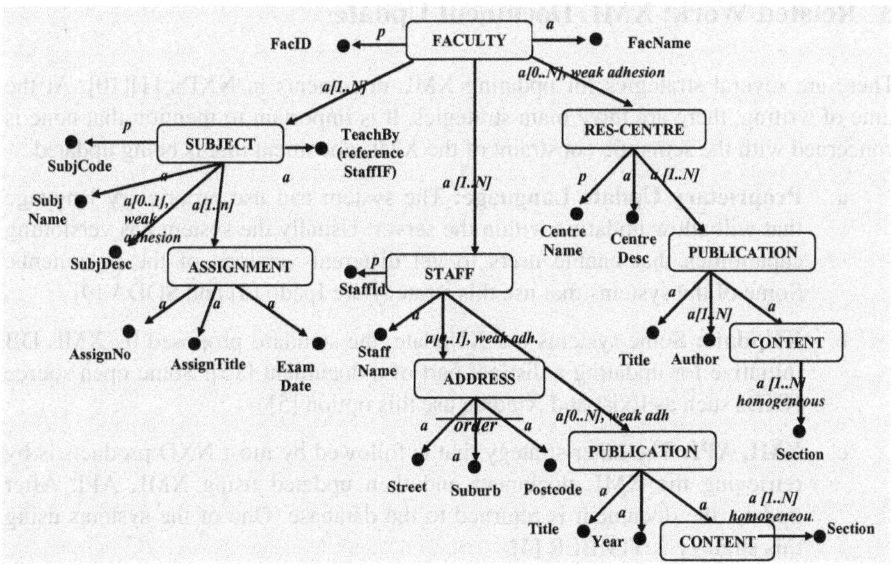

Fig. 1. Aggregation Types in XML Document Tree

Aggregation cardinality identifies the number of instances of a particular "part" component that a single instance of a "whole" component can relate with. For example in Fig 1, a *faculty* has exactly one or more *staff* [1..N] and a *staff* can have none to many *publication* [0..N]. The cardinality default is [1..1].

Aggregation adhesion identifies whether "whole" and "part" components must or must not coexist and adhere to each other. For example, *Faculty* has weak adhesion aggregation with component *research centre*, which means the existence of the latter does not totally depended on the former. Another weak adhesion example is between a *staff* and an *address*. The default for the diagram is strong adhesion.

Ordered aggregation identifies whether the "part" components compose the "whole" component in a particular order. The unordered aggregation is usually not explicitly mentioned. In the example, *address* has ordered aggregation.

Aggregation homogeneity identifies whether "whole" component is made up by either homogeneous or heterogeneous "part" component type. For example, in the *publication* node the *content* has homogeneous aggregation of *section* document.

Aggregation share-ability identifies whether instance(s) of a "part" component can be shared by more than one instance of one or more "whole" components. If they can be shared, we call it a shareable aggregation. This aggregation type cannot be depicted in any XML conceptual model including the semantic network diagram. We cannot enforce the same "part" component to be owned by more than one "whole" component. The usual practice is having the "part" components separately and linking them with the "whole" component. For example, we can assume that the *publication* component is shareable between *staff* and *research centre*.

3 Related Work: XML Document Update

There are several strategies for updating XML documents in NXDs [1][10]. At the time of writing, there are three main strategies. It is important to mention that none is concerned with the semantic constraint of the XML document that is being updated.

a. **Proprietary Update Language:** The system can use proprietary language that will allow updating within the server. Usually the system has versioning capabilities that enable users to get different versions of the documents. Some of the systems that use this strategy are Ipedo [3] and SODA [9]

b. **XUpdate:** Some systems use XUpdate, the standard proposed by XML DB initiative for updating a distinct part of a document [15]. Some open source NXDs such as Exist and Xindice use this option [5]

c. **XML API:** The other strategy that is followed by most NXD products is by retrieving the XML document and then updated using XML API. After update, the document is returned to the database. One of the systems using this strategy is TIMBER [4].

Different strategies have limited the database interchangeability. To unite these different strategies, [11] has tried to propose the update processes for XML

Documents into an XML language. These processes are embedded into XQuery and thus, can be used for any NXD that has supported this language.

XQuery is a W3C-standardized language designed for processing XML data. This query language is defined based on XQuery 1.0 and XPath 2.0 Data Model [14]. To locate the nodes, this language uses path expressions. It has high capability to combine and restructure the nodes. The most important expression is the FLWOR expressions. It contains of five clauses. FOR and LET clauses associate variables to expressions, WHERE clause filters the binding results generated by FOR and LET clauses, ORDER BY clause sorts the binding results in a binding stream, and RETURN clause builds the results (see Fig. 2).

```
FOR $binding1 IN path
    expression…
LET $binding := path
    expression…
    WHERE predicate, …
    ORDER BY predicate, …
        RETURN results
```

Fig. 2. XQuery FLOWR Expressions

```
FOR. . .LET. . .WHERE. . .
UPDATE $target{
        DELETE $child|
        INSERT content
              [BEFORE|AFTER $child]|
        REPLACE $child WITH $content|
        {,subOp}*
        }
```

Fig. 3. XQuery UPDATE Extensions

When it was first introduced, XQuery was only used for document query or retrieval. [11] introduces some primitive operations embedded in XQuery for XML document update. The update is applicable for ordered and unordered XML Documents and also for single or multiple level of nodes.

Fig.3 depicts the XQuery update extensions. The UPDATE clause specifies the node targets that will be updated. Inside the UPDATE clause, we determine the operation types. Notice that we can have nested update operations.

Nonetheless, even with this proposal there is a basic question to answer. We do not know how the update operations affect the semantic correctness of the updated XML Documents. This fact has motivated us to take the topic a step further. Table 1 depicts the comparison of the existing strategy with our methodology. The first column shows the operation types provided by different strategy. Our proposed method can accommodate three different operations. The second column shows whether the strategy utilizes any W3C-standardized features. In this case, our proposed method can be applied using XQuery standard language. The third column shows whether the strategies have concerned on preserving the semantics of the documents. In this case our proposed method is the only one that has preserved the semantics.

Table 1. Comparison of the related work with the proposed methodology

XML UPDATE	Operation			Standard	Preserve Semantics
	Delete	Insert	Replace		
Prop. language	✔	✔	✔	✗	✗
XML Update	✔	✔	✗	✔	✗
XML API	✔	✔	✗	✗	✗
Proposed method	✔	✔	✔	✔	✔

4 Mapping Aggregation Relationship to XML Schema

During XML update checking, we will require a schema to validate the document structure. Among different schema languages (XML-Data, DDML, DCD, SOX, RDF, DTD) [6], we select to use *XML Schema.* It has high precision in defining the data type, as well as an effective ability to define the semantic constraints of a document.

a. **Cardinality Constraint:** The first constraint in aggregation that can be captured by XML Schema is the cardinality constraint. We can determine the *minoccurs* and *maxoccurs*, even though it is only applicable for element. For example, *faculty* has to have at least one staff to unbounded number of staff.

b. **Adhesion Constraint:** The adhesion constraint for an attribute can be determined by using *use* specification. If the *use* is *required*, we have a strong adhesion. Otherwise, it is a weak adhesion. For an element, this constraint can be identified from the cardinality as well. If the minimum cardinality is one (1..1, 1..N), the adhesion is strong. For example, a *staff* has a strong adhesion with the attribute *staffID* and element *staffName*, but has a weak adhesion with the element *address*.

c. **Ordering Constraint:** The ordering constraint in XML Schema is defined using "sequence". The ordering is only applicable for the element and not the attribute. In general practice, the attribute is located after all the elements of the same "whole" component. For example, the elements *street*, *suburb*, and *postcode* in an *address* are in a specific order.

d. **Homogeneity Constraint:** The homogeneity constraint is not treated by using a unique specification in XML Schema. In fact, if we only declare a single element under a "whole" component, it has shown the homogenous aggregation. For example, the component *section* under a *content* is a homogenous aggregation.

e. **Share-ability Constraint:** The share-ability constraint in XML Schema will be treated as an association relationship. XML Schema provides ID/IDREF and key/keyref for this purpose. We have chosen to use the latter based on several reasons: (i) key has no restriction on the lexical space [12], (ii) key cannot be duplicated and thus facilitate the uniqueness semantic of a key node, and (iii) key/keyref can be defined in a specific element and thus, helping the implementer to maintain the reference.

5 Proposed XML Update Methodology

In this section we differentiate the XML Update methodology into three main parts: deletion, insertion, and replacement. On each of them, the checking is further differentiated based on the targeted node such as element/attribute and key/keyref.

5.1 Method for Delete Operation

Deletion of any node type can affect the cardinality and adhesion constraints. Specifically for key node, the deletion can create a referential integrity problem as well. If the key is being referred by any key reference, there will be dangling pointers. At the time of writing, XML query languages such as XQuery allows dangling references to data that is not present. However, it is actually not desirable since it can create some incomplete data retrieval. Unlike in any other data model, there has no attempt to provide referential integrity action such as cascade, nullify, or restriction.

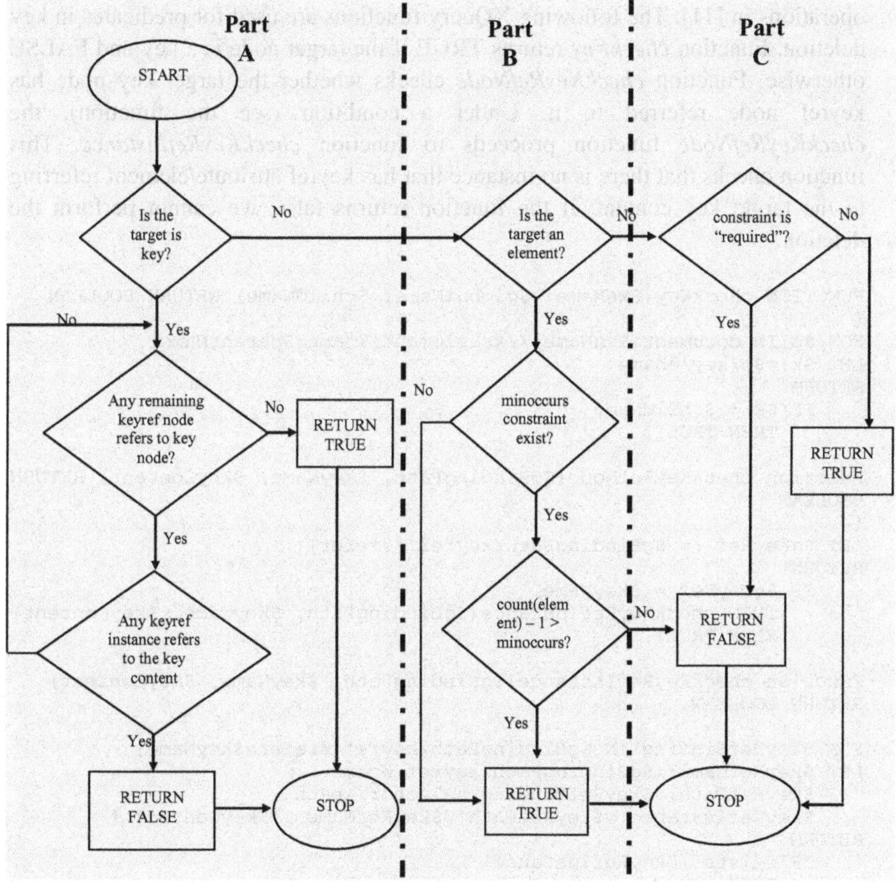

Fig. 4. Methodology for Delete Update

The chart (see Fig. 4) shows the proposed checking method for the update. It is divided into three parts. Part A shows the method for key node deletion. If the method returns TRUE, the deletion can be executed since the method has checked the semantics of the document. If it returns FALSE, we restrict the deletion since it will violate any semantics constraints. Part B shows the method for element deletion. The cardinality and adhesion constraint checking is performed. Part C shows the method for attribute deletion. The adhesion constraint checking is performed. Same with Part A, in Part B and Part C the functions might return TRUE or FALSE. The result will determine whether the deletion can be executed or not.

a. **Key Node Deletion:** For the deletion of a key node (part A), checking on instances is required. Besides avoiding integrity problem, this is also necessary to maintain the share-ability constraint in aggregation, since this constraint is implemented by using key/keyref.

   To implement this checking method, we use XQuery, utilizing the primitive operations in [11]. The following XQuery functions are used for predicates in key deletion. Function *checkKey* returns TRUE if the target node is a key and FALSE otherwise. Function *checkKeyRefNode* checks whether the target key node has keyref node referred to it. Under a condition (see the function), the *checkKeyRefNode* function proceeds to function *checkKeyRefInstance.* This function checks that there is no instance that has keyref attribute/element referring to the target key content. If the function returns false, we cannot perform the deletion.

```
FUNCTION checkKey($xsName, $globalName, $childName) RETURN BOOLEAN
{
FOR $p IN document($xsName)//xs:element[@name=$parentName],
LET $k:=$p/key/@name
RETURN
    IF($k = $childName
       THEN TRUE)}

Function checkKeyRefNode($gBindingPath, $keyName, $keyContent) RETURN
BOOLEAN
{
LET $gKeyRef := $gBindingPath/keyref/[@refer]
RETURN
    IF $gKeyRef = $keyName
       THEN checkKeyRefInstance($gBindingPath, $keyName, $keyContent)
       ELSE TRUE}

Function checkKeyRefInstance($gBindingPath, $keyName, $keyContent)
RETURN BOOLEAN
{
FOR $keyRefBinding IN $gBindingPath/keyref[@refer=$keyName]
LET $keyRefName:=$gBindingPath/keyref/@name
    $keyRefPath:=$keyRefBinding/selector/xpath
    $keyRefInstance:=$keyRefPath[@$keyRefName, "$keyContent"]
RETURN
    IF exists ($keyRefInstance)
       THEN FALSE
       ELSE TRUE}
```

b. **Non-Key Node Deletion:** Part B and part C (see Fig. 4) show the checking for deletion upon an element and an attribute respectively. In each of these methods, we perform checking for all aggregation constraints we have previously mentioned. Note that there is no specific method for keyref. It is because in deletion operation, keyref can be treated like simple data content.

For implementation, we implement a function that will return TRUE if the target node is an element. If it is an element, we proceed to another function, which checks and returns the cardinality constraint of the element. If the deletion violates the cardinality constraint, the operation is restricted. We do not show the whole queries due to the space limitation.

Example

The following example shows the key deletion *subjcode* in document "Faculty.xml". Note that if the *checkKeyRefNode* function returns TRUE, we will delete whole element and not only the key *subjcode*. It is because we do not have trigger-based delete, which will delete the whole element if the key is deleted.

```
FOR $g IN document("Faculty.xml")/Faculty(@FacID = "FSTE")
    $p IN $g/Subject(@SubjCode = "ADB21")
    $c IN $p/SubjCode
LET $cContent := "ADB21"
UPDATE $p{
WHERE checkKey("Faculty.xml", "Faculty", "SubjCode")
     UPDATE $p{
     WHERE checkKeyRefNode($g, "SubjCode", $cContent)
            UPDATE $p{
                  DELETE $p (:delete the key and the siblings:)}}}
```

5.2 Method for Insert Operation

Insertion of a node is more complicated than a deletion because not only we have to check the key, we also have to check the key reference (keyref). The following chart (see Fig. 5) classifies the mechanism into three categories. Part A shows the method for key node insertion. If it returns TRUE, the insertion can be executed. Part B checks the insertion of the keyref node. Part C checks the insertion of simple node content, covering the element node and attribute node.

a. **Key Node Insertion:** For insertion of a key node (part A), we ensure that there is no key content duplication. The problem will not be encountered during the insertion, but it will arise once we have a key reference instance that refers to the duplicated key node.

   To implement the method above, we also use XQuery language. Unlike deletion, insertion requires the constructor of new attribute or new element. We add a function that will return TRUE if the target is not duplicating an existing instance and thus, the insertion can be performed. Otherwise, the insertion should be restricted because it can create an integrity problem.

b. **Keyref Node Insertion:** For insertion of a keyref node (part B), we ensure that the inserted value refers to an existence key node instance. Besides, after this we still have to perform checking on other constraints such as cardinality, adhesion and homogeneity.

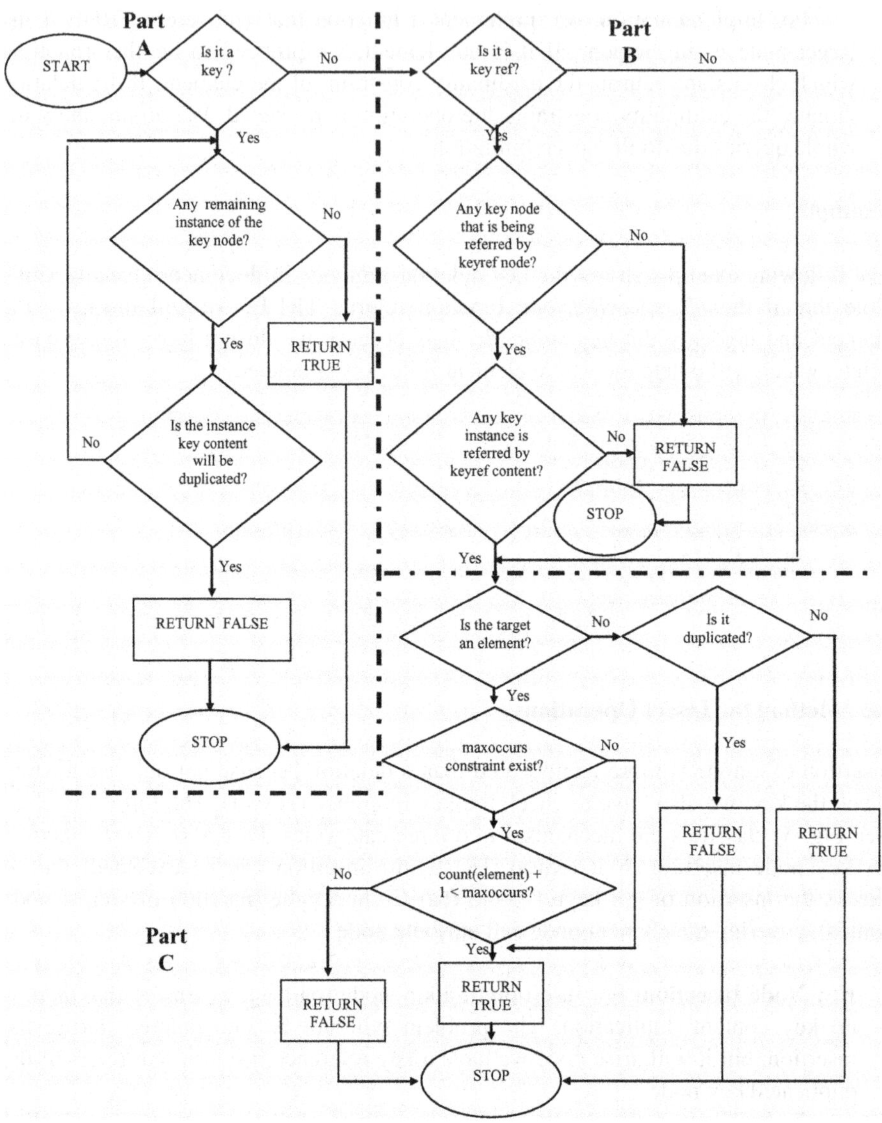

Fig. 5. Methodology for Insert Update

We propose an additional function for keyref insertion. It passes the keyref name and content, and then checks the referred key. If there is an instance being referred, it returns true and we can proceed.

c. **Non-Key Non-Keyref Node Insertion:** The last part is for simple attribute/element node insertion (part C). For attribute insertion, we add an additional function to ensure that the target attribute is not duplicated. As for element insertion, we add two additional functions to calculate the *maxoccurs* constraint of a keyref node. If the particular instance has the maximum number of keyref, we will disable the insertion of another keyref content.

5.3 Method for Replace Operation

Since replacement can be seen as a combination of deletion and insertion, we can reuse the methods we have already described in the last two sub-sections. We do not show the chart for this operation due to the page limitation.

Example

For implementation using XQuery, we want to replace node *SubjName* into "Foundation of Database System". Since the target is not a key nor a keyref, we just need to check whether the target is an element or an attribute. Once we know, we can select the appropriate statement.

```
FOR $g IN document("Faculty.xml")/Faculty(@Faculty_Name = "FSTE")
    $p IN $g//Subject(@SubjectID = "DB21")
    $c IN $p/subjname

UPDATE $p{
WHERE checkChild("Faculty.xml", "Subject", "subjname")
       UPDATE $p{
REPLACE $c WITH <subjname>Foundation of Database System</subjname>}
WHERE checkChild("Faculty.xml", "Subject", "subjname") = FALSE
       UPDATE $p{
REPLACE $c WITH new_att(subjname, "Foundation of Database System")}}
```

6 Discussions

Section 2 discusses a specific conceptual semantic in XML documents, the aggregation relationship. Using semantic network diagram [2] we can depict five constraints associated with this relationship type namely cardinality, adhesion, ordering, homogeneity, and share-ability. Even though these constraints are widely used in the object-oriented conceptual model [8], very rarely we find XML storage application uses this semantic. This work wants to extend the modeling capability of XML Database.

In section 4 we proposed the transformation of the conceptual level semantic constraint into a logical model, in this case using schema language. This step is necessary before we can proceed to the next step, which is the XML Update methodology. It is because our methodology will require the document structure validation that is provided by schema language. We have a few selection of schema language. We select XML Schema based on its modeling strengths to capture different semantics [2][12].

The only constraint that cannot be captured using XML Schema is the share-ability. We implement this constraint as an ordinary association relationship with the shared part component become a separate element and referred by the whole components.

The schema derived from the previous rules is used for the next step. Section 5 discusses the proposed methodology for updating XML document. The method is divided into three operations: deletion, insertion, and replacement. For implementation, we apply the query language XQuery. Not only because it is the most complete W3C-standardized language [14], but also because it is used by most NXD products [3][4][5][7][9].

For each update operation, we distinguish the checking based on the target node such as key/keyref and attribute/element. Our methodology has contributions compared to the current practice:

a. We have included the aggregation semantic constraints as a checking factor. By doing this the conceptual design of the documents can be preserved even after having many updates. In current practice, the updated documents might have constraints that are totally different with the original model. For example, the order of the elements might have changed, the number of instance have been exceeded, etc.

b. We avoid the possibility of database anomalies. The anomalies can be created by duplicated insertion of key node. The anomalies can also be created by inserting a keyref that refers to non-existing instance. In current practice, there is no mechanism that stops users to insert the same key node value or to insert a dangling keyref. These practices will be the potential integrity problems

To the best of our best knowledge, there is no NXD that has preserved the semantic of the XML documents during the update operations. This work has tried to maintain the semantic constraint focusing on the aggregation relationship by doing the checking during the update of the whole component and part component instances.

7 Conclusion

In this paper, we propose checking methodology to preserve semantic constraints during an XML update. The update operations are divided into deletion, insertion, and replacement. Each operation considers different type of target node such as key, key reference, and simple data content whether it is an element or an attribute.

The focus in the paper is on the aggregation relationship type. For the purpose, we deal with the checking mechanism of different constraints such as cardinality, adhesion, ordering, homogeneity, and share-ability. By doing this, we can preserve the conceptual semantic of the XML Documents. For implementation, we apply the method in the XQuery language.

Since Update requires a document structure validation, we also propose the transformation of the document structure into a schema language. For this purpose we select XML Schema. With this extension, XML query languages (in the form of XQuery) are becoming more powerful. Concurrently, it can increase the potential of using tree-form XML repository such as Native XML Database.

References

1. Bourett, R.: XML and Databases. http://www.rpbourret.com/xml/XMLAndDatabases.htm, (2003)
2. Feng, L., Chang, E., Dillon, T.S.: A Semantic Network-Based Design Methodology for XML Documents. ACM Trans. Information System, Vol. 20, No. 4. (2002) 390-421
3. Ipedo.: Ipedo XML Database, http://www.ipedo.com/html/products.html, (2004)
4. Jagadish, H. V., Al-Khalifa, S., Chapman, A., Lakhsmanan, L. V. S., Nierman, A., Paprizos, S., Patel, J. M., Srivastava, D., Wiwattana, N., Wu, Y., Yu, C.: TIMBER: A native XML database. VLDB Journal, Vol. 11, No. 4. (2002) 279-291
5. Meier, W.M.: eXist Native XML Database. In Chauduri, A.B., Rawais, A., Zicari, R. (eds): XML Data Management: Native XML and XML-Enabled Database System. Addison Wesley (2003) 43-68
6. Mercer, D.: XML A Beginner's Guide, Osborne McGraw Hill, New York (2001)
7. Robie, J.: XQuery: A Guided Tour. In Kattz, H. (ed.): XQuery from the Experts. Addison Wesley (2004) 3-78
8. Rumbaugh, J., Blaha, M.R., Lorensen, W., Eddy, F., Premerlani, W.: Object-Oriented Modelling and Design, Prentice Hall, (1991)
9. SODA Technology.: SODA. http://www.sodatech.com/products.html, (2004)
10. Staken, K.: Introduction to Native XML Databases. http://www.xml.com/pub/a/2001/10/31/nativexmldb.html, (2001)
11. Tatarinov, I., Ives, Z.G., Halevy, A. Y., Weld, D. S.: Updating XML. ACM SIGMOD (2001) 413-424
12. Vlist, E. V-D.: XML Schema, O'Reilly, Sebastopol (2002)
13. W3C: XML Schema. http://www.w3.org/XML/Schema, (2001)
14. W3C: XQuery 1.0: An XML Query Language. http://www.w3.org/TR/xquery, (2001)
15. XML DB: XUpdate – XML Update Language, http://www.xmldb.org/xupdate/, (2004)

Exploiting PageRank at Different Block Level

Xue-Mei Jiang[1], Gui-Rong Xue[2], Wen-Guan Song[1], Hua-Jun Zeng[3], Zheng Chen[3], and Wei-Ying Ma[3]

[1] Department of Information Management, Shanghai Commercial University, 2271 Zhongshan West Ave., 200235 Shanghai, P.R.China
cs_xmjiang@hotmail.com, swg@21cn.com

[2] Department of Computer Science and Engineering, Shanghai Jiao Tong University, 1954 Huashan Ave., 200030 Shanghai, P.R.China
grxue@sjtu.edu.cn

[3] Microsoft Research Asia, 5F, Sigma Center
49 Zhichun Road, Beijing 100080, P.R.China
{hjzeng, zhengc, wyma}@microsoft.com

Abstract. In recent years, information retrieval methods focusing on the link analysis have been developed; The PageRank and HITS are two typical ones According to the hierarchical organization of Web pages, we could partition the Web graph into blocks at different level, such as page level, directory level, host level and domain level. On the basis of block, we could analyze the different hyperlinks among pages. Several approaches proposed that the intra-hyperlink in a host maybe less useful in computing the PageRank. However, there are no reports on how concretely the intra- or inter-hyperlink affects the PageRank. Furthermore, based on different block level, inter-hyperlink and intra-hyperlink can be two relative concepts. Thus which level should be optimal to distinguish the intra- or inter-hyperlink? And how the ratio set between the intra-hyperlink and inter-hyperlink could ultimately improve performance of the PageRank algorithm? In this paper, we analyze the link distribution at the different block level and evaluate the importance of the intra- and inter-hyperlink to PageRank on the TREC Web Track data set. Experiment shows that, if we set the block at host level and the ratio of the weight between the intra-hyperlink and inter-hyperlink is 1:4, the retrieval could achieve the best performance.

1 Introduction

In recent years, several information retrieval methods using the information about the link structure have been developed and proved to provide significant enhancement to the performance of Web search in practice. Google's PageRank[3][14] and Keinberg's HITS[12] are two fundamental algorithms by employing the hyperlink structure among the Web page. A number of extensions to these two algorithms are also proposed, such as [1][2][4][5][6][9][10][11]. All these link analysis algorithms are

X. Zhou et al. (Eds.): WISE 2004, LNCS 3306, pp. 241–252, 2004.
© Springer-Verlag Berlin Heidelberg 2004

based on two assumptions: (1) the links convey human endorsement. If there is a link from page *u* to page *v*, then the page *v* is deemed to be valuable to the author of page *u*. Thus, the importance of page *u* can, in part, spread to the pages besides *v* it links to. (2) Pages that are co-cited by a certain page are likely to share the same topic as well as to help retrieval.

Considering the Web is a nested structure, the Web graph could be partitioned into blocks according to the different level of Web structure, such as page level, directory level, host level and domain level. We call such constructed Web graph as the *block-based* Web graph, which is shown in Fig.1 (left). Furthermore, the hyperlink at the block level could be divided into two types: Intra-hyperlink and Inter-hyperlink, where inter-hyperlink is the hyperlink that links two Web pages over different blocks while intra-hyperlink is the hyperlink that links two Web pages in the same block. As shown in Fig1, the dash line represents the intra-hyperlink while the bold line represents the inter-hyperlink. For example, when we partition the Web graph at the directory level, the web pages in the same directory are organized as a block. The hyperlinks which link two Web pages in the same directory are called as intra-hyperlink while the hyperlinks which link two Web pages over different directories are called as inter-hyperlink. There are several analysis on the block based Web graph. Kamvar et al. [18] propose to utilize the block structure to accelerate the computation of PageRank. Further analysis on the Website block could be seen in [13][15]. And the existed methods about PageRank could be considered as the link analysis based on page level in our approach. However, the intra-link and inter-link are not discriminated to be taken as the same weight although several approaches proposed that the intra-hyperlink in a host maybe less useful in computing the PageRank [7].

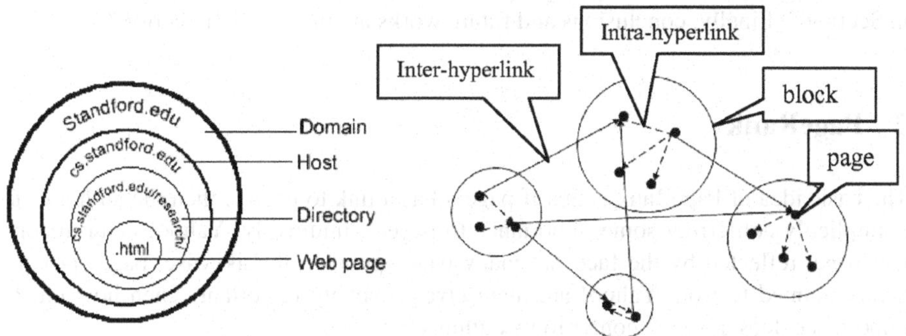

Fig. 1. Block-based Web graph

Since the intra-hyperlink and inter-hyperlink are two relative concepts based on different block level, our motivation is to analyze the importance of the intra- and inter-hyperlink to PageRank as well as find the optimal block level. Intuitively, we consider a hyperlink from a page *u* to page *v*, if *u* and *v* belong to different host then *v* will be more valuable for *u* taken an objective view, but if *u* and *v* belong to the same host then the link is considered to be probably made for convenience of the Web browsing. Therefore it will be useful for the link analysis to analyze the hyperlink, dividing them into links inside block (Intra-hyperlink) and links between the blocks (Inter-hyperlink).

In this paper, we first analyze the distribution of hyperlink at the four different block levels. Then, we construct the corresponding Web graph by leveraging the weight of the inter-hyperlink and intra-hyperlink of the block. By assigning different weight, we want to disclose which type of hyperlink are more useful to PageRank algorithm and how the ratio set between the intra-hyperlink and inter-hyperlink could achieve best performance on searching. Furthermore, we want to know which level the PageRank algorithm could be an adaptive block to leverage the intra-hyperlink and inter-hyperlink.

The contribution of this work can be summarized as follows.

- We first propose to construct the block based Web graph by partitioning Web graph into the block according to page level, directory level, host level and domain level, respectively.
- Based on the block based Web graph, the intra-hyperlink and inter-hyperlink are discriminated to be set different ratio in calculating PageRank, from which ratio 1:4 is found to be the best to ultimately improve the performance of the Web search.
- We also evaluate four different segmentation of the Web graph, and show that the host block is best level to distinguish the intra-hyperlink and the inter-hyperlink.

The rest of this paper is organized as follows. In Section 2, we review the PageRank algorithm. In Section 3, we present the characteristics about the Web graph structure. In Section 4, we show our ranking algorithm. Our experimental results are presented in Section 5. Finally, conclusions and future works are discussed in Section 6.

2 PageRank

The basic idea of PageRank is that if page u has a link to page v, then the author of u is implicitly conferring some importance to page v. Intuitively, Yahoo! is an important page, reflected by the fact that many pages point to it. Likewise, pages prominently pointed to from Yahoo! are themselves probably important. Then how much importance does a page u confer to its outlinks?

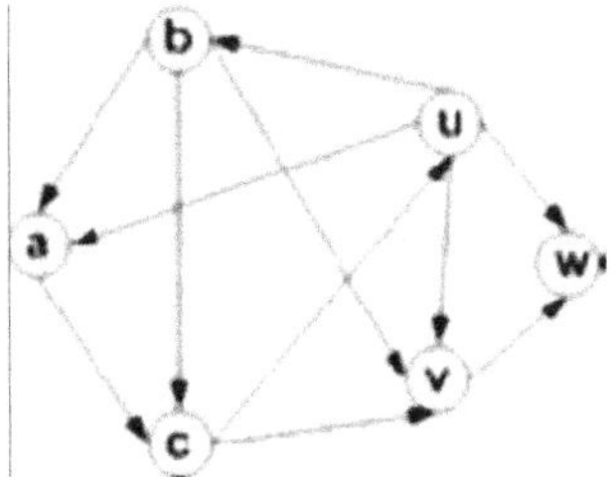

Fig. 2. Web Graph

Let N_u be the outdegree of page *u*, and let *PR* (*u*) represent the importance (i.e., PageRank) of page *u*. Then the link (*u*, *v*) confers $PR(u)/N_u$ units of rank to *v*. This simple idea leads to the following iterative fixpoint computation that yields the rank vector over all of the pages on the Web. If *n* is the total number of pages, assign all pages the initial value 1/ *n*. Let B_v represent the set of pages pointing to *v*. In each iteration, propagate the ranks as follows:

$$\forall_v PR^{(i+1)}(v) = \sum_{u \in B_v} PR^{(i)}(u) / N_u \tag{1}$$

We continue the iterations until *PR* stabilizes to some threshold. The final vector *PR* contains the PageRank vector over the Web. This vector is computed only once after each crawl of the Web; the values can then be used to influence the ranking of search results.

The process can also be expressed as the following eigenvector calculation, providing useful insight into PageRank. Let *M* be the square, stochastic matrix corresponding to the directed Web graph *G*. If there is a link from page *j* to page *i*, then let the matrix entry m_{ij} have the value $1/N_j$. Let all other entries have the value 0. One iteration of the previous fixpoint computation corresponds to the matrix-vector multiplication $M \times \overrightarrow{PR}$. Repeatedly multiplying $\overrightarrow{PR}$ by *M* yields the dominant eigenvector $\overrightarrow{PR}$ of the matrix *M* . In other words, *PR* is the solution to

$$\overrightarrow{PR} = M \times \overrightarrow{PR} \tag{2}$$

Because M^T is the stochastic transition matrix over the graph *G*, PageRank can be viewed as the stationary probability distribution for the Markov chain induced by a random walk on the Web graph.

However, in practice, many pages have no in-links (or the weight of them is 0), and the eigenvector of the above equation is mostly zero. Therefore, the basic model is modified to obtain an "actual model" using *random walk*. Upon browsing a webpage, with the probability 1-ε, a user randomly chooses one of the links on the current page and jumps to the page it links to; and with the probability ε, the user "reset" by jumping to a web-page picked uniformly and at random from the collection. Therefore the ranking formula is modified to the following form:

$$\forall_v PR^{(i+1)}(v) = \frac{\varepsilon}{n} + (1-\varepsilon) \sum_{u \in B_v} PR^{(i)}(u) / N_u \tag{3}$$

Or, in the matrix form:

$$\overrightarrow{PR} = \frac{\varepsilon}{n} \vec{e} + (1-\varepsilon) M \overrightarrow{PR} \tag{4}$$

where $\vec{e}$ is the vector of all 1's, and ε ($0<\varepsilon<1$) is a parameter. In our experiment, we set ε to 0.15. Instead of computing an eigenvector, the simplest iterative method—Jacobi iteration is used to resolve the equation.

Table 1. Terminology using the sample URL http://cs.standford.edu/research/index.html

Term	Example: cs.standford.edu/research/index.html
Domain	Standford.edu
Host	cs.standford.edu
Directory	cs.standford.edu/research/
Page	cs.standford.edu/research/index.html

3 Block Structure of the Web

The key terminology we use in the remaining discussion is given in Table 1.

As we known, the whole Web is a graph structure where the Web pages represent the nodes and hyperlink between the Web pages represents the edge between nodes. Such Web graph looks like a flat. All the nodes are considered as the same level and all the hyperlinks are set equal weight in existed method about PageRank.

The fact is that the Web is also a hierarchical structure based on the organization of the Web page, for example the website structure. Hence the Web graph is also a hierarchical structure ranged from the Web page to the domain. We could partition the Web graph into the blocks according to the four different views: page level, directory level, host level and domain level. On the basis of different blocks, the hyperlink could be divided into two types: Intra-hyperlink and Inter-hyperlink.

According to the analysis on Section 1, the weight of the hyperlink should be set different weight when we compute the PageRank. The basic intuition is that the hyperlink within the same block is mainly for navigation while the link over the blocks is for recommendation. So we should give the different weight to the two types of link. In order to testify the intuition, we perform the PageRank on the modified Web graph over the four different block levels Web graph.

To investigate the structure of the block based Web, we run the following simple experiment. We take all the hyperlinks in the .GOV collection [20] , and count how many of the links are "Intra-hyperlink" and "Inter-hyperlink" at different block level.

Table 2. The Number of intra-hyperlink and inter-hyperlink at different level

Level	Intra-hyperlink	Inter-hyperlink
Domain	7342031 (97%)	227322 (3%)
Host	6506578 (86%)	1062775 (14%)
Directory	2956566 (39.1%)	4612787 (60.9%)
Page	0 (0%)	7569353 (100%)

As shown in Table 2, the number of the intra-hyperlink and the inter-hyperlink at four different level is different, so we also should evaluate which block level to distinguish the intra-hyperlink and the inter-hyperlink could achieve the higher performance than other three levels.

4 PageRank at Different Level

In this section, we consider the different weight of the hyperlink according to the link that belongs to the same block or across two different blocks. First, we construct a matrix to represent the link graph, where each represents the weight of the link; then, a modified link analysis algorithm is used on the matrix to calculate the importance of the pages. Finally, we re-rank the Web pages based on two kinds to re-ranking mechanics: order-based re-ranking and score-based re-ranking.

4.1 Matrix Construction

The Web can be modeled as a directed graph $G = (V, E)$ where $V = \{p_i \mid 1 \le i \le n\}$ is the set of vertices representing all the pages in the web, and E encompasses the set of links between the pages. $l_{i,j} \in E$ is used to denote that there exists a link between the page p_i and p_j.

We propose to construct a new *block-based* Web graph instead of the original *page-based* Web graph. This new graph is a weighted directed graph $G' = (V, E')$, where V is same as above and E' encompasses the links between pages. Furthermore, each link $l_{i,j} \in E'$ is associated with a new parameter w_{ij} denoting the weight of the page p_j to page p_i, where the weight is calculated according to the hyperlink that is in the block or between the block. In this paper, we tune the weight of the link by value w_{ij}:

$$w_{ij} = \begin{cases} \alpha & p_i, p_j \text{ in same block} \\ \beta & p_i, p_j \text{ in different blocks} \end{cases} \quad (5)$$

Where α and β are the parameters. In this paper, we tune the α and β as the ratio between inter-hyperlink and intra-hyperlink to evaluate how the different types of the links affect the PageRank of the pages.

4.2 Modified PageRank

After obtaining the block-based Web structure, we apply a link analysis algorithm similar to PageRank to re-rank the web-pages. We construct a matrix to describe the graph. In particular, assume the graph contains n pages. The $n \times n$ adjacency matrix is denoted by A and the entries $A[i, j]$ is defined to be the weight of the links $l_{i,j}$.

The adjacency matrix is used to compute the rank score of each page. In an "ideal" form, the rank score PR_i of page p_i is evaluated by a function on the rank scores of all the pages that point to page p_i :

$$PR_i = \sum_{j:l_{ji} \in E} PR_j \cdot A[j,i] \tag{6}$$

This recursive definition gives each page a fraction of the rank of each page pointing to it—inversely weighted by the strength of the links of that page. The above equation can be written in the form of matrix as:

$$\overrightarrow{PR} = A\overrightarrow{PR} \tag{7}$$

However, in practice, many pages have no in-links (or the weight of them is 0), and the eigenvector of the above equation is mostly zero. Therefore, the basic model is modified to obtain an "actual model" using *random walk*. Upon browsing a web-page, with the probability 1-ε, a user randomly chooses one of the links on the current page and jumps to the page it links to; and with the probability ε, the user "reset" by jumping to a web-page picked uniformly and at random from the collection. Therefore the ranking formula is modified to the following form:

$$PR_i = \frac{\varepsilon}{n} + (1-\varepsilon) \sum_{j:l_{j,i} \in E} PR_j \cdot A[j,i] \tag{8}$$

or, in the matrix form:

$$\overrightarrow{PR} = \frac{\varepsilon}{n}\vec{e} + (1-\varepsilon)A\overrightarrow{PR} \tag{9}$$

where $\vec{e}$ is the vector of all 1's, and ε ($0<\varepsilon<1$) is a parameter. In our experiment, we set ε to 0.15.

4.3 Re-ranking

The re-ranking mechanism is based on two types of linear combination: the score based re-ranking and the order based re-ranking. The score based re-ranking uses a linear combination of content-based similarity score and the PageRank value of all web-pages:

$$Score(w) = \lambda Sim + (1-\lambda)\, PR \quad (\lambda \in [0, 1]) \tag{10}$$

where *Sim* is the content-based similarity between web-pages and query words, and *PR* is the PageRank value.

The order based re-ranking is based on the rank orders of the web-pages. Here we use a linear combination of pages' positions in two lists in which one list is sorted by similarity scores the other list is sorted by PageRank values. That is,

$$Score(w) = \lambda O_{Sim} + (1-\lambda) O_{PR} \quad (\lambda \in [0, 1]) \tag{11}$$

where O_{Sim} and O_{PR} are positions of page *w* in similarity score list and PageRank list, respectively.

We have conducted the experiments that the order based re-ranking could achieve higher performance than the score based re-ranking. So in this paper, we just impose the order based re-ranking method for evaluation.

5 Evluation

In this section, several experiments were performed to compare four block level link analysis algorithms, i.e. domain-based PageRank, host-based PageRank, directory-based PageRank and traditional PageRank.

5.1 Experimental Environment

By 1999, link analysis and Web search in general have become a "hot" topic and a special "Web Track" in the annual TREC benchmarking exercise [20] was dedicated to Web search related tasks [19]. Topic Distillation task [6] is mainly evaluated using the measure of precision at Top 10 and the goal of which is to find a small number of key resources on a topic as opposed to the more conventional (ad-hoc) listing of relevant pages. Topic Distillation, although not that far removed from ad-hoc is perhaps more suited to Web search evaluation because it has been found that over 85% of users never look beyond the first page of the results from any Web search [17].

In order to support the experiments of participants, TREC distributes test collections that consist of three components: a set of documents, a set of queries (called topics) and a set of relevance judgments for each query.

In this paper, we do the analysis on the .GOV collection used in 2002(and 2003 also) TREC Web track, which are better reflect today's WWW. The collection consists of 1,247,753 documents from a fresh crawl of the Web pages made in early 2002. Among them, 1,053,372 are text/html, which are used in our experiment. Finding for TREC-2002 illustrate that for some participants, the application of link analysis did indeed improve retrieval performance in the new Topic Distillation task. Link analysis can provide some extra useful information for ranking. This situation is much like the real world Web search. So the corpus and queries are very suitable in evaluating different link analysis algorithm.

They are totally 50 queries. The number of relevant pages (based on human judgment) for each query ranged from 1 to 86 with average 10.32. Among them 31 queries have less than 10 relevant pages, so the average P@10 is a litter bit low.

5.2 Relevance Weighting

In our experiments, we use BM2500 [16] as the relevance weighting function. It is of the form:

$$\sum_{T\in Q}\omega\frac{(k_1+1)tf(k_3+1)qtf}{(K+tf)(k_3+qtf)} \tag{12}$$

where Q is a query containing key terms T, tf is the term frequency in a specific document, qtf is the frequency of the term within the topic from which Q was derived, and w is the Robertson/Sparck Jones weight of T in Q. It is calculated by

$$\log\frac{(r+0.5)/(R-r+0.5)}{(n-r+0.5)/(N-n-R+r+0.5)} \tag{13}$$

where N is the number of documents in the collection. n is the number of documents containing the term, R is the number of documents relevant to a specific topic, and r is the number of relevant documents containing the term. In our experiment, the R and r are set to zero. In the equation 12, K is calculated by

$$k_1((1\text{-}b)+b\times dl/avdl) \tag{14}$$

where dl and $avdl$ denote the document length and the average document length. In our experiments, we tune the k_1=4.2, k_3=1000, b=0.8 to achieve the best baseline (we took the result of using relevance only as out baseline). The average precision is 0.1285. The P@10 is 0.112. Compared with the best result of TREC 2003 anticipants (with P@10 of 0.128), this baseline is reasonable. TREC 2003 did not report the average precision.

5.3 Performance of 50 Queries on .GOV Collection

In order to evaluate the importance of the intra-hyperlink and inter-hyperlink based on the four block levels, we construct the Web graph by tuning the ratio between α and β from 5:1 to 1:10 and calculate the p@10 average precision of 50 queries on the Web TREC data.

Meanwhile, we combined the relevance rank with PageRank of four levels. We chose the top 1000 results according to the relevance, and then we sorted these 1000 results according to their PageRank values. Thus, we get two ranking list. One is according to the relevance and the other is according to importance. We tune the parameter λ in equation 11 from 0.76 to 0.9. The results of P@10 precision with λ are shown in Fig 2, Fig 3, and Fig 4. When the ratio between α and β is set as 1:1, the algorithm of the other three levels are performed as traditional PageRank algorithm.

As we can see from the Fig 3, Fig 4, and Fig 5, the different weight of the intra-hyperlink and inter-hyperlink is sure to affect the performance of the P@10 precision. Generally, the performance is better when the weight of the intra-hyperlink is lower than that of the inter-hyperlink.

From the Fig 3, the directory-based PageRank could achieve the highest performance when we set the ratio between α and β as 1:7 while λ as 0.81.

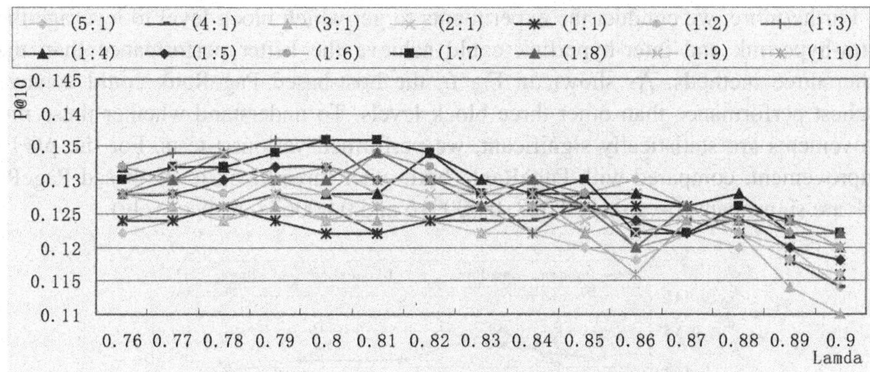

Fig. 3. Performance of directory-based PageRank

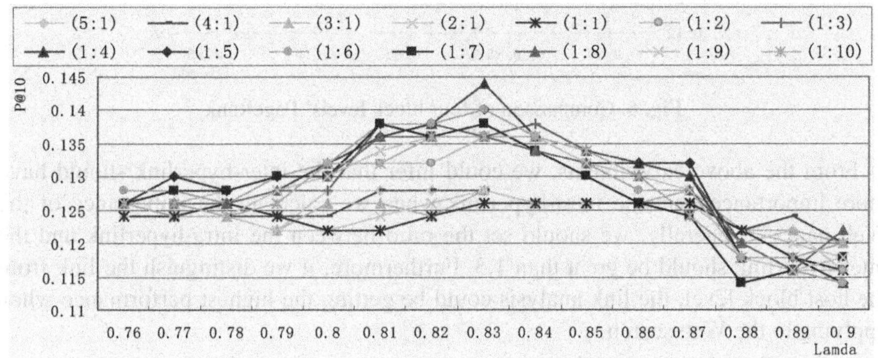

Fig. 4. Performance of host-based PageRank

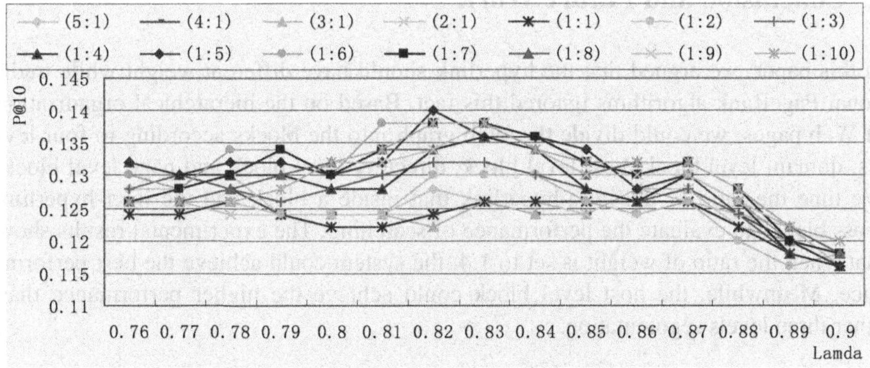

Fig. 5. Performance of domain-based PageRank

From the Fig 4, host-based PageRank could achieve the highest performance when we set the ratio between α and β as 1:4 while λ as 0.83.

From the Fig 5, domain-based PageRank could achieve the highest performance when we set the ratio between α and β as 1:5 while λ as 0.81.

Furthermore, we conduct the experiments to get which block level to leverage the intra-hyperlink and inter-hyperlink could achieve the better performance than the other three methods. As shown in Fig 6, the host-based PageRank could achieve highest performance than other three block levels. To understand whether these improvements are statistically significant, we performed various t-tests. For the p@10 improvement, compared with PageRank, both other three block levels based PageRank are significant (p-value is 0.028, 0.000916 and 0.000674, respectively).

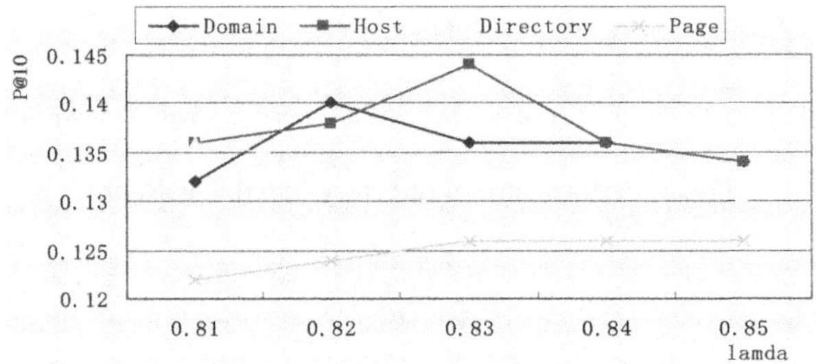

Fig. 6. Comparison of four block levels' PageRank

From the above experiments, we could infer that the inter-hyperlink should have more importance than the intra-hyperlink when we calculate the importance of the Web pages. Generally, we should set the ratio between the intra-hyperlink and the inter-hyperlink should be great than 1:3. Furthermore, if we distinguish the link from the host block level, the link analysis could be getting the highest performance when applying to the Web search.

6 Conclusion and Future Work

In this paper, we argued that the hyperlink should have different weight while traditional PageRank algorithms ignored this fact. Based on the hierarchical organization of Web pages, we could divide the Web graph into the blocks according to four levels: domain level block, host level block, directory level block and page level block. We tune the ratio of the intra-hyperlink that inside a block and the inter-hyperlink cross blocks to evaluate the performance of searching. The experimental results show that when the ratio of weight is set to 1:4, the system could achieve the best performance. Meanwhile, the host level block could achieve the higher performance than other three levels segmentation.

References

[1] B. Amento, L. Terveen, and W. Hill. Does "authority" mean quality? predicting expert quality ratings of web documents. In Proc. of ACM SIGIR 2000, pages 296-303.

[2] K. Bharat and M. R. Henzinger. Improved algorithms for topic distillation in a hyperlinked environment. In Proc. of the ACM-SIGIR, 1998.
[3] S. Brin and L. Page, "The anatomy of a large-scale hypertextual Web search engine", In The Seventh International World Wide Web Conference, 1998.
[4] S. Chakrabarti, B. Dom, D. Gibson, J. Kleinberg, P.Raghavan, and S. Rajagopalan. Automatic resource list compilation by analyzing hyperlink structure and associated text. In Proc. of the 7th Int. World Wide Web Conference, May 1998.
[5] S. Chakrabarti, Integrating the Document Object Model with hyperlinks for enhanced topic distillation and information extraction, In the 10th International World Wide Web Conference, 2001.
[6] S. Chakrabarti, M. Joshi, and V. Tawde, Enhanced topic distillation using text, markup tags, and hyperlinks, In Proceedings of the 24th annual international ACM SIGIR conference on Research and development in information retrieval , ACM Press, 2001, pp. 208-216.
[7] Christof Monz, Jaap Kamps, and Marrten de Rijke, The University of Amsterdam at TREC 2002.
[8] Brian D. Davison. Recognizing nepotistic links on the Web. In Artificial Intelligence for Web Search, pages 23--28. AAAI Press, July 2000.
[9] G. Flake, S. Lawrence, L. Giles, and F. Coetzee, Self-organization and identification of web communities, IEEE Computer, pp. 66-71, 2002.
[10] D. Gibson, J. Kleinberg, and P. Raghavan. Inferring web communities from link topology. In Proceedings of the 9th ACM Conference on Hypertext and Hypermedia (HYPER-98), pages 225--234, New York, June 20--24 1998. ACM Press.
[11] T.H. Haveliwala. Topic-sensitive PageRank. In Proc. of the 11th Int. World Wide Web Conference, May 2002.
[12] J. Kleinberg, Authoritative sources in a hyperlinked environment, Journal of the ACM, Vol. 46, No. 5, pp. 604-622, 1999.
[13] Krishna Bharat, Bay-Wei Chang, Monika Rauch Henzinger, Matthias Ruhl. Who Links to Whom: Mining Linkage between Web Sites. 1st International Conference on Data Mining (ICDM) 51-58 (2001).
[14] L. Page, S. Brin, R. Motwani, and T. Winograd, The PageRank citation ranking: Bringing order to the web, Technical report, Stanford University, Stanford, CA, 1998.
[15] Nadav Eiron and Kevin S. McCurley, Locality, Hierarchy, and Bidirectionality on the Web, Workshop on Web Algorithms and Models, 2003.
[16] S. E. Robertson, Overview of the okapi projects, Journal of Documentation, Vol. 53, No. 1, 1997, pp. 3-7.
[17] Silverstein C, Henzingger M, Marais J and Moricz M. Analysis of a Very Large AltaVista Query Log. Digital SRC Technical Note 1998-014.
[18] S. Kamvar, T. Haveliwala, C.Manning and G. Golub, Exploiting the Block Structure of the Web for Computing PageRank. In Proc. of the 12th Int. World Wide Web Conference, May 2003.
[19] Hawking D, Overview of the TREC-9 Web Track. In Proc. of the 9th Annual TREC Conference, pp.87-102.
[20] TREC http://trec.nist.gov/.

Multi-type Features Based Web Document Clustering

Shen Huang[1], Gui-Rong Xue[1], Ben-Yu Zhang[2], Zheng Chen[2], Yong Yu[1], and Wei-Ying Ma[2]

[1] Department of Computer Science and Engineering, Shanghai Jiao Tong University, 1954 Huashan Ave., Shanghai, 200030, P.R.China
{shuang, yyu}@cs.sjtu.edu.cn, grxue@sjtu.edu.cn
[2] Microsoft Research Asia, 5F, Sigma Center
49 Zhichun Road, Beijing, 100080, P.R.China
{byzhang, zhengc, wyma}@microsoft.com

Abstract. Clustering has been demonstrated as a feasible way to explore the contents of document collection and organize search engine results. For this task, many features of Web page, such as content, anchor text, URL, hyperlink etc, can be exploited and different results can be obtained. We expect to provide a unified and even better result for end users. Some work have studied how to use several types of features together to perform clustering. Most of them focus on ensemble method or combination of similarity. In this paper, we propose a novel algorithm: Multi-type Features based Reinforcement Clustering (MFRC). This algorithm does not use a unique combine score for all feature spaces, but uses the intermediate clustering result in one feature space as additional information to gradually enhance clustering in other spaces. Finally a consensus can be achieved by such mutual reinforcement. And the experimental results show that MFRC also provides some performance improvement.

1 Introduction

World Wide Web grows with an unbelievable speed [12]. In such situation, autonomous or semi-autonomous methods for Web document clustering become more and more indispensable [21]. Clustering helps users tackle the information overload problem in several ways [7]: explore the contents of a document collection; organize and browse the result list returned by search engine; group duplicate and near duplicate documents. However, such unsupervised method can hardly achieve a good performance when evaluated using labeled data [7]. On the other hand, Web document has many different types of features including content, anchor text, URL, hyperlink etc. Using different kinds of feature, the clustering result will be somewhat different. We dedicate to find the optimal method which effectively exploits all kinds of features to get more consistent and better clustering results.

Many research focus on clustering using multi-type features. One intuitive way to combine results based on different features is called as *ensemble clustering* [4][10][15][16], which combines multiple partitionings of objects without accessing

X. Zhou et al. (Eds.): WISE 2004, LNCS 3306, pp. 253–265, 2004.
© Springer-Verlag Berlin Heidelberg 2004

the original features. Such algorithms do not care how to get the different sets of partitions and can be smoothly exploited by clustering based on multi-type features. Ensemble clustering attempts to solve the problem that no original features available and only label information can be used to get a consensus result. Different with these work, what we try to solve is how to effectively combine multi-type features. Another method is to combine the similarity based on different features. For example, the similarity based on hyperlink feature has been integrated with content similarity in some work to improve clustering [5][18][19]. The main problem for similarity combination is the weights of different features are hard to determine. Linear regression is a choice, but as we show in experiment section, it does not work well in clustering task.

The ideas of Co-Training [1] and Co-EM [11] enlighten us to propose a new combination method. Co-Training is applied to learning problems that have a natural way to divide their features into subsets each of which are sufficient to learn the target concept. Co-EM is a semi-supervised, multi-view algorithm that use the hypothesis learned in one "view" to probabilistically label the examples in the other one. Similarly, we use the intermediate clustering result in one feature space as additional information to enhance clustering in other spaces. Thus different types of features are taken into account simultaneously and reinforce each other. We call it *mutual reinforcement*. Figure 1 shows an example for this idea: two Web pages are similar in URL feature space and help us find some implicitly related terms in their content. In step 1, this information can be exploited by the clustering in content space. Vice versa, in step 2, the newly found related URL terms will benefit the clustering in URL space.

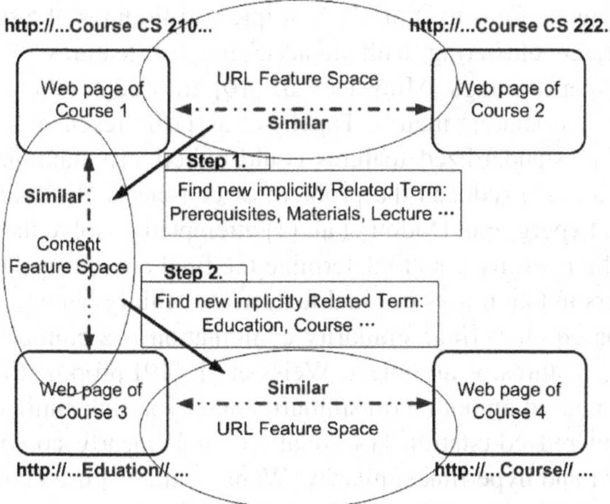

Fig. 1. An example for mutual reinforcement relation between content and URL feature.

We implement the mutual reinforcement idea in two steps. First, we transfer the similarity among different feature spaces by feature construction method. Then, we borrow the idea in [8] to generate *pseudo class* using the new feature vectors created in the first step. With such class label, supervised feature selection[1] can be done to improve performance. Feature construction and pseudo class based feature selection are both implemented in an iterative way. So they can be well integrated into an iterative clustering algorithm, such as K-means. We call such method *Multi-type Features based Reinforcement Clustering (MFRC)*. The main contributions of this work are:

- A novel reinforcement method is proposed to combine multiple clustering results based on multi-type features. The intermediate clustering results are considered to be useful for the clustering in the next iteration.
- Feature construction and feature selection are performed during the mutual reinforcement process. The feature dimensions can be reduced largely and clustering is speed up while performance is improved.
- This method is evaluated using two WebKB benchmarks and one ODP dataset. Experimental results showed that our approach can work well in most cases.

The rest of the paper is organized as follows: Section 2 presents some related work. In Section 3, we propose the general idea of mutual reinforcement clustering. Section 4 introduces feature construction and pseudo class based feature selection in MFRC. Section 5 shows the experimental results on three datasets. Finally, we give the conclusion and the directions of future work in Section 6.

2 Related Work

Ensemble clustering attempts to combine multiple partitionings of a set of objects into a single consolidated clustering without accessing the features or algorithms that determined these partitionings. Minaei et al. [10] showed how consensus function operated on the co-association matrix. Topchy et al. [16] presented a consensus function in the space of standardized features could effectively maximize mutual information. Strehl et al. [15] reduced the problem of consensus clustering to finding the minimum cut of a hypergraph. Dudoit et al. [4] attempted to solve the correspondence problem and used a majority vote to determine the final consensus partition. Our idea in this paper differs in that it uses original features to achieve better performance.

In similarity-based clustering, similarity combination is a common method to exploit the different features of an object. Weiss et al. [19] proposed a new document similarity function based on both term similarity and hyperlink similarity factor. He et al. [5] also considered co-citation [14] relations and linearly combined co-citation similarity with text and hyperlink similarity. Wang et al. [18] used co-citation and co-coupling [6] to build combined feature vectors for K-means clustering. To our best knowledge, previous approaches get unique combined similarity for clustering, which is not used in our method. We take several different features into account simultaneously and let them reinforce each other in an iterative way.

[1] In this paper, feature selection is limited in single-type feature. Different types of features are selected separately.

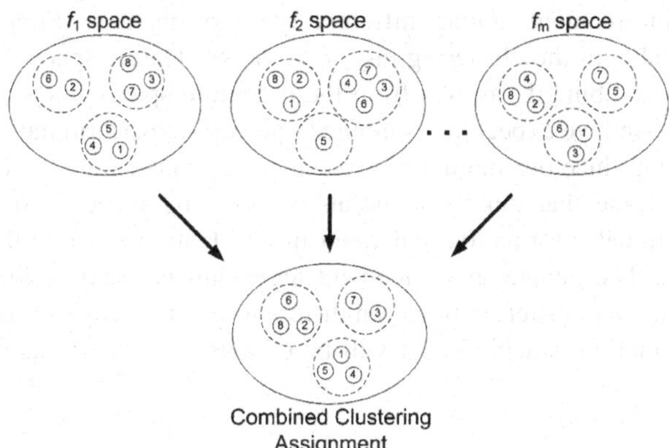

Fig. 2. Multi-type feature based clustering: combine clustering results in different feature spaces.

Blum and Mitchell [1] assumed that the description of each example could be partitioned into several distinct "views", each of which is sufficient for learning. All of the views can be used together to allow inexpensive bootstrapping. Co-EM [11] also explores the knowledge acquired in one view to train the other view. The major difference is that Co-EM uses a probabilistic model and does not commit to a label for the unlabeled examples. The "view" is similar to the different types of features discussed in this paper and we attempt to exploit the information acquired during the clustering procedure. We adopt a mutual reinforcement idea which has some relation to [17][22]. Zeng [22] and Wang [17] et al. introduced novel frameworks to cluster the heterogeneous data simultaneously. Under the frameworks, relationships among data objects are used to improve the cluster quality of interrelated data objects through an iterative reinforcement clustering process. Different from their work, our idea aims to clustering the same type of data objects. The mutual reinforcement is applied among multiple types of features, not heterogeneous types of data.

Traditional unsupervised feature selection method which does not need the class label information can be easily applied to clustering, such as Document Frequency (DF) and Term Strength (TS) [20]. Recently, there are some newly proposed methods, for example, entropy-based feature ranking method is proposed by Dash and Liu [3]. Martin et al. [9] introduced an Expectation-Maximization algorithm to select the feature subset and the number of clusters. For supervised feature selection, Liu et al. [8] used some methods to iteratively select features and perform text clustering simultaneously since no label information is available in clustering. Our idea differs with previous work in that we let feature selection in one feature space optimized by intermediate information generated in other spaces.

3 Problem Description and Mutual Reinforcement Clustering

Before introducing feature construction and feature selection in multi-type features based clustering, we first describe the multi-type features based combination problem and mutual reinforcement among different types of features. Suppose *m* feature spaces are available in the clustering task, f_k is the *kth* feature space. What we try to solve is how to combine the results from the *m* feature spaces into a unified one, as Figure 2 shows. And we expect the combined one will outperform the single ones.

Next, we'll introduce our mutual reinforcement mechanism to combine multi-type features. We assume that during an iterative clustering process, such as K-means clustering, additional information generated in one feature space will help the clustering in others. The general reinforcement algorithm is listed in Figure 3. In this algorithm, we first let clustering based on different features progress separately. Once some new information is achieved, it will be exploited by other features in the next iteration.

```
Loop for n iterations
{
  Loop for m features space
  {
    For kth feature space
    If it's the first iteration then use original fea-
    ture vector fkorig to do clustering
    Else use both original vector fkorig and new vector
    fknew to do clustering
  }
  Construct or revise new feature vector fknew for each
  object
  Loop for m features space
  {
    For kth feature space
    Get combined pseudo class and select features (Op-
    tional)
    Calculate New Centroids using both fkorig and fknew
  }
}
```

Fig. 3. Mutual reinforcement algorithm. Feature construction and selection are integrated into iterative clustering

4 Feature Construction and Feature Selection

4.1 Feature Construction for MFRC

In this section, we present how to exploit the intermediate information during the clustering in MFRC. We use Vector Space Model (VSM) to measure the similarity between document vectors constructed by TF×IDF [13]. After one iteration of clustering, each data object will be assigned to a cluster. The new feature is composed by the similarity between a data object and the centroids of different clusters. Suppose we should categorize data objects into l clusters in feature space k, then we can get a new feature vector for each object like formula (1).

$$f_k new = [f_k CSim_1, f_k CSim_2, ..., f_k CSim_l] \quad . \tag{1}$$

where $CSim_l$ is the similarity between a object and centroid l, f_k means the feature in space k. For clustering algorithm using geometric metric, this can be explained intuitively as Figure 4 shows: two data objects locate very near will have very similar $f_k new$ in formula (1). If the centroids are enough, the objects having similar vectors will also locate very near. For the task only few clusters should be formed, we choose some additional representative objects from each cluster and get new vector in formula (2):

$$f_k new = [f_k CSim_1, f_k CSim_2, ..., f_k CSim_l, f_k RSim_1, f_k RSim_2, ..., f_k RSim_r] \quad . \tag{2}$$

where $RSim_r$ is the similarity between a object and representative object r. The experiment shows that about 1% samples from the dataset are enough to assure the performance of clustering.

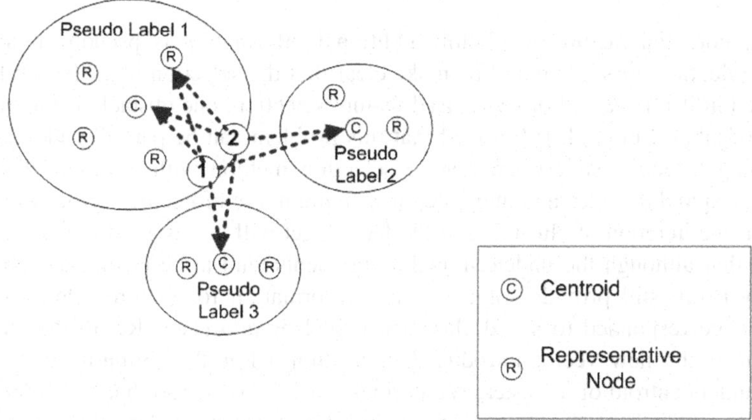

Fig. 4. The closeness of two points can be characterized using centroids and some other representative nodes.

After that, data objects in space k will get a combined vector like formula (3).

$$[...][f_{k-1} CSim_1, ..., f_{k-1} RSim_r] f_k orig [f_{k+1} CSim_1, ..., f_{k+1} RSim_r][...] \quad . \tag{3}$$

where $f_k orig = [f_k v_1, f_k v_2, \ldots, f_k v_n]$ is the original vector in space k. Finally each centroid should be updated using this combined vector. Using cosine metric, the combined similarity between an object o and centroid c in space k should be calculated using equation (4), where α and β are the weights of combination, m is available feature spaces, $ComSim_k(o,c)$ is the combined similarity in feature space k, $f_k Sim(o,c)$ is original vector similarity and $f_i Sim(o,c)$ (i k) is the new vector similarity. With the combined similarity, objects will be reassigned in the next iteration, as algorithm in Figure 3 shows.

$$\begin{cases} ComSim_k(o,c) = \alpha \times f_k Sim(o,c) + \beta \times \dfrac{\sum_{i=1}^{m} f_i Sim(o,c) \quad (i \neq k)}{m-1} (\alpha = 0.7, \beta = 0.3) \\ f_k Sim(o,c) = \dfrac{f_k orig(o) \bullet f_k orig(c)}{\sqrt{|f_k Orig(o)|^2 + |f_k Orig(c)|^2}} \\ f_i Sim(o,c) = \dfrac{f_i new(o) \bullet f_i new(c)}{\sqrt{|f_i New(o)|^2 + |f_i New(c)|^2}} \end{cases} \quad (4)$$

By equation (4), different feature space will generate different clusters in following iterations of clustering. However, similarity between any two objects in one feature space will be propagated to other spaces in low cost. The result sets will gradually converge to a unified one. The combination weights will control the speed of convergence. We'll show this in experiment section.

4.2 Feature Selection

Another potential method to exploit additional information is pseudo class based feature selection. First, it should be make clear that the selection of each type feature is limited in itself space. For supervised feature selection, one obstacle is the unavailability of label. Liu et al. [8] proved that this problem can be partially addressed by combining effective supervised feature selection method with iterative clustering. Here we expand this idea and integrated it with mutual reinforcement process.

After one iteration of clustering, each data object will be assigned to a cluster. We assume that although the undetermined assignments tend to be erroneous, such preliminary result still provide some valuable information for feature selection. Each cluster is corresponded to a real class and called *pseudo class*. Recall that each dimension of the new vector introduced in Section 4.1 is the similarity between an object and a centroid of a cluster. We normalized such vector so that the sum of each dimension is 1.0. Each dimension is treated as the confidence a data object belongs to corresponding cluster. For example, given a new vector [0.34, 0.23, 0.71], the normalized one will be [0.27, 0.18, 0.55]. That means the confidence that an object belong to cluster 1, 2 and 3 are 0.27, 0.18 and 0.55 respectively. If we match the clusters in different feature spaces, we can get a combined confidence that an object belong to a cluster, or pseudo class. The combined pseudo class is the one with max combined confidence. And it is used to conduct feature selection.

To combine pseudo class, the correspondence of clusters should be solved. We use a F1-Measure to estimate the degree of match between two clusters. For any two clusters C_1 and C_2, let N_1 be the number of objects belong to both cluster C_1 and C_2, N_2 be the number of objects belong to cluster C_1 and N_3 be the number of objects belong to cluster C_2:

Precision(C_1, C_2) = N_1 / N_2, Recall(C_1, C_2) = N_1 / N_3

$$F(C_1,C_2)=\frac{2PR}{P+R} \quad . \tag{5}$$

where F is F1-Measure, P is Precision and R is Recall. Actually, *Precision* and *Recall* are not appropriate names here. But we don't use new ones to avoid confusion. This measurement is also used to evaluate the clustering performance in our experiments.

Again, suppose we should categorize data objects into l clusters using m feature spaces. We get combined pseudo class using following equation:

$$\begin{cases} Conf_k(C_j \mid o)=\dfrac{f_k Sim(o,c_j)}{\sum_{i=1}^{l} f_k Sim(o,c_i)} \\ ComConf_k(C_j \mid o)=\alpha\times Conf_k(C_j \mid o)+\beta\times\sum_{i=1}^{m} Conf_i(C_j \mid o) \quad (i\neq k) \qquad (\alpha=0.7,\beta=0.3) \\ C_k(o)=\arg\max_j(CombConf_k(C_j \mid o)) \end{cases} \quad . \tag{6}$$

where c_j is the centroid of cluster C_j, $Conf_k(C_j \mid o)$ is the confidence that object o belong to cluster C_j in space k, $ComConf_k(C_j \mid o)$ is the combined confidence that o belong to cluster C_j in space k, $C_k(o)$ is combined pseudo class for o in space k.

Having the label information, we do feature selection using Information Gain (IG) and χ^2 statistic (CHI) [20]. Information gain measures the number of bits of information obtained for category prediction by the presence or absence of a feature in a document. Let l be the number of clusters. Given vector $[f_k v_1, f_k v_2, \ldots, f_k v_n]$, the information gain of a feature fv_n is defined as:

$$\begin{aligned} IG(fv_n) = & -\sum_{i=1}^{l} p(C_i)\log p(C_i) \\ & +p(fv_n)\sum_{i=1}^{l} p(C_i \mid fv_n)\log p(C_i \mid fv_n) \\ & +p(\overline{fv_n})\sum_{i=1}^{l} p(C_i \mid \overline{fv_n})\log p(C_i \mid \overline{fv_n}) \end{aligned} \quad . \tag{7}$$

χ^2 statistic measures the association between the term and the category. It is defined to be:

$$\begin{cases} \chi^2(fv_n,C_i)=\dfrac{N\times(p(fv_n,C_i)\times p(\overline{fv_n},\overline{C_i})-p(fv_n,\overline{C_i})\times p(\overline{fv_n},C_i))^2}{p(fv_n)\times p(\overline{fv_n})\times p(C_i)\times p(\overline{C_i})} \\ \chi^2(fv_n)=\operatorname{avg}_{i=1}^{m}\{\chi^2(fv_n,C_i)\} \end{cases} \quad . \tag{8}$$

After the feature selection, objects will be reassigned, features will be re-selected and the pseudo class information will be re-combined in the next iteration. Finally, the iterative clustering, feature selection and mutual reinforcement are well integrated.

5 Experiment

We conducted experiments to demonstrate that MFRC can improve the clustering performance when evaluated by entropy and F-Measure. K-means was chosen as our basic clustering algorithm. For this algorithm tends to influenced by selection of initial centroids, we randomly selected 10 sets of initial centroids and averaged the performances in the 10 times as the final result. TF×IDF [13] with "ltc" scheme was used to calculate the weight of each vector dimension.

5.1 Data Sets

Our evaluation approach measures the overall quality of generated clusters by comparing them with a set of categories created manually. We use three test sets:

- Co-Training (CT): A subset of the 4 Universities dataset containing web pages and hyperlink data[2]. It's used for the Co-Training experiments by Blum et al. [1].
- WebKB (WKB): A data set consisting classified Web pages[3] for Web->KB project[4].
- Open Directory Project (ODP): A data set in Open Directory Project[5], including user access log of it from MSN search engine. We use the user access as one feature for Web document clustering.

The information about these data sets is shown in Table 1:

Table 1. The test collections and some statistics. "Feature Type Num" means the number of different feature types.

Test Set	Class Num.	Doc Num.	Terms Num.	Average Terms Per Doc	Feature Type Num.
CT	2	1,051	38,991	37.1	3 (content, URL, anchor text)
WKB	4	5,396	205,683	38.1	2 (content, URL)
ODP	15	8,071	109,569	13.6	3 (content, URL, user access)

5.2 Performance Measures

Two kinds of measurements, entropy and F-Measure were used to evaluate the clustering performance. Entropy is based on the entropy in information theory [2], which measures the uniformity or purity of a cluster. Specifically, given a cluster A and category labels of data objects inside it, the entropy of cluster A is defined by

[2] http://www.cs.cmu.edu/afs/cs.cmu.edu/project/theo-51/www/co-training/data/
[3] http://www.cs.cmu.edu/afs/cs.cmu.edu/project/theo-20/www/data/
[4] http://www-2.cs.cmu.edu/~webkb/
[5] http://www.dmoz.org

$$H(A) = -\sum_j p_j \cdot \log_2 p_j \quad . \tag{9}$$

where p_j should be the proportion of *jth* class's data in the cluster.

F-Measure has been used in [7][17]. Since each cluster always consists of documents from several classes, we use an overall F-Measure as follows:

$$OverallFMeasure = \frac{\sum_{j=1}^{l}(|C_j| \arg\max_i F(C_j, Class_i))}{\sum_{j=1}^{l}|C_j|} \quad . \tag{10}$$

where $F(C_j,Class_i)$ is the F-Measure of cluster C_j when class i is used as the correct categorization to evaluate C_j. $|C_j|$ is the number of documents in cluster C_j. F-Measure can also be used to measure the degree of match between two clusters, as mentioned in Section 4.2.

5.3 Results and Analysis

To combine clustering based on different types of feature, we expect to get a unified result set. First, let's have look at the convergence of feature construction. We Use micro F1-Measure to compare two sets of clustering result, 1.0 means the two sets are totally equal. In most of the tests (>90%), F1-Measure becomes larger than 0.99 within 10 iterations, which means the different features get a consensus quickly. Figure 5 shows the convergence on three data sets.

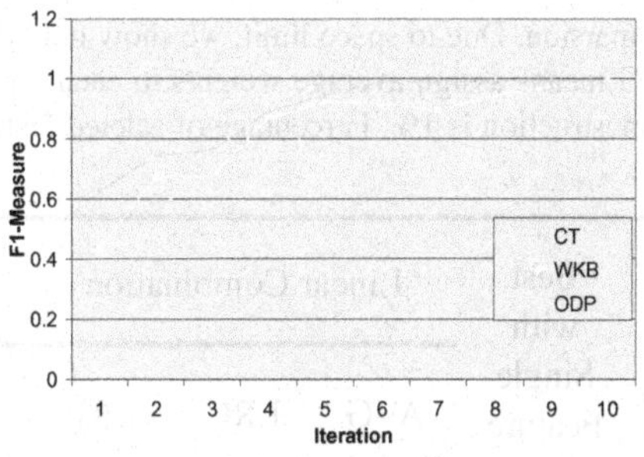

Fig. 5. The convergence of feature construction. The weights of combination are α = 0.7, β = 0.3. Given n types of features, n(n-1)/2 F-Measure values exist. We use the average one.

As to feature selection method, the consensus can't be achieved. As Liu et al. showed in [8], 10 iterations are enough for the iterative feature selection to get a good performance. We try similar test and use the combined pseudo class in the 10th iteration as the final result. Different percentages of selected features are tested and Figure 6 is obtained. In most cases, 2-percentage selection will get best performance.

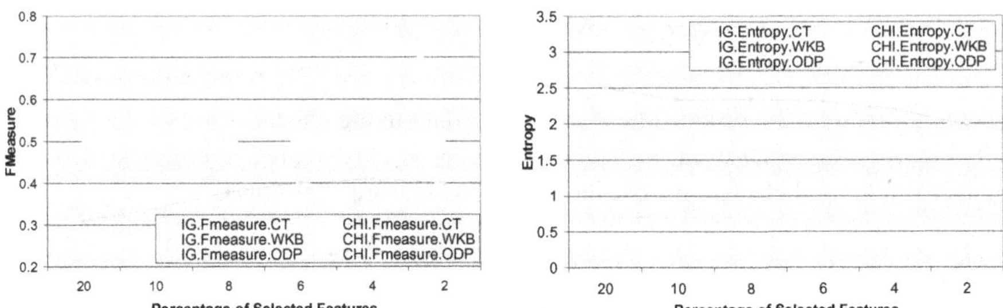

Fig. 6. FMeasure and entropy comparison on three data sets with different percentage of selected features.

In Table 2, we compare the performance of our approach with other methods, including the ones using single feature and linear combination of similarity. Besides averagely assigning weights to different types of feature, we use *linear regression* to choose the weights for similarity combination. However, we find it's not easy for clustering task to get training samples. With manually labeled data, i.e. the answer for evaluation, we use two methods to build samples. The first one uses the distance between a data object and class centroid as input, 1 (object belongs to this class) or 0 (object doest not belong to this class) as output. The second one uses the distance between any two objects as input, 1 (the two objects belong to the same class) and 0 (the two objects belong to different class) as output. We call the two methods LRC and LRP respectively. For both methods, the residues in linear regression are not small enough. Using the weight chosen by such methods, the performance may even worse than the best one based on single type of feature.

Table 2. Performance Comparsion. Due to space limit, we show only the best performance for single type of feature. AVG means assign average weights to each type of feature. The representive nodes in feature concstruction is 1%. Percentage of seleted features in feature selection is 2.

Test Sets	Measure	Best with Single Feature	Linear Combination			MFCMR		
			AVG	LRC	LRP	FC (1%)	FS (2%)	
							IG	CHI
CT	FMeasure	0.69	0.67	0.66	0.65	0.72	0.71	0.71
	Entropy	0.65	0.72	0.73	0.73	0.63	0.60	0.61
WKB	FMeasure	0.46	0.42	0.44	0.44	0.53	0.50	0.51
	Entropy	1.28	1.30	1.29	1.32	1.30	1.21	1.19
ODP	FMeasure	0.27	0.20	0.23	0.24	0.36	0.39	0.38
	Entropy	2.68	2.65	2.77	2.67	2.32	1.98	2.19

6 Conclusion and Future Work

We proposed Multi-type Feature based Reinforcement Clustering (MFRC), a novel algorithm to combine different types of features to do Web document clustering. It contains two main parts: feature construction and pseudo class based feature operations. We use the intermediate clustering result in one feature space as additional information to enhance clustering in other spaces. Besides, pseudo class is used for feature selection to improve performance. The two parts are all implemented in an iterative way and can be well integrated into an iterative clustering algorithm.

In future, we need to prove the convergence of feature construction and test MFRC on more data sets. Besides, the reinforcement idea will be tested using some clustering algorithms other than K-means, e.g. soft clustering, hierarchical clustering and density-based clustering.

References

1. Blum, A. and Mitchell, T.: Combining Labeled and Unlabeled Data with Co-Training. In Proceeding of the Conference on Computational Learning Theory, 1998.
2. Cover, T. M. and Thomas, J. A.: *Elements of Information Theory*, Wiley, 1991.
3. Dash, M. and Liu, H.: Feature Selection for Clustering. In Proceeding of 4th Pacific-Asia Conference on Knowledge Discovery and Data Mining, 2000.
4. Dudoit, S. and Fridlyand, J.: Bagging to Improve the Accuracy of a Clustering Procedure. Bioinformatics, 2003.
5. He, X., Zha, H., Ding, C. and Simon, H. D.: Web Document Clustering Using Hyperlink Structures. *Computational Statistics and Data Analysis*, 45:19-45, 2002.
6. Kessler, M. M.: Bibliographic coupling between scientific papers. American Documentation, 14:10-25, 1963.
7. Larsen, B., Aone, C.: Fast and Effective Text Mining Using Linear-time Document Clustering. In Proceedings of the 5th ACM SIGKDD International Conference, 1999.
8. Liu, T., Liu, S., Chen, Z. and Ma, W.-Y.: An Evaluation on Feature Selection for Text Clustering. In Proc. of the 20th International Conference on Machine Learning, 2003.
9. Martin, H. C. L., Mario, A. T. F. and Jain, A.K.: Feature Saliency in unsupervised learning, Technical Report, Michigan Sate University, 2002.
10. Minaei, B., Topchy, A., Punch, W. F.: Ensembles of Partitions via Data Resampling. In Proceeding of the International Conference on Information Technology, 2004.
11. Nigam, K. and Ghani, R.: Analyzing the Effectiveness and Applicability of Co-Training. In Proceeding of Information and Knowledge Management, 2000.
12. Ntoulas, A., Cho, J. and Olston, C.: What's New on the Web? The Evolution of the Web from a Search Engine Perspective. To appear: the 13th International WWW, 2004.
13. Salton, G.: Automatic Text Processing: The transformation, analysis, and retrieval of information by computer. Addison-Wesley, 1989.
14. Small, H.: Co-citation in Scientific Literature: A new measure of the relationship between two documents. *Journal of the American Society for Information*, 1973.
15. Strehl, A. and Ghosh, J.: Cluster Ensembles – A Knowledge Reuse Framework for Combining Multiple Partitions. *Journal on Machine Learning Research*, 2002.

16. Topchy, A., Jain, A. K. and Punch, W.: A Mixture Model of Clustering Ensembles. To appear in Proceedings of the SIAM International Conference on Data Mining, 2004.
17. Wang, J., Zeng, H.-J., Chen, Z., Lu, H., Li, T. and Ma, W.-Y.: ReCoM: Reinforcement Clustering of Multi-Type Interrelated Data Objects. In Proc. of the 26th SIGIR, 2003.
18. Wang, Y. and Kitsuregawa, M.: Clustering of Web Search Results with Link Analysis. Technique report, 1999.
19. Weiss, R., Velez, B., Sheldon, M. A., Namprempre, C., Szilagyi, P., Duda, A. and Gifford, D. K.: HyPursuit: A Hierarchical Network Search Engine that Exploits Content-Link Hypertext Clustering. In 7th ACM Conference on Hypertext, pages 180-193, 1996.
20. Yang, Y. and Pedersen, J. O.: A Comparative Study on Feature Selection in Text Categorization. In Proceedings of 14th International Conference on Machine Learning, 1997.
21. Zamir, O., Etzioni, O.: Web Document Clustering: A Feasibility Demonstration. In Proceeding of the 21st Annual International ACM SIGIR Conference, 1998.
22. Zeng, H.-J., Chen, Z. and Ma, W.-Y.: A Unified Framework for Clustering Heterogeneous Web Objects. In Proc. of the 3rd International Conference on WISE, 2002.

Clustering Transactional XML Data with Semantically-Enriched Content and Structural Features

Andrea Tagarelli and Sergio Greco

DEIS, University of Calabria
Via Bucci 41c, 87036 Rende (CS) – Italy
{tagarelli,greco}@deis.unical.it

Abstract. We address the problem of clustering XML data according to semantically-enriched features extracted by analyzing content and structural specifics in the data. Content features are selected from the textual contents of XML elements, while structure features are extracted from XML tag paths on the basis of ontological knowledge. Moreover, we conceive a transactional model for representing sets of semantically cohesive XML structures, and exploit such a model to effectively and efficiently cluster XML data. The resulting clustering framework was successfully tested on some collections extracted from the DBLP XML archive.

1 Introduction

XML is touted as the driving-force for exchanging data on the Web. Several approaches to mining XML data have been recently devised, mostly focusing on clustering XML documents by structure. For instance, [12] proposes an XML-aware edit distance to measure structural similarity among XML documents, and applies a standard hierarchical clustering algorithm to evaluate how closely cluster documents correspond to their respective DTDs. More recently, it has been raised the importance of defining a suitable notion of XML cluster prototype, i.e. a summarization of the relevant features of XML documents belonging to a same cluster. In [9], documents are represented by a structure graph summarizing the relations between elements within documents.

The need for organizing XML data according to both their content and structural features has become challenging, due to the increase of heterogeneity of XML sources. However, mining XML data from a content/structure combination viewpoint is still in a preliminary stage. A first attempt is given in [5], which proposes to apply a partitional clustering technique to XML documents represented by textual and tag-based features. Generation of features for XML data is more deeply investigated in [15], where annotations, structure and ontological information are combined together. However, the focus here is on building appropriate features for purposes of supervised classification of XML documents.

In this paper, we investigate how to cluster XML data according to a space of semantically-enriched features extracted by an in-depth analysis of content and structural specifics. Our contributions can be summarized as follows:

X. Zhou et al. (Eds.): WISE 2004, LNCS 3306, pp. 266–278, 2004.
© Springer-Verlag Berlin Heidelberg 2004

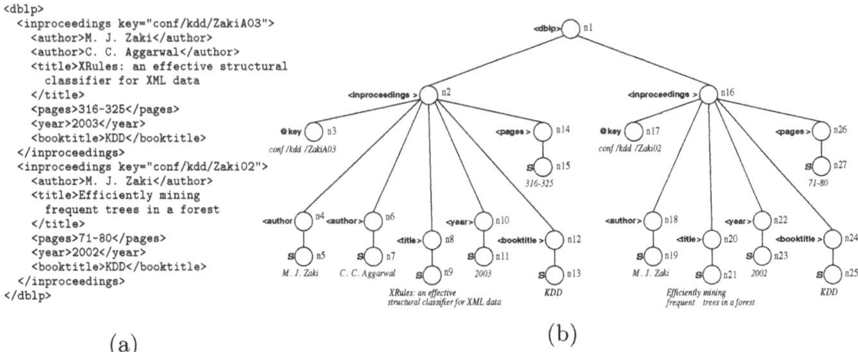
<dblp>
<inproceedings key="conf/kdd/ZakiA03">
<author>M. J. Zaki</author>
<author>C. C. Aggarwal</author>
<title>XRules: an effective structural classifier for XML data
</title>
<pages>316-325</pages>
<year>2003</year>
<booktitle>KDD</booktitle>
</inproceedings>
<inproceedings key="conf/kdd/Zaki02">
<author>M. J. Zaki</author>
<title>Efficiently mining frequent trees in a forest
</title>
<pages>71-80</pages>
<year>2002</year>
<booktitle>KDD</booktitle>
</inproceedings>
</dblp>
(a)
(b)

Fig. 1. A sample DBLP XML document and its tree

1. We define suitable features for the representation of XML elements, focusing on two informative contribution: syntactic and semantic information extracted from textual elements, and structural information derived from tag paths and enriched with ontological knowledge.
2. We propose the notion of *XML tree tuples* to mine sets of semantically cohesive structures from XML documents.
3. We conceive a transactional model for representing XML tree tuples and exploit such a model to effectively and efficiently cluster XML data.

2 Preliminaries

XML Trees and Paths. A *tree* T is a tuple $T = \langle r_T, N_T, E_T, \lambda_T \rangle$, where $N_T \subseteq \mathbb{N}$ denotes the set of nodes, $r_T \in N_T$ is the distinguished root of T, $E_T \subseteq N_T \times N_T$ denotes the (acyclic) set of edges, and $\lambda_T : N_T \mapsto \Sigma$ is the node labeling function. Let Tag, Att, and Str be alphabets of tag names, attribute names, and strings respectively. An *XML tree* XT is a pair $XT = \langle T, \delta \rangle$, where: *i)* T is a tree defined on the alphabet $\Sigma = Tag \cup Att \cup \{\mathtt{S}\}$, where symbol $\mathtt{S} \notin Tag \cup Att$ is used to denote the `#PCDATA` content of elements; *ii)* given $n \in N_T$, $\lambda_T(n) \in Att \cup \{\mathtt{S}\} \Leftrightarrow n \in Leaves(T)$; *iii)* $\delta : Leaves(T) \mapsto Str$ is a function associating a string to every leaf node of T. Internal nodes of an XML tree have a unique label, which denotes the tag name of the corresponding element. Each leaf node corresponds to either an attribute or the `#PCDATA` content of an element, and is labeled with two strings: name and value of the attribute, or symbol S and the string corresponding to the `#PCDATA` content. Fig.1(a) shows a simplified fragment from the DBLP archive [4]. The fragment is an XML document representing two conference papers, and is graphically represented by the XML tree in Fig.1(b).

An *XML path* p is a sequence $p = [s_1, \ldots, s_m]$ of symbols in $Tag \cup Att \cup \{\mathtt{S}\}$. Symbol s_1 corresponds to the tag name of the document root element. An XML path can be categorized into two types, namely *tag path* and *mixed path*, depending on whether $s_m \in Tag$ or $s_m \in Att \cup \{\mathtt{S}\}$.

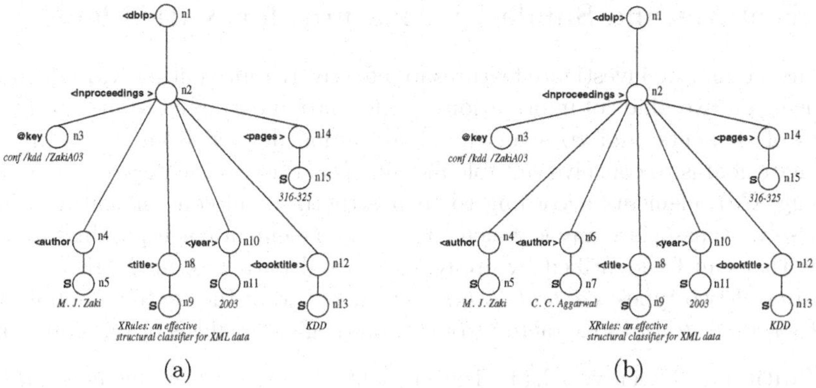

Fig. 2. Two subtrees of the XML tree of Fig.1(b)

The application of a path $p = [s_1, \ldots, s_m]$ on an XML tree XT identifies the set of nodes $p(XT) = \{n_1, \ldots, n_h\}$ such that, for each $i \in [1..h]$, there exists a sequence of nodes $n_{i_1}, \ldots, n_{i_m}$ with the following properties: $n_{i_1} = r_T$ and $n_{i_m} = n_i$; $n_{i_{j+1}}$ is a child of n_{i_j}, for each $j \in [1..m\text{-}1]$; $\lambda(n_{i_j}) = s_j$, for each $j \in [1..m]$. We define the *answer* $XT.p$ of a path p applied to XT as the set $p(XT)$ of node identifiers or the set $\{\delta_T(n) \mid n \in p(XT)\}$ of string values, respectively if p is a tag path or a mixed path. For instance, in the tree of Fig.1(b), path *dblp.inproceedings.title* yields the set $\{n_8, n_{20}\}$, whereas the answer of path *dblp.inproceedings.author*.S is the set {*"M. J. Zaki"*, *"C. C. Aggarwal"*}.

Tree Tuples. Tree tuples resemble the notion of tuples in relational databases and have been recently proposed to extend functional dependencies to the XML setting [1,7]. In a relational database, a tuple is a function assigning each attribute with a value from the corresponding domain. Given an XML tree XT, a *tree tuple* τ is a maximal subtree of XT such that, for every path p that can be applied to XT, the answer $\tau.p$ contains at most one element [7][1]. Loosely speaking, a tree tuple groups together nodes of a document which are semantically correlated, according to the structure of the tree representing the document. The benefits from using tree tuples will be clarified later in this paper.

Consider the XML tree of Fig.1(b). The subtree shown in Fig.2(a) is a tree tuple, but the subtree of Fig.2(b) is not. Indeed, the latter is not a tree tuple as there are two distinct nodes (i.e. n_4 and n_6) which correspond to the same path *dblp.inproceedings.author*. As a consequence, the subtree of Fig.2(b) contains two tree tuples, each of which corresponds to one of the paper authors. Suppose now that node n_3 is pruned from the subtree of Fig.2(a): in this case, the resulting tree is no more a tree tuple as it is not maximal.

[1] In [7], an XML document is assumed to conform to a predefined DTD. However, in our context, the presence of a schema is not necessary to derive a tree tuple.

3 Features and Similarity Measures for XML Elements

In this section, we investigate features for effectively representing XML elements, focusing on two kinds of information: *i)* information extracted from textual contents of elements, and *ii)* structural information derived from tag paths. The ultimate goal is to conceive suitable measures that assess the degree of matching among XML elements according to their structure and content features. More precisely, we associate any leaf element e, i.e. an element corresponding to a leaf node that can be identified by applying a mixed path p to an XML tree, with features of two types: *content features* extracted from the textual content $\delta(e)$, and *structure features* extracted from an ontological analysis of tag names in p.

Definition 1. Given two XML leaf elements e_i and e_j, the *element matching function* is defined as

$$match(e_i, e_j) = f \times sim_S(e_i, e_j) + (1 - f) \times sim_C(e_i, e_j),$$

where sim_S (resp. sim_C) denotes the similarity among the parts composed by structure (resp. content) features in the elements, and $f \in [0..1]$ is a factor that tunes the influence of the structural part to the overall similarity. □

3.1 Structural Features Based on Ontological Knowledge

A peculiar characterization of documents coded with a semistructured format, such as XML, cannot leave structural patterns out of consideration. Such patterns can be naturally extracted from elements forming tag paths. However, although important information can be inferred from XML tags, subjective factors brand the authorship in coding information to XML, thus they do not guarantee any informative consistency among XML data. The key-idea lies in going beyond a free-context use of mere terms, i.e. tag names, by mapping them into semantically related concepts. Each concept belongs to an ontological space and is represented by a semantic meaning, or *sense*, to be associated to a tag name. We now focus our attention on how to exploit ontology knowledge to semantically enrich features that can be extracted from XML tag names.

In our context, the ontology knowledge base is *WordNet* [6,10]. This electronic thesaurus groups words with the same meaning into equivalence classes, called *synsets* (sets of synonyms). Each synset represents one underlying lexical concept and is described by one or more short textual descriptions, called *glosses*. Synsets are explicitly connected to each other through existing relations. These relations connect senses of words that are used in the same part-of-speech. For instance, noun synsets are connected through *is-a* relations (hypernym/hyponym) and *part-of* relations (meronym/holonym). We consider only the noun portion of WordNet, since nouns are much more heavily used to annotate XML data. Indeed, as a practical matter, nouns capture fine grained distinctions among related concepts better than verbs, adverbs, and adjectives.

The structural similarity between two XML leaf elements e_i and e_j is computed by comparing their respective tag paths, i.e. paths composed of tag symbols only. For the sake of simplicity, we denote these paths with $p_i = [t_{i_1}, \ldots, t_{i_n}]$

and $p_j = [t_{j_1}, \ldots, t_{j_m}]$, respectively. In order to semantically enrich structure features from tag paths, we associate each tag t with a pair $(t.tn, t.\sigma)$, where $t.tn$ denotes a string representing the tag name of t and $t.\sigma$ denotes the most appropriate sense for $t.tn$ selected from WordNet.

Definition 2. Given two XML leaf elements e_i and e_j, the structural similarity between e_i and e_j is defined as

$$sim_S(e_i, e_j) = \frac{1}{n+m}\left[\sum_{t \in p_i} sim(t.\sigma,\ best\_match_{p_j}(t).\sigma) + \sum_{t \in p_j} sim(t.\sigma,\ best\_match_{p_i}(t).\sigma)\right],$$

where $sim(t.\sigma,\ best\_match_{p_j}(t).\sigma)$ computes the similarity between the sense assigned to tag t and the sense assigned to the tag with which t has the best matching, that is $best\_match_{p_j}(t) = t' \in p_j\ s.t.\ \nexists t'' \in p_j,\ t'' \neq t',\ sim(t.\sigma, t''.\sigma) > sim(t.\sigma, t'.\sigma)$. □

Viewed in this respect, two issues need still to be investigated: *i)* which features can be exploited to define a suitable measure of similarity between tag name senses, and *ii)* which word sense disambiguation approach can be applied to assign a tag name with the most appropriate sense.

Measures of similarity between tag name senses. To assess the similarity between tag name senses, we aim at exploiting both lengths of paths in the noun taxonomy and co-occurrences of senses. This approach lies on two main observations.

In a hierarchy of concepts, path-based measures allow for determining the degree to which two concepts are related. However, path lengths should be interpreted differently depending on where they are located in the hierarchy, since the higher a concept in a hierarchy the more general itself. A suitable path-based similarity measure is defined in [13]. Here, the focus is on the depth of the most specific sense, hereinafter called lowest common subsumer (*lcs*), that the two senses share.

Besides the semantic relatedness among word senses, we are also interested in estimating the specificity of a sense. More precisely, we estimate the specificity of a sense σ through the occurrences of every tag name associated with σ in a given corpus. Faced with the above observations, we compute the similarity between tag senses σ_1 and σ_2 by combining path-based and co-occurrence measures.

Definition 3. The similarity between two tag senses σ_1 and σ_2 w.r.t. a given corpus $\mathcal{C}$ is defined as

$$sim(\sigma_1, \sigma_2) = \frac{2 \times depth(lcs(\sigma_1, \sigma_2))}{depth(\sigma_1) + depth(\sigma_2)} \times \frac{freq(\sigma_1, \sigma_2, \mathcal{C})}{freq(\sigma_1, \mathcal{C}) + freq(\sigma_2, \mathcal{C}) - freq(\sigma_1, \sigma_2, \mathcal{C})},$$

where $freq(\sigma_i, \mathcal{C})$ is the number of XML data in $\mathcal{C}$ containing a tag t_i such that $t_i.\sigma = \sigma_i$, and $freq(\sigma_1, \sigma_2, \mathcal{C})$ denotes the number of XML data in $\mathcal{C}$ containing both a tag t_i and a tag t_j such that $t_i.\sigma = \sigma_1$ and $t_j.\sigma = \sigma_2$. □

Word Sense Disambiguation. In natural languages often words have many senses. Word sense disambiguation is the process of assigning a word with a sense based on the context in which the word appears. An effective approach consists in choosing word meanings from an existing sense inventory by exploiting measures of semantic relatedness. The underlying assumption on relatedness among concepts relies on the number of shared words appearing in the dictionary glosses that describe the senses associated with the concepts.

In this work, we adopt a strategy similar to that proposed in [2], where measures of semantic relatedness exploit both glosses associated with synsets and hierarchies of concepts in WordNet. To score the comparison of two glosses, [2] proposes to sum the sizes of the distinct overlaps between the glosses, where an overlap is detected as the longest shared sequence of words. Given two input synsets a and b, such a mechanism of scoring is used to compare not only $gloss(a)$ with $gloss(b)$ but also $gloss(r_i(a))$ with $gloss(r_j(b))$, for each pair of WordNet relations $r_i, r_j \in \mathcal{R} = \{r_1, r_2, r_3, r_4\} = \{\texttt{hypernym}, \texttt{hyponym}, \texttt{meronym}, \texttt{holonym}\}$.

We maintain the above mechanism of scoring but consider a restricted number of relations between synsets. In effect, tag names in an XML path are related by an order which allows for inferring concept hierarchies, or even lattices. This suggests us to limit the combinations of WordNet relations. Given two input synsets a and b, we choose to compare glosses corresponding to the following pairs of synsets: a-b, a-$r_1(b)$, $r_2(a)$-b, $r_3(a)$-b, a-$r_4(b)$, and $r_i(a)$-$r_i(b)$ for each $r_i \in \mathcal{R}$. We denote this set of pairs of synset relations with $\mathcal{RP}(a, b)$.

Let w§`IDsense` denote a word w and the identifier `IDsense` assigned in WordNet to one of the possible meanings for w. Each pair w§`IDsense` corresponds to a distinct synset in WordNet, thus it identifies a specific word sense. The key-idea of our approach to the disambiguation of senses for tag names consists in selecting the most appropriate senses w.r.t. a *path-context*. A path-context is represented by a semantic network between all the possible senses associated to the tags of a particular path. Given a tag path $p = [t_1, \ldots, t_n]$, we employ a directed weighted graph $SG(p)$, called *synset graph* of p, such that:

- nodes are synsets $t_i.tn$§u, for each $i \in [1..n]$, $\texttt{u} \in senses(t_i.tn)$; moreover, additional nodes *source* and *sink* are given for purposes of convenient visits through the graph;
- edges are connections between synsets $(t_i.tn\S\texttt{u},\ t_{i+1}.tn\S\texttt{v})$, for each $i \in [1..n\text{-}1]$, $\texttt{u} \in senses(t_i.tn)$, $\texttt{v} \in senses(t_{i+1}.tn)$; moreover, edges $(source, t_1.tn\ \S\texttt{u})$ and $(t_n.tn\S\texttt{v}, sink)$ hold, for each $\texttt{u} \in senses(t_1.tn)$, $\texttt{v} \in senses(t_n.tn)$;
- edge weights are computed as $weight(t_i.tn\S\texttt{u},\ t_{i+1}.tn\S\texttt{v}) = \max_{rp}\{score(rp)\}$, where $rp \in \mathcal{RP}(t_i.tn\S\texttt{u}, t_{i+1}.tn\S\texttt{v})$, for each $i \in [1..n\text{-}1]$, $\texttt{u} \in senses(t_i.tn)$, $\texttt{v} \in senses(t_{i+1}.tn)$; moreover, weights on edges involving either *source* or *sink* are set to be 0.

In the above definition, *score*() is a function that accepts as input two glosses, finds their overlaps and computes a score as previously described. We aim at disambiguating senses for the tags in p by finding a maximum-weight path in the associated synset graph $SG(p)$. Since weights on edges have always non-negative values, we adopt an efficient implementation of the Dijkstra algorithm for solving the standard problem of finding shortest paths in a weighted graph. This guarantees that, when the right sense has to be decided for the name of tag $t_i \in p$, the ambiguities for all tags preceding t_i in p have been already treated.

3.2 Content Features

Texts associated with the #PCDATA contents can be suitably represented by means of a conventional bag-of-words model, where each feature corresponds to a distinct word which survived language-specific text-preprocessing operations (such as, removal of stopwords and word stemming) [11]. Word relevance is typically weighed according to information on frequency of occurrence of the word. The most commonly-used term weighting function, namely *tf.idf*, computes the relevance of a term as a combination of its frequency of occurrence within a document and its rarity across the whole document collection [11]. In our context, a document is referred to as a "textual content unit" (u) which indicates the text extracted from a #PCDATA element content.

Conventional term weighting functions take into account only lexical information to assess the relevance of a term. Our idea is to enrich the tf.idf function by exploiting the *semantic rarity* of a term. We define this notion by resorting to the degree of polysemy of a term, in such a way that the relevance of a term is reduced as many meanings as the term has. Formally, the semantic rarity of a term w is evaluated as $s\text{-}rarity(w) = 1 - \frac{|senses(w)|}{\text{MAX\_POLYSEMY}}$, where $senses(w)$ denotes the set of meanings of w and MAX_POLYSEMY is a constant denoting the number of meanings of the most polysemous word in WordNet.

The semantic rarity function is invariant w.r.t. the term location in the collection of textual content units. Therefore, for each term w_j, the same value $s\text{-}rarity(w_j)$ can be combined with the tf.idf value associated to any pair (w_j, u_i).

Definition 4. The relevance weight of a term w_j w.r.t. a textual content unit u_i is computed as $relevance(w_j, u_i) = tf.idf(w_j, u_i) \times s\text{-}rarity(w_j)$. □

A measure particularly suitable for assessing similarity between documents is the *cosine similarity* [14]: it computes proximity in terms of the cosine of the angle that two generic documents form in a multidimensional space. In our context, any textual content unit u_i can be associated with a term vector $\boldsymbol{u}_i$ whose j-th component contains the value $relevance(w_j, u_i)$. Given two XML elements e_i and e_h, we compute the content similarity between e_i and e_h by measuring the cosine similarity between the term vectors associated with their respective #PCDATA contents: $sim_C(e_i, e_h) = \frac{\boldsymbol{u}_i \cdot \boldsymbol{u}_h}{\|\boldsymbol{u}_i\| \times \|\boldsymbol{u}_h\|}$.

4 XML Transactional Clustering

In the huge amount of available structured data, a relevant portion is represented by *transactional data*, i.e. variable-length tuples of objects with categorical attributes. The interest in analyzing this particular domain raises from many challenging application problems (e.g. analysis of web access logs) that can be formalized using transactional data.

Clustering is the task of organizing a collection of label-less objects into meaningful groups, namely *clusters*, based on interesting relationships discovered in the data. The goal is that the objects in a cluster are to be each other highly similar, but very dissimilar from objects in other clusters.

Our key-idea for addressing the problem of clustering XML data stems in exploiting a profitable transactional model to represent XML tree tuples in the space of features defined in the previous section. For this purpose, notions used in the transactional domain need to be revised in our context. Then, on the basis of the proposed model, we describe our approach to clustering XML tree tuples which exploits an efficient transactional clustering algorithm.

4.1 A Transactional Model for XML Tree Tuples

Given a set $\mathcal{I} = \{e_1, \ldots, e_m\}$ of distinct categorical values, or *items*, a transactional database is a multi-set of transactions $tr \subseteq \mathcal{I}$.

In our setting, the item domain is built over all the leaf elements in a collection of XML tree tuples, i.e. the set of distinct answers of mixed paths applied to the tree tuples extracted from a collection of XML data. A transaction is modeled as the set of items associated to the leaf elements of a specific tree tuple. The intuition behind such a model lies mainly on the definition of tree tuples itself: each path applied to a tree tuple yields a unique answer, thus each item in a transaction indicates information on a concept which is distinct from that of other items in the same transaction.

Formally, given a tree tuple τ extracted from an XML tree, a *tree tuple item* is defined as a pair $e = (p, \tau.p)$, where p is a mixed path and $\tau.p$ is a string value corresponding to the answer of p applied to τ. Let $\mathcal{I}_\tau$ denote the set of items of a tree tuple τ. The *item domain* $\mathcal{I}_{\mathcal{XT}}$ associated to a collection $\mathcal{XT} = \{XT_1, \ldots, XT_n\}$ of XML trees is the union of the sets $\mathcal{I}_\tau$ relative to all the tree tuples extracted from the trees in $\mathcal{XT}$, that is $\mathcal{I}_{\mathcal{XT}} = \bigcup_{i=1}^{n} \bigcup_j \{\mathcal{I}_{\tau_{i_j}}\}$.

Given a tree tuple τ, whose l leaf elements yield the set of items $\{e_{j_1}, \ldots, e_{j_l}\}$, the corresponding transaction is denoted as $tr = \langle e_{j_1} e_{j_2} \ldots e_{j_l} \rangle$. A transactional representation of the tree tuples in the XML tree of Fig.1(b) is shown in Fig.3.

In a sense, when comparing two transactions we are searching for the shared items. Intuitively, we could evaluate the similarity between two transactions as directly proportional to the number of common items and inversely proportional to the number of different items. The *Jaccard coefficient* [14] allows for computing the similarity between two sets as the ratio of the cardinality of their intersection to the cardinality of their union. However, exact intersection between transactions of tree tuple items may turn out to be not effective. Indeed, two items may share relevant structural or content information, even though they are not identical. Therefore, we need to enhance the notion of standard intersection between transactions with one able to capture even minimal similarities from content and structure features of XML elements. In particular, we can ex-

path (p)	$\tau_1.p$	*node ID*
dblp.inproceedings.@key	"conf/kdd/ZakiA03"	n_3
dblp.inproceedings.author.S	"M. J. Zaki"	n_5
dblp.inproceedings.title.S	"XRules: an effective ..."	n_9
dblp.inproceedings.year.S	"2003"	n_{11}
dblp.inproceedings.booktitle.S	"KDD"	n_{13}
dblp.inproceedings.pages.S	"316-325"	n_{15}

path (p)	$\tau_2.p$	*node ID*
dblp.inproceedings.@key	"conf/kdd/ZakiA03"	n_3
dblp.inproceedings.author.S	"C. C. Aggarwal"	n_7
dblp.inproceedings.title.S	"XRules: an effective ..."	n_9
dblp.inproceedings.year.S	"2003"	n_{11}
dblp.inproceedings.booktitle.S	"KDD"	n_{13}
dblp.inproceedings.pages.S	"316-325"	n_{15}

path (p)	$\tau_3.p$	*node ID*
dblp.inproceedings.@key	"conf/kdd/Zaki02"	n_{17}
dblp.inproceedings.author.S	"M. J. Zaki"	n_{19}
dblp.inproceedings.title.S	"Efficiently mining ..."	n_{21}
dblp.inproceedings.year.S	"2002"	n_{23}
dblp.inproceedings.booktitle.S	"KDD"	n_{25}
dblp.inproceedings.pages.S	"71-80"	n_{27}

(a)

item ID	*corresponding node IDs*
e_1	n_3
e_2	n_5, n_{19}
e_3	n_9
e_4	n_{11}
e_5	n_{13}, n_{25}
e_6	n_{15}
e_7	n_7
e_8	n_{17}
e_9	n_9
e_{10}	n_{23}
e_{11}	n_{27}

(b)

tr_1	e_1 e_2 e_3 e_4 e_5 e_6
tr_2	e_1 e_7 e_3 e_4 e_5 e_6
tr_3	e_8 e_2 e_9 e_{10} e_5 e_{11}

(c)

Fig. 3. Representation of all tree tuples extracted from the XML tree of Fig.1(b): (a) paths and answer paths in the tree tuples, (b) item domain, and (c) transaction set

ploit the element matching function proposed in Section 3 to define a notion of transaction matching w.r.t. a threshold of similarity among tree tuple items.

Definition 5. Given two transactions tr_1, tr_2, and a similarity threshold $\gamma \in [0..1]$, we define the Jaccard similarity coefficient between two transactions as

$$sim_J^{\gamma}(tr_1, tr_2) = \frac{|match^{\gamma}(tr_1, tr_2)|}{\max\{|tr_1|, |tr_2|\}},$$

where $match^{\gamma}(tr_1, tr_2)$ denotes the set of pairs of γ-shared items and is defined as $\{(e_i, e_j) \mid e_i \in tr_1, e_j \in tr_2, match(e_i, e_j) \geq \gamma,\ \nexists e_h \in tr_2, match(e_i, e_h) > match(e_i, e_j),\ \nexists e_l \in tr_1, match(e_l, e_j) > match(e_i, e_j)\}$. □

We also define $match_{lin}^{\gamma}(tr_1, tr_2) = \{e_i \mid \exists(e_i, e_j) \in match^{\gamma}(tr_1, tr_2) \vee \exists(e_j, e_i) \in match^{\gamma}(tr_1, tr_2)\}$ as the set of γ-shared items within $match^{\gamma}(tr_1, tr_2)$. In practice, the set of γ-shared items resembles the intersection among transactions at a degree greater or equal to a similarity threshold γ.

4.2 An Efficient Algorithm for XML Transactional Clustering

XML tree tuples, modeled as transactions, can be efficiently clustered by applying a partitional algorithm conceived for the transactional domain.

Generally, a partitional clustering problem consists in partitioning a set $\{x_1, \ldots, x_n\}$ of objects in k non-empty groups C_j such that each group contains a homogeneous subset of objects. An important class of partitional approaches is based on the notion of *centroid*: each object x_i is assigned to a cluster C_j according to its distance $d(x_i, c_j)$ from a value c_j, called centroid of C_j.

The *TrK-means* algorithm [8] provides suitable notions of cluster centroids defined on the basis of a compact representation model. Starting from the intersection of transactions within a cluster C, a greedy heuristic refines the approximation of the centroid by iteratively adding the most frequent items, w.r.t. C, until the sum of the Jaccard distances cannot be further decreased. Experiments showed that in most cases the heuristic computes the actual centroid and, in each case, provides an effective and compact representation of the cluster.

TrK-means is devised into two main phases. In the first phase, it works as a traditional centroid-based method to compute $k+1$ clusters: starts choosing k objects as the initial cluster centroids, then iteratively reassigns each remaining object to the closest cluster until all cluster centroids do not change. The $(k+1)$-th cluster, called trash cluster, is created to contain unclustered objects, i.e. objects having an empty intersection with each cluster centroid and so are not assigned to any of the first k clusters. The second phase is in charge of recursively splitting the trash cluster into a minimal number of clusters. For further details about the TrK-means algorithm, the reader is referred to [8].

We revised TrK-means to suitably adapt it to our setting, and called the resulting algorithm as *XTrK-means*. Here, Jaccard distance is set to the 1's complement of the similarity function defined in Section 4.1, i.e. $d_J = 1 - sim_J^{\gamma}$. Moreover, the centroid of each cluster C is computed by starting from the enhanced intersection among the transactions in C, i.e. the set of γ-shared items in C. Finally, it is worth noticing that the tree tuples chosen as initial cluster centroids are constrained to come from different XML documents. This allows us to favor an appropriate choice of the initial centroids.

5 Preliminary Experimental Studies

We aimed at evaluating the proposed clustering approach w.r.t. some prior knowledge on the similarity of selected XML documents. Here prior knowledge is referred to as the conformance of a document to a group with a specific level of structural and/or content homogeneity.

In this section, we present preliminary experiments performed on the DBLP archive [4], a digital bibliography on computer science. The XML version of this archive is represented by a unique huge document. According to the element type definition of the root element in the DBLP DTD, the document was decomposed in 512,131 XML documents concerning: journal articles, conference

Table 1. Quality of clustering results

dataset	classes	f	γ	clusters	precision	recall	F-measure
Data♯1	5	0.7	0.6	5	0.834	0.93	0.879
Data♯1	5	0.8	0.8	5	0.856	0.944	0.897
Data♯1	5	0.9	0.8	5	0.8	0.883	0.839
Data♯2	14	0.3	0.8	13	0.786	0.895	0.833
Data♯2	14	0.2	0.7	14	0.849	0.946	0.894
Data♯2	14	0.1	0.8	14	0.86	0.962	0.908
Data♯3	23	0.6	0.8	23	0.821	0.945	0.878
Data♯3	23	0.5	0.6	23	0.86	0.968	0.91
Data♯3	23	0.5	0.8	23	0.917	0.983	0.948
Data♯3	23	0.4	0.6	23	0.833	0.953	0.888

papers, books and book chapters, and theses. From these documents, we selected and extracted 3 tree tuple collections for which predefined "ideal" classifications were devised. Each ideal classification corresponds to a collection whose classes are homogeneous from a structure and/or content viewpoint:

- Data♯1 collects 586 tree tuples (232 original documents) and was constructed to test the ability of the XTrK-means algorithm in distinguishing structurally homogeneous classes, e.g. "conference papers", "journal articles", "books".
- Data♯2 contains 651 tree tuples (222 original documents) and was exploited to identify classes of tree tuples that share the same topic, e.g. "knowledge discovery in databases", "computational logics", "pattern analysis".
- Data♯3 is composed of 871 tree tuples (286 original documents) and was exploited to detect classes of tree tuples that both cover common topics and belong to the same structural category. For example, tree tuples concerning "computational logics" should be grouped in distinct clusters depending on whether they correspond to conference papers, journal articles, or books.

Experiments were performed in order to shed light on the effectiveness of our approach in matching the ideal classification of each such collection, by significantly tuning parameters f and γ. Quality of clustering results were evaluated by means of traditional precision, recall and F-measure criteria [11].

Table 1 summarizes quality results obtained from the main experiments. Experimental evidence highlights the overall accuracy of our approach in distinguishing among classes according to a specific degree of similarity. As we can see, tests involving Data♯1 show good quality, thus indicating an appropriate behavior of XTrK-means, for high values of f, in clustering tree tuples by structure only. We obtained distinct clusters for papers of proceedings, articles of journals, chapters of books, and so forth.

High quality results characterized also experiments related to Data♯2, with $f \in [0.1, 0.3]$: as we expected, groups of tree tuples having similar contents (but not structure) were detected. We observed that terms appearing in tags `<title>`, `<book title>`, `<journal>`, `<author>`, and `<publisher>` were particularly discriminative in raising relevant topics. For instance, tree tuples concerning conference papers, journal articles, and books written by "Jeffrey D. Ullman" were grouped into a distinct cluster.

As far as Data♯3 is concerned, XTrK-means exhibits an excellent behavior in recognizing groups of tree tuples having both similar content and structure. The intuition devised for such a kind of experiment was surprisingly confirmed by the results obtained by equally weighing the importance of the content features w.r.t. the structure features, i.e. by setting f to values close to 0.5.

As a final remark, we observe from Table 1 that the quality of clustering results is functional to γ, and is maximized when γ ranges between 0.6 and 0.8. Such values moderately high (but not too close to 1) suggest that our notion of enhanced intersection between tree tuple transactions, i.e. γ-shared tree tuple items, allows for effectively capturing relevant structural or content information shared from even different items.

6 Conclusions

We presented a novel approach to cluster XML data, which addresses the issue of defining XML structure and content features. Such features are effectively able to represent both structural and content information extracted from a collection of XML documents, with the support of an ontology knowledge base. By exploiting the notion of XML tree tuple, we proposed a transactional model underlying an efficient partitional clustering algorithm. We also defined a notion of transaction matching w.r.t. a predefined threshold of similarity among tree tuple items, to detect XML elements sharing relevant structural and/or content information. The resulting clustering framework was tested on some collections extracted from the DBLP archive, revealing high effectiveness.

Nevertheless, the role played by ontological knowledge in supporting the detection of structural and content similarities among XML data needs to be deeply investigated. For this purpose, rigorous experiments on larger and heterogeneous datasets are currently being carried out and evaluated.

References

1. Arenas, M., Libkin, L.: A Normal Form for XML Documents. *ACM Transactions on Database Systems* 29(1) (2004) 195–232
2. Banerjee, S., Pedersen, T.: Extended Gloss Overlaps as a Measure of Semantic Relatedness. In: *Proc. 18th IJCAI* (2003) 805–810
3. Budanitsky, A., Hirst, G.: Semantic Distance in WordNet: An Experimental Application-oriented Evaluation of Five Measures. *Workshop on WordNet and Other Lexical Resources, 2nd meeting of NAACL* (2001)
4. DBLP XML Records (2004). Available at `http://dblp.uni-trier.de/xml/`
5. Doucet, A., Myka, H. A.: Naive Clustering of a Large XML Document Collection. In: *Proc. 1st INEX Workshop* (2002) 81–87
6. Fellbaum, C.: *WordNet: An Electronic Lexical Database.* MIT Press (1998)

7. Flesca, S., Furfaro, F., Greco, S., Zumpano, E.: Repairs and Consistent Answers for XML Data with Functional Dependencies. In: *Proc. 1st XSym Symp.* (2003) 238–253
8. Giannotti, F., Gozzi, C., Manco, G.: Clustering Transactional Data. In: *Proc. 6th PKDD Conf.* (2002) 175–187
9. Lian, W., Cheung, D. W., Mamoulis, N., Yiu, S.-M.: An Efficient and Scalable Algorithm for Clustering XML Documents by Structure. *IEEE Transactions on Knowledge and Data Engineering* 16(1) (2004) 82–96
10. Miller, G. A.: WordNet: A Lexical Database for English. *Communications of the ACM* 38(11) (1995) 39–41
11. Moens, M. F.: *Automatic Indexing and Abstracting of Document Texts.* Kluwer Academic Publishers (2000)
12. Nierman, A., Jagadish, H. V.: Evaluating Structural Similarity in XML Documents. In: *Proc. 5th WebDB Workshop* (2002) 61–66
13. Resnik, P.: Semantic Similarity in a Taxonomy: An Information-based Measure and its Application to Problems of Ambiguity in Natural Language. *Journal of Artificial Intelligence Research* 11 (1998) 95–130
14. Strehl, A., Ghosh, J., Mooney, R.: Impact of Similarity Measures on Web-page Clustering. In: *Proc. AAAI Workshop on AI for Web Search* (2000) 58–64
15. Theobald, M., Schenkel, R., Weikum, G.: Exploiting Structure, Annotation, and Ontological Knowledge for Automatic Classification of XML Data. In: *Proc. 6th WebDB Workshop* (2003) 1–6

Schema-Less, Semantics-Based Change Detection for XML Documents

Shuohao Zhang[1], Curtis Dyreson[1], and Richard T. Snodgrass[2]

[1] Washington State University, Pullman, Washington, U.S.A.
{szhang2, cdyreson}@eecs.wsu.edu

[2] The University of Arizona, Tucson, Arizona, U.S.A.
rts@cs.arizona.edu

Abstract. Schema-less change detection is the processes of comparing successive versions of an XML document or data collection to determine which portions are the same and which have changed, without using a schema. Change detection can be used to reduce space in an historical data collection and to support temporal queries. Most previous research has focused on detecting structural changes between document versions. But techniques that depend on structure break down when the structural change is significant. This paper develops an algorithm for detecting change based on the semantics, rather than on the structure, of a document. The algorithm is based on the observation that information that *identifies* an element is often conserved across changes to a document. The algorithm first isolates identifiers for elements. It then uses these identifiers to associate elements in successive versions.

1 Introduction

Change detection is a process that identifies changes between successive versions of a document or data collection. At the logical level, change detection aids in understanding the temporal behavior of data. Putting data into the context of its evolution usually entails more meaningful information. This is particularly true of data on the web, which often has a high rate of change [2,6]. At the physical level, change detection helps an archival system reduce space by storing only the changes to a new version because the size of the change is generally a small fraction of the entire version. In systems where storage is not a concern but data is shipped across a network, change detection can reduce network traffic, since often only the changes, and not the entire document, can be transferred.

Change detection is also significant in *temporal query support* and *incremental query evaluation*. In contrast to queries that are issued against a single version of the data, temporal queries can involve both current and past versions [11,12]. Temporal queries that access more than one version are important in mining historical facts and predicting future trends. The semantics of many temporal queries depends on identifying which data has changed and which has continued to reside unchanged in a database. Incremental query evaluation, when applicable, can significantly reduce the cost

X. Zhou et al. (Eds.): WISE 2004, LNCS 3306, pp. 279–290, 2004.
© Springer-Verlag Berlin Heidelberg 2004

of query evaluation. Some *continuous* (and non-continuous) queries can be incrementally evaluated, just by using the change. A continuous query is re-evaluated when *new* data arrives, for instance, as the query reads from a data stream [15,16]. For certain types of queries it is sufficient to combine the result of the query on the changed data with the previous result, rather than re-evaluate the query on the entire database.

This paper is organized as follows. Section 2 presents an example that motivates this research. We show that when the structure of a document changes while the data remains the same, a new method is needed to associate nodes in successive versions of a document. Related work in structural change detection is presented in Section 3. Section 4 formalizes the notion of *semantic identifiers* for Extensible Markup Language (XML) documents and outlines an algorithm for computing identifiers. Next, the paper shows how to use the semantic identifiers to detect changes in XML by matching elements based on their identifiers. A match means that an element has retained its semantic identity across successive versions. The paper then concludes with a discussion of future work.

2 Motivation

Fig. 1 shows an XML document. Fig. 2 shows the next version of the document. The change from the old version to the new version can be effected in two steps: an update and an insertion. The underlined parts in Fig. 1 and Fig. 2 reflect the change. The rest of the new version is an *exact* copy of the old version.

But consider a different, more substantial change. Fig. 3 shows an alternative version of the document fragment in Fig. 1. It is an alternative version in the sense that it has basically the same information, just arranged in a different schema. What has changed from Fig. 1 to Fig. 3? The two fragments are far from identical. Intuitively, it requires a significant number of element insertions and deletions.

The high cost of change in this particular situation, however, is not our primary concern. Regardless of how large the change is, the cost is always an order of the size of the document. The problem lies in the fact that significant structural change makes it difficult to *associate* elements in different versions. An association is a correspondence between elements in successive versions. The association establishes that an element in one version has a successor in the next version of the document. The association is possibly a new version of the element. For instance, the Pocket Star <publisher> element in Fig. 3 should be associated with the Pocket Star <publisher> element in Fig. 1; ostensibly, it is a new version of that element. But each <publisher> is structurally very different and therefore cannot be associated by change detection processes based on recognizing structural copies. This creates an obstacle for temporal query or incremental query evaluation. If we are unable to appropriately associate elements in successive versions, these applications cannot be implemented correctly. The example sketched above suggests that if the structural change is significant, even though semantically the same data is present, it becomes difficult to associate elements.

```
<author>
  <name>Dan Brown</name>
  <book>
    <title>The Da Vinci Code
    </title>
    <publisher>Doubleday
    </publisher>
    <listprice>$24.95
    </listprice>
  </book>
  <book>
    <title>Angels & Demons
    </title>
    <publisher>Pocket Star
    </publisher>
    <listprice>$7.99</listprice>
  </book>
</author>
```

Fig. 1. The original version

```
<author>
  <name>Dan Brown</name>
  <book>
    <title>The Da Vinci Code
    </title>
    <publisher>Doubleday
    </publisher>
    <saleprice>$14.97</saleprice>
    <isbn>0385504209</isbn>
  </book>
  <book>
    <title>Angels & Demons
    </title>
    <publisher>Pocket Star
    </publisher>
    <listprice>$7.99</listprice>
  </book>
</author>
```

Fig. 2. A new version

```
<publisher>Doubleday
  <book>
    <title>The Da Vinci Code</title>
    <author>
      <name>Dan Brown</name>
    </author>
    <listprice>$24.95</listprice>
  </book>
</publisher>
<publisher>Pocket Star
  <book>
    <title>Angels & Demons</title>
    <author>
      <name>Dan Brown</name>
    </author>
    <listprice>$7.99</listprice>
  </book>
</publisher>
```

Fig. 3. An alternative new version

At issue is how to define “change.” Previous research considered two documents, or portions thereof, the same if and only if they are *identical* (see Section 3 for a review of previous research). This requires not only textual equality but structural as well. Some researchers have considered unordered trees as the basis of comparing versions, which unlike the XML data model, ignores order among siblings.

This paper proposes a semantics-based change detection framework. Nodes that are *semantically equivalent* are considered unchanged and will be associated, regardless of their structural contexts. Finding all such associations between two versions has two important benefits: (1) it allows elements to exist across successive versions of a document (thus providing good support for temporal queries, for example), and (2) it detects semantic changes (which also includes “easier” changes, i.e., those that do not involve significant amounts of structural change).

3 Related Work

Early work in change detection mainly deals with string matching [1,14,18,19,23]. The subject is thus “flat” (plain-text) documents without hierarchical structures like those in SGML or XML. Plain-text change detection does not work well for XML because it is insensitive to hierarchical structure. It is also poorly-suited to finding semantic change, which is the goal of this paper. There has been some research in change detection for HTML [8] and general hierarchical structured documents [5,7]. To achieve efficiency, some simplifying assumptions are made. For example, [7] assumes that any leaf in one version has at most one leaf in another version “close” enough to be its match. This may not be true for such XML documents, as illustrated in Fig. 3.

In almost all research on XML, the data model is considered or presumed to be a tree. It is thus natural to make use of the results from tree matching (sometimes also called tree correction) [13,17,20] in XML change detection. It is important to point out that most research adopts an *ordered, labeled tree* data model [4]. The best known algorithm for general ordered labeled tree matching is by Zhang and Shasha [24]. To the best of our knowledge, only a few papers have considered the scenario where XML is modeled as an unordered labeled tree [22,26], in part because the tree matching problem for unordered labeled trees is NP-complete [25]. Due to space limitations, we omit presenting the complexities of the algorithms mentioned above since they all consider structural equality for a match while we focus on semantic equivalence.

Our semantic change detection technique is based on finding a (*semantic*) *identifier* for each node in an XML data model. An identifier is like a *key* for XML, but does not play a role in validation. Buneman et al. define a key as the pairing of a *target path* with a set of *key path expressions* [3]. Both the target path and key path expressions are *regular expression queries* (similar to XPath queries) on the data model for the document. Our work on identifiers differs from Buneman et al.'s research in that it is possible for the identifiers (but not keys) of two nodes to evaluate to the same value (when they have the same semantics) and we focus on a method to compute and use identifiers to associate nodes across multiple versions of a document's data model.

4 Semantic Identifiers

This section develops an algorithm for computing semantic identifiers. Basically, an identifier is a query expression that can be used for element identity, that is, to distinguish one element from another. Semantic identity is related to identity based on structure alone, but some elements can have exactly the same structure, yet be semantically different.

4.1 Structural Identity

In a given XML data model, each element and text node is of a specific *type*, which we will denote as *T*. The type is the concatenation of labels (element names) on the path from the root to a node, separated by a '/'. The type has been referred to in the literature as the *signature* [22]. A text node and its parent (an element node) will have the same type, but they are distinguished by the fact that they are different *kinds* of nodes. We will refer to the final label in the type as the *abbreviated type*. It suffices to use the abbreviated type except when two types happen to have the same abbreviation.

The structure of an element node is its type and the set of all its descendants (assuming lexical order is not important, a list of descendants otherwise). We will consider a pair of elements to be *structurally different* if the elements are of different types or if there is some descendant of one element that is structurally different from every descendant of the other element. Otherwise, the elements are considered to be *structurally identical.*

4.2 Relating Semantic to Structural Identity

This section develops a notion of semantic identity as different from, but related to, structural identity. We give two axioms that capture the intuition with which we reason about semantic identity. Thus these axioms serve as a bridge that connects intuitive understanding to the rigor necessary for computer processing.

Axiom I: *Nodes that are structurally different are semantically different.*

Let's consider text nodes first, and then element nodes. The structure of a text node is its type and value. Axiom I states that two text nodes are considered to be different, semantically, when their structures are different. As an example, consider the document in Fig. 3. The text nodes corresponding to "Angels & Demons" and "The Da Vinci Code" are different in semantics because they are textually different. But the text nodes corresponding to "Dan Brown" are structurally identical, and therefore could be semantically identical. Each <book> element has <title>, <author> and <listprice> subelements. Since the two text children of *title* nodes are "The Da Vinci Code" and "Angels & Demons," the two <book> nodes are semantically different regardless of the <author> or <listprice> nodes.

If two element nodes are semantically different, it is not necessarily the case that they are structurally different. In fact, it is possible for two element nodes to be structurally identical but semantically different. This is stated in the following axiom.

Axiom II: *Nodes that are structurally identical are semantically identical if and only if their respective parents are semantically identical, or if they are both root nodes.*

Axiom II states that nodes that have the same structure also have the same semantics if and only if their parents are semantically the same. Axiom I distinguishes nodes that have different content; but when nodes have exactly the same content, Axiom II offers an alternative to distinguish them by their *context.* The context is the semantic identity of the parent node. For example, the two <name> nodes in the data model for the XML document in Fig. 3 both have a text child "Dan Brown" and are thus structurally equivalent. Are they semantically equivalent? It depends on their context. If we inspect their parents' semantics, we find that the two <author> nodes are structurally different (in the <book> subelement, or similarly, in <listprice>), and so by Axiom I are semantically different. Therefore the two <name> nodes are structurally identical but semantically different since each is in the context of a different book.

If two structurally equivalent nodes have semantically identical parents, then they are regarded as identical. This is reasonable because we cannot semantically distinguish two exact copies when they are enclosed in the same context.

4.3 Identifiers

This section defines several terms that are important to the algorithm for semantics-based change detection presented in the next section.

An identifier is based on the evaluation of XPath expressions [21] so we first define what it means to evaluate an XPath expression.

Definition [XPath evaluation]. Let *Eval(n, E)* denote the result of evaluating an XPath expression *E* from a context node *n*. Given a list of XPath expressions, $L = (E_1, \ldots, E_k)$, then $Eval(n, L) = (Eval(n, E_1), \ldots, Eval(n, E_k))$. ▮

Since an XPath expression evaluates to a list of nodes, *Eval*(*n*, *L*) evaluates to a list of lists.

Definition [Identifier]. An *identifier* for a type, *T*, is a list of XPath expressions, *L*, such that for any pair of type *T* nodes, *x* and *y*, *x* and *y* are semantically different if and only if $Eval(x, L) \neq Eval(y, L)$. ▮

An identifier serves to distinguish nodes of the same type. Two nodes are considered semantically the same if and only if their identifiers evaluate to the same result. Two lists are considered equivalent if they have the same cardinality and are equal at each position.

The choice of XPath expressions as the basis for specifying an identifier is a means rather than an end. It could be any mechanism that is able to properly locate nodes in a data model. We use XPath since it is widely adopted and supported.

Definition [Identifier map]. An *identifier map* (denoted *M*) is a relation that maps each type to its corresponding identifier (an XPath expression list), i.e.,

$$M = \{(T, L) \mid L \text{ is an identifier for type } T\}. \quad ▮$$

Identifiers are constructed from XPath expressions that locate values (text nodes) in the subtree rooted at a node.

Definition [Type-to-leaf path list]. The *type-to-leaf path list* for a type, *T*, denoted *typeL*(*T*), is a list of XPath expressions such that *typeL*(*T*) is a sorted list of XPath expressions, **sort**(*S*), where

- $E = \{e \mid e \text{ is of type } T\}$ is a set of all of the elements of type *T* in a document,
- $D = \{d \mid d \text{ is a text descendant of some } e \in E\}$ is a set of all of the text descendants of type *T* elements (if *T* is a text type then self() is the only descendant), and
- $S = \{s/\text{text()} \mid s = \textbf{suffix}(T, T') \text{ where } T' \text{ is the type of some } d \in D\}$ is a set of all of the relative XPath expressions that locate a text descendant from a context node of a type *T* element. (Note that if *T* and *T'* are the same then *S* includes text().) ▮

A type-to-leaf path list is a specific list of XPath expressions that locate text values that are descendants of nodes of a particular element type. In a given XML document, each type *T* has exactly one *typeL*(*T*). In the document shown in Fig. 1, for example, *typeL*(*author/book*) = (title/text(), publisher/text(), listprice/text()).

Note that for the document shown in Fig. 1, *typeL(book)* should contain one more XPath expression: text(). We believe that trivial text nodes, i.e., text nodes whose contents are all white-space characters, are insignificant in semantics. Thus the expression text() appears in a type-to-leaf path list *typeL(T)* only if there exists at least one type *T* node with a non-trivial text child.

Definition [unique with respect to *typeL(T)*]. Suppose that node *n* is of type *T*. Then *n* is *unique with respect to typeL(T)*, if and only if *typeL(T)* is an identifier for type *T*. That is, if and only if for any *n'* of type *T*,

$$Eval(n, typeL(T)) \neq Eval(n', typeL(T)).$$ ∎

4.4 Computing Identifiers

The algorithm to compute identifiers will operate in a bottom-up fashion, working from the leaves towards the root of the tree. The following definitions describe positions in the bottom-up traversal. We use the term "floor" to evoke the idea that the algorithm ascends the tree like a person might climb floors in a building.

Definition [Floor-0 node]. All text nodes and only text nodes are *floor-0 nodes*. ∎

Definition [Floor-*k* node]. A node is a *floor-k node* if and only if the maximal floor among its children is *k*-1. ∎

Note that not all nodes of a certain type are of the same floor, and not all nodes of the same floor are of the same type. Types are computed top-down while floors bottom-up in the data model tree. Both concepts are important in computing identifiers.

Definition [local identifier]. An identifier is a *local identifier* if the XPath expressions evaluate to descendants of the context node; otherwise it is non-local. ∎

An identifier contains XPath expressions that evaluate to some leaf nodes in the document tree. It is either a local identifier or a non-local identifier. A non-local identifier locates at least one leaf node that is not a descendant of the context node. For example, the <name> node in Fig. 1 is identified by its text content, Dan Brown; so (text()) is a local identifier for <name>. On the other hand, the two <name> nodes in Fig. 3 have identical contents. It is impossible for the identifier of this type to contain only descendants of the <name> nodes. Thus <name>'s identifier must be non-local.

The algorithm for computing identifiers is shown in Fig. 4. The algorithm consists of two phases. Phase 1 finds all local identifiers, working bottom-up from the floor-0 nodes. This phase corresponds to Axiom I. When Phase 1 terminates, all semantically distinct nodes that Axiom I can determine are found. Phase 2 recursively computes the identifiers for the remaining types. This corresponds to Axiom II. When Phase 2 terminates, all semantically distinct nodes are found. Any remaining node is a redundant copy of another node in the document.

The total cost of the algorithm is bounded by $O(n*\log(n))$ where n is size of the document tree.

Pre: $M = \{(T_k, ())\}$ ($1 \le k \le$number of different types)

Post: $M = \{(T_k, L_k) \mid L_k$ is a identifier for type $T_k\}$

Phase 1: find local identifiers

1) $i = 0$;
2) For each floor-i node n of type T such that $M(T) = ()$, if every type T node is unique with respect to $typeL(T)$, add $(T, typeL(T))$ to M and for each type T' that is a prefix of T, add (T', **suffix**(T', T)/$typeL(T)$) to M;
3) $i = i + 1$; terminate Phase 1 if the next floor is the root, or go to 2).

Phase 2: expand with non-local identifiers

Starting from the root and working down the tree, for each node n of type T such that n is not unique with respect to $typeL(T)$, add (T, Id) to M where Id is a list obtained by appending to $typeL(T)$ the identifier of n's parent.

Fig. 4. Algorithm for computing identifiers

5 Semantic Change Detection

We are now able to semantically identify a node in an XML document. In this section, we discuss how nodes in different versions can be matched based on their identifiers. Once all semantically identical nodes are matched, we regard the unmatched elements as change participants.

5.1 Semantic Node Matching

The following definitions assume that element nodes p and q are both of type T and reside in different versions V_p and V_q of an XML document. ID(p) is p's identifier.

Definition [Type Territory]. The territory of a type T, denoted T_T, is the set of all text nodes that are descendants of the least common ancestor, denoted $lca(T)$, of all of the type T nodes. ∎

Within the type territory is the territory controlled by individual nodes of that type.

Definition [Node Territory]. The territory of a type T node p, denoted N_p, is T_T excluding all text nodes that are descendants of other type T nodes. ∎

The type territory of T contains all the information that might be useful in identifying any type T node. The territory of a specific node of that type is contained in the type territory, but does not contain any node that is a descendant of another type T node.

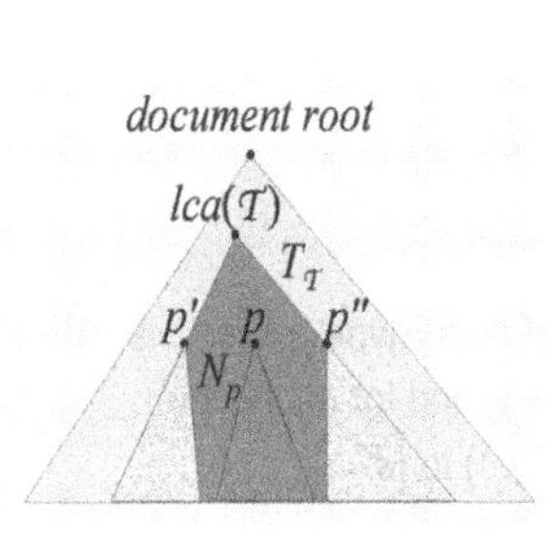

Fig. 5. Node territory

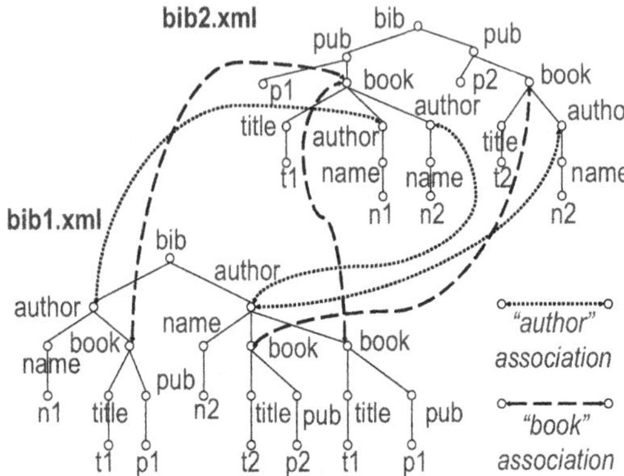

Fig. 6. Part of the match between bib1.xml and bib2.xml

Fig. 5 visualizes the idea of type territory and node territory. Suppose there are three type *T* nodes, *p*, *p*' and *p*''. The type territory of *T*, T_T, is the subtree rooted at the node *lca*(*T*). The node territory of *p*, N_p, is the area shaded dark in the figure. N_p is T_T excluding the two subtrees rooted at *p*' and *p*'' (represented by the striped areas).

The type territory of *book* in Fig. 5, for example, is (Dan Brown, The Da Vinci Code, Doubleday, $24.95, Angels & Demons, Pocket Star, $7.99). The node territory of the leftmost *book* node is (Dan Brown, The Da Vinci Code, Doubleday, $24.95).

Now we are ready to match nodes in successive versions.

Definition [Admits]. *q admits p* if *Eval*(*q*, ID(*q*)) $\subseteq N_p$. ∎

In general, *Eval*(*p*, ID(*p*)) is a list of lists because each XPath expression in the identifier evaluates to a list of values. Here in semantic matching we implicitly convert (flatten) it to a list of distinct values. This is because only the values are important in our semantic matching.

Definition [Node match]. Nodes *p* and *q* are *matched* if and only if *p* and *q* admit each other. ∎

Intuitively, admission and match can be described as follows. *q* is identified by a list of text values $q_1, \ldots, q_n$ in V_q. If a node *p* in V_p has at least as much information as *q* does, then *p* should have a group of text values $q_1, \ldots, q_n$ in its own territory N_p. A match implies semantic equality between two nodes, thus it requires admissions in both directions.

5.2 Semantic Matching for Sample Documents

We now show how nodes are matched based on the criteria described above. Fig. 6 shows bib1.xml and the next version, bib2.xml, in which there has been significant structural change. The document versions are displayed as tree diagrams rather than textually to better illustrate how the nodes are matched. The change between the two versions is similar to that presented in Fig. 1 and Fig. 3. Intuitively, we can tell that the semantics of the two versions are the same insofar as they contain the same information, but arranged to different schemas.

First we need to compute the identifiers for each node in both versions. We are then able to evaluate the value of each node's identifier. For example, the values of <book>'s identifiers in both versions are shown in Table 1. The territory of the leftmost <book> in bib2.xml is (p1, t1, n1, n2, p2); the identifier of the leftmost <book> in bib1.xml evaluates to (n1, t1). Hence the leftmost <book> in bib1.xml admits the leftmost <book> in bib2.xml. Similarly, the first <book> in bib2.xml admits the first <book> in bib1.xml. Therefore, the first <book> in bib1.xml and the first <book> in bib2.xml match. This is represented in Fig. 6 by a dashed line connecting the two.

All matches for *book* and *author* are shown in Fig. 6. (Two matched *author* nodes are connected by a dotted line.) To preserve the clarity of the figure, we do not show matches for all of the nodes. It turns out that each node is matched to one or more nodes in the other version. For a change (insertion, deletion or update) to occur, there has to be at least one unmatched node in one version. We can thus conclude that there is no semantic change from bib1.xml to bib2.xml for *book* and *author* elements.

Table 1. Values of identifiers for *book*

bib1.xml	**Value of Identifier**
leftmost *book*	((n1), (t1))
middle *book*	((n2), (t2))
rightmost *book*	((n2), (t1))
bib2.xml	**Value of Identifier**
leftmost *book*	((t1))
rightmost *book*	((t2))

5.3 Complexity Analysis

Let P and Q denote numbers of nodes in two documents to which nodes p and q belong, respectively. Deciding whether node q admits node p is bounded by $O(P*\log(P))$. Thus deciding whether q and p match takes $O(P*\log(P)+ Q*\log(Q))$.

For entire document matching, it would take $O(P*Q*(P*\log(P)+ Q*\log(Q)))$ if we try to directly match all possible pairings of nodes in two documents. To reduce the time cost of matching, we use the following heuristic. If the identifier for a node type remains the same, then we can base our matching solely on the values of the evaluated identifiers, effectively skipping the expensive test to search for a match in the node's territory. The notion of node territory is crafted to help match nodes when their identifiers are different; two nodes match if each node's territory includes the other's evaluated identifier. However, if the identifier for a node type remains unchanged, we can in fact base our matching solely on the evaluated identifiers. In this case, two nodes match if and only if their evaluated identifiers are the same. There is no need to compute node territories. In most real-world applications, the extent of change over versions is usually small. Hence, it is reasonable to expect that the identifiers of most of the types remain the same over versions. Based on this assumption, the number of direct matching attempts is often relatively small. For large documents, computing node territories will take a major portion of the processing time.

6 Conclusions and Future Work

This paper proposes a new approach to detect changes in successive versions of XML documents. The approach is novel because it utilizes semantic change; previous work focused on structural change. We first define the notion of a semantic identifier, which is an expression that serves to distinguish elements of a particular type. This paper then sketches an algorithm to efficiently compute these identifiers. Changes in successive versions are obtained by matching nodes based on their semantic identifiers. Our approach is to observe that the information that identifies an element is conserved across changes to a document. We provide an algorithm that matches a pair of nodes by looking for the identifying information of one node in the territory of the second node. The advantage of our approach is that we can match nodes even when there has been significant structural change to a document. Compared to conventional structural change detection, our semantics-based technique is able to detect semantic change in various conditions, without prior knowledge of schema.

The next stage of this research is to implement the algorithm in C and integrate the code into the Apache web server to support server-side versioning of XML documents [9]. Another task is to devise a metric to measure the quality of a semantic match, and to develop an algorithm to compute the metric mechanically. With this refined framework of semantics-based node association in place, we then plan to build a transaction-time XML repository and implement a system such as *TT*XPath [10] to support transaction-time XPath queries.

References

1. A. Apostolico and Z. Galil, editors. *Pattern Matching Algorithms.* Oxford University Press, 1997.
2. B. Brewington and G. Cybenko. "How Dynamic is the Web?" In *Proc. of the 9th International World Wide Web Conference*, Amsterdam, Netherlands, May 2000, 257–276.
3. P. Buneman, S. Davidson, W. Fan, C. Hara, and W. Tan. "Keys for XML". In *Proc. of the 10th International World Wide Web Conference*, Hong Kong, China, 2001, 201–210.
4. G. Cobéna, S. Abiteboul, A. Marian. "Detecting Changes in XML Documents". In *Proceedings of ICDE*, San Jose, February 2002, 41–52.
5. S. Chawathe and H. Garcia-Molina. "Meaningful Change Detection in Structured Data". In *Proceedings of SIGMOD Conference*, June 1997, 26–37.
6. Cho, J. and H. Garcia-Molina. "The Evolution of the Web and Implications for an Incremental Crawler". In *Proc. of VLDB Conference*, Cairo, Egypt, Sep. 2000, 200–209.
7. S. Chawathe, A. Rajaraman, H. Garcia-Molina and J. Widom. "Change Detection in Hierarchically Structured Information". In *SIGMOD Conference*, Montreal, Canada, June 1996, 493–504.

8. F. Douglis, T. Ball, Y. F. Chen, E. Koutsofios. "The AT&T Internet Difference Engine: Tracking and Viewing Changes on the Web". *World Wide Web*, 1(1): 27–44, Jan. 1998.
9. C. Dyreson, H. Ling, Y. Wang. "Managing Versions of Web Documents in a Transaction-time Web Server". In *Proc. of the 13th International World Wide Web Conference*, New York City, May 2004., 421–432.
10. C. Dyreson. "Observing Transaction-time Semantics with TTXPath". In *Proceedings of WISE*, Kyoto, Japan, December 2001, 193–202.
11. Fabio Grandi. "Introducing an Annotated Bibliography on Temporal and Evolution Aspects in the World Wide Web". *SIGMOD Record*, Volume 33, Number 2, June 2004.
12. D. Gao and R. T. Snodgrass. "Temporal Slicing in the Evaluation of XML Queries". In *Proceedings of VLDB*, 2003, 632–643.
13. C. M. Hoffmann, M. O'Donnell. "Pattern Matching in Trees". *JACM*, 29: 68–95, 1982.
14. V. I. Levenshtein. "Binary codes capable of correcting deletions, insertions, and reversals". *Cybernetics and Control Theory*, 10: 707--710, 1966.
15. L. Liu, C. Pu, R. Barga, and T. Zhou. "Differential Evaluation of Continual Queries". *Proc. of the International Conference on Distributed Computing Systems*, 1996, 458–465.
16. L. Liu, C. Pu, and W. Tang. "Continual Queries for Internet Scale Event-Driven Information Delivery". *IEEE Trans. Knowledge Data Engineering*, 11(4), 610–628, 1999.
17. S. Lu. "A tree-to-tree distance and its application to cluster analysis". *IEEE Trans. Pattern Analysis and Machine Intelligence*, 1(2): 219–224, 1979.
18. W. Masek, M. Paterson. "A faster algorithm for computing string edit distances". *J. Comput. System Sci.*, 1980, 18–31.
19. E. Myers. "An O(ND) Difference Algorithm and Its Variations". *Algorithmica*, 1(2): 251–266, 1986.
20. K. C. Tai. "The Tree-to-Tree Correction Problem". *JACM*, 26: 485–495, 1979.
21. "XML Path Language (XPath) 2.0". *W3C*, `www.w3c.org/TR/xpath20/`, current as of August 2004.
22. Y. Wang, D. DeWitt, J.-Y. Cai. "X-Diff: An Effective Change Detection Algorithm for XML Documents". `www.cs.wisc.edu/niagara/papers/xdiff.pdf`, current as of August 2004.
23. R. A. Wagner, M. J. Fischer. "The string-to-string correction problem". *JACM*, 21: 168–173, 1974.
24. K. Zhang and D. Shasha. "Simple Fast Algorithms for the Editing Distance between Trees and Related Problems". *SIAM Journal of Computing*, 18(6): 1245–1262, 1989.
25. K. Zhang, R. Statman, D. Shasha. "On the Editing Distance between Unordered Labeled Trees". *Information Processing Letters*, 42: 133–139, 1992.
26. K. Zhang. "A Constrained Edit Distance between Unordered Labeled Trees". *Algorithmica*, 205–222, 1996.

Discovering Minimal Infrequent Structures from XML Documents

Wang Lian, Nikos Mamoulis, David W. Cheung, and S.M. Yiu

Department of Computer Science and Information Systems,
The University of Hong Kong, Pokfulam, Hong Kong.
{wlian, nikos, dcheung, smyiu}@csis.hku.hk

Abstract. More and more data (documents) are wrapped in XML format. Mining these documents involves mining the corresponding XML structures. However, the semi-structured (tree structured) XML makes it somewhat difficult for traditional data mining algorithms to work properly. Recently, several new algorithms were proposed to mine XML documents. These algorithms mainly focus on mining frequent tree structures from XML documents. However, none of them was designed for mining infrequent structures which are also important in many applications, such as query processing and identification of exceptional cases. In this paper, we consider the problem of identifying infrequent tree structures from XML documents. Intuitively, if a tree structure is infrequent, all tree structures that contain this subtree is also infrequent. So, we propose to consider the minimal infrequent structure (MIS), which is an infrequent structure while all proper subtrees of it are frequent. We also derive a level-wise mining algorithm that makes use of the SG-tree (signature tree) and some effective pruning techniques to efficiently discover all MIS. We validate the efficiency and feasibility of our methods through experiments on both synthetic and real data.

1 Introduction

The standardized, simple, self describing nature of XML makes it a good choice for data exchange and storage on the World Wide Web. More and more documents are wrapped in XML format nowadays. To process large amount of XML documents more efficiently, we can rely on data mining techniques to get more insight into the characteristics of the XML data, so as to design a good database schema; to construct an efficient storage strategy; and especially for enhancing query performance. Unlike traditional structured data, XML document is classified as semi-structured data. Besides data, its tree structure always embeds significant sementic meaning. Therefore, efficiently mining useful tree structures from XML documents now attract more and more attention.

In recent years, several algorithms that can efficiently discover frequent tree structures are available. However, discovering infrequent tree structures is also a very important subject. In fact, infrequent tree structures carry more information than frequent structures from the information theory point of view. There are many applications that can make use of the infrequent tree structures such as query optimization, intrusion detection and identification of abnormal cases. Unfortunately, as far as we know, there are no papers that formally address this problem. In this paper, we present our work

X. Zhou et al. (Eds.): WISE 2004, LNCS 3306, pp. 291–302, 2004.
© Springer-Verlag Berlin Heidelberg 2004

in mining infrequent structures. Because any superstructure of an infrequent structure must be infrequent, identifying all infrequent structures is impractical as the number of them will be huge. On the other hand, we propose to discover a special kind of infrequent structure: the *Minimal Infrequent Structure* (MIS), which is itself infrequent but all its substructures being frequent. The role of MIS is similar to that of negative border on itemsets [8]. Based on MIS, we can easily identify all infrequent structures by constructing superstructures from MIS.

Several methods have been proposed for the problem of mining frequent tree structures in semi-structure data [2][6] [10][12]. Most of them are based on the classical Apriori technique [1], however, these methods are rather slow when applying to find MIS (the number of MIS is rather small, whereas the number of frequent structures is very large, a lot of time is spent on counting the support of frequent structures). In order to accelerate the discovery of MIS, we propose the following three-phase data mining algorithm. In phase one, we scan the data to derive the edge-based summary (signature) of each XML document. In phase two, we run Apriori on the summaries to quickly generate a set of frequent structures of size k. In phase three, we remove the frequent structures so as to identify the minimal infrequent structures. Experimental results demonstrate that this three-phase data mining algorithm indeed achieves a significant speed improvement.

The contribution of this paper is two-fold:

– We introduce a useful structure: Minimal Infrequent Structure as a base for representing all infrequent structures in XML documents.
– We propose an efficient level-wise data mining algorithm that discovers Minimal Infrequent Structures in XML data, which can also be used in other mining applications.

The rest of the paper is organized as follows. Section 2 provides background on existing work. In Section 3, we present the data mining algorithm that finds all MIS. In Section 4, we evaluate our proposed methods on both synthetic and real data. Finally, Section 5 concludes the paper with a discussion about future work.

2 Related Work

According to our knowledge, there are no papers that have discussed the problem of mining infrequent tree structures in XML documents. On the other hand, there are several algorithms for mining frequent tree structures in trees [2][6] [10][12] based on Apriori [1]. Starting from frequent vertices, the occurrences of more complex structures are counted by adding an edge to the frequent structures of the previous level. The major difference among these algorithms is on the candidate generation and the counting processes.

In [2], a mining technique that enumerates subtrees in semi-structured data efficiently, and a candidate generation procedure that ensures no misses, was proposed. The tree enumeration works as follows: for each frequent structure s, the next-level candidate subtrees with one more edge are generated by adding frequent edges to its rightmost path. That is, we first locate the right most leaf r, traverse back to the root, and extend each node visited during the backward traversal. This technique enumerates the occurrences of trees relatively quickly, but fails to prune candidates early, since the final goal is to discover frequent structures. A similar candidate generation technique is applied in TREEMINER [12]. This method also fails to prune candidates at an early stage, although the counting efficiency for each candidate is improved with the help of a special encoding schema.

In [6], simple algorithms for canonical labeling and graph isomorphism are used, but they do not scale well and cannot be applied to large graphs. In [10], complicated pruning techniques are incorporated to reduce the size of candidates, however the method discovers only collections of paths in ordered trees, rather than arbitrary frequent trees. Our work is also related to FastXMiner [11], discovers frequently asked query patterns and their results are intelligently arranged in the system cache in order to improve future query performance. This method is also Apriori-like, however, it only discovers frequent query patterns rooted at the root of DTD, whereas our mining algorithm does not have this limitation.

Among the studies on association rule discovery, the Maxminer in [3] is the most related work to this paper. Maxminer is equipped with an efficient enumeration technique based on set-enumeration tree to overcome the inefficiency of lattice-based itemset enumeration. On the other hand, our data mining method uses the enumeration method in [2] to generate the candidates level-by-level, but we apply more effective pruning techniques to reduce the number of candidates; a generated candidate is pruned if any of its substructures are not in the set of frequent structures generated in previous level. Furthermore, we use a novel approach which performs counting on a SG–tree [7], a tree of signatures, to quickly identify possible large frequent structures of a particular size. The mining algorithm on the exact structures then counts only candidates which are not substructures of the frequent structures already discovered. This greatly reduces the number of candidates that need to be counted and speeds up the mining process significantly. The details of the new data mining method will be described in the next section.

Other related work includes [8] and [5]. In [8], the concept of negative border is introduced, which is a set of infrequent itemsets, where all subsets of each infrequent itemset are frequent. Conceptually, MIS is similar to negative border. In [5], WARMR is developed on first-order models and graph structures. This algorithm can be applied for frequent tree discovery, since tree is a special case of graph structures. However its candidate generation function is over-powerful, it produces many duplicated candidates.

3 Discovery of MIS

3.1 Problem Definition

Before defining our data mining problem, we introduce some concepts that are related to the problem formulation.

Definition 1. *Let L be the set of labels found in an XML database. A* ***structure*** *is a node-labelled tree, where nodes are labels from L. Given two structures, s_1 and s_2, if s_1 can be derived by removing recursively $l \geq 0$ nodes (which are either leaf nodes* *or root nodes) from s_2 then s_1 is a **substructure** of s_2. In this case we also say that s_2 **contains** s_1, or that s_2 is a **superstructure** of s_1. Finally, the size of a structure s $size(s)$ is defined by the number of edges in it.*

If a structure contains only one element, we assume the size of it is zero. Assuming that $L = \{a, b, c, d, e\}$, two potential structures with respect to L are $s_1 = (a(b)(c(a)))^*$ and $s_2 = (a(c))$; s_2 is a substructure of s_1, or s_1 contains s_2.

Definition 2. *Given a set D of structures, the **support** $sup(s)$ of a structure s in D is defined as the number of structures in D, which contain s. Given a user input threshold ρ, if $sup(s) \geq \rho \times |D|$, then s is **frequent** in D, otherwise it is **infrequent**.*
*(1) If $size(s) \geq 1$ and $sup(s) < \rho \times |D|$, and for each substructure s_x of s, $sup(s_x) \geq \rho \times |D|$, then s is a **Minimal Infrequent Structure(MIS)****.*
(2) If $size(s) = 0$ and $sup(s) < \rho \times |D|$, then s is a MIS.

In practice, some MIS could be arbitrarily large and potentially not very useful, so we restrict our focus to structures that contain up to a maximum number of k edges. Note that the set D in Definition 2 can be regarded as a set of documents. Now, we are ready to define our problem formally as follows:

Definition 3. (problem definition): *Given a document set D, and two user input parameters ρ and k, find the set S of all MIS with respect to D, such that for each $s \in S$, $size(s) \leq k$.*

The following theorem shows the relationship between MIS and an infrequent structure.

Theorem 1. Let D be a document set, and S be the set of MIS in D with respect to ρ and k. If an infrequent structure t contains at most k edges then it contains at least one MIS.

Proof. In the cases where $size(t) = 0$ or all substructures of t are frequent, t itself is an MIS (of size at most k), thus it should be contained in the set of MIS. Now let us examine the case, where t has at least one infrequent proper substructure t'. If t' is MIS, then we have proven our claim. Otherwise, we can find a proper substructure of t' which is infrequent and apply the same test recursively, until we find a MIS (recall that a single node that is infrequent is also an MIS of size 0). □

Based on the above theorem, we can easily: (i)construct infrequent structures by generating superstructures from MIS. (ii)verify whether a structure is infrequent by checking whether it contains a MIS or not.

Finally, in order to accelerate the data mining process we make use of a document abstraction called *signature*, which is defined as follow:

* We use brackets to represent parent/child relationship.

** From now on, we use MIS to represent both Minimal Infrequent Structure and Minimal Infrequent Structures.

Definition 4. *Assume that the total number of distinct edges in D is E, and consider an arbitrary order on them from 1 to E. Let $order(e)$ be the position of edge e in this order. For each d $\in D$, we define an E-length bitmap, $sig(d)$, called* ***signature****; $sig(d)$ has 1 in position $order(e)$ if and only if e is present in d. Similarly, the signature of a structure s is defined by an E-length bitmap $sig(s)$, which has 1 in position $order(e)$ if and only if e is present in s.*

The definition above applies not only for documents, but also for structures. Observe that if s_1 is a substructure of s_2, then $sig(s_1) \subseteq sig(s_2)$. Thus, signature can be used as a fast check on whether or not a structure can be contained in a document. On the other hand, it is possible that $sig(s_1) \subseteq sig(s_2)$ and s_1 is not a substructure of s_2 (e.g., $s_1 = (a(b(c))(b(d)))$, $s_2 = (a(b(c)(d)))$. Thus, we can only use the signature to find an *upper bound* of a structure's support in the database.

3.2 Mining MIS

We consider the problem of mining MIS as a three-phase process. The first phase is *preprocessing*. The document in D is scanned once for two purposes. (1) Find out all infrequent elements, infrequent edges and all frequent edges. The set of all frequent edges are stored in FE. We will use M to store the discovered MIS. (2) Compute signatures of all the documents and store them in an array SG. Besides the signature, SG also store the $support$ of the signature in D, which is the number of documents whose signatures match the signature. Since many documents will have the same signature, SG in general can fit into the memory; otherwise, the approach in MaxMiner[3] could be used to store SG on disk.

The second phase of the mining process is called *signature-based counting*, and is described by the pseudocode in Figure 1. In this phase, given a fixed k, we will compute the set of size-k frequent structures in D. These frequent structures will be stored in F_k. In the third phase, F_k will be used to narrow the search domain of MIS because no subset of a frequent structure in F_k can be an MIS. Note that k is a user input parameter which is the same as the maximum size of MIS that we want to mine.

```
/* Input k, the maximum number of edges in a MIS*/
/* Output F_k, all size k frequent structures*/
F_prev = FE
for i=2 to k
    candidates = genCandidate(F_prev, FE)
    if candidates == ∅ then break; F_prev = ∅
    for each c in candidates
        if sigsup(c) ≥ ρ × |D| w.r.t SG then move c to F_prev
scan documents to count the support of each c ∈ F_prev
for each c in F_prev
    if sup(c) ≥ ρ × |D| then insert c into F_k
return F_k
```

Fig. 1. The Mining Algorithm – Phase 2

The algorithm in Figure 1 computes the frequent structures in an Apriori-like fashion. The procedure $genCandiates$ uses the method proposed in [2] to generate the candidates. Frequent structures of the previous level (F_{prev}) and the edges in FE are used to generate candidate structures for the current level (line 3). Note that if the signature of a structure does not have the enough support, then it cannot be a frequent structure. (The reverse is not necessary true.) Therefore, we can use the information to remove many inadmissable candidates during the generation. Using SG to prune the candidates in F_{prev} will not wrongly remove a true frequent structure but may have false hits remaining in F_{prev}. Therefore, a final counting is required to confirm the candidates reminds in F_{prev} (line 9).

The third phase is *structure counting*. We will find out all MIS in D and this step is described in Figure 2. The key steps are in lines 5–7. We again build up the candidates from FE by calling $genCandidates$ iteratively (line 3). The function $prune()$ removes a candidate if anyone of its substructure is found to be infrequent by checking it against the frequent structures from the previous iteration stored in F_{prev} (line 3). Subsequently, for a candidate c, we check if it is a subset of a frequent structure in F_k. This will remove a large number of frequent structures (line 7). For the reminding candidates, we scan D to find their exact support (line 9). If it is not frequent, then it must be an MIS and it will be stored in M (line 13).

```
/* Input int k, the maximum number of edges in a MIS*/
/* Input F_k, all size k frequent structures*/
/* Output M, the set of MIS up to size k*/
1).  F_prev = FE; M = ∅
2).  for i=2 to k
3).      candidates = prune(genCandidate(F_prev, FE))
4).      if candidates == ∅ then break; F_prev = ∅
5).      for each c in candidates
6).          if c is a substructure of an structure in F_k then
7).              candidates.remove(c); insert c into F_prev
8).      for each c in candidates
9).          update sup(c) w.r.t D
10).             if sup(c) ≥ ρ × |D| then
11).                     candidates.remove(c); insert c into F_prev
12).     for each c in candidates
13).         if sup(c) > 0 then insert c into M
14). return M
```

Fig. 2. The Mining Algorithm – Phase 3

3.3 Optimizations

In this section we describe several optimizations that can improve the mining efficiency.

First Strategy: Use distinct children-sets. During the first scan of the dataset, for each element we record every distinct set of children elements found in the database. For example, consider the dataset of Figure 3, consisting of two document trees. Observe that element a has in total three distinct children sets; $((a)(b))$, $((c)(d))$, and $((d)(f))$. The children sets $((a)(b))$, $((c)(d))$ are found in doc1, and the children sets $((a)(b))$, $((d)(f))$ are found in doc2. When an element a having d as child is extended during candidate generation, we consider only f as a new child for it. This technique greatly reduces the number of candidates, since generation is based on extending the frequent structures by adding edges to their rightmost path.

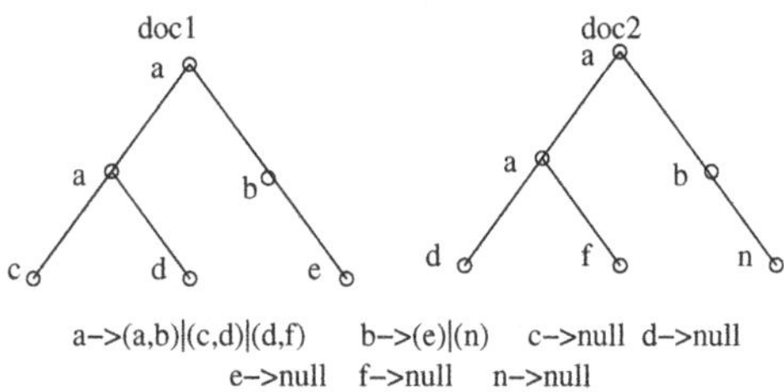

Fig. 3. Summary of Children-sets

Second Strategy: Stop counting early. Notice that we are searching for MIS rather than frequent structures, thus we are not interested in the exact support of frequent structures. During the counting process, when the support of a candidate is greater than the threshold, the structure is already frequent. Thus, we do not need to count it anymore; it is immediately removed from $candidates$ and inserted to F_{prev}. This heuristic is implemented in Lines 8–9 in Figure 1 and Lines 10–11 in Figure 2.

Third Strategy: Counting multiple levels of candidates. After candidate pruning, if the number of remaining ones is small, we can directly use them to generate the next level candidates and count two levels of candidates with a single scan of the documents. This can reduce the I/O cost at the last phases of the data mining process.

Fourth Strategy: Using the SG–tree in phase-two counting. In Figure 1, we obtain the supports of candidates by sequentially comparing their signatures to those of all documents. This operation is the bottleneck of the second phase in our mining algorithm. Instead of comparing each candidate with all document signatures, we can employ an index for document signatures, to efficiently select only those that contain a candidate.

The SG–tree (or *signature* tree) [7] is a dynamic balanced tree similar to R–tree for signatures. Each node of the tree corresponds to a disk page and contains entries of the form $\langle sig, ptr\rangle$. In a leaf node entry, sig is the signature of the document and ptr stores the number of documents sharing this signature. The signature of a directory node entry is the logical OR of all signatures in the node pointed by it and ptr is a pointer to this node. In other words, the signature of each entry *contains* all signatures in the subtree pointed by it. All nodes contain between c and C entries, where C is the maximum capacity and $c \geq C/2$, except from the root which may contain fewer entries. Figure 4 shows an example of a signature tree, which indexes 9 signatures. In this graphical example the maximum node capacity C is three and the length of the signatures six. In practice, C is in the order of several tens and the length of the signatures in the order of several hundreds.

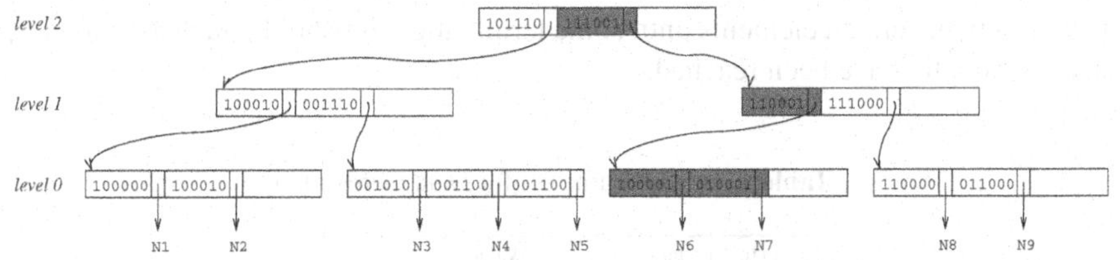

Fig. 4. Example of a Signature Tree

The tree can be used to efficiently find all signatures that contain a specific query signature (in fact, [7] have shown that the tree can also answer *similarity* queries). For instance, if $q = 000001$, the shaded entries of the tree in 4 are the qualifying entries to be followed in order to answer the query. Note that the first entry of the root node does not contain q, thus there could be no signature in the subtree pointed by it that qualifies the query.

In the first phase of our mining algorithm, we construct an SG–tree for the set SG of signatures, using the optimized algorithm of [7] and then use it in the second phase to facilitate counting. Thus, lines 5–6 in Figure 1 are replaced by a depth-first search in the tree for each candidate c, that is to count the number of document signatures containing the signature of c. As soon as this number reaches the threshold $\rho \times |D|$, search stops and c is inserted into F_{prev}. Note that we use a slight modification of the original structure of [7]; together with each signature g in a leaf node entry we store the number of documents $sup(g)$ having this signature (in replacement of the pointer in the original SG–tree).

4 Performance Studies

In this section, we evaluate the effectiveness and efficiency of our methodology using both synthetic and real data. The real data are from the DBLP archive [13]. First, we describe how the synthetic data is generated. Then, we validate the efficiency of our data mining algorithm on both synthetic and real data. All experiments are carried out in a computer with 4 Intel Pentium 3 Xeon 700MHZ processors and 4G memory running Solaris 8 Intel Edition. Java is the programming language.

4.1 Synthetic Data Generation

We generated our synthetic data using the NITF (News Industry Text Format) DTD [14]. Table 1 lists the parameters used at the generation process. First, we parse the DTD and build a graph on the parent-children relationships and other information like the relationships between children. Then, starting from the root element r of the DTD, for each subelement, if it is accompanied by "*" or "+", we decide how many times it should appear according to a Poisson distribution. If it is accompanied by "?", its occurrence is decided by a biased coin. If there are choices among several subelements of r, then their appearances in the document follow a random distribution. The process is repeated on the newly generated elements until some termination thresholds, such as a maximum document depth, have been reached.

Table 1. Input Parameters for Data Generation

Name	Interpretation	Value
N	total number of docs	10000–100000
W	distribution of '*'	Poisson
P	distribution of '+'	Poisson
Q	probability of '?' to be 1	a number between 0 & 1
Max	distribution of doc depth	Poisson

4.2 Efficiency of the Mining Algorithm

In the first set of experiments, we compare the total running cost (including the I/O time) of our mining algorithm (denoted by MMIS) with the algorithm in [2](denoted by MFS). The efficiency of the two techniques is compared with respect to three sets of parameters: (1) the support thresholds, (2) the maximum size k of the mined MIS, (3) the number of documents.

The synthetic data used in the experiments were generated by setting the parameters of the distribution functions to: W=3, P=3, Q=0.7, Max=10. Except experiments in Figure 7 and 10, N = 10000 in synthetic data set and N = 25000 in real data set.(where documents were randomly picked from the DBLP archive.)

Varying the Support Threshold

Figures 5 and 8 show the time spent by MMIS and MFS on the synthetic and real data respectively. The support threshold varies from 0.005 to 0.1. We set k=10 for the real dataset and k=15 for the synthetic one. Both figures show the same trend: as the support threshold increases, the improvement of MMIS over MFS decreases. This is because the number of frequent structures decreases, which degrades the pruning effectiveness of F_k. The improvement in the DBLP data is smaller than the improvement in the synthetic data, because these documents are more uniform.

Note that in lines 5 – 7 of the algorithm in Figure 2, a large number of candidates would be pruned in the course of finding the MIS. Figure 11 shows for k=15, ρ=0.01, the percentage of candidates in the synthetic data, which are pruned because of this optimization. The amount is in the range of 84% to 97%, which is significant saving.

Varying k

Figures 6 and 9 show the time spent by MMIS and MFS on synthetic and real data respectively, for various values of k and $\rho = 0.01$. Observe that as k increases, the speedup of MMIS over MFS increases. The reason for this is that once k goes beyond the level at which the number of candidates is the maximum, the number of frequent structures in F_k becomes smaller. Yet, the optimization from the pruning still have noticeable effect on the speed.

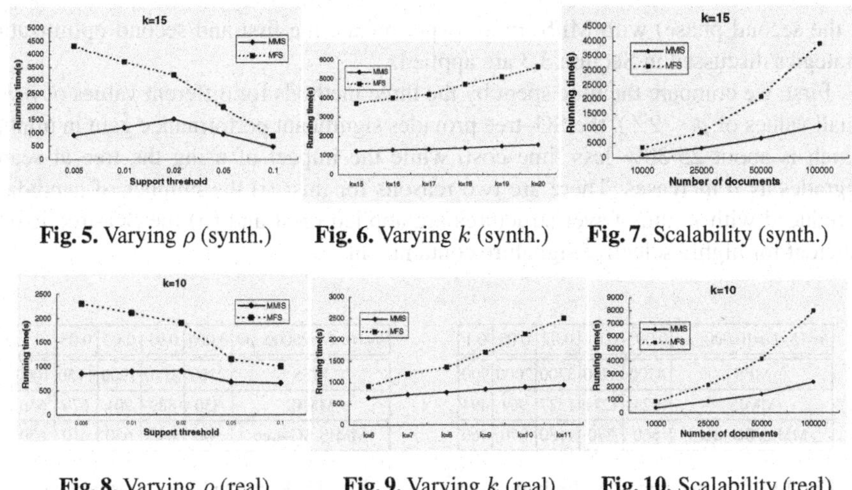

Fig. 5. Varying ρ (synth.) **Fig. 6.** Varying k (synth.) **Fig. 7.** Scalability (synth.)

Fig. 8. Varying ρ (real) **Fig. 9.** Varying k (real) **Fig. 10.** Scalability (real)

Figures 12 and 13 show the number of MIS discovered for various k on the synthetic and real dataset, respectively. The numbers unveil: First, the total numbers of MIS in both cases are small. Secondly, the number of MIS do not grow much while k increases. Therefore, even if k is very large, the time to mine MIS is still acceptable. (Even if we mine *all* the MIS of any size.) This is also confirmed by the results in Figures 6 and 9.

size of candidates.	8	9	10	11	12	13
% pruned candidates	84	85	90	90	95	97

Fig. 11. Effectiveness in 2nd Phase

k	15	16	17	18	19	20
MIS	321	325	340	342	342	348

Fig. 12. MIS (Synth.)

k	6	7	8	9	10
MIS	69	73	75	78	78

Fig. 13. MIS (Real)

Varying the Number of Documents

Figures 7 and 10 show the time spent by MMIS and MFS on synthetic and real document sets of various cardinalities. For this experiment, k=10 for real data and k=15 for synthetic data, while $\rho = 0.01$ in both cases.

In both cases the speedup of MISS over MFS is maintained with the increase of problem size, showing that MMIS scales well. We observe that for the DBLP data, the speedup actually increases slightly with the problem size. This is due to the fact that DBLP documents have uniform structure and the number of distinct signatures does not increase much by adding more documents.

Mining MIS Using SG–Tree

As we have discussed the usage of SG-tree as an optimization techniques, here we show the improvement achieved by SG-tree measured in running time. In the experiments, we compare the total running time (Including the I/O time) of two versions of our mining technique (a) MMIS and (b) MMIS-SG–tree (which is MMIS equipped with SG–tree in the second phase) with MFS. In all experiments, the first and second optimization strategies discussed in Section 3.3 are applied.

First, we compare the time spent by the three methods for different values of ρ. For small values of $\rho(\leq 2\%)$, the SG–tree provides significant performance gain in mining, which is about 25-30% less time cost, while the impact of using the tree at search degrades as ρ increases. There are two reasons for this: (i) the number of candidates is reduced with ρ, thus fewer structures are applied on it and (ii) the SG–tree is only efficient for highly selective signature containment.

k=15, D=10,000, ρ=	0.005	0.01	0.02	0.05	0.1
MFS	4300	3700	3200	2000	900
MMIS	923	1211	1527	967	494
MMIS-SG–tree	660	870	1180	870	460

Fig. 14. Running Time on Synthetic Data

k=10, D=25000, ρ=	0.005	0.01	0.02	0.05	0.1
MFS	2300	2110	1900	1150	1000
MMIS	850	889	901	679	650
MMIS-SG–tree	600	640	650	610	630

Fig. 15. Running Time on Real Data

k=15, ρ=0.01 D=	10000	25000	50000	100000
MFS	3700	8700	21000	39000
MMIS	1211	3300	6610	10910
MMIS-SG–tree	900	2400	4700	7400

Fig. 16. Running Time on Synthetic Data

k=10, ρ=0.01 D=	10000	25000	50000	100000
MFS	900	2200	4200	8000
MMIS	400	889	1460	2400
MMIS-SG–tree	280	630	1080	1750

Fig. 17. Running Time on Synthetic Data

Next, we show the time spent by the three methods for different values of D, where ρ=0.01. In Table 16 and 17, again the advantage of using the SG–tree is maintained for small ρ for about 25-30% less time cost.

5 Conclusion and Future Work

Besides discovering frequent tree structures in XML documents, mining infrequent tree structures is also important in many XML applications such as query optimization and identification of abnormal cases. In this paper, we initiate the study of mining infrequent tree structures. Since all superstructures of an infrequent tree structure are always infrequent, it does not make sense to find all infrequent tree structures. We introduced the concept of Minimal Infrequent Structures (MIS), which are infrequent structures in XML data, whose substructures all are frequent. Based on MIS, it is easy to construct all infrequent tree structures.

In order to efficiently find all MIS, we developed a data mining algorithm which can be several times faster than previous methods. In addition, our algorithm is independent to the problem of indexing MIS. It can be used for other data mining applications (e.g., discovery of maximum frequent structures).

In the current work, we have focused on the applicability of our techniques in databases that contain a large number of XML trees (i.e., documents). However, our methodology could be adapted for arbitrarily structured queries (e.g., graph-structured queries with wild-cards or relative path expressions), by changing the definitions of the primary structural components (e.g., to consider relative path expressions like $a//b$, instead of plain edges), and the graph matching algorithms. Some preliminary work has been done on considering relative edges in [12], we plan to combine the encoding schema in [12] with our three phase algorithm in our future research.

Another interesting direction for future work is the incremental maintenance of the set of MIS. A preliminary idea towards solving this problem is to change the mining algorithm of Figure 1 to compute the exact counts of frequent structures of size k (instead of stopping as soon as the mininmum support has been reached). Then given a set ΔD of new XML documents, we apply the first and second phases of our algorithm for ΔD, to count the frequencies of all frequent structures of size k there. Having the exact count of frequent structures of size k in the existing and new document sets, we can then directly use the algorithm of [4] to compute the exact count of all frequent structures of size k in the updated document set $D + \Delta D$ and simply apply the third phase of our algorithm to update the MIS set. Integration of value elements within MIS and incrementally updating MIS are two interesting problems for further investigation.

References

1. R. Agrawal and R. Srikant. Fast algorithms for mining association rules. In *Proc. of VLDB Conf.*, 1994.
2. T. Asai, K. Abe, S. Kawasoe, H. Arimura, and H. Sakamoto. Efficient Substructure Discovery from Large Semi-structured Data. *Proc. of the Annual SIAM symposium on Data Mining*, 2002.
3. R. Bayardo. Efficiently Mining Long Patterns from Databases, *Proc. of SIGMOD Conf.*, 1998
4. D.W. Cheung, J. Han, V. Ng, and C.Y. Wong. Maintenance of Discovered Association Rules in Large Databases: An Incremental Updating Techniques. *Proc. of ICDE Conf.*, 1996.
5. L. Dehaspe, H. Toivonen, and R. D. King. Finding frequent substructures in chemical compounds. *Proc. of KDD Conf.*, 1998.
6. M. Kuramochi and G.Karypis. Frequent subgraph discovery. *Proc. of ICDM Conf.*, 2001.
7. N. Mamoulis, D. W. Cheung, and W. Lian. Similarity Search in Sets and Categorical Data Using the Signature Tree. *Proc. of ICDE Conf.*, 2003.
8. H. Toivonen. Sampling large databases for association rules. *Proc of VLDB Conf.*, 1996.
9. S. M. Selkow. The tree-to-tree editing problem. *Information Processing Letters*, 6(6):184–186, 1977.
10. K. Wang and H. Liu. Discovering Structural Association of Semistructured Data *IEEE Transactions on Knowledge and Data Engineering*, 12(3):353–371, 2000.
11. L. H. Yang, M. L. Lee and W. Hsu. Efficient Mining of XML Query Patterns for Caching. *Proc. of VLDB Conf.*, 2003.
12. M. J. Zaki. Efficiently Mining Frequent Trees in a Forest. *Proc. of SIGKDD Conf.*, 2002.
13. DBLP XML records. *http://www.acm.org/sigmod/dblp/db/index.html*. Feb. 2001.
14. International Press Telecommunications Council. News Industry Text Format (NITF). *http://www.nift.org*, 2000.

Temporal Web Page Summarization

Adam Jatowt and Mitsuru Ishizuka

University of Tokyo, 7-3-1 Hongo, Bunkyo-ku, 113-8656 Tokyo, Japan
{jatowt, ishizuka}@miv.t.u-tokyo.ac.jp

Abstract. In the recent years the Web has become an important medium for communication and information storage. As this trend is predicted to continue, it is necessary to provide efficient solutions for retrieving and processing information found in WWW. In this paper we present a new method for temporal web page summarization based on trend and variance analysis. In the temporal summarization web documents are treated as dynamic objects that have changing contents and characteristics. The sequential versions of a single web page are retrieved during predefined time interval for which the summary is to be constructed. The resulting summary should represent the most popular, evolving concepts which are found in web document versions. The proposed method can be also used for summarization of dynamic collections of topically related web pages.

1 Introduction

Web pages can change their contents any number of times. It is tempting to analyze the changing content retrieved from temporally distributed versions of web documents. The amount of data available for summarization could be increased by considering dynamic and static content of a web document. In this paper we provide methods for summarization of multiple, spread in time versions of a single web document.

Our aim is to provide a summary of main concepts and topics discussed in the web page over given time period. There is an important difference between multi-document summarization and the summarization of multiple versions of a single web page. Usually for the former one there are several documents discussing the same event or topic. However temporal versions of a single web page do not always contain the same concepts. The stress is put here more on the time dimension and the evolution of the content due to the temporal character of data. Therefore for temporal summarization one should use text mining techniques that can help with extracting common, related information which is distributed in some defined time interval. We assume here that the scope of topics and the structure of a document in question do not change rapidly so that a short-term summarization can be performed.

There are several situations when single or multi-document temporal summaries can be of some use. For example a user can be interested in main changes or popular topics in his favorite web page, web site or the collection of pages during given period. It can happen that for some reasons he may not be able to track all changes in

X. Zhou et al. (Eds.): WISE 2004, LNCS 3306, pp. 303–312, 2004.
© Springer-Verlag Berlin Heidelberg 2004

the chosen web page or the group of pages. Moreover, due to the large size of new content it may be impossible to manually compare each document version. Thus automatic methods for the summarization of temporal contents of web pages could be helpful. Such summaries could be also beneficial from the commercial point of view. For example companies may want to gather and summarize important information from their competitors' websites.

The summarization approach proposed here is suitable for dynamic or "active" type of web pages, which have enough changing content so that successful summaries can be constructed. The applicability of a web document for such a summarization can be simply estimated by calculating the average change frequency and the average volume of changes of the document during the desired period.

Additionally, apart from analyzing single web documents, our algorithm can be applied for multi-document temporal summarization. This task assumes summarization of topically related collections of web pages over some time intervals [7], [9].

This paper is organized as follows. In the next section we discuss the related research work. Section 3 explains the method used for term scoring. In Section 4 we introduce the sentence selection and the sentence ordering algorithms. In the next section the results of our experiment are presented. We conclude and discuss future research in the last section.

2 Related Research

Summarization of web pages is particularly useful for handheld devices whose size limitations require converting web documents to more compact forms. The straightforward approach utilizes textual content of web documents in question [4], [5] together with additional structural or presentational information like HTML tags. This method works well for web documents which contain enough textual content and few multimedia. On the other hand, there are also context-based methods which are making use of hypertext structure of the Web [3], [6]. They typically exploit parts of content like anchor texts which are found in documents linking to the chosen web page. Usually anchor texts contain useful information about target web documents or their summaries.

Recently, summarization of temporal versions of web documents has been proposed as a way of describing distributed in time content and topics of web pages [8]. This approach can be used to summarize web documents which have frequently updated content. Consecutive web page versions are combined together as an input for summarization instead of analyzing only momentary snapshots of web documents' content.

On the other hand, temporal summarization in web collections of related pages has been proposed in [9] and [7]. ChangeSummarizer [9] is an online summarization system for detecting and abstracting popular changes in the groups of web documents which uses temporal ranking of web pages. In [7] a sliding window is applied on retrospective collection of web documents whose content changes are separated into deletion and insertion type.

Topic Detection and Tracking (TDT) [2] is another research area that is close to our work. TDT focuses on detection, clustering and classification of news articles from online news streams or retrospective corpora. Temporal summarization of news events was presented in [1] where novelty and usefulness of sentences retrieved from newswire streams are calculated for the construction of a summary.

Statistical methods have been used by some researchers for detecting trends and mining textual collections. In [12] comparison of probability distributions was done for trend detection in news collections. On the other hand, regression method was used in [11] to enhance IR efficiency by considering the changing meaning of words in long time spans. Lent et al. [10] proposed a query searching of shapes of trends by using Shape Definition Language (SDL) in a patent database.

3 Term Scoring

First, a user has to specify the length of an interval *T* for which he requires a summary of the selected web page (Figure 1). Additionally, the sampling frequency for fetching web page versions should be defined. This frequency determines the number of web document samples and hence, the amount of available content to be analyzed. High sampling frequency results in higher probability of detecting all changes, which have occurred in the web page during the period *T*. It is especially critical for fast-changing web documents. Therefore the user should choose a tracking scheme which is appropriate for his web page. Document versions will be automatically downloaded during the interval *T* and their content will be extracted by discarding HTML tags. We have limited our focus to the textual contents of web documents. Thus pictures and other multimedia are rejected. In the next step frequent words are eliminated by using stop-word list. Then, each word is subjected to stemming. Except for single words we also use bi-grams as basic features for the summarization. Thus the final pool of terms contains single words and bi-grams which have been filtered by stop-word list and stemmed.

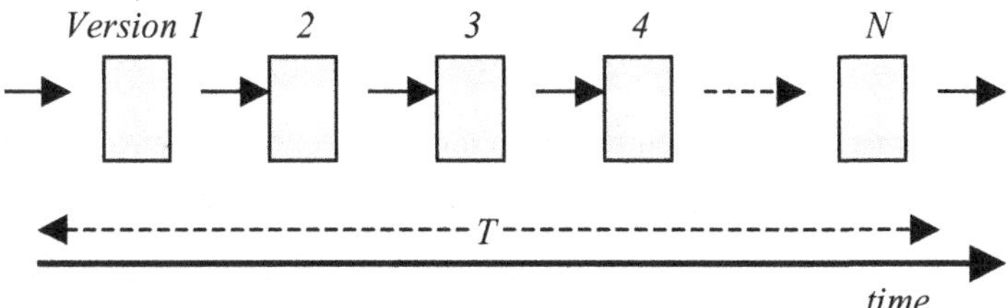

Fig. 1. Temporal versions of a web page

For each term its frequencies are calculated for every web page version. Because the document size may change in time term frequencies are divided by the total number of terms in the given web page sample. Consequently, term weight will reflect the relative importance of the term in the page version. Thus the weight of a term, which has fixed frequency in the collection, can change if the document size varies in different versions of the web page. For example, when a large part of the document has been deleted then the relative importance of a given term will increase even if the frequency of this term has not changed.

As it was mentioned before, temporal summary of the collection of multiple, related web pages can also be created using the proposed method. In this case instead of calculating the frequency of a term in each web page version one should use the document frequency of the term. Document frequency is a ratio of the number of web pages that contain the term to the whole number of different web documents in a given time point of tracking process. After calculating document frequencies of terms for all points during T we may observe how their importance was changing in time.

In the next step terms are scored according to their distributions in web page versions. We are looking for a scoring scheme, which would favor popular and active terms in the collection. If some concept or topic is becoming popular then it is usually often discussed throughout the collection of web page versions. However, just only the level of popularity estimated as the average term frequency does not reflect properly the significance of the term. Terms, which occur frequently in many web page versions, do not have to be important from the point of view of the temporal summarization. For example high but equal frequency of a word in the large number of consecutive versions may indicate that no change has occurred in concepts or events associated with this term.

To represent long-term changes in the frequency of a term during the interval T we apply simple regression analysis. Regression is often used to summarize relationships between two variables, which in our case are: time and the frequency of a term. We have restricted our analysis to simple regression because of its simplicity and the sparseness of our data. However some better fitting regression would be necessary to more correctly approximate changes in the importance of a term. The slope S and the intercept I are calculated for every term so that scatter plots of terms can be fit with regression lines. Slope value informs whether term frequency is stable, rising or decreasing during the specified period. Intercept point, on the other hand, can be used to check how popular a given term was at the beginning of the web page monitoring. Additionally for every term, its variance V is calculated. Variance conveys information about the average magnitude of changes in the term importance for the interval T. To determine which terms are significant for the summary we need to compare their statistical parameters. The slope of a term different from zero is an indicator of an emerging or disappearing event or concept. A term that has a clearly rising trend whose value of the slope is much higher than zero should have a high score assigned. If additionally such a term has a low intercept point we can conclude that there is a high probability for the term to discuss a new, emerging topic. A falling trend, on the other hand, may indicate a term, which is associated with an already accomplished event or with a concept that is no longer important. The score of such a term should have a low value assigned providing that a user is interested only in emerging or ongoing events. However if the user wants to construct a general summary of any popular concepts in the web page then terms with evidently falling trend lines could also be useful. On the other hand, a term with nearly horizontal slope is probably not an active word in the sense that its average importance remains on the same level throughout the summarization period. To test this hypothesis the term variance should also be examined. The low value of variance together with the slope value being close to zero indicates a term, which probably was static in the document versions throughout the interval *T*. Its importance remained on the same level because it was occurring mostly in the static parts of many web page versions. Finally, the intercept plays a role of a novelty indicator showing how popular given terms were before the beginning of the interval *T*. Thus the intercept allows us to choose terms that are not only popular but also novel during tracking process.

In general the score of a term is defined by the following formula.

$$W_i = \alpha * \frac{S_i^r}{N_s^r} + \beta * \frac{V_i^r}{N_v^r} + \delta * \frac{I_i^r}{N_I^r} . \quad (1)$$

The score W_i of a term *i* is expressed as a linear combination of the ranks of this term S_i^r, V_i^r, I_i^r in the respective ranking lists of slopes, variances and intercepts. Terms are ordered in an increasing way in the first two ranking lists according to their values of slopes and variances. However the list of intercept ranks is sorted decreasingly so that the terms with low intercepts have high values of ranks and thus have an increased influence on the final score. N_s^r, N_v^r and N_i^r denote the numbers of different ranks for all three lists while weights α, β and δ specify the strength of each variable. The choice of the weights depends on what kind of terms should have the highest scores assigned. In general any combination of weighs can be used for obtaining a desired type of a summary. According to the weighting scheme discussed above the weights have following values.

$$\begin{aligned} \alpha &= \frac{\left|2 * S_i^r - N_s^r\right|}{N_s^r} \\ \beta &= 1 - \alpha \\ \delta &= 0 \end{aligned} . \quad (2)$$

In this case the score of a term is dependent on the value of the slope if the rank of the slope is close to the maximum or minimum term slope in the web page. This is the situation of a rising or a falling trend. If the value of the slope is close to the average slope value for all terms, then the term score becomes more influenced by the variance of the term. Therefore “active” terms with horizontal regression lines will have higher scores than low variance terms with the same slope values.

It is important to note that the above statistical parameters are calculated for the whole contents of the web page versions in each time point rather than for new, inserted parts only. Some web documents have only minor changes. Therefore if we had analyzed only dynamic parts occurring in page versions then the importance of a static text would be neglected. However in some cases the longer a given content stays in the web page the more important it is. Additionally, it is also difficult to distinguish whether sentences have informational or other purposes like for example a structural one. Therefore we adopt a simplified and general approach where equal significance is given to the static and the changing data in web documents. In general we consider overall frequencies of terms in consecutive time points without distinction for unchanged, inserted or deleted type of content.

In this section we have described long-term scores of terms considering their statistics over the whole tracking interval. However for each web page version terms can have also so-called momentary scores computed. They are calculated using the local and neighboring frequencies of a term. After the term scoring has been completed important sentences can be selected for the inclusion into the summary. The algorithm for selecting and ordering sentences and the momentary scoring scheme are discussed in the next chapter.

4 Sentence Selection and Ordering

The algorithm for the sentence selection presumes the identification of points in time when particular terms have their highest importance. Every term will have its momentary score assigned for each page version depending on the local values of its frequency. The peak momentary score of a term would point to the web page version where the biggest frequency change has occurred. We believe that in such a page version there is a higher probability of the onset of an event or emergence of a concept associated with the term. Therefore it is advisable to select sentences whose terms have the highest local scores. The momentary weighting function has the following form.

$$M_i^j = \left(1 + \frac{\left(F_i^j - F_i^{j-1}\right)}{F_i^{\max}}\right) * \frac{F_i^j}{F_i^{\max}}. \tag{3}$$

Terms are weighted maximally in the web page versions where the frequency of the term i expressed as F_i^j has increased significantly in comparison to the frequency F_i^{j-1} in the previous version of the document. The momentary term score M_i^j in the version j will also increase when the term frequency has a high value in this version compared to the maximum term frequency $F_i^{\max}$ for all the page versions.

For constructing a summary we will select informative sentences, which have the highest sentence scores. The easiest way to estimate the score of a sentence is to compute its average term score. The score of contributing terms in this case could be calculated by multiplying their momentary scores by the long-term scores introduced in Equation 1. In this way the momentary score would be regarded as an indicator of the relative strength of a term in a particular web page version. Thus, when estimating scores of sentences we consider not only the words that they contain but also the web page versions in which these sentences appear.

Another way for selecting important sentences is to take n terms with the highest average long-term scores and use them as a base for the sentence extraction. Let Vi denote a page version when a given top-scored term i has its peak momentary score. From all the sentences containing the term i in Vi the one with highest average long-term score will be chosen for the summary. The same procedure is followed for the next top terms if they are not present in any of already selected sentences. In case they have already been included, the algorithm checks if the differences of their maximal momentary scores M_i^{max} and the momentary scores in those sentences are lower then some predefined threshold. If the threshold condition is met then the next term is examined and the value of n is increased by one. The sentence selection algorithm is summarized below.

```
1. Define an empty set Z of sentences which will be in-
   cluded into summary
2. For each term i from 1 to n:
      a. For each sentence Sj from Z:
            i. if term i exists in sentence Sj then
                  1. if (M_i^max - M_i^j < Threshold) then in-
                     crease n by one and go to (2.)
      b. Find page version Vi where the term i has the
         highest M_i^j
      c. Choose a sentence from Vi which contains term i
         and has the highest average long-term score, and
         insert it into Z if it has not been already in-
         cluded
3. Return Z
```

The above algorithm ensures that a specified number n of the top terms will be represented in the summary. On the other hand if the sentence selection is based on the average term score then there is a possibility that some top-terms will not occur in the final summary. Thus the presented sentence selection algorithm could be used in the case when a user requires all the top-scored terms to be included into summary.

For redundancy elimination, the comparison of vectors of candidate sentences can be done in order to eliminate similar sentences. Because sentences are selected from different web page versions their local contexts can be different. To increase the coherence of the summary we also extract and include the preceding and the following sentences for all the sentences that have been selected by our algorithm. Additionally we employ a sentence ordering method, which is a combination of a temporal and a content ordering (Figure 2). The first one orders sentences according to the sequence of web page versions in which they appear. The latter one arranges sentences according to their relative positions in the document. Each sentence has its insertion and deletion time points that restrict the period during which the sentence can be found in the document. Thus, for temporal ordering one needs to check in which versions the sentence occurs. The combined ordering algorithm works in the following way. First the selected sentences are ordered according to the timestamps of page versions from which they have been extracted. In order to detect if it is necessary to reverse the order of two neighboring sentences from different versions we must make sure if the latter sentence occurs also in the same web page version as the former one. If they occur then the sentences are ordered according to the sequence in which they appear in this web page version. In other words, sentences are sorted by two keys. The first key is the timestamp of a sentence in its earliest web page version and the second one is the position of the sentence in this document sample.

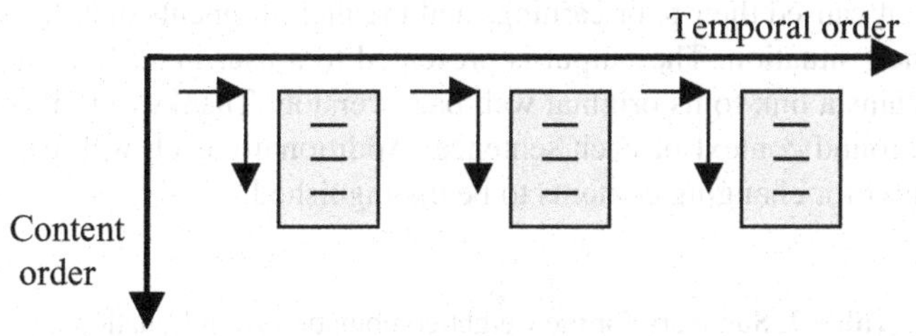

Fig. 2. Temporal and content ordering

Table 1. Top terms for different combinations of the values of weights α, β and δ

$\alpha=1$ $\beta=0$ $\delta=0$	$\alpha=0$ $\beta=1$ $\delta=0$	$\alpha=0$ $\beta=0$ $\delta=1$	α, β, δ as in Eq. 2.
washington	airlin	chicago	airport
chicago	airport	bag	secur
servic	secur	detroit	flight
fare	carrier	hare	travel
airport	associ	code	fare
offer	flight	impact	airlin
washington_po	associ_press	chicago_hare	servic
price	press	staff	press
profit	travel	access	carrier
increas	blue	lake	associ
detroit	war	dozen	associ_press
work	industri	spirit	long
bag	fare	tower	blue
fort	journal	public	atlanta
northwest	atlanta	missil	war
program	servic	hartsfield	industri
end	sar	kuwait	journal
access	cut	arm	profit
flight	long	trend	sar

5 Results

We show the example of a summary of "USATODAY.com – Travel - Today in the Sky" web page in Table 2. This page contains news about airline industry. We have collected 20 web page versions for the period of 3 months starting from 15th April

2003. In Table 1 the ranking lists of the top terms for different values of α, β and δ are displayed.

The summary contains information about financial problems of major US airlines, the reasons that caused their poor earnings and the measurements that the airlines take to improve their situation. The output is presented to a user in such a way that every sentence contains a link to its original web page version. Thanks to it, it is possible to see the background context of each sentence. Additionally each web page may contain colored text for changing contents to be distinguished.

Table 2. Summary for the weight combination from Equation 2

Bankrupt United announced today that it lost $1.3 billion during the first quarter, topping American's $1 billion loss for the same period. Not surprisingly, the airline blamed the war in Iraq and SARS fears for driving down traffic.
The proposed cuts simply "move Delta pilots from industry-leading pay to, well, industry-leading pay," J.P. Morgan analyst Jamie Baker told The Atlanta Journal-Constitution. He said that even if Delta's pilots agree to the cuts — as expected — their wages will still be about 12.5% higher than at United and up to 22% more than at American.
While the carrier still faces hurdles — witness today's announcement that United lost $1.3 billion — some say the airline has a decent shot to survive. "I'm much more optimistic now about United than I was a few weeks ago," said Phil Roberts, a consultant with Unisys R2A. "If it all comes together the way they'd like, they would emerge a very powerful carrier."
Airlines are slowly beginning to restore flights to their schedules after weeks of cutbacks due to war, a viral outbreak and the economic downturn, USA TODAY reports. U.S. carriers made some of the deepest cuts during the war on international routes, according to flight-schedule data provided by OAG.
"To convince passengers that the national carrier is free from SARS, we would pay $100,000 to any passenger who can prove he or she got SARS from flying Thai." — Thai Airways chairman Thanong Bidaya to The Associated Press.

6 Conclusions

In this paper we have presented a sentence extraction method for temporal summarization of web pages based on comparison of statistical parameters of text features. Temporal summarization of web documents attempts to summarize the contents of web pages spread in time. We have applied trend analysis and variance measure to reveal the main concepts of a web page during specified time period. Additionally we have proposed the sentence selection algorithm which identifies sentences where given terms have the highest local importance. The algorithms presented here can be extended to summarizing entire web sites or the collections of related web documents.

There are some limitations of the proposed method that we would like to consider in the future research. A better fitting regression could help to approximate more correctly changes in the evolution of the importance of terms. Additionally, it would be beneficial to employ some more sophisticated concept representation. Lastly, we would like to make experiments with different kinds of web pages and to provide solutions, which are more specialized to the diverse types of documents.

References

1. Allan, J., Gupta, R. and Khandelwal, V.: Temporal Summaries of News Topics. Proceedings of the 24th Annual ACM SIGIR Conference on Research and Development in Information Retrieval, New Orleans, USA (2001) 10-18
2. Allan, J. (ed.): Topic Detection and Tracking: Event-based Information Organization. Kluwer Academic Publishers, Norwell, MA USA (2002)
3. Amitay, E., and Paris, C.: Automatically Summarizing Web Sites: Is There Any Way Around It? Proceedings of the 9th International Conference on Information and Knowledge Management, McLean, Virginia USA (2000) 173-179
4. Berger, A. L., and Mittal, V. O.: Ocelot: a System for Summarizing Web Pages. Proceedings of the 23rd Annual International ACM SIGIR Conference on Research and Development in Information Retrieval, Athens, Greece (2000) 144-151
5. Buyukkokten, O., Garcia-Molina, H., and Paepcke, A.: Seeing the Whole in Parts: Text Summarization for Web Browsing on Handheld Devices. Proceedings of the 10th International World Wide Web Conference, Hong Kong (2001) 652-662
6. Glover, E. J., Tsioutsiouliklis, K., Lawrance, S., Pennock, D. M., and Flake, G. W.: Using Web Structure for Classifying and Describing Web Pages. Proceedings of the 11th International World Wide Web Conference, Honolulu USA (2002) 562-569
7. Jatowt, A., and Ishizuka, M.: Summarization of Dynamic Content in Web Collections. Proceedings of the 8th European Conference on Principles and Practice of Knowledge Discovery in Databases, Pisa, Italy (2004)
8. Jatowt, A., and Ishizuka, M.: Web Page Summarization Using Dynamic Content. Proceedings of the 13th International World Wide Web Conference, New York, USA (2004) 344-345
9. Jatowt, A., Khoo, K. B., and Ishizuka, M.: Change Summarization in Web Collections. Proceedings of the 17th International Conference on Industrial and Engineering Applications of Artificial Intelligence and Expert Systems, Ottawa, Canada (2004) 653-662
10. Lent, B., Agrawal, R., and Srikant, R.: Discovering Trends in Text Databases. Proceedings of the 3rd International Conference on Knowledge Discovery and Data Mining, Newport Beach, California, USA (1997) 227-230
11. Liebscher, R., and Belew, R.,: Lexical Dynamics and Conceptual Change: Analyses and Implications for Information Retrieval. Cognitive Science Online, Vol. 1, http://cogsci-online.ucsd.edu (2003) 46-57
12. Mendez-Torreblanca, A., Montes-y-Gomez, M., and Lopez-Lopez, A.: A Trend Discovery System for Dynamic Web Content Mining. Proceedings of the 11th International Conference on Computing, Mexico City, Mexico (2002)

Web Pre-fetching Using Adaptive Weight Hybrid-Order Markov Model

Shengping He, Zheng Qin, and Yan Chen

Department of Computer Science, Xi'an Jiaotong University, 710049, Xi'an, Shaanxi, China
heshengping@21cn.com, {Zhqin,chenyan}@xjtu.edu.cn

Abstract. Markov models have been widely utilized for modeling user web navigation behavior. In this paper, we propose a novel adaptive weighting hybrid-order Markov model - HFTMM for Web pre-fetching based on optimizing HTMM (hybrid-order tree-like Markov model). The model can minimize the number of nodes in HTMM and improve the prediction accuracy, which are two significant sources of overhead for web pre-fetching. The experimental results show that HFTMM excels HTMM in better predicting performance with fewer nodes.

1 Introduction

Web pre-fetching is an effective way to reduce latency in WWW, which deduce the forthcoming page accesses of a client based on previous accesses. Markov models have been used for studying and understanding stochastic processes, and were shown to be well suited for modeling and predicting a user's behavior on a web-site. Since lower-order Markov models do not look far and higher-order models do not cover enough into the past to correctly discriminate user's behavioral modes [1-4], an hybrid-order tree-like Markov model (HTMM) has been proposed to overcome these limitation [5].

Although HTMM is an advanced model for Web pre-fetching, there are too many nodes in the model which resulting in longer prediction time and higher space complexity. In addition, the prediction accuracy is depressed due to its accuracy voting method, which combines prediction results of multiple models with assigning fixed weight. In this case, to optimize HTMM is necessary.

One of optimization approach is to reduce the nodes inside HTMM, that is the set of 1~N order TMM (tree-like Markov model). A *k*-order TMM is a multi-player tree formed from a historical Web access sequence database, where each node denotes a visited page. Every node in the model records the page's URL and count, where count means how many times that a user has visited the node along the same route. Due to the fact that user access Web page randomly, a lot of nodes append into the model with a small transition probability. To filter these nodes can not only decrease computational complexity but also improve prediction accuracy of the model.

X. Zhou et al. (Eds.): WISE 2004, LNCS 3306, pp. 313–318, 2004.
© Springer-Verlag Berlin Heidelberg 2004

Another optimization approach is to improve the decision method by combining multiple predictors' results. HTMM introduces accuracy voting method that defines fixed weight for each Markov model according to historical accuracy of the predictor. It provides a fixed weight without inspecting predictor 's reliability to a sample. The model needs to be modified obviously.

In this paper, we adopted these two approaches to optimize HTMM. A novel adaptive weighting hybrid-order Markov models for frequent patterns set (HFTMM) is also proposed.

2 A Hybrid-Order Markov Model: HFTMM

Let *L* be a Web log file passed data cleaning, whose user access session is divided by user's MFP. *DB* is a historical Web access sequence database generated by *L*. ω is a page's *id*, a page's *id* maps to the page's URL. *U* is a set of Web pages in *L* and *U** is the *envelope* of *U*. Let *s* be a web access sequence. If *s* is record of *DB*, then $s \in U^*$.

Definition 1: Pattern.
If *s1* is a sequence segment of *s*, *Count*(*s*1) returns user access count of *s1*. Then *s1* is a "Pattern" while $Count(s1) > \delta$, where δ is a threshold. A "pattern" is also called high frequent access sequence segment that can be treated as correlative pages set that user usually browse them in order.

Then we define a set whose elements are those user frequent patterns. The set is called *FS* in short and denoted as *X*. Let α be a homepage of a certain web-site, *X* can be defined recursively as follow.

Definition 2: User frequent patterns set *X*.

(1) $\alpha \in X$;

(2) Let ω be a pattern, if
$\exists \zeta((\zeta = prefix(s,1), \omega \in s, length(s) = 2, s \in U^*) \cap (\xi \in X))$ and $Pr(\omega \mid \xi) \geq \delta_1$, δ_1 is a threshold, and $Count(\omega) > \delta_2$, δ_2 is another threshold, then $\omega \in X$.

Here the functions are defined as follow.

1. length(s), return length of s. The length is the number of states in s.
2. prefix(s,i), returns the subsequence comprised of the first *i* elements of s . If s'=prefix (s, i), then we take s' as the prefix of s .[6]

Let $\overline{X}$ be a Set whose element are those pages rarely accessed by user. If $\omega \notin X$, then $\omega \in \overline{X}$. Obviously, $\overline{X} = U - X$.

Theorem 1: If $\omega \in X$, $\xi \in X$, and there is only one access path from ω to ξ, then all nodes on the path are elements of *X*.

Theorem 2: If $\omega \in X$, $\xi \in X$, and there are more than one foreword access path from ω to ξ. Then there is at least one frequent access path from ω to ξ.

Definition 3: Tree-like frequent patterns set.
A Tree-like frequent patterns set is a weighted directed tree. The weights are transition probability of nodes and the edges are transition path. In fact, a Tree-like frequent patterns set has constructed a tree-like Markov model for frequent pattern sets, we call this model as FTMM. The model is shown as Fig. 1.

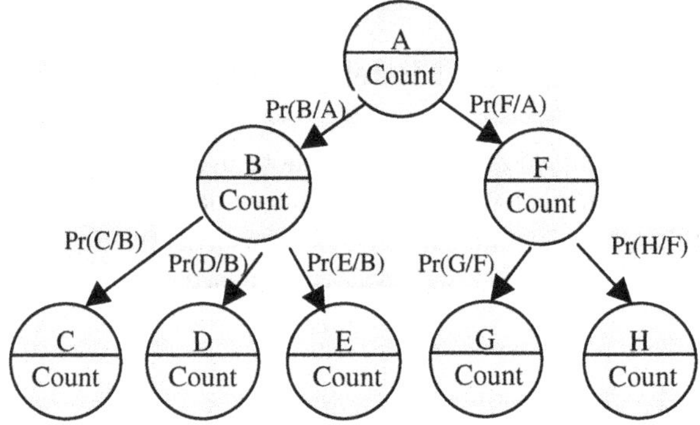

Fig. 1. Structure of a tree-like Markov model for frequent patterns sets (FTMM)

The algorithm of creating *k*-order FTMM is shown as follow. Here δ_1 is threshold of transition probability between two nodes and δ_2 is threshold of count of a node.

```
Algorithm: Create k-order FTMM
     Input k-order TMM
     Output k-order FTMM
     TMM-Pruning (k-order TMM root)
     { If  Current = NULL
           Return
       Else
           If  (Count of Current nodes) / Count of Current
node's child nodes) < δ1 )
           or (( Count of  Current node's child nodes) < δ2)
           Then
              Delete the child nodes and all its child nodes
                   If  (Current has other children) then
                         Current =Current's another child
                         TMM-Pruning (Current)
                   Endif
                   Else
                         Current = This child node
           Endif
       Endif
     }
```

3 Adaptive Weight Method: Combining Multiple Models Prediction Results

Pre-fetching is a speculative process. If the prediction is not correct, the pre-fetching work is useless. Hence, prediction should be as accurate as possible. *Accuracy vote* method [5] is a linear weighted algorithm for prediction results of multiple models. It defines fixed weight for every Markov model according to historical accuracy of the predictor. Although the *accuracy vote* method has taken accuracy of each model into account, it has a serious shortcoming because it provides a fixed weight without inspecting predictor 's reliability to a sample.

In this paper we propose a novel adaptive weight model for online assigning multiple weight of multiple Markov models. It improves prediction accuracy owe to fusing much online information.

An accurate evaluation for a predictor should based on combining both current and history behavior. In our *adaptive weighting* method, the weight of every Markov model is not fixed. Assumed there are *J* models. For model *j(1 <k<N),* its weight determined by two parameters: (1) $E_{p_j}(t)$: stands for the model prediction errors during recent sampling periods ; (2) $EA_j(t)$: stands for the model prediction errors during a longer interval. For a page pre-fetching prediction model *j*, the following definitions are given.

Definition 4: Prediction weight.

At *n* time point, the prediction weight of model *j* is: $W_j = \beta \bullet E_{p_j}(n) + (1-\beta) \bullet EA_j(n)$.

Where $\beta \in [0,1]$, and its value indicates the important degree of recent predictions. .

Having calculated the weight of all *1~N* Markov models, making a decision becomes easy. The rest computational steps are similar to *accuracy voting* method.

Let $PS = \{P_1, P_2, ... P_N\}$ represent the prediction set, where $P_k (1 \le k \le N)$ is the result of *k*-order Markov model. Then $Prediction(PageX) = \sum_{i=1}^{N} (S_i \times W_i)$,

Where $PageX \in PS$, $S_i = \begin{cases} 1(P_i = PageX) \\ 0(P_i \ne PageX) \end{cases} (0 \le i \le N)$, $P_i (0 \le i \le N)$ is element in PS, and $W_i (0 \le i \le N)$ is prediction weight of P_i.

The reliability of predicting result of a model equals to its weight. If there are several models $\{M_{i_1}, M_{i_2}, ... M_{i_j}, ... M_{i_m}\}$ outputting same predicting page P_k, then $\sum_{j=1}^{m} W_{i_j}$ is taken as output reliability of P_k.

4 Performance Evaluation

All experiment data comes from an educational web-site(in Shaanxi Normal University of RPC. The Web log used in the study include between 20:00 on 12 February 2002 and 11:00 on 20 May 2002. There are altogether 3997 different IPs and 7436 different accessed pages with 491367 browse times. There are 141346 user sessions extracted and divided two parts: 80% of them acts as train-set and the rest part is test-set.

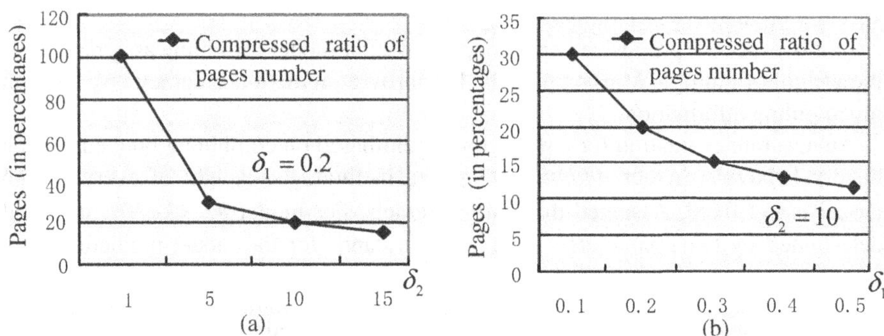

Fig. 2. Compressed ratio about number of pages in *1*-order FTMM, (a) Curves when $\delta_1 = 0.2$; (b) Curves when $\delta_2 = 10$

Firstly, *1~6* order FTMM are generated under the threshold $\delta_1 = 0.2, \delta_2 = 10$. The *1*-order FTMM contains 1147 pages, and 327136 browse times. The number of pages in FTMM has been compressed as 19.8% of total, however, their accessed times is up to 83.8% of total. Most of rarely accessed pages are filtrated by FTMM, which is shown as Fig. 2.

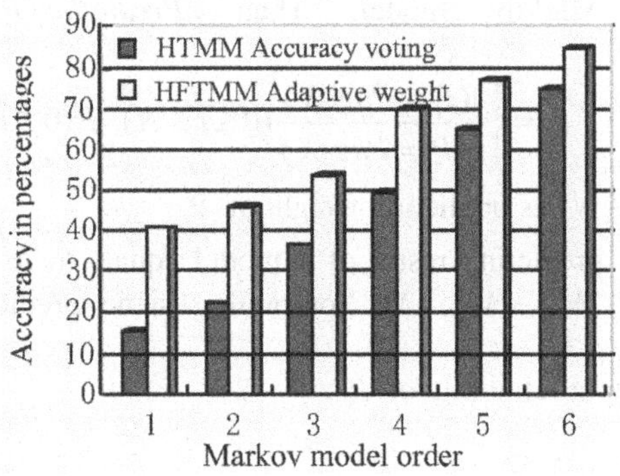

Fig. 3. Two models accuracy comparison curves. The HFTMM adaptive model gets ahead

The second evaluation experiment is prediction accuracy comparison of two methods. *1~6* order HTMM *accuracy voting* method and our HFTMM *adaptive weight* method are used to predict following accessed pages. We also take into account the fact that HFTMM refusing pre-fetching. HFTMM is taken as making mistake when it refuses pre-fetching and HTMM predicts a correct behavior, whereas HFTMM should be given score. As Fig. 3 shows, HFTMM is more accurate than HTMM.

The last one is prediction time comparison of two models. Obviously, HFTMM costs less time than the HTMM as shown in Fig. 4.

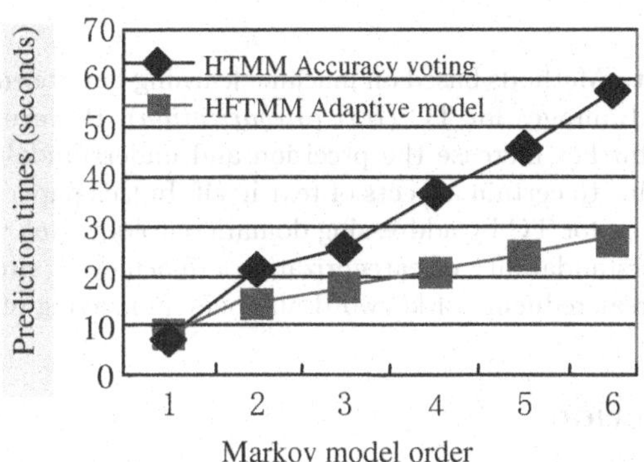

Fig. 4. Prediction time comparison curves. The HFTMM Adaptive model costs less time

5 Conclusion

In this paper, we have presented an adaptive weighting hybrid-order Markov model - HFTMM for Web pre-fetching. Owe to its pattern filtering mechanism and adaptive assigning weight for *1~N* order models, HFTMM consume less space and time than HTMM, as well as achieves higher performance. Besides, this method can be easily extended to the other prediction applications.

References

1. Pirolli P., Pitkow J.: Distribution of surfers' Paths through the World Wide Web: Empirical characterization, World Wide Web (1999) 2(1-2): 29-45
2. Duchamp D.: Prefetching Hyperlinks, In: Proc of USENIX Symp.Internet Technologies and Systems (1999) 127-138
3. Palpanas T., Mendelzon A.: Web Prefetching Using Partial Match Prediction, In: Proc of Fourth Web Caching Workshop (1999)
4. Xin C., Zhang X.D.: A Popularity-Based Prediction Model for Web Prefetching, IEEE Trans on Computer (2003) 36(3): 63-70: 396-402
5. Xing D.S., Shen J.Y.: A new Markov Model for Web access prediction, IEEE Trans on Computer in Science & Engineering (2002) 4(6): 34-39
6. Spiliopoulou M.: The laborious way from data mining to web log mining, International Journal of Computer Systems Science and Engineering (1999) 14(2): 113-126

Text Categorization Based on Domain Ontology

Qinming He[1], Ling Qiu[2*], Guotao Zhao[1], and Shenkang Wang[1]

[1] College of Computer Science
Zhejiang University, Hangzhou, China 310027
hqm@cs.zju.edu.cn
[2] School of Information Systems
Singapore Management University, Singapore 259756

Abstract. Methods based on machine learning have been proposed with certain advantages for TC (*text categorization*). However, it is still difficult to further increase the precision and understandability of categorization due to certain aspects of text itself. In this paper, we propose an architecture for TC by addressing domain ontology. Not only more effect and understandability of categorization are achieved, simulation results show a great reducing of keyword numbers and saving of system costs.

1 Introduction

Currently *text categorization* (or TC for short, also known as *text classification*) is being widely applied in many contexts covering document indexing, document filtering, word sense disambiguation, etc. However, the study of TC can be dated back to 1960s. Before the early 1990s, *knowledge engineering* (or KE for short) was the main tool deployed by the most popular approaches to TC. But from the early 1990s, with the drastically increased number of electronic documents, there was an urgent demand for high quality of TC with various classification criteria. Approaches originated from KE have increasingly lost popularity due to some technical limitations, whereas methods based on *machine learning* (or ML for short) come onto the stage at this time. ML approaches are advantageous over KE methods in terms of high degree of automation, stability of performance, flexibility, accuracy comparable to that achieved by human experts, and considerable savings of expert labor power [5].

Normally an ML approach obtains the classifiers by analyzing training documents, but there still exists several difficulties for TC. Firstly, there lacks semantical support. For example, if the classification is done word by word as the basic object, it is impossible to match the concepts the words represent, especially in the cases where a concept is represented by a phrase in the context. Secondly, there exists multi-presentation of information. Usually the same concept in a document appears in different presentations, but unluckily they are

* The author acknowledges the School of Mathematics & Computer Science at Fujian Normal University, Fuzhou, China, for the support and convenience provided for teaching, research and accommodation during his visiting, and is also thankful to the group members of Zhejiang University for the productive and cheerful collaboration.

X. Zhou et al. (Eds.): WISE 2004, LNCS 3306, pp. 319–324, 2004.
© Springer-Verlag Berlin Heidelberg 2004

treated as different words. Thirdly, there is a paucity of related information. Incomplete information about a concept in a document will cause incomplete results of machine learning.

Due to the above reasons, in this paper, we introduce domain ontology to the TC system, aiming to overcome the above difficulties and to improve the precision of classification. We construct an architecture of the TC system, i.e., *Text Categorization Agency* (or TCA for short). We deploy COSA algorithm [3] in our architecture for the extraction of valid concepts, greatly reducing the number of key words to be searched and thus saving a lot of system costs. This is an attempt by introducing ontology to TC, however, our simulation results show that our method is competitive to others (e.g., Naive Bayes, RIPPER [1]) in terms of precision and recall of categorization.

The remaining part of the paper is organized as follows. In Section 2, we present the architecture of TCA and describe in detail how it performs its functionality. Following that in Section 3, the testing results are given, which aim to show the feasibility and effectiveness of TCA. Finally in Section 4, we conclude the paper and point out research directions for future study.

2 Architecture of TCA

Recently, ontology is intensively applied by research community of computer science and engineering for the presentation of domain knowledge [6]. By introducing ontology to TC, we propose an architecture for our TC system, namely *Text Categorization Agency* (or TCA for short henceforth). Based on the structural information extraction from structure ontology, TCA firstly extracts structural information from texts and afterwards processes them uniformly. This is helpful to eliminate the heterogeneity of texts. The domain ontology addressed in the system is used for categorization on a basis of semantics. The TCA also adopts the COSA algorithm [3] to sieve up those concepts with extremely low or extremely high supports, and thus saves a lot of system costs by greatly reducing the number of key words to be searched. Figure 1 gives the skeleton of the architecture, which contains three layers, namely ontology definition layer, structurization layer, and categorization layer. In what follows, we will describe the core components of each layer and how they perform their functions.

2.1 Ontology Layer

This layer is comprised of structure ontology, domain ontology, and domain vocabulary. The structure ontology defines the structures of various heterogeneous texts, and provides the methods for the uniformly processing of heterogeneous texts (see [7] for details). We adhere to the presentation of ontology as a *six*-tuple [3]. The structure ontology is organized as a tree [7]. By applying the *Left Filtering Maximization* algorithm [2], the matching of expressions extraction is unique. With the support of domain vocabulary, the domain ontology provides related domain knowledge, including concepts, associations, entities, attributes, etc. It is also the basis for semantic extraction and sieving of key words.

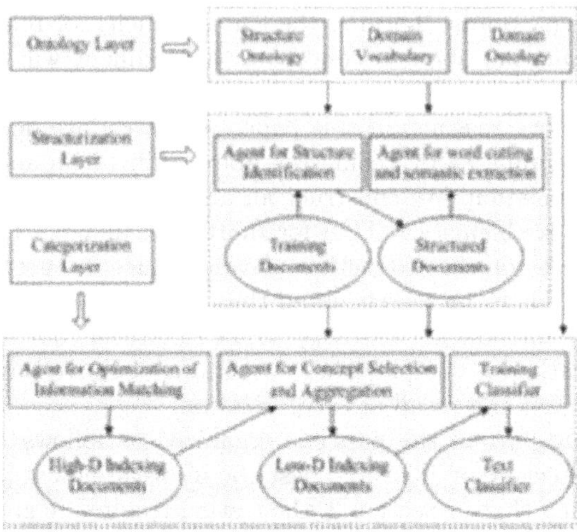

Fig. 1. Architecture of TCA

2.2 Structurization Layer

This layer is the portal of input texts waiting for categorization. Input texts are pre-processed (structurized and then vectorized) in this layer. With two agents as its main components, this layer functions as follows. Firstly, assisted by the ontology layer, training documents (possibly heterogeneous from each other) are processed by the agent for structure identification. Thus we get well formatted (structured) documents as outputs. Then these documents are passed to the agent for word cutting and semantic extraction. Secondly, the agent for word cutting and semantic extraction cuts the structured documents into meaningful words (or phrases) defined by the domain vocabulary, and extracts the semantics based on the domain ontology. After this process, all documents can be represented by a vector space with a clear definition of semantics. Here the vector space is a set of vectors each of which represents the aspects (and the corresponding weight of each) of certain type of text. The value of each dimension of the vector can be an integer, a string, or an array of attributes [1].

The first stage work is finished here, and the results are forwarded to categorization layer for further optimization and aggregation, and finally the training classifiers are obtained. With the classifiers, an unknown document (after preprocessing) can be sent to the categorization layer for classification.

2.3 Categorization Layer

This layer performs two main functions. Firstly, the generation of classifiers. With the output from structurization layer, we first optimize the information matching, then convert the high dimensional indexing documents to low dimensional indexing documents with the assistance of certain mechanism, and lastly we obtain the training classifiers. Secondly, categorization for unknown documents. The training classifiers are now used as classifiers for the categorization of an input document. In what follows, we describe these procedures.

- *Agent for Optimization of Information Matching*

Due to the complexity of semantic extraction, ambiguity of semantics is commonly encountered during this process. However, with the support of ontology, some of the ambiguity can be eliminated by some heuristics reasoning rules.

TCA adopts two rules to eliminate ambiguity [7]: (1) *Association Rule.* If a text (or a small part of a text, e.g., a sentence in the text) matches several attributes of certain domain, then the key word closely associated with the attribute is used for decision. For example, let us consider the sentence "He is at the age of 40". Here number 40 might match either attribute *age* or attribute *weight* in the ontology because both attributes appear in the form of numbers. However, an associated word *age* appears nearby, which tells us that number 40 should match attribute *age* in this case. (2) *Ontology Constraint Rule.* All the matching values should satisfy the constraints of the domain ontology, such as the range of value defined by the ontology.

- *Agent for Concept Selection and Aggregation*

With domain vocabulary, a structured document set is converted to an indexing document set, whose elements are represented as vectors with many dimensions. We name this set as *high-dimensional indexing document set* (or HDIDS). The main goal of this agent is to lessen the dimension number of HDIDS, and the result is referred to *low-dimensional indexing document set* (LDIDS).

We adopt COSA algorithm [3] for sieving of concepts. Those concepts with extremely low frequency of occurrence are abandoned, whereas those with extremely high frequency of occurrence are further divided into sub-concepts. After such processing by COSA, the set of concepts is more identifiable. This concept set, together with the attributes of the corresponding concepts and their parent concepts in domain ontology, and the associations among these concepts, form the vector space of LDIDS. A transform matrix, namely dimension-lessening matrix, fulfils the mapping from an HDIDS to an LDIDS. Readers are referred to [7] for the details of mapping function.

- *Agent for Training Classifiers and Text Categorization*

After the above processes, the set of heterogeneous training documents are presented as the LDIDS of low-dimensional vector space. In TCA, RIPPER [1] is deployed here for the rule set learning with LDIDS as the input[1]. RIPPER is a method for rule set learning. It can filter out noisy data. It is competitive to C4:5 algorithm [4] in terms of precision, but is faster than C4:5 for large amount of data with noises [5]. The training classifiers are obtained after this process, and are further used as classifiers for text categorization in next step.

[1] Other methods (e.g., Naive Bayes) can also be deployed here for the rule set learning. We have actually applied RIPPER and Naive Bayes in our simulations for the comparison of categorization performance. See Section 3.

Table 1. Performance under RIPPER and Naive Bayes with/without ontology

Methods	Dimensions of vectors	*Precision*(%)	*Recall*(%)	*F*1(%)
Naive Bayes	859	95.3	89.9	92.5
RIPPER	859	97.2	92.5	94.8
TCA+Naive Bayes	397	96.1	97.7	96.9
TCA+RIPPER	397	97.7	97.7	97.7

2.4 Categorization for an Unknown Document

The TC process for an unknown document is almost the same but relatively simpler as compared with the training process. The first several steps are the same. In structurization layer, the previous training document (refer to Figure 1) is now replaced by the unknown document as the input. Then the next several steps are done as what we have done in training process. However, the last step is different. Once we get the LDIDS for an unknown input text which is waiting for classification, we just apply the classifiers we have already obtained from training to this text and do the categorization on it.

3 Testing Results

We obtained personal information from some university websites, which includes staff's basic information, e.g., name, title, office, email, etc. All staff are classified into academic staff and non-academic staff. In total, we have collected 57 documents in our test set, among which 39 are academic and 18 are non-academic. In what follows, we are going to compare the performance of categorization under the methods of RIPPER and Naive Bayes *with* and *without* ontology.

We get the ontology of staff in a CS department from an open website (`http://www.daml.org`), but with minor revision for our experiments. At the same time, we define a domain vocabulary, and the mapping from texts to corresponding ontology concepts. The testing results are given in Table 1.

In Table 1, *precision rate* denotes the accuracy of classification, which is defined as the percentage of the number of documents correctly classified into a category among the total number of documents classified into the category (some documents not belonging to the category are wrongly included); and *recall rate* denotes the percentage of the number of documents classified into a category among the total number of documents that should be classified into the category (some documents of the category are missed out); whereas $F1$ denotes an overall consideration of precision and recall rates, which is defined as follows:

$$F1 = \frac{2 \times Precision \times Recall}{Precision + Recall} \times 100\%.$$

By definition, $F1$ reveals the deviation of *precision* and *recall*. It can be seen from Table 1, the performance of categorization increases about 2% on average with the applying of ontology in TCA.

Here we have an interesting finding. When directly applying RIPPER, we get a classification rule as follows:

`if:` vpi $\leqslant 0$, `then:` non-academic staff.

This is actually a false rule, because as a word in the text, word *vpi* is meaningless when it is taken out from the context of the document. The occurrence of such false rules lies on that we do not provide sufficient number of counterexamples in our training, which results in that the false rules cannot be eliminated from the classifiers. However, when we combine RIPPER together with TCA, the classification rule we obtained is

`if:` CONCEPT_professor $\leqslant 0$, `then:` non-academic staff.

The latter rule shows that those non-professor related documents would be put into non-academic staff. This finding tells that domain ontology is more effective in terms of better understanding of documents and classification performance.

4 Conclusions

Based on ML mechanism, we have proposed an architecture, namely TCA, for text categorization by addressing ontology to it. Supported by the testing results, our approach has been proven to be a successful attempt in terms of addressing ontology to TC with ML approaches. As compared with several other methods of TC, such as Naive Bayes and RIPPER, our attempt has shown its advantages in terms of uniformly processing of heterogeneous documents, less number of key words, saving of system costs, and lastly yet still an increase of categorization performance. For future study, more tests should be conducted to verify the robustness. Another promising direction should be in autonomous learning.

References

1. Cohen, W. W. Learning trees and rules with set-valued features. In *Proceedings of the 13th National Conference on Artificial Intelligence (AAAI'96)*, pages 709–717, Portland, Oregon, USA, 1996.
2. Davulcu, H., G. Yang, M. Kifer, and I. V. Ramakrishnan. Computational aspects of resilient data extraction from semistructured sources. In *Proceedings of the 19th ACM SIGMOD-SIGACT-SIGART Symposium on Principles of Database Systems (PODS'2000)*, pages 136–144, Dallas, Texas, USA, May 15–17, 2000.
3. Hotho, A, A. Mädche, and S. Staab. Ontology-based text document clustering. *Künstliche Intelligenz*, 16(4):48–54, 2002.
4. Quinlan, J. R. *C4:5: Programs for Machine Learning.* Morgan Kaufmann Publishers, Inc., USA, 1993.
5. Sebastiani, F. Machine learning in automated text categorization. *ACM Computing Surveys*, 34(1):1–47, March 2002.
6. William, S. and T. Austin. Guest editor's introduction: ontology. *IEEE Intelligent Systems*, 14(1):18–19, 1999.
7. Zhao, G. The study of ontology applied in text categorization. Master's thesis, College of Computer Science, Zhejiang University, Hangzhou, China, 2004.

AC-Tree: An Adaptive Structural Join Index

Kaiyang Liu and Fred H. Lochovsky

Department of Computer Science
Hong Kong University of Science and Technology
Hong Kong
{jamesliu, fred}@cs.ust.hk

Abstract. All existing indices for structural join focus on indexing the encoding information of XML elements so as to improve the XML query performance. Consequently, such indices utilize only data characteristics, but ignore query characteristics that are important for the further improvement of the query performance. In this paper, we propose AC-tree (Adaptive Cluster-tree), which is a fully workload-aware structural join index, to provide a simple but efficient way to exploit the XML query characteristics for query performance improvement. To the best of our knowledge, AC-tree is the first structural join index to take the workload into consideration. An extensive set of experiments confirms that AC-tree outperforms competitors significantly for common XML queries.

1 Introduction

Among proposed query-processing techniques for XML queries, *structural join* (SJ) is the most efficient one for simple path expressions. Its basic idea is to divide a path expression[1] into a series of basic operations, with each basic operation identifying the pair of XML elements that satisfies the child/descendant relationship. Although a number of variants of SJ have been proposed by employing different index structures to index the encoding information of XML elements, none of them has taken the query workload into consideration. However, query workload characteristics may have a significant impact on the performance of SJ, as illustrated by the following simple example. Assume Fig. 1 represents a fragment of an XML document. For a typical path expression "//A/C" or "//B/C", all existing index structures for SJ would require visiting all leaf nodes, as C elements are nested under A and B elements alternately. However, if most submitted queries involving C are either in the form "//A/C" or "//B/C", it is desirable to derive a workload-aware index so that elements that are frequently accessed by individual queries are placed adjacent to each other to further improve the query performance.

In light of the above discussion, we propose a workload-aware index, AC-tree (*A*daptive *C*luster-tree), to index the structural encoding information of XML elements. The basic idea of an AC-tree is: whenever a subset of elements are

[1] For simplicity, we will not distinguish between path expressions and XML queries in the sequel, as the core part of XML queries are path expressions.

X. Zhou et al. (Eds.): WISE 2004, LNCS 3306, pp. 325–336, 2004.
© Springer-Verlag Berlin Heidelberg 2004

```
<A>
    <C><\C><\A>
<B>
    <C><\C><\B>
<A>
    <C><\C><\A>
<B>
    <C><\C><\B>
```

Fig. 1. An XML example

accessed by an individual query, we try to store them adjacently, i.e., we place as many of them as possible into a single leaf node in the AC-tree. To achieve this goal, we partition XML elements according to the queries that access them and project the elements to a higher dimensional space so that elements can change their partition dynamically. Then we employ our AC-tree to index the partitions. One benefit of such a clustering approach is to reduce the number of disk pages visited for evaluating a path expression, as many of the elements contributing to the result will reside in the same disk pages.

There are a few issues that deserve more elaboration. Firstly, to form the partitions we have to define a distance measure between two elements, as well as divide elements into partitions based on the distance measure. By considering some unique characteristics of both XML data and XML path expressions, we develop an efficient dynamic partition scheme. Secondly, as we project elements to a multi-dimensional space and divide elements into partitions, it is possible that the ordering relationship among partitions no longer holds, i.e., a minimum bounding box (MBR) which encloses all elements in a certain partition may overlap another one. As illustrated in this paper, our AC-tree is preferable to a multi-dimensional access method, such as R-tree. Furthermore, to further improve query performance, we employ a heuristic to filter out as early as possible elements that may not contribute to the result of a path expression.

The rest of this paper is organized as follows. Section 2 discusses the related work. Our clustering algorithm and the AC-tree index are introduced in Section 3. Next, we present the experimental analysis in Section 4, and conclude the paper in Section 5. Due to space limitations, we omit the update algorithm and more extensive experimental analysis. These can be found in the full paper [10].

2 Related Work

Structural join is by far the most efficient secondary-memory based query processing technique for discovering all occurrences of a given structural relationship between two sets of elements. The basic structural join algorithms include MP-MGJN [20], $\varepsilon\varepsilon/\varepsilon A$-Join [9] and Stack-Tree-Desc/Anc [1]. Variants of these basic algorithms have been proposed to further improve the performance of structural join by utilizing different index structures, such as B^+-tree [4] and XR-tree [7]. The basic idea of these index-based approaches is to skip those ancestors (or descendants) that do not contain (or are not contained by) any descendants (or ancestors). XR-tree is an optimum solution for the structural join as it incorporates a stabbing-list for each descendant, which enables the quick location of the next ancestor potentially contributing to the final result. [6] proposes a cost-based, mixed-mode XML query processing technique, which tries to combine structural join and graph-based navigation to further improve the query performance. However, their work mainly focuses on a single path axis. Furthermore, it is unknown how their work performs compared with other techniques.

Another family of XML query processing techniques is twig pattern match, which uses a selection predicate on multiple elements. Usually, we represent a twig pattern as a node-labelled tree, and find all occurrences of the pattern in the XML database by doing twig pattern matching. [2] is the first to propose a merge-based holistic twig join. [15] proposes a cost-based query evaluation technique which emphasizes the join order selection when a twig pattern is evaluated with the traditional decomposition approach. The most recent work in [8] is an improved twig join algorithm utilizing XR-tree and several heuristics.

All the above techniques only consider the data characteristics of XML documents. They index XML elements according to the *structural relationship* among XML elements. Another important aspect, *query characteristic*, which has the potential to greatly improve the query performance, has been completely ignored and is the focus of this paper.

3 AC-Tree: An Adaptive Index for Structural Join

3.1 Motivating Examples

All existing indices for SJ focus on the XML data characteristics, but completely ignore the impact of the workload on the query performance. The example in Fig. 2 illustrates the inefficiency of existing indices for SJ, assuming a workload $W = \{$"//A/C", "//B/C"$\}$. The structural encoding information (pre-order/region encoding [20])[2] of some A, B, and C elements (represented as a_i, b_i and c_i, respectively) is shown in Fig. 2(a). The values of the elements' projection onto the X axis imply the nesting relationship among them. For example, c_1 is the child of a_1, c_2 is the child of b_1, and so on. For clarity of illustration, we use solid circles to represent those c_is that are children of b_is.

A typical index for C elements is presented in Fig. 2(b) (assuming the node capacity is 2), where we can observe that C elements that are children of different types of parent elements are put into the same leaf node regardless of W. To evaluate a simple query, $Q =$ "//B/C", although only three C elements are to

[2] In this paper we adopt the region encoding $< start, end >$, with *start*/*end* corresponding to the start/end position of an element in an XML document according to a pre-order traversal of the document elements.

be retrieved, we have to perform three disk seeks and three disk page reads. Generally, even if only one element stored in a certain disk page satisfies the path expression, the whole page has to been retrieved.

To overcome such inefficiency of existing approaches, one possible solution is to cluster elements that are frequently accessed by the same queries so that they can be retrieved by fewer disk accesses. By considering the impact of W, the index T_2 in Fig. 2(c) is a B^+-tree which groups as many solid circles (elements that are children of only B elements) as possible into the same leaf node, thus reducing the access cost of Q to two disk seeks and two disk page reads. However, there is one abnormality with T_2: we do not know how to set the key for the root node. The reason is that elements in the leaf nodes are no longer ordered according to their encoding, but according to the access patterns of queries, which makes it infeasible to utilize a normal B^+-tree. T_3 in Fig. 2(d) proposes a tree to index the elements by using a range to indicate the encoding information of elements in the corresponding subtree. In this way, T_3 supports the location of an element by checking the ranges stored in the internal nodes. In fact, our AC-tree employs this basic idea of T_3, and also includes other structural information for an element to further improve the query performance.

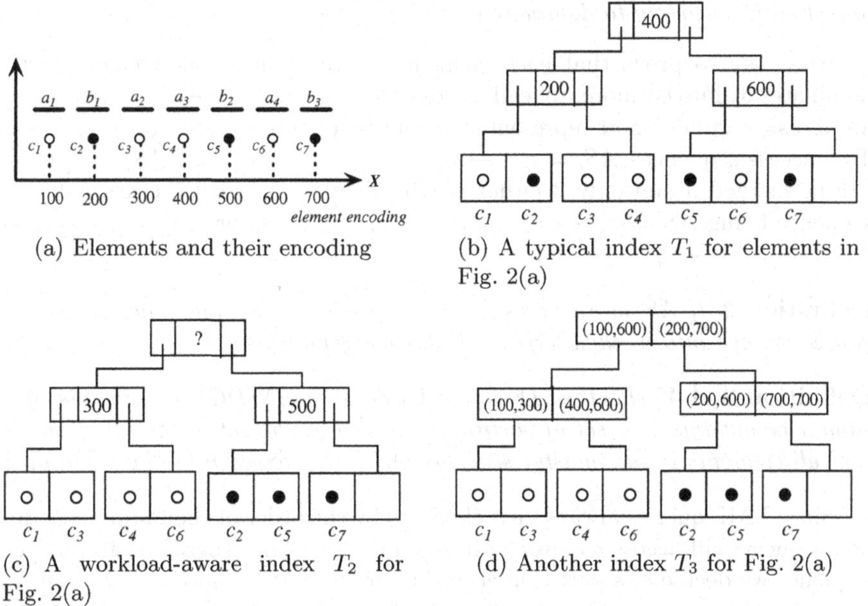

(a) Elements and their encoding

(b) A typical index T_1 for elements in Fig. 2(a)

(c) A workload-aware index T_2 for Fig. 2(a)

(d) Another index T_3 for Fig. 2(a)

Fig. 2. Workload-aware indices for XML elements

3.2 *Y*-Shortest Distance Clustering

To reflect changes in a workload, a dynamic clustering is preferable to a static one. Our approach to achieve dynamic clustering is to project each XML element

e_i of interest to a higher dimensional space to record the extra information about the clustering relationship between e_i and all other elements of the same element type[3]. Normally, e_i is assigned a region encoding of the form $< start, end >$ [20], which can be regarded as a line in a one-dimensional space. Instead, we represent e_i in a two-dimensional space, with its X value recording its region encoding and its Y value recording its clustering relationship with other elements and assigned the value of $e_i.start$ initially. Subsequently, the Y-axis is used to discover what elements should be grouped into one partition. Initally, if most queries that access e_i will also access e_j, grouping e_i and e_j would increase the overall query performance. To reflect such a query characteristic, we change e_j's position along the Y-axis such that $|e_i.Y - e_j.Y|$ is reduced. Before we define our simple clustering approach, namely *Y-shortest Distance Clustering*, we first introduce a few essential definitions.

Definition 1 *Given two elements e_i and e_j of the same element type ($e_j.start > e_i.start$), if the distance between e_i and e_j along the Y axis $|e_j.Y - e_i.Y|$ satisfies the following requirement: $\forall k, |e_j.Y - e_i.Y| \leq |e_j.Y - e_k.Y|$ ($k \neq j \bigcap e_k.start > e_i.start$), then e_i dominates e_j (represented as $e_i \longmapsto e_j$), and we denote $DM(e_j) = e_i$. If there is more than one e_i that dominates e_j, we choose the one with the lowest start encoding to dominate e_j.*

It is easy to prove that each element e_j has at most one element e_i that dominates it. Furthermore, we call a series of $e_i \longmapsto e_j, e_j \longmapsto e_k, \ldots, e_m \longmapsto e_n$ an *access sequence* and represent it as $AS = e_i \longmapsto e_j \longmapsto e_k \ldots e_m \longmapsto e_n$. Two access sequences $AS_i = e_i \longmapsto e_j \longmapsto e_k \ldots \longmapsto e_n$ and $AS_j = e'_i \longmapsto e'_j$ can be merged if and only if either $e_i = e'_j$ or $e_n = e'_i$, with the merged access sequence being $AS'_i = e'_i \longmapsto e_i \longmapsto e_j \longmapsto e_k \ldots \longmapsto e_n$ or $AS'_i = e_i \longmapsto e_j \longmapsto e_k \ldots \longmapsto e_n \longmapsto e'_j$.

Definition 2 *If AS is an access sequence such that no other access sequence can be merged into it, then AS is called a master sequence.*

Definition 3 *A Y-shortest Distance Clustering (YsDC) of elements of the same element type is a set of partitions induced by the set of master sequences, i.e., all elements in one master sequence AS_i are grouped into one partition P_i.*

Since XML queries always visit elements by the order of their *start* encoding, i.e., a query will access e_j after e_i if $e_i.start < e_j.start$, therefore, in an access sequence we decide e_j's partition according to e_i. Furthermore, e_j's Y value can be updated as needed to reflect workload changes, which can cause e_j to be dynamically adjusted to another partition.

Fig. 3 illustrates the basic idea of dynamic update using the elements in Fig. 2(a). Initially, we assign $c_i.start$ to $c_i.Y$, as presented in Fig. 3(a). After considering a given workload, we observe that two queries access c_5 and c_7 sequentially. Consequently, we twice shorten the distance between c_5 and c_7 along

[3] We only cluster elements of the same element type, i.e., they have the same element name in the XML document.

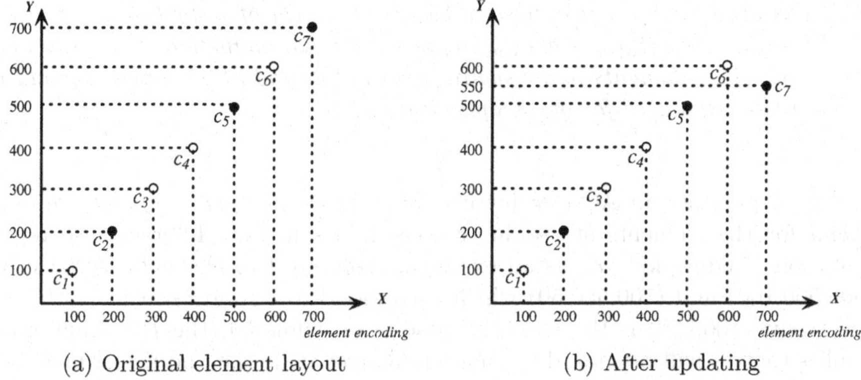

(a) Original element layout (b) After updating

Fig. 3. Workload-aware indices for XML elements

the Y axis by a factor of α, so that now $c_7.Y = 550$ as shown in Fig. 3(b)[4]. The shorter the distance between c_5 and c_7, the greater the chance that c_5 and c_7 will belong to the same partition. One fact deserves more elaboration. Our clustering approach considers the whole workload, instead of a single query. Therefore, if there is a sufficient number of queries that access both c_5 and c_7, (for our example, we need 2 queries), then we will get $DM(c_7) = c_5$.

3.3 AC-Tree

In the preceding section we introduced our clustering scheme, Y-shortest distance clustering. Our next task is to develop a simple index structure that supports XML element partitioning efficiently. Although YsDC requires projecting XML elements to a higher dimensional space, essentially it is still a one-dimensional problem. The reason is that evaluating an XML path expression only requires checking $e_i.X$ (i.e., $e_i.start$), while $e_i.Y$ is used for partitioning. Therefore, instead of utilizing a multi-dimensional access method, such as an R-tree, we propose our AC-tree to index the partitions. As confirmed by our experiments, the AC-tree achieves very good performance.

Definition 4 *An AC-tree is a multi-way tree such that:*

- *Its leaf nodes contain entries in the form of* <$e_i.start$, $e_i.end$, $e_i.Y$, $e_i.PT$>, *where* $(e_i.start, e_i.end)/e_i.Y$ *correspond to* e_i*'s region encoding/*Y *value, and* $e_i.PT$ *(Partition Threshold) is used to decide when to change an element's partition.*

[4] α is a parameter that determines how much the distance between two elements should be shortened when a query accesses both of them. For illustrative purpose, we use $\alpha = 0.5$ in Fig. 3. The optimal value of α can be determined experimentally as discussed in Section 4.3 in the full paper [10].

– *Its internal nodes, n, contain entries in the form of* <$start_{Min}$, $start_{Max}$, *ES*>, *where* $start_{Min}/start_{Max}$ *represent the minimum/maximum start encoding of all elements in the subtree rooted at n, and ES (Element Signature) is a bit-string used for query optimization.*

Fig. 4 presents an AC-tree for Fig. 3(b). Since $c_i.start = c_i.end$, we omit $c_i.end$ for the elements stored in the leaf nodes in Fig. 4 for concise representation. Taking node n_6 as an example, there are two elements stored in it: (500,500,100) and (700,550,50) which correspond to c_5 and c_7 in Fig. 3(b), respectively. (700,550) is the $start/Y$ value of c_7, while 50 (the PT value of c_7) implies that c_7 will be moved to another AC-tree node (i.e., no longer clustered with c_5) if and only if the addition of some query leads to $|c_7.Y - c_i.Y| < 50$. In other words, PT specifies when we should consider changing an element's partition. Finally, the first record in n_5 in Fig. 4 is easy to understand, as 500/700 are the min/max $start$ value in its subtree.

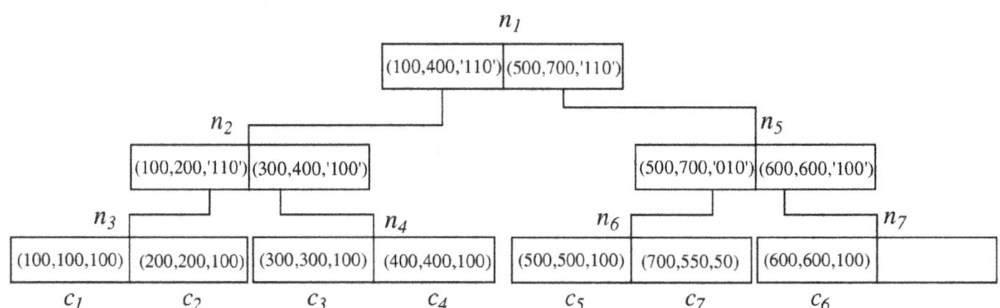

Fig. 4. AC-tree for Fig. 3(b)

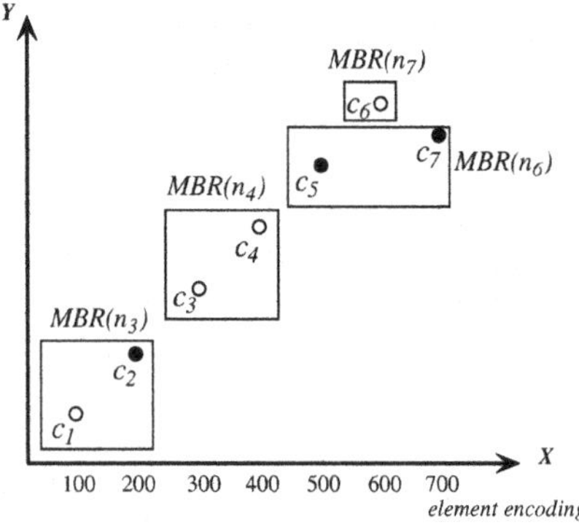

Fig. 5. MBRs of leaf nodes in Fig. 4

As we cluster elements according to their Y values, which reflects the query characteristics in a workload, it is possible that the leaf nodes in an AC-tree may overlap along the X-axis. Fig. 5 illustrates such an example for the AC-tree in Fig. 4. Recall that we use solid/hollow circles to represent C elements that satisfy "//A/C" and "//B/C", respectively. When we try to evaluate "//A/C", we cannot avoid visiting n_6. Since c_6 is a child of a A element, there exists a a_i such that $a_i.start < c_6.start = 600 < a_i.end$. Consequently, the range $(a_i.start, a_i.end)$ intersects with $MBR(n_6)$ along the X-axis, which implies we have to visit n_6 to evaluate "//A/C" according to the structural relationship between two elements, although no element in n_6 satisfies "//A/C".

We can avoid such accesses by a careful examination of XML query characteristics. In real life, most XML queries involve the child/descendant axis. Therefore, for a certain element type E, queries that access elements of type E have the form either of "$\ldots/E$" or "$\ldots//E$". Another observation is that each XML element has only one parent according to the definition of XQuery [18]. Consequently, each element can belong to only one partition induced by a simple path expression, i.e., a path expression of the form "$//E_1/E_2/E_3\ldots/E_n$". In light of these observations, we employ a data structure – ES (*Element Signature*) – for the entries in the non-leaf nodes in an AC-tree to help optimize query processing.

Definition 5 *Assume DOC represents an XML document, and the number of element types in DOC is N_{ET}. Then an ES in a non-leaf entry $entr_k$ is a bit-string of length N_{ET}, with the ith bit in $entr_k.ES$ (i.e., $entr_k.ES^i$) corresponding to the ith element type. If any element in the subtree rooted at $entr_k$ would be accessed by a query of the form either "$\ldots/E_i/E_n$" or "$\ldots//E_n$", then $entr_k.ES^i$ is set to 1, otherwise $entr_k.ES^i$ is set to 0.*

Let us take the node n_5 in Fig. 4 as an example, and assume $ES^1/ES^2/ES^3$ is for element type $A/B/C$, respectively. The ES of n_5's first entry (500,700,'010') is '010', which states that all elements in the subtree rooted at the first entry are children of some B elements. Therefore, query "//A/C" does not need to visit n_6, since '010' implies no element in n_6 is the child of some A elements. However, both "//A/C" and "//B/C" have to visit n_3, since the corresponding ES in the first entry in n_2 is '110'. Finally, a query "//C" will traverse the whole tree in Fig. 4, no matter what is the ES. In conclusion, a structural join using an AC-tree involves not only the check of the structural relationship (i.e., whether an element is a child/descendant of another element), but also the check of each ES if possible as well to avoid unnecessary node accesses.

Due to space limitations, we omit the analysis of the space cost of ES and our update algorithm. These can be found in the full paper [10].

4 Experimental Evaluation

4.1 Experimental Setup

Our AC-tree is a generalized index structure which can be utilized by any structural join based algorithm. Generally, there are two kinds of XML queries, i.e., non-branching and branching queries, which can be most efficiently evaluated by SJ-XR [7] and XRTwig [8], respectively. To illustrate how much performance gain can be achieved by utilizing the AC-tree for the above XML queries, we compare SJ-AC and ACTwig[5] with SJ-XR and XRTwig, respectively. In addition, as XRTwig can employ three heuristics, namely, top-down, bottom-up and max-distance, we implement all these heuristics in our ACTwig algorithm, represented as ACTwig(TD), ACTwig(BU) and ACTwig(MD), respectively.

As commonly adopted by real database systems, we only build AC-trees for some key elements, such as those elements that are frequently visited. Therefore, our experimental strategy is to first choose an element as the "key" element, for example, e_{key}, and then randomly generate a set of queries of size 100 with different distribution characteristics around e_{key}. Specifically, there are two kinds of query sets: non-branching queries $//e_1/e_2/.../e_{key}$ and branching queries $//e_1/e_2/.../e_{key}(/e'_1/e'_2/.../e'_k)$. Employing the same strategy as in [3], two query distribution methods are used: random and normal distribution. To simulate normal distribution, we first number the queries from Q_1 to Q_{100} and then repeat each Q_i $\lfloor \frac{100}{\sqrt{2\pi}} e^{-\frac{(i-50)^2}{2\sigma^2}} \rfloor$ times. Our experimental strategy is to update the partitions of elements indexed by the AC-tree simultaneously when evaluating the 100 queries one by one. However, the update cost and the query cost are recorded separately. Two datasets are utilized, a real dataset Play and a synthetic one XMark, with the statistics shown in Table 1.

Table 1. XML data sets

Data Set	nodes	edges	labels
Play	48818	48817	21
XMark	167865	185390	78

All the following experiments were conducted using a PC with an Intel PIII 1G CPU, 256Mb RAM and running Windows XP. Two performance indicators are used: page fault and CPU time. Page fault measures the I/O behavior of an algorithm. To get rid of disk access influence when we measure CPU time, we ran all algorithms several times to ensure that all data has been read into main memory. Whenever total cost (in terms of CPU time) is shown, 10ms is charged for each page access.

4.2 Non-branching and Branching Queries

In this section we present the performance comparison between the approaches using our AC-tree with competitors. For all experiments, we set $\alpha = 0.5$[6]. Specif-

[5] SJ-AC and ACTwig are SJ and twig algorithms which utilize the AC-tree index.

[6] Experiments on the value of α show that a value of 0.5 achieves the best overall performance [10].

ically, we compare SJ-AC with SJ-XR for non-branching queries, and ACTwig with XRTwig for branching queries.

Table 2 and Table 3 present the performance comparison for Non-Branching/ Branching Queries with Uniform distribution (NBQU/BQU). Generally, SJ-AC performs better than does SJ-XR. However, it can be observed that the performance gain is not very significant. The reason can be explained by the unform distribution of queries, as elements tend to be accessed with equal frequency, which prevents the AC-tree from efficiently clustering elements. Similarly, the family of ACTwig algorithms outperform all XRTwig algorithms as illustrated by Table 3. By comparing the results in Table 2 and those in Table 3, we observe that the speedup of AC-tree over competitors for branching queries is lower than that for non-branching queries. We will explain this later. Further, as Play has a much smaller size than does XMark, the performance gain of AC-tree on Play is marginal. As this phenomenon exists for all the rest of the experiments, in the sequel we will only present the experimental results on XMark. Moreover, we notice that the CPU cost is insignificant compared with the IO cost. Therefore, we will only present the IO cost for the rest of the experimental results.

Table 2. Query cost for NBQU (#sec)

Data Set	SJ-ACB (I/O)	SJ-ACB (CPU)	SJ-XR (I/O)	SJ-XR (CPU)
Play	2.4	0.25	2.8	0.34
XMark	20.6	3.6	29.6	4.8

Table 3. Query cost (I/O) for BQU (#sec)

Data Set	XRTwig(TD)	XRTwig(BU)	XRTwig(MD)
XMark	78.6	83.5	79.3
Data Set	**ACTwig(TD)**	**ACTwig(BU)**	**XRTwig(MD)**
XMark	63.7	64.5	62.3

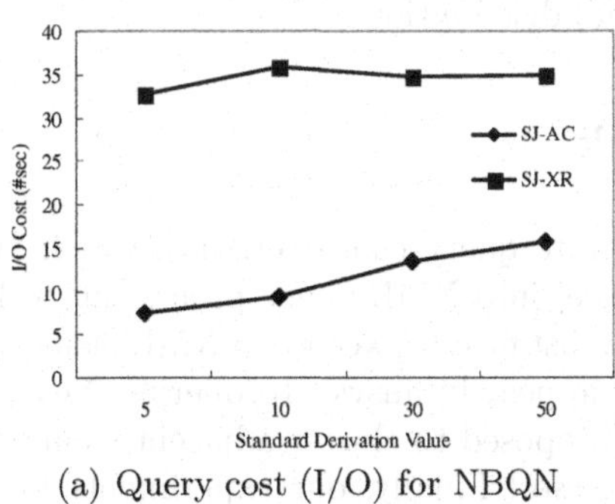

(a) Query cost (I/O) for NBQN

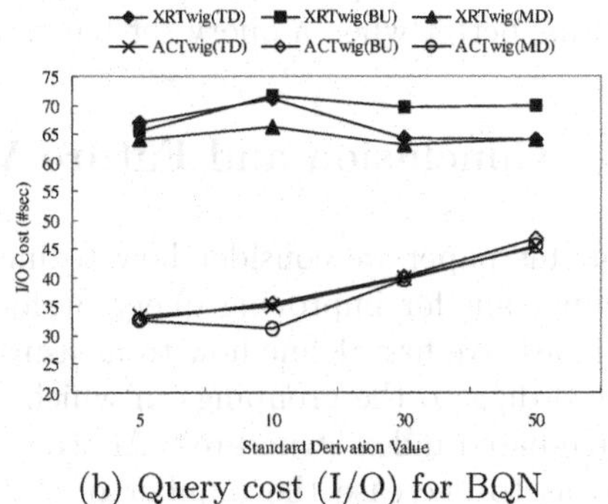

(b) Query cost (I/O) for BQN

Fig. 6. Performance comparison for queries with a normal distribution

Our next experiment set compares the performance for NBQN (Non-Branching Queries with a Normal distribution) and BQN (Branching Queries with a Normal distribution), whose result is illustrated in Fig. 6. Obviously, SJ-ACB outperforms SJ-XR greatly in Fig. 6(a). Note that the numbers along the X-axis represent the σ values for the different normal distributions used in the experiments. Unlike NBQU, in NBQN some queries will repeat, which enables the AC-tree to cluster elements more efficiently than for queries in NBQU. This explains why SJ-ACB achieves a much higher performance gain for NBQN than for NBQU. Similarly, as illustrated by Fig 6(b), all algorithms using AC-tree outperform those using XR-trees.

By comparing the speedups achieved for non-branching queries with those for branching queries we observe that the performance gain achieved by ACTwig over XRTWig is much smaller than that achieved by SJ-AC over SJ-XR. To explain this, we need some further investigation into the different characteristics possessed by non-branching and branching queries. Assume there are two non-branching queries nbq_1 and nbq_2. Then it can be proved that the result of nbq_1 either contains that of nbq_2 or is disjoint with that of nbq_2, i.e., $R(nbq_1) \subseteq R(nbq_2)$ or $R(nbq_1) \cap R(nbq_2) = \emptyset$. Such an observation can be easily verified by the fact that each XML element has only one parent. A detailed proof can be found in [3]. On the contrary, branching queries do not possess such a characteristic, and the result sets of two branching queries can overlap. Clearly, the nice containment relationship among result sets of non-branching queries enables an AC-tree to cluster elements more efficiently than that for branching queries.

In addition, we notice that different σ values have little impact on the performance of SJ-XR/XRTwig, as the XR-tree will not be affected by the different query sets. On the contrary, as AC-tree will adjust itself according to the query characteristics, its performance varies with the change of σ values. The smaller the σ value, the smaller is the number of queries and the higher is the occurrence of some queries resulting in more efficient clustering of the AC-tree elements. Consequently, the AC-tree performs worse with the increasing value of σ.

In conclusion, our experiments have confirmed that by clustering XML elements according to the query characteristics we can greatly improve the query performance, especially for non-branching queries. Furthermore, AC-tree performs better when a query set has a normal distribution.

5 Conclusion and Future Work

In this paper we consider how to incorporate query characteristics, which are important for improving query performance, into XML query processing techniques. We first define how to measure the distance between two XML elements according to the groupings in which they appear in answer to queries. Next, a tree-based index structure – AC-tree – is proposed to cluster adjacent elements so as to decrease the number of disk accesses. Finally, our experiments have confirmed that our AC-tree can significantly improve the query performance for common XML queries with different query characteristics.

As we adopt a rather simple distance measurement, Y−shortest distance clustering, in future we may consider more complex distance measures. For example, we could use a statistics-based distance measurement for developing an off-line index structure that captures query characteristics more accurately. Another promising future research direction is to extend our basic idea of indexing elements of the same type to that of combing indices built on elements of different types, so as to further improve the performance. Finally, we believe that focusing on query characteristics opens a new research direction for XML queries.

References

1. S. Al-Khalifa, H. Jagadish, N. Koudas, J. Patel, D. Srivastava, and Y. Wu. Structural Join: A Primitive for Efficient XML Query Pattern Matching. ICDE'02, pp. 141-152.
2. N. Bruno, D. Srivastava, and N. Koudas. Holistic Twig Join: Optimal XML Pattern Matching. SIGMOD'02, pp. 310-321.
3. C. W. Chung, J. K. Min, and K. Shim. APEX: an adaptive path index for XML data. SIGMOD'02, pp. 121-132.
4. S. Chien, Z. Vagena, D. Zhang, V. Tsotras, and C. Zaniolo. Efficient Structural Joins on Indexed XML Documents. VLDB'02, pp. 263-274.
5. http://www.oasis-open.org/cover/genealogy.html
6. A. Halverson, J. Burger, L. Galanis, A. Kini, R. Krishnamurthy, A. N. Rao, F. Tian, S. D. Viglas, Y. Wang, J. F. Naughton, and D. J. DeWitt. Mixed Mode XML Query Processing. VLDB'03.
7. H. Jiang, H. Lu, W. Wang, and B. C. Ooi. XR-Tree: Indexing XML Data for Efficient Structural Join. ICDE'03.
8. H. Jiang, W. Wang, H. Lu, and Y. J. Xu. Holistic Twig Join on Indexed XML Documents. VLDB'03.
9. Q. Li, and B. Moon. Indexing and Querying XML Data for Regular Path Expressions. VLDB'01, pp. 361-370.
10. K. Liu, and F. Lochovsky. *AC-Tree: An Adaptive Structural Join Index.* Technical Report HKUST-CS04-07, 2004 (http://ihome.ust.hk/~jamesliu/paper/ac_tree.pdf).
11. J. McHugh, and J. Widom. Query Optimization for XML. VLDB'99, pp. 315-326.
12. F. Rizzolo, and A. Mendelzon. Indexing XML Data with ToXin. WebDB'01, pp. 49-54.
13. W. Wang, H. Jiang, H. Lu, and Y. J. Xu. PBiTree Coding and Efficient Processing of Containment Join. ICDE'03.
14. W. Wang, H. Jiang, H. Lu, and Y. J. Xu. Containment Join Size Estimation: Models and Methods. SIGMOD'03, pp.145-156.
15. Y. Wu, J. M. Patel, and H. V. Jagadish. Structural Join Order Selection For XML Query Optimization. IEEE ICDE'03, pp. 443-454.
16. http://monetdb.cwi.nl/xml/
17. http://www.w3c.org/TR/xpath
18. http://www.w3c.org/TR/xquery
19. http://www.w3c.org/XML
20. C. Zhang, J. Naughton, D. DeWitt, Q. Luo, and G. Lohman. On Supporting Containment Queries in Relational Database Management Systems. SIGMOD'01, 425-436.

Approximate Query Answering for a Heterogeneous XML Document Base*

Federica Mandreoli, Riccardo Martoglia, and Paolo Tiberio

Università di Modena e Reggio Emilia,
Dip. di Ingegneria dell'Informazione, Modena, Italy
{tiberio.paolo, mandreoli.federica, martoglia.riccardo}@unimo.it

Abstract. In this paper, we deal with the problem of effective search and query answering in heterogeneous web document bases containing documents in XML format of which the schemas are available. We propose a new solution for the structural approximation of the submitted queries which, in a preliminary schema matching process, is able to automatically identify the similarities between the involved schemas and to use them in the query processing phase, when a query written on a source schema is automatically rewritten in order to be compatible with the other useful XML documents. The proposed approach has been implemented in a web service and can deliver middleware rewriting services in any open-architecture XML repository system offering advanced search capabilities.

1 Introduction

In recent years, the constant integration and enhancements in computational resources and telecommunications, along with the considerable drop in digitizing costs, have fostered development of systems which are able to electronically store, access and diffuse via the Web a large number of digital documents and multimedia data. In such a sea of electronic information, the user can easily get lost in her/his struggle to find the information (s)he requires. Heterogeneous collections of various types of documents, such as actual text documents or metadata on textual and/or multimedia documents, are more and more widespread on the web. Think of the several available portals and digital libraries offering search capabilities, for instance those providing scientific data and articles, or those assisting the users in finding the best bargains for their shopping needs. Such repositories often collect data coming from different sources. The documents are *heterogeneous* for what concerns the structures adopted for their representations but are *related* for the contents they deal with. In this context, XML has quickly become the de facto standard for data exchange and for heterogenous data representation over the Internet. This is also due to the recent emergence of wrappers (e.g. [1,2]) for the translation of web documents into XML format. Along with

* The present work is partially supported by the "Technologies and Services for Enhanced Content Delivery" FSI 2000 Project.

X. Zhou et al. (Eds.): WISE 2004, LNCS 3306, pp. 337–351, 2004.
© Springer-Verlag Berlin Heidelberg 2004

XML, languages for describing the structures and data types and for querying XML documents are becoming more and more popular. Among the several languages proposed in recent years, the syntax and semantics of XML Schema [3] and of XQuery [4] are W3C recommendations/working drafts, for the former and the latter purposes respectively. Thus, in a large number of heterogeneous web collections, data are most likely expressed in XML and are associated to XML Schemas, while structural queries submitted to XML web search engines are written in XQuery, a language expressive enough to allow users to perform structural inquiries, going beyond the "flat" bag of words approaches of common plain text search engines.

In order to exploit the data available in such document repositories, an entire ensemble of systems and services is needed to help users to easily find and access the information they are looking for. Sites offering access to large document bases are now widely available all over the web, but they are still far from perfect in delivering the information required by the user. In particular, one of the issues which is still an open problem is the effective and efficient search among large numbers of "related" XML documents. Indeed, if, from one side, the adoption of XQuery allows users to perform structural inquiries, on the other hand, such high flexibility could also mean more complexity: Hardly a user knows the exact structure of all the documents contained in the document base. Further, XML documents about the same subject and describing the same reality, for instance compact disks in a music store, but coming from different sources, could use largely different structures and element names, even though they could be useful in order to satisfy the user's information need. Given those premises, the need for solutions to the problem of performing queries on all the useful documents of the document base, also on the ones which do not exactly comply with the structural part of the query itself but which are similar enough, becomes apparent.

Recently, several works took into account the problem of answering approximate structural queries against XML documents. Much research has been done on the instance level, trying to reduce the approximate structural query evaluation problem to well-known unordered tree inclusion (e.g. [5,6]) or tree edit distance [7] problems directly on the data trees. However, the process of unordered tree matching is difficult and extremely time consuming; for instance, the edit distance on unordered trees was found in [8] NP hard. On the other hand, a large number of approaches prefer to address the problem of structural heterogeneity by first trying to solve the differences between the schemas on which data are based (e.g. [9,10,11]). However, most of the work on XML schema matching has been motivated by the problem of schema integration and the fundamental aspect of query rewriting remains a particularly problematic and difficult to be solved aspect [12]. Conversely, most of the works on query rewriting do not actually benefit from the great promises of the schema matching methods, and, while presenting interesting theoretical studies [13], they generally do not propose practical ways of efficiently performing the rewriting operation itself.

In this paper, we propose an effective and efficient approach for *approximate query answering* in heterogeneous document bases in XML format. Instead of working directly on the data, we interpret the structural component of the query by exploiting a reworking of the documents' schemas. In particular, our approach relies on the information about the structures of the XML documents which we suppose to be described in XML Schema. A *schema matching* process extracts the *semantic* and *structural* similarities between the schema elements which are then exploited in the proper query processing phase where we perform the *rewriting* of the submitted queries, in order to make them compatible with the available documents' structures. The queries produced by the rewriting phase can thus be issued to a "standard" XML engine and enhance the effectiveness of the searches. Such an approach has been implemented in a web service, named XML S^{3}MART (XML Semantic Structural Schema Matcher for Automatic query RewriTing), we are integrating in the context of the ongoing Italian MIUR Project "Technologies and Services for Enhanced Content Delivery" (ECD Project), whose aim is the production of new and advanced technologies enabling the full exploitation of the information available in web document collections or digital libraries, offering enhanced contents and services such as advanced search engines with a cutting-edge search effectiveness.

The paper is organized as follows: In Sect. 2 we give a brief overview of the XML S^{3}MART service motivations and functionalities and introduce how such a module can work in an open-architecture web repository offering advanced XML search functions. Then, in Sections 3 and 4 we specifically analyze the matching and rewriting features. The results of some of the experiments we conducted are discussed in Sect. 5. Finally, Sect. 6 concludes the paper.

2 Overview of the Matching and Rewrite Service

From a technological point of view, the principle we followed in planning, designing and implementing the matching and rewriting functionalities was to offer a solution allowing easy extensions of the offered features and promoting information exchange between different systems. In fact, next generation web systems offering access to large XML document repositories should follow an *open* architecture standard and be partitioned in a series of modules which, together, deliver all the required functionalities to the users. Such modules should be autonomous but should cooperate in order to make the XML data available and accessible on the web; they should access data and be accessed by other modules, ultimately tying their functionalities together into services. For all these reasons, XML S^{3}MART has been implemented as a *web service* and makes use of SOAP which, together with the XML standard, give the architecture an high level of inter-operability.

The matching and rewriting services offered by XML S^{3}MART can be thought as the middleware (Fig. 1) of a system offering access to large XML repositories containing documents which are heterogenous, i.e. incompatible, from a structural point of view but related in their contents. Such middleware

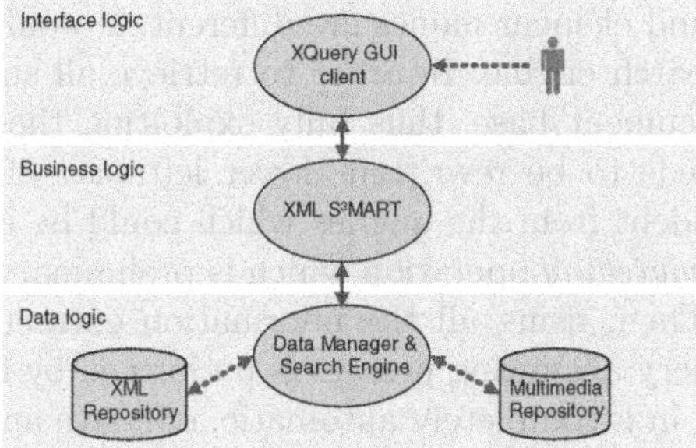

Fig. 1. The role of schema matching and query rewriting open-architecture web repository offering advanced XML search functions

Original query...

```
FOR $x IN /musicStore
WHERE $x/storage/stock/compactDisk
        /albumTitle = "Then comes the sun"
RETURN $x/signboard/namesign
```

... rewritten query

```
FOR $x IN /cdStore
WHERE $x/cd/cdTitle = "Then comes the sun"
RETURN $x/name
```

Document in Repository

```
<cdStore>
    <name>Music World Shop</name>
    <address> ... </address>
    <cd>
        <cdTitle>Then comes the sun</cdTitle>
        <vocalist>Elisa</vocalist>
    </cd>
    ...
</cdStore>
```

Fig. 2. A given query is rewritten in order to be compliant with useful documents in the repository

interacts with other services in order to provide advanced search engine functionalities to the user. At the interface level users can exploit a graphical user interface, such as [14], to query the available XML corpora by drawing their request on one of the XML Schemas (named *source schema*). XML S^{3}MART automatically rewrites the query expressed on the source schema into a set of XML queries, one for each of the XML schemas the other useful documents are associated to (*target schemas*). Then, the resulting XML queries can be submitted to a standard underlying data manager and search engine, such as [15], as they are consistent with the structures of the useful documents in the corpus. The results are then gathered, ranked and sent to the user interface component. Notice that the returned results can be actual XML textual documents but also multimedia data for which XML metadata are available in the document base.

Let us now concentrate on the motivation and characteristics of our approximate query answering approach. The basic premise is that the structural parts of the documents, described by XML schemas, are used to search the documents as they are involved in the query formulation. Due to the intrinsic nature of the semi-structured data, all such documents can be useful to answer a query only if, though being different, the target schemas share meaningful similarities with the source one, both *structural* (similar structure of the underlying XML tree) and *semantical* (employed terms have similar meanings) ones. Consider for instance the query shown in the upper left part of Fig. 2, asking for the names of the music stores selling a particular album. The document shown in the right part of the figure would clearly be useful to answer such need, however, since its structure and element names are different, it would not be returned by a standard XML search engine. In order to retrieve all such useful documents available in the document base, thus fully exploiting the potentialities of the data, the query needs to be rewritten (lower left part of Fig. 2). Being such similarities independent from the queries which could be issued, they are identified by a *schema matching* operation which is preliminary to the proper query processing phase. Then, using all the information extracted by such analysis, the approximate query answering process is performed by first applying a *query rewriting* operation in a completely automatic, effective and efficient way.

As a final remark, notice that, some kind of approximation could also be required for the values expressed in the queries as they usually concern the contents of the stored documents (texts, images, video, audio, etc.), thus requiring to go beyond the exact match. We concentrate our attention only on the structural parts of the submitted queries and we do not deal with the problem of value approximation, which has been considered elsewhere (for instance in [16]).

3 Schema Matching

The schema matching operation takes as input the set of XML schemas characterizing the structural parts of the documents in the repository and, for each pair of schemas, identifies the "best" matches between the attributes and the elements of the two schemas. It is composed by three sub-processes, the first two of which, the structural expansion and the terminology disambiguation, are needed to maximize the effectiveness of the third phase, the real matching one.

Structural Schema Expansion. The W3C XML Schema [3] recommendation defines the structure and data types for XML documents. The purpose of a schema is to define a class of XML documents. In XML Schema, there is a basic difference between complex types, which allow elements as their content and may carry attributes, and simple types, which cannot have element content and attributes. There is also a major distinction between definitions which create new types (both simple and complex), and declarations which enable elements and attributes with specific names and types (both simple and complex) to appear in document instances. An XML document referencing an XML schema uses (some of) the elements introduced in the schema and the structural relationships between them to describe the structure of the document itself.

In the structural schema expansion phase, each XML schema is modified and expanded in order to make the structural relationships between the involved elements more explicit and thus to represent the class of XML documents it defines, i.e. the structural part of the XML documents referencing it. As a matter of fact, searches are performed on the XML documents stored in the repository and a query in XQuery usually contains paths expressing structural relationships between elements and attributes. For instance the path `/musicStore/storage/stock` selects all the `stock` elements that have a `storage` parent and a `musicStore` grandparent which is the root element. The resulting expanded schema file abstracts from several complexities of the XML

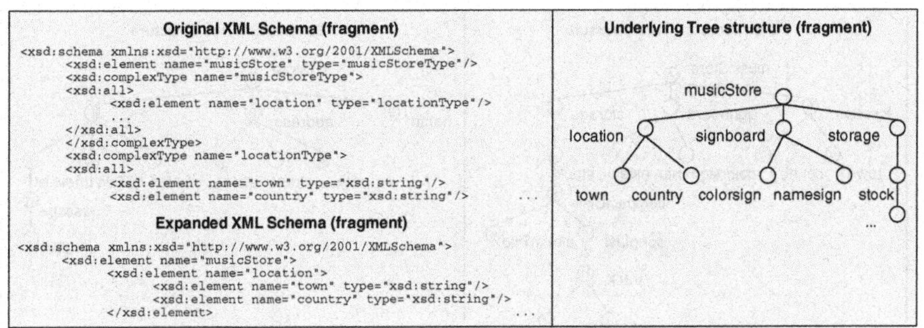

Fig. 3. Example of structural schema expansion (Schema A)

schema syntax, such as complex type definitions, element references, global definitions, and so on, and ultimately better captures the tree structure underlying the concepts expressed in the schema.

Consider, for instance, Fig. 3 showing a fragment of an XML Schema describing the structural part of documents about music stores and their merchandiser, along with a fragment of the corresponding expanded schema file and a representation of the underlying tree structure expressing the structural relationship between the elements which can appear in the XML documents complying with the schema. As can be seen from the figure, the original XML Schema contains, along with the element definitions whose importance is definitely central (i.e. elements `musicStore`, `location`), also type definitions (i.e. complex types `musicStoreType`, `locationType`) and regular expression keywords (i.e. `all`), which may interfere or even distort the discovery of the real underlying tree structure, which is essential for an effective schema matching. In general, XML Schema constructions need to be resolved and rewritten in a more explicit way in order for the structure of the schema to be the most possibly similar to its underlying conceptual tree structure involving elements and attributes. Going back to the example of Fig. 3, the element `location`, for instance, is conceptually a child of `musicStore`: This relation is made explicit only in the expanded version of the schema, while in the original XML Schema `location` was the child of a `all` node, which was child of a complex type. Further, every complex type and keyword is discarded.

In the resulting expanded schema, every element or attribute node has a name. Middle elements have children and these can be deduced immediately from the new explicit structure. On the other hand, leaf elements (or attributes) can hold a textual value, whose primitive type is maintained and specified in the "type=..." parameter of the respective nodes of the output schema.

Terminology disambiguation. After having made explicit the structural relationships of a schema with the expansion process, a further step is required in order to refine and complete even more the information delivered by each schema, thus maximizing the successive matching computation's effectiveness. This time the focus is on the *semantics* of the terms used in the element and attribute definitions. In this step, each term is disambiguated, that is its mean-

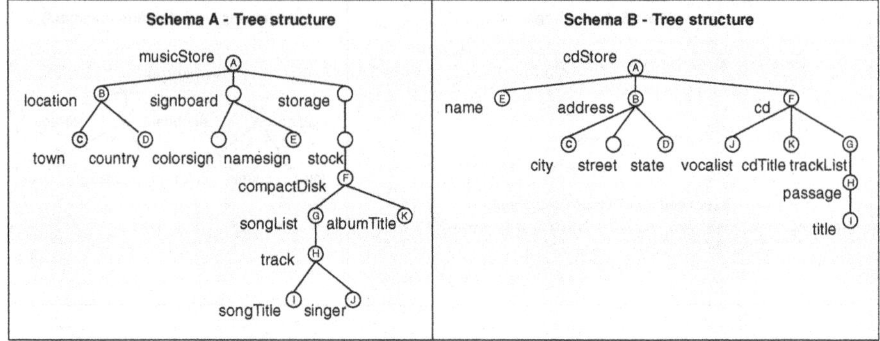

Fig. 4. Example of two related schemas and of the expected matches

ing is made explicit as it will be used for the identification of the semantical similarities between the elements and attributes of the schemas, which actually rely on the distance between meanings. To this end, we exploit one of the most known lexical resources for the English language: WordNet [17]. The WordNet (WN) lexical database is conceptually organized in synonym sets or *synsets*, representing different meanings or *senses*. Each term in WN is usually associated to more than one synset, signifying it is polysemic, i.e. it has more than one meaning. At present, term disambiguation is implemented by a semi-automatic operation where the operator, by using an ad-hoc GUI, is required to "annotate" each term used in each XML schema with the best candidate among the WN terms and, then, to select one of its synsets.

Matching Computation. The matching computation phase performs the actual matching operation between the expanded annotated schemas made available by the previous steps. For each pair of schemas, we identify the "best" matchings between the attributes and the elements of the two schemas by considering both the structure of the corresponding trees and the semantics of the involved terms. Indeed, in our opinion the meanings of the terms used in the XML schemas cannot be ignored as they represent the semantics of the actual content of the XML documents. On the other hand, the structural part of XML documents cannot be considered as a plain set of terms as the position of each node in the tree provides the context of the corresponding term. For instance, let us consider the two expanded schemas represented by the trees shown in Fig. 4. Though being different in the structure and in the adopted terminology, they both describe the contents of the albums sold by music stores, for which the information about their location is also represented. Thus, among the results of a query expressed by using Schema A we would also expect documents consistent with Schema B. In particular, by looking at the two schemas of Fig. 4, a careful reader would probably identify the matches which are represented by the same letter. At this step, the terms used in the two schemas have already been disambiguated by choosing the best WN synset. As WordNet is a general purpose lexical ontology, it does not provide meanings for specific context. Thus, the best choice is to associate terms as `albumTitle` and `songTitle` for Schema

A and `cdTitle` and `title` for Schema B with the same WN term, i.e. `title`, for which the best synset can thus be chosen. In these cases, which are quite common, it is only the position of the corresponding nodes which can help us to better contextualize the selected meaning. For instance, it should be clear that the node `albumTitle` matches with the node `cdTitle`, as both refer to album title, and that `songTitle` matches with the node `title`, as both refer to song title.

The steps we devised for the matching computation are partially derived from the ones proposed in [11] and are the following:

1. The involved schemas are first converted into directed labelled graphs following the RDF specifications [18], where each entity represents an element or attribute of the schema identified by the full path (e.g. `/musicStore/location`) and each literal represents a particular name (e.g. `location`) or a primitive type (e.g. `xsd:string`) which more than one element or attribute of the schema can share. As to the labels on the arcs, we mainly employ two kinds of them: `child`, which captures the involved schema structure, and `name`. Such label set can be optionally extended for further flexibility in the matching process. From the RDF graphs of each pair of schemas a *pairwise connectivity graph (PCG)*, involving node pairs, is constructed [11] in which a labelled edge connects two pairs of nodes, one for each RDF graph, if such labelled edge connects the involved nodes in the RDF graphs.
2. Then an initial similarity score is computed for each node pair contained in the PCG. This is one of the most important steps in the matching process. In [11] the scores are obtained using a simple string matcher that compares common prefixes and suffixes of literals. Instead, in order to maximize the matching effectiveness, we chose to adopt an in-depth semantic approach. Exploiting the semantics of the terms in the XML schemas provided in the disambiguation phase, we follow a *linguistic approach* in the computation of the similarities between pairs of literals (names), which quantifies the distance between the involved meanings by comparing the WN hypernyms hierarchies of the involved synsets. We recall that hypernym relations are also known as IS-A relations (for instance "feline" is a hypernym for "cat", since you can say "a cat is a feline"). In this case, the scores for each pair of synsets (s_1, s_2) are obtained by computing the depths of the synset in the WN hypernyms hierarchy and the length of the path connecting them as follows:
$$\frac{2 * \text{depth of the least common ancestor}}{\text{depth of } s_1 + \text{depth of } s_2}.$$
3. The initial similarities, reflecting the semantics of the single node pairs, are refined by an iterative fixpoint calculation as in the similarity flooding algorithm [11], which brings the structural information of the schemas in the computation. In fact, this method is one of the most versatile and also provides realistic metrics for match accuracy [19]. The intuition behind this

computation is that two nodes belonging to two distinct schemes are the more similar the more their adjacent nodes are similar. In other words, the similarity of two elements propagates to their respective adjacent nodes. The fixpoint computation is iterated until the similarities converge or a maximum number of iterations is reached.

4. Finally, we apply a stable marriage filter which produces the "best" matching between the elements and attributes of the two schemas. The stable marriage filter guarantees that, for each pair of nodes (x, y), no other pair (x', y') exists such that x is more similar to y' than to y and y' is more similar to x than to x'.

4 Automatic Query Rewriting

By exploiting the best matches provided by the matching computation, we straightforwardly rewrite a given query, written w.r.t. a source schema, on the target schemas. Each rewrite is assigned a score, in order to allow the ranking of the results retrieved by the query. Query rewriting is simplified by the fact that the previous phases were devised for this purpose: The expanded structure of the schemas summarizes the actual structure of the XML data where elements and attributes are identified by their full paths and have a key role in an XQuery FLWOR expression paths. At present, we support conjunctive queries with standard variable use, predicates and wildcards (e.g. the query given in Fig. 2). Due to the lack of space, we will briefly explain the approach and show some meaningful examples. After having substituted each path in the `WHERE` and `RETURN` clauses with the corresponding full paths and then discarded the variable introduced in the `FOR` clause, we rewrite the query for each of the target schemas in the following way:

1. all the full paths in the query are rewritten by using the best matches between the nodes in the given source schema and target schema (e.g. the path `/musicStore` `/storage/stock/compactDisk` of Schema A is automatically rewritten in the corresponding best match, `/cdStore/cd` of Schema B);
2. a variable is reconstructed and inserted in the `FOR` clause in order to link all the rewritten paths (its value will be the longest common prefix of the involved paths);
3. *a score* is assigned to the rewritten query. It is the average of the scores assigned to each path rewriting which is based on the similarity between the involved nodes, as specified in the match.

Fig. 5 shows some examples of query rewriting. The submitted queries are written by using Schema A of Fig. 4 and the resulting rewriting on Schema B is shown on the right of the figure. Query 1 involves the rewriting of a query containing paths with wildcards: In order to successfully elaborate them, the best matches are accessed not exactly but by means of regular expressions string matching. For instance, the only path of the tree structure of

Original Query on Source Schema A	*Automatically Rewritten Query on Target Schema B*
Query 1	
FOR $x IN /musicStore WHERE $x/storage/*/compactDisk//singer = "Elisa" AND $x//track/songTitle = "Gift" RETURN $x/signboard/namesign	*FOR $x IN /cdStore* *WHERE $x/cd/vocalist = "Elisa"* *AND $x/cd/trackList/passage/title = "Gift"* *RETURN $x/name*
Query 2	
FOR $x IN /musicStore/storage/stock /compactDisk/songlist/track WHERE $x/singer = "Elisa" AND $x/songtitle = "Gift" RETURN $x	*FOR $x IN /cdStore/cd* *WHERE $x/vocalist = "Elisa"* *AND $x/trackList/passage/title = "Gift"* *RETURN $x/trackList/passage*
Query 3	
FOR $x IN /musicStore WHERE $x/storage/stock/compactDisk = "Gift" AND $x/location = "Modena" RETURN $x	*FOR $x IN /cdStore* *WHERE ($x/cd/vocalist = "Gift"* *OR $x/cd/cdTitle = "Gift"* *OR $x/cd/trackList/passage/title = "Gift")* *AND ($x/address/city = "Modena"* *OR $x/address/street = "Modena"* *OR $x/address/state = "Modena")* *RETURN $x*

Fig. 5. Examples of query rewriting between Schema A and Schema B

Schema A satisfying the path `/musicStore/storage/*/compactDisk//singer` is `/musicStore/storage/stock/compactDisk/songList/track/singer` and the corresponding match in Schema B (label J in Fig. 4) will be the one used in the rewrite. When more than one path of the source schema satisfies a wildcard path, all the corresponding paths are rewritten and put in an `OR` clause. Query 2 demonstrates the rewriting behavior in the variable management. The value of the `$x` variable in the submitted query is the path of the element `track` in Schema A and the corresponding element in Schema B is `passage` (label H in Fig. 4). However directly translating the variable value in the rewritten query would lead to a wrong rewrite: While the elements `singer` and `songTitle` referenced in the query are descendants of `track`, the corresponding best matches in Schema B, that is `songTitle` and `vocalist`, are not both descendants of `passage`. Notice that, in these cases, the query is correctly rewritten as we first substitute each path with the corresponding full path and then we reconstruct the variable, which in this case holds the value of path `cdStore/cd`. In example 3 an additional rewrite feature is highlighted concerning the management of predicates involving values and, in particular, textual values. At present, whenever the best match for an element containing a value is a middle element, the predicates expressed on such element are rewritten as `OR` clauses on the elements which are descendants of the matching target element and which contain a compatible value. For instance, the element `compactDisk` and its match `cd` on Schema B are not leaf elements, therefore the condition is rewritten on the descendant leaves `vocalist`, `cdTitle` and `title`.

5 Experimental Evaluation

In this section we present a selection of the most interesting results we obtained through the experimental evaluation performed on the prototype of XML S³MART. Since in our method the proper rewriting phase and its effectiveness is completely dependent on the schema matching phase and becomes quite

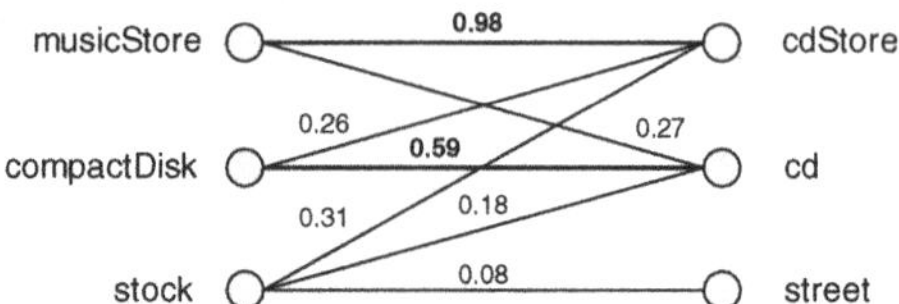

Fig. 6. A small selection of the matching results between the nodes of Schema A (on the left) and B (on the right) before filtering; similarity scores are shown on the edges.

straightforward, we will mainly focus on the quality of the matches produced by the matching process. We are currently evaluating the effectiveness of our techniques in a wide range of contexts by performing tests on a large number of different XML schemas. Such schemas include the ones we devised ad hoc in order to precisely evaluate the behavior of the different features of our approach, an example of which is the music store example introduced in Fig. 4, and schemas officially adopted in worldwide DLs in order to describe bibliography metadata or audio-visual content. Due to space limitations, in this section we will discuss the results obtained for the music store example and for a real case concerning the schemas employed for storing the two most popular digital libraries of scientific references in XML format: The DBLP Computer Science Bibliography archive and the ACM SIGMOD Record.

For the music store schema matching, we devised the two schemas so to have both different terms describing the same concept (such as `musicStore` and `cdStore`, `location` and `address`) and also different conceptual organizations (notably `singer`, associated to each of the tracks of a cd in Schema A, vs. `vocalist`, pertaining to a whole cd in Schema B). Firstly, we performed a careful annotation, in which we associated each of the different terms to the most similar term and sense available in WordNet. After annotation, XML S^3MART iterative matching algorithm automatically identified the best matches among the node pairs which coincides with the ones shown in Fig. 4. For instance, matches A, E, F and G between nodes with identical annotation and a similar surrounding context are clearly identified. A very similar context of surrounding nodes, together with similar but not identical annotations, are also the key to identify matches B, C, D, H and J. The matches I and K require particular attention: Schema A `songTitle` and `albumTitle` are correctly matched respectively with Schema B `title` and `cdTitle`. In these cases, all four annotations are the same (*title*) but the different contexts of surrounding nodes allow XML S^3MART to identify the right correspondences. Notice that before applying the stable marriage filtering each node in Schema A is matched to more than one node in Schema B; simply choosing the best matching node in Schema B for each of the nodes in Schema A would not represent a good choice. Consider for instance the small excerpt of the results before filtration shown in Fig. 6: The best match for `stock` (Schema A) is `cdStore` but such node has a better match with `musicStore`. The same applies between `stock` - `cd`, and `cd` - `compactDisk`. Therefore, the matches for `musicStore` and `compactDisk` are correctly selected (similarities in bold), while `stock`, a node which has no correspondent in Schema B, is ultimately matched

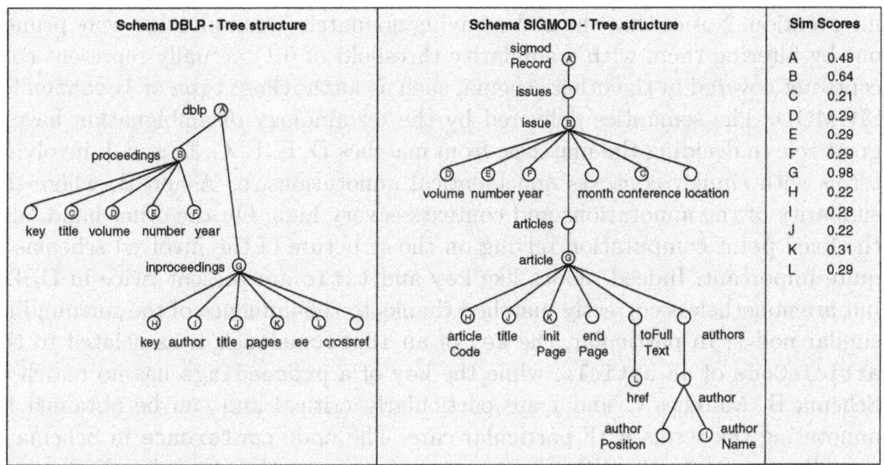

Fig. 7. Results of schema matching between Schema DBLP and Schema SIGMOD. Each match, represented by a letter, is associated to a similarity score (shown on the right).

with `street`. However, the score for such match is very low (< 0.1) and will be finally filtered out by a threshold filter.

As to the tests on a real case, Fig. 7 shows the two involved schemas, describing the proceedings of conferences along with the articles belonging to conference proceedings. Along with the complexities already discussed in the ad-hoc test, such as different terms describing the same concept (`proceedings` and `issue`, `inproceedings` and `article`), the proposed pair of schemas presents additional challenges, such as an higher number of nodes, structures describing the same reality with different levels of detail (as for `author`) and different distribution of the nodes (more linear for DBLP, with a higher depth for SIGMOD), making the evaluation of the matching phase particularly critical and interesting. In such real cases the annotation process is no longer trivial and many terms could not have a WN correspondence: For instance DBLP's `ee`, the link to the electronic edition of an article, is annotated as *link*, `inprocedings`, a term not available in WN, as *article*. In general, we tried to be as objective and as faithful to the schemas' terms as possible, avoiding, for instance, to artificially hint at the right matches by selecting identical annotations for different corresponding terms: For instance, terms like `procedings` (DBLP) and `issue` (SIGMOD) were annotated with the respective WN terms, `dblp` was annotated as *bibligraphy* while `sigmodRecord` as *record*.

After annotation, XML S^{3}MART matcher automatically produced the matches shown in Fig. 7. Each match is identified by the same letter inside the nodes and is associated with a similarity score (on the right). The effectiveness is very high: Practically all the matches, from the fundamental ones like B and G, involving articles and proceedings, to the most subtle, such as L involving the link to electronic editions, are correctly identified without any manual intervention. Notice that the nodes having no match (weak matches were pruned out by filtering them with a similarity threshold of 0.1) actually represent concepts not covered in the other schema, such as `authorPosition` or `location` for SIGMOD. The semantics delivered by the terminology disambiguation have a great role in deciding the matches, from matches D, E, F, G, L, and J, involving terms with similar contexts and identical annotations, to A and B, where the similarity of the annotations and contexts is very high. On the other hand, also the fixed point computation relying on the structure of the involved schemas is quite important. Indeed, nodes like `key` and `title` are present twice in DBLP but are nonetheless correctly matched thanks to the influence of the surrounding similar nodes: In particular, the `key` of an `inproceedings` is associated to the `articleCode` of an `article`, while the `key` of a `proceedings` has no match in Schema B. Matches C and I are particularly critical and can be obtained by annotating the terms with particular care: The node `conference` in Schema B actually represents the *title* of a given conference, and as such has been annotated and correctly matched. The same applies for the node `author` in Schema A, representing the *name* of an author. In this regard, we think that a good future improvement, simplifying the process of making annotations of complex terms like these, would be to allow and exploit composite annotations such has "the title of a conference", "the name of an author", or, for nodes like Schema B `articles`, "a group of authors". Further, an additional improvement, this time to the matching algorithm, might be to enable the identification of 1:n or, even more generally, of m:n correspondences between nodes: For instance match K is not completely correct since the node `pages` would have to be matched with two nodes of Schema B, `initPage` and `endPage`, and not just with `initPage`.

We performed many other tests on XML S^{3}MART effectiveness, generally confirming the correct identification of at least 90% of the available matches. Among them, we conducted "mixed" tests between little correlated schemas, for instance between Schema B and DBLP. In this case, the matches' scores were very low as we expected. For instance, the nodes labelled `title` in Schema B (title of a song) and DBLP (title of articles and proceedings) were matched with a very low score, more than three times smaller than the corresponding DBLP-SIGMOD match. This is because, though having the same annotation, the nodes had a completely different surrounding context. Finally notice that, in order to obtain such matching results, it has been necessary to find a good trade-off between the influence of the similarities between given pairs of nodes and that of the surrounding nodes, i.e. between the annotations and context of nodes; in particular, we tested several graph coefficient propagation formulas [11] and we found that the one delivering the most effective results is the inverse total average.

6 Conclusions

In this paper, we have considered the problem of query answering for a document base storing documents in XML format and we have proposed a method for structural query approximation which is able to automatically identify semantic and structural similarities between the involved schemas and to exploit them in order to automatically rewrite a query written on a source schema towards other available schemas. The proposed approach has been implemented in a web service prototype, XML S^{3}MART, which is currently under testing and evaluation and represents a versatile solution since it accepts as input any query in the XQuery standard and, by means of rewriting, is able to enhance the effectiveness of the standard available XML search engines. The preliminary experimental results on query rewriting effectiveness are promising; as we expected, the rewriting efficiency is also particularly encouraging, thanks to the "lightness" of our method which relies on schema information alone and does not require explicit navigation of the XML data. In the near future, we plan to enhance both the schema matching, such as automatic structural word sense disambiguation, and the query rewriting by studying automatic deduction of the schema underlying the submitted queries and ad-hoc rewriting rules.

References

1. Baumgartner, R., Flesca, S., Gottlob, G.: Visual Web information extraction with Lixto. In: Proc. of the Twenty-seventh Int. Conference on Very Large Data Bases. (2001)
2. Crescenzi, V., Mecca, G., Merialdo, P.: RoadRunner: automatic data extraction from data-intensive web sites. In: Proc. of the 2002 ACM SIGMOD Int. Conference on Management of Data (SIGMOD-02). (2002)
3. Thompson, H.S., Beech, D., Maloney, M., Mendelsohn, N.: XMLSchema. W3C Recommendation (2001)
4. Boag, S., Chamberlin, D., Fernández, M.F., Florescu, D., Robie, J., Siméon, J.: XQuery 1.0: An XML Query Language. W3C Working Draft (2003)
5. Ciaccia, P., Penzo, W.: Relevance ranking tuning for similarity queries on xml data. In: Proc. of the VLDB EEXTT Workshop. (2002)
6. Schlieder, T., Naumann, F.: Approximate tree embedding for querying XML data. In: Proc. of ACM SIGIR Workshop On XML and Information Retrieval. (2000)
7. Guha, S., Jagadish, H.V., Koudas, N., Srivastava, D., Yu, T.: Approximate XML joins. In: Proc. of ACM SIGMOD. (2002) 287–298
8. Zhang, K., Statman, R., Shasha, D.: On the editing distance between unordered labeled trees. Inf. Process. Lett. **42** (1992) 133–139
9. Do, H., Rahm, E.: COMA – A system for flexible combination of schema matching approaches. In: Proc. of the 28th VLDB. (2002) 610–621
10. Madhavan, J., Bernstein, P.A., Rahm, E.: Generic Schema Matching with Cupid. In: Proc. of the 27th VLDB. (2001) 49–58
11. Melnik, S., Garcia-Molina, H., Rahm, E.: Similarity Flooding: A Versatile Graph Matching Algorithm and ist Application to Schema Matching. In: Proc. of the 18th ICDE. (2002)
12. Rishe, N., Yuan, J., Athauda, R., Chen, S., Lu, X., Ma, X., Vaschillo, A., Shaposhnikov, A., Vasilevsky, D.: Semantic Access: Semantic Interface for Querying Databases. In: Proc. of the 26th VLDB. (2000) 591–594
13. Papakonstantinou, Y., Vassalos, V.: Query rewriting for semistructured data. In: Proc. of the ACM SIGMOD. (1999) 455–466

14. Braga, D., Campi, A.: A Graphical Environment to Query XML Data with XQuery. In: Proc. of the 4th Intl. Conference on Web Information Systems Engineering. (2003)
15. Castelli, D., Pagano, P.: A System for Building Expandable Digital Libraries. In: Proc. of the Third ACM/IEEE-CS Joint Conference on Digital Libraries. (2003)
16. Theobald, A., Weikum, G.: The index-based XXL search engine for querying XML data with relevance ranking. Lecture Notes in Computer Science **2287** (2002) 477
17. Miller, G.: WordNet: A Lexical Database for English. In: CACM 38. (1995)
18. Lassila, O., Swick, R.: Resource Description Framework (RDF) model and syntax specification. W3C Working Draft WD-rdf-syntax-19981008 (1998)
19. Do, H., Melnik, S., Rahm, E.: Comparison of schema matching evaluations. In: Proc. of the 2nd Int. Workshop on Web Databases. (2002)

Optimization of XML Transformations Using Template Specialization

Ce Dong and James Bailey

Department of Computer Science and Software Engineering
The University of Melbourne
{cdong, jbailey}@cs.mu.oz.au

Abstract. XSLT is the primary language for transforming and presenting XML. Effective optimization techniques for XSLT are particularly important for applications which involve high volumes of data, such as online server-side processing. This paper presents a new approach for optimizing XSLT transformations, based on the notion of template specialization. We describe a number of template specialization techniques, suitable for varying XSLT design styles and show how such specializations can be used at run time, according to user input queries. An experimental evaluation of our method is undertaken and it is shown to be particularly effective for cases with very large XML input.

1 Introduction

XML is rapidly becoming the de facto standard for information storage, representation and exchange on the World Wide Web. The eXtensible Stylesheet Language Transformations (XSLT) standard [3, 16] is a primary language for transforming, reorganizing, querying and formatting XML data. In particular, use of server side XSLT [15] is an extremely popular technology for processing and presenting results to user queries issued to a server-side XML database.

Execution of XSLT transformations can be very costly, however, particularly when large volumes of XML are involved and techniques for optimization of such transformations are therefore an important area of research. In this paper, we propose a new method for optimization of XSLT programs, based on the technique of program specialization. The underlying idea is that server-side XSLT programs are often written to be generic and may contain a lot of logic that is not needed for execution of the transformation with reference to given user query inputs. Such inputs are passed as parameters to the XSLT program at run-time, often using forms in a Web browser. For example, a user reading a book represented in XML might pass a parameter to an XSLT program referring to the number of the chapter they wish to see presented (i.e. transformed from XML to HTML by the XSLT). The XSLT program may obviously contain logic which is designed for presenting the contents of other chapters, but it will not be needed for this user query. Given knowledge of the user input space, it is instead possible to automatically (statically) create different specialized versions of

X. Zhou et al. (Eds.): WISE 2004, LNCS 3306, pp. 352–364, 2004.
© Springer-Verlag Berlin Heidelberg 2004

the original XSLT program, that can be invoked in preference to the larger, more generic version at run-time. In our book example, specialized XLST programs could be created for each chapter. Since the specialized versions can be much smaller than the original program, important savings in execution time and consequently user response time are possible.

In the paper, we describe methods for i) automatically creating a set of specialized XSLT programs (small XSLTs) based on an original generic (big) XSLT program ii) selecting an appropriate small XSLT at run-time according to a cost analysis of the user input. Our contributions in this paper are:

- An optimization approach for XSLT Transformations based on template specialization.
- Four novel principles that can be used for XSLT template specialization: 1)Branch_Principle, 2)Position_Principle, 3)Kin_Principle, 4)Calling_Principle.

Presentation of experimental results demonstrates the effectiveness of specialization for XSLT. We are not aware of any other work which uses the concept of specialization to improve the performance of XSLT programs.

2 Background

We begin by briefly reviewing some concepts regarding DTDs, (server-side) XSLT and XPath, assuming the reader already has basic knowledge in these areas.

2.1 DTDs and *DTD-Graph*

An XML DTD [2] provides a structural specification for a class of XML documents and is used for validating the correctness of XML data (An example is shown in Fig.1(a)).

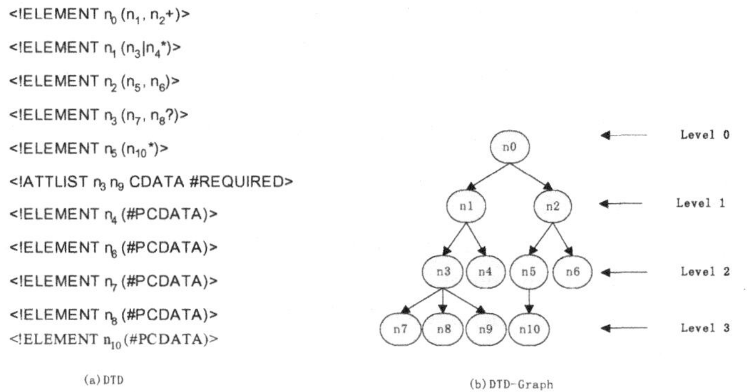
<!ELEMENT n_0 (n_1, n_2+)>
<!ELEMENT n_1 (n_3|n_4*)>
<!ELEMENT n_2 (n_5, n_6)>
<!ELEMENT n_3 (n_7, n_8?)>
<!ELEMENT n_5 (n_{10}*)>
<!ATTLIST n_3 n_9 CDATA #REQUIRED>
<!ELEMENT n_4 (#PCDATA)>
<!ELEMENT n_6 (#PCDATA)>
<!ELEMENT n_7 (#PCDATA)>
<!ELEMENT n_8 (#PCDATA)>
<!ELEMENT n_{10} (#PCDATA)>
(a) DTD
n0
n1
n2
n3
n4
n5
n6
n7
n8
n9
n10
Level 0
Level 1
Level 2
Level 3
(b) DTD-Graph

Fig. 1. The DTD and its corresponding *DTD-Graph*

Based on the DTD, we can create a data structure to summarize the hierarchical information within a DTD, called the *DTD-Graph*. It is a rooted, node-labeled graph, where each node represents either an element or an attribute from the DTD and the edges indicate element nesting. We assume that the DTD contains no IDs and IDREFs, and is acyclic. The *DTD-Graph* is similar to the *Dataguide* structure described by Goldman and Widom in 1997[8]. It will be used to explain the *XSLT Template Specialization Principles* in section 3. From the example of the *DTD-graph* in Fig.1.(b), n_0 to n_{10} (except n_9) denote the names of elements which may exist in the XML document and n_9 denotes the name of an attribute of element n_3.

2.2 Templates in XSLT

An XML document can be modeled as a tree. In XSLT, one defines templates (specified using the command *<xsl:template>*) that match a node or a set of nodes in the XML-tree[16], using a *selection pattern* specified by the *match* attribute of the *<xsl:template>* element. We require a matched node to exist in the *DTD-Graph*. The content of the template specifies how that node or set of nodes should be transformed. The body of a template can be considered to contain two kinds of constructs: i) constant strings and ii) *<xsl:apply-templates>*(or *<xsl:for-each>*). We ignore the branch commands *<xsl:if>* and *<xsl:choose>*, since they cannot directly trigger the application of another template. Constant strings can be inline text or generated XSLT statements (e.g. using *<xsl:value-of>*). The XSLT instruction *<xsl:apply-templates>* has critical importance: without any attributes, it "selects all the children of current node in the source tree, and for each one, finds the matching template rule in the stylesheet, and instantiates it"[12]. A *construction pattern* can optionally be specified using the *select* attribute in *<xsl:apply-templates>*, to select the nodes for which the template needs to match. Our specialization methods support XSLT programs that make use of the elements *<xsl:template>*, *<xsl:apply-templates>*, *<xsl:for-each>*, *<xsl:if>*, *<xsl:choose>*, *<xsl:value-of>*, *<xsl:copy-of>*, *<xsl:param>*. This represents a reasonably powerful and commonly used fragment of the language. For the *<xsl:param>* element, we assume that the parameters corresponding to the user inputs are declared at the top level in the XSLT program.

2.3 Server-Side XSLT

Server-side XSLT is a popular solution for data exchange and querying on the Web. It is often deployed in e-commerce, e-publishing and information services applications. A typical server-side processing model is sketched in Fig.2 below. Transforming the content on the server has advantages such as providing convenience for business logic design and code reuse, cheaper data access and security and smaller client downloads [13]. A problem that can occur in the use of server-side XSLT, is when a generic XSLT program is designed so that it can handle many possible inputs from the user. At run-time, given specific user input values, much of the logic of the generic XSLT program may not be required. Execution of an XSLT program which is larger than required may result in increased run-time. The main theme of this paper is to propose methods for automatically creating smaller XSLT programs, which are specialised to handle specific combinations of user input values. The *user query* is modelled as a set of parameters, each of which corresponds to an element in the DTD. e.g. The input "Chapter1 Section2" might indicate the user wishes to see the contents of section 2 in Chapter 1 displayed (converted from XML to HTML).

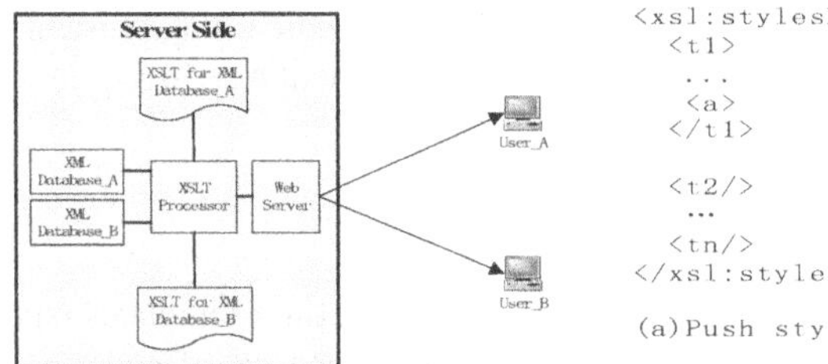

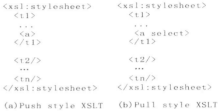

Fig. 2. The Server-Side XSLT model

```
<xsl:stylesheet>            <xsl:stylesheet>
  <t1>                        <t1>
   ...                         ...
   <a>                         <a select>
  </t1>                       </t1>

  <t2/>                       <t2/>
  ...                         ...
  <tn/>                       <tn/>
</xsl:stylesheet>           </xsl:stylesheet>

(a)Push style XSLT          (b)Pull style XSLT
```

Fig. 3. The XSLT design styles

2.4 XSLT Design Styles

The simplest way to process an XML source tree is to write a template rule for each kind of node that can be encountered, and for that template rule to produce the output required, as well as calling the *<xsl:apply-templates>* instruction to process the children of that node [12]. We call this style of processing *recursive-descent* style or *push* style. A skeleton of a *push* style XSLT is shown in Fig.3.(a). Here, <t> denotes *<xsl:template>* and <a> denotes *<xsl:apply-template>*.

We also can design instructions to explicitly select specific nodes. This makes the instruction more precise about which node to process. This is *pull* style design. The XSLT template instruction *<xsl:apply-templates>* with the value of *select* attribute as the *construction* pattern, is the normal form of a *pull* style processing and *<xsl:for-each>* is also commonly used. A skeleton of *pull* style XSLT is shown in Fig.3.(b). The most general style of XSLT design is the *hybrid* style. It is a combination of *push* and *pull* styles together.

Our specialization methods can be used for any style of XSLT, though our experimental results will refer to these design classifications. An example of a *hybrid* style XSLT program, *XSLBench.xsl*, is given in Fig.4. Looking at Fig.4, the template match for *"FM"* and *"SPEECH"* uses *<xsl:apply-templates>* (*push* style) as the implicit instruction to retrieve child nodes in the source tree and the template match for *"PLAY"* gives an explicit instruction *<xsl:apply-template select="FM|PERSONAE|ACT">* (*pull* style) to retrieve node sets of *FM*, *PERSONAE* and *ACT* in the source tree. An XSLT (program input) parameter is declared by the *<xsl:param>* element with the *name* attribute indicating the name of parameter. This example is from Kevin Jones' XSLBench test suite and it was also used by XSLTMark[4]as a test case for testing the processing of *match* and *select* statements (we have added the parameter declarations to model user input). The corresponding XML source input to *XSLBench.xsl* is a well-known XML document, *shakespeare.xml*[4], consisting of the 37 plays of Shakespeare. These will be used in examples throughout the remainder of the paper.

```
<xsl:stylesheet version="1.0"
xmlns:xsl="http://www.w3.org/1999/XSL/
Transform">
  <xsl:output encoding="utf-8"/>
  <xsl:param name="p0"/>
  <xsl:param name="p1"/>
  <xsl:param name="p2"/>
  <xsl:param name="p3"/>
  <xsl:param name="p4"/>
  <xsl:param name="p5"/>
  <xsl:param name="p6"/>
  <xsl:param name="p7"/>
  <xsl:param name="p8"/>
  <xsl:param name="p9"/>
  <xsl:param name="p10"/>
  <xsl:template match="PLAY">
    <html>
      <body>
        <xsl:apply-templates
select="TITLE"/>
        <xsl:apply-templates
select="FM|PERSONAE|ACT"/>
      </body>
    </html>
  </xsl:template>
  <xsl:template match="TITLE">
    <xsl:if test="$p0">
      <font style="ITALIC" color="RED">
        <xsl:value-of select="TITLE"/>
      </font>
    </xsl:if>
  </xsl:template>
  <xsl:template match="FM">
    <xsl:if test="$p1">
      <i>
        <xsl:apply-templates/>
      </i>
    </xsl:if>
  </xsl:template>
  <xsl:template match="PERSONAE">
  <xsl:if test="$p2">
    <h2>
      Parts - <xsl:value-of select="TITLE"/>
    </h2>
    <xsl:apply-templates select=".//
PERSONA"/>
    </xsl:if>
  </xsl:template>
  <xsl:template match="PERSONA">
    <xsl:if test="$p3">
      <p><b><i>
        <xsl:value-of select="."/>
      </i></b></p>
    </xsl:if>
  </xsl:template>
  <xsl:template match="ACT">
    <xsl:if test="$p4">
    <h3>
      <xsl:value-of select="TITLE"/>
    </h3>
    <xsl:apply-templates select="SCENE"/>
    </xsl:if>
  </xsl:template>
  <xsl:template match="SCENE">
    <xsl:if test="$p5">
    <h3>
      <xsl:value-of select="TITLE"/>
    </h3>
    <xsl:apply-templates select="SPEECH"/>
    </xsl:if>
  </xsl:template>
  <xsl:template match="SPEECH">
    <xsl:if test="$p6">
      <xsl:apply-templates/>
    </xsl:if>
  </xsl:template>
  <xsl:template match="SPEAKER">
    <xsl:if test="$p7">
      <p><b>
        <xsl:value-of select="."/>
      </b></p>
    </xsl:if>
  </xsl:template>
  <xsl:template match="LINE">
    <xsl:if test="$p8">
      <xsl:value-of select="."/>
      <br/>
    </xsl:if>
  </xsl:template>
  <xsl:template match="STAGEDIR">
    <xsl:if test="$p9">
      <xsl:value-of select="."/>
      <br/>
    </xsl:if>
  </xsl:template>
  <xsl:template match="SUBHEAD">
    <xsl:if test="$p10">
      <xsl:value-of select="."/>
      <br/>
    </xsl:if>
  </xsl:template>
</xsl:stylesheet>
```

Fig. 4. The *Hybrid* style XSLT Stylesheet *XSLTBench.xsl*

2.5 XPath Expressions

XPath is a language for locating nodes in an XML document using path expressions. In XSLT, *selection patterns* [15, 17] are specified using a *subset* of XPath and can be used in the *match* attribute of *<xsl:template>* elements. *Construction patterns* are specified using the *full* XPath language and can be used in the *select* attribute of the elements *<xsl:apply-templates>*, *<xsl:for-each>* and *<xsl:value-of>*. XPath also defines a library of standard *functions* for working with *strings*, *numbers* and *boolean* expressions. The expressions enclosed in '[' and ']' in an XPath expression are called *qualifiers*. In this paper, we disallow the use of functions and qualifiers inside construction patterns.

3 XSLT Template Specialization Principles

Specialization is a well-known technique for program optimization [10] and can reduce both program size and running time. In our context, a specialization S, of an XSLT program P, is a new XSLT program containing a subset of the templates contained in P. The templates chosen be included in S may also need to undergo some modification, to eliminate dangling references and to make them more specific. Section 3.3 will later describe the modification process. Execution of S will yield the same result as execution of P, for certain combinations of user inputs.
We now describe two broad kinds of XSLT specialization schemes: one is *Spatial Specialization,* which creates a number of specializations based on consideration of the spatial structure of the XML document and the likely patterns of user queries. The other is *Temporal Specialization,* which creates specialized program versions based on the expected (temporal) calling patterns between program templates. The overall aim of specialization is to construct groupings of templates likely to be related to one another. i.e. A specialization corresponds to a possible sub-program of the original, generic one.

3.1 Spatial Specialization

We describe three different principles for spatial specialization. Spatial specialization groups templates together according to the "nearness" of nodes they can match within the DTD. It is intended to reflect the likely spatial locality of user queries. i.e. Users are likely to issue input queries containing terms (elements) close to one another in the *DTD-Graph.*

Branch_Principle(*BP*): Templates are grouped together according to sub-tree properties in the *DTD-Graph*. Each node N in the *DTD-Graph* can induce a specialization as follows: Suppose N is at level k, it forms a set Q_N consisting of N + all descendants of N + all ancestors of N along the shortest path to the root node. Q_N is now associated with a set of templates S. For each node in Q_N, find all templates in the XSLT program which contain a *select pattern* that matches the node and place these in S. We say S is now a specialization at branch level *k*.
Example: In Fig 1 (b), for each different *branch level*, nodes in the *DTD-Graph* can be grouped as below. Each of these node sets Q_i would then be associated with a set S_i of templates which can match at least one of these nodes.

- Level 0: All nodes
- Level 1: 2 sets: Q_1={n0, n1, n3, n4, n7, n8, n9}, Q_2={n0, n2, n5, n6, n10}.
- Level 2: 4 sets: Q_1={n0, n1, n3, n7, n8, n9}, Q_2={n0, n1, n4}, 3), Q_3={n0, n2, n5, n10}, Q_4={n0, n2, n6}
- Level 3: 4 sets: Q_1={n0, n1, n3, n7}, Q_2={ n0, n1, n3, n8}, Q_3={ n0, n1, n3, n9}, Q_4={ n0, n2, n5, n10}.

Kin_Principle(*KP*): Templates are grouped together based on the ancestor-descendant relationships of the corresponding elements in the *DTD-Graph.* Given a kin generation number *k,* each node N in the *DTD-Graph* can induce a specialization as follows: Construct a set Q_N consisting of N + all descendants of N of shortest distance at most k-1 edges from N. Q_N is now associated with a set of templates S in the same way as for the branch principle, above.
Example: In Fig 1, suppose the kin generation number is 3, we get three node sets, namely, Q_1={n1, n3, n4, n7, n8, n9}, Q_2={n2, n5, n6, n10} and Q_3={n0, n1, n2, n3 n4, n5, n6}.

Position_Principle(*PP*): Templates are grouped together based on the minimum distance (in any direction) between the corresponding elements in *DTD-Graph.* This differs from the kin-principle in that groupings are no longer ancestor/descendant dependent. Given a distance parameter *k*, each node N in the *DTD-Graph* can induce a specialization as follows: Construct a set Q_N consisting of N + all elements of shortest distance at most *k* edges from N. Q_N is then associated with a set of templates S in the same way as for the branch principle above.
Example: Looking at Fig. 1, suppose the distance parameter is 1. Some of the node sets are Q_0 = {n0,n1,n2}, Q_1 = {n1,n0,n3,n4}, Q_2 = {n2,n0,n5,n6}, Q_5 = {n5,n2,n10}. Any sets which are subsets of other sets are removed.

3.2 Temporal Specialization

We now describe a single principle for temporal specialization. A temporal specialization is intended to reflect the expected execution sequence of templates at run-time, based on static analysis of calling relationships within the XSLT program. This reflects, in part, the program designer's view of which collections of templates are related.

Calling_Principle(*CP*): Templates in an XSLT are grouped together by the different calling relationship paths between templates. Work in [7] described the use of a structure known as the *XSLT Template and Association Graph(TAG).* This is a graph where the templates are nodes and there is an arc from node x to node y if template x may call template y. Based on this structure, we form specializations which model the maximal calling sequences between templates.
Example: Suppose there are five templates t1, t2, t3, t4 and t5 in an XSLT program and the possible calling paths in the *TAG* are: t1->t2, t1->t3 and t1->t4->t5. This gives the specializations: S_1={t1, t2}, S_2={t1, t3} and S_3={t1, t4, t5}

3.3 Summary of Specialization Processing

The process of *XSLT Specialization* is described by Fig 5. Due to space constraints we sketch, rather than present in detail the various components.

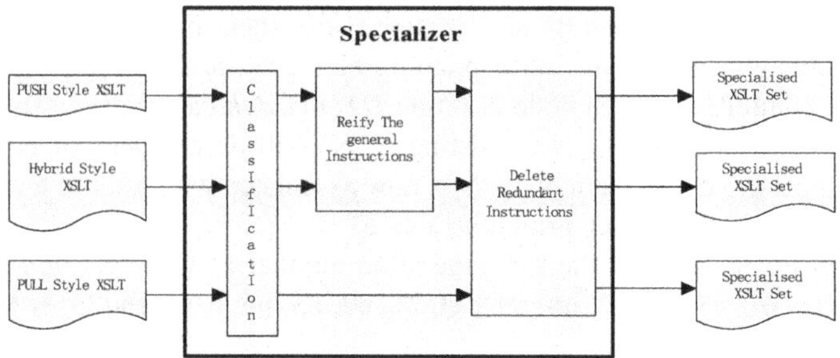

Fig. 5. Specialization process

In Fig 5, the templates of different style XSLTs are classified (grouped) using the specialization schemes(e.g *BP*, *KP*, *PP* and *CP*). Reification is then applied to any *push* style templates. In this case, any templates that contain a *<xsl:apply-templates>* instruction without a *select* attribute, have a *select* attribute added so that any possible children in the specialization are called explicitly. For *pull* style XSLT templates, *<xsl:apply-templates>* instructions are deleted if there do not exist any corresponding templates that could match the s*elect* attribute (removal of dangling references). For *hybrid* templates, we need to apply both *reify* and *delete* steps. The XSLT shown in Fig 6 is one of the possible XSLTs specialized from the original XSLT in Fig 4, using the *Branch Principle* (level 1). We call this program *SpeXSLBench.xsl.* It can be used to do the transformation if the user query is about the title of the play.

```
xsl:stylesheet version="1.0" xmlns:xsl="http://
www.w3.org/1999/XSL/Transform">
  <xsl:output encoding="utf-8"/>
  <xsl:param name="p0"/>
  <xsl:template match="PLAY">
    <html>
      <body>
        <xsl:apply-templates select="TITLE"/>
      </body>
    </html>
  </xsl:template>
  <xsl:template match="TITLE">
    <xsl:if test="$p0">
      <font style="ITALIC" color="RED">
        <xsl:value-of select="TITLE"/>
      </font>
    </xsl:if>
  </xsl:template>
</xsl:stylesheet>
```

Fig. 6. The specialized XSLT

4 Overview of XSLT Specialization Process

We give an overview of the *XSLT Specialization Process* in Fig 7. Fig 7(a) describes the steps performed statically and Fig 7(b) describes the steps performed at run time. Looking at Fig.7.(a), we parse the DTD into the *DTD-Graph*, parse the XSLT into an *XSLT-Tree* and *TAG* (containing information about the calling relationships [7]) and parse the XML into an *XML-Tree*. Observe that we assume existence of the XML DTD and XML data source for static analysis. This is a realistic assumption for server side XML. Next, we use the template specialization principles to specialize the original XSLT into a set of specialized XSLTs. After that, we apply an *XSLT Transformation Cost Model(XTCM)* to evaluate each specialization and label it with an expected cost. This cost determination considers four parameters: *Scan_Size* (the expected number of nodes examined during program execution), *Access_Nodes* (the expected size of the output), *Num_of_Templates* (the number of templates in XSLT) and *XSLT_File_Size*. We omit the details of the cost model due to space constraints, but note that any cost model which produces an estimate of execution time could be used.

At runtime (Fig 7 (b)), based on the user query, an XSLT template index (a simple B+ Tree data structure) is used to select the best (lowest cost) individual specialization for each term in the user query. If all terms have the same best specialization, then this specialization is used instead of the original XSLT program to answer the query. Otherwise, if different terms have different best specializations, then the original XSLT will be selected to run the transformation instead (the default case).

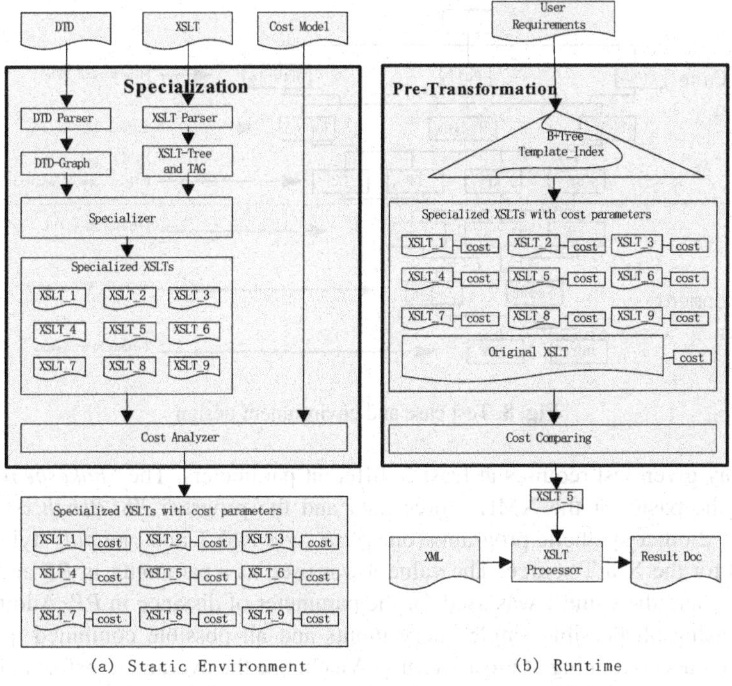

Fig. 7. The overview of XSLT specialization process

Recall that specializations were created under the assumption that the user query is likely to contain related terms. However, if the user query includes two or more unrelated topics, then it is unlikely they will be covered by the same best specialization. In this case, a combination of two or more specializations might be more effective than using the original XSLT program. We leave this as a topic for future research.

5 Experimental Results

We now experimentally investigate the effectiveness of the XSLT specializations. There are a variety of parameters which need to be considered: 1)Different XSLT styles such as *push*, *pull* and *hybrid*, 2)Different XSLT sizes: big size(consists of more than 30 templates), medium size(consists of 10 to 30 templates) and small size(consists of 10 or less templates), 3)Different *XSLT Template Specialization Principles:* including *BP*, *KP*, *PP* and *CP*. Fig 8(a) describes the space of possibilities. The test environment includes three situations 1) Different sizes of XML data: big size(14MB), medium size(7MB) and small size(4MB), 2)Different XSLT processors: Xalan-j v2.5.1 and Saxon v6.5.3, 3)Different systems(hardware and OS): Dell PowerEdge2500 (two P3 1GHz CPU and 2G RAM running Solaris 8(X86)) and an IBMeServer pSeries 650 (eight 1.45GHz CPU, 16GB RAM, running AIX5L 5.2). All of these considerations are shown in Fig.8(b).

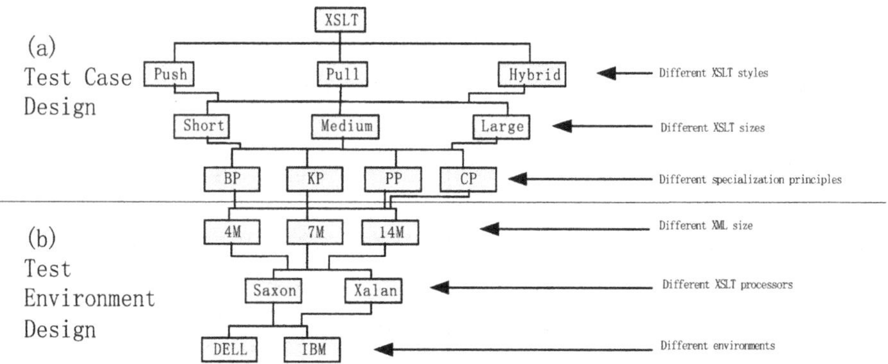

Fig. 8. Test case and environment design

So, any given test requires at least 6 different parameters. The *Shakespeare.xml* is used as the basis for the XML source data and the program *XSLBench.xsl* (shown earlier) + 2 other synthetic programs (one *push* style XSLT and one *pull* style XSLT) are used for the XSLT source. The value 3 was used as a parameter in *BP* and *KP* respectively and the value 1 was used for the parameter of distance in *PP*. Additionally, we test using all possible single query inputs and all possible combined query parameter inputs containing at most 3 terms. We choose the average transformation time over all such queries. For example, if there are 3 possible parameter values, p1, p2 and p3 (representing 3 different query terms), we test the specialization by giving the parameter p1, p2, p3, p1-p2, p1-p3, p2-p3 and p1-p2-p3 respectively and then calculate the average transformation time over all queries.

We show charts below summarising the improvements. We concentrate on contrasting 1)different XSLT styles, 2)different template specialization principles, 3)different size XML data sources. Average time saving improvement compared to the original program is given. e.g. If we want to determine the effect of specialization for different size XML inputs, we classified all test results by the test parameter of

XML size(there are three in this paper: 4MB, 7MB and 14MB). And for each group of test results we generate the average value as the final time saving improvement. Then we build a bar chart to compare the effect of different groups.(some sub-classifications are setup to display more information of contrast. e.g. under each group of different XML sizes, we make the sub-classification of different XSLT processors.)

In Fig.9.(a) we see that template specialization is effective across the three different XSLT design styles, with the *pull* style XSLT giving the greatest savings. *Pull* style obtains the most improvement, since pull style templates require more expensive access to the XML data, due to the need for explicit XPath expressions in *construction patterns*. From Fig.9.(b), we see all specialization principles give improvements in the average transformation time. The *Branch_Principle* is the most effective, since it generates the most specializations and hence one is more likely to cover the query. Conversely, the *Calling Principle* is the least effective, since it generates the fewest specializations (due to not few calling paths existing in the program). From Fig.9.(c) we see that the technique of template specialization is effective for varying XML sizes and is most effective for bigger size XML data size, because evaluating XPath expressions takes more time for large XML input and the specializations contain fewer XPath expressions than the original XSLT program.

Considering the XSLT transformation time [15], it can be broken into a number of parts shown in Fig. 10.

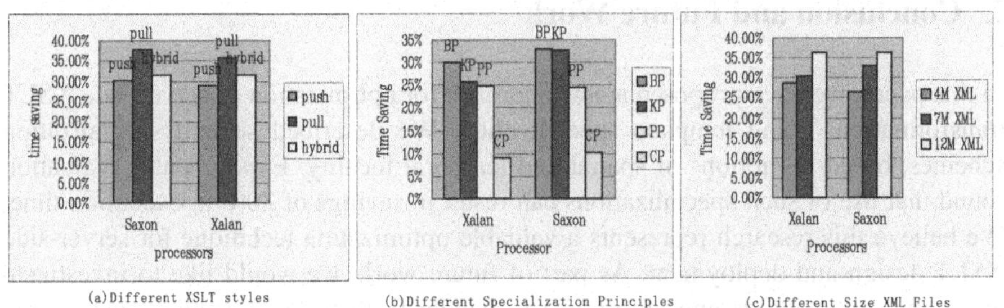

Fig. 9. The summarized experimental results

XML Parsing	XSLT Parsing	XSLT Compiling	XSLT Scanning	XSLT Instructions Evaluation	XML Scanning	Content Transformation	Document Output

Fig. 10. The different parts of time spend on XSLT transformation

Among all these components, the times for XML parsing, content transformation (assuming the same document output) and document output serialization are unalterable, given a specific XSLT processor and XML source. Oppositely, the times for XSLT parsing, XSLT compiling, XSLT scanning and XML scanning are all alterable. Each specialization contains fewer templates than the original XSLT program. Consequently XSLT parsing, XSLT compiling and XSLT scanning is expected to take less time. Furthermore, the specializations are likely to require less time in XML scanning, since the scanning time is related to the XPath expressions of select attributes for template instructions in *<xsl:apply-templates>*. These can be changed during the specialization process. Since we treat the XSLT processor as a black box it isn't possible to more accurately analyse the savings for each component.

6 Related Work

To the authors' knowledge, there is no other work which considers specialization for XSLT programs. There is of course a rich body of work on specialization for various kinds of programs [10, 16]. The difference for the XSLT scenario, compared to, say, functional or logic programs, is that XSLT is data intensive and a DTD is provided. XSLT based optimization has been considered by Z. Guo, M. Li et al in 2004[9]. They use a streaming processing model *(SPM)* to evaluate a subset of XSLT. By *SPM*, an XSLT processor can transform an XML document to other formats without using extra buffer space. However, some strong restrictions on the XSLT syntax and design are made, limiting the applicability. XPath based XML query optimization has been considered in a large number of papers, e.g. S. Abiteboul and V. Vianu in 1997, A. Deutsch and M. Fernandez et al in 1999, Li and Moon in 2000.[1, 5, 6, 14]

7 Conclusion and Future Work

In this paper, we have proposed a new approach for optimization of server-side XSLT transformations using template specialization. We described several specialization schemes, based on notions of spatial and temporal locality. Experimental evaluation found that use of such specializations can result in savings of 30% in execution time. We believe this research represents a valuable optimization technique for server-side XSLT design and deployment. As part of future work, we would like to investigate extending our methods and algorithms to handle further XSLT syntax, such as the wider use of built-in templates, and functions within *construction patterns*. We also plan consider the possible cost models in more detail and analyse methods for combining specializations.

References

[1] S. Abiteboul and V. Vianu. Regular path queries with constraints. In *the 16th ACM SIGACT-SIGMOD-SIGSTART Symposium on Principles of Database Systems*, AZ, 1997.

[2] T. Bray, J. Paoli, and C. M. Sperberg-McQueen, and E. Maler (2000): W3C Recommendation. Extensible Markup Language (XML) 1.0

[3] J. Clark. (1999): W3C recommendation. XSL Transformations (XSLT) version 1.0

[4] http://www.datapower.com/xmldev/xsltmark.html

[5] A. Deutsch and V. Tannen. Containment and integrity constraints for XPath. In *Proc. KRDB 2001,* CEUR Workshop Proceedings 45, 2003.
[6] A. Deutsch, M. Fernandez, D. Florescu, A. Levy and D. Suciu. A query language for XML. In *Proc.of 8th Int'l. World Wide Web Conf,* 1999.
[7] C. Dong and J. Bailey. The static analysis of XSLT programs. *Proc.of The 15th Australasian Database Conference*, Vol.27, Pages 151-160, Dunedin, New Zealand, 2004.
[8] R. Goldman and J. Widom. DataGuides: Enabling query formulation and optimization in semi-structured database. *Proc. Int'l Conf on VLDB*, Athens, Greece, 1997.
[9] Z. Guo, M. Li, X. Wang, and A. Zhou, Scalable XSLT Evaluation, *Proc. of APWEB 2004*, HangZhou, China, 2004.
[10] N. Jones. An Introduction to Partial Evaluation. *ACM Computing Surveys*, 1996.
[11] M. Kay. (2000): Saxon XSLT Processor. http://saxon.sourceforge.net/.
[12] M. Kay. Anatomy of an XSLT Processor, 2001.
[13] C. Laird. XSLT powers a new wave of web, 2002.
[14] Q. Li, B. Moon. Indexing and querying XML data for regular path expressions. In *Proc. Int'l Conf on VLDB,* Roma, Italy, 2001.
[15] S. Maneth and F. Neven Structured document transformations based on XSL. Proceedings of *DBPL'99*, Kinloch Rannoch, Scottland, 2000.
[16] W3C. XSL transformations(XSLT) version 2.0. http://www.w3.org/TR/xslt20/.
[17] World Wide Web Consortium. XML Path Language(XPath) Recommendation. http://www.w3.org/TR/xpath.

Materialized View Maintenance for XML Documents

Yuan Fa, Yabing Chen, Tok Wang Ling, and Ting Chen

{fayuan, chenyabi, lingtw, chent}@comp.nus.edu.sg

Abstract. XML views are often materialized for improving query performance. Their consistency needs to be maintained against the updates of the underlying source data. In this paper, we propose a novel approach to incrementally maintain the materialized view for XML documents based on a semantically rich data model – ORA-SS. This approach introduces a new concept – update tree to identify the changes to source and view. This approach computes the view update tree according to the source update tree. Then the view update tree is merged into the existing materialized view tree to produce the complete updated view. This approach supports more complex XML views than other works, such as views involving swap, join and aggregation of source data.

1 Introduction

XML is rapidly emerging as a standard for publishing and exchanging data on the Web. It is natural to construct XML views on heterogeneous data source in order to exchange these data on the Internet. Moreover, XML views are often materialized to speed up the query processing. It is important to keep the contents of the materialized view consistent with the contents of the source data as the source data are updated. XML views are more complex than relational views because of their hierarchical structures. Thus, it is more difficult to incrementally maintain the materialized XML views than relational views. Currently, there are several works on materialized view maintenance for XML documents. [2] examines the view maintenance for semi-structured data based on the Object Exchange Model (OEM) [5] and the Lorel query language [1]. An algebraic approach to maintain the views for semi-structured data is proposed in [6], in which the designed view is limited to select-project queries and only simple update such as insertion is considered. [7] studies the graph structured views and their incremental maintenance. Similarly, it can only handle very simple views that consist of object collections, even without edges. In this paper, we propose a novel approach to maintain materialized views for XML documents. In this approach, we express XML views through schema mapping based on a semantically-rich data model – ORA-SS [4]. The views are defined to have selection, drop, join, swap and aggregation of nodes over multiple source XML documents. Thus, the views are more powerful than those handled in the existing works. Having the complex view, we use four steps to maintain materialized XML views. First, we compute the source update tree. Second, we check the relevance of the update. Third, we compute the view update tree. Fourth, we merge the view update tree into the existing materialized view to produce the completely new materialized view.

X. Zhou et al. (Eds.): WISE 2004, LNCS 3306, pp. 365–371, 2004.
© Springer-Verlag Berlin Heidelberg 2004

The rest of the paper is organized as follows. In section 2, we introduce the ORA-SS data model. In section 3 we introduce the view specification using ORA-SS. Section 4 presents the approach to incrementally maintaining the materialized views for XML documents. We conclude this paper in Section 5.

2 The ORA-SS Data Model

The data model used in this paper is ORA-SS (Object-Relationship-Attribute model for Semi-Structured data) [4]. We adopt ORA-SS because it is a semantically richer data model that has been proposed for modeling semi-structured data compared to OEM or Dataguide. Using ORA-SS, we can define flexible XML views, and develop efficient incremental view maintenance algorithm. There are three main concepts in the ORA-SS data model, which are **object class**, **relationship type** and **attribute** (of object class or relationship type). There are two main diagrams in the ORA-SS. One is the **ORA-SS instance diagram**, and the other is **ORA-SS schema diagram**. The ORA-SS instance diagram represents the real XML data. And the ORA-SS schema diagram represents the schema and semantics of the XML document. The following example illustrates ORA-SS instance and schema diagrams.

Example 2.1. Figure 2.1 shows two ORA-SS instance diagrams that represented two XML documents. The XML document 1 in Figure 2.1(a) contains information on suppliers, parts supplied by each supplier, and projects that each supplier is supplying each part to. The XML document 2 in Figure 2.1(b) contains information on projects and the department that each supplier belongs to. Figure 2.2 shows two ORA-SS schema diagrams extracted from the two ORA-SS instance diagrams in Figure 2.1. In the schema diagram *s1*, there are one binary relationship type *sp* between *supplier* and *part*, and one ternary relationship type *spj* among *supplier*, *part* and *project*. There is a label *spj* on the incoming edge of *quantity*, indicating *quantity* is the attribute of the relationship type *spj*. This attribute *quantity* contains the number of *part* provided by each *supplier* to a specific project.

3 View Specifications

In this section, we define XML views based on ORA-SS schema. The views defined in ORA-SS are more flexible than views in other works. In particular, they support the following semantic operations in source schema. ***Selection***: A selection condition is a predicate associated to an object or attribute in the ORA-SS schema diagram.
Drop: In order to make the view contain interested data only, we can drop the uninterested object class or attribute from the source ORA-SS schemas and only keep the interested data in the view. ***Join***: The views can be designed by joining a set of source schemas. In particular, we can combine two source schemas by joining two semantically equivalent object classes in them. ***Swap***: The nature of XML is hierarchical. Thus, it will be natural to interchange the positions of two object classes of an ORA-SS schema. ***Aggregation***: Aggregate functions can be applied to the attributes of the object classes or the relationship types to derive new attributes.

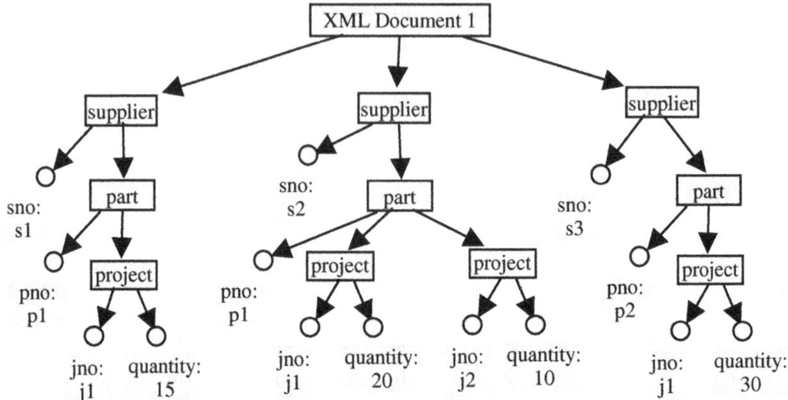

(a) ORA-SS instance diagram for XML document 1

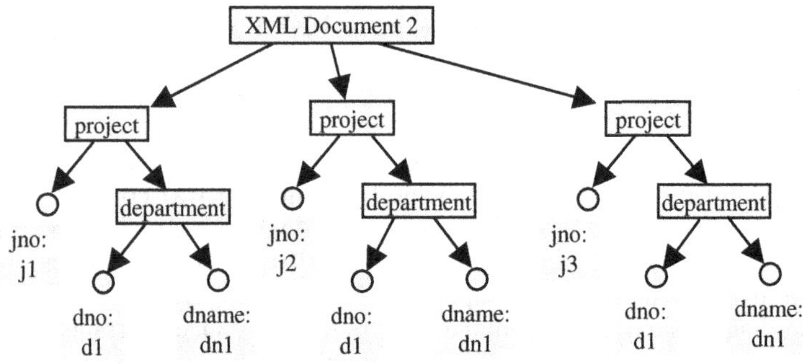

(b) ORA-SS instance diagram for XML document 2

Fig. 2.1. XML supplier-part-project database

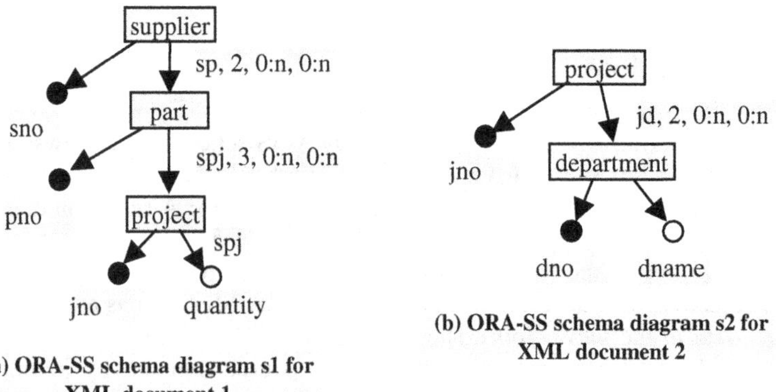

(a) ORA-SS schema diagram s1 for XML document 1

(b) ORA-SS schema diagram s2 for XML document 2

Fig. 2.2. ORA-SS schema diagrams

Example 3.1. Figure 3.1 depicts a view based on the two source schemas in Figure 2.2 by using schema mapping method. The view swaps, joins and drops the object classes in the source schemas. It shows information of *project*, *part* of each *project*, and the *department* that each *project* belongs to. *supplier* is dropped from the source schema 1. *part* and *project* are swapped. A new relationship type *jp* is created between *project* and *part*. A new attribute called *total_quantity* is created for *jp*, which is the sum of *quantity* of a specific part that the suppliers are supplying for the project. Source schema *s1* and *s2* in Figure 2.2 are joined together by the value of object class *project*. One selection condition is specified such that only the projects of *department* dn1 are selected. Obviously, with the combination of *swap*, *join*, and *drop* operators, we design a very flexible XML view based on ORA-SS.

In this paper, we adopt view transformation strategy in [3] to produce materialized views based on the view schema. Figure 3.2 depicts the materialized view for the view schema in Figure 3.1. To emphasize the importance of aggregation, we can see from this example, in the materialized view, the value of *total_quantity* for *part* p1 is 35 for *project* j1, which is the sum of *quantities* 15 and 20 supplied by *supplier* s1 and s2 in source XML document 1.

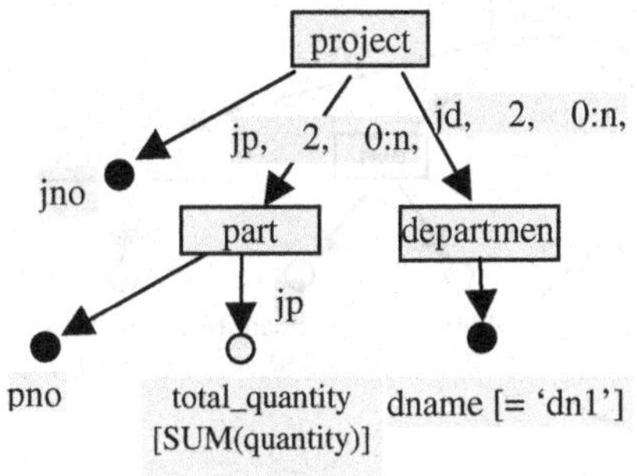

Fig. 3.1. ORA-SS schema diagram of the view over source schemas in figure 2.2

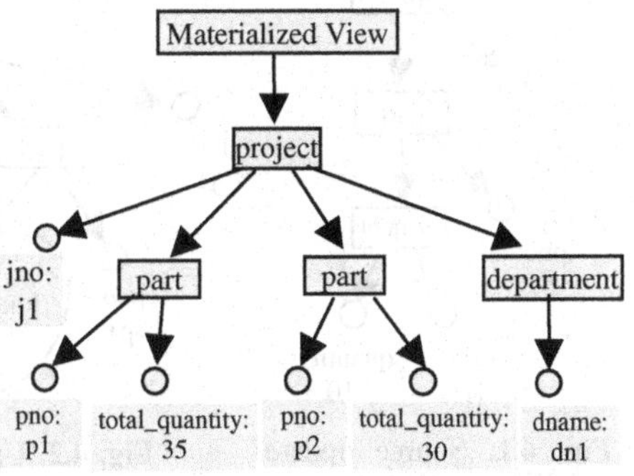

Fig. 3.2. Initial content of the materialized view specified in Figure 3.1

4 Incremental Maintenance of XML View

After the view is materialized, it is ready to accept updates to the source XML documents and incrementally maintain the materialized view. The source update can be an insertion, a deletion or a modification. The insertion operation inserts a sub-tree into a source XML document. The deletion operation deletes a sub-tree from a source XML document. The modification operation modifies the value of attribute of an object class or a relationship type.

Definition 4.1. *A path in a source XML document is said to be in a* ***source update tree*** *iff it is from the root of the updated source XML document to the updated sub-tree in source, or to the object class or the relationship type with the modified attribute. A source update tree contains the update information and conforms to the source ORA-SS schema.*

Definition 4.2. *A path in an XML view is said to be in a* ***view update tree*** *iff it is from the root of view to the updated sub-tree in the view, or to the object class or the relationship type with the modified attribute. A view update tree contains the update information and conforms to the view ORA-SS schema.*

The task of our incremental maintenance is to find the update part of the view (view update tree) according to the update of the source (source update tree), and maintain the view properly. We will first give an example on the source update tree, followed by the detailed algorithm of incremental view maintenance.

Example 4.1. Using the database in Figure 2.1 and the view in Figure 3.1, suppose *supplier* s3 is going to supply *part* p1 to *project* j1 with a quantity of 10. The source update tree in this case is shown in Figure 4.1, which contains the path from *supplier* s3 to *project* j1. The *total_quantity* of *part* p1 of *project* j1 will be increased by 10. The updated view is shown in Figure 4.2 with the updated part in the dashed circle.

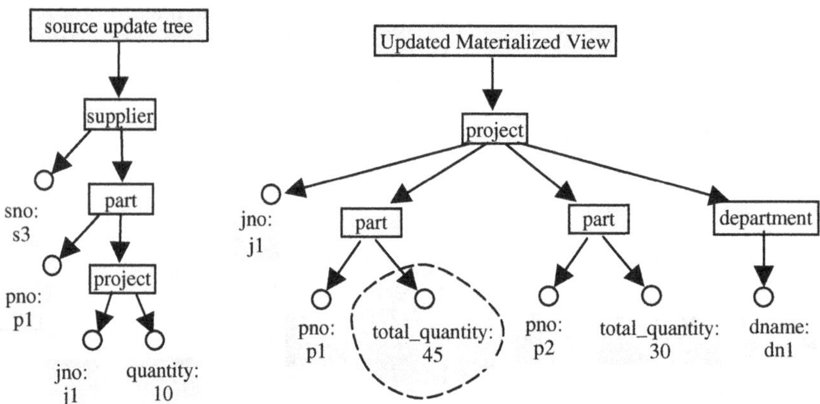

Fig. 4.1. Source update tree in Example 4.1

Fig. 4.2. Updated materialized view in Example 4.1

The **View_Maintenance algorithm** receives as input an update on one source XML document, the source XML documents, the ORA-SS schemas of the source, the existing materialized view, and the existing materialized view. The View_Maintenance algorithm constains the following four procedures:

1. The **procedure GenerateSourceUpdateTree** receives as input an update *U* to a source XML document *D*, *D* itself, and the ORA-SS schema *S* of *D*. The procedure generates the source update tree, which contains the update information to *D* upon *U*. Example 4.1 specifies a source update which is an insertion on the source XML document 1. The tree conforms to the ORA-SS schema diagram of XML document 1 in Figure 2.2 (a) as well.

2. The **procedure CheckSourceUpdateRelevance** receives as input the source update tree, the source ORA-SS schemas and the view ORA-SS schema. It checks whether the source update will have impact on the existing materialized view. We call the update which will affect the view as the relevant update. Only the relevant source update will be processed further. We do the relevance checking by consider the selection conditions specified in the view. According to the selection condition in the

view, the source update tree in Example 4.1 is relevant as *project* j1 belongs to *department* d1.

3. The **procedure GenerateViewUpdateTree** generates the view update tree which contains the update information to the view. It receives as input the relevant source update tree *SUT* in source XML document D_1, the un-updated source XML documents and the ORA-SS schema of the view (S_V). It uses the view transformation technique in paper [3]. It uses the source update tree instead of the source document D_1, so that the output is the update to the view instead of the initial content of the view. The view update tree for source update in Example 4.1 is shown in Fig. 4.3.

4. The **procedure MergeViewUpdateTree** receives as input the view update tree, the view ORA-SS schema, and the existing materialized view *MV*. It merges the view update tree into the *MV* and produces the updated materialized view. The view update tree in Fig. 4.3 is merged into the existing view to produce the updated view as shown in Fig. 4.2.

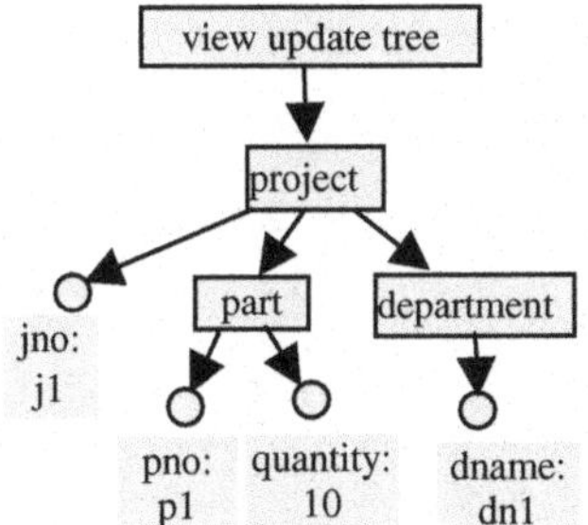

Fig. 4.3. View update tree for Example 4.1

5 Conclusion

In this paper, we proposed an incremental view maintenance algorithm for XML documents, which supports immediate refresh of the views when source XML documents are updated. The views supported in our work involve flexible semantics, such as selection, drop, join and swapping elements on multiple source schemas. The approach supports updates like insertion and deletion of sub-tree from the source XML document. Most importantly, we introduce the concept of update tree provides us a chance to handle transaction. In the future, we will enable multiple changes to be specified in one single update tree. The view update tree can be derived together at one time. The performance of view maintenance will certainly be improved.

References

1. S. Abiteboul, D. Quass, J. McHugh, J. Widom, and J. Wiener. The Lorel Query Language for Semistructured Data. Journal of Digital Libraries, 1(1), Nov. 1996.
2. S. Abiteboul, J. McHugh, M. Rys, V. Vassalos, and J. Wiener. Incremental Maintenance for Materialized Views over Semistructured Data. In VLDB, pages 38-49, 1998.
3. D. Luo, T. Chen, T. W. Ling, and X. Meng. On View Transformation Support for a Native XML DBMS. In 9th International Conference on Database Systems for Advanced Applications, Korea, March 2004.

4. G. Dobbie, X. Y. Wu, T. W. Ling, M. L. Lee. ORA-SS: An Object – Relationship - Attribute Model for Semistructured Data. Technical Report TR21/00, School of Computing, National University of Singapore, 2000.
5. Y. Papakonstantinou, H. Garcia-Molina, and J. Widom. Object Exchange across Heterogeneous Information Sources. In Proceedings of the 11th International Conference on Data Engineering, pages 251-260, Taipei, Taiwan, Mar. 1995.
6. D. Suciu. Query Decomposition and View Maintenance for Query Language for Unstructured Data. In VLDB, pages 227-238, Bombay, India, September 1996.
7. Y. Zhuge and H. Garcia-Molina. Graph Structured Views and Their Incremental Maintenance. In Proceedings of the 14th International Conference on Data Engineering (DE), 1998.
8. World Wide Web Consortium, "XQuery: A Query Language for XML", W3C Working Draft, 2002. http://www.w3.org/XML/Query
9. XSLT 2.0. http://www.w3.org/Style/XSL

An Efficient Algorithm for Clustering XML Schemas*

Tae-Woo Rhim[1], Kyong-Ho Lee[1], and Myeong-Cheol Ko[2]

[1] Dept. of Computer Science, Yonsei Univ.
134 Shinchon-dong, Sudaemoon-ku, Seoul 120-749, Korea
twrhim@icl.yonsei.ac.kr, khlee@cs.yonsei.ac.kr,

[2] Dept. of Computer Science, Konkuk Univ.
322 Danwol-dong, Chungju-si, Chungbuk 380-701, Korea
cheol@kku.ac.kr

Abstract. Schema clustering is important as a prerequisite to the integration of XML schemas. This paper presents an efficient method for clustering XML schemas. The proposed method first computes similarities among schemas. The similarity is defined by the size of the common structure between two schemas under the assumption that the schemas with less cost to be integrated are more similar. Specifically, we extract one-to-one matchings between paths with the largest number of corresponding elements. Finally, a hierarchical clustering method is applied to the value of similarity. Experimental results with many XML schemas show that the method has performed better compared with previous works, resulting in a precision of 98% and a rate of clustering of 95% in average.

1 Introduction

With the widespread use of XML(Extensible Markup Language) [1] documents, the volume of XML schemas also grows at a rapid speed. For the integration of heterogenious information, there is a growing interest in XML schema[1] clustering and integration of which the process is shown in Fig. 1. This paper proposes an efficient method for schema clustering that is prerequisite to the integration of schemas.

As summarized in Table 1, XML clustering is studied in two approaches: document clustering [5][6] and schema clustering [3][4]. An XML document is an instance of a schema and doesn't have any cardinality indicators and choice operators. Therefore, previous methods targeting XML documents may not handle XML schemas.

Since most of previous works for clustering XML schemas are based on just structural and lexical similarities among elements, their clustering results might be inappropriate for schema integration. In this paper, we propose a similarity between schemas based on the cost to integrate the schemas and apply a hierarchical clustering to the similarities among schemas. Experimental results with a large volume of schemas show that the proposed method has performed better compared with previous works.

* This work was supported the Korea Research Foundation Grant(KRF-2003-003-D00429)

1 In this paper, the term "XML schema" means both XML Schema [2] and XML DTD (Document Type Definition)[1].

X. Zhou et al. (Eds.): WISE 2004, LNCS 3306, pp. 372–377, 2004.
© Springer-Verlag Berlin Heidelberg 2004

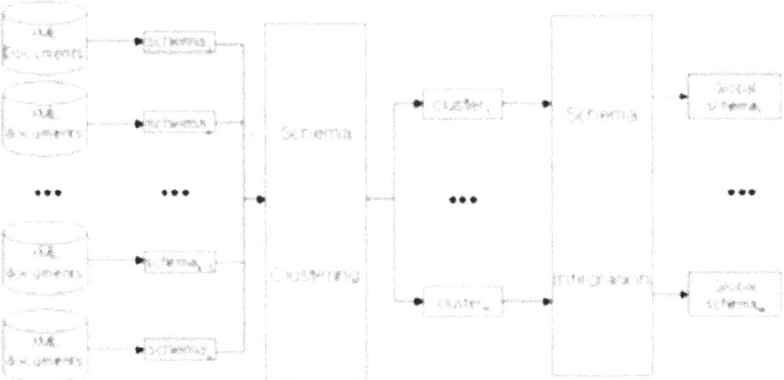

Fig. 1. The process of schema clustering and integration.

Meanwhile, XML schemas are mainly made up of declaration of elements and attributes. Element declarations define not only the names, cardinalities, and content types of elements, but also hierarchical structure among elements. An element may contain child elements and/or attributes that characterize the element.

This paper proposes a document model based on a tree structure. We call the tree representarion of an XML schema as a schema tree. Each node of a schema tree represents an element of an XML schema. It may have an element name as a label, and the datatype and cardinality as attributes.

2 The Proposed Clustering Algorithm

The proposed clustering method consists of three steps: simplification of a schema tree, computation of similarities, and hierarchical clustering.

2.1 Simplification of a Schema Tree

First of all, XML schemas are modeled as a schema tree. Because a choice operator(|) in a schema makes it possible to generate several schema trees, a choice operator is transformed into a sequence operator(,). The proposed method applies the transformation rules proposed by Lee et al. [3].

2.2 Computation of Similarity

A global schema covers all schemas in a cluster. The proposed similarity between schemas depends on how much it cost to generate a global schema. The less it cost to transform two schemas into a global schema, the more similar they are. Specifically, the similarity is defined by the ratio of a common structure.

Table 1. A brief survey of clustering methods of XML schemas and documents

Target	Author	Year	Characteristic
XML Schema	Lee et al. [3]	2002	Compute DTD similarity by using the lexical and structural similarities among nodes and hierarchically cluster DTDs based on the similarity. The method is relatively accurate because it considers contextual aspect. However, time complexity is greater than other methods.
	Jeong And Hsu [4]	2001	Propose schema integration system for an efficient information retrieval. Calculate the schema similarity by using the length of transformation operator between two schemas, and cluster XML schemas based on the similarities.
XML Document	Francesca et al. [5]	2003	Compute the document similarity based on the size of common structure between document trees.
	Nierman and Jagadish [6]	2002	Define a distance between documents as the edit script of minimal cost, and cluster documents based on the distance.

Before computing a structural similarity between schema trees, a node similarity between two nodes, Ns and Nt, is computed. As shown in Equation 1, the node similarity is defined as the weighted sum of a name similarity, a cardinality similarity, and a data type similarity. In the case of XML DTDs, w_3 becomes zero because an XML DTD has no type attribute.

$$\text{NodeSimilarity(Ns, Nt)} = w_1 \times \text{NameSimilarity(Ns, Nt)} + w_2 \times \text{CardinalitySimilarity(Ns, Nt)} + w_3 \times \text{DatatypeSimilarity(Ns, Nt)} \quad (w_1 + w_2 + w_3 = 1). \tag{1}$$

The name similarity is determined by a function, NameSimilarity(Ns, Nt), which computes the degree of similarity between labels of two nodes Ns and Nt. Specifically, the function computes the similarities of constituted tokens of the two nodes as follows:

$$\text{NameSimilarity(Ns, Nt)} = \frac{\Sigma\ \text{similarity}(Ns_i, Nt_j)}{|Ns| + |Nt|} \tag{2}$$

Ns_i : token of source node, $1 \le i \le n$, Nt_j : token of target node, $1 \le j \le m$

Labels are tokenized by using capital letters or special characters as delimiters. For more accuracy, abbreviation and synonym dictionaries are used. If token are in the abbreviation dictionary, they are replaced by their full names before computing similarities. If two tokens are identical, the similarity between the two tokens is 1.0. Otherwise, we find the two tokens in a synonym dictionary [7]. If two tokens are in a synonym list, the value of similarity is 0.8.

Leaf nodes of a schema tree have data types. Since the transformation between nodes with different data types may cause some information loss, the similarity between data types is proposed based on the degree of information preservation. The data type similarity is classified into four groups by the degree of information loss: exact transformation, transformation without loss, transformation with some loss, and impossible transformation. Exact transformation is assigned the highest similarity and impossible transformation is assigned the lowest similarity.

The cardinality of node is represented by kleene operators(?, +, and *) or attributes minOccurs and maxOccurs. The cardinality similarity with two kleene operators is assigned from 0.7 to 1.0 based on the degree of information loss. In the case of attributes, if one of the value of minOccurs and maxOccurs are equal, the cardinality similarity is 0.9. Otherwise, the similarity is 0.7.

For computing similarity between trees, we extract all paths from the root node to leaf nodes, SPathi, 0 i n, and TPathj, 0 j m. Then, we calculate LCSs [8] among all paths. The LCS between paths is extracted by one-to-one matching of paths. The parent-child order should be preserved.

We find one-to-one matchings among paths with the greatest sum of LCSs for extracting the common structure of two schemas. Then, the total of LCSs is defined as the GCS(Greatest Common Subset) of the trees. For computing GCS, we model the paths and LCSs as graph G(V,E). In G(V,E), vertex means each path and edges are weighted with the length of LCSs between paths. The vertexes are classified into source and target vertexes. So, the graph G(V,E) with n source paths and m target paths is considered as a weighted bipartite graph Kn,m. Therefore, we regard the computation of GCS as finding maximal bipartite matching [9] of Kn,m.

Dividing the size of GCS by the number of source and target node, we get the similarity between two schema trees as folloes.

$$\text{Similarity between schema trees} = \frac{|Tgcs|}{|Ts| + |Tt| - |Tgcs|} \quad (3)$$

2.3 Hierarchical Clustering

The proposed method clusters schemas based on the similarity values among schemas. We use a hierarchical clustering method [10], where the schemas with the highest similarity are merged first. First of all, schemas generate each cluster. Then, the clusters with the highest similarity are merged and their similarity value is modified to 0. When all clusters with higher similarity than a threshold are merged, the clustering process are terminated.

If a higher threshold is applied, many schemas are clustered independently. Otherwise, they are merged into a few large clusters.

3 Experimental Results

We have experimented with the schemas used in XClust of Lee et al. The data set consists of 109 schemas on 4 domains: Travel, Patient, Publication, and Hotel. The weights w_1, w_2, and w_3 are assigned with 0.7, 0.3, and 0 because an XML DTD has no type attribute.

We propose two measures for evaluating performance. Precision is defined as the ratio of schemas clustered into its original cluster. The other measure is a clustering rate, which is the ratio of schemas clustered actually. For effective clustering, both measures are important. As the threshold is raised, the precision is improved and the clustering rate is decreased.

The precision and the clustering rate of XClust and the proposed method while varing thresholds are shown in Fig. 2. Consequently, the two methods have similar precision. Meanwhile, XClust is immoderately sensitive in terms of a clustering rate. As the threshold increases, the clustering rate is rapidly decreased and the experiment result becomes worse.

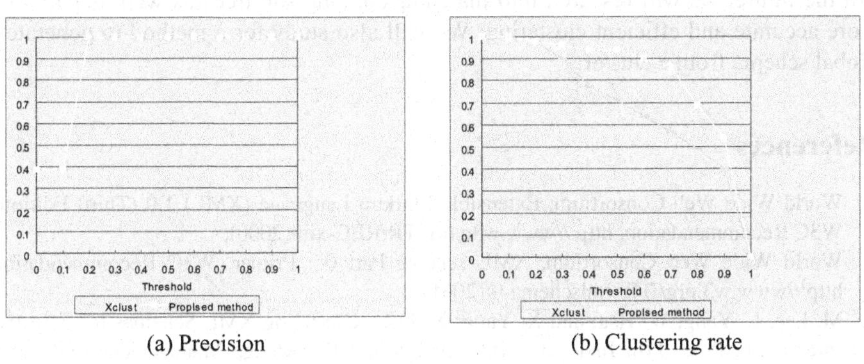

(a) Precision (b) Clustering rate

Fig. 2. The precision and clustering rate of XClust and propose method.

We compute a recall of representative clusters for evaluating the quality of clustering. The representative cluster is the cluster which has most schemas for a specific domain. The recall is the ratio of schemas included in representative clusters. Higher recall means that the schemas in same domain tend to be clustered into a cluster. Experimental results show that the recall of the proposed method of 0.84 is better than the recall of XClust of 0.79.

Meanwhile, we cannot compare with the method proposed by Jeong and Hsu because we cannot get the experimental data and results.

Table 2 shows the time complexity of the proposed method, XClust, and the method by Jeong and Hsu. The proposed method uses a path extraction method, so it has the time complexity of $O(n^2e^3)$.

Table 2. Comparison of the method with previous works in terms of time complexity

	XClust	Jeong and Hsu	The proposed method
Computation of similarity	$O(n^2m^2e^3)$	$O(n^2Km^2)$	$O(n^2e^3)$
Hierarchical clustering	$O(n^3)$		
n : number of schemas, m : number of nodes, e : number of leaf nodes K : number of children			

4 Conclusions and Future Works

This paper presents the clustering algorithm that is a prerequisite of XML schema integration. Since most of previous researches consider just lexical and structural similarity of nodes for measuring similarity, they are not suitable for schema integration. The proposed method clusters the schemas based on the size of common structure between two schemas. Abbreviation and synonym dictionaries are used for more precise matchings between nodes.

The proposed method also improves the time complexity by matching paths. Experimental results on the schemas used in previous research show that, comparing with previous work, our method has similar precision and better performance in the quality of clustering.

In the future, we will research into matchings among sub-trees as well as paths for more accurate and efficient clustering. We will also study for a method to generate a global schema from a cluster.

References

1. World Wide Web Consortium, Extensible Markup Language (XML) 1.0 (Third Edition), W3C Recommendation, http://www.w3c.org/TR/REC-xml(2000).
2. World Wide Web Consortium, XML schema Part 0 : Primer, W3C Recommendation, http://www.w3.org/ TR/xmlschema-0/(2001).
3. M. Lee, L. Yang, W. Hsu, and X. Yang: XClust : Clustering XML Schemas for Effective Integration, Proc. 11th Int'l Conf. Information and Knowledge Management(2002) 292-299.
4. Euna Jeong and Chun-Nan Hsu: Induction of Integrated View for XML Data with Heterogeneous DTDs, Proc. 10th Int'l Conf. Information and Knowledge Management(2001) 151-158.
5. F. De Francesca, G. Gordano, R. Ortale, and A. Tagarelli: Distance-based Clustering of XML Documents, Proc. First Int'l Workshop on Mining Graphs, Trees and Sequences(2003) 75-78.
6. A. Nierman and H. V. Jagadish: Evaluate Structural Similarity in XML Documents, Proc. Fifth Int'l Workshop on the Web and Databases(2002) 61-66.
7. George A. Miller: WordNet: A Lexical Database for English, Communications of the ACM, Vol. 38, No. 11(1995) 39-41.
8. Claus Rick: Simple and Fast Linear Space Computation of Longest Common Subsequence, Information Processing Letters, Vol. 75, Issue 6(2000) 275-281.
9. Robert Sedgewick: Algorithm in C++, Part 5 Graph algorithm(2001), 3rd edition, Addison Wesley.
10. E. Gose, R. Johnsonbaugh, and S. Jost: Pattern Recognition and Image Analysis(1996), Prentice Hall.

Google's "I'm Feeling Lucky", Truly a Gamble?

Roelof van Zwol and Herre van Oostendorp

Center for Content and Knowledge Engineering
Utrecht University
Utrecht, The Netherlands
{roelof,herre}@cs.uu.nl

Abstract. With huge quantities of multimedia information becoming available on the Internet everyday, our foremost mechanisms to find information still rely on text-based retrieval systems with their keyword-based query interfaces. However little to nothing is known about the retrieval performance and/or the quality of the user interface of these search engines.
Often when a retrieval system is developed the evaluation focuses either on the retrieval performance analysis of the retrieval strategy, or on the usability testing of the interface offered by the retrieval system. Both experiments are time consuming to set up and often require the same preconditions to be fulfilled, i.e. a test reference collection, and in the case of usability testing respondents, to be available.
The contribution of this article is twofold. It discusses a testbed for the evaluation of a wide variety of retrieval systems that allows both a usability and a retrieval experiment to be conducted in the same platform. Besides greatly reducing the effort needed to set up and perform such experiments, it also allows for the investigation of the relationship between usability testing and retrieval performance analysis of retrieval systems. Secondly, it presents the results of a case study with the testbed, comparing three major search engines available on the Internet.

1 Introduction

Information retrieval systems, like the popular search engines such as Google, AllTheWeb, Vivisimo and many others, form the gateway to the Internet and other on-line digital libraries that allow users to find relevant pieces of information. Often a user specifies his information need through a simple interface and the retrieval systems returns a list with relevant documents.

To evaluate a retrieval system two types of experiments are frequently used. Through *usability testing* of the interface provided by the search engine valuable information regarding the interaction of the user with the retrieval systems can be derived. Based on the methodology used, the experiment provides information about the usability of the retrieval system, in terms of *effectivity*, *efficiency*, and *satisfaction* experienced by the user. On the other hand *retrieval performance experiments* are used to measure the performance of the retrieval strategy implemented by the retrieval system in terms of *recall* and *precision*, irrespective of user' experiences.

X. Zhou et al. (Eds.): WISE 2004, LNCS 3306, pp. 378–389, 2004.
© Springer-Verlag Berlin Heidelberg 2004

Often, when a retrieval system is developed the evaluation focuses either on the retrieval performance analysis of the retrieval strategy, or on the usability testing of the interface offered by the retrieval system. Both experiments are time consuming to set up and often require the same preconditions to be fulfilled, i.e. the availability of a test reference collection, and respondents/experts.

This article discusses TERS, a testbed for the evaluation of a wide variety of retrieval systems that allows both usability and batch experiments to be conducted in the same environment. Besides greatly reducing the effort needed to set up and perform such experiments, it also allows for the investigation of the relationship between usability testing and retrieval performance analysis of retrieval systems.

In literature both types of evaluation are described extensively in [1,2,3]. In particular Turpin and Hersh also investigated the differences between usability testing and batch evaluation in [4]. Their assessment showed that systems with superior results in batch experiments did not gain better performance when real users were put to the test. E.g. systems with a lower retrieval performance were still evaluated higer in terms of usability. They conclude that it was most likely due to users being able to adequately find and utilise relevant documents, though they were ranked further down the output list. The results of our case study however contradict with this point of view, as discussed in Section 6.

1.1 Case Study

To demonstrate the testbed a case study is setup that compares three major search engines available on the Internet: Google[5], AllTheWeb[6] and Vivisimo[7]. The choice of Google seems obvious, as many Internet users currently consider Google as their first choice. AllTheWeb, which is based on the indexes of Yahoo!, provides similar end-user functionality as Google. In that sense, one can expect similar results when it comes to the methodology fo searching. Finally, the last choice is Vivisimo, a clustering meta search engine[8] that differs from both Google and Yahoo in both the retrieval strategy and the user interface that offers a clustering of documents, based on related terms that were found in the document.

One of Google's features, i.e. the "I'm Feeling Lucky"-button of the query interface, allows a user to directly jump to the first document in the ranking for a particular information request. This is based on the assumption that Google's retrieval strategy is capable to retrieve a relevant document at the number one position in the ranking. Is this true, or truly a gamble?

1.2 Organisation

The remainder of this article is based on the following organisation. Section 2 introduces TERS, the *T*estbed for the *E*valuation of *R*etrieval *S*ystems. The next two sections discuss the particularities of the two types of experiments that are hosted by the testbed. Section 3 will discuss in more detail the methodology behind the usability experiment, while Section 4 will explain the methodology used for the retrieval performance experiment. Sections 5 and 6 will discuss what is needed to setup both experiments using the testbed and discuss the outcomes of the case study with the Internet search engines. Finally the conclusions and future work are discussed in Section 7

2 TERS – Testbed for the Evaluation of Retrieval Systems

Usability testing or retrieval performance analysis of a retrieval system alone, does not provide the full picture[4,9]. If time and resources permit, a complete evaluation of a retrieval system should take both aspects into account. However as argued in the previous section, research shows that the outcomes of the experiments can contradict each other. With TERS we aim at providing a controlled platform that allows us to investigate this aspect.

A seamless integration of the two approaches should provide more insight in the aspects of the evaluation that might cause a contradiction. A strict procedure is setup and supported by TERS to gain control of the parameters that might influence the outcome of the experiments. Two important parameters that are considered of influence are respondents and topics, e.g. if the same respondents and topics are used for both experiments the subjectivity of respondents and the complexity of the topics can be filtered from the outcomes of the experiments. In Section 5 this procedure is described in more detail.

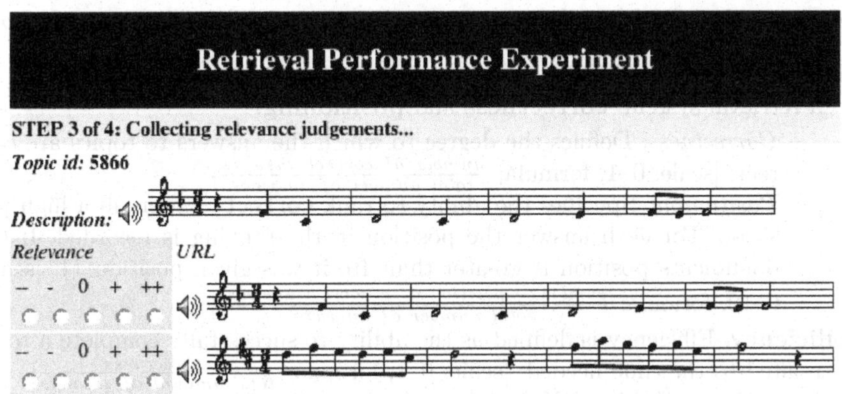

Fig. 1. Fragment of the interface of the retrieval performance experiment.

2.1 Application Domains

The aim of the testbed is to provide a platform that can be used for the evaluation of a wide variety of retrieval systems. The testbed is already used for the evaluation of three different classes of retrieval systems. First of all TERS is used for the case study of the three search engines, as described in this article.

Furthermore, TERS has been used for the evaluation of a music retrieval system[10]. Figure 1 shows a snapshot of the interface used by the retrieval performance experiment to gather the relevance judgements for the music fragments retrieved by the system. The task here is to judge the relevance of each piece of music given a topic (query), which in this case also is a music fragment. On a scale of one to five the expert judges the relevance of the fragment, and assigns a score of one if the fragment is completely irrelevant, up to five, if the fragment is highly relevant.

The third application domain for which TERS has been used is to test the usability of XML query languages[11]. We also plan to use TERS for the evaluation of content-based XML retrieval systems, like the systems that are built for INEX[12].

3 Usability Experiment

The methodology behind usability testing is extensively described in [2,3]. Below the measures commonly used for usability engineering are discussed in more detail.

Measures

To determine the usability of the retrieval system TERS offers 3 measures, which are frequently used for usability testing: *effectivity*, *efficiency*, and *satisfaction*.

Effectivity. Within TERS, two measures are used to express the effectivity of a retrieval system: **correctness** and **positioning**.

- *Correctness.* Defines the degree to which the answers to topics are correct. [scale: 0–1, formula: $\frac{number\ of\ correct\ answers}{total\ number\ of\ answers}$]
- *Positioning.* Specifies the ability to rank **correct** answers in a high position. For each answer the position in the ranking is recorded. If the documents position is greater than 10, it was given position 11. [scale: 0–10, formula: $\frac{sum(11\ -\ position\ of\ a\ correct\ answer)}{total\ number\ of\ answers}$]

Efficiency. Efficiency is defined as the ability to successfully complete a topic related to the time needed. [scale: 0–1, formula: $\frac{correctness}{total\ amount\ of\ seconds}$]

Satisfaction. Within TERS the user's satisfaction is measured through a survey. An overall satisfaction score is calculated by averaging the scores of the questions that are associated with a retrieval system. [scale: 0–7, $\frac{sum(score)}{total\ number\ of\ related\ questions}$]

Additional measures. A number of additional statistics can easily be calculated on demand, since all data collected, is available upon running the evaluation scripts. Background information on the respondents and a classification of the topics provide additional information, crucial for so called 'within subjects analysis'.

4 Retrieval Performance Experiment

The methodology used for the retrieval performance experiment is based on the blind-review pooling method as commonly accepted in TREC, CLEF, and INEX. TERS gratefully adopts this methodology and provides the functionality needed to host a retrieval performance experiment.

Measures

The measures **recall** and **precision** are most frequently used to measure the retrieval performance in an experiment, evaluating an IR system in batch mode. Given an *information request* I, taken from the test reference collection. Let R be the set of relevant documents for that specific information request, then $\mid R \mid$ refers to the number documents in this set. Let A be the answer set of documents found by the retrieval strategy for information request I. Then $\mid A \mid$ is the number of documents in the answer set. Further, let $\mid R_a \mid$ be the number of documents in the intersection of the sets R and A. The measures for recall and precision are then calculated as:

Recall. [scale: 0–1, $\frac{|R_a|}{|R|}$]
Precision. [scale: 0–1], $\frac{|R_a|}{|A|}$]

The 'perfect' IR system would have a recall and precision of both 1. Unfortunately such systems do not exist. Furthermore, basing the retrieval performance solely on these two measures would neglect the fact that the answer set of a specific information request is ranked. Retrieval strategies that rank relevant documents higher should be rewarded for that. This is normally expressed in a *precision versus recall curve.* This curve is calculated by introducing 11 standard recall levels, for which the precision is calculated. This results into a curve, as shown in figure 3.

Alternatively, the average precision at given *document cut-off levels* can be computed. This approach provides additional information with respect to the retrieval performance of the ranking algorithm. The result is a curve that shows the average precision of the retrieval strategy when for example 5, 10, ... , 100 documents are seen. More information about measures for the evaluation of retrieval systems can be found in [1,13].

5 Configuring the Testbed

To setup the testbed for both a usability and a retrieval performance experiment a number of tasks have to be performed:

Identify Retrieval Systems to Be Evaluated
The configuration of the testbed requires the unique identification of each system that will be evaluated. In the case-study the search engines are referred to as 'Alltheweb', 'Google', and 'Vivisimo'. In addition a URL is

needed for the usability experiment that links to the user interface of the search engine.

Creation of Topics

As part of the test reference collection, a set of topics is defined that will be used for both experiments. A topic, i.e. a search assignment, consists of four fields: an unique ID, title, description, and narrative. This approach is fully compliant with the approaches used for TREC and INEX. When defining topics, it is recommended to investigate how well a topic fits within the document collection, e.g. for our case-study this is the Internet, and to pay attention to the specificity of the topic[14]. Table 1 shows one of the forty topics used in the case study.

Table 1. Example topic

```
<topic id='10' title='Pollution problems'>
 <description>
  What treatments can be suggested to lower the pollution caused by cars?
 </description>
 <narrative>
  Documents describing methods or treatments like using hybrid cars,
  the development of cleaner fuel, the fuel cell are considered relevant.
  Documents that describe pricing or specific technological terminology
  are not relevant.
 </narrative>
```

Compose Survey Questions

A survey within TERS usually consists of several sections. One section contains questions of a general nature, which is used to determine the background of the respondents participating in the experiment. Table 2 shows the general questions that are used for the case-study. The general questions are presented to the respondents prior to the experiment.

An additional section is introduced for each retrieval system that is evaluated. Once a respondent has performed the topics within the usability experiment for a particular system, he/she is requested to complete the relevant section of the survey.

For the case study we used the following set of five questions for each of the search engines. The respondents were requested to express their satisfaction on a scale of 1 – 7. Figure 2 illustrates how these questions cover the different aspects of a retrieval system.

1. Are you satisfied with the search options offered by the search engine?
2. How satisfied are you with the presentation of the results?
3. Are you satisfied with using this search engine for your search as a whole?
4. How satisfied are you with the relevance of the retrieved documents?
5. Are you satisfied with the response time of the search engine?

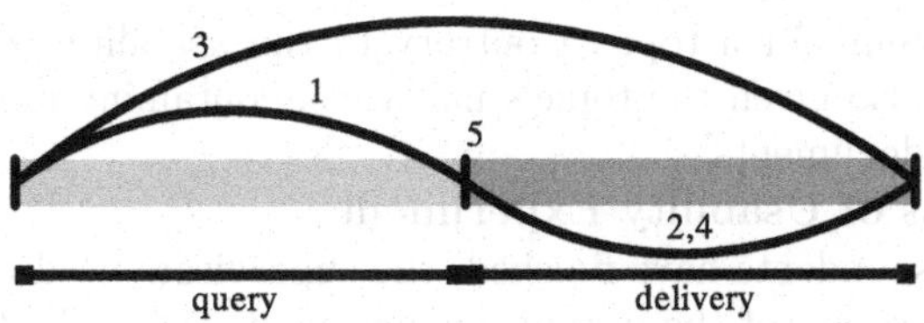

Fig. 2. Survey questions – coverage

Gather the Runs
For the retrieval performance experiment a run should be constructed for each of the retrieval systems in the testbed. A run contains the top N results obtained for each topic. In TREC-like experiments the top 500 documents are often obtained for each topic, while INEX uses the top 100 documents. For the case-study only the top 20 documents were taken from the results, due to the limited amount of time available for the respondents to provide the relevance judgements. Furthermore, common practise learns that in the case of web-based search a user will rather refine his search, than browse through the documents that are not high in the ranking.

Divide the Workload over the Respondents
To be able to compute the relation between the usability of the retrieval system and its retrieval performance, it is desirable that the respondent provides the relevance judgements for the same topics in the retrieval performance experiment that he/she has carried out in the usability experiment. To streamline the organisation, this process can be stored in the respondents matrix. For the case study, the experiment consisted of forty topics, four search engines and twenty respondents.
The twenty respondents participated in both experiments, where they carried out eight topics within the usability experiment. The topics were carried out using the same search engine for each pair of topics, equally spread over the different search engines and participants. Next a respondent was requested to provide relevance judgements for two out of (the same) eight topics for the retrieval performance experiment.

Perform the Usability Experiment
A respondent ideally starts with a usability experiment, before entering the retrieval performance experiment. This ensures that the respondent has no prior knowledge about relevant documents/information for a particular topic of the experiment.
The respondent starts with the general section of the survey and then continues with an example topic to become acquainted with the interface of the experiment. Next the respondent is requested to perform a number of topics using the different retrieval systems in the experiment. Finally, the respondent completes the remaining sections of the survey.

Perform the Retrieval Performance Experiment
The final task for the respondent is to provide relevance judgements for a (sub)set of topics, containing the randomised results of the participating

retrieval systems for a topic. Contrary to the usability experiment the respondent is also given the topic's narrative, containing hints about criteria for relevant documents.

Judge Results of Usability Experiment
Once the respondents have finished, the supervisors need to inspect the results for the topics of the usability experiment. Using the topic's narrative, they judge, as experts, the correctness of the results.

Run the Evaluation Scripts
The evaluation scripts provide the raw results of the experiments. In the case of usability testing these results provide a rough indication of the outcome, but additional analysis is often needed to identify the significant differences between the systems. The evaluation script for the retrieval performance experiment is based on the TREC evaluation script. It produces the data needed for the recall-precision curves that are commonly used to analyse the differences between the retrieval strategies.

6 Results of the Case Study

In this section the results of the case study are presented. Table 2 provides some background information about the respondents participating in the experiment. It shows how the respondents answered the general section of the survey. Interesting to see is that although they frequently use the Internet to find information, the advanced options of the query interface are not essential for their search.

Table 2. General information about the experimental setup

	avg	std
What kind of search engine user are you? (beginner – expert)	4.7	1.63
How often do you use the Internet to find information? (monthly – daily)	5.5	1.67
Does your search for information always lead to satisfying results? (never – always)	4.85	1.39
How often do you use the advanced options of the query interface? (never – always)	3.25	1.92

In total 20 respondents participated in both experiments. They can be categorised in three user groups: *beginner* (5), *novice* (8), and *expert* (7). A so called 'between subjects' analysis, based on Manova repeated measurements was performed. A significant difference[1] (0.02) for efficiency (number of correct answers per second) was found between the novice (avg: 0.003, std: 0.01) and expert user (avg:0.008, std: 0.01) groups. The analysis also found a significant difference (0.03) between the novice (avg:4.58, std: 0.25) and expert (avg:5.46, std:0.26) users, based on satisfaction.

[1] Using a threshold of $p<0.05$

In total 40 topics were defined, but due to the limited availability of the respondents only 37 topics are taken into account when computing the outcomes of the experiment. The methodology used for the analysis of the results of the usability experiment is described in detail in [2].

Based on the criteria of Rouet [14] the topics can be divided into 18 specific topics, and 19 topics of a generic nature. Topic 10 of Table 1 is a clear example of a generic topic, since various answers are valid. No significant differences between the search engines were found for a 'within subjects' (material/topic) analysis based on Manova repeated measurements. However the between subjects analysis shows a marginal significant difference between the specific and generic topics, in favour of the specific topics. This is in-line with the results found by [14].

6.1 Usability

In this section the outcomes of the usability experiment for the three search engines is discussed, based on summary statistics, effectivity, efficiency, and satisfaction.

Summary Statistics

The summary statistics of Table 3 show that Google out performs the other search engines on all aspects of the usability experiment.

Table 3. Summary statistics (means) for usability experiment

	Alltheweb	Google	Vivisimo
effectivity			
correctness	0.78	***0.95***	0.73
positioning	6	***7.68***	4.92
efficiency	0.0056	***0.0061***	0.0048
satisfaction	4.32	***5.97***	4.55

Effectivity and Efficiency

Based on the raw results of the usability experiment both a user and material analysis are carried out, using Manova repeated measurements. Only the outcome of the user analysis is discussed here, since they both showed the same trend for the three search engines.

The repeated measurements analysis showed a significant difference (0.04) between AllTheWeb (avg: 0.78, std: 0.42) and Google (std: 0.95, std: 0.23) based on the correctness measure. Based on positioning an even stronger significant difference (0.01) was found between AllTheWeb (avg: 6,std: 3.88) and Google (avg: 7.68, std: 3.07). No significant differences between the search engines were found based on efficiency.

Satisfaction

The survey provided the input used to calculate the satisfaction of the users with the user interface offered by the search engines. Table 4 presents the

Table 4. Mean satisfaction per search engine

	AllTheWeb		**Google**		**Vivisimo**	
	avg	**std**	**avg**	**std**	**avg**	**std**
(search options) 1.	4.35	1.63	5.8	1.01	4.65	1.46
(presentation of results) 2.	4.35	1.35	5.8	0.77	4.65	1.63
(satisfaction as a whole) 3.	4.25	1.55	6.1	0.85	4.35	1.50
(relevance of retrieved documents) 4.	4.15	1.6	5.95	1.00	4.5	1.32
(response time) 5.	4.5	1.64	6.2	0.70	4.6	1.54
Overall	4.32	1.53	**5.97**	**0.87**	4.55	1.47

Table 5. Summary statistics for retrieval performance experiment

	AllTheWeb	**Google**	**Vivisimo**
retrieved	703	738	733
relevant	611	611	611
relevant retrieved	206	236	241
recall	0.337152	0.386252	***0.394435***
precision	0.29303	0.319783	***0.328786***

results of the survey, showing Google as the overall winner on all aspects. However we cannot assume that the respondents were entirely subjective, due to Google's popularity and the background experiences of the respondents. The Manova repeated measurement analysis showed on overall satisfaction a significant difference (0.01 and 0.00, resp.) between the search engines AllTheWeb (avg: 4.32, std: 1.53) and Google (avg: 5.97, std: 0.87), and Google (avg: 5.97, std: 0.87) and Vivisimo (avg: 4.55, std: 1.47).

6.2 Retrieval Performance

The discussion of the results of the retrieval performance analysis is limited here to a discussion of the *summary statistics* and the *precision at document cutoff levels*. However a complete analysis is available, using the TREC evaluation scripts.

Summary Statistics
The summary statistics (Table 5) show that after evaluating the results of 37 topics, AllTheWeb, Google, and Vivisimo retrieved respectively 703, 738, and 733 documents. More importantly, the retrieval strategy of Vivisimo, i.e. a meta-search approach [8], leads to a higher recall and precision, than achieved by AllTheWeb and Google.

Precision at Document Cutoff Levels
A more closer look into the ranking mechanisms of the three search engines, shows that for the lower document cutoff levels (>10) the search engines have the same performance in terms of precision (Figure 3. However, the higher document cutoff levels (<5) clearly show that Vivisimo and AllTheWeb perform significantly better than Google. Apparently, the meta search approach,

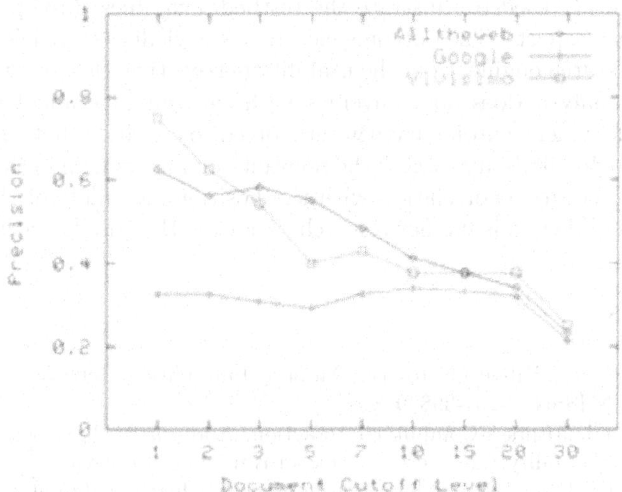

Fig. 3. Precision at document cutoff levels.

i.e. combination of results found by different search engines, allows Vivisimo to more frequently rank the relevant documents at the first position of the list, than Google and even AllTheWeb.

6.3 Usability Versus Retrieval Performance

The results of case study show a discrepancy between the outcomes of the usability experiment and the retrieval performance experiment, like found by Turpin[4]. Based on the retrieval performance experiment, Turpin might be correct to suggests that users are likely to browse in documents down the list to find relevant information. However the positioning measure of the usability experiment shows that users are very well capable of finding the relevant information within the top ranked documents. This is not in-line with Turpin's findings. We observed that users would rather refine their search than browse through the lower ranked documents.

7 Conclusions and Future Work

The evaluation of retrieval systems is a time consuming and complex task, that often reaches beyond the expertise of the researcher. TERS aims to provide a generic platform that can be used for the evaluation of different classes of retrieval systems. In addition it allows to investigate the correlation between the two types of evaluation supported by TERS: *usability testing* and *retrieval performance analysis*. Future work will include a tighter integration of the experiments and more extensive support for the analysis of the raw results, such as described above.

The case study used to illustrate the testbed, examines three public search engines on both aspects. The outcome clearly acknowledges Google's position as most popular search engine, from the usability perspective. However the retrieval performance analysis does not converges with this outcome and based on the precision-at-document-cutoff curves we are forced to conclude that this is mainly caused by Google's inability to rank the relevant documents high in the result list. This reveals a negative correlation with the positioning results of the usability experiment, and demands further research. Knowing this, do you still feel lucky?

References

1. Baeza-Yates, R., Ribeiro-Neto, B.: Modern Information Retrieval. ACM Press (1999) ISBN_ISSN: 0-201-39829-X.
2. Preece, J., ed.: Human-Computer Interaction. Addison-Wesley (1994)
3. Nielsen, J.: Usability Engineering. Morgan Kaufmann Publishers (1994)
4. Turpin, A.H., Hersh, W.: Why batch and user evaluations do not give the same results. In: Proceedings of the 24th annual international ACM SIGIR conference on Research and Development in Information Retrieval, ACM Press (2001) 225–231
5. Google: Case study search engine. `http://www.google.com/ncr` (1998)
6. Alltheweb: Case study search engine. `http://www.alltheweb.com/` (1999)
7. Vivisimo: Case study search engine. `http://www.vivisimo/` (2000)
8. Zhao, D.J., Lee, D.L., LuoA, Q.: Meta-search method with clustering and term correlation. In: Proceedings of DASFAA 2004. (2004) 543–553
9. Jansen, B., Spink, A., Saracevic, T.: Real life, real users, and real needs: A study and analysis of user queries on the web. Information Processing and Management **36** (2000) 207– 227
10. Typke, R., Veltkamp, R.C., Wiering, F.: Searching notated polyphonic music using transportation distances. In: proceedings of ACM Multimedia 2004. (2004)
11. Graaumans, J.: A qualitative study to the usability of three xml query languages. In: Proceedings of the Dutch chapter Special Interest Group for Computer-Human Interaction - SIGCHI.NL. (2004)
12. INEX: Initiative for the evaluation of xml retrieval. `http://inex.is.informatik.uni-duisburg.de:2004/` (2004)
13. van Zwol, R.: Modelling and searching web-based document collections. Ctit ph.d. thesis series, Centre for Telematics and Information Technology (CTIT), Enschede, the Netherlands (2002)
14. Rouet, J.F.: What was I looking for? The influence of task specificity and prior knowledge on students search strategies in hypertext. Interacting with Computers **15** (2003) 409–428

A Knowledge-Based Framework for the Rapid Development of Conversational Recommenders

Dietmar Jannach and Gerold Kreutler

Institute for Business Informatics and Application Systems
University Klagenfurt
Universitätsstraße 65
9020 Klagenfurt, Austria
{dietmar.jannach, gerold.kreutler}@uni-klu.ac.at

Abstract. Web-based sales assistance systems are a valuable means to guide online customers in the decision-making and product selection process. Conversational recommenders simulate the behavior of an experienced sales expert, which is a knowledge-intensive task and requires personalized user interaction according to the customers' needs and skills. In this paper, we present the ADVISOR SUITE framework for rapid development of conversational recommenders for arbitrary domains. In the system, both the recommendation logic and the knowledge required for constructing the personalized dialog and adaptive web pages is contained in a declarative knowledge-base. The advisory application can be completely modeled using graphical tools based on a conceptual model of online sales dialogs. A template mechanism supports the automatic construction of maintainable dynamic web pages. At run-time, a controller component generically steers the interaction flow. Practical experiences from several commercial installations of the system show that development times and costs for online sales advisory systems can be significantly reduced when following the described knowledge-based approach.

1 Introduction

Customers are increasingly overwhelmed by the variety of comparable products or services available on the market. Unlike in real buying environments where sales experts with adequate experience and knowledge support customers in selecting the optimal product, in the online channel customers are generally not provided with good sales assistance. Thus, online customer assistance is not only a means to reach a competitive advantage by offering an additional value to the customers, in e-commerce it is even a necessity. Web-based sales assistance and recommendation systems are used to guide online customers in their product selection process. In order to be of real value, such systems have to simulate the behavior of a human sales assistant, i.e., elicit the customer's needs and preferences in a personal dialog ([1], [2]) and come up with one or more suitable proposals. In addition, adequate explanations for the recommendation are required in order to increase the customer's confidence in his buying decision. Such dialogs have to be carried out in a *conversational* style ([3], [4]), i.e. with a mixed-initiative interaction.

X. Zhou et al. (Eds.): WISE 2004, LNCS 3306, pp. 390–402, 2004.
© Springer-Verlag Berlin Heidelberg 2004

In a real world conversation, there are two types of knowledge that an experienced sales assistant exploits. First, there is the basic recommendation knowledge to determine the suitable product according to the customer's needs and preferences. Second, the sales assistant needs to know *how* to acquire the real customer's needs. Intuitively, he will therefore adapt his conversation style to the customer's skills and then ask different questions or offer adequate explanations, depending on the current situation.

The goal of the ADVISOR SUITE project was to develop a framework and corresponding tools for rapidly building intelligent, maintainable conversational recommenders for arbitrary domains. Using an *expert system* is the natural choice for such a problem, as the expert's knowledge is made explicit and stored in a declarative knowledge base that is strictly separated from domain-independent recommendation algorithms. In order to fully exploit the benefits of a knowledge-based system, the expert knowledge about the different conversation styles also has to be formalized. This, however, leads to the problem that the user interface of such an application has to be extremely flexible and dynamic; during an interactive advisory session, the customer's characteristics have to be continuously evaluated based on the answers to different questions, and the dialog flow as well as the presentation style has to be adapted dynamically.

There are some important requirements to be respected in the design of such a recommendation system. First, the dialog pages must be robust against changes in the knowledge base, i.e., the questions to be displayed to the customer, the possible answers, as well as other personalized text fragments have to be dynamically retrieved from the repository. Second, these dynamic pages have to be simple, comprehensible, and maintainable by a web developer who has to adapt the layout using standard HTML and style sheets, such that it is aligned e.g., with the company's corporate design. Finally, there have to be adequate tools and intuitive conceptual models, such that the typically costly process of making the expert's knowledge explicit is simplified.

The software framework presented in this paper illustrates a practical application where several best-practices from the field of Web Engineering (e.g., [5], [6], [7], [8]) are implemented for a specific kind of web applications, i.e., conversational recommenders. In the following sections, the main architecture, implementation details, as well as practical experiences from commercial applications of the system are described and a comparison with other approaches in the area is drawn.

2 Overall Architecture

Figure 1 sketches the overall architecture of the system. All of the required expert knowledge is stored in a common repository built on top of a relational database system ([9], [10]). The ADVISOR SUITE system comprises a set of graphical knowledge acquisition tools that are used by the knowledge engineer and the domain expert for modeling the recommendation logic as well as the interaction and personalization knowledge. The "user characteristics", i.e., his/her preferences, needs, and wishes are the main pieces of knowledge which are elicited in an advisory dialog either by direct questioning the online customer or by indirect reasoning. These characteristics determine the products to be proposed as well as the interaction and presentation style.

Based on the modeled information about the dialog, e.g., the definition or the dialog screens, questions, questions' styles or dialog sequences, the *GUI Generation Module* is used to automate the web page development process. Therefore, this module automatically constructs the source code for the corresponding dynamic web pages by using a *template* mechanism which is described in a later section.

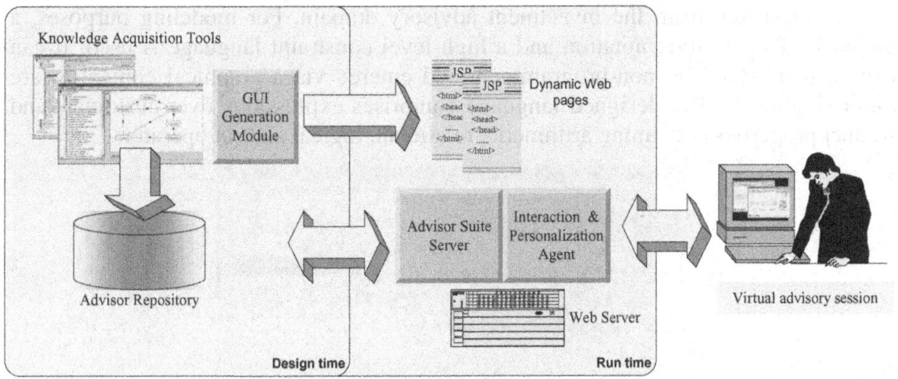

Fig. 1. Architecture of the framework

At run-time, the sales advisory application runs on a standard web server. For each customer session, an *Interaction and Personalization Agent* manages the interaction with its client and forwards the user to the correct dialog screens. The agent also communicates with a *Server Module* that implements the core reasoning logic, e.g., product recommendation based on the customer's characteristics. The Server module itself loads the knowledge from the repository on start-up and also stores information to the repository, like all interaction data, customer properties, session statistics, and other information collected by the interaction agent.

3 Modeling the Sales Assistance System

When developing an expert system, elicitation and formalization of the expert knowledge are the critical tasks. As such, it is important to have an adequate and intuitive form of knowledge representation that can be easily understood by domain experts. The whole advisory process in the ADVISOR SUITE system is driven by the customer properties which are modeled as variables that can take one or more predefined values from a given domain. One simple example is the *user expertise*, i.e., the customer could be asked for a self-assessment of his knowledge level at the beginning of the dialog. Corresponding to the variable's domain, possible values are for instance *"beginner"*, *"advanced"*, or *"expert"*. The customer's answers (i.e., his profile) consequently influence both the set of products to be recommended as well as the subsequent dialog steps, as different questions for experts and beginners could be defined. Note that in some domains the real user characteristics cannot be acquired based on self-assessment by direct questioning alone, e.g., when determining the risk class of a customer in investment advisory. For such cases, ADVISOR SUITE also supports indirect reasoning on customer properties based on expert knowledge.

In this paper, we do not go in detail of the constraint-based recommendation algorithms. Basically, the domain expert defines *filtering rules* that relate customer characteristics to product properties like "*If the customer is a beginner and has no adequate financial background, do not recommend investment products with a high risk*", an example taken from the investment advisory domain. For modeling purposes, a classical "if-then" style notation and a high-level constraint language is used. It can also be understood by non-programmers and entered via a graphical context-aware editor (Figure 2). The designed language comprises expressions over customer- and product properties containing arithmetic, relational, logical and set operators.

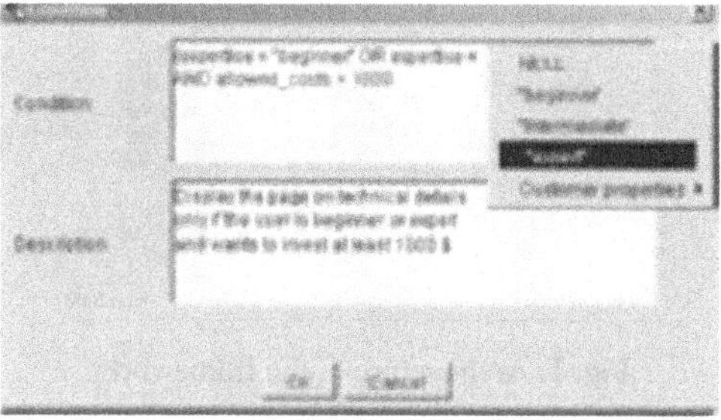

Fig. 2. Context-aware condition editor

After the application of all filter constraints, possibly no suitable products could remain. In this case, we use an algorithm based on Hierarchical Constraint Satisfaction [11] for priority-based filter relaxation. Furthermore, in order to increase the customer's confidence, the sets of applied and relaxed filters are used to construct an explanation of the recommendation. Finally, for computing a personalized ranking of the remaining products that takes the user's preferences and interests into account, a standard multi-attribute utility technique (MAUT, [12]) is applied.

The acquisition of the customer characteristics by direct questioning and indirect reasoning is done in an interactive advisory session. Therefore, these characteristics are also the starting point for designing the personalized dialog flow. In order to simplify this modeling step, we base it on a generic, conceptual model of a sales advisory application and a corresponding graphical notation. There were two driving factors in the design of that conceptual model. First, we have to use a terminology and a notation that is understandable by domain experts, but still has a defined semantics for automating the application construction process in later steps. Intentionally, we did not rely on standard methods for modeling application dynamics like UML State Diagrams [13] or Petri Nets for representation purposes, because from our experiences domain experts are not acquainted with defined technical terms like "state" or "transition". Second, the gap between the model of the application and the resulting web pages and other components has to be kept small in order to be able to directly relate changes in the model to changes in the application.

Figure 3 sketches conceptual model of a sales assistance application in a UML class diagram. The advisory application consists of a set of dialog pages, whereby on each page a set of questions and their possible answers can be displayed in a given style, e.g., as radio buttons. Note that these questions and answers can correspond both to customer characteristics and product properties, i.e., the customer can also state his requirements on the basis of technical product features. Further, for questions and answers explanatory texts in multi-lingual versions can be defined. In order to model the dialog flow, each page has a set of possible successor pages, whereby for each of them a transition condition over the customer properties can be defined. These conditions are again modelled using the system's constraint language with a context aware editor (see Figure 2) and are evaluated at run-time by the *Interaction and Personalization Agent* that determines the next dialog page. Furthermore, the whole dialog can be organized in phases, which is typically used to provide the customer feedback about the dialog's progress or additional navigation possibilities.

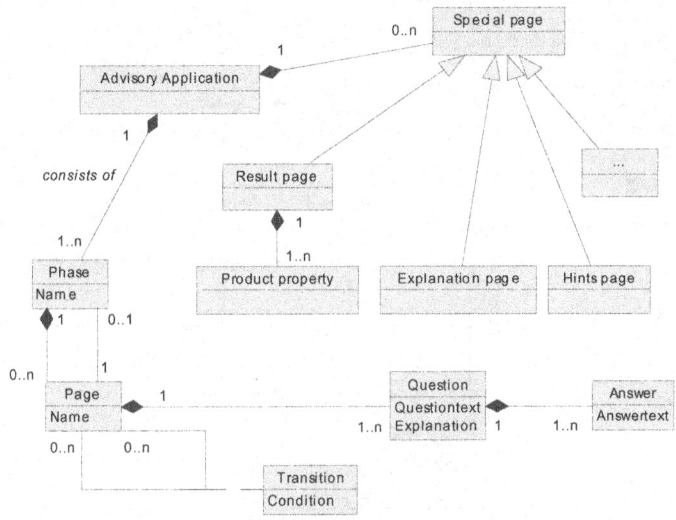

Fig. 3. UML model of an advisory application

In addition to application-specific pages, there are also domain-independent *special pages*, like a page where the results are displayed or where the explanations for the proposal are presented. In most cases, these pages are quite similar for different domains and only differ in the set of product properties to be displayed or in the layout and positioning of the elements. For instance, one special page is the one where *hints* are displayed during the dialog. We allow domain experts to model conditions when the standard dialog flow should be actively interrupted by the system. Typically, this is done when the customer's answers are conflicting, or in situations when an experienced sales assistant would provide additional explanations or hints. This feature is also commonly used for cross-selling and up-selling purposes. The interruption of the dialog depends on the current customer's characteristics and the corresponding conditions that are again evaluated by the Interaction Agent at run-time.

In order to support the domain experts in modeling the interaction flow, graphical modeling tools are integrated in the ADVISOR SUITE system. Figure 4 shows a screenshot of this tool with a simple page flow from the domain of digital cameras.

4 User Interface Generation

One of the major goals of the ADVISOR SUITE project was to automate the development process for the web application as far as possible. This feature should allow us to reduce the overall development and maintenance times, guarantee consistent high quality of the web application, and provide rapid prototyping facilities without the need for highly skilled web developers.

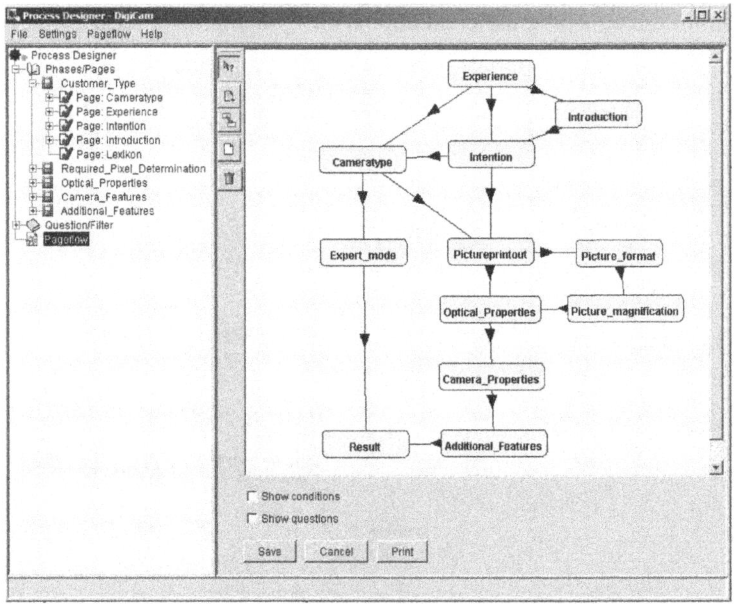

Fig. 4. Dialog modeling tool

The approach taken in the ADVISOR SUITE system relies on two basic techniques. First, we make extensive use of *Custom Tags* [14] in the generated dynamic *Java Server Pages (JSP)*[1]. *Custom Tags* are syntactically similar to standard HTML tags and can be included in the application's HTML code. Internally, however, they implement arbitrary application-specific functionality and behavior. This technique strictly separates static HTML code from Java code or other scripting code that determines the dynamics of the page. Therefore, one consistent "programming" model is used.

The listing fragment in Figure 5 shows how custom tags are included in standard HTML code. In this example, predefined tags are used to display a question corresponding to a customer characteristic together with the possible answers in an HTML table element. Internally, the custom tag evaluates the current customer's characteristics and retrieves the personalized question text and the possible answers that are defined in the knowledge base and displays the corresponding information, e.g. in the language of the current customer. The tags also transparently manage the communi-

[1] see http://java.sun.com

cation with the Interaction Agent, e.g. for steering the dialog flow. The implementation details of the tags, however, are completely hidden for the web developer. The ADVISOR SUITE framework provides such tags for most of the functionality typically required in sales advisory applications, e.g., displaying the result products, explanations, or dialog hints. Note that using this technique, no changes in the HTML code are needed, if the contents in the knowledge base change.

The second mechanism exploited for automated application development is based on page assembly and parameterization using adaptable *templates*. This assembly task is performed by the *GUI Generation Module* after maintenance activities on the knowledge base, e.g., when a new dialog page is inserted into the page flow. In our framework, each dialog page consists of a set of predefined areas like headers, navigation area, or an area for displaying a question (see Figure 6). For these areas, small HTML templates with no more than thirty lines of HTML code are provided, that can be adapted by the web-developer, in case that the style or positioning has to be changed or additional HTML content should be included in the page.

```
<advise:question name="$QUESTION_NAME$">
<table class=QUESTIONDISPLAY>
   <tr><td>
      <advise:questiontext/>
   </td></tr>
   <advise:answers>
      <tr><td>
         <advise:radio/> <advise:optiondisplay/>
      </td></tr>
   </advise:answers>
</table>
</advise:question>
```

Fig. 5. HTML fragment with custom tags

In fact, the listing in Figure 5 is such a template for displaying a question with radio buttons for the answers, whereby the radio buttons are arranged vertically in table rows. A typical layout change in the template, for instance, would be a horizontal arrangement of the radio buttons, which only causes a small change in the template. Nevertheless, the placement of questions on pages as well as the display style like using radio buttons is defined in the process modeling tool without changes in the templates. The *GUI Generation Module* then generates one Java Server Page for each page defined in the conceptual model and replaces the placeholders (e.g., $QUESTION_NAME$ in the example) with correct values.

The described template mechanism is robust against repeated generation of pages after maintenance activities, as the changes are done in the templates. In cases when very specific functionality that cannot be generalized to all pages has to be implemented, the generated but still readable pages can be edited. On repeated generation of the application, the changed page can be prevented from being overwritten by the Generation Module. Note that we also make extensive use of predefined Cascading Style Sheets (CSS) within the standard templates, which allows us adapt the presentation style like layout of the elements as well as positioning independently from the knowledge base content.

5 Implementation and Practical Experiences

The whole ADVISOR SUITE framework including the knowledge-based recommendation and personalization engine was built using Java and HTML technology and runs on standard web servers and relational database management systems. The integration of external data sources like pre-existing electronic product fact sheets can be done on the basis of a Java database connectivity (JDBC) interface or an XML-based data exchange format.

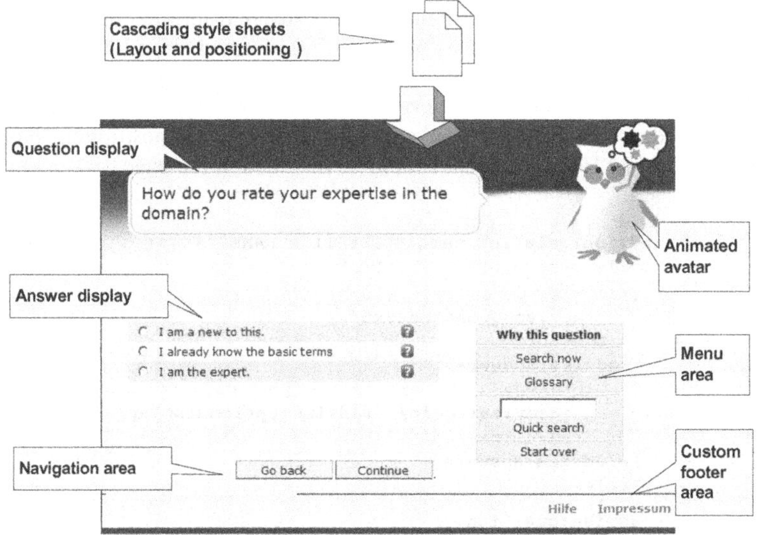

Fig. 6. Structure of a generated page

From the point of view of development, we experienced that the consistent use of technologies significantly increases the quality of the software and the interoperability between the individual components. This holds both for the internal quality of the framework as well as for the generated sales advisory web applications. In order to avoid maintenance problems in the highly interactive web application, we also minimized the usage of client-side scripting technology like *JavaScript*. Furthermore, typical performance issues that potentially arise in Java-based applications are addressed by extensive data caching. In addition, a pre-compilation mechanism for fast processing of filtering rules and personalization conditions increases performance. In a practical setting with an installation on one of Austria's largest e-commerce web sites[2], around twenty thousand full advisory sessions in the first few days did not cause any performance problems, whereby only standard hard- and software for the Web server was used.

Besides increased customer satisfaction by the value adding service, companies offering online sales assistance systems also profit from the new information provided by the system. As mentioned before, the ADVISOR SUITE framework collects information gathered during the customer dialog, e.g., interaction data, session data, or cus-

[2] With respect to unique daily visits, http://www.geizhals.at

tomer characteristics. Thus, companies can learn about their customers and their preferences and desires, which is necessary for a successful Customer Relationship Management (CRM, [15]). As an example, the information about the customers' self-assessment of the expertise can be useful in order to tailor the online service to this target group. On the other hand, the evaluation of click-behavior of the online users can be helpful to improve the advisory application itself, e.g., it is possible to determine if the dialogue is terminated by the users prematurely. Such an analysis can be supported by advanced Web Mining techniques [16], which will be part of our future work.

Up to now, several commercial sales assistance systems were built with the ADVISOR SUITE framework, whereby the application areas range from technical products like digital cameras or video projectors, to complex domains like investment advisory in private banking, as well as to "quality and taste" domains like fine cigars or vacation planning. Our experiences show that the overall development times (and the corresponding costs) for the sales assistance application are extremely short. For most domains, the initial setup of the knowledge base including the basic design of the dialog can be done in very few workshop days with the help of a knowledge engineer. Although the provided development tools were typically not directly used by the domain expert for the initial setup and prototyping phase, they served as a good basis for communication in these phases. Later maintenance activities, however, required the help of the knowledge engineer only in few cases.

The development times for the final web user interface varied with the specific requirements on the layout that was mostly determined by the existing web site. In some cases, only minor changes in the generated application's layout were required, in other cases more efforts had to be spent for the implementation of domain-dependent, specific application-behaviour or for a smooth integration into an existing web site. Our experiences show that the realization of the advisory service in a "wizard-style" separate application window was well appreciated by the users mostly because the recommendation process can be experienced as an easy-to-follow and focused task. From a technical point of view, easy integration of our system into existing web sites is ensured by the consistent use of standard technologies.

In all cases, however, we found that the maintenance or extension of the generated pages was no problematic issue and could be done by a web developer without advanced programming skills. In fact, by using the described Custom Tags and standard HTML, the generated pages remain small and readable and the developers soon understand how the pages are assembled. Note that specific extensions for a customized behaviour of the application can be incorporated into the application by adding arbitrary *Java Server Pages* code to the generated pages or the templates, whereby also an Application Programming Interface (API) for the communication with the advisory server is provided.

As a result, the quality of the web pages of the application remained at a high level, as many tasks like maintenance of multi-lingual version, management and automatic logging of user inputs in the HTTP session, or communication with the web server are already automated. Moreover, the given structure of the generated web application guarantees that the clear separation of the underlying model, the page flow control, as well as the presentation style with style sheets in the sense of the Model-View-Controller concept [17] is consequently obeyed.

6 Related Work

Applications that are built with ADVISOR SUITE belong to the class of conversational recommender systems (see, e.g., [3] and [4]) which have the advantage that the user can be guided in the decision process in a personalized dialogue. When compared to the work of [4], differences can be found for instance with respect to the possible complexity of dialogues, which is somewhat more restricted in our work. Bridge [4], for instance, focuses on a formal "dialog grammar", drawing ideas from Conversational Analysis for defining conversational dialogs. Although more complex dialogs can be modeled, we argue that this formal, domain-independent approach is problematic with respect to knowledge acquisition, because it is harder to understand for domain experts. In addition, when the dialogs become more "natural", some systems suffer from the problem that end users attribute to the system more intelligence than is warranted. Overall, in this paper we have mainly focused on the engineering and maintenance aspects of conversational recommender systems than on the personalization or recommendation functionality itself. Some functional features of our system, however, like the generation of adequate explanations which are made possible by the consistent knowledge-based approach, cannot be found in other conversational recommender systems.

In the field of *Web Engineering*, several approaches have been presented over the last years that aim at applying state-of-the-art Software Engineering practices to the development of such web applications, or extend such common methods to fit the specific requirements of these applications. The main goal is to support a better design, structuring, and understanding of data-intensive web applications by the use of abstractions, corresponding conceptual models, and graphical notations.

The Web Modeling Language (WebML) ([5], [18][3]), for instance, defines a *data model* that extends Entity/Relationship diagrams to capture relevant entities and relationships in the domain; a *hypertext model*, that specifies the content units that make up the page; and *links* that express navigation possibilities. Another approach, HDM/OOHDM (Object Oriented Hypermedia Design, [6]) uses an extended UML [13] notation to model the data view and introduce *navigational classes* (nodes, links and access structures) and *navigational contexts* for the critical part of navigation modeling in web applications in order to separate it from data and interface design. In recent work (e.g., [7]), an even more general architecture for building different families of web applications is introduced. Furthermore, some existing modeling methods are extended in order to support the conceptual design of web applications, for instance UML using stereotypes [19] or the OO-Method [8]. The main focus of these approaches is a smooth integration of web application specific concepts into a general software production process, which enables automatic generation of parts of the code on the basis of the conceptual models.

Our work differs from the above-mentioned approaches insofar, as we do not aim at providing a comprehensive methodology for developing web applications in general, but rather limit ourselves to conceptual modeling and development support for a specific family of applications in the sense of [7], i.e., web-based sales assistance systems. Nonetheless, several concepts of such general *Web Engineering* approaches are instantiated in a particular form in the ADVISOR SUITE system. First, there is a

[3] See also http://www.webml.org

clear separation of the different aspects of the application, whereby the application is not data-intensive, but knowledge-driven. Therefore, the underlying *model* is not a data model in terms of a class diagram describing data structures, but rather a knowledge-base consisting of expert rules over problem variables. The model of the application's dynamics – the dialog flow – is quite similar to the above-mentioned approaches and is in our case based on a model of the application's web pages and navigational links between them. In contrast to general approaches, however, we did not chose a technically oriented notation like *state diagrams*, but we utilize a problem-oriented, proprietary notation for the target users, i.e. domain experts, who usually have not sufficient expertise in standard conceptual modeling techniques.

The separation of the page content and its presentation in our framework is very rigid. In the modeling phase only the phases, pages, and the questions to be displayed as well as the basic presentation template is chosen. The actual layout and presentation style is determined by the style sheets and is not influenced by changes in the dialog flow. Nevertheless, the limitations of the Model-View-Controller concept in the context of interactive hypermedia techniques [7], where the navigational logic is in many cases mixed with interface layout, are addressed by the use of a knowledge-based, generic controller component that dynamically computes navigational links and page successor relations in the context of the current user's characteristics. The usage of one generic dialog model instead of several contextual models also allows us also to keep it at a manageable size.

Because of their targeted level of generality, the automated page and application generation mechanism of ADVISOR SUITE can not be found in the general approaches. However, compared to the WebML approach, the basic structure of the dialog pages can be seen as part of an instance of the *hypertext model* that pre-defines the individual units of which a page consists. The UML model describing the general structure of the generated application (Figure 3) can be regarded as an *instance* of a conceptual model or a typical pattern of a sales assistance application, and could also be expressed in the notation of [18] or [19].

In addition to the work of existing approaches from the Web Engineering field, we also see extended tool support during the whole development cycle as an important issue. The modeling tools provided in the ADVISOR SUITE framework enables rapid prototyping cycles during the analysis (knowledge acquisition) phase, which has shown to be extremely helpful. Moreover, the quality of the resulting applications can be increased by the usage of properly engineered HTML templates and custom tags. Finally, the presented framework also provides basic tool support for HTML-editing and resource management consistently into the web development process, as it is explicitly mentioned as a focus of the work in [8].

Some correspondence can also be found to the field of *Domain-Specific Modeling* – DSM ([20], [21], [22]). In contrast to general modeling languages like UML, domain-specific modeling languages are based on concepts and the specific semantics of the particular application domain and serve as starting point for automated code generation. Beside that increased automation of the software development process, these approaches have also the advantage that the domain-specific notation and terminology can be more easily understood by the domain experts. The domain-oriented modeling techniques and the code generation capabilities of ADVISOR SUITE can be seen as such an DSM approach that enables domain experts to express their knowledge on a high abstraction level that can be exploited to generate a executable web-based application.

7 Conclusions

In this paper we have described a framework for rapid development of maintainable conversational recommenders. We follow a consistent knowledge-based approach both for the core recommendation task as well as for the design of a web interface that has to support complex and personalized user interaction. The usage of graphical knowledge acquisition tools, a conceptual model of the application, and automated web page generation based on templates allowed us to significantly reduce development efforts, whereby also the internal quality of the generated web application can be kept at a high level.

Compared with popular approaches from the area of Web Engineering, the work presented in this paper in many facets can be regarded as an implementation of best-practices from different methods with a difference of a knowledge-driven underlying problem and an end-user oriented notation and terminology.

Future work will include data mining techniques to be able to better exploit the information collected during the customer interactions, both for supporting CRM-related analysis tasks as well as to increase the quality of the recommendation process by analyzing user behavior. Further research will also be done towards the generalization of the presented techniques for dialog and navigation modeling for other application domains that require personalized user interactions.

References

1. Ardissono, L., Felfernig, A., Friedrich, G., Goy, A., Jannach, D., Petrone, G., Schäfer, R., and Zanker, M.: A Framework for the Development of Personalized, Distributed Web-Based Configuration Systems, *AI Magazine*, 24 (3), Fall 2003, 93-110.
2. Ardissono, L., Felfernig, A., Friedrich, G., Goy, A., Jannach, D., Petrone, G., Schäfer, R., and Zanker, M.: Personalizing on-line configuration of products and services, *Proceedings 15th European Conference on Artificial Intelligence*, Lyon, France, IOS Press, 2000.
3. Thompson, C.A., Göker, M.H., Langley, P.: A Personalized Systems for Conversational Recommendations, *Journal of Artificial Intelligence Research*, 21, 2004, pp. 393-428.
4. Bridge, D.: Towards Conversational Recommender Systems: A Dialogue Grammar Approach, *Procs. of the Workshop in Mixed-Initiative Case-Based Reasoning*, Workshop Programme at the Sixth European Conference in Case-Based Reasoning, pp. 9-22, 2002.
5. Ceri, S., Fraternali, P., and Matera, M.: Conceptual Modeling of Data-Intensive Web Applications. *IEEE Internet Computing*, 6 (4), pp. 20-30.
6. Rossi, G., Schwabe, D., Esmeraldo, L., Lyardet, F.: Engineering Web Applications for Reuse, *IEEE Multimedia*, 8 (1), 2001, pp. 20-31.
7. Jacyntho, M.D., Schwabe, D., Rossi, G.: A Software Architecture for Structuring complex Web Applications, *Journal of Web Engineering*, 1 (1), October 2002, pp. 37-60.
8. Gomez, J., Cachero, C., Pastor, O.: Extending a Conceptual Modelling Approach to Web Application Design, *Proc. of the 1st International Workshop on Web-Oriented Software Technology*, Valencia, Spain, June, 2001.
9. Jannach, D.: Advisor Suite – A knowledge-based sales advisory system, *Proc. of the 16th European Conference on Artificial Intelligence – 3rd Prestigious Applications Intelligent Systems Conference*, Valencia, Spain, 2004, pp. 720-724.
10. Jannach, D., Kreutler G.: Building on-line sales assistance systems with ADVISOR SUITE, *Proc. of the 16th International Conference on Software Engineering and Knowledge Engineering (SEKE 04)*, Banff, Canada 2004, pp. 110-116.

11. Schiex, T., Fargier, H., Verfaille, G.: Valued Constraint Satisfaction Problems: Hard and Easy Problems, Proc. of *International Joint Conference on Artificial Intelligence (IJCAI'95)*, Montreal, Canada, 1995, pp. 631-639.
12. von Winterfeldt, D., Edwards, W.: Decision Analysis and Behavioral Research, Cambridge University Press, Cambridge, UK, 1986.
13. Rumbaugh, J., Jacobson, I., Booch, G.: The Unified Modeling Language Reference Manual, Addison-Wesley, 1998.
14. Goodwill, J.: Mastering JSP Custom Tags and Tag Libraries, Wiley Publishers, 2002.
15. Berson, A., Smith, S., Thearling, K.: Building data mining applications for CRM. McGraw-Hill, New York, 2000.
16. Kosala, R., Blockeel, H.: Web mining research: A survey. *SIGKDD Explorations* 2 (1), 2000, pp. 1-15.
17. Krasner G.E., Pope S.T.: A Description of the Model-View-Controller User Interface Paradigm in the Smalltalk-80 System. ParcPlace Systems Inc., Mountain View, 1988.
18. Ceri, S., Fraternali, P., Bongio, A.: Web Modeling Language (WebML): a Modeling Language for Designing Web Sites, *Computer Networks*, 33, 2000, Elsevier, pp. 137-157.
19. Conallen, J.: Building Web Applications with UML, Addison Wesley, Reading, 2000.
20. Gray, J., Rossi, M., Tolvanen, J.-P. (Eds.): Domain-Specific Modeling with Visual Languages, *Journal of Visual Languages & Computing* 15 (3-4), June-August 2004, pp. 207-330.
21. Tolvanen, J.-P., Kelly, S.: Domänenspezifische Modellierung, *ObjektSpektrum*, 4/2004, pp. 30-35.
22. MetaCase Corp.: Domain-specific modeling: 10 times faster than UML. White Paper, available online at http://www.metacase.com/, August 2004.

Categorizing Web Information on Subject with Statistical Language Modeling

Xindong Zhou[1], Ting Wang[2], Huiping Zhou, and Huowang Chen

National Laboratory for Parallel and Distributed Processing,
Changsha, Hunan, P.R.China 410073
[1] zhouxindong@sohu.com, [2] wonderwang70@hotmail.com

Abstract. With the rapid growth of the available information on the Internet, it is more difficult for us to find the relevant information quickly on the Web. Text classification, one of the most useful web information processing tools, has been paid more and more attention recently. Instead of using traditional classification models, we apply *n*-gram language models to classify Chinese Web text information on subject. We investigate several factors that have important effect on the performance of *n*-gram models, including various order *n*, different smoothing techniques, and different granularity of textual representation unit in Chinese. The experiment result indicates that bi-gram model based on word and tri-gram model based on character outperform others, achieving approximately 90% evaluated by *F1* score.

1 Introduction

With the volume of information available on the Internet continues to increase, the need for tools that can help users easy to find, filter and manage the information quickly on the Web is growing accordingly [1]. Many tasks related to free-text processing, such as document retrieval, categorization, routing and filtering systems or agents, are usually based on text classification. A number of classification models have been developed and worked well in practice, which include Rocchio relevant feedback algorithm [2], Naive Bayes classifier [2], Decision Tree classifier [3], Regression methods [3], Neural networks [3], and Example-based classifier [3].

Statistical language modeling [4] has been widely used in many fields, including speech recognition, OCR, and machine translation. Most of the previous works use statistical language modeling in the field of text categorization and mainly focus on exploiting collocation or co-occurrence with the forms of bi-gram or tri-gram so as to present documents textual more precisely, or avoiding the word segmentation issues that always arise in Chinese or other Asian language. Peng [5] proposed Chain Augmented Naive Bayes classifier (CAN), which allows a local Markov chain depended on the context in calculating the class conditional probability of documents belong to categories in Naive Bayes model, relaxing some of the independence assumptions.

This paper applies the statistical language modeling—*n*-gram models [6] as text classifiers directly, treating documents as random observation sequences while traditional classifying models look documents as bag of words, the category in which a document can be observed with the biggest probability is considered as the result of

X. Zhou et al. (Eds.): WISE 2004, LNCS 3306, pp. 403–408, 2004.
© Springer-Verlag Berlin Heidelberg 2004

classification. The goal of learner is to construct a language model for each category on its training corpus, which is quite different to traditional classifying models that based on representing documents as points in a multi-dimension vector space.

We investigate several factors that have impact on the performance of the *n*-gram models, including various order *n*, alternative granularity unit in Chinese textual representation, and the effect of different smoothing methods. Especially for Good-Turing smoothing [4], we adapt it to being used independently in language models.

2 Statistical Language Modeling

Statistical language modeling [6] has been widely used in the research of natural language processing. From the view of statistical language modeling, any string (can be imagined as the combination of words) could be accepted, and the distinction among them is the different possibility of acceptance. There are a few types of statistical language modeling, including *n*-gram Language Models [6], Hidden Markov Model [7], Probabilistic Context Free Grammar [6], and Probabilistic Link Grammar [8]. Among them the most widely used model, by far, is *n*-gram models. In our experiment, we will apply it as text classifier.

2.1 *n*-Gram Language Models

The *n*-gram language model has been used successfully in many fields; it captures the local constraint of natural language successfully [9]. Assuming there is a document *d*: $w_1w_2 \ldots w_n$, where w_i means the textual presentation unit in a specified language. How can we calculate its observed probability in a certain category *c*: $P_c(d)$? In *n*-gram models, according the chain rule, we can calculate it as follow:

$$P_c(d) = P_c(w_1 w_2 \cdots w_n) = p_c(w_1) p_c(w_2 \mid w_1) \cdots p_c(w_n \mid w_1, \cdots, w_{n-1}) \tag{1}$$

2.2 Smoothing Methods

Now the problem we should deal with is how to calculate the conditional probability: $p(w_i|w_1 \ldots w_{i-1})$. Usually we use the maximum likelihood estimate (MLE):

$$p(w_i \mid w_1 \cdots w_{i-1}) = \frac{p(w_1 \cdots w_i)}{p(w_1 \cdots w_{i-1})} \approx \frac{C(w_1 \cdots w_i)}{C(w_1 \cdots w_{i-1})} \tag{2}$$

where *C*(*s*) means the frequency of *s* occurs in training corpus. As the number of parameters that need to be estimated is tremendous, an unavoidable and crucial problem is how to deal with the case that *C*(*s*)=0, namely the problem of sparse data [9]. Smoothing techniques, tending to make distribution more uniform by adjusting low probabilities such as zero probabilities upward and high probabilities downward, are needed. There are several types of smoothing techniques: additive [4], discounting [4][5], back-off [4][5], and interpolation [4].

Here we introduce a novel variation of Good-Turing (GT) smoothing method, and our purpose is making this smoothing method can be used independently and generating probabilities more detailed and reliable. We pre-define a threshold of frequency for observed events, for the grams with frequency higher than it, we use MLE, for others, we use GT smoothing to discount probabilities a little. Let n_i denotes the number of events, which occur exactly i times in training corpus. As the case $n_i = 0$ would not occurs for infrequent grams, thus it can be used independently, Let k be the threshold, for a specified gram $w_1 \ldots w_n$, if its frequency is r and $0<r<k$, then the discounting probability that gets from this specified gram is:

$$\tilde{p}_r = \frac{r - r^*}{N} = \frac{r \times n_r - (r+1)n_{r+1}}{N \times n_r} \tag{3}$$

Finally the mass of discounting probability is: $\sum_{0<r<k} n_r \times \tilde{p}_r$

How to determine the best threshold value k? The optimal value of k is chosen based on empirical observations and related to the size of training corpus closely.

3 Applying *n*-Gram Models as Text Classifiers

Text classification is a task that assigns documents to a certain category according to its contents. Since we look document as a random observed sequence, well then the appearance of words and the sequence of them can be seen as a type of language combining modes, which is very closely related to the document contents itself. The *n*-gram models are exactly the tools that attempt to reveal or capture the language combining modes for different categories. The formal definition can be described as follow: for a new document d, $d = w_1 w_2 \ldots w_n$, we can calculate the probability of d that would appears in category c as:

$$P_c(d) = P_c(w_1 \cdots w_n) \approx \prod_{i=1}^{n} p_c(w_i \mid w_{i-N+1}^{i-1}) \propto \sum_{i=1}^{n} \log p_c(w_i \mid w_{i-N+1}^{i-1}) \tag{4}$$

and the decision rule is $\arg\max_{c \in |C|} P_c(d)$.

4 Experiment Results

The corpus used in our experiments is obtained from Fudan University. Most of them are Chinese Web pages collected from Internet, consisting of news, papers, and articles. All experiment results that given below are evaluated by *F1* score.

The implementing of various smoothing techniques in our experiments is: in additive smoothing methods, the size of vocabulary is the number of distinct events occurred in training corpus, and the adjustment coefficient λ is 0.1. For absolute discounting, d is assigned to $n_1/(n_1+2*n_2)$. For adaptive Good-Turing smoothing, the threshold k is 5 for tri-gram models, and 10 for bi-gram models.

Table 1. Results on categorizing Web information (CB, additive and discounting smoothing)

n	Laplace	Lidstone	Absolute	Linear	Good-Turing	Witten-Bell
1	83.72%	83.85%	83.44%	83.29%	**83.89%**	83.61%
2	84.78%	86.6%	86.78%	86.73%	86.66%	**86.93%**
3	81.43%	86.79%	89.88%	89.37%	89.14%	**90.11%**
4	76.48%	79.07%	80.85%	81.43%	81.02%	**81.58%**

Table 2. Results on categorizing Web information (WB, additive and discounting smoothing)

n	Laplace	Lidstone	Absolute	Linear	Good-Turing	Witten-Bell
1	85.16%	85.21%	85.28%	85.49%	86.04%	**86.12%**
2	80.03%	85.09%	89.35%	89.09%	89.72%	**89.94%**
3	77.33%	82.17%	85.06%	85.18%	85.42%	**86.24%**

4.1 Experiments on Character-Based (CB) Models

One advantage of using CB n-gram models is avoiding the problem of word segmentation in Chinese. Another advantage is that there are fewer parameters need to be estimated compared with Word-Based language models, so the reliability of model parameters is higher than the WB language models with the same order n.

4.2 Experiments on Word-Based (WB) Models

In Chinese, words have been considered as the smallest unit that can carry meanings; so breaking words into characters lead to lose information inevitably. To make a language model capture more information, we investigate WB language models.

4.3 n-Gram Models Versus Traditional Classifying Models

In order to compare the performance between n-gram models and traditional classifying models, we also construct and test Rocchio classifier and Naive Bayes classifier on the same corpus.

Fig. 1 shows the *F1* scores achieved by WB bi-gram model (89.94%) and CB tri-gram model (90.11%) are higher than Rocchio classifier (86.38%) and Naive Bayes classifier (86.54%). For traditional models, feature selection is a crucial step, and there are several other factors such as weighting strategy, etc, can also affect the performance. On the other hand, all the factors mentioned above need not to be considered in n-gram models any more, so the stability of n-gram models is better than traditional models.

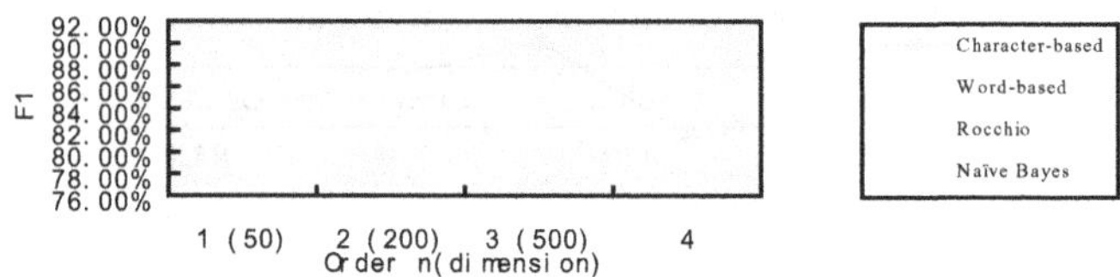

Fig. 1. Results of n-gram models (Witten-Bell smoothing), Rocchio classifier, and Naive Bayes classifier

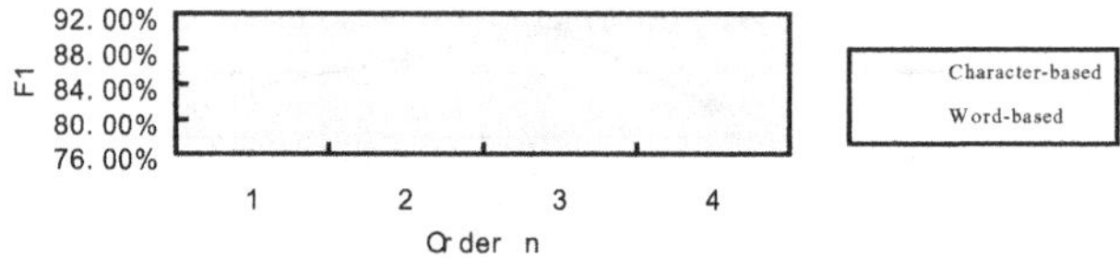

Fig. 2. Relations between $F1$ score and order n (Witten-Bell smoothing)

5 Analysis of Experiment Results

There are several important factors that can significantly affect the quality of n-gram models in Chinese. From the experiment results, we will analyze the influence of each individual factor, and give the conclusions accordingly.

5.1 Effects of Order n and CB Models Versus WB Models

The order n is a key factors that relating to the quality of language models.

For the CB models, the sparse data problem is not as serious as the WB models', so the $F1$ score increases up to the 3-gram, while WB models decreases at 3.

5.2 Effects of Smoothing Techniques

Smoothing technique is another important factor that can affect the performance of the language models, especially for the higher order models.

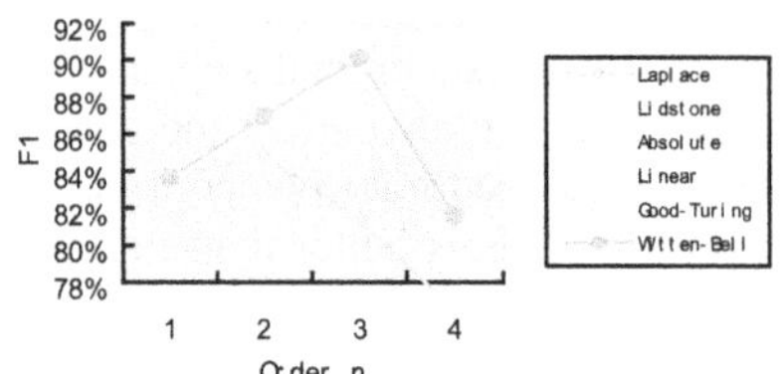

Fig. 3. Performance of smoothing techniques with CB models

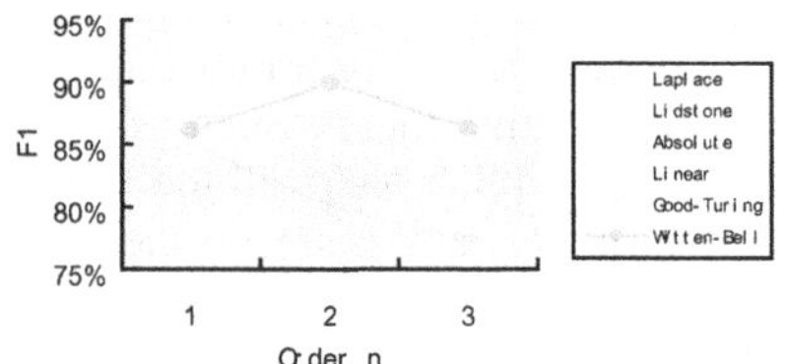

Fig. 4. Performance of smoothing techniques with WB models

We can find that Laplace smoothing is the most sensitive to the perplexity of model parameters. Lidstone smoothing has the moderate performance, and other smoothing methods' performance in parameters estimating have little difference, including our adaptive Good-Turing smoothing method.

6 Conclusions

In this paper, we apply *n*-gram language models as text classifiers directly. We also investigate several important factors that can affect the quality of statistical language models and compare the performance of *n*-gram models as classifiers with traditional classifiers on the task of Web information classification. The experiment result shows that the performance of *n*-gram language models in Chinese text classification is better than traditional classifying models.

Acknowledgement. This research is supported in part by the National High Technology Research and Development Program and the National Natural Science Foundation of China.

References

1. Aas, K. & Eikvil, L: Text Categorization: A Survey. Technical Report #941, Norwegian Computing Center, (1999)
2. Thorsten Joachim: A Probabilistic Analysis of the Rocchio Algorithm with TFIDF for Text Categorization. Processing of ICML-97□14th International Conference on Machine Learning. (1996) 143-151
3. Fabrizio Sebastiani: Machine Learning in Automated Text Categorization. ACM Computing Surveys, Vol. 34, No.1, March (2002) pp. 1-47
4. Stanley F. Chen, Joshua Goodman: An Empirical Study of Smoothing Techniques for Language Modeling. Proceedings of the Thirty-Fourth Annual Meeting of the Association for Computational Linguistics
5. Peng, F., Schuurmans, D. and Wang, S: Augmenting Naïve Bayes Classifiers with Statistical Language Models. Information Retrieval, September (2004) vol. 7, no. 3-4, pp. 317-345 (29)
6. Rosenfeld R. Two decades of Statistical Language Modeling: Where Do We Go From Here? Proceedings of the IEEE, (2000), 88 (8)
7. Christopher D Manning, Hinrich Schutze: Foundations of Statistical Natural Language Processing. London: The MIT Press, (1999)
8. Daniel Sleator and Davy Temperley: Parsing English with a Link Grammar. Carnegie Mellon University Computer Science technical report CMU-CS-91-196, October (1991)
9. Katz, Slave M: Estimation of probabilities from sparse data for the language model component of a speech recognizer. IEEE Transactions on Acoustics, Speech and Signal Processing, March (1987), ASSP-35 (3): 400-401

Optimizing Web Search Using Spreading Activation on the Clickthrough Data

Gui-Rong Xue[1], Shen Huang[1], Yong Yu[1], Hua-Jun Zeng[2], Zheng Chen[2], and Wei-Ying Ma[2]

[1] Department of Computer Science and Engineering, Shanghai Jiao Tong University, 1954 Huashan Ave., 200030 Shanghai, P.R.China
grxue@sjtu.edu.cn, {shuang, yyu}@cs.sjtu.edu.cn

[2] Microsoft Research Asia, 5F, Sigma Center
49 Zhichun Road, Beijing 100080, P.R.China
{hjzeng, zhengc, wyma}@microsoft.com

Abstract. In this paper, we propose a mining algorithm to utilize the user click-through data to improve search performance. The algorithm first explores the relationship between queries and Web pages and mine out co-visiting relationship as the virtual link among the Web pages, and then Spreading Activation mechanism is used to perform the query-dependent search. Our approach could overcome the challenges discussed above and the experimental results on a large set of MSN click-through log data show a significant improvement on search performance over the DirectHit algorithm as well as the baseline search engine.

1 Introduction

Approach based on keywords in existing Web search engines often works well when users' queries are clear and specific. However, the performance of Web search engines is often deteriorated by that search queries are often short [1] and ambiguous, and Web pages contain a lot diverse and noisy information [3][6]. This problem can be partially solved by using external evidence to enrich the content of existing Web pages – the so-called *surrogate document* approach. One of such examples is to use anchor texts as additional description of target Web pages. This is because anchor texts represent the view of a Web page by other Web editors rather than its own author. Another solution is to introduce additional description by using click-through data, which has not been extensively studied.

User click-through data can be extracted from the logs accumulated by Web search engines. These logs typically contain user-submitted search queries and the URL of Web pages clicked by users in the corresponding search results. Many valuable applications have been proposed along this direction, such as term suggestion [2][12], query expansion [3], and query clustering [4][8].

Derived from the co-citation and co-coupling methods [7][10] to find the similar papers, we propose to use the analogous method co-visiting, which is used to exploit

X. Zhou et al. (Eds.): WISE 2004, LNCS 3306, pp. 409–414, 2004.
© Springer-Verlag Berlin Heidelberg 2004

the relationship between the Web pages and the queries in the clickthrough data, to find the association relationship among the Web pages. If the two Web pages are clicked by many same queries, they are similar. We take such co-visiting relationship as the virtual link between the Web pages. Additionally, there is a weight associated with the link represent the degree of the similarity between two Web pages. Finally, the Spreading activation approach is proposed, which impose the co-visiting relationship among the Web pages, to re-rank the search result.

2 Spreading Activation on the Clickthrough Data

2.1 Problem Description

We define click-through data as a set *Session*, each of which is defined as a pair of a query and a Web page the user clicked on. We assume that Web pages *d* is relevant to the query *q* in each session for most users usually are likely to click on a relevant result.

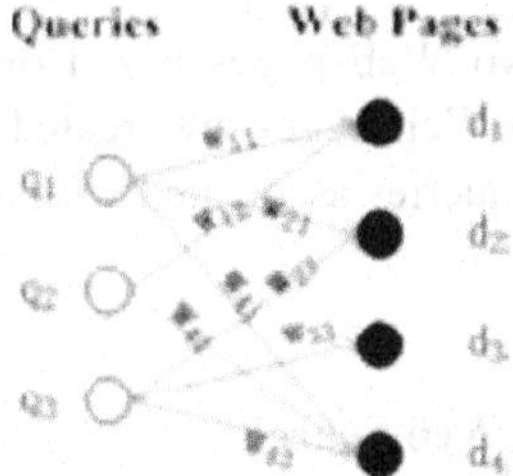

Fig. 1. Interrelations between queries and Web pages

By merging same queries and Web pages in the above sessions, click-through data could be modeled as a weighted directed bipartite graph $G=(V, E)$, where nodes in V represent Web pages and queries and edges E represent the click-throughs from a query to a clicked Web page. We can divide V into two subsets $Q=\{q_1, q_2, \ldots, q_m\}$ and $D=\{d_1, d_2, \ldots, d_n\}$ where Q represents the queries and D represents the Web pages.

Then, the problem is to efficiently find the relationship between the nodes in D by mining the bipartite graph G. Here we propose a co-visiting mining algorithm to solve the problem.

2.2 Co-Visiting Mining (CVM)

It is easy to demonstrate that DirectHit method could achieve good performance if the query click-through data is complete, i.e. each query is associated with all the related documents. But unfortunately, in the real world, each query will randomly be associated with only a few individual documents instead of whole list. This data incompleteness problem makes the performance of the DirectHit algorithm drop significantly. Deriving from the co-citation in the scientific literature [7][10][15], we develop an analogous approach to find similar Web pages. As shown in Fig.1, if the two Web pages are clicked by mostly the same queries, it is possible that two Web pages are similar. We define Web pages with such relationship as ***co-visiting*** Web pages.

Next we describe how to measure the similarity of two co-visiting Web pages using the click-through information. Precisely, the number of visit times of a Web page d_i, denoted as $visiting(d_i)$, refers to the number of the sessions containing Web page d. The number of co-visiting times of a two Web pages pair (d_i, d_j) visited by the same query, denoted $visiting(d_i, d_j)$.

Then, the similarity S between two Web pages d_i and d_j based on the co-visiting relationship can be computed as:

$$S(d_i, d_j) = \frac{visiting(d_i, d_j)}{visiting(d_i) + visiting(d_j) - visiting(d_i, d_j)} \tag{1}$$

The measure is scaled to [0, 1].

If the similarity between two Web pages based on co-visiting is greater than a minimum threshold σ, the two Web pages are treated as similar. Later experiments will show that the precision of queries associated with a given page is highest when σ is equal to 0.3.

2.3 Spreading Activation on Web Search

The technique of spreading activation is based on a model of facilitated retrieval [5] from human memory [1][9] and has at least once been implemented for the analysis of hypertext networks structure by [13]. The model assumes that the coding format of human memory is an associative network in which the most similar memory items have strongest connections [16]. Retrieval by spreading activation is initiated by activating a set of cue nodes which associatively express the meaning of the nodes be retrieved. Activation energy spread out from the cue nodes to all other related nodes modulated by the network connection weights.

Derived from the definition of spreading activation approach, we propose to use this method to re-rank the result of Web search by utilize the co-visiting information among the Web pages.

First, the user submits the query Q to the search engine and the system returns the result set D that matching the query terms. The degree of match between a Web page d_i in D and Q is computed by the retrieval system (In this paper, we take the BM2500 as relevance measurement between the query and Web pages). We denote the similarity between the d_i and Q as $sim(d_i, Q)$.

Then, we use the spreading activation approach to propagate the similarity between the d_i and Q to the co-visiting Web pages of d_i through a certain number of cycles using a propagation factor. To simplify the problem, we use a simplified version with only one cycle. In that case, the final retrieval status value of a Web page d_i that co-visiting with *m* Web pages is computed according to the following equation:

$$sim(d_i, Q) = sim(d_i, Q) + \lambda \sum_{j=1}^{m} sim(d_j, Q) \quad (2)$$

Finally, the search result is re-ranked according to the final similarity values between the Web pages and query.

3 Experiments

3.1 Data Set

Our experiments are conducted on a real click-through data which is extracted from the log of the MSN search engine [11] in August, 2003. It contains about 1.2 million query requests recorded over three hours.

Before doing experiment, all queries are converted into lower-case, stemmed by the Porter algorithm; stop words are removed in process. The query sessions sharing a same query are merged into a large query session, with the frequencies being summed up. After preprocessing, the log contains 13,894,155 sessions, 507,041 pages and 862,464 queries. We use a crawler to download the content of all Web pages contained in this log. After downloading the pages, Okapi system [14] is used to index the full text using BM25 formula.

3.2 Evaluation Criteria

The *Precision* in IR is applied to measure the performance of our proposed algorithm. Given a query *Q*, let *R* be the set of the relevant pages to the query and $|R|$ be the size of the set; let *A* be the set of top 20 results returned by our system. *Precision* is defined as:

$$Precision = \frac{|R \cap A|}{|A|} \quad (3)$$

In order to evaluate our method effectively, we also propose a new evaluation metric *Authority*. Given a query, we ask the ten volunteers to identify top 10 authoritative pages according to their own judgments. The set of 10 authoritative Web-pages is denoted by *M* and the set of top 10 results returned by search engines is denoted by *N*.

$$Authority = \frac{|M \cap N|}{|M|} \quad (4)$$

3.3 Performance

We fixed several parameters for the rest experiments. i.e. minimum similar threshold as 0.3 and the weight of the original similarity as 0.4, which are determined by extensive experiments.

First, the volunteers were asked to evaluate the *Precision* and *Authority* of search results for 20 queries. Fig. 2 shows the comparison of our approach with content based search (Content) and DirectHit (DH).

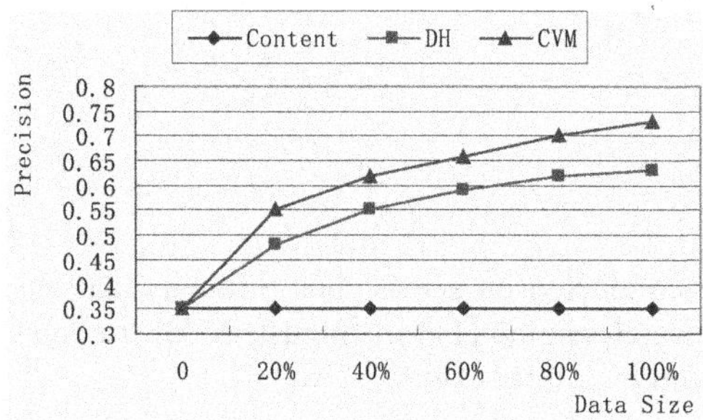

Fig. 2. The precision on different data

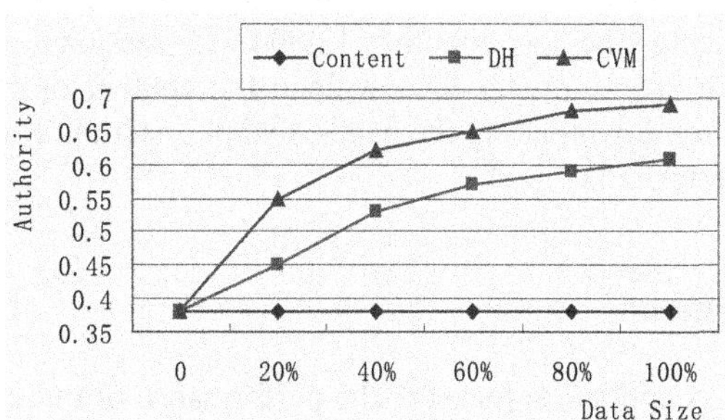

Fig. 3. The authority on different data sizes

From Fig. 2 and Fig. 3, we found that the performance of the full text search technique is poor, demonstrating the gap between the document space and the query space. When click-through data is introduced, the search performance is improved. The more click-through data is introduced, the higher is the performance of search. Co-visiting method has a highest performance in all the algorithms. Co-visiting method outperforms the DirectHit method by fully mining the implicit link relationship among the Web pages.

4 Conclusions

In this paper, we propose a novel mining algorithm to utilize click-through data. The algorithm could fully explore the interrelations between heterogeneous data objects, and effectively find the virtual link between Web pages, thus deal with the above issues. Experiment results on a large set of MSN click-through data show a significant improvement of search performance.

References

[1] A.M.Collins and E.F.Loftus. A Spreading Activation theory of Semantic Processing. Psychological Review, 82:407-428,1975.

[2] Chien-Kang Huang, Lee-Feng Chien, and Yen-Jen Oyang. Relevant term suggestion in interactive Web search based on contextual information in query session logs. *JASIST* 54(7): 638-649,2003.

[3] Cui H., Wen J.R., Nie J.Y., and Ma W.Y., Query Expansion by Mining User Logs, *IEEE Transaction on Knowledge and Data Engineering*, Vol. 15, No. 4, July/August 2003.

[4] D. Beeferman and A. Berger. Agglomerative clustering of a search engine query log. In *Proceedings of the sixth ACM SIGKDD International Conference on Knowledge Discovery and Data Mining*, pages 407-415, 2000.

[5] D.E. Meyer and R.W. Schvaneveldt. Facilitation in Recognition Pair of Words: Evidence of a dependence between Retrieval Operations. Jounal of Experimental Psychology, 90:227-234,1971.

[6] Funas, G.W., Landauer,T.K., Gomez,L.M. and Dumais, S.T. 1987. The vocabulary problem in human-system communication. *Communications of the ACM* 20,11, Pages 946-971, Nov.1987.

[7] H. Small. Co-citation in the scientific literature: A new measure of the relationship between two documents. *Journal of the American Society for Information Science*, 24:265–269, 1973.

[8] J.-R. Wen, J.-Y. Nie, and H.-J. Zhang. Clustering user queries of a search engine. In *Proceedings of the Tenth International World Wide Web Conference*, Hong Kong, May 2001.

[9] John R. Anderson. A spreading activation theory of memory. Journal pf Verbal Learning and Verbal Behaviours, 22:261-295,1983.

[10] M. M. Kessler. Bibliographic coupling between scientific papers. *American Documentation*, 14:10–25, 1963.

[11] MSN Search Engine,

[12] Nicolas J. Belkin, Helping people find what they don't know, *Communications of the ACM*, v.43 n.8, p.58-61, Aug. 2000.

[13] Peter Pirolli, James Pitkow, and Ramana Rao. Silk from a sow's ear: Extracting usable structure from the Web. In Proc. of CHI'96 (ACM), Human Factors in Computing Systems, Vancouver, Canada, Apirl 1996, ACM.

[14] Robertson, S.E. et al. Okapi at TREC-3. In *Overview of the Third Text REtrieval Conference(TREC-3)*, 109-126, 1995.

[15] R. R. Larson. Bibliometrics of the World-Wide Web: An exploratory analysis of the intellectual structure of cyberspace. In *Proceedings of the Annual Meeting of the American Society for Information Science*, Baltimore, Maryland, October 1996.

[16] W.Klimesch. The Structure of Long Term Memory: A connectivity Model of Semantic Processing. Lawrence Erlbaum and Associates, Hillsdale,1994.

AVATAR: An Advanced Multi-agent Recommender System of Personalized TV Contents by Semantic Reasoning

Yolanda Blanco-Fernández, José J. Pazos-Arias, Alberto Gil-Solla, Manuel Ramos-Cabrer, Belén Barragáns-Martínez, Martín López-Nores, Jorge García-Duque, Ana Fernández-Vilas, and Rebeca P. Díaz-Redondo

Department of Telematic Engineering, University of Vigo, 36310, Spain
{yolanda,jose,agil,mramos,belen,mlnores,jgd,avilas,rebeca}@det.uvigo.es

Abstract. In this paper a recommender system of personalized TV contents, named AVATAR[1], is presented. We propose a modular multi-agent architecture for the system, whose main novelty is the semantic reasoning about user preferences and historical logs, to improve the traditional syntactic content search. Our approach uses Semantic Web technologies – more specifically an OWL ontology – and the TV-Anytime standard to describe the TV contents. To reason about the ontology, we have defined a query language, named LIKO, for inferring knowledge from properties contained in it. In addition, we show an example of a semantic recommendation by means of some LIKO operators.

1 Introduction

Nowadays, a migration from analogue to digital TV is taking place in TV. This change has two main implications: the capacity to broadcast more channels in the same bandwidth, and the possibility to send software applications mixed with audiovisual contents. The TV recommenders play a key role in this scenario because they can help the users to find interesting contents among a large amount of irrelevant information.

Several different approaches have appeared in the field of TV recommender systems, such as Bayesian techniques [7], content-based methods [8], collaborative filtering [9], decision trees [10]. In this paper, a new recommender system is presented, named AVATAR, that combines different strategies to improve the success of recommendations. Among others, we use Bayesian techniques, semantic reasoning and profiles matching. Here the semantic reasoning approach is described, as we think it is a novel and promising method to enhance the elaborated suggestions by our system.

Such a reasoning process requires a high degree of normalization. In this regard, we use the TV-Anytime standard (*www.tv-anytime.org*), which normalizes descriptions of generic TV contents, concrete instances of programs and user profiles. On the other hand, our personalization tool needs a knowledge base to feed the reasoning process. This work extends the use of the Semantic Web [6] technologies to the TV context. So, we have implemented an ontology about TV contents according to the OWL language.

[1] Work supported by the Ministerio de Educación y Ciencia Research Project TSI2004-03677.

X. Zhou et al. (Eds.): WISE 2004, LNCS 3306, pp. 415–421, 2004.
© Springer-Verlag Berlin Heidelberg 2004

Finally, note that we conceive our system as a MHP interactive application, downloaded from the service provider through the transport stream, achieving a wide deployment.

This paper is organized as follows. Sect. 2 describes the architecture of the TV recommender proposed. In Sect. 3, we focus on different issues referred to the semantic reasoning and in Sect. 4 we show how it can be used in the context of personalized TV through an example. Finally, we present some conclusions and discuss future work.

2 The Architecture of the AVATAR Recommendation Service

In this section, the main design decisions of the AVATAR architecture are presented. We propose an open and modular architecture that allows to update the modules that generate recommendations and to add new ones that compute suggestions by other strategies.

2.1 The AVATAR Recommender System: A MHP Interactive Application

As commented in the introduction, the system must be flexible enough to be updated frequently. For this reason, we conceive our system as a MHP interactive application.

In the DVB MHP standard, applications are executed in the context of concrete services or events in a service, and, usually, they do not survive after finishing that context (*event final* or *service change*). Taking into account that AVATAR needs to record all the viewers actions beyond a concrete service, our approach integrates a special agent, named *local agent*, to know the user viewing behavior all the time.

Our prototype uses the TV-Anytime standard to store the historic logs of the users and their personal preferences about TV contents. The real format of the data stored by the *local agent* might be private and in this case, the procedure of access the information must be normalized. So, we propose a new MHP API (TV-Anytime MHP API) to provide a neutral way to access information described with TV-Anytime metadata, even though the local agent does not use this format to store these data.

2.2 AVATAR: A Modular Multi-agent Recommender System

As we said previously, we propose a modular architecture, in which the recommender is divided into two parts. The first one is related to the local software of the STB, that requests the personal data and user preferences, and records information about the TV contents already watched. This information would be accessible for the recommender through the TV-Anytime MHP API. For the second part, the MHP application implements the functionality of the recommendations service. It consists of three modules:

Recommenders. They are agents that implement the different strategies to make personalized recommendations. Fig. 1 shows three of them: an agent based on Bayesian techniques, another one based on semantic reasoning and the last one, based on profiles matching. Their recommendations are mixed by the combiner module, that is a neural network [1]. This recommendation is stored as private data and compared with the user choices to improve future suggestions. The semantic agents need a knowledge base to reason about TV contents and user preferences. The knowledge base in our system is

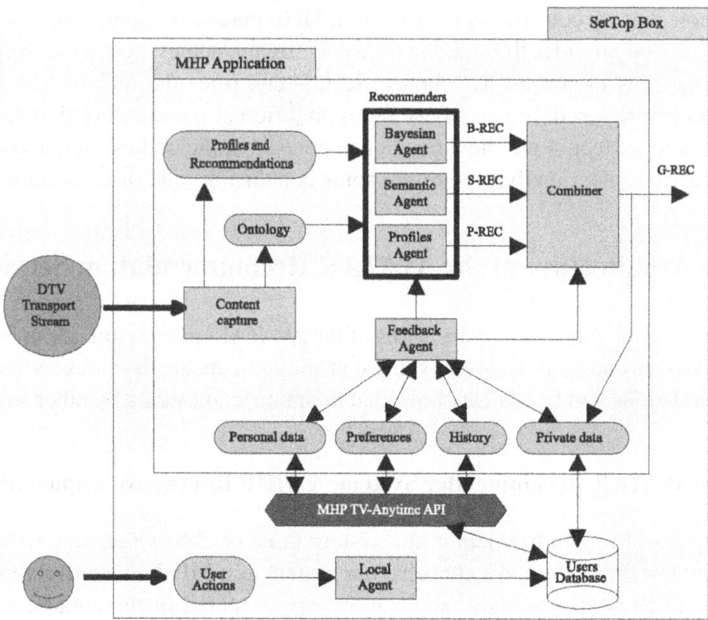

Fig. 1. The architecture of a broadcast recommender system

an OWL ontology (*http://avatar.det.uvigo.es/ontology*) that allows to share and reuse information efficiently in a multi-agent architecture [5].

Capture and classification of information. The goal of this module is the capture of the TV contents, described by TV-Anytime metadata, and their classification into the appropriate ontological classes. Besides, the tool receives a set of prototypical profiles together with recommendations for each one of them in order to reuse suggestions previously made for viewers with analogous profiles.

The feedback system. The feedback agent accesses to the feedback information stored in a user database by the TV-Anytime MHP API, updates the user profiles and feeds the recommender agents with information for the inference process.

The modular character of the architecture proposed ensures its openness. Thus, only small changes would be necessary to add new strategies to make recommendations.

3 The Semantic Reasoning Approach

The Semantic Web is a novel approach that intends to get the computers can "understand" the handled information [6]. Just like it happens in TV recommender systems, one of the main goals is to attain a high degree of personalization in the services offered to the Web users. On the other hand, the Semantic Web thinks of the Web as a repository of knowledge [2], so that there exist mechanisms to share and manage the knowledge efficiently, such as ontologies [4]. For that reasons, we propose the application of Semantic Web technologies in the domain of TV.

Table 1. The query operators of the LIKO language

Operator	*Input Parameter*	*Description*
$\triangleright$	A superclass that can also be a subclass in the ontology.	Returns a set of subclasses whose superclass is indicated in the field parameter.
$\triangleleft$	A subclass that can also be a superclass in the ontology.	Returns a set of superclasses of the subclass indicated as input parameter.
$>>$	A superproperty defined in the ontology.	Returns the subproperties of the indicated property.
$<<$	A subproperty defined in the ontology.	Returns a set of superproperties of the indicated property.
$>\Leftarrow$	Instances of classes of the ontology.	Returns the properties where the domain contains the indicated class.
$>\Rightarrow$	Instances of classes of the ontology and values of Datatype properties.	Returns a set of properties where the range contains the indicated parameter.
$>\odot$	Instances of classes or Datatype properties values.	Returns properties inferred from the transitive properties of the ontology.
$>\oplus$	Instances of classes or Datatype properties values.	Returns properties inferred from the functional properties in the ontology.
$>\ominus$	Instances of classes or Datatype properties values.	Returns the properties inferred from the inverse functional properties.
$>\hookleftarrow$	Instances of classes or datatype properties values.	Returns a set of properties inferred from symmetric properties of the ontology.

So, the OWL ontology that we have implemented is a tree with several levels. The root node is named "TV Contents". The second level consists of general programs (such as "Movies" and "Documentaries"), the third level are more specialized contents (i.e. "Action Movies" and "Nature Documentaries") and so on. The reasoning process is carried out in two phases. Firstly, AVATAR must choose a set of general contents (programs in the tree second level) according to the user profile. For that purpose, AVATAR uses a query language, named *LIKO* (see Table 1) , to reason about classes and properties contained in the TV ontology. Finally, the tool must select the appropriate instances of the chosen classes to enhance the offered recommendations.

These operators can be combined by unions or intersections. The operators that infer knowledge from transitive, functional, inverse functional and symmetric properties are implemented by the rest of *LIKO* operators. It is obvious that to infer data with the $>\odot$ operator by the ontological transitive properties, is necessary to analyze the properties range and domain (through $>\Rightarrow$ and $>\Leftarrow$, respectively), to make reasonings such as *IF* $a \to b$ *and* $b \to c$ *THEN* $a \to c$. A use example of the $>\odot$ operator is shown in Sect. 4.

4 An Example of Recommendation Based on Semantic Reasoning

In this section, we show how the AVATAR system applies the *LIKO* query operators about some properties contained in the ontology.

Assume that a user registers in AVATAR. He is married and works as a doctor. Besides, he has watched "Safaris in Kenya" (a documentary) and "CNN News".

Table 2. Applied operators to reason about the user's job

Query operators	*Obtained properties and classes*
Doctor $>\Rightarrow \cup$ Doctor $>\Leftarrow$	Doctor $\leftarrow$ WorksIn $\rightarrow$ Hospitals
Hospitals $>\Rightarrow \cup$ Hospitals $>\Leftarrow$	IncidentsNews $\leftarrow$ hasSynopsis $\rightarrow$ "Hospitals strike in Madrid"
Incidents News $\lhd$	News
News $\lhd$	Informative Programs

Table 3. Applied operators to reason about the user's marital status

Query operators	*Obtained properties and classes*
Married People $>\Rightarrow \cup$ Married People $>\Leftarrow$	Married People $\leftarrow$ interestedIn $\rightarrow$ Cruises
Cruises $\lhd$	Travels
Travels $\lhd$	Advertising Products
Advertising Products $\lhd$	NULL
Cruises $>\Rightarrow \cup$ Cruises $>\Leftarrow$	Advertising Product $\leftarrow$ hasDescription $\rightarrow$ "Cruise on the Nile" Advertising Product $\leftarrow$ hasDescription $\rightarrow$ "Cruise on the Caribbean"
Advertising Product $>\Rightarrow \cup$ Advertising Products $>\Leftarrow$	Advertising $\leftarrow$ hasProducts $\rightarrow$ Advertising Products

Firstly, AVATAR reasons about the user's job as seen in Table 2. The first two *LIKO* operators relates the user's working place to the "Incidents News" class. Next, AVATAR locates one personalized content of interest for the user because it is related to his job.

AVATAR also reasons about the user marital status. So, as seen in Table 3, the first operator finds that the cruises are appealing to the married people. Later, AVATAR must choose an appropriate region for the cruise. Next, the system finds out the superclass referred to the "Cruises" class, until to get the "Advertising Products" superclass. When the reasoning by the search of superclasses is not possible, AVATAR uses other operator about "Cruises". So, the system establishes relations to the "Advertising" category.

Once the "Advertising" and "Informative Programs" classes have been chosen, the tool will not consider all the ontological categories in the following reasoning phase, reducing greatly the complexity of the inference process. Next, the system uses information about the user's view history so as to find relations between the watched programs and the TV contents computed previously. Remember that the user view history contains news and documentaries. AVATAR allows to add brief personalized subtitles during the viewing of the programs selected by the user, related to news of interest. So, AVATAR recommends subtitles referred to a strike in hospitals.

AVATAR continues reasoning by means of the datatype property *"Safaris"* $\leftarrow$ *hasDescription* $\rightarrow$ *"Safaris in Kenya."*. Next, AVATAR uses the $>\odot$ operator as shown in Table 4 to reason about the transitive property "isIn" by exploring its range and domain.

Table 4. An example of reasoning involving the $>\odot$ query operator

Query operators	*Obtained properties*	*Inferred knowledge*
Kenya $>\Rightarrow$	NULL	
Kenya $>\Leftarrow$	Kenya $\leftarrow$ isIn $\rightarrow$ Africa	
Africa $>\Rightarrow$	Egypt $\leftarrow$ isIn $\rightarrow$ Africa	
Africa $>\Leftarrow$	NULL	
Egypt $>\Rightarrow$	Nile $\leftarrow$ isIn $\rightarrow$ Egypt	Nile $\leftarrow$ isIn $\rightarrow$ Africa and Kenya $\leftarrow$ isIn $\rightarrow$ Africa

After applying the $>\odot$ query operator, the system has discovered a common nexus between Kenya and the Nile: both regions are in Africa. This way, AVATAR can include in the informative subtitles previously described news about incidents happened in Africa. Remember that AVATAR had found two interesting commercials about cruises (see Table 3). The relation between the Nile and Africa allows to choice an appropriate region for this cruise. Taking into account that the user had watched a documentary about Kenya, a region in Africa, it is most appropriate to suggest a cruise on the Nile.

In a real scenario, we should need a knowledge base with a large amount of data, to obtain recommendations by means of discovering relations between users personal data and information contained in the TV ontology. For that reason, we are focusing on the implementation of a LIKO-based semantic matching algorithm to find out semantic associations among the users favourite programs and other TV contents.

5 Conclusions and Further Work

In this paper we have presented a TV recommender system, named AVATAR, conceived as a MHP application. For this system, we have described an open multi-agent architecture that allows to include modules with additional functionalities easily to enhance the made recommendations. Our approach is novelty so that improves the previous TV recommendation tools by incorporating reasoning capabilities about the content semantics. For that purpose, we have used the TV-Anytime initiative to describe the TV contents and a TV ontology to share and reuse the knowledge efficiently [3]. To discover semantic associations among different TV contents, the system employs a query language that infers data from the AVATAR knowledge base.

Our future work is related to the application of the Description Logics to improve the semantic reasoning by incorporating new inference rules into our knowledge base.

References

1. Ardissono L. et al. *Personalized Digital TV: Targeting Programs to Individual Viewers*, chapter 5. 2004.
2. Daconta M. et al. *The Semantic Web: A Guide to the Future of XML, Web Services and Knowledge Management.* John Wiley & Sons, 2003.
3. Davies J. et al. OntoShare: Using Ontologies for Knowledge Sharing. In *Proceedings of the 11th International WWW Conference WWW2002*, 2002.
4. Davies J. et al. *Towards the Semantic Web: Ontology-driven Knowledge Management.* John Wiley & Sons, 2003.

5. Decker S. et al. Ontobroker: Ontology Based Access to Distributed and Semi-Structured Information. In *DS-8*, pages 351 – 369, 1999.
6. Geroimenko V. et al. *Visualizing the Semantic Web*. Springer Verlag, 2003.
7. Heckerman D. Bayesian networks for data mining. *Data Mining and Knowledge Discovery*, pages 79–119, 1997.
8. Mouaddib A. et al. Knowledge-based anytime computation. In *Proceedings of IJCAI*, 1995.
9. Resnick P. et al. Grouplens: An open architecture for collaborative filtering of netnews. In *Proceedings of Conference on Computer Supported Cooperative Work*, 1994.
10. Sekine S. et al. A decision tree method for finding and classifying names in japanese texts. In *Proceedings of the Sixth Workshop on Very Large Corpora*, 1998.

An Online Adaptive Method for Personalization of Search Engines

Guanglin Huang and Wenyin Liu

Department of Computer Science, City University of Hong Kong, Hong Kong SAR, China
hwanggl@cs.cityu.edu.hk, csliuwy@cityu.edu.hk

Abstract. A personalized search engine combines a user's interest into its ranking algorithm and can therefore improve its performance for that particular user. In this paper, we present such a personalized search engine, in which we collect the user's interest implicitly and dynamically from the user's profile and measure the similarity at the semantic level. Preliminary experiment results show that our method can achieve a promising improvement after collecting sufficient profile data of a particular user.

Keywords: Search Engine, Personalization, User Profiling, Clickthrough Data, Thesaurus

1 Introduction

Recently, many commercial and research search engines have achieved great successes. However, most of these information retrieval systems tend to use only static and general term information, e.g., term frequency and backlink, in their ranking algorithm. Therefore, they pose a performance drawback when the user varies. Different users probably have different interests and ranking criteria. A document relevant to A may be totally irrelevant to B for the same query. This situation calls for personalization of search engines.

Personalized information retrieval system is not new in the literature; example systems are Striver [3], Nutch [7], and LASER [8]. Practically, personalization algorithm should setup a profile, which records the user's preference or interest, for the user. This procedure is known as User Profiling [4][11]. The key problem of personalizing a search engine is how to learn from the user's behavior and do re-ranking. Boyan et al. [8] employed simulated annealing in their LASER system. Joachims [3] reported a Support Vector Machine based approach in his Striver system. Fan and Pathak [10] tested their genetic programming method on TREC data and showed a promising result. However, their approaches are intended for offline use, not adequate for online.

In this paper, we present a research prototype system built on Google's Web APIs [1]. It redirects the search keywords to Google and retrieves the search results. By recording the user's "clickthrough data", it implicitly collects the user's feedback to infer his/her interest and construct the user's profile dynamically. It re-ranks the Google's result items online according to their semantic meanings in the WordNet thesaurus. Unlike the search engine systems mentioned above, our system implicitly collects feedback and builds the user's profile dynamically. It can learn online and

X. Zhou et al. (Eds.): WISE 2004, LNCS 3306, pp. 422–427, 2004.
© Springer-Verlag Berlin Heidelberg 2004

incrementally, and is therefore adaptive to the user's interest, without any extra user participation.

The definition to "clickthrough data" was given by Joachims [3]. It can be regarded as a triplet (***q***, ***r***, ***c***) consisting of the query ***q***, the ranking list ***r***, and the set ***c*** of links the user has clicked on. We assume a normal user of our system would not click the result links at random; instead, the clicked links should contain some salient words that let him/her make the decisions. WordNet [5] is an electronic thesaurus that models the lexical knowledge of English language. Here we only use its nouns portion, because nouns are much more heavily used in information retrieval than other classes of words. In WordNet, words with the same meaning are grouped into a "synset". All synsets are organized in a hierarchical way by the "hypernym/hyponym" relation, making WordNet as a lexical inheritance system.

The rest of this paper is structured as follows. The next section presents our method of dynamic profiling and relevancy assessment. Experiments and results are shown in Section 3. Section 4 presents conclusions and future work.

2 Dynamic Profiling and Semantic Relevancy Assessment Method

Two issues should be tackled in our method. One is dynamic profiling, that is, how to build and update a user's profile from his/her clickthrough data dynamically; the other is re-ranking, i.e., given the user profile as prior knowledge, how to evaluate the relevancy of a document. After introducing our prototype system, they are addressed in the subsequent sub-sections respectively. In our system, a user's profile is composed of the words he/she has browsed. One entry of user's profile is represented by a triplet ***p***=(***w***, ***r***, ***t***), where ***w*** is the word in the clickthrough data; ***r*** is a [0, 1] value reflecting the user's preference to this word; ***t*** denotes the time when ***p*** is generated and can be viewed as the measure of "age" of this triplet.

2.1 The Prototype System

Our prototype system consists of two major parts: browser part and search part. The browser part is a mini-IE browser. The search part provides the user with an interface where he/she can initiate queries and get the results. By calling the Google Web APIs, the search part works as a client of Google. Typically, a Google search result item mainly contains the following parts 1: **title** of the searched page**, URL** of the searched page, **summary** of the searched result, and **snippet**, i.e. a text excerpt from the results page. Consistently, the search part of our system also presents the user these four parts, which form the content ***r*** in the clickthrough data.

2.2 Dynamic Profiling

In our method, user's profile data is mined and constructed from his/her clickthrough data. Generally, clicking a link is a positive feedback to this link but not vice versa. We build the construction model based on the following 5 observations:

1) User usually scans the search results in the order they are listed.
2) User usually only reads several top pages.
3) Clicking on an item of the search results indicates that the title, summary, or snippet of this item is relevant to the query.
4) User may be deceived by the summary or snippet of this webpage then click an irrelevant link. Therefore the staying time in this webpage is an important clue to infer the user interest.
5) When a user clicks a result item, the preceding items are more irrelevant than the clicked one.

The user's profile is built as follows. First of all, stopword filtering together with stemming is performed in all clickthrough data entries. In addition, all non-noun words are wiped.

Second, for each clicked result item, the words in its title, summary and snippet are regarded as relevant to user's interest according to Observation 3, and are therefore given a relevancy r=1, forming a new profile data entry.

After the user clicks a link of the result item, he/she usually will read the linked webpage, whose content provides additional information about the user's interest. Because the word number of the webpage may be large, we use the traditional TF-IDF [13] technique to select some salient words to represent this webpage. The words with top N (N=100 in our implementation) maximum TF-IDF values are regarded as the salient words. These words' relevancies are calculated as follows based on Observation 4:

$$r_i = \begin{cases} 1 & t_s > t_1 \\ 0 & t_s < t_0 \\ (t_s - t_0)/(t_1 - t_0) & otherwise \end{cases}$$

where t_s is the user's staying time in this webpage, t_0 and t_1 are two thresholds. We adopt t_0=1s and t_1=3s in our experiments.

Finally, un-clicked result items are considered based on the principle of Observation 5. We divide the total result items into several groups according to the positions of the clicked items. Except for the last group, every other group contains one clicked item which lies on the last of the group. Similar to the method of 7, the relevancies of the words in the un-clicked item j, are modeled as an exponential decay process: $r_j = r_i \times \gamma^{|rank(i) - rank(j)|}$, where i is the clicked item in the group containing j, r_i is the relevancy of i, which is calculated in the previous step, *rank(i)* and *rank(j)* indicate Google's original ranks of i and j, γ is a constant ranged (0,1) to control the decay ratio (γ =0.8 in our practice).

After getting all the words as well as their corresponding relevancies, we add the time information to them and form a bunch of user profile data entries. Therefore, the user's profile is dynamically updated.

2.3 Re-ranking Approach

A straightforward solution to the re-ranking problem is to compute the semantic similarity between the result item and the user's profile using the statistical term based approaches [13]. However, using word matching directly will lose its semantic information thus yield poor performance. Therefore, we adopt the approach proposed by Yang et al. [9] in their CBIR system.

Nouns words with the same meaning are grouped into a synset in WordNet, and synsets are organized in a hierarchical lexical tree by their semantic relations, as exemplified in Figure 1.

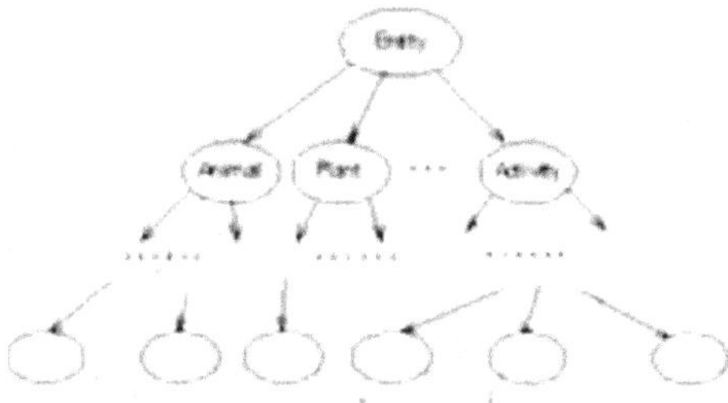

Fig. 1. The lexical tree of nouns in WordNet.

Any synset residing in a leaf node of the tree has a link to its super-ordinate synset, e.g., oak @-> tree @-> plant @-> organism @-> entity. The "@->" operation can be viewed as an upward movement in the lexical tree; it goes from specific to generic.

We use two measures to calculate the word similarity based on the synset hierarchy of the lexical tree. In this paper, "similarity" refers to similarity of the semantic meanings of words, e.g. "football" is more similar to "basketball" than "animal". In the first measure, the similarity between two words is assessed in terms of the depth of their maximal co-ancestor, which is the root of the minimal tree that contains both the two words. Formally, it reads:

$$sim(c_i, c_j) = \begin{cases} \dfrac{d(c^*)}{max_{c_k}[d(c_k)]}, & if \quad c_i \neq c_j \\ 1, & otherwise \end{cases}$$

where $\boldsymbol{c_i}$ and $\boldsymbol{c_j}$ are the synsets to which the two words belong respectively, $\boldsymbol{c^*}$ is the maximal co-ancestor of $\boldsymbol{c_i}$ and $\boldsymbol{c_j}$, $\boldsymbol{d(c)}$ stands for the depth of the synset $\boldsymbol{c}$, and $\boldsymbol{c_k}$ ranges over all the synsets in the synset hierarchy, it is used for normalization. Intuitively, when $\boldsymbol{c_i}$ and $\boldsymbol{c_j}$ are the same, the similarity is set to be 1.

The second measure is introduced to penalize the generic word, similar to the IDF term of TF-IDF measure. It also measures the property of the two words' maximal co-ancestor:

$$sim(c_i, c_j) = \begin{cases} log\left(\dfrac{1}{p(c^*)}\right), & if \quad c_i \neq c_i \\ 1, & otherwise \end{cases}$$

where $p(\boldsymbol{c})$ represents information content of the synset $\boldsymbol{c}$, and it can be approximated by the sum of the probability of occurrence of the keywords corresponding to that synset and to all its descendant synsets in an external static corpus (Reuters-21578). Similarly, the similarity is set to 1 when $\boldsymbol{c_i}$ and $\boldsymbol{c_j}$ are identical.

We combine the two measures by a linear normalized weighted formula, and finally obtain the overall words similarity at the semantic level.

The relevancy of a result item ***i*** relevancy is defined as:

$$r_i = \frac{1}{N \times M} \sum_{c_i \in i} \sum_{c_j \in j} sim(c_i, c_j) \times age(c_j) \times rel(c_j)$$

where, ***j*** denotes the words recorded in user's profile, ***N and M*** are the word numbers in result item ***i*** and the user's profile, respectively, *rel*(c_j) is the relevancy of ***j*** stored in the profile; *age*(c_j) is a normalized measure on how "old" the word recorded in the profile is.

Finally, we re-rank top ***M*** (***M***=100 in our implementation) search result items according to their relevancy metrics and obtain a new semantic rank list. We linearly combine this semantic rank list with the Google's PageRank list to produce the final rank by a weighted summation formula.

3 Experiments and Results

We collect 50 clickthrough data entries by one user during his actual web searching as usual. The number of query keywords ranges from 1 to 5, and the topics of queries are kept consistent. This user is asked to evaluate the precision of the original and modified ranking based on the top 20 result items. Here the experiment results are evaluated only in terms of the precision metric, just as Selberg [2] suggested. Figure 2 shows them.

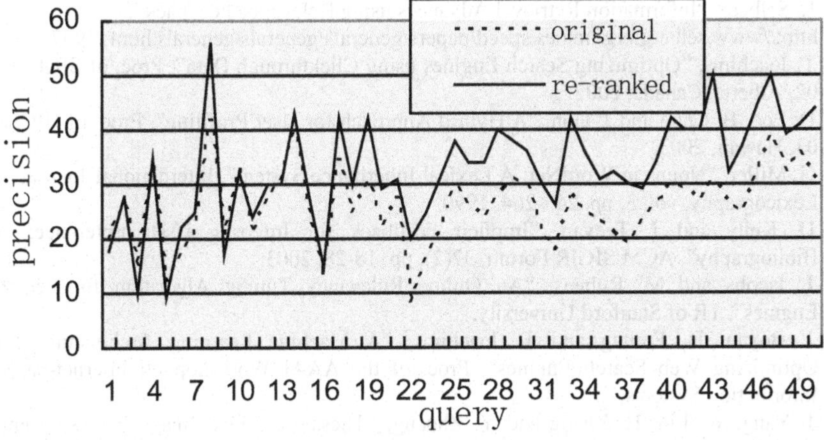

Fig. 2. The experiment results

As we can see from Figure 2, initially, the precision of re-ranked list is closed to the original one, or even lower, because the user's profile data have not been collected enough. As the times of query increase, more and more clickthrough data are collected, and the precision of our re-ranked list is improved smoothly. After learning from the data from about 20 queries, our re-ranking gets a precision that is greater than the original precision remarkably.

4 Conclusion and Future Work

In this paper, we propose an online method to personalize the search engine by dynamic profiling and semantic understanding techniques. The main advantage of our approach is the online and incremental inference to the user's interest, without any extra activity from the user. Our method is easy to implement and bears a low computational complexity. Preliminary experiment result has shown that our method can yield a promising enhancement after collecting sufficient data from the user.

There are several aspects that our system can improve in the future. In the implementation of the system, we simply assume every word has only one meaning and thus belongs to only one synset. This assumption is inappropriate. We will seek a solution based on the contextual information. Furthermore, the word relation model we use is a bit simple. Actually, beside the "hypernym/hyponym" relation, there are some other complex relations between words. We will further investigate this problem using other techniques.

Acknowledgement. The work described in this paper was fully supported by a grant from City University of Hong Kong (Project No. 7001462).

References

1. Google Corporation, Google Web APIs, http://www.google.com/apis/.
2. E. Selberg, "Information Retrieval Advances using Relevance Feedback", http://www.selberg.org/homes/speed/papers/generals/generals/generals.html, 1997.
3. T. Joachims, "Optimizing Search Engines using Clickthrough Data", Proc. of SIGKDD 02, Alberta, Canada, 2002.
4. D. Poo, B. Chng and J. Goh, "A Hybrid Approach for User Profiling", Proc. of HICSS 03, Hawaii, 2003.
5. G. Miller, "Nouns in WordNet: A Lexical Inheritance System", International Journal of Lexicography, vol. 3, pp. 245-264, 1990.
6. D. Kelly and J. Teevan, "Implicit Feedback for Inferring User preference: A Bibliography", ACM SIGIR Forum, 37(2), pp. 18-28, 2003.
7. J. Jacobs and M. Rubens, "An Online Relevancy Tuning Algorithm for Search Engines", TR of Stanford University.
8. J. Boyan, D. Freitag and T. Joachims, "A Machine Learning Architecture for Optimizing Web Search Engines", Proc. of the AAAI Workshop on Internet-based Information Systems.
9. J. Yang, W. Liu, H. Zhang and Y. Zhuang, "Thesaurus-Aided Image Browsing and Retrieval", Proc. of ICME 01, pp. 313-316, Japan, 2001.
10. W. Fan and P. Pathak, "Personalization of Search Engine Services for Effective Retrieval and Knowledge Management", Proc. of 21st ICIS, pp. 20-34, Queensland, Australia, 2000.
11. S. Stewart and J. Davies, "User profiling Techniques: A Critical Review", 19th Annual BCSIRSG Colloquium on IR Research, pp. 8-9, 1997.
12. K. Bradley, R. Rafter and B. Smyth, "Case-Based User Profiling for Content Personalisation", Proc. of AH 2000, pp. 62-72, Trento, Italy, 2000.
13. D. Harman, "Information Retrieval: Data Structure and Algorithms", Prentice-Hall, 1992.

Management of Serviceflow in a Flexible Way

Shuiguang Deng, Zhaohui Wu, Li Kuang, Chuan Lin, Yueping Jin, Zhiwei Chen, Shifeng Yan, and Ying Li

College of Computer Science, Zhejiang University,
310027 Hangzhou, China
{dengsg, wzh, kuangli,lingchuan,jinyp, chenzw,yansf,liying}@zju.edu.cn

Abstract. With the emergence of technologies and standards supporting the development of web services, more and more services are becoming available on the Internet. But almost all of them are single and simple functional units. Composing existing services into new functionality becomes very essential for enterprises. We call a service composition "Serviceflow". This paper presents the DartFlow framework aimed to build, execute and manage serviceflow. Due to the similarity between serviceflow and workflow, we use workflow technology in DartFlow to compose services dynamically and flexibly. A detailed comparison between serviceflow and workflow is introduced in this paper. Semantic technology is also adopted to resolve some basic issues about services, such as service description, service registration and automatic service discovery in DartFlow.

1 Introduction

Service has grown to be the hottest research topic nowadays [1, 2]. With the development of technologies related to services, a large number of services become available on the Internet. Service is becoming the focus of business today. On one hand, more and more enterprise applications are built based on services. On the other hand, enterprises are willing to encapsulate their functionalities into services to attract their business partners. Composing existing single and simple services into large and complex ones will help enterprises to realize their business goals with minimal effort. We call a service composition "serviceflow" that is composed by multiple single services according to data flow and control flow among them. Workflow is the automation of processes, in whole or part, during which documents, information or tasks are passed from one participant to another for action, according to a set of procedural rules [3]. Workflow has been evolved into a primary technology in managing processes. Making a comparison between serviceflow and workflow, we found that there was much similarity between them. For example, they both need languages to model processes; both handle data dependency and control dependency; both require dynamism characteristic, and so on. A detailed comparison between serviceflow and workflow is presented later. Due to the similarity between them, we can use workflow technology

X. Zhou et al. (Eds.): WISE 2004, LNCS 3306, pp. 428–438, 2004.
© Springer-Verlag Berlin Heidelberg 2004

to deal with serviceflow. While establishing a framework to build, execute and manage serviceflow, there are still some essential issues related to services needed to be considered carefully, such as service description, service registration and service discovery. To date, however, the activities concerning the above issues have been handled mostly at syntactic level. The limitation of such a rigid approach is that it does not support dynamic service composition. In fact, the dynamic characteristic is very important for serviceflow to allow businesses to dynamically change partners and services. Thus those issues must be considered at semantic level.

In this paper, we employ technologies from semantic web, web service, and our earlier research in workflow management [4, 5] to build a new framework called "DartFlow" offering the functions of building, executing and managing serviceflow.

2 Serviceflow Versus Workflow

The use of serviceflow and workflow are both to integrate existing resources to automate or semi-automate various business processes. These resources include man, equipments, and services, etc. There are two major stages in both of workflow and serviceflow management: one is the build-time stage, and the other is the run-time stage. While building a serviceflow, it mainly needs to specify the flow of service invocations (i.e., the services to be invoked, their input and output data, and their execution dependencies). Similarly, while building a workflow, it must specify the flow of work (i.e., the work items to be executed, their input and output data, and their execution dependencies) [6]. Both serviceflow and workflow need definition languages to represent actual business processes in the first stage. While a serviceflow or a workflow is put into execution in the run-time stage, an engine is needed both for them to interpret flow definitions, and to invoke corresponding activities or services. Concerning the similarity between serviceflow and workflow, we can regard serviceflow as a special kind of workflow. With the wide application of workflow technology, the mechanism of workflow modeling, workflow execution and workflow exception handling have been evolved to be more mature and more advanced. Thus, we can use workflow technology to help constructing, executing and managing serviceflow in a flexible and efficient way.

Though serviceflow is similar to workflow to such a great extent, there is still some difference between them, which we must take into consideration while importing workflow technology into serviceflow. Firstly, serviceflow is composed by services, which are distributed in a global area, but workflow is composed by activities in a local area, for example, within an enterprise. So it is important and necessary for serviceflow to locate, match and discovery services from a tremendous number of services on the Internet. Secondly, unlike traditional workflow, serviceflow have to cope with a highly dynamic environment. Due to the continuously change of services on the Internet, serviceflow is apt to change frequently. Thus serviceflow needs more flexible mechanism to handle changes. Thirdly, the execution of serviceflow is more automatic than workflow. Executing a serviceflow is to invoke outer services automatically without human's intervention. But for a workflow, in general, it requires a human with a special role to participate in the corresponding work item at each step. Therefore, a framework for managing serviceflow needs more automatism than a workflow management system.

3 A Serviceflow Management System: DartFlow

Workflow can be defined, executed and managed through a workflow management system (WFMS). Similarly, serviceflow also need a system to define, execute and manage them. We call such a system "Serviceflow Management System (SFMS)". Besides the above three major functions must to be realized in a SFMS, a SFMS will also offer some basic essential functions, such as service registration, service discovery and so on. Thus, a SFMS needs a graphic definition tool to model serviceflow, needs an execution engine to interpret serviceflow definition and to execute serviceflows, needs tools to monitor the execution status. Furthermore, a SFMS needs additional components to realize the above basic functions. As an implementation of a serviceflow management system, the architecture of DartFlow is illustrated in fig 1.

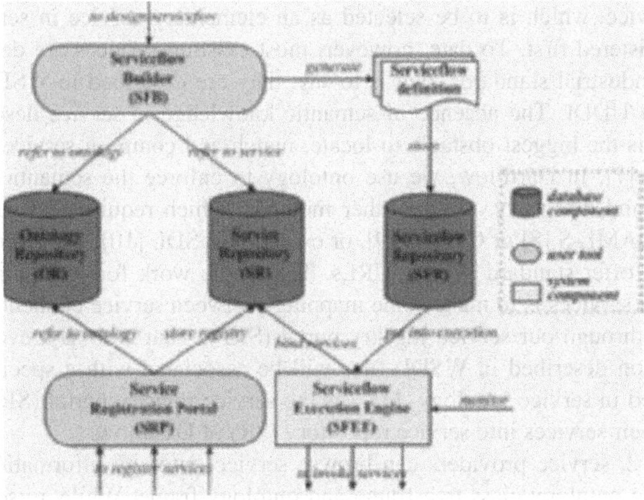

Fig. 1. The architecture of DartFlow

As the figure 1 shows, there are three major functional parts in DartFlow: service registration, serviceflow definition, serviceflow execution. Each functional part is implemented based on several components. The service registration part includes the following three ones: Service Registration Portal (SRP), Ontology Repository (OR) and Service Registry (SR); the serviceflow definition part includes Serviceflow Builder (SFB), OR, SR and Serviceflow Repository (SFR); the serviceflow execution includes Serviceflow Execution Engine (SFEE) and SR.

Serviceflow in DartFlow is divided into three categories: *static serviceflow*, *dynamic serviceflow* and *synthetic serviceflow*. The first type means all the elementary services to be composed are determined at design time; the second type means all the elementary services to be composed are determined at run time; the last type means that some elementary services can be determined at design time, but others at run time. For those three different types, the complexity in themselves, the difficulty to manage and the flexibility to deal with changes are compared in table 1. DartFlow support all of the three types of serviceflow in both build-time and run-time stages.

Table 1. Comparison between three types of serviceflow

Serviceflow Category	*Complexity*	*Difficulty*	*Flexibility*
Static Serviceflow	Low	Low	Low
Synthetic Serviceflow	Middle	Middle	Middle
Dynamic Serviceflow	High	High	High

3.1 Service Description and Registration in DartFlow

For any service, which is to be selected as an elementary service in serviceflow, it must be registered first. To date, however, most existing services are developed according to industrial standards, that is to say, they are described in WSDL files and registered in UDDI. The absence of semantic knowledge in service description and registration is the biggest obstacle to locate, match and compose services accurately and quickly [7]. In DartFlow, we use ontology to enforce the semantics in service registration and discovery. Unlike other methods, which require services to be described by DAML-S [8] or OWL-S [9], or extended WSDL [10], we just need service providers to offer standard WSDL URLs. The whole work for service providers to register their services is to make some mappings between service elements and ontology classes through our service registry portal (SRP). That is to say, every message part, operation described in WSDL files will be associated with a specific class already defined in service ontology. Fig.2 is the service registry portal (SRP) for users to register their services into service repository (SR) of DartFlow.

In figure 2, service providers can browse service ontology information stored in OR using the ontology class tree frame and ontology frame. While a user inputs his WSDL URL in the "Address" textbox and then clicks on the "OK" button, he can brows every service element of WSDL in the WSDL tree frame and service operation frame. Using SRP, service providers can map service elements into service ontology classes. For example, in fig.2, one input part named "Location" of the weather service is mapped into the "City" ontology class and the other is into the "Date" class. After a service provider click on the "Register" button, SRP will automatically generate a file formatted in Ontology Service Description Language (OSDL). OSDL is designed to store the mapping information between service elements and ontology classes, and to be used in service discovery latter. Figure 3 shows the snapshot of OSDL file associated with the "Weather" service shown in figure 2.

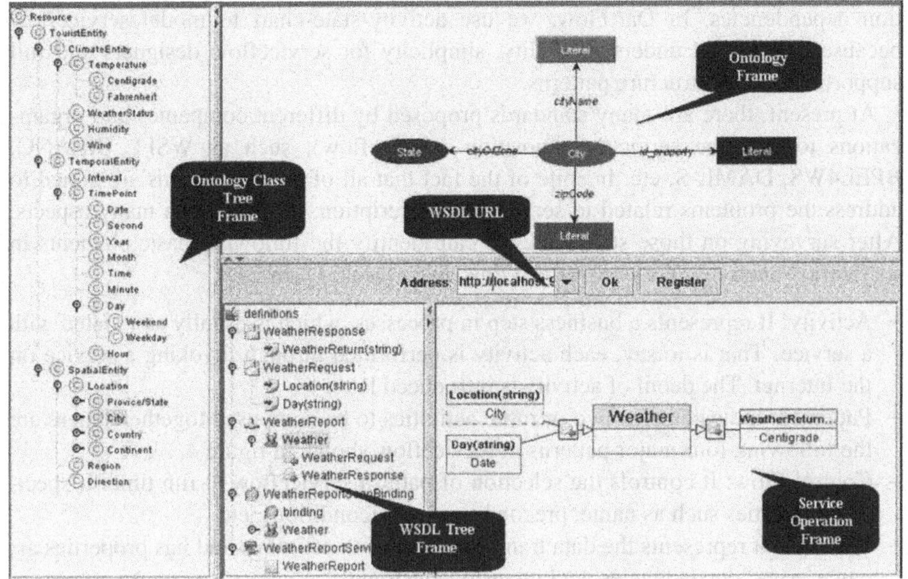

Fig. 2. Service registration portal in DartFlow

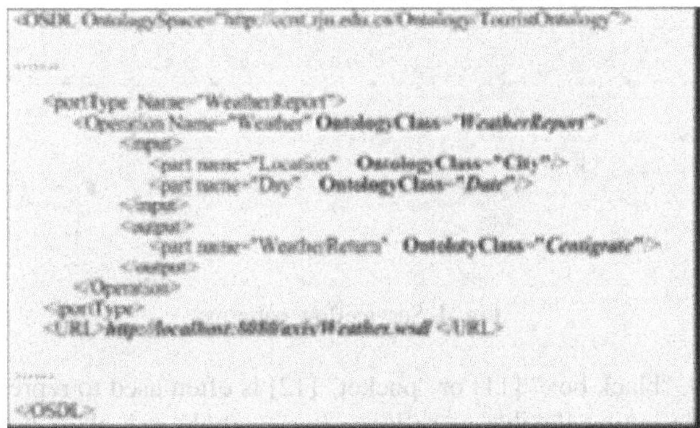

```
<OSDL OntologySpace="http://ccnt.zju.edu.cn/Ontology/TouristOntology">
......
  <portType Name="WeatherReport">
    <Operation Name="Weather" OntologyClass="WeatherReport">
        <input>
            <part name="Location"   OntologyClass="City"/>
            <part name="Day"   OntologyClass="Date"/>
        </input>
        <output>
            <part name="WeatherReturn"   OntolotyClass="Centigrate"/>
        </output>
    </Operation>
  </portType>
  <URL>http://localhost:8080/axis/Weather.wsdl</URL>
......
</OSDL>
```

Fig. 3. A snapshot of the OSDL file

Based on those ontology information embodied in OSDL files, we can make ontology inference automatically in service discovery and service matching latter.

3.2 Design Serviceflow in DartFlow

After services are registered into DartFlow, users can build their own serviceflows. Using the serviceflow builder (SFB) in DartFlow to design a serviceflow, a user needs to specify which services to be invoked, their input and output data, and their execution dependencies. In DartFlow, we use activity-state-chart to model serviceflow because of its good understandability, simplicity for serviceflow designers and full support of enough structure patterns.

At present, there are many standards proposed by different companies and organizations to describe service composition (serviceflow), such as WSFL, XLANG, BPEL4WS, DAML-S, etc. In spite of the fact that all of these standards are aimed to address the problems related to serviceflow description, they differ in many aspects. After surveying on those standards, we can identify the following basic elements in serviceflow: activity, *pattern*, *control flow*, *message* and *provider*.

- Activity: It represents a business step in processes, which is usually associated with a service. That is to say, each activity is performed through invoking a service on the Internet. The detail of activity is introduced later.
- Pattern: It indicates how two or more activities to be composed together. There are the following four major patterns in serviceflow shown in figure 4.
- Control Flow: It controls the selection of path in serviceflow at run time. It specifies properties such as name, preconditions, postconditions, etc.
- Message: It represents the data transferred between activities and has properties as: name, parts, dependencies, and integrity constraints.
- Provider: It describes a party offering concrete services, which can be invoked at runtime to carry out activities. It specifies properties such as name, description, capabilities, cost, quality, URI, services and so on.

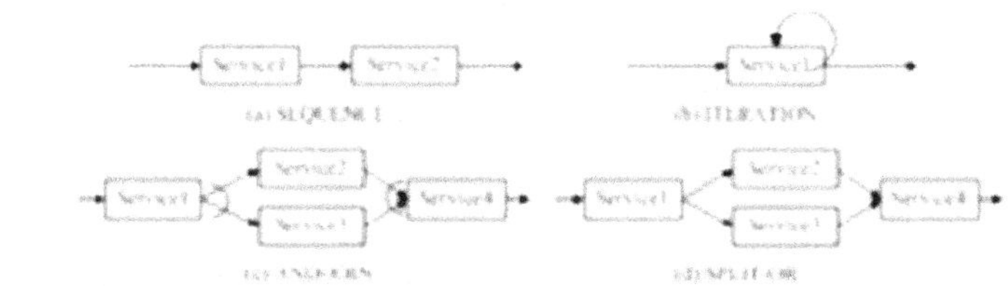

Fig. 4. Serviceflow patterns

In workflow, "black box" [11] or "pocket" [12] is often used to represent uncertain factors while designing flexible workflows. For example, use black box to represent an uncertain activity. When those workflows are put into execution, "black box" or "pocket" is replaced with concrete things. This mechanism is called "later binding". In DartFlow, we also use this method to improve the flexibility for serviceflow. Thus, there are two kinds of activity node in serviceflow: one is *concrete service node*; the other is *abstract service node*. A concrete service node is bound with a specified WSDL of a concrete service and one of its operations. In general, if a user knows the target service and operations in the service definitely, he can specify the activity as a concrete service node. While designing a concrete service node in serviceflow, a user can use SFB to browse all the services registered in SR and then select one as the binding with that node. As an example, figure 5 shows the partial specification of one concrete service node.

```
<Activity  name="Weather Report">
    <Node-Type>Concrete Service Node</Node-Type>
    <WSDL-URL>http://ccnt.zju.edu.cn:8080/axis/Weather.wsdl</WSDL-URL>
    <Operation>WeatherQuery</Operation>
</Activity>
```

Fig. 5. An example of concrete service node

When a user does not know which service is the target one or he wants the activity node to be bound to a target service at run time, he can specify this activity node as an abstract service node. An abstract service node is associated with an abstract specification of a type of service, instead of a concrete one. The abstract specification is described by Ontology Service Query Language (OSQL), which is designed to describe the requirements of users when querying services registered in service repository (SR) at run time. OSQL statements are constructed based on ontology classes. While designing an abstract service node, a user browses the service ontology stored in OR first and then constructs an OSQL statement for this node. Figure 6 illustrates an example of OSQL statement and the specification of an abstract service node. From the OSDL statement in figure 6, we can see that the user want to query such a service that has two inputs (City and Date) and one output (Temperature) when the activity "Weather Report" is put into execution.

```
<!--------an OSQL statement for WeatherReport-------->
<OSQL name="OSQL for a WeatherReport">
    <OntologySpace>
        http://ccnt.zju.edu.cn/Ontology/TouristOntology
    </OntologySpace>
    <Input-Parts-List>
        <Input-Part>City</Input-Part>
        <Input-Part>Date</Input-Part>
    </Input-Parts-List>
    <Output-Parts-List>
        <Output-Part>Temperature</Output-Part>
    </Output-Parts-List>
</OSQL>

<!------an abstract service node bound with the above OSQL statement -------->
<Activity  name="Weather Report">
    <Node-Type>Abstract Service Node</Node-Type>
    <OSQL-Statement>http://ccnt.zju.edu.cn:8080/axis/Weather.wsdl</OSQL-Statement>
</Activity>
```

Fig. 6. An example of abstract service node

3.3 Execute Serviceflow in DartFlow

When a serviceflow is selected from SFR and is put into execution, as shown in figure 1, the serviceflow execution engine (SFEE) will interpret the serviceflow definition, and invoke corresponding services for each activity.

Serviceflow execution engine (SFEE) is the heart of a serviceflow management system. It is the same as the workflow engine to a workflow management system.

Besides the functions referred in workflow engine, such as interpreting process definitions, initiating a process instance, invoking corresponding applications, controlling the execution routing, and so on, a serviceflow execution engine is also responsible for service locating, service matching, service binding. In DartFlow, a serviceflow execution engine is divided into four major functional units: Serviceflow Interpreter, Service Matcher, Ontology Inference Engine and Service Invoker. Figure 7 shows the relationship between the four functional units.

- Serviceflow Interpreter is responsible for interpreting serviceflow definition files, generating serviceflow instances and activity instances, making routing decisions.
- Service Matcher is responsible for making service queries in Service Registry (SR) according to OSQL statements, making a sort between the results, and also responsible for binding the most appropriate concrete service to an activity. It updates the corresponding serviceflow definition according to the binding information.
- Ontology Inference Engine is used to make ontology inference while Service Matcher wants to do service matching. For example, Service Matcher wants Ontology Inference Engine to infer the relationship between two ontology classes.
- Service Invoker performs the invoking to concrete services. It sends out the input messages to a target service and gets corresponding responses. It is also responsible for catching and handling exceptions while invoking. If an invoking is overtime before getting any response or an exception is thrown out, the service Invoker will inform the Service Matcher to make a new service binding. After the service matcher returns a new service, it will try to invoke later.

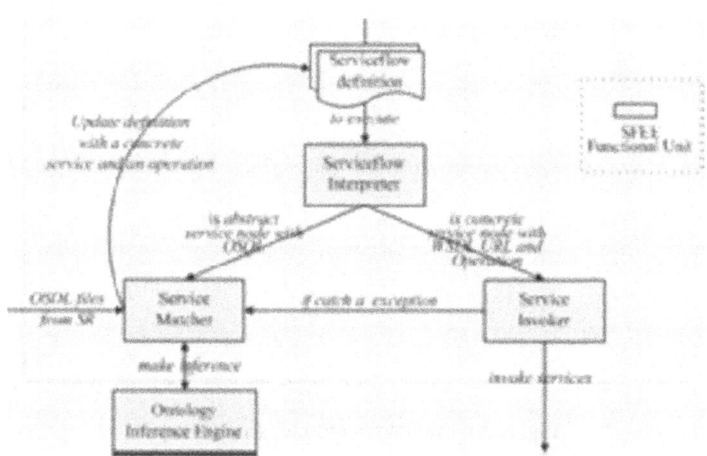

Fig. 7. Architecture of serviceflow execution engine (SFEE)

When an instance of serviceflow runs to an abstract service node, the Service Matcher will ask the Ontology Inference Engine for service discovery and service matching. In DartFlow, the service discovery and matching is carried out between OSQL statements of abstract service nodes and services registered in SR. As the previous sections have described, OSQL statement is constructed according to ontology classes; and ontology is used in the process of service registration. Thus, it is feasible to make ontology inference while making service matching. At present, we use the algorithm presented in [13] to make service matching.

3.4 Key Features of DartFlow

- Enriches service and service composition semantically. We import ontology into the process of service registration (OSDL), service matching (Ontology Inference) and service composition (OSQL).
- Realizes visual and flexible composition of services. All the operations related to serviceflow design are carried out in graphic environment.
- Allows dynamically change partners and services by later binding of services. Use abstract service node with an OSQL statement to represent uncertain services at build-time. A concrete service is bound to this node after making a service binding operation automatically at run-time.
- Ensure the successful execution through handling exceptions while invoking outer services.

4 Related Work

Service composition is a hot area today. Building a framework to compose service has allured much attraction from many researchers and organizations. In this section, we give a survey on some related projects and prototypes.

eFlow [2, 6, 17] is a framework that allows registering, composing, deploying service. It also uses workflow technology to model and execute service compositions. Processes are modeled as graph that defines the control and data flow. The nodes represent services in the process. eFlow supports dynamic service composition using service templates and later binding technology. But unlike DartFlow, neither the service registration, service discovery mechanism nor the service template in eFlow is semantically enriched.

SELF-SERV [15] is a platform where web services are declaratively composed and executed in a peer-to-peer environment. Then the composition can be executed in a P2P fashion with the help of peer software components -coordinators for each constituent web service. Although the concept of "service community" is proposed to realize dynamic service composition, it does not perform dynamic discovery very well. The user has to discover services and then define composition using state-chart diagrams. Moreover, it is hard to control the execution of composition when some exceptions occur in P2P environment.

METEOR-S [14] is a project initiated by the Large Scale Distributed Information Systems (LSDIS) Lab at the University of Georgia. In METEOR-S, they build a framework to address the problems of semantic web service description, discovery and composition. They use semantic service template and semantic process template to capture the semantic characteristics of services and processes. But they require service providers to register their services using an extended WSDL specification [10]. That is to say, they need services to be specified by extended WSDL, not the standard service definition language- WSDL. Furthermore, METEOR-S does not support dynamic composition indeed. This is because that all semantic service templates in a composition are bound to concrete services before the composition is put into execution.

A DAML-S based prototype for semi-automatic composition of services is proposed in [16]. It provides a composer that will help the user to select services for each activity in the composition and to create flow specifications to link them. Upon selecting a service, the services that can produce output that could be fed as the input of the selected service are listed after filtering based on profile descriptions. The user can manually select the service that he wants to fit in at a particular activity. After selecting all the services, the system generates a composite process in DAML-S. But this prototype does not support dynamic service composition. Furthermore, using the composer of this prototype to design a composition, user can only specify SEQUENCE and AND-JOIN structure patterns.

5 Conclusion and Future Work

Composing existing services on the Internet will bring much added-value for enterprises. Building such a framework that supports service registration, service discovery, service composition and service deployment will become an emergent thing. Our work is to combine technologies from workflow, web service and semantic web to build such a framework- DartFlow. Since there is so much similarity between workflow and service composition, it is natural to use workflow technology to resolve corresponding problems in service composition. On the other hand, the use of ontology in service description, service registration, service discovery and service composition allows much richer description of activity requirements and more effective way of locating services to carry out the activities in service composition. DartFlow provides the possibility to compose, custom, and deploy services in a very flexible and efficient way. However, at present we do not consider any QOS factor in service composition. In fact, with the number of services growing larger on the Internet, QOS is more and more important for users. Moreover security access in serviceflow is another factor that should not be ignored. Thus QOS and security in service composition is the focus of our future work.

Acknowledgement. This work is supported in part by subprogram of the Fundamental Technology and Research Program, China Ministry of Science and Technology, and Chinese 211 core project: Network-based Intelligence and Graphics.

References

1. B. Benatallah, M.Dumas, etc. Overview of Some Patterns for Architecting and Managing Composite Web Servces. ACM SIGECOM Exchanges 3.3. 9-16,2002.
2. F. Casati, M. C. Shan. Dynamic and adaptive composition of e-services. Information system 26, 3, 143-162. 2001.
3. Workflow Management Coalition. WfMC-TC00-1003 1996, Reference model and API specification.
4. S.G. Deng, Z. Yu, Z.H. Wu. Enhancement of Workflow Flexibility by Composing Activities at Runtime. Proc. of the Annual ACM Symposium on Applied Computing. 2004
5. S.G. Deng, Z.H. Wu.Yu Z. etc. A Secure Process-Service Model. Proc. of International Conference on Computational Science. 2004.
6. F. Casati, M.C. Shan. Definition, Execution, Analysis, and Optimization of Composite E-Services. Bulletin of the IEEE Computer Society Technical Committee on Data Engineering. 29-34,2001.
7. B. Benatallah, M. Hacid, etc. Towards Semantic Reasoning for Web Services Discovery. Proc. of the International Semantic Web Conference. 2003.
8. A. Ankolekar, M. Burstein, etc. DAML-S: Web Service Description for the Semantic Web. Proc. of the International Semantic Web Conference, 2002.
9. OWL Services Coalition. OWL-S: Semantic Markup for Web Services. 2004. OWL-S White Paper http://www.daml.org/services/owl-s/1.0/owl-s.pdf.
10. K. Sivashanmugam, K. Verma, etc. Adding Semantics to Web Services Standards. Proc. of the International Semantic Web Conference, 2003.
11. P. Heinl, S. Horn, S. Jablonski. A comprehensive approach to flexibility in workflow management systems. Proc .of International Joint Conference on Work Activities Coordination and Collaboration, 2001.
12. S. Sadiq, W. Sadiq. Pockets of Flexibility in Workflow Specifications. Proc .of International Conference on Conceptual Modeling, Yokohama Japan, 2001.
13. L. chuan, W. Zhaohui, D. shuiguang. Service Matching and Discovery Based on Ontology. submitted to the International Conference on Grid and Cooperative Computing 2004
14. K. Sivashanmugam, J. A. Miller, A. P. Sheth. Framework for Semantic Web Process composition. International Journal of Electronic Commerce. 2004.
15. B. Benatallah, M.Dumas, Q.Z. Sheng. The SELFSERV Environment for Web Services Composition. IEEE Internet Computing. 17(1):40-48, 2003.
16. E. Sirin, J. Hendler, B. Parsia. Semi-automatic composition of web services using semantic descriptions. Proc. of the International Conference on Enterprise Information Systems, 2002.
17. F. Casati, M. Sayal, etc. Developing E-Services for Composing E-Services. Proc. Of International Conference on Advanced Information Systems Engineering. 2001.

Recovery Nets: Towards Self-Adaptive Workflow Systems*

Rachid Hamadi and Boualem Benatallah

School of Computer Science and Engineering
The University of New South Wales
Sydney, NSW 2052, Australia
{rhamadi,boualem}@cse.unsw.edu.au

Abstract. A workflow management system (WfMS) provides a central control point for defining business processes and orchestrating their execution. A major limitation of current WfMSs is their lack of support for dynamic workflow adaptations. This functionality is an important requirement in order to provide sufficient flexibility to cope with expected but unusual situations and failures. In this paper, we propose Self-Adaptive Recovery Net (SARN), an extended Petri net model for specifying exceptional behavior in workflow systems at design time. SARN can adapt the structure of the underlying Petri net at run time to handle exceptions while keeping the Petri net design simple and easy. The proposed framework also caters for high-level recovery policies that are incorporated either with a single task or a set of tasks, called a recovery region.

1 Introduction

In a workflow process, each task can fail, e.g., its execution produces unexpected results [1]. Therefore, exception handling must be part of the workflow process. If we want to model a workflow that takes into account and reacts to failures adequately, then the exception handling part ends up dominating the normal behaviour part [2]. Existing workflow modeling languages such as traditional state machines, statecharts, and Petri nets [3] are not suitable when the exceptional behaviour exceeds the normal behaviour since they do not, as such, have the ability to reduce modeling size, improve design flexibility, and support exception handling at design time.

There are two main approaches that deal with exceptions in existing WfMSs: (i) the *Ad-Hoc* approach and (ii) the *Run Time* approach. The former integrates all expected exceptions within the normal behavior of the business process. This makes the design of the workflow complicated and inconvenient. The latter deals with exceptions at run time, meaning that there must be a workflow expert who decides which changes have to be made to the workflow process in order to handle exceptions (see, e.g., [4]).

* This work is partially supported by the ARC SPIRT grant "Managing Changes in Dynamic Workflow Environments".

X. Zhou et al. (Eds.): WISE 2004, LNCS 3306, pp. 439–453, 2004.
© Springer-Verlag Berlin Heidelberg 2004

One solution is to use high-level recovery policies that are incorporated either with a *single* task or a set of tasks that we will call hereafter a *recovery region*. These recovery policies are *generic constructs* that model exceptions at design time together with a set of primitive operations that can be used at run time to handle the occurrence of exceptions. Note that our proposed approach concentrates on handling exceptions at the instance level and not on modifying the workflow schema such as in [5].

We identified a set of recovery policies that are useful and commonly needed in many practical situations. Our contribution is twofold:

- *Self-Adaptive Recovery Net (SARN).* An extended Petri net model for specifying exceptional behavior in workflow systems at design time. This model can adapt the structure of the underlying Petri net at run time to handle exceptions while keeping the Petri net design simple and easy.
- *High-level recovery policies.* These recovery policies are generic constructs that model exceptions at design time. They are incorporated with either a single task or a set of tasks called a recovery region. Note that this list of recovery policies is not exhaustive. Indeed, new (customized) recovery policies can be added.

Handling exceptions introduces two major aspects. First, the system should provide support (i.e., a set of recovery policies) to enable the flexibility to deal with expected exceptions. Second, expected exceptions should only be allowed in a valid way. The system must ensure the correctness of the modified SARN w.r.t. consistency constraints (such as reachability and absence of deadlock), so that constraints that were valid before the dynamic change of SARN are also valid after the modification.

The rest of the paper is organized as follows. Section 2 introduces the proposed model SARN along with a motivating example. Section 3 presents the task-based recovery policies. Their extension to a recovery region is given in Sect. 4. Finally, Sect. 5 reviews some related work and concludes the paper.

2 Self-Adaptive Recovery Net

Petri nets [3] are a well-founded process modeling technique that have formal semantics. They have been used to model and analyze several types of processes including protocols, manufacturing systems, and business processes. A Petri net is a directed, connected, and bipartite graph in which each node is either a *place* or a *transition*. Tokens occupy places. When there is at least one token in every place connected to a transition, we say that the transition is *enabled*. Any enabled transition may *fire* removing one token from every input place, and depositing one token in each output place. For a more elaborate introduction to Petri nets, the reader is referred to [6,3].

SARN extends Petri nets to model exception handling through *recovery* transitions and *recovery* tokens. In SARN, there are two types of transitions: *standard* transitions representing workflow tasks to be performed and *recovery* transitions

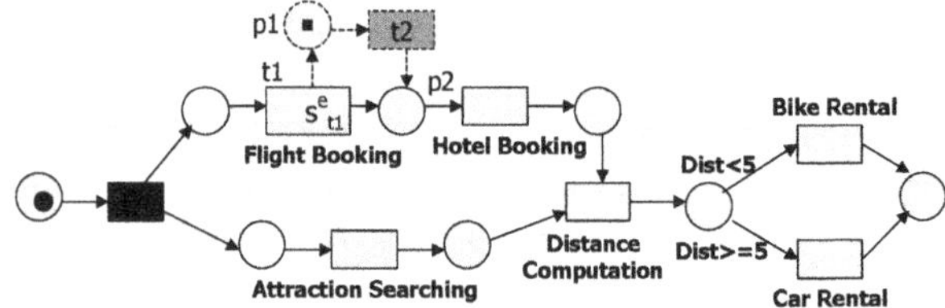

Fig. 1. *Travel Planning* Workflow as a SARN

that are associated with workflow tasks to adapt the recovery net in progress when a failure event occurs. There are also two types of tokens: *standard* tokens for the firing of standard transitions and *recovery* tokens associated with recovery policies. There is one recovery transition per type of task failure, that is, when a new recovery policy is designed, a new recovery transition is added. When a failure (such as a time out) within a task occurs, an event is raised and a recovery transition will be enabled and fired. The corresponding sequence of basic operations (such as creating a place and deleting an arc) associated with the recovery transition is then executed to adapt the structure of SARN that will handle the exception.

2.1 A Motivating Example

A simplified *Travel Planning* workflow specified as a SARN model is depicted in Fig. 1. In this workflow process, a sequence of a *Flight Booking* task followed by a *Hotel Booking* task is performed in parallel with an *Attraction Searching* task. After these booking and searching tasks are completed, the distance from the attraction location to the accommodation is computed, and either a *Car Rental* task or a *Bike Rental* task is invoked. The symbol S^e_{t1} within the *Flight Booking* task means that a *Skip* recovery policy is associated with it (see Sect. 3.1 for details about the *Skip* recovery policy).

The part drawn in dotted lines is created after the sequence of primitive operations associated with the *Skip* recovery transition has been executed. When a *Skip* failure event e (e.g., e="no response after one day") occurs during the execution of the task *Flight Booking*, the *Skip* recovery transition appears and the operations associated with it are executed.

Note that, in this paper, exceptions constitute events which may occur during workflow execution and which require deviations from the normal business process. These events can be *generic* such as the unavailability of resources, a time-out, and incorrect input types, or *application specific* (i.e., *dependent*) such as the unavailability of seats for the *Flight Booking* task in the *Travel Planning* workflow. In this latter case, events must be defined by the workflow designer.

2.2 Definition of SARN

In the following, we will give the formal definition of SARN.

Definition 1 (SARN).
A Self-Adaptive Recovery Net (SARN) is a tuple $RN = (P, T, Tr, F, i, o, \ell, M)$ *where:*

- P *is a finite set of places representing the states of the workflow,*
- T *is a finite set of standard transitions* ($P \cap T = \varnothing$) *representing the tasks of the workflow,*
- Tr *is a finite set of recovery transitions* ($T \cap Tr = \varnothing$ *and* $P \cap Tr = \varnothing$) *associated with workflow tasks to adapt the net in-progress when a failure event occurs. There is one recovery transition per type of task failure such as Skip and Compensate,*
- $F \subseteq (P \times (T \cup Tr)) \cup ((T \cup Tr) \times P)$ *is a set of directed arcs (representing the control flow),*
- i *is the input place of the workflow with* ${}^{\bullet}i = \varnothing$,
- o *is the output place of the workflow with* $o^{\bullet} = \varnothing$,
- $\ell : T \to \mathcal{A} \cup \{\tau\}$ *is a labeling function where* $\mathcal{A}$ *is a set of task names.* τ *denotes a silent (or an empty) task (represented as a black rectangle), and*
- $M : P \to \mathbb{N} \times \mathbb{N}$ *represents the mapping from the set of places to the set of integer pairs where the first value is the number of standard tokens (represented as black small circles within places) and the second value the number of recovery tokens (represented as black small rectangles within places).* □

In the SARN model, there are some primitive operations that can modify the net structure such as adding an arc and disabling a transition (see Table 1). Several of these basic operations are combined in a specific order to handle different task failure events. The approach adopted is to use one recovery transition to represent one type of task failure. Thus a recovery transition represents a combination of several basic operations.

In the example depicted in Fig. 1, the *Skip* recovery policy S^{e}_{t1} is associated with eight basic operations: (1) `DisableTransition(t1)`, (2) `CreatePlace(p1)`, (3) `AddRecoveryToken(p1)`, (4) `CreateArc(t1,p1)`, (5) `CreateTransition(t2)`, (6) `SilentTransition(t2)`, (7) `CreateArc(p1,t2)`, and (8) `CreateArc(t2,p2)`. It should be noted that this sequence of operations must be executed as an atomic transaction.

In SARN, when a task failure occurs, a recovery token is injected into a place and the set of primitive operations associated with the recovery policy are triggered.

2.3 Enabling and Firing Rules in SARN

In ordinary Petri nets, a transition is enabled if all its input places contain at least one token. An enabled transition can be fired and one token is removed from each of its input places and one token is deposited in each of its output places. The tokens are deposited in the output places of the transition once the corresponding task finishes its execution, that is, the tokens remain hidden when the task is still active. Upon the completion of the task, the tokens appear in the

Table 1. Primitive Operations

Operation	Effect
`CreateArc(x,y)`	An arc linking the place (or transition) `x` to the transition (or place) `y` is created
`DeleteArc(x,y)`	An arc linking the place (or transition) `x` to the transition (or place) `y` is deleted
`DisableArc(x,y)`	An arc linking the place (or transition) `x` to the transition (or place) `y` is disabled
`ResumeArc(x,y)`	A disabled arc linking the place (or transition) `x` to the transition (or place) `y` is resumed, i.e., will participate in firing transitions
`CreatePlace(p)`	A place `p` is created
`DeletePlace(p)`	A place `p` is deleted
`CreateTransition(t)`	A transition `t` is created
`SilentTransition(t)`	An existing transition `t` is replaced by a silent transition
`ReplaceTransition(t,t')`	An existing transition `t` is replaced by another transition `t'`
`DeleteTransition(t)`	A transition `t` is deleted
`DisableTransition(t)`	A transition `t` will not be able to fire
`ResumeTransition(t)`	A disabled transition `t` is resumed, i.e,
`AddToken(p)`	A standard token is added to a place `p`
`RemoveToken(p)`	A standard token is removed from a place `p`
`AddRecoveryToken(p)`	A recovery token is added to a place `p`
`RemoveRecoveryToken(p)`	A recovery token is removed from a place `p`

outgoing places. If no task failure events occur, SARN will obey this enabling rule.

Besides supporting the conventional rules of Petri nets, some new rules are needed in SARN as a result of the new mechanisms added (recovery transitions and tokens). Here is what will happen when a task failure event occurs:

1. The recovery transition corresponding to this failure event will be created and a recovery token is injected in the newly created input place of the recovery transition.
2. Once a recovery token is injected, the execution of the faulty task will be paused and the system will not be able to take any further task failure event.
3. Once a recovery transition is created, the basic operations associated with it will be executed in the order specified. The net structure will be modified to handle the corresponding failure. Note that this sequence of basic operations does not introduce inconsistencies such as deadlocks.
4. When all operations associated with the recovery transition are executed, all the modifications made to the net structure in order to handle the failure will be removed. The net structure will be restored to the configuration before the occurrence of the failure event.

5. The recovery tokens generated by the execution of the operations will become standard tokens and the normal execution is resumed. The enabled transitions will then fire according to the standard Petri net firing rules.

2.4 Valid SARN Models

SARN must meet certain *constraints* in order to ensure the correct execution of the underlying workflow at run time. Each transition t must be *reachable* from the initial marking of the SARN net, that is, there is a valid sequence of transitions leading from the initial marking to the firing of t. Furthermore, we require that from every reachable marking of the SARN net, a final marking (where there is only one standard token in the output place o of the SARN net) can be reached, i.e., there is a valid sequence of transitions leading from the current marking of the net to its final marking.

To verify the correctness of our SARN model, we utilize some key definitions for Petri net behavior properties adapted from [6].

Definition 2 (Reachability).
In a SARN net $RN = (P, T, Tr, F, i, o, \ell, M)$ with initial marking $M_0 = i$, a marking M_n is said to be reachable from M_0 if there exists a sequence of firings that transforms M_0 to M_n. A firing or occurrence sequence is denoted by $\sigma = M_0 t_1 M_1 t_2 M_2 \dots t_n M_n$ or simply $\sigma = t_1 t_2 \dots t_n$. In this case, M_n is reachable from M_0 by σ and we write $M_0[\sigma\rangle M_n$. □

Definition 3 (Liveness).
A SARN net $RN = (P, T, Tr, F, i, o, \ell, M)$ is said to be live, if for any marking M_n that is reachable from $M_0 = i$, it is possible to ultimately fire any transition of the net by progressing some further firing sequence. □

A SARN model that satisfies the above properties is said to be *valid.*

2.5 Task States

Each task in a workflow process contains a task state variable that is associated with a task state type which determines the possible task states [1]. A transition from one task state to another constitutes a primitive task event. Figure 2 shows the generic task states. At any given time, a task can be in one of the following states: `NotReady`, `Ready`, `Running`, `Completed`, `Aborted`, or `Frozen`.

The task state `NotReady` corresponds to a task which is not yet enabled. When a task becomes enabled, i.e., all its incoming places contains at least one token, the task state changes into `Ready`. A firing of a task causes a transition to the `Running` state. Depending upon whether an activity ends normally or is forced to abort, the end state of a task is either `Completed` or `Aborted`. The `Frozen` state indicates that the execution of the task is temporarily suspended. No operations may be performed on a frozen task until its execution is resumed.

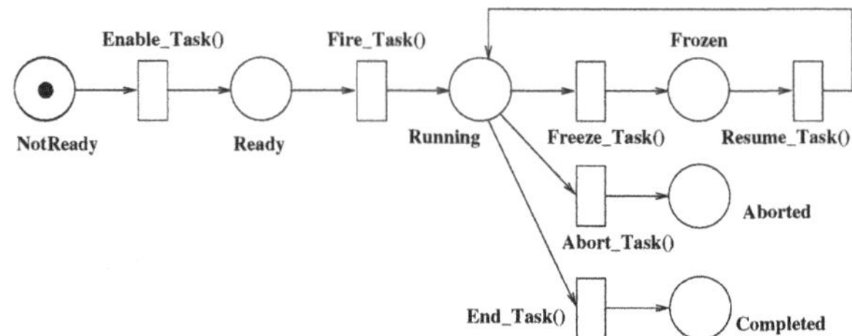

Fig. 2. Generic Task States

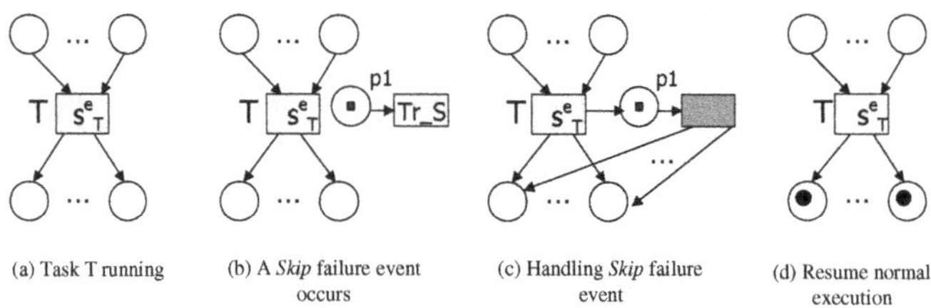

Fig. 3. *Skip* Recovery Policy

3 Task-Based Recovery Policies

In what follows, we will discuss some task-based recovery policies. We will first informally describe the recovery policy, then give a formal definition, and finally, give an example to illustrate how the workflow system modelled as a SARN behaves at run time. We will distinguish between nine recovery policies, namely, *Skip*, *SkipTo*, *Compensate*, *CompensateAfter*, *Redo*, *RedoAfter*, *AlternativeTask*, *AlternativeProvider*, and *Timeout*. Due to lack of space, we will only give details of the *Skip* and *Compensate* recovery policies. For details about other recovery policies see Table 2 and [7].

3.1 Skip

The *Skip* recovery policy will, once the corresponding failure event occurs during the execution of the corresponding task `T`: (i) disable the execution of the task `T` and (ii) skip to the immediate next task(s) in the control flow. This recovery policy applies to running tasks only.

Formally, in the context of SARN, a `Skip(Event e, Transition T)` recovery policy, when executing a task `T` and the corresponding failure event `e` occurs, means (see Fig. 3):
Precondition: *state*(`T`) = `Running`.
Effect:

1. `DisableTransition(T)`, i.e., disable the transition of the faulty task,
2. `CreatePlace(p1)`: create a new place `p1`,
3. `CreateTransition(Tr_S)`: create a *Skip* recovery transition,
4. `CreateArc(p1,Tr_S)`: `p1` is the input place of the *Skip* recovery transition,

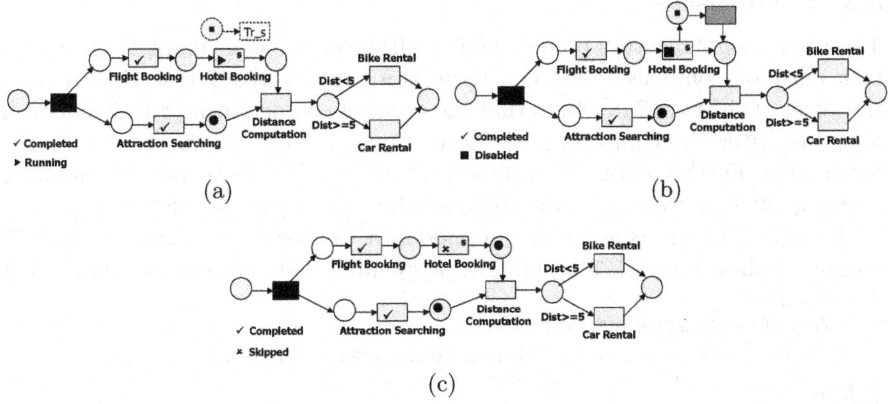

Fig. 4. *Skip* Recovery Policy Example

5. `AddRecoveryToken(p1)`: inject a recovery token into the input place of the *Skip* recovery transition (see Fig. 3(b)),
6. execute the basic operations associated with the *Skip* recovery transition to modify the net structure in order to handle the exception (see Fig. 3(c)),
7. execute the added exceptional part of the SARN net,
8. once the exceptional part finishes its execution, i.e., there is no *recovery* token within the added structure, the modifications made for the task failure event are removed, and
9. resume the normal execution by transforming the recovery tokens on the output places of the skipped task into standard tokens (see Fig. 3(d)).

The operations associated with a *Skip* recovery transition, in order to complete step (7) above, are as follows (see Fig. 3(c)):

(a) `CreateArc(T,p1)`: add an incoming arc from the skipped task to the input place of the recovery transition,

(b) `SilentTransition(Tr_S)`: replace the *Skip* recovery transition with a silent transition (i.e., a transition with no associated task or an empty task), and

(c) $\forall$ `p` $\in$ `T`$^\bullet$ `CreateArc(Tr_S,p)`: add an outgoing arc from the silent transition to each output place of the skipped task `T`.

For instance, in the *Travel Planning* workflow example (see Fig. 1), we associate with the task *Hotel Booking* a *Skip* recovery policy at design time. Upon the occurrence of a skip failure event (for instance, "no response after one day") while executing *Hotel Booking* task, the resulting SARN net will look like Fig. 4(a). After executing the set of basic operations corresponding to the *Skip* recovery policy, the SARN net will become like Fig. 4(b). Once the skip failure is handled, the SARN net will look like Fig. 4(c).

3.2 Compensate

The *Compensate* recovery policy removes all the effects of a completed task. The task must be compensatable, i.e., there is a `compensate-T` task that removes the effect of the task `T` [8]. Note that the event of compensating a task can occur any time after the completion of the task and before the workflow execution terminates. Furthermore, we assume that there is no data flow dependencies between the task to be compensated and the subsequent completed task(s).

Formally, in the context of our model, a `Compensate(Event e, Task T)` recovery policy of a task `T` when its corresponding failure event `e` occurs means:
Precondition:
- *state*(T) = `Completed` and
- `T` is *compensatable*, i.e., there is a `compensate-T` task of `T`.

Effect:
1. $\forall\, \mathtt{t} \in T \mid (\mathtt{t},\mathtt{T}) \in F^{+} \;\wedge\; \mathit{state}(\mathtt{t}) = \mathtt{Running}$ *do* `DisableTransition(t)`, so that *state*(`t`) = `Frozen`, hence all running subsequent task(s) of the task to be compensated are disabled (recall that T is the set of transitions, i.e., tasks of the workflow),
2. `CreatePlace(p1)`: create a new place `p1`,
3. `CreateTransition(Tr_C)`: create a *Compensate* recovery transition,
4. `CreateArc(p1,Tr_C)`: `p1` is the input place of the *Compensate* recovery transition,
5. `AddRecoveryToken(p1)`: inject a recovery token into the input place of the *Compensate* recovery transition,
6. execute the primitive operations associated with the *Compensate* recovery transition,
7. execute the exceptional part of the SARN net,
8. remove the modifications made for the task failure event, and
9. resume the execution of the workflow.

The operations associated with a *Compensate* recovery transition are as follows:
(a) `ReplaceTransition(Tr_C,compensate-T)`: associate to the *Compensate* recovery transition the task `compensate-T` that removes the effects of the task `T` and
(b) $\forall\, \mathtt{t} \in T \mid \mathit{state}(\mathtt{t}) = \mathtt{Frozen}\ \forall\, \mathtt{p} \in {}^{\bullet}\mathtt{t}$ *do* `CreateArc(compensate − T,p)`: add an outgoing arc from the `compensate-T` transition to each input place of the suspended running task(s).

Figure 5 gives an example of the *Compensate* recovery policy where the *Flight Booking* task was compensated while the system was executing the *Distance Computation* task. At design time, we associate with the task *Flight Booking* a Compensate recovery policy. When a compensate failure event, for instance, "cancel flight", occurs while executing the task *Distance Computation*, the resulting SARN net will look like Fig. 5(a). After executing the set of basic operations associated with the *Compensate* recovery policy, the SARN net will appear like Fig. 5(b). Finally, once the *Compensate* exception is handled, the *Travel Planner* workflow will look like Fig. 5(c).

Table 2 gives a summary of the other task-based recovery policies.

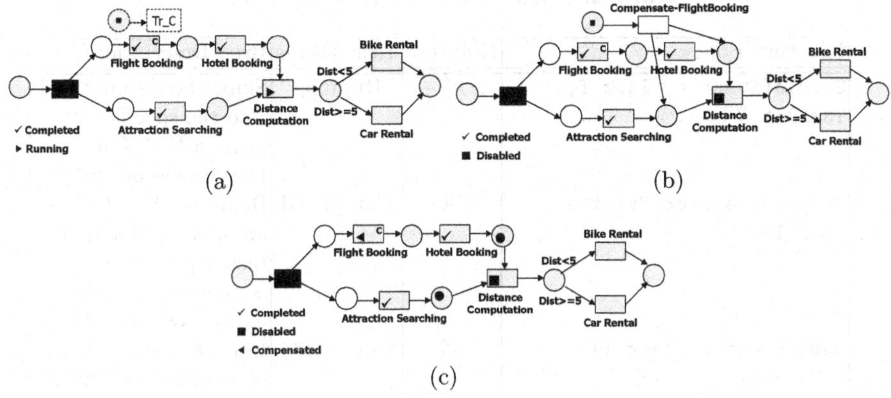

Fig. 5. *Compensate* Recovery Policy Example

4 Region-Based Recovery Policies

The recovery policies defined in the previous section apply to a single task only. In this section, we will extend them to a *recovery region*, i.e., a set of tasks. We will first define the notion of recovery region and then extend some of the single task-based recovery policies to be applied to a recovery region.

4.1 Recovery Region

A *recovery region* is a connected set of places and transitions. Recovery regions are required to have a certain structure. We require that a recovery region has one input place and one output place. The output place of a recovery region is typically an input place for the eventual next recovery region(s). To make the definition of recovery regions clear, we will separate them in such a way that, between the output place of a recovery region and the input place of the eventual subsequent recovery region(s), a silent transition will occur transferring the token from a recovery region to its subsequent recovery region(s). This will cause a non-overlapping of recovery regions, hence making them clearly separated.

A *recovery region* is then a subworkflow that can be seen as a unit of work from the business perspective and to which a set of recovery policies may be assigned. As such, a recovery region is more than a traditional subworkflow. Formally, a *recovery region* is defined as follows.

Definition 4 (Recovery Region).
Let $RN = (P, T, Tr, F, i, o, \ell, M)$ be a SARN net. A recovery region is a subnet $R = \langle P_R, T_R, F_R, i_R, o_R, \ell_R \rangle$ of RN where:

- *$P_R \subseteq P$ is the set of places of the recovery region,*
- *$T_R \subseteq T$ denotes the set of transitions of the recovery region R,*
- *$i_R \in P_R$ is the input place of R,*

Table 2. Other Task-Based Recovery Policies

Recovery Policy	Notation	Task Status	Brief Description
`SkipTo(Event e, Task T, TaskSet` $\mathcal{T}$`)`	$ST^{e}_{T,\mathcal{T}}$	Running	Skips the running task `T` to the specific next task(s) $\mathcal{T}$ if the event `e` occurs
`CompensateAfter(Event e, Task T)`	CA^{e}_{T}	Completed	Removes the effect of an already executed task `T` just after completing it if the event `e` occurs
`Redo(Event e, Task T)`	R^{e}_{T}	Completed	Repeats the execution of a completed task `T` if the event `e` occurs
`RedoAfter(Event e, Task T)`	RA^{e}_{T}	Completed	Repeats the execution of a completed task `T` just after finishing it if the event `e` occurs
`AlternativeTask(Event e, Task T, Task T')`	$AT^{e}_{T,T'}$	Running	Allows an alternative execution of a task `T` by another task `T'` if the event `e` occurs
`AlternativeProvider(Event e, Task T, Provider P)`	$AP^{e}_{T,P}$	Running	Allows an alternative execution of a task `T` by another provider `P` if the event `e` occurs
`Timeout(Task T, Time d)`	T^{d}_{T}	Running	Fails a task `T` if not completed within a time limit `d`. The execution is frozen

– $o_R \in P_R$ *is the output place of* R,
– $\ell_R : T_R \rightarrow \mathcal{A} \cup \{\tau\}$ *is a labeling function, and*
– *Let* $T_R = \{t \in T \mid t^{\bullet} \cap P_R \neq \varnothing \ \wedge \ {}^{\bullet}t \cap P_R \neq \varnothing\}$. *Then* R *must be connected (i.e., there is no isolated place or transition).* □

R represents the underlying Petri net of the recovery region that is restricted to the set of places P_R and the set of transitions T_R.

4.2 Region-Based Recovery Policies

In what follows, we will discuss some region-based recovery policies. They are mainly based on an extension of their corresponding task-based recovery policies.

We will distinguish between eight region-based recovery policies, namely, *SkipRegion*, *SkipRegionTo*, *CompensateRegion*, *CompensateRegionAfter*, *RedoRegion*, *RedoRegionAfter*, *AlternativeRegion*, and *TimeoutRegion*. We will only

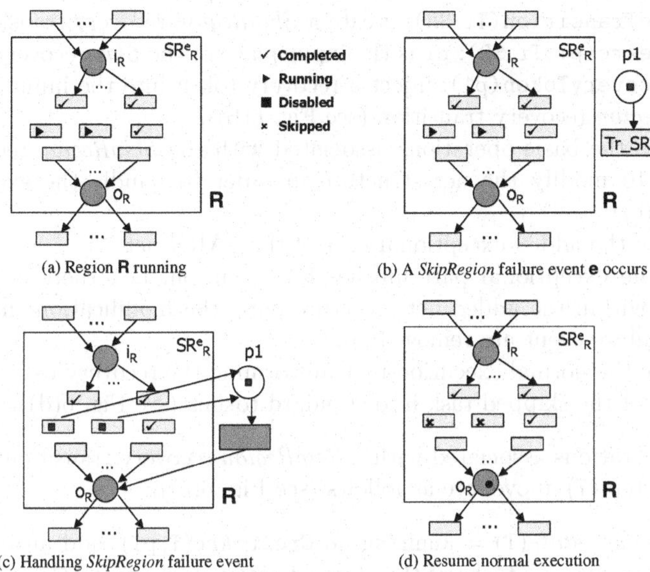

Fig. 6. *SkipRegion* Recovery Policy

describe the *SkipRegion* recovery policy (refer to [7] for details about other region-based recovery policies).

Note also that region-based recovery policies should only be allowed in a valid way. The system must ensure correctness of the modified SARN with respect to consistency constraints (reachability and liveness), so that these behavior properties that were valid before the dynamic change of SARN are also preserved after the handling of the exception.

SkipRegion. The *SkipRegion* recovery policy will, when the corresponding failure event occurs during the execution of the corresponding recovery region `R`: (i) disable the execution of the running tasks within the recovery region `R` and (ii) skip the non-completed tasks of the recovery region `R` to the immediate next task(s) of `R`. This recovery policy applies to running recovery regions only, i.e., there are tasks within the recovery region `R` that are still running. This means that, eventually, some tasks within the recovery region are completed while others have not yet executed.

Formally, in the context of SARN, a `SkipRegion(Event e, Region R)` recovery policy when executing tasks of the recovery region `R` and the corresponding failure event `e` occurs means (see Fig. 6):

Precondition: $\exists$ `T` $\in T_R \mid$ *state*(`T`) = `Running`.

Effect:

1. $\forall$ `T` $\in T_R \mid$ *state*(`T`) = `Running` *do* `DisableTransition(T)`: disable all running tasks of the recovery region `R`,
2. `CreatePlace(p1)`: create a new place `p1`,

3. `CreateTransition(Tr_SR)`: create a *SkipRegion* recovery transition,
4. `CreateArc(p1,Tr_SR)`: `p1` is the input place of the *Skip* recovery transition,
5. `AddRecoveryToken(p1)`: inject a recovery token into the input place of the *SkipRegion* recovery transition (see Fig. 6(b)),
6. execute the basic operations associated with the *SkipRegion* recovery transition to modify the net structure in order to handle the exception (see Fig. 6(c)),
7. execute the added exceptional part of the SARN net,
8. once the exceptional part finishes its execution, i.e., there is no *recovery* token within the added net structure part, the modifications made for the task failure event are removed, and
9. resume the normal execution by transforming the recovery tokens on output places of the skipped task into standard tokens (see Fig. 6(d)).

The operations associated with a *SkipRegion* recovery transition, in order to complete step (7) above, are as follows (see Fig. 6(c)):

(a) $\forall$ `T` $\in T_R \mid state($`T`$) =$ `Running` *do* `CreateArc(T,p1)`: add an incoming arc from the running tasks of the skipped recovery region to the input place of the recovery transition,
(b) `SilentTransition(Tr_SR)`: replace the *SkipRegion* recovery transition with a silent transition, and
(c) `CreateArc(Tr_SR,`o_R`)`: add an outgoing arc from the silent transition to the output place o_R of the recovery region `R` to skip.

4.3 Correctness Preservation

The SARN net generated by using the previously defined task- and region-based recovery policies is a consistent net that satisfies the behavior properties defined in Sect. 2.4 (i.e., reachability and liveness).

Proposition 1 (Correctness Preservation).
The SARN net RN of a workflow obtained after handling an exception using the above defined task- and region-based recovery policies is valid, i.e., the reachability and liveness properties are preserved. □

Proof. Immediate consequence of Definition 1 and of the task- and region-based recovery policies defined previously. □

5 Related Work and Conclusions

Some studies have considered the problem of exception handling and recovery from activity failures in WfMSs, such as [9,5,10,4,11]. Leymann [12] introduced the notion of *compensation sphere* which is a subset of activities that either all together have to be executed successfully or all have to be compensated. The fact that spheres do not have to form a connected graph leads to very complicated semantics. The model of Hagen and Alonso [2] uses a similar notion of sphere to specify atomicity and focuses on the handling of expected exceptions and the integration of exception handling in the execution environment. Grigori et al. [13] focus on the analysis, prediction, and prevention of exceptions in order to reduce their occurrences. In contrast, our aim is to model the recovery from an exception at design time. In addition, an extensive amount of work on flexible recovery in the context of advanced transaction models has been done, e.g., in [14,15]. They particularly show how some of the concepts used in transaction management can be applied to workflow environments.

In this paper, we proposed the Self-Adaptive Recovery Net (SARN) model for specifying exceptional behavior in WfMSs at design time. SARN allows the handling of prespecified events at run time while keeping the Petri net design simple and easy. For existing models to realize the same functionality, the design effort could be tremendous. We also identified a set of high-level recovery policies that are incorporated with either a single task or a recovery region.

To illustrate the viability of our approach, we are currently developing SARN simulator as part of *HiWorD* (HIerarchical WORkflow Designer), a hierarchical Petri net-based workflow modeling tool [16,17].

References

1. Georgakopoulos, D., Hornick, M., Sheth, A.: An Overview of Workflow Management: From Process Modeling to Workflow Automation Infrastructure. Distributed and Parallel Databases **3** (1995)
2. Hagen, C., Alonso, G.: Exception Handling in Workflow Management Systems. IEEE Transactions on Software Engineering (TSE) **26** (2000) 943–958
3. Peterson, J.: Petri Net Theory and the Modeling of Systems. Prentice Hall, Englewood Cliffs (1981)
4. Reichert, M., Dadam, P.: ADEPT flex: Supporting Dynamic Changes of Workflows without Losing Control. Journal of Intelligent Information Systems **10** (1998) 93–129
5. Casati, F., Ceri, S., Pernici, B., Pozzi, G.: Workflow Evolution. Data and Knowledge Engineering **24** (1998) 211–238
6. Murata, T.: Petri Nets: Properties, Analysis and Applications. In: Proceedings of the IEEE. Volume 77(4). (1989) 541–580
7. Hamadi, R., Benatallah, B.: Policy-Based Exception Handling in Business Processes. Technical Report CSE-TR-2004-28, The University of New South Wales, Sydney, Australia (2004)
8. Benatallah, B., Casati, F., Toumani, F., Hamadi, R.: Conceptual Modeling of Web Service Conversations. In: Proceedings of CAiSE'03. Volume 2681., Klagenfurt, Austria, Springer Verlag (2003) 449–467
9. Ellis, C., Keddara, K., Rozenberg, G.: Dynamic Change within Workflow Systems. In: Proceedings of COOCS'95, Milpitas, USA, ACM Press (1995) 10–21
10. Joeris, G., Herzog, O.: Managing Evolving Workflow Specifications. In: Proceedings of CoopIS'98, New York, USA (1998)
11. Klingemann, J.: Controlled Flexibility in Workflow Management. In: Proceedings of CAiSE'00, Stockholm, Sweden (2000)

12. Leymann, F., Roller, D.: Production Workflow — Concepts and Techniques. Prentice Hall (2000)
13. Grigori, D., Casati, F., Dayal, U., Shan, M.C.: Improving Business Process Quality through Exception Understanding, Prediction, and Prevention. In: Proceedings of the 27th Very Large Data Base Conference (VLDB'01), Rome, Italy (2001)
14. Georgakopoulos, D., Hornick, M., Manola, F.: Customizing Transaction Models and Mechanisms in a Programmable Environment Supporting Reliable Workflow Automation. IEEE TKDE **8** (1996) 630–649
15. Wächter, H., Reuter, A.: The ConTract Model. In Elmagarmid, A., ed.: Database Transaction Models for Advanced Applications, Morgan Kaufmann (1992) 219–264
16. Benatallah, B., Chrzastowski-Wachtel, P., Hamadi, R., O'Dell, M., Susanto, A.: HiWorD: A Petri Net-based Hierarchical Workflow Designer. In: Proceedings of ACSD'03, Guimaraes, Portugal, IEEE Computer Society Press (2003) 235–236
17. Chrzastowski-Wachtel, P., Benatallah, B., Hamadi, R., O'Dell, M., Susanto, A.: A Top-Down Petri Net-Based Approach for Dynamic Workflow Modeling. In: Proceedings of BPM'03. Volume 2678., Eindhoven, The Netherlands, Springer Verlag (2003) 336–353

Structuring the Development of Inter-organizational Systems

Frank G. Goethals, Jacques Vandenbulcke, Wilfried Lemahieu, and Monique Snoeck

F.E.T.E.W. – K.U.Leuven – Naamsestraat 69, B-3000 Leuven, Belgium
{Frank.Goethals, Jacques.Vandenbulcke, Wilfried.Lemahieu, Monique.Snoeck}@econ.kuleuven.be
Tel. +32 16 326880 Fax. +32 16 326732
SAP-leerstoel Extended Enterprise Infrastructures

Abstract. In this paper we argue that there are two basic types of Business-to-Business integration (B2Bi), each of which requires a different information systems development approach. A framework is set up to structure the development of intra and inter- organizational systems. The framework has three dimensions, the first one showing business and ICT (Information and Communication Technology), the second one showing strategic, tactical and operational management levels, and the third one showing different levels of systems integration: Enterprise Application Integration, Extended Enterprise Integration, and Market B2Bi. The meaning of the so-created cells and their relationships are investigated.

1 Introduction

Enterprises and the Web services they are offering and using are constantly changing. Changing an enterprise from the current AS-IS state to a desired TO-BE state is a complex task. A company cannot be seen as an entity that can easily be transformed as an integrated, harmonious unit from the current architecture into a new desired architecture. In this paper we want to stress the fact that individual projects, such as Web services development projects, should be seen as a part of a bigger whole. This paper deliberately gives a high-level view on B2Bi (Business-to-Business integration) approaches, so as not to obscure the image with details. We believe such a high-level view is interesting for both practitioners and researchers who live in the middle of a complex reality. The paper at hand shows that there exist different types of B2Bi, and that different development approaches can and need to be used to deal with each.

In what follows, we first discuss two basic types of B2Bi, namely Extended Enterprise integration and Market B2Bi. Next, in Section 3, we add two other dimensions to the discussion of realizing B2B systems. These are (1) the classic problem of Business-ICT alignment, and (2) the alignment and the integration of short term project plans with long term enterprise-wide plans. The three-dimensional structure that is formed by combining these issues structures the architecture problem companies are currently confronted with. The structure makes it possible for practitioners and researchers to pinpoint the problems they are dealing with.

X. Zhou et al. (Eds.): WISE 2004, LNCS 3306, pp. 454–465, 2004.
© Springer-Verlag Berlin Heidelberg 2004

2 Three Basic Types of Systems Integration

From the theory on the network form of organizations (see e.g. [1, 2]), it is clear that companies may be involved in three basic types of *organizational* integration:

- at the level of the *individual enterprise* the different departments have to be integrated,
- at the level of the *Extended Enterprise* the companies that make up the Extended Enterprise have to be integrated. An Extended Enterprise (EE) is *a collection of legal entities ($N \geq 2$) that pursue repeated, enduring exchange relations with one another* [11].
- at the level of the *market* a very loose coupling is established with companies in the environment (other than those within the Extended Enterprise). In contrast with the Extended Enterprise situation, no long term relationship is envisioned with these companies.

Contingency theory reveals that there should be a fit between an organization's structure, its technology, and the requirements of its environment (see e.g. [4]). Hence, companies are confronted with three basic types of information systems integration (see [2] for a detailed motivation). First, companies have to deal with the integration of their internal systems (the so-called Enterprise Application Integration, or EAI for short). Secondly, there is an integration with the systems of partnering companies within the Extended Enterprise. This is called EEi (Extended Enterprise integration). Thirdly, companies may want to integrate their systems with those belonging to other companies than close partners. This practice is called Market B2Bi. While the existence of these three types of systems integration has been recognized earlier (see [2]), it is interesting for the purpose of this paper to dig further into the meaning of each type of B2Bi.

Transaction cost economics shows that an *Extended Enterprise* is usually set up for transactions that are more likely to involve uncertainty about their outcome and that require transaction-specific investments [5]. Web services may be developed for use by one specific partner, and fairly complex choreographies of Web services may be built. In the case of the Extended Enterprise the development of new Web services requires coordination, and the physical distance between user and developer – which is usually large in a Web services context – will be lowered artificially. This can result in the implementation of radically new business practices in ICT systems. While standards are the only option for Market B2Bi, bilateral agreements (even at technology level) may be used in the Extended Enterprise. For example, while SOAP is becoming *the* way to communicate with systems of other companies, partnering companies do *not have to* use SOAP.

In *Market B2Bi*, network effects play. Network effects are based on the concept of positive feedback, i.e., the situation in which success generates more success. The value of connecting to a network depends on the number of other people already connected to it (i.e., you can connect to). Market B2B transactions are in essence isolated events; there is no fixed counterparty in such transactions. ICT can then only be used if it allows for the flexible replacement of one counterparty in an automated transaction by another one. With a 'flexible replacement' we mean that the necessary adaptations should be easily manageable, and should not be expensive nor time-consuming. Therefore, Market B2Bi Web services are generic, standard services that can be used by, and are being offered by many counterparties. Companies will not coordinate or negotiate the development of Market B2Bi Web services, but will use (preferably vendor-neutral) standards.

Clearly, developing Web services for close partners does more resemble the development of classic systems than Market B2Bi Web services development does. Moreover, although an Extended Enterprise is usually not a real enterprise from a legal (financial) point of view, it is noticeable that an Extended Enterprise conceptually forms a new enterprise. After all, the organizations share and redesign processes, data, etcetera. This new enterprise has a starting point and an endpoint (in time) and can be architected. Hence ideas from the Enterprise Architecture discipline can be applied [3].

During the life of an Extended Enterprise, Web services may be designed, implemented, used, and decommissioned[1]. Consequently, the Extended Enterprise Web services lifecycle is encompassed by the lifecycle of the Extended Enterprise (which is in turn usually encompassed by the lifecycles of the Extended Enterprise's constituting companies). This is not the case for Market B2Bi Web services, which are standardized services that have been designed for use by a generic combination of companies. The Market B2Bi Web services lifecycle encompasses the duration of the relationship between parties in Market B2Bi. This is illustrated in Figure 1.

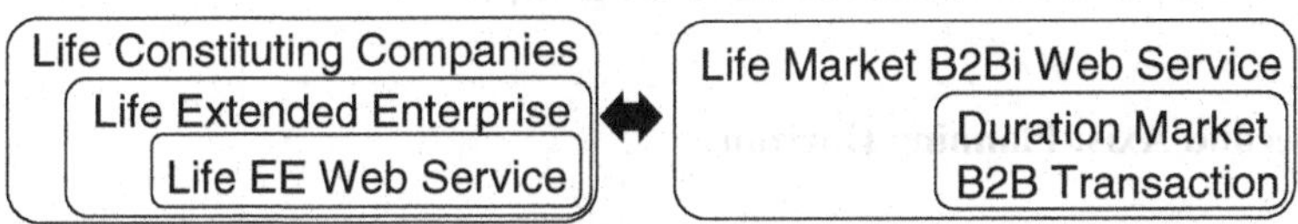

Fig. 1. Life cycle comparisons

Of course, services developed for use by one specific partner may, after some time, be generalized and be made available for use to all companies in the marketplace. Furthermore, novel Web services developed in creative Extended Enterprises may be copied, and practices that once seemed innovative may thus become de facto standard practices, or even formalized standards.

3 Structuring the Architecture Problem in a Framework

Enterprises are constantly changing. Changing an enterprise basically means moving it from the current AS-IS state to a desired TO-BE state (see e.g. [6] for a discussion on this from the Enterprise Architecture discipline). This is illustrated in Figure 2.

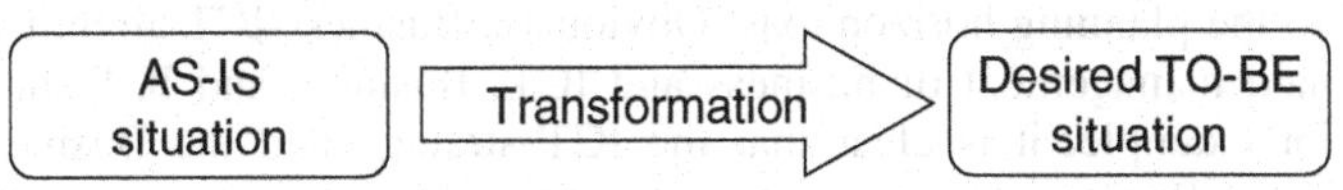

Fig. 2. Moving from the AS-IS situation to a desired TO-BE situation

[1] The lifecycle of entities in general and of enterprises in specific has been discussed in the GERAM (the Generalised Enterprise Reference Architecture and Methodology) [7].

This picture is a tremendous simplification of the reality if the enterprise under consideration is a 'modern' enterprise (i.e., an enterprise that pursues B2Bi). In what follows, we argue that changing an enterprise concerns changing many different issues that should be aligned and integrated. We present three types of 'concerns' which we place on three axes of a cube. One of these axes shows the three types of systems integration mentioned above. This axis is added to the discussion last (i.e., in Section 3.3) because it is by coupling this axis to the two other axes that new insights are developed. The two other axes show two issues that have been discussed extensively in literature in the context of traditional isolated enterprises. Considering these two axes has proved important for traditional enterprises, and now we argue these dimensions are also present and important at a B2B level.

3.1 First Axis: Business Versus ICT

Most companies are using ICT to support their business. Clearly, the business side and the ICT side of a company should evolve in harmony. As the business (departments) should be integrated, the ICT systems they are using should be integrated as well [4]. Alignment between business and ICT is not an easy task and has been the topic of major discussions (see e.g. [8]).

3.2 Second Axis: Planning Horizon

We notice that people may be involved 1) in the *execution* of operations, and 2) in the *management* of operations. In this paper we mainly focus on the latter because this is where the engineering happens. Typically three levels of management are discerned, namely strategic, tactical and operational (see e.g. [9]). At strategic level the desired future of the enterprise is puzzled out. Decisions made at strategic level typically cover a long time horizon of about five years. The mission, the vision, important principles, etcetera are defined. Clearly decisions at this level are not detailed at all, they are vague by nature. At the tactical level a planning is made to structure the different projects that will be executed during the following year. It is important to note that these projects are placed and fitted within the total enterprise architecture. That is, an enterprise-wide viewpoint is taken to define the projects. Hence, this level is fundamental for companies to achieve an *integrated* enterprise. At operational level a detailed planning is made to execute the projects that were foreseen. At this level the focus is on a single project, not on the entire enterprise. Next the project is executed, i.e., the software is programmed, people are trained, etcetera.

We notice the presence of the three management levels both at the business side and at the ICT side of a company; hereby indicating that the Business-ICT axis is orthogonal to the planning horizon axis. Obviously, Business-ICT alignment requires the intertwined management of business and ICT. Business and ICT should be co-evolving. For example, it is clear that the ICT strategy and the Business strategy should fit. If the Business strategy is to automate public processes (i.e., processes in which the company interacts with partners), the ICT vision should not be directed to the use of proprietary protocols, but to the use of open standards such as SOAP.

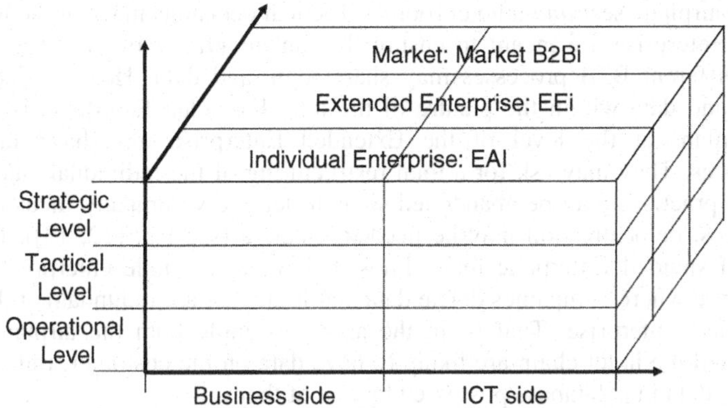

Fig. 3. A three-dimensional classification of architecture issues

3.3 Third Axis: The Three Types of Systems Integration

The third axis represents the three types of systems integration described in Section 2. First, there is the integration of the systems within the firewall. Secondly, the systems of the companies that make up the Extended Enterprise may need to be integrated. Thirdly, companies may want to integrate their systems with those belonging to other parties than close partners (Market B2Bi).

3.4 The Three Axes Together

If we bring the three axes together, we get Figure 3.

The 'Individual Enterprise' cross-section of the cube is not that new[2]. Still, it should be noted that the Tactical ICT cell has been neglected in the past, resulting in disintegrated information systems. That is, while ICT systems used to be developed for use by one specific user group (often one department), it has been admitted (especially in the Enterprise Architecture discipline; e.g. [10]) that an enterprise-wide point of view is needed to get different computer systems to share data and logic.

At the level of the Extended Enterprise operational, tactical and strategic decisions can be made that relate to the collection of companies that make up the Extended Enterprise. Companies may define new concepts and processes which do only exist at the level of the Extended Enterprise, and not at the level of an individual enterprise. Imagine two collaborating companies: an airplane booking company and a hotel chain. They may decide to offer a Web service which allows customers to make a reservation for both an airplane seat and a hotel room in one transaction. This service (which does only exist at the level of the Extended Enterprise, not at the level of the individual enterprises) may produce data such as 'the number of trips booked that

[2] Actually, it fits with the ideas of Maes [11] concerning the vertical extension of the Strategic Alignment Model of Henderson and Venkatraman [8]. While Henderson and Venkatraman focuss on the strategy and the operations, Maes stresses the importance of a 'structure' level (in addition to the strategic and operational levels), which we call "tactical" level.

include an airplane seat *and* a hotel room'[3]. Tactical decisions made at the level of the Extended Enterprise are meant to ensure that an *integrated* Extended Enterprise is created. Different B2B processes may share logic and data. Hence, structuring all processes and data within the picture of the total Extended Enterprise is important. Strategic plans at the level of the Extended Enterprise may have far-reaching consequences. They may ask for a total restructuring of the individual enterprises. A number of practices may be abandoned so as to let every company focus on its core competences, delocalization may be needed, etcetera (see e.g. [12, 13]). In extreme cases the Extended Enterprise may almost behave as a single enterprise. Still, the cases are rare where companies delete data and logic that are redundant at the level of the Extended Enterprise. That is, in the above example both the airplane booking company and the hotel chain are likely to have data on the customer, rather than just storing this data in a database possessed by one of them.

At the level of Market B2Bi, companies have (per definition) a short term relationship with each other, and they do not sit together around the table to make plans. Actually, these plans are likely to be made by standardization organizations or the legislator. The operational plans are existing (horizontal or vertical) standards, such as individual RosettaNet PIPs. Tactical plans show how the standardization organizations see those operational plans coming together (e.g., linking standards such as WSDL, BPEL4WS, WS-coordination, and WS-security). Of course, these standardization organizations have a strategy as well, a vision (e.g., the 'semantic web' is for the most part still a vision). At the level of Market B2Bi, standardized processes and standardized vocabularies may be available (ontologies) which can be used by all companies within some sector for example. Enterprises could then map their proprietary terminology to the standardized vocabulary.

Furthermore, for all three types of integration, business and ICT are expected to be aligned. Doing B2Bi is not just about 'playing' with new ICT standards; it is about developing Web services that are useful for future service-consumers [14] (i.e., ICT departments should become consumer-oriented just like business departments). Alignment is thus also needed across company borders. Interestingly, also at the Market B2Bi level there is a business side and an ICT side to the picture. Some standards are being developed that purely arrange business practices (e.g., CPFR, Collaborative Planning, Forecasting, and Replenishment [15]), while others purely concern ICT matters (e.g., SOAP). Clearly, both types of standards alone will not break any bricks; complementary and explicitly linked standards are needed.

Standards can be very useful, and ease the job of integrating systems, but they can only be used to the extent that they fit with the specific situation of a company. Of course, not everything is being standardized. When it comes to technology, it is only where interoperability is important that standards are developed. Features that cause customer dissatisfaction or hinder industry growth[4] evolve into standards, while features on which differentiation is valuable to the customer do not tend to evolve into standards. Furthermore, the demand for standards usually comes from the users and

---

[3] The Web service would then use two smaller Web services provided by the individual companies. While the choreography of the Web services is something that is negotiated at the B2B level, the internal functioning of the two smaller Web services is something that is realized at the level of the individual enterprises (see the example in Section 3.5).

[4] This may also be the 'software industry' of course. COTS (Commercial Of The Shelf) software is in this sense standardized software.

customers of the technology who experience the confusion caused by the lack of standards [16]. As stated earlier it may become interesting for businesses to use Web services that were initially developed for use by one specific partner, for integration with other counterparties as well. The users then experience the importance of having a standard way to realize this B2B process, and the B2B process may be standardized so as to make it a Market B2B practice. In this context it is also interesting to have a look at COTS software (such as the SAP software packages, for example). In the past, COTS packages were focused on the inside of the company. Now COTS packages are starting to incorporate standard B2Bi practices as well. B2B processes could be entirely realized by individual participants in the business process. That is, the individual participants could implement the Web services internally, and the execution of a choreography of Web services could arise naturally from sending messages from one company to the other (and back), without intervention of a central choreography engine. Standard Web services and standard Web services choreographies could be implemented in COTS software. Furthermore, if some central component is needed, this could be offered by COTS vendors, or standardization organizations. An example of this is the public UDDI registry (which is aimed at Market B2Bi). This registry is offered by companies such as Microsoft, IBM and SAP and can be used to publish and to search Web services.

Note that the Web services concept may seem understandable to business people, but that a business person's perception of a Web service is different from an ICT person's perception. By an ICT person a Web service can be seen as '*a component that is callable by anyone in a loosely coupled style over the Internet using XML and SOAP*' [17]. As such, Web services may exist that do not offer 'business functionality' [14]. Furthermore, for business people, the fact that some functionality is offered by *a software component* is not relevant; they are only interested in the service that is offered (i.e., in the functionality). In fact, one software component may offer several operations that are accessible via SOAP. However, for a business person this is transparent; he sees several services (i.e., functionalities that are offered). Also, the other way around, functionality demanded by business people is not restricted by the borders of existing software systems.

3.5 Discussion and Example

The cube presented in Figure 3 places the development of B2Bi systems within the larger context of 'changing enterprises'. Enterprises may consist of a formal and an informal part. The informal part is usually given shape by things like 'culture'. The formal part concerns the issues that are being actively managed. It should be noticed that ICT systems are deterministic (i.e., their behaviour needs to be specified entirely before they can function). Therefore, ICT systems can only be used to support formal (aspects of) business processes. If personnel wants freedom, and wants to behave in an unpredictable and creative way, it cannot expect information systems to fully support their practices. The only things that can be supported are the deterministic, stable (subparts of) processes. At the moment a process becomes too unstable (i.e., unmanageable), it does not make any sense anymore to formalize the process and to restrict employees that way.

Informal practices bring along uncertainty. For as long as abstraction can be made of the uncertainty (i.e., you only need to know *what* will be done, not *how* it will be done), uncertainty causes no problems. However, in a B2B process companies have to agree on *how* the public process will execute. Companies participate in a shared process (they share the *how*), and uncertainty cannot be abstracted and must be avoided. This – together with the fact that businesses were not concerned about designing B2B processes – is why at a B2B level practices have been stable for many years. Now, to automate B2B processes, the B2B processes need to be formalized, and explicit agreement on the desired TO-BE situation is desirable. In an Extended Enterprise setting, companies may sit together around the table to develop a new B2B process. For Market B2Bi only standardized B2B processes can be used, at least for as long as no software agents do exist that can validate, negotiate, and steer choreographies of Web services. It is needless to say that the development of such agents will take many years, and that such agents require many standards. Software agents that offer such functionality are still a vision (i.e., this concept is still situated at the Market B2Bi Strategic ICT level, where it is linked to the vision of the semantic web) and the infrastructure for such B2Bi practices needs to be developed (i.e., the Market B2Bi Tactical ICT level needs to be planned, and systems and standards need to be put into operation).

The formal part of an entity may or may not be made explicit in 'architectural descriptions'. These architectural descriptions could model the AS-IS situation, or a desired TO-BE situation which needs to be realized. In the Extended Enterprise, we expect the application of "Extended Enterprise Architecture" to gain momentum. Especially now companies are developing more and more Web services, and their B2Bi practices become complex, it becomes important to keep things manageable by having good documentation. For Market B2Bi standardization organizations build generic models, and these can be instantiated by companies for use. Please note that some argue that in the future it will become possible to automatically generate ICT systems from models (see e.g. [18]). As an illustration, the ARIS tool that will be part of the next version of the SAP NetWeaver platform is said to enable business people to change business processes and the underlying ICT systems by dragging and dropping boxes in a graphical user interface. The MDA (Model Driven Architecture) also fits with this vision [14]. While architectural descriptions always have been handy for supporting communication among people and to maintain systems, they would now become directly useful for generating the system. Making the architecture explicit would then not only prove useful in the long term any more, but also in the short term. Of course, when working with standards code generation becomes less of an issue because standard mappings can be made available. Models such as RosettaNet PIPs could for example (partly) be made executable by creating standard mappings to software platforms (e.g., to Microsoft's Biztalk Accelerator).

The theory presented in this paper can be illustrated with a (simplified) hypothetical example of the development of a Web service by an Extended Enterprise. While the text that follows pays attention to the decisions that are made within the cells of the framework, Figure 4 shows the communication between cells. Clearly this image is not complete; much more arrows could be added to the picture (e.g., arrows going back up so as to change unrealistic project plans).

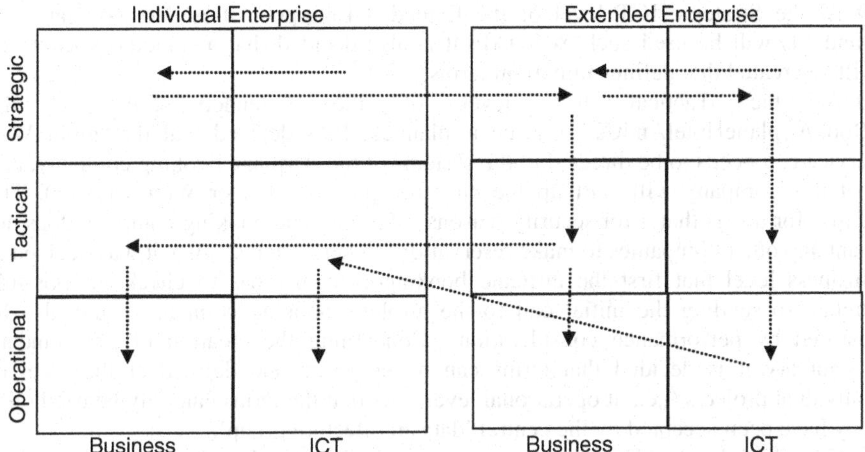

Fig. 4. Example of Extended Enterprise integration

We consider the situation of a hotel chain (the 'Individual Enterprise') which is part of an Extended Enterprise composed of an airplane booking company, a car rental company, and the hotel chain.

At the Strategic ICT level of the hotel chain it is discussed that the ICT department needs to make itself 'useful' to the company. A discussion is started with the people at the Strategic Business level of the company to show that new B2Bi technologies make it possible to cut costs and to create new opportunities.

→ A new Business Strategy is developed for the Individual Enterprise: to use ICT to cut costs and to seize opportunities at a B2B level.

→ Negotiation with the partners within the Extended Enterprise results in a new Extended Enterprise Business Strategy: to offer services to customers by using ICT.

→ A first test Web service is planned at Tactical Business level of the Extended Enterprise. This service should allow customers to book hotel rooms, airplane seats, and cars in one automated transaction via the Internet.

→ This service is further detailed at the Operational Business level of the Extended Enterprise. First, the current phone-and-fax way of working is adapted to the new computerized way of working: While the customer used to be able to go to the party of his choice first (the hotel booking company, the airplane booking company or the car rental company) automated requests of the customer will automatically be sent to the airplane booking company first. It is decided that this company has to be contacted first because the timing of the flights will determine the moment a car can be picked up, and the moment a hotel room is needed (a transcontinental flight may take 20 hours or more, making an extra night in the hotel necessary or unnecessary). Once one or more airplane seats have been put into reservation state for one or more flights, the car rental company and the hotel chain can be contacted to make reservations. Next, a number of proposals (all-in arrangements) are sent to the customer. Once an answer is received from the customer, or 36 hours have past by without any notice from the customer, the reservations are cancelled or confirmed. Finally, an invoice is sent to the customer.

→ At the Strategic ICT level of the Extended Enterprise it is decided that open standards will be used such as SOAP. It is also decided that a standard vocabulary will be created that defines important terms.
→ At the Tactical ICT level of the Extended Enterprise the 'BookAirplaneHotelAndCar' service is planned. It is decided that the initial Web service call needs to be directed to the systems of the Airplane booking company, and that this company will start up the choreography (of smaller Web services). The reason for this is that – for security reasons - the Airplane booking company does not want any other companies to make reservations in her systems. Also, it was decided at Business level that first the airplane booking company has to check for possible flights, so sending the initial call to the airplane booking company could also be justified by performance considerations. Concerning the creation of the standard vocabulary it is decided that terms can be proposed and defined at the level of individual projects (i.e., at operational level), but that the terms can only be used once they have been accepted by the central 'data architecture group'.
→ The 'BookAirplaneHotelAndCar' service is further detailed at the Operational ICT level of the Extended Enterprise. The Web service could be realized in many different ways. The partnering companies choose for the following approach (a motivation for this 'serialized' way of working can be found in [3]). As was decided at Tactical ICT level, the initial Web services call goes to the airplane booking company. This company makes a number of reservations, and sends a request to the car rental company to book both cars and hotel rooms. The car rental company makes a reservation (or sends a rejection to the airplane booking company) and sends a request to the hotel chain for hotel rooms. Once the hotel chain has made reservations it sends a number of proposals to the customer. The customer replies to the hotel chain, which confirms and cancels the necessary rooms, and communicates the confirmation to the car rental company (which also makes the necessary confirmations and cancellations) which in turn communicates the decision to the airplane booking company. Once the necessary airplane seats have been confirmed, an invoice is sent to the customer.
A standard vocabulary is defined for parameters that will be used. It may for example be necessary to define what is meant with the tag 'departure date'. For the airplane booking company this may for example be the day the client leaves his home, while for a hotel chain a 'departure date' would typically be the day the client leaves the hotel. Clearly, a standard vocabulary needs to be defined.

At the level of the Individual Enterprise (the hotel chain) the following is noticed:
→ At Tactical Business level it is believed that this project has no 'restructuring' consequences (e.g., no people will need to be moved from one department to another).
→ At Operational Business level the old operational process of renting rooms will remain valid. Still, the people responsible for making reservations will now also have to check 'alerts' fired by the system concerning special requests of customers who try to book a room via the Internet automatically.
→ At Tactical ICT level it is decided that the company needs to develop a generic RoomRental service. This service should be generic in that it can handle requests that come from the customer directly, requests that come from the partnering car rental company (in which case airplane seats may have been booked already) and requests that come from the partnering airplane booking company (in which case airplane seats will already have been reserved, but no car is needed). It is noticed that this Web service can use functionality from the existing integrated 'room booking system'.

→ At Operational ICT level, the Web service itself is realized. A SOAP wrapper is created for the existing 'room booking system', and an 'alert mechanism' is created that allows the people in the lobby to check and to handle special requests.

The above example is (of course) a simplification of reality, but it illustrates the roles of the cells in the framework.

4 Conclusions

The contribution of this paper is that it brings two classic topics (Business-ICT alignment, and the different management levels) together in one framework with a new (third) dimension to take B2B practices into consideration. Putting the three axes together brings structure to the B2B domain and shows a number of basic viewpoints on integration practices. The framework is high-level in that it talks about 'business' and 'ICT' rather than about specific roles within these categories (such as CIO, business analysts, programmers, configuration managers, etcetera). Also, we did not further dig into the six aspects identified by Zachman [10] that need to be architected in an enterprise. (Basically, the data, processes, locations, persons, timing and motivation should be architected in each cell of Figure 3.) This may be seen as a negative point. However, including these ideas was expected to obscure the total picture this paper wants to draw. We have shown that changing a modern enterprise actually boils down to changing a number of different issues harmoniously. Communication between cells in the framework is necessary to realize required changes. We believe it would be very interesting to research the relationship between the performance of a company and (1) the effort put in each cell (as stated the tactical ICT level of individual companies has been neglected for years, resulting in EAI projects now), (2) the information that is communicated across cells (which is necessary to achieve alignment and integration), and (3) the absence or presence of models explicitly showing formal issues (as having models of something from different points of view makes it easier to manage and to communicate that something, and to automatically generate systems).

We believe that identifying the concerns of different people in an integration effort is important. Architectural descriptions made from different viewpoints (i.e., that make different abstractions of the reality) should be linked to each other. Concepts such as 'private processes', 'public processes', 'Web services choreographies', 'Web services orchestration', 'executable processes', and 'abstract processes' actually all relate to viewpoints (and to the concerns of someone looking from that point of view). Also, ICT standards such as WSDL, BPEL4WS, BPML, and business standards such as CPFR can be related to viewpoints. A clear definition of all concepts needed to do B2Bi is only possible once the necessary viewpoints have been identified. Clearly, with BPEL4WS a Web services process can be described, but this gives only a description from one point of view. Several points of view are needed to develop an entire enterprise (and its relationships with the outer world). Also, to generate programming code different viewpoints on the system and the relationships between those viewpoints should be documented. This paper has structured the domain of B2Bi, offering a number of basic viewpoints on B2Bi.

Acknowledgements. This paper has been written as part of the 'SAP-leerstoel'-project on 'Extended Enterprise Infrastructures' sponsored by SAP Belgium.

References

1. Podolny, J., Page, K.: Network forms of organization. ARS 24 (1998): 57-76.
2. Goethals, F., Vandenbulcke, J., Lemahieu, W., Snoeck, M., Cumps, B.: Two Basic Types of Business-to-Business Integration. International Journal of E-Business Research, Forthcoming (2005).
3. Goethals, F., Vandenbulcke, J., Lemahieu, W., Snoeck, M., De Backer, M., and Haesen, R.: Communication and Enterprise Architecture in Extended Enterprise Integration. ICEIS 2004 conference proceedings, Volume 3, 332-337.
4. Borgatti, S.: Organizational Theory: Determinants of structure. Retrieved from http://www.analytictech.com/mb021/orgtheory.htm on March 4, 2003 (2001).
5. Picot, A., Ripperger, T., Wolff, B.: The Fading Boundaries of the Firm: The Role of Information and Communication Technology. JITE (1996), 152(1), 65-79.
6. CIO Council: A Practical Guide to Federal Enterprise Architecture. Retrieved from http://www.cio.gov/archive/bpeaguide.pdf on June 9, 2004 (2001).
7. Bernus, P., Nemes, L., Schmidt, G: Handbook on Enterprise Architecture, Springer-Verlag, 778 (2003).
8. Henderson, J., Venkatraman, N.: Strategic Alignment: Leveraging Information Technology for Transforming Organizations. IBM Systems Journal (1993) Vol 32, no 1, 4-16.
9. Proper, H., Bosma, H., Hoppenbrouwers, S., Janssen, R.: An Alignment Perspective on Architecture-driven Information Systems Engineering. Proceedings of the Second National Architecture Congres, Amsterdam, The Netherlands (2001) 11.
10. Zachman, J.: A framework for information systems architecture. IBM Systems Journal (1987) Vol. 26, No.3, 276-292.
11. Maes, R.: A Generic Framework for Information Management. PrimaVera Working Paper (1999) 99-03, 22.
12. Bowersox, D., Closs, D., Stank, T.: How to Master Cross-enterprise collaboration. Supply Chain Management Review (July/August 2003) 18-27.
13. Liedtka, J.: Collaborating across lines of business for competitive advantage. Academy of Management Executive (1996) 10(2), 20-34.
14. Frankel, D., Parodi, J.: Using Model-Driven Architecture to Develop Web Services. Retrieved from http://www.omg.org/ on January 29, 2003 (2002).
15. The Collaborative Planning, Forecasting and Replenishment Committee: VICS CPFR model. Retrieved from http://www.cpfr.org/ on June 14, 2004.
16. Cook, M.: Building Enterprise Information Architectures. Prentice-Hall (1996) 179.
17. van der Lans, R.: SAI-workshop, Webservices - Hét nieuwe webparadigma (2002).
18. Smith, H., Fingar, P.: A New Path To Business Process Management. Optimize (October 2002) 55-61.

Contemplating Open Source Enterprise Systems

Alexander Dreiling, Helmut Klaus, Michael Rosemann, and Boris Wyssusek

Queensland University of Technology
Faculty of Information Technology
Centre for Information Technology Innovation (CITI)
GPO Box 2434, Brisbane Qld 4001, Australia
{a.dreiling, h.klaus, m.rosemann, b.wyssusek}@qut.edu.au

Abstract. Until recently, integration of enterprise systems has been supported largely by monolithic architectures. From a technical perspective, this approach has been challenged by the suggestion of component-based enterprise systems. Lately, the nature of software as proprietary item has been questioned through the increased use of open source software in business computing in general. This suggests the potential for altered technological and commercial constellations for the design of enterprise systems, which are presented in four scenarios.

1 Introduction

The development of integrated enterprise information systems shows that the proprietary paradigm of contemporary enterprise systems development is a major obstacle preventing these systems from ever meeting the promises made by their proponents as well as meeting the expectations of the companies implementing them. An alternative appears in the paradigm of open source software development, which could be extended into the development of enterprise systems.

2 Integration: Architecture Between Developer and User

Commercial software is a rather recent phenomenon in the computer and services industry, which emerged simultaneously with the separation of expertise from a single supplier [1]. In the 1950s and 1960s, hardware and software used to be bought and experts used to be hired—en bloc—from vendors such as IBM. Software became a commodity only after IBM's monopoly power had been legally challenged, and software and hardware had to be unbundled [2]. Subsequently, diversity and incompatibility of hard- and software prevailed, yet this situation was soon superseded by large-scale developers controlling architectures [3], while taking advantage of common standards.

X. Zhou et al. (Eds.): WISE 2004, LNCS 3306, pp. 466–471, 2004.
© Springer-Verlag Berlin Heidelberg 2004

The control of architecture is prevalent today in the enterprise system software industry. This suggests that the commodity form of large-scale business applications should be accounted for, when their 'match' with 'business needs' is contemplated. The leading rationale of enterprise systems—integration, having already been the "holy grail of MIS" since the 1960s [4, 5]—is a contentious issue. In terms of software, the objection was that integration implied that enterprise systems had a "monolithic architecture" [4, 6]. This was due to them being commercial products, covering the requirements and complexities of a variety of industries and organisations. Subsequent adaptation through configurations effected ever more options and parameters entering the code: specialised applications, such as Finance, Human Resources, or Logistics became large modules through incremental evolution [6]. Technical integration became an issue in that interfaces had to be developed for combining enterprise systems software with in-house and legacy applications, and add-ons by third-party developers (ibid). However, it might have been against the interests of large software developers to offer truly open interfaces that would allow for combining their products with that of a competitor. Third-party developers overcame these obstacles by designing enterprise application integration software (ibid).

The technical integration dilemma and the perceived imposition of developers' business models on users [7], occasioned the proposal of an "alternate minimalist strategy ... [that] relies on composing large systems from largely independent components that are assembled to meet situation-specific requirements" [4]. The new software 'paradigms' of object orientation and distributed computing, combined with concern for user organisations' 'actual' requirements provided 'technology and business imperatives' for a reversal of the architectural, and necessarily commercial conditions of enterprise computing applications [8]. The architecture that should deliver the desired fit between technology and business, firstly meant changing the current fundamentals in terms of hardware: client-server technology was supposed to be supplanted by distributed object architecture (ibid). Next, components were envisaged that could be assembled with ease into applications covering specialised processes, and providing high adaptability, in terms of current and future special requirements. Their integration within the distributed system was to be accomplished by middleware—a logical layer providing coordination. Correspondingly, component development should become the domain of specialised developers that were close to their clients and the processes in their industries (ibid). The accomplishment of the distributed architecture, both in terms of software as well as in terms of the software industry structure, relied heavily on standardisation that ensured interoperability of components and middleware (ibid).

The vision for a new kind of enterprise systems was based on the premise that "[the] monopoly model where a company provides a bundled, monolithic package will not work in the future" (ibid). It would have entailed a swift re-orientation of the computer and services industries. From today's perspective, the promise of the "component model of software engineering [...] introducing the market-mechanism to software engineering", and by that providing "better products, and lower costs [... and] breaking large monopolies and generating high efficiencies" (ibid), remained unfulfilled. The (relative) openness of application interfaces, since being a strategy by large developers to increase usage of their products, was certainly not a suitable means to shake-up the structure of an industry that is dominated by a handful of 'global players'. The latter could also control either through cooperation or through rivalry the development of the crucial standards that would have allowed or disallowed software engineering principles to be mirrored in industry structure. For users, the implications of moving from comprehensive packages from big developers to components from a diverse market would have implied strengthening the internal IT-expertise, as informed purchaser and wise manager of a tailored portfolio of applications [4]. However, the increased interest in outsourcing, not only of information technology, but also of business processes, has reduced this expectation to another ambition unfulfilled.

Integration in enterprise systems appears to be only viable by accommodating with the circumstance that systems development remains in the hands of a few 'global players', interpreting standards according to their interest. Yet, while managing complexity from a central control perspective may have too many trade-offs to be acceptable for good, software engineering principles and open standards are only a necessary but not sufficient condition for enterprise software development becoming less constrained by the politics of 'global players', responsive to user interests, and benefiting regional industries. As the first step of commodifying software was a legal matter, attempting to dissolve the proprietary nature of contemporary enterprise systems development may open an opportunity to address some deficiencies of enterprise systems. The abandonment of proprietary software development is open source development. The possible consequences of a change in the legal status of enterprise systems software towards open source will be elaborated on in the following.

3 Open Source Versus 'Closed Source'

Free in the context of open source refers to its legal status and not to its use being free of charge. "Free software is a matter of the users' freedom to run, copy, distribute, study, change and improve the software" [9]. Consequently, "free" does not preclude that free software or open source software can be commercial products. Software that comes free of charge may still be protected by intellectual property rights. Similarly, the general availability of the source code does not imply that it can be used by everyone. The principal distinction between open source and 'closed source' software lies in the development process. The open source software development model can be referred to as "bazaar" as opposed to "cathedral" representing the classical one of proprietary software development. The bazaar model is characterised by the openness of the source code which allows basically everyone to participate in the development of open source software; the cathedral model is characterised by a limited number of people having exclusive access to the software under development [10] (thus "closed source"). Even if the general public has access to the source code of proprietary software it does not mean that it is free. On the other hand, this does not preclude that open source software can be commercial software.

Due to its distinct characteristics open source software development has major consequences on the outcome of the development process, e.g., it:

- supports the development of open standards; it is possible for other parties to provide extensions to existing software;
- implies open data formats; users can access data without being bound to proprietary software that may not be available in the future;
- supports customisability; users can tailor software to meet their specific requirements; e.g., localisation which has been neglected by most proprietary software in addressing the needs of profitable markets only;
- supports improved quality; the development of the source code is not bound to a limited group of developers it becomes easier to detect bugs and the like;
- can help to speed up development processes, since the number of developers involved in an open source software development project is not limited.

The effects of 'bazaar style' software development process on its outcome point to the deficiencies of the 'cathedral style', the software development process for enterprise systems. These can be corroborated by the acknowledgement of many economists that dominant companies, such as those in the enterprise software industry, are less disposed to respond to articulated customer requirements, and that monopolies as well as oligopolies tend to stifle product and service innovation.

Dissatisfaction with enterprise systems can be explained by the constellation between developers and users, which is in favour of the developers, and a significant cornerstone for that is the proprietary nature of software licensed to organisations. Positing the proprietary nature of software as determinant of the dissatisfaction with enterprise systems simply means to shift the attention to the mode of production, rather than being focussed on the point of application. Considering the interests of developers and their control of production allows for recasting client dissatisfaction according to the following examples:

- *Insufficient standardisation of enterprise systems functionality*: Standardisation of enterprise systems functionality would enable easy creation of, e.g., enterprise systems web services. However, why would an enterprise systems developer be interested in such standards if this meant opening his client-base to competition?
- *Insufficient differentiation of technical and business expertise*: Separation of technical expertise from business expertise would enable smaller companies to enter the market by offering business expertise for existing technical expertise or the other way around. However, if a large proprietary company offers both in an integrated way and implementing consultants operate accordingly, why would they foster such a development of technology and expertise?
- *Insufficiently opened architecture*: Open architectures would allow for easy integration between business partners. However, if a proprietary enterprise systems vendor developed an entirely open architecture, migration would be facilitated and he would make it simpler to replace his product components.
- *Cultural misfit of enterprise resource planning packages*: Different cultures need enterprise systems with different functionality. However, how can enterprise systems developers solve a particular issue of a region if they do not operate there?

Open source 'bazaar style' software development can successfully address a number of deficits of contemporary enterprise systems. Neither are these deficiencies of enterprise systems unknown to developers nor are they insurmountable in principle, since alternative architectures and standards have already been proposed. The problem is the way how software is developed within the constraints of the proprietary 'closed source' model. If the legal status of software developed changes, the unwanted consequences of the 'cathedral style' development process will most likely disappear as well. Thus, transferring enterprise software into the legal status of open source software gives developers the opportunity to address a range of deficiencies of contemporary enterprise systems.

4 Enterprise Systems and Open Source Software Development

Viable alternatives to the contemporary prevailing mode of enterprise system development can be made apprehensible by scenarios that show potential constellations of 'cathedral style' (i.e., proprietary) and 'bazaar style' (i.e., open source) software development. The decomposition of enterprise systems into an architecture layer and a business application layer combined with the 'cathedral style' and 'bazaar style' development paradigms leads to four scenarios of interaction between architecture layer and business application layer. The case of enterprise systems as monolithic blocks without evident separation between architecture and business applications is included as well. These scenarios of decomposition are defensible, since similar developments took place in the past with computer systems, e.g., with the separation of operating systems and applications. All scenarios, except for the status quo, require open interfaces between the architecture and business application layers.

- The *monolithic ES Package* scenario is the status quo. There are many examples of such enterprise systems on the market.
- In the *solely proprietary* scenario, both business applications and architecture are proprietary. Splitting monolithic enterprise system packages into architecture and business application layers would result in such a constellation.
- In the *open source business applications on proprietary architecture* scenario the proprietary architecture layer serves as a communication and integration medium between open source components. Open source software is highly dependent on the vendor of the proprietary architecture.
- In the *proprietary business applications on open source architecture* scenario, the open source architecture layer provides a truly open platform for proprietary business applications.
- In the *solely open source* scenario, both the architecture and business application layers are open source. The product nature of the enterprise systems software has disappeared entirely, giving way to a focus on the service by which installations are delivered to users.

5 Conclusions and Outlook

Proceeding not by extrapolating from the past of enterprise systems development but by questioning whether the enterprise system's underlying integration concept and development paradigm are dimensions that due to their inherent antinomies might be susceptible to change has shown that:

- Technical possibilities for novel constellations of integration and development are inherent in the architecture for enterprise systems, where the emergent vertical split of enterprise systems into architecture and business applications can be observed.
- Simultaneously, the open source paradigm suggests a novel approach to development, coexisting with the proprietary one. The vertical split of enterprise systems may show some potential for the extension of open source into that area. Given the central tenets of enterprise systems, there are several reasons for an open source enterprise systems development being preferable over its proprietary counterpart.

The recent rise of interest in open source software warrants further investigation into the viability of the open source software development paradigm for enterprise system development. This investigation must heed to the technical, legal and commercial constellations of the software industry, which, as the past has shown, can be subject to unanticipated changes. These kinds of analyses should not be left to commercial industry analysts, who are interested in 'constructing' expectations and the 'market'.

References

1. Campbell-Kelly, M.: From airline reservations to Sonic the Hedgehog: a history of the software industry. MIT Press, Cambridge, MA (2003)
2. Scarbrough, H.: Problem-solutions in the management of information systems expertise. Journal of Management Studies 30 (1993) 939–955
3. Morris, C. R., Ferguson, C. H.: How Architecture Wins Technology Wars. Harvard Business Review (1993) 86–96
4. Kumar, K., Hillegersberg, J. v.: ERP experiences and evolution. Communications of the ACM 43 (2000) 22–26
5. Haigh, T.: Software in the 1960s as concept, service, and product. IEEE Annals of the History of Computing 24 (2002) 5–13
6. Sprott, D.: Componentizing the enterprise application packages. Communications of the ACM 43 (2000) 63–69
7. Davenport, T. H.: Putting the enterprise into the enterprise system. Harvard Business Review (1998) 121–131
8. Fan, M., Stallaert, J., Whinston, A. B.: The adoption and design methodologies of component-based enterprise systems. European Journal of Information Systems 9 (2000) 25–35
9. Free Software Foundation: The free software definition. Retrieved 10 July 2004, from http://www.gnu.org/philosophy/free-sw.html
10. Raymond, E.: The Cathedral and the Bazaar. Knowledge, Technology & Policy 12 (1999) 23–49

Managing Changes to Virtual Enterprises on the Semantic Web

M.S. Akram and A. Bouguettaya

Department of Computer Science
Virginia Tech
{salman,athman}@vt.edu

Abstract. The Web has become the universal medium of interactions between distributed entities. It is changing the way virtual enterprises are being represented from the traditional single entity to a collaboration of Web accessible services called *Web services*. Web services are enabling virtual enterprises by integrating partners from across organizational boundaries. These enterprises will *evolve* over time by automatically managing changes in their environment. In this paper, we present a change management approach for virtual enterprises on the Semantic Web. We combine *Web services*, *ontologies*, and *agents* to cater for the management of changes.

1 Introduction

Virtual enterprises are a prime candidate to take advantage of the current Web revolution. A virtual enterprise (*VE*) is a conglomeration of outsourced services that collaborate to achieve a shared goal [1]. The Web began as a platform solely for scientific collaboration. Because of its ubiquity and ease, it was ultimately adopted by other communities, such as the business community and the government. A prime example is the large number of businesses that migrated their operations online during the last decade. The resulting increase in service volume on the Web has prompted enterprises to *outsource* non-core tasks and/or provide *value-added* services to consumers (e.g., *Amazon*, *Dell*). Current trend in service outsourcing and advances in *service oriented* computing are poised to make a profound impact on VEs.

One of the issues in enabling a VE is the integration of data and services from heterogeneous sources. The accessibility of these services is strictly dependent on the type of host platform. Common standards and platform independence are a prerequisite to successfully integrate VEs on the Web. The *Semantic Web* is taking center stage in providing such standards. The Semantic Web is an extension of the current Web in which information is given well-defined meaning to better enable computers and people to work in cooperation [2]. It is poised to take the concept of VEs to a higher level through the deployment of *Web services*, *agents*, and *ontologies*. A Web service is an interface that describes a collection of operations that are accessible using standard XML messaging [2]. An agent is

X. Zhou et al. (Eds.): WISE 2004, LNCS 3306, pp. 472–478, 2004.
© Springer-Verlag Berlin Heidelberg 2004

a software that acts autonomously based on the parameters provided by humans or other intelligent entities. An ontology is a specification of a conceptualization.

One of the fundamental challenges in enabling VEs on the Semantic Web is *change management*. Change management is the *detection*, *propagation*, and *reaction* to significant changes in the VE environment. We expect that VEs would only thrive if they are able to quickly and automatically adapt to changes in the environment. Current methods of change management are usually *ad hoc* and require significant human involvement (e.g., business process re-engineering, continuous process improvement). *Workflows* have traditionally been used to model and enact organizational business logic. In this approach, tasks are mapped to business units for enactment. These units are usually part of one single enterprise. The enterprise's internal structure is fairly static and the rate of organizational change is usually very slow. Therefore, changes in workflows have usually been modeled as *exceptions*. In contrast, Semantic Web based VEs consider changes as the rule, and any solution to change management would need to treat them as such. In this paper, we propose change management techniques in loosely coupled VEs. The paper is organized as follows. We describe a categorization of changes in section 2. Section 3 presents our change management approach. Finally, section 4 concludes the paper.

2 Categorizing Changes

Changes are categorized into three layers: *business*, *ontological*, and *service* (Figure 1). Each business layer change describes a type of change that is of interest to the entrepreneur. These "abstract" changes map to the ontological layer. The ontological layer consists of the changes that can be executed in the VE and subsequently mapped to the service layer. The service layer describes the changes to the participant Web services and service environment.

Business changes are further classified into three types. The first type of business change is the change in enterprise *efficiency*. Efficiency is the ratio of

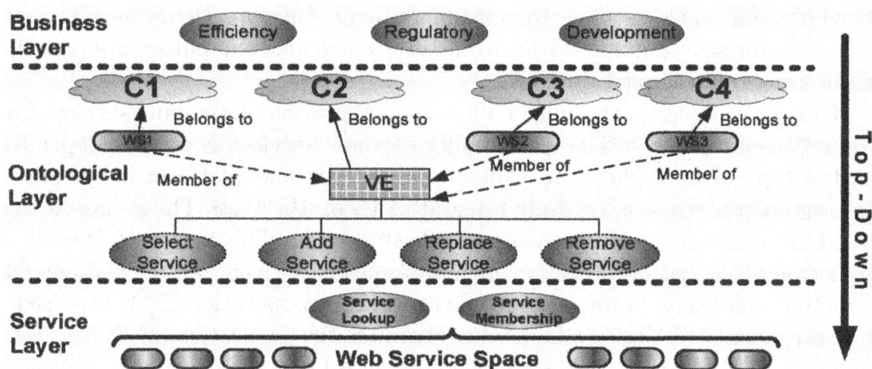

Fig. 1. The Mapping of Change Management Layers

the VE's output versus the input resources. As a VE expands, the magnitude of user transactions are poised to grow substantially. This influx of transactions may be focussed on a specific service, and prove as a potential bottleneck. In essence, the request overload at a specific service consumes resources, such as time and bandwidth, that could be used elsewhere. To rectify this problem, an additional *instance* of that service may be added to distribute the request load. Alternatively, a VE may determine in the future that multiple instances of a service are no longer required. In this case, only a single instance of the service would suffice, and the additional instances will be removed. The second type of change is managed through *business development*. Business development is a process that the VE executes throughout its lifecycle, and consists of business expansion, retention, and attraction. Business *expansion* is the process an established VE goes through when increasing the size of its operations, its customer base, or its geographic operating area. *Attraction* is defined as the effort of a VE acting independently to secure the business of a third party by offering the most favorable terms. A VE promotes business attraction through the *dynamic* selection of partners. Similarly, *retention* is enforced by dynamically offering services to users. The third type of business change in a VE is *regulatory*. While the previous two changes deal with the performance and economic factors of the environment, respectively, regulatory changes are derived from the governance of the enterprise. These changes are initiated by new government *legislations* or by changes in organizational *regulations*. Regulatory changes are explicitly introduced in the VE.

Each business layer change is mapped to the *ontological* layer. An *ontology* defines a collection of Web services that share the same domain of interest. The ontological layer consists of changes that are applied to the ontological organization of the VE and its environment. We divide the *ontological space* into *communities* and ontological *operations* (Figure 1). A community is a collection of Web services that provide similar functionalities. The semantic description of a Web service determines the type of services it provides and the community it belongs to. A Web service may belong to more than one community at a given instance. Business partners in a VE are dynamically selected from the respective communities. In turn, the VE itself is a member of a community. The business operations of *select*, *add*, *remove*, and *replace* correspond to the type of business change.

The ontological changes are finally mapped onto the service layer. The service layer consists of the actual Web services and the service registries that comprise the Semantic Web. The service layer is the one that is physically present in the virtual enterprise environment. Hence, the VE must propagate changes to this layer for execution. For example, if a service is removed from the VE, the appropriate registries in the web service space must be updated to reflect the change in VE membership. Service layer changes are, thus, concerned with updating the appropriate registries (e.g., service registry, ontology).

3 Managing Changes

An enterprise may experience numerous types of business changes. Furthermore, changes could also occur in a *implicit* form, which is only initiated by the successive execution of business changes. Change in VE identity is an example of such a change. We limit our discussion to the three abstract changes categorized earlier. These changes are mapped to the ontological layer, and finally executed at the service layer. An important aspect of change management is service discovery. Therefore, we first discuss our service selection approach, and then describe the change management mechanisms.

Organizing Web Services

Service location is a prerequisite to Web service orchestration. The problem of discovering the services necessary to manage changes is particularly challenging in the dynamic Web services context. Services required by a VE must be searched from an *exploratory* service space. Exploratory refers to the *non-deterministic* process of identifying the necessary Web services [3]. Web services are *a priori* unknown and may only be determined dynamically, i.e., after their need is established. Our approach to the problem is based on organizing Web services into communities.

The UDDI registry in the standard Web service framework does not suffice in dynamically discovering appropriate Web services. UDDI uses `tModels` to categorize a service into a reusable taxonomy [4]. These taxonomies are predefined and it is necessary to have *a priori* knowledge of a `tModel` in order to search for it. Furthermore, `tModels` do not provide a framework to establish relationships with other `tModels` that can promote efficient location of services. For our solution, we use *DAML-S* (DARPA Agent Markup Language for Web services) to complement the standard *WSDL* (Web Service Description Language) description of Web services. DAML-S provides the ability to organize Web services into ontological communities [2]. DAML-S divides service descriptions into the service *profile*, *model*, and *grounding*. The service profile provides a high level description of a Web service. It expresses the required input of the service and the output the service will provide to the requester (i.e., input/output parameters). The service model defines the operations and their execution flow in the Web service. Service grounding provides a mapping between DAML-S and the WSDL, and describes how the service is physically invoked.

The service profile provides sufficient information for discovery of a community that hosts a certain Web service. A service profile is divided into a *description* of the service, the *functionalities*, and the *functional attributes*. The description provides human understandable information about the Web service. For example, a description includes the name of the service and its textual description. A functionality in DAML-S describes properties like input, output, precondition, effect, etc. The functional attributes provide information such as response time and costs [2].

Web services required to fulfill VE goals are discovered using descriptions provided in DAML-S registries. The *semantic* criteria for the service is first extracted from the *schema* of the VE. The `schema` is an XML representation of the VE's *business strategy*, which defines the business objectives, goals, organizational structure, and competence of components of an enterprise. After the successful discovery of the Web services, each service description is registered with the `schema`.

Detecting Changes

Change *detection* is the awareness that a change has occurred and the subsequent identification of its cause. All significant changes must be detected for the successful execution of a VE. Changes are detected by monitoring interactions between the (i) user and VE, and (ii) participant services. Business changes, such as development and efficiency, are determined through the user's interaction with the enterprise. User interactions must be monitored to detect these changes. For instance, the VE monitors a growing trend that users are targeting a specific group of services. Therefore, the VE detects the need for adding a *composite* service that represents the service group. In turn, the VE modifies its `schema` and adds the composite service to accomplish business development. The description of such a service is generated by extracting the description of the existing services from the `schema`. Similarly, a participant Web service that does not contribute to the development of the VE is also detected through user interactions. Consequently, the `schema` of the VE is modified to remove the service.

Interaction between participant Web services is also monitored to determine the changes to the VE. All services that have direct P2P conversations with other participant Web services establish their conversational protocols with mutual agreements [5]. These mutual agreements are predefined in a machine-understandable format and stored in the VE `schema`. The VE must be cognizant of such protocols, as they may affect the levels of internal traffic. Let us consider two participant Web services that have P2P conversations. In this case, these services frequently exchange information. To determine a change in the efficiency of the VE, we monitor the increase or decrease in conversations. The VE searches for an additional service instance in case for increase, or removal of existing instance if conversations decrease. Changes are, therefore, detected by deploying monitoring agents between participant Web services, and between users and Web services.

Propagation

The `schema` is the prime mechanism for change propagation in the VE. It consists of references to all participant Web services, in addition to other relevant VE information. Changes are propagated by (i) adding, (ii) removing, or (iii) replacing service descriptions from the `schema`. The `schema` is updated each time a change is detected. The update involves the removal of the service reference from the `schema`, in case of the ontological change of remove service. If a service addition is required, the description of the Web service is added to the `schema`. Similarly, if a service must be replaced, the reference of the existing service is replaced with the reference of the newly selected service. Since a service reference must be present in the `schema` before it can be invoked, the service reference maintains the membership of a service with the VE.

Reaction

Reaction to changes depends on the (i) type of service change and (ii) availability of alternate services. In case of a service addition or replacement, the service selection stage is initiated and provided with the description of the required service. At this point, the quick and dynamic discovery of alternate services is crucial to the successful execution of the VE. If an appropriate service does not exist (or cannot be located), the VE must be paused by freezing conversations in the system and notifying the user. In the meanwhile, the enterprise searches for services in *similar* or *overlapping* communities [1]. If an alternate service cannot be selected from *any* community, the VE must abort the relevant requests and terminate its services. This *dissolution* of a VE requires the enterprise to be "unregistered" from all service registries and any pending requests being cancelled. However, if an alternate service is selected successfully, it is registered with the `schema` and service orchestration may be resumed.

Selecting an alternate service *during* the execution of the enterprise is complex. We propose that a VE is *versioned* to accommodate the alternate service for future requests. However, any on-going request will be executed to its graceful completion. Virtual enterprise versioning is the process where the `schema` of the enterprise is temporarily described as more than one instance. The older version of the `schema` is destroyed as soon as all previous requests are completed.

Change Management Algorithm

The change management algorithm requires the `schema` parameter as input. The `schema` contains the list of all Web services that are currently participating in the system. The algorithm executes for the lifetime of the VE. It starts by managing the business change of efficiency. Second, it determines the business development strategy of enterprise. Third, the regulatory changes are extracted from the `schema`. Finally, these changes are physically executed in the Web service space.

4 Conclusion

We proposed a change management technique for virtual enterprises on the Semantic Web. Change management is enabled by monitoring agents that detect, propagate, and react to changes. We use ontologies to locate and select alternate partner services. Change managements allows enterprises to maintain competitiveness by dynamically selecting partners.

References

1. Medjahed, B., Benatallah, B., Bouguettaya, A., Elmagarmid, A.: WebBIS: An Infrastructure for Agile Integration of Web Services. International Journal on Cooperative Information Systems **13** (2004) 121–158
2. McIlraith, S.A., Martin, D.L.: Bringing Semantics to Web Services. IEEE Intelligent Systems (2003)
3. Akram, M.S., Medjahed, B., Bouguettaya, A.: Supporting Dynamic Changes in Web Service Environments. In: First International Conference on Service Oriented Computing, Trento, Italy (2003)
4. Curbera, F., Ehnebuske, D., Rogers, D.: Using WSDL in a UDDI Registry 1.05. Technical report, IBM, Microsoft, http://www.uddi.org/pubs/wsdlbestpractices-V1.05-Open-20010625.pdf (2001)
5. Casati, F., Shan, E., Dayal, U., Shan, M.: Business-oriented management of web services. Communications of the ACM **46** (2003) 55–60

A Reflective Approach to Keeping Business Characteristics in Business-End Service Composition

Zhuofeng Zhao[1,2], Yanbo Han[1], Jianwu Wang[1,2], and Kui Huang[1,2]

[1]Institute of Computing Technology, Chinese Academy of Sciences, 100080, Beijing, China
[2]Graduate School of the Chinese Academy of Sciences, 100080, Beijing, China
{zhaozf, yhan, wjw, huangkui}@software.ict.ac.cn

Abstract. Business-end service composition can be best characterized as a user-centric approach to web application construction and promises to better cope with spontaneous and volatile business requirements and the dynamism of computing environments. The mapping of business-end service composites into software composites is a key issue in realizing business-end service composition, and a corresponding reflective approach is proposed in the paper. It is also investigated how to keep the business characteristics of business-end service composites during the mapping and how to adapt to changes of the correlation information for mapping. Basic components and patterns for keeping business characteristics are designed first. Then, using the principle of reflection, the contents for keeping business characteristics and the correlation information for mapping are combined and maintained on a meta-level. The result following the approach is a system implemented for mapping business-end service composites to software composites.

1 Introduction

Service composition implies a new way of application construction. A number of approaches to service composition have been proposed, for example BPEL4WS [2], BPML [3], SELF-SERV [5], SWORD [15], SAHARA [16] and so on, covering different aspects of service composition, such as modeling, language, system implementation, etc. However, these works are mainly from software perspectives, and require professional knowledge to develop business applications [14]. Most of them are still weak in dealing with a spectrum of application scenarios that require Web services be quickly composed and reconfigured by non-IT professionals in order to cope with the spontaneity and volatility of business requirements. Examples of such application scenarios include dynamic supply chain, handling of city emergency, and so on. Business-end service composition, as a novel way for service composition, promises to better cope with spontaneous and volatile business requirements. It can be best characterized as a user-centric approach to application construction and an effective way to achieve service composition from business perspectives.

Motivated by the above-stated considerations, we have designed a user-centric, business-end service composition language – VINCA [7]. VINCA specifies the following four aspects of business requirements in a process-centric manner: VINCA process, VINCA business services, user contexts and interaction patterns. However,

X. Zhou et al. (Eds.): WISE 2004, LNCS 3306, pp. 479–490, 2004.
© Springer-Verlag Berlin Heidelberg 2004

VINCA only provides a way for modeling service composition from business perspective. In order to realize business-end service composition completely, business-end service composites in VINCA have to be mapped to IT-end composites supported by standard service composition technologies, such as BPEL4WS that is used in fact as an IT-end service composition language in our paper. To solve this problem, we propose a reflective approach which result in a system for the mapping.

The rest of the paper is organized as follows: Section 2 highlights the main issues for solving the mapping problem through a reference example. In section 3, the conceptual model of the reflective approach is presented. System implementation for the reflective approach is given in section 4. In section 5, we briefly discuss the related work. Section 6 concludes the paper and discusses some future works.

2 Problem Statement with a Reference Example

In this section, we discuss the issues of the mapping problem through a simplified example excerpted from the FLAME2008 project[1]. The example is shown in Fig. 1, it is a simple business process: *Mr. Bull is going to visit Beijing during the Olympic Games. He schedules two activities for his first day in Beijing before the Olympic Games: ordering a restaurant for dinner after booking a sightseeing tour from a travel agency.*

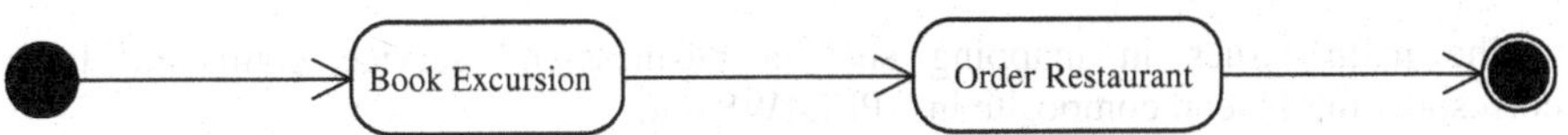

Fig. 1. Business Process of the Reference Example

Assume that Mr. Bull builds a business-end service composite for the above-stated example using VINCA. A VINCA process is defined, which contained *Book Excursion* activity and *Order Restaurant* activity. *Travel Agency* business service[2] and *Restaurant* business service are arranged to fulfill the two activities respectively. Furthermore, Mr. Bull would like to book the cheapest travel agency by means of configuring *Travel Agency* business service flexibly. In addition, he plans to order a restaurant near his location in the evening, so he configures the *Order Restaurant* activity as a context-awareness activity. The VINCA specification of this example is shown in Fig. 2.

From this example, we can first sense the importance of business-end service composition. Furthermore, we can note that the resulted business-end service composite in VINCA shows the following characteristics:

- **Context-awareness**. User contexts can be used to serve as a sort of implicit inputs in defining and executing a VINCA process, such as the *Order Restaurant* activity.

---

1 FLAME2008 is a project for developing service-oriented applications that provide integrated, personalized information services to the public during the Olympic Games 2008.

2 Business service is the core mechanism in VINCA. It supports service virtualization through abstracting Web services into business services so that the technical details of Web services can be hidden.

- **Dynamic composition of services.** Services composed in a VINCA process can be determined dynamically at runtime, such as the *Travel Agency* business service used in *Book Excursion* activity.
- **Flexible support of user interaction.** Users are allowed to appoint special places in a VINCA process for interaction during process execution, e.g. Mr. Bull can decide to interact after execution of the *Book Excursion* activity.

```
<VINCAProcess name="Bull's Travel">
  ...
  <SequentialActivity>
    <BizActivity name="Book Excursion">
      <Inputs>...</Inputs>
      <Outputs>...</Outputs>
      <QoSConstraint>
        <Cost>cheapest</Cost>
      </QoSConstraint>
      <ReferredBizService>.../TravelAgency</ReferredBizService>
    </BizActivity>
    <BizActivity name="OrderRestaurant"
      <Inputs>
        <BizEntity name="location" source="User Context">
        ...
      </Inputs>
      <Outputs>...</Outputs>
      <QoSConstraint/>
      <ReferredBizService>.../Restaurant</ReferredBizService>
    </BizActivity>
  </SequentialActivity >
</VINCAProcess>
```

Fig. 2. Snippet of the VINCA Specification of the Reference Example

The main issues in mapping such a business-end service composite to a corresponding IT-end composite in BPEL4WS are:

- **Maintenance of business characteristics**. BPEL4WS does not provide support for above-stated three business characteristics of VINCA directly. So, how to keep the business characteristics of business-end service composites during the mapping is an important issue to be solved.
- **Adaptability of correlation information**. The mapping from VINCA to BPEL4WS needs to follow a set of correlation information between them, specifying for example how an element in VINCA is mapped to elements in BPEL4WS. However, BPEL4WS is in progress and evolving. Furthermore, the business characteristics of VINCA may be augmented to adapt to a new business domain. These mean that the correlation information will change over time. How to adapt to changes of the correlation information is another important issue.

3 Conceptual Model of the Reflective Approach

To deal with the above-stated two issues, we propose a reflective approach. In this section, we will first introduce the conceptual model of the approach.

The principle of reflection [6, 11] has been one of the most useful techniques for developing adaptable systems, and it opens up in the possibility of system inspecting and adapting itself using appropriate metadata. To solve the problems introduced in section 1, we consider designing some special components and patterns for keeping business characteristics first. Then using the reflection principle to maintain the correlation information in an adaptive way.

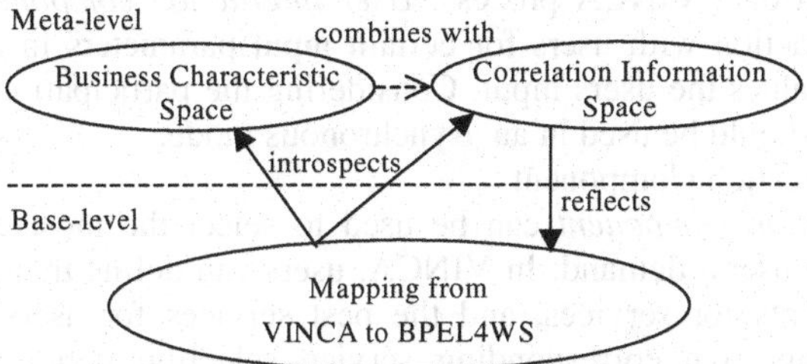

Fig. 3. Conceptual Model of the Reflective Approach

As shown in Fig. 3, the key elements of the reflective approach are *Business Characteristic Space* and *Correlation Information Space* on the meta-level, which are put forward to deal with the issues of maintaining business characteristics and adaptability of correlation information respectively. They can be used to introspect and reflect the concrete mapping from VINCA to BPEL4WS on the base level. Since BPEL4WS of current version requires static binding of Web services to flow, some special services for keeping business characteristics and its' usage patterns have to be provided. The metadata about these service components and patterns are maintained in *Business Characteristic Space*. Furthermore, the goal of Correlation Information Space is to reify and control the mapping behavior from VINCA to BPEL4WS through maintaining the correlation information. At the same time, through combining the contents in Business Characteristic Space with the correlation information in Correlation Information Space, the business characteristics can be kept during the mapping controlled by Correlation Information Space. In the following subsection, we detail these two key elements on the meta-level respectively.

3.1 Business Characteristic Space

Business Characteristic Space contains metadata about contents of keeping business characteristics. The metadata can be divided into two categories. One is about the special service components for keeping business characteristics; another is about the patterns for using the components to keep business characteristics. The metadata about components includes component name, textual description, operation interface, access address, etc; the metadata about patterns includes pattern name, textual description, condition for using, address of pattern file, etc.

Components for Keeping Business Characteristics

With respect to the three business characteristics of VINCA, we design the following components to keep business characteristics:

➢ Context Collection Component

User contexts are represented in terms of key-value pairs in VINCA. Keys are called dimensions and may take static values (such as name and birth date) or dynamic values (such as the location of user at a certain time point). *Context collection component* can be used to get both kinds of contextual values according to the designed context dimensions.

➢ User Interaction Component

User interaction in VINCA is defined to allow a user to input parameters during the execution period of a VINCA process. *User interaction component* can be used to trigger the interaction with users for certain input parameters in a VINCA process, and return the values the users input. Considering the participation of human beings, this component should be used in an asynchronous mode.

➢ Service Selection Component

Service selection component can be used to select the most appropriate service according to the users' demand. In VINCA, users can define their demands in terms of QoS constraints for services, and the best services for users' demands can be chosen according to a corresponding service selection policy. Service selection component implements the service selection policy.

➢ Service Invocation Component

Service invocation component acts as a proxy for invoking services dynamically. It can be used to invoke a service according to the access information of the service and returns the results after the invocation.

Patterns for Keeping Business Characteristics

Patterns for keeping business characteristics define the default pattern of using the above-listed components to keep business characteristics of VINCA. Each pattern that may include one or more components is designed specially for one category of business characteristics. Accordingly, there are three patterns for VINCA:

➢ Context-Awareness Pattern

Context-awareness pattern defines the usage pattern of context collection component to keep the business characteristic of context-awareness. This pattern can be used when context-aware business activities are defined in a VINCA process.

➢ User Interaction Pattern

User interaction pattern defines the usage pattern of user interaction component to keep the business characteristic of user interaction. This pattern can be used when there are business activities that need user interaction in a VINCA process.

➢ Dynamic Composition Pattern

Dynamic composition pattern defines the usage pattern of service selection component and service invocation component to keep the business characteristic of dynamic composition. This pattern contains two components. It can be used when there are business services that are used in the dynamic mode in a VINCA process.

The detailed representation of the three patterns in BPEL4WS will be given in section 4.1.

3.2 Correlation Information Space

In order to adapt to changes of the correlation information, including information about keeping business characteristics given above, *Correlation Information Space* is set to maintain the correlation information between VINCA and BPEL4WS. Table 1 shows an overview of the correlation information in Correlation Information Space.

The correlation information is represented as the mapping relationship between VINCA and BPEL4WS in terms of metadata of VINCA and BPEL4WS with constraints. Note that the correlation information has three parts as shown in the table: metadata of VINCA, metadata of BPEL4WS, and constraints on the mapping relationship. The metadata of VINCA and BPEL4WS can be gotten from the basic constructs of VINCA and BPEL4WS languages. Some constructs of VINCA and BPEL4WS can be mapped directly, such as control logic. However, the mapping relationships from VINCA to BPEL4WS are not always one to one indeed, e.g. when the business characteristics need to be kept, constraints are provided to express the complicated mapping relationships. In this way, the patterns for keeping business characteristics can be defined as constraints on the correlation information. As such the contents in *Business Characteristic Space* can be combined with the correlation information. Besides, some basic constraints can be defined, such as constraints for transformation of elements' name from VINCA to BPEL4WS. Due to the space limitation, the complete correlation information is not listed here.

Table 1. Overview of Correlation Information between VINCA and BPEL4WS

Metadata of VINCA	Metadata of BPEL4WS	Constraints
VINCA Process	BPEL4WS Process	Basic constraints
Business Service	PartnerLink	Basic constraints, Dynamic composition keeping pattern
Business Activity	Invoke, Receive, Reply	Basic constraints, Context-awareness keeping pattern, User interaction keeping pattern
Business Entity	Variables	Basic constraints
Control Logic (same as BPEL4WS)	Sequence, Flow, While, Switch	Null

4 Implementation and Application

In this section, we discuss the implementation of the reflective approach. Fig. 4 shows the system architecture of implementation. There are two layers in the architecture:

- *Reflective Platform*, it maintains all the contents on meta-level introduced in the previous section and affects the function of Transformation Engine in Transformation Platform.
- *Transformation Platform*, it is in charge of transforming the VINCA specifications of business-end service composites into BPEL4WS specifications of IT-end service composites.

4.1 Reflective Platform

As shown in Fig.4, the Reflective Platform has two main parts: auxiliary service set and Metaobjects.

Auxiliary Service Set

Auxiliary service set is composed of a set of services corresponding to the components for keeping business characteristics introduced in section 3.1. For our purposes, four kinds of services are defined, namely context collection service (*ContextCollectionServ*), user interaction service (*UserInteractionServ*), service

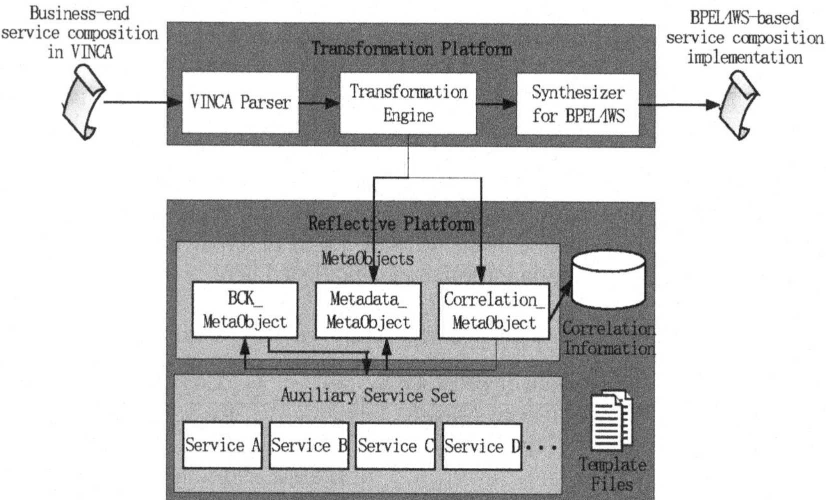

Fig. 4. System Architecture of the Reflective Approach

selection service (*ServiceSelectionServ*) and service invocation service (*ServiceInvocationServ*). These services are implemented as Web services so that they can be used in BPEL4WS directly.

```
<invoke partnerLink="ContextCollectionServ"
          portType=" getUserContextPT"
          operation=" getUserContext"
          inputVariable="varContextNames"
          outputVariable="varContextValues">
</invoke>
<invoke>
    ......  // Invoke activity corresponding to
             business activity
</invoke>
```

Fig. 5. Context-Awareness Pattern in BPEL4WS

```
<invoke partnerLink="UserInteractionServ"
          portType=" getUserInputPT"
          operation=" getUserInputs"
          inputVariable="varInputNames">
</invoke>
<receive partnerLink="UserInteractionServ"
          portType=" getUserInputCBPT"
          operation="returnUserInputs"
          Variable="varInputValues">
</receive>
<invoke>
    .....  // Invoke activity corresponding to
          business activity
</invoke>
```

Fig. 6. User Interaction Pattern in BPEL4WS

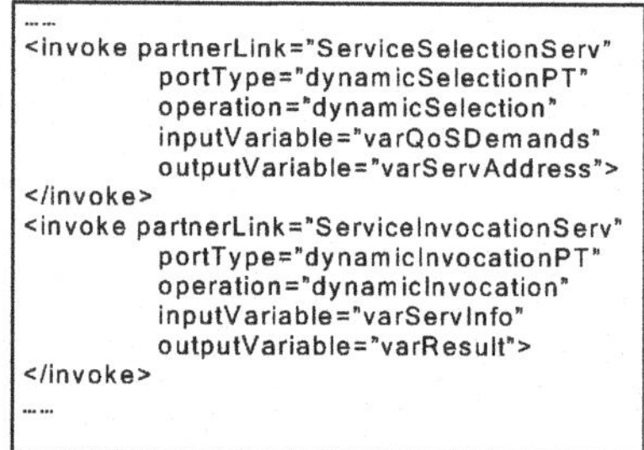

```
......
<invoke partnerLink="ServiceSelectionServ"
          portType="dynamicSelectionPT"
          operation="dynamicSelection"
          inputVariable="varQoSDemands"
          outputVariable="varServAddress">
</invoke>
<invoke partnerLink="ServiceInvocationServ"
          portType="dynamicInvocationPT"
          operation="dynamicInvocation"
          inputVariable="varServInfo"
          outputVariable="varResult">
</invoke>
......
```

Fig. 7. Dynamic Composition Pattern in BPEL4WS

Table 2. Fuctional Operations of BC_Metaobject

Operation	Function
addBCKS(ServiceDesc service)	Add a service for keeping business characteristic into Business Characteristic Space
addBCKP(Pattern pattern)	Add a pattern for keeping business characteristic into Business Characteristic Space
getBCKS(String serviceName)	Get a service for keeping business characteristic
getBCKP(String patternName)	Get a pattern for keeping business characteristic

Table 3. Fuctional Operations of MetaData_Metaobject

Operation	Function
buildMetaData(String dataName, String dataType, Vector dataAttrs)	Build a metadata of VINCA or BPEL4WS
buildAttribute(String attrName, String attrValue, String attrType)	Build an attribute of a metadata
getMetaData (String dataName)	Get a metadata according to its name
getAttribute (MetaData data, String attrName)	Get an attribute of a metadata according to its name

With these services, patterns for keeping business characteristics introduced in section 3.1 can be defined in the BPEL4WS format. Context-awareness pattern is defined as shown in Fig. 5, where an additional *invoke* activity for invoking *ContextCollectionServ* is inserted before the *invoke* activity corresponding to the business activity of context-awareness. User interaction pattern is defined as shown in Fig. 6. User interaction component should be used in an asynchronous mode as we have mentioned before, so the pattern defines the usage of *UserInteractionServ* by inserting an *invoke* activity and a *receive* activity before the *invoke* activity corresponding to the business activity that needs user interaction. Fig. 7 shows the dynamic composition pattern defined in BPEL4WS, which contains two *invoke* activities, invoking *ServiceSelectionServ* and *ServiceInvocationServ* respectively. These patterns are stored as XML files and will be used as target templates by transformation platform when producing service composites in BPEL4WS.

Metaobjects

Metaobject is viewed as an effective means to implement reflection [8]. In this paper, three Metaobjects are designed to maintain the contents on the meta-level of our reflective approach. They form the kernel of the reflective platform.

(1) BC_Metaobject (Business Characteristic Metaobject)

BC_Metaobject is responsible for maintaining the metadata in *Business Characteristic Space*. As shown in Table 2, it provides functional operations for getting and setting metadata about the services and patterns for keeping business characteristic.

(2) MetaData_Metaobject

MetaData_Metaobject is responsible for maintaining the metadata of VINCA and BPEL4WS in Correlation Information Space. The functional operations provided by MetaData_Metaobject are given in Table 3.

(3) Correlation_Metaobject

Correlation_Metaobject is responsible for maintaining the correlation information between metadata of VINCA and BPEL4WS in Correlation Information Space. It is implemented based on above two Metaobjects. Correlation_Metaobject provides functional operations for defining and acquiring correlation information, which are shown in Table 4.

Table 4. Fuctional Operations of Correlation_Metaobject

Operation	Function
buildMetaDataCorrelation(String corrName, Vector vecLeftMetaData, Vector vecRightMetaData, String strConstraint)	Build correlation between metadata of VINCA and BPEL4WS
buildAttributeCorrelation(String corrName, String strLeftAttr, String strRightAttr, String strConstraint)	Build correlation between attributes of metadata of VINCA and BPEL4WS
getMetaDataCorrelation(String metadataName)	Get correlation between metadata according to metadata name
getAttributeCorrelation (String metadataName, String attrCorrName)	Get correlation between attributes of metadata according to its name

The correlation information between VINCA and BPEL4WS maintained by these three Metaobjects is saved persistently in our implementation. These Metaobjects can be used to support the implementation of Transformation Engine in the Transformation Platform and affect the function of Transformation Engine by changing the correlation information.

4.2 Transformation Platform

The Transformation Platform collects the VINCA specifications of business-end service composites from users, and transforms them into BPEL4WS specifications of IT-end service composites. The output from the Transformation Platform can be exported for direct execution by a BPEL4WS engine. The components - VINCA Parser, Synthesizer for BPEL and Transformation Engine are the core components of the Transformation Platform. VINCA parser is in charge of parsing VINCA file and making preparations for the transformation; VINCA synthesizer for BPEL4WS produces the BPEL4WS file in the XML format. Transformation Engine is the central element of the Transformation Platform, which is realized with the help of MetaData_Metaobject and Correlation_Metaobject. It does not use BC_Metaobject directly. Instead, Correlation_Metaobject uses BC_Metaobject implicitly. The algorithm of the transformation engine is given as follows:

Transformation Algorithm

```
INPUT: bizApp  //The parsing result object of business-end service composite in VINCA
OUTPUT: bpelApp  //The transformation result object for synthesizer for BPEL4WS
{
  bpelApp = new Vector(); //Produce the space for storing bpelApp
  for every element in bizApp
  {
    sourceElement = bizApp(i); //Get an element in bizApp
    /*Get the metadata of VINCA that the element belongs to*/
    Metadata metadata = MetaData_Metaobject.getMetaData(sourceElement.type);
    /*Get the correlation information about the obtained metadata*/
    correlations = Correlation_Metaobject.getMetaDataCorrelation(metadata);
    /*Do transformation according to the obtained correlation information*/
    for every correlation in correlations
```

```
    {
        Correlation correlation = correlations(j);
        /*Produce bpelApp element according to correlation information*/
        targetElement = transformation(correlation, sourceElement);
        bpelApp.add(targetElement);
    }
  }
  return bpelApp;
}
```

According to this algorithm, Transformation Engine can be implemented in an adaptive way through utilizing MetaData_Metaobject and Correlation_Metaobject.

4.3 Application

With the mechanisms and implementation discussed so far, the business-end service composite of the reference example in VINCA given in section 2 can be transformed to the IT-end composite in BPEL4WS now. *Book Excursion* activity in VINCA process, which refers to *Travel Agency* business service in the dynamic mode, is mapped to two *invoke* activities for invoking *ServiceSelectionServ* and *ServiceInvocationServ* services according to the dynamic composition pattern in BPEL4WS. The *Order Restaurant* activity, which is context-aware, is mapped to a corresponding *invoke* activity, but an additional *invoke* activity for invoking *ContextCollectionServ* service is inserted according to the context-awareness pattern in BPEL4WS. In this way, the resulted BPEL4WS specification of the example keeps the business characteristics defined in the business-end service composite in VINCA. Due to space limitation, the resulted BPEL4WS specification of the example is omitted here.

The above example shows that business characteristics of business-end composites in VINCA can be kept through the presented patterns. The following advantages can be gained: the shortage of BPEL4WS for supporting business characteristics can be complemented by special services and the information for keeping business characteristics can be maintained in an explicit way. Furthermore, when VINCA and BPEL4WS evolve, e.g. augmenting new business characteristics in VINCA, it is easy to adapt to changes through reconfiguring the reflective meta-space. We can reconfigure the correlation information including the information about business characteristics through the Metaobjects to achieve the adaptability. In this way, it needs not recode the Transformation Engine any more.

The approach and implementation proposed in this paper are experimenting in a real world project called FLAME2008 to facilitate business-end service composition.

5 Related Work

Though concepts of business-end service composition are relatively new and unexplored, there are a number of outstanding research efforts in this area. The research work in [17], with the goals like ours, also aims at supporting service composition from business perspectives. It provides a Business Process Outsourcing Language to capture business requirements. Then, the business-level elements can be mapped into Web services flow to achieve on-demand Web services composition. The correlation between business requirements described in BPOL and Web services flow composition is not specified explicitly and is wired in codes directly.

In [4, 12], the authors raised the level of abstraction for developing service composition implementations in BPEL4WS, following an MDA approach. The correlation between a specific UML profile for BPEL4WS and constructs in BPEL4WS is defined and managed. However, because the UML profile is defined for BPEL4WS specially and do not support more business characteristics.

In [9, 10], a model-driven approach is proposed to transform platform-independent business models into platform-specific IT architectural models. The core mechanism for transformation is that special business patterns of business-level model are abstracted and assigned with corresponding IT implementation. However, the contents for keeping business characteristics and mapping are not maintained explicitly and need to be hard-coded when realizing the approach. An important contribution of this approach is the consistency checking of transformation, which will be considered in our ongoing work.

The work on model transformation shares some methodological similarity with our work. In [13], a framework for model transformation is given. A transformation scheme is defined in UML through extending the CWM Transformation metamodel. Through the transformation scheme, transformation can be represented explicitly. In [1], authors emphasized the importance of a high-level model transformation language. With this language, the behavior of model transformers can be formally specified. As such, the representation and the implementation of the behavior of transformers can be separated, and the development or maintenance of these transformers gets easier.

6 Conclusion

In this paper, we present a reflective approach to mapping business-end service composites in VINCA to IT-end service composites in BPEL4WS. The focuses are on: how to keep the business characteristics during the mapping; how to adapt to changes of the correlation information for the mapping. The approach provides the following valuable contributions:

- It allows representing the correlation information between VINCA and BPEL4WS on the meta-level explicitly. As such the correlation information can be maintained in an adaptive way and it is easy to adapt to new versions of VINCA and BPEL4WS.
- It can achieve the goal of keeping business characteristics through special components and patterns. By combining the contents about the components and the patterns with the correlation information on the meta-level, the business characteristics can be maintained in an adaptive way.
- It results in a lightweight and extendable Transformation Engine. It is lightweight because it “interprets” the Metaobjects to transform VINCA into BPEL4WS; it is extendable in the sense that it is easy to extend the transformation function by modifying the correlation information through the Metaobjects.

In our current work, the IT-end composites in BPEL4WS mapped from business-end composites in VINCA are still proprietary. How to support more sophisticated function of BPEL4WS, such as compensation, except handling, etc, is one of the important goals of our undergoing research work. How to express these contents in the correlation information and how to maintain them through Metaobjects are still open questions. Furthermore, we will also address the deployment and load-balancing of the services for keeping business characteristics to ensure effective usages.

References

1. A. Agrawal, Metamodel Based Model Transformation Language to Facilitate Domain Specific Model Driven Architecture, In OOPSLA'03, Anaheim, California, USA, 2003.
2. T. Andrews, F. Curbera et al, Business Process Execution Language for Web Services, http://www-106.ibm.com/developerworks/webservices/library/ws-bpel/, 2003.
3. A. Arkin, Business Process Modeling Language - BPML1.0, http://www.bpmi.org, 2002.
4. J. Amsden, T. Gardner et al, Draft UML 1.4 Profile for Automated Business Processes with a mapping to BPEL 1.0, IBM, 2003.
5. B. Benatallah, Q. Z. Sheng, and M. Dumas, The Self-Serv Environment for Web Services Composition, IEEE Internet Computing, 7(1): 40-48.
6. D. Edmond and A.H.M. Hofstede, Achieving Workflow Adaptability by means of Reflection, In The ACM Conf. Computer Supported Cooperative Work (Workshop on Adaptive Workflow Systems), Seattle, USA, 1998.
7. Y. Han, H. Geng et al, VINCA - A Visual and Personalized Business-level Composition Language for Chaining Web-based Services, In First International Conference on Service-Oriented Computing, Trento, Italy, 2003, LNCS 2910, 165 - 177.
8. G. Kickzales, J. Rivieres, and D. G. Bobrow, The Art of the Metaobject Protocol, MIT Press, Cambridge, Massachusetts, 1991.
9. J. Koehler, G. Tirenni, and S. Kumaran, From Business Process Model to Consistent Implementation, In Proceedings of EDOC'02, Switzerland, 2002, IEEE, 96-108.
10. J. Koehler, R. Hauser et al, A Model-Driven Transformation Method, In Proceedings of EDOC'03, Brisbane, Australia, 2003, IEEE, 186-197.
11. P. Maes. Concepts and Experiments in Computation Reflection, ACM SIGPLAN Notices, 1987, 147-155.
12. K. Mantell. Model Driven Architecture in a Web services world: From UML to BPEL, http://www-106.ibm.com/developerworks/webservices/library/ws-uml2bpel/, 2003.
13. J. Oldevik, A. Solberg et al, Framework for model transformation and code generation, In Proceedings of EDOC'02, Lausanne, Switzerland, 2002, IEEE, 181-189.
14. B. Orriens, J. Yang, and M. P. Papazoglou, Model Driven Service Composition, In First International Conference on Service-Oriented Computing, Trento, Italy, 2003, LNCS 2910, 75 - 90.
15. S. R. Ponnekanti and A. Fox, SWORD: A Developer Toolkit for Building Composite Web Services, In The Eleventh International World Wide Web Conference, Honolulu, Hawaii, USA, 2002.
16. B. Raman, Z. M. Mao et al, The SAHARA Model for Service Composition across Multiple Providers, In Proceedings of the First International Conference on Pervasive Computing, Zurich, Switzerland, 2002, LNCS 2414, 1-14.
17. L. J. Zhang, B. Li et al, On Demand Web Services-Based Business Process Composition, In International Conference on Systems, Man & Cybernetics, Washington, USA, 2003.

A Domain Framework for Representation of Web System Impacts

Norazlin Yusop, David Lowe, and Didar Zowghi

University of Technology, Sydney
PO Box 123 Broadway NSW 2007, Australia
{norazlin, didar}@it.uts.edu.au, david.lowe@uts.edu.au

Abstract. In web systems development, the business environment, processes and the related Web systems are interdependent. The business domain not only drives the identification of system needs, but the business is fundamentally changed by the introduction or evolution of the system. This results in Web systems that are highly volatile with complex inter-dependencies with the business domain. In this paper we describe a framework which allows us to describe and structure these interdependencies, particularly focusing on the concept of *mutual constitution*. The result is a consistent terminology and a basis for more effective reasoning about the business consequences of introducing and changing Web systems.

1 Introduction

A key characteristic of many Web systems[1] (as well as various other software systems) is that the introduction of the system has a fundamental impact on the nature of the business processes and business models which are being supported by the system. In other words, the business environment and processes not only drive the definition of the system needs, but are in turn fundamentally changed by the system. In effect, the business "problem" defines the nature of the technical system "solution" that is desired, but the solution itself changes the characteristics of the problem space, resulting in systems and business processes which co-evolve. This can be described as solutions and problems being mutually constituted Z. Zhao et al. a concept well understood in the area of social informatics [1] and requirements engineering [2]. Whilst this concept of mutual constitution Z. Zhao et al. or its expression as a technical solution leading to substantial changes in the problem space – is typical of almost all systems development, it is particularly significant with Web systems. This is due in large part to the scale and immediacy of the impacts that web systems can have on their domain.

[1] Whilst we use the term *Web system* throughout this paper, we recognise that this terminology is still somewhat ill-defined within the literature (which includes terms such as Web applications, web-based systems, online systems, as well as a host of domain specific terms such as business-to-business (B2B), business-to-consumer (B2C), etc.). In this paper we use the term *Web system* to refer to those system which utilise web technologies as an integral element of a functionally complex system which typically incorporates interfaces beyond the organisational boundaries.

X. Zhou et al. (Eds.): WISE 2004, LNCS 3306, pp. 491–502, 2004.
© Springer-Verlag Berlin Heidelberg 2004

Whilst there has been a significant body of work looking at specific impacts of Web system, the results have not been drawn together into an overall framework. In this paper we describe a framework which allows us to describe and structure the impacts (and hence interdependencies) between Web systems and their organisational contexts. Such a framework can provide benefits such as ensuring a consistent terminology and a basis for more effective reasoning about the business consequences of introducing and changing Web systems.

2 Related Work

There is a significant body of work that discusses specific impacts of Web systems and technologies. For example, [3] discusses ways in which e-commerce technology has a positive impact on the supply chain as it allows information visibility, which in turn allows companies to integrate their system components on production planning and scheduling and inventory control, and implement that through the supply chain thus getting into just-in-time service/product delivery.

In [4], Osmonbekov, et al state that using electronic commerce tools such as Internet electronic data interchange (EDI), less costly extranets and intranets, web storefronts, web-based products, or service information can reduce the systems and transaction cost that the organisations will have to bear. These tools enable the buyers and sellers to get shared information on updated information pertaining to inventories, orders and shipments This is a positive impact for both parties as it eliminates the need to install and maintain expensive proprietary networks, (such as the old EDI networks) which leads to substantial cost savings which can effectively be passed on to the end user.

Web systems development can pose negative impacts to the organisation and its systems. With new technology, such as web systems, new forms of threats are encountered regularly. These threats include intrusion and illegal access to proprietary data, virus attacks, denial of service attacks, and illegal acquisition or distribution of data that is copyrighted. Some of these problems are more critical with intranet system where there is lack of full implementation of firewalls and encryption technology [5]. The threats that the organisation face also impact on the organisation's system, whereby the system needs to be safeguarded with sophisticated security measures that support mutual authentication, fine grain authentication, communication integrity, confidentiality, non-repudiation, and authorization. Security poses a high impact on the organisation and the system development because there is no security technology that can secure the system effectively [6] [7].

Another significant impact pertains to e-business interfaces. Common e-business interfaces refer to industry-level specifications for the interactions among IT applications at different enterprises which are needed to coordinate a business process involving multiple supply chain roles [8]. Some of the B2B interface specifications include Microsoft Biztalk, Ariba cXML, Open buying on the Internet (OBI), EDI/XML, OASIS ebXML, Common Business Library (CBL), and Information and Content Exchange (ICE) among others. These electronic interfaces impact on fundamental supply chain capabilities, which in turn would reduce misalignments between supply chain partners and increase the opportunities through flexible integration of supply chain processes. These supply chain capabilities are:

coordination capabilities; plug and play capabilities; and knowledge creation and sharing capabilities [8]. These e-business interfaces therefore have a positive impact on the organisation and its systems.

The literature discussed above tends to highlight aspects such as the impact of electronic commerce tools on the reduction of business costs [4] and changes to business processes – particularly as they relate to aspects such as supply chains. These impacts can be both positive (such as increased customer satisfaction) and negative (such as increased vulnerability to security breaches). E-business interfaces are critical in any web system projects as it aligns the supply chain processes. However, it is also critical that organisations ensure that the different web applications and tools can be integrated seamlessly with the organisation's system and the system of its trading partners. Any development of a new system, particularly web systems will pose a significant impact on the other system components that are already in place. Despite this, there has been little research on systemizing or structuring the nature of these impacts.

3 Dimensions of Impact

From the web system impacts discussed in the literature (examples of which are shown in Table 1) it can be observed that different web systems have different impacts on the business environment. In this paper our focus will be on describing the characteristics of the domain of mutual influence – i.e. those characteristics of the system environment which affect the system, but are in turn affected by the system. We have identified six dimensions of these impacts, which are as follows:

- Affecting Characteristics: The system characteristics which has an affect on its domain, or a domain characteristic which has an effect on the system;
- Affected Characteristics: the characteristic of system or its domain which is affected.
- Types of Web Systems: The types of system for which this impact applies. e.g. internet, intranet and extranet.
- Facet of the Domain Impacted: Whether the characteristics that are impacting, and which are impacted upon, are part of the system, the organisation, or the external environment (e.g. OvS indicates an organisational characteristic and a system characteristic which impact on each other).
- Effect: whether the impact is viewed as having a positive or a negative effect on business operations;
- Level: extent of the impact, e.g. high, medium, low.

Table 1 shows an example of data compiled using this framework, which specifically depicts the characteristics of the domain that are mutually influenced. The numbers in brackets ( ) displayed on each characteristic correspond to the numbers in Figure 2. The numbers displayed on this table is not in sequence as this table is extracted from a complete table, which is discussed in detail in [9] to illustrate characteristics of the domain which are mutually influenced (shown in the Facets of the Domain Impacted column). It is necessary to include the numbers this way for the purpose of cross-referencing in Figure 3.

Table 1. Example characteristics of the business environment that impact and/or are impacted by the web system

	Characteristics that affect	Characteristics that are affected	Types of systems / Facet of domain / Effect / Level	Sources
2	Supply chain intermediation and disintermediation in (6) Access levels differentiation (7) Customer value (8)	Value Exchange (9)	Extranet O↔S Positive Medium for all aspect EXCEPT High for value offering	[11] [14] [16] [17]
3	Service personalization (10) Robots to monitor (11) promotion activities Multiple response generations (12)	Scalability (13)	Internet/Extranet S↔S Negative High for System	[18] [19] [20] [21]
4	Real time access, easy to use interfaces, interactivity (14)	Usability (15)	All S↔S Positive Medium (all aspects)	[22] [23] [24]
7	Security threat to org. proprietary data (20) Internet infrastructure security threat (21)	Security (22)	All O↔S Negative High (all aspects)	[4] [12] [25]
15	Management and improving organisation's relationship with customer and supplier (38)	Relationship Management (39)	Extranet/ Internet O↔S Positive Medium (all aspects)	[15]

Key:

Facets of the Domain Impacted:

O↔S: Organisation characteristic that impacts on the System characteristic but which is in turn directly impacted by the system. Hence the organisation and system characteristics are mutually influenced, thus identified as being the characteristic in the Domain of Mutual Influence

S↔S: System characteristic that are mutually influenced by another system characteristic

Explanations for Level of Impact:

High: Significant Impact. Impact that changes the business model, business process, customer-supplier relationships, value offering, organization structure and system

Medium: Impact that changes some parts of the business model, business process, customer-supplier relationships, value offering, organization structure and system

Low: Minimal impact. Impact that does not change the business model but causes a minimal change to the business process, customer-supplier relationships, value offering, organization structure and system

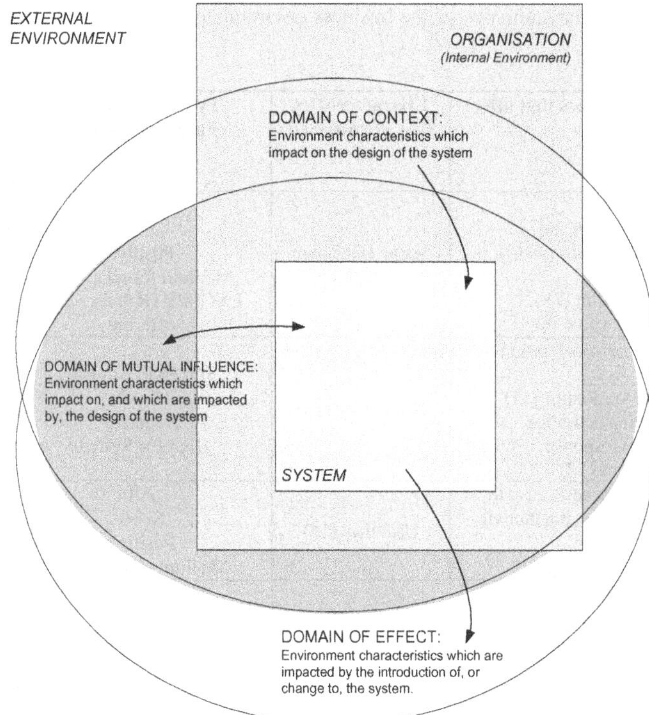

Fig. 1. Domain of Context, Domain of Influence, Domain of Effect

4 Impact Framework

As discussed above, we have argued that a Web system and its problem domain are mutually constituted - i.e. they are inter-dependent such that they impact each other. This problem domain involves characteristics of both the organisation hosting the system and external environment that relates to it. These characteristics can be grouped into several sub-domains, which are useful in understanding and reasoning about the inter-dependencies. These are shown in Figure 1.

The *Domain of Context* is made up of those characteristics of a systems domain, which provide a context for the system (i.e. affect the design of the system in some direct and immediate way). For example, both existing business processes and a legal regulatory framework may affect the design of the system. The *Domain of Effect* is made up of those characteristics of a systems domain which are impacted upon in some direct and immediate way by the introduction of the system. For example, both existing workflows and customer expectations will often be impacted upon by the system, and are therefore part of the domain of effect. The *Domain of Mutual Influence* is the intersection of the domain of context and the domain of effect - i.e. it is made up of those characteristics of a systems domain which both impact the design of the system, and which are potentially impacted upon by the introduction of the system. Taking the previous example, existing business process are likely to be part of the domain of mutual influence (since they influence the system design, but will also be changed by the system) but legal frameworks will not (since, whilst they affect the system design, they are unlikely to be directly impacted upon by the system).

4.1 Domain of Mutual Influence

From the Impact Framework described above, the characteristics of the *Domain of Mutual Influence* are those characteristics of the domain which affect the system, but which are in turn directly and immediately affected by the system (e.g. business processes, or – for most web systems – the external customers). Some of the key characteristics are discussed below.

Value exchange processes and activities between the organisation and its intermediaries are identified as a characteristic of the organisation that impact on the system. In e-business, process of intermediation and disintermediation presents specific e-business risks for traditional sellers [11]. For example; intermediaries such as brokers might easily disappear or re-appear in an e-business environment. This is because buyers might decide to use a middle person (intermediary) to increase their combined buying power and seek better negotiations with the sellers. Due to this issue, it is important to show who is doing what with whom as e-business is more flexible [11]. This will have significant impacts on the e-business project if there is no differentiation in the value offered by the different entities. An important issue in e-commerce business design is the assignment of value activities to actors.

Web systems offer the customers a distinct customer service value, compared to traditional business systems. The types of customer service offered via the web systems include answering customer enquiries, providing search and comparison activities, providing technical information to customers and allowing customers to track order status [10]. Most banks and financial institutions allow their customers to view their account balance, status of stock portfolio, loan application anywhere and at any time via an extranet. As shown in Table 1, row 2, the facets of the domain impacted are labelled as OvS, which explains that the characteristics of the organisation facet and the characteristics of the system facet are mutually influenced.

Integration of different web applications and tools can lead to complex problems for an organisation and its trading partners. It is therefore important that different systems within the organisations and with external parties are able to interoperate with each other. Poor integration of the web applications and tools will lead to negative impact for both the organisation and the system. Any development of a new system, particularly web systems will pose a significant impact on the other system components that are already in place. It is critical that the system components are able to interoperate with each other. The issue of interoperability has shifted from the level of applications to the level of standards. A trading partner has to deal with several standards at the same time. In case where one trading partner exchanges messages across industries, the variety of standards is likely to increase even more. One solution to deal with such problem is through the use of B2B protocol and integration engines. These execute actual message exchanges according to various standards [6].

Bussler et al [13] state that B2B e-business integration is a complex issue and web services are used as a solution for many significant integration problems. There is currently little research or lessons learned that report on the deployments that could advance web services technology functionality. SOAP (Simple Object Access Protocol) is the implementation technology for web services. SOAP messages can be easily exchanged over the Internet. As such, SOAP can be proposed to be a superior way to implement B2B interactions between companies (inter-enterprise) [13].

5 Impacts and the Domain Boundary: Real World Examples

As discussed above (and shown in Figure 1) we can identify the domain of context, the domain of effect, and the intersection of these two – the domain of mutual influence. In order to identify where the various characteristics lie with respect to these domains we have developed the Impact and Domain Diagram (refer to Figure.2). Let us illustrate the diagram with two real world cases which were analysed from the literature.

Figure 2 shows that characteristics 1, 2, 3 and 4 are characteristics of the organisation which impact on characteristic 5, which is a characteristic of the system domain.. In a real world example discussed in Turban et al [10] Adaptec, Inc. is a large microchip manufacturer supplying critical components to electronic equipment makers. The organisation needed to improve on its product delivery cycle time as it required up to 15 weeks delivering products to customer, while competitors took only 8 weeks. The longer delivery time was mainly caused by the need to coordinate design activities between Adaptec, Inc. headquarters in California and its three principal fabrication factories in other countries. In order to solve this problem, Adaptec, Inc. adopted extranet and enterprise-level supply chain integration software, which incorporates automated workflow and EC tools. E-mail was used to communicate with manufacturers across several time zones, thereby automatically starting the flow of raw materials. This in turn reduced invoicing and shipping times. Due to the organisation's need to reduce design cycle time, the implementation of the extranet and web applications impact on the organisation's system. The system developers needed to ensure seamless integration of these applications and tools. As the implementation of the extranet and web application tools were a success, it therefore impacted positively on the organisation as it benefited from the reduced time required to generate, transmit and confirm purchase orders [14].

In another example, Figure 2 shows that characteristic 38 is a characteristic of the organisation that impact on characteristic 39, which is a characteristic of the system. Table 1 shows that management and improvement of organisation's relationship with customer and supplier is a characteristic of the organisation (characteristic 38) that impact on process of relationship of management (characteristic 39) which is conducted and facilitated in the web system. Web systems facilitate relationship management activities and operations between customers and suppliers over the Internet and extranet. In a case study extracted from a literature pertaining to relationship management, Dignum [15] cited an experience report, which is conducted by Eindhoven University of Technology in cooperation with 11 partners in the region of Eindhoven. In a customer relationship management project embarked by a trucking company in Eindhoven, Netherlands, DAF trucks use the Internet to get feedback from their customers on the product and on the transaction of performance.

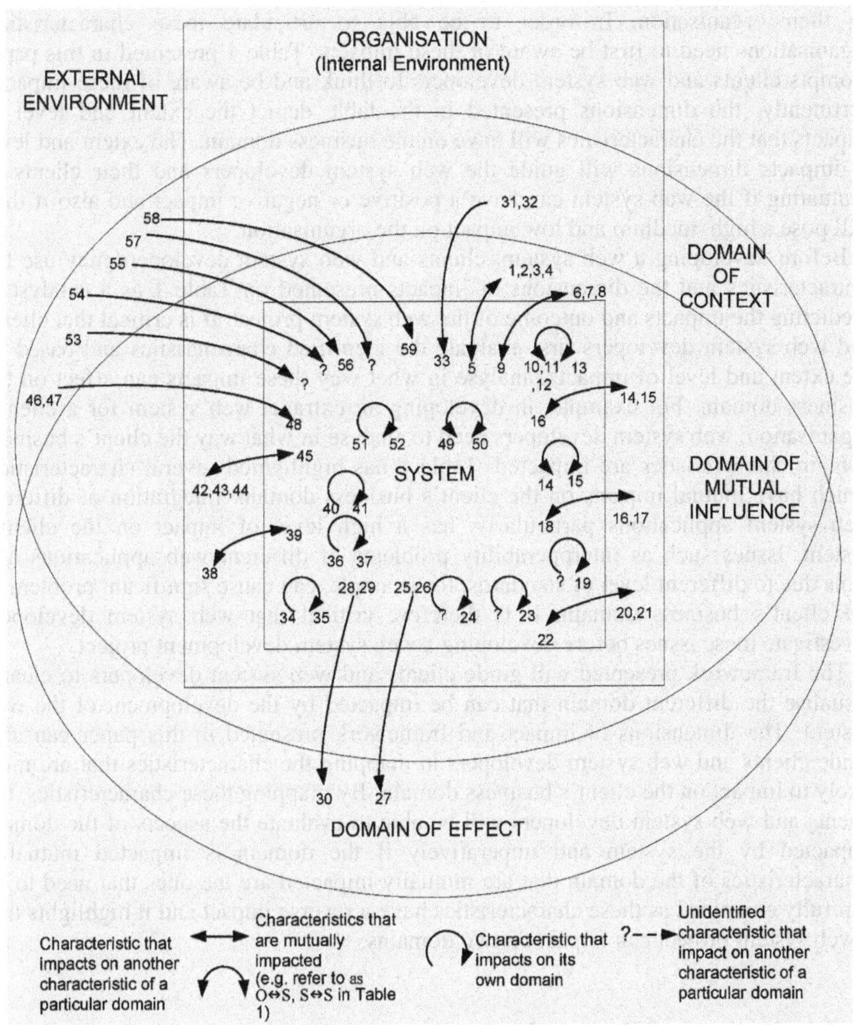

Fig. 2. Impact and Domain Diagram

This means that the feedback from a customer can be processed together with the customer's profile by the departments of the company that are most affected by the feedback. This has significant impact on the system, whereby the organisation's information systems that are used internally have to be connected and synchronised, due to the use of an enterprise resource planning system throughout the company.

6 Implications for Organisations

From the framework and illustrated examples, therefore it is critical for clients to know and articulate the characteristics of the business domain that are going to impact on their organisation. In order to be able to articulate these characteristics, organisations need to first be aware of these impacts. Table 1 presented in this paper prompts clients and web system developers to think and be aware of these impacts. Pertinently, the dimensions presented in the table depict the extent and level of impacts that the characteristics will have on the business domain. The extent and level of impacts dimensions will guide the web system developers and their clients in evaluating if the web system can have a positive or negative impact and also if they will pose a high, medium and low impact on the organisation.

Before developing a web system, clients and web system developers may use the characteristics and the dimensions of impacts presented on Table 1 as a catalyst in predicting the impacts and outcome of the web system project. It is critical that clients and web system developers first evaluate the identified characteristics and based on the extent and level of impacts, analyse in what way these impacts can affect on the business domain. For example, in developing an extranet web system for a client's organisation, web system developers need to analyse in what way the client's business domain characteristics are impacted. Table 1 has highlighted several characteristics, which have mutual impacts on the client's business domain. Integration of different web system applications particularly, has a high level of impact on the client's system. Issues such as interoperability problems of different web applications and tools due to different level of standards, for example, can cause significant problem to the client's business domain. It is therefore critical that web system developers investigate these issues before developing a web system development project.

The framework presented will guide clients and web system developers to clearly visualise the different domain that can be impacted by the development of the web system. The dimensions of impact and framework presented in this paper can also guide clients and web system developers in mapping the characteristics that are most likely to impact on the client's business domain. By mapping these characteristics, the clients and web system developers will be able to evaluate the aspects of the domain impacted by the system and imperatively if the domain is impacted mutually. Characteristics of the domain that are mutually impacted are the ones that need to be carefully examined as these characteristics have a reverse impact and it highlights that a web system project can impact on two domains.

7 Limitations of Research

In identifying inter-dependencies between web systems and their environment, we undertook a broadly-focused analysis of literature from diverse disciplines including: marketing; management; logistics; engineering; information systems; information technology; and manufacturing. These findings are then used to formulate a framework which comprises of six dimensions of the web systems impacts. As the literature was sourced from diverse disciplines, it may be seen as a limitation to this research as the results obtained are broad. However, the literature that we have selectively surveyed is rich in information and represents various disciplines which are critical to the development of web system. The generic types of impacts that have been collected and characterised from the literature become the basis of questions to be used in the second stage of data gathering, which is the case study. The case study is conducted to triangulate the data collected from the literature. A series of industrial case studies will be conducted on organisations that have adopted web systems for their businesses in recent years. There is a limitation to the case study in which we acknowledge that most web system development projects are developed within a short time frame and web system developers need to complete the project within a limited time as well. In order to obtain a richer data, the case study needs to ideally be a longitudinal case study, particularly looking at several domains. We attempt to address this limitation by focusing on organisations that have recently developed web based enterprise systems which have had a direct impact on their trading partners, such as the suppliers and customers.

8 Conclusion and Future Work

In this paper we have described a framework for structuring information about Web impacts. The application of this framework in collating specific impacts is described elsewhere [9]. This framework is designed based on key characteristics of these impacts, and can support specific reasoning about these impacts. For example, once a data repository has been populated with information on potential impacts, it becomes possible to address questions such as: "if we make a change to the security support in the design of an intranet, then what aspects of the business operations might be most significantly affected?"

Ongoing work is focusing on commercial case studies which are providing us with significant data on business impacts which can be structured according to this framework. This can subsequently support organisations in developing strategies for the co-evolution of web systems and business processes. The nature, extent and dimensions of the impacts identified from the organisations will serve as value-added knowledge for the companies in understanding how to best manage their Web development projects.

The purpose of the case studies is to identify and analyse specific impacts from the web system development projects. In particular the goal is to develop a clearer understanding of the mutual dependency between application solutions and the organisational context of the web applications. It is also the goal of the study to reaffirm from practice the type and level of impacts found in the literature. In addition, there may be more specific and fine-grained impacts and characteristics that will be discovered from the organisation that could complement the literature survey and hence the framework that we have developed in this study.

A prototype tool is currently being developed from the repository of the knowledge captured in this paper. This tool aims at allowing industry users (for example, web system developers and their clients) to query for information such as the web systems impacts and their domains with ease. The premises of the tool are to help identify and assess the impacts and their extent, and to identify characteristics typical to various web systems, such as the Internet, extranet and intranet. This tool will also increase awareness of risks involved in design. Pertinently, it will assist in strategic decision making of various stages of web systems development.

References

1. Sawyer, S., Rosenbaum, H.: Social informatics in the information sciences. Informing Science 3 (2000) 89–96
2. Carroll, J.: Scenarios and design cognition. In: International Requirements Engineering Conference, Essen, Germany (2002) 3–5
3. Golicic, S., Davis, D., T.M., M., Mentzer, J.: The impact of e-commerce on supply chain relationships. International Journal of Physical Distribution and Logistics Management 32 (2002) 851–871
4. Osmonbekov, T., Bello, D.C., Gilliland, D.I.: Adoption of electronic commerce tools business procurement: enhanced buying center structure and processes. Journal of Business & Industrial Marketing 17 (2002) 151–166
5. Scott, G., Walter, Z. : Management problems of Internet systems development: System Sciences, HICSS. Proceedings of the 35th Annual Hawaii International Conference, 7-10 Jan. (2002)
6. Medjahed, B., Benatallah, B., Bouguettaya, A. Ngu, A.H.H., Elmagarmid, A.K.: Business-to-business interactions: issues and enabling technologies, The International Journal on Very Large Data Bases, 12(1) (2003) 59-85
7. Yang, J., Papazoglou, M.P.: Interoperation support for electronic business, Communication of the ACM, 43(6) (2000), 39-47
8. Gosain, S., Malhotra, A., El Sawy, O., and Chehade, F.: The impact of common e-business interfaces. Communications of the ACM, 46(12), December (2003), 186-195
9. Yusop, N., Zowghi, D., Lowe, D.: An analysis of e-business systems impacts on the business domain. In: The Third International Conference on Electronic Business (ICEB 2003)., Singapore (2003)
10. Turban, E., Lee, J. King, D & Chung, H.M.: Electronic Commerce: A managerial perspective, Prentice-Hall (2000)
11. Gordijn, J. and Akkermans, H.: Designing and Evaluating E-business models, Intelligent Systems, 16 (4) (2001) 11-17
12. Murray, J.: Choosing the right web services management platform, Fawcette Technical Publications, (2003) Available online: http://devresource.hp.com/drc/topics/web_services_mgt.jsp#techpapers
13. Bussler, C.,Maedche, A. & Fensel, D.: Web services: Quo Vadis, IEEE Intelligent Systems, (2003)
14. Turban, E., Lee, J. King, D & Chung, H.M.: Electronic Commerce: A managerial perspective (2nd ed), Prentice-Hall (2002)
15. Dignum, F.: E-commerce in production: some experiences, Integrated Manufacturing Systems, 13(5) (2002) 283- 294
16. Gordijn, J., Akkermans, H., Vliet, H.V.: What is an electronic Business Model, Proceeding Knowledge Engineering and Knowledge Management, 12th International Conference (EKAW 2000), Springer Verlag, (2000) 257-274
17. John. I., Muthig, D., Sody, P. & Tolzmann: Efficient and Systematic Software Evolution Through Domain Analysis, Proceedings of the IEEE Joint International Conference on Requirements Engineering (RE02) (2002)
18. Arlitt, M., Diwakar, K., Rolia, J.: Characterising the scalability of a large web-based shopping system", ACM Transactions on Internet Technology, 1(1) (2001) 44-69
19. Arlitt, M., Jin, T.: Workload characterisation of the 1988 World Cup Web site, IEEE Network, 14(3) (2000) 30-37
20. Challenger, J., Iyengar, A., Witting, K., Ferstat, C., Reed, P.: A publishing system for efficiently creating dynamic web content, Proceedings of IEEE INFOCOM 2000, (2000)
21. Fielding, R.T., Taylor, R.N.: Principled design of the modern Web architecture, In Proceedings of the 2000 International Conference on Software Engineering (ICSE 2000), Limerick, Ireland, June 2000, (2000) 407-416

22. Hansen, S.: Web information systems- The Changing landscape of management models and web applications", in Proceedings of Conference SEKE 02, July 15-19 (2002)
23. Teo, H.H., Oh, LB., Liu, C., Wei, K.K.: An empirical study of the effects of interactivity on web user attitude, International Journal of Human-Computer Studies, 58(3) (2003) 281-305
24. Morris, M.G., Turner, J.M.: Assessing users' subjective quality of experience with the world wide web: an exploratory examination of temporal changes in technology acceptance, International Journal of Human-Computer Studies, 54(6) (2001) 877-901
25. Chakrabarti, A., Manimaran, G.: Internet Infrastructure Security: A Taxonomy, IEEE Network, November/December (2002) 13-21
26. Ardagna, D. and Francalanci, C.: A cost-oriented methodology for the design of web based IT architectures, Proceedings of the 2002 ACM symposium on Applied computing, (2002) 1127 – 1133

Knowledge Management in the Business Process Negotiation

Melise Paula[1], Jonice Oliveira[1], and Jano Moreira de Souza[1,2]

[1] COPPE/UFRJ - Computer Science Department, Graduate School of Engineering, Federal University of Rio de Janeiro, Brazil.
{mel, jonice, jano}@cos.ufrj.br
[2] DCC-IM/UFRJ - Computer Science Department, Mathematics Institute, Federal University of Rio de Janeiro, Brazil

Abstract. With the fast growth of electronic commerce, there is increased demand and greater potential for online negotiation services. Negotiation is the means through which participants arrive at a specific agreement under conditions of strategic interaction or interdependent decision making. Furthermore, negotiation environment information, knowledge about both parties, and previous experience in negotiations can be useful in new negotiations. This scenario requires a management model which should be able to capture and manage this knowledge, disseminating it to the negotiators, providing the right knowledge at the right time during a negotiation, and improving the results. Our approach proposes an environment to support negotiation processes, which combines a business process model, a negotiation protocol and a workflow-based architecture to facilitate cooperation among users, managing the acquired knowledge in each negotiation and disseminating it to the organization.

1 Introduction

According to [15] electronic business enforces completely new infrastructures for doing business, and negotiation certainly bears its part in it. In negotiations, the negotiator often needs to be in contact, and to interact, with people belonging to diverse, and sometimes conflicting, organizational cultures, thereby diversifying his form of behavior and allowing the process to flow in a common direction among parties until agreement is reached. Another decisive factor present at the negotiation table is the negotiator's own experience: the successful or unsuccessful past experiences can improve the quality of future negotiations and decisions.

Current work on the technologies supporting consumers and businesses in making negotiation decisions leads in the development Negotiation Support Systems (NSS). The technologies found in the literature on negotiation support systems present great possibilities for information exchange, automation and support to the decision-making process in negotiation, but little effort has been made toward using technology to capture and manage the acquired knowledge during the negotiation. Hence, the challenge of this work is to use the Knowledge Management and related technology to capture, store and making knowledge available and accessible so that the

X. Zhou et al. (Eds.): WISE 2004, LNCS 3306, pp. 503–509, 2004.
© Springer-Verlag Berlin Heidelberg 2004

negotiators can make use of that knowledge and apply it in the attempt to optimize the results obtained in the negotiations.

The remainder of this paper is organized as follows: The section 2 describes the Business Process Model where the phases that compose a business process are identified, inclusively the negotiation that is the focus of this work. The Section 3 presents some concepts on the negotiation process that will be indispensable for the understanding of this work. Section 4 describes how the KM can be applied in the negotiation. In section 5, the architecture for supporting business negotiation process through KM is presented. Finally, future works and the conclusion are shown in section 6.

2 Business Process Model

In this work, the business model process presented was based on two models found in the literature: the Value Chain Model [7] and Consumer Behavior Buying [12].

A business process consists of a number of e-business phases. These phases define the first level of abstraction of model and are successively executed in time for buyers and for sellers. We distinguish three phases: Information Phase, Execution Phase and Evaluation Phase.

Each phase consists of specific activities for a stage of the e-business process. In the **Information Phase**, general preparations are made and informations are provided. This phase consist of different activities for the buyer and for the seller (Figure 1).

In the Need Identification activity, buyer and seller becoming aware of some unmet need.

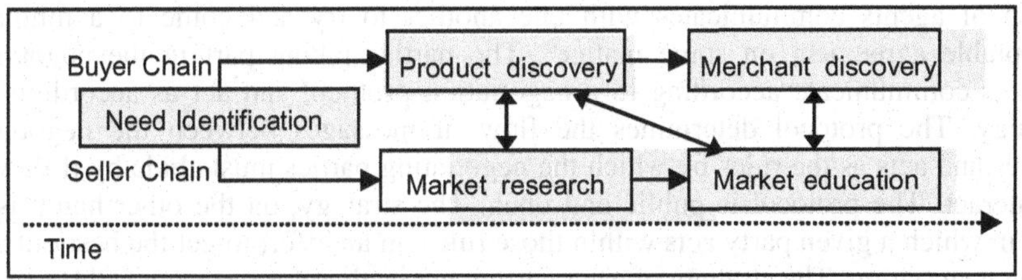

Fig. 1. Information Phase – Second level of Abstraction

From the point of view of a buyer, the following activities are the Product Discovery and Merchant Discovery. In product discovery, the buyer searches for products that will meet his need. The Merchant Discover Activity combines the information from the previous stage with merchant-specific information to help determine whom to buy from. This includes the evaluation of merchant alternatives based on consumer-selected criteria (e.g., price, warranty, availability, delivery time, reputation, etc.).

From the point of view of a seller, the Marketing Research and Marketing Education Activities are to be followed. Marketing Research include the planning, collection, and analysis of data relevant to marketing decision making, and the communication of the results of this analysis to management. Marketing Education is the study of how the marketing process seeks to determine and satisfy the needs and wants of people who buy goods, services and ideas.

The **Execution Phase** starts after that necessity is identified and the trading partners are coupled. In this phase, the negotiation activities begin and the trading partners negotiate to arrive at an agreement and formalize a contract. In negotiation, it may be established a long-term relationship between the buyer and the seller that leads to a continuing business process. This phase is represented in Figure 2.

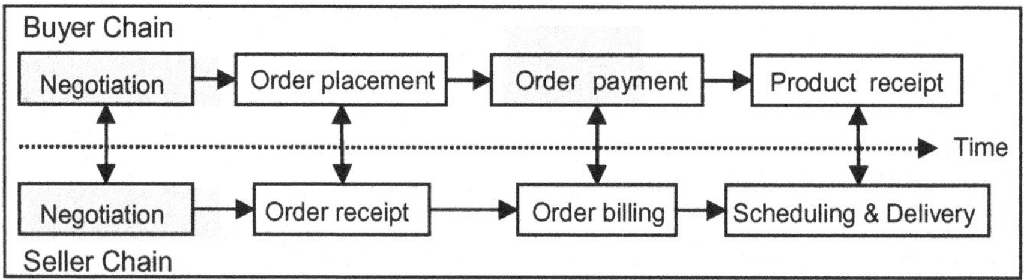

Fig. 2. Execution Phase – Second level of Abstraction

In this work, we focus on negotiation activity. Hence, in the next section, we present some concepts about negotiation and the sub-activities that compound the process.

3 Negotiation Process

According to Lomuscio *et. al.* [8], negotiation can be defined as: "Process by which a group of agents communicates with one another to try and come to a mutually-acceptable agreement on some matter". The parties taking part in the negotiation process communicate according to a negotiation protocol and act as according to a strategy. The protocol determines the flow of messages between the negotiating parties and acts as the rules by which the negotiating parties must abide by if they are to interact. The protocol is public and open. The strategy, on the other hand, is the way in which a given party acts within those rules, in an effort to get the best outcome of the negotiation. The strategy of each participant is, therefore, private [1][4].

As every process, a negotiation can be divided in phases. In Kersten and Noronha [6], the authors suggest three phases of the negotiation: pre-negotiation, conduct of negotiation and post-settlement.

In the **Pre-Negotiation Phase**, the objective is the understanding of the negotiation problem. This phase involves the analysis of the situation, problem, opponent, issues, alternatives, preference, reservation levels and strategy. Moreover, in this phase, negotiators plan the agenda of the negotiations and develop their BATNA[4].

The second phase of the negotiation, **Conduct of Negotiation**, involves exchanges of messages, offers and counter-offers based on different strategies. The **post-settlement analysis phase** involves the evaluation of the negotiation outcomes generated, and, afterwards, the negotiation activity. These outcomes include the information about the compromise and the negotiators' satisfaction.

4 KM Applied in Negotiation

Through negotiation process analysis, it was possible to verify that the knowledge creation occur in each one of the stages described by Kersten *et. al.* [6] and the negotiation process can be mapped on the knowledge creation process proposed by Nonaka and Takeuchi [10].

In the pre-negotiation phase, new knowledge is created by data search and analysis and information rising. At this phase, there is intense data collection, analysis and manipulation, and this data can be classified and used in a new context, similar to the Combination process. After the Combination process, the analyzed data imparts a new meaning to the negotiator, just like the process of Internalization, in which the explicit knowledge is acquired and can be transformed into tacit knowledge. Eventually, explicit knowledge is regarded as insufficient and other allied negotiators and experts about the domain are consulted. New knowledge can be created from this interaction, akin to the Socialization process.

One of the results of the pre-negotiation phase is the BATNA, which can be seen as knowledge externalization. Each negotiator bears experiences, sensations and own negotiation characteristics which are, somehow, documented on the planning and elaborating of this document type. In other words, each BATNA comprises knowledge externalization of the negotiation process on a domain.

Negotiation conduction is found in the second phase of the negotiation, a strong interaction between the parties, so that new knowledge about decisive facts can be acquired. Personal opinions, trends and the opponent's features, learned through contact and mutual actions can be cited as decisive factors here. This learning process is represented by socialization. The post-negotiation phase involves the evaluation and documentation of the results achieved, this step comprising an Externalization process.

5 Proposed Architecture

The proposal for elaborating a computational environment for knowledge management in negotiations arose with the aim of following up on the negotiation process, so as to capture and manage the knowledge regarding this process, rendering it available and accessible, so that the negotiators can acquire this knowledge and apply it in the attempt of optimizing the results obtained in the negotiations in e-commerce. In the design of this work, a number of negotiation tools available for training were analyzed, as [2], [13], [5], [9], [14].

The architecture of the proposed environment is distributed in two layers: i) The Process Layer and ii) The Knowledge Layer.

5.1 Process Layer: Tools for Supporting the Negotiation Process

The Process Layer is responsible for implementing the cooperative negotiation protocol and for permitting the interaction among negotiators, which will be facilitated through the use of CSCW' technologies and Groupware [3].

The support to the activities in the preparation phase can be divided in two levels: user level and decision level. In the user level, every user will have an exclusive individual access area, in which all the important information about the negotiation such as the BATNA can be stored. In the decision level, the available knowledge can facilitate decision-making when more than one business opportunities have been found.

After the preparation, one of the users may wish to start the contact. Electronic mail, Instant Messenger, Bulletin Board and the E-meeting tool resource allow for informal communication. Moreover, the users involved in a negotiation will have access to a common area, in which they can include important negotiation information, such as, for instance, the negotiation agenda.

In a general way, following the agreement, the next step in the negotiations is the signing of the commitment term or agreement. To facilitate the elaboration of the term, the electronic form of agreement (EFA) begins to be generated automatically when the users confirm their interest in the negotiation. Thus, the system is responsible, for it increases the following information: identification of the involved users (name, position, Agency) and the description of the subject of negotiation.

All process is supported by a Workflow Management System (WfMS), to define processes and roles, to deliver work items to users, and to support work performance by invoking appropriate specific applications and utilities during the negotiation process. Agents are used to monitor communications between buyers and sellers. Aiming to capture knowledge in each step in a negotiation process and providing the right knowledge in the right moment and to right people, our architecture has the Knowledge Level described bellow.

5.2 Knowledge Level: KM Support Tools

In this case, use is made a computational environment, named Epistheme [11], for the management and selective dissemination of the knowledge in the negotiation process stages.

The Knowledge Acquisition Module has as its purpose the capturing of knowledge through the interaction of Epistheme with people and its storage in structured form. To do so, Epistheme bears three sub-modules: Center of Practices, Center of Competences and Yellow Pages.

In the center of Best Practices and Worst Practices, specialists and experts in negotiation can render a successful or an unsuccessful project available, as well as information on its elaboration, with the modeling of the entire executed process becoming useful for greater knowledge exchange between negotiators.

Centers of Competences are communities providing a forum for the exchange and acquisition of tacit knowledge referring to a domain, enabling negotiators to interact with one another and exchange knowledge. Knowledge extracted should later be formalized and inserted in the knowledge base, a task to be executed by the knowledge identification module. The Knowledge Identification module is still comprised of tools for finding relevant information, experts on an issue, and information categorization.

The Yellow Pages tool is used to facilitate finding data suppliers and internal customers, as well as to carry through quality control and regularity of the supplied data.

Automatic knowledge creation is carried out by "Case-Based Reasoning" (Knowledge Creation module), capable of identifying the same, or similar, cases broached in the past, thus generating new conclusions based on already-existing knowledge. A case is a formal description of an offer, a counter-offer, negotiation model and plan. A specialist in the validation module verifies these conclusions.

Data and information can frequently be strongly associated to many areas, even though they are treated with different names, according to the applied domain. Therefore, it is necessary to identify the data and information correlated in different areas, this being the responsibility of the integration layer through the use of ontology. The Knowledge Integration module is responsible for creating and editing domain ontology in a collaborative way, solving conflicts in a model edition.

All information or data is distributed automatically to users, considering the kind of data inserted in the knowledge base and the way it can be useful, meanwhile taking into account the user's profile.

6 Conclusion and Future Works

Negotiation is an important, potentially profitable part of electronic commerce. We have analyzed the question of how to manage knowledge to facilitate negotiations in e-commerce. The use of CSCW and KM tools has been analyzed in the proposed environment. Thus, we could identify tools and functions associated to those areas which can be appropriately adapted to each step of the negotiation process.

It is important to emphasize that a culture fostering collaborative work and increase of organizational knowledge constitutes the major factor for the success of this kind of approach, and the adoption of this environment does not provide a singular solution to all problems faced in an e-Commerce negotiation process. It is a resource to improve the decisions and knowledge flow.

Therefore, this work addresses a new context in which information technology (IT) can add value, through KM and CSCW, by providing support to the Negotiation Process between organizations, and facilitating process integration among them. As future works, we have the development, implementation, adaptation and evaluation of this environment in an experimental scenario. Currently, two areas are being analyzed: negotiation for hydraulic resource allocation in river basin and negotiation in the supply chain. In the former, there is negotiation of raw data and information analysis among research institutions, and the latter shows a current scenario in an e-Business process.

References

[1] Bartolini, C., Preist., C. and Kuno, H., "Requirements for Automated Negotiation", http://www.w3.org/2001/03/ WSWS/popa/. Accessed: March, 2002.

[2] Cybersettle: http://www.cybersettle.com, Accessed: Feb, 2004

[3] Ellis, C.A., Gibbs, S. and Rein, G.L, “Groupware: Some Issues and Experiences”, Communications of the ACM - January-Vol.34.No 1. 1991

[4] Fisher, R. E, Ury, W., and Patton, B, “Getting to Yes: negotiating agreement without giving in”. 2 ed., USA: Penguin Books, 1991.

[5] INSPIRE: http://interneg.org/interneg/tools/inspire/index.html, Accessed: Feb, 2004

[6] Kersten, G. E and Noronha, S. J., “Negotiations via the Word Wide Web: A Cross-cultural Study of Decision Making”. Group Decision and Negotiations, 8, p. 251-279, 1999.

[7] Kersten, G. E. and S. Szpakowicz. "Modelling Business Negotiations for Electronic Com- merce". Intelligent Information Systems, A. M. M. Klopotek, Z. W. Ras, Ed., Malbork, Po- land, IPI PAN: 17-28, 1988.

[8] Lomuscio, A.R, Wooldridge and M. and Jennings, N. R, “A classification scheme for negotiation in electronic commerce”. In: Agent-Mediated Electronic Commerce: A European Agent Link Perspective, p. 19-33, 2001.

[9] Negoisst: http://www-i5.informatik.rwth-aachen.de/enegotiation/. Accessed: Feb, 2004

[10] Nonaka, I. E, Takeuchi, H., "The Knowledge-Creating Company: How Japanese Companies Create the Dynamics of Innovation". Oxford Univ. Press. 1995.

[11] Oliveira,J., Souza, J. and Strauch, J., "Epistheme: A Scientific Knowledge Management Environment", ICEIS, Angers, France. 2003.

[12] R.H. Guttman, A.G. Moukas and P. Maes 'Agent-mediated electronic commerce: a survey' Knowledge Engineering Review, 13 vol 13. no. 2 143—152, 1988.

[13] Smartsettle: http://www.smartsettle.com, Accessed: Feb, 2004

[14] WebNS: http://pc-ecom-07.mcmaster.ca/webns/, Accessed: Feb, 2004.

[15] Zlatev, Z. and Eck, P. van. “An Investigation of the Negotiation Domain for Electronic Commerce Information Systems”. In: Proceedings of the 5th ICEIS 2003.

A Web Service Oriented Integration Approach for Enterprise and Business-to-Business Applications

Sam Chung[1], Lai Hong Tang[1], and Sergio Davalos[2]

[1] Computing & Software Systems, Institute of Technology
University of Washington Tacoma
Tacoma, WA 98402
{chungsa, letang}@u.washington.edu

[2] Milgard School of Business
University of Washington Tacoma
Tacoma, WA 98402
sergiod@u.washington.edu

Abstract. The purpose of this paper is to propose a web service oriented approach of integrating applications for both Enterprise Application Integration (EAI) and Business-to-Business (B2B) application integration. For this purpose, four service-oriented integration approaches for both EAI and B2B are described in terms of private and shared public web service registries, synchronous and asynchronous interaction protocols, and vertical extensible markup languages. As a case study, one of the integration approaches for EAI and B2B, which can be implemented by using the current available web services platforms, is applied to a Supply Chain Management example in retail business. The empirical results show that the service-oriented application integration is seamless whether it is done within an organization or across organizations since the web services can be employed for implementing business logics regardless of integration types such as EAI and B2B.

1 Introduction

The Service-Oriented Computing (SOC) paradigm has been considered to be effective for Business-to-Business (B2B) application integration projects that require interoperable operations between heterogeneous applications [1, 2]. However, an Enterprise Information System (EIS) [3] needs two types of application integration strategies depending on where the integration occurs: Enterprise Application Integration (EAI) within the organization that the EIS belongs to and B2B application integration between an organization and its business partners. If we can use the same application integration approach for both EAI and B2B, we can streamline the application integration process not only within an organization but also between organizations. To accomplish this, we must address the following two issues: 1) which service-oriented approaches based upon SOC are possible for enterprise and B2B appli

X. Zhou et al. (Eds.): WISE 2004, LNCS 3306, pp. 510–515, 2004.
© Springer-Verlag Berlin Heidelberg 2004

cation integration? 2) How can we apply one of the approaches to a real business example that requires both EAI and B2B?

The purpose of this paper is to propose a web service oriented approach of integrating applications for EAI and B2B. We propose four such service-oriented approaches based on Service-Oriented Architecture (SOA) with variations in terms of service registries, interaction protocols, and vertical eXtensible Markup Language (XML) protocols. One of these approaches, which can be implemented by using the current available web services platforms such as .NET and J2EE [5, 6], is applied to a Supply Chain Management (SCM) [7] in retail business.

2 Related Works

Since protocols and specifications of the current SOA are still evolving, new SOAs may be proposed in the near future. Papazoglou and Georgakopoulos extend the current SOA to include service layers, functionality, and roles and proposed an extended SOA in [3]. Alonso and et al. proposed an internal SOA for wrapping existing internal functionality as web services and an external SOA for integrating the wrappers [1].

Since the basic SOA is supported by current commercial web service platforms, it can be employed for developing a service-based information system. However, the main purpose of the basic SOA was to show how to integrate applications between organizations, not within an organization. The extended SOA supports various higher-level protocols and specifications. However, its protocols and specifications are not currently available in terms of implementation and it is not known which protocols and specifications can be accepted by standardization organizations in the future. Internal and the external SOAs open the application of web services for both EAI and B2B. However, the architectures for EAI and B2B are not identical: the external architecture is similar to the basic SOA. But, the internal SOA is the extension of the conventional middleware architecture with web services.

3 Service-Oriented Architecture for Both EAI and B2B

There are two different types of application integration depending upon where the integration occurs: EAI and B2B. Since the web service technology supports standard interfaces for integration and general protocols for interactions regardless of homogeneous or heterogeneous applications with current commercial web services platforms, we propose four different types of service-oriented integration approaches based upon basic SOAs for both EAI and B2B, which are variants of the basic SOA in Section 2: Basic SOA Type I, Type II, Type III, and Type IV.

In the Basic SOA Type I, which is shown in Figure 1, basic features of the SOA are used. Synchronous binding is used between a service requestor and a service provider. For B2B, the web services are published onto an external web service registry that can be accessed by any organizations that participate in business transactions. To interchange data, a domain specific XML format is employed. (In this paper, since we consider a retail SCM example, IxRetail is used for data interchange [8].) However, web services for EAI are not published onto a service registry because we can assume that a service requestor knows where they are located and this assumption is possible within the same organization. As the number of available web services for EAI grows, a service requestor may have difficulty in discovering a web service. The main idea of the Basic SOA Type I is the fact that we can apply the SOC computing paradigm to both EAI and B2B with minimal middleware support.

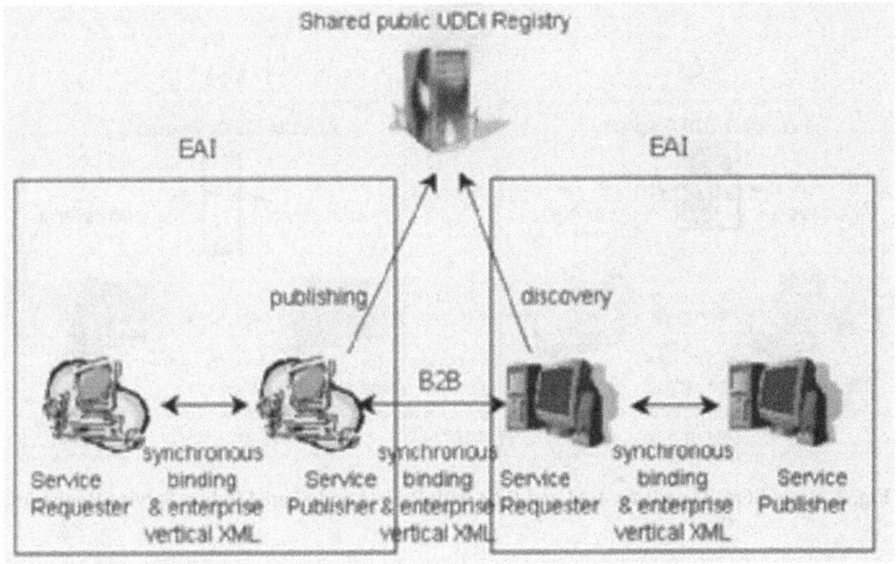

Fig. 1. Basic SOA Type I for EAI and B2B without/with Service Registries.

In the Basic SOA Type II, web services are employed for both EAI and B2B with two different types of web service registries: a private web service registry for EAI and a shared public web service registry for B2B. Web services in the private registry can be invoked by other client applications of the same organization. Web services in the shared public registry can be invoked by other client applications of any organizations with an agreement between each other. Figure 2 shows the application of SOA to EAI and B2B using private and shared public web service registries.

In the Basic SOA Type III, different protocols for binding a web service between a service requestor and a service provider are used for EAI and B2B, respectively. Since the B2B transactions are being done across organizations, the results of the binding cannot be returned as soon as the services are invoked. Therefore, asynchronous protocols such as Simple Object Access Protocol (SOAP) with Simple Mail Transfer Protocol (SMTP) are more suitable for the B2B transactions instead of using synchronous protocols such as SOAP with HyperText Transfer Protocol (HTTP).

The Basic SOA Type IV expands the Type III by considering more meaningful message exchange formats for B2B transactions. Contrary to the EAI transactions, more semantics such as policies, business agreements, XML to internal database mapping, etc. need to be considered in the B2B transaction. For this purpose, a standardized vertical XML in the business domain needs to be considered. For example, Electronic Business using eXtensible Markup Language (ebXML) can be used as a standard vertical XML for the B2B transactions [9].

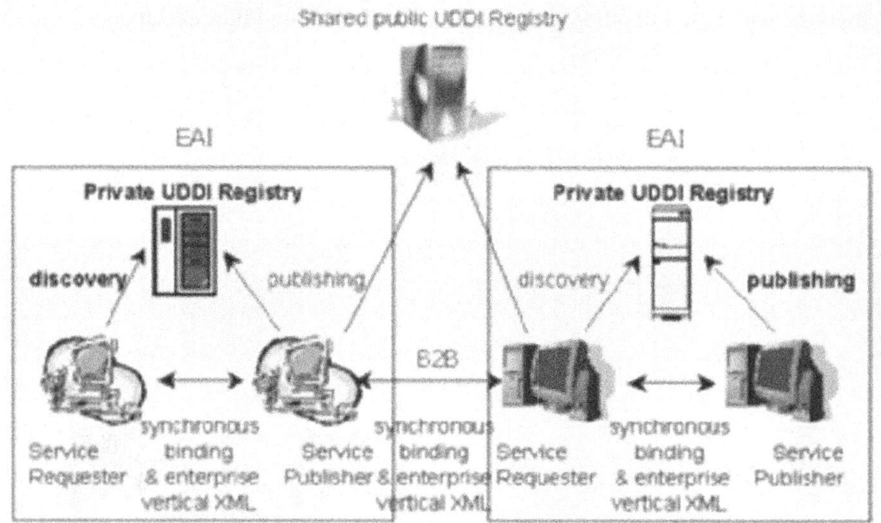

Fig. 2. Basic SOA Type II for EAI and B2B with Private and Shared Public Service Registries.

4 Case Study: EAI and B2B in Retail SCM

In order to demonstrate how a service oriented application integration approach can be applied to both EAI and B2B, the transactions between retailer and supplier enterprise information systems are considered. The retail SCM process is described with four use case scenarios: retailer's purchase order entry, supplier's purchase order retrieval, supplier's invoice entry, and retailer's invoice retrieval. The use cases of retailer's purchase order entry and supplier's invoice entry are conducted within the retailer's and the supplier's enterprise information systems, respectively. However, the other two use cases for supplier's purchase order and retailer's invoice retrievals are done across both organizations.

The four use cases are described as follows: The retailer's purchasing department enters the purchasing order that will be saved into the retailer's database. The retailer sends the purchasing order form to the supplier's sales department. The supplier's sales department looks over the purchase order and processes the order. Then the supplier's shipping department fulfills the order and updates the purchasing order to show the number of items shipped. Once that step is complete, the purchasing order becomes an invoice. That invoice is then sent to the retailer's inventory department. The retailer looks over the invoice to confirm the quantity ordered, quantity shipped and to verify that the prices are correct. If everything appears accurate, the invoice can then be closed. Otherwise the retailer can then contact the supplier with a listing of the discrepancies.

5 Service-Based BIS Development in Retail SCM

The SCM process cannot be completely demonstrated without a starting and ending point in the B2B transaction. Before implementing B2B transactions as web services, service-oriented Business Information Systems (BIS) have to be implemented for retailer and supplier, respectively. The retailer BIS would initialize the SCM process by creating a purchase order. The supplier BIS would take the purchase order and update that into an invoice. Once the invoice is ready, the retailer can retrieve it through its BIS. The BISs use SOA to implement the systems so that the applications will be easier for B2B application integrations.

Once the BISs are complete, a standard based interoperable Electronic Data Interchange (EDI) format for heterogeneous retail SCM systems, which we call a service-oriented XML generator (SoRetailXMLGen), is developed. It translates relational schemas of the Association for Retail Technology Standards (ARTS) Data Model into a standard external retail data representation for marshalling and unmarshalling called IxRetail and vice versa. The implemented methods are declared as web services. The web services were published on Microsoft's Universal Description, Discovery and Integration (UDDI) web service registry. While we were implementing this SCM system with .NET platform, a private UDDI service registry was not available. Recently, Microsoft Windows 2003 server supports the UDDI service function. Therefore, we use the Basic SOA Type I for this implementation. The internal or private web services are not published onto any service registry. We assume that a service requestor know the endpoints of the web services. However, external or public web services are published onto Microsoft's UDDI web service registry.

Among the four use cases, the supplier's purchase order use case is selected for explanation purpose: A supplier retrieves the purchase order from the retailer. To initialize the process, the supplier goes out and checks for new purchase order available through a web interface. The web interface will display a list of retailers from the supplier's database using a private web service called SupplierWS. The supplier will select the desired retailer and the site will retrieve a list of purchase order dates from the retailer's database through a method from the public web service published by the retailer called RetailerDB2IxRetailWS. Then the supplier selects the date of the purchase order requested. This will retrieve the purchase order from the retailer and convert the data into IxRetail format following the IxRetail_PO schema. SoRetailXMLGen will create an XML file and use that file to convert the IxRetail data into the supplier's database structure. The file will be inserted into the supplier's database through a method in the private web service called IxRetail2SupplierDBConverterWS.

6 Results and Discussions

The completion of this project shows how a service-oriented integration approach can be applied to both EAI and B2B. The retailer's BIS is created with a Windows client application. It is bound to a private web service that contains all methods to communicate with the retailer's database. The supplier's BIS is created with an ASP.NET web client application, which is bound to a private web service that contains all methods to communicate with the supplier's database. Combining the BISs and applying the service-oriented approach to B2B resulted in the SoRetailXMLGen system. The system contains two public and two private web services. The public web services are made available for discovery through a shared public UDDI registry.

The empirical results show that the service-oriented integration approach brings significant benefits to both EAI and B2B. First of all, application integration is seamless whether it is done within an organization or across organizations since web services can be employed for implementing business logics regardless of integration types such as EAI and B2B. Web services enhance reusability of methods in an Enterprise Information System (EIS). It also enhances interoperability of methods across EISs since they are published to a public UDDI registry and can be accessed from any EIS. Secondly, the openness and the reusability of internal software components are enhanced for both EAI and B2B since the standardized interfaces of the web services can be published onto service registries for both EAI and B2B requestors. Lastly, these empirical results of the service oriented approach in retail SCM will be useful for the SOC community since there are currently very few examples of applying SOC concepts and architectures to real business applications.

References

1. Gustavo Alonso, Fabio Casati, Harumi Kuno, and Vijay Machiraju. *Web Services Concepts, Architectures and Applications*. Springer Verlag. 2004.
2. Olaf Zimmermann, Mark Tomlinson, and Stefan Peuser. *Perspectives on Web Services: Applying SOAP, WSDL, and UDDI to Real-World Projects*. Springer Verlag. 2004.
3. Mike. P. Papazoglou and Dimitrios Georgakopoulos. "Service-Oriented Computing" *Communication of the ACM*. October 2003. Vol. 46, No. 10. pp. 25-28.
4. Enterprise Information System. J2EE v1.4 Glossary.
5. Joseph Williams. The Web services debate: J2EE vs. .NET. *Communications of the ACM*. June 2003. Vol. 46, No. 6. pp. 58-63.
6. Gerry Miller. The Web services debate: .NET vs. J2EE. *Communications of the ACM*. June 2003. Vol. 46, No. 6. pp. 64-67.
7. Kuldeep Kumar. Technology for Supporting Supply Chain Management. *Communications of the ACM*. June 2001. Vol. 44, No. 6. pp. 58-61.
8. The Association for Retail Technology Standards (ARTS) of the National Retail Federation.
9. ebXML.

A Two-Phase Sampling Technique to Improve the Accuracy of Text Similarities in the Categorisation of Hidden Web Databases

Yih-Ling Hedley[1], Muhammad Younas[1], Anne James[1], and Mark Sanderson[2]

[1] School of Mathematical and Information Sciences, Coventry University,
Priory Street, Coventry CV1 5FB, UK
{y.hedley, m.younas, a.james}@coventry.ac.uk
[2] Department of Information Studies, University of Sheffield,
Regent Court, 211 Portobello St, Sheffield, S1 4DP, UK
m.sanderson@shef.ac.uk

Abstract. The larger amount of high quality and specialised information on the Web is stored in document databases, which is not indexed by general-purpose search engines such as Google and Yahoo. Such information is dynamically generated as a result of submitting queries to databases — which are referred to as Hidden Web databases. This paper presents a *Two-Phase Sampling (2PS)* technique that detects Web page templates from the randomly sampled documents of a database. It generates terms and frequencies that summarise the database content with improved accuracy. We then utilise such statistics to improve the accuracy of text similarity computation in categorisation. Experimental results show that 2PS effectively eliminates terms contained in Web page templates, and generates terms and frequencies with improved accuracy. We also demonstrate that 2PS improves the accuracy of text similarity computation required in the process of database categorisation.

1 Introduction

Hidden Web databases or searchable databases [4, 1] maintain a collection of documents such as archives, user manuals or news articles. These databases dynamically generate document lists in response to users' queries which are submitted through search interfaces. In recent years, general-purpose or specialised search engines provide services for information searches on the Hidden Web. However, as the number of databases increases, it has become prohibitive for these services to individually evaluate databases in order to answer users' queries. Therefore, current research strives to identify databases that contain information most relevant to queries.

Techniques such as database selection [2, 7, 10] and database categorisation [4, 8] have been developed in order to assist users in the search of information from Hidden Web databases. As knowledge about the contents of underlying databases is often unavailable, current approaches acquire such knowledge through sampling documents from databases [2, 7, 10]. For instance, the query-based sampling technique [2] queries databases with terms that are randomly selected from those contained in

X. Zhou et al. (Eds.): WISE 2004, LNCS 3306, pp. 516–527, 2004.
© Springer-Verlag Berlin Heidelberg 2004

sampled documents. The techniques in [7, 10] sample databases with terms contained in Web logs to retrieve additional topic terms. A major issue associated with existing techniques is that they extract terms irrelevant to queries. A number of the extracted terms are often found in Web page templates that contain navigation panels, search interfaces and advertisements. Consequently, the accuracy of terms and frequencies generated from sampled documents has been reduced.

This paper presents a sampling and extraction technique, referred to as *Two-Phase Sampling* (*2PS*), which is built on our previous work [6]. 2PS aims to extract information from Web document databases that is relevant to queries. Our technique accomplishes the sampling process in two phases: First, it randomly selects a term from the Web interface pages of a database to initiate the process of sampling documents. Subsequently, 2PS queries databases with terms that are randomly selected from those contained in the documents previously sampled. Second, 2PS detects Web page templates in order to extract information relevant to the respective queries. This generates statistics (i.e., terms and frequencies) from the sampled documents, which summarises the content of the database. Such statistics are then utilised in the process of categorisation in which text similarities are computed between the statistics and a pre-defined set of subject categories.

2PS utilises the terms contained in the Web interface pages of a database to initiate the sampling process. This differs from query-based sampling, which carries out an initial query with a frequently used term. Furthermore, 2PS extracts terms that are relevant to queries. By contrast, [2, 7, 10] extract all terms from sampled documents, which may also contain terms used in Web page templates. Moreover, our technique is applied to the categorisation of databases, whilst query-based sampling is proposed for the purpose of database selection.

2PS is implemented as a prototype system and tested on a number of real-world Hidden Web databases that contain computer manuals, health archives and general news articles. We assess the effectiveness of our technique in two respects: (i) the accuracy of extracting relevant information from sampled documents, and (ii) accuracy of text similarity computation. The latter is computed between resultant statistics and a set of pre-defined subject categories, which is required in the process of database categorisation. The results of 2PS are compared with those of query-based sampling, which has been widely adopted by other relevant studies [4, 8]. Experimental results show that our technique generates statistics with improved relevancy. The results also demonstrate that the technique obtains text similarities more accurately for a number of subject categories.

The remainder of the paper is organised as follows. Section 2 introduces current approaches to discovering information contents of Hidden Web databases. It then describes current database/document sampling techniques and their limitations. Section 3 presents the proposed 2PS technique. Section 4 describes the criteria for generating terms and their frequencies from sampled documents in order to summarise database contents. In section 5, we describe the computation of similarities between statistics generated from the sampled documents of a database and pre-defined subject categories. Section 6 illustrates experimental results. Section 7 concludes the paper.

2 Related Work

A number of research studies have attempted to automatically discover the contents of databases in order to facilitate their categorisation or selection. For instance, [3] proposes the Stanford Protocol Proposal for Internet Retrieval and Search (STARTS) protocol in order to gather information contents from database sources. However, STARTS requires cooperation from individual data sources. This approach is, therefore, considered to be less practical in the Web environment [2]. In addition, information about database contents can also be gathered by examining the textual contents of Web interface pages maintained by databases [7, 10] or by analysing their hyperlink structures [5].

An alternative approach is to collect information from actual documents contained in databases. However, in the domain of Hidden Web databases, it is difficult to obtain all documents from a database. Therefore, a number of approaches have been proposed to acquire such information from documents through sampling [2, 7, 10]. For instance, query-based sampling [2] submits queries to databases with terms that are randomly selected from those contained in previously sampled documents. The techniques in [7, 10] sample databases with terms contained in Web logs, but the selection of terms may be limited. Terms and frequencies generated from sampled documents are referred to as Language Models [2], Textual Models [7, 10] or Centroids [8].

A major issue associated with the aforementioned techniques is that they extract terms that are often irrelevant to a query, in that a number of terms retrieved are found in templates for descriptive or navigation purposes. For instance, the language model generated from the sampled documents of the Combined Health Information Database (CHID) contains terms (such as 'author' and 'format') with high frequencies. However, these terms are irrelevant to the queries but are used to describe document contents. Consequently, the accuracy of terms and frequencies generated from sampled documents has been reduced. [2] proposes the use of additional stop-word lists to eliminate irrelevant terms, but maintains that such a technique can be difficult to apply in practice.

Current approaches in the categorisation of Web document databases utilises different sources of information. These include the number of document matches returned in response to a query [4]. This approach requires database sources to provide information about the number of documents relevant to queries. However, such information might be unavailable or inaccurate in practice. [8] proposes the computation of average similarities between the concepts and each of the most relevant documents to determine the categories of databases. However, the relevancy of documents retrieved is likely to be reduced if the number of query words exceeds the limit imposed by databases [4]. In addition, the computation of text similarities, between 'centroids' (i.e., terms and frequencies) generated from sampled documents and pre-defined concepts, is also proposed in [8]. Such statistics may contain information that is irrelevant to queries.

In summary, the retrieval of documents through sampling for categorisation provides an alternative solution in view of the aforementioned limitations — particularly when the number of document matches is not available or databases are queried with the number of terms that exceed the limit. However, existing database/document sampling techniques extract terms irrelevant to queries, as these terms are often found in templates used for descriptive or navigation purposes. We, therefore, present a sampling technique that extracts information relevant to queries. This generates terms and frequencies from sampled documents with improved accuracy. Furthermore, the categorisation of databases can be enhanced as text similarities between the statistics of a database and subject categories can be attained with a higher degree of accuracy.

3 Two-Phase Sampling Technique (2PS)

This section presents the proposed technique that collects information from Hidden Web databases in two phases. In the first phase, it queries a Hidden Web database to sample a required number of documents. In the second phase, it detects Web page templates and extracts information relevant to queries from the sampled documents, from which terms and frequencies are then generated. Fig. 1 depicts the process of sampling documents and extracting query-related information from Hidden Web documents. The two phases are detailed in section 3.1 and 3.2.

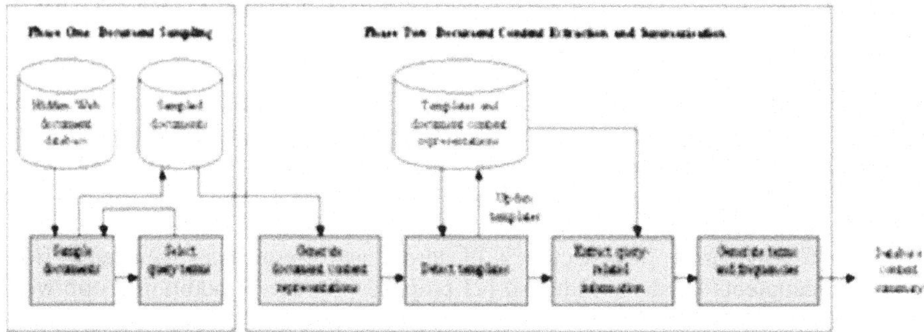

Fig. 1. The Two-Phase Sampling (2PS) Technique

3.1 Phase One: Document Sampling

A document database (such as Help Site and CHID) is first queried with a randomly selected term from those contained in its Web interface pages. This retrieves top N documents where N represents a number of documents that are most relevant to the query. A subsequent query term is then randomly selected from terms contained in the sampled documents. This process is repeated until a required number of documents are sampled, which are stored locally for further processing.

In this phase, 2PS differs from query-based sampling in respect of selecting an initial query term. The latter performs an initial query with a frequently used term. By contrast, 2PS initiates the sampling process with a term randomly selected from those contained in the Web interface pages of a database. This utilises a source of information that is closely related to its contents. Sampled documents will then be further processed locally to generate terms and frequencies.

3.2 Phase Two: Document Content Extraction and Summarisation

Documents retrieved from the first phase are analysed in order to retrieve information relevant to the queries submitted to the underlying database. This phase is carried out in the following steps:

Step 1: Generate Document Content Representations. This firstly converts the content of a sampled document into a list of text and tag segments. Tag segments include start tags, end tags and single tags. Text segments are text that resides between two tag segments. The document content is then represented by text segments and their neighbouring tag segments, which we referred to as *Text with Neighbouring Adjacent Tag Segments* (*TNATS*). The neighbouring adjacent tag segments of a text segment are defined as the list of tag segments that are located immediately before and after the text segment until another text segment is reached. Neighbouring tag segments describe how a given text segment is structured and its relation to the nearest text segments. Assume that a document contains n segments, we define a text segment, TxS, as follows:

$$TxS = (tx_i,\ tg\text{-}lst_j,\ tg\text{-}lst_k)$$

where tx_i is the textual content of text segment i, $1 \le i \le n$; $tg\text{-}lst_j$ represents p tag segments located before tx_i and $tg\text{-}lst_k$ represents q tag segments located after tx_i until another text segment is reached. $tg\text{-}lst_j = \{tg_1, \ldots, tg_p\}$, $1 \le j \le p$ and $tg\text{-}lst_k = \{tg_1, \ldots, tg_q\}$, $1 \le k \le q$. Consider the following segments in a document sampled from the CHID database. The text segment, '1. HIV and AIDS should I get tested?:.', (in bold) is represented as ('1. HIV and AIDS should I get tested?:.', {</title></head> <body> <hr><h3><b><i>}, {</i></b></h3> <i><b>}).

…
CHID Document
</title></head> <body>
<hr><h3><b><i>
1. HIV and AIDS should I get tested?:.
</i></b></h3> <i><b>
subfile:
…

Therefore, given a sampled document, d, with n text segments, the content of d is then represented as:

$$Content(d) = \{TxS_1, \ldots, TxS_n\}$$

where TxS_i represents a text segment, $1 \le i \le n$.

Step 2: Detect Templates. This process identifies Web page templates used to generate documents in response to queries. Template detection is performed as follows.

(i) Represent and analyse the contents of sampled documents based on *TNATS*.

(ii) Detect an initial Web page template through searching for identical patterns (i.e., the matched text segments along with their neighbouring tag segments) from the first two sampled documents. Identical patterns are eliminated from the document content representations. Both documents are assigned to a group associated with the template. If no repeated patterns are found, the content representations of both documents are stored for future template detection.

(iii) Detect new templates through comparing each of the subsequently sampled documents with existing templates generated or the previously stored document content representations. Assign documents to a group associated with the template from which the documents are generated. Eliminate any identical patterns from each document. In the case where no identical patterns are found in a document, its content representation is stored.

The process in (iii) is repeated until all sampled documents are analysed. This results in the identification of one or more templates. For each template, there also exist two or more documents associated with the template from which the documents are generated. Each of these documents contains text segments that are not found in their respective template. These text segments are partially related to their queries. In addition to the templates generated, the result of the process contains zero or more documents in which no matched patterns are found.

Step 3: Extract Query-Related Information. This extracts information that is related to the queries only. The set of documents generated from their respective template are analysed. This process further identifies repeated patterns from the remaining text segments of the documents. The textual content of a text segment is represented as a vector of terms with weights. A term weight is obtained from the frequencies of the term that appears in the segment. Cosine similarity [9] is computed for the text segments from different documents in order to determine their similarities. The computation of similarities is given as follows:

$$COSINE\ (TxS_i, TxS_j) = \sum_{k=1}^{t} (tw_{ik} * tw_{jk}) \ / \ \sqrt{\sum_{k=1}^{t} (tw_{ik})^2} * \sqrt{\sum_{k=1}^{t} (tw_{jk})^2} \quad (1)$$

where TxS_i and TxS_j represent two text segments in a document; tw_{ik} is the weight of term k in TxS_i, and tw_{jk} is the weight of term k in TxS_j.

This is only applied to text segments with identical neighbouring tag segments. Two segments are considered to be similar if the similarity value exceeds a threshold value. The threshold value is determined experimentally. This process results in the extraction of text segments with different tag structures. It also extracts text segments that have identical neighbouring tag structures but are significantly different in their textual content.

Step 4: Generate Terms and Frequencies. Frequencies are computed for the terms extracted from randomly sampled documents. These summarise the information content of a database, which is described in Section 4.

4 Database Content Summarisation

In the domain of Hidden Web databases, the inverse document frequency (*idf*), used in traditional information retrieval, is not applicable as the total number of documents in a database is often unknown. Therefore, document frequency (*df*), collection term frequency (*ctf*) and average term frequency (*avg_tf*) initially proposed in [2] are applied in this paper. Our technique generates terms and frequencies from the randomly sampled documents of a database, which we refer to as *Content Summary*. We consider the following frequencies to compute the content summary of a Hidden Web database.

- *Document frequency (df): df* is the number of documents in the collection of documents sampled that contain term *t*, where *d* is the document and *f* is the frequency
- *Collection term frequency (ctf): ctf* is the occurrence of a term, *t*, in the collection of documents sampled, where *c* is the collection and *f* is the frequency
- *Average term frequency (avg_tf): avg_tf* is obtained by dividing collection term frequency by document frequency (i.e., *avg_tf = ctf / df*).

The content summary of a document database is defined as follows. Assume that a Hidden Web database, *D*, is sampled with *N* documents. Each sampled document, *d*, is represented as a vector of terms and their associated weights [8]. Thus $d = (w_1, \ldots, w_n)$, where w_i is the weight of term t_i, and *m* is the number of distinct terms in $d \in D$, $1 \leq i \leq m$. Each w_i is computed using the term frequency metrics, *avg_tf*, i. e., $w_i = ctf_i/df_i$. The content summary is then denoted as *CS* (*D*), which is generated from the vectors of all sampled documents in *D*. Assume that *n* is the number of distinct terms in all sampled documents. *CS* (*D*) is, therefore, expressed as a vector of terms:

$$CS\,(D) = \{w_1, \ldots, w_n\}$$

where w_i is computed by adding the weights of t_i in all sampled documents in *D* and dividing the sum by the number of sampled documents that contain t_i, $1 \leq i \leq n$.

5 Text Similarity Computation

A previous research study [2] demonstrates that statistics generated from the randomly sampled documents of a database are sufficient to represent its content. We utilise such statistics and a pre-defined category scheme in the process of database categorisation.

We adopt a scheme from Open Directory Project (ODP), which contains a hierarchy of categories for different subject domains. This scheme is widely used by search services (such as Google). Fig. 2 depicts a subset of its category hierarchy. Cosine similarity [9] is applied to compute text similarities between the content summary of a database and subject categories. Such computation is required to determine the relevancy of databases and categories.

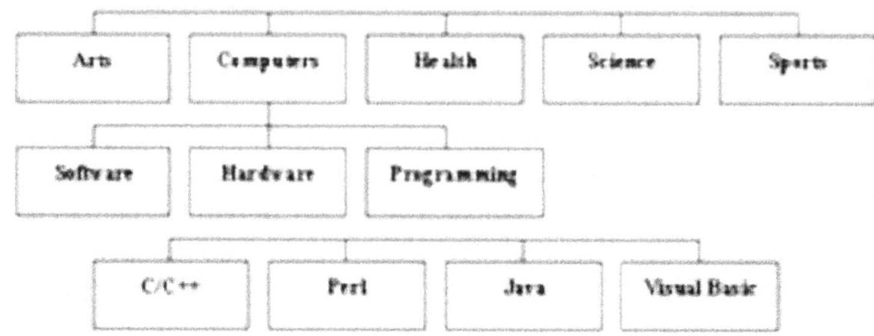

Fig. 2. A subset of the ODP category hierarchy

A previous research [8] defines the concepts of a category by its child categories. Text similarity is computed between a database centroid (i.e., terms and frequencies) and each of the categories. For instance, the set of concepts associated with category 'Programming' are 'C/C++', 'Perl', 'Java' and 'Visual Basic' as shown in Fig.2. We refer to this approach as the *Concept-Coverage* of a category. However, the concept of a category can also be specified by its parent categories, which we refer to as the *Concept-Specificity* of a category. For instance, the 'Java' category is given within the context by its two parent categories, 'Programming' and 'Computers'. We apply both *Concept-Coverage* and *Concept-Specificity* of a category to determine its similarity with a database.

The content summary (i.e., statistics) of a database, CS_i and the concepts (i.e., *Concept-Coverage* or *Concept-Specificity*) of a category, C_j, are represented as a document and a query, respectively. Each is viewed as a vector of terms. Terms are stemmed and stop words are removed. The cosine function, $COSINE(CS_i, C_j)$, is then computed as follows:

$$COSINE\ (CS_i, C_j) = \sum_{k=1}^{t} (w_{ik} * w_{jk}) \ / \ \sqrt{\sum_{k=1}^{t} (w_{ik})^2} * \sqrt{\sum_{k=1}^{t} (w_{jk})^2} \quad (2)$$

where w_{ik} is the weight of term k in the CS_i and w_{jk} is the weight of term k in the C_j.

6 Experimental Results

This section presents the experiments that assess the effectiveness of the proposed 2PS technique. In particular, we measure the effectiveness of retrieving relevant information from the documents of a Hidden Web databases through sampling. The experimental results are compared with those generated using query-based sampling (abbreviated as QS) [2]. We compare 2PS with QS as it is a well-established technique and has also been adopted by other relevant studies [4, 8].

Experiments are carried out on three real-world Hidden Web document databases including Help Site, CHID and Wired News. These provide information about user manuals, healthcare archives and news articles respectively. Table 1 summarises the their associated subjects, contents and number of templates used to generate documents. For instance, Help Site and CHID contain documents that are related to the subjects of computing and healthcare, respectively. Their information contents are homogeneous in nature. By contrast, Wired News provides information that is heterogeneous in nature as it contains articles from different subjects of interest. Where the number of templates is concerned, CHID and Wired News generate documents using one Web page template. Help Site differs from the two databases as it contains documents from other information sources that provide computing related information. Subsequently, different Web page templates are found in Help Site documents.

Table 1. 3 Hidden Web databases used in the experiment

Document databases	URL	Subject	Content	Templates employed
Help Site	www.help-site.com	Computers	Homogeneous	Multiple templates
CHID	www.chid.nih.gov	Health	Homogeneous	Single template
Wired News	www.wired.com	General news	Heterogeneous	Single template

The experiment conducted using QS initiates the first query to a database with a frequently used term. It then selects subsequent query terms from those contained in all previously sampled documents. All terms are extracted and their frequencies are updated. By contrast, 2PS initiates its sampling process with a term randomly selected from the Web interface pages of a database. The sampled documents are then processed in the second phase in order to retrieve relevant information. Terms and frequencies are generated from the documents after irrelevant information is eliminated.

This paper investigates whether our technique effectively generates terms and frequencies that are relevant to queries without extracting those contained in Web page templates. The results are compared with those obtained using QS, which extract terms (including terms used in Web page templates) from all sampled documents.

Experimental results in [2] conclude that QS retrieves approximately 80% of terms, when 300 documents are sampled and top 4 documents are retrieved for each query. In this paper, these two parameters are used to obtain results for QS and 2PS. Terms and frequencies for all sampled documents are generated after the required number of documents has been sampled. The results produced from QS provide the baseline for our experiments.

Five sets of samples are obtained for each database and 300 documents are randomly retrieved for each sample. We retrieve top 50 terms ranked according to their *ctf* frequencies for 2PS and QS to determine the relevancy of terms extracted. *Ctf* frequencies are used to analyse the results generated from both techniques. This frequency represents the occurrences of a term that appears in all documents that are sampled. The *ctf* frequency is used to demonstrate the effectiveness of information extraction from sampled documents since terms contained in Web page templates are often ranked with high *ctf* frequencies. Therefore, we compare the number of relevant terms (from top 50 terms) retrieved using 2PS with that obtained from QS. Our aim is to demonstrate whether our technique effectively extracts query-related information.

Moreover, 5 top-level categories and a total of over 8,000 categories are selected from ODP. Text similarities are computed between the categories and content summaries of databases generated by 2PS and QS. We experiment on categories in terms of *Concept-Coverage* and *Concept-Specificity*. The content summary of a database is given by terms and their *avg_tf* frequencies. *Avg_tf* frequencies are chosen as they produce the ranking of terms that is most informative [2]. Stemming techniques and stop-word removal are applied to content summaries and categories.

Experimental results for QS and 2PS are summarised as follows. Firstly, Table 2 gives the number of relevant terms (from top 50 terms ranked according to ctf) obtained using 2PS and QS for the three databases. The relevancy of a term is determined by examining whether the term is found in Web page templates. The results generated from CHID and Wired News demonstrate that 2PS retrieves more relevant terms.

For instance, in the first set of documents sampled from CHID using 2PS, the number of relevant terms retrieved is 48, whilst the number obtained for QS is 20. As CHID and Wired News generate documents using one Web page template, terms contained in the templates have been successfully detected and eliminated. By comparison, multiple templates are employed in the Help Site database (as described in Table 1). Consequently, a smaller number of terms that are found in Web page templates are eliminated from its documents.

Table 2. The number of relevant terms retrieved (from top 50 terms) ranked according to *ctf*

Sample sets	Number of relevant terms					
	Help Site		CHID		Wired News	
	QS	2PS	QS	2PS	QS	2PS
Sample set 1	46	48	20	48	14	42
Sample set 2	47	48	19	47	10	43
Sample set 3	46	48	20	47	11	39
Sample set 4	46	49	20	48	7	40
Sample set 5	47	49	20	47	7	42

Table 3 shows the top 50 terms (ranked according to their *ctf* frequencies) retrieved from the first set of sampled documents of the CHID database for QS and 2PS. As QS does not eliminate terms contained in Web page templates, a number of terms (such as 'author', 'format' and 'language') have attained much higher frequencies. By contrast, 2PS excludes such terms and therefore obtains terms (such as 'immunodeficiency', 'virus' and 'treatment') in the higher rank.

Table 4 gives the number of categories for which text similarities are correctly computed for QS and 2PS. These results are obtained based on the statistics generated from the first set of CHID sampled document. We examine the number of categories that are given incorrect similarity values as a result of statistics containing template terms. This demonstrates that the accuracy of text similarity computation is improved for the statistics of databases generated using 2PS. For instance, similarity is incorrectly computed between statistics generated (using QS) and the Concept-Specificity of a sub-category, i.e., 'Formats', which is defined by its parent categories, 'Computers', 'Software', 'Typesetting' and 'TeX'. Since 2PS eliminates terms such as 'format' (used for descriptive purposes) from the sampled documents, it results in more accurate computation of similarity.

Table 3. Top 50 terms ranked according to ctf generated from CHID for QS and 2PS

Rank	Term (QS)	Term (2PS)	Rank	Term (QS)	Term (2PS)
1	hiv	hiv	26	subfile	services
2	aids	aids	27	verification	discusses
3	health	health	28	lg	hepatitis
4	prevention	information	29	ve	persons
5	information	document	30	yr	abstinence
6	education	chid	31	ac	available
7	tb	prevention	32	mj	syndrome
8	number	human	33	code	testing
9	accession	Immuno-deficiency	34	ab	transmitted
10	author	virus	35	english	national
11	pamphlet	pamphlet	36	availability	sheet
12	format	sex	37	physical	sexual
13	language	tb	38	corporate	positive
14	human	treatment	39	pd	programs
15	document	care	40	cn	report
16	audience	community	41	www	program
17	published	public	42	http	acquired
18	update	service	43	national	individuals
19	major	transmission	44	public	http
20	descriptors	organizations	45	treatment	sexually
21	fm	risk	46	Immuno-deficiency	women
22	chid	education	47	persons	www
23	abstract	disease	48	disease	infection
24	date	professionals	49	sheet	cdc
25	description	provides	50	virus	diseases

Table 4. The number of categories for which text similarities are correctly computed when applying QS and 2PS to the CHID database

Top-level categories	Number of sub-categories	Number of categories with similarities correctly computed			
		Concept-Coverage		Concept-Specificity	
		QS	2PS	QS	2PS
Arts	1382	1354	1374	1346	1377
Computers	4093	3914	4046	2995	4022
Health	1505	1497	1505	1494	1505
Science	1088	1048	1080	951	1083
Sports	726	724	726	723	726

7 Conclusion

This paper presents a sampling and extraction technique, 2PS, in an attempt to extract query-related information and generate terms and frequencies that represent the contents of databases. Experimental results show that our technique eliminates terms contained in Web page templates, thereby obtaining relevant terms and frequencies. We then apply 2PS in the process of database categorisation and introduce the use of Concept-Specificity of a category in the computation of text similarities, in addition to Concept-coverage previously proposed. The results also demonstrate that the accuracy of text similarity computation is improved when the content summaries of databases are generated using 2PS.

Acknowledgement. This work was funded in part by the EU 6th Framework project, BRICKS: contract number IST-2002-2.3.1.12.

References

1. Bergman, M. K.: The Deep Web: Surfacing Hidden Value. Appeared in The Journal of Electronic Publishing from the University of Michigan (2001). Retrieved: 10 August, 2004, from http://www.press.umich.edu/jep/07-01/bergman.html
2. Callan, J., Connell, M.: Query-Based Sampling of Text Databases. ACM Transactions on Information Systems, Vol. 19, No. 2 (2001) 97-130
3. Fravano, L. Change, K., Garcia-Molina, H., Paepcke, A.: STARTS Stanford Proposal for Internet Meta-Searching. In Proceedings of the ACM-SIGMOD International Conference on Management of Data (1997)
4. Gravano, L., Ipeirotis, P. G., Sahami, M.: QProber: A System for Automatic Classification of Hidden-Web Databases. ACM Transactions on Information Systems (TOIS), Vol. 21, No. 1 (2003)
5. Heß, M., Drobnik, O.: Clustering Specialised Web-databases by Exploiting Hyperlinks. In Proceedings of the Second Asian Digital Library Conference (1999)
6. Hedley, Y.L., Younas, M., James, A., Sanderson M. Query-Related Data Extraction of Hidden Web Documents. In Proceedings of SIGIR (2004)
7. Lin, K.I., Chen, H.: Automatic Information Discovery from the Invisible Web. International Conference on Information Technology: Coding and Computing (2002)
8. Meng, W., Wang, W., Sun, H., Yu, C.: Concept Hierarchy Based Text Database Categorization. International Journal on Knowledge and Information Systems, Vol. 4, No. 2 (2002) 132-150
9. Salton, G., McGill, M.: Introduction to Modern Information Retrieval. McCraw-Hill, New York (1983)
10. Sugiura, A., Etzioni, O.: Query Routing for Web Search Engines: Architecture and Experiment. 9th WWW Conference (2000)

Capturing Web Dynamics by Regular Approximation

Dirk Kukulenz

Universität zu Lübeck,
Institut für Informationssysteme,
Ratzeburger Allee 160,
23538 Lübeck, Germany
kukulenz@ifis.uni-luebeck.de

Abstract. Software systems like Web crawlers, Web archives or Web caches depend on or may be improved with the knowledge of update times of remote sources. In the literature, based on the assumption of an exponential distribution of time intervals between updates, diverse statistical methods were presented to find optimal reload times of remote sources. In this article first we present the observation that the time behavior of a fraction of Web data may be described more precisely by regular or quasi regular grammars. Second we present an approach to estimate the parameters of such grammars automatically. By comparing a reload policy based on regular approximation to previous exponential-distribution based methods we show that the quality of local copies of remote sources concerning 'freshness' and the amount of lost data may be improved significantly.

1 Introduction

For diverse software systems applied in the Web it is necessary to keep track of data changes of remote sources. Web caches, developed to reduce network traffic and response time, may be optimized by estimating when the cached data are 'stale' and have to be reloaded. Web archives, mirroring a fraction of the Web over a period of time, depend on the knowledge, when new data appear and have to be stored. One main component of search engines are crawlers, responsible for finding data in the Web usually by traversing hyperlinks. The data that is found by crawlers and indexed should represent the current state of the Web. However often the data are stale or no longer available. New data often are not yet available.

The common problem of these systems is the dependence on the knowledge at what points in time data on remote and distributed sources change. Basically there exist two strategies to acquire this knowledge, denoted as the *push* and the *pull* strategy. The push strategy implies that a data source itself informs the client (crawler, cache etc.) about the times of changes. An investigation concerning the push model is presented in [10]. However a push service is difficult to realize in a heterogenous information system as the World-Wide Web. In the

X. Zhou et al. (Eds.): WISE 2004, LNCS 3306, pp. 528–540, 2004.
© Springer-Verlag Berlin Heidelberg 2004

pull model it is necessary for a client to predict remote changes in order to initiate reload operations. In order to predict changes it is first necessary to acquire information about a data source, i.e. to detect changes. Two strategies are available for this purpose. One is to reload the data source periodically and to compare previous and current data object. A higher reload frequency increases the precision of detected changes but also the costs concerning network load. A second strategy in order to detect data changes is provided by the HTTP protocol [6]. Different strategies were developed to acquire optimal cache behavior based on http-headers [7], [14]. However there are three reasons not to consider HTTP headers as a source to analyze time behavior of Web data. One reason is that e.g. a 'last-modified'-header doesn't contain information about the changes that took place before the last change, which may therefore possibly not be registered. A second reason is that 'last-modified'-headers hardly contain information about the kind of a document's change. Many changes may not be relevant for a user since the content of a page isn't changed [13]. A third reason is that HTTP headers are frequently not available; 'last-modified'-headers e.g. are only available in 65% of the pages according to [2].

In this article we assume that http-headers are not available. Documents are loaded as a whole and compared to each other. The main problem discussed in this this article is to estimate and to predict change behavior based on an observed history of changes acquired with the above method with a certain precision. The goal is to find an optimal reload policy of remote sources according to quality parameters like amount of lost data, age etc. that will be introduced in detail in section 3.

1.1 Related Research

In the fields of Web search engine design, crawler optimization, Web archives and Web cache optimization diverse statistical methods were presented in order to optimize requests for remote data sources. In [1] an introduction into search engine design and into the problems related to optimal page refresh is given. In [5] aspects of optimal (Web-)robot scheduling are discussed from a theoretical point of view, modeling page change intervals by independent Poisson processes. An empirical analysis of Web page dynamics with respect to statistical properties of intervals between data changes is presented in [2]. One main result is that the distribution of intervals between changes is similar to an exponential distribution. In the article the page download frequency of the remote source is optimized for the case that the reload frequency is the same for a number of sources. In [15] the problem of minimizing the average level of 'staleness' for web pages and the development of an optimal schedule for crawlers is analyzed mainly by assuming independent and identically distributed time intervals. One obvious estimator for an optimal page reload frequency is $\frac{X}{T}$, where X is the number of detected changes in a number successive reloads and T is the total time interval. Assuming a Poisson process for intervals between update times, in [4] an optimization of this estimator with respect to the reduction of the bias is developed. In [3] optimal reload frequencies are found by considering only a small fraction of pages from a web server and thereby estimating the dynamics of the other pages of the same server.

1.2 Contribution

When analyzing the update patterns of specific Web pages we found that an exponential distribution is a very rough approximation of time intervals between updates. Also, the assumption of an independent and identical distribution of consecutive time intervals which is usually applied in statistical approaches, is not true for many Web pages. Many examples exist in the Web where data are updated (approximately) according to a well-defined pattern, e.g. every working day, not at night and not at weekends.

In this article we present an estimation method for similar update patterns. We consider the case where the sequence of time intervals between updates may be approximated by a special kind of a regular grammar we will denote as a *cyclic regular grammar*. Regular grammar inference is a problem well-known from machine learning [8], [9]. Many algorithms were presented to learn regular grammars from positive and negative examples [11], [12]. The cyclic-regular case as defined in section 3 is simpler than the general regular inference problem and may be computed efficiently. We will apply the grammar estimation for the development of a new reload policy in order to optimize local copies of remote sources.

In section 4 we propose an algorithm for cyclic-regular inference. In section 5 we show how this knowledge of regular behavior may be applied to find optimal reload times. The estimation algorithm is illustrated by an example in section 6. In section 7 we present experiments concerning the application of the regular-grammar based reload policy to real Web data and in section 8 a summary is given and further aspects are discussed.

2 Web Change Patterns

In the literature empirical analysis of web page dynamics usually concerns a large amount of pages [2]. In contrast to this in this section we focus on a small set of pages and analyze the change behavior of these specific pages. We believe that this analysis exposes basic dynamic properties of a significant fraction of Web data. For the analysis we downloaded Web pages at a high frequency and compared previous to current data. Figure 1 shows the results for 4 web pages from the field of economics, weather and news. The x-axis denotes the course of time, the y-axis denotes the number of changed lines with respect to current copy and previously loaded copy. A value of '-1' denotes a change in the number of lines.

In page 1 (www.oanda.com) two intervals between updates of different sizes appear alternately. This page provides information related to currency exchange.

Page 2 (http://www.ghcc.msfc.nasa.gov/GOES/goeswestpacus.html) provides satellite data. The pattern reappears every 85300 sec, i.e. every day. Page 3

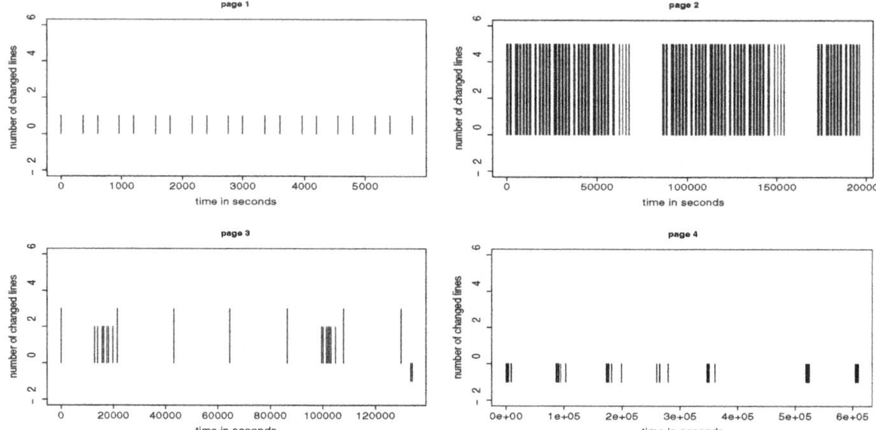

Fig. 1. Change dynamics of different Web pages. Page 1: www.oanda.com; page 2: http://www.ghcc.msfc.nasa.gov/GOES/goeswestpacus.html, page 3: www.meteo.fr, page 4: www.abendblatt.de.

(www.meteo.fr) provides information related to weather forecasts. About every two days a specific change occurs on the page. The change pattern below on the right (www.abendblatt.de) is the home-page of a newspaper. Changes appear every day in the morning except on weekends. Page 4 is not deterministic on a focused scale. However seen from a distance the pattern also appears to be regular. We will denote such patterns as *quasi regular*.

Similar change patterns are our motivation to consider the approximation of Web changes by regular grammars in the following.

3 The Model

Let $u_{p,i} \in \mathbb{R}^+$ denote the points in time at which the ith update of page p occurs, where $0 \leq u_{p,1} \leq u_{p,2} \leq u_{p,3} \leq u_{p,4} \leq \ldots u_{p,n} \leq T \in \mathbb{R}^+, n \in \mathbb{N}$. We omit the page identification p in the following because we consider only one Web page at a time, i.e. $u_i := u_{p,i}$. The interval of time between the $i-1^{st}$ and i^{th} update will be denoted by $t_i := u_i - u_{i-1}, i \in \mathbb{N}$. Let $a_1, a_2, \ldots a_m \in \mathbb{R}^+$ denote the points in time where reload operations are executed, where $0 \leq a_1 \leq a_2 \leq a_3 \ldots \leq a_m \leq T$. For $t \in \mathbb{R}^+$ let $N^u(t)$ denote the largest index of an element in the sequence u that is smaller than t, i.e. $N^u(t) := \max\{n | u_n \leq t\}$. Let $A^u(t) \in \mathbb{R}^+$ denote the size of the time interval since the last update, i.e. $A^u(t) := t - u_{N^u(t)}$. If t is the time of a reload ($t = a_i$ for $i \leq m$), we denote $A^u(t)$ as the *age* of a_i. The age of a local copy denotes how much time since the last remote data update has passed and thus how long an old copy of the data was stored although a new version should have been considered.[1]

[1] If a local copy is used as an information source for users, in the respective period of time these users receive the old instead of the new data.

Let $Q := \{t_j | j \le n \in \mathbb{N}\}$ denote the set of time intervals between updates. We assign a *symbol* $s_i, i \in \mathbb{N}_{\le n}$ to every element of Q. We call the set of symbols $\Delta := \{s_i | i \le n\}$ the *alphabet* of the sequence u.

Let S denote a starting symbol, let $r_1, r_2, \dots r_n$ denote terminals and the symbols $R_1, R_2, \dots R_n$ non-terminals. In the following we refer to a regular grammar Γ corresponding to the non-deterministic finite automaton in figure 2 as a *cyclic regular grammar*. In figure 2, 'R_0' is a starting state which leads to any of n *states* $R_1, \dots, R_n$. After this, the list of symbols is accepted in a cyclic way. Every state is an accepting state. To abbreviate this definition we will use the notation: $(r_1 r_2 ... r_n)^\circ := \Gamma$.

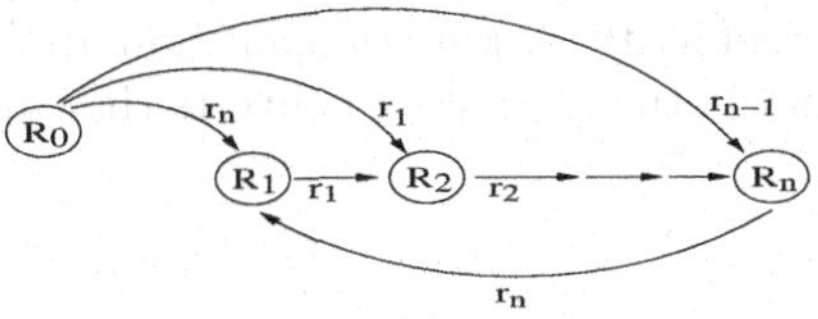

Fig. 2. Nondeterministic automaton corresponding to the grammar $(r_1 r_2 \dots r_n)^\circ$.

The first problem in the following is to describe a sequence of symbols $s_1, s_2 ...$ (corresponding to time intervals) by a cyclic regular grammar of minimal size. The second problem is to predict further states of the automaton and to find optimal query execution times. Finding the optimum means that after each update of the remote data source, the data should be reloaded as soon as possible, i.e. the sum of ages $sumage := \sum_{i=1}^{m} A^u(a_i)$ has to be minimal. The number of reloads should be as small as possible. No change of the data source should be unobserved. One problem is that due to the discussion in the introduction the exact values for the update times are not known and have to be estimated by file comparison. Moreover, it is not possible to track data back in time.

4 Estimation of Time-Regular Update Behavior

4.1 Definitions

The presented algorithm for the estimation of cyclic-regular grammars consists mainly of three components. A first component is responsible for the estimation of time intervals between successive updates. Second, a sequence of symbols has to be determined. A number of intervals correspond to the same symbol. As a motivation for this definition it may be assumed that in many cases in the Web remote update operations are executed by daemon processes after certain time periods. However due to a server and network delay, the time intervals that are actually registered on the client side are slightly different. A symbol represents these intervals providing a maximal and a minimal length estimation for the symbol length. A *symbol* is a 3-tuple $s = (i, max, min)$ consisting of a unique identifier i and two length parameters $s.max$ and $s.min$. A third component of the algorithm is responsible for the estimation of a grammar that represents the update behavior of a remote source. A *hypothesis* $H = (\Gamma, s)$ is a 2-tuple consisting of a cyclic-regular grammar Γ and the current state s of the associated finite automaton, according to the enumeration of states in figure 2. In every step of the algorithm after the detection of a symbol, the *default hypothesis* is added to the set of hypotheses. Taking the sequence of symbols registered by the system so far $(r_{i_1}, r_{i_2}, \ldots r_{i_p})$, the *default-hypothesis* is the cyclic regular grammar $(r_{i_1} r_{i_2} \ldots r_{i_p})^{\circ}$ with the corresponding automaton being in the state '1' according the enumeration of states in figure 2. This automaton accepts the sequence of input symbols. The last symbol is accepted by a transition from the last state to the first state. A *prediction* of a hypothesis which is not in the start state (R_0) is the symbol, generated by a transition to the (unique) state following the current state. A *proceed* operation applied to a hypothesis H ($H.proceed$) which is not in the start state converts the current state of H into the subsequent state.

4.2 The Algorithm

Step 1: Interval Estimation. Figure 3 shows the basic idea of the interval estimation. The data source is reloaded after constant time periods $a_i - a_{i-1}$ denoted as *sampling interval* (*sampsize*) in the following. By detecting two remote changes (update 2 and 3 in figure 3) in subsequent reload intervals (interval [3,4] and [7,8]) we acquire a maximal and a minimal estimation for the interval length (min and max in figure 3). The mean value of $|max - min|$ depends on the reload frequency and should be minimized. An obvious problem is that remote changes taking place between two successive reload operations may not be recognized. A second difficulty is to find an adequate reload frequency. We will not discuss this question here but in order to develop an automatic approach, solutions in [4] might be applied.

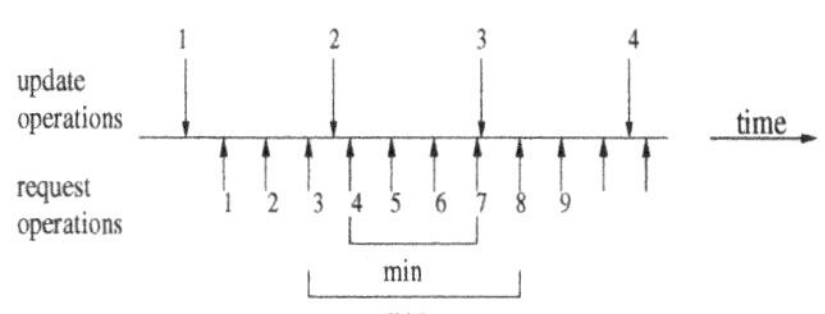

Fig. 3. Determination of a maximal and a minimal estimate for an interval length.

Step 2: symbol estimation. The previous algorithm provides us with a sequence of interval estimations some of which are similar. The problem is to find an adequate similarity measure for intervals and to apply it to the interval sequence in order to find a sequence of symbols. Figure 4 shows the algorithm component *Symbol-Assignment*, responsible for the learning of new symbols or the assigning of a new interval to a previously registered symbol. It depends on the estimation parameters of a new interval (*max* and *min*), the sampling-interval length *sampsize* and a list of previously registered symbols (*symbols*). In step 1 and 2 for each symbol in the set of symbols it is tested whether the new parameters are 'significantly different' with respect to the sampling size. If this is not true for one symbol, i.e. if the current symbol has already been detected, the respective symbol is appended to the list of symbols and returned. If the new interval-parameters are significantly different from all symbols defined so far, a

```
Symbol-Assignment( max, min, sampsize, symbols)

1    for each symbol s in symbols:
2      if |max - s.max| ≤ sampsize
        and |min - s.min| ≤sampsize
3        add s to symbols
4    define new symbol sn
     set sn.max = max
     set sn.min = min
     add sn to symbols
```

Fig. 4. Algorithm component for insertion of new symbols or assignment of new intervals to previously registered symbols. max and min are the parameters of a new interval.

```
Grammar-Estimation( symbols)

1    set hset = ∅
2    for i=1 to symbols.length()
3      symbol s := symbols.get(i)
4      add the default-hypothesis to hset
5      for each H ∈ hset do
6        if symbol not equal to prediction of H
7          delete H from hset
8        else
9          apply H.proceed
```

Fig. 5. Main algorithm component for the estimation of a cyclic regular grammar.

new symbol is inserted into the set *symbols* in step 4. The algorithm is executed for each new detected interval.

Step 3: grammar estimation. Based on the list of symbols detected so far it is now possible to develop hypotheses for the time-based grammar that generated the current symbol sequence. Figure 5 shows the algorithm which takes the sequence of symbols as the input. For every position in the sequence, the whole sequence of symbols observed prior to this position is used to create the *default-hypothesis* (as defined in section 4.1) in step 4 of the algorithm in figure 5. In steps 5 and 6 it is tested for each hypothesis H in the set of hypotheses if the prediction of H corresponds to the newly observed symbol. If not, the hypothesis is deleted from the set of hypotheses (step 7). If the prediction is consistent with the observation, the state of the hypothesis is increased in step 9 (an example is provided in section 6).

4.3 Limitations

In order to apply this algorithm, in the interval estimation step the variable *sampsize*, i.e. size of the time interval between requests $a_j - a_{j-1}$, has to be sufficiently small compared to the time between updates ($sampsize \ll \min_i t_i$). Moreover, in the symbol estimation step, the sampling size has to be smaller than the size difference between update intervals ($|t_i - t_j| > 2 \star sampsize$).

5 An Algorithm for Optimal Data Update

In this section we presume that the alphabet and the grammar have already been determined and we present an algorithm to find optimal reload times (figure 6). We assume that the current state of the automaton is already known. This 'phase' of the automaton may simply be determined by observing remote changes with a high reload frequency until the symbol sequence observed so far uniquely describes the current state of the automaton (step 1, figure 6). In steps 2 to 11 a loop is executed that determines at first the unique subsequent symbol according to the automaton H in step 3. According to this symbol an optimal reload time is computed in step 4. The system waits for the respective period of time in step 5, and reloads the remote data. High frequency reload is applied in steps 7 to 10 until a change with respect to the current and the previous version of the reloaded data is detected.

Reload-Control (Input: estimated grammar $\sim H$, sampsize)

```
1     find current state of automaton
2     do
3       find next symbol according to automaton H
4       compute optimal reload time t
5       wait until t
6       reload
7       do
8         t := t + sampsize
9         wait until t, reload
10      until change detected
11    until end of observation
```

Fig. 6. Algorithm to determine optimal reload times based on the grammar estimation in section 4.

After this change detection (step 11), the algorithm continues with the prediction of the subsequent symbol, as provided by the estimated automaton. An example for this reload policy is illustrated in a subsequent section in figure 9.

6 Example

In order to illustrate the *Grammar-Estimation* algorithm we assume that the system registers remote updates as depicted in figure 7. Impulses of length 0.7 denote reload requests, impulses of length 1 denote registered changes by the interval estimation component in the remote data source. According to figure 7, the sequence of detected symbols is *ababcab*, if the respective symbols are denoted as *a*, *b* and *c*.

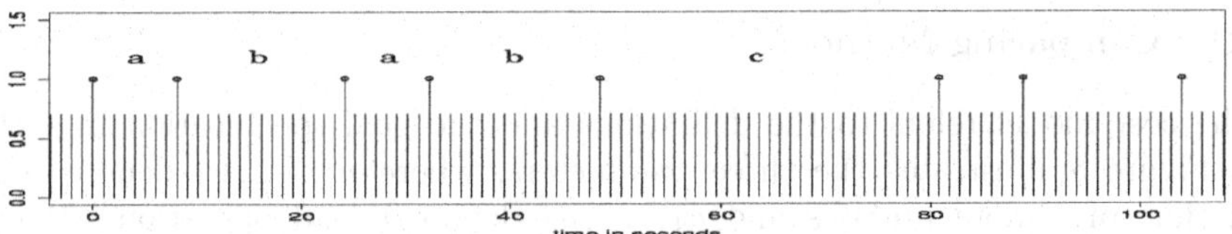

Fig. 7. Update times as registered by the *Grammar-Estimation*-algorithm with assigned symbols a,b and c.

After detecting the symbol a, the default hypothesis $H1 := (a)^\circ$ is inserted into the empty set *hset* (table 1) in step 4 of the *Grammar-Estimation* component. This hypothesis is in state 1 (figure 2). In step 2 in table 1 the second detected symbol is b which is different to the prediction of $H1$ ($H1.prectict = a$). Therefore $H1$ is deleted from *hset*. Again, the default hypothesis $H2 := (ab)^\circ$ is added to *hset*. In step 3 the symbol a is detected. In this case the prediction of $H2$ is true. Therefore the state of $H2$ is increased. The default hypothesis $H3 := (aba)^\circ$ is added to hset. This procedure continues until in step 5 the symbol c is detected. In this step $H2$ and $H4$ have to be rejected and the default hypothesis $H5 := (ababc)^\circ$ is added. After consideration of subsequent symbols this hypothesis turns out to be consistent with the sequence *ababcab* and it also turns out to be the smallest one.

Table 1. Computation steps of the *Grammar-Estimation*-algorithm for the sequence *ababc*....

step	input symbol	reject hypothesis	insert hypothesis	hypotheses/state
1	a		H1:=$(a)^\circ$	H1/state=1
2	b	H1	H2:=$(ab)^\circ$	H2/state=1
3	a		H3:=$(aba)^\circ$	H2/state=2 H3/state=1
4	b	H3	H4:=$(abab)^\circ$	H2/state=1 H4/state=1
5	c	H2,H4	H5:=$(ababc)^\circ$	H5/state=1
⋮				

7 Experiments

In this section we compare the regular-approximation policy, in the following denoted as the *regular* method, to the policy based on a constant reload frequency, denoted as the *constant* method. The latter is currently applied e.g. by Web crawlers. The issue in the literature is usually to find optimal sampling frequencies for specific Web data. Optimization refers to a specific definition of costs, which have to be minimized. In the following, first we give a precise definition of our cost model. Then we apply the cost model to dynamic Web data.

7.1 Comparing Methods

The cost model refers to the definitions and the goal specification in section 3. Figure 8 illustrates the three parameters, where $u_1, \ldots, u_4$ denote points in time of remote updates and $a_1, \ldots, a_4$ denote reload operations. Remote update u_3 is not captured, the respective information is lost. The amount of such lost data objects will be denoted as ♯loss. a_2 is a superfluous reload operation. The number of superfluous reloads is denoted as ♯superfluous. The sum of differences $a_1 - u_1$, $a_3 - u_2$ etc. is denoted as *sumage* (section 3). The different quality parameters may easily be computed from the sequence of reload operations, which is known and the sequence of remote updates, which is either known or has to be estimated by high-frequency sampling. In the latter case the quality measure is only an approximation; e.g. the ♯loss value may only be regarded as a minimal value. Figure 9 shows the application of a reload policy based on constant intervals (above) and based on the regular method (below). In the experiments we fix the number of downloads of the constant-frequency method such that it is equal to the number of downloads of the regular method.[2]

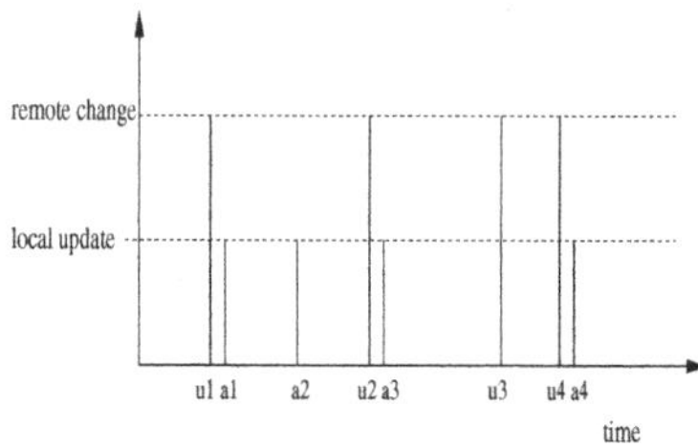

Fig. 8. The figure illustrates different quality aspects of a reload sequence of remote sources like superfluous reloads (a_2) and lost updates (u_3).

7.2 Application to Web Data

Figure 9 basically shows the experiment that was pursued for different Web data. A fix time interval of 5 days is defined. In this time interval the two reload policies are executed and the original update times are determined by fast sampling in order to compute the quality measure. The number of downloads is equal for both systems.

[2] The results in [4] suggest that a specific sampling interval should be chosen for the constant-frequency method in order to minimize ♯*loss*. However other quality

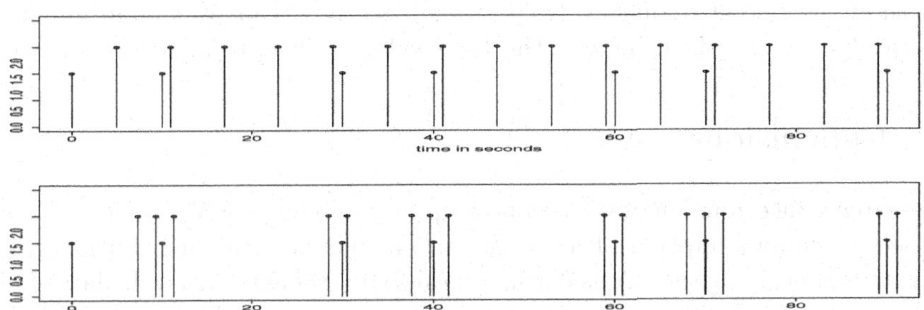

Fig. 9. Constant-frequency sampling policy (above) and regular sampling policy (below). Impulses of length 1 denote times of remote updates. Impulses of length 1.5 denote reload operations.

Table 2. Comparison of reload policies for different Web pages. Page 1 (http://www.oanda.com) provides financial data. Page 2 (http://www.sec.noaa.gov/rt_plots/xray_5m.html) provides data related to space weather. The reduction of *agesum* with regular-approximation based reload ranges from 50% to 90%.

	page	loss	superfluous	sumage (seconds)
constant method	1	0	3512	24143
regular method	1	0	3456	12960
constant method	2	0	1003	50331
regular method	2	0	992	6233

Table 2 shows the result of a comparison of the two reload policies for different Web pages. Page 1 has the URL http://www.oanda.com. It provides information related to currency exchange. Page 2 (http://www.sec.noaa.gov/rt_plots/xray_5m.html) provides data related to x-radiation from the sun. The results in table 2 show that values for lost data and superfluous data are very similar if as in this example the number of downloads is identical. The age of data (*sumage*) may be reduced from 50% up to about 80% for different pages. This significant reduction of the age of data using the regular method was expected, since due to the grammar estimation, the system roughly knows when the next update will occur.

However the regular approximation strategy has also an advantage concerning the amount of lost data. If the variance of intervals between updates is very large, this doesn't change the number of required downloads if the regular method is applied. The constant method has to consider a reload interval smaller than the smallest update interval in order to capture all updates. Since in this

---

parameters are not considered and a comparison of the methods would be difficult using this strategy.

method the reload frequency is constant, this may lead to a large number of (superfluous) reloads; otherwise the $\sharp loss$ value is likely to increase.

8 Conclusion

Research concerning the estimation of update behavior of Web data is usually based on the assumption of an identical and independent distribution of consecutive time intervals. Considering the update behavior of Web data it may however be observed that this assumption is a rough model for many Web data. Many update patterns may be approximated by a reappearing cycle of time intervals. We present an algorithm to estimate the parameters of such update behavior. The algorithm takes into account that the points in time where data sources in the Web change may usually not be registered exactly. The estimated grammar is used to determine optimal points in time for data reloads with respect to a minimization of the age of data and the amount of lost data. In the experiments it is shown that the age of data may be reduced significantly using the regular-approximation reload policy compared to a constant-frequency based method. The presented algorithm is suitable for a personal information system, where a user provides initial parameters for specific data objects. Application for crawlers considering millions of pages requires the parameters like estimation time, initial sampling rate etc. to be estimated automatically. In order to apply this method to a larger fraction of Web data, the method has to consider further statistical properties of Web data and regular and statistical properties have to be combined. In the learning phase, some update values may be missing. The algorithm should nevertheless be able to find an optimal grammar in the case of distorted input data.

References

1. A.Arasu, J.Cho, H.Garcia-Molina, A.Paepcke, and S.Raghavan. Searching the web. *ACM Trans. Inter. Tech.*, 1(1):2–43, 2001.
2. Brian E. Brewington and George Cybenko. How dynamic is the Web? *Computer Networks (Amsterdam, Netherlands: 1999)*, 33(1–6):257–276, 2000.
3. Junghoo Cho and A.Ntoulas. Effective change detection using sampling. In *proceedings of the 28th VLDB Conference, Hong Kong, China*, 2002.
4. Junghoo Cho and Hector Garcia-Molina. Estimating frequency of change. *ACM Trans. Inter. Tech.*, 3(3):256–290, 2003.
5. E. Coffman, Z.Liu, and R.R.Weber. Optimal robot scheduling for web search engines. *Journal of Scheduling*, 1(1):15–29, June 1998.
6. World Wide Web Consortium. W3c httpd. http://www.w3.org/Protocols/.
7. A. Dingle and T.Partl. Web cache coherence. *Computer Networks and ISDN Systems*, 28(7-11):907–920, May 1996.
8. P. Dupont, L. Miclet, and E. Vidal. What is the search space of the regular inference? In R. C. Carrasco and J. Oncina, editors, *Proceedings of the Second International Colloquium on Grammatical Inference (ICGI-94): Grammatical Inference and Applications*, volume 862, pages 25–37, Berlin, 1994. Springer.

9. E. Gold. Language identification in the limit. *Information and Control*, 10:447–474, 1967.
10. C. Olston and J.Widom. Best-effort cache synchronization with source cooperation. In *Proceedings of SIGMOD*, pages 73–84, May 2002.
11. J. Oncina and P.Garcia. Inferring regular languages in polynomial update time. *Pattern Recognition and Image Analysis, Perez, Sanfeliu, Vidal (eds.), World Scientific*, pages 49–61, 1992.
12. Rajesh Parekh and Vasant Honavar. Learning dfa from simple examples. *Machine Learning*, 44(1/2):9–35, 2001.
13. Sean C. Rhea, K.Liang, and E.Brewer. Value-based web caching. In *WWW 2003*, pages 619–628, 2003.
14. D. Wessels. Intelligent caching for world-wide web objects. In *Proceedings of INET-95, Honolulu, Hawaii, USA*, 1995.
15. J. L. Wolf, M. S. Squillante, P. S. Yu, J. Sethuraman, and L. Ozsen. Optimal crawling strategies for web search engines. In *Proceedings of the eleventh international conference on World Wide Web*, pages 136–147. ACM Press, 2002.

Deep Crawling in the Semantic Web: In Search of Deep Knowledge

Ismael Navas-Delgado, Maria del Mar Roldan-Garcia, and Jose F. Aldana-Montes

University of Malaga, Computer Languages and Computing Science Department, Malaga 29071, Spain,
{ismael, mmar, jfam}@lcc.uma.es,
http://khaos.uma.es

Abstract. In this paper we present Deep (Semantic) Crawling, an enhanced crawling methodology. Deep crawling allows for the analysis of semantic mark-ups in both static and dynamic pages. This unique capability offers us both a much bigger crawling space (the Deep Web) together with new applications. The paper ends with an use case to highlight the features of Deep Crawling.

1 Introduction

The main challenge of the Semantic Web is to make web content not only machine-readable but also machine understandable. To achieve this goal, the Semantic Web relies on the use of ontologies to annotate web pages, formulate queries and derive answers. Much more work must still be done; in particular, tools are needed to deal with a) information retrieval, b) information extraction, c) information visualization, and d) semantic annotation of web content.

Many researchers are building tools to introduce semantic content into HTML pages [1,2], which will allow performing intelligent searches instead of just matching basic keywords. Based on particular ontologies, the documents are edited and modified with additional tags, which are embedded in HTML pages according to the ontologies. However, most of these annotation tools only focus on (semi-) automatic annotation of static web pages and not on dynamic ones.

We previously proposed [3] a methodology to annotate static and dynamic web documents, offering two main contributions: on the one hand, the automatic generation of a function that dynamically calculates annotations for a web document (both static and dynamic ones); on the other hand, a novel approach for annotating dynamic web documents by annotating the queries enveloped in each document and their results (making use of an ontology, O_Q, which allows us to describe the structure of dynamic web documents). However, annotation of web sites is not sufficient to improve web searching and querying. It is also necessary to find these documents and efficiently store links or indexes to them and their annotations. Thus, crawlers must be developed to reach static and dynamic documents, and Semantic Web applications must be able to retrieve and store annotations embedded in both types of web documents.

X. Zhou et al. (Eds.): WISE 2004, LNCS 3306, pp. 541–546, 2004.
© Springer-Verlag Berlin Heidelberg 2004

We propose a crawler (Deep Semantic Crawler) that not only makes use of traditional crawling techniques for static and dynamic documents, but also takes advantage of semantic annotations of dynamic documents defined in [3]. Thus, our tool could reach more documents than traditional crawlers if web sites use instances of O_Q to annotate dynamic documents. Besides, better results would be obtained if web developers make public their databases and knowledge bases, because our crawlers could extract important information to query dynamic documents.

In this paper we describe how crawling can be improved making use of semantic annotations (Section 2). Section 3 shows an usage example over our web site. Finally, Section 4 presents some conclusions and future work.

2 Deep Semantic Crawling

Generally, semantic web-crawlers comprise two processes: one of them wanders around the web in search of mark-up pages following all the links found; the other one indexes downloaded pages and stores annotations in a repository (a Knowledge-base - KB - in our case). This process could arise annotations from several ontologies, so the KB stores the ontologies and the annotations that are stored as instances of the related ontology. As our crawling process should not only wander to static pages, but also reach the dynamic pages, it must take into account two different types of links:

1. Links to dynamic documents, with all their parameters instantiated. We can use the values of this parameters later in the crawling process.
2. Links to dynamic documents with some non-instantiated parameters (like a web form). In this case a traditional crawler does not know which values to use in each field of the form to generate the dynamic document. At best, it could analyze this form and could deduce which fields to use, but it does not know their types or correct values.

Thus, we have divided the crawling process into three classes, depending on the type of information that we can find in a web document (see Figure 1). These classes inherit from the Analyser class that contains a crawling method, which receives a URL and returns a vector of URLs that are links found in the web document. Each of these classes contains a different implementation of this method, depending on the type of information that the web site contains:

- First, a web document can contain HTML code with links to other documents. So, StaticCrawler implementation searches links in the document. That is, it tries to find the *a* tags (¡a .... /a¿) in the document, and reach the *href* field.
- Second, a web document could have web forms, and the target of the form is a dynamic document (JSP, ASP, PHP, etc.). DynamicCrawler must implement the crawling method using traditional techniques for analysing dynamic documents and obtain a set of links to dynamic documents with instantiated

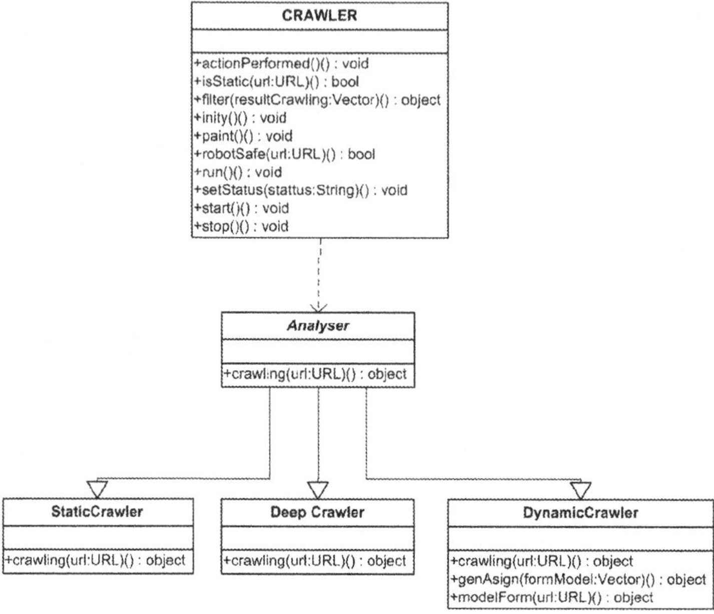

Fig. 1. Crawling Tool Classes

parameters. In a first approach we have decided to use a Label Value Set (LVS) table [4]. Each entry (or row) in the LVS table is of the form (L;V), where L is a label and V = $\{v_1, v_2, \ldots v_n\}$ is a set of values belonging to that label.

– Third, DeepCrawler implements the crawling method taking advantage of our approach to annotate dynamic documents [3]. That is, DeepCrawler searches an instance of O_Q associated with the dynamic document that is called from a web form. It is possible in this instance to find data types, allowed values and mappings with a database and/or a knowledge-base. If there are mappings with databases or knowledge bases, the crawler could find values in order to make use of the web form. However, this is not possible if databases or knowledge-bases are not public. Thus the success of this method depends on the quality of data types and allowed values. Results would be better if databases and/or knowledge-bases are made public.

We have designed a class (Crawler) that makes use of crawling classes. This class receives a start web document, and puts this document in a list of non-visited documents. Then it begins a loop that consists of several steps:

1. To extract a document (D) from a non-visited document list.
2. To add D to the visited document list.
3. To search annotations in D, and add them to a knowledge-base.
4. To index D.

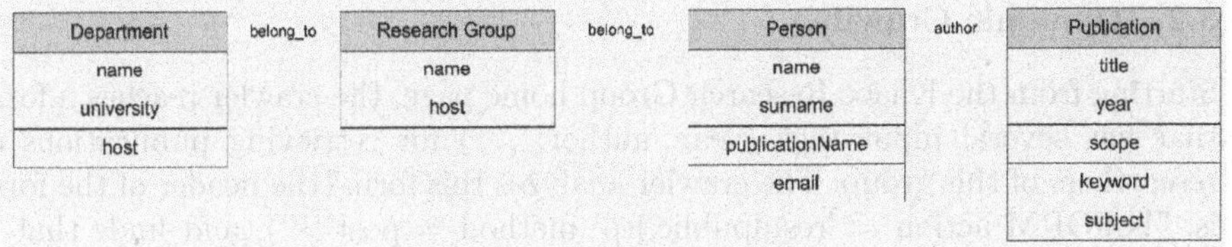

Fig. 2. Domain Ontology

(http://khaos.uma.es/khaos/eng/pgpersonal.jsp?name='Aldana',
http://khaos.uma.es/khaos/eng/pgpersonal.jsp?name='Navas',
http://khaos.uma.es/khaos/eng/pgpersonal.jsp?name='Roldan', ...)

Fig. 3. Part of the links vector

5. To search links:
   a) Using StaticCrawler
   b) Using DynamicCrawler
   c) Using DeepCrawler
6. To add links to the non-visited document list if they are not in one one of the two lists.

3 An Example of Crawling Use

In order to show how the crawler works, we present an example of each crawling process, namely Static, Dynamic and Deep crawler (Figure 1). For the example, we will use the website of the research group Khaos at the University of Málaga (http://khaos.uma.es). This website contains a set of personal web pages about people working for the research group and about their publications. As we said before, our crawler takes advantage of our annotation process. The pages are annotated according to an ontology (Figure 2). On the one hand, we have annotated static pages. On the other hand, we have some pages dynamically generated and annotated. We will describe how the crawler works in both cases.

3.1 Static Crawling

The home page is a static web document. If our crawler starts from this page, and follows several links (about us -> people), it will finally find a page that returns a list of links to personal web pages of people who belong to the Khaos research group. The crawling method of the StaticCrawler class returns a vector object containing these links, as well as all links found (see figure 3)

These links are completely instantiated, so the crawler can add them directly to its unvisited links. On the other hand, these pages are annotated pages; therefore the crawler will compile annotations and will store them in a knowledge-base.

3.2 Dynamic Crawling

Starting from the Khaos Research Group home page, the crawler reaches a form that has several input tags (year, author, ...) for retrieving publications of researchers of this group. The crawler analyzes this form (the header of the form is: "!<FORM action = 'resulpublic.jsp' method = post'>"), and finds that it performs a call to the procedure "resulpublic. jsp". However, DynamicCrawler does not know the parameter types, whether they are mandatory, the allowed values, etc. Therefore, it tries to find some possible values for these parameters. For this purpose, the crawler analyzes two sources (1) the default values for the parameters, that is, those that the pop-up menus show, and (2) the LVS table (see Section 2). In our example, we have default values for authors. After inserting these values to the LVS table it looks like Table 1. Using these values, the crawler tries to generate as many documents as possible, adding the links to the non-visited links vector and compiling annotations like in the previous case. A new value for the vector will be, among others, "http://khaos.uma.es-/khaos/eng/resulpublic.jsp?author='Aldana Montes, Jose F.".

Table 1. Partial view of LVS table

Parameter	Value
Author	(Aldana Montes, Jose F., Roldan Garcia, Maria del Mar, ...)
Year	(2003, 2004, ...)
...	...

3.3 Deep Crawling

Finally, the URL form (http://khaos.uma.es/khaos/eng/resulpublic.jsp) is sent to DeepCrawler, which searches an instance of O_Q (Section 2). This instance exists and contains the mappings between each parameter and a database column or a knowledge-base attribute. Using these mappings the crawler can query the database or knowledge-base in search of new values to use in the web form. The found values are added to the LVS table, and the crawler continues working as in the dynamic case. Note that we need query privileges on the data/knowledge-base for DeepCrawling.

4 Conclusions

In this paper we present a crawling process that introduces a novel approach: Deep Crawling. It takes advantage of an approach for dynamic document annotation that makes use of an ontology (O_Q) to annotate dynamic documents. This ontology describes the structure of dynamic web documents, describing parameters involved in the query that is used to generate the document. It also describes the mappings between these parameters and the attributes of a data/knowledge-base. These mappings enable the development of crawling systems that use databases and knowledge-bases (if they are available) to find parameter values. Therefore, dynamic documents can be generated and the annotations of these documents can be compiled. Some documents cannot be generated without the ontology and the mappings, because we do not know the values for the form parameters. Therefore, annotations can not be compiled.

This approach reaches more documents than traditional crawlers if websites use instances of the O_Q ontology to annotate dynamic documents, and if the data/knowledge-base is accessible. In the current web, where a lot of efforts are being applied to annotating (static and dynamic) web documents, it is very important to retrieve this knowledge. It is possible to assume that website owners are not going to make their databases public. However, in the Semantic Web explosion, in which a lot of knowledge is being stored in knowledge-bases, it is realistic to believe that they will be published.

Thus, in the most cases the knowledge of web document annotations from the most common type of web documents (dynamic ones) will not be retrieved with traditional techniques that make use of heuristics. However, the combination of our technique to annotate web documents with the deep crawling defined in this paper will allow for access to both dynamic information and knowledge stored in databases, thus enlarging the search space to the deep web and allowing for new kinds of applications.

Acknowledgements. This work has been supported by the MCyT grant TIC2002-04586-C04-04

References

1. Handschuh, S., Staab, A: Authoring and Annotation of Web Pages in CREAM. In Proceedings of the WWW2002 – Eleventh International World Wide Web Conference, Hawaii, USA, May 2002.
2. Kalyanpur, A., Hendler, J., Parsia, B., Golbeck, J.: SMORE- Semantic Markup, Ontology, and RDF Editor. Available at http://www.mindswap.org/papers/SMORE.pdf
3. Navas-Delgado, I., Moreno-Vergara, N., Gómez-Lora, A.C., Roldán-García, M.M., Ruiz-Mostazo, I., Aldana-Montes, J.F.: Embedding Semantic Annotations into Dynamic Web Contents. In Proceedings of Webs'04, August, Zaragoza, Spain. IEEE Computer Society, pp. 221–235.
4. Raghavan, S., Garcia-Molina, H.: Crawling the Hidden Web. In Proceedings of the 27th International Conference on Very Large Data Bases, 2001, pp. 129–138.

Designing Localized Web Sites

Olga De Troyer and Sven Casteleyn

WISE
Department of Computer Science, Vrije Universiteit Brussel, Pleinlaan 2,
1050 Brussel, Belgium
{Olga.DeTroyer, Sven.Casteleyn}@vub.ac.be, http://wise.vub.ac.be

Abstract. The term World Wide Web (WWW) emphasizes that the Web is global and many companies realize that this creates new opportunities. A considerable amount of literature on web site development stresses that, in order to attract and retain more customers, it is vital to create different versions of a web site and adapt those versions to the local communities they target. This process is usually called *globalization* and the different web site versions are called *localized* web sites. Although content management systems (CMS) for web sites provide support for multinational web sites, current web site design methodologies do not consider the issue of globalization. In general, the globalization effort is done after the web site is designed and implemented. This makes globalization much harder. In this paper, we show how to extend an existing web site design method, WSDM, to support the design of localized web sites.

1 Introduction

WWW pages are accessible from all over the world. This offers opportunities for companies and organizations to attract visitors from across the country borders and to do business with them. Two different approaches are possible to address this issue: develop one single web site to serve everyone or develop 'localized' web sites for particular localities. The 'one size fits all' approach may be appropriate for particular communities (like researchers) but in general it will be less successful. A considerable amount of literature on web site development stresses that, in order to attract and retain more customers, it is vital to localize a global web site, i.e. to create different web site versions and adapt those versions to the local communities they target. Members of a community do not only share a common language, but also common cultural conventions. Since measurement units, keyboard configurations, default paper sizes, character sets and notational standards for writing time, dates, addresses, numbers, currency, etc differ from one culture to another, it is self-evident that local web sites should address these issues. Some jokes, symbols, icons, graphics or even colors may be completely acceptable in one country, but trigger negative reactions in another country. Sometimes the style or tone of the site's text might even be considered offensive by a particular cultural entity, as a result of which the text needs to be rewritten rather than merely translated. Next to culturally differences, it may also be necessary to adapt the content to regional differences, like differences in the services and products offered, differences in price, and differences in regulations.

X. Zhou et al. (Eds.): WISE 2004, LNCS 3306, pp. 547–558, 2004.
© Springer-Verlag Berlin Heidelberg 2004

The localization issue is not new. Localization of software has been done for years and research has been performed in this context. Nielsen and Del Galdo [5] stress that localization should encompass more than a 'surface-level' adaptation, by acknowledging underlying cultural differences. The role of culture in user interface has also been addressed by Evers and Day [11]. Barber and Badre [1] detected the existence of cultural markers, i.e. web design elements that are prevalent in web sites of a particular culture (e.g. color, icons, symbols). Sheppard and Scholtz [21] and Sun [23] conducted pilot studies to determine if the absence or presence of cultural markers affects the user's preference or performance. Cultural differences have also been investigated from an anthropological perspective, looking at the intangible nuances of a culture's social hierarchy, individualism, gender roles, attitude towards uncertainty and time-orientation ([18], [10]). This type of research is commonly approached through Hofstede's cross-cultural theory [15]. According to Hofstede, cultural differences are based in deeply rooted values that can be categorized along five fundamental dimensions: power distance, collectivism-individualism, masculinity-femininity, uncertainty avoidance, and long and short-term orientation. His research is based on a large-scale survey carried out between 1967 and 1973 and which covered 53 countries representing the major regions of the world. Marcus and Gould [18] attempt to apply those dimensions to global web interface design, providing suggestions and guidelines to produce successfully localized web sites.

In the context of localization, three different terms are used: *globalization*, *internationalization* and the term *localization* itself. According to LISA (Localization Industry Standards Association) [17] localization of a thing is adapting it to the needs of a given locale. Globalization is about spreading a thing to several different countries, and making it applicable and useable in those countries. Globalization is never all encompassing; you will never cover all the 600 languages on the planet today. In the context of web sites, globalization usually indicates the process of converting a web site to different languages and communities. Internationalization consists of all preparatory tasks that will facilitate subsequent localization. The purpose of internationalization is to make localization easier, faster, of higher quality and more cost-effective. It may include: creating illustrations in which the text can easily be changed; allowing space for translation into languages that require more space; abstracting content from markup; identification and isolation of culturally specific items. Localization adds cultural context to a previously internationalized web site and includes translation. Translation is only one of the tasks of localization but because it is the most cost expensive, time consuming and most vital task it is often used in the same context as globalization, internationalization and localization.

As for classical software, web site globalization is often done once the web site is completely developed and available for a particular community. Content Management Systems (CMS) for web sites usually provide support for multinational web production [4]. However such systems don't provide a methodology for designing the web site. Nowadays, it is recognized that a proper method should be used to design professional web sites. Although, several methods to design web sites (e.g. OOHDM [22], WebML[3], OO-H [13], UWE [16], WSDM[6]) exist, as far as we are aware of, none of these methods takes globalization issues or one of its aspects (localization, internationalization or translation) into account during the design process. We believe that the globalization process could benefit from taking localization requirements into consideration while designing the web site. If web sites are designed with the need for localization in mind, it may be easier to actually realize globalization because the internationalization activities may already be considered and prepared for during the design process. For this reason, we have extended our own web site design method WSDM in order to support web localization. In this paper, we explain how this has been done. The paper is structured as follows. Section 2 provides a brief overview of WSDM. In section 3, we explain the extensions to WSDM and illustrate them with an example. Section 4 discusses the proposed solution and presents conclusions.

2 WSDM

The design process of WSDM follows an audience driven design philosophy i.e. the design is based on and driven by the requirements of the different types of users. Figure 1 gives an overview of the different phases of the method.

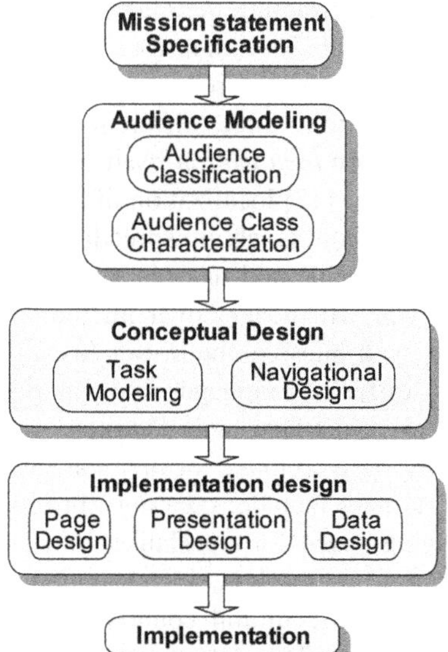

Fig. 1. Overview of WSDM

The method starts with the 'Mission Statement Specification'. The mission statement should identify the purpose, the subject and the target audience(s) of the web site. Next, the 'Audience Modeling' phase is performed. In the sub phase 'Audience Classification', the different types of users are identified and classified into so called *audience classes*. During the sub phase 'Audience Class Characterization' the different audience classes are characterized regarding age, experience level, language, etc. The next phase, the 'Conceptual Design', is composed of '*Task Modeling*' and '*Navigational Design*'. During 'Task Modeling', the requirements identified during Audience Classification are elaborated and *task models* and *object chunks* are created to model the necessary information and functionality needed to fulfill the requirements. The 'Navigational Design' is used to design the overall conceptual structure of the web site and the navigational possibilities for each audience class. The fourth phase, the '*Implementation Design*' contains three sub phases. The '*Page Design*' translates the conceptual and navigational design to an actual page structure. The look & feel of the website is defined in the '*Presentation Design*'. The '*Data Design*' is only needed for data-intensive web sites. In case the data will be maintained in a database, the database schema is constructed. It is also possible that the data will not originate from a database but provided by means of another source (e.g. XML). For pure static web pages, the data design step can be omitted; the actual data will be supplied by the designer during the last step of the method, the actual implementation of the website.

3 Designing Localized Web Sites with WSDM

We will explain how WSDM is extended to allow modeling localized web sites by indicating how each of the different (sub) phases is adapted and illustrate this with an example. For the example, suppose a company wants a web site to offer their products for sale in the US and Belgium. In addition, the product managers of the company should be able to maintain the product information through the web site.

First, we introduce a new concept: *locality*. A locality describes a particular place, situation, or location. Localities are identified by means of a name and a label. Examples of localities are: the US, Japan, and the Flemish community in Belgium.

3.1 Mission Statement Specification

The mission statement is the starting point of the design. The mission statement should identify the purpose, the subject and the target audience(s) of the web site. If we want to be able to take localization into account during the design process, the mission statement should also mention the different localities for which the web site needs to be developed.

For the example web site, we can formulate the following mission statement:

"The web site should allow to increase the sales of the company in the company's country (Belgium) as well as in the US, by allowing people to search for information about the products and to buy the products online. In addition, the web site should act as an easy user interface for the product managers (located in Flanders) to maintain the product information and to keep track of the supply"

From this statement, we can identify:

- The purpose: increase the sales and provide support for maintaining the product information and the supply
- The subject: products of the company
- The target audiences: potential buyers, and the company's product managers

- The target localities: US, Flanders and Wallonia (Flanders and Wallonia are the two main regions in Belgium each with a different language).

3.2 Audience Modeling

The target audiences identified in the mission statement should be refined into audience classes. Therefore, for each target type of user, the different functional- and informational requirements are identified. Users with the same information and functional requirements become members of the same audience class. Users with additional requirements form audience subclasses. In this way a hierarchy of audience classes can be constructed. The class *Visitor* is always the top of the audience class hierarchy, grouping the requirements all visitors have in common. During 'Audience Class Characterization' the different audience classes are characterized regarding age, experience level, language, etc.

In our extension of WSDM, we make a distinction between requirements that are typical for the audience class and requirements that are typical for a locality. Requirements that are typical for a locality will be specified separately from those typical for an audience class. Therefore, an additional sub phase called *'Locality Specification'* has been introduced. The requirements specified in the Audience Classification should be independent of the localities'. In a similar way a sub phase, called *'Locality Characterization',* is added to allow specifying the characteristics of the localities. The characteristics given for the different audience classes should be independent of the specific characteristics of the different localities. The order in which the sub phases 'Audience Classification' - 'Audience Class Characterization' and 'Locality Specification' - 'Locality Characterization' is performed is not important because the information they allow to specify is independent.

To express the relationship between the audience classes and the localities another new sub phase is introduced, the *'Locality Mapping'*. This sub phase can only be performed after finishing the four other sub phases. See figure 2 for an overview of the different sub phases of the extended Audience Modeling phase. We now describe the new sub phases into more detail and illustrate them with the example web site.

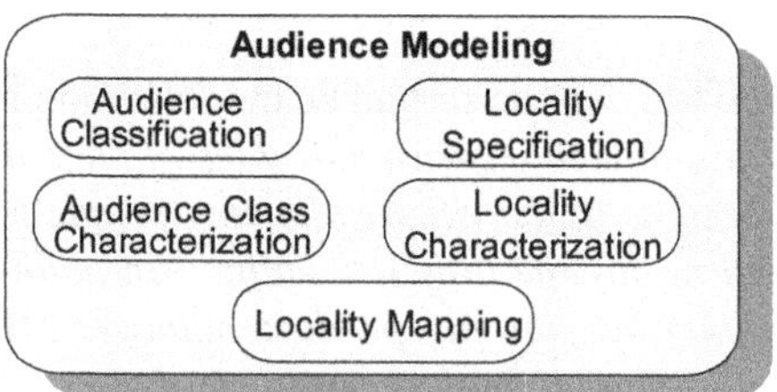

Fig. 2. Audience Modeling

Locality Specification and Characterization

The requirements and characteristics that are typical for a locality are related to the language, culture, habits or regulations of the locality. Some examples of locality requirements are: an address should always include the state; for each price it should be indicated if tax is included or not, and if it is not included the percentage of tax that need to be added should be mentioned; all prices should be expressed in EURO. Locality characteristics will typically deal with issues as language use, reading order, use of color, and use of symbols.

We illustrate the Audience Modeling phase with the example web site. There are three audience classes: 'Visitor', 'Buyer' and 'ProductManager', and there are three localities: 'US', 'Flanders' ('FL') and 'Wallonia' ('WA'). Due to space limitations we only give the most important requirements and characteristics.

- **Audience Class** 'Visitor': Need to be able to browse through the products for sale in the Visitor's country and obtain detail descriptions of those products. *Characteristics*: varying age and varying web expertise
- **Audience Class** 'Buyer': Need to be able to buy products that are for sale in the Buyer's country. *Characteristics*: varying age but older than 18 and varying web expertise
- **Audience Class** 'ProductManager': Need to be able to update information and supply information on the products for sale in both countries. *Characteristics*: familiar with the system and the Web
- **Locality** 'US': Each address should include a state; prices must be in US dollars. *Characteristics*: English speaking
- **Locality** 'FL & WA': Contact address of the company must be clearly mentioned; prices must be in EURO with tax included; it must be allowed to pay by means of bank transfer
- **Locality** 'FL': *Characteristics:* Dutch speaking
- **Locality** 'WA': *Characteristics:* French speaking

Locality Mapping

The localities need to be linked to the different audience classes. An audience class may span different localities, e.g. in the example 'Visitor' and 'Buyer' are applicable for all localities. Different audience classes may be needed for a locality, e.g. for the locality 'Flanders' we need the audience classes 'Visitor', 'Buyer' and 'ProductManager'. 'ProductManager' is only needed for the locality 'Flanders'. Therefore, in the 'Locality Mapping', for each locality the audience classes that need to be supported are enumerated. For our example, this results in the following sets. Flanders: {Visitor, Buyer, ProductManager}; Wallonia: {Visitor, Buyer}; and US: {Visitor, Buyer}. Graphically, this can be represented by drawing, for each locality, a box in the audience class hierarchy diagram that includes all the audience classes needed and label this box with the locality' label (see figure 3).

3.3 Conceptual Design

We now describe how the sub phases of the 'Conceptual Design' phase are influenced by the localization requirement.

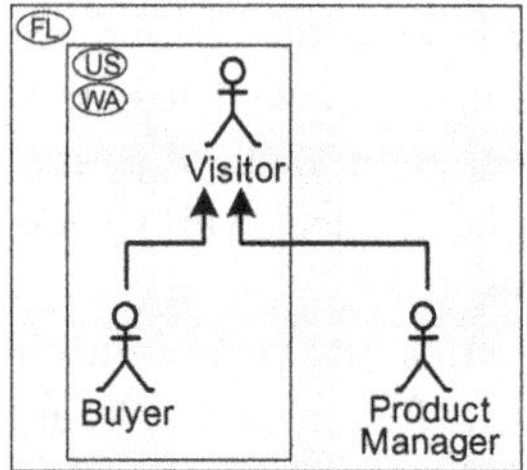

Fig. 3. Audience Modeling

Task Modeling

During 'Task Modeling', a *task model* is defined for each requirement of each audience class. This is done using an adapted version of CTT diagrams [20] (CTT+). To create such a task model, each task is decomposed into elementary tasks and temporal relationships between tasks indicate the order in which the tasks need to be performed. For each elementary task an object model, called '*object chunk*', is created modeling the necessary information and functionality needed to fulfill the requirement of the elementary task. An extended form of ORM (Object Role Model) [14] (ORM+) is used as language for the object chunks.

In our extended version of WSDM, there are also requirements for the different localities. These requirements also need to be considered during task modeling. When constructing the task models, we need to inspect the locality requirements to check if additional or different steps are needed when decomposing a task. If a task needs to be completely different for a specific locality (which is rarely the case), a different CTT must be created and labeled with this locality. If only some additional steps are needed, then these steps are labeled with the localities for which they are needed. In our example, it was specified that in Belgium it must be possible to pay by bank transfer, in the US only payment by credit card is possible. This is indicated in the subtask 'payment method' by means of the labels 'FL' and 'WA' (see figure 4).

When constructing the object chunks, again, we need to inspect the locality requirements to check if additional information is needed. If this is the case, this information is added to the object chunk and labeled with the locality for which it is needed. If the object chunk is created for an elementary task that is labeled, the object chunk itself is labeled in the same way. Figure 5 shows the object chunk 'shipping details'; the State of an Address is only needed for the locality 'US'.

In the object chunks, we should also indicate which information is dependent on the locality. E.g., the value and the currency of the price may depend on the locality. Also the available set of products may be dependent on the locality. This is indicated by labeling the object types that are locality dependent (see figure 6). The set of 'Product' is different for the localities 'US' and 'FL&WA': other products might be available in the US compared to Belgium (FL&WA). 'ProductName' has the three localities US, FL, WA denoting that names of products differ in the three localities.

In summary, the extended Task Modeling is as follows (the new steps are in italic):
For each requirement of each audience class:

1. Define a task for the requirement

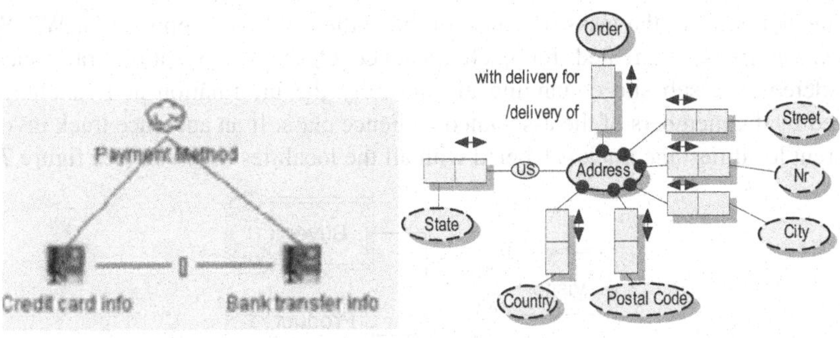

Fig. 4. CCT 'Payment Method' **Fig. 5.** Object Chunk 'Shipping Details'

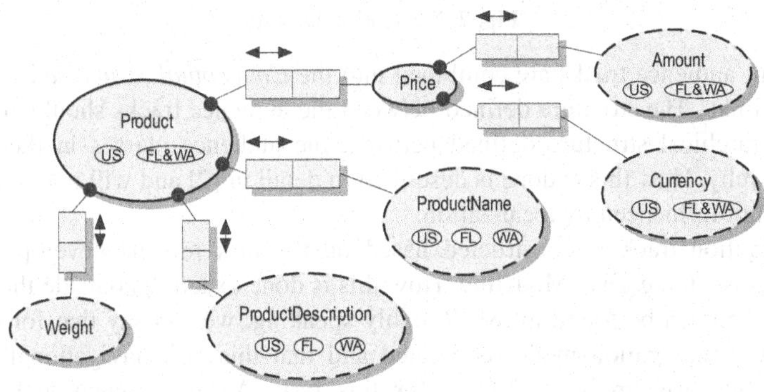

Fig. 6. Object Chunk with Locality Dependent Object Types

2. Decompose the task into elementary tasks and add temporal relations between the tasks (using CTT+).
   - *If the decomposition of the task or a sub-task depends on the locality (expressed by means of a locality requirement) then either make different CTTs and label the CTT with the appropriated locality label or label the nodes that are specific for a locality with the appropriated locality label(s)*
3. For each elementary task:
   Make an object chunk that models the information and/or functionality required by the task (using ORM+)
   - *If the elementary task is labeled, then also label the object chunk with the same labels*
   - *If a locality requires additional information or functionality (formulated by means of locality requirements) label the relationships that models these requirements with the label of this locality*
   - *If the content of an object type is dependent on the locality, label it with all the localities in which the audience class is involved*

Navigational Design

The Navigational Design defines the conceptual structure of the web site and models how the members of the different audience classes will be able to navigate through the site and perform the tasks. Because of the audience driven approach of WSDM, a *navigation track* is created for each audience class. A navigation track can be considered as a sub site containing all and only the information and functionality needed by the members of the associated audience class. If an audience track involves different localities, the track is labeled with all the localities involved (see figure 7).

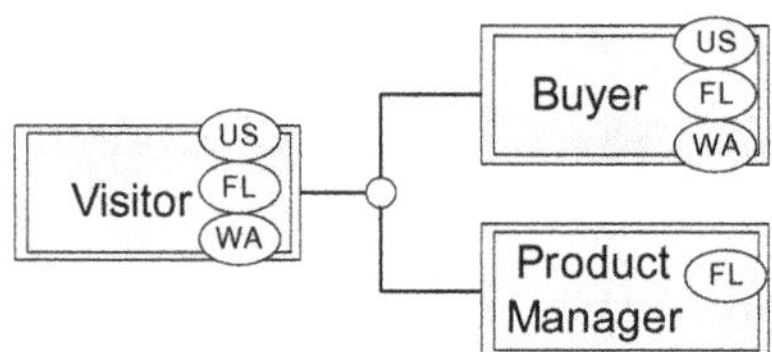

Fig. 7. Navigation Design

Next, all audience tracks are combined into the *Conceptual Structure* by means of structural links. The structure defined between the audience tracks should correspond to the hierarchical structure defined between the audience classes in the audience class hierarchy. How this is done is described in detail in [2] and will not be discussed here. It is not influenced by localization.

A navigation track is constructed based on the task models developed for the audience class in the Task Modeling. How this is done exactly is outside the scope of this paper and can be found in [8]. Roughly speaking, we can say that for each task model a task navigation model is created and that this task navigational model is based on the structure of the CTT for this task. A task navigational model is composed of *components* and *links*. Because we have labeled the tasks and sub-tasks in the task models where necessary, it is easy to indicate in the task navigational models which components and links are locality dependent.

3.4 Implementation Design

We now describe the impact on the sub phases of the 'Implementation Design'. The 'Page Design' translates the conceptual and navigational design into an actual page structure. The actual page structure is obtained by grouping (or splitting) the components and links from the navigational design into pages. Usually the page structure will be independent of the locality, i.e. for each locality the page structure will be the same. However, if some task models are very different for different localities, a different page structure may be needed. In that case, alternative page structures must be defined and each page structure must be labelled with the locality to which it applies.

The presentation design defines the general look and feel of the web site and for each page in the page design a template is constructed defining the layout of the page. Clearly, in this sub phase we must take the localization characteristics formulated in the 'Localization Characterization' into consideration. Each page belongs to exactly one audience class. Therefore, for each page and for each locality needed for this audience class, a different template should be created. How to take the localization characteristics into consideration in the presentation design is not treated here. This is described extensively in the literature about localization (see e.g. [12], [17], [19]).

When localization is needed, the easiest way to maintain the data is by means of a database (or CMS). In WSDM, the database schema is obtained (during Data Design) by integrating all object chunks into a single schema [9] and map this schema onto a database schema (see e.g. [14]). Here, we also need to take the labeling of the object chunks into consideration when mapping the object chunks into a database schema. We will do this for a mapping to a relational database. Different situations are possible:

1. **The complete object chunk is labeled**. This means that the information modeled in the chunk is only needed for the label's locality. This can be reflected by using table (and/or attribute) names that include the locality's label. E.g. TABLE ProductSupply_FL (ProductId INTEGER, ….)
2. **A relationship is labeled**. This means that the information modeled by the relationship is only needed for the label's locality. This can be reflected by using an attribute name that includes the locality's label. Furthermore, the attribute must allow for null values. E.g. TABLE DeliveryAddress (Street STRING NOT NULL, Nr INTEGER NOT NULL, … , State_US STRING)
3. **An object type is labeled**. This means that the content of the object type is dependent on the locality. We distinguish between entity types and label types:
   - For an entity type, we can add, per locality, a boolean-type attribute to the primary key to indicate if an entity should be considered in the locality or not. E.g. TABLE Product (productId INTEGER, availability_US BOOLEAN, availability_Fl&WA BOOLEAN, …). The value TRUE for the attribute 'availability_US' indicates that the product is available in the US.
   - For a label type, we have to provide an attribute per locality needed. E.g. TABLE Product (productId, …. , productName_US, productName_FL, productName_WA,…). An alternative solution is to put the locality dependent attributes in a separated table. E.g. TABLE Product_locality (productId INTEGER, locality STRING, productName STRING, price REAL, …)

Please note that the mapping described here is only one possible solution. In the proposed mapping, information for different localities is maintained in the same table. If (nearly) all information is locality dependent, it may be better to define different tables for different localities. E.g. Table Product_US (productId, …, productName, …) and Product_FL (productId, …, productName, …). In this way it is also easier to physically separate the information for the different localities in different databases.

4 Conclusions and Discussion

We have shown how to extend an existing web site method, WSDM, in order to support the localization of web sites. First, a new concept 'locality' has been introduced. A locality describes a particular place, situation, or location. Then, the different phases of the method were adapted to allow for the specification of different localities. The mission statement should also answer the question: What are the different target localities? The Audience Modeling was extended with some extra sub phases to allow to describe the specific requirements and characteristics of the different localities and to link the localities to the audience classes. During Conceptual Design, the locality requirements are taken into consideration and integrated in rest of the design. In the Implementation Design, for each locality a different Presentation Design may be needed and when using an underlying database, the Data Design should take into consideration that for some tables and attributes more than one version is needed. Although, the extension has been done for WSDM, we believe that the principle of using localities as a starting point is generally applicable and may therefore be used by other web site design methods.

We also discuss some of the limitations of the method proposed. First of all, the method is not appropriate for the 'one size fits all' approach to globalization. In that case, it is better to use standard WSDM and to mention in the audience class characterization that the members are from different localities. Then, during Presentation Design, these issues can be taking into consideration.

Sometimes, the approach needed is a mixture of localization and the 'one size fits all' approach. An example of this is our own university web site. 'Potential Students' and 'Researchers' are two of the target audiences. For researchers, we want to use the 'one size fits all' approach, but for potential students we want to localize. Our local students should be addressed in their local language; foreign students should be addressed in English and should only see information that is applicable to them (e.g. only the English programs). We can achieve this dual approach by defining two localities ('Locals' and 'Foreigners') for the audience class 'Potential Students' and no localities for the audience class 'Researchers'. In the audience characterization of the 'Researchers' we can state that the language must be English and that it is an international audience.

Next, the approach that we follow assumes that the differences in type of content and structure between the localized web sites are rather small. If the local web sites need to be substantially different, this method may not work well. In that case too many requirements from the audience classes need to be moved to the locality specification and those requirements may not all express requirements that are "specific" for the locality. Then, it may be better to define different audience classes, e.g. 'US-Tourists' and 'Europe-Tourists' instead of one audience class 'Tourists' and two localities 'US' and 'Europe'.

References

1. Barber, W. and Badre, A.: Culturability: The Merging of Culture and Usability. In: Proceedings of the 4th Conference on Human Factors and the Web, at http://www.research.att.com/conf/hfweb/proceedings/barber/ (1998)
2. Casteleyn, S. and De Troyer, O.: Structuring Web Sites Using Audience Class Hierarchies. In: Proceedings of DASWIS 2001 (ER) workshop. Yokohama, Japan (2001)

3. Ceri S., Fraternali P., and Bongio A: Web Modeling Language (WebML): a modeling language for designing Web sites. In: WWW9 Conference, First ICSE Workshop on Web Engineering, International Conference on Software Engineering (2000)
4. CMSWatch, at http://www.cmswatch.com (accessed date: May 2004)
5. Del Galdo, E. M. and Nielsen, J. (Eds.) International User Interfaces. John Wiley & Sons, New York (1996)
6. De Troyer, O. and Leune, C.: WSDM : A User-Centered Design Method for Web Sites. In: Computer Networks and ISDN systems, Proceedings of the 7th International WWW Conference, Elsevier (1998) 85-94
7. De Troyer, O.: Audience-driven web design. In: Information modeling in the new millennium, Eds. Matt Rossi & Keng Siau, IDEA GroupPublishing (2001)
8. De Troyer, O., Casteleyn, S.: Modeling Complex Processes for Web Applications using WSDM. In: Proceedings of the IWWOST2003 workshop, Oviedo, Spain (2003)
9. De Troyer, O., Plessers, P. ,Casteleyn, S.: Conceptual View Integration for Audience Driven Web Design. In: CD-ROM Proceedings of the WWW2003 Conference, Budapest, Hongary (2003)
10. Dormann, C. and Chisalita, C.: Cultural Values in Web Site Design. In: Proceedings of the 11th European Conference on Cognitive Ergonomics ECCE11 (2002)
11. Evers, V. and Day, D.: The Role of Culture in Interface Acceptance, In: Proceedings of Human Computer Interaction, Interact'97. Chapman & Hall: London, (1997) 260-267
12. Globalization, Localization, Internationalization and Translation (GLIT), at (accessed date: January 2004)
13. Gómez, J., Cachero, C., and Pastor O.: Modelling Dynamic Personalization in Web Applications, In: Third International Conference on Web Engineering (ICWE'03), LNCS 2722, pages 472-475. Springer-Verlag Berlin Heidelberg (2003)
14. Halpin, T.: Information Modeling and Relational Databases, 3rd edition, Morgan Kaufmann (2001)
15. Hofstede, G.: Cultures and Organizations: Software of the Mind. McGraw-Hill, New York (1997)
16. Koch, N and Kraus, A.:. The expressive Power of UML-based Web Engineering. In Second International Workshop on Web-oriented Software Technology (IWWOST02), Schwabe D., Pastor, O. Rossi, G. and Olsina L. (eds) (2002) 105-119
17. Localization Industry Standards Association (LISA), at (accessed date: January 2004)
18. Marcus, A. and West Gould, E.: Crosscurrents: Cultural Dimensions and Global Web User-Interface Design. ACM Interactions 2 (4) (2000) 32 – 46
19. McCracken D., D. Wolfe R.J.: User-Centered Website Development. A Human-Computer Interaction Approach, Pearson Prentice Hall (2004)
20. Paterno, Mancinii and Meniconi,: ConcurTaskTress: a Diagrammatic Notation for Specifying Task Models. In: Proceedings of INTERACT 97, Chapman & Hall (1997)
21. Sheppard, C. and Scholtz, J.: The Effects of Cultural Markers on Web Site. In: Proceedings of the 5th Conference on Human Factors and the Web (1999)
22. Schwabe, D and Rossi, R.: An Object Oriented Approach to Web-Based Application Design. Theory and Practice of Object Systems 4(4). Wiley and Sons, New York, ISSN 1074-3224) (1998)
23. Sun, H.: Building a Culturally Competent Corporate Web Site: An Exploratory Study of Cultural Markers in Multilingual Web Design. In: Proceedings of the 19th Annual International Conference on Computer Documentation. ACM Press: New York (2001).

Scaling Dynamic Web Content Provision Using Elapsed-Time-Based Content Degradation*

Lindsay Bradford, Stephen Milliner, and Marlon Dumas

Centre for Information Technology Innovation
Queensland University of Technology, Australia
{l.bradford, s.milliner, m.dumas}@qut.edu.au

Abstract. Dynamic Web content is increasing in popularity and, by its nature, is harder to scale than static content. As a result, dynamic Web content delivery degrades more rapidly than static content under similar client request rates. Many techniques have been explored for effectively handling heavy Web request traffic. In this paper, we concentrate on dynamic content degradation, believing that it offers a good balance between minimising total cost of ownership and maximising scalability. We describe an algorithm for dynamic content degradation that is easily implemented on top of existing mainstream Web application architectures. The algorithm is based on measuring the elapsed time of content generation. We demonstrate the algorithm's adaptability against two traffic request patterns, and explore behavioural changes when varying the algorithm's key parameters. We find our elapsed time based algorithm is better at recognising when the server is unloaded, that the supporting architecture limits the effectiveness of the algorithm and and that the algorithm must be configured pessimistically for best results under load.

1 Introduction

An Internet hosting facility routinely maintains a large and heterogeneous collection of publicly available services. The shared nature of the underlying computing node in conjunction with the best-effort nature of the Internet public infrastructure often yields significant delays in processing user requests, especially in the presence of bursty request cycles or during periods of sustained elevated traffic.

The shared hosting of Web applications and/or services on a single, possibly clustered, platform implies a strong relationship between the application/service provider and the administrator of the facility. Part of this relationship is the guarantee that service should not be disrupted during events such as shortage in capacity and high fluctuations in demand. Even in the presence of such events, users should ideally experience an almost regular response from the system.

* This research is funded in part by the SAP Reasearch Centre, Brisbane.

X. Zhou et al. (Eds.): WISE 2004, LNCS 3306, pp. 559–571, 2004.
© Springer-Verlag Berlin Heidelberg 2004

One approach to overcome these problems is to over-provision computing resources in the facility, typically by supplying several duplicated machines that share requests through some load balancer. This solution is not only costly, but also requires increased configuration and administration efforts.

Multiple other ways exist to address the above problems. One of them, widely used in telecommunications, is to apply denial of service when demand goes beyond designated capacity limits. Another possibility is to create digital islands of caching, fashioned after Content Delivery Networks (CDNs), in order to disseminate Web content.

Web content degradation is yet another approach to scaling Web content delivery. To date, research has mostly been focused on static and multimedia Web content in the form of degrading image and video quality under load. Very little has emerged for dynamic Web content, despite its growing usage. The research we report here is a first attempt at implementing graceful dynamic Web content degradation at a single server using a simple control feedback loop.

The main objectives of our work are: (i) to determine if benefits associated with the proposed method for dynamic Web content degradation outweigh the overhead introduced; (ii) to investigate the behavioural changes when altering the key parameters of our proposal; and (iii) to examine the impact of differing high user request patterns on a given service.

To achieve these objectives, we start by defining a simple and pragmatic framework for measuring service adequacy. We then propose a service degradation method based on a selector of service provisioning approaches parameterised by two tunable thresholds.

In order to evaluate this proposal, we undertook a prototyping effort on a cluster of machines and conducted experiments corresponding to different operating settings of an Internet hosting facility, under two patterns of service requests: steady and periodic. The experimental results show that our proposal increases service adequacy and sheds light on the impact of varying the key parameters of our proposed method.

This paper extends the approach described in [1]. Here, we introduce a memory-intensive type of content delivery to complement the CPU-intensive type described in our first publication. We also introduce the modification of key parameters in the approach selector algorithm with this paper.

Section 2 discusses prior work on scalability of service provision. Section 3 and Section 4 successively present the proposed service adequacy metrics and the technique for controlled service degradation. Section 5 describes the experimental environment while Section 6 presents experimental results. Finally, Section 7 concludes.

2 Background

When delivering static content such as basic HTML pages, network bandwidth is typically the bottleneck [2]. For dynamic Web content delivery, the resource bottleneck typically shifts to the CPU (see [3], [4], [2] and [5]).

Given that static content changes infrequently, basic Internet infrastructure allows caching of the content 'closer to the user' (via reverse-proxy caching, Web browser caching, CDNs, edge servers, etc.). This allows a degree of scalability by spreading bandwidth consumption amongst a set of remotely located caches. Resource management for bandwidth under heavy load has also been investigated and approaches typically attempt to limit certain types of bandwidth consumption (see [6] for a comparison of popular approaches) and to implement controlled degradation of service [7].

In times of extreme load, traditional static content caching techniques can be augmented with more active approaches to better meet demand [8]. Peer-to-peer caching schemes [9], adaptive CDNs [10], and cooperative networking models (where clients act as proxy cache servers to newer clients) [2] are examples of approaches to mitigate the effects of heavy request loads for static Web content.

As the Internet continues to grow, there is strong evidence that dynamic content is becoming more prevalent [11]. When attempting to scale delivery of dynamic Web content, the application of caching is less applicable. Basic Internet infrastructure offers limited support for caching results to dynamic queries, simply because it can make no guarantees on what future response might be.

Data update propagation [3], Active query caching [12] and Macro preprocessing of HTML [13] are examples of dynamic content caching. However, the applicability of dynamic content caching is limited (see [14] and [15]). Hence, minimising the resource requirements of dynamic Web content during times of heavy load should also be considered when caching is inappropriate.

Graceful service degradation is not a new concept, at least in terms of static Web pages (see [16] and [17]), the delivery of multimedia (e.g. [18]) and time-constrained neural networks (e.g. [19]). Dynamic Web content degradation, however, has only recently been catered for by a small number of adaptive Web architectures. These architectures range from using content degradation as the primary resource management technique across several nodes [20] through to using content degradation alongside a suite of other adaptive service provision techniques [21].

This paper explores using a "single server" method for dynamic content degradation, using a popular, existing Web application server. We do this to minimise the interdependence between varying pieces of Web infrastructure and to discover what limitations may exist when using popular existing architectures. We use user-perceived quality of service as our guide, and choose elapsed time of content generation to trigger decisions on when a service must alter its behaviour in delivering content (see [22] and [23]). We draw on these works to determine an appropriate target for elapsed time of responses, and as support for using content degradation for scaling dynamic Web content. We argue that the server is thus more closely aligned to its end-users in how quality of service is being judged.

Certain parallels exist between our proposal and the automatic Quality of Service (QoS) control mechanisms proposed by Menascé and Mason [24]. Their approach, however, involves modifying the configuration of the application/Web server, which usually cannot be done at runtime as required in case of sudden capacity overflow. In contrast, we focus on what the application developer may do without modifying the underlying server's configuration or API.

3 Measuring Service Adequacy

We supply a more rounded discussion of what we mean by *adequacy* in [1], but condense the discussion here to just those points needed to make the paper self-contained. A response to a given Web request is *adequate* if the response is returned to the client within one second of receiving the request. For a response to be adequate, the total *end-to-end response time* [25] must be under one second. The degree of adequacy that a particular set of measured results has is the percentage of adequate responses delivered for the total measured requests sent, and is concerned only with message latency.

We chose this one-second limit based on human–computer interface research showing that any human–computer interaction taking over a second is a noticeable delay [26]. We could vary this limit for specific circumstances. For example, it may need to be smaller for each machine that delivers a composite response for content to an end user. It could be much larger if the client waiting on the response is a machine, and not prone to boredom.

The nature of the content being delivered might also matter. There is evidence (see [26] and [27]) suggesting that the more cognitive effort a user must put into completing a task, the longer they expect to wait for a response. Users are also willing to wait longer for a response if there is obvious visual feedback on the progress being made [23]. Our experiments attempt to simulate the delivery of an average Web page, requiring little cognitive effort from the user from a server whose preference is to deliver all content for a given URL within a time-frame such that the user will not feel that they have waited.

Our measure of adequacy does not address the softer concerns of possible user "dissatisfaction" that may arise with a less "complete" service provision.

4 Design Considerations

We assume that for processing a given type of request, there are multiple *approaches* available, each with its own expected system execution time. When request traffic is low, more CPU effort can be devoted to each request, and a heavier approach is used. Conversely, when traffic at the server is high, a lighter approach is executed in an attempt to reduce load on the server and maintain an acceptable response time. Approaches are statically ranked during servlet initialisation in order of expected system time execution from heaviest to lightest.[1]

[1] We have not yet attempted to automatically rank approaches at initialisation.

4.1 The Approach Selector

The approach to be used is determined by an *approach selector* as illustrated in Fig. 1 and is implemented as a *Java servlet filter*. The approach selector assumes that a service provider would prefer to use the most costly approach possible so long as the response is timely and expects the approaches to be ranked as described above.

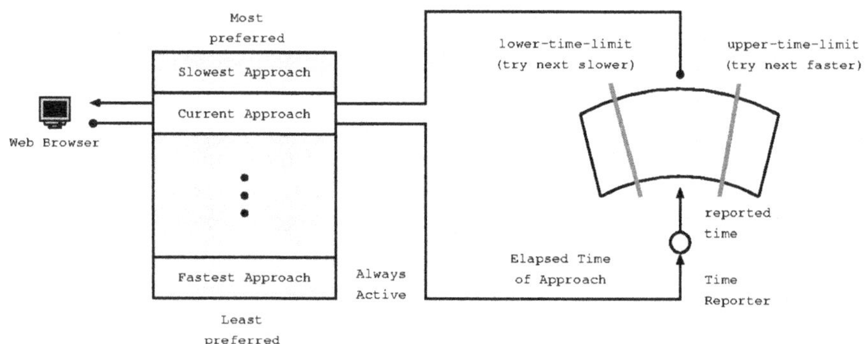

Fig. 1. The Approach Selector

The approach selector, at a given point in time, is pointing its cursor at the *current approach*. The current approach is used to process incoming requests. The approach selector delegates content production to the current approach and measures the elapsed time the current approach takes to generate and deliver a response. This elapsed time is then fed into the current approaches time reporter (discussed below).

The approach selector picks a new approach by querying the reported time of the current approach and comparing this reported time against the two key parameters defined below:

***upper-time-limit*:** The maximum elapsed time we desire for a response to be generated for any received request. Once the reported time of an approach breaches this limit, the approach selector will point its cursor at the next cheaper approach, deactivating the current approach. The cheapest approach is never deactivated, regardless of the degree to which the limit is breached.

***lower-time-limit*:** Once the reported time of an approach drops below this limit, the approach selector points its cursor at the next, more expensive approach.

The threshold *upper-time-limit* differs from the *client-time-limit* defined earlier, in that it does not take into account time outside the control of the server (such as communications overhead). Assuming that the communication delay is modelled as a constant value c, this means that *upper-time-limit* should be set to *client-time-limit* – c so that degradation occurs when inadequate responses (in terms of time) are being generated. This is not an unreasonable assumption to make given our former assumption that CPU consumption is the bottleneck, even when using the cheapest approach. We will consider a mixed model where the bottleneck shifts between CPU and bandwidth in future work.

4.2 Application Development Implications

For service degradation to be applicable, several versions of the application providing the service should be available: a "full-service" version and one or more "degraded" versions. The need for these multiple versions thus becomes a requirement in the application development process. In order to reduce the costs of handling this requirement in terms of analysis, design, coding, and testing, (semi-)automated support can be provided.

In particular, design-level support could be introduced that would allow designers to provide meta-data about the cost and importance of various processing steps. At the coding level, special directives could be inserted in the dynamic content generation scripts to indicate, for example, when not to generate certain sections of a document. The number of possibilities are large and outside the current scope of this work.

5 Experimental Environment

We designed an experimental environment to study how to deploy an application to optimise service delivery using approach selection. The experimental environment aims to study:

- the overhead associated with approach selection for graceful service degradation, and whether its costs outweighs its benefits
- the importance of the algorithm parameters in optimising the approach selection decision
- the effect of different patterns of traffic being experienced at the server
- what to expect from memory-intensive vs CPU-intensive service provision in our approach to content degradation.

We choose the URL as the level of granularity for dynamic content degradation. In other words, a number of approaches could be invoked to provide a response for a given URL depending on the approach selector algorithm.

CPU-intensive content provision is simulated by running a number of loops and performing a floating point division in each loop. We consider four approaches (or versions of a service), corresponding to 3000, 1000, 500 or 100 loops respectively. We use the 3000-loop approach as a baseline.

Memory-intensive content provision is simulated by running a number of loops and accessing a random element of a 2K block of memory in each loop. Again, we consider four approaches of 3000, 1000, 500, and 100 loops, with the

3000-loop approach being the memory-intensive baseline. The idea is to simulate a service that spends most of its time parsing requests and inserting response data into templates.

Each experiment is conducted using two request traffic patterns. The first, namely the "steady" request pattern, corresponds to a server under heavy, constant request pressure. The second, namely the "periodic" pattern, alternates between one-minute periods of request activity (exceeding the baseline's ability to respond adequately) and one-minute periods of zero traffic. This second request pattern we use to verify that the approach selector is exercising its full range of approaches for a given URL.

The experiments are carried out on a set of eight dedicated Sun boxes running Debian Linux on an isolated 100 megabit per second LAN. The testing architecture relies on a single testing server and a single target server. The testing server broadcasts UDP messages to synchronise the activity of clients in order to generate differing request patterns (specifically, to synchronise client machines for periodic traffic pattern). The target server, a Sparc Ultra-5, 192 MB, runs the Tomcat 4.1.18 application server, configured to 25 threads, with our approach selection algorithm.

Two of the test client machines are used to generate sufficient traffic to ensure the server is close to, but not actually at, the point where it will refuse incoming connections for the baseline CPU approach. These machines send a request and once the request is received, will immediately disconnect, generating the equivalent of a denial of service attack. Early tests verified that Tomcat 4.1.18 will fully process a request (except actually returning the response) of a client that deliberately breaks a connection early.

The remaining four machines send requests and wait for responses before sending new requests. The figures reported later have been derived from the data collected from these four machines. The expectation, when introducing approach selection, is that it should be able to reduce end-to-end response times, and allow significantly more timely service responses reported from the four sampling machines than when run against the baseline.

Experiments are run for one hour each to ensure the receipt of sufficient sampled data. Statistics are not collected for the first 10 minutes of each experiment to ensure the results are not skewed by warm-up time. We track the *end-to-end response time* of each client request and report the percentage that fail to fall within our *client-time-limit* of one second.

For both request patterns there is a target number of requests processed that the approach selector should tend towards. If less requests than the target are processed, the approach selector may have been overly optimistic about the workload. Similarly, if more are processed, the approach selector may have been overly pessimistic about the workload. For the steady request pattern, the target request number is the number of sampling clients times the number of seconds in the 50 minute period, which is 4 * 3000, or 12,000 requests. The periodic pattern spends only 25 minutes of the 50 sending requests, so its target is 6,000 requests.

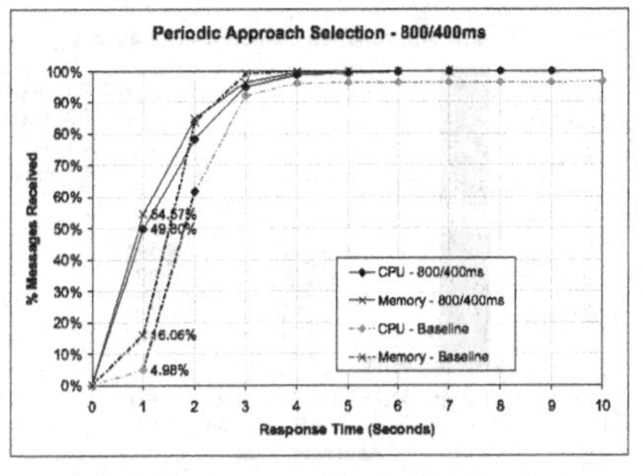

(a) Adequacy – Periodic Pattern

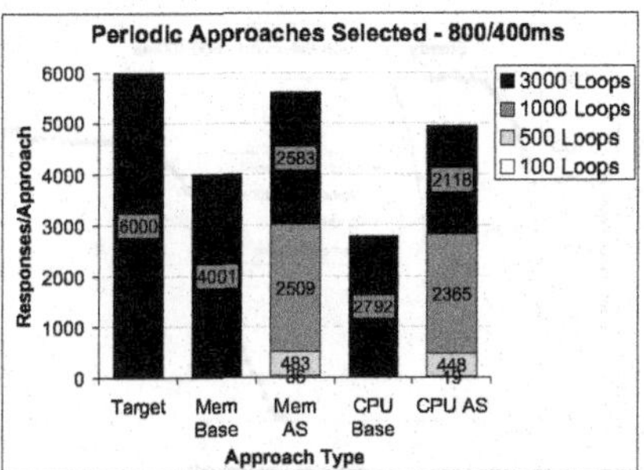

(b) Throughput – Periodic Pattern

Fig. 2. Naïve approach selection using periodic request pattern

6 Experimental Results

We conducted a total of four experiments. The first experiment runs approach selection with a naïve setting of key parameters under the periodic request pattern for both the CPU-intensive and memory-intensive approach types. The second experiment repeats this setup using the steady request pattern.

In Experiments 1 and 2, the thresholds *upper-time-limit* and *lower-time-limit*, discussed in Sect. 4 are set at 800 and 400 milliseconds (ms) respectively. The *upper-time-limit* threshold of 800 ms was chosen as a number within our one second target with an amount of time (200 ms) set aside to receive and transmit request and response messages. The 400 ms *lower-time-limit* was chosen simply as half of the *upper-time-limit*. Experiments 3 and 4 are similar to 1 and 2, varying the upper and lower time limits, in order to determine their effect on service adequacy under the periodic and steady request patterns respectively.

We display our experimental results as either histograms or bar charts. The histograms show the response times (in seconds) on the horizontal axis, and plot on the vertical axis the cumulative percentage of responses sent within a given response time limit, thereby measuring service adequacy. The percentage of requests returned in under one second represents our measure of adequacy. The bar charts, on the other hand, show for each approach (i.e. version of the service) the percentage of requests that were processed using that approach in a given experiment.

6.1 Experiment 1: Approach Selection with Periodic Pattern

Fig. 2 shows the results of running approach selection for both memory- and CPU-intensive approach types with the periodic request pattern. Figure 2(a) shows the cumulative percentage of responses returned within a number of seconds and places these adequacy results against their respective baselines. Figure 2(b) shows the actual number of requests processed against a given approach for both approach selection and the baseline. An extra column shows the target request number the server should tend towards.

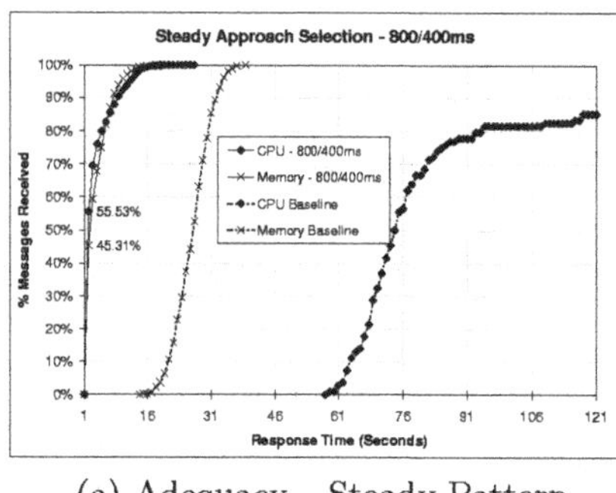

(a) Adequacy – Steady Pattern

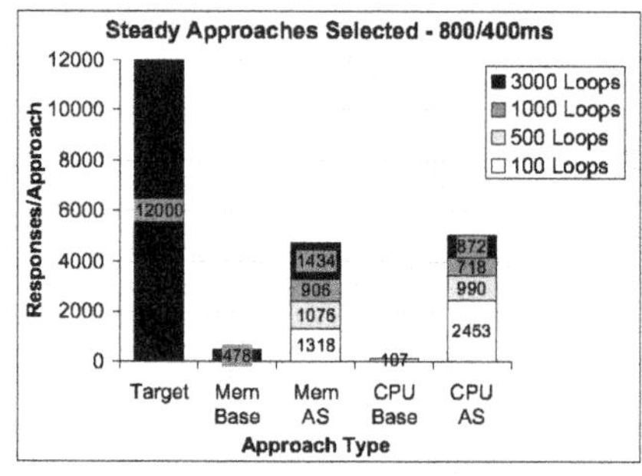

(b) Throughput – Steady pattern

Fig. 3. Naïve approach selection using steady request pattern

For the default time-limit settings of the approach selector, we see that we achieved an adequacy measure of just under 50% for both approach types. With respect to throughput, both approach types came much closer to our target throughput figure than their corresponding baselines, but still fell somewhat short. Interestingly, a large percentage of the requests were served with the most costly approach, and many of the extra requests (on top of the baseline number) were served with the next most expensive approach.

The time-limit values chosen saw the approach selector behave somewhat overly optimistically. A better result would have been to generate fewer 3000-loop responses in favour of more 1000-loop responses.

6.2 Experiment 2: Approach Selection with Steady Pattern

Fig. 3 shows the results of running approach selection for both memory- and CPU-intensive approach types with the steady request pattern. Figures 3(a) and 3(b) show the same detail for the steady pattern as Figures 2(a) and 2(b) did for the periodic pattern.

For the default time-limit settings of the approach selector, again, we see that we achieved an adequacy measure of just under 50% for both approach types. With respect to throughput, both approach types fell far short of our target throughput figure, but were significantly higher than their baselines. Of striking difference is the response times recorded. The minimum response times recorded for the the memory and CPU baselines were 14 seconds and 55 seconds respectively. The difference between the baseline and naïve approach selection is far more pronounced with this request pattern.

In these approach selection results, there was a far more even distribution of requests across the various approaches. The time-limit values chosen saw the approach selector again behave overly optimistically. In this case, a better match of approaches to the request traffic would have seen far more of the smaller approaches used than what was witnessed.

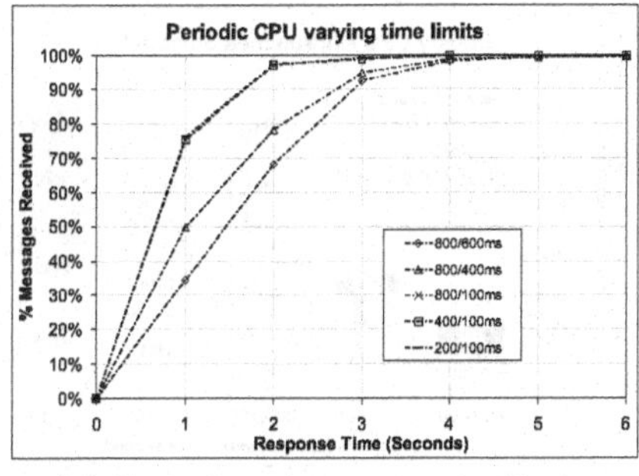

(a) Periodic adequacy w.r.t limits

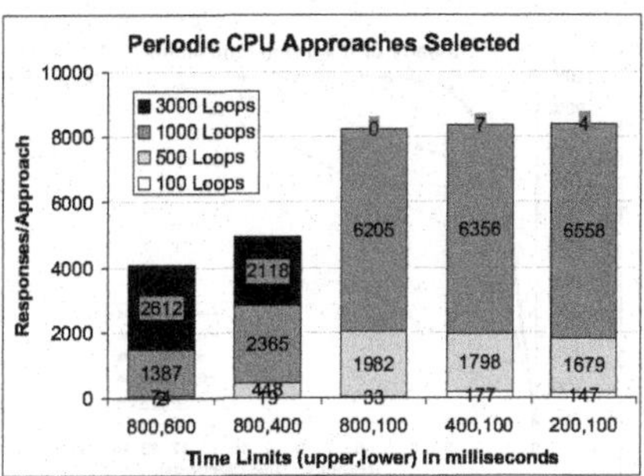

(b) Periodic throughput w.r.t limits

Fig. 4. Approach selection with periodic pattern, varying time limits (CPU)

6.3 Experiment 3: Periodic Request Pattern Varying Time Limits

In this section we present CPU approach type results only. Memory results were consistent with those gained via CPU.

Figures 4(a) and 4(b) display adequacy and throughput results for the periodic request pattern with varying upper and lower time limits. The limits are reported in the graphs with the upper limit followed by the lower limit.

We see from Fig. 4(a) that changes to the *lower-time-limit* had a significant impact on adequacy. Changes to *upper-time-limit*, however, had no noticeable impact. Turning our attention to throughput in Fig. 4(b), the *lower-time-limit* again makes a significant difference. We note that with a *lower-time-limit* of 100 milliseconds we processed far more requests than our target of 6000, but that our adequacy figure did not climb above about 75%.

A smaller *lower-time-limit* figure forces the approach selector to be more pessimistic about trying a more costly approach than the one it is currently using. An initial study of the throughput might suggest that the approach selector was too pessimistically configured for the request traffic. However, adequacy figures of only 75% suggest that the approach selector was actually overly optimistic.

There is a period of time between receipt of request and the handing of a request to the approach selector (which is where the measuring of elapsed time begins). A significant amount of time can pass between receipt of a request by the application server and its subsequent processing by the approach selector.

6.4 Experiment 4: Steady Request Pattern Varying Time Limits

Figures 5(a) and 5(b) display adequacy and throughput results for the steady request pattern using the same time limits as figures 4(a) and 4(b).

Again, we see similar trends. The *lower-time-limit* has significant impact on adequacy and throughput, the *upper-time-limit* far less so. An initial look at the throughput figures would suggest that a 100 millisecond *lower-time-limit* is about right for ensuring that measuring clients are receiving one request per

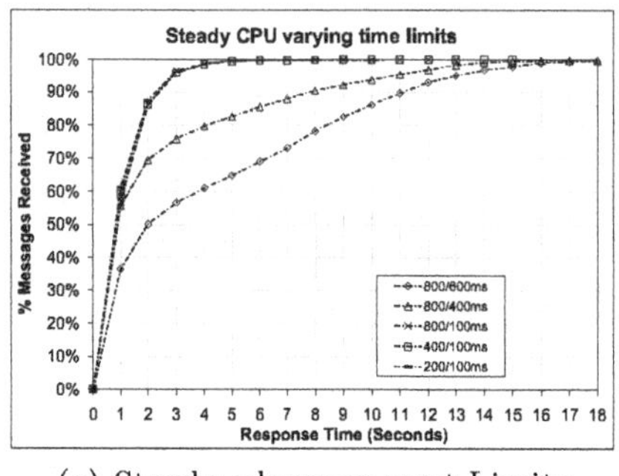

(a) Steady adequacy w.r.t Limits

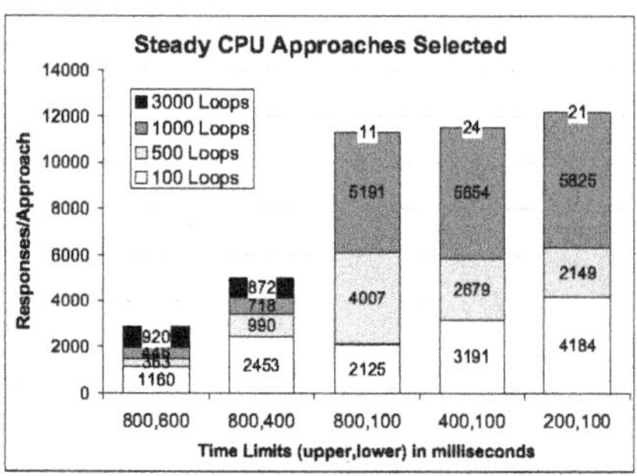

(b) Steady throughput w.r.t Limits

Fig. 5. Approach selection with steady pattern, varying time limits (CPU)

second. When we look at adequacy measures, however, again we see that the adequacy achievable via changing limits is capped and does not do as well as with the periodic request pattern.

7 Concluding Remarks and Future Work

This paper has demonstrated that the principle of controlled dynamic content degradation in times of load can deliver significant performance improvement. In addition the results provide insights for tuning a hosting facility with "capped" processing ability using content degradation.

We tested a simple, easy-to-implement method for dynamic content degradation using a popular, unmodified application server. As elapsed time is how an end-user typically judges the quality of a web service offering, our algorithm also uses elapsed time for decisions in changing server behaviour.

Our algorithm is a simple control loop with the two key parameters we name the *lower-time-limit* and *upper-time-limit*. These limits tell the algorithm when to try faster or slower approaches to content generation respectively once elapsed time goes below or above these limits. The smaller we make these values, the more pessimistic we make the approach selector.

From the results of our experiments, we conclude that:

– varying the *lower-time-limit* has significant impact: the smaller the limit, the better the service adequacy and throughput obtained
– varying the *upper-time-limit* had far less impact on both adequacy and throughput
– if significant time passes in the application server that is outside of the period of time measured by the approach selector, very little can be done by tweaking the parameters of the algorithm to lift the adequacy results further.

To maximise the benefits of our approach selector, we need a supporting environment that minimises the effort to receive requests and record as accurately as possible time of receipt of requests. Perhaps a high-volume front end "request forwarder" that marks up a request with receipt time before passing on to the main application server would be appropriate. Without a supporting environment that offers this, we should err on the side of pessimistically configuring the approach selector to somewhat compensate for the time the approach selector cannot measure.

We see a number of possible research directions. Firstly, the inclusion of further factors into the experimental setup (e.g. I/O and database access) should be considered.

Secondly, we would like to study the benefits of automatically varying the values of the thresholds and dynamically changing the approach selection heuristic itself. A secondary control loop on the *lower-time-limit* may be a good first step. We envision this requiring a modified application server as outlined above.

Thirdly, we would like to investigate ways in which degrading approaches for generating content can be obtained with minimal overhead on the application development process, for example, by extending scripting languages for dynamic content (e.g. JSP, ASP, PHP) with directives to indicate portions of code to be skipped in certain times of overload.

References

1. Bradford, L., Milliner, S., Dumas, M.: Varying Resource Consumption to Achieve Scalable Web Services. In: Proceedings of the VLDB Workshop on Technologies for E-Services (TES), Berlin, Germany, Springer Verlag (2003) 179–190
2. Padmanabhan, V., Sripanidkulchai, K.: The Case for Cooperative Networking. In: 1st International Peer To Peer Systems Workshop (IPTPS 2002). (2002)
3. Challenger, J., Iyengar, A., Witting, K., Ferstat, C., Reed, P.: A Publishing System for Efficiently Creating Dynamic Web Content. In: INFOCOM (2). (2000) 844–853
4. Kraiss, A., Schoen, F., Weikum, G., Deppisch, U.: Towards Response Time Guarantees for e-Service Middleware. Bulletin on the Technical Committee on Data Engineering **24** (2001) 58–63
5. Amza, C., Chanda, A., Cecchet, E., Cox, A., Elnikety, S., Gil, R., Marguerite, J., Rajamani, K., Zwaenepoel, W.: Specification and Implementation of Dynamic Web Site Benchmarks. In: Fifth Annual IEEE International Workshop on Workload Characterization (WWC-5). (2002)
6. Lau, F., Rubin, S.H., Smith, M.H., Trajovic, L.: Distributed Denial of Service Attacks. In: IEEE International Conference on Systems, Man, and Cybernetics. Volume 3., Nashville, TN, USA (2000) 2275–2280
7. Singh, S.: Quality of service guarantees in mobile computing. Computer Communications **19** (1996)
8. Iyengar, A., Rosu, D.: Architecting Web sites for high performance. In: Scientific Programming. Volume 10. IOS Press (2002) 75–89
9. Stading, T., Maniatis, P., Baker, M.: Peer-to-Peer Caching Schemes to Address Flash Crowds. In: 1st International Peer To Peer Systems Workshop (IPTPS 2002), Cambridge, MA, USA (2002)
10. Jung, J., Krishnamurthy, B., Rabinovich, M.: Flash Crowds and Denial of Service Attacks: Characterization and Implications for CDNs and Web Sites. In: Proceedings of the International World Wide Web Conference, ACM Press New York, NY, USA (2002) 252–262

11. Barford, P., Bestavros, A., Bradley, A., Crovella, M.: Changes in Web Client Access Patterns: Characteristics and Caching Implications. Technical Report 1998-023 (1998)
12. Luo, Q., Naughton, J.F., Krishnamurthy, R., Cao, P., Li, Y.: Active Query Caching for Database Web Servers. In Suciu, D., Vossen, G., eds.: WebDB (Selected Papers). Volume 1997 of Lecture Notes in Computer Science., Springer (2001) 92–104
13. Douglis, F., Haro, A., Rabinovich, M.: HPP: HTML Macro-Preprocessing to Support Dynamic Document Caching. In: USENIX Symposium on Internet Technologies and Systems. (1997)
14. Yagoub, K., Florescu, D., Issarny, V., Valduriez, P.: Caching Strategies for Data-Intensive Web Sites. In Abbadi, A.E., Brodie, M.L., Chakravarthy, S., Dayal, U., Kamel, N., Schlageter, G., Whang, K.Y., eds.: VLDB 2000, Proceedings of 26th International Conference on Very Large Data Bases, September 10-14, 2000, Cairo, Egypt, Morgan Kaufmann (2000) 188–199
15. Shi, W., Collins, E., Karamcheti, V.: Modeling Object Characteristics of Dynamic Web Content. Technical Report TR2001-822, New York University (2001)
16. Tarek F. Abdelzaher and Nina Bhatti: Web Server QoS Management by Adaptive Content Delivery. In: Proceedings of the 8th Internation World Wide Web Conference, Toronto, Canada (1999)
17. Chandra, S., Ellis, C.S., Vahdat, A.: Differentiated Multimedia Web Services using Quality Aware Transcoding. In: INFOCOM 2000. Proceedings of the Nineteenth Annual Joint Conference of the IEEE Computer and Communications Societies. Volume 2., IEEE (2000) 961–969
18. Hutchison, D., Coulson, G., Campbell, A.: 11. In: Quality of Service Management in Distributed Systems. Addison Wesley (1994)
19. Stochastic and Distributed Anytime Task Scheduling. In: Tools with Artificial Intelligence. Volume 10., IEEE (1998) 280–287
20. Chen, H., Iyengar, A.: A Tiered System for Serving Differentiated Content. In: World Wide Web: Internet and Web Information Systems. Volume 6., Netherlands, Kluwer Academic Publishers (2003) 331–352
21. Welsh, M., Culler, D.: Adaptive Overload Control for Busy Internet Servers. In: USENIX Symposium on Internet Technologies and Systems. (2003)
22. Ramsay, J., Barbesi, A., Peerce, J.: A psychological investigation of long retrieval times on the World Wide Web. In: Interacting with Computers. Volume 10., Elsevier (1998) 77–86
23. Bhatti, N., Bouch, A., Kuchinsky, A.: Integrating user-perceived quality into Web server design. Computer Networks (Amsterdam, Netherlands: 1999) **33** (2000) 1–16
24. Menascé, D.A., Mason, G.: Automatic QoS Control. IEEE Internet Computing **7** (2003) 92–95
25. Menascé, D.A., Almeida, V.A.F.: Capacity Planning for Web Services. Prentice Hall (2001)
26. Miller, R.: Response Time in Man–Computer Conversational Transactions. In: Proc. AFIPS Fall Joint Computer Conference. Volume 33. (1968) 267–277
27. Selvidge, P.R., Chaparro, B.S., Bender, G.T.: The world wide wait: effects of delays on user performance. International Journal of Industrial Ergonomics **29** (2002) 15–20

Component Reconfiguration Tool for Software Product Lines with XML Technology

Seung-Hoon Choi

School of Computer Science, Duksung Women's University
Seoul, Korea
csh@duksung.ac.kr
http://www.duksung.ac.kr/~csh

Abstract. A Paradigm of software product lines is to facilitate more strategic reuse by predicting and analyzing the variabilities and commonalities among the members of software family at early stage of software lifecycle. This paper proposes an automatic component reconfiguration tool that could be applied in constructing the component-based software product lines. Our tool accepts the reuser's requirement via a feature model and makes the feature configuration from which it generates the source code of the reconfigured component. The component family in our tool should have the architecture of GenVoca, and XSLT scripts provide the code templates for implementation elements. Taking the 'Bank Account' component family as our example, we showed that our tool produced automatically the component source code that the reuser wants to create. The result of this paper should be applied extensively for increasing the productivity of building the software product lines.

1 Introduction

A software product line is a set of software-intensive systems sharing a common, managed set of features that satisfy the specific needs of a particular market segment or mission and that are developed from a common set of core assets in a prescribed way [1]. A paradigm of software product lines is to facilitate more strategic reuse by predicting and analyzing the variabilities and commonalities among the members of software family at early stage of software lifecycle.

Recently the various researches on component-based software product lines are performed actively in academic and industrial fields [2]. The essential parts of component-based software product lines are the techniques to build the core software assets and to produce the specific software system by composing these assets. The software components in software product lines are required to support the variabilities. The 'variabilities' represents the features of a series of components that may be modified according to its context or purpose. This is opposite concept of 'commonalities' that represents the features which are shared by a series of components.

To analyze the commonalities/variabilities of the software components in specific domain, a lot of domain engineering methodologies were proposed [3,4,5,6]. Our

X. Zhou et al. (Eds.): WISE 2004, LNCS 3306, pp. 572–583, 2004.
© Springer-Verlag Berlin Heidelberg 2004

approach utilizes the feature model proposed in FODA(Feature-Oriented Domain Analysis) [7] as modeling tool for representing the commonalities and variabilities among the members in component family.

The crucial point in supporting the variabilities is the capability to reconfigure the functions and architectures of software asset according to its execution environment or purpose. Various approaches based on component generation have been proposed as effective mechanism to support the variabilities and construct the product lines. They include generic programming, template class based programming, aspect oriented programming, static meta-programming and intentional programming [8,9].

Our approach exploits the ideas presented in [8] which showed how to implement generators using template meta-programming called GenVoca, and [10] which demonstrated the applicability of the XML technologies to the application code generation. [11] proposed the XVCL(XML-based language) approach for managing variants in component-based product families. The differences among our approach, GenVoca and XVCL are described in Section 5. Main distinction is that our approach provides the fully-automatic support for code generation and exploits XSLT's document transformation capability that is more general technology.

Our component reconfiguration tool generates the source code of specific software component according to the set of features chosen by the reusers. This tool makes use of the generative programming and XML techniques that are emerging recently as the effective methods in building the software product lines. Our tool accepts the reuser's requirement via a feature model and makes the feature configuration from which it generates the source code of the reconfigured component. To accomplish this process, the component family in our tool should have the architecture of GenVoca.

This paper is organized as follows. Overall architecture of the component reconfiguration tool is described in section 2. In section 3, the construction process of the component family is explained using 'Bank Account' component family example. Section 4 describes the reconfiguration steps. In section 5 the evaluation of our approach is presented and in section 6 the conclusion is drawn.

2 Component Reconfiguration Tool

2.1 Feature Configuration

Feature model, the main result of domain engineering, is the requirement model that represents the commonalities and variabilities among the members of product lines at high level abstraction. 'Features' denote the functional abstractions that should be implemented, tested, deployed and maintained. So, they represent the functions or requirements which are considered to be important to customers. In feature models, the commonalities are represented by mandatory features and the variabilities are modeled by optional, alternative or free parameter features.

A *Feature configuration* represents the set of features selected by the customer to be included in a specific product [12]. A feature configuration is constructed by a

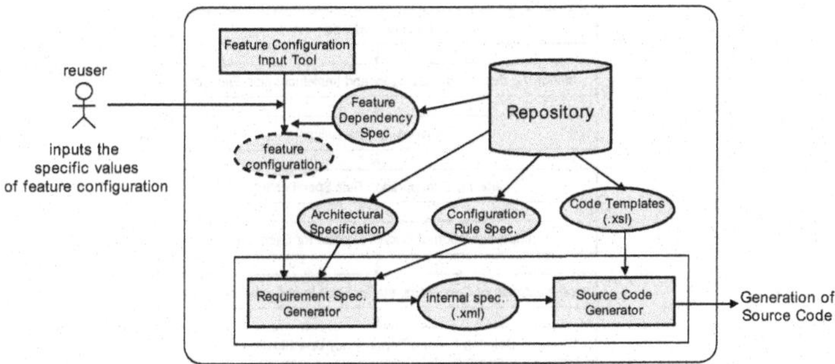

Fig. 1. Overall Architecture of Reconfiguration Tool

reuser's selecting the specific features and entering the specific values in the feature model. This configuration thus can be understood as an initial requirements specification for the specific product. Our reconfiguration tool takes in a feature configuration as input and generates the source code of reconfigured component.

2.2 Architecture of Component Reconfiguration Tool

The overall architecture of our reconfiguration tool is illustrated in Fig. 1.

2.3 Example: "Bank Account" Component

In this paper, we take the 'Bank Account' component family as our example to describe our approach to reconfigure and generate the source code of specific component from component family.

3 Component Family Construction Process

To support automatic reconfiguration, we should follow the component family construction process. Fig. 2 illustrates the overall construction process.

3.1 Feature Modeling

At first, we should build the feature model to represent the commonalities and variabilities among the members. Fig. 3 shows the feature model of bank account component family.

The meanings of the main features in Fig. 3 are as follows:

- *Personal Account:* a feature representing the target component
- *number:* a feature representing the type of account number
- *overdraft:* a feature determining whether the customer can retrieve the cash above the balance or not

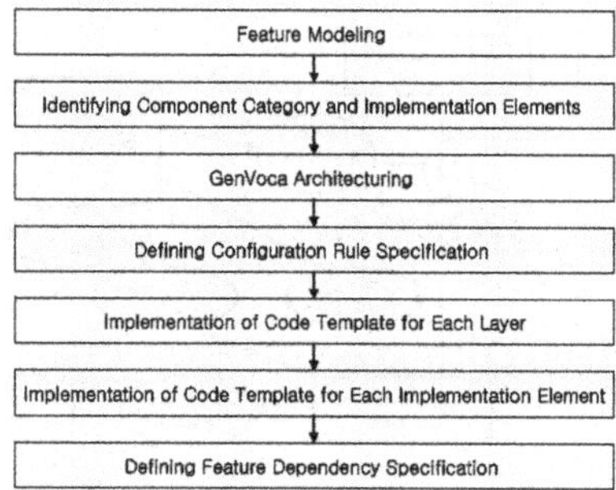

Fig. 2. Overall Component Family Construction Process

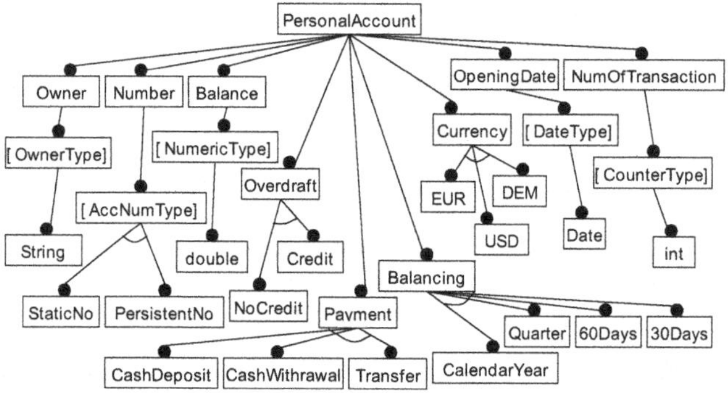

Fig. 3. Feature Model for Bank Account Component Family

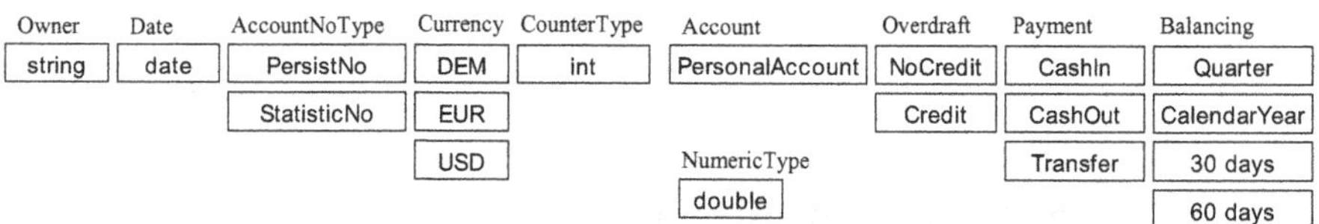

Fig. 4. Component Categories for the Bank Account Component Family

- *payment:* a feature determining the kind of main bank functions such as cash deposit, cash withdrawal and transfer
- *balancing:* determines when the interest is calculated

3.2 Identifying Component Category and Implementation Elements

In this step, the component categories are identified based on the result of previous domain engineering process. Component category represents the main responsibility or capability of the target component family. If a responsibility has more than one alternative implementation, the corresponding component category will contain an implementation element for each alternative. Component category is one layer providing the standard interfaces and all of the implementation elements in one component category have the same interfaces [8]. Fig. 4 shows the component categories and the implementation elements in each component category for bank account component family.

3.3 GenVoca Architecturing

In this step, GenVoca layered architecture[8] is defined using the component categories and implementation elements of previous step. GenVoca layered architecture is constructed by "uses" dependencies between component categories. More specific layer is located above more general layer and uses the services provided by direct lower layer. The layered architecture like this allows the composition and extension among layers through the standardized interfaces provided by each layer.

Fig. 5 displays the GenVoca architecture for the bank account component family. In this figure, the arrow represents the "uses" or "depend-on" relationship between two layers. The GenVoca architecture in Fig. 5 is stored in architectural specification file(in xml format) like Fig. 6 and used in generating the specific component.

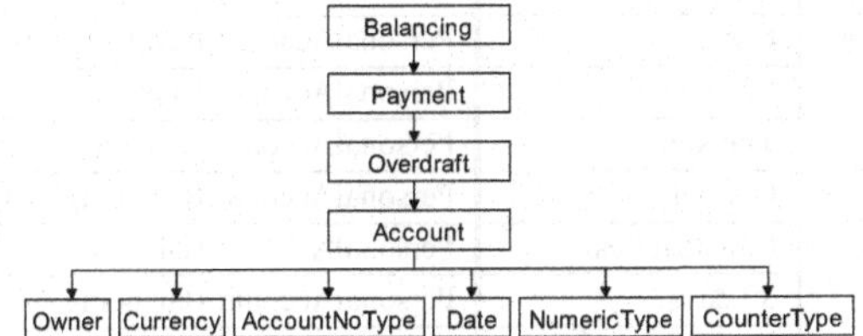

Fig. 5. GenVoca Architecture for Bank Account Component Family

```
<ComponentArchitecture>
  <layers>
   ... ...
   <Component_category name="Payment" type="mandatory" depend_on="Overdraft, Payment">
      <ImplCom name="CashIn"/>
      <ImplCom name="CashOut"/>
      <ImplCom name="Transfer"/>
   </Component_category>
   ... ...
  </layers>
</ComponentArchitecture>
```

Fig. 6. Part of Architectural Specification for Bank Account Component Family

3.4 Defining Configuration Rule

The configuration rule defines the regulation that determines which implementation elements are selected from all of the implementation elements included in each component category. The process of defining the configuration rule can be achieved easily through making the decision table that represent which implementation elements should be selected according to the value of each feature. Table 1 represents the rule that determines which implementation elements in each component category should be selected according to the specific feature configuration. The *configuration rule specification* is constructed from the decision table like table 1. Fig. 7 shows the part of configuration rule specification for 'Payment' category.

Table 1. Decision Table for Bank Account Component Family

Component Category	Implementation Element	Values of Features in Feature Configuration
Owner	v1(free parameter)	PersonalAccount.Owner.[OwnerType] = v1
	String	PersonalAccount.Owner.[OwnerType] = "String"
AccountNoType	PersistNo	PersonalAccount.accountNumberType = "PersistNo"
	StaticNo	PersonalAccount.accountNumberType = "StaticNo"
Currency	DEM	PersonalAccount.currency = "DEM"
	EUR	PersonalAccount.currency = "EUR"
	USD	PersonalAccount.currency = "USD"
Account	PersonalAccount	PersonalAccount = selected
Overdraft	NoCredit	PersonalAccount.Overdraft = "NoCredit"
	Credit	PersonalAccount.Overdraft = "Credit"
Payment	CashIn	PersonalAccount.Payment = "CashDeposit"
	CashOut	PersonalAccount.Payment = "CashWithdrawal"
	Transfer	PersonalAccount.Payment = "Transfer"
Balancing	Quarter	PersonalAccount.Balancing = "Quarter"
	CalendarYear	PersonalAccount.Balancing = "CalendarYear"
	30 days	PersonalAccount.Balancing = "30 days"
	60 days	PersonalAccount.Balancing = "60 days"

```
<Component_category name="Payment">
 <ImplCom name="CashIn">
  <OR_cond><AND_cond>CashDeposit</AND_cond></OR_cond>
 </ImplCom>
 <ImplCom name="CashOut">
  <OR_cond><AND_cond>CashWithdrawal</AND_cond></OR_cond>
 </ImplCom>
 <ImplCom name="Transfer">
  <OR_cond><AND_cond>Transfer</AND_cond></OR_cond>
 </ImplCom>
</Component_category>
```

Fig. 7. Configuration Rule for 'Payment' Category

3.5 Implementation of Code Template for Each Layer

Each component category defines the standard interfaces and the implementation elements in each component category follow those common interfaces. Through these common interfaces, two implementation elements included in distinct categories can be composed. In this step, the code templates for the standard interfaces of the each component category are defined. Fig. 8 shows the XSLT code template for the interfaces of 'Payment' category. In reconfiguration, the architectural specification and configuration rule specification are integrated with the feature configuration made by the reuser. Then, the internal specification is constructed and applied to this code template to generate the concrete interface java code. For example, the second line of Fig. 8, `select = "Layers/Component[@category='Payment']"` gets its value from the generated internal specification in XML format.

```
<xsl:template match="Specification">
public interface <xsl:apply-templates select="Layers/Component[@category='Payment']"/>
}
</xsl:template>
<xsl:template match="Layers/Component[@category='Payment']">
        <xsl:apply-templates select="@*"/>
</xsl:template>
<xsl:template match="@category">
        <xsl:value-of select="."/>
        <xsl:text> {</xsl:text>
</xsl:template>
```

Fig. 8. XSLT Code Template for the Interface of 'Payment' Category

3.6 Implementation of Code Template for Each Implementation Element

In this step, XSLT code templates for every implementation elements in each component category are developed. Fig. 9 shows the XSLT code template for *'Transfer'* implementation element in 'Payment' category.

3.7 Defining Feature Dependency Specification

The feature dependency specification defines the relationships among various features in feature model. Feature configuration input tool validates the current feature configuration using this specification. Fig. 10 displays one form of the feature dependency specification. This specification includes the inclusive relationships(two features should be selected simultaneously) and the exclusive relationships(two features should not be selected simultaneously). For example, the specification says that if *'Transfer'* feature is selected among alternative sub-features of *'Payment'* feature then *'Quarter'* and *'Credit'* feature should be included in current feature configuration and *'30days'* should not be included.

4 Automatic Component Reconfiguration

Fig. 11 illustrates using system sequence diagram of UML the scenario in which reuser generates the source code of their target component via our reconfiguration tool.

```
<xsl:template match="Specification">
public class <xsl:value-of select="Layers/Component[@category='Payment']/ImplCom"/>
extends <xsl:value-of select="Layers/Component[@category='Overdraft']/ImplCom"/>
implements Payment {
  public <xsl:value-of select="Layers/Component[@category='Payment']/ImplCom"/>() {
  }
  public void transfer(<xsl:value-of select="Configuration/Config_Component[@category=
'NumericType']"/> amount, Account toAccount) {
    if(this.currency() == toAccount.currency()){
      if (amount > 0) {
         super.debit(amount);
         toAccount.credit(amount);
      } } } }
</xsl:template>
```

Fig. 9. XSLT Code Template for ‘Transfer’ implementation element in ‘Payment’ category

```
<FeatureDependency>
  <Feature name = "PersonalAccount.Payment.Transfer">
    <inclusive>
      <Feature name = "PersonalAccount.Balancing.Quarter">
      <Feature name = "PersonalAccount.Overdraft.Credit">
    </inclusive>
    <exclusive>
      <Feature name = "PersonalAccount.Balancing.30days">
    </exclusive>
  ... ...
</FeatureDependency>
```

Fig. 10. Example of Feature Dependency Specification

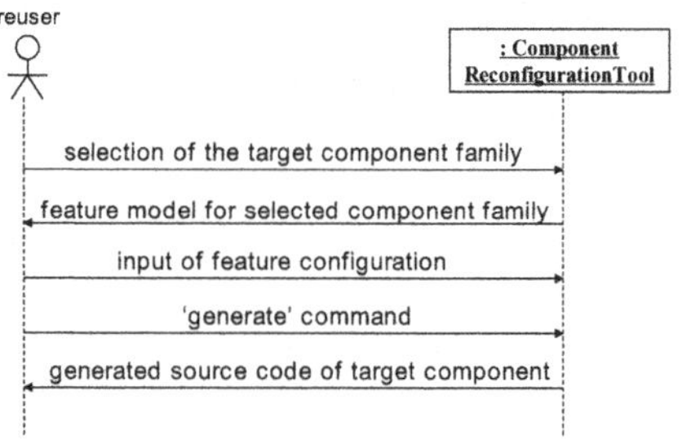

Fig. 11. System Sequence Diagram for Component Reconfiguration Process

4.1 Making Feature Configuration

As showed in Fig. 12, reuser makes his feature configuration by selecting the features and providing the required values in feature model. Making the feature configuration includes one of the following actions:

(i) For the free parameter features, the actual value should be provided.

(ii) For the optional features, the selection or de-selection should be determined.
(iii) For features with several alternative sub-features, one of them should be chosen.

In Fig. 12, the feature node with bold line represents the feature that is selected by reuser and included in current feature configuration. Small dialog box in lower left corner represents typing the value of *'OwnerType'* free parameter feature. The click of *'Make XML File'* button initiates the construction of the internal specification.

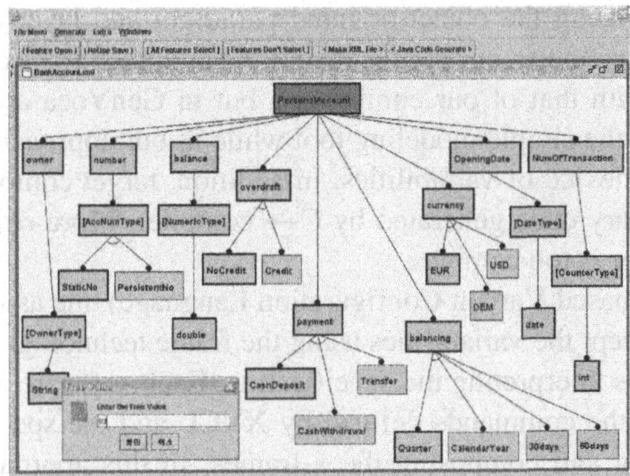

Fig. 12. GUI of Component Reconfiguration Tool

4.2 Generation of Component Source Code

After making the internal specification the click of the *'Java Code Generate'* button in Fig. 12 initiates the generation of the source code of the target component. The source codes for the specific bank account component include 17 java files in total. Fig. 13 shows the generated source code of *'NoCredit'* implementation element.

```
public class NoCredit extends PersonalAccount implements Overdraft {
  public NoCredit() {
    super();
  }
  public void debit(double amount){
    if (amount <= 0)
      return;
    if (super.balance() - amount >= 0)
      super.debit(amount);
  }    }
```

Fig. 13. Example source code of 'NoCredit' implementation element

5 Evaluation

In this chapter the evaluation of our approach is presented in two ways. In first evaluation we compare our approach with two generative techniques that are most relevant to our approach. In second evaluation we analyze the advantages and disadvantages of our approach in term of software product lines.

5.1 Comparison

In this section, the result of comparing our approach with two related works such as GenVoca[13,14] and XVCL[15,16] is presented. GenVoca is the approach to develop the code generator using the object-oriented paradigm and layer composition. GenVoca gave the motivation to our approach and the architecture of component in GenVoca is identical with that of our component, but in GenVoca approach the feature model is utilized as the simple modeling tool while in our approach the feature model is utilized as input device of variabilities. In addition, target component of GenVoca has the form of binary code generated by C++ compiler. More over, the structure of component generator is too complex.

In XVCL(XML-based Variant Configuration Language), the assets in product lines are structured to accept the variabilities using the frame technology, and the assets are customized by tool's interpreting the specification. Each software asset is represented by x-frame having the commands defined by XVCL and the specific system is created by customizing and composing the x-frames. In this approach the proprietary XVCL processor is required and the component developer or reuser should learn additionally the grammar of XVCL language. In addition, reuser has to construct the requirement with his own hands and should understand the internal structure and contents of code templates(x-frames).

Distinctions among GenVoca, XVCL and our approach are summarized in table 2.

5.2 Pros and Cons

In this section, the advantages and the limitations of our approach are presented.

5.2.1 Advantages

Our approach has the following advantages in building the core assets in component-oriented software product lines:

• *More abstract view of component*

Because target component is viewed through the feature diagram, more abstract model, the reusers can easily understand the semantic of the component to be reused without the knowledge of the internal implementation.

•*Modifiability of configuration rule and feature dependency*

To change the kind of implementation element to be included in generating the target component, only the configuration rule file should be modified. As well, due to separation of the feature dependency specification it can be modified easily.

•*Extensibility of Target Component*

To add the new functionality into the target component, we only have to develop and insert the new implementation element that follows the interfaces of the specific component category into its component category and modify the configuration rule.

Table 2. Comparisons among GenVoca, XVCL and our approach

Item	GenVoca	XVCL	Our Approach
Implementation Tech.	C++	XML / Java / JAXP	XML / Java / JAXP
Architecture	Layered Architecture	General Tree	Layered Architecture
Composition Method	Inheritance/Aggregation	Frame Technology	Inheritance/Aggregation
Form of Code Template	C++ template class	X-frames in XML (text + XVCL commands)	XSLT file (java code + XSLT elements)
Form of Variation point	parameter of C++ template class	XVCL commands	XSLT elements
Method of Requirement Input	program with reuser's own hands	requirement in XML with reuser's own hands (SPC)	feature configuration with feature modeling tool
Resolver of Variation point	C++ Compiler	proprietary XVCL processor	XSLT processor
Form of Generated Component	C++ Binary Code	Java source code (feasible in any type of software documents)	Java source code

•*Extensibility of generation process*

It is easy to extend to generation process by integrating the additional code into XSLT script file, such as the component testing code.

5.2.2 Limitations

Our approach has the following limitations:

•*Complexity in Component Family Construction*

To construct the component family in our approach, a lot of specification and code templates should be developed. This process could be assisted by additional tools.

•*Limitation in Component Architecture*

Architecture of our component is limited to GenVoca architecture and is composed only via inheritance/aggregation. More research is required to solve this problem.

•*Inflexibility in Changeable Domain*

To add new features or delete the existing features we should modify a lot of documents such as feature model, corresponding specifications and code templates. So, our approach should be more valuable in stable software development environment. This problem can be resolved by various tools.

6 Conclusion and Future Work

Software product lines paradigm is to facilitate more strategic reuse by predicting and analyzing the variabilities and commonalities among the members of software family at early stage of software lifecycle. This paper proposes an automatic component reconfiguration tool that could be applied in constructing the component-based software product lines. Our tool accepts the reuser's requirement via a feature model and makes the feature configuration from which it generates the source code of the reconfigured component. To accomplish this process, the component family has the architecture of GenVoca. In addition, XSLT scripts provide the code templates for implementation elements. Taking the 'Bank Account' component family as our example, we showed that our tool produced automatically the specific component source code that the reuser wants to create. The result of this paper should be applied extensively for increasing the productivity of building the software product lines. Future works include applying our approach to more large-scaled software and developing the various tools to assist the component family construction process.

References

1. Clements, P., Northrop, L.: Software Product Lines: Practices and Patterns", Addison-Wesley (2002)
2. Atkinson, C. et al. : Component-based Product Line Engineering with UML, Addison-Wesley (2002)
3. Bailin, S.: KAPTUR: A Tool for the Preservation and Use of Engineering Legacy, CTA Inc., Rockville, MD (1992)
4. Reenskaug, T., Wold, P., Lehne, O. A.: Working with Objects: OOram Software Engineering Method, Manning Publications Co. (1996)
5. Frakes, W., Prieto-Diaz, R., Fox, C.: DARE: Domain Analysis and Reuse Environment", (1996)
6. Griss, M., Favaro, J., d'Alessandro, M.: Integrating Feature Modeling with the RSEB, Proc. of 5th International Conference of Software Reuse (1998)
7. Kang, K., Cohen, S., Hess, J., Nowak, W., Peterson, S.: Feature-Oriented Domain Analysis(FODA) Feasibility Study, Technical Report, CMU/SEI-90-TR-21, Software Engineering Institute, Carnegie Mellon University (1990)
8. Czarnecki, K., Eisenecker, U. W.: Generative Programming: Methods, Tools, and Applications, Addison-Wesley (2000)
9. Biggerstaff, T. J.: A Characterization of Generator and Component Reuse Technologies, Proceedings of Third International Conference, GCSE(Generative and Component-Based Software Engineering), Erfurt, Germany (2001)
10. Cleaveland, J. C.: Program Generators with XML and Java, Prentice Hall (2001)
11. Zhang, H., Jarzabek, S., Swe, S. M.: XVCL Approach to Separating Concerns in Product Family Assets, Proceedings of Third International Conference, GCSE(Generative and Component-Based Software Engineering), (2001) 36-47
12. Thiel, S., Hein, A.: Systematic Integration of Variability into Product Line Architecture Design", SPLC2 2002, LNCS 2379, Springer-Verlag (2002) 130-153
13. Batory, D., et al.: The GenVoca Model of Software-System Generators, IEEE Software (1994) 89-94
14. Batory, D., Chen, G., Robertson, E., Wang, T.: Design Wizards and Visual Programming Environments for GenVoca Generators, IEEE Transactions on Software engineering (2000) 441-452
15. Soe, M.S., Zhang, H., Jarzabek, S.: XVCL: A Tutorial, Proc. 14th International Conference on Software Engineering and Knowledge Engineering (SEKE'02), ACM Press (2002) 341-349
16. Jarzabek, S., Li, S.: Eliminating Redundancies with a Composition with Adaptation Meta-programming Technique, Proc. ESEC-FSE'03, ACM Press, (2003) 237-246

Generating Multidimensional Schemata from Relational Aggregation Queries

Chaoyi Pang[1], Kerry Taylor[1], Xiuzhen Zhang[2], and Mark Cameron[1]

[1] CSIRO ICT Centre and Preventative Health National Flagship Program, Australia
{chaoyi.pang, kerry.taylor, mark.cameron}@csiro.au
[2] School of Computer Science & IT, RMIT University, Australia
zhang@cs.rmit.edu.au

Abstract. Queries on operational databases can be viewed as a form of business rules on data warehouse schema design. We propose to use such queries to automatically generate measures, dimensions and dimension hierarchies and their representation in a star schema. The schema produced with our approach has good properties such as non-redundant dimensional attributes and orthogonality among dimensions and can answer many more queries than just those it was generated from.

1 Introduction

The multidimensional model has proven extremely successful in data warehouse and On-line Analytical Processing (OLAP) applications. OLAP applications are dominated by analytical queries: rather than retrieving detailed information from a data repository about individual transactions, the main concern is to retrieve summaries of data. Designing a multidimensional schema involves deciding (1) the dimensions and attributes describing each dimension, (2) the aggregation hierarchy for the dimensions, and (3) the measure attributes and their dependent dimensions. Most current methods on schema design, such as [5], start the design process with requirements analysis and specification, then conceptual design, logical design, and finally physical design. In contrast, we treat summary queries over a source schema as the statement of requirements, and automatically derive the logical design. Our rationale is that, when collecting requirements for designing data warehouses, stakeholders can more easily formulate the knowledge or analysis they are expecting as queries over existing data resources, rather than by describing a view of the enterprise business process or research needs.

Our motivation for researching this problem is stimulated by the following observations in practice:

- Designing a multidimensional schema is difficult. Complex business processes make it hard to achieve an accurate overall picture of an enterprise to understand data analysis needs. As an alternative to the phase of requirement collection and business rules analysis employed in data warehouse design, we use the schemas and analytical queries of conventional databases as a proxy

X. Zhou et al. (Eds.): WISE 2004, LNCS 3306, pp. 584–589, 2004.
© Springer-Verlag Berlin Heidelberg 2004

for a specialist designer. A significant feature of this approach is that queries can be composed easily by business analysts and database developers with little expertise in data warehouse design.
- The schemas and analytical queries on the conventional database are essential elements in building any data warehouse. Generally, the schemas imply functional dependencies among attributes which suggest hierarchical structures within dimensions and can be used to eliminate unprofitable redundancy. In practice, functional dependencies and referential constraints are stored in system tables as metadata and may be readily available. Queries, on the other hand, associate raw data in the conventional database with the manipulated data in the data warehouse. They identify the desired application scope.
- OLAP applications are a data driven exercise where the requirements for the output often evolve as the data is extracted. Moreover, such applications are characterized by the use of many similar and repeated queries. When new demands occur, our design methodology can evolve the previously generated schemata into new schemata by integrating the new queries interpreted from the demands [12].

2 Our Method

We analyze the attributes from the given relational queries and the dependency relationships among them to design a schema with good properties such as non-redundant dimensional attributes and orthogonality among dimensions. Our designed schema can answer the queries that it was generated from and has the minimal number of dimensions for an aggregation. Furthermore, the schema can answer many more queries other than the given ones.

In the following, we compare a hand-designed schema with an automatically generated one for a running example. Our theoretical results can be explained through the following observations: (i) all the dimensional attributes are relevant; (ii) the dimensional hierarchies are properly described; (iii) aggregation-dimension relationships are defined precisely; and, as a result, (iv) aggregation-dimension relationships are non-redundant. In fact, these observations are inherited from the following properties: (1) the schema can answer the generating queries; (2) the schema can answer many more additional queries; (3) the total number of attributes in the dimensions is minimal (counting the attributes in a hierarchy relation as one attribute); and (4) the number of dimensions for aggregation is minimal. Properties (1) and (2) imply a query reuse capability of the obtained schema. Property (3) indicates that if an attribute in a dimension is removed then there is a query amongst the given queries which could not be answered from the computed schema. Property (4) indicates that any two dimensions for the same aggregation are *orthogonal* [9], which is a key design criteria for an efficient data warehouse.

We need the following steps to build a multidimensional schema from a set of queries: we first use the proposed *measure dependency* to represent each aggregate query over a source schema; then apply the *transformations* to associate the "relevant" measure dependencies together so that they can be treated in the same cube of the multidimensional schema; and lastly apply functional dependencies to define dimensions and dimensional hierarchies in a cube. Two transformations are introduced: a *referential* transformation and a *join* transformation that relies on functional dependency and recognizing query equivalence. There exist polynomial time algorithms for computing the closure of functional dependencies and recognizing query equivalence that apply [1,7]. By using the dependency relations and referential constraints between attributes, we have developed a method within a cube to determine the dimensional attributes and to group them into dimensional hierarchies.

3 Related Work

To the best of our knowledge, this is the first paper that designs data warehouse schemata using queries on a conventional database. We are not aware of any papers that use the dependency relationship and referential constraints to associate queries in designing a multidimensional schema.

Our method generalizes the procedure used in OLAP products such as Cognos, Business Objects and MicroStrategy, where a single query over a relational database is used to generate a specific, single-purpose multidimensional schema. Our idea on transformation rules for queries is different to the one used in materialized view advisors on the existing commercial products such as those from Oracle and IBM: Their methods are based on the existing data warehouse schema and extract views either to flood the schema or to materialize for efficient computation. [11] is based on the data warehouse cube.

Recently, materialized views have been explored extensively to provide massive improvements in query processing time, especially for aggregation queries over large databases [2,3,4]. These methods rely on the source database remaining intact for complete query answering, but they supplement the database with derived data to speed up query processing. This is very different from our method in which we aim to define a new data warehouse schema, with good design properties, against which data warehouse queries may be addressed without ongoing reference to the source data for query answering. Having designed the data warehouse, methods for view materialization might be applied to choose a population and maintenance strategy for the data warehouse, taking account of space efficiency and view maintenance costs.

To ensure a good design, papers such as [8,9,10] propose a *multidimensional normal form* for schema design. The normal form is used for reasoning about the quality of a schema to reduce redundancy, diminish sparsity and to retain summarizability. Sparsity relates to the dimension orthogonality, which, in turn, can be reflected by the existence of a functional dependency. We will use some of these concepts in our schema design.

4 Running Example

In the following, we use a running example to briefly describe our result on schema design. Refer to [13] for the detailed illustration and algorithm.

Table 1. A banking relational database

Branch(*branchNo*, bstreetAddress, bCity)
LoanManager(*empNo*, empName, phone, branchNo)
Customer(*custNo*, custName, profession, streetAddress, city, state)
Account(*accNo*, accType, balance,aDate, custNo)
LoanContract(*conNo*, loantype, amount, cDate, empNo, custNo)

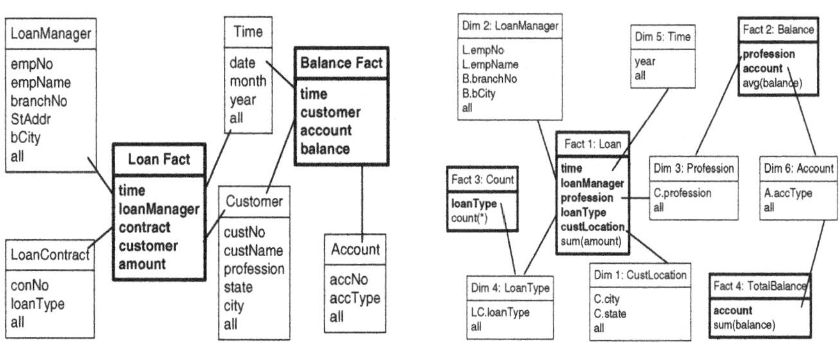

Fig. 1. The star schema: (1) by hand; (2) by queries.

We study the operational banking database as shown in Table 1, where the primary keys for each relation are underlined. Some sample queries and their SQL equivalents are given in Table 2. On one hand, we generate the warehouse schema of Figure 1(1) manually by the data warehouse design process recommended in a standard text [6]. We use the sample queries to indicate the application scope for that design. On the other hand we can design the warehouse schema directly from the queries. We therefore automatically derive the star schema of Figure 1(2) by using our method with the queries in Table 2. By assessing the two generated schemata, we have the following comments . First, the irrelevant dimensional attributes in Figure 1(1) result in poor dimension hierarchies and data redundancy in facts and dimensions; the automatically generated schemata does not include the redundant attributes such as branchName, Month, accNo and cusNo in Figure 1(1). These attributes are not referred to in any given queries and therefore they are considered inappropriate to the application scope. Including many irrelevant attributes in the dimensions could cause inefficient query execution and data storage. Moreover, due to the existence of irrelevant attributes

Table 2. Aggregation queries on the banking database.

Q1 : The total loan in 2002.

```
select sum(LC.amount)
from LoanContract LC
where LC.cDate = 2002
```

Q2 : For the types of loans with more than 10 loan contracts, the type of loan and the number of contracts.

```
select LC.loantype, count(*)
from LoanContract LC
group by LC.loantype
having count(*) > 10
```

Q3 : For each loan type, and each city and state where customers resides, the total loan amount in 2002.

```
select C.city,C.state,C.loanType,
       sum(LC.amount)
from LoanContract LC, Customer C
where LC.custNo = C.custNo and
      LC.cDate = 2002
group by C.city,C.state,C.loanType
```

Q4 : For each type of loan and each customer profession, list the total loan amount.

```
select LC.loanType,C.profession, sum(LC.amount)
from LoanContract LC, Customer C
where LC.custNo = C.custNo
group by LC.loanType,C.profession
```

Q5 : The performance (total loan amount) of each loan manager in 2002.

```
select L.empNo,L.empName,sum(LC.amount)
from LoanContract LC, LoanManager L
where LC.empNo = L.empNo and LC.cDate ≥
      2002 and LC.cDate < 2003
group by L.empNo, L.empName
```

Q6 : The total loan amount of each branch.

```
select B.branchNo, sum(LC.amount)
from Branch B, LoanManager L, LoanContract LC
where B.branchNo = L.branchNo and
      L.empNo = LC.empNo
group by B.branchNo
```

Q7 : The overall performance of each customer profession and account type.

```
select A.accType,C.profession,avg(A.balance)
from Account A, Customer C
where A.custNo = C.custNo
group by A.accType, C.profession
```

Q8 : The total loan amount for each branch and city

```
select B.bCity, B.branchNo, sum(LC.amount)
from Branch B, LoanManager L,
     LoanContract C
where B.branchNo = L.branchNo and
      L.empNo = LC.empNo
group by B.bCity, B.branchNo
```

Q9 : The average balance for each customer profession.

```
select C.profession, avg(A.balance)
from Account A, Customer C
where A.custNo = C.custNo
group by C.profession
```

Q10 : The total balance for each account type.

```
select A.accType, sum(A.balance)
from Account A
group by A.accType
```

in Figure 1(1), the dimension hierarchies of Figure 1(1) are not described properly. For example, the "Customer" dimension of Figure 1(1) is represented as two dimensions in Figure 1(2), CustomerLocation and CustomerProfession. But from the aggregation hierarchy, we can see that they are orthogonal, being two disjoint aggregation paths for the Customer dimension. cusNo and custName are not dimensional attributes in Figure 1(2). These differences mean that the design of Figure 1(2) is more compact than that of Figure 1(1). Secondly, the vague Aggregation-Dimension relationships of Figure 1(1) causes redundancy. For example, Figure 1(1) describes the dependency of the Balance measure on the Time, Customer and Account dimensions in general, leading to redundancy in the fact table due to unrelated attributes in one dimension table. Figure 1(2) describes this dependency more precisely: the Average of balance depends on the Customer Profession and Account, whereas the Sum of balance depends on the Account dimension only. Lastly, even though the queries used to generate the schema are quite simple, the obtained schema supports more complicated queries. For example, it can handle a query for "the best loan manager each year", where he is the one with the largest contract value sum.

5 Conclusion

Our future work is to improve and extend this work in several ways: to address a wider class of queries including disjunctive queries; to merge some similar dimension tables; to subdivide some attributes in order to create new measures; to capture multi-database dependencies; to automatically populate the automatically-built schema from the source database; and, more importantly, to evaluate our approach in the real world.

Acknowledgements. We would like to thank the anonymous referees for their very helpful remarks.

References

1. C. Chekuri and A. Rajaraman. Conjunctive query containment revisited. In *6th Int. Conference on Database Theory; LNCS 1186*, pages 56–70, Delphi, Greece, 1997.
2. D. W. Cheung, B. Zhou, B. Kao, H. Lu, T. W. Lam, and H. F. Ting. Requirement-based data cube schema design. In *Proc. of the 8th Intl. Conf. on Information and knowledge management*, pages 162–169. ACM Press, 1999.
3. R. Chirkova, A. Y. Halevy, and D. Suciu. A formal perspective on the view selection problem. *The VLDB Journal*, 11(3):216–237, 2002.
4. J. Goldstein and P.-Å. Larson. Optimizing queries using materialized views: a practical, scalable solution. *SIGMOD Record*, 30(2):331–342, June 2001.
5. B. Husemann, J. Lechtenborger, and G. Vossen. Conceptual data warehouse modeling. In *Design and Management of Data Warehouses*, page 6, 2000.
6. R. Kimball. *The Data Warehouse Toolkit.* John Wiley and Sons, 1996.
7. P. G. Kolaitis and M. Y. Vardi. Conjunctive-query containment and constraint satisfaction. In *Proc. of the 17th ACM SIGACT-SIGMOD-SIGART symposium on Principles of database systems*, pages 205–213. ACM Press, 1998.
8. J. Lechtenb rger and G. Vossen. Multidimensional normal forms for data warehouse design. *Information Systems*, 28(5):415–434, 2003.
9. W. Lehner, J. Albrecht, and H. Wedekind. Normal forms for multidimensional databases. In *10th Intl Conf. on Scientific and Statistical Database Management, Proc., Capri, Italy, July 1-3, 1998*, pages 63–72. IEEE Computer Society, 1998.
10. H.-J. Lenz and A. Shoshani. Summarizability in OLAP and statistical data bases. In *Statistical and Scientific Database Management*, pages 132–143, 1997.
11. T. Niemi, J. Nummenmaa, and P. Thanisch. Constructing OLAP cubes based on queries. In *Proc. of the 4th ACM international workshop on Data warehousing and OLAP*, pages 9–15. ACM Press, 2001.
12. C. Pang, K. Taylor, and X. Zhang. Multidimensional schema evolution from aggregation queries. *CSIRO ICT Centre, Technical Report*, 03(186), 2003.
13. C. Pang, K. Taylor, X. Zhang, and M. Cameron. Generating multidimensional schema from aggregation queries. *CSIRO Mathematical and Information Sciences Technical Report*, 2003.

Semantics Based Conformance Assessment of ebXML Business Processes*

Yi Luo[1], Zhiyong Peng[1], Zhe Shan[2], and Qing Li[2]

[1] State Key Lab of Software Engineering, Computer School,
Wuhan University, Wuhan, China
luo_guo02@hotmail.com, peng@whu.edu.cn

[2] Department of Computer Engineering and Information Technology,
City University of Hong Kong, Kowloon, Hong Kong
zshan0@cityu.edu.hk, itqli@cityu.edu.hk

Abstract. In the business world, the acceptance of a contract often lies beyond the agreement on price and quality of products. The conformance of respective business processes plays a significant role in the collaboration of business partners. Today, e-commerce standards such as ebXML have enabled enterprises to collaborate in the business process level. However, there is little work on the study of conformance assessment (also called matchmaking in some works) of business processes. Moreover, these e-commerce standards are syntactic rather than semantic, in which semantic constraints on interactions are represented informally. In this paper, we extend the ebXML specifications to support the semantics based conformance assessment of business processes, which transforms XML into RDF via the Semantic Web technology. The conformance criteria are mapped to OWL. The semantics based conformance criteria are defined. Furthermore, we extend the ebXML architecture by adding a conformance assessment agent to support the conformance assessment of business processes when searching the potential business partners. With its help, appropriate business partners can be discovered for the client as desired.

1 Introduction

Internet is bringing profound changes to the business world and has enabled a new way of conducting commerce - e-commerce. Through web, enterprises can lookup appropriate business partners, negotiate commodity prices and manage to obtain an e-contract. However, an agreement of a business contract lies beyond these. The conformance of respective business processes ahead of e-contract is one of key factors in the success of business cooperations, which can reduce the cost of negotiation and can also improve business efficiency in e-commerce.

* This research is supported by State Key Lab of Software Engineering (Wuhan University, China) under grant: SKLSE03-01, NSFC (National Natural Science Foundation of China) (60273072), National 863 Project (2002AA423450), Research Fund for the Doctoral Program of Higher Education (20010486029) and Hubei Natural Science Foundation for the Distinguished Youth (2002AC003).

X. Zhou et al. (Eds.): WISE 2004, LNCS 3306, pp. 590–595, 2004.
© Springer-Verlag Berlin Heidelberg 2004

ebXML[5] provides a well-defined infrastructure enabling enterprises to collaborate at the business process level. However, there is little work on the study of conformance assessment of business processes in ebXML area; what's more, they are based on XML technology, so the functions provided are primarily syntactic.

In this paper, we describe an application of Semantic Web [1] to extend the framework of ebXML and support the conformance assessment of business processes via introducing the conformance assessment agent(CAA). The related ebXML information described in XML are extended to the formal semantic constraints via extending XML description to RDF[11] description & OWL[10] ontology, whose advantages include that the conformance assessment is formally based on semantic assessment and the evaluation result is more precise.

The remainder of the paper is organized as follows. Section 2 defines conformances on content level, which is the basis of conformance assessment. Section 3 presents how to assess the conformance on process level. Section 4 shows the extended framework of ebXML for the conformance assessment and describes the assessment steps in it. Related works are discussed in Section 5, and Section 6 concludes the paper with our future work intentions.

2 Content-Based Conformance

Within ebXML, definition of business processes (BPSS)[8] of collaboration parties and involved documents, which will be exchanged in the collaboration, are both described in XML Schemata. In order to introduce the semantic extension in ebXML, we utilize RDF to model the information and OWL to express conformance criteria against these RDF description.

Since content-based conformance is the basis of conformance assessment, we first give the definitions of content-based conformance.

Definition 1. *Assume elements x and y. If x is equivalent-concept or sub-concept of y; x is said to be semantically compatible with y, termed as $x \doteq y$.*[1]

Definition 2. *Assume S is one party of a binary collaboration; $S(x)$ means that x is the document of S, who is the responding party, and $S(\overline{x})$ means that x is the document of S who is the requesting party. S_1 is said to be* ***Document Conformable*** *to S_2, (i.e. the document specification of party S_1 is compatible with that of party S_2), iff (i)In a TransactionActivity $S_1(x)$, $S_2(\overline{y})$, and $x \doteq y$; or (ii)In a NonTransactionActivity $S_1(x)$, $S_2(y)$, and $x \doteq y$; or $S_1(\overline{x})$, $S_2(\overline{y})$, and $x \doteq y$.*

Definition 3. *A RequestingActivity a_1 of the requesting party S_1 is said to be* ***Activity Conformable*** *to a RespondingActivity a_2 of the responding party S_2, iff for the documents that may be exchanged by them, S_1 is document conformable to S_2; and $a_1 \doteq a_2$, where a_1 is the activity of S_1, and a_2 is the activity of S_2.*

[1] Note that here the semantic relationship between x and y is non-inverse, i.e., $x \doteq y$ is different from $y \doteq x$.

If one document of one collaboration party specifies the quotation of product - ERP, while the corresponding document of another party specifies the quotation service - Enterprise System that is different from ERP. However, ERP is semantically compatible with Enterprise System in the practical scenario. In order to express this compatibility, a special conformance document in XML should be given against the traditional XML descriptions, which is time-consuming and inflexible. Now, if we transfer the XML description to RDF description, some formal and accurate ontology based on the elements or properties in RDF could be specified in OWL, in which the involved information are described in accurate concepts and relationship of these concepts. ERP *vs.* Enterprise System above would be described in **subClassOf** relationship. These ontology will be stored in an ontology repository, and can be processed by an OWL reasoner.

3 Process-Based Conformance

The interconnection of activities embodies the procedure of business actions. If two business parties have the business processes which are semantically compatible with each other, they can have a successful collaboration. This is called *Structure Conformance.*

In ebXML, transitions among activities are expressed as some normal transitions or pseudo states. We use combinators to formally express these transitions in definition 4, of which, ';' means two connected activities are sequential, '&' means two activities are executed in parallel, '|' means only one activity can be chosen to run, and '!' means the loop execution of the activity(s).

Definition 4. *A process $P(a_1 c_1 a_2 \ldots a_k)$ is composed of a set of activities or subprocesses $(a_1, a_2, \ldots)$, which are connected by combinators $c_1, c_2, \ldots$, such as ';', '&', '|', and '!'. The term $P \xrightarrow{a} Q$ stands for that a process P transforms to another process Q after executing activity a.*

We next give the conformance ontology in the process level.

1. $a_1; a_2$ of Party A is said to be semantically compatible with $a'_1 x a'_2$ Party B (where x stands for a combinator or a set of activities and combinators), if there exists a path from a'_1 to a'_2, a_1 is *activity conformable* to a'_1, and a_2 is activity conformable to a'_2.
2. $a_1; a_2$ of Party A who acts as the requesting role is said to be semantically compatible with $a'_1 \& a'_2$ of Party B who acts as the responding role, if a_1 is *activity conformable* to a'_1 and a_2 is activity conformable to a'_2.
3. $a_1 \mid a_2$ of Party A is said to be semantically compatible with $a'_1 \mid a'_2$ of Party B, if a_1 is activity-conformable to a'_1 or a_2 is *activity conformable* to a'_2.
4. $!a$ of Party A who acts as the requesting role is said to be responding role is said to be semantically compatible with a', if a is *activity conformable* to a'.

Definition 5. *A process P_1 of Party A and a process P_2 of Party B satisfied the binary relation $\mathcal{S}$, termed as $P_1 \mathcal{S} P_2$, iff P_1 and P_2 are semantically conformable with each other.*[2]

[2] The form of this definition originates from the simulation definition of the $\pi - calculus$, see e.g. [4].

Definition 6. *A process P_1 of Party A is said to be Structure Conformable to a process P_2 of Party B, iff $P_1 \mathcal{S} P_2$ and $\forall P_1 \xrightarrow{m} P_1' : \exists P_2 \xrightarrow{n} P_2' : P_1' \mathcal{S} P_2'$.*

Example 1. Party P_1 provides a process $A_1; B_1; C_1; D_1; H_1; E_1; F_1$. And Party P_2 supports the process $A_2; B_2; C_2; D_2 \& (E_2; G_2); F_2$.
Now $A_1 vs. A_2, B_1 vs. B_2, C_1 vs. C_2, D_1 vs. D_2, E_1 vs. E_2, F_1 vs. F_2$ are activity-conformable to each other, and in P_1 H_1 is an activity that is disrelated to any activities in P_2, likewise, in P_2 G_2 is an activity that is disrelated to any activities in P_1.
We can say that $A_1 \mathcal{S} A_2$ via Definition 5.
Since $A_1 \xrightarrow{a_1} B_1$ and $A_2 \xrightarrow{a_2} B_2$, then $B_1 \mathcal{S} B_2$ can be deduced via Definition 6;
Similarly, since $B_1 \mathcal{S} B_2$, $B_1 \xrightarrow{b_1} C_1$ and $B_2 \xrightarrow{b_2} C_2$, then $C_1 \mathcal{S} C_2$;
Since $C_1 \mathcal{S} C_2$, $C_1 \xrightarrow{c_1} (D_1; H_1; E_1)$, $C_2 \xrightarrow{c_2} (D_2 \& E_2)$ (where H_1 can be ignored), and by item 2 in conformance ontology in process level, $(D_1; H_1; E_1)$ is semantically compatible with $(D_2 \& E_2)$, then we can say $(D_1; H_1; E_1) \mathcal{S} (D_2 \& E_2)$;
Since $(D_1; H_1; E_1) \xrightarrow{e_1} F_1$, $(D_2 \& E_2) \xrightarrow{e_2; g_2} F_2$ (where G_2 can be ignored), then $F_1 \mathcal{S} F_2$.
The result of conformance assessment of Party P_1 and Party P_2 is: P_1 matches (i.e. structurally conformable to) P_2.

4 Extended Framework of ebXML for Conformance Assessment

In this section, we present the extended framework of ebXML supporting conformance assessment of business processes, which can be seen in Figure 1.

In Figure 1, dashed line steps stand for the phrases included in the original framework of ebXML. Steps 1, 2 and 3 consist of the implementation phase. Steps 9 and 10 stand for Discovery and Negotiation Phase, and Steps 11 is the real transaction phase. These steps is beyond this paper, so we do not describe them in detail.

As shown in Figure 1, CAA is add into the ebXML framework as an intermediate layer. In this extended framework, CAA interacts with two parties, namely, the client who is requesting the conformance business information and ebXML registry servers. The functional procedure of CAA, which is indicated by solid lines in Figure 1, includes the following steps :

1. **(Step 4)** As the ebXML Registry Servers are accessible to the public, Organization B, who is requesting the conformance assessment service, can also browse the registry. In particular, Organization B searches relevant business categories, and finds the common business terms and other concepts in its industry.
2. **(Step 5)** In order to find the most suitable partners to collaborate, Organization B contacts with CAA to request a conformance assessment service. It submits the target information, self business profile and its process details to CAA.
3. **(Step 6)** After CAA receives the query, it searches the registry servers for the information of those companies which satisfy the target information from the client. Then, CAA gets the information (CPP) of target organizations. According to the reference referred in the CPPs of target organizations, CAA also gets other additional information, such as business process scenarios, which are used by the target organizations.

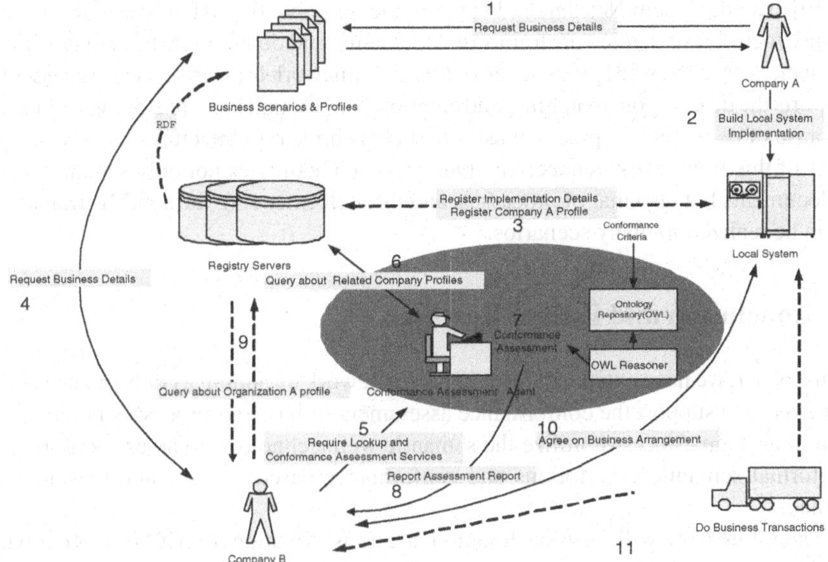

Fig. 1. Extended Framework Supporting Conformance Assessment

4. **(Step 7)** When all the necessary information is obtained, CAA assess the conformance between business process of Organization B and that of target organization one by one. The conformance assessment is directed under the predefined conformance criteria that is composed of some conformance ontology stored in the ontology repository in OWL, and is processed by an OWL reasoner.
5. **(Step 8)** As an outcome, an evaluation report is created by CAA, which records the assessment result. CAA submits the evaluation to the client organization at the end of the conformance assessment service.
6. **(Step 9)** After Organization B receives the result from CAA, it checks the report and decides the ideal business partners (e.g., Organization A). Then, it directly searches the registry server for the information of Organization A and starts to negotiate with Organization A for further work.

5 Related Work

ebXML is a recent focus of web services technology [2,6,12]. These works focus more on the interconnection between ebXML specification and local business systems. [7] is a recently released work for the matching issue of business processes in ebXML. The author eliminate the prarallelism problem in matching business processes through transformation between activity diagrams and State Transition Systems(STS). However, this approach has too many restrictions, which includes that each activity may only consist of the exchange of one document, and any nest activities must be decomposed into the atomic activities firstly, etc. All these restrictions are infeasible in most actual business cases.

[9] extends RosettaNet standard via introducing semantics to the Nile system, which mainly focus on semantic constraints of documents, and do not indicate semantic match of business processes. [3] proposes an ontology framework for web service processes that supports the description, matching, and composition through logic reasoning techniques. Because of deficiency in practical aspects such as broker architectures and tools, feasibility of this framework is uncertain. Our approach addresses not only semantic match of documents but also that of processes, and through extending the ebXML framework, it can be realized in many scenarios.

6 Conclusion and Future Research

In this paper, we have extended the ebXML framework by adding a conformance assessment agent to support the conformance assessment of business processes in the partner searching stage. Since we utilize the semantic web technology to assess conformance, the formal semantic descriptions and conformance based on semantic reasoning are formed.

Our future work will focus on the automatic transformation from XML to RDF, which would enhance the generality of our approach, and make our approach evolutionary, given that it accepts ebXML in its current form.

References

1. Berners-Lee, T., Hendler, J., Lassila, and O. The semantic web. *Scientific American*, 2001.
2. Qiming Chen, Meichun Hsu, and V. Mehta. How public conversation management integrated with local business process management. In *IEEE International Conference on E-Commerce, 2003. CEC 2003.*, pages 199–206, 2003.
3. C.Pahl and M. Casey. Ontology support for web service processes. *ACM SIGSOFT Software Engineering Notes*, 28, 2003.
4. D.Sangiorgi and D.Walker. The $\pi - calculus$ - a theory of mobil processes. *Cambridge University Press*, 2001.
5. ebXML. http://ebxml.org/.
6. HyoungDo Kim. Conceptual modeling and specification generation for b2b business processes based on ebxml. *SIGMOD Rec.*, 31(1):37–42, 2002.
7. Dennis Krukkert. Matching of ebXML business process. Technical Report IST-28584-OX-D2.3-v.2.0, TNO-FEL E-Business, 2003.
8. Business Process Project Team. www.ebxml.org/specs/ebbpss.pdf, 2001.
9. David Trastour, Chris Preist, and Derek Coleman. Using semantic web technology to enhance current business-to-business integration approaches. In *Proceedings of the Seventh IEEE International Enterprise Distributed Object Computing Conference (EDOC03)*, 2003.
10. W3C. http://www.w3.org/tr/2004/rec-owl-features-20040210/, 2004.
11. W3C. http://www.w3.org/tr/2004/rec-rdf-concepts-20040210/, 2004.
12. K. Yano, H. Hara, and S. Uehara. Collaboration management framework for integrating b-to-b and internal processes. In *Proceedings of Sixth International Enterprise Distributed Object Computing Conference*, pages 75–83, 2002.

Usage Scenarios and Goals for Ontology Definition Metamodel[1]

Lewis Hart[1], Patrick Emery[1], Robert Colomb[2], Kerry Raymond[3], Dan Chang[4], Yiming Ye[5], Elisa Kendall[6], and Mark Dutra[6]

[1] AT&T Government Solutions, Inc., {lewishart, patemery}@att.com
[2] School of Information Technology and Electrical Engineering, The University of Queensland, colomb@itee.uq.edu.au
[3] DSTC Pty Ltd, kerry@dstc.com
[4] IBM Silicon Valley Lab, Santa Jose California, dtchang@us.ibm.com
[5] IBM Watson Research Center, Hawthorne, New York
[6] Sandpiper Software, Inc., {ekendall,mdutra}@sandsoft.com

Abstract. This paper contains a taxonomy of the uses of ontologies, intended as motivation for the Ontology Definition Metamodel development effort by the Object Management Group. It describes several usage scenarios for ontologies and proposes example applications for use in these scenarios. Many of the scenarios and applications are based on efforts currently underway in industry and academia. The scenarios descriptions are followed by goals for the Ontology Definition Metamodel.

1 Introduction

Ontology is a philosophical concept which was introduced into computing by the Artificial Intelligence community to describe data models which were conceptually independent of specific applications. Over the past decade the term has introduced into several other branches of computing where there is a need to model data independently of applications. With the advent of the semantic web movement [1] and the consequent development of ontology modeling languages like OWL by the W3C, the development of ontologies has become mainstream. Consequently, in 2003 the Object Management Group issued a Request for Proposal for an Ontology Development Metamodel, for a Meta-Object Facility (MOF-2) metamodel intended to support

- development of ontologies using UML modeling tools
- Implementation of ontologies in the W3C Web Ontology language OWL
- forward and reverse engineering for ontologies

---

[1] The work reported in this paper has been funded in part by the Cooperative Research Centres Program through the Department of the Prime Minister and Cabinet of the Commonwealth Government of Australia, and funded in part through the United States Government Defense Advanced Research Program Office's DAML program.

X. Zhou et al. (Eds.): WISE 2004, LNCS 3306, pp. 596–607, 2004.
© Springer-Verlag Berlin Heidelberg 2004

The authors of this paper were the original team established by the original submitters to the RFP, who are working together to develop a draft standard scheduled for delivery to the OMG in late 2004.

Early in the process, the team realized that there was not a comprehensive analysis of what ontologies were and what they were used for. Such an analysis is essential in development of any software, so our first step was to develop a usage scenarios and goals document (to use OMG terminology).

The usage scenarios presented herein highlight characteristics of ontologies that represent important design considerations for ontology-based applications. They also motivate some of the features and functions of the ODM and provide insight into when users can limit the expressivity of their ontologies to a description logics based approach, as well as when additional expressivity, for example from first order logic, might be needed. This set of examples is not intended to be exhaustive. Rather, the goal is to provide sufficiently broad coverage of the kinds of applications the ODM is intended to support that ODM users can make informed decisions when choosing what parts of the ODM to implement to meet their development requirements and goals.

This analysis can be compared with a similar analysis performed by the W3C Web Ontology Working Group [3]. We believe that the six use cases and eight goals considered in [3] provide additional, and in some cases overlapping, examples, usage scenarios and goals for the ODM.

Table 1. Perspectives of applications that use ontologies that are considered in this analysis.

Perspective	*One Extreme*	*Other Extreme*
Level of Authoritativeness	Least authoritative, broader, shallowly defined ontologies	Most authoritative, narrower, more deeply defined ontologies
Source of Structure	Passive (Transcendent) – structure originates outside the system	Active (Immanent) – structure emerges from data or application
Degree of Formality	Informal, or primarily taxonomic	Formal, having rigorously defined types, relations, and theories or axioms
Model Dynamics	Read-only, ontologies are static	Volatile, ontologies are fluid and changing.
Instance Dynamics	Read-only, resource instances are static	Volatile, resource instances change continuously
Control / Degree of Manageability	Externally focused, public (little or no control)	Internally focused, private (full control)
Application Changeability	Static (with periodic updates)	Dynamic
Coupling	Loosely-coupled	Tightly-coupled
Integration Focus	Information integration	Application integration
Lifecycle Usage	Design Time	Run Time

2 Perspectives

In order to ensure a relatively complete representation of usage scenarios and their associated example applications, we evaluated the coverage by using a set of perspectives that characterize the domain. Table 1 provides an overview of these perspectives.

We found that these perspectives could be divided into two general categories, those that are model centric and those that are application centric. The model centric perspectives characterize the ontologies themselves and are concerned with the structure, formalism and dynamics of the ontologies, they are:

- Level of Authoritativeness – Least authoritative ontologies define a broad set of concepts, but to a limited level of detail while the most authoritative ontologies are likely to be the narrowest, defining limited numbers of concepts to a greater depth of detail. More authoritative ontologies will represent safer long term investments and thus are likely to be developed to a greater depth.
- SNOMED[2] is a very large and authoritative ontology. The periodic table of the elements is very authoritative, but small. However, it can be safely used as a component of larger ontologies in physics or chemistry. Ontologies used for demonstration or pedagogic purposes, like the Wine Ontology[3], are not very authoritative. Table 1 can be seen as an ontology which at present is not very authoritative.
- Source of Structure – The source of an ontologies structure can be defined by external sources (*transcendent*), or it can be defined by information internal to the data and using applications (*immanent*). SNOMED is a transcendent ontology defined by the various governing bodies of medicine. E-commerce exchanges are generally supported by transcendent ontologies. The set of topics used for searching a newsfeed are immanent, since they change as the news does.
- Degree of Formality – refers to the level of formality from a knowledge representation perspective, ranging from highly informal or taxonomic in nature, where the ontologies may be tree-like, involving inheritance relations, to semantic networks, which may include complex lattice relations but no formal axiom expressions, to ontologies containing both lattice relations and highly formal axioms that explicitly define concepts. SNOMED is taxonomic, while engineering ontologies like [2] are highly formal.
- Model Dynamics – Some ontologies tend to be stable, while others are likely to be modified dynamically by the agents or applications that use them. The periodic table of the elements is pretty stable, but an ontology supporting tax accounting in Australia would be pretty volatile at the model level.
- Instance Dynamics–refers to the degree that instances of classes in the information resources or knowledge bases that use the ontology change as a result of some action the application takes as it is running. The periodic table of the elements is stable at the instance level (eg particular elements) as well as the model level (eg classes like noble gasses or rare earths), while an ontology supporting an e-

[2] http://www.snomed.org

[3] http://www.w3.org/2001/sw/WebOnt/guide-src/wine.owl

commerce exchange would be volatile at the instance level but not at the model level.

Application centric perspectives are concerned with how application use and manipulate the ontologies, they are:

- Control / Degree of Manageability – refers to the scope of control of the application using one or more ontologies, and also of control over changes made in the ontologies or knowledge bases. The ontology evolution control may span organizations or operate inside a private firewall or VPN, For public ontologies there may be little to no control from an ontology evolution perspective. An e-commerce exchange may have a high degree of control over the product catalogs and terms of trade, but a low degree of control over value-added tax categories and payment regimes.
- Application Changeability – The ontologies may be applied statically, as they might be if used for database schema mapping, with periodic updates to support evolution in the schemas, or they may be applied dynamically, as in an application that composes web services at run time.
- Coupling – refers to the degree that the information resources or applications using the ontologies are coupled. In an e-commerce exchange the players are tightly coupled using the ontology, while different applications using the engineering mathematics ontology may have nothing at all in common at run time.
- Integration Focus – refers to the degree that the ontology is focused on the structure of messages implementing interoperability without regard for content (for example Electronic Data Interchange or EDI), application interoperability without regard to content (eg a shared database) or both (eg booksellers using publishers' product catalogs as ontologies focus on content as well as message structure).
- Lifecycle Usage – refers to the phase of a project life cycle in which the ontologies are used. This ranges from early design and analysis phases to being an active part of the application at run time. The engineering mathematics ontology would be used mainly in the design phase, while an e-commerce exchange may need to validate messages dynamically.

3 Usage Scenarios

As might be expected, some of these perspectives tend to correlate across different applications, forming application areas with similar characteristics. Our analysis, summarized in Table 2, has identified three major clusters of application types that share some set of perspective values:

- Business Applications are characterized by having transcendent source of structure, a high degree of formality and external control relative to nearly all users.
- Analytic Applications are characterized by highly changeable and flexible ontologies, using large collections of mostly read-only instance data.
- Engineering Applications are characterized by again having transcendent source of structure, but as opposed to business applications their users control them primarily internally and they are considered more authoritative.

Table 2. Usage scenario perspective values

Use Case Clusters		Characteristic Perspective Values									
		Model Centric					Application Centric				
	Description	Authoritativeness	Structure From	Formality	Model Dynamics	Instance Dynamics	Control	Changeability	Coupling	Focus	Life Cycle
2.1	**Business Applications**		**Outside**	**Formal**			**External**				
2.1.1	**Run-time Interoperation**	Least/Broad	Outside	Formal	Read-Only	Volatile	External	Static	Tight	Information	Real Time
2.1.2	**Application Generation**	Most/Deep	Outside	Formal	Read-Only	Read-Only	External	Static	Loose	Application	All
2.1.3	**Ontology Lifecycle**	Middle/ Broad& Deep	Outside	Semi-Formal Formal	Read-Only	Read-Only	External	Static	Tight	Information	Real Time
2.2	**Analytic Applications**				**Volatile**	**Read-Only**		**Dynamic**	**Flexible**		
2.2.1	**Emergent Property Discovery**	Broad & Deep	Inside	Informal	Volatile	Read-Only	Internal & External	Dynamic	Flexible	Information	Real Time
2.2.2	**Exchange of Complex Data Sets**	Broad & Deep	Inside	Informal	Volatile	Read-Only/ Volatile	Internal & External	Dynamic	Flexible	Information	Real Time
2.3	**Engineering Application**	**Broad & Deep**	**Outside**				**Internal**				
2.3.1	**Information System Development**	Broad & Deep	Outside	Semi-Formal Formal	Read-Only	Volatile	Internal	Changeable	Tight	Information	Design Time
2.3.2	**Ontology Engineering**	Broad & Deep	Outside	Semi-Formal Formal	Volatile	Volatile	Internal	Changeable	Flexible	???	Design Time

4 Business Applications

4.1 Run Time Interoperation

Externally focused information interoperability applications are typically characterized by strong de-coupling of the components realizing the applications. They are focused specifically on information rather than application integration (and here we include some semantic web service applications, which may involve composition of vocabularies, services and processes but not necessarily APIs or database schemas). Because the community using them must agree upon the ontologies in advance, their application tends to be static in nature rather than dynamic.

Perspectives that drive characterization of these scenarios include:

- The level of authoritativeness of the ontologies and information resources.
- The amount of control that community members have on the ontology and knowledge base evolution
- Whether or not there is a design time component to ontology development and usage
- Whether or not the knowledge bases and information resources that implement the ontologies are modified at run time (since the source of structure remains relatively unchanged in these cases, or the ontologies are only changed in a highly controlled, limited manner).

These applications may require mediation middleware that leverages the ontologies and knowledge bases that implement them, potentially on either side of the firewall – in next generation web services and electronic commerce architectures as well as in other cross-organizational applications, for example:

- For semantically grounded information interoperability, supporting highly distributed, intra- and inter-organizational environments with dynamic participation of potential community members, (as when multiple emergency services organizations come together to address a specific crisis), with diverse and often conflicting organizational goals.
- For semantically grounded discovery and composition of information and computing resources, including Web services (applicable in business process integration and grid computing).
- In electronic commerce exchange applications based on stateful protocols such as EDI or Z39.50, where there are multiple players taking roles performing acts by sending and receiving messages whose content refers to a common world.

In these cases, we envision a number of agents and/or applications interoperating with one another using fully specified ontologies. Support for query interoperation across multiple, heterogeneous databases is considered a part of this scenario.

While the requirements for ontologies to support these kinds of applications are extensive, key features include:

- the ability to represent situational concepts, such as player/actor – role – action – object – state,
- the necessity for multiple representations and/or views of the same concepts and relations, and

- separation of concerns, such as separating the vocabularies and semantics relevant to particular interfaces, protocols, processes, and services from the semantics of the domain.
- Service checking that messages commit to the ontology at run time. These communities can have thousands of autonomous players, so that no player can trust any other to send messages properly committed to the ontology.

4.2 Application Generation

A common worldview, universe of discourse, or domain is described by a set of ontologies, providing the context or situational environment required for use by some set of agents, services, and/or applications. These applications might be internally focused in very large organizations, such as within a specific hospital with multiple, loosely coupled clinics, but are more likely multi- or cross-organizational applications. Characteristics include:

- Authoritative environments, with tighter coupling between resources and applications than in cases that are less authoritative or involve broader domains, though likely on the "looser side" of the overall continuum.
- Ontologies shared among organizations are highly controlled from a standards perspective, but may be specialized by the individual organizations that use them within agreed parameters.
- The knowledge bases implementing the ontologies are likely to be dynamically modified, augmented at run time by new metadata, gathered or inferred by the applications using them.
- The ontologies themselves are likely to be deeper and narrower, with a high degree of formality in their definition, focused on the specific domain of interest or concepts and perspectives related to those domains.

For example:

- Dynamic regulatory compliance and policy administration applications for security, logistics, manufacturing, financial services, or other industries.
- Applications that support sharing clinical observation, test results, medical imagery, prescription and non-prescription drug information (with resolution support for interaction), relevant insurance coverage information, and so forth across clinical environments, enabling true continuity of patient care.

Requirements:

- The ontologies used by the applications may be fully specified where they interoperate with external organizations and components, but not necessarily fully specified where the interaction is internal.
- Conceptual knowledge representing priorities and precedence operations, time and temporal relevance, bulk domains where individuals don't make sense, rich manufacturing processes, and other complex notions may be required, depending on the domain and application requirements.

4.3 Ontology Lifecycle

In this scenario we are concerned with activity, which has as its principle objectives conceptual knowledge analysis, capture, representation, and maintenance. Ontology repositories should be able to support rich ontologies suitable for use in knowledge-based applications, intelligent agents, and semantic web services. Examples include:

- Maintenance, storage and archiving of ontologies for legal, administrative and historical purposes,
- Test suite generation, and
- Audits and controllability analysis.

Ontological information will be included in a standard repository for management, storage and archiving. This may be to satisfy legal or operations requirements to maintain version histories.

These types of applications require that Knowledge Engineers interact with Subject Matter Experts to collect knowledge to be captured. UML models provide a visual representation of ontologies facilitating interaction. The existence of meta-data standards, such as XMI and ODM, will support the development of tools specifically for Quality Assurance Engineers and Repository Librarians.

Requirements include:

- Full life-cycle support will be needed to provide managed and controlled progression from analysis, through design, implementation, test and deployment, continuing on through the supported systems maintenance period.
- Part of the lifecycle of ontologies must include collaboration with development teams and their tools, specifically in this case configuration and requirements management tools. Ideally, any ontology management tool will also be ontology aware.
- It will provide an inherent quality assurance capability by providing consistency checking and validation.
- It will also provide mappings and similarity analysis support to integrate multiple internal and external ontologies into a federated web.

5 Analytic Applications

5.1 Emergent Property Discovery

By this we mean applications that analyze, observe, learn from and evolve as a result of, or manage other applications and environments. The ontologies required to support such applications include ontologies that express properties of these external applications or the resources they use. The environments may or may not be authoritative; the ontologies they use may be specific to the application or may be standard or utility ontologies used by a broader community. The knowledge bases that implement the ontologies are likely to be dynamically augmented with metadata gathered as a part of the work performed by these applications. External information resources and applications are accessed in a read-only mode.

- Semantically grounded knowledge discovery and analysis (*e.g.*, financial, market research, intelligence operations)
- Semantics assisted search of data stored in databases or content stored on the Web (*e.g.*, using domain ontologies to assist database search, using linguistic ontologies to assist Web content search)
- Semantically assisted systems, network, and / or applications management.

- Conflict discovery and prediction in information resources for self-service and manned support operations (*e.g.*, technology call center operations, clinical response centers, drug interaction)

What these have in common is that the ontology is typically not directly expressed in the data of interest, but represents theories about the processes generating the data or emergent properties of the data. Requirements include representation of the objects in the ontology as rules, predicates, queries or patterns in the underlying primary data.

5.2 Exchange of Complex Data Sets

Applications in this class are primarily interested in the exchange of complex (multimedia) data in scientific, engineering or other cooperative work. The ontologies are typically used to describe the often complex multimedia containers for data, but typically not the contents or interpretation of the data, which is often either at issue or proprietary to particular players. (The OMG standards development process is an example of this kind of application.)

Here the ontology functions more like a rich type system. It would often be combined with ontologies of other kinds (for example an ontology of radiological images might be linked to SNOMED for medical records and insurance reimbursement purposes).

Requirements include

- Representation of complex objects (aggregations of parts)
- Multiple inheritance where each semantic dimension or facet can have complex structure.
- Tools to assemble and disassemble complex sets of scientific and multi-media data.
- Facilities for mapping ontologies to create a cross reference. These do not need to be at the same level of granularity. For the purposes of information exchange, the lower levels of two ontologies may be mapped to a higher level common abstraction of a third, creating a sort of index

5.3 Engineering Applications

The requirements for ontology development environments need to consider both externally and internally focused applications, as externally focused but authoritative environments may require collaborative ontology development.

5.4 Information Systems Development

The kinds of applications considered here are those that use ontologies and knowledge bases to support enterprise systems design and interoperation. They may include:

- methodology and tooling, where an application actually composes various components and/or creates software to implement a world that is described by one or more component ontologies.
- Semantic integration of heterogeneous data sources and applications (involving diverse types of data schema formats and structures, applicable in information integration, data warehousing and enterprise application integration).

- Application development for knowledge based systems, in general.

In the case of model-based applications, extent-descriptive predicates are needed to provide enough meta-information to exercise design options in the generated software (*e.g.*, describing class size, probability of realization of optional classes). An example paradigm might reflect how an SQL query optimizer uses system catalog information to generate a query plan to satisfy the specification provided by an SQL query. Similar sorts of predicates are needed to represent quality-type meta-attributes in semantic web type applications (comprehensiveness, authoritativeness, currency).

5.5 Ontology Engineering

Applications in this class are intended for use by an information systems development team, for utilization in the development and exploitation of ontologies that make implicit design artifacts explicit, such as ontologies representing process or service vocabularies relevant to some set of components. Examples include:

- Tools for ontology analysis, visualization, and interface generation.
- Reverse engineering and design recovery applications.

The ontologies are used throughout the enterprise system development life cycle process to augment and enhance the target system as well as to support validation and maintenance. Such ontologies should be complementary to and augment other UML modeling artifacts developed as part of the enterprise software development process. Knowledge engineering requirements may include some ontology development for traditional domain, process, or service ontologies, but may also include:

- Generation of standard ontology descriptions (*e.g.*, OWL) from UML models.
- Generation of UML models from standard ontology descriptions (e.g., OWL).
- Integration of standard ontology descriptions (e.g., OWL) with UML models.

Key requirements for ontology development environments supporting such activities include:

- Collaborative development
- Concurrent access and ontology sharing capabilities, including configuration management and version control of ontologies in conjunction with other software models and artifacts at the atomic level within a given ontology, including deprecated and deleted ontology elements
- Forward and reverse engineering of ontologies throughout all phases of the software development lifecycle
- Ease of use, with as much transparency with respect to the knowledge engineering details as possible from the user perspective
- Interoperation with other tools in the software development environment; integrated development environments
- Localization support
- Cross-language support (ontology languages as opposed to natural or software languages, such as generation of ontologies in the XML/RDF(S)/OWL family of description logics languages, or in the Knowledge Interchange Format (KIF) where first or higher order logics are required)
- Support for ontology analysis, including deductive closure; ontology comparison, merging, alignment and transformation

Table 3. Summary of Requirements

Requirement	Section
Structural	
Support ontologies expressed in existing description logic, (e.g. OWL/DL) and higher order logic languages (e.g. OWL Full and KIF), as well as emerging and new formalisms.	2.1.2 2.2.1 2.3.2
Represent complex objects as aggregations of parts	2.2.2
Multiple inheritance of complex types	2.2.2
Separation of concerns	2.1.1
Full or partial specification	2.1.2
Model-based architectures require extent-descriptive predicates to provide a description of a resource in an ontology, then generating a specific instantiation of that resource.	2.3.1
Efficient mechanisms will be needed to represent large numbers of similar classes or instances.	2.1.1
Generic concepts	
Support physical world concepts, including time, space, bulk or mass nouns like 'water', and things that do not have identifiable instances.	2.1.2
Support object concepts that have multiple facets of representations, e.g., conceptual versus representational classes.	2.1.1
Provide a basis for describing stateful representations, such as finite state automaton to support an autonomous agent's world representation.	2.1.1
Provide a basis for information systems process descriptions to support interoperability, including such concepts as player, role, action, and object.	2.1.1
Other generic concepts supporting particular kinds of domains	2.1.2
Run-time tools	
Tools to assemble and disassemble complex sets of scientific and multimedia data.	2.2.2
Service to check message commitment to ontology	2.1.1
Design-time tools	
Full life-cycle support	2.1.3 2.3.2
Support for collaborative teams	2.1.3 2.3.2
Ease of use, transparency with respect to details	2.3.2
Support for modules and version control.	2.1.3
Consistency checking and validation, deductive closure	2.1.3 2.3.2
Mappings and similarity analysis	2.1.3 2.2.2 2.3.2

- Support for import/reverse engineering of RDBMS schemas, XML schemas and other semi-structured resources as a basis for ontology development

5.6 Goals for Generic Ontologies and Tools

The diversity of the usage scenarios illustrates the wide applicability of ontologies within many domains. Table 3 brings these requirements together. The table classifies the requirements into

- structural features – knowledge representation abstract syntax
- generic content – aspects of the world common to many applications
- run-time tools – use of the ontology during interoperation
- design-time tools – needed for the design of ontologies

Associated with each requirement is the usage scenario from which it arises.

To address all of these requirements would be an enormous task, beyond the capacity of the ODM development team. The team is therefore concentrating on the most widely applicable and most readily achievable goals. In particular

- ODM is based on the OMG Meta-Object Facility (MOF), so can benefit from a wide variety of MOF-based design-time tools.
- ODM supports several widely-used modeling languages, including UML, RDFS/OWL, Entity-Relationship and Topic Maps, with inter-metamodel mapping, as well as the logic language Simple Common Logic (successor to KIF).
- MOF supports a package structure allowing optional compliance points, so that elements needed for a subclass of applications such as e-commerce can be provided, perhaps by third parties.

The resulting ODM will be not a final solution to the problem, but will be intended as a solid start which will be refined as experience accumulates.

Acknowledgement. The authors would like to thank John Kling and John Poole for review and comments.

References

1. T. Berners-Lee and M. Fischetti. *Weaving the Web : the past, present and future of the World Wide Web by its inventor* London : Orion Business 1999
2. T.R. Gruber, and G.R. Olsen. An ontology for engineering mathematics, in Jon Doyle, Piero Torasso and Erik Sandewell, eds. *Fourth International Conference on Principles of Knowledge Representation and Reasoning*, Morgan Kaufmann, 1994.
3. W3C. *OWL Web Ontology Language Usage Scenarios and Requirements*, W3C Candidate Recommendation, 18 August 2003, http://www.w3.org/TR/webont-req/

XML Schema Matching Based on Incremental Ontology Update[1]

Jun-Seung Lee and Kyong-Ho Lee

Dept. of Computer Science, Yonsei University 134
Shinchon-dong Sudaemoon-ku, Seoul, 120-749 Korea
jslee@icl.yonsei.ac.kr, khlee@cs.yonsei.ac.kr

Abstract. Schema matching is important as a prerequisite to the transformation of XML documents with different schemas. This paper presents a schema matching algorithm based on a dynamic ontology. The proposed algorithm consists of two steps: preliminary matching relationships between leaf nodes in the two schemas are computed based on the ontology and a proposed leaf node similarity, and final matchings are extracted based on a proposed path similarity. Particularly, unlike static ontologies of previous works, the proposed ontology is updated by user feedback for a sophisticated schema matching. Furthermore, since the ontology can describe various relationships such as IsA or PartOf, the method can compute not only simple matchings but also complex matchings. Experimental results with various XML schemas show that the proposed method is superior to previous works.

1 Introduction

XML(eXtensible Markup Language) [1] is widely accepted as a standard format to represent structured documents because it can embed logical structure information into documents. With this widespread use of XML documents, the volume of XML schemas[2] also grows at a rapid speed.

Since XML is so flexible that schema designers can define their own tags, several different schemas are used in the same application domain. For example, companies in an e-business field use different schemas for invoice information. A company should transform its XML documents into ones that conform to the schema of other company for the invoice interaction. An automated transformation of XML documents has therefore become an important issue.

Generally, the transformation of XML documents consists of two steps: schema matching and XSLT(eXtensible Stylesheet Language Transformations) [3] scripts generation. Schema matching computes semantic and structural relationships between two schemas and XSLT scripts are generated based on the relationships. The conventional transformation methods generate XSLT scripts from matching relationships that are created manually. However, in case of schemas with the size of

[1] This works was supported by the Korea Research Foundation Grant(KRF-2003-003-D00429)

[2] This paper uses the term "XML schema" that means both XML DTD(Document Type Definition)[1] and XML Schema[2]

X. Zhou et al. (Eds.): WISE 2004, LNCS 3306, pp. 608–618, 2004.
© Springer-Verlag Berlin Heidelberg 2004

several mega bytes, creating matchings by hand is time consuming and error prone. Therefore, computing schema matchings is prerequisite to an efficient transformation of XML documents.

Most of the recent works for schema matching use auxiliary information such as a synonym dictionary, an abbreviation dictionary, or a domain ontology. Particularly, since the domain ontologies used in previous works have been statically designed, they do not reflect new concepts and relationships, and require a high initial construction cost.

Therefore, this paper proposes a schema matching algorithm based on an ontology that is continually updated by user feedback and previous matching results. The proposed method supports more sophisticated schema matching because the ontology represents various relationships between concepts such as *IsA* and *PartOf*.

In this paper, matchings among nodes of source and target schemas are classified into two types: simple and complex matchings. A simple matching corresponds to one-to-one matching relationship between a source node and a target node. A complex matching implies one-to-many or many-to-one relationships between source and target schemas. The elements with these kind of relationships are splitted or merged during the transformation process. For instance, two elements *firstName* and *lastName* may have a many-to-one relationship with element *Name* in a target schema. As a result, the contents of *firstName* and *lastName* are merged and copied into the content of *Name*. Since the proposed ontology can represent this kind of PartOf relationship, the proposed method computes complex matchings as well as simple matchings.

Experimental results with real schemas show the proposed method is highly accurate. Furthermore, due to the dynamic nature of the proposed ontology, there has been a 13% increase in a recall.

The organization of this paper is as follows. In Section 2, a document model that represents XML schemas is introduced and a brief discussion about previous works is provided. In Sections 3, the proposed ontology and its operations are described in detail. In Section 4, the proposed algorithm is presented in two steps: producing preliminary matchings between leaf nodes and extracting final matchings based on a proposed path similarity. In Section 5, experimental results and analysis are given. In Section 6, the conclusions and future works are summarized.

2 Document Model and Related Works

In this section, we describe a document model to reprsent XML schemas. Additionally, a brief discussion about previous works concerning schema matching is presented along with their limitations.

2.1 Document Model

The document model is based on a rooted ordered tree. Specifically, each node that makes up a tree has a label and a value. Elements and attributes of a schema become nodes in the corresponding tree according to the proposed document model. A node takes the name of an element or an attribute as its label. The type of an element or an attribute is represented as the value of the corresponding node. Only leaf nodes have values.

We define a tree that is represented by the proposed document model as a schema tree. We also define a path of a leaf node as a sequence of nodes from its parent node to its root node.

2.2 Related Works

As mentioned before, we propose a schema matching algorithm based on an ontology. As shown in Table 1, several works for schema matching have been studied in various fields. Previous works for schema matching can be classified by the application domain, supporting matching types, or auxiliary information [4]. We summarize the recent works that support complex matchings.

Table 1. A brief survey of schema matching methods

Author	Feature	Type
Li and Clifton [7]	propose a machine learning approach based on a neural network.	Simple
Bergamaschi et al. [8]	compute a similarity using a synonym dictionary and structural information, and integrate schemas based on the matchings.	Simple
Milo et al. [9]	compute schema matchings between heterogeneous schemas based on rules.	Simple
Lerner [10]	proposes a schema matching algorithm between an original schema and its modified schema.	Simple
Doan et al. [11]	propose a machine learning approach for schema matching that consists of three layers.	Simple
Miller et al. [12]	propose a schema matching algorithm for heterogeneous database schemas. It supports an interactive user interface.	Simple
Madhavan et al. [13]	propose a hybrid schema matching algorithm for general schemas.	Simple
Su et al. [14]	compute matchings between two schemas as a prerequisite to an automated transformation of XML documents. They compute matchings with the minimum cost according to a proposed cost model.	Simple
Lee et al. [15]	propose a clustering method that computes a similarity between XML schemas.	Simple
Do and Rahm [16]	propose a hybrid matching algorithm using the modulation of various approaches. They support user feedback and reuse previous matchings.	Simple
Melnik et al. [17]	propose a schema matching algorithm based on the idea that a similarity of one node is influenced by adjacent nodes.	Simple
Xu and David [5]	propose a method to find complex matchings based on an ontology that includes expected patterns and lexicons.	Comple x
Dhamankar et al. [6]	propose a matching algorithm to compute complex matchings by a machine learning approach.	Comple x

Xu et al. [5] propose a schema matching algorithm to compute complex matchings using an ontology with a hierarchical structure. The ontology includes all possible concepts of a specific domain and represents the relstionships among them in a form of a directed graph. Each concepts is associated withe a list of words. However, since the ontology is managed by an human expert, it takes a lot of cost to update the ontology.

iMAP proposed by Dhamankar et al. [6] supports complex matchings using a machine learning approach. There are several classifiers trained in various perspectives to select the most appropriate matching. Specifically, iMAP can compute more complicated equations for combination of attributes by analyzing data characters of value. However, because iMAP is proposed for relational database schemas, it does not handle hierarchial schemas. iMAP also uses domain constraints that is statically predefined.

To overcome the limitation of previous works, we propose a schema matching algorithm based on a dynamically updated ontology. Since the proposed ontology is updated by user feedback from the previous matchings, the ontology reflects new concepts and relationships in a specific domain. For more efficient management of the ontology, ontology operations are also proposed. In the next sections, the proposed ontology and schema matching method are described in detail.

3 Ontology

The proposed ontology is dynamically updated by user feedbacks from the previous matching results. For computing complex matchings, the ontology is designed to formulate various relationships among concepts such as *PartOf* and *IsA*. A detailed description of the proposed ontology is as follows.

3.1 Ontology Architecture

The proposed ontology is represented by a set of trees in which nodes and arches correspond to concepts and relationships respectively. The label of each node is the name of an element or an attribute in an XML schema. There may exist three types of relationships is, *IsA*, *PartOf*, and *Similar*, which represent the traditional meaning of generalization, composition, and similarity, respectively.

The ontology describes the strength of which can be used at the matching process among nodes. The strength increases or decreases according to users' feedback. For example, if a user removes a matching relationship that already exist in the ontology, the strength of the relationship decreases.

The ontology defines operations that are associated with the type of user feedback. The proposed ontology operations enable us to add concepts, add tree, merge trees, group concepts, and delete relationships. A detailed description of ontology operations is as follows.

3.2 Ontology Operations

Ontology operations are selected by user feedback. The feedback is formulated like the following representation format according to users' feedback.

FeedBack = (SourceNodeName, TargetNodeName, IsA | PartOf | Similar | Remove).

For example, when the schema matching system computes a wrong matching, *HomeAddress* in a source schema matching with *CompanyAddress* in a target schema, and user removes the matching, the feedback is formulated as (*HomeAddress, CompanyAddress, Remove*). On the contrary, when the system could not find that *lastName* in a source schema matches with *familyName* in a target schema, and user adds the matching with a *Similar* relationship, the feedback is formulated as (*lastName, familyName, Similar*).

Adding Concepts. If the ontology includes one concept of the feedback and does not include the other of the feedback, the concept that is not included in the ontology is added to the existing tree. The relationship between the existing node and the new node follows the relationship in the feedback.

Adding Trees. If the ontology does not include both nodes in the feedback, two nodes construct a new tree that is added to the ontology. Fig. 1(a) shows an example for adding a new concept *MobilePHONE* by the feedback, (*PHONE, MobilePHONE, IsA*) and adding a new concept tree by the feedback, (*Telephone, HomePhone, IsA*). In the figure, the gray circles represent existing ontology and the white circles represent new concepts.

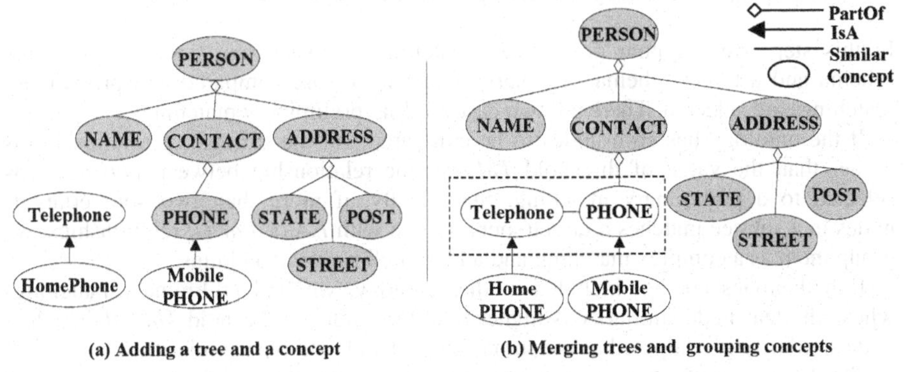

Fig. 1. An example for merging trees and grouping concepts.

Merging Trees. If two nodes of the feedback are included in different trees, those trees are merged. Fig. 1(b) shows that an example for merging the trees by the feedback that is (*Telephone*, *PHONE*, *Similar*). Since *Telephone* has a *Similar* relationship with *PHONE* in feedback and they are in different trees of the ontology, the two trees are merged into one tree.

Grouping Concepts. If adding concepts or merging trees operations is occured with *Similar* relationship, we group the concepts that have *Similar* relationships. The concepts that are grouped have identical relationships. For instance, in Fig. 1(b), after merging operations, *Telephone* has a *Similar* relationship with *PHONE*. Two concepts are grouped (represented by a spot line box). As a result of grouping, the *Telephone* has identical relationship with PHONE. In other words, the *TelePhone* has an *IsA* relationship with *MobilePHONE* and a *PartOf* relationship with *CONTACT*. And the strength of relationship is assigned an average the strength of relationships.

Deleting Relationships. If the schema matching system computes wrong matchings, users correct those matchings by user feedback with *Remove* relationship. If user inputs a *Remove* relationship as an user feedback and that relationship is in the ontology, the strength of relationship decreases. Finally, when the strength of relationship is below a threshold, that relationship is deleted.

4 The Schema Matching Algorithm

The proposed schema matching algorithm consist of two steps : preliminary matchings between leaf nodes are produced based on the domain ontology, a lexical similarity and a data type similarity, and final matchings are extracted based on a path similarity. Specifically, by the proposed ontology, we can compute not only simple matchings but also complex matchings. After the schema matching process, the ontology is updated by user feedback.

4.1 Producing Preliminary Matchings Between Leaf Nodes

In this step, we compute preliminary matchings between leaf nodes of a source schema and a target schema. All pairs of leaf nodes are compared and preliminary matchings are selected. There are two cases to find preliminary matchings.

If the ontology has both nodes to be compared and the strength of relationship is higher than the value of threshold *ThLeaf*., the relationship between two nodes is selected to a preliminary matching. Specifically, if more than two source(target) nodes in a subtree matches a target(source) node with *IsA* or *PartOf* relationships, we group them as a complex matching and add to preliminary matchings.

If both nodes are not included in the ontology, we find preliminary matchings whose the leaf node similarity is higher than the value of threshold *ThLeaf*. The leaf node similarity is computed as the sum of lexical and data type similarities.

The lexical similarity means the similarity between the labels of two nodes. At first, we compute the similarity between tokens that labels are parsed into by using special characters and capital letters as delimiters. If tokens are in the abbreviation dictionary, they are replaced by their full names before computing similarities. A similarity between tokens is computed by comparing the strings of tokens and using a synonym dictionary [18]. Finally, the lexical similarity is determined by the average similarity between tokens.

To compute leaf nodes similarity, we should compute a data type similarity. Leaf nodes of a schema tree have data types, which denote their contents. The data type similarity is defined by the degree of information preservation when a source node is transformed into a target one. The data type similarity is classified into four groups by the degree of information loss: equal transformation, transformation without loss, transformation with some loss, and impossible transformation. Equal transformation is assigned the highest similarity and impossible transformation is assigned the lowest similarity.

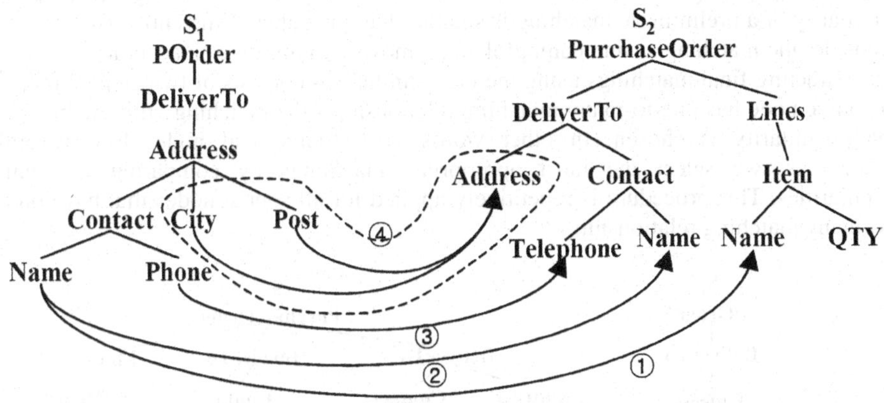

Fig. 2. An example for leaf node matchings.

Fig. 2 shows an example leaf node matchings between the source schema *S1* and the target schema *S2* that are used for invoicing. *Name* in *S1* matches with two *Name* in *S2* as matching □ and □. As you see, in the process of the leaf node matching, many-to-many matching relationships can be computed due to considering only the information of leaf nodes. In next step, we select more appropriate matching based on the path similarity.

For the matching □, *Phone* matchs with the *Telephone* using the synonym dictionary. Also, we can find the complex matching □ using the domain ontology. Since the ontology defines a concept *City* and *Post* have a *PartOf* relationship with a concept *Address*, we can find that the node *City* and *Post* in a same subtree are matched with the node *Address* as a complex matching that has a *PartOf* relationship.

4.2 Extracting Final Matchings Based on the Path Similarity

Preliminary matchings found in the previous phase have many-to-many matching relationships. In this phase, we extract one-to-one matchings based on a proposed path similarity. The path similarity between two leaf nodes which have been matched in the previous phase is computed as average of similarities of matched internal nodes in their paths. For all pairs of matchings between leaf nodes, path similarities are computed to extract final matchings.

For computing the path similarity, matchings between internal nodes on their paths should be found. To find internal node matchings, we compute the internal node similarity. The internal node similarity is computed as the sum of lexical and structural similarities. If the similarity is higher than the value of threshold *ThInternal*, they are matched.

The lexical similarity is same in the previous phase and the structural similarity represents the rate of common leaf nodes included in the subtrees rooted at the each internal node. The higher structural similarity means that the correspoding internal nodes include more matched leaf nodes.

After computing path similarities for all pairs of leaf nodes matchings, if the path similarity of a preliminary matching is smaller than the value of threshold *ThPath*, we consider the matching as unmeaningful and remove it to improve an accuracy.

Extracting final matchings using the path similarities consists of two steps. First, if a source node has one-to-many matching relationships, the matching with the highest path similarity is chosen. In other words, if a source leaf nodes has serveral matchings, we select the most appropriate matchings by comparing the path similarities. This procedure is repetitively applied for all source nodes that have one-to-many matching relationship.

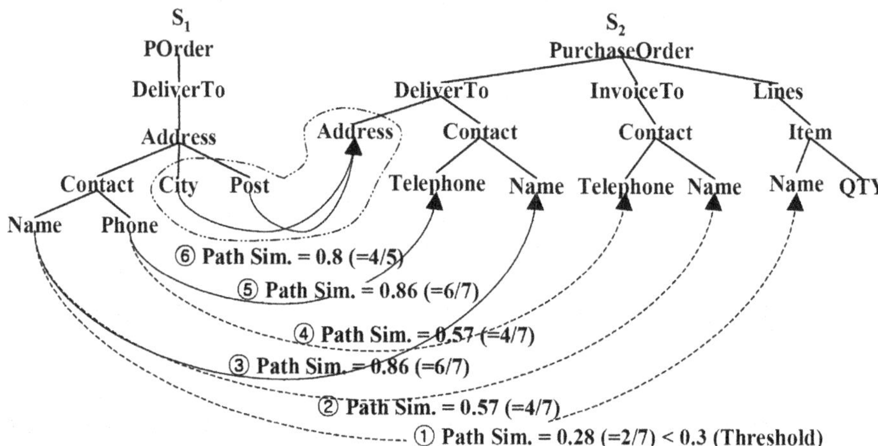

Fig. 3. An example for extracting final matchings.

After resolving one-to-many matchings for each source leaf nodes, there may still exist many-to-one matchings. Resolving many-to-one matchings is very similar to the previous step. For a target node that has several matchings, the matching with the highest path similarity is selected. If there exists more than one matching that has the highest path similarity, their leaf node similarities computed in the phase of leaf node matching are compared for a decision. Specifically, if the selected matching is a complex matching, we regard the average of the strength of relationships as a leaf node similarity.

For a instance, in Fig. 3, matching ① to ⑥ are preliminary matchings computed in the phase of leaf node matching. However, matching ① is deleted since the path similarity value(=0.28) of matching ① is smaller than *ThPath*(=0.3). In spite of deleting matching ①, the leaf node labeled Name in *S1* has two matchings ② and ③.

We select matching ③ as a final matching by comparing the path similarities. The matching ⑤ is selected because of the same reason. Because the complex matching ⑥ is regards as a single matching, it is not 2:1 matching. There is no conflict matchings, then matching ⑥ is selected for a final matching. Finally, in this case, final matchings are ③, ⑤, and ⑥.

After the system computes final matchings, users revise the matching results by removing incorrect matchings or adding missing matchings. It is used for feedback to update the domain ontology.

5 Experimental Results

To evaluate the performance of the proposed method, we have experimented with two groups of schemas that are used to represent a list of academic courses of a university and a list of houses in the real estate field. For a fair evaluation, we have used the same test set with the work of Doan [11].

Schemas for course lists include just simple matchings, but schemas for house lists include complex matchings as well as simple matchings. Fig. 4 shows a precision and a recall of each group. Experiments has been performed two times for each domain. First, only a synonym dictionary [18] has been used as an auxiliary information (A represents the experimental results without a domain ontology). Additionally, the proposed domain ontology has been applied (B indicates this case of using the ontology). As shown in Fig. 4(a)□Fig. 4(d), the dynamic nature of the proposed domain ontology has improved the accuracy of the proposed schema matching method.

In the first experiment with course schemas, which resulted in a precision of 99% and a recall of 85% on the average, the ontology did not help to improve a precision. This is because the course schemas have just simple matching relationships that can be computed by the initial domain ontology and a lexical database.

In the case for house schemas by using the domain ontology, a recall has risen from 46% to 72%. This is due to the fact that the proposed ontology improves on with users' feedback from previous matching results.

6 Conclusions and Future Works

In this paper, we have presented a schema matching algorithm based on a dynamic ontology. The proposed matching algorithm consists of two steps: preliminary matching relationships between leaf nodes in two schemas are computed based on the proposed ontology and the proposed leaf node similarity, and final matchings are extracted based on the proposed path similarity.

Since the ontologies proposed by previous works are managed by human experts, it takes a lot of cost to update them. On the contrary the ontology proposed in this paper is updated by users' feedback. This paper presented the architecture and operations of the ontology. The ontology operations are automatically generated and performed by

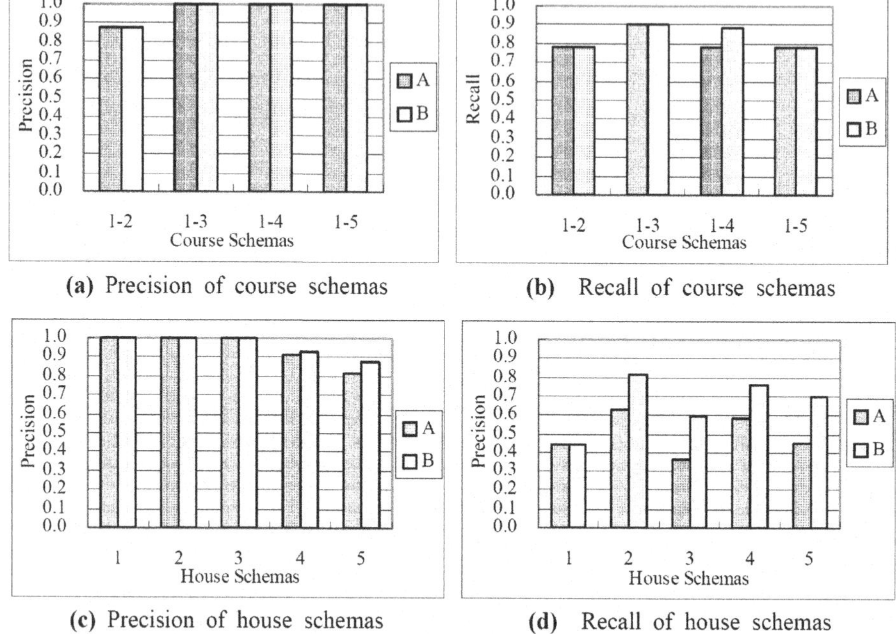

(a) Precision of course schemas

(b) Recall of course schemas

(c) Precision of house schemas

(d) Recall of house schemas

Fig. 4. Experimental Results.

the associated user feedback. As a result, the proposed ontology renews its constituent concepts and relationships in a specific domain. Particularly, since the proposed ontology presents various relationships among concepts such as *IsA* and *PartOf*, the method can find complex matchings, that is one-to-many or many-to-one matching relationships, as well as simple matchings that correspond to one-to-one matching relationships.

For an evaluation, we have experimented with the schemas that were used in the recent works that support complex matchings. Experimental results show that the proposed method is highly accurate. Specifically, there has been a 13% increase in a recall by using the proposed ontology. However, the overall accuracy of a recall has been relatively low because the names of elements and attributes of the test schemas are usually composite words with different textual patterns. Since the proposed ontology is updated with whole names (not tokens) in the previous schema matching, future works include a development of a method to update the domain ontology more efficiently based on the analysis of composite words.

References

1. World Wide Web Consortium, Extensible Markup Language (XML) 1.0 (Second Edition), W3C Recommendation, http://www.w3c.org/TR/REC-xml (2000).
2. World Wide Web Consortium, XML Schema 1.0, W3C Recommendation, http://www.w3.org/TR/xmlschema-0/ (2001).

3. World Wide Web Consortium, XSL Transformations (XSLT) 1.0, W3C Recommendation, http://www.w3.org/TR/1999/REC-xslt-19991116 (1999).
4. Erhard Rahm and Philip A. Bernstein: A Survey of Approaches to Automatic Schema Matching. VLDB Journal 10 (4) (2001) 334-350.
5. Li Xu, David W. Embley: "Discovering direct and indirect matches for schema elements."Proc. 8th Conf. DASFAA (2003) 39-46.
6. Robin Dhamankar, Yoonkyong Lee, AnHai Doan and Alon Halevy: iMAP: Discovering Complex Semantic Mappings between Database Schemas. Proc. Int``l Conf. SIGMOD on Management of Data (2004).
7. Wen-Syan Li and Chris Clifton: Semantic Integration in Heterogeneous Databases Using Neural Networks. Proc. 20th Int'l Conf. VLDB (1994) 1-12.
8. Sonia Bergamaschi, Silvana Castano, Sabrina De Capitani di Vimercati, S. Montanari, and Maurizio Vincini: An Intelligent Approach to Information Integration. Proc. Int`l Conf. on Formal Ontology in Information Systems (1998) 253-267.
9. Tova Milo and Sagit Zohar: Using Schema Matching to Simplify Heterogeneous Data Translation. Proc. 24th Int'l Conf. on VLDB (1998) 122-133.
10. Barbara Staudt Lerner: A Model for Compound Type Changes Encountered in Schema Evolution. ACM Transactions on Database Systems 25 (1) (2000) 83-127.
11. AnHai Doan, Pedro Domingos, and Alon Halevy: Learning to Match Schemas of Data Sources: A Multistrategy Approach. Machine Learning 50 (3) (2003) 279-301.
12. Renee J. Miller, Laura M. Haas, Mauricio A. Hernandez, Lingling Yan, C. T. Howard Ho, Ronald Fagin, and Lucian Popa: The Clio Project: Managing Heterogeneity. SIGMOD Record 30 (1) (2001) 78-83.
13. Jayant Madhavan, Philip A. Bernstein, and Erhard Rahm: Generic Schema Matching with Cupid. Proc. 27th Int`l Conf. VLDB (2001) 49-58.
14. Hong Su, Harumi Kuno, and Elke A. Rundensteiner: Automating the Transformation of XML Documents. Proc. 3rd Int`l Workshop on Web Information and Data Management (WIDM) (2001) 68-75.
15. Mong Li Lee, Wynne Hsu, LiangHuai Yang, and Xia Yang: XClust: Clustering XML Schemas for Effective Integration. Proc. 11th Int'l Conf. on Information and Knowledge Management (2002) 292-299.
16. Hong-Hai Do and Erhard Rahm: COMA - A System for Flexible Combination of Schema Matching Approaches. Proc. 27th Int'l Conf. VLDB (2002) 610-621.
17. Sergey Melnik, Hector Garcia-Molina, and Erhard Rahm: Similarity Flooding - A Versatile Graph Matching Algorithm. Proc. 18th Int`l Conf. on Data Engineering (2002) 117-128.
18. George A. Miller: WordNet: A Lexical Database for English. Communications of the ACM 38 (11) (1995) 39-41.

Spam Mail Filtering System Using Semantic Enrichment

Hyun-Jun Kim[1], Heung-Nam Kim[1], Jason J. Jung[1], and Geun-Sik Jo[2]

[1] Intelligent E-Commerce Systems Laboratory,
School of Computer and Information Engineering, Inha University,
253 YongHyun-Dong, Incheon, Korea, 402-751
{dannis,nami4596,j2jung}@eslab.inha.ac.kr
http://eslab.inha.ac.kr

[2] School of Computer and Information Engineering, Inha University,
253 YongHyun-Dong, Incheon, Korea, 402-751
gsjo@inha.ac.kr

Abstract. As the Internet infrastructure has been developed, E-mail is regarded as one of the most important methods for exchanging information because of easy usage and low cost. Meanwhile, exponentially growing unwanted mails in users' mailbox have been raised as a main problem. To solve this problem, researchers have suggested many methodologies that are based on Bayesian classification. The kind of system usually shows high performances of precision and recall. But they have several problems. First, it has a cold start problem, that is, training phase has to be done before execution of the system. The system must be trained about spam and non-spam mail. Second, its cost for filtering spam mail is higher than rule-based system. Third, if E-mail has only few terms those represent its contents, the filtering performance is fallen. In this paper, we have focused on the last issued problem and we suggest spam mail filtering system using Semantic Enrichment. For the experiment, we tested the performance by using the measurements like precision, recall, and F1-measure. As compared with Bayesian classifier, the proposed system obtained 4.1%, 10.5% and 7.64% of improved precision, recall and F1-measure, respectively.

1 Introduction

As the Internet infrastructure has been developed, E-mail is used as one of the major methods for exchanging information. Meanwhile, exponentially growing spam mails have been raised as a main problem and its rate in users' mailboxes is increasing every year [1]. Hence, E-mail service companies have troubles in managing their storage devices, and also users have problems that consume time to delete spam mails. According to the recent research from one of the biggest internet service companies, 84.4% of total mail were spam mails [2]. To solve the problem, there have been many studies using rule-based method [3] and probabilistic methods such as Bayesian classifier. Especially, Bayesian classifier-based systems usually show high performances of precision and recall. But they have several problems. First, they have a cold start problem, that is, training phase has to be done before execution of the system. The system has to be trained about spam and non-spam mail. Second, the cost of spam mail filtering is higher than rule-based systems [4]. Third, if an e-mail has

X. Zhou et al. (Eds.): WISE 2004, LNCS 3306, pp. 619–628, 2004.
© Springer-Verlag Berlin Heidelberg 2004

only few terms those represent its contents, the filtering performance is fallen. In this paper, we have focused on the last issued problem, and we suggest a spam mail filtering system using semantic enrichment to solve this problem. Semantic enrichment is a technique to make interpretability between heterogeneous database systems mainly used in database field, but we modified this to use in our system. When there is an e-mail with only few terms those represent its contents, we enriched conceptualized terms to that content from candidate path of a hierarchy built through training phase.

The outline of the paper is as follows. Section 2 concentrates on the related work and basic concepts related in our system, Section 3 refers to the suggested spam mail filtering system using semantic enrichment, and we explain experimental result in section 4. We conclude this study with prospects on future work in section 5.

2 Related Work

Spam mail filtering system has been developed for recent years, and there have been lots of studies to increase the performance of the system. In 1996, rule-based system is suggested to classify spam mails, but this system can be strongly dependent on the existence of key terms, therefore, specific terms can cause the failure of filtering [6][7]. On the other hand, Naïve Bayesian classifier is traditionally very popular method for document classification and mail filtering system [14][15]. It uses probabilistic method; it can compute test document d_i's possible categories, therefore, many spam mail filtering systems currently have adopted it. As we mentioned in earlier, there are several problems remained. Many researchers also suggested new systems those using other methods such as Bayesian network that enhancing the performance of Bayesian classification [8], and WBC (Weighted Bayesian Classifier) that gives weight on some key terms that representing the content's class by using SVM (Support Vector Machine) [9][10].

2.1 Bayesian Classifier Based Systems

There has been a good deal of work in automatically generating probabilistic text classification techniques using Bayesian classifier such as Naïve Bayesian classifier [16], weighted Bayesian classifier and Bayesian network in field of information retrieval and machine learning [5]. Recently, these techniques are popularly used for filtering spam mails. More generally, Weighted Bayesian classifier is used for enhancing the filtering performance by giving weights to the features representing the document [18]. Also, the filtering performance of Bayesian classifier can be increased by using Bayesian network that models the probabilistic relationships among the variables [8]. But usually performance of these probabilistic classification techniques takes an influence by several factors such as pre-processing phase, number of trained data set and each document's content. Especially, if there is too small number of terms in a context, the probability of the context is highly depend on the trained data set, and it can cause decrease of the filtering performance.

2.2 Semantic Enrichment

Originally, semantic enrichment is the process that upgrades the semantics of databases. This is usually done by remodeling database schemas in a higher data model in order to explicitly express semantics that is implicit in the data [11]. But in this paper we used this technique to enrich semantically useful terms to an e-mail that contains only few terms. Through the past research, we could find that lack of the key terms in content can decrease the performance of systems [7]. Normally, the semantic enrichment process is divide into two, structural information and semantical concepts. In section 3, we will introduce these two steps more in detail. Currently, there are several studies about semantic enrichment in information retrieval field, and usually these techniques are used with ontology [13][19].

3 Spam Mail Filtering System Using Ontology and Semantic Enrichment

As shown in Fig. 1, the proposed system is divided into two phases, training and testing. We can say training phase is ontology construction phase, and testing phase is classification phase as well.

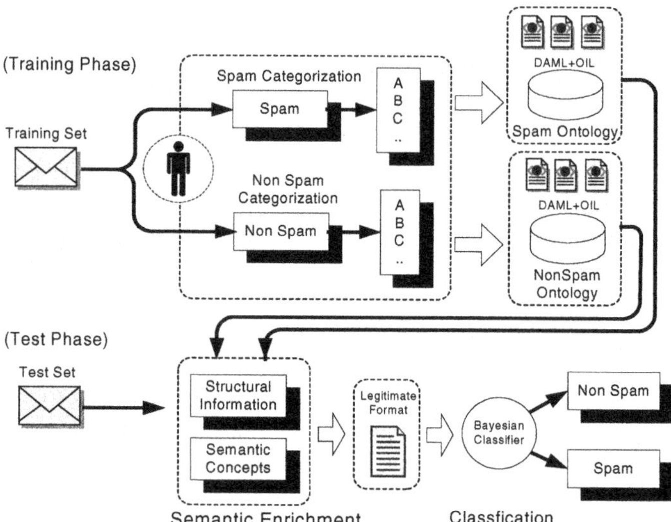

Fig. 1. Architecture of spam mail filtering system using ontology and semantic enrichment.

Usually training phase is necessary to train the system. Additionally, in our spam mail filtering system, ontology is constructed through this phase. Then, this ontology is used on testing phase for semantic enrichment. Since ontology has conceptualized classes, when there is content with only a few terms, the system enriches conceptualized terms from the classes of the ontology. In the training phase, the system learns about spam and nonspam mail by classifying them. Domain experts classify training mails as a spam and a nonspam, and they classify mails as sub classes again. Then ontology is made of these classes, and this ontology can be used in test phase.

3.1 Ontology Construction

As already mentioned, training phase makes the system filter e-mails automatically. A domain expert carries training. Also this phase creates the classes on ontology unlike the previous systems [17][20]. When the previous systems train mails, those are only trained about spam mail and nonspam mail. But in our system, we train more detailed classes. For example, let us say there are two classes, C_{Spam} and $C_{NonSpam}$. Each class also has subclasses, $C_{Spam}=\{c_1,c_2,\ldots,c_m\}$ and $C_{NonSpam}=\{c_1,c_2,\ldots,c_n\}$. Then these classes organize ontology through DAML+OIL format as shown in Fig 2 [12]. We used most common way to express each concept.

```
<daml:Class rdf:about="#Sales">
    <rdfs:subClassOf rdf:resource="#Spam"/>
</daml:Class>
<daml:Class rdf:about="#Adult">
    <rdfs:subClassOf rdf:resource="#Spam"/>
</daml:Class>
<daml:Class rdf:about="#Pirating sales">
    <rdfs:subClassOf rdf:resource="#Spam"/>
</daml:Class>
        ......
<daml:ObjectProperty rdf:about="#Sales">
    <rdfs:domain rdf:resource="#Spam"/>
    <rdfs:range rdf:resource="#Spam"/>
</daml:Class>
        ......
```

Fig. 2. An example ontology using DAML+OIL

And also, it is one of the most import parts of the proposed system to define sub classes because it can influence the system's performance. In this work, we defined these classes semi-automatically. At first, we used nearest neighbor for grouping training data set. Since the grouping result is very rough, we need to modify groups manually by domain experts. The numbers of sub classes are not same between spam and nonspam, through the experiment we found that spam class has more sub classes than nonspam sub classes. Moreover, unlike the spam sub classes, we cannot apply nonspam sub classes to every user because they are quite different from users. We consider this is personalized system, and globally applicable system will be developed in future work.

3.2 Semantic Enrichment Filtering Spam Mails

Test Phase has two steps, 'Structural Information' and 'Semantic Concepts' [13]. By using ontology constructed through training phase, the system can filter test e-mails.

If there is a e-mail with a few terms, the system makes it understandable mail in terms of the document format and the semantic content for effective filtering. Since a few terms can cause decreasing of the precision, semantic enrichment can help the system to filter well in that case. Detailed two steps are as follows.

- **Structural Information.** E-mails are text-based document, but ontology is RDF (DAML+OIL) format. So the system firstly changes E-mails into RDF format. By doing this, mapping between e-mails and ontology comes to be possible. Then the system finds candidate classes, $C_{Spam,i}$ and $C_{NonSpam,i}$ to be used for enriching semantically conceptualized terms by using cosine-similarity method [6].

When we assume E-mail as a document, document D_k contains its terms d_i, and each sub class C_m of ontology also contains its terms c_j.

$$Candidate\ \ Class = Rank\ (Sim\ (D_k, C_m)) = \frac{\sum_{m=0}^{n} D_k \times C_m}{\sqrt{\sum_{i=0}^{I} d_i^{\,2}}\sqrt{\sum_{j=0}^{J} c_j^{\,2}}} \tag{2}$$

$n = number\ of\ \ classes \qquad I,J = number\ of\ \ elements$

As shown in Eq. (2), the candidate classes are calculated by cosine similarity method. Once the similarity is computed about all classes, we use these classes according to their ranks.

- **Semantical Concepts.** This step builds the relationships between terms in a e-mail and sub classes of ontology. Then, the system enriches conceptualized terms from candidate classes. This helps a mail with a few terms become rich contents. Eq. (3) and Table 1 shows a simple example of traditionally trained filtering system. According to the table. 1, the result of traditional system is based on two classes - spam and nonspam. But it can be a problem for filtering performance because spam and nonspam is disjoint concept whereas traditionally trained systems try to learn a unified concept description [21].

$$C_i = Max(freq(C_{Spam}, d_i), freq(C_{NonSpam}, d_i)) \qquad d_i \in D \tag{3}$$

When there is a frequency matrix as shown in Table. 1, and a test mail D_k={a_1,a_2}, *k=spam*, we can get a candidate class of C_{Spam}=6 (4+2) and $C_{NonSpam}$=8 (5+3). Therefore the system will classify D_k as nonspam mail, $C_{NonSpam}$.

Table 1. Frequency matrix which the system only trained spam and nonspam mail.

	C_{Spam}				$C_{NonSpam}$			
Terms	a_1	a_2	a_3	a_4	a_1	a_2	a_3	a_4
Frequency	4	2	1	3	5	3	2	2

But if there is another frequency matrix as shown in Table 2, the result can be changed. This table contains sub classes on C_{Spam} and $C_{NonSpam}$. So we can calculate probability more precisely. The first step to classify D_k is finding candidate classes from spam and nonspam classes. The candidate class is simply computed by cosine-similarity method, and we can sort candidate classes according to their similarities. Then we can find two of most similar sub classes from spam and nonspam classes.

Table 2. Frequency matrix which the system trained spam and nonspam mail with sub classes. (Candidate class of C_{Spam} is $\{c_1\}$ and $C_{NonSpam}$ is $\{c_2, c_3, c_4\}$)

Category / Terms	C_{Spam}				$C_{NonSpam}$			
	c_1	c_2	c_3	c_4	c_1	c_2	c_3	c_4
a_1	3	0	0	1	1	2	1	1
a_2	1	0	1	0	0	1	1	1
a_3	0	1	0	0	0	1	0	1
a_4	2	0	1	0	0	1	1	0
a_5	6	1	2	1	1	5	3	3

When the candidate classes are selected, the semantic enrichment is executed to D_k. As we can see in Fig. 3, each candidate classes are enriched (underlined terms, a_i is enriched terms). Unlike the result of Table 1 we can get the most reliable class from candidate classes, its result is different (Eq. (4)). In Fig. 3, the most reliable sub class in spam class is C_2 and the most reliable sub class in nonspam is C_1. Finally, the system compares these two classes, and it will classify the document D_k as nonspam mail.

Spam : $C_1 = \{ a_2, a_3, \underline{a_4}\} = \{3,1,2\} = \mathbf{6}$

NonSpam : $C_2 = \{ a_1, a_2, \underline{a_3}, \underline{a_4}\} = \{2,1,1,1\} = \mathbf{5}$

$C_3 = \{ a_1, a_2, \underline{a_4}\} = \{1,1,1\} = 3$

$C_4 = \{ a_1, a_2, \underline{a_3}\} = \{1,1,1\} = 3$

Fig. 3. Semantic enrichment on each candidate classes and the result.

$$\begin{aligned} C_i &= Max(Max(freq(spam,\ d_i + e(cc_j)),\ Max(freq(nonspam,\ d_i + e(cc_j))), \\ e(cc_j) &= elements\ of\ the\ candidate\ class,\ cc_j \qquad d_i \in D_k \end{aligned} \tag{4}$$

Surely, this result will affect on Bayesian classifier because terms' frequencies are directly influence probability of a class. Now we just showed a simple example of semantic enrichment based on frequency table. But, since the Bayesian classifier is probabilistic model, terms' frequency has also influence directly on the result.

4 Experiment

The proposed system is implemented using Visual Basic, ASP (Active Server Page), MS-SQL Server and IIS 5.0 environments. All the experiments are performed on a 2.4GHz Pentium PC with 256M RAM, running Microsoft Window 2000 Server.

We used *lingspam* mail set which introduced by Androutsopoulos [23]. This mail set contains 4 types of mails – 'bare', 'stop-list', 'lemmatizer', 'lemmatizer+stop-list'. Each type of mails is created by pre-processing procedure. And in this experiment, we used the last type of mails, lemmatized and stop-list deleted mails for training and testing the system.

Table 3. Data sets

	Training Data	Test Data
Spam mail	329	148
NonSpam mail	247	53
Total	576	201

4.1 Performance Measure

To evaluate the performance of the proposed system, we used the most commonly used evaluation measures - precision, recall and F1-measure [22] as defined in Eq. (5).

$$\begin{aligned} Precision &= \frac{Spam\ mails\ \ which\ are\ \ classifie\ d\ as\ Spam}{Mails\ whic\ h\ are\ clas\ sified\ as\ \ Spam} \\ Recall &= \frac{Spam\ mails\ \ which\ are\ \ classifie\ d\ as\ Spam}{All\ spam\ m\ ails} \\ F1 - measure &= \frac{2*Precisio\ n*Recall}{Precision\ +Recall} \end{aligned} \tag{5}$$

4.2 Experimental Results

Experiment for evaluating the proposed system is split into three parts: one part for finding optimal threshold about a number of enriched terms during semantic enrichment phase (Fig. 4) and a second part for comparing our system against Bayesian Classifier which is widely used in text classification system as shown in Table. 4. Last part is analyzing variation of the system's performance related to the number of terms (Fig. 5).

As can be seen from Fig. 4, when the optimal threshold for the enrichment is 5, the performance achieves the highest value. This means that the performance is best when we enriched five conceptualized terms to original mail terms.

But when we enriched more than 12 terms, the performance is begun to down. This means that much of enriched terms can lead to confusion. So, finding the opti-

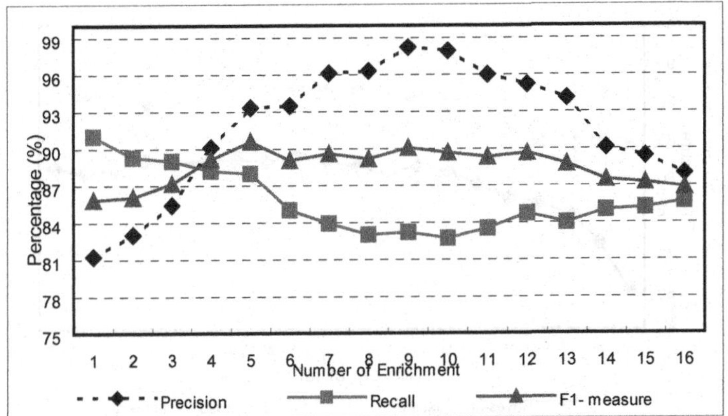

Fig. 4. Variation of the *F1-measure* as changing threshold.

mal number of terms is one of the most important parts for semantic enrichment. Therefore, we run experiments in performance comparison of semantic enrichment method with Bayesian classifier as setting enriched number of terms = 5. And table 4 shows a summary of the results.

Table 4. Comparison result between bayesian classifier and proposed system.

		Precision	Recall	F1-measure
1	Bayesian Classifier	89.21%	77.5%	82.94%
2	Semantic Enrichment	93.33%	88%	90.58%
Improved Performance		(2) 4.1%	(2) 10.5%	(2) 7.64%

Experimental result shows that precision, recall and F1-measure of our proposed method are improved 4.1%, 10.5% and 7.64% on those of Bayesian Classifier respectively.

Also, in Fig. 5, we can see the comparison result between Bayesian Classifier and Semantic Enrichment. In case of Bayesian Classifier, as the number of terms are decreases F1-measure is also decreased (from 5 to 20). But our proposed system, Semantic enrichment, shows an improved result in average 9.67%, maximum 19% compare to Bayesian Classifier. The system showed stable performance even when the number of terms is small. It covers one of major defect of Bayesian classifier. This result implied that the proposed system could make the system understandable and improve the performance of the classification.

5 Conclusions and Future Work

In this paper, we proposed a new efficient method for spam mail filtering by using Semantic Enrichment technology with ontology. The major advantage of the system

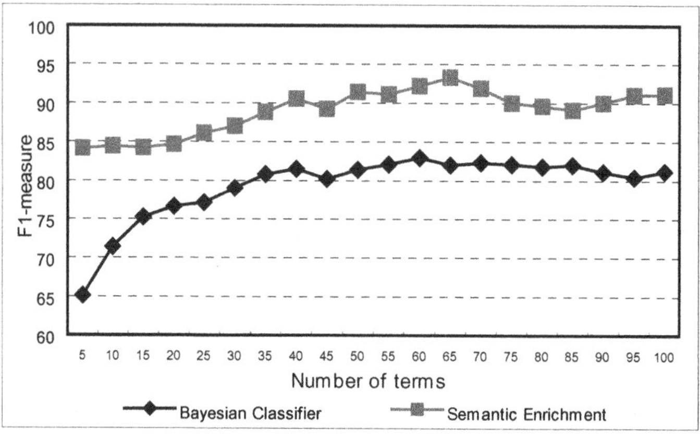

Fig. 5. Comparison result of the variation as changing number of terms in case of Bayesian Classifier with the case of Semantic Enrichment.

is that ambiguous mails can be filtered by making the system understandable. In evidence, as shown in Fig. 5, the system showed stable performance as changing the number of terms. Even when a mail has only few terms, by enriching terms, the system can understand it. The experimental results showed that the proposed method has better filtering performances compare to the Bayesian classifier. Our study provides evidence that Semantic Enrichment method can be useful method for spam mail filtering system. However, our system requires lots of effort to construct ontology because the performance of the proposed system can be influenced by the ontology. As future work, we have two plans – First, studying the issues of finding a more suitable updating schema to further improve the performance, second, we will develop automatic ontology construction procedure using concept-indexing method for getting more precise sub classes [24].

Acknowledgement. This work was supported by the Korea Science and Engineering Foundation (KOSEF) through the Northeast Asia e-Logistics Research Center at University of Incheon.

References

1. National Computerization Agency: National Informatization White Paper, (2002) 23.
2. Korean Telecom. : www.kt.co.kr (2004)
3. W. W. Cohen : Learning rules that classify e-mail, Proc. of the AAAI Spring Symp., (1996).
4. Provost, J. : Naive-Bayes vs. Rule-Learning in Classification of Email, Technical report, Dept. of Computer Sciences at the U. of Texas ay Austin, (1999).
5. L. F. Cranor and B. H. LaMacchia : Spam!, Commun. ACM, vol 41, no. 8 pp. 74-83, (1998).

6. Ricardo, B.-Y. and Berthier, R.-N. : Modern Information Retrieval, Addison-Wesley, (1999).
7. Androutsopoulos, I., Koutsias, J., Chandrinos, K. V. and Spyropoulos, C. D. : An Experimental Comparison of Naive Bayesian and Keyword-Based Anti-Spam Filtering with Personal E-Mail Messages, Proc. of the 23rd Annual International ACM SIGIR Conference on Reach and Development in Information Retrieval, (2000).
8. Sahami, M., Dumais, S., Heckerman, D. and Horvitz, E. : A Bayesian Approach to Filtering Junk E-Mail. In Learning for Text Categorization, Proc. of the AAAI Workshop, Madison Wisconsin. AAAI Technical Report WS-98-05, (1998) 55-62.
9. Thomas, G. and Peter, A. F. : Weighted Bayesian Classification based on Support Vector Machine, Proc. of the 18th International Conference on Machine Learning, (2001) 207-209.
10. Joachims, T. : Text Categorization with Support Vector Machines: Learning with Many Relevant Features, European Conference on Machine Learning, (1998).
11. Hohenstein, U., Plesser, V. : Semantic Enrichment : A First Step to Provide Database Interoperability, Proc of the Workshop Föderierte Datenbanken, Magdeburg, (1996).
12. Maedche, A. : Ontology Learning for the Semantic Web, Kluwer academic publishers, (2002) 29-55.
13. Saias, J., Quaresma, P. : Semantic enrichment of a web legal information retrieval system, Proc. of the JURIX2002, volume 89 of Frontiers in AI and Applications, London, UK, (2002) 11-20.
14. Diao, Y., Lu, H. and Wu, D. : A Comparative Study of Classification Based Personal E-mail Filtering, Proc. of PAKDD-00, 4th Pacific-Asia Conference on Knowledge Discovery and Data Mining, (2000).
15. Mitchell, T. M. : Machine Learning, Chapter 6: Bayesian Learning, McGraw-Hill, (1997).
16. Baldi, P., Frasconi, P., Smyth, P. : Modeling the Internet and the Web-Probabilistic Methods and Algorithms, Wiley, (2003) 1-4.
17. Davies, J., Fensel, D., Harmelen, F. A. : Towards the Semantic Web : Ontology-driven Knowledge Management. John Wiley & Sons, (2003).
18. J. T. A. S. Ferreira, D. G. T. Denison, D. J. Hand : Weighted naïve Bayes modelling for data mining, Technical report, Dept. of Mathematics at Imperial College, (2001).
19. Enrico, M., Simon, B. S., John, D.: Ontology-Driven Document Enrichment: Principles and Case Studies, Proc. of the 12th Workshop on Knowledge Acquisition, Modeling and Management, (1999).
20. Taghva, K., Borsack, J., Coombs, J., Condit, A., Lumos, S., Nartker, T.: Ontology-based Classification of E-mail, Proc of the International Conference on Information Technology: Computers and Communications, (2003).
21. Pádraig C., Niamh N., Sarah J. D., Mads H.: A Case-Based Approach to Spam Filtering that Can Track Concept Drift, Proc. of the ICCBR03 Workshop on Long-Lived CBR System, (2003).
22. Y. Yang, and X. Liu: A Re-examination of Text Categorization Methods, Proc. of the ACM SIGIR'99 Conference, (1999).
23. Androutsopoulos, I., Koutsias, J., Chandrinos, K.V., Paliouras, G., Spyropoulos, C.D.: An Evaluation of Naive Bayesian Anti-Spam Filtering, Proc. of the ECML 2000 Workshop on Machine Learning in the New Information, (2000) 9-17.
24. Weng, S. S., Liu, C. K.: Using text classification and multiple concepts to answer e-mails, Expert Systems with Applications, Volume 26, No. 4, (2004).

Integrating Ontology Knowledge into a Query Algebra for Multimedia Meta Objects

Sonja Zillner and Werner Winiwarter

Dept. of Computer Science and Business Informatics
University of Vienna, Austria
sonja.zillner@univie.ac.at

Abstract. Efficient access to multimedia content can be provided, if the media data is enriched with additional information about the content's semantics and functionality. For making full use of domain-specific knowledge for a specific context this meta information has to be integrated with a domain ontology. In previous research, we have developed Enhanced Multimedia Meta Objects (EMMOs) as a new means for semantic multimedia meta modeling, as well as a query algebra EMMA, which is adequate and complete with regard to the EMMO model. This paper focuses on the seamless integration of ontology knowledge into EMMA queries to enable sophisticated query refinement.

1 Introduction

Today, large collections of multimedia resources are available, e.g. commercial and private video and audio collections, repositories of technical multimedia documentations, or distributed units of multimedia learning material. However, the reuse of this wealth of material requires the efficient access to specific information items. Text-based keyword searching alone is not sufficient for retrieving multimedia data. The way how multimedia content can be searched depends on the way how multimedia content is annotated, and whether domain specific knowledge can be integrated into the retrieval. Within the EU-project CULTOS (see `www.cultos.org`), we have developed a novel approach for semantic multimedia content modeling – *Enhanced Multimedia Meta Objects (EMMOs)* [1] – suitable for the representation of InterTextualThreads (ITTs), i.e. complex knowledge structures used by researchers in intertextual studies to share and communicate their knowledge about the relationships between cultural artefacts. An EMMO constitutes a self-contained piece of multimedia content that indivisibly unites three of the content's aspects.

First, the *semantic aspect* reflects that an EMMO further encapsulates semantic associations between its contained media objects. For that purpose, we use a graph-based model similar to conceptual graphs. The links and nodes of the graph structure are labeled by *ontology objects* representing concepts of the domain ontology. Hence, an EMMO constitutes a unit of expert knowledge about multimedia content. Figure 1 shows the EMMO "Crucifixion in Popular Texts", which is used as a running example throughout this paper. The media

X. Zhou et al. (Eds.): WISE 2004, LNCS 3306, pp. 629–640, 2004.
© Springer-Verlag Berlin Heidelberg 2004

objects contained within the EMMO "Crucifixion in Popular Texts" are digital manifestations of the ancient bible text "Luke 23", the movies "Life of Brian" and "Tommy", and Madonna's video clip "Like a Prayer". The types of a media object are established through a reference to concepts of the domain ontology, e.g. *Ancient Text* or *Rock Opera.* By also labeling the associations with the corresponding concepts of the ontology, we can express that the ancient text "Luke 23" was *retold* by "Like a Prayer" and *influenced* "Life of Brian", which again *influenced* "Tommy". By modeling semantic associations and EMMOs as first-class objects, the EMMO model becomes very expressive in a way that it is possible to establish references to other EMMOs and to reify associations.

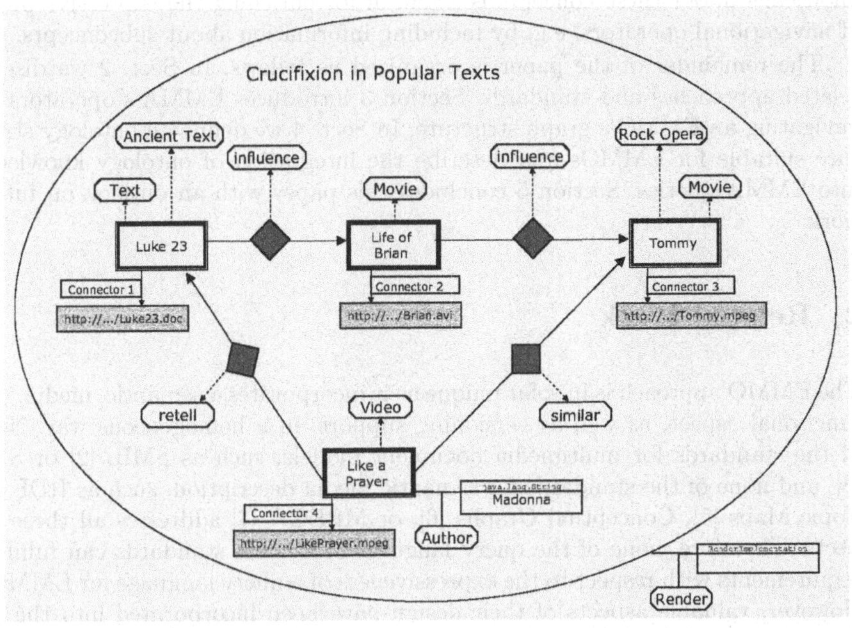

Fig. 1. Emmo "Crucifixion in Popular Texts" ($e_{popular}$)

Second, the *media aspect* describes that an EMMO aggregates the media objects of which the multimedia content consists, e.g. the EMMO "Crucifxion in Popular Texts" contains the text document "Luke23.doc", the MPEG videos "Tommy.mpeg" and "LikePrayer.mpeg", and the AVI video "Brian.avi".

Third, the *functional aspect* specifies operations on the content and on the semantic description of an EMMO that can be invoked and shared by applications; e.g. the EMMO "Crucifixion in Popular Texts" offers a rendering operation, which returns a presentation of the EMMO's content in different formats, such as SMIL or SVG.

EMMOs are *tradeable* – they can be bundled and exchanged in their entirety including media, content description, and functionality – and *versionable*, i.e. they can be modified concurrently in a distributed collaborative scenario.

To enable the efficient retrieval of EMMOs, we developed the *query algebra EMMA*, which is adequate and complete with regard to the EMMO model. By providing simple and orthogonal operators, which can be combined to formulate more complex queries, EMMA enables query optimization. Moreover, EMMA provides means to navigate through an EMMO's ontology-labeled graph structure by using navigational operators.

In order to make full use of the characteristics of the application domain, the query algebra needs to integrate *ontology knowledge*. The contribution of this paper is to present an efficient solution for the seamless integration of ontology knowledge into EMMA queries to enable sophisticated query refinement. We focus on concepts used for labeling associations, because the integration of ontology knowledge about these concepts is essential for enriching the expressive power of navigational operators, e.g. by including information about subconcepts.

The remainder of the paper is organized as follows. In Sect. 2 we discuss related approaches and standards. Section 3 introduces EMMA's operators for navigating an EMMO's graph structure. In Sect. 4 we define an ontology structure suitable for EMMOs and describe the integration of ontology knowledge into EMMA queries. Section 5 concludes this paper with an outlook on future work.

2 Related Work

The EMMO approach is in sofar unique as it incorporates a semantic, media, and functional aspect, as well as versioning support, in a homogeneous way. None of the standards for multimedia document models, such as SMIL [2] or SVG [3], and none of the standards for semantic media description, such as RDF [4], Topic Maps [5], Conceptual Graphs [6], or MPEG-7 [7] addresses all these aspects. Therefore, none of the query languages for those standards can fulfil all requirements with respect to the expressiveness of a query language for EMMOs. However, valuable aspects of their design have been incorporated into the design of the algebra EMMA. The seamless integration of ontology knowledge is essential for enriching the expressive power of EMMA's navigational operators. Navigational operators allow to traverse the semantic relationships between entities contained within an EMMO. Standards for semantic media descriptions can be used to model multimedia content by describing the information it conveys on a semantic level, similar to an EMMO's semantic aspect. Therefore, we have analyzed query languages for RDF, Topic Maps, Conceptual Graphs, and MPEG-7, with the focus on their ability to navigate the graph structure and to integrate ontology knowledge.

Although there exist several query languages for *RDF*, there is no official standard yet. RAL [8], an algebra for querying RDF, and RQL [9], a declarative query language for RDF, both provide means to navigate the RDF graph structure and enable the integration of a very simple ontology structure described by an RDF Schema [10], but they cannot deal with more elaborate ontology constructs, such as the transitivity or symmetry of relationships.

For *Topic Maps* the situation is similar to that of RDF, i.e. there exist several query languages but no standard yet. Tolog [11], a logic based query language for querying Topic Maps, provides a crude way of graph navigation and very basic ontology support, but neglects to address more sophisticated ontology constructs commonly described within ontology structures. The approaches TMPath [12] and XTMPath [13] focus on the navigation of Topic Maps. However, they are not constructed as fully fledged query languages and do not provide any features for ontology integration.

Conceptual Graphs allow to specify query graphs to formulate any database query that can be expressed by SQL [14], but to the best of our knowledge, there is no explicit query algebra for Conceptual Graphs, therefore also no formal basis for integrating ontology knowledge into queries.

The same is true for *MPEG-7*. Although there are quite a few approaches adapting XQuery for querying MPEG-7 documents [15], there is no approach focusing especially on MPEG-7's `Graphs` tool defined for the description of content semantics (allowing to describe networks of semantically interrelated media objects).

To summarize, there are several approaches, like RAL, RQL, or Tolog enabling graph navigation and allowing to integrate primitive constructs of ontology structures, such as the concept-subconcept relationship; but more elaborate constructs, such as the transitivity or symmetry of relationships, cannot be integrated. Although establishing a comprehensive syntax for the navigation of graph structures, approaches such as TMPath or XTMPath provide no features for ontology integration. Thus, also with regard to the seamless integration of ontology knowledge, none of these query languages provides sufficient functionality.

3 Navigating an EMMO's Graph Structure

The formal basis of the EMMO model are *entities*. There exist four different specializations of entities:

- *ontology objects* represent concepts of an ontology,
- *logical media parts* represent media objects or parts of media objects, e.g. video scenes or book chapters,
- *associations* model binary relationships,
- *EMMOs* aggregate semantically related entities.

Each entity can be labeled by concepts of the ontology, i.e. each entity w associates a set $types(w)$ including its labeling ontology objects. Semantic relationships between entities are described by *directed associations* specifying a *source* and *target entity* for which the relationship holds. Thus, an EMMO describes a graph-like knowledge structure of entities with associations being labeled by ontology objects (representing concepts of the domain ontology) describing the edges of the graph structure. Navigation through an EMMO is controlled by a *navigation path*, which is defined as a set of *sequences* of ontology objects. For each ontology object in a sequence, a mapping to the corresponding association within the EMMO is established to traverse the graph. We have defined *regular path expressions* over ontology objects for describing the syntax of a navigation path; and the *navigational operators* specify how those syntactic expressions are applied to navigate the graph.

For example, for a given EMMO, start entity, and regular path expression, the navigational operator *JumpRight* returns the set of all entities that can be reached by traversing the navigation path in the right direction, i.e. by following associations from source to target entities. Applying the operator *JumpRight* to the EMMO "Crucifixion in Popular Texts" ($e_{popular}$) , the starting entity "Luke 23" (l_{luke}), and the primitive regular path expression consisting of one single ontology object *influence* ($o_{influence}$) yields the logical media part representing the movie "Life of Brian" (l_{brian}), i.e.

$$JumpRight(e_{popular}, l_{luke}, o_{influence}) = \{l_{brian}\}.$$

In addition to one single ontology object, there exist two other primitive regular path expressions:

- "ε" refers to the empty entity and is interpreted by the operation *JumpRight* as absence of movement, e.g.:

$$JumpRight(e_{popular}, l_{luke}, \varepsilon) = \{l_{luke}\}.$$

- "_" refers to any arbitrary ontology object, e.g.:

$$JumpRight(e_{popular}, l_{prayer}, \_) = \{l_{luke}, l_{tommy}\}.$$

Regular path expressions may include two operators for the combination of other regular path expressions:

- Regular path expressions can be *concatenated* to specify a longer navigation path, e.g.:

$$JumpRight(e_{popular}, l_{prayer}, o_{retell} o_{influence}) = \{l_{brian}\}.$$

- "|" allows to combine two regular path expressions as alternative branches, e.g.:

$$JumpRight(e_{popular}, l_{prayer}, o_{retell} \,|\, o_{similar}) = \{l_{luke}, l_{tommy}\}.$$

Finally, there exist four unary operators to modify regular path expressions:

- "?" added to a regular path expression describes its optionality, e.g.:

$$JumpRight(e_{popular}, l_{luke}, o_{similar}?o_{influence}) =$$
$$JumpRight(e_{popular}, l_{luke}, o_{influence} \,|\, (o_{similar} o_{influence})) = \{l_{brian}\}.$$

- "+" defines an iteration of path expressions, which is interpreted as navigation along the same regular path expression any number of times, but at least once, e.g.:

$$JumpRight(e_{popular}, l_{luke}, o_{influence}+) = \{l_{brian}, l_{tommy}\}.$$

- "*" defines an iteration of path expressions, which is interpreted as navigation along the same regular path expression any number of times, e.g.:

$$JumpRight(e_{popular}, l_{luke}, o_{influence}*) =$$
$$JumpRight(e_{popular}, l_{luke}, \varepsilon \,|\, o_{influence}+) =$$
$$\{l_{luke}, l_{brian}, l_{tommy}\}.$$

- "−" allows to express the inversion of regular path expressions, i.e. to follow associations from target to source entities, e.g.:

$$JumpRight(e_{popular}, l_{luke}, o_{retell}-) = \{l_{prayer}\}.$$

Traversal along the opposite direction of associations can also be expressed with the navigational operator *JumpLeft*, e.g.:

$$JumpLeft(e_{popular}, l_{luke}, o_{retell}) = JumpRight(e_{popular}, l_{luke}, o_{retell}-) = \{l_{prayer}\}.$$

4 Integration of Ontology Knowledge

Ontologies provide a shared and common understanding of a domain and facilitate the sharing and reuse of knowledge [16]. They describe concepts, relationships, and constraints in the domain of discourse. The integration of ontology knowledge into EMMA queries has two appealing benefits. First, knowledge inherent in a domain ontology can be seamlessly integrated into queries. Therefore, the user can pose imprecise queries, which are refined by drawing inferences over the ontological knowledge. For example, if the user asks for all media objects which had been *influenced* by the ancient bible text "Luke 23", he should also receive media objects which were indirectly *influenced* by the ancient bible text, e.g. the rock opera "Tommy". This can be accomplished if the transitivity of the ontology object $o_{influence}$ is known, i.e. defined in the ontology.

Second, ontology knowledge can be used for checking integrity constraints during the design and authoring process of EMMOs, e.g. only associations can be stored in the database which conform to the specified types regarding source and target entities. The integration of constraint checking into the EMMO authoring environment is still ongoing work, and will not be further discussed in this paper.

In the following, we will focus on concepts used for labeling associations, because the integration of ontology knowledge for those concepts is essential for enhancing the expressive power of navigational operators. We define an ontology structure suitable for the EMMO model, describe how the most common modeling constructs used in standard ontology languages like DAML+OIL [17] or OWL [18] can be represented within the structure, and exemplify how the ontology knowledge can be integrated into EMMA queries.

The definition of an ontology structure for EMMOs was inspired by the ontology structure definition in [19]. Any concept of the ontology which is used for labeling entities within the EMMO model is represented as ontology object within the EMMO model. As the EMMO model treats associations as first class objects, ontology objects can be used for labeling both, the nodes and the edges, within an EMMO's graph structure. However, as mentioned before, we will only discuss ontology objects for labeling edges in the following. We specify an *ontology structure* suitable for the EMMO model as 3-tuple $\mathcal{O} = \{\Theta, \mathcal{H}^{\Theta}, \mathcal{A}^{\mathcal{O}}\}$ consisting of

- a *set of ontology objects* Θ, representing the concepts of the ontology,
- a *concept hierarchy* $\mathcal{H}^{\Theta}$ describing the subclass relationship between ontology objects, i.e. $\mathcal{H}^{\Theta}$ is a directed relation $\mathcal{H}^{\Theta} \subseteq \Theta \times \Theta$ with $\mathcal{H}^{\Theta}(o_1, o_2)$ expressing that o_1 is a subconcept of o_2.
- a set of *ontology axioms* $\mathcal{A}^{\mathcal{O}}$, expressed in first order logic.

Figure 2 illustrates a small portion of the Ontology of Intertextuality used in the CULTOS project as defined in [20].

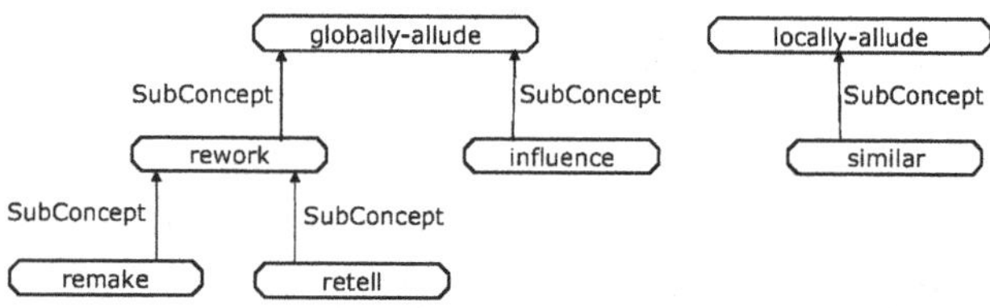

Fig. 2. Extract from the Ontology of Intertextuality

The set of ontology axioms $\mathcal{A}^{\mathcal{O}}$ allows to specify properties and restrictions of concepts, and defines relationships or properties of relationships between concepts. We can specify that some specific ontology objects are dedicated for describing associations within the EMMO model, e.g.

$$(\{o_{globally-allude}, o_{rework}, \dots, o_{similar}\} \subseteq \mathcal{CR}) \quad \in \quad \mathcal{A}^{\mathcal{O}}, \tag{1}$$

with $\mathcal{CR} = \{o \in \Theta \mid \forall w \in \Omega \land o \in types(w) \rightarrow w \in \Lambda\}$ describing the set of all ontology objects used for labeling associations, Ω the set of all entities, Λ the set of all associations, and $types(w)$ the set of ontology objects labeling the entity w.

Example 1. The hierarchical structure of concepts in Fig. 2 specifies that the concept $o_{globally-allude}$ has two subconcepts o_{rework} and $o_{influence}$. Integrating this knowledge into the EMMA query

$$JumpRight(e_{popular}, l_{luke}, o_{globally-allude}) = \emptyset$$

yields the expanded query:

$$JumpRight(e_{popular}, l_{luke}, o_{globally-allude} \,|\, o_{rework} \,|\, o_{influence}) = \{l_{brian}\}.$$

Thus, a user requesting all entities which were *globally alluded* by the ancient bible text "Luke 23", receives the logical media part "Life of Brian" because the EMMO "Crucifixion in Popular Texts" specifies that it was *influenced* by the bible text.

Example 2. However, incorporating the knowledge about the hierarchical structure of concepts into the query of a user asking for all entities being *globally alluded* by Madonna's video clip "Like a Prayer", i.e.

$$JumpRight(e_{popular}, l_{prayer}, o_{globally-allude}) \quad = \quad \emptyset.$$

yields the expanded query

$$JumpRight(e_{popular}, l_{luke}, o_{globally-allude} \,|\, o_{rework} \,|\, o_{influence}) = \emptyset.$$

still returning the empty answer set because the concept o_{retell} is not a direct subconcept of the concept $o_{globally-allude}$.

To enable also query expansion with indirect subconcepts, we can define the *transitivity of the concept hierarchy* within the set of ontology axioms, i.e.

$$(\forall o_1, o_2, o_3 \in \Theta \quad \mathcal{H}^{\Theta}(o_1, o_2) \wedge \mathcal{H}^{\Theta}(o_2, o_3) \rightarrow \mathcal{H}^{\Theta}(o_1, o_3)) \in \mathcal{A}^{O}. \quad (2)$$

Example 3. By incorporating the knowledge about the transitivity of concepts into the query of Example 2, this yields the expanded query:

$$JumpRight(e_{popular}, l_{prayer}, o_{globally-allude} \,|\, o_{rework} \,|\, o_{influence} \,|\, o_{retell} \,|\, o_{remake}) = \\ = \{l_{luke}\}.$$

Within the ontology axioms, we can also define *transitive concepts*, i.e. concepts for which an iteration of the corresponding path expression can be defined without changing the semantics of the concept, e.g.

$$(o_{influence} \in \Theta_{\mathrm{TRANS}}) \in \mathcal{A}^{O}, \quad (3)$$

with $\Theta_{\mathrm{TRANS}} = \{o \in \mathcal{CR} \,|\, \forall a_1, a_2 \in I(o) \;\; target(a_1) = source(a_2) \rightarrow \exists a_3 \in I(o) \;\; source(a_3) = source(a_1) \wedge target(a_3) = target(a_2)\}$ describing the set of all transitive ontology objects, $I(o) = \{w \in \Omega \mid o \in types(w)\}$ the set of all entities labeled by the ontology object o, and $source(a)$ and $target(a)$ the source and target entities of association a (see Fig. 3).

Example 4. Integrating the knowledge that $o_{influence}$ references a transitive concept into the EMMA query

$$JumpRight(e_{popular}, l_{luke}, o_{influence}) = \{l_{brian}\}$$

expands the query to

$$JumpRight(e_{popular}, l_{luke}, o_{influence}+) = \{l_{brian}, l_{tommy}\}.$$

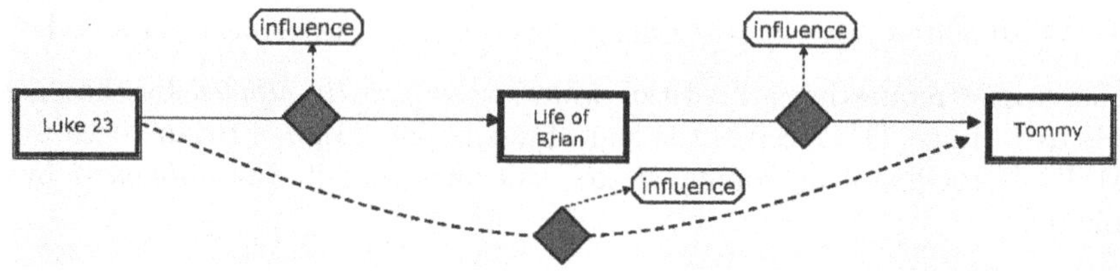

Fig. 3. Integrating the knowledge that $o_{influence}$ refers a transitive concept

In a similar way we express *symmetric concepts*, i.e. concepts for which all associations can be traversed in both directions, i.e. source and target entities can be exchanged without changing the semantics of the concept, e.g.

$$(o_{similar} \in \Theta_{\text{SYM}}) \in \mathcal{A}^{\mathcal{O}}, \tag{4}$$

with $\Theta_{\text{SYM}} = \{o \in \mathcal{CR} \,|\, \forall a_1 \in I(o)\, \exists a_2 \in I(o)\, (source(a_1) = target(a_2) \wedge source(a_2) = target(a_1))\}$ describing the set of all symmetric ontology objects (see Fig. 4).

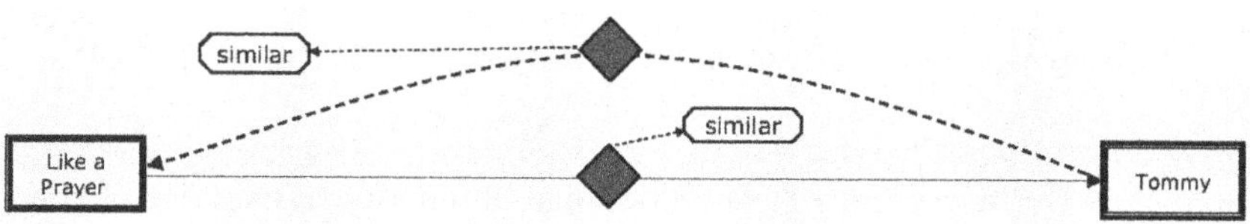

Fig. 4. Integrating of the knowledge that $o_{similar}$ refers a symmetric concept

Example 5. By incorporating the knowledge that $o_{similar}$ references a symmetric concept, the EMMA query

$$JumpRight(e_{popular}, l_{tommy}, o_{similar}) = \emptyset$$

is expanded to

$$\begin{aligned}&JumpRight(e_{popular}, l_{tommy}, o_{similar}) \cup JumpLeft(e_{popular}, l_{tommy}, o_{similar}) =\\ &JumpRight(e_{popular}, l_{tommy}, o_{similar} \,|\, o_{similar}-) =\\ &= \{l_{prayer}\}.\end{aligned}$$

Finally, we can also express that two concepts are *inverse* to each other, i.e. if an association is labeled with the inverse concept, then source and target entities have to be exchanged to keep the semantics intact, e.g.

$$((o_{retell}, o_{is-retold}) \in \Theta_{\text{INV}}) \in \mathcal{A}^{\mathcal{O}}, \tag{5}$$

with $\Theta_{\text{INV}} = \{(o_1, o_2) \in \mathcal{CR} \times \mathcal{CR} \,|\, \forall a_1 \in I(o_1)\, \exists a_2 \in I(o_2)(source(a_1) = target(a_2) \wedge source(a_2) = target(a_1))\}$ describing the set of all pairs of inverse ontology objects (see Fig. 5).

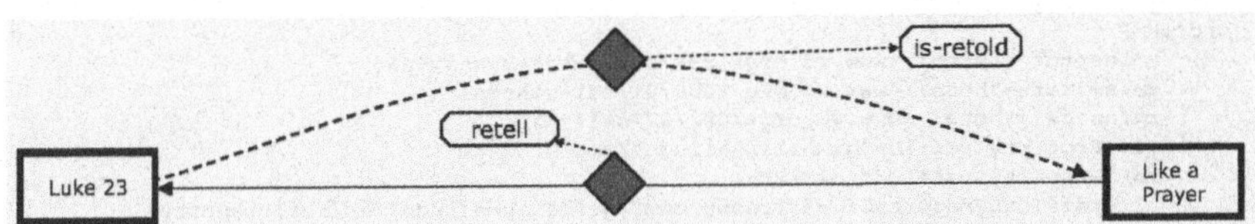

Fig. 5. Integrating the knowledge that o_{retell} and $o_{is-retold}$ reference inverse concepts

Example 6. Knowing that the ontology objects o_{retell} and $o_{is-retold}$ refer to two inverse concepts expands the EMMA query

$$JumpRight(e_{popular}, l_{luke}, o_{is-retold}) = \emptyset$$

to the query:

$$\begin{aligned}&JumpRight(e_{popular}, l_{luke}, o_{is-retold}) \cup JumpLeft(e_{popular}, l_{luke}, o_{retell}) = \\ &JumpRight(e_{popular}, l_{luke}, o_{is-retold} | o_{retell}-) = \\ &= \{l_{prayer}\}.\end{aligned}$$

Figure 6 enhances Fig. 2 by a graphical representation of the ontology axioms, i.e. the concept *influence* is marked as transitive, the concept *similar* as symmetric, and the concepts *retell* and *is-retold* as being inverse to each other.

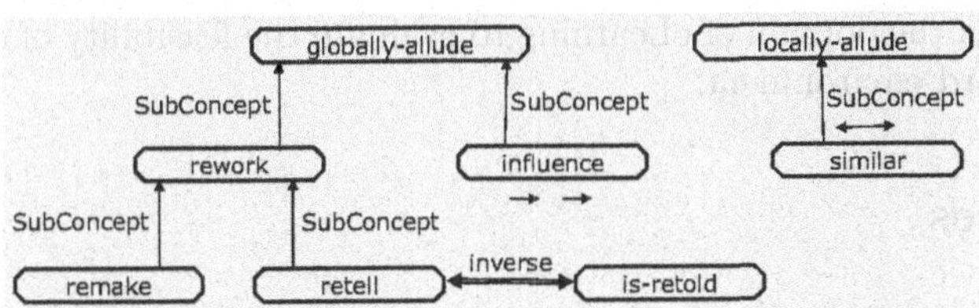

Fig. 6. Ontology of Intertextuality enhanced by Ontology Axioms

Since DAML+OIL does not provide modeling constructs for symmetric properties, it was not adequate as representation language for an ontology structure. However, OWL specifies all the modeling constructs used within an ontology structure, i.e. constructs for expressing transitive, symmetric, and inverse concepts. Therefore,we could use Protege-2000 as authoring tool for ontology, and import the resulting OWL description into an EMMO environment. Figure 7 shows the OWL representation for the ontology in Fig. 6.

However, by representing the ontology in the standard formats, such as OWL, more complex inferences drawn form the ontology knowledge cannot be integrated into EMMA queries. Therefore, we plan to develop our own ontology description language compatible with the EMMO model allowing for sophisticated reasoning on EMMOs.

```
<rdf:RDF
     xmlns:rdf ="http://www.w3.org/1999/02/22-rdf-syntax-ns#"
     xmlns:rdfs="http://www.w3.org/2000/01/rdf-schema#"
     xmlns:owl="http://www.w3.org/2002/07/owl#" >
    <rdf:Property rdf:ID="globally-allude"/>
    <rdf:Property rdf:ID="rework">
        <rdfs:subPropertyOf rdf:resource="#globally-allude"/></rdf:Property>
    <owl:TransitiveProperty rdf:ID="influence">
        <rdfs:subPropertyOf rdf:resource="#globally-allude"/></owl:TransitiveProperty>
    <rdf:Property rdf:ID="remake">
        <rdfs:subPropertyOf rdf:resource="#rework"/> </rdf:Property>
    <rdf:Property rdf:ID="retell">
        <rdfs:subPropertyOf rdf:resource="#rework"/></rdf:Property>
    <rdf:Property rdf:ID="is-retold">
        <owl:inverseOf rdf:resource="#retell"/></rdf:Property>
    <rdf:Property rdf:ID="locally-allude"/>
    <owl:SymmetricProperty rdf:ID="similar">
        <rdfs:subPropertyOf rdf:resource="#locally-allude"/></owl:SymmetricProperty>
</rdf:RDF>
```

Fig. 7. OWL representation of the Ontology of Intertextuality

5 Conclusion

We have developed the query algebra EMMA, which enables the access to all aspects regarding the EMMO model, and provide means to integrate ontology knowledge. Currently, we are in the process of integrating ontology-based constraint checking into the EMMO authoring process. Future work will focus on the development of an ontology description language that is compatible with EMMOs to offer advanced question-answering capabilities. Furthermore, we will compile a comprehensive set of use cases for query evaluation and carry out a case study in the domain of eLearning to evaluate the feasibility of our approach in a real-word environment.

References

1. Schellner, K., Westermann, U., Zillner, S., Klas, W.: CULTOS: Towards a World-Wide Digital Collection of Exchangeable Units of Multimedia Content for Intertextual Studies . In: Proc. of the Conference on Distributed Multimedia Systems (DMS 2003), Miami, Florida (2003)
2. Ayars, J., et al.: Synchronized Multimedia Integration Language (SMIL 2.0). W3C Recommendation, World Wide Web Consortium (W3C) (2001)
3. Ferraiolo, J., Jun, F., Jackson, D.: Scalable Vector Graphics (SVG) 1.1. W3C Recommendation, World Wide Web Consortium (W3C) (2003)
4. Lassila, O., Swick, R.: Resource Description Framework (RDF) Model and Syntax Specification. W3C Recommendation, World Wide Web Consortium (W3C) (1999)
5. ISO/IEC JTC 1/SC 34/WG 3: Information Technology – SGML Applications – Topic Maps. ISO/IEC International Standard 13250:2000, International Organization for Standardization/International Electrotechnical Commission (ISO/IEC) (2000)
6. ISO/JTC 1/SC 32/WG 2: Conceptual Graphs. ISO/IEC International Standard, International Organization for Standardization/International Electrotechnical Commission (ISO/IEC) (2001)

7. ISO/IEC JTC 1/SC 29/WG 11: Information Technology – Multimedia Content Description Interface – Part 5: Multimedia Description Schemes. Final Draft International Standard 15938-5:2001, ISO/IEC (2001)
8. Frasincar, F., et al.: RAL: An Algebra for Querying RDF. In: Proc. of the Third International Conference on Web Information Systems Engineering (WISE 2000), Singapore (2002)
9. Karvounarakis, G., et al.: RQL: A Declarative Query Language for RDF. In: Proc. of the 11th International World Wide Web Conference (WWW 2002), Honolulu, Hawaii (2002)
10. Brickely, D., Guha, R.: Resource Description Framework (RDF) Vocabulary Description Language 1.0: RDF Schema. W3C Working Draft, World Wide Web Consortium (W3C) (2002)
11. Garshol, L.: Tolog 0.1. Ontopia Technical Report, Ontopia (2003)
12. Bogachev, D.: TMPath – Revisited. Online Article, available under http://homepage.mac.com/dmitryv/TopicMaps/TMPath/TMPathRevisited.html (2004)
13. Barta, R., Gylta, J.: XTM::Path – Topic Map management, XPath like retrieval and construction facility. Online Article, available under http://cpan.uwinnipeg.ca/htdocs/XTM/XTM/Path.html (2002)
14. Sowa, J.: Knowledge Representation - Logical, Philosophical, and Computational Foundations. Brooks/Cole, Pacific Grove, USA (2000)
15. Manjunath, B., Salembier, P., Sikora, T., eds.: Introduction to MPEG-7. John Wiley & Sons, West Sussex, UK (2002)
16. Fensel, D.: Ontologies: A Silver Bullet for Knowledge Management and Electronic Commerce. Springer, Heidelberg (2001)
17. Connolly, D., et al.: DAML+OIL (March 2001) Reference. W3C Note, World Wide Web Consortium (W3C) (2001)
18. Schneider, P., Hayes, P., Horrocks, I.: OWL Web Ontology Language Semantics and Abstract Syntax. W3C Recommendation, World Wide Web Consortium (W3C) (2004)
19. Maedche, A.: Ontology Learning for the Semantic Web. Kluwer Academic Publishers, Massachusetts, USA (2002)
20. Benari, M., et al.: Proposal for a Standard Ontology of Intertextualtiy. Public Deliverable Version 2.0, CULTOS Consortium and Project Planning (2003)

Toward Semantic Web Services for Multimedia Adaptation

Dietmar Jannach, Klaus Leopold, Christian Timmerer, and Hermann Hellwagner

Department of Business Informatics & Application Systems,
Department of Information Technology
University Klagenfurt, 9020 Austria
{firstname.lastname}@uni-klu.ac.at

Abstract. *Universal Multimedia Access* (UMA), where users can consume any multimedia resource anywhere at any time, is the driving vision of ongoing ISO/IEC Moving Picture Experts Group (MPEG) standardization efforts. In that context, intelligent *adaptation* means that before resources are sent over the network, they are prepared according to the client's device capabilities, the network conditions, or even the user's content preferences. In this paper, we argue that *Semantic Web Services* can serve as a key enabling technology to achieve the goals of UMA. As the standards evolve, more and more specialized software tools will be available that provide specific functionalities for adapting the media in different dimensions. When the functionality of such tools is described declaratively with the means of Semantic Web Services technology, intelligent *adaptation network nodes* can be developed, capable of automatically composing multi-step adaptation sequences and dynamically integrating such services available on the Web. This paper describes the architecture and a prototypical implementation of an intelligent adaptation node that supports automatic, knowledge-based service composition which is made possible by the shared domain ontology defined in MPEG metadata standards.

1 Introduction

The increasing availability of high-speed wired and wireless networks as well as the development of a new generation of powerful (mobile) end-user devices like Personal Digital Assistants or cell phones leads to new ways in which multimedia resources can be consumed over the Web. At the same time, new standards like MPEG-7 [1] have become available, allowing us to enrich media content with semantic content annotations, which in turn facilitates new forms of multimedia experience, like search on specific topics or semantics-based content selection and filtering.

MPEG-21 is an emerging ISO/IEC standard that aims at addressing these new challenges by defining a normative open framework for multimedia delivery and consumption involving all parties in the delivery and consumption chain[1]. One of the driving visions of these efforts is *Universal Multimedia Access* (UMA), where users can consume any multimedia resource anywhere at any time. A major part of these

[1] http://www.chiariglione.org/mpeg

X. Zhou et al. (Eds.): WISE 2004, LNCS 3306, pp. 641–652, 2004.
© Springer-Verlag Berlin Heidelberg 2004

standardization efforts deals with the definition of an interoperable framework for *Digital Item Adaptation* (DIA) [2]. Adaptation in that context means that a given resource is adapted according to the user's specific requirements as well as to given device and network capabilities before it is sent over the network. Figure 1 shows a typical distributed environment where different types of end-user devices are used to consume multimedia content over heterogeneous networks.

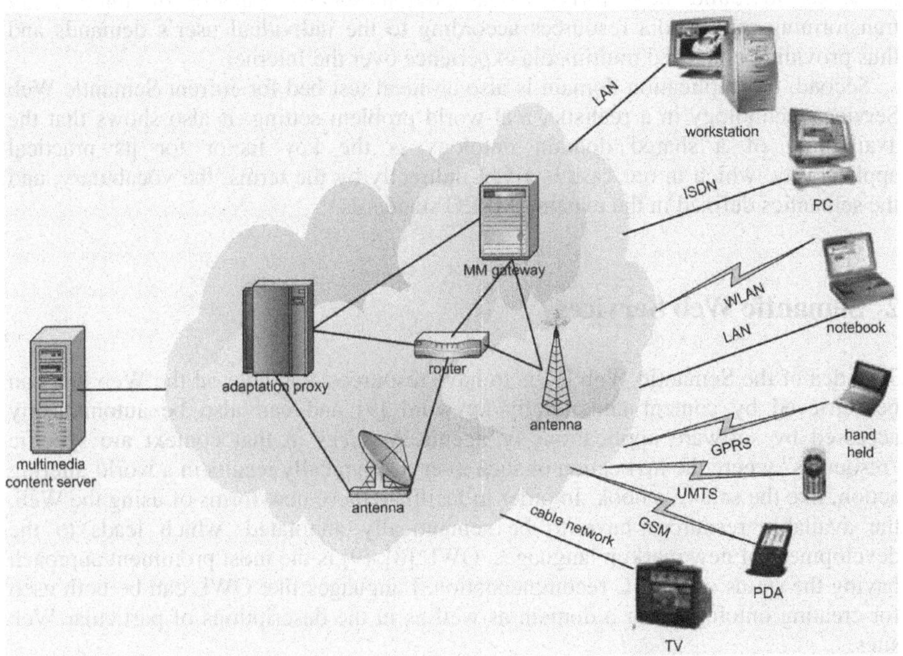

Fig. 1. Multimedia provision over the Internet

Currently, the scope of MPEG-21 standards with respect to adaptation comprises mechanisms (normative description schemes) enabling interoperability by describing the adaptation problem, like the terminal capabilities, the user preferences, or the format of the resource itself. The implementation of an engine that actually performs the required adaptation steps is left to tool vendors and is currently beyond the scope of standardization.

Nonetheless, there is a specific requirement in that context that is only marginally addressed in the current standardization efforts, i.e., the multimedia framework "... *shall support a convenient and efficient way to concatenate multiple adaptation steps*" [6]. Therefore, in order to enable efficient treatment and automatic construction of such transformation sequences by an adaptation engine, we argue that mechanisms are needed that allow us to capture the *semantics* of adaptation steps. Note that it does not seem realistic that one single software tool will be able to perform all required adaptation steps for the various user preferences, terminal capabilities, network characteristics, or even for the diverse set of coding formats. Consequently, such a mechanism has to be expressive enough and independent from the actual implementation such that interoperability among tools of different vendors is guaranteed. Finally, an open and extensible approach has to be chosen, such that no changes in the general mechanism are required when new forms of adaptation are possible as the standards evolve or new tools become available.

In this paper, we demonstrate how *Semantic Web Services* [5],[7] can serve as a key enabling technology for fulfilling these currently open requirements. The contribution of this work is twofold. First, semantic descriptions of adaptation steps allow us to build new forms of adaptation servers capable of intelligently transforming multimedia resources according to the individual user's demands and thus providing enhanced multimedia experience over the Internet.

Second, the application domain is also an ideal test bed for current Semantic Web Services technology in a realistic, real-world problem setting. It also shows that the availability of a shared domain ontology is the key factor for its practical applicability, which in our case is given indirectly by the terms, the vocabulary, and the semantics defined in the existing MPEG standards.

2 Semantic Web Services

The idea of the Semantic Web [5] is to have resources available on the Web that can be retrieved by content and not by keyword [9] and can also be automatically accessed by software applications or agents. *Services* in that context are specific "resources" where the invocation of such a service typically results in a world-altering action, like the sale of a book. In order to facilitate these new forms of using the Web, the available resources have to be semantically annotated, which leads to the development of new markup languages. OWL [8], [9] is the most prominent approach having the status of a W3C recommendation. Languages like OWL can be both used for creating ontologies for a domain as well as in the descriptions of particular Web sites.

If we look at *service*-type resources, the envisioned automation in the Semantic Web means that we need annotation mechanisms such that software agents can, e.g., search for appropriate services, invoke them with the required parameters, or even compose a complex transaction from several distributed services. A typical example from the domain of travel planning is described in [7], where a complete travel arrangement requires the invocation of multiple services, like making a hotel reservation or booking a flight. These requirements are currently addressed in OWL-S [9], which constitutes a general ontology for the domain of services.

Automatic *service composition* and *interoperation* are the most important aspects with respect to our problem domain of intelligent multimedia adaptation. (Other OWL features related to organizational aspects, e.g., service registration and publication, are not discussed in this paper.) In order to support these tasks, OWL-S comprises mechanisms to describe the functionality of a service in terms of a description of the transformation that is caused when a service is invoked. In particular, with OWL-S one can declaratively describe the *inputs*, *outputs*, *preconditions*, and *effects* (IOPE) of a service. This particular IOPE approach is also widely used for planning tasks in Artificial Intelligence.

The *Semantic Web* and its underlying technologies can therefore also change the way software is developed in a more general way, i.e., as Semantic Web proponents put it, "creating software will be just a matter of finding the right components on the

Web and a specification document linking to these components. The new software is again just a resource available on the Web"[2]

3 An Adaptation Framework Based on Semantic Web Services

The new possibilities of Digital Item Adaptation in the context of the MPEG-7 and MPEG-21 standards induce new requirements for multimedia servers which should be able to intelligently adapt the media resources according to their clients' needs:

- The system should be able to perform adaptation on various resource types (videos, images, etc.) and with respect to different dimensions, e.g., media transcoding or content selection. At the moment no tool exists that can handle all these adaptations in a single step. Therefore, multi-step adaptation chains have to be supported.
- A lot of adaptation utilities with specific functionality are already (freely) available and should be re-used by the adaptation engine. As such, the adaptation engine must provide open interfaces such that these tools can be easily incorporated.
- As the standards emerge and the corresponding tools are available, additional coding formats and forms of adaptation will become possible. Consequently, the mechanism for computing the required adaptation operations should be based on declarative specifications in order to be robust and extensible with respect to such additions.

In order to address these new requirements, we propose a knowledge-based approach [3], which is sketched in Figure 2. Here, a client requests a certain resource from a multimedia server and also provides a declarative description of its usage environment (i.e., device capabilities, network conditions, and user preferences). Together with the multimedia resource, the media server stores descriptions of the content and the available adaptation tools. These metadata are the input for the *adaptation decision taking engine* which produces a sequence of appropriate transformation steps (an adaptation plan). The adaptation plan is then forwarded to the *adaptation engine* which executes the adaptation tools on the original resource according to the adaptation plan and, thus, produces the adapted multimedia resource.

In the framework presented in this paper, we propose to model this process of constructing the adaptation plan as a classical state-space planning problem (see, e.g., [10]), where the description of the existing resource is the start state, the functionality provided by existing tools corresponds to world-altering actions, and the user requirements can be mapped to the goal state.

The following simple example sketches how transformation steps can be described in terms of inputs, outputs, preconditions, and effects (IOPE) and how a suitable adaptation plan for a given problem is constructed. We use a simplified logic notation instead of the XML notation for better readability [4].

---

[2] http://www.semanticweb.org

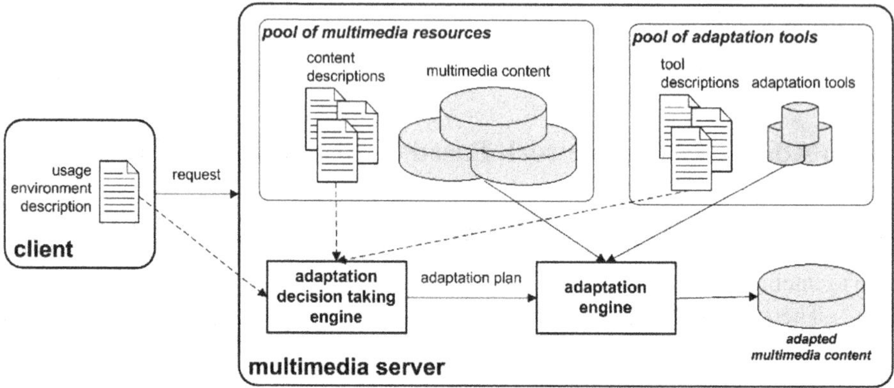

Fig. 2. Overview of knowledge-based adaptation

The existing resource is described by the following Prolog like facts:

coding_format(mpeg_4_Visual_ES). color_domain(true). frame_size(640,480).

The terminal's capabilities are as follows:

decoding_capabilities(mpeg_1). color_capabilities(false). display_size(320, 240).

Let us assume that the adaptation steps *grey scaling* and *spatial scaling* are available in an existing image transformation API, among others, such as *encoding* and *decoding*. Note that the adaptation operations as described in the following, are performed on a single image of a video. The decomposition of a video into frames is done by another tool executed by the adaptation engine.

Grey scaling (*greyscale*):

Input: *image*
Output: *greyimage*
Preconditions: *yuvImage(image), color(true).*
Effects: *yuvImage(greyimage), color(false).*

Spatial scaling (*spatialscale*):

Input: *image, x, y, newx, newy*
Output: *scaledimage*
Preconditions: *yuvImage(image), width(x), height(y)*
Effects: *yuvImage(image), width(x), height(y), horizontal(newx), vertical(newy).*

A corresponding plan can be computed by a standard state-space planner as follows, where "fb1" to "fb5" ("frame buffer") are the unified variables:

1: decode(fb1,mpeg_4_visual_es,fb2)
2: spatialscale(fb2,640,480,320,240,fb3)
3: greyscale(fb3,fb4)
4: encode(fb4,mpeg_1,fb5)

Using the IOPE approach and a logic language for modeling the functionality of adaptation services has two main advantages. First, the general approach is simple to comprehend and has a defined, commonly agreed semantic such that the automated composition of action sequences is possible. In addition, the approach is flexible, since the core planner operates on arbitrary symbols, such that new types of predicates or new actions can be easily added when they are available, without changing the implementation. Finally, there is a long history in state-space planning that showed that IOPE-style descriptions are expressive enough for a wide range of problem domains.

Note that in our specific problem setting, the IOPE modeling approach can also serve as a means for addressing further domain-specific challenges. First, as sketched in the example, frame *width* and *height* are used for describing the size of the existing resource; the client's terminal capabilities, however, are described in terms of the display size, i.e., *vertical* and *horizontal* resolution as shown in Document 1 and Document 2. Such a situation is quite common in the problem domain, as for instance different multimedia standards are involved. Such a situation can be coped with as described in the example, i.e., the ontological mapping between those terms or other (mathematical) relations can be explicitly modeled using preconditions and effects of the actions. Second, adaptation is not necessarily limited to the transformation of the media resource itself, but the same mechanism can be utilized to transform the accompanying (semantic) content descriptions, if this is needed by the client. In other words, in the adaptation process also the metadata may be updated correctly.

OWL-S 1.0 does not yet specify the rule language to be used for describing conditions or outputs of actions. Different candidates like Semantic Web Rule Language[3] are currently evaluated and will soon be part of OWL-S, as the common language and defined semantics are crucial for interoperability. However, for our problem domain we feel that in typical cases no unusual requirements on the expressiveness of the language should arise that are not within the scope of the current proposals. Another interesting aspect in our problem domain is that the level of detail of the functional descriptions of available adaptation services can vary. In the example given, each action is an atomic, single-step picture transformation. This fine-granular specification is reasonable in cases when, e.g., open-source transcoding software like *FFMPEG* or *ImageMagick*[4] should be re-used in the adaptation engine. In this scenario, the adaptation chain and the execution plan is composed of API calls to a local media processing library, showing that existing libraries can easily be integrated. On the other hand, as newer standards for semantic content annotation like MPEG-7 are increasingly established in commercial environments, specialized software companies will be able to provide such advanced adaptation functionality as (chargeable) services for their clients. With the approach described in this paper, however, the potential distributed nature of the individual services is transparent for the engine.

In our opinion, one of the most important aspects that can hamper the usage of *Semantic Web Services* is the problem of having a shared domain ontology. If we think again of the well-known travel planning problem, automatic service composition can only be done if all participants not only use the same terms like "hotel reservation", but also associate the same meaning with that term. Semantic markup languages like OWL (or its predecessor DAML+OIL) only provide a common infrastructure for defining, integrating, and reasoning about such ontologies, but cannot solve the problem of agreeing on a domain-specific ontology in a community. In fact, even for well-understood domains like business-to-business

---

[3] http://www.w3.org/Submission/2004/SUBM-SWRL-20040521/

[4] http://ffmpeg.sourceforge.net, http://www.imagemagick.org

electronic commerce or electronic supply-chain management, several competing pseudo-standards for XML-based data exchange emerged[5]. In our domain, however, such a common understanding can be reached by interpreting the existing MPEG standards as the basis for describing the functionality and semantics of the adaptation services.

4 Multimedia Standards as Domain Ontology

Multimedia standards like MPEG-7 or MPEG-21 precisely specify the way how multimedia resources and usage environments (e.g., terminal and network capabilities) can be annotated with additional information. XML Schema[6] technology is extensively used in the standards as the specification language for the shared vocabulary. Specific media resources are annotated with document instances that correspond to that standardized schema. Document 1 shows an example of how a video resource is annotated in MPEG-7; in particular it specifies the parameters *color* or the frame *size*, which we used in the planning example.

```
<Mpeg7>
  <Description xsi:type="ContentEntityType">
    <MultimediaContent xsi:type="VideoType">
      <Video>
        <MediaInformation id="news1_media">
          <!-- MediaIdentification ... -->
          <MediaProfile>
            <MediaFormat>
              <!-- Content, Medium, FileFormat, Filesize ... -->
              <VisualCoding>
                <Format        href="urn:mpeg:mpeg7:cs:VisualCodingFormatCS:2001:3.3.1"
                         colorDomain="color">
                  <Name xml:lang="en">
                         MPEG-4 Visual Advanced Simple Profile @ Level 0</Name>
                </Format>
                <Pixel aspectRatio="0.75" bitsPer="8"/>
                <Frame width="640" height="480" rate="25"/>
              </VisualCoding>
            </MediaFormat>
          </MediaProfile>
        </MediaInformation>
      </Video>
    </MultimediaContent>
  </Description>
</Mpeg7>
```

Document 1. Fragment of an MPEG-7 video description

The MPEG-21 DIA description of the end device used in the planning example is shown in Document 2.

Although not explicitly mentioned as such, the definitions in the standards implicitly form a precise ontology for the multimedia domain. The dimensions and corresponding syntactical structures in which a resource can be annotated are strictly defined. The intended semantics of the terms is specified in natural language. For the examples above, the *colorDomain* attribute describes the color domain of the video with a frame size of 640×480 pixels indicated by the *width* and *height* attributes. The

[5] http://www.ebxml.org/

[6] http://www.w3.org/XML/Schema

```
<DIA>
  <Description xsi:type="UsageEnvironmentType">
    <UsageEnvironmentProperty xsi:type="TerminalsType">
      <Terminal>
        <TerminalCapability xsi:type="DisplaysType">
          <Display>
            <DisplayCapability
                 xsi:type="DisplayCapabilityType"
                 activeDisplay="true" colorCapable="false">
              <Mode>
                <Resolution horizontal="320" vertical="240"
                 activeResolution="true"/>
                <Resolution horizontal="160" vertical="120"
                 activeResolution="false"/>
                <Resolution horizontal="80" vertical="60"
                 activeResolution="false"/>
              </Mode>
            </DisplayCapability>
          </Display>
        </TerminalCapability>
      </Terminal>
    </UsageEnvironmentProperty>
  </Description>
</DIA>
```

Document 2. MPEG-21 DIA description of a terminal with certain display capabilities

resolution and color capabilities of the rendering device are described by the *horizontal* and *vertical* attributes and the *colorCapable* attribute respectively. Please note that such a rendering device could support multiple resolutions and the resolution mode currently used is indicated by the Boolean *activeResolution* attribute.

For our multi-step adaptation problem, the representation mechanism for the resource descriptions (MPEG-7) and the client preferences (MPEG-21) is therefore already given. At the moment, the language to be used for describing the semantics of the transformation services is not within the scope of OWL-S. Quite obviously, the concepts that are used in pre-conditions and effects of the services have to correspond to those that are used in the standards.

In our current prototypical implementation, we have chosen a proprietary notation that is automatically transformed to an internal, logic-based format which can be exploited by a Prolog-based planning engine. Our experiments show that the complexity of the conditions and expressions that we need for describing a transformation service is rather low and the description can be expressed by a set of facts. This also holds for a potential extension of the approach for the problem of *Digital Rights Management (DRM)*[7]. If some transformations, like the extraction of the audio stream from a movie, require particular rights, such information can be easily incorporated in our extensible approach and encoded in the pre-conditions of the transformation functions.

Overall, we are optimistic that the rule language that is developed for OWL-S will be expressive enough for our problem domain and that compatibility of our prototype can be reached by transforming the descriptions on the syntactical level.

Note that a full re-implementation of the MPEG standards with the representation means of OWL-S is in principle possible and would allow for a consistent usage of OWL technology throughout. As a side effect, such an approach would in our opinion

[7] Open Mobile Alliance (http://www.openmobilealliance.org) and Digital Media Project (http://www.chiariglione.org/project)

also improve the comprehensibility and clarity of the standards. A first step in that direction can be the construction of an OWL-based ontology for the domain, which can serve as accompanying material that can be used for constructing the semantics descriptions for adaptation services. Figure 3 illustrates a small fraction of the object relations within an MPEG-21 document which could be translated to OWL in a straightforward manner.

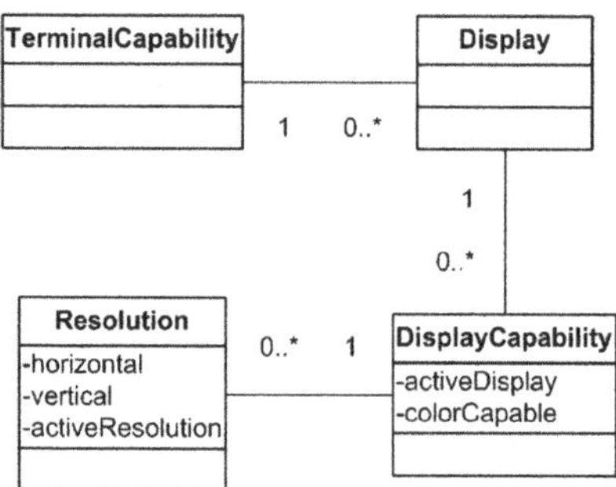

Fig. 3. Fraction of the object relations of an MPEG-21 document

5 Experimental Results

In order to evaluate the general feasibility of the described approach, we implemented a first proof-of-concept prototype. The architecture of our system corresponds to the system overview depicted in Figure 2. The intelligence required for computing the adaptation chains is implemented in a light-weight state-space planner written in SWI-Prolog[8]. Beside a small module responsible for actually executing the needed transformations on the original resource, the system consists of parsers and Java-based transformation tools for processing the XML documents and transforming them to the internal representation. With regard to computational complexity, we found that the actual planning problems were rather simple and did not cause performance problems. In particular the length of the needed plans, which is an important factor influencing the complexity of the problem space, was very small, typically no more than five to seven steps. In all of our experiments, the computation of the plan could be done in less than one second on a standard PC or the non-existence of such a plan could be proven. In addition, the planning process only takes a marginal part of the overall process of providing an adapted resource over the Web. The costly operations are typically the transformation itself or the establishment of streaming sessions, in particular when network conditions change or session mobility is involved, which means that during the resource consumption the session is migrated to another end-user device.

At the moment, we have not yet performed experiments in a real distributed environment, but rather integrated locally available transformation tools like *FFMPEG* or *ImageMagick*. Nonetheless, the usage of declarative functionality descriptions and a general function invocation mechanism already provided

[8] http://www.swi-prolog.org

significant benefits. For instance, the system is extensible as the incorporation of new transformation tools does not cause any implementation efforts; in addition, interoperability across platforms and programming languages is guaranteed as the actual tools provide an independent, XML-based invocation interface based on Web Service technology. Finally, for the implementation of a scenario where multiple adaptation servers are used that only conjointly can perform all required adaptation steps, we can then rely on existing and well-established technologies like WSDL or UDDI[9] for administrative tasks like service registration etc.

6 Related Work

Up to now, Semantic Web technology was not broadly used in the field of current multimedia-related research and only limited efforts like in [11] where spent in the direction of bringing together tools and technologies for describing multimedia content and the shared knowledge representation provided by the *Semantic Web*.

In [12] for instance, an approach towards automated, knowledge-assisted *content analysis* is described. In this work, the authors show how domain specific ontologies can be used for narrowing the semantic gap that arises when concepts and objects should be automatically extracted without human intervention from image or spatio-temporal features. They use Semantic Web technologies as a representation mechanism for modeling additional domain-specific knowledge because of the intention that the general mechanisms of knowledge representation and reasoning should be applicable for arbitrary other domains.

In [13] an approach is presented, where ontologies are serving as integrating technology for advanced concept, metadata, and content browsing and retrieval in the domain of digital museum information. In this work, a domain ontology and a semantic layer with references to the actual objects of the digital collection like 2-D or 3-D images and models was developed. Semantic Web technology was mainly used for the purpose of system integration, as the existing information like textual metadata on items is often stored in separate collections and legacy systems.

The described approaches use Semantic Web technology basically as a tool for further semantic annotations and domain-specific ontologies with the goals of better retrieval methods or content analysis. In our work, we use Semantic Web technologies at a different level as we aim at transforming the contents themselves. The shared ontology required for the integration of such adaptation services is in our case domain-independent and defined in the existing multimedia standards. As such, we also view the problem domain as a promising area for Semantic Web Services in general, as the number of reported real-world application fields is still limited.

In [14] the architecture of an adaptive proxy for MPEG-4 visual streams is described which adapts MPEG-4 resources according to terminal capabilities (display size and color capabilities) and network characteristics (available bandwidth). Therefore, an adaptor chain concept has been introduced enabling the concatenation of several adaptation steps. However, this approach is currently restricted to the MPEG-4 visual domain. While an adaptor chain is dynamically instantiated according to the usage environment, the approach lacks extensibility in the sense that new

[9] http://www.w3.org/TR/wsdl, http://www.uddi.org

adaptors must implement a predefined interface and need to be integrated into the existing system by re-compilation of the whole adaptation engine. The concept of adaptor chains follows an imperative (procedural) approach whereas our approach is declarative and therefore not restricted to a certain programming language, enabling the integration of new adaptation algorithms at run-time.

Within MPEG-21, only one tool (AdaptationQoS) which is part of the DIA specification deals somehow with the issue of adaptation decision taking. AdaptationQoS supports the selection of optimal parameter settings for media resource adaptation engines that satisfy constraints imposed by terminals and/or networks while maximizing the Quality of Service [15]. Therefore, the relationship between constraints, feasible adaptation operations satisfying these constraints, and associated utilities (qualities) is described for a certain resource. However, these relationships do not cope with the semantics of the actual adaptation process as described within this paper. Furthermore, AdaptationQoS provides only relationships for a subset of the possible adaptation operations and is always related to one particular resource. Thus, it reflects only the adaptation possibilities taken into account by the content creator or provider. On the other hand, this information can be used as a decision support mechanism by providing optimal parameter settings within one adaptation step. Additionally, it provides means for describing optimization problems allowing the adaptation engine to achieve suboptimal solutions which is currently not supported by our approach, but will become part of our future work.

7 Conclusions

In this work, we argued that Semantic Web Services technologies can serve as the technical infrastructure for future multimedia adaptation services. These technologies allow us to build a new generation of intelligent multimedia adaptation engines that fully exploit the new possibilities that arise with existing and upcoming multimedia annotation standards. With the help of semantic descriptions of the functionality of existing transformation tools and services, complex multi-step adaptation sequences can be automatically computed and executed on arbitrary media resources.

The employed mechanisms inherently support interoperability, openness, and extensibility such that independence from platforms, programming languages, or the tool implementation is guaranteed.

References

1. J. M. Martinez, R. Koenen, and F. Pereira, "MPEG-7 - The Generic Multimedia Content Description Standard, Part 1," IEEE MultiMedia 9(2):78–87, April–June 2002.
2. A. Vetro and C. Timmerer, "Overview of the Digital Item Adaptation Standard", IEEE Transactions on Multimedia, Special Issue on MPEG-21, 2004 (to appear).
3. D. Jannach, K. Leopold, and H. Hellwagner, "An extensible framework for knowledge-based multimedia adaptation", in: B. Orchard, C. Yang, M. Ali (eds.): Innovations in Applied Artificial Intelligence, LNAI 3029, Springer Verlag 2004.

4. K. Leopold, D. Jannach, and H. Hellwagner, "Knowledge-based Media Adaptation", Proceedings of the SPIE ITCom 2004, Internet Multimedia Management Systems IV, vol. 5601, 25-28 October 2004 (to appear).
5. T. Berners-Lee, J. Hendler, and O. Lassila, "The Semantic Web", Scientific American 284(5):34-43, 2001.
6. J. Bormans (ed.), "MPEG-21 Requirements v 1.5", ISO/IEC JTC 1/SC 29/WG 11 N5873, Trondheim, July 2003.
7. S. McIlraith, T.C. Son, and H. Zeng, "Semantic Web Services", IEEE Intelligent Systems, Special Issue on the Semantic Web, 16(2):46–53, 2001.
8. D. L. McGuiness and F. van Harmelen (eds.), "OWL Web Ontology Language Overview", February 2004, http://www.w3.org/TR/owl-features/.
9. The OWL Services Coalition, "OWL-S: Semantic Markup for Web Services", Technical Report, 2004, http://www.daml.org/services/owl-s/1.0/.
10. I. Bratko, *Prolog Programming for Artificial Intelligence*, 3rd Edition, Addison-Wesley 2000.
11. V. Mezaris, I. Kompatsiaris, and M. G. Strintzis, "Region-based Image Retrieval using an Object Ontology and Relevance Feedback", EURASIP Journal on Applied Signal Processing, Special Issue on Object-Based and Semantic Image and Video Analysis, 2004(6):886–901, June 2004.
12. I. Kompatsiaris, V. Mezaris, and M. G. Strintzis, "Multimedia content indexing and retrieval using an object ontology", in: G. Stamou (ed.), Multimedia Content and Semantic Web Methods, Standards and Tools, Wiley 2004.
13. M. Addis, M. Boniface, S. Goodall, P. Grimwood, S. Kim, P. Lewis, K. Martinez, and A. Stevenson, "SCULPTEUR: Towards a New Paradigm for Multimedia Museum Information Handling", Proc. of ISWC'2003, LNCS 2870, Springer Verlag 2003.
14. P. Schojer, L. Böszörmenyi, H. Hellwagner, B. Penz, and S. Podlipnig, "Architecture of a Quality Based Intelligent Proxy (QBIX) for MPEG-4 Videos", Proc. of the WWW Conference 2003, pp. 394-402, May 2003.
15. D. Mukherjee, E. Delfosse, J.G. Kim, and Y. Wang, "Terminal and Network Quality of Service", IEEE Transactions on Multimedia, Special Issue on MPEG-21, 2004 (to appear).

A Lightweight Encryption Algorithm for Mobile Online Multimedia Devices

Zheng Liu, Xue Li, and Zhaoyang Dong

School of Information Technology and Electrical Engineering,
University of Queensland, Australia

Abstract. Online multimedia data needs to be encrypted for access control. To be capable of working on mobile devices such as pocket PC and mobile phones, lightweight video encryption algorithms should be proposed. The two major problems in these algorithms are that they are either not fast enough or unable to work on highly compressed data stream. In this paper, we proposed a new lightweight encryption algorithm based on Huffman error diffusion. It is a selective algorithm working on compressed data. By carefully choosing the most significant parts (MSP), high performance is achieved with proper security. Experimental results has proved the algorithm to be fast, secure, and compression-compatible.

1 Introduction

Online mobile devices are getting popular. Similar to personal computers, online mobile devices can also access web multimedia such as image, audio and video. To control access to web multimedia, encryption is required. There are two constraints for web multimedia encryption with mobile devices. Firstly, there are various devices on the web, some does not have fast CPU and big memory, encryption algorithm must be able to work on them. In other words, lightweight encryption should be applied. Secondly, web multimedia are compressed for transmission and storage. In some devices, the encoding and decoding are done by hardware or programable circuits. It is not desired that encryption algorithm access any other data besides compressed data. In this paper, we focus on image and video, so the word "web multimedia" refers to web image and video.

People have proposed many lightweight encryption approaches to meet these requirements. They can be classified into two categories, scrambling and selective encryption. The basic idea of scrambling is to permutate multimedia data blocks or transformed data blocks. This topic is discussed in [1] in 1995 and used in some digital television solutions. Later, a frequency domain scrambling scheme is proposed in [2]. The author scramble DCT coefficients within blocks and inter blocks. In addition, the significant bit of data is encrypted to ensure security. In [3], 2D scrambling is mathematically analyzed. Accordingly, a 2D scramble algorithm is designed, which will not introduce bandwidth expansion.

Differently, selective encryption selects the most significant parts of multimedia data and encrypt them only. To improve efficiency of multimedia streaming

X. Zhou et al. (Eds.): WISE 2004, LNCS 3306, pp. 653–658, 2004.
© Springer-Verlag Berlin Heidelberg 2004

video encryption, people tried to encrypt multimedia data according to the importance. In general, low frequency DCT coefficients are considered more important. Algorithms are proposed to encrypt the first few low frequency coefficients only [4,5,6], or to encrypt the most significant bit of them [7].

However, for those network devices that does not have adequate computation resources, such as mobile devices and IP appliances, the proposed algorithm is still too complex. Further, compression/decompression in these devices are usually done by common hardware, thus, the encryption process should be independent from compression/decompression schemes if we want it to be flexible. Moreover, for network transmission consideration, encryption should not add obvious compression overhead. On the other hand, security requirements of web multimedia encryption is so critical. As we have described in [8], the security of web multimedia encryption is on entertainment level in most cases. That is to say, destroying the semantic meaning is enough, it is not necessary to conceal all static information, as for the critical level.

As a short summary, the requirements of web multimedia encryption are:

1. The encryption algorithm must be simple and fast, with low cost in computation and storage.
2. Entertainment security level is required. Destroying the quality of web multimedia is enough.
3. The algorithm should be compression independent, it should not add obvious compression overhead.

According to the requirements listed above, we designed a new lightweight encryption algorithm for web multimedia. Our algorithm is based on observations of error diffusion in variable length coding, as we described in section 2. The algorithm is illustrated in section 3, with experimental results. Finally the paper is concluded in section 4.

2 Observations on VLC Error Diffusion

There are two kind of compression algorithms in web multimedia, lossless and lossy. Lossless compression, such as GIF, PNG format, does not impact quality while compressing them. Differently, lossy compression removes redundant data which is not perceptual sensitive, thus, it can achieve higher compression ratio. In this paper, we are going to focus on lossy compression schemes, particular JPEG and MPEG.

The procedure of MPEG, the most popular video compression approach, is shown in figure 1. It consists of four stages. Firstly, the color image is converted into YUV color space. Color data (U, V) are not very important that they are sub-sampled. Then the spatial domain data are transformed using discrete cosine transformation(DCT), to frequency domain coefficients. In the next stage, DCT coefficients are quantized to round and truncate unimportant coefficients. The last stage is to compress using variable length coding(VLC). In JPEG, VLC algorithms are run-length coding and Huffman coding. For motion frames.

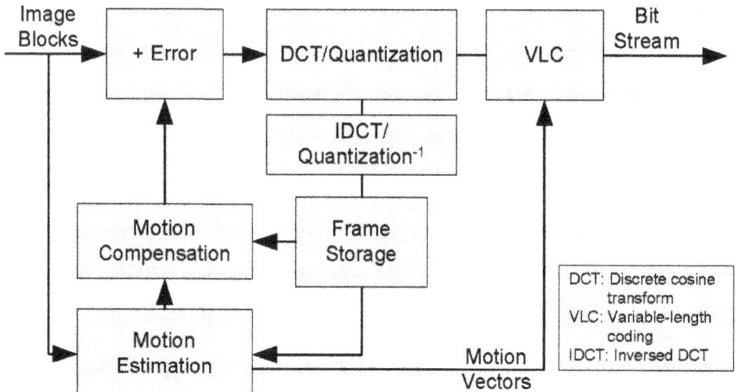

Fig. 1. Block Diagram of MPEG

They are predicted based on adjacent still frames and stored as motion vectors and compensation signals. MPEG also employ VLC coding for motion frame compression as the final stage.

As we described above, multimedia compression schemes are complex combinations of different compression algorithms. Each algorithm contributes various compression ratio to the whole compression. In table 1, some experimental results regarding compression ratio proportions are shown.

Table 1. Compression Contributions of Algorithm Employed in MPEG

Name	smq.mpg	Name	bus.mpg
original size	230400k	original size	15635k
yuv ratio	2	yuv ratio	2
runlength ratio	5.4432	runlength ratio	3.7123
huffman ratio	1.7287	huffman ratio	1.9115
motion ratio	2.07	motion ratio	3.16
compressed size	5929k	compressed size	354k
overall ratio	38.8165	overall	44.1904

In overall, multimedia data can be compressed to 1/25 or more. Therefore, it is understandable that if the compressed data is modified, the error will diffuse into a large range. Suppose that one bit is modified in compressed data, when we decompress the data, Huffman error will be raised. Although Huffman decoder can self-synchronize, it will take it a few bits to do so. Later, in run-length decoding, the error will be ulteriorly amplified. If the few error bits are in a run-value byte, the values in its full run-length will be inaccurate; If they are in a run-length byte, the length of repetition will be impacted, the synchronization of multimedia will also be destroyed. Further, in inverse DCT stage, the errors

Fig. 2. Original image vs. compression error diffused image. 1% error added.

are diffused into the macro block that they reside. The visual effect comparison of error diffused image and original image is shown in figure 2.

An experiment is designed to analysis how much the error diffuses. In the experiment, a number of web images and videos are randomly modified, then, the diffusion range is evaluated accordingly. In our experiment, we have found that the average diffusion of a bit is around 15 bits. It is to say, one bit modification on compressed media could averagely cause approximately 15 bits of error. Another result is the contribution to the error diffusion of each stage. As we prospected, the proportions are related to the compression ratio that they contribute.

3 Proposed Algorithm

According to the results we obtained in section 2, minor errors in compressed web multimedia data will result in significant visual effect. The diffusion of error can be used for encryption. With a certain extent of modification on compressed data, the visibility of multimedia data can be destroyed.

To be a reliable and fast encryption algorithm, there are two major problems to resolve. The first problem is how to select most significant encrypting bits for highest performance. Another problem is how to adjust the encryption ratio in multimedia to trade off between security and performance.

Error diffusion result is interrelated to the position of modification. For Huffman coding, modification on shorter word will cause higher diffusion. For run-length coding, modification on run-length will cause higher diffusion. Therefore, our algorithm will try to look for these two kinds of data to encrypt.

The algorithm we proposed can be described as below:

Suppose the compressed data stream is $C = c_1, c_2......c_n$;

Encryption key is K;

RunSign=FindRunSign(HuffmanTable)
p=GeneratePNbit(K)
for Each c_i in C **do**
  if c_i == RunSign **then**
    i++

```
      p=GeneratePNbit(p)
      Encrypt(c_i.MSB(2),p)
    end if
    if c_i.HuffmanLength¡=Threshold then
      p=GeneratePNbit(p)
      Encrypt(c_i.MSB(Threshold −c_i.HuffmanLength,p))
    end if
  end for
  Scramble blocks
```

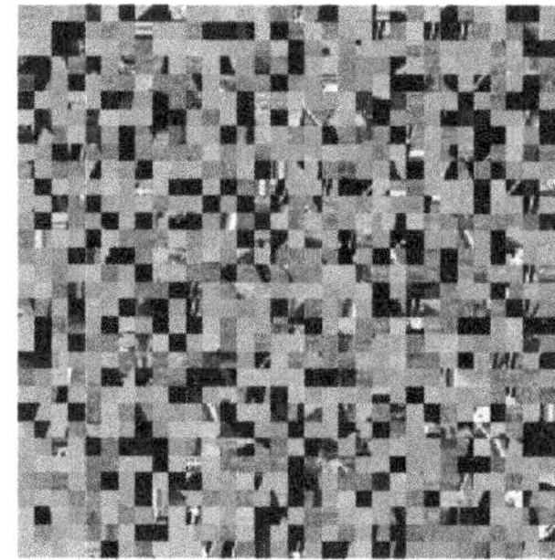

Fig. 3. Comparison of original image and encrypted image using our proposed algorithm

The algorithm is implemented in Matlab platform to encrypt JPEG compressed data stream. For assessment, we compare our algorithm to the most popular selective algorithm in three facets: performance, security, compression overhead. As it is a lightweight encryption algorithm, performance is the primary assessment criteria. We compared the performance of our proposed algorithm and selective algorithm [5]. In this experiment, IBM SEAL stream cipher [9] is used as PN generator, DES is used for selective algorithm. In our algorithm, about 1/13.1 (statical value) data needs to be encrypted. In selective algorithm, DC and first 5 ACs are selected, so there is 6/64=1/10.6 data needs to be encrypted. Regardless the performance bias between DES and SEAL, our proposed algorithm is 1.23 times faster than selective algorithm.

Furthermore, selective encryption must decode data before processing, so it will be definitely slower than shown in the figure. Figure 3 performs the encryption results of the proposed algorithm. As shown, our algorithms have provided eligible security level for entertainment requirements. There is no obvious visible information in the encrypted multimedia data.

For compression overhead, as our algorithm work on the compressed data stream, it will definitely introduce zero compression overhead. On the contrary, selective encryption will cause some enlargement to the data bandwidth, which might slow down transmission of web multimedia. Generally, our experiments has revealed that frequency domain permutation will cost 12-51% increases in compression data size, modification on significant bits will cause 2-17% increases(with 1/8 bits modified), depending on video data types, algorithms, and compression factors. It is obvious that any algorithm using any of these technology will not escape compression overhead problem, however, our algorithm can.

4 Conclusion

In this paper, we discussed a novel encryption approach for web multimedia encryption. Web multimedia data requires fast, low cost encryption algorithm without influences on transmission. To achieve this goal, we analyzed the compression scheme of web multimedia data. Based on the analysis and observations, a VLC error diffusion based encryption algorithm is proposed. The performance and security are accessed by experiments. The VLC based algorithm has shown great viability comparing to generic lightweight encryption algorithms. Another obvious advantage is that this algorithm is compression independent, which means it will not interfere compression process.

References

1. Macq, B.M., Quisquater, J.J.: Cryptology for digital tv broadcasting. (1995) Proceedings-of-the-IEEE. June 1995; 83(6): 944-57.
2. Wenjun, Z., Lei, S.: Efficient frequency domain selective scrambling of digital video, Sharp Labs. America Inc. Camas WA USA (2003) IEEE-Transactions-on-Multimedia. March 2003; 5(1): 118-29 Usa 1520-9210 Copyright 2003, IEEE.
3. D. Van De Ville, W. Philips, R.V.d.W.I.L.: Image scrambling without bandwidth expansion. IEEE Transactions on Circuits and Systems for Video Technology (2001)
4. Cheng, H.: Partial encryption for image and video communication (1998) Master's thesis, Univ. of Alberta, 1998. http://citeseer.ist.psu.edu/cheng98partial.html.
5. Agi, I., Gong, L.: An empirical study of secure mpeg video transmission (1996) In Symposium on Network and Distributed Systems Security. IEEE, 1996.
6. Qiao, L., Nahrstedt, K.: Comparison of MPEG encryption algorithms. Computers and Graphics **22** (1998) 437–448
7. Shi, C., Wang, S., Bhargava, B.: Mpeg video encryption in real-time using secret key cryptography (1999) Proc. of PDPTA '99, (Las Vegas, Nevada), 1999.
8. Liu, Z., Li, X.: Enhancing security of frequency domain video encryption (2004) ACM Multimedia 2004, October 16, 2004, New York, USA.
9. Rogaway, P., Coppersmith, D.: A software-optimized encryption algorithm. Journal of Cryptology: the journal of the International Association for Cryptologic Research **11** (1998) 273–287

Aspect-ARM: An Aspect-Oriented Active Rule System for Heterogeneous Multimedia Information

Shuichi Kurabayashi[1] and Yasushi Kiyoki[2]

[1] Graduate School of Media and Governance, Keio University
5322 Endoh, Fujisawa, Kanagawa, 252-0816, Japan
kurabaya@sfc.keio.ac.jp

[2] Faculty of Environmental Information, Keio University
5322 Endoh, Fujisawa, Kanagawa, 252-0816, Japan
kiyoki@sfc.keio.ac.jp

Abstract. An active database mechanism is important to realize new information provision in current mobile and ubiquitous computing environments. Applying an active database mechanism to multidatabase environments realizes the automatic and meaningful information provision from various and heterogeneous databases. In this paper, we propose an aspect-oriented active rule system, called Aspect-ARM, for heterogeneous multimedia information resources. The Aspect-ARM provides an ECA rule language, called an aspect-ECA rule language, in adapting the rule system to the multimedia information in active and dynamic multidatabase environments. The aspect-ECA rule language is designed on a framework of conceptual data modeling for structuring complex multimedia data from multiple viewpoints. This model focuses on two concepts: "aspects" of multimedia data and "relationships" among multimedia data. We call this data model an aspect-oriented data model. The feature of this model is to deal with meanings included implicitly in media data in active rule evaluation. By introducing aspect-ECA rules with the aspect-oriented data model, it is possible to provide the active database functionality in cross-over multimedia database environments without affecting application structures and local information system structures.

1 Introduction

Currently, an incommensurable amount of digital information is becoming available in digital libraries and on the WWW. Furthermore, we have opportunities to create various multimedia information resources with digital devices, such as digital cameras and digital music recorders. Those multimedia data are stored in passive information systems, such as web servers and relational database systems. Users must manually and periodically check the state of data to stay up-to-date on multimedia information in passive systems. By introducing the active database functionality [1] [2] into multimedia information resources in multidatabase environments, in particular, users can receive up-to-date information automatically. Active systems offer higher capability of information publishing than passive systems. However, the active database functionality have been considered mostly in centralized environments [3]. In spite of the fact that users have rapidly growing access to these information resources, users must manually compare,

X. Zhou et al. (Eds.): WISE 2004, LNCS 3306, pp. 659–667, 2004.
© Springer-Verlag Berlin Heidelberg 2004

examine and integrate different information resources to obtain objective information, because conventional systems have difficulty in supporting such comparison and examination automatically among heterogeneous multimedia information resources. In multidatabase environments, active behavior is the essential missing piece that allows the automatic and meaningful dissemination of information that matches users' implicit requirements.

Several studies have been proposed to realize active multidatabase systems [4] [5] [6] [7] [8] [9]. Generally speaking, most of the projects that try to incorporate active behavior in multidatabase environments have not dealt with active dissemination of multimedia data. Most of conventional approaches aims to detect a meaningful event from a flood of disseminated events. An event is occurrence of something interest. Otherwise, our approach deals with "situations" that relationships among multimedia data have big meanings. A situation is a state of data and a relationship among data. We have proposed the basic active multidatabase system architecture and the ECA rule language for it [10] [11]. Conventional rule languages provided very basic operators to describe situations in heterogeneous and open database environments. The aim of our approach is detecting a meaningful situations of multimedia information which change drastically and dynamically. As far as we know, there are no active rule systems suitable for distributed multimedia information.

For the new objective discussed above, we propose an aspect-oriented **A**ctive **R**ule system for heterogeneous **M**ultimedia information, called *Aspect-ARM*. The Aspect-ARM provides an abstract and conceptual data model to describe complex meanings of multimedia data from multiple viewpoints. This data model focuses on two concepts: "aspects" of multimedia data and "relationships" among multimedia data. We call this data model the *aspect-oriented data model*. The aspect represents a certain meaning of multimedia data from a specific viewpoint. The relationship represents implicit and dynamic correlation among the modeled multimedia data. We design a new generation ECA rule language, called an *aspect-ECA rule language*. The aspect-ECA rule language is able to deal with implicit situations of media data in active rule evaluation, by allowing to evaluate meanings behind the media data in the aspect-oriented data model. In this paper, we propose the Aspect-ARM and the aspect-ECA rule language with its clear semantics, which are defined with the concept of aspects, specifically adapted to the multimedia information in active and dynamic multimedia databases environments. The Aspect-ARM has two essential features: i) *Media independence* of active rules makes it possible to describe meanings of multimedia data in a simple way. Aspect-ECA rules are not affected by any low-level features of media data, such as file formats and access methods. ii) *Dynamism* of active rules, that is achieved by on-demand rule evaluation mechanism of the Aspect-ARM, provides capability of up-to-date information dissemination.

2 Aspect-ARM

The goal is to realize a system architecture for new generation dissemination of information in distributed and heterogeneous database environments. In designing the Aspect-ARM, one basic premise is that the rule model needs to be flexible and rich enough

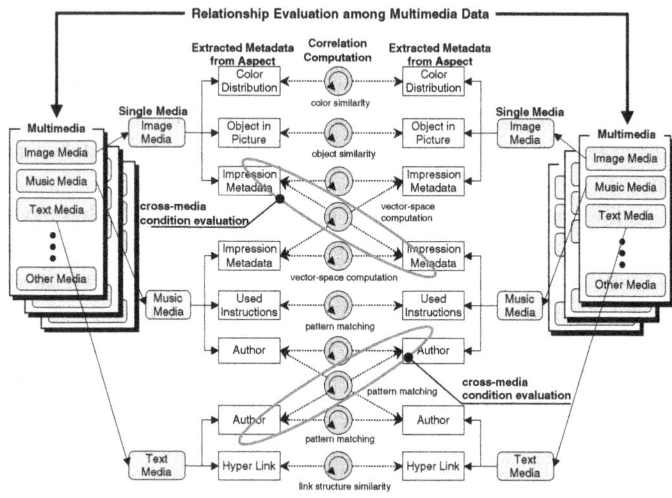

Fig. 1. Overview of the Aspect-Oriented Media Modelling Framework

to intuitively describe complex meanings of multimedia information. Furthermore, in the active multidatabase environment, where a wide variety of multimedia information resources are dynamically added and deleted, how to evaluate relationships among them in a dynamic and meaningful way is a significant issue.

2.1 Foundations

As multimedia data may have different meanings when they are modeled from different viewpoints, our premise is that the multimedia data modeling from multiple viewpoint is essentially needed for dealing with meanings behind the media. The aspect-oriented data model focuses on two concepts: "aspects" of multimedia data and "relationships" among multimedia data. An aspect determines a feature set of multimedia data, which represents represents a certain meaning from the specific viewpoint. For example, to retrieve music data, users may retrieve music by instructions used in music, or by impressions of music. In those cases, instructions used in music and impression words are aspects of music. A relationship determines computation method, which is used to evaluate implicit and dynamic relationships among multimedia data, for correlations among features extracted from the specific aspect. As shown in Figure 1, multimedia data consists of several kinds of single media. Each single media has multiple aspects, and every aspect has its own meaning. Therefore, different aspects have different features. Relationships among those multimedia data are dependent on the selected aspects. As media data has a separate meaning for every aspect, extremely wide variety of relationships exist among multimedia data. For dealing with such dynamic relationships among media data, we take an approach to describe relationships by functions which computes correlations among them. No static descriptions about relationships are introduced. In the active multidatabase environment, where a wide variety of multimedia information

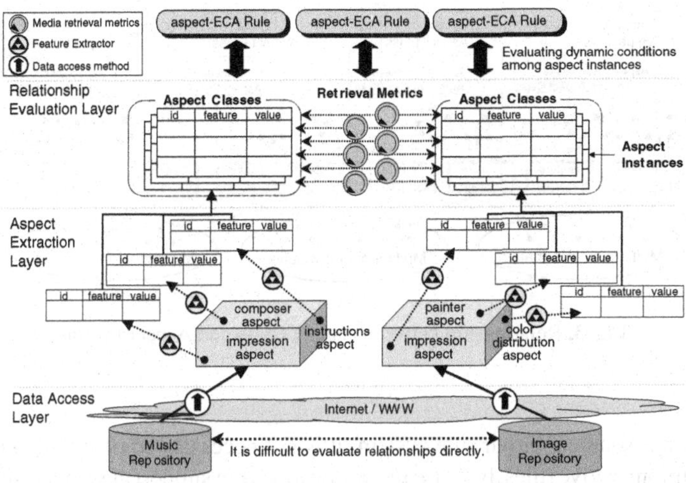

Fig. 2. Overview of the Aspect-ARM

resources are dynamically added and deleted, it is difficult to statically describe relationships among those information resources. Describing relationships with functions makes it possible to dynamically compute relationships among the multimedia data.

To describe multiple meanings of multimedia data, the Aspect-ARM employs the concept of class and instance. Aspect classes serve as uniform descriptive structures of meanings of multimedia data. An aspect instance represents a particular exemplar of an aspect class that represents a certain meaning of multimedia data. An aspect instance contains a metadata for aspect-oriented media retrieval. Aspect instances are created by extracting a particular feature set from the media data. In the Aspect-ARM, every multimedia information resource can be modeled as multiple aspect instances by applying feature extraction methods. We use an aspect instance as an atomic data element of the Aspect-ARM, and all the operators of our system are applied to a set of aspect instances. The Aspect-ARM does not deal with entities of media data but metadata of media data. The aspect-oriented data model makes aspect-ECA rules independent of underlying information systems as shown in Figure 2.

2.2 Aspect-ECA Rule Language

We have designed the aspect-ECA rule language as an extension of the conventional **E**vent / **C**ondition / **A**ction (ECA)-rule model [12] [13] for adjusting it to multimedia multidatabase environments. An event is an occurrence the system must react to. When an event occurs, all respective rules are triggered. A condition may be a query or predicate on the aspect-oriented data model. If the result of evaluation is true or non-empty, respectively, the condition is satisfied. If the condition of a triggered rule is fulfilled then its action is executed. The action specifies the reactive behavior of the rule. It may contain commands for dissemination of information from heterogeneous multimedia

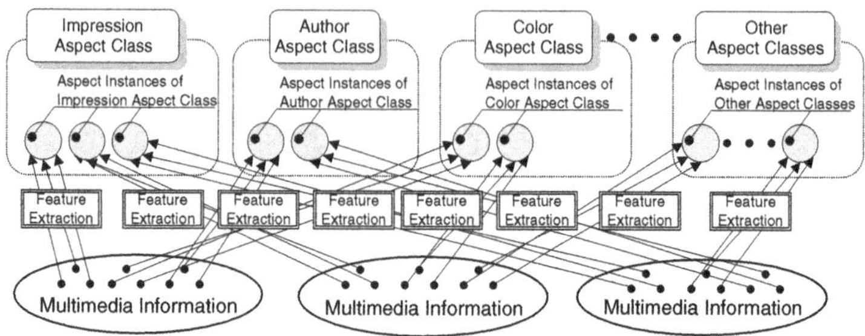

Fig. 3. Relationship between Aspect Class and Aspect Instance

information resources. In our rule system, it is not necessary to deal with any updating conflicts among active rules, because the system does not support any updating operations as actions. The aspect-ECA rules do not cause any updating conflicts among themselves. The general form of aspect-ECA rules is described in the following:

define rule *rule-name* **on** *event*
where *condition*
viewpoints of *<identifier list>*: *<set of instantiation sentence>*
do *action*

The power of aspect-ECA rule language is concentrated in the **where** clause and **viewpoints** clause. The where clause specifies conditions among sets of aspect instances. We introduce a concept of an *aspect variable* into aspect-ECA rules to manipulate arbitrary sets of aspect instances as the aspect variable. We show the usage of aspect variable as follows:

aspect variable **.** *retrieval metrics()*

The aspect variable points a set of aspect instances which belong to the same aspect class. The dot "." notation means invocation of retrieval metrics of the aspect class. The sentence of retrieval method invocation returns a set of aspect instances that satisfies the conditions specified by the retrieval metrics.

The **viewpoints** clause defines aspect variables and assigns aspect instances to aspect variables. The aspect variable is defined with media object identifier as follows: "*identifier* **.** *aspect variable*". Aspect variables which have the same identifier mean that assigned aspect instances should be created from the same media object. We show the general form of aspect instance creation sentences in the following:

new *constructor* **as** *identifier* **.** *aspect variable*

The sentence generates a new set of aspect instances, and the generated instances are assigned in the aspect variable. By invoking the constructor with several arguments, users can customize instance creation processes.

We show an example aspect-ECA rule. Assume that there are two databases which have various image data. A user, who wants to stay up-to-date on his/her favorite artist's works, can write an aspect-ECA rule as follows:

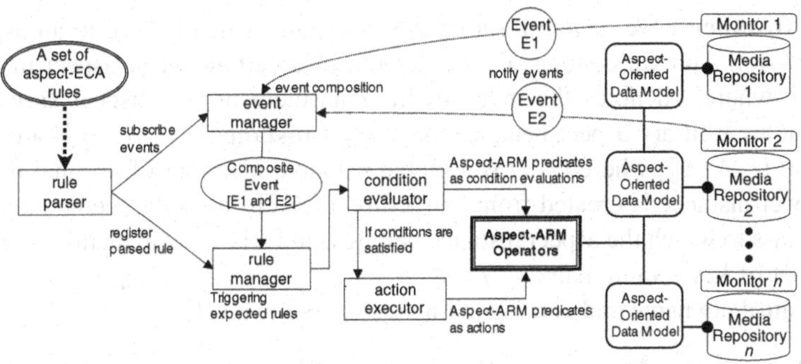

Fig. 4. Rule System Architecture

```
DEFINE RULE ON db1 OR db2 WHERE id1.author.equals("John Smith")
  AND id1.impression.inner_product("light, bright", 0.6)
VIEWPOINTS OF id1:
  NEW Author() AS id1.author, NEW ImageImpression() AS id1.impression,
DO notify(id1, "kurabaya@sfc.keio.ac.jp");
```

The where clause specifies conditions that a name of artist is "John Smith", an impression of picture is "light and bright". This example shows two important features of the Aspect-ARM. First feature is that the aspect-ECA rule specifies conditions by using various retrieval metrics. Second feature is that aspect-ECA rule is completely independent of low-level attributes of image data. This example rule deals with aspect instances of image data, and it does not deal with entities of image data. The aspect-ECA rules makes it possible to avoid the definition of method for monitoring conditions as hard-wired codes in the applications. By applying the following modification of the aspect-ECA rule, users can check the similarity between one sample image and other images without affecting application structure and local information system structure.

```
WHERE id1.impression.inner_product(id2.impression, 0.4)
VIEWPOINTS OF id1, id2: NEW ImageImpression() AS id1.impression,
 CONSTANT NEW ImageImpression( "location=http://host/query.jpg,
    filter=img_impression") AS id2.impression
```

2.3 Aspect-Oriented Data Model

In this section, we show the formal description of the aspect-oriented data model. We define three data structures: the aspect classes, the aspect instances, and the local multimedia information resources. The relationship among those three data structure is illustrated in Figure 3.

Aspect Classes: We denote all the set of aspect classes in the system as $\mathcal{A}$ and each aspect class as A_i where i is a class identifier. An **aspect class** $A_i \in \mathcal{A}$ is a two-tuple: $A_i = \{V_i, \{\Theta_1^i, \Theta_2^i, \ldots, \Theta_r^i\}\}$, where V_i is a feature set definition $V_i = \{f_1, f_2, \ldots, f_n\}$, and r-tuple Θ_r^i are functions $f : V_i \times V_i \to [0, 1]$ for calculating correlations between aspect instances that belong to the aspect class A_i.

Aspect Instances: We denote a set of aspect instances that belong to an aspect class A_i by $a(A_i)$. And we denotes a data element of a certain set of aspect instances by $a[l](A_i)$, where l denotes the index of the data element. The aspect variable a can represent an arbitrary aspect instance. An **aspect instance** $a \in a(A_i)$ is a three-tuple: $a = \{OID, A_i, v\}$, where OID is a global resource identifier of original media data. The aspect instance is created from extracting a feature from the media data. A_i is an aspect class to which the aspect instance belongs, and v is a metadata that is represented with a set of key / value pairs $< f_1, v_1 >, < f_2, v_2 >, \ldots, < f_n, v_n >$, with $f_{[1\ldots n]}$ being a attribute name and corresponding $v_{[1\ldots n]}$ being a value.

Local Information Resources: We denote all the set of local information resources connected to the system as $\mathcal{D}$ and each local information resource as D_s where s is a global resource identifier. A local information resource $D_s \in \mathcal{D}$ is two-tuple: $D_s = \{OID, \{< A_1, \mu_1 >, < A_2, \mu_2 >, \ldots, < A_n, \mu_n >\}\}$, where OID denotes a global resource identifier of this media data, and $< A_1, \mu_1 >, < A_2, \mu_2 >, \ldots, < A_n, \mu_n >$ denotes a set of aspects that the information resource has. Each $< A_n, \mu_n >$ denotes a pair of an aspect class and a corresponding feature extraction filter for creating metadata for the aspect class. A feature extraction filter $\mu_i^s : D_s \rightarrow a \in a(A_i)$ accepts a data source D_s and returns a aspect instance $a \in a(A_i)$. The Aspect-ARM deals with any information resources as a set of aspect instances, and it does not directly deal with entity of information resources. Therefore, information resources are defined with both aspects and feature extraction filters.

3 Interpretation of Aspect-ECA Rules

As illustrated in Figure 4, Aspect-ARM operators play a crucial role in the interpretation of aspect-ECA rules. We have designed four fundamental operators of the Aspect-ARM. Every operator is independent of underlying information systems.

An Operator for Aspect Instance Creation: The aspect instance creation operator $\Gamma^l_{A_i}$ creates a set of aspect instances belonging to a certain aspect class from heterogeneous multimedia information resources. We define $\Gamma^l_{A_i}$ as follows:

- *Definition*: The operator $\Gamma^l_{A_i} : D \rightarrow a(A_i)$ creates a set of aspect instances $a(A_i)$, that belongs to the aspect class A_i. The operator $\Gamma^l_{A_i}$ accepts a data set D specified with a data set constraint description l. The data set constraint description l restricts a scope of data sources.

$$\Gamma^l_{A_i}(D) := \bigcup_{j=0}^{k} \left\{ a \leftarrow \mathcal{E}(D_{[j]}, A_i) \;\middle|\; \mathcal{Q}(D_{[j]}, l) \equiv \mathbf{true} \wedge a \neq \emptyset \right\} \quad (1)$$

Note that k denotes the number of elements in the data set. The data set restriction function $\mathcal{Q}$ accepts each data element $D_{[j]}$ and the data set restriction description l, which specifies various low-level attributes of multimedia data, such as locations of data, types of data, and size of data. The function $\mathcal{Q}$ returns true value, when the data element $D_{[j]}$ satisfies the restriction description l. By specifying the special parameter "any" as l, a user can instantiate all the sets of aspect instances of the aspect class A_i. The aspect instantiation function $\mathcal{E}$ accepts a data element $D_{[j]}$, from which the feature set is to be extracted, and an aspect class A_i, that the instantiated aspect instance belongs to. The function $\mathcal{E}$ selects the the feature extraction filter μ_i to extract metadata from the data element $D_{[j]}$ by reference to the definition of local information resources described in Section 2.3. When there is no appropriate metadata extraction filters, the function $\mathcal{E}$ returns null value. The operator $\Gamma^l_{A_i}$ constructs the set of aspect instances $a(A_i)$ by accumulating each aspect instance generated by the function $\mathcal{E}$.

An Operator for Retrieval: The aspect-oriented retrieval operator Λ^t_r selects the aspect instances by applying various media retrieval metrics. The Λ^t_r operator is defined as follows:

- *Definition*: $\Lambda^t_r : a(A_i), a'(A_i) \rightarrow r(A_i)$ generates a set of aspect instances whose similarity value excesses the denoted thresholds t, by evaluating a specified relationship r between two sets of aspect instances a and a'.

$$\Lambda^t_r(a(A_i), a'(A_i)) := \bigcup_{n=0}^{j} \left\{ \bigcup_{m=0}^{k} \left(a_{[n]} \;\middle|\; \Theta^i_r(a_{[n]}, a'_{[m]}) > t \right) \right\} \tag{2}$$

Note that j denotes the number of elements in $a(A_i)$, and k denotes the number of elements in $a'(A_i)$. The function Θ^i_r calculates correlation between two aspect instances a_n and a'_m. The following example expression generates a set of aspect instances by evaluating impression relationships among image data in DB1 and DB2, where inner product value of impression metadata excesses 0.7.

$$\Lambda^{0.7}_{inner\_product}(\Gamma^{media=image,location=DB1}_{impression}(D), \Gamma^{media=image,location=DB2}_{impression}(D))$$

An Operator for Integration: The integration operator Δ_c is used for obtaining original media objects which are referred by sets of aspect instances. Every aspect instance has the pointer to its original media object as described in section 2.3. The operator Δ_c dereferences the pointer, which are sets of OID held by every set of aspect instances, to original media object. The operator Δ_c is defined as follows:

- *Definition*: $\Delta_c : a, a' \rightarrow D$ generates a set of media objects which are referred by two sets of aspect instances a and a'.

$$\Delta_c(a, a') := \bigcup_{n=0}^{j} \left(\mathcal{P}(I_n) \;\middle|\; I \leftarrow \begin{cases} \mathcal{O}(a) \cap \mathcal{O}(a'), & c \equiv \textbf{and} \\ \mathcal{O}(a) \cup \mathcal{O}(a'), & c \equiv \textbf{or} \\ \mathcal{O}(a) \setminus \mathcal{O}(a'), & c \equiv \textbf{not} \end{cases} \right) \tag{3}$$

Note that j denotes the number of elements in the set of OID I. The function $\mathcal{O} : a_i \rightarrow I$ constructs a set of OID held by a set of aspect instances a_i. The function $\mathcal{P} : I_n \rightarrow D$ dereferences the OID I_n and returns a corresponding media object D_n. Note that c determines the set operation that the operator Δ_c applies to construct the set of OID. By this operation, we can specify "and", "or", and "not" conditions among several results of Λ^t_r operator. When "**and**" is specified as c, the operator Δ_c constructs the intersection of two sets of OID held by a and a'. When "**or**" is specified as c, the operator Δ_c constructs the union of two sets of OID held by a and a'. When "**not**" is specified as c, the operator Δ_c constructs the relative complements of the OID set held by a' to the OID set of a.

4 Conclusion Remarks

In this paper, we have proposed the aspect-oriented active rule system, called Aspect-ARM, for heterogeneous multimedia information resources. The Aspect-ARM provides the aspect-ECA rule language which is designed on the aspect-oriented data model. The Aspect-ARM realizes the active database functionality in cross-over multimedia databases environments.

References

1. Dittrich, K.R., Gatziu, S., Geppert, A.: The active database management system manifesto: A rulebase of adbms features. In: Proc. 2nd International Workshop on Rules in Databases (RIDS) LNCS-985, Springer-Verlag (1995) 101–115
2. Paton, N.W., Díaz, O.: Active database systems. ACM Computing Surveys **Vol. 31** (1999) 63–103
3. von Bültzingsloewen, G., Koschel, A., Lockemann, P.C., Walter, H.D.: Eca functionality in a distributed environment. In Paton, N., ed.: Active Rules in Database Systems. Springer-Verlag New York (1999) 147–175
4. Cilia, M., Buchmann, A.P.: An active functionality service for e-business applications. ACM SIGMOD Record **31** (2002) 24–30
5. Cilia, M., Bornhövd, C., Buchmann, A.P.: Cream: An infrastructure for distributed, heterogeneous event-based applications. In: On The Move to Meaningful Internet Systems 2003: CoopIS, DOA, and ODBASE, Springer-Verlag Heidelberg (2003) 482–502
6. Koschel, A., Lockemann, P.C.: Distributed events in active database systems: Letting the genie out of the bottle. Data and Knowledge Engineering **25** (1998) 11–28
7. Risch, T., Josifovski, V., Katchaounov, T.: Functional data integration in a distributed mediator system. In Gray, P., Kerschberg, L., King, P., Poulovassilis, A., eds.: Functional Approach to Data Management - Modeling, Analyzing and Integrating Heterogeneous Data. Springer-Verlag (2003) 211–238
8. Kantere, V., Mylopoulos, J., Kiringa, I.: A distributed rule mechanism for multidatabase systems. In: On The Move to Meaningful Internet Systems 2003: CoopIS, DOA, and ODBASE, Springer-Verlag Heidelberg (2003) 56–73
9. Heimrich, T., Specht, G.: Enhancing eca rules for distributed active database systems. In: Web, Web-Services, and Database Systems, Springer-Verlag Heidelberg (2002) 199–205
10. Kurabayashi, S., Kiyoki, Y.: A meta-level active multidatabase system architecture for heterogeneous information resources. Information Modelling and Knowledge Bases (IOS Press) **Vol. XV** (2003) 143–160
11. Kurabayashi, S., Kiyoki, Y.: An active multidatabase system architecture with an aspect-oriented media modelling framework. Information Modelling and Knowledge Bases (IOS Press) **Vol. XVI** (2004)
12. Buchmann, A.P.: Architecture of active database systems. In Paton, N.W., ed.: Active Rules in Database Systems. Springer-Verlag New York (1999)
13. Widom, J., Ceri, S.: Active Database Systems: Triggers and Rules for Advanced Database Processing. Morgan Kaufmann (1996)
14. Kiyoki, Y., Kitagawa, T., Hayama, T.: A metadatabase system for semantic image search by a mathematical model of meaning. ACM SIGMOD Record **23** (1994) 34–41
15. Kiyoki, Y., Kitagawa, T., Hitomi, Y.: A fundamental framework for realizing semantic interoperability in a multidatabase environment. Journal of Integrated Computer-Aided Engineering, John Wiley & Sons **25** (1995) 3–20

Opportunistic Search with Semantic Fisheye Views

Paul Janecek and Pearl Pu

Swiss Federal Institute of Technology – Lausanne (EPFL), 1015 Lausanne, Switzerland,
{paul.janecek,pearl.pu}@epfl.ch,
http://hci.epfl.ch/

Abstract. Search goals are often too complex or poorly defined to be solved with a single query in a web-based information environment. In this paper we describe how we use *semantic fisheye views* (SFEVs) to effectively support opportunistic search and browsing strategies in an annotated image collection. We have developed a SFEV prototype enabling rapid, interactive exploration using both keyword similarity and semantic relationships derived using WordNet. SFEVs visually emphasize and increase the detail of information related to the focus and de-emphasize or filter less important information. The contribution of the SFEV approach is the flexible definition of context as a combination of interest metrics, which can be reconfigured and combined to support a wide range of visualizations and information needs.

1 Introduction

Information seeking is often iterative, interactive, and opportunistic, especially when search goals are complex or uncertain. The results of a query may lead to the discovery of unfamiliar vocabulary and relationships that guide the future direction of search. This type of opportunistic search, which blends search and browsing behavior, is still a time-consuming and poorly-supported process in online search interfaces.

Visual Information Retrieval Interfaces (VIRI) allow users to rapidly shift between search and browsing tasks [8]. The tight coupling between visual representations and interaction make VIRIs powerful tools for discovering relationships between documents. However, as the amount of information displayed in a VIRI grows, it is increasingly difficult to represent and navigate over all of it within the constraints of screen size and access latency. As a result, a visualization is often a compromise between showing a small amount of information in detail, or a large amount of information abstractly. Furthermore, visual representations are often time-consuming to generate, but optimally supports only a small set of tasks [4,23].

Semantic fisheye views (SFEVs) are a type of interactive *focus + context* visualization technique that attempts to manage the complexity of a visual interface by fluidly adapting the representation based on the user's current focus. SFEVs

X. Zhou et al. (Eds.): WISE 2004, LNCS 3306, pp. 668–680, 2004.
© Springer-Verlag Berlin Heidelberg 2004

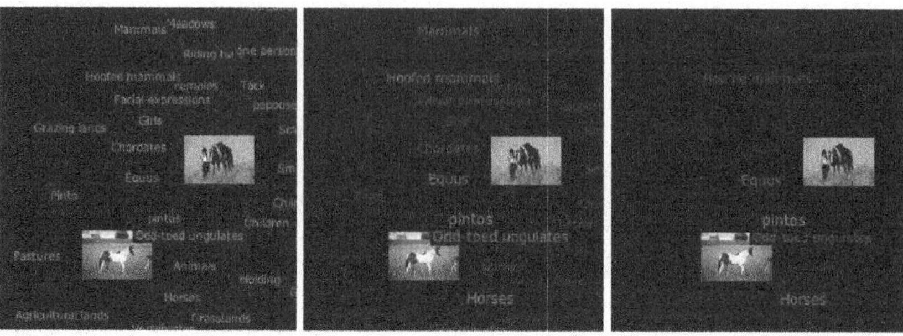

Fig. 1. Reducing visual complexity with SFEVs. This simple example shows two images and the keywords used to annotate them positioned using a spring layout algorithm. On the left, the keywords are shown without any emphasis. The figures in the middle and on the right show the keywords emphasized by their relative importance in this small collection.

can use simple visual techniques to emphasize or increase the detail of the most important information, and de-emphasize or filter less important information, where *importance* is calculated relative to some measure of the user's current focus or task [7,10]. By selectively reducing the complexity of a visualization, users are able to quickly understand and access local and global structure. For example, Fig. 1 uses these techniques to reveal a frequent theme in a collection.

In this paper[1], we describe a prototype that uses SFEV techniques to support diverse search and browsing strategies within a large collection of professionally annotated images. Researchers have identified a wide range of browsing behaviors with different goals, strategies, and at different levels of granularity [14]. For example, Bates describes information seeking as an iterative, interactive process that evolves in response to the information found, and that encompasses both directed search and browsing [2]. Furthermore, the results of information seeking are not limited to documents, but also include the *knowledge* accumulated during the search process. This knowledge is essential for understanding and using the information discovered during search [21]. This model of search differs from the more classic query/document similarity in both the diversity and granularity of the information collected, as well as its evolving nature.

The prototype directly supports two alternative search strategies. The first technique emphasizes images and keywords that are similar in content to the focus. In contrast, the second technique emphasizes information that is *conceptually* related to the focus based on WordNet, a general lexical ontology of the English language. These strategies correspond to classic search strategies used for opportunistic search over heterogeneous collections of information [1,2].

A significant contribution of this research is that it demonstrates a general method for integrating semantics directly into the interaction and visualization

[1] Color version available at http://hci.epfl.ch/website/publications/2004/janecek-wise04.pdf

of information to support opportunistic search. This approach can easily be extended to support new search strategies that take advantage of metadata and ontologies.

In the following section we describe our general framework for designing semantic fisheye views, followed by an overview of the prototype architecture. We then explain how the prototype supports similarity- and semantic-guided browsing in greater detail, and discuss how we integrated WordNet into our interactive browser. We then briefly discuss some lessons learned and findings from user studies. Finally, we discuss related research and our conclusions.

2 Semantic Fisheye Views

We have designed and developed an interactive environment for exploring a large collection of professionally annotated images using *semantic fisheye view* techniques. The prototype directly supports different search strategies with separate types of fisheye views, one based on similarity metrics and another based on semantic relationships. The prototype was designed based on our SFEV framework [10], which we will describe generally in this section. In a previous workshop paper we described how this framework could be used to support query-based opportunistic search [11]; in this paper we focus primarily on browsing.

The semantic fisheye view framework describes two components that influence the *degree of interest* (DOI) assigned to each object in the collection. The first is *a priori* interest (API), which models "landmarks" in the collection, such as frequently used keywords or representative images. Conceptually, these landmarks provide a global context for the user to browse within. The second component, the set of interest metrics, models the conceptual distance of objects from the current focus. The combination of these two components results in a DOI value for each object in the collection.

A wide range of semantic fisheye views can result from simply changing the balance and composition of these components. For example, Fig. 2 shows browsing over a collection using two different types of interest metrics. In the top row, the user focuses on an image and a similarity-based SFEV guides him to another image that is similar by content. In the bottom row, the user focuses on the keyword "Horses" and a semantic-based SFEV reveals other keywords that are semantically related, such as the "pinto" type of horse. In both cases, when the user brushes the mouse over an object it immediately begins to grow in size and detail and related information is progressively emphasized after a short delay. When the mouse moves away from an object, the related objects will slowly fade to their original state.

This example also shows how emphasis techniques modify the visual representation of information to reveal changes in degree of interest. The goal of the emphasis techniques is to align the visual weight of objects with their DOI: the most interesting objects are immediately apparent, and less interesting objects fade into the background. Emphasis techniques impose a visual order over the objects in the collection and control the global contrast and complexity of the

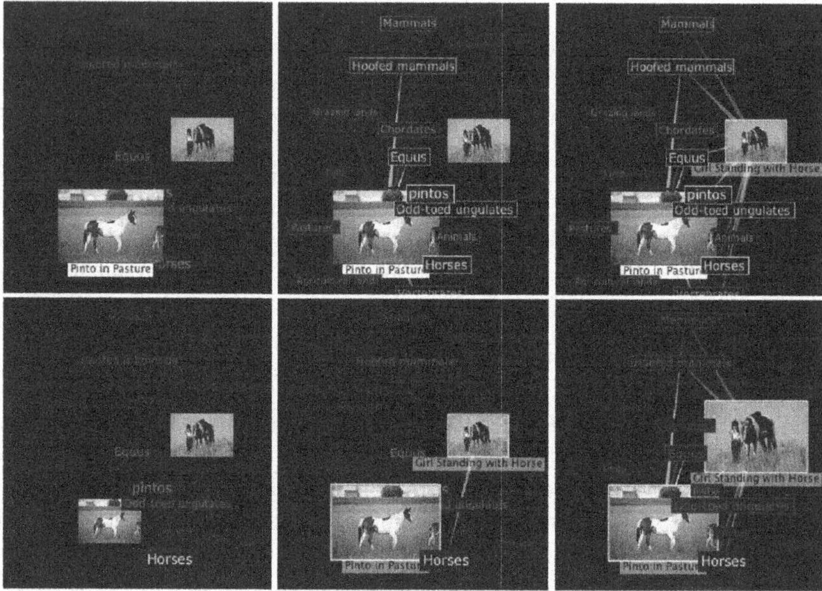

Fig. 2. Interacting with similarity (top row) and semantic (bottom row) SFEVs. Moving the mouse over an object causes related objects to smoothly increase in size and brightness based on the SFEVs interest metrics.

display. These techniques become progressively more important for exploration as the size of the collection increases. Another important aspect of SFEVs is the smooth animation that makes transitions between states understandable. In the following sections we provide greater detail about the general architecture of the prototype.

3 Architecture

The prototype is a complex Java application developed in our lab over several years to allow us to investigate the effectiveness of SFEV techniques for solving complex opportunistic search tasks in a semantically rich environment. Although the prototype does support keyword- and concept-based queries, it is primarily designed for rapid interactive exploration over the set of results. System responsiveness is critical for this type of task.

The architecture of the prototype can be divided at a high level into two parts: a client for launching queries and browsing over results, and a server that contains the image and WordNet databases. Only the relevant subset of these two large databases is loaded into the client browser to maintain system responsiveness and minimize traffic between the client and server.

Fig. 3 shows a general overview of how the prototype handles a simple query for "pintos." The bold arrows trace the optimized path from a keyword-based

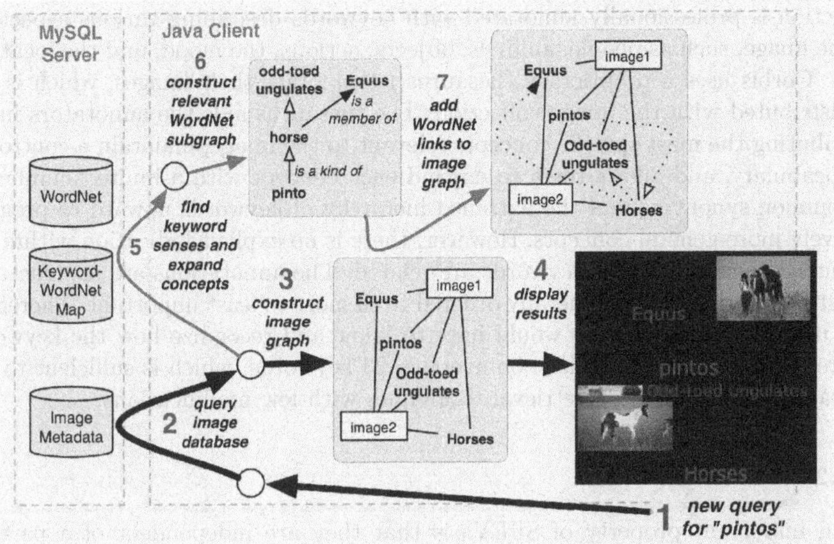

Fig. 3. The asynchronous architecture adds images to the workspace in the foreground and prepares for semantic interaction in the background. The images that match a query are quickly added to the display (1-4), while the subgraph of relevant concepts from WordNet is constructed in the background (5-7). These concepts are used during interactive exploration of the images.

query to the database (steps 1 and 2), followed by the construction of a graph from the resulting images and their keyword annotations (3), which is displayed in the view (4). The graph models images and keywords as nodes, and the links between them as edges. The importance of a keyword in an image is assigned to the weight of the edge connecting them. Small result sets will display in a few seconds and then animate as the layout algorithm places the nodes. At this point, the user can immediately begin interacting with the objects shown in the display.

The information required for semantic browsing is loaded into the browser in a second, background process shown with the smaller gray arrows (steps 5-7). For each keyword, the prototype loads the different word senses and all of their superconcepts (5) and constructs the WordNet subgraph (6). This is a query-intensive process that is done in batches rather than one keyword at a time. As concepts are loaded into the browser, they are linked to the keywords (7). The WordNet subgraph is not shown directly in the display, but is used for rapid, interactive semantic browsing.

3.1 The Annotated Image Collection

The image database contains the metadata for a diverse collection of over 56,500 images provided to us by Corbis Corp for this research. Each image in the collection is professionally annotated with keywords describing various aspects of the image, such as people, animals, objects, actions, the mood, and the location.

Corbis uses a proprietary thesaurus to annotate their images, which is not distributed with the image collection. The thesaurus aids the annotators in attributing the most specific concepts relevant to the image, maintain a controlled vocabulary, and allows them to expand each concept with a limited number of common synonyms and the flattened hierarchy of keywords upward to progressively more general concepts. However, there is no explicit indication within the annotations of how the keywords are related. The annotations are unstructured lists of words, but are generally ordered from most to least important. Therefore, a user looking at the list would have to know and recognize how the keywords are related. Each image has, on average, 23 keywords, which is sufficient to use traditional information retrieval techniques with few modifications.

3.2 Visual Layout

An important property of SFEVs is that they are independent of a particular visual representation. We have implemented both tabular and map-based layouts of image collections that use the same interest metrics and emphasis techniques [19,11]. The prototype described in this paper uses a spring layout to position the image graph.

Our layout algorithm is adapted from the implementation of the spring layout in the graphical model of the KAON library [16], however we do not use any of its functionality for managing ontologies. In general, a spring algorithm assigns a repulsive force to the nodes in a graph, and models the edges between nodes as springs with a tension based on their weight. To reduce empty space in the layout, we separated the repulsive force of each node into x and y components that varied according to the image or keyword dimensions. Furthermore, to improve legibility we exaggerated the y-component of the repulsive force for keywords. The algorithm initially places nodes randomly, and then iteratively attempts to minimize tension. The resulting layout tends to place highly connected sets of nodes into visual clusters, and minimally connected nodes drift towards the outside of the representation.

4 Similarity- and Semantic-Guided Browsing

The images and keywords that are found as the result of lexical and semantic queries are loaded into the local workspace of the prototype. The cost of accessing information in the local workspace is much lower than query-based interaction, which encourages opportunistic exploration. The prototype directly supports two different strategies for a user to browse over the collection (shown earlier in Fig. 2). The first strategy is based on content *similarity* and the direct relationships between objects in the collection. This corresponds to common keyword-based search and browsing behavior. The second strategy uses WordNet to find concepts related to the focus, which corresponds to *semantic* search and browsing behavior. In the following sections we describe how the prototype supports these strategies with different combinations of interest metrics.

4.1 Similarity-Guided Browsing

The first set of interest metrics are designed to reveal information in the collection that is similar to the current focus based on content, and is derived from the direct links between images and keywords. The metrics calculate interest by searching outward from the focus to gather a set of related images and keywords. The interest of each object in the set is based on the weight of the links that lead to it. We derive the weight of these links from the order the keywords are used to annotate an image. This heuristic works well in this collection because the keywords are generally ordered from more specific to more general concepts as a result of the thesaurus-based term expansion.

These metrics reveal similarities between objects, and create visual clusters of tightly connected nodes. When the user changes their focus, the interface recalculates the degree of interest of every object to reflect their similarity to the new focus. This supports opportunistic discovery of images that are similarly annotated, as well as the vocabulary of the collection. In the following section, we describe metrics for finding information that is conceptually related, but not similarly annotated.

4.2 Semantic-Guided Browsing

The second type of SFEV implemented in the prototype allows a user to search and browse over the image collection using semantic relationships that are modeled in an external general ontology, WordNet. WordNet was developed at Princeton in 1985 to test psycholinguistic theories of the English language [15], and has continued to evolve since then. The version this research is based on (1.7.1, August 2002) contains approximately 140,000 unique word forms with 111,000 different senses.

While searching for information, users will often apply a wide range of strategies to find conceptually related information. For example, if a search for "horse" returned too many images, a person may use a more specific query, such as "wild horse" or "foal" to find a smaller, more manageable set of images. These strategies were described by Bates as generalization and specialization tactics [1]. A problem with these strategies is that they require domain knowledge: a person would have to know the existence of more general, more specific, or related concepts and add them to the query. Implementing these strategies using SFEV techniques allows a user to simply brush over a keyword and see the related concepts that exist in the image collection.

In order to use WordNet interactively, we only load a relevant subset of the entire graph into the browser (shown in steps 5-7 of Fig. 3). There were several significant steps required to prepare WordNet and the Corbis database to support rapid interactive browsing. The first step was to create a mapping between the vocabularies of WordNet and Corbis. We discovered that there is

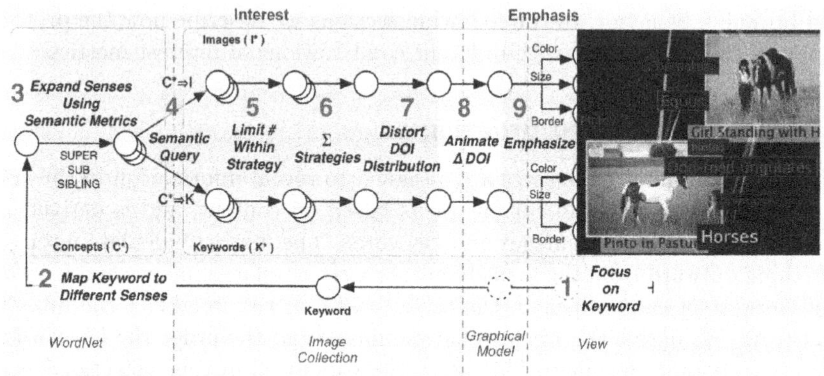

Fig. 4. Calculating interest with the SUPER, SUB and SIBLING strategies using a composite interest metric.

a significant overlap between the vocabularies and relationships in WordNet and the thesaurus used to annotate the images in the Corbis collection. This allowed us to derive links between the two vocabularies for over 90% of the most frequently occurring keywords in the Corbis collection [11].

The second step was to extract the different hierarchical relationships in WordNet (e.g., kind-of, part-of, member-of) and store them in separate tables. This allows us to rapidly access the entire path from a concept to its root in a single query over a single table, which is a critical step in constructing the subgraph related to a set of keywords. The final step was to precalculate values for images and concepts that are used in lexical and semantic queries, such as keyword frequency and inter-concept distance.

We use a single composite metric to support three of the basic search strategies described by Bates [1]: SUPER, SUB, and SIBLING. Each of these strategies is modeled as a directed search in WordNet along a particular type of hierarchical relationship. The SUPER and SUB strategies trace upwards or downwards along the kind-of, part-of and member-of hierarchies, while the SIBLING strategy finds concepts that share the same superconcept (e.g., if "pinto" was the focus, it would find other types of horse).

Fig. 4 shows a data state model tracing the flow of information in the composite metric that supports these search strategies. From left to right, this model is divided into four vertical regions: WordNet, the Image Collection, the Graphical Model, and the View. The leftmost vertical region shows operations over the subgraph of WordNet loaded into the workspace. The Image Collection region shows operations over the image graph loaded into the workspace as a result of one or more queries. The Graphical Model and View regions show operations that transform the visual representation.

When a user focuses on a keyword, the composite metric maps the keyword to different possible senses in WordNet (steps 1,2), and then expands these senses outward to find a limited set of the most closely related images and keywords

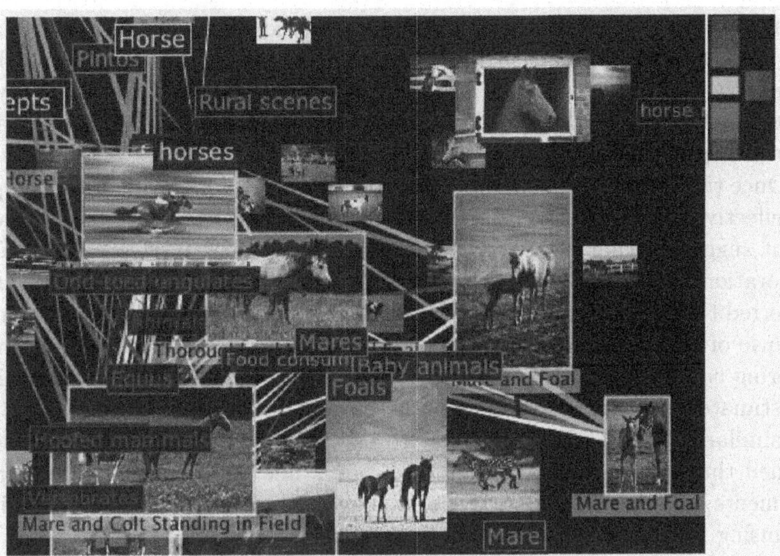

Fig. 5. Representing a sample of concepts most closely related to "horses" calculated with multiple strategies. The legend on the top right shows how colors are used to encode SUPER, SUB, and SIBLING relationships between keywords.

using the SUPER, SUB and SIBLING strategies (steps 3-6). The composite metric coordinates information common to these three strategies, such as the different senses of a keyword and aggregates their results (step 6), but each strategy operates in a separate thread to optimize performance. The results of each strategy are limited so that the final view has a representative sample from each strategy while maintaining a relatively constant amount of visual complexity in the interface.

The keywords resulting from each type of strategy are displayed in different colors: more general concepts are shown in red, more specific concepts are shown in cyan, and siblings are shown in magenta. Fig. 5 shows a part of the results from focusing on the keyword "horses" in a collection of images. The colors allow the user to find related concepts quickly without adding lines to the complex display. Showing the conceptual neighborhood helps users opportunistically discover related concepts without having to explicitly search for them or navigate over a complex semantic model.

4.3 User Evaluation

Interaction is a critical component of fisheye views that was not originally addressed in our framework. During the development of the prototype, feedback from early users highlighted a significant problem of interaction that had to be overcome before we could conduct a formal user evaluation. Users were confused if too much information changed at the same time, but frustrated if information changed too slowly. Smoothly animating transitions and improving responsiveness with multiple threads helped, but the real solution was more subtle. We eventually found that we could support both rapid scanning detailed analysis by immediately showing the focus in greater detail and then progressively adding information after a short delay.

Once the prototype was usable, we conducted a formal evaluation comparing the effectiveness of the two types of browsing behavior. The results of this experiment suggested that the WordNet-based fisheye is more effective for complex exploration tasks [12]. The vast majority of users in the experiment strongly preferred the semantic interface over the similarity interface for this type of task because of the structure it provided for navigating over the collection and discovering new concepts. However, several people commented that it was difficult to estimate relative distances with the current emphasis techniques. Although the similarity-based SFEV was easy to use and understand, many people complained that it was more difficult to discover new information. In general, the comments were highly supportive and suggest that the SFEV approach is very promising for opportunistic search.

5 Related Work

Furnas first described fisheye views as a technique for selectively reducing the information in a display to show the most interesting items, where interest was calculated as a tradeoff between *a priori* importance and relevance to the user's current task [7]. Furnas suggested that this general technique could be used to create compact views in a variety of different domains by redefining the function that calculates *degree of interest (DOI).*

Researchers have since developed a wide range of fisheye or *focus + context* techniques. *Distortion techniques* [13] use geometric transforms to magnify the area near the focus in the view. *Graphical* fisheye views [22] increase the size or detail of information related to the focus within the structure and constraints of a graphical model. The effectiveness of both distortion techniques and graphical fisheye views for specific search tasks depends largely on whether distance within the view or graphical model corresponds to the information needs of the user.

Semantic fisheye views, on the other hand, calculate interest based on *conceptual* distance from the focus to each object within one or more related data models, and then correspondingly modify the detail or emphasis [7,10]. In this case, the usefulness of the emphasized information depends on the data model rather than any particular visual representation. Our approach to SFEVs extends Furnas' original proposal in two important ways: the direct support for multiple contexts and emphasis techniques.

There are a number of examples of these techniques applied to hypertext. The ScentTrails [17] prototype calculates the *DOI* of links in a Web page based on the user's current search goals, the hypertext path distance to relevant information, and a spreading activation model of Information Scent [18,6]. The visual weight of the links is then adjusted to indicate relative interest by modifying the underlying HTML. The ZoomIllustrator [20] calculates *DOI* based on user interaction within a hypertext of human anatomy, and then adjusts the transparency and detail of relevant objects in a related illustrative graphical model.

The prototype we describe in this paper differs from these examples in several important ways. First, we use both similarity and semantic metrics to calculate *DOI*. The semantic metrics, in particular, are designed to provide a diverse sample for browsing rather than a narrow match. Second, the collection is dynamically constructed from the results of a query rather than a static hypertext. Third, the *focus* of the fisheye dynamically follows the mouse to support rapid brushing over the result collection rather than deliberate hypertext navigation, similar to the behavior of glosses in Fluid Documents [5].

Hollink, et al. recently developed a prototype that integrates four ontologies for searching within and annotating an image collection [9]. The link between ontologies is generated by hand, which increases precision over our technique but also limits its scalability. Our approach, in contrast, compensates for incomplete or ambiguous annotations using visualization techniques that place similarly annotated images near each other and interaction to support rapid exploration in both the collection and related ontology.

6 Conclusion

Opportunistic search and sensemaking in large information collections are highly interactive tasks that are poorly supported in current interfaces. These types of search activities require rapidly discovering, analyzing, and navigating between the relationships within information collections. However, a significant obstacle for users to effectively search over unstructured collections is their lack of domain knowledge, such as the vocabulary and semantic structure of the collection. To overcome this obstacle, researchers have proposed that interfaces should support search strategies to guide users over information in a collection.

The relationships within information collections are often too complex to be displayed in a single representation. We propose semantic fisheye views as an interactive visualization technique to support effective guided exploration over unstructured collections of information. Fisheye views reduce the visual complexity of displays by selectively emphasizing the most important information in a representation and deemphasizing or filtering less important information. The measure of importance is based on the user's current focus and activity. An advantage of fisheye view techniques is that the metrics to determine importance are flexible, and can therefore interactively support a wide range of search strategies over the same visual representation.

The main contribution of this research is the extension of focus + context techniques to effectively support multiple search strategies within a visualization. Initial experimental results suggest that semantic fisheye views are promising techniques for opportunistic search, and that semantic-guided search may be more effective than similarity-guided search for complex sensemaking tasks.

Acknowledgements. This research was funded by grant 2000-066816 from the Swiss National Science Foundation. Corbis Corporation generously supported this research by giving us direct electronic access to their archive of annotated images. We greatly appreciate the helpful comments of the anonymous reviewers.

References

1. M. J. Bates. Information search tactics. *Journal of the American Society for Information Science*, 30:205–214, 1979.
2. M. J. Bates. The design of browsing and berrypicking techniques for the online search interface. *Online Review*, 13(5):407–424, 1989.
3. M. J. Bates. Where should the person stop and the information search interface start? *Information Processing and Management*, 26(5):575–591, 1990.
4. Stephen M. Casner. A task-analytic approach to the automated design of graphic presentations. *ACM Transactions on Graphics*, 10(2):111–151, 1991.
5. Bay-Wei Chang, Jock D. Mackinlay, Polle T. Zellweger, and Takeo Igarashi. A negotiation architecture for fluid documents. In *Proceedings of the ACM Symposium on User Interface Software and Technology*, Enabling Architectures, pages 123–132. ACM Press, 1998.
6. Ed Huai-hsin Chi, Peter Pirolli, K. Chen, and James Pitkow. Using information scent to model user information needs and actions on the web. In *Proceedings of the ACM Conference on Human Factors in Computing Systems*, pages 490–497, Seattle, WA, 2001. ACM.
7. G. W. Furnas. Generalized fisheye views. In *Proceedings of the SIGCHI conference on Human factors in computing systems*, pages 16–23. ACM Press, 1986.
8. George W. Furnas and Samuel J. Rauch. Considerations for information environments and the navique workspace. In *Proceedings of the third ACM conference on Digital libraries*, pages 79–88. ACM Press, 1998.
9. Laura Hollink, A. Th. (Guus) Schreiber, Jan Wielemaker, and Bob Wielinga. Semantic annotation of image collections. In *Proceedings of the KCAP'03 Workshop on Knowledge Capture and Semantic Annotation*, Sanibel, Florida, 2003. ACM Press.
10. Paul Janecek and Pearl Pu. A framework for designing fisheye views to support multiple semantic contexts. In *International Conference on Advanced Visual Interfaces (AVI02)*, pages 51–58, Trento, Italy, 2002. ACM Press.
11. Paul Janecek and Pearl Pu. Searching with semantics: An interactive visualization technique for exploring an annotated image collection. In Robert Meersman and Zahir Tari, editors, *OTM Workshops*, volume 2889 of *Lecture Notes in Computer Science*, pages 185–196, Catania, Italy, 2003. Springer.
12. Paul Janecek and Pearl Pu. An evaluation of semantic fisheye views for opportunistic search in an annotated image collection. *Journal on Digital Libraries*, 4(4), October 2004. Special Issue on Information Visualization Interfaces for Retrieval and Analysis.
13. Y. K. Leung and M. D. Apperley. A review and taxonomy of distortion-oriented presentation techniques. *ACM Transactions on Computer-Human Interaction*, 1(2):126–160, 1994.
14. G. Marchionini. *Information Seeking in Electronic Environments.* Cambridge University Press, Cambridge, MA, 1995.

15. George A. Miller. Wordnet: a lexical database for english. *Communications of the ACM*, 38(11):39–41, 1995.
16. Boris Motik, Alexander Maedche, and Raphael Volz. A conceptual modeling approach for semantics-driven enterprise. In *Proceedings of the First International Conference on Ontologies, Databases and Application of Semantics (ODBASE-2002)*, LNAI. Springer, 2002.
17. Christopher Olston and Ed Huai-hsin Chi. Scenttrails: Integrating browsing and searching on the web. *ACM Transactions on Computer-Human Interaction*, 10(3):177–197, 2003.
18. Peter Pirolli. Computational models of information scent-following in a very large browsable text collection. In *Proceedings of SIGCHI Conference on Human Factors in Computing Systems*, volume 1 of *PAPERS: Finding What You Want I*, pages 3–10. ACM, 1997.
19. Pearl Pu and Paul Janecek. Visual interfaces for opportunistic information seeking. In Constantine Stephanidis and Julie Jacko, editors, *10th International Conference on Human Computer Interaction (HCII '03)*, volume 2, pages 1131–1135, Crete, Greece, 2003. Lawrence Erlbaum Associates.
20. Michael Ruger, Bernhard Preim, and Alf Ritter. Zoom navigation: Exploring large information and application spaces. In *Workshop on Advanced Visual Interfaces (AVI96)*, pages 40–48, New York, 1996. ACM Press.
21. Daniel M. Russell, Mark J. Stefik, Peter Pirolli, and Stuart K. Card. The cost structure of sensemaking. In *Proceedings of the SIGCHI conference on Human factors in computing systems*, pages 269 – 276, Amsterdam, 1993. ACM.
22. Manojit Sarkar and Marc H. Brown. Graphical fisheye views. *Communications of the ACM*, 37(12):73–84, 1994.
23. Jiajie Zhang and Donald A. Norman. Representations in distributed cognitive tasks. *Cognitive Science*, 18:87–122, 1994.

A Graphical XQuery Language Using Nested Windows

Zheng Qin, Benjamin Bin Yao, Yingbin Liu, and Michael McCool

University of Waterloo
School of Computer Science, Waterloo, Ontario, Canada N2L 3G1
{zqin, bbyao, ybliu, mmccool}@uwaterloo.ca

Abstract. A graphical XQuery-based language using nested windows, GXQL, is presented. Definitions of both syntax and semantics are provided. Expressions in GXQL can be directly translated into corresponding XQuery expressions. GXQL supports `for`, `let`, `where`, `order by` and `return` clauses (FLWOR expressions) and also supports predicates and quantifiers. This graphical language provides a powerful and user-friendly environment for non-technical users to perform queries.

1 Introduction

XML is now being used extensively in various applications, so query languages have become important tools for users from many different backgrounds. However, the use of query languages can sometimes be difficult for users not having much database training. A graphical query language can potentially be very helpful. With a graphical interface, users do not have to remember the syntax of a textual language, all they need to do is select options and draw diagrams.

In this paper, a graphical XQuery-based language is described. Early graphical query languages for XML included G [7], G+ [8], G+'s descendant Graphlog [6], G-Log [11], WG-Log [4], and WG-Log's descendant XML-GL [3,5]. In these visual languages, a standard node-edge graphical tree representation is used to visualize the hierarchical structure of XML documents. The nodes represent elements and attributes in the documents, and the edges represent relationships between the nodes. Research has also been performed into form-based query languages, such as Equix [2], and nested-table based query languages, such as QSByE (Query Semi-structured data By Example) [9]. The BBQ language used a directory tree visualization of the XML tree [10].

Most of these visual languages were developed before XQuery. A recent graphical XQuery-based language, XQBE (XQuery By Example) [1], extends XML-GL to XQuery, and also overcomes some limitations of XML-GL. The XQBE query language is good at expressing queries, but there are some problems with it. First, XQBE defines many abstract symbols. For instance, there are two kinds of trapezoids, lozenges of two different colors, circles of two different colors, and so on. It is difficult to remember which abstract symbol represents what concept. Second, all relationships are mapped onto a uniform tree structure. This is also true of other systems otherwise similar to ours (such as BBQ).

X. Zhou et al. (Eds.): WISE 2004, LNCS 3306, pp. 681–687, 2004.
© Springer-Verlag Berlin Heidelberg 2004

Representing all relationships with a common visual formalism can lead to confusion. For instance, when a node points to another node via an edge, does it mean a parent-child relation, a cause-result relation, or an attribute relation? Third, there are some XQuery expressions that cannot be easily expressed by XQBE, for example, quantifiers.

We have designed a nested window XQuery-based language, called GXQL (Graphical XQuery Language). GXQL has fewer symbols than XQBE, and these symbols are visually suggestive. We use nested windows to represent parent-child relationships. Child elements and attributes are also visually distinguished. The visualization of a document in GXQL in fact resembles a real document. The query interface in GXQL is user-friendly. Users do not have to input everything textually or need to draw queries from scratch. Like BBQ, in our visual notation windows and icons can be dragged around to construct new nodes or copy nodes. The interface also allows users to visualize only the parts of the document structure they need to perform a query. GXQL is also more expressive than XQBE. Some queries hard to express in XQBE are easy in GXQL, and some queries impossible to express in XQBE are possible in GXQL. For instance, in XQBE predicates of a node in a `return` clause can only affect its parent node, whereas in GXQL, predicates can affect arbitrary nodes.

Since we want to compare GXQL directly with XQBE, the sample XML document and the example queries in this paper are taken from the XQBE paper [1]. Due to space limitations only two simple examples are included here; the rest of the examples are available in a technical report [12].

2 Visualization Interface

The schema of the sample document we will be using for our example queries is represented by GXQL in Figure 1 (a). Each rectangle represents an element that can have a URI, attributes and subelements. The URI indicates the location of the document. In the sample document, element `<bib>` is at the outermost level, and element `<book>` includes attribute `year` and some children.

Rectangles representing children are enclosed completely in their parent rectangle. The borders of these rectangles can be drawn in various styles. These will be explained in the next section.

Initially, only the parent node and its immediate children are represented. However, users can expand elements inline by double clicking on them. Already expanded elements can be zoomed to fill the window by double-clicking on them again. When an attribute is expanded, information about that attribute, such as its data type, will be added to the representation. When an element is expanded, it will remain the same width but will get longer, and its attributes and children will be drawn nested inside it. If an element is zoomed, its corresponding rectangle and all its children will zoom out to fill the window. If the window is not big enough to display all its elements, a scroll bar will be added to the window and users can scroll to view all the elements. Right clicking on an attribute or element will pop up a right click menu. Choosing the "`predicate`" menu item

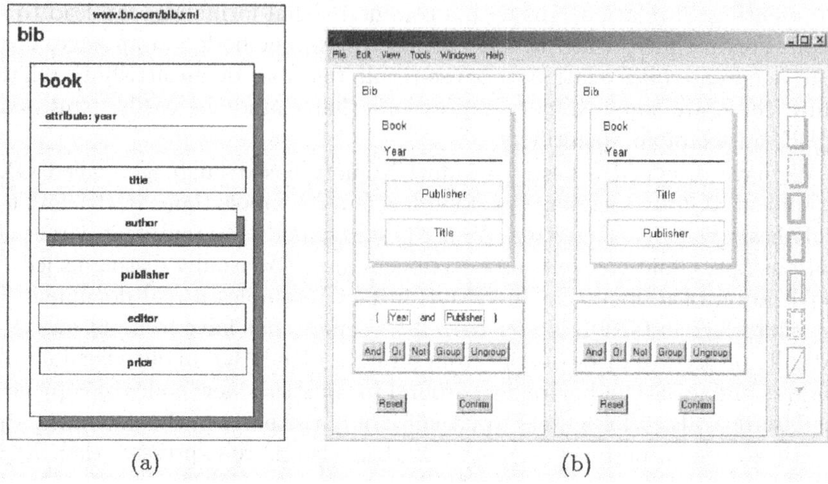

(a) (b)

Fig. 1. (a) GXQL representation of the sample document. (b) Query interface of GXQL. Retrieval is on the left, construction is on the right.

will bring up a window showing information (such as name, type and full path) about that attribute or element and allows the entry of predicates.

Drag actions are also used as part of the query interface, but these are distinguished from the clicking actions described above because in a drag action, the button up event happens outside the window.

3 Query Interface

The query interface of GXQL looks like Figure 1 (b). There are three parts in the main window. On the left, the retrieval pane represents the schema or input document. It allows users to select the subset of the input they want to query. In the middle, the construction pane allows users to structure the query results. On the very right of the interface there is a symbol bar containing all the symbols used in GXQL. These are used to create new elements from scratch in the construction pane.

In the retrieval pane, when users choose a document or document schema, GXQL will visualize its structure. At first, only the outermost node and its children are shown, but users can zoom into or expand subelements to see detail. We chose this design because we want the interface to give users some way to browse the document structure, so they do not have to remember the names of elements and attributes, but we do not want to overwhelm them with detail. Our design also allows large documents to be visualized incrementally.

We will call elements or attributes "nodes". Users can select (or deselect) any node by left clicking on it. Selecting nodes by clicking avoids errors caused by misspelling. By default, all nodes are first drawn with a light blue color indicating that they exist, but have not been selected yet. Selecting nodes will change their color to black. After users set up a query, clicking on the "`confirm`" button executes the query. All selected nodes will participate in the query, while unselected elements will be ignored.

When users want to input predicates for nodes, they need to right click on a node. A window will pop up asking for the predicate, and will provide a menu of options. After the predicates are confirmed, each predicate will be shown in a panel. Both the retrieval pane and construction pane have their own predicate panel.

In the construction pane, there are two ways to construct a node: either by dragging a symbol from the symbol bar, or by dragging a node from the retrieval pane. After dragging a symbol from the symbol bar, the new element is empty, and the user must input the name for it. When dragging a node from the retrieval pane, the node (including all its descendants) are dragged into the construction pane, forming a new node there. Users can then select the nodes they want or delete (by a right click menu selection) the ones not needed. Users can also drag the nodes around and switch their order. The results will be given based on this order. The frame border of nodes can also be changed via a right click menu.

Some rectangles have single-line frames and some have shadowed frames. Other frame styles are possible; a complete set of symbols representing the relations between nodes used in GXQL is given in Figure 2. Each frame style has a specific meaning suggested by its visual design. Symbol 1 indicates that node B is the single immediate child of node A. Symbol 2 indicates there are multiple B subelements wrapped within one A node, and all Bs are immediate children of A. Symbol 3 has the same meaning as symbol 2, except when users set up predicates for B, only some elements B satisfy the predicates. Symbol 4 indicates that the B subelements are descendants of A. There may be multiple Bs that are descendants of A. They do not have to be immediate children of A. Symbol 5 has the same meaning as symbol 4, except that when users set up predicates for B, only some elements B satisfy the predicates. Symbol 6 indicates that the B subelements are descendants of A with only one intermediate path in between. There may be multiple Bs that are descendants of A. Symbol 7 has the same meaning as symbol 6, except that when users set up predicates for B, only some elements B satisfy the predicates. Symbol 8 has the same meaning as symbol 1, except that when users set up predicates for B, they want the complement of the results. This is just one example of complementation. Any symbol from 1 to 7 can be complemented in the same way.

4 Examples

The sample XML document and the example queries used in this paper are taken from the XQBE paper [1]. We are going to show how two of these queries, 1 and 5, are expressed in GXQL, with modifications in Query 5 to demonstrate queries not supported by XQBE. The rest of the queries are demonstrated in our technical report [12].

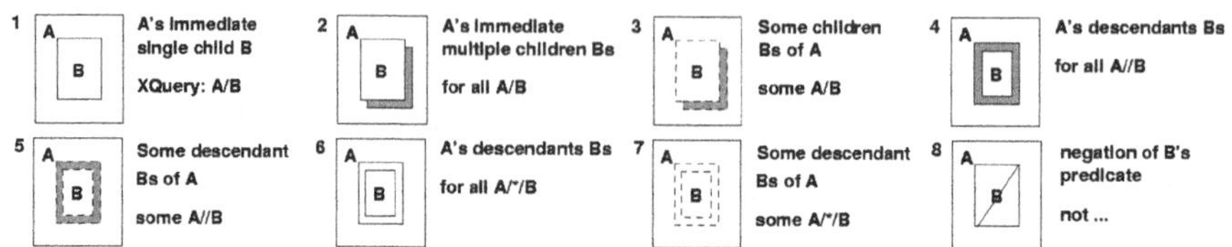

Fig. 2. Symbols used in GXQL.

Query 1: *List books published by Addison-Wesley after 1991, including their year and title.*

This query shows how to represent "for" "where" and "return" in GXQL. In the XQuery textual language, this query can be expressed as follows:

```
<bib>
{   for $b in document("www.bn.com/bib.xml")/bib/book
    where $b/publisher="Addison-Wesley" and $b/@year>1991
    return <book year="{$b/@year}"> { $b/title } </book> }
</bib>
```

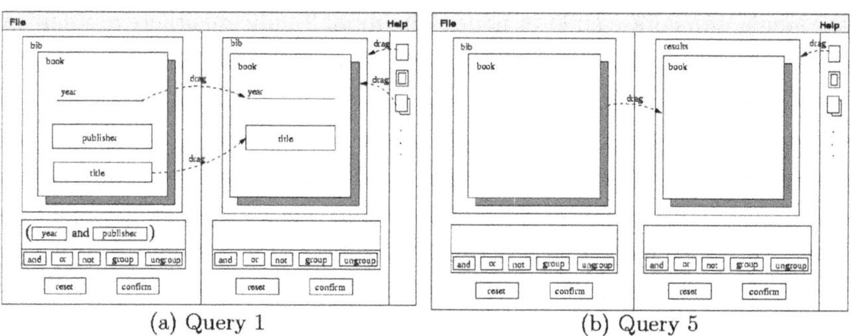

(a) Query 1 (b) Query 5

Fig. 3. GXQL expressions for queries 1 and 5.

Query 1 is represented by GXQL as in Figure 3 (a). In the retrieval pane, users first zoom into `<book>`, so the attribute `year` and all subelements will show up. Right clicking on `year` will pop up a window. This window will show the name (with full path) and data type of the attribute and will prompt for predicates. Once a predicate is set, the predicate object will show up in a predicate panel below the main figure. Predicates can be combined together by Boolean operations. All Boolean operations are supported, such as `or` and `not`. This cannot be done in XQBE, which can only represent `and` relations.

To express the example query, in the construction pane users first drag an icon with a single frame from the symbol bar to create a new element `<bib>`, then drag an icon with a shadowed frame for element `<book>`. Then users can drag `year` and `<title>` from the retrieval pane to the construction pane. When the "`confirm`" button is clicked, appropriate textual XQuery language will be generated and passed down to the processing pipeline. The query should be read from the outermost rectangle toward the innermost rectangles.

Query 5: List all the books in element `<bib>` and wrap them within one `<results>` element.

We modified this example so that it uses the `let` clause. The `let` clause is not supported in XQBE, so there is no example using `let` in the XQBE paper. XQBE can wrap multiple elements within a single element, but the query is always translated into `for` clause. The modified XQuery is given as follows:

```
let $b := document("www.bn.com")/bib/book,
return <results> { $b } </results>
```

Query 5 is represented by GXQL in Figure 3 (b). In this example, the `<book>` element is first dragged from the retrieval pane to the construction pane. Note that the `<book>` rectangle has a shadowed frame. This means all the retrieved `<book>` elements will be wrapped together in one `<results>` element in the result.

5 Semantics

To implement a query in GXQL, we have to translate a given GXQL diagram into a corresponding XQuery FLWOR expression. In the construction pane, when users set up rectangles by dragging icons from the symbol bar, it corresponds to constructing new nodes in the result. In the retrieval pane, each shaded double-line frame, if not dragged to the construction pane, corresponds to a "`for`" clause with a "`//`" path, e.g. "`for $b in bib//book`". If such a frame is dragged to the construction pane, it corresponds to a "`let`" clause, e.g. "`let $b = //book`", and the result of "`$b`" is wrapped within a single parent tag. Each double-line unshaded frame works the same way as shaded double-line frame, except that it represents the path "`/*/`". Each shadowed frame, if not dragged to the construction pane, also corresponds to a "`for`" clause with a path containing only "`/`", e.g. "`for $b in bib/book`". If such a frame is dragged to the construction pane, it corresponds to a "`let`" clause, e.g. "`let $b = /bib/book`", and the result of "`$b`" is wrapped within a single parent tag. Each single-line frame corresponds to a child "`/`", e.g. "`$f = bib/book`". If a frame has a dashed border, it corresponds to use of the "`some`" quantifier, e.g. "`some $b in //book satisfies`". If a rectangle is crossed, it corresponds to the use of "`not`" in all predicates, e.g. "`not ($b = ''Jack'')`".

So to perform translation, the construction pane should be analyzed first to find out what nodes are new and which nodes are copied from the retrieved results. The next step is to analyze the retrieval pane, going from the outermost rectangle to the innermost rectangle and binding variables to expressions according to how they are going to be used in the "`return`" clause. The last step is to construct FLWOR expressions based on the construction pane.

6 Conclusions

In this paper, we have described the design of GXQL, a graphical query language using nested windows to visualize hierarchy. Representations in GXQL can be directly translated into corresponding "`FLWOR`" clauses. GXQL also supports predicates, different path patterns, and quantifiers. GXQL is also easy to expand to support more XQuery features.

More features of XQuery might eventually be supported in GXQL, such as conditional expressions, type casting, functions, and so on. However, being both powerful and clear is a challenge to graphical languages. The system should not have so many features added to it that it becomes too difficult for a user to learn. For future work, we need to complete the implementation and perform user testing to validate our design.

We would like to thank Frank Tompa for suggesting that we submit this paper for publication. He also suggested the notation for negation.

References

1. D. Braga and A. Campi. A Graphical Environment to Query XML Data with XQuery. In *Fourth Intl. Conf. on Web Information Systems Engineering (WISE'03)*, pp. 31–40, 2003.
2. S. Cohen, Y. Kanza, Y. A. Kogen, W. Nutt, Y. Sagiv, and A. Serebrenik. Equix Easy Querying in XML Databases. In *WebDB (Informal Proceedings)*, pp. 43–48, 1999.
3. S. Comai, E. Damiani, and P. Fraternali. Computing Graphical Queries over XML Data. In *ACM Trans. on Information Systems, 19(4)*, pp. 371–430, 2001.
4. S. Comai, E. Damiani, R. Posenato, and L. Tanca. A Schema Based Approach to Modeling and Querying WWW Data. In *Proc. FQAS*, May 1998.
5. S. Comai and P. di Milano. Graph-based GUIs for Querying XML Data: the XML-GL Experience. In *SAC, ACM*, pp. 269–274, 2001.
6. M. P. Consens and A. O. Mendelzon. The G+/GraphLog Visual Query System. In *Proc. ACM SIGMOD*, 1990, pp. 388.
7. I. F. Cruz, A. O. Mendelzon, and P. T. Wood. A Graphical Query Language Supporting Recursion. In *Proc. ACM SIGMOD*, 1987, pp. 323–330.
8. I. F. Cruz, A. O. Mendelzon, and P. T. Wood. G+: Recursive Queries without Recursion. In *2nd Int. Conf. on Expert Database Systems*, pp. 335–368, 1988.
9. I. M. R. Evangelista Filha, A. H. F. Laender, and A. S. da Silva. Querying Semistructured Data by Example: The QSByE Interface. In *2nd Int. Conf. on Expert Database Systems*, pp. 335–368, 1988.
10. K. D. Munroe and Y. Papakonstantinou. BBQ: A Visual Interface for Integrated Browsing and Querying of XML. In *5th IFIP 2.6 Working Conf. on Visual Database Systems*, 2000.
11. P. Peelman, J. Paredaens and L. Tanca. G-log: A Declarative Graph-based Language. In *IEEE Trans. on Knowledge and Data Eng.*, 1995.
12. Z. Qin, B. B. Yao, Y. Liu and M. McCool. A Graphical XQuery Language Using Nested Windows. Technical Report CS-2004-37, School of Computer Science, University of Waterloo, August, 2004.

Grouping in MetaXQuery

Hao Jin and Curtis Dyreson

Washington State University
Pullman, Washington
U.S.A.
{hjin, cdyreson}@eecs.wsu.edu

Abstract. Metadata plays an important role in describing and proscribing data in both traditional and XML applications. In this paper, we present an extension of the XML data model and XQuery query language to support grouping of data and metadata. We focus in particular on grouping because of its importance but lack of explicit support in querying and restructuring XML. Typically elements that have the same data are grouped together, but when metadata is present, the metadata must also be evaluated to determine group membership.

1 Introduction

This paper outlines an extension to XQuery [19] to support grouping of both data and *metadata*. Metadata is "data about data". Metadata is usually *descriptive*, but some metadata, especially security metadata, is also *proscriptive* in the sense that it restricts access to data. We present a collection of XQuery functions to support grouping with metadata. XQuery does not currently have a grouping construct or clause, though the *distinct-value* function can be used to effect grouping. We introduce an explicit *data-group* function. But grouping by data values alone is insufficient when metadata annotates the data since the metadata has semantics that must be enforced during grouping. So we also introduce a *meta-group* function.

This paper is organized as follows. The next section presents an example that motivates this research. We then outline the XQuery extensions. Finally, we present related work and conclusions.

2 Motivating Example

Our motivating example comes from the W3C XQuery and XPath Full-Text Use Cases document [20]. The example scenario is a collection of book information that has both data and metadata. The metadata includes a book's title, list of authors, and subject in several different languages. The data is the content of the book. We adopt a unified data model that supports proscriptive metadata, is able to distinguish data from metadata, and yet also capture their relationship. Suppose that a publisher wants to make information about new books available only to on-line subscribers. The publisher annotates the book data with *security* metadata. The security is intended to limit

X. Zhou et al. (Eds.): WISE 2004, LNCS 3306, pp. 688–693, 2004.
© Springer-Verlag Berlin Heidelberg 2004

access to only the user Joe. The publisher also wants to archive the book information and so decides to record the *transaction time* of the book data. The transaction time is the system time when the data is available to Joe. The publisher adds meta-metadata to record the lifetime of Joe's changing access rights. An example of such a metadata-aware data model is shown in Fig. 1. The metadata and data in the model are separated into different, yet related scopes. The key difference between our metadata-enhanced model and a normal XML data model is the directed edge from book to metadata and from user to meta-metadata. These directed edges represent the relationship between data and its metadata. By following an edge, the user jumps to its metadata scope. The scope limits the search performed by a "wild card". For instance a query that follows the descendant axis from the book node will not descend into the metadata.

Now let's take a look at the challenges that we have. The first challenge is grouping. In the current XPath and XQuery, there's no explicit grouping construct such as the GROUP BY clause in SQL. To effect grouping a user employs the `distinct-value` function to first determine which nodes (of a particular kind) have unique values (the "value" is the concatenation of the values of its descendants).

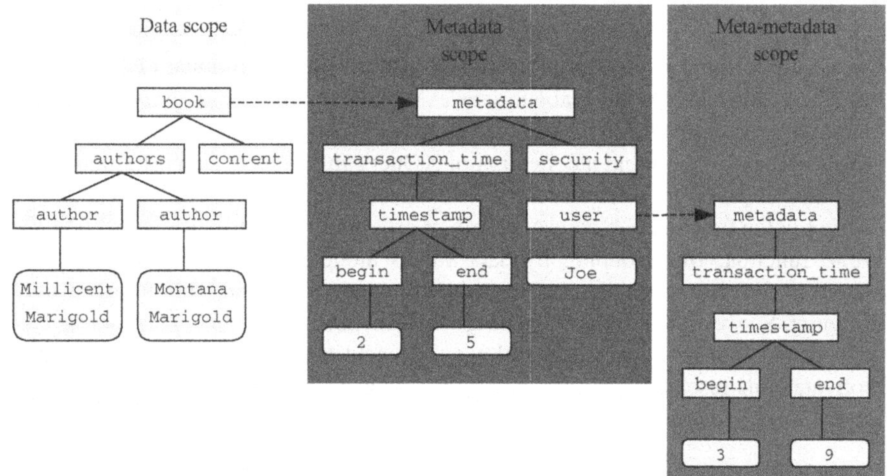

Fig. 1. A sample metadata-aware data model for an online publisher

There are two limitations in doing grouping this way. First, the `distinct-value` function only returns the first node in document order from the set of nodes that have the same value, discarding the others. Sometimes the discarded members of the group are needed, for instance the size of each group. Also, a group could be "merged" into a single node, retaining all children of the original group (e.g., if we want to group only by an author's birthplace, assuming each author has a birthplace sub-elements). Secondly, when we add metadata to the data model, the metadata could change the grouping. For instance we may not want to group data that appears in different versions of a document, i.e., that have different transaction time metadata.

3 Grouping in MetaXQuery

This section presents extensions to XQuery to support grouping of both data and metadata. We adopt the notation used by the W3C [19] to express all XQuery extensions here. The extensions include a meta axis in XPath, and a set of functions for explicit grouping. These functions can be implemented by extending an XQuery processor, or in programming languages like Java and loaded into XQuery as external functions. Parts can also be written directly in XQuery as user functions. We will leave it to the MetaXQuery implementation to decide how to achieve these functions.

3.1 MetaXPath

In order to make the metadata available to users of MetaXQuery we adopt the same approach used in MetaXPath [8]: we add a new axis, the *meta* axis, to XPath expressions. The meta axis follows the meta property of the context node to its metadata. We will use the notation "meta::" to denote the meta axis. For example, "meta::node()" will locate the metadata's root node from the context node. The meta axis will be abbreviated as "^".

The meta axis is orthogonal to all other XPath axes. In other words, the metadata can only be located through the meta axis. This ensures the separation of scope between data and metadata. So if we want to ask a query such as "When was book 1 in the document?", it can be constructed in MetaXPath as follows.

```
//book[@number="1"]^/transaction_time
```

Note that a traditional XPath expression can still be evaluated in our metadata-aware data model by simply ignoring the metadata. So it's fully backwards-compatible to current XPath and XQuery.

3.2 Grouping

The grouping function is divided into several sub-functions. We make these sub-functions available to users of MetaXQuery in order to provide fine-grained control in grouping. The sub-functions are data-group and meta-group. The data-group function groups nodes based on their data values. The meta-group function groups nodes based on their metadata values. The output of data-group is typically input to meta-group. The nodes ended up in the same group could be further merged and coalesced. Due to the limitation of space, we will refer the readers to [12] for further details.

Both data-group and meta-group function keeps all the nodes in a group so they can be utilized for further computations. And with the definition of the meta-group function, we are able to group nodes based on both their data and metadata conditions.

Our data-group function groups nodes that have the same value. The value is computed by XQuery's `distinct-value` function, but unlike distinct-value, all of the nodes with the same value are retained in a group (in document order).

The type *meta-dm:node()* denotes a node in the metadata data model. Note that the return type of the function is a list of groups, which is an extension of XQuery's

Sequence type so it is in the *meta-dm* namespace. In a list of groups, each group is internally in document order, but the order of the groups is implementation defined.

Definition [data-group]. The data-group function takes a Sequence of nodes and returns a list of groups, where each group is a Sequence.

```
ext-fn:data-group($seq as meta-dm:node()*) as (meta-dm:node()*)*
```

$$= (s_1, s_2, \ldots, s_n) \mid s_i = (v_{i1}, v_{i2}, \ldots, v_{im})$$

$$\text{where } \mathit{fn{:}distinct\text{-}value}(s_i) = \mathit{fn{:}distinct\text{-}value}(v_{i1}) \wedge \forall j,k, 1 \leq j,k \leq n, j \neq k,$$
$$(\mathit{fn{:}distinct\text{-}value}(s_j) \neq \mathit{fn{:}distinct\text{-}value}(s_k))$$

■

The result of data grouping is passed on to the meta-group function for further partitioning based on their metadata. Sometimes the metadata might prevent grouping. For example, two identical temperatures with different metadata, one in the Celsius scale, and the other in degrees of Fahrenheit, should be placed into different groups. The meta-group function partitions a group into subgroups based on the metadata. The semantics of meta-grouping is parameterized by the type of metadata.

Definition [meta-group]. The meta-group function takes a sequence of nodes and returns a list of sequences. All nodes in a sequence have the "same" data and metadata.

```
meta-fn:meta-group($fn as meta-dt: MetaFNHash,
        $seq as meta-dm:node()*) as (meta-dm:node()*)*
```

$$= (s_1, s_2, \ldots s_n) \mid \forall i, \ (s_j \subseteq \texttt{\$seq} \wedge (\forall v_j, v_k \in s_i, (\mathit{meta\text{-}fn{:}meta\text{-}match}(\texttt{\$fn}, v_j, v_k))))$$

■

Internally, meta-group calls the meta-match function, which compares the metadata to determine if a pair of nodes can be in the same group.

Definition [meta-match]. The meta-match function takes an operation matrix and a pair of nodes, and evaluates whether the metadata in the nodes "matches".

```
meta-fn:meta-match($fn as meta-dt:MetaFNHash,
                   $node1 as meta-dm:node(),
                   $node2 as meta-dm:node()) as xs:Boolean
```

$$= \left\{ \begin{array}{ll} \mathit{True} & \text{If } (\mathit{fn{:}exists}(\texttt{\$node1\^{}/*} \mid \texttt{\$node2\^{}/*}) \Rightarrow (\forall m \in \texttt{\$node1\^{}/*} \mid \texttt{\$node2\^{}/*}, \\ & \quad \texttt{\$fn} \rightarrow \{m\}(\texttt{\$node1\^{}}/m, \texttt{\$node2\^{}}/m)) \wedge \\ & \quad \mathit{meta\text{-}fn{:}meta\text{-}match}(\texttt{\$fn}, \texttt{\$node1\^{}}/m, \texttt{\$node2\^{}}/m))) \\ \mathit{False} & \text{Otherwise.} \end{array} \right\}$$

■

The following definitions are for metadata-specific matching functions.

Definition [metadata-specific matching functions]. These functions are used to match specific kinds of metadata. The True function always reports a successful match and group-equality tests for equality of two metadata values.

```
meta-fn:group-equality($node1 as meta-dm:node(),
                       $node2 as meta-dm:node()) as xs:Boolean
```

$$= \begin{cases} \textit{True} & \text{If } \textit{meta-fn:meta-value}(\texttt{\$node1}) = \textit{meta-fn:meta-value}(\texttt{\$node2}) \\ \textit{False} & \text{Otherwise.} \end{cases}$$

■

4 Related Work

RDF is perhaps the most widely used language for annotating a document with metadata [18]. It has also become an important language for supporting the Semantic Web [1]. Several strategies for unifying the representation of XML and RDF have been proposed [15], but query languages have largely targeted either RDF or XML. There have been several RDF query languages proposed in the literature including RQL [13], SeRQL [3], and etc. For a comparison of these RDF query languages, please refer to [11]. Discussions are ongoing about accessing and querying RDF data [17], but in general RDF query languages use a very different data model than XML query languages.

Support for particular kinds of metadata has been researched. Two of the most important and most widely discussed types of (proscriptive) metadata are temporal and security metadata. Temporal extensions of almost every W3C recommendation exist, for instance, *TT*XPath [6], τXQuery [9], τXSchema [4]. Grandi has an excellent bibliography of time-related web papers [10]. Security in XML management systems has also been researched, e.g., [2] and [5]. Our approach is to build infrastructure that supports a wide range of different kinds of metadata in the same vein as our previous efforts with the semistructured data model [7] and XPath data model [8].

In this paper we focus on grouping that we did not address previously. While grouping is important, it has not received much attention in the research community. Paparizos et. al showed that the lack of an explicit grouping construct in XQuery forces users to employ inefficient strategies when grouping [14]. They proposed improving the efficiency of grouping by adding an explicit grouping operator to the TAX algebra in the context of the TIMBER [16] native XML database system. We focus instead on grouping with metadata.

5 Conclusion

In this paper, we outline an extension to the XML data model that supports data annotated with metadata. Different semantics can be given to different kinds of metadata. We also present part of a query language, called MetaXQuery, for the extended data model. We focus in particular on the grouping aspects of MetaXQuery. MetaXQuery extends XPath with an additional "meta" axis, and extends XQuery with additional functions to group data and metadata. The grouping-related functions provide rich expressive power to our query language.

References

1. T. Berners-Lee. "Why RDF Model is Different from the XML Model", 1999. Available at www.w3.org-/DesignIssues/RDF-XML.html.
2. E. Bertino, S. Castano, E. Ferrari, and M. Mesiti. "Specifying and Enforcing Access Control Policies for XML Document Sources". World Wide Web Journal, 3(3): 139-151, 2000.
3. J. Broekstra and A. Kampman. "SeRQL: An RDF Query and Transformation Language". Submitted to the International Semantic Web Conference, 2004.
4. F. Currim, S. Currim, C. E. Dyreson, and R. T. Snodgrass. "A Tale of Two Schemas: Creating a Temporal XML Schema from a Snapshot Schema with τXSchema". In *Proceedings of EDBT*, pp: 348-365. Crete, Greece, March 2004.
5. E. Damiani, S. De Capitani di Vimercati, S. Paraboschi, P. Samarati. "A Fine-Grained Access Control System for XML Documents". ACM Transactions on Information and System Security, 5(2): 169-202, May 2002.
6. C. E. Dyreson. "Observing Transaction-time Semantics with *TT*XPath". In *Proceedings of WISE*, pp: 193-202. Kyoto, Japan, December 2001.
7. C. E. Dyreson, M. H. Böhlen, and C. S. Jensen. "Capturing and Querying Multiple Aspects of Semistructured Data". In *Proceedings of VLDB*, pp: 290-301. Edinburgh, Scotland, September 1999.
8. C. E. Dyreson, M. H. Böhlen, and C. S. Jensen. "METAXPath". In *Proceedings of the International Conference on Dublin Core and Metadata Applications*, 2001. pp. 17-23.
9. D. Gao and R. T. Snodgrass. "Temporal Slicing in the Evaluation of XML Queries". In *Proceedings of VLDB*, 632--643, 2003.
10. F. Grandi. "Introducing an Annotated Bibliography on Temporal and Evolution Aspects in the World Wide Web". SIGMOD Record, 33(2), June 2004.
11. P. Haase, J. Broekstra, A. Eberhart, and R. Volz. "A Comparison of RDF Query Languages". Available at www.aifb.uni-karlsruhe.de/WBS/pha/rdf-query.
12. H. Jin and C. E. Dyreson. "Capturing, Querying and Grouping Metadata Properties in XML". In preparation.
13. G. Karvounarakis, S. Alexaki, V. Christophides, D. Plexousakis, and M. Scholl. "RQL: a declarative query language for RDF". In *Proceedings of WWW*, pp: 592-603. Honolulu, Hawaii, USA, May 2002.
14. S. Paparizos, S. Al-Khalifa, H.V. Jagadish, L. Lakshmanan, A. Nierman, D. Srivastava, and Y.g Wu. "Grouping in XML". XML-Based Data Management and Multimedia Engineering - EDBT 2002 Workshops, Pages: 128-147. Prague, Czech Republic, March 2002.
15. P. F. Patel-Schneider, and J. Siméon. "The Yin/Yang Web: A Unified Model for XML Syntax and RDF Semantics". In IEEE Transactions on Knowledge and Data Engineering, 15(4), pp: 797-812. July/August 2003.
16. University of Michigan, TIMBER native XML database. www.eecs.umich.edu-/db/timber.
17. W3C RDF Data Access Working Group. Available at www.w3.org/sw/DataAccess.
18. World Wide Web Consortium. "RDF Primer", W3C Recommendation, Feb. 2004. www.w3.org/TR/2004/REC-rdf-primer-20040210.
19. World Wide Web Consortium. "XQuery 1.0: An XML Query Language", W3C Working Draft, Nov. 2003. www.w3.org/TR/2003/WD-xquery-20031112.
20. World Wide Web Consortium. "XQuery and XPath Full-Text Use Cases", W3C Working Draft, Feb. 2003. www.w3.org/TR/2003/WD-xml-query-full-text-use-cases-2003.

Search in Unstructured Peer-to-Peer Networks

Zhaoqing Jia, Xinhuai Tang, Jinyuan You, and Minglu Li

Department of Computer Science and Engineering,
Shanghai Jiao Tong University, Shanghai 200030, China
jiazhaoqing@hotmail.com

Abstract. Unstructured Peer-to-Peer (hence P2P) applications, such as KaZaa, Gnutella, etc. are very popular on the Internet over the last few years. Search method is a major component of these distributed systems and its efficiency also does influence the systems performance. An efficient technique for improving performance of search method is to replicate file location information in P2P networks. Unstructured P2P topology has power-law characteristic in the link distribution, so we present a replica spread mechanism utilizing high degree nodes in this paper. Based on this spread mechanism, we proposed two search methods. Extensive simulation results show that they performs very well on the power-law networks, achieve high success rates, and are robust to node failure.

1 Introduction

In the last few years, Peer-to-Peer networking has been growing rapidly. It is a new paradigm of sharing the resources available at the edges of the Internet. In general, we classify P2P architectures into two categories: Structured P2P and Unstructured P2P. Structured P2P applications have strict structure, and require the files to be placed at specified location. Highly structured P2P designs are prevalent in research literature, such as Chord [1], CAN [2]. Unstructured P2P applications are very popular, such as Gnutella [3], KaZaa [4], Napster [5]. They are designed for sharing files among the peers in the networks. Today, bandwidth consumption attributed to these applications amounts to a considerable fraction (up to 60%) of the total Internet traffic [6]. It is of great importance to reduce the total traffic of them for the user and the broad Internet community.

A search for a file in a P2P network is successful if it discovers the location of the file. The ratio of successful to total searches made is the success rate of the algorithm. The performance of an algorithm is associated with its success rate, while its cost relates to the number of messages it produces.

At present, existed search methods for unstructured P2P can be categorized into two kinds: blind and informed. In blind search, each node has not any information about file location, and randomly chooses some neighbors and forwards query message to them. Current blind methods waste a lot of bandwidth to achieve high success rate, such as flooding search, or have low success rate, such as random walks search. In informed search, some nodes cache information that relate to files, and can choose

X. Zhou et al. (Eds.): WISE 2004, LNCS 3306, pp. 694–705, 2004.
© Springer-Verlag Berlin Heidelberg 2004

"good" neighbors to forward query to. In general, most informed search methods improve the success rate. However they produced a lot of update messages in changing P2P environment.

Unstructured P2P networks display a power-law distribution in their nodes degree [7] [8], so that we propose a replica spread mechanism utilizing high degree nodes for improving search in unstructured P2P. Combing it with random walk search or high degree walk search, we present two different search algorithms. With spreading file location information through high degree walk, the high degree nodes in unstructured P2P network form a "directory server group". Query messages can easily arrive at the "directory servers" through random walk or high degree walk, so that the target file location information can be easily found. The two algorithms achieve high success rates with low bandwidth consumption, and are robust to node failure.

This paper makes the following contributions:

1. We present a replica spread mechanism to improve search in unstructured P2P. We describe its idea, its spread scheme, and analyze its performance.
2. Combining our spread mechanism with random walk search or high degree walk search, we define two search algorithms, HRWS, which combines our spread mechanism and random walk search, and HHDWS, which combines our spread mechanism and high degree walk search. We describe their search procedures and analyze their performances.
3. We perform extensive simulations, and our search methods achieve great results in the success rates, message production, load balance and robustness to high degree nodes failure. Comparing our search methods with the method in [9], our methods have higher success rates.

2 Related Works

In recent years, many search algorithms for unstructured P2P networks have been proposed. Gnutella is a real-world P2P system, and employs flooding scheme for searching object. Each query request produces O(<k>N) messages, hence it is very difficult to scale for Gnutella [3].

Ref. [10] proposed a variation of flooding search. In this method, nodes randomly choose a ratio of their neighbors to forward the query to. It certainly reduces the average message production compared to flooding search. But it still contacts a large number of nodes.

In [11], authors proposed a random walks search method. The requesting node sends out several query messages to an equal number of randomly chosen neighbors. Each query message is forwarded to a randomly chosen neighbor node at each step by intermediate nodes. In this algorithm, message production is largely reduced. But its success rate is very low.

Ref. [9] proposed a search algorithm based on random walks, which utilized high degree nodes. Each node indexes all files on its neighbors, and when a node forwards a query message, it chooses the highest degree neighbor node to forward. In this algorithm, the probability is that the files on the low degree nodes can not be found.

3 Algorithms

3.1 Some Assumptions and Definitions

Consider N nodes in a network, the following assumption about them:

1. Each node has a local directory (LocalDir) that points the shared files on this node. Each node has total control over its local files and its local directory.
2. Each node has a file information database (FileInfoDB). The location information of the remote files managed by other nodes can be stored in this database. An entry of this database is a pair (*filename*, *metadata*), and the metadata includes file name, file size, and file descriptor. The file descriptors are used for keyword matches in querying. For simplicity, we only examine filename-based query, and the request only includes file name.
3. Each node has a message cache (MessCache). An entry of the message cache is a pair (*messageId*, *nodeId*).

We have the following definitions about our algorithms:

Random walk is a well-known technique, which forwards a query message to a randomly chosen neighbor at each step until the object is found. This message is known as "random walker". If the query message is forwarded to the highest degree neighbor at each step, then we call this message a "high degree walker".

Definition 1. FileInformation(*messageId*, *filename*, *metadata*, *ttl*) is a message. It is sent by a node to spread the *metadata* information of the file *filename*. MessageId is used to identify a unique message in networks. The message can be only forwarded to at most *ttl* steps. The FileInformation is also known as "spread walker

Definition 2. QueryRequest(*messageId*, *filename*, *ttl*) is a query message sent by a node to query file *filename*. The message can be only propagated at most *ttl* nodes. The QueryRequest is also known as "search walker".

Definition 3. Response(*messageId*, *filename*, *loc*) is a reply message. If the location information of the target file *filename* is found on certain node, then a reply message is return to the request node. Field *loc* indicates the address of the file *filename*.

Definition 4. Neighbors(*s*) is a node set which is formed by the neighbors of node *s*.

Definition 5. Degree(*s*) denotes the degree of the node *s*.

3.2 Spread Mechanism

Gnutella' notoriously poor scaling is because it employs flooding search mechanism and produces huge query traffic. Random walk is an effective search technique for reducing message production and good solution to search in unstructured P2P. However, pure random walk search has low success rate, and it is required to improve its performance by other ways. In power-law networks, only a few nodes have high degrees. Assuming that p(k) is the probability that a randomly chosen node has degree k, a random edge arrives at a node with probability proportional to the degree of the node, i.e., kp(k). It is obvious that the probability that random walks arrive at high degree node is high. So, random walks in power-law networks naturally gravitate towards the high degree nodes. If file location information is placed on the high degree nodes, then it will be easily found through random walk. Unstructured P2P topology has power-law characteristic in the link distribution, and this reflects the presence of central nodes which interact with many others and play a key role in relaying information. Hence, we design a replica spread method employing high degree walk for placing files information on the high degree nodes in unstructured P2P.

Program 1 detailedly describes the High Degree Walk SPREAD mechanism (HDWSPREAD). Each node which wants to share its files spreads those files' metadatum through high degree walk, so all files' metadatum are stored on the high degree nodes and the high degree nodes form a "directory server group". The size of high degree walk is c (c<<N) and c is a constant. With increasing c, more nodes join the "directory server group" and answer query request, so search algorithm is more robust to node failure and the load of each high degree node is also reduced. Hence by increasing the value of c we can reduce the load of each high degree node and enhance algorithm's reliability. Our simulations validate the above analysis.

Program 1. HDWSPREAD Mechanism (Node *sId* spreads the metadata of the file *filename*).

Spread Procedure on Source Node *sId*:

```
add filename to LocalDir;
fi = New FileInformation(fmId, filename, metadata, c);
choose a node ni, (ni∈Neighbors(sId)) And (∀m ∈ Neigh-
bors(sId) Degree(m) ≤ Degree(ni));
forward fi to node ni;
add (fmId, ni) to MessCache;
```

Spread Procedure on Intermediate Node *ni*:

```
receive FileInformation(fmId, filename, metadata, ttl)
from node n1;
add (fmId, n1) to MessCache;
if filename not in LocalDir {
  if filename not in FileInfoDB {
    Add (filename, metadata) to FileInfoDB;
  }
}
if ttl>0 {
  construct node set S(s): S(s)=(s∈Neighbors(ni) And
((fmId, s) not in MessCache));
  if Size(S(s))>0 {
    choose a node n2, (n2∈S(s)) And (∀m∈S(s) Degree(m)
≤ Degree(n2));
    forward FileInformation(fmId, filename, metadata,
ttl-1) to node n2;
    add (fmId, n2) to MessCache;
  }
}
```

3.3 Search Methods

In this section, we present two search methods: HRWS, which combines HDWSPREAD with Random Walk Search, and HHDWS, which combines HDWSPREAD with High Degree Walk Search. Program 2 describes HRWS' search mechanism. When a node starts a query, it sends out *b* (such as 16, 32 or 64) query messages to an equal number of randomly chosen neighbors. Each of these messages follows its own path, having intermediate nodes forward it to a randomly chosen node at each step.

Program 2. Search Mechanism of HRWS (Node *rId* locates file *filename*).

Query Procedure on Request Node *rId*:

```
if filename not in FileInfoDB
  for I=1 to b {
    randomly choose a node nj, nj∈Neighbors(rId);
    forward QueryRequest(qmId,filename,ln(N)) to node
nj;
  }
else
  return Response(rmId, filename, loc);
```

Query Procedure on Intermediate Node *nj*:

```
receive QueryRequest(qmId,filename,ttl) from node n1;
if filename in LocalDir
  return Response(rmid, filename, nj) to node rId;
if filename in FileInfoDB
  return Response(rmid, filename, loc) to node rId;
if ttl>0 {
  randomly choose a node n2, n2∈Neighbors(nj);
  forward QueryRequest(qmId,filename,ttl-1) to node n2;
}
```

The average path length of a random graph is proportional to ln(N)/ln(<k>) where <k> is the average degree of the graph, so in our search algorithms time-to-live (TTL) value of a query message is set at ln(N). Messages per request is O(bln(N)) for random walk search.

Program 3 displays HHDWS' search mechanism. When a node starts a query, it sends out a query message with TTL=ln(N) to the highest degree node of its neighbors. This query message is always forwarded to the highest degree neighbor node at each step. So this query message will walk through those high degree nodes in power-law network. Hence, the target file information on the high degree nodes can be easily found. For high degree walk search, the message production per request is O(ln(N)).

Program 3. Search Mechanism of HHDWS (Node *rId* locates file *filename*).

Query Procedure on Request Node *rId*:

```
if filename in FileInfoDB
  return Response(rmId, filename, loc);
else {
  qr=New QueryRequest(qmId,filename,ln(N));
  choose a node nj, (nj∈Neighbors(rId)) And (∀m ∈
Neighbors(rId) Degree(m) ≤ Degree(nj));
  forward qr to node nj;
  add (qmId, nj) to MessCache;
}
```

Query Procedure on Intermediate Node *nj*:

```
receive QueryRequest(qmId,filename,ttl) from node n1;
add (qmId, n1) to MessCache;
if filename in LocalDir
  return Response(rmId,filename,nj) to node rId;
if filename in FileInfoDB
  return Response(rmId,filename,loc) to node rId;
if ttl>0 {
  construct node set S(s):S(s)=(s∈Neighbors(nj) And
((qmId,s) not in MessCache));
  if Size(S(s))>0 {
    choose a node n2, (n2∈S(s)) And (∀m∈S(s) Degree(m)
≤ Degree(n2));
    forward QueryRequest(qmId,filename,ttl-1) to node
n2;
    add (qmId, n2) to MessCache;
  }
}
```

4 Simulations

4.1 Simulation Setup

M.A. Jovanovic presented node degree power-law exponent of 1.6 for the Gnutella topology [8], and Clip2 reported the power-law exponent of 2.3 [7], so we used two groups of power-law graph models with different power-law exponents. Each group has five power-law graphs with different sizes, and the sizes of them are 4000, 8000, 12000, 16000 and 20000. Innet-3.0[12] produced the first group of power-law random graphs with exponent γ=2.3 in the Table 1 and Pajek[13] produced the second group of power-law random graphs with exponent γ=1.6 in the Table 2.

We used 1000 files in all simulations. All files are equally popular and be accessed at same probability. In simulation, we model query distribution strategy and replication distribution strategy using uniform distribution.

Table 1. The First Group of Graphs (Produced by Innet-3.0)

Graph Name	I4000	I8000	I12000	I16000	I20000
Graph Size	4000	8000	12000	16000	20000
Average Degree	3.32	3.87	4.35	4.80	5.26
Maximum Degree	855	1502	2086	2635	3159

Table 2. The Second Group of Graphs (Produced by Pajek)

Graph Name	P4000	P8000	P12000	P16000	P20000
Graph Size	4000	8000	12000	16000	20000
Average Degree	6.68	6.69	6.72	6.70	6.64
Maximum Degree	822	910	1258	1252	927

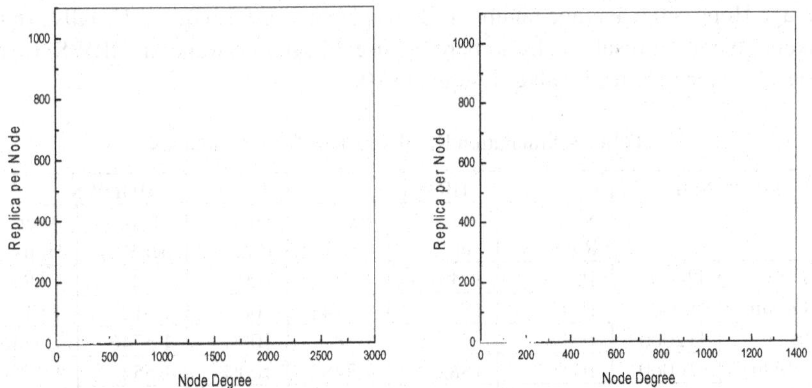

(1) Replica Distribution on Graph I16000 (2) Replica Distribution on Graph P16000

Fig. 1. Replica Distribution on Graph I16000 and Graph P16000 at Spread Steps=10.

4.2 Simulation Results of Spread Mechanism

Fig.1. depict replica distribution on the graph I16000 and the graph P16000, after 1000 files information spread over the two graphs through high degree spread walk with steps=10. The figures show that the five highest nodes of each graph have almost all files information, and they form a "directory server group". Even though the two graphs have different exponent and different nodes degrees, power-law in link distribution makes them have same replica distribution.

Table 3. Number of Nodes with over 80% Files Information at Different Spread Steps

Spread Steps	1	5	10	15	20	25	30
I16000	0	3	5	7	8	9	10
P16000	0	3	5	7	7	9	9

Table 3 displays the number of nodes with over 80% files information at different spread steps on the graph I16000 and the graph P16000. This table shows that more nodes join "server group" with increasing the size of spread walk. It also shows that the exponent and nodes degrees of one graph have little influence on the number of nodes with over 80% replica information.

4.3 Performance of Search Methods

In this section, we carried out the simulations on the two groups of power-law graphs and focus on three metrics: Success Rates, Messages per Request and Average Hops. Average Hops is the average number of hops per successful request. Usually, 16 to 64 walkers give good results [11], so here we use 32 random walks in HRWS. In simulations, the size of spread walker is equal to 10.

Table 4. Simulation Results of Two Search Methods

Graph Name		HRWS			HHDWS		
		Succ. Rates	Mess. per Req.	Aver. Hops	Succ. Rates	Mess. per Req.	Aver. Hops
First Group of Graphs	I4000	100%	171.3	1.6857	100%	1.58	1.58
	I8000	100%	186.9	1.7748	100%	1.6177	1.6177
	I12000	100%	191.76	1.78	100%	1.5746	1.5746
	I16000	100%	188.2	1.7487	100%	1.554	1.554
	I20000	100%	184.25	1.7151	100%	1.5143	1.5143
Second Group of Graphs	P4000	100%	244.0	1.9874	99.96%	1.9105	1.9104
	P8000	99.95%	263.4	2.2492	100%	2.0332	2.0332
	P12000	99.94%	300.4	2.5385	99.95%	2.1529	2.1527
	P16000	99.88%	305.5	2.6038	99.96%	2.1833	2.1832
	P20000	99.74%	313.4	2.8737	99.85%	2.2647	2.2539

Table 4 shows that the two methods achieve high success rates on all graphs, and over 90%. In HRWS, each request produces about hundreds of messages and several messages in HHDWS. In contrast to graphs sizes Query cost is very low, and increases very slowly with increasing graph size for the same method. The average hops are less than 3.

The success rates on the first group of graphs are slightly higher than those on the second group of graphs for HRWS and HHDWS. This is because the degrees of the high degree nodes in the first group of graphs are higher than those in the second group of graphs. Hence a query message can more quickly arrive at the high degree nodes in the first group of graphs and this also causes that the messages per request and average hops on the first group of graphs are lower.

In general, with several random walkers, HRWS can gain more response results, but it produces more traffic cost than HHDWS does.

4.4 Load Balance

In this section we present that the load balance among the high degree nodes can be improved by increasing the size of spread walker.

Fig.2. shows that the loads are reduced by increasing the steps of spread walker. For simplicity, only the curves of request ratios of the first and the second highest degree nodes are drawn in the two figures, for the changes of the load of the other nodes are small. Fig.2(1). displays the request distribution of HHDWS on the graph I16000 and the graph P160000, and it shows that the load of the first highest degree node is largely reduced (from 75.25% to 47.74% on the graph I16000 and from 76.16% to 52.96% on the graph P16000). Fig.2(2). displays the request distribution of HRWS and also shows that the reductions of the load are relative small.

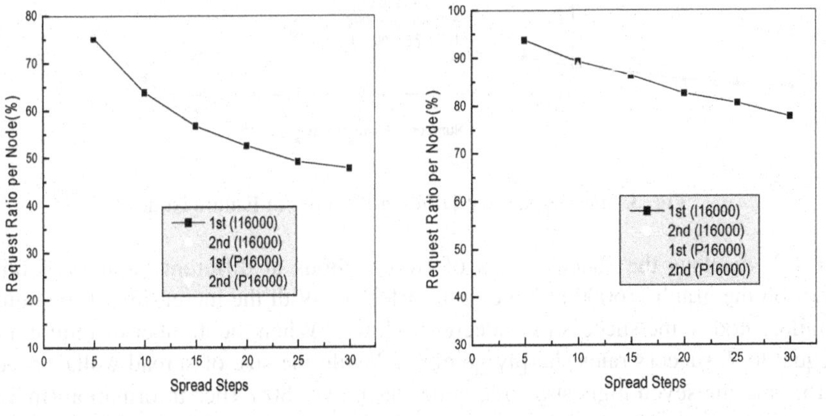

(1) Request Distribution of HHDWS (2) Request Distribution of HRWS

Fig. 2. Request Distribution on Graph I16000 and Graph P16000 with Different Spread Steps

The above results show that increasing the size of spread walker is good for HHDWS. In HHDWS, a query message is forwarded to the highest degree neighbor node at each step, and the probability that high degree walk arrives at a node relates the order of the degree of this node. With increasing the steps of spread walker, more high degree nodes join "directory server group", more query messages can be answered before they arrive at the first highest degree node. But, in HRWS a query message is forwarded to a randomly chose node at each step, so increasing size of spread walker has a little influence on the load balance of HRWS.

4.5 Robustness to High Degree Nodes Failures

Usually, the high degree nodes with heavy load are prone to failure. On the one hand, we can prevent the high degree nodes from failure by enforcing that only high capacity nodes become highly connected [14] [15]. On the other hand, our algorithm is robust to high degree nodes failure, and we can also enhance its robustness by increasing the size of the spread walker.

In this section, we carried out robustness tests of HHDWS and HRWS on the graph I16000 and the graph P16000. The size of the spread walker is equal to 15. At first, the state of the first highest degree node is set at failure, and then the two highest degree nodes, and till that the states of the ten highest degree nodes are set at failure.

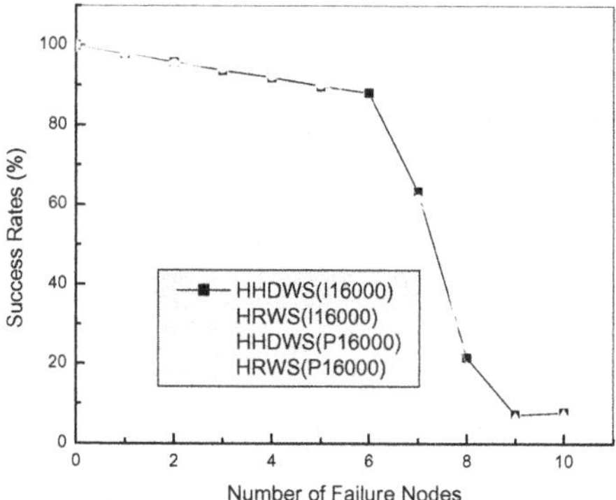

Fig. 3. Success Rates at Different Number of Failure Nodes

Fig.3. displays the success rates of two methods at different number of failure nodes on the graph I16000 and the graph P16000. With the increasing of the number of failure nodes, the success rates decrease slowly. When the number of failure nodes is equal to 7, success rates sharply go down. While the size of spread walker is equal to 15, only the seven highest degree nodes have over 80% files information (in Table 3) for each graph. Hence, when the seven highest degree nodes are failure, the success rates fall sharply. By increasing the steps of the spread walker, more high degree nodes have over 80% files information, and the algorithms will be more reliable.

4.6 Comparison with Ref. [9] Algorithm

Table 5 displays simulation results of Ref. [9] algorithm. Comparing it with table 4, success rates of Ref. [9] algorithm are very low, especially on the graph P16000. Messages per request and average hops of this algorithm are also higher than those of HHDWS. In this algorithm, each node indexes the files on its neighbors, so the high degree nodes have the information about the files on their neighbors, but they have not any information about the files on many low degree nodes which do not neighbor on them. When query messages walk along the high degree nodes, the files on the low degree nodes can not be found. But in our search method, the information of the files on the network spread over the network through high degree walk, so the files on the low degree nodes can be found. Hence, success rates of HRWS and HHDWS are higher than those of algorithm in [9].

Table 5. Simulation Results of Ref. [9] algorithm

Metrics	Success Rates	Messages per Request	Average Hops
Graph P16000	14.62%	9.12	4.04
Graph I16000	47.76%	6.94	3.59

The degrees of the high degree nodes in the graph I16000 are higher than those in the P16000, so the high degree nodes in the graph I16000 have more neighbor nodes, and this causes that success rate of Ref. [9] algorithm on the graph I16000 is higher than that on the graph P16000.

5 Conclusion

This paper presents an effective spread mechanism for improving search in unstructured P2P. By spreading files information over networks through high degree spread walk, the high degree nodes in unstructured P2P form a "directory server group", so the files can be easily located through random walk or high degree walk. We proposed two search methods: HRWS and HHDWS. Extensive simulations show that HRWS and HHDWS achieve high performance on a variety of environments. The means, increasing the size of spread walker, is proposed for improving the load balance among the high degree nodes, and our simulations show it is very effective for HHDWS. We also point out that HRWS and HHDWS are robust to high degree node failure, and their robustness can be improved by increasing the size of spread walker. Finally, comparing HRWS and HHDWS with Ref. [9] algorithm, HRWS and HHDWS have two times higher success rates.

Acknowledgements. This paper is supported by 973 project (No.2002CB312002) of China, ChinaGrid Program of MOE of China, and grand project of the Science and Technology Commission of Shanghai Municipality (No. 03dz15026, No. 03dz15027 and No. 03dz15028).

References

1. I. Stoica, R. Morris, D. Karger, M. Frans Kaashoek, H. Balakrishnanm, Chord: A Scalable Peer-to-peer Lookup Protocol for Internet Applications. ACM SIGCOMM Computer Communication Review. Volume:31 Issue 4: Oct. 2001. Pages: 149-160.

2. S. Ratnasamy, P. Francis, M. Handley, R. Karp, and S. Schenker. A Scalable Content-Addressable Network. ACM SIGCOMM Computer Communication Review. Volume:31 Issue 4: Oct. 2001. Pages: 161-172.
3. Gnutella website: http://gnutella.wego.com.
4. Kazaa website: http://www.kazaa.com.
5. Napster wensite: http://www.napster.com.
6. Sandvine Inc. An Industry White Paper: The Impact of File Sharing on Service Provider Networks. Dec. 2002.
7. Clip2.com. Gnutella: To the Bandwidth Barrier and Beyond. Nov. 2000.
8. Mihajlo A. Jovanovic. Modeling Large-scale Peer-to-Peer Networks and a Case Study of Gnutella. Master Thesis. Apr. 2001.
9. L.Adamic, R. Lukose, A. Puniyani, and B. Huberman. Search in Power-Law Networks. Phys. Rev. E64(2001), 046135.
10. V. Kalogeraki, D. Gunopulos, and D. Zeinalipour-Yazti. A Local Search Mechanism for Peer-to-Peer Networks. In CIKM, 2002.
11. Qin Lv, Pei Cao, Edith Cohen, Kai Li and Scott Shenker. Search and Replication in Unstructured Peer-to-Peer Networks. ICS'02. Jun.2002. Pages: 84-95.
12. C. Jin, Q. Chen, and S. Jamin. Inet: Internet Topology Generator. Technical Report CSE-TR443-00 , Department of EECS, University of Michigan,2000.
13. Pajek website: http://vlado.fmf.uni-lj.si/pub/networks/pajek/.
14. Q. Lv, S. Ratnasamy, and S. Shenker. Can Heterogeneity Make Gnutella Scalable?. Lecture Nodes in Computer Science. 2002. Volume 2429. Page:94-103.
15. Yatin Chawathe, Sylvia Ratnasamy and Lee Breslau. Making Gnutella-like P2P Systems Scalable. SIGCOMM'03. Aug.2003.

A Formal Model for the Grid Security Infrastructure*

Baiyan Li, Ruonan Rao, Minglu Li, and Jinyuan You

Department of Computer Science and Engineering, Shanghai Jiao Tong University, Shanghai 200030, China
libaiyan@sjtu.edu.cn

Abstract. The Grid Security Infrastructure (GSI) proposed and implemented in Globus Toolkit has been a widely accepted solution for the security of grids in recent years. But there is no formal analysis or modelling on security mechanisms of GSI emerging in the literature yet. In this paper, we propose a formal logic, and formalize those primary security mechanisms using the logic. Our formalism not only is useful in understanding GSI but also provides us a substantial theoretic basis for some high-level security mechanisms to be developed based on GSI for the emerging service-oriented grid.

1 Introduction

The grid computing is mainly concerned with the problem of resources sharing within the Virtual Organization (VO) [1, 2]. So the protection to the shared resources of VO is clearly a critical task of a secure grid environment. As the most important solution for the security of computational grid, Grid Security Infrastructure (GSI) [3, 4, 5] has received much attention since it was proposed in Globus project in 1997. However, since the emergence of Open Grid Services Architecture (OGSA) [6], the research interests for grid computing have shifted from the high-performance computational grid to the service-oriented grid rapidly. The GT3, whose security mechanisms were implemented using WS-Security, WS-Trust, WS-SecureConversation and SOAP, is a vivid instance of this tendency [4]. In the service-oriented grid, various computing resources and facilities are abstracted and implemented in a unified form: the grid service. So the security mechanisms in GSI that is originally designed for computational grid should be significantly adjusted or integrated with some high-level security mechanisms such as *published security policy* [4], or *role-based access control*, to fill the requirements of new environments.

As the first step to extend the security mechanisms of GSI, we shall investigate the security mechanisms of GSI in detail, and evaluate the feasibilities of various GSI extensions in a strict manner. For these purposes, we propose a

* This work is supported by 973 project (No.2002CB312002) of China, ChinaGrid Program of MOE of China, and grand project of the Science and Technology Commission of Shanghai Municipality (No. 03dz15027)

X. Zhou et al. (Eds.): WISE 2004, LNCS 3306, pp. 706–717, 2004.
© Springer-Verlag Berlin Heidelberg 2004

formal logic, and establish a formal model for the key security mechanisms in GSI using the logic.

Our logic uses *trust*, a kind of relationships between entities, as a core concept. Its formulas can be interpreted using Kripke's *possible-worlds* semantics [7]. In our context, the grid is a dynamic VO formed by a large number of entities connected by networks for resources sharing. These entities may be hosts, services, user proxies, or even public keys. All the entities in a grid are regarded as agents in a Kripke structure. The primitive propositions such as "read file foo", form the world about which we wish to reason. The primary idea of our logic is that an entity would believe in statements made by another if it trusts that entity with respect with these statements. For example, if a grid user trusts his root Certification Authorization (CA), he would believe in the authenticity of all of the certificates issued by the CA. Furthermore, our logic has a strong ability in encoding various credentials and policies as logic formulae. So many security mechanisms such as the authentication and the decision of access control can be expressed as a procedure of logical reasoning on a set of formulas that are translated from credentials and policies.

The rest of this paper is organized as follows. In Section 2, we give an overview of the security mechanisms in GSI. In Section 3, we introduce the syntax and semantics of our logic. In Section 4, we formalize the primary security mechanisms of GSI using the logic, and discuss some important issues related to the future of GSI. Finally, we give the conclusion of this paper in Section 5.

2 An Overview of GSI

As a crucial component of the well-known Globus Project, GSI is an implementation of grid security architecture using the currently existing standards [3]. It has been widely accepted by the security community as a solution for security of the computational grid in the past few years [4].

GSI is built up on the Public Key Infrastructure (PKI) technologies. It provides many capabilities and features such as the single sign-on, proxy credentials, user-controlled delegation, mapping to local security mechanisms, and Generic Security Service application programming interface (GSS-API).

Currently, there are two important implementations of Globus Toolkit available: the GT2 for computational grid and the GT3 for service-oriented grid. In GT2, the GSI is implemented using SSL/TLS protocol and the proxy certificate, an extension of the standard X.509 certificate. In GT3, however, the OGSA compatible implementation of GSI uses the specifications for Web services security, including WS-Security, WS-Trust, WS-SecureConversation, XML-Signature, XML-Encryption, and so on.

At high-level, GSI uses Grid Security Service API as its programming interface. It also has the ability to integrate with local security solutions. In current implementations, GSI maps an authenticated user into a local user account through a simple grid-map file at servers.

3 The Logic of Trust

There is no a widely accepted definition for *trust* in the literature [8, 9]. In this section, we give the *trust* a specific definition in term of *belief* and develop a theory of trust based on the modal logic $\mathbf{K45}_n$ [7].

3.1 Syntax and Semantics

A logic of any kind needs a language to define its well formed formulas (*wffs.*). Given a nonempty set Φ of primitive propositions, which we typically label p, q, $\cdots$, and a set of n agents whose names are denoted A_1, A_2, $\cdots$, A_n, we define a modal language $\mathcal{L}_n(\Phi)$ to be the least set of formulas containing Φ, closed under negation, conjunction, and modal operators $B_1, B_2, \cdots, B_n$. In other words, the formulas of $\mathcal{L}_n(\Phi)$ are given by rule $\phi ::= p \mid \neg\phi \mid \phi \wedge \phi \mid B_i p$ where p ranges over elements of Φ and $i = 1, \cdots, n$. We use the classical abbreviations $\varphi \vee \psi$ for $\neg(\neg\varphi \wedge \neg\psi)$ and $\varphi \supset \psi$ for $\neg\varphi \vee \psi$; we take *true* to be an abbreviation for some valid formula such as $\neg p \vee p$, and define *false* as the negation of *true*. Especially, the modal operator B_i in the rule is read as "agent A_i believes". In this paper, the formulas $B_i p$ and A_i *believes* p are semantic equivalence, and can be used alternatively for the sake of convenience.

In order to interpret the semantics of formulae in $\mathcal{L}_n(\Phi)$, we define a semantic model for the language.

Definition 1. *A frame for modal language $\mathcal{L}_n(\Phi)$ is a tuple $\Gamma = (S, \mathcal{K}_1, \cdots, \mathcal{K}_n)$ where S is a nonempty set, and $\mathcal{K}_i$ is an accessibility relation set on S for $i = 1, \cdots, n$. A model for $\mathcal{L}_n(\Phi)$ is a pair $M = (\Gamma, \pi)$, where Γ is a frame, and π is a truth assignment to the primitive propositions in Φ for each states $s \in S$ (i.e., $\pi(s) : \Phi \rightarrow \{true,\ false\}$ for each state $s \in S$).*

The model M, usually denoted $M = (S, \pi, \mathcal{K}_1, \cdots, \mathcal{K}_n)$, is a typical Kripke structure for n agents [7]. Intuitively, we say that $(s, t) \in \mathcal{K}_i$ iff agent A_i considers state t possible at state s where $s \in S$ and $t \in S$. The conditions on $\mathcal{K}_i$ enforce certain axioms associated with belief. For example the fact that $\mathcal{K}_i$ is serial means that agent A_i always considers some world possible and cannot believe in falsehood. By modifying those conditions, one can get different axioms for belief.

A formula in $\mathcal{L}_n(\Phi)$ *is true at a state* s in a model $M = (S, \pi, \mathcal{K}_1, \cdots, \mathcal{K}_n)$ can be defined as following:

$(M, s) \models p$ iff $\pi(s)(p) = true$ (for $p \in \Phi$)
$(M, s) \models \varphi \wedge \psi$ iff both $(M, s) \models \varphi$ and $(M, s) \models \psi$
$(M, s) \models \neg\varphi$ iff $(M, s) \not\models \varphi$
$(M, s) \models B_i\varphi$ iff $(M, t) \models \varphi$ for all t such that $(s, t) \in \mathcal{K}_i$

The first three definitions correspond to the standard clauses in the definition of truth for propositional logic. The last definition formalizes the idea that agent A_i believes φ in global state s exactly if and only if φ is *true* in all the global states that A_i consider possible in state s.

Formally, we say that a formula φ is valid in M, and write $M \models \varphi$, if $(M, s) \models \varphi$ for every state $s \in S$; we say that φ is satisfiable in M if $(M, s) \models \varphi$

for some state $s \in S$. We say φ is valid with respect to a class $\mathcal{M}$ of structures and write $\mathcal{M} \models \varphi$, if φ is valid in all structures in $\mathcal{M}$, and say φ is satisfiable with respect to $\mathcal{M}$ if it is satisfiable in some structure in $\mathcal{M}$. We use $\mathcal{M}_n$ to denote the class of all Kripke structures for n agents.

The term "modal logic" is used broadly to cover a family of logics with similar rules and a variety of different symbols. In this paper, we adopt the well-known $\mathbf{K45}_n$ [7, 10] as axiom system for our logic. The $\mathbf{K45}_n$ consists of following axioms and inference rules:

A1. All instances of tautologies of the propositional calculus.
A2. $(B_i\varphi \wedge B_i(\varphi \supset \psi)) \supset B_i\psi,\ i = 1, \cdots, n$
A4. $B_i\varphi \supset B_iB_i\varphi,\ i = 1, \cdots, n$ *(introspection of positive belief)*
A5. $\neg B_i\varphi \supset B_i\neg B_i\varphi,\ i = 1, \cdots, n$ *(introspection of negative belief)*
R1. From φ and $\varphi \supset \psi$ infer ψ *(modus ponens)*
R2. From φ infer $B_i\varphi,\ i = 1, \cdots, n$ *(generalization)*

The soundness and completeness of $\mathbf{K45}_n$ with respect to $\mathcal{M}^{et}$, the class of transitive and Eucilidean Kripke structures, has been well-known [7, 10]. So it provides us a substantial basis for modeling belief and trust. Now we give an intuitive definition to the trust relationship between two agents in models of $\mathcal{M}^{et}$.

Definition 2. *Let $M^{et} = (S, \pi, \mathcal{K}_1, \cdots, \mathcal{K}_n)$ be a transitive and Eucilidean Kripke structure. Let A_i and A_j $(1 \leq i,\ j \leq n)$ be a pair of agents in $\mathcal{M}^{et}$. Let R be a set of formulas in $\mathcal{L}_n(\Phi)$. We say A_i trusts A_j regarding R, denoted by formula $A_i \succ_R A_j$, iff A_i believes that A_j could determine the truth values of every formula in R. Formally, $A_i \succ_R A_j \equiv (B_j\varphi \supset B_i\varphi) \wedge (B_j\neg\varphi \supset B_i\neg\varphi)$ where variable φ ranges over elements of R.*

In this way, we defined a restricted trust relationship between agents with agent's beliefs. We will give the semantics of this kind of trust the model M^{et}. Before that, we define a state set for a given state $s \in S$

$$\mathcal{K}_i(s) = \{t \mid \forall t \in S \text{ if } (s,t) \in \mathcal{K}_i\},\quad i = 1, \cdots, n.$$

We also define a mapping $\theta^* : S \to S$ that takes states to a subset of the original states where * represents some set of formulae. Given a set $S_0 \subseteq S$ and a set R of formulae, we define

$$\theta^R(S_0) = \{s_0 \mid \forall s_0 \in S_0,\ \text{if } (M^{et}, s_0) \models \varphi \text{ for all } \varphi \in R\}$$

We now use notation $\neg R$ to represent the negation of R. So we have that $\neg R = \{\neg\varphi \mid \forall \varphi \in R\}$. Then, the semantic definition of *trust-regarding* relationship is given as following:

$$\begin{aligned} M^{et} &\models A_i \succ_R A_j \text{ iff} \\ \forall s \in S,\ \theta^R(\mathcal{K}_i(s)) &\subseteq \theta^R(\mathcal{K}_j(s)) \text{ and} \\ \theta^{\neg R}(\mathcal{K}_i(s)) &\subseteq \theta^{\neg R}(\mathcal{K}_j(s)). \end{aligned}$$

Symmetrically, we define a *speaks-for-regarding* relationship between agents in M^{et} based on the definition of the *trust-regarding* relationship.

Definition 3. *A_i speaks for A_j regarding R, denoted $A_i \overset{R}{\Rightarrow} A_j$, if and only if $A_j \succ_R A_i$.*

We use "$\succ$" and "$\Rightarrow$ to represent the abbreviation of "$\succ_R$" and $\overset{R}{\Rightarrow}$ respectively if R is the universe of all *wffs.* of $\mathcal{L}_n(\Phi)$.

In order to devise a mechanism to derive new beliefs from existing beliefs and trust relationships, we define the concept of logical consequence.

Definition 4. *Let Σ be a set of formulas in a modal language $\mathcal{L}_n(\Phi)$ and φ a single formula of $\mathcal{L}_n(\Phi)$. We say φ is a logical consequence of Σ, denoted $\Sigma \vdash \varphi$, if φ is valid in every $\mathcal{L}_n(\Phi)$ structure M in which every $\psi \in \Sigma$ is valid.*

If we represent beliefs of an agent with a collection of formulas, then a logical consequence of these formulas is a derived belief of that agent.

Theorem 1. *Let Σ be a formula set of modal language $\mathcal{L}_n(\Phi)$; let φ, ψ and ϕ be formulas of $\mathcal{L}_n(\Phi)$. Then we have that $\Sigma \vdash \phi$ if $\Sigma \vdash \varphi$, $\Sigma \vdash \psi$, and $\{\varphi, \psi\} \vdash \phi$.*

Proof. Omitted

This theorem provides us the rationality to invent some inference rules for the belief deriving.

3.2 Inference Rules

We now give the major inference rules of our logic as following:

$$\frac{B_i(A_i \succ_R A_j) \quad B_i B_j \varphi}{B_i B_i \varphi} \tag{1}$$

$$\frac{B_l(A_i \succ_R A_j) \quad B_l(A_j \succ_V A_k)}{B_l(A_i \succ_{R \cap V} A_k)} \tag{2}$$

$$\frac{B_i(A_i \succ_R A_j) \quad B_j(A_j \succ_V A_k)}{B_i(A_i \succ_{R \cap V} A_k)} \tag{3}$$

In the above rules, notations A_i, A_j, and A_k $(1 \le i,\ j,\ k,\ l \le n)$ represent agents. Letters R and V represent formula set of $\mathcal{L}_n(\Phi)$. The symbol φ represents a variable that ranges over elements of R. The soundness proofs of these inference rules with respect to $\mathcal{M}^{et}$ can be found in the appendix of this paper.

3.3 The Encoding

Our logic has a strong ability in encoding credentials and security policies. In our context, the credentials refer to various signed certificates issued by entities in the grid. In order to encode certificates, we devise a way to represent the public keys. For instance, we use $k_A = (k_A^{+1},\ k_A^{-1})$ to represent the public-key pair of agent A with the public part k_A^{+1} and the private part k_A^{-1}. We regard a public key as an agent that speaks for the agent who owns it. So if k_A is a public key of agent A, we may immediately encode the fact in formula $k_A \Rightarrow A$ or $A \succ k_A$.

Furthermore, if a CA, say $CA1$, signs a certificate to bind k_A with agent A using its private key k_{CA1}^{-1}, we express the certificate as $[k_A \Rightarrow A]_{k_{CA1}^{-1}}$, and encode it in formula k_{CA1} *believes* $k_A \Rightarrow A$.

We adopt the Lampson's method [11] to deal with certificate expiration. We assume that an agent will never issue a negative credential such as k_A *is not a public key of agent A*. This assumption ensures the monotonicity of our reasoning system. If a CA cancels some certificate, we just treat the certificate as a time expired one. We encode basic privileges such as "read file foo", as primitive propositions. We use formula $A \succ B$ to represent that entity A delegates a set of privileges, denoted R, to entity B.

Our logic can also encode many basic security policies. For instance, if agent A regards $CA1$ as trusted CA, we encode the fact as $A \succ_{ID-Key} CA1$ where the $ID-Key$ represents a formula set that contain all the bindings of identities and keys. We could restrict the set of $ID - Key$ further if necessary. For instance, the $ID-Key.PC$ in next section represents the set of identity-key bindings only in the proxy certificate.

4 A Formal Model for GSI

In this section, we will establish a formal model for the major security mechanisms in GSI using the logic introduced in Section 3. Our formalism mainly focuses on issues related to the authentication, the authorization, the certificate and the delegation.

4.1 Basic Security Mechanisms

The crucial entities closely related to the security of the grid include but are not limited to the CAs, users, proxies and keys. Nevertheless, the entities in a grid may belong to different trust domains [3]. When they interact with each other, the entities in different trust domains are required to mutually authenticate while those in the same trust domains not.

One of the remarkable features of GSI is that it supports an authorization delegation mechanism to access resources across multiple organizations. The mechanism allows a user to distribute jobs to remote grid machines and let them distribute their child jobs to other machines under the user's security policy. In the delegation model of GSI illustrated in Fig.1, the CA is responsible for verifying grid users and issuing the End Entity Certificate (EEC) to them. A grid user can dynamically create a proxy and delegate his privileges to a proxy by signing a Proxy Certificate (PC) [12]. With the PC, the proxy can access resources in remote machines on behalf of the user. In fact, the proxy is allowed to delegate the privileges to another proxy further by signing a PC if necessary. The proxies with delegation relationship form a chain as shown in Fig. 1. The final proxy submits a signed request, a Request Certificate (RC), to the server who represents the requested resource. If the server has identified the grid user and properly checked the privilege information of all the certificates in the chain, it would map the user to a local account using the information in a grid-map file.

In GSI, an extension of standard SSL/TLS is used for mutual authentication between two entities in different trust domains. Similarly, the PC is also an extension of standard X.509 certificate (version 3) [11]. It uses extension fields to carry privilege information, and implement a restricted delegation mechanism in GSI.

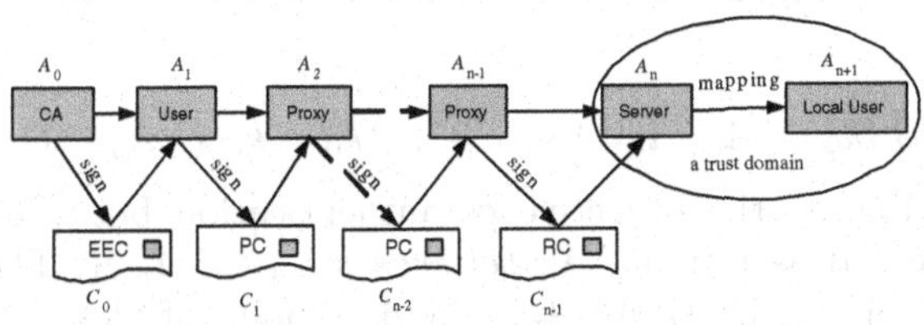

Fig. 1. The delegation model of GSI (n≥3)

4.2 The Certificate

The certificates and their major contents are shown in Fig.2. For instance, the User-ID represents the identifier of the user who owns the certificate; the k^{+1}_{User} represents the public part of the user's public key pair. The T_{valid} represents the valid period of a certificate, and the R represents the privilege information in a certificate. The three kinds of certificate are signed by k^{-1}_{CA}, k^{-1}_{User}, and k^{-1}_{Proxy} respectively.

Now, using the encoding methods introduced above, we express the certificates shown in Fig.1 with a uniform format as following:

$C_0 = [k_1 \Rightarrow A_1,\ A_0 \succ_{ID-Key.PC} A_1]_{k_0{}^{-1}}$

$C_1 = [k_2 \Rightarrow A_2,\ A_1 \succ_{R_1} A_2,\ A_1 \succ_{ID-Key.PC} A_2]_{k_1^{-1}}$

$C_2 = [k_3 \Rightarrow A_3,\ A_2 \succ_{R_2} A_3,\ A_2 \succ_{ID-Key.PC} A_3]_{k_2^{-1}}$

$\vdots \quad \vdots \quad \vdots$

$C_{n-2} = [k_{n-1} \Rightarrow A_{n-1},\ A_{n-2} \succ_{R_{n-2}} A_{n-1},\ A_{n-2} \succ_{ID-Key.PC} A_{n-1}]_{k_{n-2}^{-1}}$

$C_{n-1} = [R_{n-1}]_{k_{n-1}^{-1}}$.

Obviously, those certificates can be translated into formulae in our logic immediately without too much effort. For a delegation chain of m proxies, there will be $3m + 3$ formulae needed to be deal with in the delegation model of GSI.

4.3 Authentication

The GSI uses SSL/TLS protocol (in GT2) and SecureConversation protocol (in GT3) to implement the authentication between entities in different domains. Before formalizing the authentication mechanism in GSI, we give following formulas as conventional beliefs of entities shown in Fig.1:

$$B_i(A_i \succ_{ID-Key} A_0) \quad i = 1 \cdots n+1 \quad (A_0 = CA) \tag{4}$$

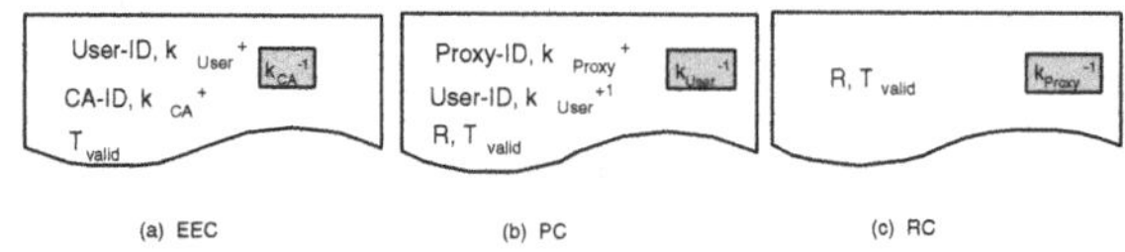

Fig. 2. The three kinds of certificates in GSI

$$B_i(k_0 \Rightarrow A_0) \quad i = 1 \cdots n+1 \quad (k_0 = k_{CA},\ A_0 = CA) \tag{5}$$

As shown in Fig. 1, the objective of authentication between A_n and A_{n-1} can be represented as formula A_n *believes* $k_{n-1} \Rightarrow A_{n-1}$. The logical proofs through which A_n authenticate A_{n-1} in A_n's point of view (A_n's beliefs) can be expressed as following reasoning:

(I_1) k_0 *believes* $k_1 \Rightarrow A_1$ (from C_0)
(I_2) k_0 *believes* $A_0 \succ_{ID-Key.PC} A_1$ (from C_0)
(I_3) A_0 *believes* $k_1 \Rightarrow A_1$ (from (5), (I_1), (1))
(I_4) A_0 *believes* $A_0 \succ_{ID-Key.PC} A_1$ (from (5), (I_2), (1))
(I_5) $k_1 \Rightarrow A_1$ or $A_1 \succ k_1$ (from (4), (I_3), (1))
(I_6) $A_n \succ_{ID-Key.PC} A_1$ (from (4), (I_4), (3))
(I_7) k_1 *believes* $k_2 \Rightarrow A_2$ (from C_1)
(I_8) k_1 *believes* $A_1 \succ_{ID-Key.PC} A_2$ (from C_1)
(I_9) A_1 *believes* $k_2 \Rightarrow A_2$ (from (I_5), (I_7), (1))
(I_{10}) A_1 *believes* $A_1 \succ_{ID-Key.PC} A_2$ (from (I_5), (I_8), (1))
(I_{11}) $k_2 \Rightarrow A_2$ or $A_1 \succ k_1$ (from (I_6), (I_9), (1))
(I_{12}) $A_n \succ_{ID-Key.PC} A_2$ (from (I_6), (I_{10}), (3))
$\vdots \quad \vdots \quad \vdots$
(I_{6n-11}) k_{n-2} *believes* $k_{n-1} \Rightarrow A_{n-1}$ (from C_{n-2})
(I_{6n-10}) k_{n-2} *believes* $A_{n-2} \succ_{ID-Key.PC} A_{n-1}$ (from C_{n-2})
(I_{6n-9}) A_{n-2} *believes* $k_{n-1} \Rightarrow A_{n-1}$ (from (I_{6n-13}), (I_{6n-11}), (1))
(I_{6n-8}) A_{n-2} *believes* $A_{n-2} \succ_{ID-Key.PC} A_2$ (from (I_{6n-13}), (I_{6n-10}), (1))
(I_{6n-7}) $k_{n-1} \Rightarrow A_{n-1}$ (from (I_{6n-12}), (I_{6n-9}), (1))

4.4 Authorization

The authorizaton is another important security mechanism in GSI. For the sake of convenience, we use R, $R = R_1 \cap R_2 \cap \cdots \cap R_n$, to replace each R_i, $i = 1 \cdots n$. It is obviously that such a substitution will not affect the final results of our logical reasoning. One of the policies in grid-map file of A_n can be encoded in following formula where $A_1 \overset{R}{\Leftrightarrow} A_{n+1} \equiv (A_1 \overset{R}{\Rightarrow} A_{n+1}) \wedge (A_{n+1} \overset{R}{\Rightarrow} A_1)$.

$$A_n \text{ believes } (A_1 \overset{R}{\Leftrightarrow} A_{n+1}) \wedge (A_n \succ_R A_1) \tag{6}$$

The authorization decision of A_n for a request r from A_{n-1} depends on whether A_n can derive the formula A_n *believes* r ($\forall r \in R$) from existing

credentials and its policies. Such procedure of logical reasoning is shown as follows:
(S_1) k_1 *believes* $A_1 \succ_R A_2$ (from C_1)
(S_2) A_1 *believes* $A_1 \succ_R A_2$ (from (I_5), (S_1), (1))
(S_3) $A_n \succ_R A_2$ (from (6), (S_2), (3))
(S_4) k_2 *believes* $A_2 \succ_R A_3$ (from C_2)
(S_5) A_2 *believes* $A_2 \succ_R A_3$ (from (I_{11}), (S_4), (1))
(S_6) $A_n \succ_R A_3$ (from (S_4), (S_6), (3))
$\vdots \quad \vdots \quad \vdots$
(S_{3n-8}) k_{n-2} *believes* $A_{n-2} \succ_R A_{n-1}$ (from C_{n-2})
(S_{3n-7}) A_{n-2} *believes* $A_{n-2} \succ_R A_{n-1}$ (from (I_{6n-11}), (S_{3n-8}), (1))
(S_{3n-6}) $A_n \succ_R A_{n-1}$ (from (S_{3n-9}), (S_{3n-7}), (3))
(S_{3n-4}) k_{n-1} *believes* r (from C_{n-1})
(S_{3n-3}) A_{n-1} *believes* r (from (I_{6n-7}), (S_{3n-4}), (1))
(S_{3n-2}) A_n *believes* r (from (S_{3n-6}), (S_{3n-3}), (1))

4.5 Some Discussions on GSI

With our formal model of GSI, we could easily learn some remarkable features of GSI. For example, the mechanism of restricted privilege delegation can reduce the damage due to being compromised or abuse of trust since a proxy trusts another only regarding a limited collection of privileges.

In the meantime, we also find several points on which the security mechanisms of GSI need to be extended for the service-oriented grid:

- A mechanism that support large-scale PKIs so that two entities in different PKI domains can interact with each other, for instance, the *cross-certification* that relies on the interoperability of existing PKIs.
- A general mechanism for evaluating credentials and policies in the grid environment to support more feasible security solution, for instance, the *published security policy* [4].
- A more powerful and general mechanism than grid-mapfile for mapping resource requests to authorization mechanisms such as *role-based access control* systems.

In fact, the primary motivation of our proposal is to provide a theoretic basis for solutions of above problems. By now, we are working on a *trust engine* that is responsible for deriving logical consequences from a fixed set of formulas based on the theory introduced in this paper. Our goal is to enhance abilities of GSI to handle the diversity of credentials and policies in the service-oriented grid without loss of its original merits.

5 Conclusion

In this paper, we propose a well-defined logic that can reason about trust based on Kripke semantics, and establish a formal model for the key security mechanisms of GSI using the logic. As we have seen, our formalism not only is useful in understanding GSI but also provides us a substantial theoretic basis for some high-level security mechanisms to be developed based on GSI for the emerging service-oriented grid.

References

1. Foster, I., Kesselman, C.,(eds.): The Grid: Blueprint for a new computing infrastructure. Morgan Kaufmann (1999)
2. Foster, I., Kesselman, C., Tuecke, S.: The anatomy of the Grid: enabling scalable virtual organizations. International Journal of High Performance Computing Application **15(3)**, (2001) 200–222
3. Foster, I., Kesselman, C., Tuecke, S.: A security architecture for computational grid. Proc. 5th ACM Conference on Computer and Communications Security Conference, (1998) 83–92
4. Welch, W., Siebenlist, F., Foster, I., Bresnahan, J., Czajkowski, K., Gawor, J., Kesselman, C., Meder,S., Pearlman, L., Tuecke, S.: Security for grid services. Twelfth International Symposium on High Performance Distributed Computing, Seattle Washington, (2003) 48–57
5. Foster, I., Kesselman, C., Intl, J.: Globus: A metacomputing infrastructure toolkit. Super-computer Applications **11(2)**, (1997) 115–128
6. Foster, I., Kesselman, C., Nick, J., Tuecke,S.: The physiology of the grid: An open grid services architecture for distributed systems integration. Open Grid Service Infrastructure WG, Global Grid Forum, (2002)
7. Halpern, J.Y., Moses Y.: A guide to completeness and complexity for modal logics of knowledge and belief. Artificial Intelligence **54**, (1992) 319–379
8. Grandison, T., Sloman, M.: A survey of trust in Internet applications. IEEE Communications Surveys (2000)
9. Chuchang, L., Maris, O.A.: Trust in secure communication systems-the concept, representations and reasoning techniques. 15th Australian Joint Conference on Artificial Intelligence Canberra (2002) 60–70
10. Rangan, P.: An axiomatic basis of trust in distributed systems. Proc. of the IEEE CS Symp. on Research in Security and Privacy (1988) 204–211
11. Abadi, M., Burrows, M., Lampson, B., Plotkin, G.: A calculus for access control in distributed systems. ACM Transactions on Programming Languages and Systems **15(4)** (1993) 706–734.
12. Tuecke, S., Engert, D., Foster, I., Thompson, M., Pearlman, L., Kesselman, C.: Internet X.509 Public Key Infrastructure-Proxy Certificate Profile Internet Draft, (2001)

A Soundness Proof for Inference Rule (1)

Theorem 2. *Given arbitrary agents A_i and A_j $(1 \leq i,\ j \leq n)$, if R is a set of formulas in modal language $\mathcal{L}_n(\Phi)$ we have that $\{B_i(A_i \succ_R A_j)\} \cup \{B_i B_j \varphi\} \vdash B_i B_i \varphi$ where φ ranges over elements of R.*

Proof. Omitted.

B Soundness Proof for Inference Rule (2)

Theorem 3. *Let R and V be sets of formulas in modal logic language $\mathcal{L}_n(\Phi)$. Let A_i, A_j, A_k and A_l ($1 \leq i,\ j,\ k,\ l \leq n$) be agents. Then we have that* $\{B_l(A_i \succ_R A_j)\} \cup \{B_l(A_j \succ_V A_k)\} \models B_l(A_i \succ_{R\cap V} A_k)$.

Proof. It is easy to know that $B_l(A_i \succ_R A_j)$, $B_l(A_j \succ_V A_k)$, and $B_l(A_i \succ_{R\cap V} A_k)$ are *wffs.* in $\mathcal{L}_n(\Phi)$. For the sake of convenience, we denote the intersection of R and V by T. Let $M^{et} = (S, \pi, \mathcal{K}_1, \cdots, \mathcal{K}_n)$ be an arbitrary $\mathcal{L}_n(\Phi)$ structure where both formulas $B_l(A_i \succ_R A_j)$, $B_l(A_j \succ_V A_k)$ are valid. Then it follows immediately that $(M^{et}, t) \models A_i \succ_T A_j$ and $(M^{et}, t) \models A_j \succ_T A_k$ for any given states $s \in S$, $t \in S$ if $(s, t) \in \mathcal{K}_l$. By the semantics of the *trust-regarding* relationship we have the following valid constraints in M^{et}:

$$\theta^T(\mathcal{K}_i(t)) \subseteq \theta^T(\mathcal{K}_j(t)) \tag{7}$$

$$\theta^{\neg T}(\mathcal{K}_i(t)) \subseteq \theta^{\neg T}(\mathcal{K}_j(t)) \tag{8}$$

$$\theta^T(\mathcal{K}_j(t)) \subseteq \theta^T(\mathcal{K}_k(t)) \tag{9}$$

$$\theta^{\neg T}(\mathcal{K}_j(t)) \subseteq \theta^{\neg T}(\mathcal{K}_k(t)) \tag{10}$$

From above constraints we have

$$\theta^T(\mathcal{K}_i(t)) \subseteq \theta^T(\mathcal{K}_k(t)) \tag{11}$$

$$\theta^{\neg T}(\mathcal{K}_i(t)) \subseteq \theta^{\neg T}(\mathcal{K}_k(t)) \tag{12}$$

So it follows that $(M^{et}, t) \models A_i \succ_T A_k$. Due to the way by which we pick the states s and t, we know that $M^{et} \models B_l(A_i \succ_T A_k)$. Therefore, formula $B_l(A_i \succ_{R\cap V} A_k)$ is a logical consequence of formulas $B_l(A_i \succ_R A_j)$ and $B_l(A_j \succ_V A_k)$.

C Soundness Proof for Inference Rule (3)

Theorem 4. *Let A_i, A_j, and A_k ($1 \leq i,\ j,\ k \leq n$) be agents. Let R and V be sets of formulae in modal language $\mathcal{L}_n(\Phi)$. Then we have that* $\{B_i(A_i \succ_R A_j)\} \cup \{B_j(A_j \succ_V A_k)\} \models B_i(A_i \succ_{R\cap V} A_k)$.

Proof. It's easy to know that $B_i(A_i \succ_R A_j)$, $B_j(A_j \succ_V A_k)$, and $B_i(A_i \succ_{R\cap V} A_k)$ are in $\mathcal{L}_n(\Phi)$. Suppose that $M^{et} = (S, \pi, \mathcal{K}_1, \cdots, \mathcal{K}_n)$ be an arbitrary $\mathcal{L}_n(\Phi)$ structure in which both formulas $B_i(A_i \succ_R A_j)$ and $B_j(A_j \succ_V A_k)$ are valid. Now, we will try to prove that $M^{et} \models B_i(A_i \succ_{R\cap V} A_k)$.

For the sake of convenience, we denote the intersection of sets R and V by T. For the accessibility relations related to agent A_i, only the following cases are possible:
Case 1: $\mathcal{K}_i = \emptyset$,
Case 2: $\mathcal{K}_i \neq \emptyset$ i.e., $\exists s \in S, \exists t \in S$ such that $(s, t) \in \mathcal{K}_i$.

For Case 1: Agent A_i considers no state possible at any state of S in M^{et}. So A_i will believe in any *wff.* by the semantic of modal operator "B_i". Hence, we have that $M^{et} \models B_i(A_i \succ_{R\cap V} A_k)$ in this case.
For Case 2: Since $(s,t) \in \mathcal{K}_i$, it follows that $(M^{et},t) \models A_i \succ_T A_j$. The semantics of $(M^{et},t) \models A_i \succ_T A_j$ can be interpreted as that the following constraints:

$$\theta^T(\mathcal{K}_i(t)) \subseteq \theta^T(\mathcal{K}_j(t)) \tag{13}$$

$$\theta^{\neg T}(\mathcal{K}_i(t)) \subseteq \theta^{\neg T}(\mathcal{K}_j(t)) \tag{14}$$

are in effect between A_i and A_j in M^{et}. In M^{et}, it is easy to learn that all states of S can be divided into following non-overlapped sets:
$G_0 = \{g \mid \forall g \in S, \text{ if } (M^{et},g) \models \varphi \text{ for all } \varphi \in T\}$
$G_1 = \{g \mid \forall g \in S, \text{ if } \exists \varphi \in T \text{ such that } (M^{et},g) \models \varphi \text{ and } (t,g) \in \mathcal{K}_j\}$
$G_2 = \{g \mid \forall g \in S, \text{ if } \exists \varphi \in T \text{ such that } (M^{et},g) \models \varphi \text{ and } (t,g) \notin \mathcal{K}_j\}$
$G_3 = \{g \mid \forall g \in S, \text{ if } (M^{et},g) \models \neg\varphi \text{ for all } \varphi \in T\}$
For any state g in set G_0 or G_3 we have that $(t,g) \in \mathcal{K}_j$ if $(t,g) \in \mathcal{K}_i$ by constraints (13) and (14). For any state g in group G_1, we immediately have that $(t,g) \in \mathcal{K}_j$ no matter whether $(t,g) \in \mathcal{K}_i$ or not. However, for the states in G_2, things become somewhat complicated. We now start out to show that $(t,g) \notin \mathcal{K}_i$ if g is a state of G_2.

By $(M^{et},t) \models A_i \succ_T A_j$ and the fact $T \subseteq R$ we have that $(M^{et},t) \models A_i \succ_T A_j$. Let g be a state ranging over elements of G_2, φ be a formula in T such that $(M^{et},g) \models \varphi$. Then we have that $(M^{et},t) \models A_i \succ_{\{\varphi\}} A_j$ from $(M^{et},t) \models A_i \succ_T A_j$. Now we suppose that $(t,g) \in \mathcal{K}_i$. Then we will have that $g \in \theta^{\{\varphi\}}(\mathcal{K}_i(t))$ and thereby $g \in \theta^{\{\varphi\}}(\mathcal{K}_j(t))$ according to the semantics of $(M^{et},t) \models A_i \succ_{\{\varphi\}} A_j$. This result obviously conflicts with hypothesis $(t,g) \notin \mathcal{K}_j$. So we have that $(t,g) \notin \mathcal{K}_i$ if g is a state in G_2.

Now we have shown that $(t,g) \in \mathcal{K}_j$ if $(t,g) \in K_i$ for any state $g \in S$. We can draw a useful conclusion: if agent A_i thinks some state, denoted g, possible at state t in M^{et}, it must be true that $(t,g) \in \mathcal{K}_j$ i.e., if $(t,g) \in K_i$ then $(M^{et},g) \models A_j \succ_T A_k$.

By the premise $M^{et} \models B_i(A_i \succ_T A_j)$ and the fact that M^{et} is transitive, we have that $\mathcal{M}^{et} \models B_iB_i(A_i \succ_T A_j)$. So for any state g if $(t,g) \in K_i$ we have that $(\mathcal{M}^{et},g) \models A_i \succ_T A_j$, $(M^{et},g) \models A_j \succ_T A_k$ and $(s,g) \in \mathcal{K}_j$. Hence, we have that $(M^{et},g) \models A_i \succ_T A_k$ by applying Theorem 3 to those conditions.

On the other hand, from the fact that M^{et} is Euclidean, that $(s,t) \in \mathcal{K}_i$, and that $(t,g) \in \mathcal{K}_i$, we have that $(g,t) \in \mathcal{K}_i$. Then through the similar steps as that we get $(M^{et},g) \models A_i \succ_T A_k$, we can derive that $(M^{et},t) \models A_i \succ_T A_k$ as well.

Now we have shown that if $(s,t) \in K_j$ then $(M^{et},t) \models B_i(A_i \succ_T A_k)$. So the formula $B_i(A_i \succ_T A_k)$ is valid in M^{et} in this case.

As we have seen, if formulae $B_i(A_i \succ_T A_j)$ and $B_j(A_j \succ_T A_k)$ are valid in some M^{et} the formula $B_i(A_i \succ_T A_k)$ will also be valid in it. So formula $B_i(A_i \succ_{R\cap V} A_k)$ is a logical consequence of formulae $B_i(A_i \succ_R A_j)$ and $B_j(A_j \succ_V A_k)$.

SPSS: A Case of Semantic Peer-to-Peer Search System

Fei Liu, Wen-ju Zhang, Fan-yuan Ma, and Ming-lu Li

Department of Computer Science and Engineering, Shanghai Jiaotong University, Shanghai, P. R. China, 200030
{fliu, zwj2004, ma-fy, li-ml}@cs.sjtu.edu.cn

Abstract. Traditional search system approaches have either been centralized or use flooding to ensure accuracy of the results returned which have bad performance. This paper presents SPSS (Semantic Peer-to-Peer Search System) that search documents through the P2P network hierarchically based on document semantic vector generated by Latent Semantic Indexing (LSI) [1]. The search cost for a given query is thereby reduced, since the indices of semantically related documents are likely to be co-located in the network. SPSS organize contents around their semantics in a P2P network. This makes it achieve accuracy comparable to centralized search systems. CAN [2] and range addressable network are used to organize the computing nodes. Owning to the hierarchical overlay network, the average number of logical hops per query is smaller than other flat architectures. Both theoretical analysis and experimental results show that SPSS has higher accuracy and less logic hops.

1 Introduction

Peer-to-peer technologies widely emerged through the last years. Several peer-to-peer approaches such as for distributed storage (CFS, Oceanstore, PAST) and distributed content (CAN, Pastry, Chord, Tapestry), which were all based on high level routing, have been developed. A number of P2P systems provide keyword search, including Gnutella [3] and KaZaA [4]. These systems use the simple and robust technique of flooding queries over some or all peers. The estimated number of documents in these systems is 500 million [5]. Documents are typically music files, and searches examine only file meta-data such as title and artist. These systems have performance problems [6] even with workloads much smaller than the Web and bad accuracy. Another class of P2P systems achieves scalability by structuring the data so that it can be found with far less expense than flooding. These are commonly called distributed hash tables (DHTs) [7, 8, 9]. DHTs are well-suited for exact match lookups using unique identifiers, but do not directly support text search. The fundamental problem that makes the above P2P search systems difficult is that documents are randomly distributed. Given a query, the system either has to search a large number of nodes or the user runs a high risk of missing relevant documents. We use LSI in P2P system to address the problem. VSM and LSI are used to represent documents and queries as vectors in a Cartesian space. The cosine of the angle between documents vectors and queries vectors are the similarity between a query and a document. Owning to the flat

X. Zhou et al. (Eds.): WISE 2004, LNCS 3306, pp. 718–723, 2004.
© Springer-Verlag Berlin Heidelberg 2004

architecture of P2P, performance of query of P2P is a problem. Range Addressable Network is used in our paper to solve the problem.

2 Latent Semantic Indexing (LSI)

Literal matching schemes such as Vector Space Model (VSM) suffer from synonyms and noise in document. LSI overcomes these problems by using statistically derived conceptual indices instead of terms for retrieval. It uses singular value decomposition (SVD) [10] to transform a high-dimensional term vector into a lower-dimensional semantic vector. Each element of a semantic vector corresponds to the importance of an abstract concept in the document or query.

Let *N* be the number of documents in the collection and *d* be the number of documents containing the given word. The inverse document frequency (*IDF*) is defined as

$$IDF = \log[\frac{N}{d}] \tag{1}$$

The vector for document *Do* is constructed as below

$$Do = (T_1 * IDF_1, T_2 * IDF_2, ..., T_n * IDF_n) \tag{2}$$

Where T_i takes a value of 1 or 0 depending on whether or not the word i exists in the document *Do*. The vectors computed for documents are used to form a documents matrix *S.* Suppose the number of returned documents is *m,* the documents matrix *S.* is constructed as $S=[S_1,S_2,...S_m]$. Based on this document matrix *S,* singular value decomposition (SVD) of matrix is used to extract relationship pattern between documents and define thresholds to find matched services. The algorithm is described as follow. Since *S* is a real matrix, there exists SVD of S:$S=U_{m\times m}\Sigma_{m\times n}V^T_{n\times n}$ where *U* and *V* are orthogonal matrices. Matrices *U* and *V* can be denoted respectively as $U_m=[u_1, u_2,...,u_m]_{m\times m}$ and $V_n=[v_1, v_2,...,v_n]_{n\times n}$, where $u_i(i=1,...,m)$ is a m-dimensional vector $u_i=(u_{1,i},u_{2,i},...u_{m,i})$ and $v_i(i=1,...,m)$ is a n-dimensional vector. $v_i=(v_{1,i},v_{2,i},...,v_{3,i})$ Suppose $rank(S)=r$ and singular values of matrix *S* are: $\beta_1 \geq \beta_2 \geq ... \geq \beta_r \geq \beta_{r+1} = ... = \beta_n = 0$. For a given threshold ε $(o < \varepsilon \leq 1)$, we choose a parameter k such that $(\beta_k - \beta_{k-1}) / \beta_k \geq \varepsilon$. Then we denote $U_k=[u_1, u_2,...,u_k]_{m\times k}$, $V_k=[v_1, v_2,...,v_k]_{n\times k}$, $\sum_k = diag(\beta_1, \beta_2, ...\beta_k)$, and $S_k=U_k\Sigma_kV_k^T$. S_k is the best approximation matrix to *S* and contains main information among the documents. In this algorithm, the documents matching queries are measured by the similarity between them. For measuring the documents similarity based on S_k, we choose the *ith* row R_i of the matrix Σ_kV_k as the coordinate vector of documents *i* in a k-dimensional subspace:

$$R_i = (u_{i,1}\beta_1, u_{i,2}\beta_2, ...u_{i,k}\beta_k) \quad i = 1, 2, ..., m$$

The similarity between document *i* and query *j* is defined as:

$$sim(R_i, R_j) = \frac{|R_i.R_j|}{\|R_i\|_2 \|R_j\|_2} \tag{3}$$

3 Generating and Deploying the Indices in SPSS

P is defined to be an *m*-dimensional CAN overlay network and let $P=[p_1,p_2,\ldots p_z]$ P_i is one of the nodes in *P* that is regarded as directory node. We assume d_i is a document. From the introduction in section 1, we can set the dimension of semantic vector of d_i to be 10**m* by adjusting ε in order to resolve match between CAN and semantic vector, where *m* is the number of dimension of CAN. We calculate the temp semantic vector of d_i using LSI and denote the temp semantic vector of d_i is $tv(d_i)$. We use average algorithm and $tv(d_i)$ to generate semantic vector of d_i --- $tv(d_i)$ as follows:

$$v(d_i) = \left(\frac{\sum_{j=1}^{10} tv(d_i).x_j}{10}, \frac{\sum_{j=11}^{20} tv(d_i).x_j}{10}, \ldots, \frac{\sum_{j=10m-10}^{10m} tv(d_i).x_j}{10}\right) \tag{4}$$

We assume point $v(d_i)$ is in the space controlled by P_i. $index(d_i)$ denotes the index of document d_i includes the semantic vector of a document and a reference (URL) to the document. Nodes $p_1,p_2,\ldots p_y$ in CAN are used as root nodes of Range Addressable Network (Fig. 1).

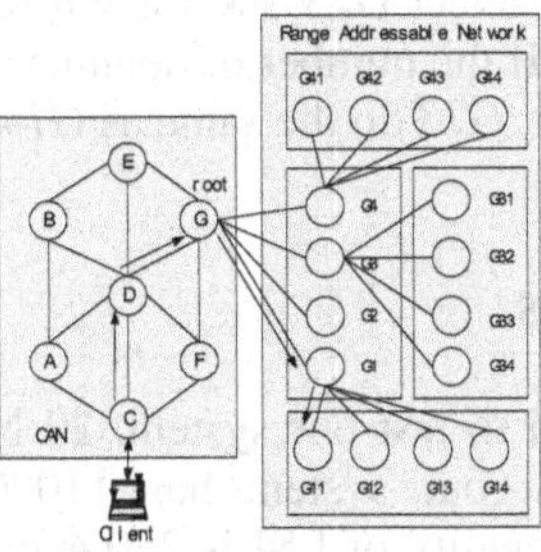

Fig. 1. The topology of SPSS

We define $R(p_i)$ to be the Range Addressable Network which root is p_i and each node in $R(p_i)$ has at most 4 son nodes. If the number of nodes in $R(p_i)$ is *f* then the depth of tree topology of $R(p_i)$ is $\log 4^f$. Indices of documents are stored in leaves of $R(p_i)$. We divide the space SP_i controlled by P_i into *s*(*s* is the number of son nodes of P_i and smaller than 5) parts--- $sp(p_{i1}),\ldots,sp(p_{is})$ equally. P_i makes its sons to hold the above *s* space respectively. If the son node of P_i is not leaf, it does the same as P_i. Otherwise it holds the space. Accord to above algorithm, the spaces are held by leaves in RAN.

4 Querying with Semantic Vector in SPSS

Fig. 2 shows an example of querying document. We want to explain the process of querying by this example. The client that knows directory node *B* sends a query *q*. After *B* receives *q*, it generates the semantic vector of *q* by LSI and average algorithm. Then *B* sends *v(q)* to *G* for the space controlled by *G* contains point *v(q)*. After *G* receives *v(q)*, it transmits them to one of its son node which holds the space containing the point *v(q)*.

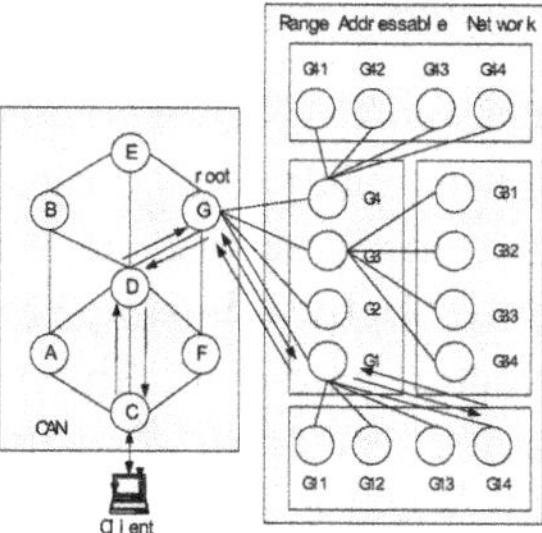

Fig. 2. Querying documents in SPSS

In this example *v(q)* is transmitted to node *G1*. Because *G1* is not a leaf, it transmits *v(q)* to one of its son node *G14* which controls the space containing the point *v(q)*. Besides *G14* is a leaf, *G14* computes $sim(v(q),d_{141}),sim(v(q),d_{142}),\ldots,sim(v(q),d_{14h})$ and select *k* documents with the first *k* highest similarities. The *k* documents are the result of this query to be sent to client. If the number of indices stored by *G14* is smaller than *k*, *G14* reports *G1*. Owning to *v(q)* is nearest to the space held by *G13* among the sons of *G1* exclude *G14*, *G1* select *G13* ask for *k-h* (*h* is the number of documents supplied by *G14*) documents. If the number of documents supplied by *G13* and *G14* is not enough for client's request, *G13* do the same as *G14*.

5 Experimental Results

20 Newsgroup dataset is used to test our system. 20 Newsgroups consists of 20000 messages. In our experiment our system has 11000 nodes those contain 1000 directory nodes. The dimensionality of LSI is 250 and the dimensionality of CAN is 25. The number of returned documents for a query is 10. Fig. 3 and Fig. 4 show the effect on the number of logic hops and the accuracy of the search results when varying the number of system nodes. The results are averaged over 50 queries. From Fig. 3 we can find that as the system size increases, the number of logic hops only increases slightly. From Fig. 4 we can find that as the system size increases, the accuracy of system decrease slightly. SPSS with 2000 range addressable network nodes and 200 directory nodes can achieve an accuracy of 96%. However our system with 10000 range addressable network nodes and 1000 directory nodes can reach 83%.

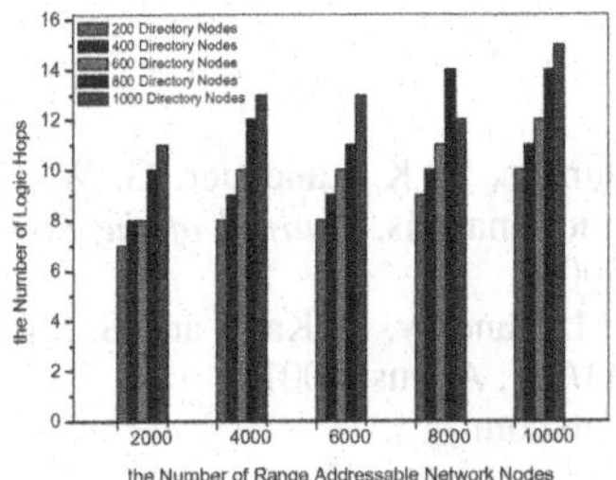

Fig. 3. The effect of varying system size on the number of logic hops

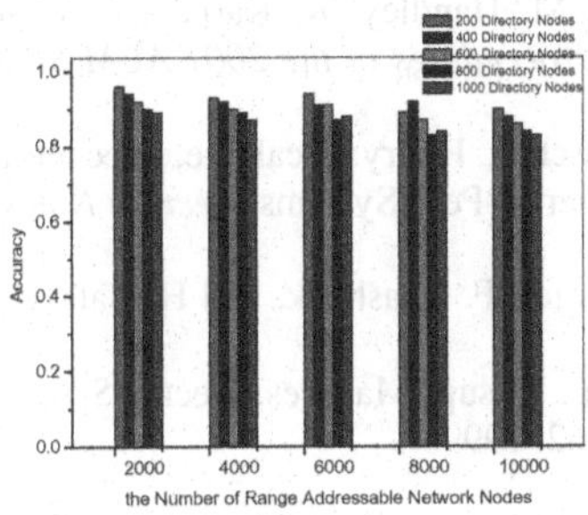

Fig. 4. The effect of varying system size on the accuracy

6 Conclusions and Future Work

With the rapid growth of online information, distributed search system has become one of the key techniques to deal with digital information. One fundamental problem that confronts distributed information retrieval is to efficiently obtain higher accuracy and less logic hops while handling large-scale tasks in the real world. Owning to P2P being resistant, scalable and robust, more and more researchers use P2P to organize information retrieval system. This paper presents SPSS that search document through the P2P network hierarchically based on document semantic vectors and Cartesian of CAN. SPSS uses CAN and Range Addressable Network organize nodes into a hierarchical overlay network to reduce number of logical hops. Owning to SPSS use LSI, it has better accuracy. Both theoretical analysis and experimental results show that SPSS has higher accuracy and less logic hops. However, there are still some problems to be explored. Can we add more directory nodes to reduce the load of directory nodes? We will explore these issues in the future.

Acknowledgements. This paper is supported by 973 project (No.2002CB312002) of China, ChinaGrid Program of MOE of China, and grand project of the Science and Technology Commission of Shanghai Municipality (No. 03dz15026, No. 03dz15027 and No. 03dz15028).

References

1. S. C. Deerwester, S. T. Dumais, T. K. Landauer, G. W. Furnas, and R. A. Harshman. Indexing by Latent Semantic Analysis. *Journal of the American Society of Information Science*, 41(6):391–407, 1990
2. S. Ratnasamy, P. Francis, M. Handley, R. Karp, and S. Shenker. A scalable -addressable network. In *ACM SIGCOMM'01*, August 2001
3. Gnutella. http://gnutella.wego.com
4. Kazaa.
5. Ingram: Record Industry Plays Hardball with Kazaa. http://www.globeandmail.com/
6. Why Gnutella Can't Scale. No, Really. http: //www.darkridge.com/˜jpr5/doc/gnutella.html
7. S. Ratnasamy, P. Francis, M. Handley, R. Karp, and S. Shenker. A Scalable Content Addressable Network. In *Proceedings of the 2001 ACM SIGCOM Conference*, Berkeley, CA, August 2001
8. A. Rowstron and P. Druschel. Pastry: Scalable, Decentralized Object Location, and Routing for Large-Scale Peer-to-Peer Systems. *Lecture Notes in Computer Science*, 2218, 2001
9. I. Stoica, R. Morris, D. Karger, F. Kaashoek, and H. Balakrishnan. Chord: Scalable Peer-To-Peer
10. M. Berry, Z. Drmac, and E. Jessup. Matrices, Vector Spaces, and Information Retrieval. *SIAM Review*, 41(2):335–362, 1999

An Efficient Broadcast Algorithm Based on Connected Dominating Set in Unstructured Peer-to-Peer Network

Qianbing Zheng, Wei Peng, Yongwen Wang, and Xicheng Lu

School of Computer Science, National University of Defense Technology
Changsha 410073, China
nudt_zhengqianbing@hotmail.com

Abstract. Flooding-based broadcast algorithm is very inefficient for Gnutella-like unstructured peer-to-peer network due to generating a large amount of redundant traffic. So far, few research has been done to make an efficient broadcast in unstructured P2P network. In this paper, we present an efficient broadcast algorithm-*BCDS* (Broadcast based on Connected Dominating Set). We also build some P2P overlay graphs based on scale-free model and simulate *BCDS* algorithm in the P2P overlay graphs. Experimental results show that *BCDS* algorithm reduces redundant messages greatly, while maintaining the same coverage as flooding. Furthermore, it shows better performance with the increase of source broadcast node degree and graph density.

1 Introduction

Many P2P systems have come forth since 1999. Gnutella-like decentralized, unstructured P2P systems have a large amount of Internet users, causing significant impact on Internet traffic. Flooding-based algorithm is the main way to search in the unstructured P2P network, and it produces vast redundant messages and wastes enormous bandwidth. To address the flooding problem in Gnutella-like unstructured P2P systems, researchers have proposed many statistics-based solutions for efficient search. However, these solutions produce the Partial Coverage Problem[1] and can't be used for broadcast.

In fact, broadcast is an important operation. Using broadcast, not only the Partial Coverage Problem can be solved, but also users can search with arbitrary queries, make group communication, as well as collect global information. Flooding algorithm is very inefficient for broadcast. So far, research [2] on broadcast mainly focuses on the structured P2P network. At present, few research has been done to make an efficient broadcast in unstructured P2P network. Researchers [3] construct the tree-like sub-overlay called *FloodNet*, and propose an efficient algorithm-LightFlooding with the objective to minimize the number of redundant messages and retaining the same message propagating scope as that of standard flooding. But the disconnected components that it generates can't ensure that every node would receive the message.

X. Zhou et al. (Eds.): WISE 2004, LNCS 3306, pp. 724–729, 2004.
© Springer-Verlag Berlin Heidelberg 2004

In this paper, we present an efficient broadcast algorithm-*BCDS* (Broadcast based on Connected Dominating Set) in unstructured P2P overlay network. It reduces redundant messages to a great extent while ensuring every P2P node can receive the broadcast message.

The rest of this paper is organized as follows. In section 2, we describe the algorithm in details. In section 3, we make two experiments in simulation environment and discuss the results. Finally, we end with conclusions in section 4.

2 *BCDS* Algorithm

We consider a P2P overlay network as an undirected graph in which the nodes correspond to P2P nodes in the network and the edges correspond to connections maintained between the nodes. The graph is defined as $G = (V, E)$, where V is the node set and E is the edge set. Two nodes u and v are called *neighbors* if there is a direct connection between the nodes. A node set C in $G(V, E)$ is a CDS(*Connected Dominating Set*) if all the nodes in $G(V, E)$ are either in C or neighbors of nodes in C and the sub-graph induced by the set is connected. The CDS of an undirected graph is not unique. A node is called a *dominating node* if it is in C. In this paper, a *dominating node* is also called *forwarding node* which takes charge of forwarding broadcast message to its neighbors.

In flooding-based broadcast algorithm, every node is a *forwarding node*, thus a lot of duplicate messages are generated. It is a natural idea that we can reduce the duplicate messages through decreasing the number of forwarding nodes. This problem can be resolved by finding a minimum CDS(Connected Dominating Set) in a general graph. We propose a distributed algorithm to approximate the minimum CDS effectively by each node maintaining its two-hop topology information.

BCDS algorithm selects forwarding node along with the process of broadcast. Each forwarding node u computes two node sets:forwarding node set $DN(u)$ and receival node set $BN(u)$. $DN(u)$ contains the forwarding nodes within the local topology of u. $BN(u)$ contains the nodes which u will broadcast message to. $BN(u)$ is a subset of neighbor set of u.

The main process of our algorithm is as follow. The source broadcast node is s. s computes $DN(s)$ and $BN(s)$ and forwards a broadcast message with $DN(s)$ to nodes belonging to $BN(s)$. When a node u receives the broadcast message, it can learn whether it is a forwarding node. If true, it will compute $DN(u)$ and $BN(u)$ and forwards message with $DN(u)$ to nodes belonging to $BN(u)$. Otherwise, it will not do anything. This process will not stop until there is not a new forwarding node set computed by a forwarding node.

Our algorithm is a modification on PL algorithm[4] which was originally used in the broadcast of mobile Ad Hoc Network. The behavior of executing a broadcast is different at mobile Ad Hoc Network and P2P network[5]. In order to make this algorithm adapted to the P2P network and improve its performance, we add the computation of the node set $BN(u)$ to reduce the number of duplicate messages. The calculation of $BN(u)$ enables forwarding nodes send message to only part of its neighbors while ensure the correctness of broadcast, so duplicate messages can be reduced to a great extent. Meanwhile, we simplify the message handling process for each forwarding node and reduce the information carried by each message.

Assuming that the set which node u receives from node r is $DN(r)$, and u is a forwarding node for it belongs to $DN(r)$. The process of computing $DN(u)$ and $BN(u)$ is as follow:

1. if u has received the message before, stop; else u simplifies its local topology
   - remove nodes in $DN(r)$ excluding u from the local topology and cut down the edges and nodes associating with these nodes
   - cut down the edges between two neighbors of u from the local topology
   - remove nodes with degree=0 from the local topology
2. Let $S1$ is the neighbor set of u in its simplified topology, and $S2$ is the set of nodes which can be reached by two hops from u.
3. if $S2$ is not empty, then
   - if there is a node with degree=1 in $S1$
   - then u selects the node v as the forwarding node and puts it into $DN(u)$
   - else u selects a node v whose degree is the max as the forwarding node and puts it into $DN(u)$
   - remove nodes adjacent to v from the simplified topology
   - go to 2
4. else $BN(u) = S1 \cup DN(u)$, stop.

$BN(u)$ is the neighbor set of u in its simplified two-hop neighbor graph. The simplification of the graph cuts redundant links between nodes and removes redundant nodes within the range of two hops, so $BN(u)$ is subset of the neighbor set of u. Thus the duplicate broadcast messages generated by the redundant links are reduced.

The dynamic behavior of P2P network results in the frequent change of the local topology information which one node maintains, each node can obtain its two-hop topology information through periodically exchanging their neighbor sets with their neighbors. The approach which proves the dominating node set computed by $BCDS$ forms a CDS of G is similar to that of [4], so we don't discuss it in detail.

3 Experimental Setup and Results

Recent measurements and researches show that Gnutella-like unstructured networks have power-law degree distribution[6,7,8], which have similar characteristics to the scale-free model[9]. The scale-free model can be used to simulate Gnutella-like P2P overlay network.

There are two experiments to evaluate the performance of $BCDS$ algorithm in our simulation. Furthermore, another algorithm-LightFlood[3] is involved in for comparison. In the simulation, We choose policy $(1, *)$, $(2, *)$, $(3, *)$ and the optimal policy $(4, *)$.

The target of the first experiment is to evaluate the message coverage of algorithms. For broadcast, the message coverage should be 100%. Ten P2P overlay graphs are generated by Barabais Graph Generator. These graphs have the same average node degree, with $|V|$ ranging from 5,000 to 5,0000. The message coverage and the latency time of these algorithms are logged. The former is the ratio of the number of nodes which receive the message and $|V|$, and the latter is equal to the max value of message hops within which 100% of nodes in P2P overlay could be reached or algorithm stops.

The results of the first experiment are illustrated in Figure 1. From Figure 1, we notice that *BCDS* algorithm covers the whole nodes in these overlay graphs, but only Lightflood policies with $M > 2$ can approximate to the coverage of *BCDS* algorithm due to the disconnected components that it generates. Though the optimal policy $(4, *)$ can cover the whole nodes of overlay graphs, it doesn't reduce duplicate messages nearly. And the more coverage is, the less duplicate messages which Lightflood policies reduce. Furthermore, experimental results show these algorithms cost the similar latency time.

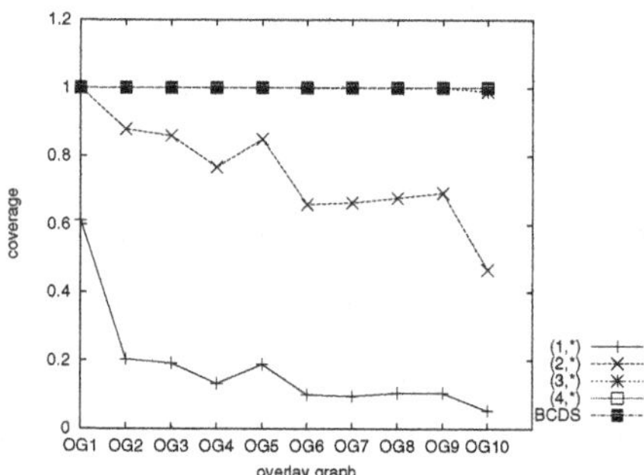

Fig. 1. The message coverage of these algorithms in ten overlay graphs with $|V|$ ranging from 5,000 to 5,0000.

We make the second experiment to explore the influence of the source broadcast node degree and graph density ρ on *BCDS* algorithm. Nine overlay graphs with different graph density which have about 5,000 nodes are generated.

The metric γ is defined to evaluate the improvement of new algorithm over flooding algorithm.

$$\gamma = \frac{d_f - d_n}{d_f}$$

where d_f is the number of duplicate messages which flooding algorithm generates, and d_n is that of new algorithm.

From the results of the second experiment, we compare *BCDS* algorithm with the Lightflood policies whose coverage can exceed 99% and γ beyond 1%.

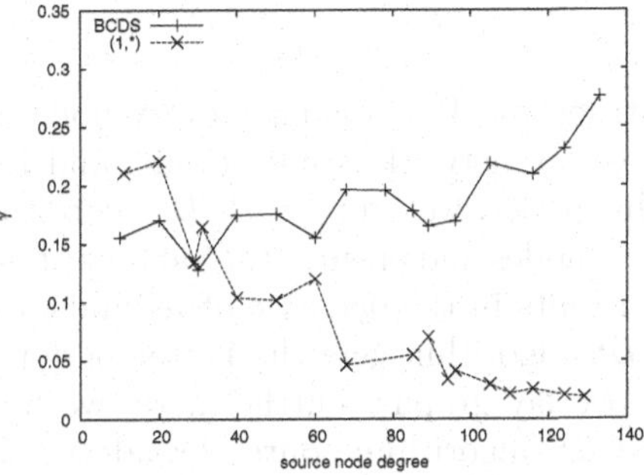

Fig. 2. γ vs. source node degree in a Gnutella-like overlay

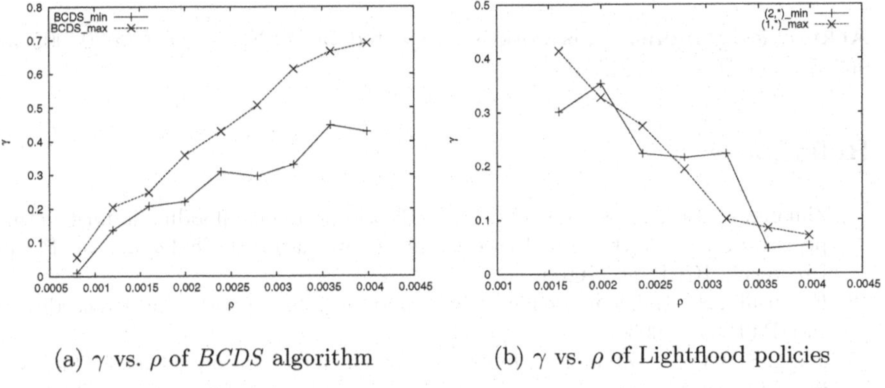

(a) γ vs. ρ of *BCDS* algorithm

(b) γ vs. ρ of Lightflood policies

Fig. 3. Performances of these algorithms change with graph density ρ

From Figure 2, we can conclude that source node degree influences the performance of algorithms. With the increase of source node degree, γ for *BCDS* algorithm almost grows linearly, on the contrary, γ for Lightflood policies decreases with the increase of source node degree. Compared with Lightflood policies, *BCDS* algorithm gets the better performance. γ for *BCDS* algorithm ranges between 15% and 27%, and its mean value is 18.6%. γ for Lightflood policies varies from 1% and 21%, and its mean value is 10.3%. The results indicate a node with high degree is adapted to be chosen as source broadcast node in *BCDS* algorithm.

Another influencing factor is graph density ρ. *BCDS* algorithm and Lightflood policies run with the source nodes having maximal degree and minimal degree respectively. As we can see from the results in Figure 3, γ for *BCDS* algorithm almost increases linearly with the increase of ρ. This is because the more ρ is, the more likely the graph has redundant paths.

On the other hand, γ for $(1,*)$ declines sharply for high graph density makes Lightflood policies generate more disconnect components.

4 Conclusions

In Gnutella-like unstructured P2P systems, every node forwards the broadcast message. The P2P overlay network is not acyclic, and it generates vast redundant messages. In this paper, we propose *BCDS* algorithm based on CDS that reduces the forwarding nodes and ensures the validity of broadcast. The decrease of forwarding nodes results in the decrease of redundant messages. Experimental results show *BCDS* algorithm gets the better performance than Lightflood policies in the P2P overlay graphs. Furthermore, we find there are two influencing factors for *BCDS* algorithm: source broadcast node degree and graph density ρ. The former provides the selective standard for source broadcast node, and the latter indicates *BCDS* algorithm can perform well in the P2P scientific collaboration network[10].

Acknowledgement. This work is supported by NSFC project 90204005 and 863 project 2003AA121510.

References

1. Zhuang, Z., Liu, Y., Xiao, L., Ni, L.M.: Hybrid periodical flooding in unstructured peer-to-peer networks. In: Proceedings of International Conference on Parallel Processing ICPP'03. (2003)
2. El-Ansary, S.: Efficient broadcast in structured p2p networks. In: Proceedings of the IPTP'03. (2003)
3. Jiang, S., Guo, L., Zhang, X.: Lightflood: an efficient flooding scheme for file search in unstructured peer-to-peer systems. In: Proceedings of International Conference on Parallel Processing. (2003)
4. Peng, W., Lu, X.: Efficient broadcast in mobile ad hoc networks using connected dominating sets. Journal of Software **12** (2001) 529–536
5. Rüdiger Schollmeier, I.G., Finkenzeller, M.: Routing in mobile ad hoc and peer-to-peer networks . a comparison. In: Networking 2002, International Workshop on Peer-to-Peer Computing, Pisa, Italy (2002)
6. Ripeanu, M., Foster, I., Iamnitchi, A.: Mapping the gnutella network: Properties of large-scale peer-to-peer systems and implications for system design. IEEE Internet Computing Journal **6-1** (2002)
7. Jovanovic, M., Annexstein, F.S., Berman, K.A.: Modeling peer-to-peer network topologies through "small-world" models and power laws. In: Proceedings of the TELFOR. (2001)
8. DSS, C.: Gnutella: To the bandwidth barrier and beyond. Technical report, http://dss.clip2.com (2000)
9. Barabasi, A.L., Albert, R.: Emergence of scaling in random networks. Science **509** (1999)
10. Iamnitchi, A., Ripeanu, M., Foster, I.: Locating data in (small-world?) p2p scientific collaborations. In: Proceedings of the IPTPS'02. (2002)

A Time-Based Peer Trust Evaluation in P2P E-commerce Environments

Yan Wang and Vijay Varadharajan

Department of Computing
Macquarie University
Sydney, NSW 2109
Australia
{yanwang, vijay}@ics.mq.edu.au

Abstract. In P2P e-commerce environments, as lack of central management, it is rational to investigate the trust status of unknown peers before interacting with them for possible transactions. This paper presents a novel peer trust evaluation model for P2P systems. In the model, we adopt a probabilistic approach with time dimension for evaluating the transaction trust of unknown peers according to their transaction history.

1 Introduction

As an application of P2P technologies, P2P based e-commerce (EC) is now increasingly drawing more and more interests. However, in P2P and P2P-based e-commerce environments, any peer can join and leave the community anytime. As lack of a central management in most P2P systems, the dynamic status of each peer as well as the network causes trust evaluation a very important issue. Before interacting with an unknown peer, it is rational to doubt its trustworthiness. Therefore, to enable the trust evaluation prior to interacting with a set of unknown peers makes the transaction securer. In particular, when P2P network is used for e-commerce applications, the trust evaluation becomes extremely a prominent issue.

In this paper we present a novel peer trust evaluation model. In our method, the trustworthiness of a certain peer can be determined by investigating its transaction history with other peers if the end-peer has no previous transactions with it. After the investigation, the probability of a given threshold of trust value for a peer can be calculated. With these results, a set of "good" peers can be chosen that satisfy the requirement of the end-peer. After that, the end-peer can interact with them for their offers. Meanwhile, a time-based evaluation is added in this model that fresh transactions will weighted more than old transactions.

2 Related Work

Regarding trust evaluation in P2P environments, there are some notions of trust and different kinds of trust satisfying different properties that can be established differently [1].

X. Zhou et al. (Eds.): WISE 2004, LNCS 3306, pp. 730–735, 2004.
© Springer-Verlag Berlin Heidelberg 2004

In terms of computer security, trust is considered as a fundamental concept. An entity is trustworthy if there is sufficient credible evidence leading to believe that the system will meet a set of given requirements. Trust is a measure of trustworthiness, relying on the evidence provided [2]. A complex mechanism is proposed in [3] as the process of trust negotiation, where the two parties need to open the respective authentication policy to each other and exchange their required credentials [3]). It is valuable for initial trust establishment for two strangers.

On the other hand, trust can be defined in terms of trust belief and trust behavior [4]. Trust belief between two parties is the extent to which a party believes that the other party is trustworthy in a certain situation. Trustworthy means one is willing and able to act in the other party's interests. Trust behavior between two parties is the extent to which a party depends on the other in a given situation with a feeling of relative security, even though negative consequences are possible.

[1] proposed a PeerTrust model considering the trust belief between two peers in a P2P environment. But in this model, each peer will give only an evaluation as Satisfaction (S) or Complaint (C) to another peer after their transactions. Other work can be found in [5] and [6]. However, trust evaluation should be time-relevant. Old histories should not be weighted the same as fresh one.

3 Peer Trust Evaluation

In our method, the trustworthiness of an unknown peer can be determined by investigating its transaction history with other peers. After the investigation, the probability of a given threshold of trust value can be calculated. With this method, a set of peers can be chosen for possible transactions that satisfy the requirement of the end-peer. In the following context, we assume that feedbacks are collected from a large number of peers.

3.1 Trust Metrics

1. For an individual peer, its degree of satisfaction with another peer which is a service provider in a transaction can be a real number among a predefined scope (e.g. $[0, 1]$), not just simply 1 or 0. The value results from the service quality, and the recognition by the end-peer. The final trust value is the cumulative sum of of a large number of feedbacks from peers for a relative long period.
2. As far as the trust of a peer is concerned in the e-commerce environments, it should be more concrete other than an abstract notation only. We can further decompose it into several aspects for conducting the investigation against an unknown peer. For example, the end peer may consider some of the follows:
   a) did any cheating transaction occur with other peers?
   b) was the delivery as quick as claimed?

c) is the the payment correct for each transaction with the peer?
d) is the peer online most of time?

3. Moreover, the trust value should reflect more on the 'fresh' status of a given peer being investigated. Recent transactions weight much in the computation of new trust value.

3.2 Peer Investigation

Now suppose an end-peer A hopes to have a transaction with an unknown peer X. To evaluate the trust status of X, A will have to investigate other peers which have transaction histories with X.

In the request from peer A, each peer will be asked to evaluate the performance of peer X considering the attributes in list x given by A. Say,

$$a = \{a_1, a_2, \ldots, a_n\}$$

Now we assume that the evaluation given by peer Y against X for attribute a_i is denoted as $E_{Y\rightarrow X}(a_i) \in [0,1]$ where "1" means the highest satisfaction degree while "0" means the lowest one.

After obtaining a set of feedbacks from other peers, A can initially *filter* these peers according to its *rules*. For instance, if some cheating transactions occurred with a peer, it will be deleted from the peer list. After the filtering process, the trust value of X (if retained in the peer list) by peer Y can be obtained as:

$$T_{Y\rightarrow X} = \sum E_{Y\rightarrow X}(a_i) * w_{a_i} \tag{1}$$

where w_{a_i} is the weight for attribute a_i given by end peer A and $\sum w_{a_i} = 1$.

3.3 Trust Evaluation Method

Suppose the end peer A has collected feedbacks from a set of intermediate peers $\{M_1, M_2, \ldots, M_k\}$:

$$\{T_{M_1\rightarrow X}, T_{M_2\rightarrow X}, \ldots, T_{M_k\rightarrow X}\}$$

The *mean trust value* $\bar{T}$ can be calculated as

$$\bar{T} = \frac{1}{k}\sum_{i=1}^{k} T_{M_i\rightarrow X}$$

Accordingly, the *sample variance* is

$$S^2 = \frac{1}{k-1}\sum_{i=1}^{k}(T_{M_i\rightarrow X} - \bar{T})^2$$

Let $\mu = \bar{T}$, $\sigma^2 = S^2$. Since $T \sim N(\mu, \sigma^2)$, for any random variable T and a given value v, according to the theory of Gauss Distribution [7], we have the distribution function as follows

$$F(v) = P(T \leq v) = \frac{1}{\sqrt{2\pi}\sigma} \int_{-\infty}^{\frac{v-\mu}{\sigma}} e^{-\frac{x^2}{2}} dx \tag{2}$$

Likewise, we have

$$P(T > v) = \frac{1}{\sqrt{2\pi}\sigma} \int_{\frac{v-\mu}{\sigma}}^{\infty} e^{-\frac{x^2}{2}} dx \tag{3}$$

After having collected $\{T_{M_1 \to X}, T_{M_2 \to X}, \ldots, T_{M_n \to X}\}$, *the probability of* X*'s trust value in a given scope* $(v_1, v_2]$ $(v_1 < v_2, v_1, v_2 \in [0,1])$ is

$$P_\alpha^X(v_1, v_2) = P(v_1 < T \leq v_2) = \frac{1}{\sqrt{2\pi}\sigma} \int_{\frac{v_1-\mu}{\sigma}}^{\frac{v_2-\mu}{\sigma}} e^{-\frac{x^2}{2}} dx \tag{4}$$

Definition 1. From equation (4), peer A could calculate *the probability that peer* X*'s trust value is better than a given value* $v \in [0,1]$.

$$P_\beta^X(v) = P(T > v | T \in (0,1]) = \frac{P(v < T \leq 1)}{P(0 < T \leq 1)} = \frac{\int_{\frac{v-\mu}{\sigma}}^{\frac{1-\mu}{\sigma}} e^{-\frac{x^2}{2}} dx}{\int_{-\frac{\mu}{\sigma}}^{\frac{1-\mu}{\sigma}} e^{-\frac{x^2}{2}} dx} \tag{5}$$

To get more accurate trust value of the peer reflecting the 'fresh' trust status, time property should be considered. Here it is not required that each peer should have a transaction with X in any time period.

Suppose peer A is the end-peer collecting the feedbacks from a set of peers P about the trust status of peer X during period $[t_{start}, t_{end}]$. If $t_{end} - t_{start}$ is divided into different sub-periods $\{t_1, t_2, \ldots, t_m\}$ $(t_l < t_{l-1},\ t_{l+1} - t_l = \Delta t)$, the returned values from a peer Y $(Y \in P)$ are denoted as

$$\{T_{Y\to X}^{t_1}, T_{Y\to X}^{t_2}, \ldots, T_{Y\to X}^{t_m}\}$$

$$\textit{where}\ \ T_{Y\to X}^{t_l} = \begin{cases} null & \textit{if Y has no transaction with X during period } t_l \\ v \in [0,1] & \textit{otherwise} \end{cases}$$

After having collected $\{T_{M_1\to X}^{t_l}, T_{M_2\to X}^{t_l}, \ldots, T_{M_n\to X}^{t_l}\}$ $(l = 1, \ \ldots, \ m)$ from a set of intermediate peers $\{M_1, M_2, \ldots, M_n\}$ *the probability of* X*'s trust value in a given scope* $(v_1, v_2]$ *at period* t_l $(v_1 < v_2, v_1, v_2 \in [0,1])$ is

$$P_\alpha^{X(t_l)}(v_1, v_2) = P(v_1 < T \leq v_2) = \frac{1}{\sqrt{2\pi}\sigma(t_l)} \int_{\frac{v_1-\mu(t_l)}{\sigma(t_l)}}^{\frac{v_2-\mu(t_l)}{\sigma(t_l)}} e^{-\frac{x^2}{2}} dx \tag{6}$$

where $\mu(t_l) = \bar{T}(t_l) = \frac{1}{n}\sum_{i=1}^{n} T_{M_i\to X}^{t_l}$
and $\sigma^2(t_l) = S^2(t_l) = \frac{1}{n-1}\sum_{i=1}^{n}(T_{M_i\to X}^{t_l} - \bar{T}(t_l))^2$.

Table 1. An example

PEER	$w_1 = 0.05$	$w_2 = 0.075$	$w_3 = 0.125$	$w_4 = 0.30$	$w_5 = 0.45$	mean	$P_\beta^{X_{t_1}^{t_5}}(v)$	order
X_1	0.10	0.20	0.30	0.45	0.60	0.33	0.49	1
X_2	0.30	0.30	0.30	0.30	0.30	0.30	0.30	2
X_3	0.25	0.25	0.45	0.35	0.20	0.30	0.28	3
X_4	0.60	0.45	0.30	0.20	0.15	0.34	0.23	4
X_5	0.15	0.15	0.15	0.15	0.15	0.15	0.15	5

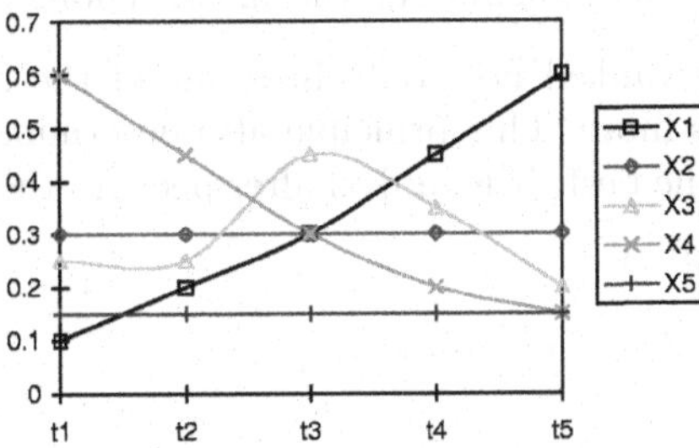

Fig. 1. Example 1

Definition 2. From equation (6), peer A could calculate $P_\beta^{X(t_l)}(v)$, *the probability that peer X's transaction trust value is better than a given threshold $v \in [0,1]$ in a certain period t_l*

$$P_\beta^{X(t_l)}(v) = P(T > v | T \in [0,1]) = \frac{P(v < T \leq 1)}{P(0 < T \leq 1)} = \frac{\int_{\frac{v-\mu(t_l)}{\sigma(t_l)}}^{\frac{1-\mu(t_l)}{\sigma(t_l)}} e^{-\frac{x^2}{2}} dx}{\int_{-\frac{\mu(t_l)}{\sigma(t_l)}}^{\frac{1-\mu(t_l)}{\sigma(t_l)}} e^{-\frac{x^2}{2}} dx} \tag{7}$$

For evaluating the trust in a certain period $\{t_1, t_2, \ldots, t_m\}$ (where $t_1 < t_2 < \ldots < t_m$, $t_{l+1} - t_l = \Delta t$), the end peer A can specify the weight allocation, where recent observations are given more importance than older ones.

Definition 3. With all $P_\beta^{X(t_l)}(v)$ $(l = 1, \ldots, m,\ t_l < t_{l+1},\ t_{l+1} - t_l = \Delta t)$, the end peer A can specify the time-based weight allocation as $\{w_{t_l}\colon l = 1, \ldots, m, \sum_{l=1}^{m} w_{t_l} = 1$, and $w_{t_l} \leq w_{t_{l+1}}\}$ and evaluate *the probability that peer X's transaction trust value is better than a given threshold $v \in [0,1]$ in a certain period* $[t_1,\ t_m]$ as follows:

$$P_\beta^{X_{t_1}^{t_m}}(v) = \sum_{l=1}^{m} w_{t_l} \cdot P_\beta^{X(t_l)}(v) \tag{8}$$

4 Experiment

This experiment illustrates the properties of equation (7) and (8).

Table 1 lists an example where the values of $P_{\beta}^{X_{t_1}^{t_5}}(v)$ for peers in set $\{X_1, X_2, X_3, X_4, X_5\}$ were given. Each peer has different features with respect to the probability distribution among period t_1 to t_5. From Fig. 1, we could observe that peer X_1's probability $P_{\beta}^{X(t_i)}(v)$ increases from t_1 to t_5 while the trend of peer X_4 is in a reverse way. Peer X_2 and X_5 have stable $P_{\beta}^{X(t_i)}(v)$ with different values while X_3's value varies in different periods.

As $w_{x_{i+1}} > w_{x_i}$, this benefits X_1 the most. Though the average of X_4 is better than X_1, it is ranked no.4 only in terms of the final value $P_{\beta}^{X_{t_1}^{t_5}}(v)$ as a recent value affects more. This principle also determines that peer X_3's final value cannot not be the best. It is ranked after peer X_2 though their mean values are the same.

5 Conclusions

In this paper, we have presented a peer trust evaluation method using a probabilistic approach considering the time based trust variation. For an individual trust evaluation, some transaction attributes are taken into account with the criteria given by the end peer. After a transaction, peers will become known to each other and evaluations can be done according to the behaviors in the occurred transactions [8].

References

1. L. Xiong and L. Liu, "PeerTrust: A trust mechanism for an open peer-to-peer information system," Tech. Rep. GIT-CC-02-29, Georgia Institute of Technology, 2002.
2. M. Bishop, *Computer Security: Art and Science.* Addition-Wesley Press, 2003.
3. T. Yu, M. Winslett, and K. E. Seamons, "Interoperable strategies in automated trust negotiation," in *Proceedings of ACM Conference on Computer and Communications Security 2001*, pp. 146–155, 2001.
4. D. H. Knight and N. L. Chervany, "The meaning of trust," Tech. Rep. WP9604, Universoty of Minnesota, Management Information Systems Research Center, 1996.
5. K. Aberer and Z. Despotovic, "Managing trust in a peer-2-peer information system," in *Proceedings of CIKM 2001*, pp. 310–317.
6. S. D. Kamvar, M. T. Schlosser, and H. Garcia-Molina, "The eigentrust algorithm for reputation management in P2P networks," in *Proceedings of WWW2003*, (Budapest, Hungary), May 2003.
7. G. Grimmett, *Probability: An Introduction.* Oxford University Press, 1986.
8. Y. Wang and V. Varadharajan, "Interaction trust evaluation in decentralized environments," in *Proceedings of 5th International Conference on Electronic Commerce and Web Technologies (EC-Web'04)*, vol. LNCS 3182 (Zaragoza, Spain), August-September 2004.

Fault Resilience of Structured P2P Systems

Zhiyu Liu[1], Guihai Chen[1], Chunfeng Yuan[1], Sanglu Lu[1], and Chengzhong Xu[2]

[1] National Laboratory of Novel Software Technology, Nanjing University, China
[2] Department of Electrical and Computer Engineering, Wayne State University, USA

Abstract. A fundamental problem that confronts structured peer-to-peer system that use DHT technologies to map data onto nodes is the performance of the network under the circumstance that a large percentage of nodes join and fail frequently and simultaneously. A careful examination of some typical peer-to-peer networks will contribute a lot to choosing and using certain kind of topology in special applications. This paper analyzes the performance of Chord [7] and Koorde [2], and find out the crash point of each network through the simulation experiment.

1 Introduction

Peer-to-peer systems are distributed systems without any centralized control or hierarchical organization. However, unlike traditional distributed systems, nodes in peer-to-peer system are continuously joining and leaving the system. Thus, data items must migrate as nodes come and go, and routing tables must be updated constantly.

To deal with these problems that arise over time, all realistic peer-to-peer systems implement some kind of stabilization routine which continuously repairs the overlay as nodes come and go, updating control information and routing tables to ensure that the overlay remains connected and support efficient lookups. However, when facing large percentage of nodes joins and leaves, different peer-to-peer proposals may have very different performance due to the geometric properties of the topology they are built up on.

In general, there is a tradeoff between degree and resilience. High degree usually induces strong connectivity and therefore good resilience, vice versa. However, other aspects like clustering properties also have impact on resilience, so, through careful design, even network with constant degree can perform well under a certain percentage of node failure. Now there is the question: if we know how often the nodes come and go, given the demanding fault tolerance, which kind of peer-to-peer network should we choose?

A lot of related work addressed to this problem has been done. Some [4,6,3,5] did execellent theoretical analysis and some did careful selected simulation [3].So far, however, simulation of dynamic peer-to-peer systems to detect their crash point hasn't been done yet. For there is no widely accepted definition of crash point, we here define it as follows: If x percent of nodes fails, and half (50%) look-ups failed, then x is defined as the **crash point**. By this definition, we can ignore the difference between two kinds of crash. One kind is a node become

X. Zhou et al. (Eds.): WISE 2004, LNCS 3306, pp. 736–741, 2004.
© Springer-Verlag Berlin Heidelberg 2004

isolated, all look-ups from/to it will fail. The other kind is the whole network break up into some disconnected subnets, look-ups between each net will fail, however look-ups within the subnet can still success. Then we can compare different protocols under the same criterion.

In this paper we will simulate to find out the crash point of 2 typical kind of networks Chord [7] and Koorde [2].

2 Related Works

Fault tolerance of peer-to-peer networks is an important topic. Liben-Nowell *et al.* [4] examine error resilience dynamics of Chord when nodes join/leave the system and derive lower bounds on the degree necessary to maintain a connected graph with high probability. Fiat *et al.* [8] build a Censorship Resistant Network that can tolerate massive adversarial node failures and random object deletions. Saia *et al.* [9] create another highly fault-resilient structure with $O(\log 3N)$ state at each node and $O(\log 3N)$ hops per message routing overhead. Unfortunately, very few studies examine the resilience of existing graphs in comparison with each other, especially when nodes join/leave at a high rate. We are aware of only few comparison study, including that Gummadi *et al.* [3] find that ring-based graphs (such as Chord) offer more flexibility with route selection and provide better performance under random node, and Dmitri Loguinov *et al.* [5] do some theoretical analysis of the existing graph.

3 Analysis

One of the reasons DHTs are seen as an excellent platform for large scale distributed systems is that they are resilient in the presence of node failure. This resilience has two different aspects [3]:

Static resilience: we keep the routing table static, only delete the items of failed nodes to see whether the DHTs can route correctly. Thus, static resilience gives a measure of how quickly the recovery algorithm has to work.

Routing recovery: they repopulate the routing table with live nodes, deleting the items of failed nodes.

Later you will see, Chord and Koorde nearly have the same routing recovery algorithm. However, since Koorde has only $(\log 1)$ neighbor, it has much weaker static resilience than Chord. Even if it increases its neighbors to $O(\log n)$, it is still not as good as Chord, because unlike Chord, the geometry of Koorde (de bruijn graph) doesn't naturally support sequential neighbor.

Let's first discuss flexibility and path overlap, which have impact on static resilience.

3.1 Flexibility

When basic routing geometry has been chosen, more flexibility means more freedom in the selection of neighbors and routes. Let's discuss in turn:

Neighbor Selection. DHTs have a routing table comprised of neighbors. Some algorithms make purely deterministic neighbors (i.e., Koorde), others allow some freedom to choose neighbors based on other criteria in addition to the identifiers; most notably, latencies have been used to select neighbors. (i.e., ChordFingerPNS).

Route Selection. Given a set of neighbors, and a destination, the routing algorithm determines the choice of the next hop. However, when the determined next-hop is down, flexibility will describe how many other options are there for the next-hop. If there are none, or only a few, then the routing algorithm is likely to fail.

Then we examine Chord and Koorde from the aspect of flexibility.

Chord. Chord provides both neighbor selection flexibility and routing selection flexibility.

Gummadi *et al.* [3] mentioned that Chord has 2^i possible options in picking its ith neighbors for a total of approximately $n\{(\log n)/2\}$ possible routing tables for each node, and having selected one of its possible routing tables, the flexibility in route selection now available is $(\log n)!$ for two nodes that are initially $O(n)$ distance apart.

What's more, Chord also allows paths that are much longer than $\log n$. This is accomplished by taking multiple hops of smaller spans instead of a single hop of large span. For example, one could take two successive hops using $(i-1)th$ neighbors of span 2^{i-1} each instead of a single hop using ith neighbor of span 2^i. This feature will reduce the probability of path failure when large percentage nodes fails.

Koorde. Koorde has no flexibility in either neighbor selection or route selection. When large percentage of nodes fails simultaneously, the lookup through de Bruijn path will easily fail. Fortunately like finger pointers in Chord, Koorde's de Bruijn pointer is merely an important performance optimization; a query can always reach its destination slowly by following successors. Because of this property, Koorde can use Chord's join algorithm. Similarly, to keep the ring connected in the presence of nodes that leave, Koorde can use Chord's successor list and stabilization algorithm.

However, when facing a large percentage of nodes leaving, the path length will increase fast, and more failure due to time out will happen.

3.2 Path Overlap

Dmitri et.al [5] have done simulation to compare the path overlap of Chord and de Burijn graph. They drew the conclusion that de Bruijn graph select backup

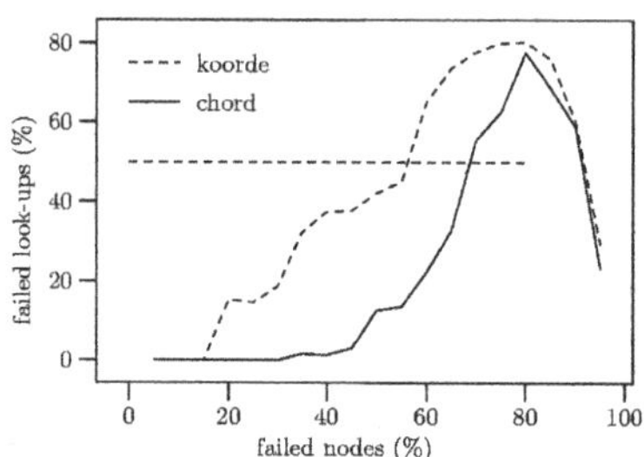

Fig. 1. Percentage of failed lookups for varying percentage of node failures across Chord and Koorde. Koorde has 8 fingers, which is equal to Chord with 256 nodes. The stabilization time are both 20s. Successors are both 4.

paths that do not overlap with the best shortest path or with each other, while Chord has certain neighbors that show tendency to construct shortest paths that always overlap with the already-failed ones. However, in sparse Koorde, one real node is responsible for forwarding request for many imaginary nodes. It's another kind of path overlap. Unfortunately, in Koorde, all neighbors of a certain node usually have the same predecessor. The advantage of non-overlap path could only be seen in dense de Bruijn graph.

4 Simulation

Since Chord and Koorde use the same stabilization algorithm, We will see from the simulation: when Chord and Koorde execute the stabilization routine under the same frequency, which one has a better performance.

To speed up the development, we build the simulators on top of an existing tools—p2psim [1]. The protocol of Chord and Koorde are already implemented, we rewrite parts of code, mainly the `eventgenerator()` to do the experiments in this paper.

To test how Chord and Koorde perform when mass nodes fail simultaneously, we use the same network events but with different protocols. The network events includes "join","fail","look-up". First, we build a stable network of 256 (2^8) nodes. Each node executes look-up events which are exponentially distributed about the given meantime (0.5 second). At the 5th second we randomly select $p-percentage$ of nodes. And from the 5th second till the end of the experiment, these nodes will fail or join simultaneously every 20 seconds. That is to say at the 5th second, they all fail, then at the 25th second, they all join, and so on. p is variated from 5-percent to 95 percent in increments of 5 percent.

The total simulation time is 120s, during which the network is continuously changing, and we record the percentage of failure lookups.

It is obviously that Chord performs better than Koorde under the same network circumstance (see Figure 1), which are not surprising after our discussion above. By our definition, the crash point of Koorde is 55%, while the crash point of Chord is about 70%. And in Koorde, when 15% nodes fails, failure start

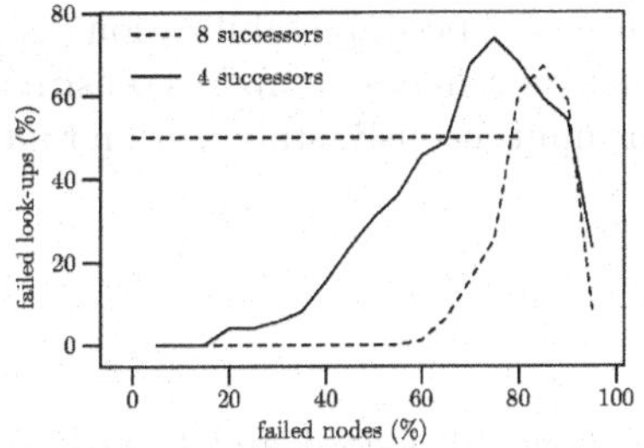

Fig. 2. Chord: Percentage of failed lookups for varying percentage of node failures. When successors increase from 4 to 8, the crash point increases from 65% to 80%

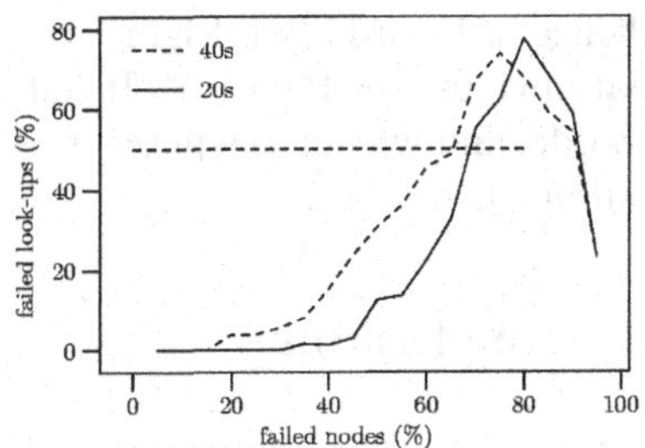

Fig. 3. Chord: Percentage of failed lookups for varying percentage of node failures. When stabilization time decrease from 40s to 20s, the crash point increases from 65% to 70%

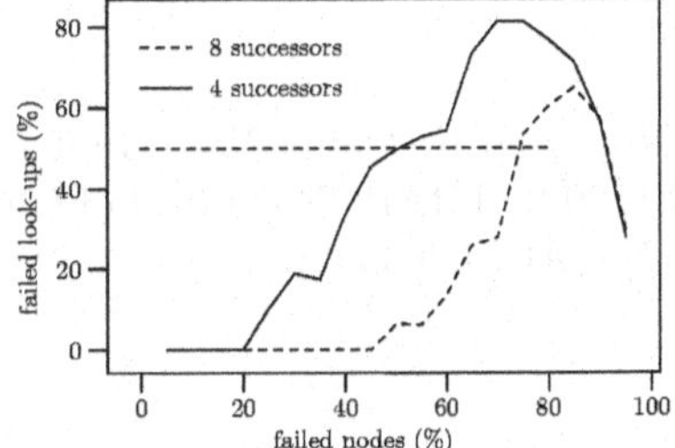

Fig. 4. Koorde: Percentage of failed lookups for varying percentage of node failures. When successors increase from 4 to 8, the crash point increases from 50% to 75%.

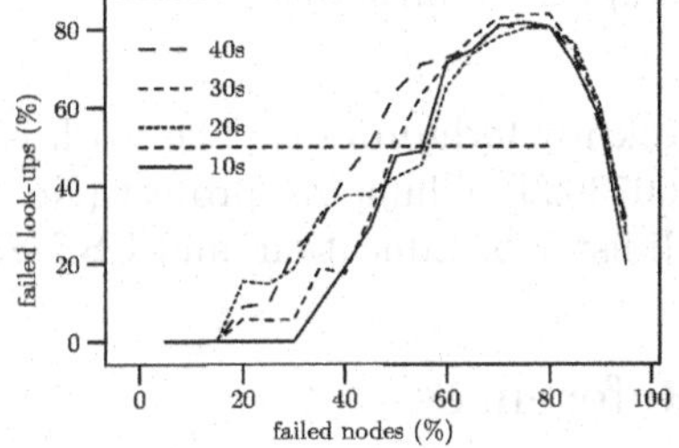

Fig. 5. Koorde: Percentage of failed lookups for varying percentage of node failures with different stabilization time:10s, 20s, 30s and 40s

to emerge. While in Chord, look-up failures are very few when failed nodes are under 40%. This can be attributed to successor back-ups, when 40% nodes fail, the probability of a node losing all it four successors is only $0.4^4 = 0.025$.In both protocols when the number of fail nodes increases, the percentage of look-up failure increasing fast. It is because when lots of fingers are not correct, the path length is growing fast, and more nodes are contacted, hence, the probability of encountering failed nodes increases fast. When the failed nodes are above 80%, the failed look-ups are decreasing because at this time, most of the nodes are failed, the number of look-ups are very few, and some nearby look-ups can reach its destination quickly.

Then let us have a look at how "increasing successors" and "speedup stabilization" have impact on the performance of Chord and Koorde. The result get from the simulation is that both "increasing successors" and "speedup stabilization" obviously enhance the fault resilience of Chord (see Figure 2 and Figure 3). However, in Koorde while "increasing successors" greatly enhances the fault resilience of Koorde (see Figure 4), the influence of "speedup stabilization" is not that obvious (see Figure 5). It tells that "concurrent nodes failure" is sensitive to Koorde, and when large percent of nodes fail simutaneously, stabilization routine couldn't help a lot.

5 Conclusions

In this paper, we compare the dynamic resilience of Chord and Koorde from theoretical analysis and simulation. The result is that: Chord has better dynamic resilience than Koorde. We also find out the crash point of both protocol under some given circumstance. However we haven't compare the path overlap through simulation. This is left for further work. Due to time limitation, we just finish some initiating work in comparing the fault resilient of different peer-to-peer networks, Further work will be done to compare more networks under more complex circumstance.

Acknowledgement. The work is partly supported by China NSF grant (No. 60073029), China 973 project (No. 2002CB312002), TRAPOYT award of China Ministry of Education, and US NSF grant (No. ACI-0203592).

References

1. http://pdos.lcs.mit.edu/p2psim/howto.html
2. M. F. Kaashoek and R. Karger: Koorde: A simple degreeoptpimal distributed hash table. In 2nd International workshop on P2P Systems(IPTPS'03),(2003)
3. K.P. Gummadi, R. Gummadi, S.D. Gribble, S. Ratnasamy, S. Shenker, and I. Stoica: The Impact of DHT Routing Geometry on Resilience and Proximity. ACM SIGCOMM (2003)
4. D. Liben-Nowell, H. Balakrishnan, and D. Karger: Analysis of the Evolution of Peer-to-Peer Networks. ACM PODC (2002)
5. D. Loguinov, A. Kumar, V. Rai, S. Ganesh: Graph-Theoretic Analysis of Structured Peer-to-Peer Systems: Routing Distances and Fault Resilience. ACM SIGCOMM (2003)
6. J. Aspnes, Z. Diamadi, and G. Shah: Fault-Tolerant Routing in Peer-to-Peer Systems. ACM PODC (2002)
7. I. Stoica, R. Morris, D. Karger, M.F. Kaashoek, and H. Balakrishnan: Chord: A Scalable Peer-to-Peer Lookup Service for Internet Applications. ACM SIGCOMM (2001)
8. A. Fiat and J. Saia: Censorship Resistant Peer-to-Peer Content Addressable Networks. ACM/SIAM Symposium on Discrete Algorithms (2002).
9. J. Saia, A. Fiat, S. Gribble, A.R. Karlin, and S. Saroiu: Dynamically Fault-Tolerant Content Addressable Networks. IPTPS (2002).

Author Index